ISBN 978-1-5278-4496-4
PIBN 10891372

English
Français
Deutsche
Italiano
Español
Português

www.forgottenbooks.com

Mythology Photography **Fiction**
Fishing Christianity **Art** Cooking
Essays Buddhism Freemasonry
Medicine **Biology** Music **Ancient**
Egypt Evolution Carpentry Physics
Dance Geology **Mathematics** Fitness
Shakespeare **Folklore** Yoga Marketing
Confidence Immortality Biographies
Poetry **Psychology** Witchcraft
Electronics Chemistry History **Law**
Accounting **Philosophy** Anthropology
Alchemy Drama Quantum Mechanics
Atheism Sexual Health **Ancient History**
Entrepreneurship Languages Sport
Paleontology Needlework Islam
Metaphysics Investment Archaeology
Parenting Statistics Criminology
Motivational

McELROY'S

LADELPHIA DIRECTORY

FOR

1847:

ED. 10

CONTAINING

NAMES OF THE INHABITANTS, THEIR OCCUPATIONS,
PLACES OF BUSINESS, AND DWELLING HOUSES;

ALSO,

A LIST OF THE STREETS, LANES, ALLEYS,

THE

OFFICES, PUBLIC INSTITUTIONS, BANKS, &c.

Tenth Edition.

es of Subscribers, in this edition, are printed in Capitals, and the same
course will be pursued in all future editions.]

EE ADVERTISEMENTS AT THE END OF THIS BOOK.

SHOWING THE SITUATION OF THE WARDS IN THE CITY AND NEIGHBOURING TOWNSHIPS.

F
8547
.5 2

1847

	6th Street.	
Penn Township.		Northern Liberties.

RIVER SCHUYLKILL—OR WESTERN BOUNDARY OF THE CITY.		SEVENTH STREET.—Or Middle Boundary of the Wards.		RIVER DELAWARE—OR EASTERN BOUNDARY OF THE CITY.
	VINE		STREET.	
	North Mulberry Ward.		Upper Delaware Ward.	
	RACE OR		SASSAFRAS STREET.	
	South Mulberry Ward.		Lower Delaware Ward.	
	ARCH OR		MULBERRY STREET.	
	North Ward.		High Street Ward.	
	MARKET OR		HIGH STREET.	
	Middle Ward.		Chestnut Ward.	
	CHESTNUT		STREET.	
	South Ward.		Walnut Ward.	
	WALNUT		STREET.	
	Locust Ward.		Dock Ward.	
	SPRUCE		STREET.	
			Pine Ward.	
	Cedar Ward.		PINE STREET.	
			New Market Ward.	
	SOUTH OR		CEDAR STREET.	

Moyamensing.		
Passyunk.	Passyunk road.	Southwark.

REGULATIONS

OF THE STATE HOUSE BELL IN CASE OF FIRE.

NORTH,	· · ·	One,	One,	One.
SOUTH,	· · ·	Two,	Two,	Two.
EAST,	· · ·	Three,	Three,	Three.
WEST	· · ·	Four,	Four,	Four.
NORTH-EAST,	· ·	One, three,		One, three.
NORTH-WEST,	· ·	One, four,		One, four.
SOUTH-EAST,	· ·	Two, three,		Two, three.
SOUTH-WEST,	· ·	Two, four,		Two, four.

ALMANAC,

FOR THE YEAR OF OUR LORD

1847.

MONTHS.	Sunday.	Monday.	Tuesday.	Wednesday.	Thursday.	Friday.	Saturday.	MONTHS.	Sunday.	Monday.	Tuesday.	Wednesday.	Thursday.	Friday.	Saturday.
JANUARY...						1	2	JULY......					1	2	3
	3	4	5	6	7	8	9		4	5	6	7	8	9	10
	10	11	12	13	14	15	16		11	12	13	14	15	16	17
	17	18	19	20	21	22	23		18	19	20	21	22	23	24
	24	25	26	27	28	29	30		25	26	27	28	29	30	31
	31														
FEBRUARY..		1	2	3	4	5	6	AUGUST.....	1	2	3	4	5	6	7
	7	8	9	10	11	12	13		8	9	10	11	12	13	14
	14	15	16	17	18	19	20		15	16	17	18	19	20	21
	21	22	23	24	25	26	27		22	23	24	25	26	27	28
	28								29	30	31				
MARCH....		1	2	3	4	5	6	SEPTEMBER.				1	2	3	4
	7	8	9	10	11	12	13		5	6	7	8	9	10	11
	14	15	16	17	18	19	20		12	13	14	15	16	17	18
	21	22	23	24	25	26	27		19	20	21	22	23	24	25
	28	29	30	31					26	27	28	29	30		
APRIL....					1	2	3	OCTOBER...						1	2
	4	5	6	7	8	9	10		3	4	5	6	7	8	9
	11	12	13	14	15	16	17		10	11	12	13	14	15	16
	18	19	20	21	22	23	24		17	18	19	20	21	22	23
	25	26	27	28	29	30			24	25	26	27	28	29	30
									31						
MAY.....							1	NOVEMBER..		1	2	3	4	5	6
	2	3	4	5	6	7	8		7	8	9	10	11	12	13
	9	10	11	12	13	14	15		14	15	16	17	18	19	20
	16	17	18	19	20	21	22		21	22	23	24	25	26	27
	23	24	25	26	27	28	29		28	29	30				
	30	31													
JUNE.....			1	2	3	4	5	DECEMBER..				1	2	3	4
	6	7	8	9	10	11	12		5	6	7	8	9	10	11
	13	14	15	16	17	18	19		12	13	14	15	16	17	18
	20	21	22	23	24	25	26		19	20	21	22	23	24	25
	27	28	29	30					26	27	28	29	30	31	

LENGTH OF SQUARES EAST AND WEST.

Beginning at Schuylkill low water mark on Cedar street.

Thence to Water street		400	Amount brought forward,	78	646
Water street width	60		Twelfth street width	50	
Square to Willow,		620	Square		396
Willow street	50		Eleventh street	50	
Square		267	Square		396
Beach street	50		Tenth street	50	
Square		240	Square		396
Ashton street	50		Ninth street	50	
Square		273	Square		396
Front street	60		Eighth street	50	
Square		396	Square		396
Second street	50		Seventh street	50	
Square		495	Square		396
Third street	50		Sixth street	50	
Square		396	Square		397 6
Fourth street	50		Fifth street	50	
Square		396	Square		400
Fifth street	50		Fourth street	50	
Square		396	Square		395 9
Sixth street	50		Third street	50	
Square		396	Square		500
Seventh street	50		Second street	50	
Square		396	Square		402
Eighth street	50		Front street	60	
Square		396	Square		130
Broad street	113		Penn street	50	
Square		250	Square		78
	—	—	New Water street	30	
From Sch. to Broad, inclusive,	733	5317	To the end of wharf		205
	—	—	From Broad to Delaware,	768	5530 3
Juniper street	28			733	5317
Square		250		1501	10,947 3
Thirteenth street	50				1,501
Square		396	Total feet from Schuylkill		
	—	—	to Delaware,		12,448 3
Amount carried forward,	78	646			

LENGTH OF SQUARES NORTH AND SOUTH.

Vine street width	50		Amount brought forward,	447	2765
Square		632	Walnut street width	50	
Sassafras street	50		Square		370
Square		288	Locust street	50	
Cherry street	40		Square		400 3
Square		288	Spruce street	50	
Mulberry street	66		Square		473 3
Square		307	Pine street	51	
Filbert street	51		Square		282
Square		306	Lombard street	50	
High street	100		Square		322
Square		484	Cedar street	51	
Chestnut street	50			749	4622 6
Square		225			749
George street	40				
Square		235	Total feet,		5371 6
Amount carried forward,	447	2765			

A. M'ELROY'S

PHILADELPHIA DIRECTORY,

FOR THE YEAR 1847.

ABBREVIATIONS.

Ab above, acct. accountant, al alley, att'y and coun. attorney and counsellor, av avenue, bel below, bet between, (B H) Bush Hill, b h boarding house, c. h. (counting house,) c corner, ct court, E East, F Frankford, (F M) Fairmount, (F V) Francisville, gent. gentleman, gentw. gentlewoman, G T Germantown, h house, K Kensington, l lane, lab labourer, M Moyamensing, manuf. manufacturer and manufactory, mer. merchant, mers. merchants, mr maker, n near, N North, N L Northern Liberties, O Y Old York, P Passyunk, P T Penn Township, R Ridge, S South, Sch. Schuylkill, W West, whf wharf or wharves, wid widow, (W P) West Philadelphia.

Abbatt Martha, 71 New Market

Abbett Ezekiel M., bonnet presser, 109 N 5th

ABBETT LYDIA, inn, S E Sch Beach & Walnut

Abbey Chas., gold-beater, 24 Pear, h 71 Spruce

Abbey Roswell, machinist, 261 N 8th

Abbot Saml., druggist, S E Sch 6th and Chancellor

Abbott Ann, Union ab Franklin

Abbott Catharine, 5 Gaskill

Abbott Charles H., merch., 16 N 4th, h 11 Sansom

ABBOTT C. H. & G., hardware, 16 N 4th

Abbott & Conard, hardware, S E 2d and Coates

Abbott Edward, Marshall ab Parish

Abbott Francis, bricklayer, rear Carpenter bel 8th

Abbott George, mer., 16 N 4th, h 183 Mulberry

Abbott Isaiah, bricklr., Tyler st

Abbott Jacob, shop, 33 M road

Abbott James, mer., 127 High, h 245 Walnut

Abbott James G., mer., Marshall ab Parrish

Abbott Joel, dealer, S W 4th and Marriott

Abbott John, grocer, N E Broad and Sassafras, h Sassafras bel Broad

Abbott Johnes & Co., silk goods, 153 High

Abbott Joseph, gent, Wharton ab 4th

Abbott Leonard, bonnet presser, Clark bel 4th

Abbott Mary, wid. of James, 55 New

Abbott Nathan S., 1 Scheetz

Abbott Redman, mer., 153 High

Abbott Saml. A., mer., Marshall ab Parish

Abbott Samuel W., 10 Girard

Abbott Theodore, carp., 1 Shaffer's ct

Abbott Thomas, carman, rear 4 Charlotte

Abbott William, leather-dealer, 78 S Front, h 189 S 3d

Abbott Wm. real estate broker, 95½ Walnut, h 19 S 10th

Abbott William, hardware, 2d and Coates, h 23 Coates

Abbott Wm. H., atty. at law, 24 George

A'Beckett Thos., comedian, 3 Jefferson

Abel Anthony, shoemr., 21 Rachel

ABEL & BICKNELL, brushmrs., 20 N 3d

Abel Catharine, gentw., 10 Brown

Abel Catharine, wid. of Joseph, Ulrich

Abel Charles J., mer., 20 N 3d, h 5 Lodge

Abel Chas. R., tinsmith, 380 N 2d, h 450 N 4th

Abel Edwin, shoemr., 33 Sheaff's al

Abel George, cordwainer, Crown ab Bedford

Abel Jacob, nailor, Front bel Master (K)

Abel James, labourer, Wharton ab 4th

Abel John, cordw., rear 21 Chatham

Abel John, chairmr. Kennedy's ct

Abel John, shoemr., 19 Rachel (N L)

Abel John, stone-cutter, Wallace bel 13th

Abel Joseph, cordw., 143 Poplar

Abel Mary, wid. of John, Allen bel Palmer (K)

Abel Peter, 27 Apple tree al

Abel Peter, cordw., Union ab Franklin (K)

Abel Peter, carp., rear 575 N Front

Abel Robert K., watchcase mr., Alder bel Girard av

Abel Samuel, brassfounder, 5 York ct

Abel Susan, 491 N 5th

Abel, Wilson & Co., forwarding mers., 1st whf bel Vine, Delaware

1

Abel Wm. W. brassfounder, 16 Rose al
Abell A. B., coach-painter, 234 Catharine
Abell F., tailor, rear 382 S 3d
Abell Joseph A., cooper, Lancaster ab Keefe
Abels Hester, 292 S Front
Abercrombie Christiana, 167 S 11th
Abercrombie Mary, wid. of James, 6 Portico sq
Abernethy John, carter, Sch 8th n Willow
Abraham Elizabeth, Apple ab Poplar
Abrahams David, vict., 5th ab George (N L)
Abrahams Elias, tailor, 4 S 6th
Abrahams Isaac, vict., 263 Green
Abrahams Isaac, jr., butcher, 10th ab Catharine
Abrahams Moses, trimmings, 42 Apple
Abrahams Moses, tailor, 257 N 2d, h 481 N 2d
Abrahams Moses, gent., N W Coates and St John
Abrahams & Vandegrift, tailors, 4 S 6th
Abram Robert, drayman, Sch 3d ab Lombard
Abram Wm., vict., Hanover ab Franklin (K)
Abrams Joseph, att'y and coun., 43 N 5th
Accoo Jesse, coachman, 13 Watson's al
Accoo Wm., lab., Madison ct
Acheson Charles, flour mer., 387 High
Acheson James, baker, Sch 2d and Wood
Acheson Jos., weaver, Philip ab Jefferson (K)
Acheson Mary, 9 Passmore's pl
Acheson & Rommell, flour mers., 387 High
Ackerman David, cordw., Charlotte ab Beaver
Ackley Elizabeth, 244 S Front
Ackley John N., stoves, Sp Garden, h Centre ab Brown
Ackley Josiah, optician, 83 Sassafras
Ackley Lorenzo, boots and shoes, Wood ab Sch 6th
Ackley Lydia, 421 N 4th
Ackley Moses B., shoemr., rear Vienna above Franklin (K)
Ackley Norman, shoemr., 61 Apple bel Poplar
Ackley & Waters, stoves, 9th and Sp Garden
Ackley Wm., paper-boxmr., Beaver ab St John (K)
Acor Stephen, 465 N 4th
Acroyd Jeremiah, dyer, 22 W Cedar
Adair Robert Rev., Carpenter ab 3d
Adair Robert, coachmr., Carlton n Sch 8th
Adaire Ann, b. h., Marlborough ab Duke (K)
Adams Alex., brushes, 31 High, h 232 Green
Adams Alex., drayman, Walnut al
Adams Amos, cordw., rear 492 N 3d
Adams And. W., mer., 45 High, h 47 Mulberry
Adams Andw. W. & Co., mers., 45 High
Adams A. Mrs., paper ruling, 36 N 6th, h 37 Zane
Adams Catharine, rear Pleasant bel 10th
Adams C. L., printer, cards, of. 118 Chestnut, h Courtlin pl
Adams & Co., package express, 80 Chestnut
Adams C. W., cabinetmr., 186 N 5th
Adams David, waiter, 10 Bird's ct
Adams David, grocer, S E 2d and Poplar
Adams Eleanor, layer out of the dead, rear 9th ab Coates
Adams Eliza, 3 Young's al
Adams Francis, carp., rear 5 Ogden

Adams George, vict., Lemon ab 12th
Adams George, cordw., 4 Rose al
Adams George, carp., Crown ab Bedford (K)
Adams Henry, machinist, 471 N 5th
Adams Henry S., broker, 95½ Walnut
Adams Jacob, mer., 73 S whfs., h 94 Union
Adams James, lab., Pearl n Nixon
Adams Jas., carp. weaver, Clinton ab Norris (K)
Adams James B., grocer, 166 S 13th
Adams James C., clerk, 129 Gaskill
Adams Jas. W., machinist, Nectarine bel 11th
Adams John, bookbinder, 4 Charles pl
Adams John, blacksmith, Locust and Juniper
Adams John, cooper, 2 Silva's ct
Adams John, fisherman, Cherry ab Queen (K)
Adams John, b h, 40 Penn
Adams John, carman, 10 Cox's al
Adams John, carp. weaver, Otter n Front (K)
Adams John, carpenter, 53 Perry
Adams John, seaman, 5 Twelve Feet al
Adams John B., provisions, 310 Sassafras
Adams John Q., mer., 40 S Front, h 371 Sassafras
Adams John Q. & Co., com mers., 40 S Front
Adams John S., Mt Vernon House, 95 N 2d
Adams Joseph, fisherman, Cherry ab Queen (K)
Adams Joseph, waterman, 270 N 2d
Adams Martha, McKean's ct
Adams Mary, 19 Julianna
Adams Mary Ann, b h, 319 Chestnut & 9 S 11th
Adams Mrs. Robt., gentw., 182 Chestnut
Adams Nathan, shipcarp., Queen ab Cherry (K)
Adams Priscilla, rear 23 John st (S)
Adams Rebecca, dry goods, 330 Sassafras
Adams Reuben, seaman, 63 Mulberry
Adams Robt., Rose bel School (K)
Adams Robt., mariner, 30 Beck (S)
Adams Robt., mer., 123 Walnut, h 20 Girard
Adams Robt., coal dealer, N E Water and Callowhill, h 39 Coates
Adams Robert, weaver, Wagner's al
Adams Robert H., hatter, 324 High, h 214 S 8th
Adams Samuel, b h, 22 S 2d
Adams Samuel, clerk K. Bank, h Queen below Shackamaxon (K)
Adams Samuel C., brickmr., S Garden ab 12th, h Barker and Sch 2d
Adams Sarah Ann, dressmr., 162 Pine
Adams Thomas, cordwainer, Queen ab Hanover (K)
Adams Thomas, blacksmith, Phœnix ab 2d (K)
Adams Thomas, mer., 220 Sassafras
Adams Thomas, lab., Wood ab Nixon
Adams Thomas F., printers' ink manufactory, 28 Dock
Adams Timothy, machinist, 11th ab Coates
Adams Wm., cordw., Howard bel Franklin (K)
Adams Wm., carp., Duke ab Hanover (K)
Adams Wm., collector, 26 Old York Road
Adams William, fisherman, Queen ab Cherry
Adams William, gent., Mantua Village
Adams Wm., lab., Jones w of Sch 8th
Adams Wm. D., tobacconist, 5th ab Brown
Adams Wm. H., sec. Gr. Lodge, Hall S 3d
Adams Wm. M., drayman, Crown ab Queen (K)

Adams Wm. M., grocer, 427 N Front
Adams Wm. R., stove mr., Thompson n Sch 8th
Adamson H., lumb. mer., N W 11th and Pine, h Washington ab 11th
Adamson James, carpet weaver, 125 N 6th, h Carlton bel 13th
Adamson John L., blacksmith, 9th bel Poplar, h 12th and Pleasant
Adamson Thomas, grocer, 5th & George (N L)
Addicks John E., mer., 159 High, h 203 N 6th
ADDICKS, VAN DUSEN & SMITH, shoes, 159 High
Addis Charles, brickmr., Shippen la bel Cedar
Addis Jacob, carp., 377 Pine
Addis John, brickmr., Sch 7th bel Helmuth
ADLER GEO. S., leather manufacturer, 64 N Market, h 4 Margaretta
Adler John, morocco dresser, 53 Green
Adler Samuel, dry goods, 534 N 2d (K)
Adolph Eliz., wid. of John, 254 St. John
Adolph G., carp., 24 Coates
Adolphus Abraham, corn-doctor, 235 Spruce
Adrian Ellen, rear 12 Cresson's al
Adriance G. W., periodicals, 28 and 29 Arcade, h Carpenter rear Arcade
Aechternacht F. A., tailor, 5th and Pine
Aertsen Jas. M., mer, 8 S Front, h Pine ab 13th
Aertsen John P., mer., 100 George
Aertsen Robert B., mer., 81 S Front
Affalder Augustus, cordw., 433 N 3d
Afflerbach George, wheelwright, 4 Harrison's ct (K)
Afflerbach Henry, starch mr., Marlborough ab Duke (K)
Afflerbach Henry J., cordw., M'Avoy's ct
Afflerbach Wm., gunsmith, 621 N 2d (K)
Afflick James, tavern, Lancaster pike (W P)
Afflick Morris E., bricklayer, 290 N 7th, coal yard 9th ab Poplar
Agasstorff Christian, cabinet mr., Grim's ct
Ager Wm., wheelwright, 7 Blackhorse al
Agin Isaac, currier, 22 Elfreth's al
Agin Wm., lab., Bedford
Agnew & Co., fancy dry goods, 26 S 2d
Agnew Dennis, weav., Hancock bel Master (K)
Agnew Edward, cordw., Moon's ct
Agnew Henry, dyer, rear G T road bel Master (K)
Agnew Henry O., blacksmith, Sch 6th & Jones, h Sch 6th ab Pine
Agnew Isabella, dry goods, 97 N 9th
Agnew John, Franklin works, 340 Vine, h 12 Morgan
Agnew John, lab., Master and Hancock (K)
Agnew Michael, weaver, Hancock ab Morris (K)
Agnew Samuel, publisher, 12 N 11th
Agnew Wm., mer., 26 S 2d
Agnew Wm. G. E., teacher, 48 N 7th
Ahern Daniel, grocer, N W 4th and Shippen
Ahern Patrick, 17 Fayette
AHRENFELT C. & Co., fancy goods, 16 N 4th
Aigen Catherine, shop, 3d and Queen
Aikens David, lab., Shippen n Front
Aikman Jno., hat blockmr., 33 Dock, h 162½ S 2nd

Ailes Alexander H., shoemr., High w of Sch 6th
Ailes Catherine, shoemr., S 5th bel Queen
Aim E. Mrs. milliner, Beach ab Ken Market
Ainscow Thos., weaver, Duke ab Hanover (K)
Airey John, soap-boiler, 228 N Front
Airey Richard, gent., 17 Wood
Airley Peter, weaver, G T road ab Master, (K)
Aitken Amelia, widow of Wm. P., Elizabeth ab Poplar
Aitken Charles C., boot manf., 19 Edward (K)
Aitken & Co., boot and shoe manf., 14 Bank
Aitken Jos., manf., 14 Bank, h Front ab Otter
Aitken Thos. P., tailor, Otter bel G T road
Akers Irwin, tailor & vari. store, 16 Strawberry
Akers Thomas, china & queensware, 317 High
Akin Alexander, carman, Callowhill ab 13th
Akin John, brushmr., Perry and Lombard
Akin Ophelia, 18 Prune
Akins James, cabinetmr., 94 German
Akins John, shoemr., 4 Charles
Alberger Edward, bookbinder, 496 S 2d
Alberger Jacob, butcher, 174 S Water
Alberger Mary, rear 575 N Front
Albert Henry, skin-dresser, Schleisman's al
Albert John, lab., 1 Myers' ct
Albert Peter, tavern, 243 S 6th
Albert Rainerd, tanner, Clymer ab Mud la (K)
Alberti Geo. F., cupper, Clair bel Carpenter
Albertie Beulah, trimmings, Lemon ab 10th
Albertson Benj., mer., 19 High, h 45 N 6th
Albertson Eliza, gentw., 15 Harmony ab 4th
Albertson Enoch, cordw., 25 Paul st
Albertson Gilbert, lab., 2d ab Greenwich
Albertson Isaac, 173 N 4th
Albertson James, saddler, P road ab Carpenter, h Carpenter bel 7th
Albertson James, shipwright, Marlborough ab Bedford (K)
Albertson Joseph, shoes, Queen bel Marlboro' (K)
Albertson Lewis, tavern, 89 Plum st
Albertson Marmaduke, shipwt., Beach ab Marlborough (K)
Albertson Mary, sempstress, 4 Humphrey's ct
Albertson Samuel, carp. M'Clung's ct.
Albertson Thos. S. cordw. 68 N 3d, h 16 Clarke
Albertson Wm., cordw. Marlborough bel Bedford (K)
Albertson Wm., blacksm. 2d and Mary
Albrecht J. F. shoemr. 297 Mulberry.
Albright C. collector, 18 S 3d
Albright Frances, dressmr. Sch 8th ab Sassafras
Albright Jacob, sen. lab. 80 German
Albright Jacob, watchman, 20 Duke
Albright Jacob, packer, James ab Charles
Albright John, carter, rear 373 N 3d
Albright John W. tailor, 60 Walnut, h 347 S 3d
Albright Maria, rear 525 N 4th
Albright Peter, tavern, 404 N 2d
Albright Samuel, carp. 7th ab Parrish
Albright Thos. F. clock & watchmr. 246 High
Alburger Abraham, painter, 651 N 2d (K)
Alburger Abraham, victualler, 281 Callowhill
Alburger Christian, victualler, Powell bel Vineyard (F V)

Alburger Henry, vict. Ogden ab Sch 7th
Alburger Jacob, wheelwt. George ab 3d (N L)
Alburger John G. vict. 259 Callowhill
Alburger Susan & Eliz. teachers, 125 M road
Alburger & Stratton, painters, 651 N 2d (K)
Alburger Wm. M. plumber, N W Marshall and Noble, h 64 Marshall
Alcorn Andrew, weaver, Sch 5th bel Filbert
Alcorn George, lab. Winter bel Sch 8th
Alcorn George, cigarmr. 7 Flower ct (S)
Alcorn James, coachman, 16 Pratt
Alcorn James, bookseller, 46 N 5th
Alcorn Samuel, carter, Bickham and Sch 7th
Alcorn Samuel, baker, 10th and Ogden
Alcorn Thomas R. victualler, Thompson ab Sch 8th
Alcorn Wm., lab. Montgomery bel 2d (K)
Alden D. P. musical academy, 351 High
Alden Jonathan, cashier Globe Insurance and Trust Co. 435 N 2d, h 218 N 7th
Alderdice Wm., weaver, Pearl bel Sch 6th
Alderman Joel, watchman, Allen's ct
Alderman Joseph, tailor, P road & Carpenter
Aldred George, glue boiler, rear of Marshall ab Poplar
Aldred George H. varnisher, rear 16 Ogden
Aldrich Cynthia, b h, 231 Spruce
Aldridge George, lab. Hutchinson ab Poplar
Aldridge Peter, cordw. 7 State st
Aldridge Samuel H. salesman, 382 N 8th
Aldworth John, lab. 203 N Front
Aldworth Richard, bootmr. 2 Ridgway's ct
Alexander Andw. stonecut. Parrish bel 12th
Alexander Ann, widow of Richard, 24 Plum
Alexander Benjamin W. furniture, 82 Green
Alexander & Carver, mer. N W 3d & Mulberry
Alexander Charles, printer, Franklin pl, h 141 N 10th
Alexander C. widow, 14 Tammany
Alexander Edward, millwt. 4 Garret's ct
Alexander Elenor, widow, 35 Shippen
Alexander Elizabeth, 26 S 13th
Alexander George, blk. sm., Wood ab Sch 6th
Alexander George, watchman, 20 Swanson
Alexander George, grocer, N E 3d & Coates
Alexander Henry, lapidist, Clark ab 3d
ALEXANDER HUGH, mer. 5 S 2d, h 107 Pine
Alexander Hugh, combmr. Crown bel Franklin (K)
Alexander Isaac, ostler, 129 N Juniper
Alexander James, manuf. Filbert n Sch 8th
Alexander James, Mrs., 10 Montgomery
Alexander James, baker, 201 N Front
Alexander John, shoemr. 207 Locust
Alexander John, porter, 614 N 2d (K)
Alexander John, painter, 43 M road
Alexander John, 43 N 11th
Alexander John, lab. 4 Hunter
Alexander John, weaver, St Andrew's st.
Alexander Joseph, printer, 101 Christian
Alexander Jos. D., machinist, 60 S 13th, h Marshall ab Poplar
Alexander Lewis, porter, 6 Pryor's ct.
Alexander Martin W, clerk, 145 N 7th

Alexander M. S., mer., 139 Filbert
Alexander Robert, weaver, 34 Harmstead
Alexander Samuel, Washington ab 5th
Alexander Samuel D., brushmaker, Morris ab Christian
Alexander Thos., seaman, rear Carpenter ab 8th
Alexander Wallace, machinist, Marshall ab Poplar
Alexander Wm., cooper, 43 M road (S)
Alexander Wm., Buttonwood W of 13th
Alexander Wm., painter, Coombes' al
Alexander Wm., collector, 15 Jefferson row
Alexander Wm., baker, 27 Green (N L)
Alexander Wm., home missionary, 117 M. road
Alexander Wm., machinist, 60 S 13th
Alexander Wm. G., acct., 314 S Front
Alexander Wm. G., shop, Dean and Locust
Alexander Wm. G., bootma., 4 Randall's ct.
Alexander Wm. L., mer., 61½ N 3d, h 10 Marshall
Alford Mary, 14 Wallace
Alford Wm., book keeper, 120 Christian
Algeo John H., cooper, 5 Linden
Algie Daniel, block cutter, Sch 8th n Wood
Algie Wm., weaver, 14 Myers' ct
Algier Joseph, agent, Carlton bel Sch 5th
Allanesse John, boot black, 1 Little Pine
Allardice Peter, gent., 82 W. Willow
Allaway Alex T., cabinetmr., 6 John (S)
Allchin George, bookbinder, Jay bel Coates
Allebach Amos, porter, George ab 2d (K)
Alleborn Jacob, M. D., 464 N 4th
Allee James, b h, 96 N Front
Allen Aaron R., bricklayer, rear Schleisman's al
Allen Albert, hatter, 56 Fitzwater
Allen Albert G., clerk, 3 Jacoby
Allen Albertus, carp., 145 Queen, h Washington ab 5th
Allen Alfred W., cordw., 481 N 4th
Allen Andrew, moulder, Lancaster bel Reed
Allen Andrew, foreman, Crown bel West (K)
Allen Ann, beer house, 125 Swanson
Allen Ann, b h, 309 Chestnut
Allen Anna, 117 S 4th
Allen Anna, dressmr., 10th and Wood
Allen Bartholomew, porter, Traquair's ct.
Allen Benjamin, bootmr., 2 Lodge pl
Allen & Brother, drygoods, N W 4th & Spruce
Allen Chs., coachmr., Orange ab Washington
Allen Charles G., lampmr., 383 Sassafras
Allen Charles J., teacher, N E 6th & Prune, h 146 Pine
Allen Clapton, tailor, N E 2d and Chestnut, h 160 Cherry
Allen Edward, trader, 5 Emeline
Allen Edward, shoemr., Barron bel Gaskill
Allen Edwin, b h, 207 N 8th, japanner, 158 Sassafras
Allen Eleanor C., 29 O Y road
Allen Elizabeth, 18 Strawberry
Allen Elizabeth, 25 Franklin
Allen Enoch, tailor, 9th and High, h 10 N 9th
Allen Ephraim, cordw., 22 Castle
Allen Franklin, bricklayer, 3 Stanley
Allen George, chairmr., 166 Swanson

Allen George, boots and shoes, 326 High
Allen George, lab., Hancock ab Norris (K)
Allen Geo., prof., Univ. Pa., h Walnut & Sch 6th
Allen Geo. W., M. D., 28 S 6th, h 77 Wood
ALLEN G. F., druggist, S W 13th & Cedar
Allen Harriet, b h, 63 Shippen
Allen Henry, sparmr., 353 N Front
Allen Isabella, grocer, Queen ab Bishop (K)
Allen James, plasterer, Filbert bet Sch 5th & 6th
Allen James, baker, Vine ab Broad
Allen James, plasterer, S. E. Sch 6th & Filbert
Allen Jarvis, bookbinder, 184 Queen
Allen John, waiter, 29 Elizabeth
Allen John, mariner, 13 Tamarind
Allen John, lab., 211 Shippen
Allen John, bricklayer, 8th ab Cedar
Allen John, lab., 496 N 4th
Allen John, gent., 204 S 3d
Allen John B. A., mer., 10 S whfs., h Pine and Fothergill
Allen John C., druggist, 180 S 2d
Allen John M., tinsmith, 123 N 11th
Allen Joseph, clerk, Duke n Hanover (K)
Allen Joseph, cabinetmr., 119 Spruce
Allen Joseph, gilder, Raspberry al
Allen Jos., carp. weaver, Master & Pink (K)
Allen Jos., weaver, Perry bel Phoenix (K)
Allen Jos. H., confectioner, 12 Shippen
Allen Jos. L., carp., 34 John (S)
Allen Jos. W., barber, Baltimore House
ALLEN JOSIAH J., mer., 6 S Water, h 22 George
Allen J. M., M. D., 43 S 10th
Allen Martha, sewer, 382 S 3d
Allen Mary, 3 Hickory
Allen Mary, tobacco, 271 S 4th
Allen & Morgan, sailmrs., Spruce st whf.
Allen Richard S., clerk, 7 New Crown
Allen Robert, mer., 140½ High, h 469 Mulberry
Allen Robert, weaver, Franklin ab Front (K)
Allen Robt., distil., S W 3d & Plum, h 276 S 3d
Allen Samuel, mer., 7 S whfs., h 145 Franklin
Allen Samuel, teacher, 134 S Front
Allen Samuel, lab., Flower
Allen Samuel, lab., 6 Flytax al
Allen & Scattergood, tailors, S W 6th & Haines
Allen Thomas, carp., Marshall ab Parrish
Allen Thomas, mariner, 13 Mead
Allen Thomas, mariner, 13 Mead
Allen Thomas, cordw., 28 Harmony
Allen Thomas G., Rev., h 14 Jefferson Row
Allen Thomas H., collector, 202 S Front
Allen Thomas, weaver, Bedford bel Broad
Allen Walter, weaver, 13th ab Fulton
ALLEN WILLIAM & J., furniture, 119 Spruce
Allen Wm., weaver, Mariner
Allen Wm., moulder, Corn ab Mackey
Allen Wm., baker, Crown n West (K)
Allen Wm., carp., 462 S 4th
Allen Wm., machinist, 324 N 8th
Allen Wm., sailmr., Lombard st wharf, h 91 Prime
Allen Wm., hair dress., 6 S 9th, h 14 Watson's al
Allen Wm., lab., Robinson's ct (K)
Allen Wm. jr., cabmr., 119 Spruce, h Prune

Allen Wm. C., wooden ware, 1 Chestnut, h 12 Melon
Allen Wm. G., weighmaster, 34 S whfs., h 229 Spruce
Allen Wm. H., hardware, 31 High
Allen Wm. M., tailor, S W 6th and Hains, h 150 E Cedar
Allen Wm. N., clerk, 34 John (S)
Allen Wm. N., trimmings, 10th and Poplar
Allen, Wilson & Co., dry goods, 140½ High
Allen & Wyand, japanners, 158 Sassafras
Alleson Hannah, gentw., 24 George
Allhiser John, ship. carp., Franklin bel Cherry (K)
Allibands John, coachmr., 24 Branch
Allibone Samuel A., mer., 17 S whfs.
ALLIBONE THOS. & Co., commission mers., 8 S whfs.
Allibone Thomas, mer., 8 S whfs., h W. P.
Alligum Gregg, lab., Sch Bank bel Pine
Allingham Thos., carp., Jones E Sch 4th
Allingham Wm., carp., Jones W Sch 5th
Allingham Wm., jr., carp., Jones W Sch 5th
Allington Aaron, stationery, 512 N 2d (K)
Allinson Geo. B., civil engr., Locust ab Sch 8th
Allinson Samuel, gent., Locust ab Sch 8th
Allis & Hyde, bakers, 314 N 5th
Allis Wells P., baker, 314 N 5th
Allison Andrew, weaver, Perry's ct
Allison D. M., M. D., 24 Plum
Allison James, painter, 1 Short ct
Allison James, tailor, 316 High, h 186 N 12th
Allison John, manf., Hope bel Master (K)
Allison John, lab., Pearl ab 13th
Allison Joseph, atty. at law, N E 7th and Noble
Allison Rebecca, gentw., Concord st
Allison Sarah, Pearl bel Broad
Allison Thomas, tailor, 127 S 12th
Allison Walter, carp., Chancellor W Sch 7th
Allison W. C., wheelwright, Broad n Vine, h 520 Vine
Allman & Brock, flour mers., S E 2d & Shippen
Allman Edward, hatter, 12th ab Sp Garden
Allman Joseph, hatter, 223 High, h 20 S Garden
Allman Meux, 91 R road
Allman & Robinson, hatters, 223 High
Allman Thos., mer., 214 E Walnut
Allmendinger Chas., trimmings, 341 N 2nd, h 109 Noble
Allmendinger Wm., baker, 71 Crown
Alloway Geo. W., painter, Hanover ab Bedford (K)
Alloway Isaac, cordw., Scott's ct
Alloway Isaac, tavern, O Y road and Button-wood
Alloway Lewis, waterman, rear 12 Brown
Alloway Wm., drayman, Charlotte ab George
Allebrook Samuel, hosier, 4th & G T road (K)
Alonan J. M., shoemr., Vine bel 12th
Alp David, cordw., Hope ab Phoenix (K)
Alrich Peter, collector, 453 Vine
Alrich Saml., lab., Marlboro' & West (K)
Alrich Saml., blacksm., Beach ab Palmer (K)
Alrich & Son, blacksms., Beach ab Palmer (K)
Alsop Amy, 93 S 4th

Alsop Robert, att. at law, 6th n Green
Alsop Saml., cabinetmr., Bedford ab 12th
Alsop Thomas, lab., Ann n 13th
Altamatt Jcrome, cordw., School st
Altemus Benj. C., tailor, Green bel 12th
Altemus Geo., blksmith, 202 G T road (K)
Altemus James, skin-dresser, 527 N 2d ab Otter, (K)
Altemus Joseph T., bookbinder, 44 N 4th, h 426 Coates
Altemus Nich., blacksm., rear 372 S 3d
Altemus Pamelia, matron, City Hospital
Altemus Saml. T., mer., 78 High, h 145 Dillwyn
Altemus Sandford, chairmr., 3 Mead
Altemus Susan, G T road bel Phoenix (K)
Altemus Thomas, Phila. Bank, h City Hospital
Altemus Wm., starch manuf., 2d and Oxford, h 669 N 2d (K)
Altemus Wm., wheelwright, rear 486 N 3d
Alter Charles cordw., 3 Vernon st
Alter Jacob, grocer, 30 N whfs. & 59 N Water, h 404 N 6th
Alter Solomon, mer., 247 High, h 328 N 6th
Althouse Jacob, cordw., Cherry n Duke (K)
Altins Henry, cordw., Wood ab Sch 4th
Alvord Christopher, agent, 20 Chester
Alward Henry M., shoemr., 466 E Vine
Aman Jacob, dry goods, 346½ High
Ambler David, Lewis ab Poplar
Ambler Jno., tinsm., S W Marshall and Sp Garden
Ambrose Charlotte, hair-dresser, 253 S 7th
Ambrosi Thomas C., painter, High and 12th
Ambruster John, bricklayer, Wallace bel 10th
Amer Ann, Carlton bel Sch 7th
Amer James, weaver, rear Carpenter ab 9th
Amer John, hatter, rear 216 Noble
Amer Jos., weaver, Mariner ab 13th
Amer Nancy, Carpenter ab 8th
AMER JOSEPH H., machinist, 50 N 6th and James bel 13th, h Wood n Sch 7th
AMER WM., morocco dresser, N W 3d & Willow, h Green bel Franklin
Ames John, carter, Clymer ab Mud lane (K)
Ames Josiah, ship master, 152 Catharine
Amey Olis, plasterer, 31 Charlotte
Amies Margaret, b h 10 N 6th
Amies Richard, paper dealer, rear 24 Catharine
Amies Thomas K., mer., 331 S 2nd
Ammidon Otis, Treasurer Lehigh Coal and Navigation Co., 82 S 2d, h 171 S 3d
Amon Christian, baker, Beach ab Maiden (K)
Amone John, cordw., 1 Mechanic
Amos Charles T., stoves, 197 N 2d, h 116 New Market
Amos Christian, lab., Fraley's al (K)
Amos Diana, 73 G T road (K)
Amos & Ditzler, stoves, 197 N 2d
Amos Elizabeth, 116 New Market
Amos Jacob, carp., Coates al, h 67 New
Amos John, Carlton bel Sch 7th
Amos Jonathan, tailor, Poplar ab 10th
Amos Robt., cordw., rear 30 St John
Amos Wm., jr., carpenter, 2 Porter's ct
Amtor Andrew, cabtmr., 13 Caliowhill

Anberry Caspar, gent., rear 7 Mead al
Anderfuhrer John, tailor, 86 St John
Anders John, bootmr., 314 Sassafras
Anders Margaret, Mechanics' ct (N L)
Anderson Abigail, dressmr., 127 Green
Anderson Amelia, dressmr., 154 Union
Anderson Andrew, brickmr., M'Duffie n Sch 2d
Anderson Andw., mariner, Swanson bel Queen
Anderson Cecilia, 312 Cedar
Anderson Charles, lab., rear 160 Queen
Anderson Charles, drayman, Howard bel Master (K)
Anderson Chas., butcher, 2nd bel Wharton
Anderson Chas. W., barber, 29 S 3d, h 6 Portland lane
Anderson Christian, gent., 3 Lombard ct
Anderson Christiana, Culvert ab 4th
Anderson Christopher, porter, 2 Juniper la
Anderson Daniel, tailor, Carpenter bel 6th
Anderson David, plasterer, Parrish ab Sch 8th
Anderson Edward, mer., 28 N 3d, h 209 S 2d
Anderson Edward, stone-cutter, 3 Gray's ct (K)
Anderson Eliza, widow, Amber ab Phœnix (K)
Anderson Elizabeth, confect., 321 Pine
Anderson Elizabeth, 88 Crown (C)
Anderson Geo., lab., 5th and George (N L)
Anderson Geo., cooper, rear 499 Vine
Anderson Geo., cordw., Fraley's al (K)
Anderson Geo. W., editor, 79 Dock
Anderson Geo. R., cabt. mr., Higgins' ct
Anderson Henry, seaman, rear 115 Queen
Anderson Henry, shoemr., 12th bel Pine
Anderson Jacob S., tailor, 618 N 3d
Anderson Jacob W., hair-dresser, 9th ab Poplar
Anderson James, engineer, 622 N 8th (K)
Anderson James, weaver, Callowhill n Sch 2d
Anderson James, weaver, 12th ab Pine
Anderson James, brickmr., Brumen ct (K)
Anderson James, carter, High w Sch 3d
Anderson James, weaver, Hanover ab West (K)
Anderson James, weaver, Lydia bel William (K)
Anderson James, ostler, 28 Bread
Anderson Jane, washer, Ball al
Anderson John, tailor, 10 Spruce
Anderson John, lab., Mulberry n Broad
Anderson John, weaver, Vine n Sch
Anderson John, chandler, 353 Callowhill
Anderson John, cordw., Morris bel Catharine
Anderson John, boot-black, 48 S 4th, h Morris bel Catharine
Anderson John B., blindmr., 9 S. 13th
Anderson John D., mariner, Washington ab 2d
Anderson John R., tailor, 451 S 2d
Anderson John W., grocer, Palmer & Duke (K)
Anderson Joseph, blacksm., 28 Lebanon
Anderson Joseph, musician, 252 Lombard
Anderson La Fayette, combmr., Marlborough ab Franklin
Anderson Levi, file manuf., Palmer ab Franklin (K)
Anderson Lewis, lab., Beach ab Warren (K)
Anderson Margaret, sempstress, 46 George (S)
Anderson Marg., Loud st
Anderson Mary, S W 3d and Catharine
Anderson Mary, Hunter's ct, rear 535 Vine

Anderson Mary, trimmings, 182 Pine
Anderson Matt., grocery, Front ab Master
Anderson Michael, drayman, Small bel 6th
Anderson M., M. D., S E 5th and Pine
Anderson Nicholas, glass-cutter, Marlboro' ab Franklin
Anderson Philip, whitewasher, 98 N 4th
Anderson Philip P., 9th ab Catharine
Anderson Rebecca, 5 Lytle's ct
Anderson Robert, cordw., rear 390 Sassafras
Anderson Robert, wheelwt., Filbert bel 12th, h 15 Morgan
Anderson Rosanna, 3 Lyndall's al
Anderson Sarah, trimmings, 6th bel Green
Anderson Sarah H., wid. of Sl. V. 152 N Front
Anderson Stephen, 27 Prosperous al
Anderson Stephen D., tailor, Poplar ab 4th
Anderson Thomas, sailor, Riley's ct
Anderson Thomas, Charlotte n Creek
Anderson Thomas, b h, 122 N 4th
Anderson Westley, barber, 6 Portland la
Anderson, White & Lippincott, grocers, 10 N whfs., and 17 N Water
Anderson Wm., seaman, Clare st
Anderson Wm., weigher, 16 Duke
Anderson Wm., carp., Charlotte bel Thompson (K)
Anderson Wm., drayman, Orchard ab George (N L)
Anderson Wm. B., blindmr., Beach bel Marlborough (K)
Anderson Wm. D., house painter, 12 N 12th
Anderson Wm. V., mer., 17 N Water, h 242 Spruce
Andes F. J., turner, 11 West st
ANDRADE JOSEPH, mer., 28 Walnut, h 141 Spruce
Andress Conrad B., bricklayer, Coates ab 2d
Andress & Durell, trimmings, S W 2nd and Coates
Andress Michael, bricklayer 20 Noble
Andress Michael, jr., bricklayer, 11 York ct
Andress Saml., bricklayer, 123 Brown
Andrews Alex., drayman, Sch 8th ab Sassafras
ANDREWS BENJAMIN, trunk manuf., 86 High, h 75 N 5th
Andrews David, milkman, 620 N 3d
Andrews David, weaver, Phoenix bel Front (K)
Andrews E. W., mer., 53 N 6th
Andrews George, cabinet mr., 11 Freed's av
Andrews Henry, moulder, Franklin ab Front
Andrews Henry W., com. mer., 99 S whfs., h 18 W Walnut
Andrews Isaac, lab., Hope bel Phoenix (K)
Andrews Isabella, spooler, 4th ab Master (K)
Andrews Jacob, clothing, 45 Chestnut, h 324½ Cedar
Andrews James, stove finisher, 9 Parker
Andrews John, cordwr., Fisher ab Carpenter
Andrews Joseph, moulder, rear Orchard
Andrews Joseph B., lumber merchant, N W 10th and Cedar, h 292 Pine
Andrews Joshua, bricklayer and measurer, 12th and Washington

Andrews J. & J. B. & Co., lumber, N W 10th and Cedar
Andrews Little, lab., Callowhill ab Broad
Andrews Lyon, clk, rear 126 S 6th
Andrews Lyon, pawnbroker, 250 Cedar
Andrews Rebecca, milliner, 15 S 8th
Andrews Robert, lab., Sch 3d and Willow
Andrews Robert, labourer, Pearl ab 13th
Andrews Robert, warehouse-man, 5 Myers' ct
ANDREWS R. S. R., stoves, 82 N 6th, h 30 Madison
Andrews Saml., mer., 10 High
Andrews Samuel R., bricklayer, 13th bel High
Andrews Sarah, washer, 3 Acorn al
Andrews Thos., sailor, Relief st
Andrews Thomas Cecil, music store, Sp Garden ab 7th
Andrews Thomas A., gilder, 132 S 6th
Andrews & Thorne, grocers, 10 High
Andrews Wm., lab., Willow bel 12th
Andrie J., bootmr., Willow ab 6th
Ang Eli, cordw., rear 24 Rose al
Angel Adam, lab., Federal bel M road
Angel Meyer, pedler, Justice's ct
Angel Sarah, R road bel Buttonwood
Angelo John, blksm., 29 Marriott
Angelo Reb., gentw., 378 S 3d
Anger Charles, lab., Clymer
Anger Charles, cordw., Wood bel 3d
Angerer Charles, shoemr., 97 Callowhill
Angle Christian, lab., Otter bel G T road (K)
Angney Cath., wid. of John, Brown bel Vienna
Angney & Dickson, druggists, N E 5th and Spruce
Angney John R., druggist, N E 5th & Spruce
Angue Albert D., corks and liquors, 109 N 2d
Angue John, jr., wines and cordials, 30 N 3d
Anna Fredk., shoemr., rear 1 Clymer
Annadown Thomas, clerk, 9th ab Coates
Annadown Thomas, shoemr., 49 N 2d
Annadown Wm., clerk, 16 Magnolia
Anneley Wm., harness mr., 5th n German
Anners Henry F., bookseller, 141 Chestnut
Anning John D., painter, P road bel Federal
Annis Josiah, waiter, 216 Lombard
Ansbey George, silver plater, 5 Kenworthy's ct
ANSEL MYER, exchange broker, 74 S 3d
Ansis William, M. D., 165 Pine, h 2 Twelve Foot al
Ansley Isabella, gentw., Jackson ab Adams
Ansley John, plasterer, 3 Howard pl
Ansley William, plasterer, Jackson ab Adams
Anson Louis, 181 12th bel Willow
ANSPACH, BROTHER & CO., dry goods, 90 N 3d
Anspach John, mer., 90 N 3d, h 345 N 6th
Anspach Wm., mer., 90 N 3d, h 326 N 6th
Anstice William, trimming store, 5th ab Poplar
Antelo A. J., mer., 21 S whfs., h 257 S Front
Anthony Chas., soil makr., Carpenter ab 8th
Anthony David, bootmaker, 2 Juniper lane
Anthony Elizabeth, 10 Kenworthy ct
Anthony Geo., plasterer, rear 19 Elizabeth (N L)

Anthony George W., seaman, 15 Ellen
Anthony Joseph, blindmaker, 283 S 3rd
Anthony Joseph, carp., Sarah n Bedford, (K)
Anthony Jos., carp., Penn ab Poplar, h Sarah bel Bedford, (K)
Anthony Joseph W., machinist, 627 S 2d
Anthony Saml., cordw., rear 31 Charlotte
Anthony Simon, cordwainer, rear 31 Charlotte
Anthony Wm., clothes, 43 Chest., 15 Little Pine
Antrim Eliza, 1 Clymer st
Antrim Charles, watchmr., Clinton ab Brown
Antrim P., dentist, 63 S 2nd
Apker Henry, lab., Hughes' ct (S)
Apkey Henry, rope mak., Marriott, n 6th
App George, pumpmr., F road bel Franklin, (K)
App George, sen., pumpmr., 46 F road n Queen, (K)
App Jacob, cabinetmr., Hanover bel Franklin, (K)
App Rosanna, shop, 332 St. John, (K)
App Samuel, watchmaker, F R n Queen, (K)
Appelbia John, tailor, 104 Lombard
Apple Chas., brushmr., 12th bel Callowhill
Apple Elizabeth, N E 4th and Brown
Apple Henry, cooper, Christian ab 9th
Apple Henry, cooper, 59 S Water, h 94 S Front
Apple Henry, blacksmith, 8th n Willow
Apple Henry, wheelwright, 8th and Willow
Apple Jacob, 10 Barber's row
APPLE JOHN, alderman, 360 N 3rd
Apple John, jr., cigar mak., 16 School
Apple Mrs. Mary Ann, Sch Front, ab Mulberry
Applegate Daniel T., bricklayer, 92 S 12th, h 143 N 12th
Applegate Edw., lab., rear Beach ab Poplar, (K)
Applegate Francis, tavern, 135 S Water
Applegate Jediah, baker, 480 N 4th
Applegate John, carter, 574 S 2d
Applegate Robert, bricklayer, 2 Beldin row
Applegate Sarah, 2 Furlong's ct
Applegate John, mariner, rear 92 Christian
Applegate John, carter, Sp Garden, ab 8th
APPLETON C. W., M. D., N E 12th and Filbert
Appleton D., cordw., c Sheaff's al and Madison
Appleton George S., bookseller, 148 Chestnut
Appleton George W., tailor, 43 N 6th, h 8th bel Poplar
Appleton Jno. W., hatter, Madison & Sheaff's al
Appley Luther, bookseller, 10 Arcade
Apt Charles, harness maker, rear Coates bel 9th
ARALL PHILIP, blacksm., 3 Cressman's ct
Arbuckle David, shoemr., N E 13th & Locust
Arbuckle Joseph, watchmaker, 37 Mechanic
Arbuckle Samuel, paper carrier, 2 Greble's ct
Arbuckle Thomas, lab., Dunton bel Franklin (K)
ARBUCKLE WILLIAM, Western Hotel, 288 High
Arbuckle Wm., lab., Murray, n Sch 2d
Archambault Joseph, tavern, 130 N 2d
Archambault V. E., dry goods, N E 11th & High
Archer Abel, furniture car, Dunton ab Otter (K)
Archer Ben., ferry house, Callowhill

Archer Charles, brushmr., Marriott ab Fisher
Archer Chas., carter, rear 25 Allen (K)
ARCHER ELLIS S., oil and lamps, 32 & h 55 N 2d
Archer George S., mer., 8 S Water
Archer Isaac, drayman, Sarah n Bedford, (K)
Archer James, weaver, Cadwalader ab Jefferson, (K)
Archer Jeremiah, porter, Bedford bel 8th
Archer Job, brushmr., Queen ab F road, h Crown bel Franklin, (K)
Archer John, tailor, Hutchinson ab Poplar
Archer Pearce, carter, Poplar n 10th
Archer William, weaver, Oxford ab Front (K)
Archibald Jno., silver plat., Duke ab Cherry (K)
Archibald Robert, sailmr., Washington ct
Ardis George, lab., 15 Reckless
Ardis John W., carp., 69 Carpenter (S)
Ardis Wright B., carp., 5th and Wharton
Ardley Alexander, drugt., 76 S 2d, h 62 S 5th
Ardley Charles, 62 S 5th
Arensfelt Henry, locksmith, 19, & h 9 Norris' al
Arey E. Mrs., 153 S 9th
Arey Henry W., att'y and coun., 153 S 9th
Arey John, paper hanger, 36 Prune
Arey Rebecca, R road below Buttonwood
Arfford Conrad, blacksmith, Washington ct
Argue David, plasterer, Poplar bel 9th
Arick Jno., gunsmith, Phœnix bel G T road (K)
Arkins Mary, 9 Union sqr
Arkins George, acct., 9 Union sqr
Armbrust Charles, baker, 2 Helmuth ct
Armbruster Amelia, Carpenter ab 3rd
Armbruster John G., brushmr., 136 Callowhill
Armbruster Joseph, carter, O Y road ab Tammany
Armbruster Peter, brushmaker, 223 N 3d, h 81 Callowhill
Arment Wm., coach painter, Nectarine bel 9th
Armitage Joseph, foreman, Allen & Shackamaxon (K)
Armitage Thomas, blacksmith, Vine n 12th, h Carlton ab 12th
Armitage Thomas J., ven. blindmr., 23 N road
Armitage John, painter, 141 N 12th
Armitage Jos., lumber mer., Callowhill ab Sch 3rd
Armitage Robt., bootmr., N 8th bel Vine
Armor Alex., carp., 13th ab Spring Garden
Armour Jacob, bootmr., 31 Apple
Armour Wm., gent., 267 Coates
Armrod Thos., manuf., Frankford road, n Marlborough (K)
Armstrong Alex., stonema., 13th and Catharine
Armstrong Andrew, seaman, 9 Union st (S)
Armstrong Andw., tobac., 51 S Front, h Sch 6th and Pine
Armstrong Allen, mer., 11 N Water
Armstrong Ann, shop, Pearl ab 12th
Armstrong Benj., tailor, 343 N Front
Armstrong Chas., tailor, 464 N 2d
Armstrong Dav., bricklr., Howard ab Master (K)
Armstrong Edward, att'y and coun., 108 S 4th
Armstrong Elizabeth, dressmr., 139 Locust

Armstrong Francis, manuf., 141 G T road
Armstrong George H., beer house, 327 Cedar
Armstrong Geo. W., clk., 12 Richard
Armstrong Henry, porter, 5 Little Pine
Armstrong Jackson, lab., Perry bel Phœnix (K)
Armstrong Jacob, Wood ab 12th
Armstrong Jacob, Myrtle bel 12th
Armstrong Jacob, clk., rear Nectarine ab 10th
Armstrong James, carp., Juniper ab Cedar
Armstrong James, carter, Orchard
Armstrong Jas., weaver, G T road, bel Phoenix (K)
Armstrong James, weaver, Front ab Master (K)
Armstrong Jas., hatter, Otter n Frankford road (K)
Armstrong Jas. J., cabinetmr., 19 Dock ·
Armstrong John, weaver, Sch Front ab Filbert
Armstrong John, blacksm., Clay av (K)
Armstrong John, lab., Fitler bel Harrison (K)
Armstrong Jos. T., carp., 8 John st (S)
Armstrong Littleton, clothing, 125 N 2d, h 5 Lebanon
Armstrong Lybella, 64 S 11th
Armstrong M'Kimmey, clothing, 50 N 2d, h 5 Lebanon st
Armstrong Peter, dealer, 58 Tammany
Armstrong Rebecca, wid., 302 S 10th
Armstrong Robert, lab., Clay bel Beach
Armstrong Robert, 13th ab Shippen
Armstrong Robert, blacksm., rear 9th ab Coates
Armstrong Saml., currier, 343 N Front
Armstrong & Taylor, paper dealers, 336 N Front
Armstrong Thos., fireman, Jefferson ab Front (K)
Armstrong Thos. G., dentist, 88 Mulberry
Armstrong William, M. D., 53 Union
Armstrong Wm., cabinetmr., 22 Walnut
Armstrong Wm., tailor, 343 N Front
Armstrong Wm., weaver, 13th ab Fitzwater
Armstrong Wm., weaver, Murray
Armstrong Wm. G., engraver, 25 Minor
Arney Elizabeth, 343 Lombard
Arnold Ann, sempstress, 33 R road
Arnold Catharine, 30 Union
Arnold Conrad, baker, Thompson and Sch 7th
Arnold E., mer., 10 Bank, h 16 Chatham
Arnold Francis, baker, Shippen bel 8th
Arnold Frederick F., baker, Parrish ab 13th
Arnold Gottlieb, confect., G T road ab Jefferson (K)
Arnold Jacob, cordw., Noble bel 9th
Arnold John, tailor, rear 114 Cherry
Arnold John H., bookbinder, 5 Logan
Arnold John W., shoemr., 14 Swanwick st
Arnold I., dry goods, 106 N 3d, h 79 Union
Arnold Maria, rear 41 Chester
Arnold Mayer, mer., 63 & 65 High, h 275 N 6th
Arnold Michael, tavern, 233 Callowhill
Arnold Morris, mer., 68 N 3rd
Arnold Mrs., wid. of Jacob, 258 N Front
Arnold Samuel, cordw., rear 493 N 3rd
Arnold, Springer & Co., dry goods, 10 Bank
Arnold Wm., shoemaker, Pine and Quince
Arnold Wm G., bookbinder, 4 Marble pl
Arnot Geo. J., marble cut., Carlton ab Sch 6th

Arnot Jas., mariner, 2 Braceland's ct
Arnoux Joseph P., oysters, N W 11th & Pine
Aronheimer A., clothing store, 246 Callowhill
Arrants Richard B., sea capt., 108 Coates
Arrison Henry D., blacksmith, 77 Dillwyn, h 60 Tammany
Arrison John C., brickmr., Montgomery pl
Arrison John P., sashmaker, 4 State
Arrison Joseph, watchman, 52 W Cedar
Arrison Matthew, jr., bricklr., Ogden ab Sch 7th
Arrison Matthew, gent., Sch 7th and Poplar
Arrott Colin, M. D., 16 S 12th
Arrowsmith E., capt., 110 N 6th
Arthur & George, sashmrs., Broad and Paper al
Arthur Jas., bookbinder, Arcade, h 8 Jefferson row
Arthur James, weaver, Bank (pl) bel Pine
Arthur Mary, 107 N 10th
Arthur Robert, confr., Poplar ab Charlotte
Arthur Robt., sashmr., Broad and Paper al
Arthur T. S, gent., (W P)
Arthur Wm. C., clerk, 4 Flower st
Arthurs Andrew, shoemr., High n Sch 5th
Artsen Richard, lab., Hancock ab Phoenix (K)
Arundel R J., att'y and coun., 89 Sassafras, h 122 S 10th
Asay Abraham M., dentist, 329 Sassafras
Asay Charles, lab., 56 Washington av
Asay John, shoes, 13 N 8th
ASBURY SAM'L & CO., com. mer., 85 S Front
Asch Aaron, dry goods, 6th and Spruce
Asch Joseph M., mer., 100 High, h 103 Spruce
Asch & Pincus, umbrellas, 100 High
Ascough John, blacksmith, Front bel Maiden, h 14 Laurel
Ascough Thos., blacksmith, G T road and Haydock
Ascough Wm., blacksmith, 143 New Market
Asendorph Catharine, 10th ab Ogden
Ash Charles, victualler, Apple ab George (N L)
Ash C. I., boots and shoes, 146 S Front
Ash Franklin, carp., 33 Brandywine
Ash F. T., coal mer., 15 Walnut
Ash Geo. W., goldbeater, Hubbell ab Catharine
Ash George W., alderman, 194 N 6th
Ash George W., carp., Melon bel 10th
Ash Jacob, carter, Vaughan n Walnut
Ash James, tavern, 184 Callowhill
Ash John, lab., 16 M'Duffie
Ash Joseph, porter, 220 S 7th
Ash Joshua P., com. mer. 22 and 24 N 2d
Ash Joshua W., M. D., 45 S 5th
Ash J. T., carp., Swanson ab Christian
Ash Michael W., atty. and coun., 66 S 6th
Ash Morgan, broker, 79 S 3rd, h Sch 6th ab Walnut
Ash Robert, carp., Brown bel 10th
Ash Sebastian, confectioner, 171 Green
Ash Thomas, carp., c 10th and Washington
Ash William, tavern, N W Coates and Kesler
Ash Wm., baker, 78 Spruce
Ash Wm. R., clerk, Oneida pl
Ashbridge Thomazin Mrs., 321 Mulberry
Ashbrook James, grocer, S E 2d and Queen, h 54 M. road

2

Ashbrook Joseph, sailmr., 113 Christian
Ashbrook J. & Co., grocers, S E 2d and Queen, h 54 M. road
Ashbrook Thos., carp., 70 M. road
Ashbrook Thomas C., tailor, 1 Wood
Ashburn James C., jeweller, 61 Dock, h 166 Christian
Ashburner Adam, mer., Poplar ab 10th
Ashburner Algernon E., mer., 6 S whfs, h 15 S Sch 7th
Ashburner Benjamin, clerk, Woodland (W P)
Ashburner Wm. E., teacher, 239 S 9th
Ashby Albert, lab., 11 Cox
Ashby Franklin, hatter, S E 4th and High, h 116 N 5th
Ashby & Rocap, batters, S E 4th and High
Ashcraft Hugh, gardener, Bedford bel Hanover (K)
Ashcraft Joseph, tailor, M. road ab Carpenter
Ashcraft Josiah, carter, N E Reed and Church
Ashcraft M., milliner, 172½ S 2d
Ashe Wm. J., music store, 68 S 4th
Ashenfelder Josiah, wheelwright, 2d bel Phœnix (K)
Ashenfelder Sarah, mantua maker, St John ab George (K)
Asher Michael, dyer and scourer, 208 Cedar
Ashford Jno. R., glove manf., Coates & Marshall
Ashford Wm. H., ladies' shoe st., 18th Parrish
ASHHURST JOHN, mer., 80 High, h 129 S 6th
Ashhurst Lewis R., mer., 80 High, h Walnut W Broad
Ashhurst Rich'd, mer., 80 High, h 263 Mulberry
Ashhurst Richard & Sons, mers., 80 High
Ashhurst W. H., mer., 80 High, h 248 Chestnut
Ashley Thomas, rigger, 7 Wilson
Ashman Jas. A., cordw., Grubb st.
Ashman James J., stair rod manuf., 12 Loud
Ashman John, lab., G T road bel Master
Ashman Peter, oysterman, bel Washington bet 6th and 7th
Ashman Peter, ice dealer, R road, ab Sp Garden
Ashman Susanna, ladies' shoes, 115 N 2d
Ashman & Taylor, ladies' shoes, 115 N 2d
Ashman William, tailor, 384 N 3d
Ashmead A. S., druggist, S E 12th and Pine
Ashmead Charles J., conveyancer, 72 S 5th
Ashmead Geo., druggist, 235 High, h 247 Mulberry
Ashmead Geo. & Co., druggists, 235 High
ASHMEAD GEORGE L., atty. and coun., 106 S 4th
Ashmead Isaac, printer, rear 146 Chestnut, h 7th ab Spring Garden
Ashmead John, gent., Gaskill and 3d
Ashmead John B., cabinetmr., 65 N 4th
Ashmead John W., atty. and coun., 60 S 6th, h 130 Pine
Ashmead Samuel, mer., 61 Walnut
Ashmead Samuel B., mer., 61 Walnut
Ashmead Samuel & Son, finding st., 61 Walnut
Ashmead Thomas E., mer., 24 N Front, h S E Sch 8th and Chestnut

Ashmead Wm., M. D., 247 Mulberry
ASHMEAD WM. E., druggist, 12th and Pine
ASHMEAD WM. L., Pine n 3d
Ashmore Abraham V., carver, 393 S 6th
Ashmore John, cutler, 50 N 2d
Ashmore Luther M., coach paint., 162 Marshall
Ashton Ann, Randall's ct
Ashton Danl. R., teacher, 46 N 5th, h 98 S Front
Ashton George, druggist, 257 N 7th
Ashton Geo., drug & spice deal., Poplar bel 6th
ASHTON ISAAC M., hats, 200 High, h 144 N 12th
Ashton Isaac S., carp., h 247 S 9th
Ashton James, mariner, Front bel Catharine
Ashton John, tailor, 16 and 18 High
Ashton John, waiter, 2 Little Pine
Ashton John, jr., tailor, 30 High, h 185 S 5th
Ashton Joseph S., Beach bel Shackamaxon (K)
Ashton J., grocer, N W Front and Reed
Ashton J. R., clerk, 134 Catharine
Ashton Richard, carp., F road and Montgomery
Ashton Samuel, cooper, 266 N 2d, h 76 New st
Ashton Samuel, 472 Callowhill
Ashton Samuel K., M. D., Lombard and 10th
Ashton Susan, shop, Brown and Marshall
Ashton Mrs. S., 370 S 4th
Ashton Thos., currier, Carpenter bel 9th
Ashton Thomas, boarding, 134 N 8th
Ashwald Stephen, Callowhill ab Sch 8th
Ashworth James, plasterer, Ogden bel Ridge R
Ashworth Thos., mariner, Hope bel Master (K)
Askin Richard, carp., 10 Helmuth
Askings Ann, layer out of dead, 298 S Front
Askins Jas. H., shoe store, 522 High st
Aspden John, machinist, 97 S Front
Aspell George, tailor, 10th ab Poplar
Aspinall Nathan, cabinetmr., Pratt
Aspinwall Geo. W., mer., Dock st wharf, h 260 Walnut
ASSON WM. T., mer., 9 Commerce, h 78 Walnut
Astic Peter, vict., Conrad's ct (N L)
Atack Danl., carp. weaver, Hope n Jefferson
Atcheson Joseph, weaver, Cadwalader ab Phœnix (K)
Atherby John, dealer, Allen ab Shackamaxon (K)
Atherholt Chris., jr., brickmr., rear G T road ab 5th (K)
Atherholt Isaac, brickmr., 6th bel G T road (K)
Atherholt Jacob, brickmr., 6th bel G T road (K)
Atherton Henry, atty. and coun., 325 Chestnut
Atherton Henry, broker, Walnut ab 6th
Atherton Humphrey, real estate, Walnut n 6th
ATHERTON H. & SON, real est. broker, Walnut ab 6th
Atherton Nathan, carp. Perry bel Pine
Atherton Nathan, watchmaker, 113 S 12th
Atkins Charles, carp., 28 Blackberry al
Atkins James B., cabinetmr., Marion ab 2d
Atkins Juliana, 10th ab James st
Atkins Rich'd, tavern, Front and Shippen
Atkins Robert, plasterer, Watt
Atkins Wm., flour inspector, 67 Wood
Atkinson Arch'd, carter, Hancock ab Master

Atkinson Bennet J., painter, rear 101 Dillwyn
Atkinson B. G., tailor, 64 Chestnut
Atkinson Charles, grocer, N E Cedar & Water, h 74 Swanson
Atkinson Eliza, stock store, 52 N 8th
Atkinson George, weaver, 6th ab Master (K)
Atkinson Isaac S., umbrellamr., 77 Cedar
Atkinson Joel, Cherry W of 10th
Atkinson John, drayman, 14 Juniper la
Atkinson John C., lab., 12 Kenworthy's ct
Atkinson Joseph L., bricklayer, 413 S 2d
Atkinson Mary, washer, Crown ab Duke (K)
Atkinson Rebecca, 279 Marshall
Atkinson Saml., botanic physician, 633 N 2d (K)
Atkinson Thomas, weaver, 18 Lloyd's ct (K)
Atkinson T. B., baker, Washington (W P)
Atkinson Wm. W., painter, rear 80 Green
Atlee David, lab., 8 Burd's ct
Atlee Edwin A., M. D., Sp Garden bel 13th
Atlee W. L., M. D., 3 Colonnade Row
Atmore Edward, jeweller, 59 Gaskill
Atmore Frederick, grocer, 175 Buttonwood
Atmore John B., carp., Nectarine & Moore's ct
Atmore R. jr., grocer, N W 10th & Buttonwood
ATMORE R. & F., grocers, N W 10th and Buttonwood
Attmore Marshall, mer., 7 High, h 18 N 5th
Attmore & Shumway, boots and shoes, 7 High
Attmore Wm. P., carp., 21 Sergeant
ATWOOD & CO., dry goods, 124 High
Attwood Wm. N., dry goods, 18 N 8th
Atwood James, mer., O Y road n Green
Atwood John M., mer., 124 High, h 362 Walnut
Atwood Origen, 441 High
Auble David, tavern, Vine bel 12th
Auble Nathan, shoe store, Franklin & Callowhill
Auck Jesse, weaver, School opp Edward (K)
Audenreid A C., 254 N 7th
Audenreid Lewis, coal mer., 61 Dock
Auffort Fred'k, cordw., Wood ab Queen (K)
Auffort Fred'k, jr., cordw., Dyott's ct (K)
Auffort Geo., fisherman, Wood ab Queen (K)
Augee Wm., stationery, 69 Green
August Anthony, lab., Mechanic ab Franklin (K)
August Jacob, lab., Wood ab Franklin (K)
Augustin Joseph, stevedore, 1 Warner's ct
Augustin Lewis, tinplate-worker, N E Juniper and High, h 88 North 11th
Augustin Mary F., confectioner, 123 S 3d
Augustin Peter, bricklayer, 46 Washington av
Augustus Eliza, washer, 7 Richards
Augustus Mary, ice cream, 9 Park
Augustus Samuel, lab., Liberty ct
Auld Andrew, weaver, Bedford bel Broad
Aull Wm., stone cutter, 9 Wall
Auner C. H., stationer, 79 Cherry
Auner G. A., carp., Minor, h 60 S 11th
AUNER JOSEPH G., bookseller, 333 High, h 382 Walnut
Auner Wm., watchman, 13th ab Olive
Austie Henry, mer., 139½ High, h 197 Walnut
Austin Alexander, 55 Shippen
Austin Alvah, tinsm., 33 Carlton
Austin Ann, tailoress, Ross ct
Austin Anna, n c Wood and West (K)

Austin Charles, carter, 6 Poplar
Austin Collins, sen., b. h., Sch 8th ab Sassafras
Austin Collins J., tinsm., 462 Sassafras
Austin David, carter, Herrices' ct
Austin Eliza, gentw., 222 Spruce
Austin Franklin, tinsm., Division bel 12th
Austin George, cordw., rear Apple ab George
Austin Hosea, oysterman, 332 S 5th
Austin John B., acct., 11 Jefferson Row
Austin John E., hatter, 48 Noble, h 9 Green (N L)
Austin Margaret, confectioner, 364 S 2d
AUSTIN SAMUEL H., atty. and coun. 193 Walnut
Austin Seth, tavern, N E Front and Otter (K)
Austin Wm., grocer, S E Flower and Fitzwater
Austin Wm., tinsm., S W 13th and Callowhill
Autz Adam, carpet weaver, G T road n 4th (K)
Averell Israel G., baker, 332 Sassafras
Averley Jacob, Front bel Master (K)
Avery Henry, dentist, 88 Mulberry
Avery Isaac, straw manuf., 88 Mulberry
Avery Lydia Ann, teacher, N 10th
Avery Sylvian, gentw., 10th bel Parrish
Avis George, h 214 N 5th
Avis John W., lab., Court al
Avy Lewis, blacksm., 59 Mead al
Awl Ann C., 21 St John
Awl Jacob, lithograph, 165 S 11th
Awll C. W., 110 Crown
Axe Joseph, combmr., Charlotte bel George
AXFORD E. J., mer. tailor, 165 Spruce
Ayars Jas. B. Rev., Wallace bel 10th
Ayars Samuel, painter, St John and Coates, h 88 Poplar
Ayars Zebul. I., harnessmr., rear 9 Charlotte
Ayers Saml. W., tobac., 59 S 3d, h 224 S Front
Aykroyd Henry, vict., Brown ab 12th
Aylesbury & Miller, milliners, N W 3d & Green
Ayres Cabel, carp., Prospect al
Ayres Charlotte, washer, 26 Mayland
Ayres Elizabeth, 5 Warner's ct
Ayres George, porter shop, Cedar bel Front
Ayres Geo. R., mer., 57 N whfs, h 40 Palmyra sq
AYRES & HAWKINS, coal, 11th and Willow
Ayres Henry, coachman, Pearl ab 13th
Ayres Henry R., trimmings, 49 N 8th
Ayres Hiram, coal office, 11th and Willow, h 40 Palmyra sq ab Wood
Ayres Jacob, tailor, 97 E Lombard
Ayres John, smith, 20 E North, h Cresson's al
Ayres John, stock. weav., rear 10th ab Coates
Ayres Jonathan B., blacksm., Olive bel 13th
Ayres Joshua, lab., 34 Bird's ct
Ayres Robt., Dunton n Otter
Ayres Robert, tailor, 161 E Lombard
Ayres Samuel, painter, 94 New Market
Ayres Wm., carter, Vineyard (F V)
Ayres Wm., mer., 42 N 3d
Azen Rachel, Coates n Sch
Azpell Thomas T., teacher, 35 Spruce

————

Babb Peter, mer., Pleasant bel 10th

Babb Samuel, grocer, 6th and Christian

Babbit Wm. W., mer. 7 Commerce, h. 26 Madison

Babcock N. L., machinist, 14 Whitehall st

Babcock John H., cordw., 436 N 3d

Babe George, hatter, 303 N 2d

Babe John, hatter, 56 N 2d

Babe Owen, weaver, Crown ab Franklin (K)

Babington John, brushmr. 163 Christian

Babneu Joseph, carp. 6 Jenning's row

Bach Louisa, Apple ab Poplar

Bach Peter, cabinetmaker, New Market and Young's al

Bache Franklin, M. D., S. E. Juniper & Spruce

Bache Frederick A., carp. 6 Kessler's al

Bache Hart, U. S. A. 97 George, h. 13th ab Pine

Bacher John D., baker, 127 Callowhill

Bachley Adam, baker, Hanover op. Bedford (K)

BACHMAN HENRY, tavern, 323 High

Bachman Jacob, carp. 184 St. John

Bachman Jacob jr., rear 406 N 3d

Backes John, tailor, Smith's al (N L)

Backus E. F., gent. 161 Walnut

Backus Frederick R., 44 N whfs., h 17 Vine

Bacon Alexander, broker, 60 Walnut, h Ogden ab 10th

Bacon Allyn, paper-boxmr., 20 Spruce, h 43 Shippen

Bacon Benj. Curtis, Sp Garden, 8 doors bel 11th

Bacon Benj. R., undertak. Queen b Marlboro'

Bacon Chas. C., engineer, Fraley's ct (K)

Bacon Chas. W., gent. 269 Green

Bacon Chas. W., clerk, 7th n Green

Bacon Chas. W. jr., mer. 4 S Water, h 16 New Market

Bacon David, carp. 192 N Front

Bacon Dennis, lab. 2 Eagle ct

Bacon Edmond P., flour, 24 High, h 3 Green

Bacon Edward, mer. 10 S 2d

Bacon Enos, tailor, 6 Boyd's av

Bacon Francis, hatter, 50 N 6th, h 117 Sassafras

Bacon Franklin, mer. 13 S Front

Bacon G. V., convey'r. 206 Arch, h 16 N 11th

Bacon & Hallwell, hats, &c. 173 High

Bacon Hosea H., lab. Elizabeth bel Poplar

Bacon Isaac, shingle shaver, West ab Marlboro'

Bacon James, lab. 18 Raspberry

Bacon Job, waterman, 2 Swanson ct

Bacon Job, mer. High ab 5th, h Locust E Sch 8th

Bacon John, gent. office 74 S 3d, h 117 Sassafras

Bacon Joseph, flour, 24 High, h 192 N Front

Bacon Jos. W., bricklr. Beach bel Palmer (K)

Bacon Josiah, mer. 127 High, h 61 Marshall

Bacon J. & E. P., flour and grain, 24 High

Bacon Richard, carp. and undertaker, c Queen and Han over (K)

Bacon Rich'd. W., mer. 131 High, h 91 Marshall

Bacon Samuel, 188 N Front

Bacon Samuel, cordw., Cadwalader bel Phœnix (K)

Bacon Sarah, Hamilton village

Bacon Smith, 364 S 4th

Bacon Wm., waiter, 10 Acorn al

Bacon Wm., coachman, Fox's ct

Bacon Wm. C., carp., 149 G T road

Bacon Wm. H., mer. 173 High, h 231 Vine

Badger Benj., cooner, Wheat ab Wharton

BADGER SAMUEL, notary public, 60½ Walnut, h Sch 7th n Spruce

Badger Samuel jr., atty. & coun. 139 S 5th, h 163 S 9th

Badger Wm., atty. & coun. office 60½ Walnut, h N W 9th and Pine

Badlum Joseph, trimmings, 63 Pine

Baeder Chas., glue, 86 High, h G T road ab 5th

Baer Charles, 388 Coates

Baell Wm., blacksm. rear 531 N 4th

Baen Margaret, shoebinder, 8 Hallowell st

Baenheimer Lazarus, pedler, Roney's ct (K)

Bagge Elizabeth, 7 John (S)

Baggs James B., tailor, S W 4th and Chestnut, h 409 Mulberry

Baggs Thomas, lab. 289 S 6th

Baggs Thomas G., dentist, 409 Mulberry

Bagiot Julies, bootmaker, rear 360 S 2d

BAGLEY, MAKENZIE & Co., Columbia House, 207 Chestnut

Bagwell Edward, bricklayer, rear 72 Christian

Bagwell Ric'd., bricklayer, rear 72 Christian

Baier Andrew, store, 313 Callowhill

Baildon John, weaver, 2d bel Phœnix (K)

Bailey Anthony, tinware, 362 Cedar

Bailey Caroline, Cherry ab 13th

Bailey Daniel, brickmr. Master ab 3d (K)

Bailey David, carp. Carlton ab 12th

Bailey Edward, carp. 7 Quarry, h Noble & New Market

Bailey Evan, carp. Cherry n 13th

Bailey E. Westcott, 407 Mulberry

Bailey James, 272 Callowhill

Bailey John, waterman, rear 19 Beaver (K)

Bailey John, weaver, South ab 11th

Bailey John, weaver, Cedar ab 7th

Bailey John H., steward, Carpenter ab 13th

Bailey Jos. stonecutter, Franklin & O'Neal (K)

Bailey Joseph, 12 Penn av

BAILEY J. T., jeweller, 136, & h 441 Chestnut

Bailey Lydia R., printer, 26 N 5th

Bailey Nathan, conveyancer, 33 N 5th

Bailey Orin, clerk, 5th and Chestnut

Bailey Peter, shoemr., George n Sch 7th

Bailey Phebe, Shield's al

Bailey Rachel, milliner, 143 Beach (K)

Bailey Sam'l., conveyancer, Beach ab Maiden(K)

Bailey Sam. B., lumber, 20 Laurel (C) h 239 S 3d

Bailey Wm., Vine ab Sch 8th

Baille James, mer. 81 Dock

Bailleul George, printer, Relief

Bailleul N. C., painter, 7 S 6th, h 135 S 9th

Baily & Brother, dry goods, N W 13th & High

Baily S. L., dry goods, 477 High, h 153 Filbert

Baily Thomas L., mer. 477 High

Baily Wm., watchmr. 216 High, h 7th ab Sp Garden

Baily Wm., dyer, rear 591 N Front (K)

Bain M. Mrs., milliner, 268 Chestnut

Bainbridge Radcliffe, cordw. Atherton

Bainbridge Susan, 320 Walnut

Bainger Henry, tailor, 526 N 2d (K)

Bains Edward, 76 Crown

Bains Geo. B., trunkmr. 8 N 4th, h 412 9th

Baird Alexander, printer, 9 George, h 10th bel Buttonwood

Baird A., grocer, Sch 7th and Carlton

Baird George, carp. 8 St. Joseph av

Baird James, grocer, N W 13th and Shippen

Baird James, carp. 13th ab South

Baird James, st. cut, 7 Perry

Baird John, st. cut, Brown bel

Baird John, grocer, Otter and School (K)

Baird John, collector, 57 Green

BAIRD JOHN, Marble Works, R road bel Green

Baird Jos., teacher, Brown bel Broad

Baird Matt., machinist, 10th ab Washington

Baird Thomas, lab. Brown bel R road

Baird Thos R., brushmr. 122 N 3d, h 41 Franklin

Baird Wm., manuf. 122 High, h Beach n Shack-amaxon (K)

Baird Wm. M., mer. 46 S whfs., h 76½ Lombard

Baisley John, whf. build. Crown ab Queen (K)

Baisley M., grocer, 243 N Front

Baisley Sam'l., whf. build. Crown ab Queen (K)

Baitzel George, printer, 87 O Y road

Bakeoven Elizabeth, Queen ab Vienna (K)

Bakeoven John, fisherman, Queen ab Vienna

Bakeoven Louisa, Vienna ab Queen (K)

Bakeoven Peter, fisherman, Queen ab Vienna

Bakeoven Wm., fisherman, Bishop bel Queen (K)

Baker Abigail, Swanson bel Christian

Baker Abraham, mer. S W 5th and High

Baker Ann S., nurse, 1 Hause's ct

Baker Benj., pilot, rear 205 S 5th

Baker Catharine, 307 Lombard

Baker Catharine, 47 New Market

Baker Cath., shoebinder, 71 F road (K)

BAKER CHALKLEY, tavern, N W 9th and Cherry

Baker Charles, cabinetmr. Winter ab George

Baker Chas., cordw. Vienna bel Franklin (K)

Baker Chas. H., mer. 40 Walnut, h 310 Mulberry

Baker Christian, cordw. 45 New Market

Baker Christ., lab. Hanover ab Franklin (K)

Baker Conrad, waterman, Bishop bel Queen (K)

Baker Cond. P., waterman, Queen ab Vienna (K)

Baker Cor's., combmr. 3 Cadwalader ab Franklin (K)

Baker C. M., painter, 69 Race, h Elizabeth and Poplar (K)

Baker Daniel, currier, 10 Logan

Baker Daniel, rear 87 S 6th

Baker Daniel, pilot, 15 Mead

Baker Danl. M., combmr. Hope and Franklin

Baker David, police office, 166 S 10th

Baker David, carp. Paul ab 6th

Baker Edward, lampmr. 7 Quigg's ct n Vine

Baker Edwin G. A., jeweller, 7 Cherry

Baker Engard, Rugan ab Callowhill

Baker Eliza, Palmer bel Queen (K)

Baker Eliza, milliner, G T road bel 6th (K)

Baker Eliza, Brown bel 7th

Baker Elizabeth, 8th ab Master (K)

Baker Elizabeth, milliner, 165 Cedar

Baker Elizabeth J., Weccacoe ab Queen

Baker Frederick, hatter, 272 N 7th

Baker George, hair dresser, 215 Chestnut

Baker George, vict. 122 New Market

Baker Geo., carter, Franklin ab Front (K)

Baker Geo., wheelwright, Dorothy n Sch 4th

Baker Geo., tailor, rear Marriot bel 6th

Baker George A., tavern, 13 Spruce

Baker George C., fisherman, Queen bel Cherry

Baker George N., lumber mer. 106 Marshall

Baker G. N. & B., lumber, S W 5th and Brown

Baker Henry, lab. Locust ab 6th

Baker Henry, cabinetmr. 217 St. John

Baker Isaac F., lamp manuf. 176 Chestnut, h 393 Mulberry

Baker Isaac N., currier, 10th ab Ogden

Baker Jacob, victualler, 32 Brown (N L)

Baker Jacob, brickmr. 7th ab Master (K)

Baker Jacob, fisherman, Queen ab Vienna (K)

Baker Jacob, cigarmr. 34 Laurel (K)

Baker Jacob, 672 N 2d (K)

Baker Jacob G., carp. Miller's ct (N L)

Baker James, cordw. Cobb's ct

Baker James, coachman, 9 Raspberry

Baker James, grocer, 49 Gaskill

BAKER JAMES, mer. 43 N whfs., h 49 Gaskill

Baker Jane, 74 Brown (N L)

Baker Jesse, bankboxmr. 22 Bank

Baker J. & Co., grocers, 43 N whfs.

Baker John, ropemr. Franklin bel Cherry (K)

Baker John, waterman, 10 Callowhill

Baker John, acct. 17 Spruce

Baker John, lab. Mackey ab 2d

Baker John, oysterman, Sch Willow ab Spruce

Baker John, shoemr. 45 Currant al

Baker John G., lab. rear 402 N 2d

Baker Jno. H., office S E Chestnut and 3d, h 342 S 4th

Baker John L., conveyancer, Pine W Sch 7th

Baker John M. S., painter, 361 S 6th

Baker John R., mer. 150 High, h 24 N 11th

BAKER JOHN W., 9 N whfs., h 166 Mulberry

Baker Joseph, hardware mer. 473 N 2d, h 179 G T road (K)

Baker Joseph, acct. Sch 8th ab Vine

Baker Joseph, carp. Perkenpine ct

Baker Jos. E., combmr. 459 N 3d

Baker Joshua, patternmr. Washington ab 5th

Baker Louisa, tailoress, 176 Marshall

Baker Margaret, gentw. 272 N 7th

Baker Maria, 17 Penn

Baker Mary, 3 Ronaldson

Baker Mary, dressmr. F road opp Otter

Baker Mary A., 84 Beach bel Maiden (K)

Baker M. V., mer. 215 High, h 166 Mulberry

Baker Michael, ropemr., F road ab Franklin (K)

Baker Michael, agent, 66 S 12th

Baker Michael, gent., 166 Mulberry

Baker Michael, clerk, Elizabeth ab Poplar

Baker Moses, mer., 211 N 2d

Baker Mrs., Sch 6th bel High

Baker Peter, clerk, Buttonwood bel 13th

Baker Samuel, waterman, Queen ab Palmer (K)

Baker Samuel, cordw., Poplar bel 7th

Baker Susannah, 74 Crown

Baker Thomas U., printer, Rutter & Federal

Baker Valentine, tailor, S W Water & Walnut, h 5 Relief

Baker Valentine, fisherman, Palmer bel Queen

Baker William, cordw., 8 J. Baker's ct
Baker William, tailor, 62 Oak
Baker Wm., painter, 7 Rachel (N L)
Baker Wm., ship carp., Hanover ab Queen (K)
Baker Wm., segar mr., 2 Little Green (K)
Baker Wm. D., att'y, 65 S 3d, h 131 Vine
Baker Willam G., wad. manuf., Charlotte ab George
Baker Wm. S. & C. M., paint. & glaz., 69 Race
Bald R., engraver, h 4 S 10th
Bald Wm. R., grocer, 2d and Poplar
Baldinger Jacob, tailor, Mercer and Warren
Baldt Elizabeth, widow, Crown ab Duke
Baldt Frederick, whipmr., Hanover and Franklin (K)
Baldt Frederick, Hanover ab Franklin (K)
Baldt Fred'k., jr., cordw., rear 296 St John
Baldt Mary, Hanover bel Franklin (K)
Baldt John, carp., West bel Vienna (K)
Baldt John, shoemr., Frankford road n Cherry (K)
Baldt Wm., carp., Hanover and Franklin
Baldwin Adam, carter, Vienna bel Franklin (K)
Baldwin Elizabeth, b. h., 385 N 4th
Baldwin John N., painter, 9 Buttonwood, h 83 Buttonwood
Baldwin Joseph, chair painter, Hall's avenue.
Baldwin Joseph B., cordw., 72 Washington av bel Brown
Baldwin M. M., engraver, 116 Chestnut
BALDWIN M. W., machinist, locomotive and engine builder, Broad and Hamilton, h 160 S 10th
BALDWIN STEPHEN, mer., S W Front and Walnut, h 258 Walnut
Baldwin Thomas, teacher, rear 49 N 7th
Bales Mary, spooler, Phoenix ab Cadwalader (K)
Bale Israel, saddler, Beckett st
Balfe Joseph, Rev., Willing's al
Balfe Sarah, Prospect al
Balfe Thomas, bootmr., 7 N 7th
Baley Bart., skin dresser, Sarah & Bedford (K)
Baley John, lab., 438 N Front
Ball Alexander, bootmr., 6 Kelly's ct
Ball Ann, 12 Knight's ct
Ball Anna Maria, Baxter's av
Ball & Dilkes, tailors, 126 N 13th
Ball Elizabeth, washer, Loud bel 10th
Ball Frederick, clerk, 36 Callowhill
Ball George, cabinetmr., 514 N Front
Ball George W., gent., 411 Spruce
Ball Geo. W. J., 1 Baxter's avenue
Ball Henry, 163 Wood
Ball Israel R., grocer, N W 2nd and Catharine
Ball Jacob, shoemr., 8 Coomb's al
Ball James, shoemr., 8 Coomb's al
Ball Jesse R., type founder, 205 Pine
Ball John, mer., 42 N 4th, h 292 10th bel Melon
Ball John, carp., 10 Filbert, h 23 Rittenhouse
Ball John, boot fitter, Harper's pl
Ball John R., carp., Carpenter's ct
Ball Laetitia, Rush's ct
Ball Samuel H., drayman, Hope bel Master (K)
Ball Sarah, sempstress, 119 Plum
Ball Stephen H., engineer, G T road ab 6th

Ball Wm., rigger, Workman's ct
Ballard Hagar, S E Locust and Quince
Ballard John, waiter, 33 Prosperous al
Ballenger Wesley, carp., 164 Cherry
Ballentine Robt., carp., Moon's ct
Ballentine Samuel, weaver, 9 Myers' ct
Ballier John B., tavern, 235 S 4th
Ballinger John, shoemr., rear 32 Catharine
Ballinger John W., bootmr., 317 S 2d
Ballinger Thomas, skin dresser, 335 Callowhill
Ballinger Thos., plasterer, Washington bel 6th
Ballinger Wm., plasterer, Washington bel 6th
Balshaw Wm., brk. mr., Lombard ab Sch Front
Baltz Daniel, cabinetmr., 4 Pearl
Baltz Fred'k., farmer, Lily al. ab Green
BALTZ J. P., tavern, 340 N 3rd
Baltzer George, varnisher, Poplar ab 9th
Balz Henry W., carp., Bridge (M V)
Balz John, weaver, Bridge b Village
Balzer Lewis, lab., Alder ab Poplar
Bamber Margaret B., shop, 326 S 6th
Bamford John, bookseller, 27 S 8th
Bamar Wm., vict., Mechanic ab George
Bamont Mary, rear 448 Sassafras
Banagan Jas., weav., Charlotte ab Thompson (K)
Bance Anthony, shoemr., 262 S 6th
BANCKER CHARLES G., Sec'y. Franklin Fire Ins. Comp. 163½ Chestnut
Bancker Charles N., Prest. Franklin Fire Insurance Comp., 163½ Chestnut
Bancroft Addison, dry goods, 32 Bank
Bancroft Daniel, sea captain, 183 Christian
Bancroft Gideon K., blacksmith, 13 Decatur, h 51 Carpenter ab 3d
Bancroft John, blacksmith, 125 Christian
Bancroft John, dyer, 4th below Franklin, h 442 N 4th
Bancroft John, jr., soap and candle manuf., 19 Wood, h 24 St. John
Bancroft M., tailor, 101 Cherry
Bancroft Reuben F., blacksmith, 13 Decatur, h 374 S 5th
Bancroft R. F. & G. K., blacksmiths, 13 Decatur
Bancroft Thos., flannel manuf., 6th ab Master
Bancroft T. H., paint. & glaz., Filbert n Sch 7th
Bancroft Wm., book-keeper, 65 Tammany
Bane Henry, shoemr., 553 S 2d
Bane John C., lab., Scott's ct (N L)
Baner Mark, carter, New Crown bel Green
Baner Wm., cordw., N 12th ab Vine
Banes Mrs. Ann, b. h. 10 S Broad st
Banes Benj. C., carp., Mechanic ab George
Banes Charles, turner, 184 Poplar
Banes Euphemia, shoe bind., rear 211 St. John
Banes James, carp., 347 N 6th
Banes James, cordw., 13 Laurel
Banes Thomas, coach sp. mr., 130, & h 132 New Market
Banfield Martha, Orchard
Banford James, tavern, 195 S 6th
Banger Timothy, 15 N 12th
Banger Thomas, pocket book mr., 2 Moore's ct
Banister Edward, carpet warehouse, 269 High, h 9 Carlton sq

Banker Wm., Christian ab 7th
Banks Archibald, weav., Philip ab Jefferson (K)
Banks Edward, waiter, 5 Lyndall al
Banks H. O. D., druggist, Washington (W P)
Banks John, teacher, 5 Miles al
Banks John, 159 N 7th
Banks Mary, 126 N 2d
Banks Solomon, porter, 33 Cherry
Banks Wm., whitewasher, 56 Perry
Banks Wilson, blacksmith, Broad bel Vine, h 1 State st
Bankson Lloyd, gilder, 108 N 4th
Bankhead Robt., weaver, Oxford bel Front
Bankhouse Peter, cabt. makr., Palmer n West (K)
Bannen Joseph, carp., rear 90 Cherry, h 3 Valley's ct
Bannen Wm. R., carp., Lewis ab Poplar
Banning Wm. L., att'y & coun., 207 N 6th
Bannister Z., dry goods, 174 Sassafras
Banner John, carp., 201 Callowhill
Bannon Simon, carp., Dutch ct
Banton William, bootmr., 166 S 5th
Banton Wm. D., boot black, S W 3d & Walnut
Baptiste Eugene, cabinet mr., 129 Locust
Baratet Amelia, dress mr., 94 S 8th
Barbazett Sophia, shop, 308 S 4th
Barbe Francis, tobacco'n't, 140½ Chestnut ab 6th
Barbelin Rev. Felix J., St. Joseph's church
Barben Tobias, carp., rear 7 Elizabeth (N L)
Barber Alexander, cordw., 33 N 11th
Barber Edward, paint. & glaz., 7th bel Poplar
Barber Edward, weaver, G T road bel Master (K)
Barber Edw. & H. A., painters, 242 Green
Barber Geo. C., mer., 46 N 2d
Barber H. A., painter, 220 N 11th
Barber James, bricklayer, State n Sch 7th
Barber Jas., clocks, 238 High, h 10 Franklin
Barber James, grocer, Lombard ab Sch 2d
Barber Joseph, machinist, 1 Beldin Row
Barber Joseph, cordw., Poplar ab 7th
Barber Robt. V., bricklr., Beach bel Palmer (K)
Barber Saml., tailor, 112 N 8th
Barber, Slack & Lee, dry goods, 46 N 2d
Barber Wm., optician, 83 Sassafras
Barber Wm. L., cordw., Beach bel Palmer (K)
Barbier Francis, tailor, 154½ Sassafras
Barbier Maria, widow, 129 Buttonwood
Barbier Stephen, jeweller, 7 Boyd's av
Barbin Wm. M., confect., Jefferson ab 4th (K)
Barclay Andrew C., mer., 40 N wharves, h 147 Mulberry
Barclay Benj. S., music teacher, 92 Walnut
Barclay Corah, 12 Wharton
Barclay George, paver, Sch 7th n Vine
Barclay Henry, carp., 9 Perry
Barclay James J., att'y and coun., N W 7th and Walnut, h 219 Spruce
Barclay John M., 14 Portico sq
Barclay John K., trader, 400 High, h 484 Sassafras
Barclay John K., grocer, 10th and Vine

Barclay Margaret, gentw., N W 3d & Callowhill
Barclay Mary, tailoress, rear 202 Lombard
Barclay Robt., cordw., rear 517 N 3d
Barclay Valentine, boot crimper, rear 214 St. John
BARCROFT, BEAVER & CO., dry goods, 163 High
Barcroft S. B., mer., 163 High, h 359 Sassafras
Barcroft Tunis Q., grocer, cor. Tammany & Old York road
Barcus John, lab., Sch 7th n Cherry
Barcus Stephen, carp., 11 Bickham st
Barcus Stephen, Sch 7th ab Mulberry
Bard Allen, carp., 7th ab Poplar
Bard Conrad, silversmith, 205 Mulberry, h 267 Callowhill
Bardeer Jackson, plasterer, Lewis ab Poplar
Bardeer Saml., coach trimr., Parrish ab 13th
Bardin Amos, tailor, Cadwalader and Franklin
Bardin A. Z., M. D., 151 O Y road
Bardin Levi, shipmas., 361 S Front
Bardon B., wid. of Nicholas, dealer, 249 Cedar
Bardon Mary, 1 Humphrey's ct
Bardsley John, books, 46 Mulberry
Bardsley John, spinner, 84 S Water
Barford Wm., shipmaster, 3 Young's place
Barge Mary, tailoress, 447 N 3rd
Barger Benj., cooper, M'Dewitt's av (K)
Barger Benj., cust. house, Shield's ct
Barger Chas., carp., Monroe and Cherry (K)
Barger Charles, cordw., 5th bel Camac
Barger George, watchman, Buttonwood bel 6th
Barger Geo., parchment manuf., 5 Warner's ct
Barger Jacob, jr., cooper, Cadwalader bel Master (K)
Barger Jacob, cooper, G T road bel Master (K)
Barger John, printer, Bledisloe pl
Barger John, brickmr., 464 N 3d
Barger Martha, shoe bind., rear Orchard ab Rawle
Barger Samuel, brickmr., Alden ab Poplar
Barger Thomas, pressman, 266 N 5th
Barger William, paint. and glaz., 26 W North
Barger Wm. H., brickmr., Alden ab Poplar
Barker Abraham, broker, 16 S 3d, h 176 S 10th
BARKER, BROTHERS & CO., exch. brokers, 16 S 3d
Barker Calvin H., lumber merch., Shaxamaxon ab Queen, (K)
Barker Daniel, boatman, Lombard n Sch Bank
Barker David, cabmr., 1 Fisher's ct
Barker James, cordw., Charlotte bel Beaver
Barker James, mariner, 5th bel Christian
Barker James, tailor, R road bel S Garden
Barker John, shoemr., Catharine bel Flower
Barker John R., mer., 161 High, h 518 Chestnut
Barker Joseph, tailor, P road ab Carpenter
Barker Peter, saddler, 434 N Front
Barker Richard, acct., 155 Queen (S)
Barker Wm., tobacconist, 78 George (S)
Barker Wm., waterman, Sch Beach ab Spruce
Barlow Hillyard, spinner, Callowhill bel Sch 3d
Barlow John, machinist, Otter & F road (K)
Barlow Joseph, grocer, Ann n R road (F V)
Barlow Joseph, plasterer, Cobb

Barlow Thos., blacksm., Mariner bel Front, h
  Queen ab Sarah (K)
Barn John, weaver, Phillips ab Jefferson (K)
Barnard Chas. G., coal, Franklin bel Marlboro'
Barnard James, tailor, Dean ab Bedford (K)
Barnard Joseph C., store, 81 R road
Barnard Robert W., printer, 127 Christian
Barnard Samuel, tailor, 23 Pratt
Barnard S. E., dressmr., 179 S 11th
Barnard Thomas, stonecutter, 179 S 11th
Barnard Wm., printer, 48 Mead.
Barnay Charles, lab., Juniper ab Lombard
Barndollar Daniel, cooper, 48 Laurel (N L)
Barndt Henry, grocer, N E Green and 9th
Barned A., milliner, 2d bel Beaver (K)
Barnes Abraham, drayman, 5th n George (N L)
Barnes Albert, Rev. 123 S 8th
Barnes Andrew, cooper, 37 Christian
Barnes Andrew J., carp., Westford av
Barnes Anna, 81 N 5th
Barnes Barnet, cordw., Horstman's ct.
Barnes Catharine, nurse, 15 Nectarine
Barnes Charles, carp., Centre ab Brown
Barnes & Co., oyster cellar, 242 N 2d
Barnes Daniel, cordw., Brown's ct
Barnes George W., painter, 59 Apple
Barnes Henry, tavern, 5th and Master (K)
Barnes Henry W., brewer, 35 Chester
Barnes Jacob, carp., Parrish ab 9th
Barnes James, moulder, 5 Scott's ct
Barnes James, mariner, 68 Queen
Barnes Jas., boatman, Mulberry & Sch Front
Barnes Jas. M., watch case maker, 4 Ellet's av
Barnes John, carp., 4th ab Jefferson (K)
Barnes John, pawnbroker, 349 Cedar
Barnes John, weaver, Front ab Master (K)
Barnes John B., shoemr., 35 Strawberry
Barnes Joseph, hatter, Washington av
Barnes Joseph, confectioner, 300 Coates
Barnes Joseph, plasterer, Parrish ab 9th
Barnes Joseph S., boat builder, Prime n Front
Barnes Martha, rear 2 Charlotte
Barnes Matilda, washer, 50 German
Barnes Merrick, band box manuf., 6 Bread
Barnes M, Mrs., 2 Ranstead pl
Barker Maria, rear Marriott ab 5th
Barker Sarah, Christian ab 6th
Barker Thos., farmer, Rorndaffer's ct
Barnes Oliver A., band box mr., 33 Jones' al
  (C) h 2 Ranstead pl
Barnes Rufus L., map mounter, N E 7th and
  High, h 142 N 10th
Barnes R., wheelwt., George bel 5th
Barnes R., gentw., 165 Walnut
Barnes Samuel, hatter, Carlton bel Sch 6th
Barnes Sanford, blacksmith, Mechanic ct
Barnes Sarah, b h, 123 Green
Barnes Spencer, 28 John (S)
Barnes Shermon D., shoemr., 81 N 5th
Barnes Thornton, capt., Sch 7th ab Cherry
Barnes Thomas S., turner, Mechanic bel Culvert
Barnes Wm., bricklayer, 64 George (S)
Barnes Wm., skin dresser, Haydock bel Front
Barnes Wm., painter, 276 N 7th
Barnes Wm., combmr., 9 Rachael st

Barnes Wm. Rev., 30 Sch Rittenhouse
Barnes Wm. B., carp., 61 Mulberry
Barnes Wm. C., carp., George bel Apple
Barnes Wm. D., att'y., 47 S 4th, h 9th bel Fitz-
  water
Barnes Wm. W., printer, Marriott ab 3d
Barnestead Thomas, mast yard, Mead al (S) h
  28 Catharine
Barnet Joseph, com. merchant, 129 N Water, h
  241 N 7th
Barnett, Nesbit & Garretson, com. mers., 62 N
  whfs. and 129 N Water
Barnett Wm., watchman, Fox's ct
Barnett Wm. P., trunkmr., 151 Race, h 118
  N 5th
Barney Alonzo, tailor, 5 Filbert av
Barney Charles, gas fixer, Juniper ab Lombard
Barney Martin M., type founder, 634 S 2d
Barnholt Elizabeth, gentw., 237 St John
Barnholt Geo., vict., Parrish bel Sch 7th
Barnholt P., vict., Parrish bel 12th
Barnett Jacob, engineer, 89 St John
Barnett John, weaver, Dorothy n Sch 3d
Barnett Mary, tailoress, 89 St John
Barnett & Pyke, pen manuf., 138 S 2d
Barnholt Wm., vict., Pleasant av
Barnhurst Joseph, brass founder, Francis n Sch
  5th (F V)
Barnhurst Joseph, jr., umbrella furniture manu-
  facturer, Francis n Sch 5th (F V)
Barnhurst Wm., Brown bel Broad
Barns Paul, oak cooper, 293 S Front
Barns Wm. W., baker, Catharine & P road
BARNWELL JOHN, tavern, 6 Decatur
Barnwell Robert, bonnet presser, 5 N 10th
Baroux Nathaniel T., combmr., 30 N 6th
Barr Ann, 2 Holmes' al
Barr Benjamin, mer., 81 N 3d
BARR DANIEL, tavern, 139 N Front, & Cal-
  lowhill n Bridge
Barr Daniel, lab., 123 Swanson
Barr Geo, carp., Ross ab Queen (K)
Barr Hugh, oyster house, 95 N 3d
Barr Hugh, grocer, N E 4th and Sassafras
Barr Jas., bookseller, 53 S 12th, h 45 Perry
Barr Jas., clerk, 4 York ct
Barr Jane, shop, 116 S 10th
Barr John, lab., Pearl bel Nixon
Barr John, grocer, High W Sch 7th
Barr John, carter, Sharbon's ct
Barr John, cabinetmr., 131 N 6th, h 8 Magnolia
Barr John, cabinetmr., 131 N 6th
Barr Michael, clothier, 131½ N 2d
BARR OWEN, tavern, 141 N 2d
Barr Peter, gardener, 5 Poplar ct
Barr Philip, 7 Mineral pl
Barr Robert, grocer, Charles & Buttonwood
Barr Samuel, lab., Pearl bel Nixon
Barr Susan, 8th bel Catharine
Barr Thomas, tobacconist, High bel Sch 5th
Barr Wm., tailor, Carlton n Sch 2d
Barr Wm., 4 Mint ct
Barr Wm., grocer, Lombard bel 13th
Barr Wm., bricklayer, 53 Rose al n Coates
Barras John, lab., Poplar st

Barras John.B., tailor, 222 High, h Franklin n Green
Barras John M., cordw., Barker E of Sch 4th
Barras Jos. J., jeweller, 20 Franklin pl
Barras & Walter, clothing, 222 High
Barras Wilhelmina D., 73 Logan
Barratt T. E., min. painter, 136 and 150 Mulberry
Barrel Moses, carp. weav., 440 N 3d
Barrett C. B., printer, 34 Carter's al, h 259 N 8th
Barrett Dan., glass bl., Vienna ab Queen (K)
Barrett Edward, 108 Gaskill
Barrett Elizabeth, gloves, rear 443 N 3d
Barrett H., cordw., 220 N 5th
Barrett James, brushmr., 1 Wagner's ct
Barrett James, com. mer., 86 S whfs., h 63 Pine
Barrett Jacob, lab., Emeline
BARRETT & JONES, publishers of Sun, 67 S 3d, and printers, 34 Carter's al
Barrett Joseph, seaman, Vine bel Franklin
Barrett Joseph, coachmr., 73 Queen
Barrett Lydia, washer, Gillis' al
Barrett Matilda, Cilles' al
Barrett Moses, lab., 95 Coates
Barrett Richard, butcher, Ontario ab Poplar
Barrett Riley, oysterman, Shoemaker's ct
Barrett Robert, carp., Shippen n Broad
Barrett Robert, bricklayer, 493 Vine
Barrett Thomas H., gymnasium, 274 High, h 146 S 10th
Barrett Wm., saddler, 5 Fayette
Barrett Wm. P., printer, Crawford's ct
Barrington Catharine, 7 W North ab 10th
BARRINGTON CHARLES, real estate broker, 79 Dock, h Chestnut n Sch 4th
Barrington Edmond, printer, 293 High, h Sch 6th n George
Barrington Ed. P., clerk, 133 N 10th
BARRINGTON & HASWELL, booksellers, 293 High (up stairs)
Barrington Martha, wid. of Charles, 152 N 9th
Barrington Samuel, M. D., U. S. Navy, 70 S.12th
Barron Benj. M., pilot, Marlborough bel Bedford (K)
Barron George, mer., 174 N 3d, h 336 N 6th
Barron John, shoemr., Ohio & 12th
Barron John, weaver, Camac & G T road (K)
Barron Michael, carp., Queen bel Vienna (K)
Barrott Samuel H., barber, 107 N 9th
Barrow J. D. & Co. mers., 20 Bank
Barrow Rebecca, gentw., Ann (F V)
Barry David H., cedar cooper, 7 Brooke
Barry Eliza, gentw., 15 Brown (N L)
Barry Jane S., b h, 376 Chestnut
Barry Job R., machinist, Broad n Brown, h 11 Hamilton pl (K)
Barry John, cedar cooper, 11 Elizabeth (N L)
Barry John, weaver, G T road and Lloyd's ct
Barry J. B., conveyancer, 127 Walnut, h 251 S 10th bel South
Barry L. Mrs. 40 Madison
Barry Mary, 9th bel Poplar
Barry Mary, 161 Pine
Barry Matthias, dealer, 1 Farmer's row
Barry Samuel, messenger, 1 Bonsall
Barry Samuel, lab., Callowhill ab Sch 5th

Barry Thomas, lab., Ann E Sch 3d
Barstow Wm., baker, Vine ab 13th
BARTALOTT & BLYNN, hatters, 304 High
Bartalott George, hatter, 304 High
Bartels Henry C., stove finisher, 202 N 2d
Bartenback John, baker, 354 S 2d
Barth Ann, b h, Clinton ab Parrish
Barth Gottlieb M., machinist, rear 13 Ogden
Barth John F., pat. bal. manuf., 3 Drinker's al
Bartholomew Henry, turner, Say st ab Sch 8th
Bartholomew A., acc't., 18 N 9th
Bartholomew Chas., lampmr., 13th and Brown
Bartholomew George, lampmr., Ann n R road (F V)
Bartholomew John, silv. pl. rear Lemon bel 11th
Bartholomew Thos., 14 Marion st
Bartholomew Wm., lampmr., 1 Nectarine
Bartle Catharine H., 470 Callowhill
Bartle Elijah, lab., Allen bel Marlboro' (K)
Bartle Frederick, milkman, rear Hanover ab Franklin (K)
Bartle Henry, cordw., Path and Moore's al
Bartle Jacob, stonemason, 6th & Franklin
Bartle Jacob, stonemason, Howard ab Oxford
Bartle Jacob, cooper, Coates n 13th
Bartle Jesse, cooper, Coates n 13th
Bartle John, pumpmr., Landell's ct (K)
Bartle Wm., pumpmr., Landell's ct (K)
Bartle Wm. jr., pumpmr., F road op Otter (K)
Bartleman John W., acc't., Catharine n 3d
Bartleson Amelia, teacher, 88 Buttonwood
Bartleson James, stonemason, 9 Franklin row
Bartlett Edward M., silversm., 326 S 4th
Bartlett Elizabeth, sempstress, 1 Harmony ct
Bartlett Geo. W., vict., 147 N 5th
Bartlett James, seaman, 187 S 4th
Bartlett Job, bricklayer, 11th ab Callowhill
Bartlett John, bandbox manuf., 67 Coates
Bartlett Thomas H., lab., F road and Franklin
Bartlett Wm., lab., rear Carpenter bel 10th
Bartley Henry, grocer, N W Sch Water & Cedar
Bartley Philip, b. h., 362 N 2d
Bartley Samuel, 29 Pratt
Bartley Wm., brickmr., Front ab Cedar
Bartling Jane, N W 4th and Walnut
Bartman Jacob, carp., Perry ab Franklin (K)
Barton Albert G. W., currier, Parrish bel Broad
Barton Edmond, clerk, 191 S 9th
Barton Eleanor, music teacher, Poplar ab 13th
Barton Elizabeth, sempstress, 1 Harmony ct
Barton George, hatter, 29 German
BARTON G. W., atty. & coun. 14 Washington square
Barton Henry, dealer in soap, &c., 294 Cedar
Barton Isaac, mer. 29 and h 27 S 2d
BARTON ISAAC, grocer, S E 2d and Sassafras
BARTON ISAAC & CO., dry goods, 29 S 2d
Barton James, grocer, 123 Wood
Barton John, b. h., 153 Cherry
Barton John, hatter, 38 George, h 201 S 4th
Barton John W., chemist, 4th bel G T road (K)
Barton Joseph, hatter, George and Shippen
Barton J. Rhea, M. D., S W Juniper & Chestnut
Barton Rebecca, 172 S 4th
BARTON ROBERT, importer, 50 Chestnut

Barton Samuel & Co., grocers, 243 N 2d, h 67 Vine
Barton & Smiley, grocers, 431 High
Barton Thos., hatter, 38 George (S) h 57 Shippen
Barton Thos. I., tailor, 29 N 13th
Barton Thos. P., gent., 318 Chestnut
Barton Wm. cabinetmr., 6 Norris' al
Barton Wm. C., acct., 29 N 13th
Barton Wm. P. C., M. D., 519 Chestnut
Bartram Isaac, gent., 92 N Front
Barwell Ann, 23 Morgan
Barwell John, vict., Franklin ab 4th (K)
Barwell William, tobacconist, 64 N 8th
Bascon Rosarnio, mariner, 37 Mead
Baskerville John, tailor, St Mary bel 7th
Basketter John, feed, Bedford bel Broad
Bass Mary, b. h., Vaughn n Locust
Bass Samuel, hair dresser, 12th bel Spruce
Basset A., carter, rear 150 N Front
Bassett Jacob, lab., 313 Cherry
Bassett Jacob, ship joine., Dean ab Bedford (K)
Bassett James, lab., 24 Pegg st
Bassett Maria, 81 Green
Bassett Susan, tailoress, 3 Washington pl
Basso Daniel, printer, 1 Young's pl
Bastable Danl., mason, Linden n Sch 7th
Bastert Geo., musician, Westford av
Bastian Anthony, paper sta., Ronaldson
Bastian George, gent., S E 7th and Spruce
Bastian John, potter, 13th bel Rose
BASTIAN JOHN, mer., 129 S Front, h 77 Spruce
Bastian Joseph, seaman's b. h., 24 Swanson
Baszley Saml., wharf builder, Crown bel Bedford (K)
Batchelder Alex. S., messenger, 6 Haines
Batchelor John, tobac., Coates c Washington av
Batchelor John, chemist, 87 St Johns
Bateman Esli, wood, Poplar st whf., h Penn bel Maiden (K)
Bateman Joel, seaman, 33 Green

Bates Susanna, gentw., 309 Pine
Bates Wm., combmr., Mechanic bel George
Bates William, brewer, Jones n Sch 5th
Bates William, mer., 9th bel Pine
Bateson John, carp., Cedar bel 10th
Baton Augustus Mrs., 344 S 4th
Batson E., Pearl ab Sch 8th
Batt Chalkley, drayman, rear School ab Rose (K)
Batt Elijah, cordw., 526 N 2d (K)
Batt John P., cooper, School ab Rose (K)
Batt Wm., bootmr., rear 33 German
Battau P., bootmr., Buttonwood bel 6th
Battell F., agent, 1 Minor
Batties Charles, lab., Pearl ab 12th
Battin J., sculptor, 477 Chestnut st
Battin Samuel, grocer, 304 N 2d
Battis Nicholas, oysterman, 31 Prime
Battis Susan, Allen bel Hanover (K)
Battis Wm. H., baker, 96 German
Batts John, St Mary ab 7th
Batts John, carp., Carlton bel Sch 7th
BATTURS EDWARD F., hardware, 14 Commerce
Batzig John, drayman, Cherry ab Duke (K)
Batzold Gotleib, furrier, 151 Poplar
Bauer Christian, vict., Queen ab Palmer (K)
Bauer Fred, huckster, 124 Charlotte
Bauer George M., baker, 187 Callowhill
Bauer G. L., baker, 79 Buttonwood
Bauer Jacob, lab., 2 Garrigues' ct (K)
Bauer John, sausage mr., Charlotte bel Thompson (K)
Bauer John, cabinetmr., 87 St John
Bauer John, lab., Brown ab 9th
Bauer John A., cab mr., 157 S 2d
Bauer Philip, cabinetmr., 36 Pegg st
Bauersachs John N., 260 High
Bauersachs L. C., importer, 170 High
Baugh Daniel, M. D., 67 N 10th
Baugh George K., cabinetmr., 213 N 3d
Baugh Harman, turner, 10 and 11 Elfreth's al

Baxter Isaac B., gent., N E 5th & Washington
Baxter Isaac B. jr. hardw. 244 S 2d, h 316 S 4th
Baxter James, waiter, Shippen ab 12th
Baxter James C., carp., 6 Townsend's av
Baxter John, grocer, S E 6th and Green
Baxter Thos., carp., rear Mulberry bel Sch 6th
Baxter Thos., painter, Catharine ab 9th
Baxter Thos. E., hardware, 244 S 2d
Baxter Willey Ann, N E Allen and F road (K)
Bayard Charles P., saddler, S W 2d and Queen
Bayard C. P., broker, 79 Dock
Bayard George, gent., 12th n Washington
Bayard George jr., carp., Wharton ab 4th, h 12th n Washington
Bayard James, atty. and coun. 159 Walnut
Bayard Thos., carp., 363 S 6th
Bayles Eve, Henderson's ct
Bayles John E., omnibus driv., Alden ab Poplar
Bayley Robt., clerk., N W Parrish and Marshall
Bayley Wm. R., musician, 12th ab Vine
Baylis & Brooker, auctioneers, 6 N 3d
Baylis John, hardw., 6 N 3d, h Catharine ab 4th
Baylis Isabel, milliner, 323 Pine
Baylis Joseph, 10th ab Catharine
Baylis. William, carp., 323 Pine
Bayliss Jos., wire worker, Marshall ab Poplar
Baylitts Davis, cordw., rear 365 S 5th
Bayman Jos., cordw., rear 198 Christian
Baynard Wm. C., shoemr., Sch 3d ab Spruce
Bayne James, bookbinder, 472 S 4th
Bayne John D., cabinetmr., 472 S 4th
Bayne Joseph, rule manuf., 18 Rittenhouse
Bayne Nathl. turner, 20 E North, h 4 Lombard ct
Bayne Rich'd S., Carleton ab Sch 3d
Baynon N. E., currier, 79 Mulberry, h 18 Marshall
Bea John, tailor, Mechanic ab Poplar
Beach Elizabeth, sempstress, 2 Nicholson
Beach Wm., agricultural impl., 366 High, h 34 Rittenhouse
Beachel John, broker, 66 Vine
Beagle Henry, blacksm., c Willow and Magnolia, h 224 N 5th
Beal Chas., clerk, 58 Chestnut
Beal Wm. L., dealer, Weaver's row (K)
Beale Charles, driver, N W Parrish and Ontario
Beale Chas., driver, G T road ab 4th (K)
Beale Edwin, dentist, George n Broad
Beale Francis, lab., Fitzwater bel Broad
Beale Jacob, sugar-refiner, Penn ab Cedar, h Nectarine n 10th
Beale John H., mer., 70 S Front
Beale Stephen T., dentist, 335 Walnut
Beale Wm. A., tailor, 51 S 8th, h 483 Vine bel Broad
Beall Jos., lab., Cherry n West (K)
Beam Chas., tobacconist, 10th ab Willow
Beam George, bootmaker, 60 S 4th
Beam Jacob, sign painter, S E 5th and Walnut
Beam Jesse B., bricklar., Mary st (W P)
Beam John, cordw., 354 N 10th ab Parrish
Beam Sam., lab., 6 Point Pleasant ct (K)
Beamer George, blacksm., Webb's al
Beamish John, clerk, Franklin bel Cherry (K)
Bean Catharine, Lisle ab Fitzwater

Bean Charles, grocer, Clinton bel Poplar (K)
Bean Ellen, sempstress, 58 Fitzwater
Bean Jas., cordw., Fitler st (K)
Bean Wm. S., machinist, Wood bel Sch 7th
Beans Catharine, 92 N 6th
Beans John, saddler, R road bel Green
Beans Matthew, saddler, Poplar ab 13th
Beans Rebecca, nurse, 274 St John
Beans Saml., saddler, Poplar ab 13th
Beans Sarah, New Crown bel Green
Bear Isaiah, millwright, 3 Demery ct
Bear Wm., trader, Hatter's ct
Beard Adeline, 49 Perry (K)
Beard James, stone cutter, 7 Perry (K)
Beard James, tavern, 2d and German
Beard Mary, 15 Noble
Beard Nathan, waiter, 166 Locust
Beard Nicholas, vict., 5th bel Camac (K)
Beard Thos. D., confectioner, 624 S 2d
Beard Wm., vict., 36 Charlotte
Beardman John, blacksm., 87 St John st
Beasten Geo., com. mer., 48 S whfs, h Catharine bel 7th
Beates H., apothecary, Sp Garden bel 8th
Beath David, warper, 13th n Fitzwater
Beath Robert, manuf., 404 High, h Lombard n Sch 5th
Beath Robert, lab., Patterson ct
Beath Wm., cordw., 39 Apple
Beaton Mary, milliner, 163 S 10th
Beattey Hannah, 11 Paynter's ct
Beattis Jacob, coach trimmer, 347 S 5th
Beatty Adam, manuf., 353 Pine
Beatty Andrew, tavern, Federal and Front
Beatty Daniel, cordw., Thorn's ct
Beatty George, cordw., Cadwalader bel Phœnix (K)
Beatty George, lab., George ab Sch 7th
Beatty Henry, provision, Callowhill bel Sch 7th
Beatty Isabella, Brasier ab Lloyd
Beatty Jas., manuf., 2d ab Master (K)
Beatty Jas., drayman, 247 S 5th
Beatty John, lab., G T road ab Master (K)
Beatty John, contractor, 2d bel Master
Beatty John, grocer, Sch 2d and Lombard
Beatty Jos., telegraph off., 159 Wood bel 11th
Beatty K., weaver, Sch 4th and M'Duffie
Beatty Patrick, porter, 58 New Market
Beatty Robert, lab., F road ab Franklin (K)
Beatty Robt., manf., 355 Pine
Beatty Samuel, manuf., 353 Pine
Beatty Samuel, baker, 91 Cedar
Beatty Samuel, watchman, Smith's ct
Beatty Samuel, cabt. mr., 231 Shippen
Beatty Wm., machinist, Penn ab Maiden
Beatty Wm., weaver, Lombard n Sch 2d
Beaugureau Jean, teacher, 193 S 9th
Beaugureau Philibert, teacher, 404 High, h 193 S 9th
Beaumont Davis, 11th bel Sp Garden
Beaumont G. H., M. D., 230 Pine
Beaumont William, bricklayer, R road ab Sp Garden
Beaver G. Robinson, grocer, 4th & Franklin (K)
Beaver Jacob, cap mr., Cherry bel Brown (K)

Beaver Robt., Philip ab Master (K)
Beaver Thos., mer., 163 High, h 191 N 6th
Beavers Charles, tailor, 3 Castle
Becher Joseph, harnessmr., G T road opp 6th (K)
Bechler John, grocer, Crown and Wood
Bechtel Abraham, mer., 235 N 3d, h 278 N 7th
Bechtel Catharine, b h, 10 S 7th
Bechtel C., b h, 74 S 2d
Bechtel C. G., baker, 10 Perry
Bechtel Fredk. W., baker, 449 N 2d
Bechtel George, cordw., 34 Green st
Bechtel Eve, wid. of Geo., gardener, West ab Palmer
Bechtel Jacob, tavern, R road ab Broad
Bechtel John, carter, 12th bel Parrish
Bechtel Samuel, tavern, Vine n Sch
Bechtell Martin, cottage garden, G T road (K)
Bechter A., brewer, N E 7th and Coates
Bechtold G. C., baker, 9 Elfreth's al
Bechtold S., provisions, 211 Sassafras
Beck Allen, lab., 6 Miller's ct
Beck Andrew, cabinetmr., 586 N 3d
Beck & Burns, tobacconists, 290 High
Beck B. Thos., mer., Water ab Vine, h 18 Ellen st (N L)
Beck Catharine, rear 219 St John
Beck Charles, dry goods, 85 Cedar and 1 S 9th
BECK CHARLES F., M. D., 310 Chestnut
Beck Charles W., painter, 179 O Y road
Beck Danl. W., shoemr., 27 W Howard
Beck D. B., painter, O Y road ab Green
Beck Euhard, cabinetmr., 54 Sassafras
Beck George, coach mr., Brown ab 4th, h 14 Charlotte
Beck George, baker, G T road ab Jefferson (K)
Beck George, lab., Parrish bel 10th
Beck Godfrey, lab., rear 4th bel Jefferson (K)
Beck Henrietta, b h, 115 N 5th
Beck Henrietta, b h, 290 N 3d
Beck Henry, shoemr., Corn ab Mackey
Beck Henry, stoves, 45 Walnut, h Orleans
Beck Henry, combmr., 13th ab Poplar
Beck Henry, paper stainer, Cherry n Sch 8th
Beck Henry A., lumb. mer., 135 Sp Garden
BECK HENRY PAUL, 347 Chestnut
Beck Isaac, engineer, Bush hill
Beck Jacob, turner, 3d ab Washington
Beck Jacob, trunkmr., 13 Quarry
Beck Jacob, carp., 275 N 7th
Beck Jacob, mer., 64 N Front, h 5 Comptroller
Beck Jacob, hatter, rear 22 Brown
Beck Jacob & Co., tobacco warehouse, 64 N Front
Beck Jacob S. carp., 15 Duke
Beck Jacob J. carp., Washington ab 6th
Beck Jacob Wm., crock. ware, 125 Locust
Beck Jas., pumpmr., 275 N 5th
Beck John, hatter, Wharton ab 2d
Beck John, calico printer, Coates n Fairmount
Beck John, drover, Cherry n West (K)
Beck John A., dentist, 290 N 3d
Beck John O., jeweller, 3d ab Washington
Beck Levi, tobacconist, 290 High
Beck Lewis, victualler, Buttonwood ab 10th

Beck Lewis D., baker, Beach bel Shackamaxon (K)
Beck Maria, 224 N Front
Beck Margaret, Sassafras ab Sch 7th
Beck Mary, sempstress, Clawger's ct
Beck Mary, rear 219 St John
Beck Michael, carter, G T road bet 6th & 7th (K)
Beck Peter, cabtmr., S Garden ab Franklin
Beck Peter, victualler, Buttonwood ab 10th
Beck Richard, reed mr., 244 N Front
Beck Walter, lab., 189 N Front
Beck Wm., carter, 26 Fitzwater
Beck Wm., carp., 533 Coates
Beckel James C., organist, 11th ab Buttonwood
Beckenbach Robert, boot and shoe maker, 171 St John
Becker Fred., 10 Emlen's ct
Becker Geo. J., teach, 121 Filbert
Becker Harriet, rear of 20 Rose al
Becker Henry, weaver, Front ab Franklin (K)
Becker Jacob, cordw., Parrish bel 10th
Becker Philip, saddles and harness, 182 N 3d
Beckers Louis, chemist, 34 O Y road
Becket Wm., tailor, 611 S 2d
Beckett Elizabeth, 1 Warren
Beckett Isaac, lab., Helmuth ct
Beckett T. J., superintendant N F Hall, 70 Locust
Beckhorne Garrett, 72 Catharine
Beckhorne Mary, shop, 428 S Front
Beckley Jacob F., tavern, Callowhill bel Sch 3d
Beckman Christian, baker, Carpenter n Broad
Beckman Daniel, carrier, Winter
Beckman Geo., R road bel Sp Garden
Beckman James W., bootmr., 148 St John
Beckman Joseph, grocer, 11 Cherry
Beckman Thos., planemr., Winter
Becks W. G., brewer, 113 Vine
Beckworth Wm., waterman, Court al
Becraft Alex., stock store, 342 S 2d
Bedell & Pearce, importers, 50 N 3d
Bedell Wm., jr., mer., 50 N 3d
Bedford Anna Maria, rear 114 Dillwyn
Bedford Benjamin W., painter, 48 Duke
Bedford Isaac T., bricklayer, 107 Dillwyn
Bedford Thos., health office, h Clinton av
Bedlock Edward, conveyancer, S E 3d & Walnut
Bedlock & Paschall, conveyancers, S E 3d and Walnut
Bedlock Wm. J., collector, Sch 6th ab Locust
Bedloe Thos. H., agent, 38 Strawberry
Bee Joseph, farmer, Union ab Franklin (K)
Beebe Boyd C., painter, Traquair ct
Beebe Stuart, mer., 163 High
BEEBE WM. N., oysters, 257 S 2d, h 409 High
Beech A. B., potter, Franklin bel 2d (K)
Beech Hester, Carpenter ab 6th
Beecher Hannah, b h, Mantua vil
Beecher Wm., mer, 81 N 5d, h 110 N 10th
Beechy Obadiah B., gardener, Brown ab Cherry
Beecroft Geo., blacksm., rear 19 N 7th
Beedle Mrs., 6 Plumston's av
Beehler & Beader, glue manf, 86 High

Bechler Charles H., carter, P road n Marriott
Bechler Tobias, mer., 86 High, h Marshall bel Green
Beck Ann, 1 Providence ct
Beckman Thos., 40 Currant al
Been Susan, wid., 214 S 7th
BEENKEN JOHN, groc.,329 N 2d, h 101 St John
Beer H., French and English sem., 65 Spruce
Beer John, carp., 146 Poplar
Beers Andrew, tinsm., Palm bel Brown
Beers David, painter, rear 450 N 4th
Beers James B., atty. & coun., S W 4th and Mulberry
Beers John, weaver, Front bel Master (K)
Beers John D., dentist, 212 S 3d
Beesley Edward, butcher, rear 6th ab Poplar
Beesley Edward, peg maker, 273 St John
Beesley Jacob, pattern mr., 273 St John
Beesley Jas., cordw., 503 Mulberry
Beesley Rawle, cabt. mr., Charlotte bel George
BEESLEY THEOPH. E., M. D., N W 10th and Mulberry
Beesley Wm., tailor, Wharton and Caroline
Beeson Maria, gentw., 10th ab Christian
Beggs John, blacksm., 69 St John, h 139 New Market
Begley Chas., painter, 57 Walnut
Begley S. M'M., lastmr., 45 Franklin
Begley Thos., lastmr., 57 Walnut
Begley Wm. H., lastmr., rear 63 Plum
Behler Cassamer, hat colourer, 43½ Noble
Behringer Matthias, lab., Buttonwood ab 13th
Beickley Henry, carter, Locust n Sch 5th
Beidelman Abraham 157 Green
Beidelman Charles, Nectarine bel 10th
eidelman Dan., grocer, 273 High, h 33 Jacoby
Beideman Danl. S., coal dealer, 53 Chestnut & Green st whf, h 53 Vine
Beideman George, shoemr., 6th n G T road (K)
Beideman Jacob, tobacconist, 6th bel G T road
Beideman Samuel C., ship carp., Warren above Beach (K)
Beideman Wm., glass-bl., Vienna ab Queen
Beideman Wm., dealer, 3 Seybold's ct
Beidemiller John, butcher, 6th ab Master (K)
Beilmix Eliza, widow, rear 104 New Market
Beisel Simon, black & whitesmith, G T road ab 5th (K)
Beisswanger Geo., carpet weaver, Coates bel 12th
Beisswanger Jacob, baker, 20 N Sch 8th
Beisswanger John C., cordw., Coates bel 12th
Beitel Jacob, baker, 114 N 8th
Beitel James, morocco dresser, 18 Duke
Beiteman George, carman, 6th bel G T road (K)
Beitler Abraham, tavern, High W Sch 7th
Beitler Daniel B., livery stable, High n Sch 7th
Beker Fred., 10 Emlen's ct
Belair James J., tobacconist, 85 Queen (K)
Belair Lewis D., scrivener, 150 Coates
Belch Mary, 11 Castle
Belcher H., boots and shoes, 4 N 3d
Beldin Joseph, huckster, Ashton and Sassafras
Bele Saml., lab., Shippen ab 13th
Belfield Henry, brass founder, James ab R road

Belfield H., brass founder, Wood ab 13th
Belford Cecilia, spooler, Phoenix bel Front (K)
Belford Geo., waiter, Rose al
Belford Michael, lab., Marriott's la ab 4th
Belk Wm., basketmr., Franklin bel Vienna (K)
Belin Chas. A., coal mer., Broad bel Walnut
Bell Aaron, lab., Callowhill ab 12th
Bell Alex., clerk, Oak and Till (W P)
Bell Alexander, grocer, 26 Pratt
Bell Alex. W., calico engr., 190 Callowhill ab Sch 6th
Bell Ann, sempstress, 118 Filbert
Bell Arthur, weaver, Master and Penn (K)
Bell Charles, gent., Morris
Bell Charles, jr., Morris
Bell David H., cabinetmr., 20 Barker
Bell David M., Richard and Sch 7th
Bell Edward, prov. store, 93 W Callowhill
Bell Elijah, coachmr., 31 Federal
Bell Eliza, 21 Flower
Bell Eliza, confect., 150 N 8th
Bell Elizabeth, b h, 313 S 3d
Bell Hannah, gentw., 9 Powell
Bell Harriet, Hope bel Phoenix
Bell Harriet, wid. of Wm. R., 73 St John
Bell Hester, Pearl n 12th
Bell Isaiah, jr., flour and feed, 326 N Front, h 6, Green
Bell Isaiah, Sch 8th n Vine
Bell Israel, carter, Cadwalader ab Jefferson
Bell James, labourer, Dorothy n Sch 3d
Bell James, patternmr., Sch 3d ab Sassafras
Bell James, warper, 4th n Creek
Bell James, distiller, N W 6th and Cedar
Bell James, sexton, 145 Queen
Bell James, manuf., Front bel Master (K)
Bell James, chair manuf., N 6th
Bell James Henry, 55 Queen
Bell James S., plasterer, Washington ab Front
Bell Jane E., shop, Franklin ab Front (K)
Bell John, planemr., Willow ab 2nd, h 88 Dillwyn
Bell John, M. D., 227 Spruce
Bell John, lab., Sch Willow bel Spruce
Bell John, coachman, Eagle ct
Bell John, lab., Cherry ab Queen
Bell John, confect., 60 N 8th
Bell John A., clerk, 181 Christian
Bell John M., tailor, 88 S 2d, h 18 Lombard
Bell John W., painter, 50 Charlotte
Bell Julianna, 20 Jefferson row
Bell Leonard K., clerk, 74 N 5th
Bell Levi H., flour and feed, 35 Lombard
Bell Lewis M., ship carp., Reckless ct
Bell Margaret, gentw., 333 Chestnut
Bell Maria, Carlton bel Sch 7th
Bell Mary, shop, 20 Green (C)
BELL ROBERT, office 79 S 3d, h 109 S 4th
Bell Robert, weaver, Jefferson ab 2d (K)
Bell Robert F., cooper, 18 Little Water, h 57 Penn
Bell Robert R., printer, 214 S 3d
Bell Rosetta, milliner, 87 N 7th
Bell Samuel, flour, 338 N 2d, h 119 New Market
Bell Samuel, distiller, 20 Jefferson row

Bell Samuel, distiller, S W 8th and Shippen
Bell Sandford, M. D., 47 Gaskill rear 124 S 2d
Bell Sarah, shopkeeper, Sch 4th and High
Bell Thomas, gent., 10th ab Christian
Bell Thomas, grocer, 2d and Edward (K)
BELL THOMAS, mer., 32 Church al., h 114 S 3d
Bell Wm., flour mer., 338 N 2d, h 22 Duke
Bell Wm., bricklayer, Orange bel Melon
Bell Wm., hairdresser, 211 & h 200 G T road
Bell Wm., trunkmr., 3d bel German
Bell Wm., lab., Perry ab Phœnix (K)
Bell Wm., shoemr., 2 Passmore's ct
Bell Wm. W., clerk, 402 S 3d
Bell W. D., com. mer., 53 N whfs, and 111 N Water, h 59 S 12th
Bellamgee Thomas, mer., 27 S 2d
Bellangee Isaac, bricklayer, 134 Green
Bellas James, mer., N W Broad and Cherry, h Sch 8th ab Cherry
Bellis Thomas, com. & forw. mer., 35 N Sch 8th
Bellerjeau Henry, brushmr., 72 N 3d
Bellerjeau Jacob, brushmr., William ab 4th
Bellerjeau & Rhoads, brush manuf., 72 N 3d
Bellerjeau Susan, dry goods, Beach ab Poplar (K)
Belling Andrew, combmr., Apple ab George
Bellis George, mer., 50 N whfs., Beach above Marsh (K)
Bellis George & Co., grocers, 50 N whfs
BELLOWS MARTIN, boot manuf., 13 Commerce, h 8th bel Brown
Bellows Wm. K., printer, Elizabeth ab Parrish
Bellsterling John F., combmr., 134 New Market
Belmer Philip, storekeeper, 2 Pleasant row
Belnap Stephen, jeweller, 13 Melon
Belrose John, 82 Chestnut
Belrose Louis, paper hangings, 100 Chestnut, h 102 S 5th
Belshaw Richard, lab., M'Duffie n 2d
Belsinger Samuel, variety store, 299 N 2d
Belt Edward, cordw., Briton bel 11th
Bendel Catharine, nurse, Alden ab Poplar
BENDER C. W., Star Hotel, 71 Dock
Bender E., carp., Dillwyn & Tammany, h 219 Marshall
Bender John, carp., 28 Tammany
Bender John A., carp., 43 Chatham
Bender Leonard, 12 Emlin's ct
Bender & Morris, carps., Dillwyn & Tammany
Bender Nathaniel, dealer, 80 W Willow
Bender R. P., tailor, rear 118 Dillwyn
Bender Wm., painter, York pl
Bender Wm. F., druggist, 224 Callowhill
Bendernagel Philip, baker, 458 S 4th
Bene John, lab., Palm ab Brown
Benedict J. C., 38 S whfs., h 455 S Front
Benedict Nathan D., M. D., Spruce ab Juniper
Benedict Samuel, hatter, 466 S 4th
Beneke Chas. H., mer., 87½ S Front, h 287 Green
Benerman Oliver, 20 Appletree al
Benesole Chas., hairdresser, Buttonwood ab 8th
Benezet John S., 27 N 12th
Benfer John, tailor, 109 Apple (N L)
Benfer J. C., 14 Coates
Benjamin C. D., broker, 92 N 5th

Benjamin Elizabeth, sempstress, 444 Sassafras
Benjamin Henry, Sch 3d and Wood
Benkert C., bootmr., 40 S 4th
Benkert Geo., bootmr., 20 Marion
Benkert John, tailor, 4 Cox
BENKERT LEONARD, bootmr., 209 Chestnut
Benner Adam, actor, G T road ab Jefferson
Benner Andrew, carter, Sch 8th ab Locust
Benner A. G., blacksmith, Carlton bel 13th
Benner B. J., cooper, 365 N 2d
Benner Charles, biscuit baker, 22 Vine
Benner Charles, grocer, Washington (W P)
Benner George, carp., Linden bel Green
Benner Henry, carter, Vaughn ab Locust
Benner Henry, collect., 338 St John (K)
Benner Henry, coach smith, 19 Shippen
Benner Henry L., earthen manuf., 39 German, h 377 S 3d
Benner Henry L., salt inspector, 110 Walnut
Benner Isaac, conf., 411 N 4th
Benner Jacob, brickmr., Bedford bel 13th
Benner Jacob, lab., rear Charlotte ab Thompson (K)
Benner John, brickmr., 205 Locust
Benner John, baker, 31 Noble
Benner Lewis, weaver, Ann ab R road (F V)
Benner Matthias, brickmr., Spruce ab 13th
Benner Ralston, locksmith, 16 Fayette
Benner Sarah, washer, 10th bel Catharine
Benner Sarah, wash., S E Lebanon and Fitzwater
Benner Sarah, gent., 365 N 2d
Benner Thos., ostler, G T road bet 6th & 7th (K)
Benner Elizabeth, 57 New
BENNERS, GEORGE & JAMES, wines and liq., 117 N 2d
Benners Geo., wine mer., 117 N 2d, h 219 Coates
Benners Henry B., mer., 35½ S Front
Benners Jas., wine mer., 117 N 2d, h 211 Coates
Benners John, vict., 13th and Wood
Benners Jos., blacksm., Wood bel Sch 3d
Benners, Smith & Campbell, manufs., 85½ S Front
Benners Wm. J., distiller, 117 S 2d, h N W Logan and Green
Bennett E., waterm., Queen & Cherry (K)
Bennett Alfd., watches, lard lamps 125 Chestnut
Bennett Andrew, mariner, 166 Swanson
Bennett Ann, 4th and Noble
BENNETT & CALDWELL, watchmakers and jewellers, 140 Chestnut
Bennett Catharine, wid. of Wm., Marlborough bel Bedford (K)
Bennett Charles, car driver, Fraley's ct (K)
Bennett Charles, broker, 48 Chester
Bennett Chas., coachman, rear Paschal's ct
Bennett Christine, lab., Carlton ab Sch 8th
BENNETT & Co., tailors, 192 High
Bennett David, ship carp., Bishop bel Queen (K)
Bennett Edward, mer., 28 N Front
Bennett Edward, weaver, Harmony ct (K)
Bennett Edward, clerk, 10th ab Washington
Bennett Eliza, nurse, rear 382 S 3d
Bennett Eliza, trimmings, German ab 5th
Bennett Eliza'th., wid. of Purnell, 7 Sommers' ct
Bennett George, grocer, Penn ab Poplar (K)
Bennett Geo. W., carter, Bedford bel Crown (K)

Bennett Henry, mariner, Swanson bel Queen
Bennett Henry, hardware mer., h Chancellor n Sch 6th
Bennett Henry, fisherman, Queen n Cherry (K)
Bennett Hiram, cordw., rear 308 St John
Bennett Horatio, lab., 5 Little Pine
Bennett Hugh, lab., Linn's row n (F M)
Bennett Jacob, brickmr., Mary ab F road (K)
Bennett Jacob, jeweller, 53 S 5th
Bennett Jacob, waterman, Queen bel Bishop(K)
Bennett James, lab., Dyott's ct (K)
Bennett James M., mer., 140 Chestnut, h 8 S Penn sq
Bennett Jeremiah, pilot, Front & Washington
Bennett John, shoemr., 478 N 2d
Bennett John, capmr., 1 S 8th
Bennett John, trunkmr., 85 Coates
Bennett John R., salesman, 77 Franklin
Bennett Joseph, carp., Bedford n Shackamaxon
Bennett Joseph, seaman, Gilles' al
Bennett Jos., draym., rear Front bel Phœnix(K)
Bennett Jos. M., tailor, 192 High, h 54 Filbert
Bennett Joshua J., carp., 13th ab Poplar
Bennett Mary, wid. of Abel, Queen ab Cherry(K)
Bennett Mary, Stoy's ct (K)
Bennett Mary W., stock and linen manuf., 89 Mulberry
Bennett & Martin, wood dealers, 28 N Front
Bennett Stephen, printer, 7th n Washington
Bennett Thomas, dyer, 2d ab Jefferson (K)
Bennett Wm. H., cordw., Haig's ct (K)
Bennett Wm. H., painter, Penn ab Maiden, h Queen bel Palmer (K)
Bennett Wm. P., carp., 69 Apple
Bennett Wm. J., saddler, 108 Christian
Bennett Wm. W., carp., 7th ab Brown
Bennett Wm. V., flour and feed, F road & Montgomery (K)
Bennett Witman R., miller, F road ab Oxford(K)
Bennis M., clerk, 15 Julianna
Bennis Henry, rear 121 Mulberry
Bennis John, cordw., 9th bel Coates
Bennison Joseph, carter, Spruce ab Sch 5th
Bensell & Allen, weigh masters, 34 S whfs
Bensell E. S., weigh master, 34 S whfs., h 415 Walnut E Sch 8th
Benson Alex., broker, 2 S 3d, h 103 S 8th
BENSON ALEXANDER & Co., stock and exchange brokers, 2 S 3d
Benson Catharine, S W 3d and Willing's al
Benson Gustavus S., broker, 2 S 3d, h 113 S 4th
Benson John, waiter, Jefferson ab 5th (K)
Benson John, plasterer, Harmony ct
Benson John, shoemr., rear Swanson bel Queen
Benson John, porter, 38 Prosperous al
Benson Stewart, stone cut., Bedford bel Clifton
Benson Thomas, carp., 68 George (S)
Bensted John M., chairmr., 34 Elfreths
Bentley Ann, shop, 497 N 3d
Bentley David & Sons, coppersmiths, 162 N 3d
Bentley David B., coppersmith, 162 N 3d, h 1 Logan
Bentley John, coppersmith, 62 Vine
Bentley John, gent., 3 Harmony ct
Bentley J. B., coppersmith, 162 N 3d
Bentley Mary Ann, gentw., 5 School

Bentley Wm., cigarmr., Green's ct (N L)
BENTON ALBERT, & CO., lumber mer., Carpenter and 4th, h 260 Swanson
Benton Edwin H., 383 N 13th
Benton John, brassfounder, 11 Gebhard
Bentz Matilda, N W St John and George (K)
Benyard E. C., jeweller, 396 S 5th
Bera Ferdinand, jeweller, 4 Starr al
Berens Augustus, prof. of music, 119 Race
BERENS BERNARD, M. D., 114 Mulberry
Berens Joseph, M. D., 242 N 6th
Beresford John, lab., Penn ab Poplar (K)
Beresford Richard, printer, 35 S 8th, h Shield's al
Beresford Robert, printer, 35 S 8th, h Federal ab 2d
Beresford Robert H., collector, 164 S 10th
Beresford R. & R., printers, 35 S 8th
BERG CHRISTIAN, boot and shoemr., 51 S 4th
Berg Gotlieb, baker, 435 N 3d
Berg Henry, tobacconist, 2 Lee's ct (N L)
Berg Joseph F. Rev., 8th ab Brown
Berg Leon, clothing, 26 Bank, h 124 Lombard
Bergenstock Reuben, lab., Mechanic ab Culvert
Berger Augustus, carp., Buttonwood ab 12th
Berger C. F., min. & port., painter, 116 Chestnut, h. Wood ab 10th
Berger Fred., spr. beer, G T road & Otter (K)
Berger Jacob, tavern, 228 N 2d
Berger John, butcher, 109 Poplar
Berger John T., engineer, 6 Wheelock pl (K)
Berger William, 34 St John
Berger Wm., com. mer., 53 N whfs., h 34 St John
Berghauser Jacob, mer., 30 Church al, h 2 Chatham
Bergman Sarah, finding store, 301 N 2d
Bergmann H. A., grocer, 65 Franklin
Bergin Lewis, carp., Beckett st
Bergin Wm., lab., rear 194 Cherry
Bergin William, drayman, Pike
Bering Harriet, gentw., 8 Pratt
Bering James, hosiery, 20 S 8th
Beringer John, drayman, Apple ab Poplar
Berkheimer Jesse, mason, Ogden bel 10th
Berkey Geo., carter, Ogden bel 10th
Berkleback Christy Ann, Alder ab Girard av
Berkleback Wm., planemr., rear G T road and 7th (K)
Berks John, grocer, N W 2d & Willow, h 346 N 6th
Bernadou J. B., mer., 89 S whfs., h 263 S Front
Bernard Edwd., trunkmr., 72 N 7th
Bernard John, sea capt., 138 Catharine
Bernard Wm. H., mer., 60 S Front
Bernardo Mary, dressmr., 1 St. Johns st
Bernd Adolph, tailor, 425 N 2d
Bernd Levi, mer., 425 N 2d
Bernhard Joseph, brass founder, 262 High
Bernhardt C. J., bootmr., 44 Brown (N L), h 195 N 5th
Bernheimer, Einstine & Co., dry goods, 63 & 65 High
Bernheimer Isaac, mer., 63 and 65 High
Bernheimer Lazarus, peddler, Roney's ct (K)
BERRELL & BURR, auctioneers, 297 High
BERRELL & FIELD, auctioneers, 445 High

Berrell George R., auctioneer, 445 High
Berrell Hannah, b. h., 347 High
Berrell Sarah, gentw., 5th bel Master (K)
Berrell Wm. S., auctioneer, 297 High, h 139 N 11th
Berringer John G., tavern, G T road bet 5th & 6th (K)
Berrow John, brass founder, G T road bel Master (K)
Berry Benj., blacksmith, 678 N Front (K)
Berry Benj. L., clerk, 481 S 2d
Berry Caspar, agt., Flickwir's ct
Berry Charles, oysterman, 32 Queen
Berry Chas., currier, 26 Shippen
Berry Edwd., blacksmith, rear 372 S 3d
Berry Eleanor, 75 Penn
Berry Eliza Jane, 26 Shippen
Berry Marg., shop, P road ab Carpenter
Berry & Mcgary, oysters, 117 Chestnut
Berry Oliver, bootmr., 36 Mulberry
Berry James, bookbinder, 51 Garden
Berry James, weav., G T road ab 4th (K)
Berry John, tailor, 115 German st
Berry Joseph, farmer, 51 M road
Berry Joseph, flour and feed, 603 S 2d
Berry Richard, Reed bel 2d
Berry Samuel, carter, 680 N Front (K)
Berry Samuel, hatter, 164 Christian
Berry Samuel, watchman, Front bel Master (K)
Berry Saml., bootmr., Wharton ab 3d
Berry Wm. B., chair manuf., 53 N 6th
Berry Wm., carp., rear 5th ab Christian
Berryman Charles, blacksmith, Palmer & Franklin (K), h 66 Coates
Berryman James, blacksm., Powell Row ab Front
Berryman John, carp., Powell row
Berryman Matthew W., cabinetmr., 5 M road
Bersch Elizabeth, baker, P road bel Marriot's l
Berson Wm., b. h., 152 N 2nd
Berstler J., mer., 17 Commerce, h Brown ab 10th
Bert Chas., 8 Danaker's ct
Bert Edward G., confectioner, 84 Mulberry
Bertron G. W., tobacconist, High bel Sch 5th
Berwind John, cabinetmr., George ab Sch 8th
Bessan Jacob, cabinetmr., Marlborough below Franklin (K)
Besselievre Jno. A., jewelr., Washington bel 8th
Besser Edward, cabinetmr., 526 N 2d (K)
Bessig John, lab., rear Fitler n Montgomery (K)
Bessire John, wharf builder, 17 Cresson's al
Besson John M., mer., 52 S 2d
Besson Louisa, mer., 52 S 2d
BESSON L. & SON, dry goods, 52 S 2d
Bessonett Ann, Gray's ct
Bessonett John, jr., clerk, 48 S 2d
Best F., lab., 15th n Shippen
Best Hiram, tailor, 7 Jackson's ct
Best James, weaver, 13th bel Shippen
Best Jane, Passmore's pl
Best John, cordw., Pearl n Sch 6th
Best John, lab., Passmore's pl
Beswick Joseph, tavern, 138 Sassafras
Betancourt Alonzo, gent., 284 N 6th
Bethel Jno., milkman, rear Charlotte bel Poplar
Bethell John, cordw., 13th and Brown

Bethell Joshua, collector, 143 Beach (K)
Bethell J. P., M. D., office 304 N 3d
Bethell Robert, att'y, 208 N 6th, h 258 S Garden
Bethune George W. Rev., N W 13th & Walnut
Betson Robt. W., cordw., Christian ab 6th
Betton John S., trimmer, 170 Shippen
Bettle J. Rebecca, 131 N 9th
Bettle Samuel, jr., mer., 73 N 10th
Bettle Samuel, senr., 14 S 3d
Bettle W., tavern, 244 N 6th
Betts James, N E 11th and Walnut
Betts James, lab., Carlton ab Sch 6th
Betts Richard K., carpenter, Filbert n Sch 8th, h 22 N Sch 8th
Betts Ruth Ann, 3 W North
Betts Sarah, manuf. of supporters, N E 11th & Walnut
Betts Thomas, blacksmith, 7 Farries' ct
Betz Christian, cordw., Broad bel Poplar
Betz G., tavern, 174 St John
Betzold C. F., cab mr., 18 Noble
Beuerle T. F., baker, Master bel 4th (K)
Beusse John H., 7th bel Poplar
Bevan D., painter, S E 3d and High, h 3d bel Christian
Bevan Geo., gent., 173 Catharine st
BEVAN & HUMPHREYS, mers., 5 Walnut
Bevan Jas., blacksm., 3d ab Franklin (K)
Bevan John, paint. & glaz., N W Front & Pine
Bevan John S., carter, Front bel Wharton
Bevan Matt. L., mer., 5 Walnut, h 349 Mulberry
Bevan Thos., weaver, 5 Eyre's ct (K)
Beverlin Sheridan, barber, 426 S Front
Bevins Charles, stone cutter, 9 Vernon
Bewley Danl., lab., Marriott bel 5th
Bewley Elizabeth, 9 Sommer's ct
Bewley Isaac, grocer, N E 3d & Cedar, h Federal ab 5th
Bewley Isaac K., clerk, Ogden, ab 10th
Bewley Jesse, watchman, Catharine ab Lebanon
Bewley John, mason, R road ab Ann (F V)
Bewley Jona. P., spice grinder, Callowhill ab Sch 8th
Bewley Joseph, hairdresser, 440 N 4th
Bewley, Vanhorn & Co., spice & drug mill, Sch 8th ab Willow
Bewley William, coachman, 25 Quince
Bewley & Wilson, clothing, 96 S 2d
Beyer G. T., gent., 365 Pine
Beylard John, jr., mer., 23 Church al
Beylle M. L., gentw., 184 Spruce
Beyrer John G., baker, 459 S 2d
Bezard John, bootmr., 17 S 9th
Bhedermann Geo., tailor, West ab Palmer (K)
Bias Alexander, sawyer, Stevenson's ct
Bias James J. G., dentist, 157 S 6th
Bibens Hezekiah, seaman, 176 Locust
Bibens Jno., shoemr., 6 Osborne's ct
Bibens Thos., shoemr., Eagle ct
BIBIGHAUS CHARLES H., M. D., 94 Green
Bibighaus Henry, D. D., 83 Dillwyn
Bibighaus S. H., hardware, 220 N 2d, h 31 Green
Bible Sophia Mrs., Marion bel 2d
Bickel Conrad, cabinetmr., rear 467 N 4th
Bickel Daniel, b. h., 378 N Front

Bickel John A., cabinetmr., Elizabeth ab Poplar
Bickel John A., flour store, 3d and Tammany
Bickel John A., 9th ab Parrish
Bickerton Benj., clerk, 19 Harmony
Bickerton Joseph, piano tuner, 146 S 13th
Bickerton Sarah, b. h., Howard and Linden
Bickerton Thos., cooper, 57 S Water, h 36 Almond
Bickham George, cordw., Rose al n Coates
Bicking Chas. R., printer, 56 N 3d, h 281 N 8th
BICKING, CHUR & CO., dry goods, S W Front and Chestnut
Bicking Geo. H., mer., S W Front and Chestnut, h 1 Virginia Row
Bicking & Guilbert, printers, 56 N 3d
Bickley Daniel, gent., 30 Callowhill
Bickley H., city contract'r, Locust bel Sch 6th
Bickley Joseph, carter, 6 S Rittenhouse
Bickley Joseph, clerk, 100 Union
Bickley Mary, S 7th bel Fitzwater
Bicknell Robt. M., brushmr., 20 N 3d, h 7th bel Coates
Bicknell Robt. T., 1 Colonnade Row
Bicknel Rufus, M. D., Washington & Till (W P)
Biddle Abraham, cordw., 486 N 3d
Biddle Alexander, 50 S 3d, h 8 York Buildings
Biddle Chapman, 47 S 5th
Biddle Charles, trader, 18 Mechanic
Biddle Charles, waiter, 15 Hurst
Biddle Chas., trader, F road bel Master
Biddle Chas. W., morocco dr., Schleisman's al
Biddle Clement, gent., 164 Mulberry
BIDDLE CLEMENT, jr., att'y & coun., office 8 York Buildings
Biddle Clement C., Prest. Saving Fund, h Spruce and Quince
BIDDLE CRAIG, att'y & coun., 128 Walnut
Biddle C. J., att'y & coun., 72 S 6th, h 237 Pine
Biddle Edward C., 17 Washington sq
Biddle Edward C., publisher, S W 5th & Minor, h 304 Mulberry
Biddle Elizabeth B., Sch 8th and Locust
BIDDLE E. C. & J., booksellers, 6 S 5th
BIDDLE GEO. W., att'y & coun., 47 S 5th, h N W Sch 7th and Spruce
Biddle Hannah, Brinton bel 11th
Biddle Hannah, near 34 Bonsall
Biddle Henry J., stock broker, 50 S 3d
Biddle Jesse, carter, 2 Acorn al
Biddle Jno., booksel'r, 6 S 5th, h 6 Palmyra row
Biddle John W., jr., painter, 96 N Juniper
Biddle John B., M. D., Spruce ab 11th
BIDDLE J. WILLIAMS, att'y at law, 7 York Buildings, h 175 Walnut
Biddle Margaret, Sch 8th n Sassafras
Biddle Mary A., gentw., N E 8th and Locust
Biddle Robt., mer., 29 High, h 341 Sassafras
BIDDLE R. & W. C., hardware, 29 High
Biddle R. S., druggist, 13th & R road
Biddle Sarah C., wid. of James C., S W Juniper and Spruce
Biddle Thomas, stock broker, 50 S 3d, h 8 York Buildings
Biddle Thos. A., st. brok., 50 S 3d, h 351 Spruce
BIDDLE THOS. & CO., stk. brokers, 50 S 3d

Biddle Wm., druggist, N W 11th & Mulberry
Biddle Wm. C., mer., 29 High, h 431 Sassafras
Biderman Mary, shop, 305 S 5th
Bieg Jacob, lab., rear Pleasant ab 10th
Bier J., barber, 40 Pegg
Bierbraier Francis, butcher, 3d n Creek
Bierly Isaac, shipcarp., Wood bel Franklin (K)
Bierly Jacob, shipcarp., Elm bel Franklin (K)
Bierly John, shipcarp., Queen ab Marlboro' (K)
Bierly Theodore, shipcarp., yard foot Palmer st, h Elm bel Franklin
Bigan John, stove finisher, 209 S Front
Bigarty Hannah, Pearl bel 13th
Bigelow Thos., sen., carp., 158½ Cherry, h 13th bel Callowhill
Bigelow Thos., jr., carp., 305½ Callowhill
Biggard John, oysterhouse, Peach bel Coates
Biggard John, lab., rear 495 N 3d
Biggard Saml., shoemr., Dunton n Franklin (K)
Biggard Wm., wharf builder, Federal ab 2d
Biggard Wm., cordw., Ontario bel Parrish
Bigger Aaron W., bootmr., 65 Smith's pl
Biggin Thos., cooper, Jefferson ab 5th (K)
Biggins John, mason, Pearl ab Sch 8th
Biggs Henry, bootmr., 7 Benton's av
Biggs Robert, lab., Centre ab 12th
Bigler Jacob, sailmr., h 542 N 3d
Bignell Catharine, trimmings, 269 St. John
Bignell John, hatter, 174 N 5th
Bigonet Jacob, druggist, 158 Lombard, h 10th ab Fitzwater
Bilbrough Joseph, carp., Vine ab Sch 2d
Bilbrough Samuel, carp. weaver, Shackamaxon n F road (K)
Bilbrough Thomas, manuf., Willow bel Pine
Bilderback E., widow, 13 Rose al
Biles Israel, painter, High n Sch 7th
Biles Joseph T., carpenter, 21 Dugan
Biles Thos., drug mill, Sch 7th & Jones, h (W P)
Bilger Isaac, grocer, 142 N 2d
Billard Charles, shoemr., 6th bel G T road (K)
Bille de Steen, charge de affairs from Denmark, h 9 Colonnade row
Billet Lewis, oysterman, Mechanic ct (N L)
Billharz F. W., ostler, rear Mechanic ab Poplar
Billings Asa, upholsterer, Marion n 15th
Billings Thos., printer, Queen bel Brown (K)
Billingsfelt Thomas, carp., 5 Gebhard
Billmeyer John, 139 Sp Garden
Billmeyer Samuel, 139 Sp. Garden
Billmeyer Wm. M., printer, Harvey's ct (K)
Bills Jeremiah, shipcarp., Marion ab 2d
Bilslem John, lab., Cooper n Sch 3d
Bilyeu Aaron P., bricklayer, Sp Garden bel 9th
Bimmer G., cordw., 243 St John
Binder Daniel, cabinetmr., 188 Poplar
Binder Frederick W., hotel, 10 S 5th
Binder George, carp., 268 Coates
Binder George A., carp., 7th ab Poplar
Binder J. & G. A., carps., 7th ab Poplar
Binder Peter, M. D., 16 Sp Garden
Binder Wm., hatter, 7th ab Poplar
Bing James, carp., Ogden bel R road
Bingaman Susan, rear 3 Shield's al

Bingham Amos, Rev., 132 N Juniper
BINGHAM & BROTHER, dry goods, 66 N 3d
Bingham James, stonecut., Winter ab Sch 3d
Bingham James, jeweller, 112 Chestnut, h 24 Jacoby
Bingham James, mer., 66 N 3d, h 104 N 11th
Bingham John, mer., 66 N 3d, h 18 N 11th
Bingham John, cabinetmr., N E 13th & Sassafras
Bingham Richard, grocer, S E Steward and Fitzwater
Bingham Samuel, porter, Fairview ab Sch 8th
Bingham Thomas, forward. and commis. mer., 276 High, h 51 N 11th
Bingham Thomas, trunkmr., 24 Jacoby
Bingham Wm., turner, Paul bel 7th
BINGHAMS, DOCK & STRATTON, forwarding mers., 276 High
Binker John, farmer, Allen ab F road (K)
Binker Thomas, cordw., 75 F road (K)
Binley John, carp., Allen bel Palmer (K)
Binner Wm., shoemr., Duke n Hanover (K)
Binney Charlotte, gentw., 190 S 9th
BINNEY HORACE, coun., office 85, h 83 S 4th
BINNEY HORACE jr., atty. & coun., 131 S 6th
Binney J., locksm., 73 S 5th
Binnin Edward, lab., Filbert n Sch 4th
Binns Benj. F., clerk, Sch 6th bel High
BINNS JOHN, commissioner to take depositions in Pennsylvania, and nearly all the states, 116 Walnut
BINNS JOHN P., atty. and coun., 116 Walnut, h Noble ab 8th
Binns Moses, carp., 147 N Juniper
Binny Wm., plumber, Chestnut rear Sch 5th, h 353 E Lombard
Bioren & Ladd, dentists, 282 Chestnut
Bioren Mary, trimmings, 7th & Callowhill
Bioret Charles, cabinetmr., N W 3d & Lombard

Bird Thomas, lab., rear 455 N 3d
Bird Walter, millwt., 123 Juniper
Bird Wm., brushmr., 95 N 9th
Bird Wm. E., printer, Higgins' ct
Birkenbine H. P. M., machinist, 38 S Juniper
Birkett James, capt., 95 Pine
BIRKEY JOHN, dentist, 79 S 6th
Birkey John, sen., dry goods, 67 S 5th
BIRKEY Wm., J. A., M. D., dentist, S E 8th & Locust
Birks John, trimmings, 123 Locust
Birmingham Chs., groc., 7th & Poplar
Birmingham James, razor strop manuf., Parrish ab Sch 8th
Birmingham Pariset W., ivory carver & turner, Poplar ab 7th
Birmingham Sarah, grocer, N E 7th & Poplar
Birmingham Thos. lab. Hanover bel F road (K)
Birnbaum Charles, baker, 316 Pine
Birnbaum Geo. W., grocer, 370 N 4th
Bisbee Asaph, cordw., 197 G T road (K)
Bisbing Henry, carter, Wagner's ct
Bisbing Jacob, farmer, 116 St John
Bisbing Jacob H., carp., Walnut al., h 18 Rittenhouse
Bisbing John, lime burner, Darby road (W P)
Bisbing P., carpet weaver, 160 St John
Bishing Sam., lime burner, Darby road (W P)
Bishing Stephen, copper plate printer, Myrtle
Bishing Elizabeth, gentw., 63 N 4th
Bishaboy A., printer, Cherry ab 13th
Bishlag Geo., vict., Woodland (W P)
Bishlag Thos., vict., Vineyard (F V)
Bishop Abnor, porter, Clifton
Bishop Baird, Vine ab Nixon
Bishop Benj. F., jeweller, 232 E Cedar
Bishop Caroline, 215 S 7th
Bishop Charles, hatter, 25 Crotes ct

Bispham John E., U. S. N., 7 Belmont row
Bispham J., auctioneer, 34 S Front, h N W.
   Spruce & Sch 8th
Bispham Samuel, groc., 261 High, h 171 N 6th
Bisset James, gardener, 20 Pratt
Bissex Henry, bootmr., Sch 2d and Vine
Bisson Samuel S., carp., rear 159 St John
Bissont Francis, cordw., rear Marshall ab Poplar
Bitler Joseph, moulder, Sch Front ab Vine
Bitter Bernhart, barber, 45 Penn (S)
Bitter Henry, tailor, 110 Crown
Bitters Ephraim L., wheelwt., rear G T road
   ab 2d (K)
Bitters Lorenzo C., cordw., Tammany
Bitting Andrew, tailor, Melon bel 10th
Bitting George W., carp, 9th ab Poplar
Bitting Hiram, 220 High, h 139 Buttonwood
Bitting H. & L., grocers, 220 High
Bitting Jordan D. conveyancer, 2 Carpenter's ct,
   h Coates ab 13th
Bitting Knight, blacksm., Harrison pl
Bitting Lewis, groe., 220 High, h 10th ab Green
Bitting Lewis, tailor, 442 N 3d
Bitting Lewis, sen., grocer, 78 Green
Bitting & Mattson, tailors, 442 N 3d
Bitting & Morris, grocers, 166 N 3d
Bitting Philip, salesman, 184 Swanson
Bitting Thos. R., grocer, 166 N 3d
Bitting Walter, blacksmith, Poplar ab 6th, h
   Lewis ab Poplar
Biven John, whipmr., rear 143 Franklin
Bivens Samuel, Bedford bel 12th
Bixenstein Frederick, baker, 284 Coates
Black Alex., weav., Cadwalader ab Phœnix (K)
Black Ann, 98 George
Black Ann, S 12th ab Cedar
Black Catharine, Vine ab 12th
Black Cyrus, clothing, 91 N 2d, h 272 Shippen
Black David, lab., Carlton bet Sch 7th & 8th
Black Ebenezer, scourer, 14 Elizabeth
Black Ellen, wid. of Jas., O'Neal (K)
Black E., gentw., Federal ab Front
Black Harriet C., dressmr., 99 Mulberry
Black Isaac, stonecutter, Dean ab Locust
Black James, blacksmith, 6th bel Carpenter
Black James, painter, 311 S 6th
Black James, carver, 173 Cherry
Black James, barber, Sp Garden bel 7th
Black Jesse, porter, Bonsall
Black John, distiller, Sch 2d and Wood
Black John, cooper, Jefferson & Apple (K)
Black John, waiter, 6 Lombard row
Black John, watchmaker, 64 Cedar, h Wash-
   ington bel 4th
Black John H., agent, 151 S 11th
Black John L., pumpmr., 524 S Front
Black John R., gold beater, 20 Swanwick
Black Joseph, dealer, 84 Swanson
Black Matthew, bootmr., Helmuth n 6th
Black Prince, waiter, 50 Quince
Black Rebecca, dry goods, 398 Sassafras
Black Robert, blacksm., Marriott's la ab 5th
Black Robert, carp., 253 S 3d
Black Robert, shoemr., 12th ab Shippen

BLACK R. & J., grocers, High & Sch 8th, and
   S W Sch 6th & High
Black Samuel, gent., 168 S 4th
Black Samuel, weaver, 3 Phillips (K)
Black Samuel W., teacher, 263 N 7th
Black Silas, clothes, 272 Shippen
Black Thomas, lab., Lombard bel 11th
Black Thompson, grocer, N W Broad & Chest-
   nut
Black Wm., warper, Shippen ab 12th
Black Wm., lab., 1 Gabell's ct
Black Wm., lab., Cedar ab Sch 4th
Black Wm. D., black and white smith, 3d bel
   Wharton
Blackburn John, tin plate worker, High ab Sch
   8th, h Sch 7th n Pine
Blackburn John, tailor, Warner's ct
Blackburn Jno., cordw., rear Carlton ab Sch 6th
Blackburn Wm., collector, Wood bel Sch 7th
Blackburne C. J., com. mer., 24 Church al, h S
   E 10th and Filbert
Blackburne Francis, cloth, 63 High, h Sch 5th
   ab Mulberry
Blackburne Wm., president Washington Mining
   Company, 81 Dock
Blackford George, tailor, 34 Parrish
Blackford George, bricklayer, 358 Pine
Blackie James, marble cut., 30 Parker
Blackiston G. K., coal, Broad ab Sassafras
Blackman Catharine, Poplar ab 4th
Blackson Ellen, Middle al
Blackson Ellen, washer, 37 Prosperous al
Blackstone Thomas, gent., 68 N 11th
Blackwell Mary, 50 Mechanic
Blackwood John, hatter, 7 Cresson's al
Blackwood Joseph, mer., 111 Chestnut
Blade James R., cordw., Elm bel Franklin (K)
Bladen Aaron, dyer, rear 20 S 8th
Bladen Ann, 364 N Front
Bladen Martha, 334 Vine
BLADEN WASHINGTON L., biscuit baker, 87
   N Water
Bladen Wm. E., biscuit baker, 165 N Water, h
   186 N Front
Blaess Philip, tavern, Green and St John
Blaher Joseph, hatter, 8th and Brown
Blaikie John, shipjoin., Beach bel Shackamaxon
   (K)
Blaikie T. L., plumber, Warren bel Queen (K)
Blain Sarah, gentw., 357 Walnut
Blair Edward, dry goods, 152 S 4th
Blair Edw. J., cordw., 112 N 10th
Blair Elizabeth, washer, Lombard ab 12th
Blair Francis, Cedar ab 12th
Blair Henry C., druggist, S W 8th and Walnut
Blair Henry J., currier, 2 Tamarind
Blair James, manuf., c 3d and G T road (K)
Blair James, carp., 31 Perry (N)
Blair James W., machinist, 120 G T road (K)
Blair John, clerk, Vienna and Wood (K)
Blair John, whipmr., Charlotte ab Thompson
   (K)
Blair John, manuf., N 2d bel Master (K)
Blair John, lab., Washington ab 11th

Blair Joseph, tailor, 8 Roberts
Blair Robert, vict., G T road ab 3d (K)
Blair Robert, shoemr., 50 Carpenter (C) h 182 Lombard
Blair Samuel, gas-fitter, 30 N 10th, h 18 Union
Blair Sarah, 18 Union
Blair Steward, bonnet presser, 94 Fitzwater
Blair Wm., drayman, N W Sch 6th & Chestnut
Blair Wm. H., tea dealer, 33 S Front, h 13 N 10th
Blaisey Adam, cooper, 271 N Front
Blake Andrew, blacking manf., 340 Pine
Blake Ann, 9 Hirst
Blake Eliza, 1 Swanwick
Blake George E., music store, 13 S 5th
Blake H., lab., Wood bel Sch 7th
Blake Henry G., stove store, Cedar ab 8th
Blake James, bricklayer, rear 125 Green
Blake John, watchman, rear 108 N 2d
Blake Levin, shoemr., 219 Shippen
Blake Mary, millinery, 291 Coates
Blake Mary Ann, 61 Currant al
Blake Robt. B., carp., 226 Sassafras, h 5 Ogden
Blake & Rogers, carps., 226 Sassafras
Blake Ruth, washer, 50 Quince
Blake Susannah, nurse, rear 75 N 8th
Blake T., shop, 110 S Swanson
Blake Thos., brickmr., 6th bel G T road (K)
Blake Wm., lab., 54 Currant al
Blake Wm. R., comedian, 184 S 9th
Blakemore Francis, locksmith, 41 S 8th
Blakemore Henry, japanner, 7 Appletree al, h Washington ab 10th
Blaker Adam, tailor, 8 Freed's av
Blaker John, saddler, Marshall and Callowhill
Blaker Ulysses, plumber, 9th & Parrish
Blaker Ulysses, lab., Ogden's ct

Bland Benjamin, tailor, 14 Norris' al
Bland Saml., watchmr., 441 N 6th, h 2 Chatham
Blandford Wm., watchman, Sch 3d n Locust
Blaney Mary, Prospect al
Blaney Rich'd, corkmr., 166 S 6th
Blank Aletha, Brighton, E of Sch 8th
Blankley James, moulder, Winter
Blankman Anna, Lombard ab Sch 6th
Blankman George, painter, 6 Cypress
Blase Geo. F., sugar refiner, 14 Mulberry al
Blashouf John, bedstead mr., 1 Margaretta pl
Blatner Maria Ann, wadding manuf., Coates bel 10th
Blattenberger J., cooper, High ab Sch 4th
Blaylock John, barber, 5th & Carpenter
Blayney Eliza, Wood ab Broad
Blayney Robert, boot and shoemr., Phoenix bel G T road (K)
Blayney Robt., jr., cordw., rear Fittler bel Harrison (K)
Bleacher Zachariah, lab., 238 St John
Bledenhuyser John, sheet iron work., 490 S 2d
Blee Charles, brickmr., Ann n Sch 3d
Blee Edward, weaver, Jones n Sch 4th
Blee Francis, brickmr., Watt
Blee George, brickmr., Spruce n Sch 4th
Blee John, brickmr., Sch. 5th and Rittenhouse
Blee Latham, weaver, Jones n Sch 4th
Bleeker John, cooper, Union ct
Bleich Fred., tobacconist, G T road & Franklin
Bleich John, morocco dr., 105 Poplar
Bleight John D., atty. at law, 35 S 5th, h N E 13th & Chestnut
Bleight Mary Mrs., 13th and Chestnut
Bleil Fred., baker, Coates bel 10th
Blennerhasset Wm. W., bookbinder, 15 New
Bleterman M., tailor, 3 Lily al

Bloom John F., baker, 47 Brown
Bloomer Jas., shop, Milton bel 11th
Bloomer Joseph, lab., Milton ab 10th
Bloomer Lawrence, carter, 25 Lebanon
Bloomer Thos., lab., Milton ab 10th
Blow Margaret, 3d bel Thompson (K)
Blowe Geo., watchcase mr., 17 Reckless
Bloxom Mary, Clare st
Blum B., 82 Vine
Blum Saml., tailor, 148 E Cedar
Blume John, coal, 96 N 4th, h N 7th ab Coates
Blummer Chas. E., tobacconist, 44 New
Blummer Henry C., engine manuf., 134 Vine, h N 12th ab Vine
Blunden Jas., carpet weaver, 317 S 3d
Blunden Jonathan M., lab., 2 Jones' pl
Blundin John, druggist, 14 Filbert
Blundin Wm. F., overseer pen., St Andrew's st
Blust Francis B., cigarmr., 426 N 4th
Blydenburg & Hyde, machinists, 1 Fetter la
Blydenburg Samuel, 1 Fetter la, h 121 Noble
Blyes A. W., dry goods, 260 N 2d
Blyes Henry, 260 N 2d
Blynn Henry, hatter, 40 Chester
Blynn Michael, hatter, 504 High, h 43 N Sc 8th
Blythe Calvin, att. and coun., 4 George
Blythe Mary Ann, b h, Owen
Boak Robert, manuf., Philip and Master (K)
Boak Eliza, shop, F road bel Master (K)
Boardley George, clothing, 347 Lombard
Boardley Sarah, cook, Dean's al
Boardman Ann, huckster, rear 96 Filbert
Boardman F. H. Dr., 6 Chancery la
Boardman Henry A. Rev., 375 Spruce
Boardman Henry S., manuf., 104 N 3d
Boardman John, manuf., Frankford road opp Queen (K)
Boardman Robt., cabinetmr., Howard's pl
Boardman Robert, satchelmr., Marlborough bel West (K)
Boarnman Henry, vict., Union bel Franklin (K)
Boas Patrick, lab., 3 Braceland's ct
Boate George, upholsterer, 123 S 2d
Boate M., 27 Franklin
Boate Wm. collector, Parrish ab 6th
Boats Fred, 191 N 8th
Bobb Peter, brickmr., Spruce ab 13th
Bock Frederick, carp., 19 Logan
Bock Saml., Wood bel R road
Bockius Charles R., mer., 67 N 2d
Bockius Christopher, saddler, 50 High, h Wallace n 8th
BOCKIUS C. & G., fancy leather manufs., 27½ Margaretta and 30 Willow
Bockius C. G., mer., N E 3d and High, h 29 New Market
Bockius C. G. & J. C., brushmrs., N E 3d and High
Bockius & Gorgas, china, 67 N 2d
Bockius Hannah, crockery, 535 High
Bockius Henry J., carp., 213 S 9th
Bockius Isaiah, sad'r, 50 High, h Green ab 11th
Bockius Jacob U., saddler, 50 High, h Wallace n 8th
Bockius John, carp., 7 Quarry, h 34 Bread

Bockius John, carp., 18 Flower st
Bockius J., brushmr., 208 N 2d
Bockius Wm., vis. of poor, 217 S 9th
Bockius Wm., baker, High, n Sch 6th
BOCKIUS, SELLERS & Co., saddlers, 50 High
Bodder Levi D., M. D., 171 N 4th
Boddy Charles, barber, Cedar bel 9th
Boddy John, patternmr., 444 Sassafras
Boden Hannah, wid. of Josiah, Wood ab 12th
Bodenhoeffer Joseph, varnish manuf., 405 N 3d
Bodenmuller L., manuf., 16 Bread
Bodin Jas., tailor, Wood ab 12th
Bodin Joseph, tobacconist, N W 2d and Dock, h 77 Green
Bodine, Baeder & Co., glue manufs., 750 O Y road and 86 High.
Bodine Budd S., sand, Poplar st whf., h 14 Maiden (K)
Bodine Elizabeth, Oneida pl
Bodine George, lab., Hanover ab Queen
Bodine Jesse E., 65 Sassafras
Bodine J. F., clerk, 131 N 13th
Bodine Samuel T., Queen bel Shackamaxon
Bodle John, weaver, Front ab Phoenix (K)
Boehm A. W., mer., 61 N Front, h 248 Mulberry
Boehm Harietta, widow, 15 Brandywine
Boehn Henry, shoemr., 35 O Y road
Boehrer Sebastian, machin., Nectarine rear 11th
Boers J. F. A, 85 Shippen
Bofenger Fred., beer-house, 449 N Front
Boffield Nich., cordw., 2d ab G T road
Bogan Walter, ladies' shoemr., N W Green and Marshall
Boger John, tavern, N W James and Charles
Boggs David, pianomr., 24 Marion
Boggs F. M., mer., 40 N whfs, h 20 Union
Boggs Geo., chairmr., Queen bel Hanover (K)
Boggs Geo. W., hatter, Pine ab Sch 6th
Boggs James, 374 Chestnut
Boggs James, chairmr., 85 N Front, h Queen ab Marlboro' (K)
Boggs James, Allen ab Marlboro' (K)
Boggs John, lab., Carlton ab 13th
Boggs John Rev., rear Emeline
Boggs John, varnisher, Church and Reckless
Boggs Samuel, ship carp., F road n Otter (K)
Boggs Samuel, wheelwright, 208 St John
Boggs Wm., tavern, 326 S Front
Boggs Wm. L., mer., 17 N 5th, h 18 Merchant
Bogia Angelo, engineer, 215 N 10th
Bogia Francis, cordw., 10th bel Catharine
Bogle Amelia, teacher, Pine ab 10th
Bogle Ralph, dyer, Shippen ab Shippen la
BOGUE & FAWCETT, wigmrs., 174 Chestnut
Bogue Thos. haircutter & wigmr., 174 Chestnut
Bohlen Henry, mer., 69 S 4th, h 393 Walnut
Bohlen John, mer., 67 S 4th, h 238 Walnut
Bohlen John jr. atty. & coun. N W 6th & Walnut
Bohler John J. whipmr. 4 N 4th, h Poplar ab 4th
Bohn Christian, tailor, Marshall ab 4th (S)
Bohn George, cordw., 10 Collins' al
Bohn Jacob N., stevedore, 56 Penn
Bohn Richard, mariner, 5 M'Ginley's ct
Bohnert A., cordw., 239 N Front
Bohney Wm., shoemr. 146 St John

Bohrer Fred. & Jas., 106 Crown
Bohrer Henrietta, dressmr., 106 Crown
Boiether Julius, painter, 212 S 9th
Boileau Edwin B., convey'r, 145 Walnut, h 570 N 2d (K)
Boileau Isaac, alderman, 570 N 2d (K)
Boileau Isaac jr., clerk, 536 N 2d
Boileau John, shoemr., rear 164 Queen (S)
Bok Frederick, tailor, Cobb bel Catharine
BOK JOHN, tailor, 91 S 3d
Bok John G., confectioner, 178½ Sassafras
Boker & Brothers, mers., 82 High
Boker C. S., Pres. Girard Bank, h 110 S 3d
Boker Joseph, mer., 82 High, h 92 New
Boker W. C., mer., 82 High, h 185 N 6th
Boland John, bootmr., 122 N 4th, h 216 Noble
Boland Wm., weaver, Harrison's ct
Bolden James, mariner, Callowhill ab William
Bolden Mary, 11th and Barley
Bolden Robert, waiter, 6 Blackberry al
  olden Spencer, waiter, 61 Currant al
Boldin George, mer., 141 High, h 26 N 9th
Boles Wm., waiter, 12th bel Carpenter
Boley Frederick, cooper, 19 High, h 280 N 3d
Boley Fred. jr., reg. of dry measures, 280 N 3d, h Green ab 6th
Bolivar G. W., gent., S 9th bel Fitzwater
Bollen Ann, 497 N 3d
Boller & Beitel, mor. manuf., 31 Margaretta
Boller Catharine, gentw., 21 New Market
Boller H. J., mer. 78 S Front, h Spruce ab Broad
Boller Wm., mer., Margaretta, h 26 Jacoby
Bolt John, carp., 16 Cherry
Bolton John, lab., Carlton ab Sch 8th
Bolton Jos. D., cabinetmr. 4th ab Thompson (K)
Bolton Jos. R., 400 N 10th
Bolton Mary A., 110 N Front
Bolton Rachel Ann, 7 Franklin row (S G)
BOLTON WM. P., carver, 55 N 8th, h 7th ab Poplar
Bombershine John, carp., 8th ab Camac (K)
Bomeisler Lewis, mer., R road n Buttonwood
Bomeisler S., 177 N 10th
Bonart Jos., baker, F road and Marlboro' (K)
Bond Adam J., cordw., 129 Christian.
Bond Alexander, tailor, Vine ct
Bond Ann, 11 Path
Bond Benj. F., trunkmr., Sassafras n 4th
Bond Charles, fruiterer, 285 N 2d
Bond George, printer, Juniper al
Bond Henry, shoemr., 7 Charles
Bond H., M. D., 1 N 9th, 3d door bel Filbert
Bond H. Calvin, clerk, 8th ab Buttonwood
Bond James, druggist, S E 10th and Locust
Bond James F., grocer, 5th and Catharine
Bond Jane, washer, Stiles ct
Bond Joseph, carp., 577 Sassafras
Bond Jos., nail mr., rear 13th bel Buttonwood
Bond Joseph, vict., Sch 8th ab Wood
Bond Joseph, glassblower, Wood bel Duke (K)
Bond Joseph A., grocery, 6th and Paul
Bond Josiah, undertaker, Orange ab Washington
Bond Levi, mer., 136 N 13th
Bond Lewis, watchman, 3 Rose al
Bond Richard L., carpenter, 339 Callowhill

Bond Robert, lab., Liberty ct
Bond Thos., horse dealer, Hope bel Master (K)
Bond Thomas, cabinetmr., rear 90 Cherry, h Smith's ct
Bond Thomas, weaver, 29 Lebanon
BOND THOMAS, mer. 41 S Water, h 359 N 6th
Bond Wm., lab., N Market n Laurel
Bond Wm., grocery, Washington and Parker
Bondfield George, mer., 53 Penn (C)
Boner Danl., carp., George n Sch 3d
Bones Geo., 559 Vine
Bones John W., carp., George bel 10th, h S W 9th and Sassafras
Bonfield Baker, stone mason, Penn bel Broad
Bonfield G. R., artist, 28 Walnut, h 10th bel Sp Garden
Bonfield James, plasterer, 75 Smith's pl
Bongard Margaret, Sassafras ab Sch 8th
Bonhom John, relief court
Bonhom Harriet, shop, 188 S 6th
Boning Wm., jeweller, 70 Chestnut
Bonnaffon Eliza, 6 N 11th
Bonnaffon Sylvester, dry goods, 91 High
Bonnar James, B. D., George ab Sch 6th
Bonneiul Peter, gent. 72 Union
Bonnell Samuel, 99 Vine
Bonner Jas., lab., 10 Abbott's ct
Bonner John, lab., Sch 2d n Cedar
Bonner Michael, tavern, Water & Sassafras
Bonner Michael, lab., Lynn (F M)
Bonner Sarah, 332 N 3d
Bonnin Letitia Linn (F M)
Bonsall Edmund C., jeweller, 72½ High, h 298 S 5th
BONSALL E. H., conveyancer, 5th & Library, h 35 Jacoby
Bonsall Henry, conveyancer, 48 S 4th
Bonsall Isaac M., brickmr., Sch 5th n Lombard
Bonsall James S. printer, Washington ab 6th
Bonsall Jesse, tailor, 6 Richards
Bonsall John, convey. offi., 48 S 4th, h 22 Girard
BONSALL JOHN & CO. conveyancers, 48 S 4th
Bonsall Sarah, rear 4 Fetter la
Bonsall J & Scheer, jeweller, 72½ High
Bonsall T. L. booksel., 33½ High, h 27 Mulberry
Bonsall Wm., weigher, C. H., h 290 S 5th
Bonsall Wm. S., tin and sheet iron worker, 146 S 9th
Boodner Fred., locksm., Franklin bel Front (K)
Book George H. upholsterer, 52 Chester
Book Mary Ann, Rose ab School (K)
Booker Cornelius, blacksm., 22 Lebanon
Booker John, blacksm., 18 Lebanon
Bookhammer Jacoby, bootmr., 23 State st
Bool Janet, widow, rear Apple bel Franklin
Boon Charles, hatter, 62 Dock
Boon & Davis, wood & sand, Catharine st whf
Boon Geo., blacksm., Willing ab Mulberry
Boon Henry L., omnibus, Washington (W P)
Boon Horace, 4 Bird's ct
Boon Morris, whf build., Otter n G T road (K)
Boon Peter, tav'n, Beach n Shackamaxon (K)
Boon Thomas, 27 Coates al
Boon Wm., tavern, Washington (W P)

Boon Wm., chemist, Spruce n Sch 3d
Boon Wm., dyer, Master bel G T road (K)
Boon Wm., sea capt., 351 N Front
Boone Rebecca, 394 Vine
Boone Robt. shoes, 209 S 2d, h 7th bel Fitzwater
Boone Wm. F., atty. & coun., 59 S 7th
Booskirk Benj., chairmr., 17 Eutaw
Booth Abigail C., gentw., 115 Brown
Booth Benjamin, harnessmr., 131 N 5th
Booth & Boye, chemists, 27 N 7th
Booth Edmond, machinist, 222 S Juniper
Booth Edwin, mer., 108 High, h 199 N 9th
Booth Edwin & Co., cloths, &c., 108 High
Booth Isaac, oak cooper, rear 378 S 2d
Booth Isaac H., collector, 8 Franklin row
Booth James C., prof. chemistry, 300 Pine, office Old Mint
Booth Jno., dry goods, S W Sch 7th & Lombard
Booth Keziah, shopkeeper, 620 S 2d
Booth Margaret, b. h., Wheat bel Marion
Booth Thomas, cordw., Sch 3d bel High
Booth Thos. L., groc., Laurel opp Rachel (N L)
Booth Zarah, shoemr., 5 Relief
Boothryde Abm., spin., Marlboro' bel Duke (K)
Booz James, porter, 8 Barley
Boozer Adam, boot fitter, Streeper's ct
Boraef Henry, vict. 13th ab Wallace
Boraef Martin, vict. 13th ab Washington
Boraef Valentine, vict., Brown bel Broad
Boraeff Ann, Cherry ab Broad
Boran Francis, seaman, 16 Pine al
Borbek Philip, bookseller and blank books, 8 S 4th, h 12 Elfreth's al
BORBIDGE THOMAS, forwarding and com. mer. 278 High, h 32 North Rittenhouse
Borden E. P., atty. & coun. 104 S 5th
Borden Samuel, mer., 43 High, h N E Sp Garden & Marshall
Border James, shoemr., rear 100 Dillwyn
Bordman Robt., cabinetmr., 9 Howard's pl
Borer Joseph, b. h., 36 O Y road
Borhek Charles, prof. of music, 52 Gaskill
Borhek Edward, jeweller, 52 Chestnut, h 141 Queen (S)
Borhek Fred. R., 4 Miller's ct
Borie A. E., mer., 45 Dock, h 329 Spruce
Borie Chas. & Henry, mers., Front and Chestnut
Borie Charles L., mer., Front & Chestnut, h 329 Spruce
Borie Francis, blacksm., Fothergill, h 145 Catharine
Borie Henry, mer., Front & Chestnut
Borie J. J., Mrs., 97 S 4th
Borland David, shoemr., Walnut bel Sch 3d
Borland Wm., shoemr., N E Sch 8th & High
Born Baltzer, baker, Rose al n Green
Born B., baker, 127 Brown
Born Geo., weav., Bedford opp Union (K)
Born Geo., carpet weav., Lemon bel Orange
Born Geo., weaver, Front ab Franklin (K)
Born Joseph, glassblower, Franklin bel Vienna (K)
Bornman Benj., dyer, Charlotte bel Thompson (K)
Bornman Catharine, gentw., Oldham's ct

Bornman Elizabeth, Gay's ct (K)
Bornman John, vict., 5th bel Master (K)
Bornman John, jr., vict., 5th bel Master, (K)
Bornman Lewis, vict., 4th bel Master (K)
Bornman Lewis, boot crimper, 120 G T road
Bornman Nich., vict. Cadwalader ab Phœnix (K)
Borns Louis, weaver, Shackamaxon n Franklin (K)
Borradaile Thomas, restaurant, High st Ferry
Borthwick Robt. cabinetmr., 3d n Spruce, h 147 Catharine
Bose Martin, lab., Hutchinson ab Poplar
Bosee Alfred, waterman, 10 Beck (S)
Boshart George, carp., Parrish ab 6th
Boshart Geo., hair sieve manuf., 1 Sheppard's al
Boshart John, cooper, 101 Crown
Bosler John, vict., 602 N 2d
Bosler John, jr., butcher, 602 N 2d (K)
Bosler Joseph, brass founder, 477 Vine
Boss Jas., jeweller, 99 Mulberry
Bossardet F., jeweller, 79 Gaskill
Bosser John, lab., 42 N. Market
Bossert Chas., pianomr., 57 N 8th, h 126 Cherry
Bossert Henry, shoemr., Oliver bel 13th
Bossert Henry, framemr., 544 N 3d
Bossert Joseph F., fur. car., 12th ab Sassafras
Bossert Sarah, b h., 39 N 4th
Bossinger John, bar tender, 3d ab George
Bossordet Peter, jeweller, 79 Gaskill
Bostock Peter, machinist, Scott's ct
Boston Ann, tailoress, 254 Sassafras
Boston Ann, Christian ab 7th
Boston Elizabeth, 48 Currant al
Boston Grace, washer, 3 Farmers' row
Boston Jacob, whitewasher, 58 Gaskill
Boston James B., painter, Oliver bel Broad
Boston John, carter, 15 Emlen's ct
Boston John, carter, rear 237 St John
Boston Mich., mor. dress., Charlotte ab George
Boston Wm., shoemr., Winter n Creek
Boswell Andrew, painter, 33 W North
Boswell Charles, lab., Lancaster bel Wharton
Boswell Geo., tinsmith, 58 N 2d, h Thomas's al
Boswell Jacob, skin dress., Poplar ab 3d
Boswell James J., mer., 50 High, h 108 Spruce
BOSWELL JAMES J. & Co., dry goods, 50 High
Boswell Wm. R., printer, Harmony ab 4th
Bothwell James, weaver, McDuffie n Sch 2d
Bothwell John, cooper, 40 Laurel
Bothwell Wm., brickmr., Mary n Beach
Botner Wm., printer, 478 Sassafras
Botsch John George, lab., 6 Stearly's ct
Botsford Alva, stone cutter, Jones E Sch 5th
Botsford Alva, jr., pearl manf., Sch 4th bel High
Botsford John, bricklayer, 1 Short ct
Botten Stephen, baker, Palmer ab Franklin (K)
Bottomley James, wool dealer, 53 N Water, h 103 Lombard
Boucher Benj., wheelwright, 160 Marshall
Boucher James, tailor, 2 Short ct
Boucher Joseph, wheelwright, Green bel 9th
Boucher Sarah, nurse, 83 N 9th
Boudwin John, wheelwrt., Fisher bel Marriott
Boudwin Peter, marketman, 13 Queen (S)

Bouffard Mrs. & Miss, dressmrs., 86 Locust
Boulter Charles J., potter, 13th ab Vine
Boulter Henry C., hairdress., 459 Vine
Boulter Jehu R, cordw., 155 N 2d
Boulter Mary, shop, 13th ab Vine
Boulton Benj. F., shoe st., Beach bel Maiden
Boulton Giles, druggist, N E 2d and Catharine
Boulton John, gent., Walnut bel Sch 7th
Bounds James, carp., Washington ab 12th
Bounds John, boot and shoemr., rear Carpenter bel 9th
Boureau Henry, coal mer., Front bel Maiden, h 7th bel Poplar
Bourgeis Sarah, 298 S 4th
BOURHILL ROBERT F., 354 High
Bourk James, bootmr., 74 S 11th
Bourke Edward J., sexton, 39 Union
Bourke Michael, clerk, 139 N 6th
Bourne Ezra, mer., 11 N Front and 12 N Water, h 337 Sassafras
Bournonville A., M. D., 59 N 4th
Bourquin Charles F., lithog. printer, 194 Pine
Bourquin Eveline, dressmr., 43 Spruce
Bourquin Frederick, undertaker, 304 Callowhill
Bourquin Frederick, lithog. printer, 194 Pine
Boustead James, currier, N E 8th and Willow, h 10th ab Washington
Bousted Thomas, weaver, 27 Lebanon
Boutcher Martha, sempstess, N Market ab Duke
Bouvier David, butcher, Evans
Bouvier John, office 10 N 7th, h 11 Logan sq
Bouvier Michael, mahogany and marble, 93 S 2d, h 80 S Front
BOUVIER M. & Co., mahog. & marble, 93 S 2d
Bouvier Peter, butcher Marion bel M road
Bouvier Peter, jr., butcher, Federal bel M road
Bouvier Philip, butcher, rear 91 P road
Bovard Wm., tailor, Parrish bel 11th
Bowden James, carp., M'Bride's ct
Bowden John, plasterer, R road ab Buttonwood
Bowden Wm., mariner, 76 German
Bowdle Tristram, mer., 34 N Front, h 427 Sassafras
Bowen A. J., cabinetmr., 43 Dock, h 330 Catharine
Bowen Benj., trunkmr., Morris ab Christian
Bowen David, shoemr., Queen bel Marlboro'
Bowen David H., cabinetmr., 415 S 2d
Bowen Eliza, white washer, 25 Paschal's al
Bowen E., hatter, 176 High, h 134 N 12th
Bowen James, Rev., Hallowell's ct
Bowen J. E., tailor, Beach ab Walnut
Bowen J. T., lithogr., 12 S Broad
Bowen Martha, 389 Spruce
Bowen Nicholas, waiter, 76 George
Bowen Phineas A., oysters, 8 High, h 9 Charle's pl
Bowen Samuel, tavern, Washington & Green
Bowen Smith, mer., 12 Church al, h 164 N 5th
Bowen S. R., mer., 58 Walnut
Bowen Thos. S., grocer, F road & Oxford (K)
Bowen Wm., cabinetmr., F road bel Franklin (K)
Bowen Wm., E., mer., 30 Chestnut, h Spruce W Sch 8th
Bowen Wm. M., druggist, New Market & Brown
Bowen Wm. M., printer, R road n 10th

Bowen Wm. M., U. S. mint, h 278 Wood
Bower Abraham, bootmr., Mayland
Bower Frederick, hotel, 332 Callowhill
Bower George, carp., Phœnix bel G T road (K)
Bower Geo. C., druggist, 3d and G T road (K)
Bower Henry A., druggist, N E 6th and Green
Bower John, sashmr., 4 Union sq
Bower John, cabinetmr., Bryan's ct
Bower John, baker, Parrish bel 11th
Bower Mary, Penn ab Marsh (K)
Bower Robt F., combmr., rear of Phoenix N of F road (K)
Bowers Chas. P., vict., (F V)
Bowers Christian, Sch 6th bel Pine
Bowers Christian, vict., Queen ab Palmer (K)
Bowers David, wheelwrt., 24 Brown (N L)
Bowers Ellen, milliner, 138 S Juniper
Bowers George, coal mer., Davis's landing, h 455 N 3d
Bowers Henry, shoemr., 121 Melon
Bowers John, lab., rear 175 Coates
Bowers John C., clothes, 71 S 2d
Bowers John D., lab., Fairview ab Sch 8th
Bowers Joseph, bricklayer, Beach ab Shacka. maxon (K)
Bowers Jos. T., combmr., Union ab Franklin (K)
Bowers Martha, b h., 163 S 9th
Bowers Michael, lab., rear 21 Charlotte
Bowers Peter G., supt., 402 N 3d
Bowers Samuel, tailor, Benton's av
Bowers Solomon, boatm., Sch 3d bel George
Bowers Thomas, saddler, Clinton ab Parrish
Bowers Thomas, tailor, 71 S 2d, h 355 Lombard
Bowers Wm., coal mer., N W Broad and Callow. hill, h 424 N 5th
Bowers Wm., b h., 39 N 5th
Bowers Edward, weaver, 6th ab Master (K)
Bowes Jacob, chairmr., Sanderson's ct
Bowes Wm., weaver, rear 125 Charlotte
Bowie James A., mer., 282 S 2d
Bowie John, mer., 282 S 2d
Bowie Roswell, hatter, Front ab Franklin
Bowl John, engineer, Marlboro' ab Allen (K)
BOWLBY & BRENNER, hardware, 69 High
Bowlby Catharine, gentw., 165 S 3d
Bowlby E. jr., mer., 69 High, h 399 Sruce
Bowlby Samuel L., stock and note broker, 5 Walnut, h 165 S 3d
Bowles M., variety store, 242 S 2d
Bowles James, jr., carp., 13th bel Melon
Bowles John L., coffee roaster, 89 Queen (K)
Bowman Chas., mariner, Higgin's pl
Bowman Christ., blacksm., Charlotte & George
Bowman Geo. W., shoemr., 100 Carpenter (S)
Bowman Goliah, seaman, Helmuth
Bowman Henry F., 113 N 7th
Bowman Jacob, lab., F road bel Franklin
Bowman Jacob, M. D., Lombard ab Sch 4th
Bowman Jas. S., brickmr., 8th ab Carpenter
Bowman John, lab., Olive bel 13th
Bowman John, clerk, 24 Combe's al
Bowman John, salesman, Castle bel 11th
Bowman John, stevedore, Mariner ab 13th
Bowman John, butcher, 399 S Front
Bowman John, 7 Quigg's ct

Bowman Joseph K., locksmith, 344 Sassafras
Bowman Martha, 16 Dean
Bowman Moses, mer., 108 Sassafras
Bowman & Moore, mers., 108 Sassafras
Bowman Samuel, printer, 18 Beck pl
Bowman Sarah, milliner, 55½ N 2d
Bowman & Seltzer, grocers, S W 2d and Callowhill
Bowman Thomas, mer., 32 Mulberry
Bowman Wm. H., paper and rags, 15 Commerce, h 525 Coates
Bown Abraham, hatter, 381 N Front
Bowness James, Mulberry n Sch Front
Bowser David B., sign painter, 177 N 4th
Bowyer John, carp. weaver, Cadwalader below Phœnix
Boxter Wm., painter, 2 Concord
Boyce Andrew, watchman, Cooper n Sch 3d
Boyce Ann, corsets, 69 Mulberry
Boyce Elizabeth, Hansel's ct
Boyce Henry, lab., Prime ab 2d
Boyce John, cordw., 21 Mulberry al
Boyce John, painter, 126 Plum
Boyce John E., machinist, Cadwalader below Phœnix (K)
Boyce Joseph, shop, 3 Cresson's al
Boyce Mary, milliner, 348 Sassafras
Boyce Samuel, grocer, N E 13th and Carrol
Boyce Sarah, 12 Gray's al
Boyce Wm. H., livery stable, 338 Callowhill, h Wood ab Vine
Boyd Alexander, acct., 7 Wood
Boyd Alex., lab., Watman's ct
Boyd Alex., shoemr., Shippen ab 13th
Boyd Albert, painter, rear Carlton ab Sch 6th
Boyd Andrew, bookbinder, 211 Lombard
Boyd Andrew, carp. weaver, Nixon ab Vine
Boyd Ann, washer, Sycamore ab Locust
Boyd Catharine, 219 Christian
Boyd Charles, mer., 56 S 13th
Boyd Charles, stonecutter, 7 Callowhill
Boyd Charlotte C., 185 Spruce
Boyd Cornel, brickmr., Hancock ab Norris (K)
BOYD & CUMMINGS, dry goods, 103 High
Boyd David, gent., Sch 5th and Hamilton
Boyd David K., printer, 4 N 9th
Boyd Edward, carp., rear 611 N 6th
Boyd Elizabeth, gentw., 167 Pine
Boyd Elizabeth, S W Sch 7th and Mulberry
Boyd Elizabeth, 79 Tammany
Boyd Emelia S., upholsterer, 125 N 5th
Boyd Hugh, tailor, Smith's ct
Boyd George, grocer, S W 8th and Green
Boyd Hugh, Front bel Master (K)
Boyd Hugh, tailor, 514 N 2d, h Front bel Master (K)
Boyd James, lab., Thorn's ct
Boyd James, gardener, Jones n Sch 4th
Boyd James F., dyer, Shippen ab 13th
Boyd Jane, 64 Garden
Boyd John, ropemr., 21 Federal
Boyd John, machinist, Hope ab Jefferson (K)
Boyd John, tailor, 150 N Water, h Maria bel 5th
Boyd John, stonecutter, Ogden ab 9th
Boyd John, lab., Pearson's ct

Boyd John J., stone-cutter, 33 Dugan
Boyd John Oliver, merchant, 103 High, h 168 Mulberry
Boyd John S., mer., 125 High, h 317 Lombard
Boyd John W., clerk, 277 N 5th
Boyd Rebecca, tavern, 11 Decatur
Boyd Robert, weaver, Clare st
Boyd Robert, bookbinder, 327 Pine
Boyd Samuel, tailor, N W Water and Mulberry, h 21 Sassafras
Boyd Thomas, carp., 4 Sugar al
Boyd Thomas, bootmr., Sch 4th n M'Duffie
Boyd Thomas, mer., High ab 5th, h Washington (W P)
Boyd Thomas, lab., Benton and William (K)
Boyd Thomas, stonecut., rear Olive bel Broad
Boyd William, conveyancer, 91 Walnut
Boyd Wm., tallow chandler, 121 N 5th
Boyd Wm., grocer, 408 High
Boyd Wm., waiter, Pearl ab 13th
Boyd Wm A., M. D., 62 S 11th
Boyd Wm. S., grocer, 7 and 9 S Water, h 128½ Spruce
Boye M. H., chemist, 27 N 7th
Boyer Abraham, carp., Poplar bel Broad
Boyer Charles, agent, 522 S Front
Boyer Christ., vict., Vineyard ab R road (F V)
Boyer C. R., M. D., 158 N 9th
Boyer Daniel L., tobacconist, 1 S 3d, h 109 N Juniper
Boyer Ellen, b h, S W 4th and Walnut
Boyer Evan, ship carp., Church ab Washington
Boyer Franklin, agent, rear Irvine st
Boyer George, Willow bel Spruce
Boyer Henry, lab., Fox's ct
Boyer Henry, shop, Franklin ab Front (K)
Boyer Hiram L., bricklayer, 7th and Coates
Boyer Jacob, carp., Franklin ab 4th
Boyer Jeremiah, weaver, 674 N 2d (K)
Boyer Jesse, saddler, Orleans
Boyer Jno., carp., Orchard ab George, h 6 Wood
Boyer Richard, lab., 4th ab Thompson (K)
Boyer Rosanna, dry goods, 33 S Garden
Boyer Sarah L., Clark ab 3d
BOYER WM., house furnisher, 355 High, h 11th ab Green
Boyes B. C., machinist, Brandywine ab 13th
Boyland John, weaver, rear Hope ab Otter (K)
Boyle Andrew, manuf., Wood bel Sch 2d
Boyle Barney, lab., Washington (W P)
Boyle Bernard, oysters, 73 Locust
Boyle Charles, weav., Hancock ab Phœnix (K)
Boyle Charles, lab., George ab Sch 7th
Boyle Daniel, seaman, 118 S Front
Boyle Geo., dyer, Charlotte bel Thompson (K)
Boyle Henry, weaver, Nixon st
Boyle Henry, chairmr., N Market ab Laurel
Boyle Henry, stone cutter, 6 Farries' ct
Boyle Hugh, tailor, 63 S 5th
Boyle Hugh, weaver, Murray ab Sch 3d
Boyle James, lab., Walnut n Sch 3d
Boyle James, lab., Nixon ab Hamilton
Boyle & Jeffries, coachmrs., 7 Green (C)
Boyle John, printer, 2d and Brown, h 494 N 3d
Boyle John, lab., Cooper n Sch 3d

Boyle John, waterman, Reed bel Church
Boyle Michael, chandler, Laurel opp Bachel
Boyle Neal, weaver, Spruce n Sch Front
Boyle Patrick, lab., Beach n Locust
Boyle Patrick, carter, 27 Hirst
Boyle Patrick, weaver, 10th bel Christian
Boyle Patrick, lab., Ann ab Sch 5th
Boyle Robert, stonecut., Carlton bel Sch 5th
Boyle Robert, dealer, 6 Jones, W Sch 8th
Boyle Sarah, 82 Swanson
Boyle Samuel, carp., 11th and Castle
Boyle Thomas, ironfounder, 7th bel Federal
Boyle Thomas, dyer, 4th ab Franklin (K)
Boyle Thomas, cordw., 5th ab Poplar
Boyle Thomas, dry goods, 82 N 11th
Boyle Wellington H., chemist, Lemon
Boyle Wm., cedar cooper, N W 9th and High, h Barker n Sch 5th
Boyle Wm., weaver, 2d ab Master (K)
Boyle Wm., grocer, 97 P road
Boyle Wm., lab., Watson's al
Boyle William V., grocer, 35 S Water, h 9 S Penn sq
BOYLEN JAMES, tavern, 48 S 8th
Boyles James, bookbin., 9½ George, h 31 ON 7th
Boyles Wm., painter, 470 Sassafras
Boyron John, weaver, Hope ab Otter (K)
Boys George, confec., S W 12th and Spruce
Boys Wm., dry goods, 451 N 2d
Bozarth Ann, 6 Martin's ct (K)
Bozorth Richard, machinist, Grange ab Washington
Bozorth Wm., carp., Poplar n 10th, h Lewis ab Poplar
Brabant Francis, 74 Vine
Brace John, stove finisher, rear 27 Green
Brace Thomas, tinman, 3 Oldham's ct
Braceland Bridget M., upholsterer, 153 Walnut
Braceland Charles, lab., Filbert n Sch Front
Braceland John, lab., Cooper n Sch 3d
Braceland John, rear 15 Prosperous al
Braceland J., tobacconist, 397 S Front
Braceland Margaret, Marshall's ct
Bracken James, polisher, 122 Locust
Bracken Margaret, 261 Green
Bracken Thos., printer, 194 W Callowhill
Brackenridge Henry, 112 Frankford road (K)
Brackin Henry, machinist, 15 Perry
Brackin Richard, carp., Wetherell's ct
Brackin Samuel, cabinetmr., Ten foot al
Brackney Archer, painter, 25 Concord and 95 Walnut
Brackney Charles, weaver, 14 Shippen
Brackney Isaac A., tailor, 3 Sheaff's al
Brackney Saml., tinsmith, 69 Logan sq
Bracy Charles, lab., 5 Carollne pl
Bracy Thos., lab., Gales' ct
Bradan Wm., weaver, Milton bel 11th
Bradburry Ed., machinist, 2d bel Jefferson
Bradburry Wm., bootmr., 11 Relief
Bradbury C. M., captain, 5th and Marriott
Bradbury Joseph P., mer., 350 Pine
Bradbury Mary, G T. road opp 4th (K)
Bradbury Matthew, doubler and twister, Amber ab Phoenix (K)

Bradbury Robert, pedler, 19 Cherry
Braddock Darnold, carp. Franklin ab Front (K)
Braddock Ira, shoemr., Fraley's ct
Braddock L., painter, 334 Sassafras, h Vine ab Sch 6th
Braden Andrew, stonemason, Shippen ab Broad
Brades & Co., com. mers., 54 S whfs
Bradfield George W., brass founder, 71 N 8th
Bradfield Oliver, machinist, Vernon bel 11th
Bradfield Thos. C., cordw., 13th and Olive
Bradford Alfred D., gent., 433 Sassafras
Bradford Cornelius I., acct., Washington ab 11th
Bradford Elizabeth, eating house, 481 High
Bradford Hannah, Marriott ab 5th
Bradford Hira, mer., 42 N 2d
Bradford James, M. D., 347 Walnut
Bradford Samuel, Treas. Phil. and Reading railroad Co., 95½ Walnut, h Walnut n Sch 6th
Bradford Sarah Ann, b h, 48 W Cedar
Bradford Selby, eating house, 246 High
BRADFORD THOMAS, atty. and coun., 5 Sansom
Bradford T. & V. L., attys. and couns. 5 Sansom
Bradford Vincent L., att'y at law, 5 and h 22 Sansom
Bradford Walter, teacher, 139 S 11th
Bradford Wm., att. at law, 5 Sansom
Bradley Bernard, lab., Spruce ab Ashton
Bradley Christiana, gentw., 288 N 7th
Bradley Daniel, rear 5 Bread
Bradley David, trader, 2d bel Reed
Bradley Dominick, lab., rear 27 Quince
Bradley Edw., lab., rear 94 N 11th
Bradley Elizabeth, Logan ab Green
Bradley George, cordw., 246 Christian
Bradley Gurdon, india-rubber goods, 13 S 4th
Bradley Hugh, waiter, Spruce ab Sch Front
Bradley James, baker, 407 High
Bradley James, weaver, 13th ab Brinton
Bradley Jeremiah, 20 College av
Bradley John, tailor, 295 S 3d
Bradley John, mariner, 61 German
Bradley John, watchman, 2 Watson's al
Bradley John O., shoemr., 3 Clair
Bradley Joshua, machinist, 286 Wood
Bradley Mary, b h, 296 High
Bradley Nathaniel, carter, Quince & Lombard
Bradley Nathan, lab., High n Sch 2d
Bradley Peter, cabman, S E 10th & Sassafras
Bradley Thos., lab., Wash. av bel Brown
Bradley Wm. G., drover, Carpenter bel 6th
Bradnack Wm., victualler, 7th bel Federal
Bradshaw & Dyson, turners, rear 112 Walnut
Bradshaw Edmund, 306 N 8th
Bradshaw Ellen, milliner, 172 S 2d
Bradshaw Joseph, bootmr., 80 S 5th
Bradshaw Nathaniel, agent, Marlboro' n Bedford (K)
Bradshaw Sarah, rear 245 N Front
Bradshaw Wm. A., watchman, Liberty al
Bradshaw Wm. K., 74 Union
Bradshaw Wm. M., turner, rear 112 Walnut
Bradway Isaac, 320 N 8th
Bradway Mark D., paper carrier, 118 N 11th
Brady A. E., shop, R road and Francis

Brady Charles, stables, 13 Willing's al
Brady & Degroot, grocers and ship chandlers, Sch Beach bel Chestnut
Brady D. C. E. mer., 26 N Front, h Marshall ab Green
Brady Edward, bootmr., 161 Lombard
Brady Edward F., 49 Buttonwood
Brady Francis, manf., G T road ab Master, (K)
Brady Fred., 96 Catharine
Brady Hannah, 129 Queen
Brady James, cabm., 10 Nectarine
Brady James, lab., Sch Front ab High
Brady James, grocer, Sch 4th and Lombard
Brady James, candles and soap, 110 S 12th
Brady John, lab., 1 Reid's ct n German
Brady John, tavern, N E 5th and Prune
Brady John, blindmr., Hanover bel West (K)
Brady John, moulder, rear Wood ab Broad
Brady John, lab., 4 Rudolph's ct
Brady Martha, rear 127 N Market
Brady Mary, 3 Traquair's ct
Brady Mat., manuf., G T road bel Jefferson (K)
Brady Mat. J., carp., School n Franklin (K)
Brady Michael, cabtmr., 342 Sassafras
Brady Patrick, shop, 222 Shippen
Brady Patrick, grocer and ship chand., Beach bel Chestnut
Brady Patrick, lab., Sch Front n Mulberry
Brady P., mer., 26 N Front, h 397 Mulberry
Brady P. & Co., mers., 26 N Front
Brady Robert, carter, West Sch ab Walnut
Brady Rosanna M., matron, 403 Chestnut
Brady Rosanna, 177 G T road
Brady S. A. & Co., liqu., 141 N 3d, h 46 Crown
Brady Thomas, lab., 87 N 10th
Brady Thomas, lab., 4th bel G T road (K)
Brady Thomas, tailor, 360 N 2d
Brady Thos., lab., Sch 3d n Lombard
Brady Thos. F., mer., 107½ High
Brady William, gold beater, 80 N 6th, h 13 E North
Brady Wm., lab., Sch 8th ab Vine
Brady Wm., coach lace weaver, 13 Elder
Brady Wm., shoemr. 5 Smith's pl
Braeger Rudolph, susp. weaver, 43 Pegg
Bragdin Mary, Sch 3d ab High
Bragg & Warner, milliners, 62 Vine
Brainard Adams, clothing, N W 2d and Spruce, h 6th n Lombard
Brainard John, 8 Logan sq
Brainerd Thos. Rev., Green Hill & Sch 7th
Bramall Benj., colourist, Warren ab Beach (K)
Bramall Joseph, cabinetmr., Queen ab Palmer
Braman Eliza, Franklin ab Front (K)
Braman Peter, watchman, Sycamore ab Locust
Bramble Joseph, moulder, 468 N Front
Bramble Wm., 50 Gaskill
Branch Lewis H., mer., 30 S whfs
Branchley Rachel, shop, Vine n Schuyl
Branard John, broker, 21 Scheetz st
Brand Albert C., tinsmith, 343 High, h 90 N 11th
Brand Geo., tinman, 99 High, h 85 Buttonwood
Branden Thos., lab., Barker n Sch 6th
Brandsetter G. J., barber, 43 Callowhill
Brandstetter H., gentw., 43 Callowhill

Brandt Chas., bricklayer, 622 Front (K)
Brandt Jas., carp., Front ab Phœnix (K)
Brandt John, baker, 114 Swanson
Brandt Sophia, b. h., 130 Beach (K)
Brandt Thomas, bricklayer, 622 N Front
Brandt Wm., baker, 253 S 7th
Branin Abijah, carp., Charlotte n Creek
Brankin Edward, weaver, 4th bel G T road
Brannan Jas., lab., 356 N Front
Brannan John, 15 Fayette
Brannan John, carter, 6th ab Franklin
Brannegan Daniel, carter, 4 Braccland's ct
Brannegan Danl., weaver, G T road bel Jefferson
Brannegan Francis, weav., 4th bel G T road (K)
Brannegan Jno., lab., Charlotte ab Thompson (K)
Brannegan Patrick, weaver, Baker's ct (K)
Brannegar John, bedstead mr., 10th n Milton
Branner Frederick, Olive ab 13th
Brannin Jas., weaver, Murray n Sch 3d
Brannin Patrick, lab., Mulberry n Ashton
Brannin Thos., weaver, 209 Shippen
Brannin Thos., tinsmith, G T road ab Master (K)
Brannin Thos., lab., 13th and Mariner
Branning Patrick, weaver, 6 Van Buren ct (K)
Brannon Chas., carter, P road and 8th
Brannon Matthew, stone cutter, rear 517 N 3d
Brannon Michael, lab., Fleming's row
Bransby Wm., cooper, R road ab Wallace
Branson Ann, Brinton ab R road
Branson John, carter, 27 Emlin's ct
Branson John, cordw., Lewis ab Poplar
Branson & Offerman, gents. furn'g. store, 76 S 8th
Branson Peter, brass founder, Brinton ab R road
Branson Rebecca, milliner, 115 Sassafras
Branson Samuel, cordw., rear 16 Ogden
Branson Samuel, mer., 59 High
Branson Thos., coal dealer, Broad n Spruce, h Chancellor n Sch 7th
Brant Josiah, painter 77 Mulberry
Brantis George, brickmr., Sch 3d and Lombard
Brasier Amable Joseph, gent., office 117½ S 3d
Brassington John, brassfounder, 641 N 2d (K)
Bratten Isaac, carp., Parrish and Elizabeth
Braugh Michael, Perry ab Franklin (K)
Bray Charles, cap and hat store, 60 Cedar
Bray Daniel, mer., 163 High, h 217 Vine
Bray Elizabeth, Sch 6th bet Market & Chestnut
Bray Elkanah, shipmaster, 81 Christian
Bray James H., glass cutter, Allen bel Marlborough (K)
Bray John, grocer, S W Franklin and Coates
Bray John, clerk, 160 Marshall
Braynard J. D., broker, 42 Walnut, h 21 Scheetz
Brayton Oliver, carp., 25 N 13th
Brazao Joseph, shoemr., Jenning's row E side
BRAZER CHRISTOPHER, alderman, 69 N 5th
Brazer John, tailor, 190 S 3d
Breach Wm., basketmr., 27 Pratt
Brealey John, printer, 1 Scott's ct
Brearley R., widow, 3 Lancaster
Brearley Wm., shipcarp., 602 S Front
Brearly James, sawmr., 3 Fries' ct
Breason Neal, cordw., 10th bel Christian
Breban J. J., mer., 56 Walnut, h Spruce W Broad
Berchemin Lewis, jeweller, 120 S 2d

Breck Samuel, gent., Mulberry ab Broad
Breckenridge Andrew, lab., W High n Ashton
Breckenridge D., weaver, 21 M'Duffie
Breckenridge Hugh, lab., Grubb st
Breckenridge Jas., lab., Hope ab Otter (K)
Breed Samuel D., boots and shoes, 532 High
Breen Ann, distiller, 143 S 10th
Breen David, lab., 2d ab Master
Breen Jas. F., carp., Wood ab 13th
Breeson Jas., weaver, Milton ab 11th
Bregg Francis A., teacher, Broad bel Poplar
Brehm Francis, brewer, 131 Coates
Breidenhart & Co., wine mers., 115 S Front
Breidenhart E., gentw., 140 N 13th
Breidenhart George A., liquors, 115 S Front, h 106 S Front
Breidenhart John C., mer., 115 S Front
Breining Jacob, grocery, 85 Franklin
Breintnall Jane, 287 Walnut
Breintnall Thomas Rev., 10th and Wallace
Breish John, butcher, Master bel 4th (K)
Breish Joshua, tavern, S W Poplar and Apple
Breish Sarah, tavern, G T road bel Master
Breish Sarah, G T road ab Thompson
Breish Wm., butcher, Coates ab 9th
Breiter A. R., musician, 327 Sassafras
Brelsford Chapman, shoemr., Lyndall's al
Brelsford Francis, oyster house, 9th & Depot st
Brelsford John, potter, New Market and G T road, h 525 N 2d
Brelsford Joseph, blacksmith, Locust ab 12th
Brelsford Wm., plasterer, Harrison ab Fitler
Bremeyer Geo. W., mer., 54 S whfs.
Bremer Lewis, tobacconist, 190 N 3d
BREMOND & FLORENCE, hatters, N E 6th and Chestnut
Bremond J., hatter, N E 6th and Chestnut, h 47 S 4th
Brendlinger Hannah Ann, b. h., 54 Sassafras
Brenizer J. A., tailor, 21 Turner
Brenner Fred'k, baker, Franklin ab Elm (K)
Brenner Geo., Queen n Vienna (K)
Brenner Henry, baker, Queen n Vienna (K)
Brenner John, machinist, Irvine
Brenner John G., mer., 69 High, h S Logan sq

Brewster Edmund, p. painter, Rye & Wharto
Brewster Francis E., att'y and coun., 50 S 6th
BREWSTER FRED'K C., att'y and coun Sy S 6th
Brewster Joseph S., att'y and coun., 65 S 5th
Brewster M. H., 1 Sansom
Brewster Wm., weaver, Bedford and 13th
Brewton Ann, Agt. Ladies' Depos., 289 Chestnut, h S E 8th and Sansom
Brewton Daniel, seaman, Washington ab 4th
Breyer L., bootmr., 153 Mulberry
Breyer Martha, 18 Charles' pl
Brian Wm., tailor, 330 High, h Charles n Buttonwood
Brick Daniel, cordw., 10th bel Christian
Brick John R., boots & shoes, N E 6th & High, h 213 Spruce
Brick Samuel R., bricklayer, 14 Dillwyn
Brick Wm. W., morocco dr., 360 S 2d
Brickett Enoch, coach trimmer, 73 Carpenter
Brickman George, mer., 10th ab Parrish
Brickner Michael, tailor, rear 603 N 6th
Bridge Christ., trader, G T road ab Master (K)
Bridge J. C., gent., 456 Vine
Bridge Samuel, waiter, White's ct
Bridges Calvin, shoemr., 8th bel Green
Bridges Edwin, 262 High
Bridges John, waiter, Sch 4th ab Sprue
Bridges N W., 167 Walnut
Bridges Robert, M. D., Clinton bel 11th
Bridges Wm. C., broker, 62 Walnut, h Clinton bel 11th
Bridport Hugh, 239 Spruce
Brierley Thos., carp., 8th bel Shippen
Briggs Andrew, machinist, Washington bel 13th
Briggs Edmund, lab., Phœnix bel Front (K)
Briggs Edward, wool spinner, rear Charlotte ab Culvert
Briggs Ethan, gunsmith, Sarah n Queen (K)
Briggs G. E., Sch 4th ab Cedar
Briggs G. W., collector, 2 Hause's ct
Briggs John, cordw., 12 Tammany ct
Briggs John, bleeder, 47 N 7th
Briggs John, hosier, rear 487 N 3d

Brightwell Sarah, shopkeeper, 46 New Market
Brill Geo., turner, Shackamaxon ab Bedford (K)
Brill John H., cordw., Dungan's av (K)
Brimmer Elizabeth, 132 S 9th
Brimmer John, printer, 10 S Broad
Brinckle Joshua G., att'y & coun., 152 Walnut
Brinckle J. R., mer., 15 S Front, h 335 Chestnut
Brinckle T. R., M. D., 94 S 8th
Brinckle Wm. D., M D., 335 Chestnut
Brinckle Wm. H., att'y and coun., 53 S 5th
Brinckley G. W., musician, 6th bel Catharine
Brinckley Richard, lab., rear Mariott's la ab 5th
Brinckley Robert, waiter, 5 Portland la
Brindel John F., gunsm., Sarah bel Bedford (K)
Brines Thomas, lab., La Fayette ab 9th
Bringhurst John, druggist, S E 10th & Chestnut
Bringhurst J. H., sawmr., 4th and Franklin, h 671 N 2d (K)
Bringhurst John K., printer, S W 4th & Shippen
Bringhurst & Kurby, saw & knife mks., Franklin bel 4th (K)
Bringhurst Robt. R., undertaker, 239 Mulberry
Brinkworth Wm., carp., Bank bel Pine
Brinley Edward L., mer., 24 N 2d, h Spruce ab Broad
Brinnisholt Henry, wharf builder, 77 M road
Brint Nelson, lab., Sassafras ab Sch 3d
Brinton & Ely, coal mers., Broad & Willow
Brinton Elizabeth, mantuamr., 122 Chestnut
Brinton Emily, nurse, 1 Raspberry la
Brinton George, 1 S Broad
Brinton Jacob L., coal mer., 277 Marshall
Brinton R. B., mer., 103 High, h Pine n 8th
BRINTON & SHACKELFORD, silks, 103 High
Brintzinghoffer Chas., 369 High
Brisbane Wm. H., publisher, 46 N 5th
Briscoe A. H., dentist, 214 Walnut
Briscoe James H., dentist, 247 Walnut
Brison James, carter, Ruddack's ct
Brister Chas., lab., Portland bel 7th
Brister Elizabeth, Lombard bel 11th
Brister Hannah, 52 Currant al
Bristol Abraham, painter, 37 Coates' al
Bristol Andrew, 177 Lombard
Bristol Augustus, dealer, 148½ Cedar
Bristol Charles, clothes, 97 S 2d, h 177 Lombard
Bristol James, wood sawyer, 95 Lombard
Bristol Jas., waiter, Spooner's ct
Britin Jacob, tobacconist, 494 N 2d
Britsch Philip, baker, 365 N 3d
Britt Patrick, lab., Beach ab Hanover (K)
Brittain Thos., cordw., 13th bel Brown
Brittin J. B., 24 Logan
Brittner Joseph, book fitter, 3 Carlisle ct
Brittner Peter, barber, O Y road bel Coates
Britton Abraham, blindmr., Washington bel 6th
Britton Austin, bricklar., Carroll bel 13th
Britton A., nurse, rear 392 Sassafras
Britton Edmd., cordw., Apple ab Brown
Britton Ellen, dry goods, S W 13th & Pine
Britton Hall, Dr., 13th bel Rose
Britton Jacob, 3 Boyle's ct
Britton James, '19 Mulberry
Britton John, blacksm., Queen n 3d
Britton John, Mrs., Chestnut (W P)

Britton Letitia, rear 15 New Market
Britton Samuel, blacksm., Ross ab Queen (K)
Britton Thomas, U. S Mint, h 34 Jacoby
Britton Wm., saddler, Concord
Britts Isaac, ship carp., Hanover ab Queen
Broadbent Daniel W., lab., Derringer's av (K)
Broadbent Elijah, ostler, Littleboy's ct
Broadhurst Jas., weav., Montgomery ab F road
Broadhurst John, carp. weav. 2d bel Oxford (K)
Broadwater Daniel, fisher, Wood ab Queen (K)
Broadwater Wm., cordw., Bagg's ct
Brobson Wm., bookbinder, 384 S 3d
Brobston Joseph, acct., 443 High
Brock Charles C., mer., 108 N 3d
Brock Charles N., machinist, 6 Lagrange pl, h 30 N 10th
Brock Charles W., 52 St John
Brock George E., 97 & 99 N 3d
Brock & Hough, flour store, 194 N 3d & 226 N 2d
Brock John, groc., 97 & 99 N 3d, h 149 N 4th
BROCK JOHN, SONS & Co., groc., 97 and 99 N 3d
Brock J. P., atty. & coun., 149 N 4th
Brock Samuel Z., mer., 194 N 3d
Brock Wm., cabinetmr., 56 P road
Brock Wm. Penn, 91 & 99 N 3d
Brock Wm., butcher, 50 St John
Brock Wm., 52 St John
Brockerman John, driver, 3 William's ct
Brockman Benj., iron dealer, 563 N Front
Brockway Philip, weav. Beach bel Bishop (K)
Brodback John, baker, 71 F road (K)
Brode George, cordw., 97 Crown
Brode John, whipmr., Sansom's al ab Willow
Brode Walter, brickmr., 171 Green
Brodhead James, dyer, 17 Shriver's ct
Brodie Andrew, machinist, 4th bel Master (K)
Brodie James, metalic roofer, 9 St James, h 62 Coates
Brodie Robert C., druggist, Sp Garden & 12th
Brodrick Patrick, Sch Front ab Spruce
Brogan Patrick, moroc. dr., P road bel Cedar
Brogdon Wm., porter, 6 Barley n 11th
Brognard Joseph R., com. mer., 16 N Front, h 384 N 6th
Brognard N. L. mer. 22 Church al, h 306 Coates
Broker Jacob, Brown ab Cherry (K)
Brolaskey S., 419 Chestnut
Bromel Benj., sailmr., 28 Elfreth's al
Bromley Arthur, bleacher, Beach ab Palmer (K)
Bromley John, weaver, rear G T road ab 5th
Bromley Wm., blacksm., King bet Sassafras & Cherry
Brong Andrew, lab., Pearl bel Broad
Bronin Thos., tinsmith, G T road ab Master (K)
Bronstrap F., blacksm., 427 Noble
Bronson Cha., agent, Shackamaxon n Franklin
Bronwell Fred., blk. sm., Dunton bel Otter (K)
Brook Richard S., oyster house, 261 Callowhill
Brook Wm. F., machinist, 5 Ulrich (K)
Brookbank & Lewry, gasfitters, Willow bel 3d
Brookbanks Wm., gasfitter, 54 Coates

Brook Catharine E., 7 Carlton sq
Brooke Charlotte P., 34 N 9th
BROOKE C. WALLACE, atty. & coun., 144 Walnut
Brooke Hiram, mer., 77 N 3d
Brooke James, grocer, S W Sch 7th & Pine
Brooke Jas. J., paper & rags, 29 Commerce
Brooke John F., M. D., 403 Spruce
Brooke Jonas, tavern, 227 Walnut
Brooke Lewis P. mer. 72 N 3d, h 8 Montgomery
Brooke Margaret, dressmr., 79 Green
Brooke Nathan, carp., Brown bel 7th
Brooke S. H., mer., 140 High, h 34 N 9th
BROOKE, TYSON & RHEN, mers., 140 High
Brooker Benj. C., auctioneer, 6 N 3d, h 114 Catharine
Brooker Charles, machinist, Penn bel R road
Brooker Elizabeth, pawn broker, 186 Cedar
Brooker John, cordw., Hallowell n 7th
Brookfield Jos., M. D., Juniper & Filbert
Brookfield Wm., stone cr., Buttonwood & R road
Brookman Geo., lab., Lombard n Sch
Brookman Henry, tavern, 60 Penn (C)
Brooks David, brickmr., Pine ab 4th
Brooks Elias S., umbrellas, 68 S 2d
Brooks Elizabeth, 33 N Sch 8th
Brooks Elizabeth, 28 Perry
Brooks George, agent, 2 N 9th
Brooks Hannah, Lewis ab Poplar
Brooks Henry, grocer, 21 N 2d
Brooks Isaac jr., brickmr., Jefferson
Brooks Isaac, grocer, 11th & Vine
Brooks James, twister, 181 G T road (K)
Brooks Jane, grocer, Sch 7th & Helmuth
Brooks John, carp., 281 N 7th
Brooks John, cooper, 75 S Water, h 5 Norris' al
Brooks John F., carter, Lombard ab 7th
Brooks John H., clerk, 24 Wash. Market pl
Brooks John, lab., Franklin ab Front (K)
Brooks Jonathan, iron cast. Bedford & Union (K)
Brooks Joseph, cab driver, 15 Dannaker's av·
Brooks Jos., tobacco, Apple ab George
Brooks Jos. H., druggist, Beach ab Maiden (K)
Brooks J. M., 18 Church al, h 90 New
Brooks Margaret, dealer, 30 Shippen
Brooks Mary, Walnut ab 13th
Brooks Oliver & Co., bat'rs, S W 3d & Walnut
BROOKS OLIVER, hats & caps, S W 3d and Walnut, h 180 S 9th
Brooks Phebe, Christian and Stewart
BROOKS & ROACH, com. mers., 18 Church al
Brooks Samuel, mer., 7 S whfs., h 228 Walnut
Brooks Samuel, oysterman, N E Sch 8th and Chestnut

Brooks Wm., Shippen bel 4th
Brooks Wm., carp., Crown bel Duke (K)
Brooks Wm. J., carpet weaver, rear Filbert bel Sch 5th
Brooks Wm. K., grocer, 5th & Wash. Market pl
Broom Ann, matron Christ Church Hospital, 3 Cherry
Broom Christopher, 11 Noble
Broom George L., sugar refiner, 15 Bread, h 0 Y read bel Green
Broom Isaac, lab., 23 Dugan
BROOM JACOB, atty. and coun., 70 S 6th, h (W P)
BROOM JAMES M., atty. & coun., 103 Walnut, h N E 3d & York ct
Broom Thomas, ship carp., 101 Prime
Broom Wm., sugar refiner, 11 Noble
Broomall Lewis R., watchmr., 166 Sassafras
Broome Thos., morocco casemr., 46 Chestnut
Broomel Peter, bookbind. Hubbell ab Catharine
Broomel Wm., police, 20 Bonsall
Brophy John, weaver, Murray n Sch 3d
Bross Edmond R., cordw., 44 Chester
Brostin Dennis, hatter, rear 8th bel Carpenter
Brothers Charles, hatter, 27 N 3d, h 182 N 4th
Brothers Thaddeus, lab., Elizabeth ab Poplar
Brothers Thaddeus, lab., 17 Harrison
Brotherton Hugh, dry goods, 136 N 13th
Brough Mich., blacksm., Perry ab Franklin (K)
Brough Samuel, blacksm., 3d ab Beaver
Broughton Thomas, machinist, Perry ab Franklin (K)
Broughton Thomas G., mer., 38 N whfs., h 10 Belmont pl
Brous Wm., cordw., 2d bel Oxford (K)
Brower Ann, tailoress, 299 S Front
Brower Barnet, machinist, 25 N 4th
Brower Christian, Poplar, ab 11th
Brower David E., mer., 193 High
Brower, Hays & Co., booksellers, 193 High
Brower Nathan P., mer., 193 High
Brower Peter B., ladies' shoemr., Bond's ct
Browers Jacob, potter, rear 5 Brooke
Browfey Michael, weaver, Lombard n Sch 7th
Browfey Peter, weaver, Helmuth
Brown Abraham, barber, 1 S 11th
Brown Achor, harnessmr., Filbert n Sch Front
BROWN ALEXANDER, gent., 387 Walnut
Brown Alexander, mariner, 10 Liberty ct
Brown Alexander, silversm., 18 Minor
Brown Alexander, lab., Linden ab Sch 7th·
Brown Allen, lab., Hancock ab Phoenix
Brown Andrew, 85 Cherry
Brown Andrew, 353 S 6th

Brown Catharine, S W 13th and Spruce
Brown Cephas, cordw., 173 S 11th
Brown Charles, weav., rear Hanover bel Duke
Brown Charles, Rev., Callowhill n Sch Front
Brown Charles, watchman, Brooks' ct
Brown Charles, bookseller, 14 Girard
Brown Chas. B., blacksm., rear 107 N Market
Brown Chas. H. jr., tailor, 18 Ogden
Brown Chris. D. paper stainer, Pearl bel Sch 6th
Brown C., washer, St Mary
Brown C. A. & Co., booksellers, 36 N 6th
Brown Daniel, grocery, 49 Fitzwater
Brown Daniel, lab., Lombard ab Sch 6th
Brown Daniel H., tavern, Hanover n F road (K)
Brown David, carp., 32 Strawberry
Brown David, Green ab R road
Brown David, weaver, 13th & Rose
Brown David, runner, rear 62 Gaskill
Brown David Paul, atty & coun., N W 9th and Pine
BROWN DAVID S., com. mer., 38 S Front, h 274 Walnut
BROWN DAVID S. & Co., domestic goods, 38 S Front
Brown Deborah, gentw., 295 Chestnut
Brown Delos W. dry goods, 81 N 8th & 21 Bank
Brown Ebenezer, 6 Bank, h Sp Garden bel 11th
Brown Edmond, capmr., 5 Bank, h 364 N 10th
Brown Edward, teacher, 61 Prune, h 12th ab Cherry
Brown Edward, bar tender, 8 Loxley's ct
Brown Edward, machinist, 6 Lagrange pl
Brown Eleanor, Fitler bel Harrison (K)
Brown Elias, marble mas., Broad & Lombard
Brown Elijah, gent., 51 S 5th
Brown Eliza, Morris bel Catharine
Brown Eliza, washer, rear, 394 Sassafras
Brown Eliza, Vine ab Broad
Brown Eliza, b h, Julianna and Wood
Brown Elizabeth, gentw., Jackson ab Adams
Brown Elizabeth, shop, 77 George
Brown Emanuel D., collector, 25 Merchant
Brown Emeline, b h, 14 N 9th
Brown E. M., cooper, Pleasant bel 10th
Brown Enos, lab., 20 Wash. Market pl
Brown Francis, weaver, Philip ab Jefferson
Brown Francis, ice dealer, rear 116 Christian
Brown Frank, clerk, 1 Linden st (K)
BROWN FREDERICK, druggist, N E Chest. and 5th, h 70 S 5th
Brown Fredk., blacksm., Orange bel Citron
Brown George, chairmr., Rule bel Wheat
Brown George, carp., Sch 6th ab Pine, h Sch 3d n Lombard
Brown George, watchman, rear Washington ab Coates
Brown George, carp., 2 Galbraith's ct
Brown George, oak cooper, 13 Beck
Brown George, cordw., 160 Poplar
Brown George, matmr., Carpenter ab 8th
Brown George, weaver, Fitler bel Harrison (K)
Brown George, hatter, 13th ab Wood
Brown George, barber, 4 Walnut
Brown George B., atty. and coun., 68 S 6th, h 161 E Pine

Brown George D., blacksm., 450 S 4th
Brown George W., grocer, 9th and Locust, h 84 Locust
BROWN & GODWINS, com. mers. 73 S whfs
Brown Gotleib, baker, F road ab Franklin
Brown Gowen A., cordw., 450 S 4th
Brown Hans, wafer and sealg. wax manuf., 127 Vine
Brown Harriet, shop, P road bel Washington
Brown Henry, lab., 26 Quince
Brown Henry, baker, rear Willow bel 8th
Brown Henry, cedar cooper, 40 Julianna
Brown Henry, Russell bel Shippen
Brown Henry, cabtmr., F road n Cherry (K)
Brown Henry H., velocipedemr., Davis' ct
Brown Henry W., stonecut., Carpenter ab 13th
Brown Henry W. soap boiler, R road ab George
Brown & Hicks, tailors, 286 High
Brown Horace A., dentist, Hyde ct
Brown H. A., printer, 76 Chestnut
Brown H. J., M. D., 570 N 3d
Brown Isaac, waiter, Rawle
Brown Isaac, carp., 8th bel Poplar
Brown Isabella, N E Fitzwater and Shippen la
Brown Jacob, vict., F road bel Master (K)
Brown Jacob, lab., rear F road n Queen (K)
Brown Jacob, Poplar and Charlotte
Brown Jacob, porter, 3 Acorn al
Brown Jacob, jr., paperhanger, 88 Charlotte
Brown James, waiter, 23 Green (C)
Brown James, lab., Vine ab Broad
Brown James, mer., 19 Church al, h 13th bel Locust
Brown James, drover, Prospect pl
Brown James, seaman, 1 E Catharine
Brown James, drayman, 6 Fries' ct
Brown James, porter, 97 Lombard
Brown James, wheelwright, Clark bel 4th
Brown James, weaver, n Mary ab F road (K)
Brown James, teacher, 282 Chestnut
Brown James, carter, 4 Norris' ct
Brown James, lab., Fitler ab 2d (K)
Brown James, weaver, 2d ab Master (K)
Brown James, coachman, Bedford ab 12th
Brown James, Eagle Hotel, 195 Chestnut
Brown James, waiter, Morris bel Catharine
Brown James D., coal mer., Broad bel Walnut, h N W 11th and Washington
Brown James D., art. flower manuf., 351 N 2d
Brown James E., saddler, 4 S 4th, h 163 S 5th
Brown James R., bellhanger, Cobb
Brown James W., mer., 136 High, h 417 Chestnut
Brown Jane, Sycamore ab Locust
Brown Jer., mer., 19 Chestnut, h 110 Mulberry
BROWN JEREMIAH & CO., mers, 19 Chestnut
Brown Jno., groc., 277 High, h George ab Sc 6th
Brown John, coachman, 27 Prosperous al
Brown John, lab., M'Duffie n 3d
Brown John, weaver, Sch 5th n Lombard
Brown John, gent., 21 Green
Brown John, shoes, 232 S 4th
Brown John, painter, 303 Walnut, h 14 S 10th
Brown John, waiter, Barley n 6th

Brown John, lab., Webb's al
Brown John, blacksm., rear 109 N 13th, h Callowhill ab Sch 2d
Brown John, carp., 193 Cherry
Brown John, janitor 28 Watson's al
Brown John, salesman, 155 S 3d
Brown John, weaver, Lombard E Sch 7th
Brown John, porter, 6th ab Carpenter
Brown John, lab., 4 Railroad ct
Brown John, millwright, 3d ab Washington
Brown John, 199 N Front
Brown John, whitewasher, 2 Barley
Brown John, manuf., Charlotte bel George
Brown John, lab., Shippen ab 8th
Brown John, carter, 6 Lawrence
Brown John, bootmr., 2 St Mary
Brown John, printer, Dorothy n Sch 4th
Brown John A., cordw., 53 M road
Brown John A., mer., 30 Chestnut, h S E 12th and Chestnut
Brown John A. T., presser, 10 Carlton
Brown John D., printer, 69 Gaskill
Brown John H., blksm., 18 Maria
Brown John H., teacher, 10th ab Washington
Brown John H., mer., 136 High, h Pine ab 7th
Brown John H. & Co., dry goods, 136 High
Brown John J., tailor, Amber ab Phoenix (K)
Brown John T., alderman, 185 St John
Brown John T., coachmr., Fetter la
Brown John T., jr., brushmr., 505 N 2d, h Wistar's ct (K)
Brown John W., mach., Clinton ab Franklin (K)
Brown John W., cordw., Garden ab Callowhill
Brown Jonathan, grocer, James bel 10th
Brown Joseph, shoemr., 397 S 4th, h 21 Harmony
Brown Joseph, mer., 11 Bank, h 16 Carter's al
Brown Joseph, mer., 73 S whfs., h 209 S 2d
Brown Joseph, lab., 9 Mayland
Brown Joseph, engineer, Beach ab Maiden (K)
Brown Joseph, weaver, Morris n William
Brown Jos., shipwr., Hanover ab Beach (K)
Brown Jos., carp., Perry ab Franklin (K)
Brown Jos., watchman, Brooks' ct
Brown Jos., shoemr., 35 Prosperous al
Brown Joseph D., gent., office 13 Minor, h 167 Mulberry
Brown Joseph S., turner, S Garden bel 9th
Brown Josephus R., cordw., W Penn sq ab High
BROWN J. D., & Co., coal mers., Broad bel Walnut
Brown J. Henry, min. painter, 96 Walnut
Brown J. Pemberton, bookseller, 36 N 6th
Brown J., clothes, 99 S 2d, h 217 Lombard
Brown Lewis, vict., Palmer ab Duke (K)
Brown Lewis, dry goods, 146 High, h S E 6th and Vine
Brown Lorenzo D., blksm., 8 Wagner's ct
Brown Lydia, b h, Barker n Sch 6th
Brown Marcus, lab., 6 Bonsall
Brown Mary, b h, 13th ab Spruce
Brown Mary, M'Mackin's ct
Brown Mary, milliner, 351 N 2d
Brown Mary Ann, Wesley ab 3d
Brown Margaret, widow, Filbert n Sch Front

Brown Matthew, lab., 5 Grape ct
Brown Matthew, lab., 25 Union (S)
Brown Matthew, cordw., 19 Fitzwater
Brown Michael, pedler, 125 Plum
Brown Michael, cabman, George ab 10th
Brown Miller, 254 Sassafras
Brown Minus, porter, Emeline st
Brown Morris Rev., 154 Queen
Brown Morris, engineer, N E 12th and Cherry
Brown Moses, mer., 20 N 4th, h 108 Mulberry
Brown M., shoemr., 359 Cedar
Brown Nathan, 99 G T road, bel 2d (K)
Brown Nathaniel, sweep, 417 N 4th
Brown Nathaniel P., reporter, 9th ab Coates
Brown Neal, lab., Atherton
Brown Nicholas, carter, 63 Rawle
Brown Nicholas, tailor, 7th bel Parrish
Brown Nicholas, lab., 3 John's ct
Brown Nicholas, teacher, 15 Elizabeth
Brown Patrick, lab., Nixon bel Callowhill
Brown Paul S., mer., 10th bel Melon
Brown Pemberton, bookseller, 36 N 6th
Brown Peter, sugar boiler, rear 13 Brooke
Brown Peter, basketmr., G T road bet 6th and 7th
Brown Peter, 44 Wood
Brown Peter, ironfound., Franklin ab Hanover
Brown Phineas, b h, 3 Carlton
Brown Quintus C., groc., N E 10th & Lombard
Brown Rachel, shoebr., rear 73 G T road (K)
Brown Rachel, cook, Madison ct
Brown Rebecca, washer, Carpenter ab 8th
Brown Rebecca, ready. made linen, 66¼ S 4th
Brown Richard, painter, Lombard ab 13th
Brown Richard, lab. 2 Bedford
Brown Richard, sexton, Wharton bel 5th
Brown Richard, lab., Eagle's ct
Brown Richard H., ship carp., Duke ab Hanover (K)
Brown Robert, whitewasher, 149 Locust
Brown Robert, lab., Centre n Dean
Brown Robt., carp., Lombard n Sch 5th, h Sch 5th bel Lombard
Brown Robert, ostler, 13 Mary's ct
Brown Robert, carp., George ab Sch 6th
Brown Robert, waiter, 241 Shippen
Brown Robert P., barber, 11 S 6th, h 31 Currant al
Brown Roger, distiller, High ab Sch 7th, h 17 Howard
Brown Samuel, gent., 238 Spruce
Brown Samuel, Shippen ab 12th
Brown Samuel, carpet weaver, Sch 3d & Chestnut
Brown Samuel, pumpmr., P road bel Washington
Brown Samuel, bell hanger, 12th n Washington
Brown Samuel, painter, 90 Sassafras
Brown Samuel, lab., 5 Clare
Brown Samuel, tavern, 68 Washington av
Brown Samuel, mariner, Front and Federal
Brown Samuel, lab., Leyden's ct
Brown Samuel, waiter, White's ct
Brown Sarah, Poplar ab 9th
Brown Sarah, sempstress, 8 Providence ct

Brown Solomon, lab., 42 Bread
Brown Susan, 5 Hermitage pl
Brown Susan B., gentw., 350 Chestnut
Brown Susan, Willow ab Marshall
Brown Thos., mer., 42½ S Front, h Nixon ab Callowhill
Brown Thos., waterman, 58 Queen
Brown Thos., barber, 125 N 2d
Brown Thomas, ship carp., Franklin ab Hanover (K)
Brown Thomas, oysterman, 80 Tammany
Brown Thomas, seaman, 19 Prosperous al
Brown Thomas, lab., 14 Gray's al
Brown Thomas, boots & shoes, 18 and 44 High, h 7th ab Poplar
Brown Thomas, grocer, N W Spruce & Dean
Brown Thomas, boot fitter, rear 175 Brown
Brown Thomas, brickmr., rear G T road ab 5th
Brown Thomas, cordw., 196 S 2d
Brown Thomas, sawyer, F road bel Phoenix (K)
Brown Thos., carp., 15 Jones' al., h 9 Chancery lane
Brown Thomas, carp., 10 Swanson
Brown Thomas, tailor, 10th ab Christian
Brown Thomas W., cabinetmr., Mechanic (S)
Brown Timothy, boot fitter, 13 Charlotte
Brown T. Mrs., gentw., S W 13th and Spruce
Brown Walter, missionary, 142 S Juniper
Brown Walter, mer., 451½ Mulberry
Brown Wash., mer., 40 N Front, h 473 Mulberry
Brown Wm., waterman, rear 137 Christian
Brown Wm., jeweller, St John ab George (K)
Browm Wm., lab., McDuffie n Sch 2d
Brown Wm., fur. car., Filbert ab Sch 8th
Brown Wm., brushmr., 4 Elfreth's al
Brown Wm., photographist, 144 Chestnut, h 6 Marshall
Brown Wm., cordw., 142 Lombard
Brown Wm., waterman, 11 Burd
Brown Wm., cordw., 2 Roach ct (K)
Brown Wm., tailor, 286 High, h 8th ab Green
Brown Wm., carp., Callowhill ab Sch 5th
Brown Wm., plumber, 9 S 7th, h Washington bel 7th (S)
Brown Wm., blacksmith, 2d ab G T road, h Edward n 2d (K)
Brown Wm., ladies' shoemr., Jackson pl
Brown Wm., hosier, 6 Parker
Brown Wm., grocer, 277 High, h Sch 8th ab Chestnut
Brown Wm., carp. weav., Sch 3d and Chestnut
Brown Wm., carter, n Sch 6th
Brown Wm., stock'g. fr. mr., Weavers' row (K)
Brown Wm., acct., 53 N 4th
Brown Wm., lab., Miller's al
Brown Wm., hatter, 196 High
Brown Wm., carp., 6th ab Camac (K)
Brown Wm., seaman, Shippen bel 4th
Brown Wm. A., carp., 404 S 3d
Brown Wm. A., mer., 19 Chestnut
Brown Wm. A., shoemr., 431 S 2d
Brown Wm. G., brass founder, G T road ab 5th
BROWN WILLIAM H. & Co., domestic goods, 20 N 4th
Brown Wm. & John, grocers, 277 High

Brown Wm. H., mer., 77 N 3d
Brown Wm. H., plast., 34 Hazel
Brown Wm. H., mer., 20 N 4th, h 148 S 9th
Brown Wm. H., marble yard, Broad bel Cedar, h Carpenter ab 13th
Brown Wm. Linn, coun. & att'y., 208 Pine
Brown W. L., rigger, 11 Noble
Brown Zebedee, carter, Ohio
Browne Alex., register of wills, State House, h 429 N 5th
Browne Aquila A., att'y. & coun., 307 Walnut
Browne Elizabeth, b h., N W 8th and Chestnut
Browne Hannah, gentw., 90 Marshall
Browne Joseph, lastmr., 71 Sassafras
Browne N. B., att'y., 141 Walnut
Browne Peter A., gent., 331 Walnut
Brownhill Daniel B., barber, R road & Brinton
Brownholtz John, lime dealer, 8th bel Poplar
Browning & Brothers, druggists, 33 High
Browning Charles, mer., 33 High, h 406 Vine
Browning Geo. W., mer., 221 Chestnut
Browning G., mer., 33 High, h 406 Vine
Browning John, carter, G T road ab Master (K)
Browning Maurice, drug., 33 High, h 88 N Front
Browning Saml., tavern, c Marsh & Penn (E K)
Browning Wm., carter, G T road ab Master
Brownnewell John C., clerk, 94 Dillwyn
BROWNS & BOWEN, mers., 30 Chestnut
Browns Wm., waiter, 208 S 7th
Bruce George F., carp., 605 S Front
Bruce Joseph, bricklayer, 605 S Front
Bruce Luke, waiter, 6 Elizabeth
Bruce Matthew W., carp., Wharton ab 4th
Bruce Wm., baker, 15 Wharton
Bruce Wm., waiter, 10th bel Fitzwater
Bruder George, cordw., 350 N 2d
Bruen James, gent, 499 Chestnut bel Sch 7th
Bruff Jno. M., tailor, Gulielma
Bruff Robert, currier, Elm ab Franklin (K)
Brulte Joseph, painter, 4 Lytles' ct
Brumer John, oak cooper, 257 St John
Brumley Robert W. C., lab., Clark ab 3d
Brummer H., tailor, 6th ab Poplar
Brundeag Susan, tobacco, 63 Christian
Brundydge Swain, tobacconist, Shippen ab 7th
Brunell Andrew, rigger, Marlborough bel Duke
Bruner Henry, shoemr., 144 N Front
Bruner Henry, wool dealer, 7 Margaretta
Bruner Isaac, sugar refiner, 8 Carberry's ct
Bruner John, books, 8 Wallace
BRUNER J. P., wool dealer, 6 Willow, h N 6th
Bruner Philip, cordw., Orchard ab Rawle
Bruner Wm., parchment manuf., and wool warehouse, 4 Pegg & 7 Willow
BRUNER W. & SON, skindressers and wool dealers, 7 Margaretta
Brunet John, confect., 207 S 2d
Brunner Abraham, watchman, Ogden ab 10th
Brunner George, founder, Marshall ab Brown
Brunner John K., doorkr. U S Mint, h 3 Division
Brunner Manassa, bookseller, 139 N 3d, h 15 Branch
Brunt John, weaver, 13th ab Shippen
Brunt Thomas, drayman, 336 S Front
Brusstar G. H., baker, 276 S 4th

Bruester Sarah, Queen ab F road (K)
Brustche J., milliner, 218 Walnut
Bruster Anna, 31 Brown
Bruster Charles, b. h., 17 S 10th
Bruster John, ship carp., Allen ab Shackamaxon (K)
Bruster Thomas, cordw., Queen ab Crown (K)
Bruten Albert, cordw., rear G T road ab 2d
Bry Daniel, carp., Parrish ab 10th
Bryan Catharine, Cooper's ct
Bryan & Ferree, dry goods, 172 High
Bryan Geo. H., mer., 12 S Water, h 9 Franklin row
Bryan George S., mer., 172 High
Bryan Isaiah, cabinetmr., 3 Whitaker's ct
Bryan Jacob, commissioner, 29 Montgomery
Bryan James, M. D., N E 10th and Mulberry
Bryan John, gunsmith, Derringer's ct
Bryan John, cabm., 71 N 6th
Bryan J. R., M. D., Sp Garden ab 11th
BRYAN & M'ILHENNY, com. mers. 12 S Water
Bryan Maria H., 401 Mulberry
Bryan Moses, tailor, 83 Brown
Bryan Robt., Say st
Bryan Samuel, cutler, Washington (W P)
Bryan Thos., cordw., rear 198 Christian
Bryan T. M., mer., 12 S Water
Bryan Wm., lab., rear Carpenter ab 7th
Bryant Deborah, nurse, 443 N 3d
Bryant Jacob, 17 Paschall's al
Bryant James, lab., 30 Barker
BRYANT JOHN, Salutation House, 23 S 3d
Bryant Rachel, Sch 6th bel Cherry
Bryant Wm., carp. weaver, c Locust and Sch Beach, h 114 German
Bryant Wm. H., cabinetmr., 5 Schuylkill av
Bryden John, carp., Mulberry n Broad, h 115 N Juniper
Brynan Edward, umbrella mr., 6th and Chestnut
Brynan John, mer., 210 S 2d

Buchanan Sarah P., teacher of music, 38 Palmyra sq
Buchanan Sophia, Lombard ab Sch 2d
Buchanan Thomas, b. h., Sch 3d ab Callowhill
Buchanan Thos. H., insp., High W Sch 7th
Buchanan Wm., dyer, Lloyd ab Fitzwater
Buchanan Wm., porter, 21 Acorn al
Buchanan Wm., Carlton n Sch 5th
Buchanan Wm., lab., Dorothy n Sch 4th
Buchanan John, blacksm., Hope bel Phœnix(K)
Buchannan Geo. R., clerk, Juniper bel Spruce
Buchey Mrs., seminary, 240 Spruce
Buck, Bossert & Rufsnyder, cab. mr., 446 N Front
Buck Catharine, 2 Lister's pl
Buck Chas., lab. rear Carpenter bel 9th
Buck Chauncey, tinplate worker, 447 High
Buck Christo'r., shoemr., 324 High & 467 N 4th
Buck C. N., president of Columbia Insu. Co., & consul general of Hamburg, 5 Merchant's Exchange, h S W Broad and Chestnut
Buck Ebenezer, b. h., 449 High
Buck Francis N., president of Little Sch Nav., R. R. and Coal Co., 80 Walnut, h 218 Sassafras
Buck Frederick, engineer, Front ab Master (K)
Buck Geo., cooper, 419 N 2d, h Pearson's ct(K)
Buck Geo., lab., Orchard
Buck Henry, mariner, Wilson's ct
Buck Henry E., machinist, 363 N 6th
Buck Hugh, blacksm., 174 Shippen
Buck Isaac, mariner, 36 S 3d
Buck James, carter, S 11th ab Pine
Buck James, barber, 1 Emeline
Buck Jasper, tinsm., 408 High, h 118 N Juniper
Buck Jeremiah, mer., 57 High
Buck Jere. M., 13 N 3d, h 94 Vine
Buck John, ostler, 6 Farmer
Buck Joseph, vict., Perry ab Phœnix (K)
Buck Joseph, 28 John (S)

Buckley M. Brooke, gent., N W 10th & Clinton
Buckley Thomas, tinsm., Morris bel Fitzwater
Buckley Wm., carpet weav., Linn's ct n F M
Buckley Wm., wool sorter, 13th bel Brown
Buckman Benj., hatter, 16 Catharine
Buckman Jacob, lab., 9 Bosler's row (K)
Buckman Morris, coal mer., 92 Marshall
Buckman Wm., carp., Alden ab Poplar
Bucknell Jos., mili. plum. and box., Coates bel Broad
Bucknell Wm. jr., 5 Summer's ct
Bucknor A. J., mer., 41 N Water, h 374 N Front
Buckwalter David, mer., 274 N 7th
Buckwalter Jacob, millwright, 134 N Juniper
Budd Benjamin, mer., 23 N Water
Budd Henry, mer., 137 N Water
Budd Isaac, bricklayer, 27 Dugan
Budd Isaac D., broker, 30 S 3d, h 161 Spruce
Budd James, cordw., G T road bel Phœnix
Budd John, soap boiler, Marshall ab Poplar
Budd John, combmr., Beaver ab 2d (K)
Budd John M., waterman, rear 109 Christian
Budd Joseph, tailor, 162 Sassafras
Budd J. B., com. mer., 39 Dock, h 9 Walnut ab Broad
Budd J. D., dentist, 502 Chestnut
Budd Susan, Sassafras n Sch 8th
Budd Susan, gentw., 105 Pine
Budd Thomas A., atty. & coun., 169 Walnut
Budd Wm., bricklayer, 17 Dugan
BUDD WM. A. exch. bro. 30 S 3d, h 61 Spruce
Buddy Isaiah, carp., Broad ab Olive
Buddy John, baker, 24 Walnut
Buddy Lewis, biscuit baker, 198 N Front, h 254 N 7th
Buehler Christian, b. h., Buttonwood rear 13th
Buddy Peter, tavern, N W 9th and Green
Buehler James R., inspector customs, 99 S whf., h 292 S 5th
Buehler John, mer., 195 High, h 227 N 9th
Buehler Martin, hardware, 195 High, h 350 N 6th
BUEHLER MARTIN & BROTHER, hardware, 195 High
Buehler P. N. spices & mustard, 23½ Lagrange
Buehler Wm., mer., 98 High, h 472 Vine
Buel Ann, 33 Vine
Buffington Isaac, cabinetmr., 87 S 11th
Buffington Lee W., M. D., N E Mulberry and Sch 8th
Buffington Wilson, mason, 418 Poplar
Bugals Jas., cordw., Brown bel 13th
Buist David, florist, 94 S 12th
Buist Eliza, gentw., Buist ct
Buist James, carp., Fitzwater ab 12th
Buist R., florist, S 12th bel Lombard, nursery Shippen bet 11th and 12th, store 84 Chestnut
Bujac P. J., importer, 101 S Front, h Walnut ab Broad
Bukster Thos., lab., Poplar bel 10th
Bulfinch Thos., baker, Cedar ab 12th
BULKLEY CHAUNCEY, atty. and coun., and alderman, 96½ S 3d, h 20 Prune
BULKLEY CHARLES, hat., 128 Chestnut, h 275 S 10th

Bulkley Elizabeth, 20 Prune
Bulkley James H., hatter, 424 Sassafras
Bulkley M. S., tobacconist, Green bel 9th
Bull Coleman J., grocery, 348 High
Bull Eborn, baker, 25 Parham
Bull Francis, porter, 30 Burd's ct
Bull John, oysterman, Union bel Front
Bull Lewis G., gent., Sch 6th n George
Bull Oliver, barber, 7 N 8th
Bull Wm. M., atty. and coun., 189 Walnut
Bullard Edwin C., bookbinder, 187 S 3d
Bullass Jane, gentw., Hallowell ab 6th
Buller Saml., tailor, Carlton bel 13th
Bullin Rich'd, iron mould., Carpenter bel 9th
Bullinger John V., shoemr., Phoenix bel Front (K)
Bullmer G., tailor, 400½ N 2d
BULLOCK BENJ., wool warehouse, 32 N 3d
Bullock David, tailor, 21 Shippen
Bullock Janet M., corsetmr., 23 N 10th
Bullock Jonathan, carp., 16 Farmer, h 23 N 10th
Bullock J., M. D., 126 S 8th
Bullock J. & Co., coal, Broad and Sassafras
Bullock J. W., coal, 7th bel Vine
Bullock Mary E., 5th bel Camac (K)
Bullock Wm., millwright, Lewis ab Poplar
Bulmer Richard, spinner, Mary, Sch
Bulz Jacob, basket mr., 20 Lily al
Bumbah Chs. A. M. paint. and glaz. 2 Lytle's ct
Bumbaugh A., painter, rear 331 N 3d
Bumgard John, cordw., Marlboro' bel Franklin (K)
Bumm Chris'n, coppersm., Dean ab Crown (K)
Bumm Elizabeth, Duke n Palmer (K)
Bumm Geo., contractor, Vaughn bel Walnut
Bumm George S., carter, Lombard E Sch 5th
Bumm Hannah, Marlboro' ab Bedford (K)
Bumm John, whipmr., Palmer ab Franklin (K)
Bumm John S., silverplat., Marlboro' bel Franklin (K)
Bumm Jos., lab., Madison's av
Bumm W., whipmr., Union n F road
Bundes Adam, shoemr., 38 Pegg
Bundick J. S., shoe store, 37 Spruce
Bundy Ephraim, waiter, 59 Currant al
Bundy Levi, bootmr., Gulielma
Bundy Peter, waiter, 24 Burd's ct
Bundy Thomas, waiter, 168 Pine
Bunghart Wm., carter, Lewellen's av (K)
Bunker Ann, confectioner, 145 Coates
Bunker B. M., mer., 71 S. Whfs.
Bunker Henry, carp., 9 Christian
Bunn Albert G., spinner, 495 N 3d
Bunn Alexander J., exch. broker, 103 N 3d, h 483 N 4th
Bunn Saml., ship caulker, Union n Franklin (K)
Bunn S. M., dry goods, 74 N 3d, h 158 N 5th
Bunting Chas. W., lamps, 99 N 2d, h 8th ab Parrish
Bunting Daniel, police officer, 6 Drinker's al
Bunting Elizabeth, Conrad's ct
Bunting Jacob T., mer., 14 S whfs., h 65 Pine
Bunting John, skindresser, Conrad's ct.
Bunting Joshua, 183 Pine
Bunting Joshua, 104 S 4th
Bunting Lewis E., paper hanger, Depot ab 9th

Bunting Mary Ann, rear 13 Rose al
Bunting Richard, ship join., Otter bel G T road
Bunting Samuel C., real estate agent, 104 S 4th, h 356 Walnut
Bunting Spencer, carp., Trinity pl
Bunting Thomas C., M. D., S W 7th & Sassafras and 14 S 7th
Bunting Thomas H., com. mer., 112 S Front
Burall Jos., bricklayer, 6th ab Franklin
Burbeck Wm., teacher, 8 N 6th
Burble Wm., gent., 34 Almond st
Burbridge Wm., tallow chandler, rear 337 N 3d
Burch John, clothes, 5 Gulielma
Burch Joseph G., bricklayer, Wharton ab 4th
BURCH THOMAS Jr., comb and variety store, 183 High, h Sch 5th and Mulberry
Burchard Jabez, U. S. dep. marshal, Washington n 6th
Burchell Henry, plasterer, 617 S 2d
Burd Edward S., S W 9th and Chestnut
Burd Samuel S., carp., Melon ab 13th
Burd S., gentw., 231 Chestnut
Burden Alexander, keeper M. Prison, 5th and Shippen
Burden Jesse R., Sch 8th ab Pine
Burden Joseph, clerk, 5th and Shippen
Burden Rebecca, b h, 85 Chestnut
Burdett Samuel D., 142 Franklin
Burdick Ephraim N., carp., Townsend's av.
Burdick Jane, rear 112 Christian
Burdick Samuel, sail maker, rear 112 Christian
Burdsall Wm. H., 350 Mulberry
Burgaine Thomas, cordw., 519 N 4th
Burge Sarah, rear 465 N 4th
Burger Charles, baker, 10th and Melon
Burgess G. W., canemaker, 390 High, h 151 Wood
Burgess Henry E., acct., 25 Logan
Burgess James C., 23 Paul
Burgin George H., M. D. and mer., 46 N Front, h 175 S Fifth
Burgin James, cedar cooper, 9th bel Brown
Burgin & Pearsall, green glassware, 46 N Front, Glass Works, Cherry ab Franklin (K)
Burgison Israel, Division (F V)
Buritt Charles, cabinetmr., 184 S 3d
Burk Anthony, lab., 20 Marion
Burk Edmund, machinist, 12th bel Buttonwood
Burk Eli, bricklayer, 5th ab Poplar
Burk Enoch, cordw., 22 Green ct
Burk Isaac, tailor, 294 Lombard
Burk James, mer., 224 N Front
Burk James, lab., Spafford
Burk James A., mer., 77½ High
Burk John, lab., rear 1 Paschal's al
Burk John, County Comm., State House, h G. T. road ab Master
Burk Joseph, bottler, Roset and 13th
Burk Lewis, tobacconist, Beck's ct (N L)
Burk Mary, grocer, Ann and R. road, (F V)
Burk Matthew, shop, 139 N 6th
Burk Patrick, gardener, 3 Sharpless' ct
Burk Patrick, waiter, 4 Lyndall's al
Burk Paul, blacksm., Howard bel Master (K).
Burk Peter, rear 10 Noble

Burk Peter W., saddler, 5 Furlong's ct
Burk Raymond, tailor, Evan's ct
Burk Thomas, lab., George bel 3d.
Burk Thomas, coach trimmer, 567 Vine
Burk Thomas, grocer, c 2d and Franklin (K)
Burk Wm., clerk, 2 St. Stephen's place
Burk Wm. A., mer. 77½ High, h 12th bel Spruce
Burk Wm. G., druggist, 244 Lombard
Burkart Adam L., 287 N 10th
Burkart A. L., turner, 49 Spring Garden
Burkart E. W., turner, 105 Crown, h 10th bel Melon
Burkart Henry & Thos., turners, Spring Garden above 8th.
Burkart Valentine, clerk, 163 Mulberry
Burke Dennis, cordw., R. road ab Francis (F V)
Burke Jacob, 523 N Front
Burke Jeremiah, 1 Traquair's ct
Burke John, weaver, Clay and Willow
Burke John B., 523 N Front
Burke John F., grocer, N E 3d and Cedar
Burke Thomas, lab., 7 Poplar place
Burke Thomas, dry goods, 6 N 2d
Burke Wm., ink manuf., 16½ Bread
Burke Wm. C., tailor, 16½ Bread
Burkelow, Elizabeth, gentw., 12 Brown
Burkett Charles, cabinetmr., 2d and G. T. road
Burkett Henry, waiter, Brown's ct
Burkhard Melchor, chairmr., 305 S Front
Burkhard M. W., chairmr., 59 N Front
Burkhardt Geo. Jacob, carp., Logan n. Wallace
Burkhardt Henry, gent., Green and Logan
Burkhardt H. jr., baker, Green and Logan
Burkhardt Julius, barber, 113 Callowhill
Burkhart Eleanor, teacher, Marshall bel Green
Burkhart Henry, turner, 1 Weaver
Burkhart Peter, 283 Sassafras
Burkhart Robert, carp., 25 Franklin place
Burkhart Robert, dentist, 72 N Front
Burkhart Samuel, brushmr., 122 N 4th, h Green ab 11th
Burkhart T., 119 N 5th
Burkhimer Mary, 83 N 7th
Burkiett Robert, carp., 10 Paynter's ct
Burkitt Joseph, bootmr., Cobb's ct
Burkitt Joseph, turner, 98 German
Burkley John, 3 Diligent av.
Burklow D., shop, 6 Apple
Burkman Wm., carp., St. John ab Poplar
Burley A., cabs, 39 Bonsall
Burling B. S., mer., 45 N whfs, h 4 Palmyra sq
Burling & Dixon, mers., 45 N whfs
Burlock Samuel D., bookbinder, 123 Melon
Burmester Henry, 4 Seneca ct
Burn Arthur, 15 Vine
Burn Farmer, 12th and Spring Garden
Burn John, lab., Hope and Phœnix (K)
Burn John, grocer, Locust, (W. P.)
Burnar John, baker, 2 Howard
Burnell Ben, gent., Sch 3d ab Race
Burnell W. W., M. D., 34 Logan's sq
Burnet George, mer., 10th bel Cedar
Burnet L. W., teacher, N. W. 4th and Vine, h O. Y. road ab Callowhill
Burnet Mary, Barker n Sch 3d

Burnet Samuel, cordw., Crown n Bedford (K)
Burnet Wm., dry goods, 327 S 2d
Burnett Abby, b h, 96 S 11th
Burnett Eli S., dry goods, 3 S 4th, h 399 High
Burnett John, sign painter, Crown n Bedford (K)
Burnett John, tanner, Roger's ct
BURNETT JOHN W., real est. agent, 74 S 3d, h 96 S 11th
Burnett J. S., mer., 110 High, h 338 Mulberry
BURNETT & SEXTON, dry goods, 3 S 4th
BURNETT, WITHERS & CO., dry goods, 110 High
Burney Patrick, rear Pleasant ab 12th
Burnham George, clerk, 13th bel Green
Burns Abraham, watchman, Walnut & Vaughan
Burns Ann, 2 Stamper's alley
Burns Ann, washer, Bedford ab 6th
Burns Charles, lab., 2 Robert's ct.
Burns Charles, cabman, Prospect al
Burns Charles E., tavern, 270 S 6th
Burns Charles M., mer., 210 Spruce
Burns Dennis, hatter, 6th bel Carpenter
Burns Edward, drayman, Sch. 3d and Vine
Burns Edward, broker, Morris ab Christian
Burns Edward, iron founder, 12 Clark
Burns Felix, weaver, Perry bel Master (K)
Burns Hugh D., grocer, Shackamaxon and Bedford (K)
Burns James, brushmr., 137 S 4th
Burns James, lab., 11 W. Cedar
Burns James, carp., Lewis n Sch. 6th
Burns James, lab., 7 Grape ct
Burns John, seaman, 387 S Front
Burns John, lab., 5 Gray's alley
Burns John, lab., Carleton bel Sch. 2d
Burns John, lab., Duke n F. road (K)
Burns John, lab., 84 Gaskill
Burns John, manuf., Hanover ab West (K)
Burns John, carpet weaver, Weaver's row (K)
Burns Joseph, weaver, Lafayette n 10th
Burns Lawrence, soap fat, Hope ab Otter (K)
Burns Martin, blacksmith, Ferris ct
Burns Mary H., washer, Ann (F V)
Burns Michael, lab., G T road ab Jefferson (K)
Burns M. & E., ready made linen, 55 S 7th
Burns Patrick, tailor, Reed bel Front
Burns Thomas, lab., Sch. 8th ab Vine
Burns Wm., tobacco, 290 High, h 31 Carlton
Burns Wm., carter, 54 P. road
Burnson Ellen, Logan n Wallace
Burnwood Alex., printer, 12 S Penn sq
Burnwood S. harnessmr. rear Carlton ab Sch 6th
Burr Benj., 281 Sassafras
Burr George W., grocer, S W Cadwalader and Phœnix (K)
Burr Elizabeth S., b h, 74 N Front
Burr Hudson S., dentist, 135 Walnut
BURR H. COOPER, tailor, 202 Chestnut, h Sch 8th ab Filbert
Burr Israel R., bricklayer, N E 10th and Coates
Burr John P., barber, 113 S 5th
BURR JOSEPH, Ridgway House, High st ferry
Burr Joseph jr., S W 6th and Haines, h 2 Comptroller
Burr Joseph S., auct., 297 High, h 139 N 11th

Burr J., painter and glazier, 490 Callowhill
Burr M. L., 185 S 9th
Burr P. R., milliner, 65 Mulberry
Burr Richard, M. D., 120 S 4th
Burr Samuel, carp., 396 S 6th
Burr Thomas, carp., 5 Greble's ct
Burr Thomas E., tailor, 27 N 6th, h 46 Franklin
Burr Wm., manuf., Parrish and 13th
Burr W. H. & D., carps., Wood ab Broad, h 200 Mulberry
Burris Benj., carter, Centre ab Brown
Burris Elizabeth, Shippen ab Front
Burrough B., trunkmr., 56 Crown
Burrogh John, corder, Maiden st whf., h Allen bel Marlborough (K)
Burrough Thomas, carter, Apple bel George
Burroughs Enos, wheelwright, New Market bel Green
Burroughs H. N., merchant, 22 Chestnut, h 280 Spruce
Burroughs Isaac, Bevan's ct
Burroughs Jane, b. h., 435 Chestnut
Burroughs John jr., wood, Beach ab. Shackamaxon
Burrows C., umbrellas, 73 Noble
Burrows & Divine, clothing, 282 High
Burrows James, blacksmith, Mile's alley
Burrows James, U. S. Mint, h 272 Wood
Burrows Jesse, carp., Littleboy's ct, h 157 N 2d
Burrows John, cordw., 70 Apple (K)
Burrows J. L., Rev., Broad bel Poplar
Burrows J. T., bell hang. and locksm., 287 Vine
Burrows Rachel, washer, 4 Warren
Burrows Wm., 24 Howard
Burrows Wm., tailor, 282 High, h 4 Diamond
Burrows Wm., watchman, Vernon bel 11th
Burt Arthur, merchant, S. W. 6th and High, h N. W. 12th and Walnut
Burt E. R., trimmings, 162 S 2d
Burt John, carp., 22 Helmuth
Burt Michael, weaver, 3d ab Master (K)
Burtis Aaron H., plasterer, 107 Filbert
Burtis Edward T., bricklr., Sch. 7th n Sassafras
Burtis John, manuf., Beach ab Maiden (K)
Burtis, Keen & Rushton, cotton spinning, Beach bel Shackamaxon (K)
Burtman Henry C., carp., Sch. 8th ab Mulberry
Burtman & Hanna, carps., Broad ab Vine
Burton Amos, painter, 9 N 8th, h 85 N 5th
Burton Benj. C., shipwrt., Beach ab Poplar (K)
Burton Caroline, washer, 24 Mayland
Burton Catharine, 32 Currant alley
Burton Daniel, carter, Ohio E. of 12th
Burton Edward, paper hanger, 142 Mulberry, h 161 N 10th
BURTON EDWARD, office, S E 3d and Spruce
Burton Eliza, 119 S 2d
Burton E. P., grocer, 83 S whfs., h S E 3d and Pine
Burton Francis R., carp, Little Green n G T road
Burton George, lab., 17 Watson's alley
Burton George R., tailor, 119 S 2d
Burton Gideon, mer., 129 High, h 93 S 3d
Burton Guy, waiter, St. Mary bel 7th
Burton & Greis, merchants, 16 N 3d

Burton Harriet, Little Pine n 6th
Burton James, porter, 66 Garden
Burton James, porter, Bedford ab 7th
Burton James, waiter, 6 Washington
Burton Jehu, bookbinder, 107 Wood
Burton John, waiter, 167 Buttonwood
Burton John, merch., 34 S. whfs., h 62 Pine
Burton John, dry goods, 514 S 2d bel Prime
Burton John, M. D., 256 N 7th
Burton John, waiter, 46 Quince
Burton Jonathan P., dry goods, 16 N 3d, h 254 N 2d
Burton London, porter, Shippen bel 13th
Burton Lovinia, 18 Raspberry
Burton Moses, cook, Cox's al bel 2d
Burton Peter, cabinetmr., 2 Stanley ct
Burton Peter, porter, Barley n 11th
Burton Rachel, Higgin's ct
Burton Robert, mer., 34 S whfs., h 62 Pine
Burton Samuel, hatter, Vine n Sch
Burton Samuel, confectioner, 186 S 6th
Burton Wm. E., 24 N 7th
Burton & Wilt, confectioners, 52 S 10th
Burton Woolsey, shipwright, Marlborough ab Bedford (K)
Burwell Robert, hatter, rear 89 S 5th, h 204 Pine
Burwell Jackson, cordw., Christian ab Broad
Busch Miers, merchant, h 54 Pine
Buschner Cudwig, 37 Zane
Bush B., wheelwright, Carlton n Sch 3d
Bush Elizabeth, miliner, 359 N 2d
Bush Facy, Mechanic bel Culvert
Bush Frederick, paper stainer, 25 N 5th, h 13th bel Shippen
Bush Geo., dealer, 235 Christian
Bush Jos., shop, 2d bel Reed
Bush Peter, 113 Cherry
Bush Peter, grocer, George and Plum
Bush Samuel H., tobac., 230 N 3d, h 104 Noble
Busha Valeira, 10 Fetter la
Bushby Wm., carp., 11th ab Carpenter
Busher James, cooper, Rogers' ct
Bushong Andrew, distillery, Beach bel George
Buskirk Wm., goldbeater, Budden's al
Bushman John, dentist, 167 Green
BUSHNELL EDW'D. W., machinist, 31 Dock, h 24 S 2d
Bushong Philip, distiller, Sch Front bel George
Busser Jacob, car builder, Barker bet Sch 4th and 5th

Butcher Elizabeth, Fraley's al (K)
Butcher Jas., dry goods, 176 S 6th
Butcher James W., tobacconist, 157 N 2d
Butcher John, watchman, 11th ab Coates
Butcher John, mer., 49 N Water
Butcher John, butcher, Fraley's al
Butcher Jos., wheelwright, 28 Vine
Butcher Samuel, cordw., 5 Poplar pl
Butcher Saml., cordw., P road bel Washington
Butcher Theo. B., dry goods, 8 Bank, h 149 S 3d
Butcher Thomas T., mer., 49 and 51 N Water, h 307 Mulberry
Butcher Washington, mer., 49 N Water, h 155 N 6th
Butcher Wm., carp., M road bel Marion
Butcher Wm., stove & grate manuf., 11 N 11th
Butcher W. & S., agency, 24 Commerce
Butcher W. M., grocer, Front and Christian
Bute Charles L., sugar refiner, 120 Crown bel Willow
Bute & Koons, sugar refiners, Willow & Crown
Butler Andw., Sec'y of Fire Ass'n, 5th & North
Butler Cath., Stackhouse ct
Butler Catharine, 178 N 8th
Butler Charity, sempstress, 24 Lebanon
Butler Elizabeth, 12 Smith's ct
Butler Elizabeth, 9th ab Willow
Butler E., bootmr., Spruce and Little Dock
Butler E., stockmr., 47 S 3d
Butler E. H. & Co., booksellers, 23 Minor
Butler E. H., publisher, 23 Minor, h 347 Spruce
Butler George, 136 German
Butler Hannah, nurse, Marshall ab Coates
Butler Henry, printer, 27 Mary
Butler Henry W., silversmith, 77 Tammany
Butler Hen., jeweller, 5th ab Washington
Butler James, lab., Ohio
Butler Jeremiah, agent, 102 High, h Sch 7th ab Cherry
Butler John, gent., Walnut ab Sch 7th
Butler John, lab., Bedford bel 12th
Butler John, machinist, 125 Callowhill
Butler John M., copper pl. printer, N E 6th and Chestnut, h 137 Catharine
Butler Joseph, carter, 16 Carlton
Butler Joseph, shoemr., 10 Cresson's al
Butler Joshua M., coop., 63 N Water, h 74 New
Butler Judith, 6 Blackhorse al
Butler Keyrn, shoemr., 1 Howard's ct
Butler Margaret, Union al

Butler Wm. B., cooper, Clark ab 3d
Butler Wm. H., tobacconist, 39 R road
Butt Chas. H., printer, 62 Walnut, h 56 Federal
Butt Wm., printer, rear 197 Christian
Butterfield Benjamin, gunsmith, F road opp Marlboro' (K)
Butterfield, Brothers & Co., impors., 7 Church al
Butterfield Jesse S., F road ab Jefferson (K)
Butterfield Richard S., mer., 7 Church al
Butterworth Ellis M., dyer, M'Duffie, n Sch 3d
Butterworth George, weaver, rear G T road bel Jefferson (K)
Butterworth Henry W., tin plate worker, 90 High, h Charlotte ab Poplar
Butterworth Jacob, carp., 185 Poplar
Butterworth John, tin plate worker, 444 N 2d
Butterworth John, weaver, Mariner st
Butterworth Jospeh, shoemr., 140 S Water
Butterworth Willoughby, carp., Mechanic and Poplar
Butz George, brewer, 520 N 3d, h 308 N 2d
BUTZ & SCHROYER, tavern, 298 N 2d
Buxton George, dealer, 182 S 6th
Buyers Wm. D., hatter, 40 N 3d
Buzard Robert, machinist, 4 Dorr's ct
Buzby Abel, b. h., Franklin n Green
Buzby Benjamin C., mer., 157 High
Buzby G. L., mer., 19 S Water, h 360 Chestnut
Buzby Harmer B., mar. mas., R road bel Green
Buzby Hezekiah, forwd. mer., Broad ab Cherry, h W Penn square n Filbert
Buzby John L., mer., 19 S Water, h Chestnut n Broad
Buzby Mary H., cupper and leecher, 127 S 8th
Buzby Mordecai, dry goods, 212 N Front
Buzby Thomas, baker, 13th bel Brinton
Buzby Wm., cordw., R road (F V)
Buzby Wm., painter, 20 Little Pine
Buze Geo., saddler, Willow ab Marshall
Buzzard Conrad, carp., Elm bel Franklin (K)
Byard Samuel, 45 Mead al
Byard Wm., lab., Stevenson's ct
Bye Samuel, cordw., Clinton ab Poplar
Bye Samuel K., carpenter, 9th ab Poplar, h 153 Buttonwood
Byer A., basketmr., 7th ab Callowhill
Byer Harriet, washer, 18 Fayette
Byer Margaret, Cherry bel Juniper
Byerly Ann, gentw., c Mulberry and Juniper
Byerly D. Davis, mer., 28 Church al, h 12 W North
Byerly Edward, att'y & coun., Walnut ab 6th
Byerly E., mer., 35 Chestnut, h 150 Sassafras
Byerly Mary, 17 Swanson
Byerly Stephen, com. mer., 28 Church alley, h 150 Sassafras
Byerly Susan, gentw., 9 Virginia row
Byerly S. & Co., com. mers., 28 Church al
Byerly Wm., Stanley bel 4th
Byers Geo. F., coach trimmer, 8 Charles pl
Byers Henry, grocery, 22 Shippen st
Byers Hanse M. H., grocer, N E Swanson and Christian
Byers Sarah, dressmr., 63 S 5th
Byle Daniel, weaver, 112 Carpenter ab 10th

Bylisby L., printer, 10th bel Buttonwood
Byram Samuel, tavern, 95 S Water
Byrne Charles, shoemr., 409 Vine
Byrne Christopher, carp., 306 S 7th
Byrne Jas., wines & liquors, 4th bel Christian
Byrne James, tavern, wines & liquors, 121 S 2d
Byrne James, lab., 42 Plum
Byrne Morgan, lab., Lombard n Sch 2d
BYRNE THOMAS, tavern, N E Front and Almond
Byrne Timothy, grocer, 264 N 7th
Byrne Wm., cordw., 222 S Front
Byrne Wm., carp., rear 76 German
Byrne Wm., carp., 23 Dock, h German ab 3d
Byrnes Stephen, grocer, 9th & Catharine
Bywater Maurice, bookbinder, 151 Walnut
Bywaters Wm., ladies' shoemr., 106 Wood

————

Cabot Joseph, mer., 5 Walnut, h Spruce n 11th
Cadbury Joel, mer., 32 S Front, h 9 Franklin
Cade John, waterman, Lewellyn's ct
Cade Wm. M., 56 Franklin ab Noble
Cadmus Jasper, boots & shoes, S W 3d and High, h 29 North
CADMUS JASPER, shoes, 266 High
Cadmus Michael, clerk, 22 Appletree al
Cadwalader Edward, George ab R road (F V)
Cadwalader George, gent., 299 Chestnut
Cadwalader John, atty. & coun., 114 S 4th
Cadwalader Mary, widow of T. Gen., S E 9th & Mulberry
Cadwalader Sarah, b h, 21 Sansom
Cadwalader Thomas, gent., 353 Chestnut
Cady Horatio W., barber, 25 S 5th
Cafferty John J., cabmr., 75 Union
Cafferty Matthew, runner, 96 Plum
Cafferty Vanroom, bricklr., rear 112 Christian
Caffman Charles, vict., Apple ab George
Caffrey Stephen, printer, 8 Sanders' ct (K)
Cahill Daniel, lab., 10 S 13th
Cahill James, weaver, 4th ab Master (K)
Cahoon James W., wheelwright, Bruner's ct
Cain Wm., tobacconist, rear G T road ab 2d
Caines C. M. Oscar, carp., 4 Park pl
Cairl Louden S., cabmr., Simmons' ct
Cake Elizabeth, Chatham bel Green
Cake Joseph, 171 Vine
Calahan Robt., lab., 18 Burd's ct
Caldcleugh Robert, M. D., 13 Clinton sq
Caldcleugh Robert, A., gent., 13 Clinton sq
Calder Geo., agent, Cherry ab 12th
Calder Peter Y., tailor, 35 Chatham
Calder Peter Y., sen., 256 Green ab 8th
Calderhead Alexander, carpet weaver, Barker ab Sch 7th
Calderhead Wm., weav., Edward n School (K)
Caldwell A. D., carp., Brown & Front, and coal yard, Beach ab Poplar
Caldwell Chas., oysters, 31 N whfs, h 5 Carlton
Caldwell Charles P., whipmr., 4 N 4th, h 384 Coates
Caldwell C. W., agent, 168 S 4th
Caldwell David, teacher, Bickham ab Sch 7th

Caldwell David W., gent., Christian ab 9th
Caldwell Edmund B., mer., 8 S 2d, h 114 Walnut
Caldwell Edw., blacksmith, Carroll ab 13th
Caldwell E. H. Mrs., 105 S 10th
Caldwell Geo., lab., Wilson's ct
Caldwell Hannah, 44 Penn (C)
Caldwell & Harker, cloths, 8 S 2d
Caldwell H. A., com. mer., 6 N whfs
Caldwell & Keen, com. mers., 6 N whfs
Caldwell James, blacksm., Harriet & Ross
Caldwell James, plasterer, 13th bel Spruce
Caldwell James E., watchmr., 140 Chestnut, h 18 Clinton
Caldwell James S., gent., 164 N 9th
Caldwell John, clerk, 155 S 12th
Caldwell John, currier, 358 S 2d
Caldwell John, grocer, N W 3d and Plum
Caldwell John, mer., 116 S Front
Caldwell John, stone mason, 8th ab Mulberry
Caldwell Jonathan, printer, 81 N road
Caldwell Joseph, 11 Strawberry
Caldwell J. F., dentist, 118 Mulberry
Caldwell Mary and Ellen, dry goods, N E Front and Brown
Caldwell P., lab., Coates' al
Caldwell Robert, stonemas., Brazier ab Broad
Caldwell Samuel W., cashier N L bank, 405 N 5th
Caldwell Stephen B., clerk, 56 George
Caldwell Thomas, coal mer., N W 12th and Callowhill, h Sp Garden ab 10th
Caldwell Thomas, mer., 10 Chestnut, h Locust n Sch 8th
Caldwell Wm., blacksmith, Brazier ab Lloyd
Caldwell Wm., bookseller, 288 E Pine
Caldwell Wm., type-founder, Sch 6th and Jefferson
Caldwell Wm., shoemr., Coates ab Sch 7th
Caleley Edward L., coach lace weaver, St John ab Beaver
Caleley Thos., fringe weaver, 112 Vine
Calhoun Adam, lab., 29 M'Duffie
Calhoun Amy, washer, Stanley ct
Calhoun Charles, cordw., 56 Federal
Calhoun Claudius, lab., Willow n Sch
Calhoun David, butcher, 265 S 4th
Calhoun David, lab., 29 M'Duffie
Calhoun Ezra, tobacconist, 74 N 9th
Calhoun James, brickmr., Cedar ab Sch 5th
Calhoun John, machinist, Olive ab 12th
Calhoun John, lab., 29 M'Duffie
Calhoun Joseph, cordw., 306 S Front
Calhoun Mathias, printer, rear 63 Franklin
Calhoun Samuel, carter, 1 M'Duffie
Calhoun Wm., vict., 39 Shippen
Calhoun Wm., grocer, Lombard n Sch 2d
Calhoun Wm., machinist, Olive bel 12th

Callahan David, jr., weaver, rear Filbert below Sch 5th
Callahan Edw., grocer, N W Front & Pine
Callahan Janet, James ab 10th
Callahan John, stone mason, Milton bel 11th
Callahan John, 21 Union
Callahan John, grocer, Front ab Phoenix (K)
Callahan John, well digger, Carpenter ab 8th
Callahan Michael, lab., 6 Vernon
Callahan Owen, lab., Price's ct
Callahan Patrick, weaver, Shippen la ab Fitzwater
Callan David, shoemr., Hubble st
Callan John, watchman, Shippen ab 11th
Callan Wm., grocer, c Morris & Catharine
Callanan George D., police, Sch 5th n Mulberry
Callaway H. R., 344 N 13th
Callaway Jas., rear 92 Christian
Callbreath Jas. F., ladies' shoes, 59 N 8th
Callen John, lab., rear 194 Cherry
Callender Benj., carp., R road ab Green
Callin Robert, carp., Atherton
Callingham James, rigger, rear 27 Queen
Calver James, bonnet presser, G T road below Master
Calver Wm. G., bonnet presser, 81 Mulberry
Calverly & Co., manuf., 359 Callowhill
Calverly John, syringemr., Citron bel 13th
Calverly Wm., tinsmith, 9th bel Coates
Calvert Rachel, cupper & leecher, 40 N 8th
Calvert Thos., chairmr., 1 Bickim's ct
Calvert Wm., tavern, c Spruce and Willow Sch
Camac James, brickmr., Hope & Franklin (K)
Camac John, brickmr., Sch 5th bel Lombard
Camac Samuel, brickmr., 14 M'Duffie
Camblin John, lab., 68 P road
CAMBLOS CHARLES, broker, 22d S 3d, h 110 Spruce
Camblos Geo. W., Locust W Sch 6th
Cameggs Carnel, 115 Wood
Cameron Alex., tailor, 9 Eutaw
Cameron Angus, joiner, 245 Green
Cameron Angus, jr., clerk, 9 Logan
Cameron Eli, blacksmith, 12th & Pearl
Cameron Hugh, flour, Howard ab Phoenix (K)
Cameron James, weaver, Master ab Front
Cameron John, barber, 157 Catharine
Cameron John, blacksmith, 6 Boyd's av
Cameron Jonathan, watchman, 2 Dyott's ct
Cameron J. Payne, carpet store, 283 N 2d
Cameron Robert, gas fitter, 3 Lebanon
Cameron Robert, weaver, 6 Philip (K)
Cameron Saml., weaver, Philip ab Master (K)
Cameron Samuel, weaver, Hanover ab Duke
Cameron W. David, carp., 9 Logan
Cameron Wm., lab., Pearl bel William
Camm Wm., 356 Mulberry
Cammack Isaac, waiter, Portland la

Campbell Alex., distiller, Front bel Otter (K)
Campbell Alex., gent., 349 Chestnut
Campbell Alex., prison keeper, h 474 S 4th
Campbell Ann, William bel Edward (K)
Campbell Ann, dressmr., 499 Mulberry
Campbell Ann, shop keeper, 11 Blackberry al
Campbell Ann, b h, 4 Penn
Campbell Anthony, lab., William ab Benton
Campbell Archibald, brickmr., Cedar n Sch 2d
Campbell Archibald, dry goods, 443 N 2d
Campbell Archibald, lab., 8th n Carpenter
Campbell A. B., M. D., 153 S 10th, h 122 Pine
CAMPBELL A. H., oil manuf., Screw Dock (K) 54 N whfs & 109 N Water, Penn ab Maiden, h 8th bel Coates
Campbell Bernard, stone cutter 3 Mary's ct
Campbell Catharine, nurse, 290 Vine
Campbell Catharine, sempstress, 41 Currant al
Campbell Catharine, widow, 208 Queen
Campbell Charles, carp., Crans' ct
Campbell Chas. O. B., mer., 54 N whfs, h 113 S 9th
Campbell Daniel, weaver, Benton n William
Campbell David, weaver, M'Duffie
Campbell Edward, atty., 188 N 6th
Campbell Edw., carp., George ab Sch 7th
Campbell Eliza, 22 Parham
Campbell Elizabeth, N E Sch 5th and Spruce
Campbell Francis, dealer, 404 High
Campbell Francis, ostler, 12 S 10th
Campbell Geo., carter, Rule's ct
Campbell George, atty. & coun., 203 Mulberry
Campbell Graham, tavern, Front & Phoenix (K)
Campbell Henry R., engineer, 8th & Wallace
Campbell Hugh, mer., 94 High
Campbell James, lab., Sch Front n Chestnut
Campbell James, stock and exchange broker, 5 Exchange pl, h 78 N 11th
Campbell James, plasterer, 11th & Hazel
Campbell James, judge, 269 Pine
Campbell Jas., blacksm., Brown ab Cherry (K)
Campbell James, tailor, 5 Buist's row
Campbell James, stonemas., 4 Wheelock's pl
Campbell James, shoemr., Willow ab Factory
Campbell James, carter, Levy's ct
Campbell James, 156 S 10th
Campbell James, weav., Higham's ct (K)
Campbell James, coachman, 12 Quince
Campbell James A., house carp., N W 8th and Fitzwater
Campbell James D., hatter, 527 N 2d, h Rachel ab Poplar
Campbell James M., publisher, 6 Hart's Buildings, h Sch 7th bel Spruce
Campbell James R., mer., 91 High, h 122 Pine
Campbell Jane, sempstress, Carlile st
Campbell Jane, dry goods, 81 Cedar
Campbell John, tallow chand., 12 Almond
Campbell John, brickmr., Spruce bel Sch 4th
Campbell John, lab., S W Front & Green
Campbell John, weav., Jefferson n Cadwalader (K)
Campbell John, weaver, Hope ab Master (K)
Campbell John, bottler, Cedar bel Broad
Campbell John, pedler, Lombard n Sch 7th
7

Campbell John, weaver, 4th ab Master (K)
Campbell John, weaver, Clinton ab Norris (K)
Campbell John, weaver, Bedford bel Brond
Campbell John, lab., Hope ab Phoenix (K)
Campbell John, weaver, Bickham n Sch 7th
Campbell John, tobacconist, rear 458 N 3d
Campbell John H., atty'n and coun., 183 N 6th
Campbell Jonathan, carp., Poplar bel 10th
Campbell Joseph, miller, Pleasant ab 12th
Campbell Jos., ostler, rear 17 Farmer
Campbell Joshua, tailor, 3 Smith's ct n 2d
Campbell Lucinda, Carpenter ab 6th
Campbell Margaret, 11 Elmslie's al
Campbell Margaret, 199 Shippen
CAMPBELL MARTIN & Co., dry goods, 94 High
Campbell Mary, George n Sch 7th
Campbell Mary, Culvert ab 4th
Campbell Mary, 32 Crown
Campbell Michael, lab., 4 Sch Water
Campbell Michael, cordw., Sch Beach ab Walnut
Campbell Michael B., shoemr., 6 Sailor's ct
Campbell Oliver, weaver, Otter n Front (K)
Campbell Patrick, lab., Richard
Campbell Patrick, tailor, 295 S 4th
Campbell Patrick, omnibus driver, rear Beach ab Poplar (K)
Campbell Peter, weaver, Fitzwater ab 12th
Campbell Peter, weaver, Cadwalader n Oxford (K)
Campbell Quinton, pres. P. Fire Ins. Co., 134 Walnut, h 124 S 8th
Campbell Quinton jr., mer., 35½ S Front
Campbell Rachel, ½ road & Washington
Campbell Rachel, 10 Rihl's ct
Campbell Randolph U. waiter, Bedford bel 12th
Campbell Richard, capt., 295 N 7th
Campbell R. H., 113 S 9th
Campbell Samuel, lab., 13th ab Catharine
Campbell Samuel, weaver, Bedford bel 13th
Campbell Samuel, weaver, Helmuth n Sch 7th
Campbell Sarah, nurse, Front n Almond
Campbell Sarah, map col., 12, & h 137 N 5th
CAMPBELL ST. GEORGE T., atty. & coun., 94 S 4th
Campbell Susan, bookstore, Queen bel Shackamaxon (K)
Campbell Thomas, hatter, 527 N 2d
Campbell Thomas, lab., Dorothy E Sch 3d
Campbell Tristram, tailor, 119 New Market
Campbell T. & J. D., hatters, 527 N 2d
Campbell Wm., engineer, Race n Sch Front
Campbell Wm., blacksmith, 39 Lily al
Campbell Wm., weaver, Graham's ct
Campbell Wm., weaver, Cadwalader ab Franklin (K)
Campbell Wm., weaver, Perry bel Master
Campbell Wm., druggist, 10th and High, h Callowhill ab 11th
Campbell Wm., plasterer, Wood ab Sch Front
Campbell Wm. carter, rear Sch 8th ab Sassafras
Campbell Wm. machinist, F R ab Phœnix (K)
Campion John, hair dresser, 23 N 6th
Campion Joseph, 308 Mulberry

Campion Joseph H. cabinetmr. 161 & h 167 S 2d
Campion Thomas, coffee roast., 10th ab Washington
Canavan Jas. wool dealer, 5th ab Franklin (K)
Canby Caleb H., plumber, 115 Mulberry, h 63 Cherry
Canby C. H. & Sons, plumbers, 115 Mulberry
Cane Mary, washer, Chester st
Caner Margaret, 4th and Bhristian
Canfield N., broker, 51 Chestnut, h U S Hotel
Canfield P., lab., Walnut n Ashton
Cangey Cornel. plasterer, Callowhill ab Sch 3d
Cann Augustus, patternmr., 91 N 13th
Cann Conrad, coach painter, Brown ab 10th
Cann John, combmr., 84 F road
Cannavin Joseph, tailor, 2 Howard's ct
Cannell S. W. mer. 8 N Front, h 11th bel Clinton
Cannen John, painter, Leopard (K)
Cannertine John, lab., Carlton ab 13th
Canning Alexander, lab., Hope ab Otter (K)
Canning John, rear Pleasant ab 12th
Canning Mary, tailoress, 2 Scott's al
Canning Matilda, dressmr., 3 Benton
Canning Matthew, stone cutter, 1 Scott's ct
Canning M. & Co., booksellers, 272 Chestnut
Canning Wm., tavern, 89 Shippen
Cannon Daniel B., gent., 73 Pine
Cannon Dennis, grocer, 7th and St Mary
Cannon Hugh, sculptor, 7 Lodge al, h 10 Jefferson
Cannon James, lab., Dorothy n Sch 4th
Cannon James, tinsmith, 244 Callowhill
Cannon James, clerk, 12 S 10th
Cannon John, lab., Spruce n Sch 5th
Cannon Peter, brickmr., Palmer n F road (K)
Cannon Philip, lab., Pine bel Sch 6th
Cannon Rees, lab., George ab R road (F V)
Cannon Samuel T., stonecutter, Church avenue
Cannon Thomas, stonecutter, Sch 8th bel Vine
Cannon W. A., tinsmith, 2d & Laurel
Canon & Brothers, tinsmiths, 319 High
Canon George, tinsmith, 319 High
Canon James, tinsmith, 319 High
Canon John, tinsmith, 319 High, h Franklin & Callowhill
Cansler Wm. W., paper hanger, N E 7th and Mulberry
Cantay Miles, weaver, Murray n Sch 3d
Cantlin John, lab., Marriott bel 6th
Cantrell John A., druggist, 2d & Carpenter
Canty Jeremiah, weaver, White's ct
Cany Mary, gentw., 500 Vine
Capehart Henry, cordw. Hanover bel Duke (K)
Capewell & Brother, glass manuf. 11 Minor
Capewell James, mer., 11 Minor, h Kaign's P.
Capewell John, mer., 11 Minor, h Kaign's P.
Capewell Joseph, china store, 427 N 2d
Caples Robert, lab., Beach ab Poplar (K)
Capp John C., mer., 2 N whfs, h 148 N 12th
Capp Samuel, mer., 2 N whfs.
Cappell Samuel, cordw., 6th and Poplar
Cappus August, shop, 27 Tammany
Caralter Thomas, 14 Juniper la
Carberry Wm., grocer, High n Sch 4th
Carbin Elizabeth, 333 Lombard

Carbray Thomas, chandler, St Mary bel 7th
Carbray Wm., weaver, Fetter n Harrison
Carden N., tavern, 317 Callowhill
Cardera Joseph, gent., 15 Scheet's st
Cardin Thomas, lab., 14 Mark's la
Cardwell Jane, milliner, 1 N 8th
Cardwell Thomas C., mer., 34 Chestnut
Cardwell Wm., lab., Hanover & Duke (K)
Cardwell Wm., painter, Coates n Sch 6th
Cardwell Wm. C., mer., 34 Chestnut
Care James, weaver, rear 10th ab Carpenter
Care Miss M. J., b h, 212 Chestnut
Care Rachel, 4 Townsend's ct
Care Wm., currier, Linden st
Carels George, eating house, Harmony
Carels Wm., Bolivar House, 201 & 203 Chestnut
Carey Amos, carpenter, 184 St John, h rear 291 Coates n 7th
Carey Ann Eliza, teacher, Rose al
Carey Ephraim, lab., Carpenter ab 13th
CAREY & HART, booksellers, S E 4th and Chestnut
Carey Isaac, morocco dresser, Streeper's ct
Carey James, waterman, 56 Almond
Carey James, cordw., rear 386 S 2d
Carey James, waiter, George ab 10th
Carey John, drayman, Wagner's ct
Carey Maria, 290 Walnut
Carey Robert, saddle & harnessmr., 31 S 4th, h Washington bel 4th
Carey Wm., cordw., Elizabeth n Poplar
Carhart Samuel, cordw., N W Little Dock and Spruce, h 38 Almond
Cariss Wm., gilder, 1 Little Green (K)
Carl Wm., musician, 171 N 13th
Carles Joseph, framemr., 3 Raspberry la
Carleton Thomas H., carp., 8 College av, h 191 Cherry
Carlile A., clerk, 227 Coates
Carlile Wm. B., shoemr., 256 Mulberry
Carlin Andrew, artist, 595 N Front
Carlin Benj., painter, 47 S whfs
Carlin Elizabeth, Centre bel 13th
Carlin Hannah, shop, 1 Barker
Carlin Hugh, tavern, 3d & Shippen
Carlin James, Dorothy n Sch 4th
Carlin Jonathan, sawyer, S W Apple & George
Carlin Mary, shop, Bedford ab 6th
Carlin Michael, lab., Senneff's ct
Carlin Michael, lab., Sch 6th n Callowhill
Carlin Michael, shoemr., Spruce n Sch 5th
Carlin Michael, tavern, Vine & Front
Carlin Patrick, shoemr., 164 S 6th
Carlin Patrick, lab., Fitzwater ab 6th
Carlin Philip, Lebanon ab Christian
Carlin Thomas, lab., Sch 3d ab Spruce
Carlin Thomas, lab., 6th ab Master (K)
Carlin Wm., cordw., S W 6th & Lombard
Carlin W. J., tavern, Dock & Water
Carling George D., chairmr., 2 Farrie's ct
Carlis John, carp., 3 Maple
Carlisle David, 369 N 6th
CARLISLE & GASKILL, com. mers., 48 N whfs. & 97 N Water
Carlisle Henry, combmr., 304 Sassafras

Carlisle John, cordw., Chestnut bel Sch 7th
Carlisle Keziah, 67 Mulberry
Carlisle Mary Ann, 424 S 4th
Carlisle Mary Ann, 109 St John
Carlisle Wm. jr., mer., 97 N Water, h Cherry W Broad
Carll G. S., furniture, 238 S 3d
Carlley Geo. W., tobacco, square ab Rye
Carlon Charles, tailor, 36 Middle al
Carlon Charles, b h, 69 S Front
Carlton Ann, 145 Spruce
Carlyle Alex., carp., 2 Roberts' ct
Carlyle Wm., machinist, Wood ab Sch 4th
Carman Alex., millwt., 580 S Front
Carman Elizabeth, 204 Mulberry
Carman Elon, car driver, Haydock bel Front
Carman James H., saddletreemr. 9 Collins' al
Carman John, carp., 91 German
Carman Margaret, Wood bel 10th
Carman Mary, gentw., 132 S 4th
Carman Richard, bricklay. Crown bel Duke (K)
Carman Stephen, locksmith, 10 Chester
Carman Wm., saw mill, Camden, h 104 S 3d
Carman Wilson, varnishmr. 4th bel Federal
Carmichael James, oil cloth manuf., 570 N 3d, h 680 N 2d (K)
Carmick Lewis, com. mer., 125 Lombard
Carmick Mrs. wid., 125 Lombard
Carnahan D. K. Miss, teacher, 268 N 6th
Carnahan John, tailor, 13 S Sch 5th
Carnahan Sarah Ann, 1 Park av
Carnell Chas., machinist, Phoenix bel Hancock
Carnell Wm., coachmr., G T road ab 5th
Carney Arthur, tavern, Green & Washington
Carney B. L., hatter, 109 Shippen, h 278 S 4th
Carney Charles, carter, 254 S 5th
Carney Edward, tanner, rear 32 Paschal's al
Carney James, shop, Bedford bel 7th
Carney Jane, washer, Middle al
Carney John, lab., Christian bel 9th
Carney John, lab., Clare st
Carney Robert, lab., Western pl
Carney Thomas, cordw., 3 Abbott's ct
Carney Wm., lab., rear Centre bel Parrish
Carns Andrew, agent, Charlotte ab Culvert
Carns Charles W., brickmr., M'Duffie
Carns Edward, well digger, 237 S 6th
Carns Henry, shoemr., rear Beach & Poplar (K)
Carns Wm., 5th bel George (K)
Caroline Wm., cordw., Nixon n Linn (F M)
Carolus Elizabeth, cupper, 342 N 3d
Carolus Jacob, cordw., 2 Maple
Caron E. A., dry goods, 266 S 2d
Carpenter Abina, shop, 333 Vine
Carpenter Abraham, mariner, 1 Lily al
Carpenter Ann, 141 S 10th
Carpenter Ann, bookfolder, 30 Coates al
Carpenter Benj. E., 215 Coates
Carpenter Charles A., blacksm., 78 Penn (S)
Carpenter Charles R. morocco dresser, 227 St John
Carpenter C., vict., George ab R road (F V)
Carpenter & Co., bonnet manuf, 117 Chestnut
Carpenter D. H., surg. ins. mr., 643 N 2d (K)

Carpenter D. L., teacher of dancing, Assembly Buildings
Carpenter Edward, conveyancer, 56 Walnut, h Sch 8th bel Spruce
Carpenter Eliza, 25 Palmyra sq.
Carpenter Emily, gentw., Middle al
Carpenter Francis, tailor, 48 S 3d, h N W 3d & Cypress
Carpenter George, clerk, Buttonwood ab R road
Carpenter George W., carp., 14 Perry
Carpenter George W., druggist, 301 High, h Germantown
CARPENTER G. W. & Co., druggists, 301 High
Carpenter Henry M., cordw., 265 S 2d
Carpenter James, cabman, Linden n Howard
Carpenter James B., tailor, rear 11 George
Carpenter John, tailor, 159 Pine
Carpenter John, rulemr., Poplar ab 3d
Carpenter John D., blacksmith, Apple below George
Carpenter Joshua, painter, Juniper bel Spruce
Carpenter Marg., rear 45 M road
Carpenter Miles, lab., Noble n O Y road
Carpenter Powell, ice house, O Y road & Noble, h 89 Tammany
Carpenter Samuel, shoemr., 299 Walnut
Carpenter Samuel, bookbinder, 47 Wood
Carpenter Samuel H., 76½ Walnut, h 117 S 8th
Carpenter Sarah, 64 S 12th
Carpenter Sarah C., milliner, 17 S 2d
Carpenter Stephen, carp., Rose al bel Coates
Carpenter Thomas C., fancy store, 115 N 3d
Carpenter Wm., lab., 20 Shippen
Carpenter Wm., lab., 92 Bedford
Carpenter Wm., tailor, 48 S 3d, h 183 S 5th ·
Carpenter W. & F., tailors, 48 S 3d
Carpentier & Andrews, c. mers., 99 S Front
Carpentier John C., flax seed oil mill, Chestnut (W P)
Carpentier John C., mer., 99 S Front
Carpentier Lewis D., mer., 99 S Front
Carpentier Sarah K., 326 Walnut
Carr Adam, mer., 7 Commerce, h 131 S 3d
Carr Ann, shop, Wood bet Sch 6th & 7th
Carr Charles, lamp manuf., 106 Cedar
Carr Charles, weaver, 5 Brinton
Carr Daniel, grocer, 7th & Baker
Carr Danl., lab., 3 Spafford st
Carr David, engineer, 5 Harrison
Carr Edw., mer., 23 Church al, h 19 Clinton
Carr Edw'd, watchman, Chestnut n Sch 3d
Carr Edw. W., newsp. agent, 440 N 4th
Carr Elizab'th, gentw., Franklin ab Buttonwood
Carr Henry, coachman, rear 23 Appletree al
Carr Isaac, painter, 2 School
Carr Jacob, painter, 6 Penn's av
Carr Jacob B., painter, 192 Noble
Carr Jacob E., plumber, 166 N 4th, h 9th bel Melon
Carr James, grocer, 12th & Bedford
Carr James, grocer, 109 Cherry
Carr James, glass cutter, 24 Maiden (K)
Carr James, weaver, Sch 2d and Lombard
Carr James, lab., Ashton & Walnut .

Carr Jas., blacksm., Corn & Wharton
Carr James, lab., 177 S Front
Carr John, huckster, 7 Strawberry
Carr John, vict., Marlboro' n Franklin (K)
Carr John, lab., Cooper n Sch 3d
Carr John, driver, Glenat's ct (K)
Carr John, lab., rear Rose ab School (K)
Carr J. G. & G. W., dry goods, N W 4th and Poplar
Carr Lewis, atty. and coun. 66 S 6th
Carr Littleton, porter, 49 Currant al
Carr Maria, gentw., 52 Lombard
Carr Michael, weav. G T road bel Jefferson (K)
Carr Michael, waiter, 4 Garrigue's ct
Carr Michael, plumber, 10th and Bonsall
Carr Patrick, blacksm., Hays' ct (K)
Carr Robert, lab., Church ab Reed
Carr Robert, lab., Johnston's ct (K)
Carr Robert, weaver, Cedar n Sch 3d
Carr & Roberts, Misses, teachers, 118 Spruce
Carr Samuel, blacksm., Apple ab George
Carr Saml., lab., rear 482 Coates
Carr & Snyder, painters, 70 S 4th
Carr Thomas, prof. of music, 183 N 8th
Carr Wm., bootmr., 497 Vine
Carr Wm., tailor, Lewis E Sch 5th
Carr Wm., carter, 9th bel Melon
Carr Wm., engraver, 13 Pine
Carr Wm., weaver, 186 N Water
Carr William H., hardware, 6 Commerce, h 131 S 3d
Carr Wm. L., mer., Sch 7th n Vine
Carr W. R., oysters, 143 Lombard
Carragher James, lab., 62 P road
Carralho D. N., gent., 129 Lombard
Carrall David W., tavern, Beach & Maiden (K)
Carrateo Wm., vict., 6th bel G T road (K)
Carre Lewis J., tinman, Winter bel Sch 2d
Carrell James, carp., rear 116 Christian
Carrell John, tavern, Swanson and Beck
Carrick Alex., baker, High W Sch 5th
Carrick David. Callowhill n Sch 3d
Carrick Jas., grocer, Nixon bel Callowhill
Carrick Robert, lab., lab., Syracuse ab Locust
Carrick Thomas, blacksm., Callowhill ab Sch 2d
Carrigan Jacob, carp., 204 Cherry
Carrigan Jacob jr., saddlery hardware, 21 N 3d, h 5th and Buttonwood
Carrigan Matthew, dealer, 16 Acorn al
Carroll Daniel, b. h., 178 S Water
Carroll Dennis, weaver, Crown bel Duke (K)
Carroll E. A., ship and insurance broker, 14 Library, h 126 Catharine
Carroll James, harnessmr., Abbott's ct
Carroll James, stone mason, Carroll's ct
Carroll John, porter, 3 Deal's av
Carroll John, fruiterer, rear 242 Christian
Carroll Jno., lab., Salem al
Carroll Maurice, shoemr., 18 Jones' al
Carroll Michael, lab., Marriott bel 5th
Carroll Patrick, tailor, 153 Green
Carroll Patrick, porter, 11 Kenworthy's ct
Carroll Peter, blacksm., 34 Mifflin
Carroll Saml., painter, Lombard ab Sch 6th
Carroll Saml., lab., 10 Lawrence

Carroll Thomas, 4 Letitia ct and 22 High
Carroll Thos., weaver, 13th bel Brinton
Carroll Thos., weaver, 273 N Front
Carroll Wm., weaver, 118 Plum
Carrow John, jewellery manuf., 5 Bank al, h Catharine bel Grubb
Carrow Thomas, clerk, 3d bel Catharine (S)
Carsley John, blacksm., 113 N Juniper
Carson And., weaver, Jefferson ab 2d (K)
Carson Catharine, 125 New
Carson Catharine, spool., Cadwalader ab Phoenix (K)
Carson Eben'r., seaman, 246 S Front
Carson Elizabeth, 13 Julianna
Carson Eliza, 276 Wood bel Broad
Carson & Farson, carps., Elbow la
Carson Fred'k, confect., Beach bel Maiden (K)
Carson George, lab., Lombard bel Juniper
Carson George C., mer., 51 S whfs., h 10th and Clinton
Carson Hannah, Dean ab Locust
Carson Henry, carp., h 35 Vine
Carson Henry, cot. brok., S Water & Chestnut
CARSON H. L., mer., 14 N Front
Carson & Helmuth, mdz. brokers, S Water and Chestnut
Carson John, Brown ab 4th
Carson John M., Brown's ct
Carson Joseph, M. D., 53 S 13th
Carson M., weaver, Gabell's ct
Carson & Newbold, mers., 51 S whfs.
Carson Oliver, weaver, 573 N 3d
Carson Robert, weaver, Front ab Master (K)
Carson Robert, bricklayer, Dorothy E Sch 3d
Carson Saml., weaver, 255 S 3d
Carson Thomas, grocer, 207 G T road
Carson Thomas, grocer, N W 12th & Wood
Carson Thomas B., dry goods, N E 5th and Callowhill
Carstairs James, mer., 1st whf. ab Cedar, h 31 Lombard
Carswell Matthew W., 130 Franklin
Carswell Robt. B., cordw., Wood bel Sch 3d
Carter Abraham, carp., 18 Gray's al, h 30 Elfreth's al
Carter Alfred A., 11th and Buttonwood
Carter Amos, carter, Orange ab Washington
Carter Chas., M. D., 488 Chestnut
Carter Charles Ignatius H. Rev., 116 S 4th
Carter Daniel, lab., 51 Currant al
Carter Dennis, musician, Parker n Prime
Carter D. B., gent., 13th and Lombard
Carter Edw. L., M. D., S E 4th and Catharine
Carter Elizabeth, milliner, 57½ Mulberry
Carter Elizabeth, undertaker, 133 N 6th
Carter George, tobac., 90 N 5th & 372 High
Carter Harrison G., mer., 23 Church al, h 374 S 3d
Carter Isaac, lab., Perry & Phœnix (K)
Carter Jacob, oak cooper, 167 N 12th
Carter James, mer., N E 3d and Church al, h 274 N 5th
Carter James N., cooper, S E Queen & Swanson
Carter James T., straw goods, 189 High, h 39 N Sch 8th

Carter John, 33 German
Carter John, chem., 70 N 3d, h 105 S 12th
Carter John, seaman, Hancock bel Phœnix (K)
Carter J. G., cooper, 45 Commerce, h 167 N 12th
Carter Noah, waiter, Lisle
Carter Restore, mer., 11 N 3d, h 21 New
Carter Mary, shop, Palmer n F road (K)
Carter Robert T., whipmr., Carpenter bel 6th
Carter Robert W., brushmr., 74 S 2d
Carter Sarah, Conard's ct
Carter & Scattergood, chemists, 70 N 3d
Carter Tamar, washer, 55 Currant al
Carter Wm., silk dyer, 171 N 10th
Carter Wm., jeweller, 49 Catharine
Carter Wm., sailmr., 52 Brown (N L)
Carter Wm. M., waterman, Rose al ab Green
Carter Wm. T., mer., 232 N 3d, h 272 E Pine
Carteret Joseph W., undertaker, 6th & Queen
Carteret William M., com. mer., 7 Bank, h 136 Catharine
Cartledge Joseph, stone cut., Federal bel 10th
Cartridge & Cordeng, oysters, 8 High
Cartwright Henry, machinist, 456 N 8th
Cartwright Mary, 46 George (S)
Cartwright Matthew, tin worker, 456 N 3d
Cartwright Wm., tin plate worker, 456 N 3d
Carty Sumpter, cordw., 22 North
Carty S., hatter, 2 James
Carver Alexander B., conveyr., N W 9th and Filbert, h 12th bel Cherry
CARVER A. B. & CO., conveyancers, 9th and Filbert
Carver Derrick K., 270 N 7th
Carver & Hall, architects, 51 N 6th
Carver Harvey, lab, Fralev's al
Carver Isaac, turner, 8 Little Dock, h 410 S 3d
Carver Jacob, umbrellas, Palmer n F. road
Carver Jacob, conveyancer, 9th and Filbert
Carver John E., architect, 51 N 6th, h 302 Sassafras
Carver John R., carpenter, 6 Rittenhouse
Carver Mary, Palmer rear F road
Carver Samuel, atty. at law, N W 9th & Filbert
Carver Wm., weaver, reat F road ab Phœnix
Carver Wm., printer, 8th bel Parrish
Carvery Peter, lab., Pearl bel William
Carvill Sarah, Apple ab Poplar
Carvin Wm., weaver, F road bel Master (K)
Case Ambrose, cordw., rear Carlton ab Sch 6th
Case John, tailor, 1 Mary's ct
Case Samuel H., clerk, 202 Chestnut
Case Wm., cordw.; 504 Callowhill
Casely Alexander, carp., 439 S 6th
Casey Arthur, pap. stainer, Beckett st
Casey Bridget, shop, 1 Spafford st
Casey Francis, lab., Oxford ab Front
Casey & Guyant, glass cutters, rear 16 Mulberty
Casey James, tailor, 5 Stamper's al
CASEY JAMES, iron mer., 13 N Water, h 382 Mulberry
Casey Jas. D., glass cutter, rear 16 Mulberry, h Vienna ab Queen (K)
Casey John, grocer, 152 N 12th
CASEY JOHN H., bon. and caps, 116 High
Casey John T., pap. hanger, 7th bel Washington

Casey Michael, shoemr., 35 Crown
CASH ANDREW D., conveyancer, 80 Walnut, h 101 S 12th
Cash A. D. & Jones E. R., conveyancers, 80 Walnut
Cash Elizabeth, gentw., Ann (F V)
Cash Elizabeth, wid. of Thomas, 103 Franklin
Cash John S., collector, Columbia R R, h 13th ab Green
Caskel Elizabeth, b h, rear 64 N 2d
Caskey Ann, dry goods, 11th and Chestnut
Caskey James, carter, 8 Margaretta
Caskey James, weav., Cadwalader ab Jefferson
Caskey John, weaver, Hope bel Master
Caskey Joseph, groceries and flour, 446 High
Caskey Joseph, lab., Elk (K)
Caskey & Reeves, wood deals., Callowhill st whf
Caskey Samuel, lab., Sch 5th ab Callowhill
Caskey Wm., moulder, Howard bel Franklin(K)
Caslaw John, weaver, 10th bel Catharine
Casling Geo., lab, Phœnix bel G T road (K)
Cass Patrick, atty., 93 Green
Cassaday Dennis, painter, 4 Howard's ct
Cassaday Hugh, pedler, Sch Front & Chestnut
Cassaday James W., ven. blindmr., 8 S 6th, h 143 N 9th
Cassaday Patrick, weaver, Carpenter ab 10th
Cassady Dennis, tavern, Fitzwater
Cassady Edw., weaver, Milton ab 11th
Cassady Felix, carter, 2 John's ct
Cassady Felix, carp., 330 Carpenter
Cassady Francis, weav., G T road bel Jefferson
Cassady Francis, painter, 53 Carpenter (S)
Cassady Henry, segarmr., 302 S 4th
Cassady Hugh, lab., 11 Carter's al
Cassady H., dealer, 137 S 9th
Cassady James, butcher, Marriott's la ab 8th
Cassady John, baker, 130 N 4th
Cassady John, lab., rear 66 P road
Cassady John, shop, 3 Little Oak
Cassady John, carp., 328 Carpenter
Cassady John B., combmr., Otter n William(K)
Cassady Margaret, dealer, 196 Cedar
Cassady Michael, dealer, 63 S 4th
Cassady Park H., 29 Logan's sq
Cassady Patrick weav., Lloyd ab Fitzwater
Cassady Wm., tailor, 36 Strawberry
Cassan Lewis P., mariner, 10 Mary (S)
Cassary Hugh, clerk, Clare al
Casseday & Co., straw hat finis'r., 43 Lombard
Casseday Francis, weaver, G T road ab Master
Casseday James, grain mer., 121 S Water, h 27 Pine
Casseday Wm., wear., Philip ab Jefferson
Cassell Frederick, cordw., 68 Vine
Cassey Joseph, gent., 113 Lombard
Cassiday Robt., tailor 8th bel Carpenter
Cassidy Francis, carp., 23 Hurst
Cassidy Hugh, mer., 32 Walnut, h Clare al
Cassin John, provisions, 26 N Water, h 73 Union
Casteldine Ann, 307 S Front
Castels Wm., printer, 477 Vine
Castillon Giles E., mer., 28 Walnut
Castle Ann, milliner, 108 S 2d.

CASTLE JAMES H., atty. and coun., office 48 S 4th, h S Sch 8th ab Pine
Castle Wm., confectioner, 136 Mulberry
Castle Wm., lab., Hummel's row (K)
Castles Robert, shop, R road and Pleasant
Castles James, grocer, 333 S 3d
Castner Enoch, mer., 67 S whfs., h 26 Union
Castner John F., painter, 59 Dock
Castner Samuel, mer., 67 S wharves, h 269 S Front
Castner S. & E., grocers, 67 S whfs
Castor Edmund, cordw., 19 Elizabeth, (N L)
Caswell Arabella, 30 N 9th
Caterson Robt., lab., Sch 3d ab Spruce
Cathcart Alexander, cordw., 206 Queen
Cathcart James, watchman, Filbert W Sch 4th
Cathcart James, milliner, 2d and G T road
Cathcart Thos., carp., Lombard ab 11th
Cathcart Wm., cooper, 3 Mary
Cathell Josiah, hatter, 26 Catharine
Catherine James, stevedore, Essex
Catherwood Andrew J., mer., S W 13th and High, h 425 Walnut
Catherwood Hugh, gent., office S W 13th and High, h 425 Walnut
Catherwood John, weaver, Fitler n 2d (K)
Cathrall George, paper hanger, 68 Coates
Cathrell Benj., paper hanger, 9th and Brown
Cathrell Elizabeth, store, Front & Washington
Cathrell George, tobac'st., Elizabeth ab Poplar
Catlin George, musical inst. mr., 117 N 5th
Catlin Sarah, 5 N 13th
CATTELL ALEXANDER G., com. mer., 13 N whfs
Cattell David, blacksmith, 266 S Front (S), h rear 117 Queen (S)
Cattell Saml. W., painter, 60½ Walnut
Cauchlin Thos., lab., Hay's ct (K)
Cauet Armand, sugar refiner, 37 St John, h 72 Vine
Cauffman Lawrence, mer., 26 N 3d, h 125 N 9th
Cauffman Marcus, mer., 25 N 3d, h 391 N 6th
Cauffman R. S., mer., 26 N 3d, h 160 S 9th
Cauffman R. S. & Co., crockery, 26 N 3d
Cauffman T. F., mer., 26 N 3d, h 125 N 9th
Cauffman & Wolf, dry goods, 25 N 3d
Caullay C., bootmr, 141 S 6th
Caullet Sarah, Reed bel 2d
Caulk Oliver, gent., 9th ab Poplar
Caum Wm., blacksm., Alden ab Poplar
Cauvin Nicholas, gent., 49 Lombard
Cavanaugh Hugh, grocer, Almond st whf
Cavanaugh Lawrence, mason, St Joseph's av
Cavanaugh John, 23 Chatham
Cavanaugh Joseph, porter, 2 Seiser's ct
Cavanaugh Michael, gent., S E 2d and Queen
Cavanaugh Michael, lab., Filbert n Sch Front
Cavanaugh Mich., lab., Palm bel Parrish
Cavanaugh Wm., N E Juniper and High
Cave Joseph, watchmr., 10 Lagrange pl
Cavell Robt., 13th bel Callowhill
Cavender Cordelia, gentw., 243 N 7th
Cavender Curtis H., clerk, Poplar ab 8th
Cavender E. M., 25 Christian
Cavender John H., conveyancer, 348 N 5th

Cavender Mary Ann, Barker W Sch 6th
Cavender Thos. S., conveyancer, 348 N 5th, h 108 Marshall
Cavett Anna Maria, b. h., 6 S 3d
Cawley Saml. B., bricklayer, 533 Vine
Cawman John, tavern, 600 S Front
Cayley Timothy, weaver, Mariner
Cayot Henry, cabinetmr., 52 Zane
Cayser John, weaver, Otter ab School
Cehill Michael, slater, Lemon ab 10th
Celvey James, weaver, Otter ab School
Cerad Jos., trunkmr., Stackhouse pl
Certier George, watch-spring mr., Elmslie's al
Cetterson Wm., lab., cooper, n Sch 3d
Chadwick George, supt., 20 Union (S)
Chadwick Jemima, nurse, 87 S 12th
Chadwick Thos., brickmr., Pine ab Sch 3d
Chadwick T. B., baker, 83 S 12th
Chaffee James, trader, 256 Garden
Chaffee Jesse, boatmr., Sch av
Chain Ezekiel, baker, 10th and Pleasant
Chain John, tailor, 458 N 2d
Chain John, lab., 5 Poplar
Chain Thomas, barber, 67 N Front
Chalmers Ann, Parrish ab 8th
Chaloner A. D., M. D., 317 Spruce
Chaloner Deborah, gentw., 264 Marshall
Chaloner & Reynolds, mers., 423 High
Chaloner Wm., mer., 423 High, h 317 Spruce
Chamberlain C., 50 Dillwyn
Chamberlain C. R., dentist, 163 Spruce
Chamberlain Elizabeth, gentw., 279 N 7th
Chamberlain George, clerk, Fraley's ct (K)
Chamberlain Hannah, 118 Filbert
Chamberlain Henry, carp., 9 Smith's pl
Chamberlain Isaac, waterman, 56 Catharine
Chamberlain James B., cordw., rear 23 Charlotte
Chamberlain John, gauger, Nectarine ab 10th
Chamberlain John J., trader, 6 Curtis' ct
Chamberlain Theodore, mer., 135 High, h 406 Vine
Chamberlain Thos., blacksm., 100 Locust
Chamberlain Wm., carp., 74 Dillwyn
Chamberlin Britton E., teacher, c 11th and Buttonwood, h 66 N 8th
Chamberlin H. F., com. mer., 8 Bank
Chamberlin Taylor, millwrt., Penn n R road
Chambers Andrew R., leather mer., 67 & h 505 Chestnut
Chambers Asa W., com. mer., 30 S whfs., h Dungan's av (K)
Chambers David, bricklayer, Carpenter ab 3d
Chambers Edw., oysterman, 119 Swanson
Chambers Edw. W., rigger, 20 Union (S)
Chambers Elizabeth, 39 Christian
Chambers George K., grocer, N W 10th and Castle
CHAMBERS GEORGE T., manuf. flour, oat meal, &c., Willow ab 12th, h Buttonwood n 13th
Chambers G. W., M. D., S W 4th and Plum
Chambers Hannah, 250 S 6th
Chambers Isaac, waiter, 4 Mercer
Chambers James, boatm., Beach ab Marsh (K)
Chambers John, lab., Corn bel Wharton

Chambers John, stone cutter, Wood ab Sch 8th
Chambers John Rev., 360 Mulberry
Chambers John, weaver, Shippen ab Shippen la
Chambers John, R road bel Sp Garden
Chambers John C. & Son, dry goods, 54 N 2d
Chambers Joseph, bricklr., Carpenter ab 5th
Chambers Joseph, box maker, 7 Plum
Chambers Joseph C., saddle and harnessmr., R road ab 13th
Chambers J. C., mer., 54 N 2d, h 87 Wood
Chambers J. M., carp., Ogden bel Sch 7th
Chambers Lydia, washer, Smith's ct
Chambers Montgomery, M. D., 92 S 5th
Chambers N., waiter, 19 Watson's al
Chambers Peter, baker, rear 445 N 6th
Chambers Richard, mer., 54 N 2d
Chambers Samuel, carter, R road ab Girard av (F V)
Chambers Samuel, 3 Lombard row
Chambers Thomas, 4 White's ct
Chambers Wm., Milton n 11th
Chambers Wm., lab., George n Beach
CHAMBERS WILLIAM B., grocer, N W 4th & Walnut
Chambers Wm. C., 15 Dock, h 278 Walnut
Chambley B., coachman, 10 N 10th
Champion C. Collins, tailor, 2d and Dock, h 113 Wood
Champion Jehu, lab., 357 Lombard
Champion John B., real est. brok., 223 Coates
Champion Samuel, blacksm., Parrish ab 11th
Champion Thos., machinist, Sch 8th bel Willow
Champion Wm., tavern, S whfs n Cedar
Chan Isaac, clothing, 3 Paschal's al
Chance John, mariner, 11 Union (S)
Chance J. C., dry goods, 530 High
Chance Thos., waterman, N E Queen & Front
Chance Wm., blacksm, Front bel Master (K)
Chancellor Hannah, gentw., 271 Chestnut
Chancellor Wharton, 271 Chestnut
Chandlee C., carpenter, 2 Madison
Chandler Ann, 1 Taylor's al
Chandler Ann, sempstress, rear 20 P road
Chandler Edwin, agricultural warehouse, 196 High, h George ab Sch 6th
Chandler George Rev., Queen bel Palmer (K)
Chandler I. C., lab., 32 Mayland
Chandler James B., mer., 70 S 3d
Chandler John, grocer, 159 S 6th
Chandler Joseph R., editor and proprietor U S Gazette, 66 Dock, h 105 N 10th
Chandler Mary, Pleasant ab 10th
Chandler M. T. W., asst. city surv., 426 Sassafras
Chandler Wm., lab., 30 Magnolia
Chandler Wm. A., shoemr., 22 Rachel
Chapin Emma, confectioner, 441 S 2d
Chapin Luther, gunsm., Watman's ct
Chapman Ann, Beach ab Maiden (K)
Chapman Enos, carp., Cherry & Juniper, h 142 N 13th
Chapman H. B., acct., Haverford road (M V).
Chapman Jas. S., bootmr., Vine ab 12th
Chapman John, eat. house, 236 Shippen
Chapman John W., dentist 7 N 9th
Chapman Jonathan, eng., N 10th ab Buttonwood

Chapman Joseph, painter, 13th and Cherry
Chapman Joseph, carman, 8 Orchard
Chapman Julian, 11 Christian
Chapman L., M. D., Clay av
Chapman Mary, grocer, 99 Wood
Chapman & Mitchell, bookbin., rear 37 Cherry
Chapman Nathaniel, M. D., 332 Chestnut
Chapman Rebecca, St John ab Beaver (K)
Chapman Richard, M. D., Front bel Otter (K)
Chapman Richard, papermr., 513 N 2d
Chapman Sarah Ann, b. h., 151 S 10th
Chapman Susan, cigarmr., 308 St John
Chapman Theodore, bricklayer, 82 Buttonwood
Chapman Thomas, carp., George E Sch 6th
Chapman Thos. B., machinist, Beach bel Maiden h Queen n Hanover
CHAPMAN T. ELLWOOD, bookseller and binder, 74 N 4th
Chapman Wm., bricklayer, 289 N 8th
Chapman Wm., jr., dry goods, 134 N 8th
Chapman W. A., actor, Pine W Sch 7th
Chapouty Mrs. S., gentw., Sch 3d ab Sassafras
Chapouty P., furnishing store, 114 N 5th
Chapron John M., gent., 75 Spruce
CHAPRON J. B., att'y., 6th and Walnut
Chardon Sam'l R., bookselr., S E 8th & Sassafras
Charier Madame F. M., teacher, 321 S 3d
Charles Catharine, shop, Rose al
Charles George, stereotype, 9 George
Charles George, combmr., Rose al
Charlton F., carver, 3 Lebanon row
Charlton John, boot fitter, School ab Rose (K)
Charlton Mary Ann, 8 Green (C)
Charlton Martha, tavern, e 8th and Zane
Charlton Robert, hatter, 19 Mechanic
Charlton Wm., lab., Collins' ct
Charman Joseph, shoemr., 24 Strawberry
Charnley Thos., engrav., Franklin ab Crown (K)
Charnley Wm. S., stock and ex. broker, 9 S 3d, h 10 Logan's sq
Charnley & Whelen, stock and ex. broks., 9 S 3d
Charnock Thomas, cabinetmr., rear 172 Pine, h 26 Bonsall
CHARTER HENRY A., Am. hotel, 181 Chestnut
Charter Jerome, dealer, 52 Vine
Charters Samuel, boot and shoemr., R road bel Ann (F V)
Charry Peter, weaver, rear 2d bel Jefferson (K)
Chase B. W., mer., 4 S Front, h 37 Girard
Chase Daniel, waiter, Mechanic
Chase Edwin T., clerk Proth. office, District Court, h 117 North
Chase Ezra, tailor, 6 Perry st
Chase Ezra, jr., watchman, N. Y., 23 Federal
Chase Gasway, hatter, 10th & Catharine
CHASE HEBER, M. D., 4 Franklin row, 9th bel Walnut
Chase John, stonecutter, R road ab Broad
Chase John G., acct. 82 Union
Chase & Magill, com. mers., 4 S Front
Chase Philip B., com. mer., 44½ N 2d, h 4 W Penn sq
Chase Pliny E., teacher, 307 Spruce
Chase Rebecca, gentw., Ogden bel 11th
Chase Stephen, gent., 9 Union

Chase Theodore L., daguereotype, 10th & Sp Garden and 5th and Chestnut .
Chase Thos., coachman, 4 Eutaw
Chastney Jane, teacher, 37 S Sch 6th
Chatham John, cordw., Front bel Wharton
Chatham Joseph, grocer, 77 Locust
Chatham Robert, carp., N W 11th & Pine
CHATHAM ROBERT F., ladies' shoemr., 405 Chestnut
Chatham Stephen C., waterman, Rye ab Reed
Chattin Abijah, bricklayer, 10 Adams
Chattom Jas., Wood bel Sch 5th
Chauncey Chas., coun., office 85, h 87 Walnut
Chauncey Elihu, 157 Walnut
Chauncey Henry, M. D., 6 Steward
Chauncey Nathaniel, atty. & coun., 231 Pine
Chauveau A. J., mer., 242 High, h 209 Noble
Chauvenet A., grocer, N E 6th and Cedar
Chaux Theresa, Indian doctress, F R bel Phœnix
Chave George, hatter, rear 111 Brown
Cheaseman John, shoemr., 4 Burd (S)
Cheavens Wm. E., clerk, Brown bel Front
Cheesman Clinton, mariner, 1 Wilson
Cheesman Jos., huckster, 11 Monroe ct
Cheesman J. V., clerk, Noble bel 8th
Cheesman Richard, agent, Locust n Sch 2d
Cheesman Richard, mariner, rear 386 S 2d
Cheesman Thomas W., tailor, 12 N 8th
Cheetham James, hatter, Vine n Sch
Cheetham Thos., tavern, c Vine and Sch 2d
Cheetham Wm., mer,, 100 S whfs
Cheetham Wm. & Co., com. mers., 100 S whfs
CHEETHAM WM. H., carpet manuf., 270 N 2d, h 553 N 4th
Cheetham W. H., jr., carpet manuf., 5th above Poplar
Chemin A., baker, 187 S Water
CHESEBROUGH A. F., mer., 5 N whfs., h 7 Colonnade row
Chesebrough C. & Co., groceries, 16 S whfs
Chesebrough E. G., boots and shoes, 43 N 2d
Chesnut & Gravel, groceries, 6 High
Chesnut John, weaver, 9 Gay's ct (K)
Chesnut J., blacksm., 402 High, h 89 N Juniper
Chesnut Nathan, lab., Bickham n Sch 7th
Chesnut Sarah, 12th ab Pine
Chesnut Wm., grocer, c Sch 6th and Carlton
Chester Albert, carp., Queen opp Cherry (K)
Chester C. W., cordw., 39 Union (S)
Chester David, Chancellor n Sch 6th
CHESTER HENRY, att'y and coun., 85 Walnut, h 8 Clinton
Chester Hiram, bootmr., F road n Queen .
Chester Jno. ropema. rear Queen ab Palmer (K)

Chestnut Wm., grocer, 6 High, h 47 Wood
Chettle Joseph, hatter, 11 Vernon
Chevelier Wm., tinman, 5th ab Poplar
Chevers George, cabinetmr., 52 Almond
Chew Catharine, washer, Brown's ct
Chew Charles, brass founder, 48 St Mary's
Chew Henrietta, 286 Walnut
Chew Isachar J., paper stainer, Miller ab 13th
Chew I. S., batters, 275 P road
Chew Jacob, mer., 13 Sargent st
Chew Jeffery, furniture, 276 S 2d
Chew Joseph, ladies' shoemr., 39 S 8th, h 572 Poplar
Chew Joseph D., cordw., 289 S 5th
Chew John, hair dresser and wigmr., 199 Chestnut, h 9th bel Fitzwater
Chew Jonathan, cordw., 281 S 5th
Chew Nathan, buttonmr., Carleton ab Sch 4th
Chew Totten, carter, 2d ab Greenwich
Chew William, clothes, N E 2d and Walnut, h 16 Powell
Chewn Wm., seaman, 3 Cox's ct
Cheyney Charles H., ice dealer, 129 Chestnut, h S E Fitzwater and Hubbell
Chierdel Ann, 171 Pine
Child H. T., physician, 132 Green
Child John, clock and watchmr., 452 N 2d
Child Richard S., lamp black, Willow ab Broad, h Marshall and Poplar
Child Samuel T., watchmr., 248 St. John
Childs Asher M., chemist, 12th & Pleasant
Childs C. G., proprietor Com. List. Ex. Buildings, h 365 Mulberry
Childs Edmund, painter, rear 448 Sassafras
Childs G. K., silversmith, 114 Spruce
Childs Isaac, Palmer ab Duke (K)
Childs John, wheelwright, 305 N 3d, h 152 Marshall
Childs Wm., combr., Van Buren pl
Chillas Arthur, mer., 122 S 3d
Chillman James, bookbinder, Lewis ab Poplar
Chipman Chester W., M. D., 475 N 4th
Chipman George, wooden ware, 2 Chestnut, h 27 Dean
Chiquoine Servelle, pilot, F road bel Phœnix
Chism George, weaver, 12 M'Duffie
Chisholm J. A. M., tobacco, N W 8th & Lombard
Chittick Gerrard, weaver, Fulton ab 12th
Choate David L., bootmr., 24 Jone's al (C)
Choate John, saddler, S E St John & George (K)
Christian Isaac, porter, rear 3 Gray's al
Christian John, 67 Catharine
Christian John, cordw., rear 123 Plum st.

CHRISTMAN & FRY, dry goods, 45 N 2d
Christman Joseph C. D., accountant, 146 N 12th
Christman William A., mer., 45 N 2d
Christmann Edward, perfumer, 168 Chestnut
Christopher Hannah, wid., Coates ab 9th
Christopher Jesse M., acct. 423 S 6th
Christy Benjamin F., collector, 14 Union (S)
Christy Elizabeth, nurse, 2 John's ct
Christy James, bottler, S 12th n Lombard
CHRISTY JAMES C., mer., 9 Merchant
Christy John, ship rigger, Alder bel Girard av
Christy Robert, shoemr., Filbert n Sch Front
Christy Robert F., 96 S Front
Christy Sarah, dry gods, 446 N 4th
Christy Thomas, moulder, Hamell's ct
Christy Wm., umbrellamr., 438 N 4th
Christy Wm. M., stationer, 82 Chestnut, h 120 Catharine
Chubb Samuel, dry goods, 251 S 2d
Chur A. T., commis. com., Front & Chestnut, h Vine n Sch 4th
Chur Jacob, mer., 13 Sergeant
Church Fred'k H., stoves & sheet iron, 68 N 2d, h Filbert 4 doors W Broad
Church Julius, confect., 411 N 2d
Church Rebecca, shop, 61 Queen·
Churchill John, shoemr., 64 S 8th
Churchman Charles W., com. mer., 30 S Front, h Germantown
Churchman Hannah, 7th ab Parrish
Churen Samuel, mariner, 33 Union (S)
Cills Wm., tobacconist, 2d & G T road
Citti John, image mr., 80 Spruce, and 8 Arcade
Claflin Horatio S., shoemr., 196 High, h 212 Buttonwood
Claghorn E. H., auctioneer, S W Bank & High, h Franklin n Green
Claghorn John W., mer., 383 Mulberry
Claghorn J. L., auctioneer, S W Bank & High, h 77 N 10th
Claghorn Wm. C., mer., 402 Vine
Clair Margaret, b. h., 236 Wood
Clairey Danl., weaver, 2 Lloyd's ct (K)
Clamans Augustus, vict. Brown ab 13th
Clampitt John, pilot, 33 Queen
Clampitt John C., pilot, 54 Christian
Clancey John, ostler, 3 Kelly
Clancy, Timothy, tavern, 212 N Water
Claney Jeremiah, shoemr., 22 Bonsall
Claphamson John, baker, 9 Dilk's ct
Claphamson Samuel, baker, 94 N 9th
Clapier J. E., tobacconist, 434 N 2d
Clapier Mary, gentw., 216 S Front
Clapp Allen, steward, Penna. Hospital
CLAPP ENOCH, M. D., real es. agt., 72 Dock, h 152 Sassafras
Clapp N. T., mer., 8 N 2d
Clare Bartholomew, printer, 2 Mary's ct
Clare Charles, carter, Washington ab 6th
Clare John, carter, Front bel Greenwich
Clare Thomas, carter, Front and Reed
Claridge Wm. R., druggist, Queen & Hanover (K)
Clark Alex., lampmr., 9th ab Coates

8

Clark Alex., weaver, Oxford bel Queen (K)
Clark Alfred, plumber, R road & Green
Clark Alfred M., engineer, 9 Queen n F road
Clark Andrew, lab., 166 S 6th
Clark Andrew, mer., Hutton ct
Clark Anna Maria, gentw., Lombard n 13th
Clark Archibald F., carp., Poplar bel Elizabeth
Clark Arthur J., painter, 11th bel Callowhill
Clark Benj., watchmr., 1 S Front, h 115 Vine
CLARK & CADMUS, shoes, S W 3d & High
Clark Caroline, shop, Hanover bel Franklin
Clark Charles, lab., G T road ab 6th
Clark Charles, tailor, 2 Beck (S)
Clark Charles, coachman, 24 Prune
Clark Charles D., pedler, 2 Myers' ct
Clark Charles E., upholsterer, 77 S 12th
Clark Chas. S., carp., rear 5th bel Franklin (K)
Clark Clement, tailor, 163 S 2d, h 16 Beck pl
Clark & Cunningham, painters, 112 Crown
Clark Daniel, porter, 6 Little Pine
Clark David, crockery, 6th bel Catharine
Clark Deborah, millinery, 206 Green
Clark Deborah, b h, 409 Sassafras
Clark D. D., M. D. 43 Chestnut
Clark Edward, printer, rear 106 Christian
Clark Edw., lab., Cadwalader bel Phoenix (K)
Clark Eliza, milliner, 59 Cedar
Clark Elizabeth, Queen n Shackamaxon (K)
Clark Elizabeth, tailoress, 34 Maiden (K)
Clark Elizabeth H., 3d and Prime
Clark Ellen, 10th ab Buttonwood
Clark Ellis, watchmr., 142 High, h 32 Branch
Clark Ellis, jr., 30 N 4th, h 32 Branch
Clark Enoch W., exch. broker, 25 S 3d, h Pine ab 9th
Clark Ephraim, upholsterer, N W 4th & Vine, h 115 Marshall
Clark Ephraim, jr., mer., 93 S Front, h 378 Chestnut
Clark Ephraim G., sawyer, Crawford's ct
Clark Ewing, weaver, Crown ab Duke (K)
CLARK E. W. & CO., exch. brok., 25 S 3d
Clark E. W., broker, 25 S 3d, h 262 Pine
Clark F., tailoress, 2 Hyde's ct
Clark Galen, George bel 10th
Clark Geo., butcher, Sch Beach n Locust
Clark George, blacksmith, N E 13th & Olive
Clark George, boot crimper, Front bel Master
Clark George B., tailor, 1 Perry
Clark George D., iron st., 62 Coates
Clark George G., painter, Chester ct
Clark Geo. M., bookbinder, 1 Division st
Clark Gideon, engraver, Ann ab R road (F V)
Clark & Green, hotel, N W 2d & Green
Clark Hawkins, cabinetmr., 146 S 3d
Clark Henry, lab., Sch 5th & Cedar
Clark Hugh, alderman, N 4th n Master (K)
Clark Hugh, teacher, 212 Queen
Clark Hugh, grocer, 146 S 3d
Clark Isaac, carp., Carlton n Sch 8th
Clark Isaac, tanner, 345 Callowhill
Clark Isaac S., cracker baker, 22 Ellen (N L)
Clark Jacob & John, porters, Ten foot al
Clark Jacob M., painter, Olive bel 12th
Clark Jacob W., plumb., 199 N 3d, h 312 Coates

Clark James, dyer, Mechanic bel Culvert
Clark James, lab., 13th ab Christian
Clark James, tailor, F road n Master (K)
Clark James, lab., Owen ct
Clark James, medicines, Bedford bel 8th
Clark James G., gent., office 132 Mulberry
Clark Jane, gentw., 227 S Front
Clark Jane, 38 N 5th
Clark John, lab., Juniper and South
Clark John, cordw., Butler's av
Clark John, grocer, Sch 3d n Vine
Clark John, grocer, S E 5th and Prune, h 115 S 5th
Clark John, contractor, Oak ab High
Clark John, carter, Pine bel Sch Willow
Clark John, ostler, 10 Laurel (C)
Clark John, stevedore, Rose al (C)
Clark John, carpet weav., Hancock ab Phoenix
Clark John, cordw., 8 Maiden (K)
Clark John, combmr., rear 473 N 3d
Clark John, lab., Clair bel Carpenter
Clark John, skin dress., Franklin ab Crown (K)
Clark John, cordw., 238 S 4th
Clark John, porter, Ten foot al
Clark John, machinist, 10th ab Buttonwood
Clark John A., cordw., rear 399 N 3d
Clark John C., printer & stationer, 60 Dock, h 67 Locust
Clark John F., pilot, Wood bel 9th
Clark John L., mer., 2 N 3d
Clark John S., dry goods, 202 S 2d
Clark John S., stoves, 322 High, h 10 Dean
Clark John T., varnisher, 212 Queen
Clark John T., gilder, N W 7th and High, h 105 W——

Clark Rebecca, Lane's ct
Clark Reuben W., carp., 13th ab Poplar
Clark Richard, book agent, 384 S 3d
Clark Richard, lab., Linn (F M)
Clark Robert, lab., E Sch 6th
Clark Robert, jr., lumb. mer., Carpenter ab 3d
Clark Robert, cordw., 12th ab Vine
Clark Robert, hatter, 3 Butler's av
Clark Robert, distiller, Benton bel William
Clark Robt. C., com. mer., 89 S Front
Clark Robert C., druggist, R road & Wallace
Clark Robert S., gent., 8 City row
CLARK R. & W., lumber mers., 154 Christian
Clark Samuel, mariner, 64 Catharine
Clark Samuel, weaver, Shippen ab 12th
Clark Samuel, tailor, 151 S 2d
Clark Samuel, James' ct (K)
Clark Samuel, mer., 160 N 9th
Clark Samuel, lab., rear Spruce n Sch 4th
Clark Samuel H., Christ. Chron., 79 Dock, h 64 Chestnut
Clark Sarah, 33 Sansom
Clark Sarah W., 8th n Brown
Clark & Smith, clothiers, 151 S 2d
Clark Stephen, brickmr., 6th & Paul
Clark S. Mrs., b h, 104 Filbert
Clark Thomas, bookbinder, 19 St James, h 64 Zane
Clark Thomas, machinist, St John ab Beaver
Clark Thomas, foundry, Jackson's ct (N L)
Clark Thomas, carter, 439 Vine
Clark Thomas, bootmr., 102 St John's
Clark Thomas, cab mr., 14 Marion
Clark Thomas M. Rev., 47 Clinton

Clarkson Belinda, gentw., 167 Pine
Clarkson Charles, mer., 111 Chestnut, h Sch 5th bel Cherry
Clarkson George, real estate bro., 70 N 8th
Clarkson Jacob, acct., Washington (W P)
Clarkson James, weaver, Mariner ab 13th
Clarkson John, sexton, 20 Quince
CLARKSON J. G., att'y & coun., S E 6th and Walnut, h 226 Pine
Clarkson Robert, coal yard, Broad bel Vine, h Filbert W Sch 7th
Clarkson Solomon, teacher, 155 Lombard
Class Peter, copperpl. pr., 36 Farmer
Clauders Wm., coachman, Ronaldson
Clausen John G., harnessmr., 643 N 2d
Clausen Susan, 167 Coates
Clausen Wm., tobacco, 47 Chestnut, h 63 Gaskill
Clavy John, lab. 21 Cox's st
Clawges Jacob, painter, 187 Poplar
Clawges John, 21 Union sq., George
Clawges Joseph, bricklayer, 6 Wells' row
Clawges Sarah, 24 Dillwyn
Clawson Elizabeth, rear 30 St John (K)
Clawson Mary, Marlboro' ab West (K)
Claxton Edmund, bookseller, 9 N 4th, h 330 S Garden
Claxton Thos., dealer, 168 Christian
Clay Andrew mar. polisher, Myers' ct
Clay Ann, 140 S 10th
Clay Armer, driver, New Crown bel Green
Clay George, clerk Penn. Bank, h Sch 6th below Chestnut
Clay George, machinist, 218 Coates
Clay George F., drayman, 477 N 5th
Clay Henry, drayman, Green's ct
Clay James, clothier, 2d ab Race, h Linden n Sch 6th
Clay John, engineer, Prime ab Church
Clay Joseph A., att'y and coun., 47 S 5th, h Sch 8th bel Spruce
Clay J. C., Rev., Swanson bel Christian
Clay Robert, weaver, Helmuth
Clay Wm., coachman, 5 Kelly
Claypool Abraham F., agent, 3 Swarthmore pl
Claypool Abraham G., waterman, 20 Beck (S)
Claypool David C., gent., Chestnut, n Sch 4th
LAYPOOLE A. H., lad, shoemr., 17 N 4th, h 26 Duke
Claypoole Jesse D., marble mantel manuf., Callowhill & 5th
Claypoole John, cord., Dunton bel Franklin (K)
Clayton Charles, cordw., 107 Melon
Clayton Curtis, shoemr., S E cor. Sch 6th and High
LAYTON CURTIS & SON, shoe and leather store, 237½ N 3d
Clayton Edward, collector, 9 Howard
Clayton Eleanor, 3 Filbert
Clayton Henry, carp., Dunton bel Franklin
Clayton Henry M., printer, 16 Freed's av
Clayton Holmes, tailor, Palmer ab Franklin (K)
Clayton James A. B., shoemr., 99 N 9th
Clayton Jeremiah, lab., Cherry n Sch 8th
Clayton John, bout and shoemr., 9 Plum

Clayton John, att'y & coun., 48 S 4th, h 372 Chestnut
Clayton Jonathan, carp., 6 Wheat
Clayton J., sinkermr., 6th bel Little Poplar (K)
Clayton Roger, weaver, Mariner st
Clayton R., packer, 9 Fayette
Clayton Samuel, baker, Cobb bel Catharine
Clayton Samuel, printer, 75 R road, h 6 Garrigues' ct
Clayton S. Mrs., 61 N 8th
Clayton Wm., omnibus driver, Sch 4th above George (F V)
Clayton Wm., turner, 8 Blunster av
Clayton Wm., hatblockmr., 8 Drinker's al
Clear Michael, sailing master, U S Navy, 519 S Front
Clear Robt., lab., Queen & Swanson
Cleaver Elizabeth, 103 St John
Cleaver Joseph, shoemr., 6 Myers' ct
Cleaver Mary, 215 N 8th
Cleavinger Wm. S., teacher, 12th & Locust, h Woodland (W P)
Cleckner Mary, Christian bel 5th
Cleeman Gustavus, 18 and 19 Exchange, h 37 S 13th
Cleeton G., carpet weaver, 458 Vine
Cleeton Wm., carpet weaver, Wood bel 13th
Clegg Anna, Baltimore House, Front & Dock
Clegg Benj., warper, Maiden bet Front & Beach
Clegg Edward, tailor, 30 N 10th
Clegg Henry, tailor, 266 S 3d
Clegg Isaac, manuf., Hanover ab West (K)
Clegg Isaac, manuf., G T road ab Master
Clegg & Rogers, tailors, 30 N 10th
Clein Jacob, grocer, N W 9th & Sassafras
Clemens Benj. S., mus. ins. mr., 17 W North
Clemens & Baker, druggists, 187 N 3d
Clemens Geo. S., druggists, 404 N 6th
Clemens Jacob, gent., 156 Marshall
Clemens Joseph, 2 Lagrange pl
Clemens Michael, blacksmith, 13 Bank, h 73 Gaskill
Clement Aaron, smoker & curer, Shippen ab 9th, h Cedar ab 9th
CLEMENT & BROTHER, co. mers., 3 N whfs
Clement Charles W., bricklayer, 151 Spruce
Clement De Witt, c. mer., 3 N whfs
Clement James, cabinetmr., 11th bel Pine
Clement James W., jeweller, 546 S Front
Clement J. B., mer., h 39 Girard
Clement Samuel H., mer., 3 N whfs, h 8th n Lombard
Clement Samuel L., conveyancer, 223 N 6th
CLEMENT SAMUEL W., tavern, S Whfs ab Cedar
Clement Thomas, tailor, 38 Mulberry
Clements & Ashburn, jewellers, 81 Dock
Clements James, jeweller, 61 Dock
Clements John, carter, Hope & Phoenix
Clements John, bootmr., 19 Carter's al
Clements John P., carter, F road ab Bedford
Clements John W., cordw., F road bel Master
Clements Mary, gentw., 9th ab Lombard
Clements Thos., weaver, West bel Hanover
Clements Wm., porter, 3d ab German

Clendaniel Jehu, flour & provisions, 84 S whfs, h 36 Pine

Clendaniel John, lab., Mary (S)

Clendenin Mary, seminary, Wallace ab 8th

Clendenon Isaac, confect., 10 S Garden

Clendinning Jas., cordw., P road bel Christian

Clendinning Phœbe, 8th ab Catharine

Clerkas Christian, weaver, 273 N 3d

Clery Edward, hatter, 216 S 8th

Cleveland C. D., Young Ladies' School, 3 Clinton

Cleveland Orrin L., bookbinder, 203¼ Chestnut

Cleveland Richard, M. D., 133 Walnut

Cleveland Wm. A., agency, 20 S 4th

Clevenger Henry, currier, Apple ab George

Clew Jeremiah, brickmr., Cherry ab Sch 8th

Clew Peter, brickmr., Sassafras ab Sch 8th

Clew & Perlasca, lampmr., 8 Laurel (C)

Clew Wm., jr., lampmr., 8 Laurel (C) h 79 Mulberry

Cleymer James, brickmr., 50 Shippen

Cliff Daniel, engineer, 22 W Cedar

Cliff Samuel, dyer, 13 W Cedar

CLIFFORD CONSTANTINE, shop, 135½ Cherry

Clifford James, coachman, Juniper al and Juniper la

Clifford John, 13 Prosperous al

Clifford John, tinsmith, rear 291 St John

Clifford Sarah, tailoress, 6 Prospect pl

Clift Benj., cordw., rear Vienna ab Franklin (K)

Clift George, coachmr., Nectarine bel 11th

Clift Henry S., tin store, 547 S 2d

Clifton Francis F., clerk, 4 Benezet

Clifton Isaac, hatter, 11 Wood

Clifton Matthias tailor, 193 S 2d, h 528 S 2d

Clifton Robert D., tailor, 2d and Dock, h 300 S 2d

Clifton R. D. & Co., clothing, 2d & Dock

Clifton Thos., baker, N W Catharine & Lebanon

Clifton Wallace, gauger, 59 Franklin

Clifton & Wiler, tailors, 193 S 2d

Clime Jesse, mason, rear of Perry ab Phoenix

Clime Rebecca Ann, Rihl's ct

Climerson Benjamin, provisions, S W 10th and Barley

Clinch John, sailor, 43 P road

Clincher Mary, shop, 10 Fothergill

Cline Barbara, gentw., 4 Salem al

Cline Benj., tinsmith, Citron bel 13th

Cline & Brown, blacsms,, 2d and Montgomery

Cline Charles, moulder, O'Neal bel Franklin (K)

Cline Charles, silv. plat., School ab Rose (K)

Cline Clarissa, washer, rear 200 Coates

Cline Edward, tailor, O'Neal bel Franklin (K)

Cline George, carp., Irvine

Cline George, tailor, 93 N 9th

Cline John, blacksmith, Washington bel 3d

Cline John G., Sp Garden bel Broad

Cline Lewis J., tailor, 6 Norman's al

Cline Martha, milliner, 23 Hazel

Cline Peter, dealer, Spruce bel Sch 5th

Cline Philip, b h, 41 Cherry

Cline Philip, turner, 3 Little Green

Cline Philip, boatman, Carlton bel Sch 8th

Cline P. & C., silver platers, 294 Sassafras

Cline Rachel, Vienna ab Franklin

Cline Wm., dealer, Spruce bel Sch 5th

Cline Wm., stove finisher, School ab Rose (K)

Cline Wm. B., stovemr., 233 N 2d

Clinger Ann, gentw., Hamilton Vil.

Clinger Samuel, paper & rags, 28 Commerce, h 13 Pratt

Clingman John, blindmr., rear 14 Plum (S)

Clinton Edwin, brushmr., 529 N 2d

Clinton Francis, carp., 1 Paynter's ct

Clinton James, ship carp., Sarah ab Queen (K)

Clinton John, printer, 166 Buttonwood

Clinton Robert, acct., Otter n G T road

Clinton Robert H., clerk, James' ct (K)

Clinton Wm., carp., Paynter's ct

Clinton Wm., acct., 41 Gaskill

Cloak Daniel, engineer, 22 Pearl

Cloak Morris, capt., 44 Beck st (S)

Cloak Wm., carter, Parker ab Prime

Cloake Ebenezer, city watch, Perry ab Lambert

Clohosey Thomas, painter, 469 S Front

Clopp Sarah, wid. of Henry, rear 111 Brown

Clopper John C., printer, Concord ab 2d

Close Chas. S., carp., 57 Swanson, h 254 S Front

Close Edward, weav., Hope ab Phœnix (K)

Close Henry, gent., 169 Coates

Close James, carter, 62 Carlton

Close Mary, 2 Butz ct

Close Rachel, 12 Parham

Closson Mary, Division (F V)

Closson Sarah, rear 84 Walnut

Clothier Ann, Bedford bel Hanover (K)

CLOTHIER CALEB, bricklayer and flour, 35 N 5th

Clothier Jacob, cooper, Hanover ab Bedford

Clothier John, mastmr., Fraley's al (K)

Clothier John W., bricklayer, 20 Magnolia

Clothier Joseph, lab., 3 Harmony

Clothier Maria, shop, Beaver bel 3d

Clothier M. A., dressmr., Winter's ct

Clothier Sam. bricklayer, Union n Franklin (K)

Clothier Wm. brickmr. Orchard bel Jackson

Clothier Wm., Wood bel West (K)

Clotworthy Samuel, car builder, Vaughan bel Walnut

Cloud David, morocco dresser, 43 Duke

Cloud Isabella, dry goods, N W 3d & Christian

Cloud Isaac, plasterer, Perkenpine's ct

Cloud Oliver E., druggist, 302 Sassafras

Clouden Jacob, carter, Union bel West (K)

Clouden Walter, porter, 46 Currant al

Clouds John, alderman, Marlboro' bel Franklin

Clough Thomas, skin dealer, Front ab Poplar

Clouser Charles, bricklayer, Race ab Sch 8th

Clover Wm., weaver, rear Front bel Phoenix

Clowden Francis, moulder, 6th bel G T road

Clowney James, carp., rear 246 Christian

Clowney Samuel, plasterer, Wharton bel 5th

Cluley Geo. J., machinist, Nectarine ab 10th

Cluley Henrietta, trimmings, 215 S 3d

Cluley John M., chairmr., 310 S 2d

Cluley Wm., tinplate worker, 308 Sassafras

Clump Bernard, lab., Rose al

Clunet Aug. D., clk., 3d ab Washington

Clungeon Wm., boat builder, Beach ab Hanover, h Allen bel Palmer (K)
Clunn David, ship carp., Union ab Bedford
Clunn Jacob, caulker, Queen bel Hanover (K)
Clusey Peter, carp., 121 O Y road
Clutch C. R., ladies' shoemr., 429 S 2d
Clyde James, lab., Carlton pl
Clyde Theresa, b h, 6 Ogden
Clymer Andrew B., currier, 12 Spragg's av
Clymer Charles, blacksm. Evans bel Prime
Clymer David M., tailor, 317 S 4th
Clymer George, carp., 10th ab Brown
Clymer Henry, carp., Fitler bel Norris (K)
Clymer John, cooper, Fitler bel 2d
Clymer John, cooper, Gray's ct
Clymer M., M. D,, 230 Spruce
Clymer Rebecca, 10th ab Brown
Clymer Robert, carp., 9 St. James, h 10th ab Brown
Clymer Robert M., sashmr., 101 German
Clymer Wesley, machinist, Walnut al
Coachman Edwd. porter, Pearl ab 12th
Coad Patrick, patternmr., 454 S 4th
Coady Michael, lab., Poplar ab 9th
Coale Asa, printer, rear 1 Rachel (N L)
Coane Robert, cake baker, 71 S 6th
Coarse John, lab., Wharton ab 4th
Coates Andrew, mer., 9 Church al
Coates Asael, lab., F road ab West (K)
Coates A., tanner, 509 N Front, h 229 Coates
Coates & Austie, mers., 139½ High
Coates Benj., dry goods, 139½ High, h 210 Mulberry
Coates Benj. H., M. D., N W 7th & Walnut
Coates Collins, stone cutter, Wallace bel 11th
Coates George M., seed store, 49 High, h 210 Mulberry
Coates George Morrison, jr., mer., 4 N 2d, h 74 N 12th
Coates Henry,, cordw., Ruddach's ct
Coates Isaac, ship carp., Beach ab Palmer (K)
Coates Jacob B. leather inspec. 23 New Market
Coates John, printer, 416 High, h Church n Washington
Coates John W., mariner, 391 S Front
Coates Joseph P. H., seedsman, 49 High, h 72 N 12th
Coates Josiah, 49 High, h 330 Mulberry
Coates Nathan C., painter, h 242 S 4th
Coates Reynell, M. D., S E 10th & Mulberry
Coates Robert, lab., 18 Vine
Coates Sophia, Middle al n 7th
Coates Thomas, Division bel 12th
Coates Susan, 158 Swanson
Coates Wm., dry goods, Charlotte & Culvert
Coates W. C., mer., 26 Church al, h 367 Sassafras
Cobb Catharine, dressmr., Torr's ct
Cobb Daniel, waterman, 1 Catharine
Cobb Ebenezer, ict., Hanover & West (K)
Cobb Geo., carp., 430 N 5th
Cobb Henry, com. mer., 4 N whfs.
Cobb Isaac, carp., rear Hanover ab Franklin (K)
Cobb James, bricklayer, Marriott ab 5th
Cobb Mira, shop, 358 Coates

Cobb Samuel, carp., Dean ab Bedford
Cobb Wm., carp., Shackamaxon ab Franklin
Cobb Wm. sen., carp., Hanover ab Queen (K)
Cobin Wm., spooler, Diamond ab Fitzwater
Cobb Wm., carp., 10th bel Callowhill
Cobourne M. A., b h, 89 S 3d
Coburn Aaron, confect., Randall's ct
Coburn Robert, gent., 259 Pine
Coburn Wm., shoemr., Lombard ab Sch 2d
COCHRAN ANDREW, real estate broker, Walnut ab 6th, h Juniper n Pine
Cochran Andrew, tavern, S 6th n Washington
Cochran Archibald, cordw., Diligent av
Cochran Benj., drayman, rear 372 S 3d
Cochran Daniel, mer., 121 Lombard
Cochran John, blacksm., 5 Howard
Cochran John, weaver, Miller's sl
Cochran Joshua, weaver, Bedford bel 13th
Cochran Josh. superintendant, Barker n Sch 5th
Cochran J. Harvey, mer., 8 S whfs
Cochran Margaret, 314 S 7th
Cochran Patrick, painter, Brown ab Cherry
Cochran Philip, lab., rear 260 Sassafras
Cochran Richard, agent, Juniper ab Pine
Cochran Robt., seaman, 6 Workman's ct
Cochran Robt., weaver, Dorothy & Sch 3d
Cochran Samuel, waterman, rear 378 S 2d
Cochran Wm., paper carrier, Catharine bel Lebanon
Cochran Wm. G., wine mer., 72 Walnut, h 415 Chestnut
Cockerill Thomas, cigarmr., 81 Queen
Cockey John Z., tinsmith, R road ab Wallace
Cocking John, weaver, Front bel Jefferson (K)
Cockrell John, carter, Hutchinson ab Poplar
Cody Daniel, watchman, Jenney's ct n Marshall
Cody John, stonecutter, 37 Apple
Cody Mary, milliner, 83 Gaskill
Coe Mrs. Ann A., 137 N 12th
Coe R., salesman, Wood bel 8th
Coe R. jr., mer., 29 Church al, h Noble above Franklin
Coe R. G., dry goods, 323 N 2d
Coffee George F., waterman, Front ab Reed
Coffee James, machinist, Mechanic (S)
Coffee John, grocer, 184 Shippen
Coffee Mary, tobacconist, 57 Brown (N L)
Coffee Wm. F., printer, 36 Carlton
Coffey John, dealer, F road op Queen (K)
Coffin Albert, tavern, S W 2d & Lombard
Coffin Arthur G., pres. Ins. Co, N. America, S W Dock & Walnut
COFFIN, HAY & BOWDLE, glass manufs., 34 N Front
Coffman Craig, carp., Cherry bel Franklin (K)
Coffman Henry, painter, 500 N 3d
Coffin & Landell, oil, soap and candle manuf., 22 N Water, and Penn ab Maiden (K)
Coffin Lemuel, mer. 140 High, h 10th bel Cedar
Coffin Martha, 525 S 2d
Coffin Samuel L., plasterer, 525 S 2d
COFFIN T. M., mer., 22 N Water, h 1 Mulberry
Coffin Wm., mer., 34 N Front, h 351 Mulberry
Coffin Wm. C., lapidist, 25 Library, h Federal bel 2d

Cohen & Lobe, furniture, 115 S 2d
Cohen Matthew, varieties, 177 S 6th
Cohen Myer D., furrier, 140½ S 2d
Cohen Sim., manuf., 49 N Front
Cohen Solomon E., clerk, rear Juniper and Lombard
Cohill Charles, portrait painter, 86 Chestnut, h 362 Coates
Cohill George, cabinetmr., P road bel Marriott's la
Coile Mary, sempstress, 42 Almond
COIT JOHN B., mer., 31 Church al
Coke John, chemist, Front bel Oxford (K)
Colahan John B., atty. & coun., 70 S 6th
Colan John H., artist, Sch 3d & Park pl
Colbert Wm. F., clerk, rear 75 N 8th
Colburn Lyman, grocer, High n Sch Front
Colcord Enoch L., broker, 24 S 5th; h Sch 8th and Spruce
Colcord John P., collector, 99 Catharine
Colden Scotland, lab., 42 Bread
Colder Hiram, coachman, 45 Mechanic
Coldwater Ann, 12th bel Brown
Cole Charles, waiter, 34 Bonsall
Cole Clarissa, washer, Sergeant n 10th
Cole Courtland, weaver, 450 N 4th
Cole David, waiter, 13 Barley
Cole Edward, druggist, 54 High, h 8th ab Wallace
Cole Elizabeth, 41 Currant al
Cole Francis, oyster house, N E 2d and Phoenix (K)
Cole George, Callowhill ab 12th
Cole George B., porter, Poplar ct
Cole James, Nectarine ab 10th
Cole John, blacksmith, 28 Brown

Otter (K)
Coleman Patrick, shoemr., 19 Farmer
Coleman Philip, glue maker, 22 Noble
Coleman Philip, carp., 65 Coates
Coleman Samuel, bricklayer, 65 Coates
Coleman S. L., barber, 37½ S 3d
Coleman Thomas, currier, 134 Callowhill
Coleman Thomas, lab., Brown's ct
COLEMAN W., cordw., 1 Roach's ct (K)
Coleman W. H., custom house, Plum bel 5th
Coles Edward, gent., 409 Spruce
Coles Hiram, cabinetmr., Front and Linden
Coles P. B. Mrs., b. h., 8 S 5th
Coles Thomas, cordw., 59 Almond
Colesberry Isaac G., merchant, 108 High, h S E 7th and Wood
Colesberry John, saddler, 29 Cherry
Colgan John, 128 Callowhill
Colgan T. P., bookseller, 126 Queen
Colgate John, porter, 32 Bonsall
Colgate Samuel, cordw., 131 S 2d
Colhoun George, merchant, 83 S Front
Colhoun Gustavus, gent., 265 Chestnut
Colhoun Hugh, merch., 61 N Front, h 98 S 3d
Colhoun Mary M., 98 S 3d
Colhoun T. R., M. D., 167 S 10th
Colhoun Wm., merch., 61 N Front, h 98 S 3d
Colhoun Wm. & Hugh, merchants, 61 N Front
Colket Coffin, 112 N 7th
Coll Hugh, lab., Willow above Garden
COLLADAY & BROTHER, com. mers., 140 High
Colladay Chas., mer., 140 High, h Chest. (W P)
Colladay George W., carp., Wood ab 12th
Colladay Hannah, 9 Jacoby
Colladay Jacob W., carp., Vine ab Sch. 8th

Colladay Samuel R., merch., 140 High, h S. W. Franklin and Vine
Colladay Sarah W., b. h., 108 N 10th
Colladay Theodore, carp., 403 Sassafras
Colladay T. S., carp., 249 Callowhill
Colladay Wm., carp., N E Sassafras & Lybrand
Collar Jacob, fisherman, c Queen & Cherry (K)
Collar Michael, fisherman, Queen ab Cherry (K)
Collar Michael, fisherman, Cherry ab Queen (K)
Collar Samuel, fisherman, Hanover ab Queen (K)
Collard Jonathan, millinery, 129 Cedar
Collick James, carter, rear 492 S 2d
Collier Wm., seaman, 275 S Front
Colligan Bernard, carter, 82 George (S)
Collin Dennis, porter, N W 8th and Catharine
Collins Abraham, M. D., 235 Spruce
Collins Alexander, weaver, 11 Gay's ct (K)
Collins Alfred M., weigher, 44 S Water
Collins Ann, washer, 12 Elizabeth
Collins Ann B., Sassafras ab Sch.
Collins Bartholomew, weaver, 12 Lloyd's ct (K)
Collins Bernard, 11 St. Mary
Collins Bernard, livery stable, 137 Shippen
Collins Cato, oysters, 100 N 4th
Collins Chas., tailor, 234 High, h 8th ab Green
Collins Charles, shoemr., rear 119 Queen (S)
COLLINS CHARLES & SON, tailors, 234 High
Collins Charlotte, widow, 9 Tammany
Collins & Co., planing mills, High and Sch. 3d
Collins Comfort, 16 Burd's ct
Collins Daniel, lab., John's ct
Collins David, carter, 27 Pratt
Collins Edmond, caster, 5 Callowhill
Collins Edward, barber, 100 N 4th
Collins Edward, grocery, 11th n Castle
Collins Edward T., mastmr., Penn ab Marsh
Collins Elias, lab., Carpenter ab 6th
Collins Elizabeth, tailoress, Lewis W. Sch. 6th
Collins Frederick, mariner, 325 S 3d
Collins G. A., barber, 1 S 3d, h 14 Mulberry al
Collins Geo. C., atty. at law, George n Sch. 6th
Collins Henry, twister, Crown ab Duke (K)
Collins Isaac, 129 Filbert
Collins James, lab., Chestnut bet Sch. 3d & 4th
Collins James, lab., Shippen ab 12th
Collins Jas., mer., Chestnut st. whf., h 189 S 7th
Collins James C., carp., G T road ab Master (K)
Collins John, paper maker, 13th and R. road
Collins John, rope maker, R. road ab 13th
Collins John, lab., 11 Helmuth
Collins John, lab., 5 Hamell's ct
Collins John, carp., 2 Diligent av
Collins John, carp., Charlotte ab George
Collins John, weaver, Mariner
Collins John D., waterman, 31 Catharine
Collins John H., druggist, 87 High
Collins Joseph, lab., Penn bel Maiden (K)
Collins Joseph, coal, Callowhill ab Broad
Collins Joseph, printer, 472 S 2d
Collins Joseph, seaman, 72 Swanson
Collins Joseph H., bricklayer, 395 6th
Collins Margaret, shop, Mulberry n Sch. 2d
Collins Mary, sempstress, George ab 2d (K)
Collins Mary, Carpenter below 8th
Collins Matthew, lab., Pearl bel William

Collins Michael, weaver, 11 Pratt's ct
Collins Patrick, weaver, 12 Lloyd's ct
Collins Patrick, cooper, Coates ct (F M)
Collins Peter, tinsmith, 7 Marshall's ct
Collins P. G., printer, 1 Lodge alley, h 39 Zane
Collins Robert, weaver, Mary n F. road (K)
Collins Robert, oysters, 153 Locust
Collins Robert, painter, Duke below Vienna (K)
Collins Robert, carp., Sch. 4th ab Cedar
Collins Robert, rigger, 38 Beck
Collins & Rogers, coal merchants, 23 S 5th, yard Broad and Callowhill
Collins Sarah, tailoress, Charlotte ab Brown
Collins Simeon, bookseller, 100 Chestnut, h 14 Girard
Collins Thomas, carter, Spruce ab Sch. 8th
Collins T. P. & D. C., photographists, 100 Chestnut, h 14 Girard
Collins T. K., printer, 1 Lodge al h 159 N 13th
COLLINS T. K. & P. G., printers, 1 Lodge al
Collins Wm. jr., lab., Sarah ab Queen (K)
Collins Wm., tobacconist, Brown ab 3d and 220 N 6th
Collins Wm., merch., 74 and 76 S Front, h 189 S 7th
Collins Wm., shoemr., R. road ab 13th
Collins Wm., lab., Crown ab Queen (K)
Collins Wm. M., paper wareh., 33 Commerce, h 74 N 10th
COLLINS W. M. & CO., paper merchants, 33 Commerce
Collins Wm. S., tailor, 234 High, h 269 Coates
Collipp Conrad, weaver, Parrish ab Sch 8th
Collom Clement, carp., 3d and Thompson (K)
Collom Jesse, carp., Sch. 7th ab Pine
Collom John, carp., Palmer ab Beaver (K)
Collom J., waterman, 245 N Front
Collom Mary, 132 Coates
Collom Rebecca, tailoress, Perry bel Master (K)
Collom Wm., drayman, Perry bel Phœnix
Collord John, 120 Beach (K)
Collot A. G., professor, 33 S 10th
Colsher David, driver, Sassafras n Sch.
Colsher Wm., wheelwright, Sch. 7th ab Parrish
Colly Daniel, shoemr., 95 S 2d, h 58 Queen
Collyer Robt., M. D., Pine bel Sch. 6th
Colon Mrs., widow of J. R., h 7 Laurel (C)
Colson Deborah, milliner, 9 Strawberry
Colson Henry, flour and feed, Broad ab 13th
Colton Charles, porter, 207 Shippen
COLTON & CO., grocers, S W 6th & Mulberry
Colton & Code, metre makers, Jones & Sch 8th
Colton David, plane maker, 291 High, h 12 Providence ct
Colton George, victualler, 335 Pine
Colton John, clerk, 10th bel Cedar
COLTON JOHN, plane maker, 379 High, h 149 S 2d
Colton Oren, metre maker, Jones and Sch. 8th, h Sch. 7th n High
Colton Sabin W., grocer S W 10th and Mulberry and N E 8th and Sassafras
Colton & Sheneman, plane makers, 291 High
COLTON SIMON, grocer, N E 10th and Chestnut

Colton Walter Rev., 372 Chestnut
Colwell C., confectioner, Beach ab Poplar (K)
COLWELL & CO., iron mers., 53 N whfs. and 111 N Water
Colwell Matthew, carp., Shippen ab 12th
Colwell Stephen, iron manuf., 53 N whfs. and 111 N Water, h 59 S 12th
Comber & Co., stone cut's., Chestnut ab Sch. 7th
Comber Patrick, stone cut., Lewis W. Sch. 6th
Combes J. R., grocer, 7 Washington av ab Willow, h 7th bel Poplar
Combs Gilbert, teacher, Sp. Garden and 7th, h 290 N 10th
Combs John F., currier, 200 S 6th
Combs Wm., currier, 170 S 3d
Combs Wm., lab., Davies' ct
Comegys Catharine, gentw., 42 N 8th
Comer George, shingle shaver, Perkenpine's ct
Comer Thomas, lab., Flemming's row
Comfort Aaron, Thomsonian medicines, 295 High, h 194 Cherry
Comfort Cyrus C., carp., 5 Elizabeth (N L)
Comfort John, 194 Cherry
Comfort John W., M. D., 11 N 10th
Comfort Lydia, Howard House, 70 Walnut
Comfort S., exchange broker, 1 Harmony ct
Comly David, carp., 345 Sassafras
Comly Ethan, dry goods, 199 N 2d
Comly Franklin A., sec. and treas. Buck Mountain Coal Co., 82 Walnut
Comly H. & A., dry goods, 23 N 2d
Comly Henry, dry goods, 23 and h 199 N 2d
Comly John, cordw., Passmore's place
Comly Martin, boot crimper, Stiles' ct
Comly Robert, auctioneer, 44 N Front
Comly Samuel, com. mer., 42 N Front, h Poplar n Sch. 8th
Comly Thomas J., printer, 11 Wheeler's ct
Commott Benj., cordw., 5 Stiles' ct
Compton Benj., lab., rear 552 N 2d (K)
Comstock Andrew, M. D., Vocal Gymnasium, 100 Mulberry
Conally Richard, cordw., 4th and Marriott
Conard Charles, hardware, S E 2d and Coates, h 226 Green
Conard Cornelius, lab., Silvies' ct
Conard Cornelius, weigh master, Fairmount
Conard John, bricklayer, Winter's ct
Conarroe G. W., portrait painter, 392 Vine
Conarroe Richard R., 24 Callowhill
Conaway George, cordw., 9 Jenning's row
Conaway Joseph, lab., 7 Pine alley
Conde Frances, widow of Charles, 114 N 5th
Condell Thos., queensware, 210 S 2d
Condell Thos., lab., Bedford ab Marlboro' (K)
Condie D. F., M. D., 117 Catharine
Condon John, clerk, Vienna ab Queen
Condon M. G., paper merchant, 14 Decatur, h Allen ab Shackamaxon,
Condon Sarah, 8th ab Green
Condon Wm., blacksm., 2 Hoffman's al
Condy James, cordw., Christian n 7th
Condy Thos., trader, Cadwalader bel Master
Condy Wm., tailor, Joseph's al
Cone Amelia M., trimmings, 70 S 8th

Congar Charles, shoemr., S E New Market and Poplar
Congar Wm., shoemr., 82 New Market
Conger Ann, 269 Green
Conger Wm. M., umbrellamr., rear Orchard ab Bonales
Congel Ann, shop, 31 Laurel (N L)
Conkle H., cord manuf., 2 S 3d, h 4 Buttonwood
Conklin Ezra, livery stables, Lodge al
Conklin Garretson, lab., 28 St John
Conlan Bernard, weaver, 3 Ulrich's row (K)
Conlen Pat., nailer, Carlisle ct
Conley Cornelius, carp., Bevan's ct
Conley Francis, ship carp., Newton ab Wash'n
Conley Francis, carp., 11 Dilks's ct
Conley James, lab., Lemon and Orange
Conley John, shoemr., 14 Stamper's al
Conley John lab., Coates ab Sch 7th
Conliff Wm., lab., 5 Spragg's av
Conlin Alex., bootmr., 140 Lombard
Conlin Felix, weaver, 46 Fitzwater
Conlin H., lab., 12th and Willow
Conlogue Patrick, Dillwyn bel Callowhill
Conlon Thos., mach'st., Francis & Powell (F V)
Conman Jas., blacksm., Gatchell's av
Conn Andrew, weaver, Elm bel Franklin (K)
Conn James, trader, G T road ab Franklin
Conn John, trader, Beach bel Coates
Conn Thomas, weaver, Front ab Phœnix
Conn Wm. H., bootmr., 96 Filbert
Connagan Wm., weaver, Philip ab Master (K)
Connell David, weaver, 2d ab Master
Connell George, gent., Summer ab Sch 6th
Connell John, dealer, 224 Shippen
Connell John H., conveyancer, 217 N 4th
Connell Robt., printcut., Queen ab Hanover (K)
Connell Theophilus, drover, Sch 7th and Say
Connell Thos., tavern, Westford av
Connell Tristram, grocer, N W 11th & Cherry
Connelly Catharine, 1 Meredith's ct
Connelly Dennis, weaver, Reiff's ct
CONNELLY HARRY, wines and liquors, 7th and Chestnut, h Spruce ab 12th
Connelly James, cordw., Front bel Phœnix
Connelly Jane, George ab 10th
Connelly John, lab., 100 Bedford
Connelly John, cab mr., 201 Buttonwood
Connelly Joseph, lab., Locust n Sch 3d
Connelly Lawrence, 51 Chester
Connelly Margaret, huckster, Fraley's ct
Connelly Mary, 6 College pl
Connelly Mary, wid. of George, Palmer bel Duke (K)
Connelly Patrick, weaver, Phoenix ab 2d
Connelly Rhoda A., 83 Cedar
Connelly Wm., painter, Buttonwood ab 13th
Conner Barney, lab., 173 N Front
Conner D., U. S. N., 87 S 4th
Conner E. S., tragedian, 48 Lombard
Conner Flora, 141 Cherry
Conner George, seaman, Church ab Prime
Conner Isaac, driver, c High and Sch 3d
Conner Louisa, lab., Paschal's ct
Conner James, weaver, Helmuth n Sch 6th
Conner John, brickmr., 7th ab Poplar

Conner John, bootmr., 26 Parker
Conner John, b. h., 19 Litte Water
Conner John, vict., Apple bel George
Conner John H., mastmr., 6 Beck pl (S)
Conner Joshua, shoemr., 510 S 2d
Conner Michael, shoemr., 9 John's ct
Conner Michael, framemr., 387 Callowhill
Conner Peter, cabinetmr., 5 Orange
Conner Richard, lab., Dyottville
Conner Simon, driver, Grover
Conner Stephen, lab., 3 Grape ct
Conner Thomas, lab., 5 John's ct
Conner Thos., carp. weav., West bel Hanover(K)
Conner Thos., carp. weav., Cadwalader bel Jefferson
Connerry Francis, Dillwyn and Callowhill
Connolly James, tailor, 3 Clymer
Connor Bernard, weaver, Pine and Ashton
Connor Edward, cordw., Reckless ct
Connor James, lab., Clay ab Sch Willow
Connor John, lab., 100 Bedford
Connor Matthew, lab., rear Apple bel Master
Connor Mich., weaver, George and 3d
Connor Neil, weaver, Murray n Sch 3d
Connor Peter, lab., Sch Front n Chestnut
Connor Rachel, rear 16 Little Pine
Connor Richard, oysterman, 18 Union (S)
Connor Thos., weaver, 6 Diamond
Connor Thos., bootmr., Baxter's ct
Connor Thos., carp., 13th ab Poplar
Connor Thos. G., cooper and gauger, 18 Little Water, h 43 Penn
Conns James, tailor, Sch 8th ab Sassafras
onor Patrick, 7th ab P road
onover Charles, gardener, 14 Pratt
onover Jacob, combmr., Rose ab School (K)
onover Jonathan R., carp., 11 Clinton ab Brown
onover J. B., mer., 190 High, h 281 Spruce
onover J. B. & Wm. P., shoes and bonnets, 190 High
onover Lewis T., cordw., Shippen ab 10th
onover Michael F., furniture, 66 Sassafras, h 126 Christian
onover O. H. P., mer., 190 High
onover Peter, shoes and bonnets, 202 High
onover T. A., capt. U. S. N., 601 Spruce
onover Wm., shoemr., 3 Shaffer's ct
onover Wm., cabinetmr., 1 Mark's la
onover Wm. P., mer., 190 High, h 368 S 4th
onover Wm. W., tailor, 3 Winter's ct
onquest Geo., mariner, 476 S Front
onrad Ab'm., stone mason, rear 28 Paschal's al
onrad Charles, mer., 35 High
onrad David, 52 Apple
onrad D. & J. G., flour and feed, 436 N 4th
onrad Edw., boat build., Sch Front n Mulberry
onrad Elizabeth, 104 Mulberry
onrad Elizabeth, N W 4th and Brown
onrad Harry, mer., 123 N 3d, h 301 N 6th
onrad Isaiah, plasterer, R road ab Wallace
onrad Jacob G., mer., 4th ab Brown, h 49 Apple
onrad Jas. M., hardw., 203 High, h 130 N 12th
onrad John, alderman, 208 N 3d, h 40 Wood
onrad Joseph, bootmr., 31 S 5th

9

Conrad J. H. & Co., boots & shoes, 85 N 2d
Conrad Mary, tailoress, St John bel Beaver (K)
Conrad Matthew, mer., 60 High, h 25 Mulberry
Conrad M. & Co., boots and shoes, 60 High
CONRAD OSBORN, imp. of watches, 96 N 2d, h 36 N 4th
Conrad Paul, collector Willow R road, Willow ab Broad
Conrad Peter, paper carrier, 5 Gray's al
Conrad Peter, clerk market, 71 N 12th
Conrad Peter, cordw., 35 S 8th, h Baker bel 8th
Conrad Robert T., atty. and coun., 428 Sassafras
Conrad & Roberts, hardw., mers., 123 N 3d
Conrad Saml., lab., Parrish ab Sch 7th
Conrad Washington, Coates N Sch 6th
Conrad Wm., gent., c Vine and Sch 4th
Conrad Wm., blacksm., 27 Callowhill
Conrad Wm. C., mer., 60 High
Conrade David, bricklayer, 51 Almond
Conrade Wm. D., bricklayer, 382 S 3d
Conradt G., engraver and dye sinker, 129 N 4th
Conrow Chas., coachmr., Beach bel Maiden (K)
Conrow Ellis, painter and glazier, 127 Coates
CONROW WILLIAM G., alderman office, 13th and R road
Conrow Wm. G., bricklayer, 13th ab Green
Conroy John, weaver, Hope ab Phœnix
Conroy John, waiter, 37 North
Conroy Patrick, weaver, 13th ab Green, h Lombard E Sch 2d.
Conry Patrick, 57 George.
Constable John, 354 Walnut.
Constable R., gunsmith, 88 S 2d
Constable Wm., cordw., Hutchinson ab Poplar
Constant F., lab., McKean's ct
Conver Benj., lab., Oldham's ct
Converse A. Rev., editor Christian Observer, 142 Chestnut, h 8th ab Catharine
Conway Bridget, shop, 143 Cedar
Conway Charles, tailor., Boker's ct
Conway Charles, lab., 18 Farmer
Conway Charles, ostler, 2 Boyle's ct
Conway Edward, brewer, 264 S 3d
Conway Francis, soap factory, Lombard ct
Conway Hannah A., milliner, 162½ S 2d
Conway James, lab., Hallowell's st
Conway James, blacksm., Charlotte ab Poplar
Conway John, shoes, 164 S 2d
Conway John, hat., 382 High, h Lawrence
Conway John, weaver, Perry ab Phœnix
Conway John, brickmr., Cedar bel Broad
Conway John E., brass founder, Culver above Charlotte
Conway Joseph, vict., Norman's al
Conway Patrick, lab., 8 Hunter
Conway Patrick, weav., 9 Lloyd's ct (K)
Conway Philip, tavern, 9 N 11th
Conway William, saw manuf., 24 Cherry, h 1 M'Leod's pl
Conwell Arthur, weaver, Mariner ab 13th
Conwell Edw., upholsterer, 232 S 3d
Conwell George, pilot, 116 Carpenter
Conwell Patrick, clerk, 3 Boyd's ct
Conyers John, lum. mer., c High and Sch 5th, h Cherry bel Sch 6th

Conyers Walter & Co., wines, &c., N E 6th and Minor
Conyers Walter, wine, 30 Jacoby
Conyers Thos. B., combmr., Vienna n Brown
Conyers & Hamilton, feed store, High n Sch 5th
Coogan Patrick, lab., Fitler bel Harrison
Coogan Patrick, tailor, rear 5th ab Christian
Coogan Wm., cordw., rear 70 Shippen
Cook Ann, 2 Acorn al
Cook Alexander, grocer, 11th and Nectarine
Cook Ashur, bricklayer, Carlton bel 13th
Cook Charles, carp., Ogden bel 11th
Cook Charles, combmr., 67 Buttonwood
Cook Charles, hatter, 389 N 6th
Cook Charles, shoemr., 6 Swarthmore pl
Cook Charles L., jeweller, Ross ct
Cook Christopher, tailor, 169 Apple
Cook Edwin R., tobac., N E Front and Cedar, h 86 Lombard
Cook Elias, lab., Say n Sch 7th
Cook Elijah, brickmr., Parrish bel Sch 7th
Cook Elijah, chairmr., Hank's ct
Cook Elijah, chairmr., 59 Callowhill
Cook Elisha, Spruce ab Sch 7th
Cook Frederick, cordw., 11th ab Carpenter
Cook Frederick, baker, 146 New Market
Cook George, hay dealer, Mary ab F road
Cook Hannah, 11 Rogers' ct
Cook Henry, boatman, Beach ab Walnut
Cook Henry D., varnisher, 11 Pleasant Retreat
Cook James, fruiterer, S E 7th and High, h N E 10th and Cedar
Cook Jasper C., clerk, Sch 8th n Cherry
Cook Jeremiah, lab., rear 375 S Front
COOK JOEL, alderman, 189 Chestnut
Cook John, carter, Hallowell's ct (S G)
Cook John, cordw., 378 S 2d
Cook John, lab., Rugan bel Willow
Cook John, soap and candles, High E Sch 6th, h George n Sch 7th
Cook John, gent., 298 Chesnut
Cook John, col., 34 N 3d, h Callowhill ab 13th
Cook John, hay dealer, Mary ab F road
Cook John D., tobacconist, 82 Brown
Cook John E., bar tender, rear 494 N 3d
Cook John G., carp. weaver, 70 Queen
Cook John H., cordw., Beach bel Maiden (K)
Cook Joseph, lab., rear Mechanic ab George

Cook Samuel, carp., rear 16 Mechanic
Cook Samuel, tobacco, 5 Mulberry, h 555 N 3d
Cook S., letter carrier, 406 N 6t
Cook Thomas, gent., 16 Pine
Cook Thomas R., carver, 3 Goldsmith's ct
Cook Wm., combmr., 3 Mechanic (N L)
COOK WM., mer., 85 High, h 94 Marshall
Cook Wm., tobacconist, 113 Noble
Cook Wm., tailor, 3 Swanson ct
Cook Wm., carp., 7th & Poplar
Cook Wm., engineer, 14 Helmuth
Cook Wm. K., carp., New ab 2d, h 78 Mulberry
Cook W. B., clerk, Charlotte ab Thompson
Cooke Jay, ex. broker, 25 S 3d
Cooke Tamar, 96 Union
Cooke Thomas, M. D., 83 N 5th
Cooke Wm., tobacconist, 4 N Front
Cooke Wm., boots & shoes, 98 N 5th
Cooker Geo. lab., Washington ab Front
Cooker Jacob, shoemr., 6th ab Hallowell
Cooker John, shoemr., rear Washington ab 6th
Cookman Mary gentw., 361 Sassafras
Cookson Charles, tallow chand., 4 Moore's ct
Cooley A. B., mer., 57 S whfs., h Sch 8th ab Walnut
Cooley John, lab., Alden ab Poplar
Cooley John, lab., 11 Marshall ct
Cooley John, sen., lab., 12th ab Parrish
Cooley Joseph, hatter, 154 S 5th
COOLIDGE EDWIN, boots & shoes, 181 High, h 66 Franklin
Coomb Samuel, Wood bel 10th
Coombe Sarah, 5 Dugan
Coombs Adam H., sea capt., Prime ab Front
Coombs Benjamin, 1 Eutaw
Coombs Josiah, weaver, Chestnut n Sch Front
Cooness Harriet, Ohio
Cooney Anthony, 244 N Water
Cooney Christopher, lab., 7 Truxton
Cooney Patrick, lab., Filbert & Sch 8th
Cooper Aaron, ostler, 45 Currant al
Cooper Ann V., 13th n Cherry
Cooper Anna M., 246 Filbert
Cooper Anthony, 26 Garden
Cooper B. C., tailor, 130 Chestnut, h 3 Clinton square
COOPER B. C. & S. C., tailors, 130 Chestnut

Cooper Hannah, gentw., 66 Marshall
Cooper Henry, vict., 192 Callowhill ab Sch 6th
Cooper Henry, rear 38 St John
Cooper Henry, cooper, 16 Shippen
Cooper Henry C., perfumer, 222 Chestnut
Cooper Hiram T., dry goods, 393 High, h 367 Mulberry
Cooper Hugh, b. h., 39 O Y road
Cooper Isaac, lab., Perry ab Phœnix
Cooper Isaac, carp., 3 Clymer's st
Cooper Isaac, lab., South ab 11th
Cooper Isaac, lab., Carpenter bel 10th
Cooper Ignatius T., D. D. Rev., 6 Crown
Cooper Jas., cooper, 204 S Water, h 205 S Front
Cooper James M., carp., 9th bel Catharine
Cooper John, blacksmith, Marlboro' ab Queen
Cooper John, mer., 95 High, h Spruce ab 11th
Cooper John, cabinetmr., Laurel ab Spruce, h 308 S Front
Cooper John, printer, 72 George (S)
Cooper John, dealer, 253 Cedar
Cooper John, drayman, Rhil's ct
Cooper John E., carp., Wood ab Franklin (K)
Cooper John W., medicines, 20 N 12th
Cooper Jonathan, tailor, R road ab Broad
Cooper Joseph, sailmr., rear 6 Mechanic (K)
Cooper Joseph B., collector, 2 N 6th
Cooper Joseph P., dry goods, 381 High
Cooper Joseph T. Rev., 441 N 5th
Cooper Lawrence, ladies' shoemr., 199 Green
Cooper Lewis, dry goods, 29 S 2d, h 98 N 8th
Cooper Louisa, Pray's ct (N L)
Cooper Michael, collector, 13 Fitzwater
Cooper, Miller & Heyl, dry goods, 95 High
COOPER & MILLER, carps., 9th ab Christian
Cooper Philip, West ab Walnut
Cooper P. F., min. painter, 140 Chestnut
Cooper Richard T., druggist, Federal ab 7th
Cooper Samuel, weaver, 3 Philip (K)
Cooper Samuel B., boatman, 7th bel Carpenter
Cooper Sarah, teacher, 24 Perry
Cooper Sarah, washer, 2 Platt
Cooper S. C., tailor, 130 Chestnut
Cooper Thos., brushes, brooms, &c., 3 N Front, h 89 N 10th
Cooper Thomas, lab., Catharine ab 10th
Cooper Unah, porter, 26 Watson's al
Cooper Wm., chair paint., G T road bel Phœnix
Cooper Wm., watchman, 19½ Stamper's al
Cooper Wm., tavern, 172 Lombard
Cooper Wm. B., mer., 53 High, h 69 N 9th
Cooper Wm. C., grocer, 10 High, h 11 Montgomery
Cooper Wm. M., cooper, 69 & 200 S Water, h 203 S Front
Cooper Wm. Rev., 354 N 5th
Coopers & Henderson, dry goods, 53 High
Coote Owen, moulder, 15 Eutaw
Coots Reuben, shoemr., 84 S 12th
Cope Alfred, mer., 1 Walnut
Cope Caleb, mer., 165 High, h c Walnut & Quince
COPE CALEB & CO., silk goods, 165 High
Cope C., widow, 136 N 4th
Cope Edwin R., mer., 52 Commerce, h 136 Marshall

Cope Elias, carp., 6th bel G T road
Cope Francis R., mer., 1 Walnut, h 102 S 4th
Cope George, drayman, 91 Noble
Cope Hannah, shop, M road bel Prime
Cope Henry, mer., 1 Walnut, h 102 S 4th
Cope Henry, butcher, M road bel Wharton
Cope Herman, B. U. S., h 355 Walnut
COPE H. & A. & CO., mers., 1 Walnut
Cope Israel, gent., 186 Mulberry
Cope Jacob J., Cash. Com. Bank, h 138 Marshall
Cope Jasper, gent., 391 Mulberry
Cope John, 165 Marshall
Cope John, carp., Church ab Washington
Cope John, gent., 225 Marshall
Cope Levi, dealer, Juniper ab High
Cope Marmaduke C., 286 Filbert
Cope Perry, seaman, Washington bel 4th
Cope Philip, cooper, 31 Christian
Cope Thos., cabinetmr., 2d & G T road
Cope Thomas P., 272 Spruce
Cope Thomas P., dyer, 10 Sterling al
Cope Thomas P., jr., mer., 1 Walnut
Cope Wm., tavern, G T road bet 6th & 7th
Copeland Asa, carp., 99 Prime
Copeland Asa, ship joiner, Carpenter bel 7th
Copeland Ellen, gentw., Hessler ct ab Coates
Copeland Emily, Kennedy's ct
Copeland George, bricklayer, 8 Mark's la
Copeland Samuel, carp., Sch 8th & Jones, h Sch 6th ab Filbert
Copeland Wm., carp., 398 S 3d
Copes Charles, U. S. service, 17 Marion
Copes George, capt., Higgins' ct
Copia Allen, bootmr., 155 Lombard
Copia Jacob, gent., 213 Pine
Copp Geo., undertaker, 153 Vine
Coppenger John, weaver, Helmuth n Sch 6th
Copper James C., acct., 91 Wood
Copper John C., engraver, 18 Minor, h 283 N 8th
Copper Samuel, porter, 4 Farmer's row
Copple Daniel, 77 Dock, h 3 Harmony ct
Copple Jacob, brickmr., 33 Pratt
COPPLE & JONES, exchange hotel, 77 Dock
Coppuck Jos. C., mer., 30 N Front, h 120 N 10th
Coppuck Jos. W., bootmr., 187½ S 2d
Corbett John, saddler, High & Juniper, h rear 117 N 11th
CORBIT & CO., silks, 29 Church al
Corbit Henry C., mer., 29 Church al, h 153 Walnut
Corbit John, capt., Grubb st
Corbit Joseph, sug. refiner, 27 Church al, h 232 Mulberry
Corbit Sarah, 61 Union
Corbon Charles, printer, 13 Rachel (N L)
Corbyn T. J., veterinary surgeon, R road ab Vine
Corcoran John, lab., Marriott la bel 5th
Cordes Jacob, boxmr., 199 N 3d, h 598 N Front
Cordes Wm. H., carp., Sch 4th ab Callowhill
Cordiel Thomas, carp., Sassafras n Sch 8th
Corey Horatio N., mer., 157 High, h 34 Marshall
Corfield Chas., dentist, 343 N 3d
Corfield Edward D., att'y & coun., 263½ N 3d
Corfield Henry C., accountant, 320 N 3d
Corgie Barbara, gentw., 330 S 4th
Corinth Frederick W., hatter, 106 N 6th

Cork John, cooper, M'Manemy's ct
Corkery John, carp., 310 Carpenter ab 10th
Corkin Patrick, carter, rear 2d bel Master
Corkrin A. G., dry goods, S E 4th and Gaskill
Corkrin A. H., dry goods, S E 4th and Gaskill
Corlies Hannah, Locust n Sch 8th
Corliss Daniel, grocer, F road and Oxford (K)
Corliss John, blacksm., F road ab Oxford (K)
Cormany John, carp., Washington ab 7th
Cormic Margaret, Lombard n Sch 6th
Corn John, carter. M'Duffie n Sch 2d
Corndaffer Samuel, carter, Duke ab Cherry (K)
Corneal G., shoemr., Hank's ct (Rachel)
Corneau J. B. T., carp., 2 Orleans
Cornelius C., lamp and chandelier manufacturer, 4 Franklin
CORNELIUS & CO., lamps, 181 Cherry & 176 Chestnut
Cornelius Philip, lab., Barley
Cornelius R., lamps, 176 Chestnut, h 179 Cherry
Cornell & Hendry, furniture, 7 N 8th
Cornell Mary, 140 N 12th
Cornell Wm., furniture, 7 N 8th
Corney Josh., victualler, 206 Noble
Cornish Amy, Bedford bel 8th
Cornish David, waiter, 7 Lisle
Cornish Henry C., shoemr., 255 S 7th
Cornish Henry, druggist, 100 N 5th
Cornish Jas., cordw., rear Carpenter bel 9th
Cornish John, shoemr., 255 S 7th, h 14 Crabb st
Cornish Scipio, porter, Rawle ab Apple
Cornman Oliver P., painter, Wallace bel 13th
Cornog David A., visitor of the poor, 12 Madison
Corns Esther, tavern, 14 Dock
Cornwell Chas., carp., Vienna bel Franklin (K)
Cornwell James, carp., Dyott's ct (K)
Cornwell Jos., brickmr., Sch 6th bel Lombard
Cornwell Robt., carp., 16 Dyott's ct (K)
Cornwell Ruth Ann, b.h., R road bel Buttonwood
Cornwell Wm., ship carp., Wood ab Franklin
Coron Daniel, cabs, 10th and Vine
Corr Barney, weaver, 2d bel Jefferson
Corr Emeline, Juniper ab High
Corr Jas. lab., 6th ab Carpenter
Corr Joseph, grocer, Phoenix & Perry
Corr Patrick, 4th & Jefferson (K)
Correll David, blacksm., 2 Jacoby
Corrie Augustus, printer, 116 Chestnut
Corrie Geo. S., music teach., 10th ab Nectarine
Corrie Henry, organ manuf., 21 Minor, h 15 Howard
Corrigan Hugh, hostler, 313 Fitzwater
Corrin Patrick, tailor, Beach n Walnut
Corry George, glove manuf., 448 N 5th
Corry John & Co., tea store, 409 N 2d
Corsey Trim, coachman, 15 Watson's al
Corson Franklin, tavern, Prime & M road
Corson George, constable, Culvert bel 4th
Corson Hovey, waterman, Brown bel Cherry (K)
Corson Isaac M., wheelwright, Henderson's ct
Corson James, sr., shoes, 491 S 2d
Corson Jeremiah, cordw., 422 N 4th
Corson John W., shoemr., Evans st
Corson Lewis, watchman, Beach ab Warren (K)
Corson Nathan, shoemr., Lancaster ab Reed

Corson Robt., waterman, Wharton ab 2d
Corson Wm., carman, Laurel ab Front
Corvaizier Jules, boot mr., 76 S 4th
Corwine Wm. R. mould. Allen ab Shackamaxon (K)
Cory John R., 15 Lagrange pl
Coryell Wm. C., bricklayer, Sch 6th bel Cherry
Cosfeldt F., locksm., 44 Dock, h 8 Carter's al
Cosfeldt John, machinist, 256 St John
Cosgrave Daniel, morocco dresser, 87 S 5th
Cosgrove J., morocco dresser, 310 N Front
Cosh Andrew, porter, 23 Merchant
Cossart John, shoemr., Tomlin's ct
Cossart Mary, 23 Beaver (K)
Cossart Wm., cedar cooper, 60 Apple
Cost Martin F., biscuit baker, 6 Emlen's ct
Coste Raymond, chandler, 104 Cedar
Costell Mary, gent. fur'g. store, 53 S 8th
Costello John B., mer. 11th ab Shippen
Costello Michael, 6 Shoemaker
Costello Wm., weaver, Hancock ab Master (K)
Costelloy Patrick, 78 N Water
Costen Williams, hatter, Webb's al
Coten Morrell, meter mr., 5 S Sch 7th
Coster Abraham, frame mr., 132 St John, h S E Noble & Swanson's al
Coster John, segarmr., 72 Callowhill
Coster Robert, carp., 12 Pearl n Sch 7th
Coston Benton, collector, Marshall ab Poplar
Coston Ezekiel, jewellery, 45 Lily al
Coston Joseph L. M., shoemr., 281 N 10th
Cotean Mary, 90 Spruce
Cotteney Isaac, weaver, 11th & Christian
Cotter Edwin, hatter, Ellis ab Washington
Cotter James, tailor, 85 N 6th
Cotterall James, fireman, Stackhouse's ct
Cotterell John, druggist, 27 N Front, h 372 Coates
Cotterill, Hill & Co., agency, N E 5th and Commerce
Cottingham James, mariner, 22 Mead
Cottman George, tavern, 448 N Front
Cotton John S., upholsterer, 44 S 4th, h 182 S 11th
Cottrell Peter, upholsterer, 9 Pearl
Cottringer John J., clerk U. S. Navy, 64 Queen
Cottringer Joseph F., mer., 29 Church al, h 159 S 3d
Couch Wm., blacksm., rear 406 N 3d
Couchman Abraham, cordw., Hope ab Master
Cough Ridgway, lab., rear Apple bel George
Coughlin Dennis, weaver, Shippen la ab Catharine
Coughlin Francis, weaver, S W Brinton and Cochran
Coulomb Charles A., teacher of langu., 10th ab Carpenter
Coulson Elizabeth, Apple ab George
Coulson Sarah Ann, milliner, 49 Chester
Coulston Israel, carp., 66 Tammany
Coulston Nathan L., morocco dress., 484 N 4th
Coulston Wm. K., cordw., Charles ab James
Coult Joseph, foundry, 13th n Willow
Coult J. R., machinist, Pleasant ab 12th
Coulter Charles, police off., 33 Washington (M)

oulter Jane, 393 Front	Cowlings George, brewer, 40 Pratt
oulter John, paver, N E 13th & Lombard	Cownover Allen, bricklr., rear Parrish bel 10th
oulter John, waiter, 8 S 8th, h 9 Watson's al	Cownover Ferdinand, carp., Parrish bel 10th
oulter Joseph, marble polisher, 226 N 13th, h	Cownover Jacob, bricklayer, 7th and Green
Cherry bel 9th	Cowperthwait C. J., galvanic plater, h Paul ab
oulter Joshua, carp., 9th ab Coates	6th
oulter Sarah, 159 Queen	Cowperthwait E., upholsterer, 15 S 5th, h 276
oulton Andrew J., cordw., St John ab Beaver	Lombard
oulton James, carp., Fitler ab 2d (K)	Cowperthwait H., mer., 253 High, h 134 Mul-
oulton Wm., lob., Fitler ab 2d (K)	berry
ouncil Joseph, bricklr., Shippen ab Shippen la	Cowperthwaite Edwin, mer., 139½ High
ouncil Thomas, hatter, 38 Julianna	Cowperthwaite Samuel, 204 N Front
ountiss Hannah, 493 S 2d	Cowperthwaite Wm., plasterer, 119 S Fifth
ountryman Wm., tobacconist, 215 Queen	Cowpland Ann, milliner, 144½ S 2d
oursault G. A. & A. G., collectors, h 319 S 6th	Cowpland Ann, milliner, 327 S 5th
oursault Leopold P., cabinetmr., 203 S 2d	Cowpland Joshua, fancy hardware, 14 N 4th, h
oursey Eliza, 4th ab Christian	Cherry n Sch 6th
ourt Edw., clothing, 65 S 2d, h 6th n Lombard	Cox Aaron F., printer, Sch 8th n Vine
ourter Jacob, saddler, rear 31 Charlotte	Cox Ann, milliner, G T road ab Master (K)
ourter Peter, blacksm., Coates bel 12th	Cox Catharine, Barker bel Sch 6th
ourtney James, rigger, 41 Beck st (S)	Cox Charles, lime mer., N E 9th & Coates
ourtney Joseph, carpenter, 8 Farmer	Cox Charles, carter, State
ourtney Patrick, lab., 263 N Front	Cox Chas., shop, Broad ab Cedar
ourtney Samuel P., tanner and currier, Hano-	Cox Charles D., refectory, 40 S 5th
ver ab Franklin (K)	Cox Clement, coachman, 25 Prosperous al
ourtney Thomas, trader, Filbert W of Sch 7th	Cox & Cross, coal yd., Broad & Willow
ourtwright Isaac, coal dealer, 57 Pegg	Cox Daniel, painter, rear 454 S Front
ouse Catharine, trimmings, N E 10th & Wood	Cox D. J., tobacconist, 536 N 2d
ousins Charlotte, 29 Perry	Cox Elizabeth, c 7th and Sassafras
ousland & Co., engravers, 74 Chestnut	Cox Elizabeth, widow, 57 Apple
ousland & Taylor, tobacconist, 209 Chestnut	Cox George, cabinetmr., rear 27 Cresson's al
ousty Eliza B., grocer, 78 S 2d	Cox Geo. M., pattern mr., Vienna & Duke (K)
ousty John, grocer, N E Callowhill & Garden	Cox George S., ship joiner, F road ab Otter
outurier Frederick, dyer, 163 Vine	Cox Gideon, wooden and variety st., 335 High,
oyeley Henry, bricklayer, rear Locust n Beech	and dry goods N W 8th & High
overdale David S., shoemr., Wharton ab 3d	Cox Isaac, blacksmith, 141 St John, h 159 St
overdale Elias, porter house, 6th & Christian	John
overt Isaac jr., ivory turner, Traquair's ct, h	Cox I., carp., Vienna bel 11th
223 N 10th	Cox Jacob, ladies' shoemr., Harvey's ct (K)
ovey James, carp., Bache st	Cox James, U. S. Court, h 49 S 5th
ovington Isaac, watchman, 7 Freed's av	Cox James, mariner, 6th bel Carpenter
ovington Wm., cordw., 19 Reckless	Cox James, Pres. Lehigh Coal & Nav. Co., 32 S
owan C., cordwainer, 16 Green (C)	2d, h Walnut n Sch 8th
owan Jas. W., clerk, George n Sch 6th	Cox James E., mer., 74 Wood
oward Chas. W., trunkmr., 9 Stampers' al	Cox Jesse, mer., 76½ S and h 84 N Front
oward Elizabeth, 66 N 5th	Cox John, insp. custom-house, Vine n Sch 2d
oward H., gilder, 59 Fitzwater	Cox John, farmer, Shippen ab Broad
oward Jas., carp., rear 13 Mead	Cox John jr., lime dealer, G T road ab Laure ,
oward John, shoemr., 26 Castle	h 151 New Market
oward Joseph, tailor, Federal ab 2d	Cox John, weaver, Otter n Front (K)
oward Samuel T., pattern mr., 106 Coates	Cox John, weaver, Charlotte bel Thompson
oward William, trader, Logan ab Green	Cox John, mason, 13th bel Spruce
oward Wm., millwright, Franklin ab Crown	Cox John, blindmr., Prime bel Front
(K)	Cox John C., mer., 177½ High
owden Cath., gentw., 306 E Cedar	Cox John S., carp., 138 N Juniper
owden James, carp., Federal ab 7th	Cox Jonathan J., carp., Vernon bel 11th
owdrick Charles H., plater, 61 Tammany	Cox Joseph, combmr., 100 Cherry
owdrick Edward, bricklayer, Lewis ab Poplar	Cox Joseph, stone cutter, Brazier ab Lloyd
owell Henry, mer., S W 7th and Chestnut	Cox Joseph, 5 Swarthmore pl
owell John V., mer., S W Chestnut and 7th, h	Cox Joseph G., wire worker, 48 N Front
128 S 8th	Cox Lawrence, Budd n Juniper
owell J. V. & Son, dry goods, S W 7th and	Cox Lewis W., combmr. 465 N 3d
Chestnut	Cox & Lynn, carps., Penn ab Poplar
owell & Stone, tinsmiths, 57 N Front	Cox Margaret, millinery, 314 Pine
owen Henry, porter, rear 10 Quince	Cox Martin M., mer. 23 N Water

Cox Mary Ann, trims. 6 Arcade, h 15 Mead
Cox Richard P., tailor, 101 Chestnut
Cox Samuel, teacher, 281 S 10th
Cox Sarah, 476 Sassafras
Cox Sarah, ladies' shoemr., 35 N 8th
Cox Samuel C., coal yard, Broad and Willow, h 147 G T road
Cox Terence, lab., rear Charlotte ab Thompson
Cox Thomas, oysters, Smith's al (N L)
Cox Thomas, weaver, G T road ab Master
Cox William, ship joiner, 78 N. Market
Cox Wm., carter, 2d bel Franklin (K)
Cox Wm., blacksm., 6th and Hallowell
Cox Wm., coachmr., G T road ab Thompson
Cox Wm., bricklayer, Callowhill ab 13th
Cox Wm., dry goods, 262 N 2d
Cox Wm., lab., Mariner & 13th
Cox Wm., carp., rear 266 S 4th
Cox Wm. jr., atty. and coun., 167 Spruce
Cox W. P, coal mer., 86 S 3d, h 9 Franklin
Coxe Charles S., judge, Spruce ab Sch 8th
Coxe Charles W., mer., Chestnut, h 30 Wood
Coxe Daniel W., gent., 233 Chestnut
Coxe Edmund S., atty. & coun., h Walnut ab 6th
Coxe John R., M. D., c Pine and Broad
Coxe Jos., acct., 30 Wood
Coxey James, shop, Washington (W P)
Coxey Thomas, superintendent of penitentiary, shoe st., R road ab Frances
Coxey Wm., carp., Elizabeth (N L) ab Poplar
Coxhead John, 277 Walnut
Coxhead William R., tailor, 88 S 8th
Coxon Jonathan, potter, Perry ab Franklin (K)
Coyle Charles, japanner, 199 Noble
Coyle Edward, carp., Murray n Sch 3d
Coyle Edward, weaver, G T road ab Master (K)

Craft Gershom, printer, 52 Penn
Craft Harvey, shoemr., rear 121 Queen
Craft Jeremiah, blacksm., Front bel Otter
Cragg Rose, 519 N 3d
Cragg Wm., sexton and undertaker, 10 College av., and 11 Watson's al
Craig Alex., gardener, Sch 5th bel Spruce
Craig Alex., gardener, Carleton bel Sch 2d
Craig Andrew, lab., 11 Middle al
Craig Andrew, weaver, Perry n Pine
Craig Andrew, carpenter, 1 Hubbell
Craig Andrew, stone cutter, Division (F M)
Craig Andrew C., mer., S W 13th and High
CRAIG ANDREW C. & Co., wine and liquor mers., S W 13th and High
CRAIG, BELLAS & Co., com. & forw. mers., N W Cherry and Broad
Craig & Cameron, flour, 439 N 2d
Craig David, blacksmith, Fitzwater opp Adams. h 7 Clymer
Craig Elias D., tinsm., High n Sch 5th
Craig Ellen, Cadwalader ab Phœnix
Craig George, manuf., Philip ab Master (K)
Craig George, framemr., Gay's ct
Craig Henry K., U. S. A., Sch 7th ab Spruce
Craig Hester, Perry bel Vine
Craig Hyland, lab., Carroll bel 13th
Craig Hugh, mer., N W Broad and Cherry, h Sch 6th n Cherry
Craig James, 345 Vine
Craig Jas., weaver, Howard ab Phoenix (K)
Craig James, carp. rear 10 S 5th, h Vine n 10th
Craig James, weaver, Edward n School (K)
Craig James, watchman, 7th & Cedar
Craig James, carp., Citron bel 13th

Craige & Stevenson, grocers. N W 2d & Co te
Craige Thomas, riding school and livery stable, 4th ab Wood, h 520 N Front
Craige Thomas H., 12 N 4th, manu., h Mulberry W of Broad
Cram Samuel, acct., 12 Union sq
Cramer Bernard, lab., Sch 8th bel Cherry
Cramer David, carp., 5 Bread, h Parrish ab 7th
Cramer James, cot. spinner, Shackamaxon near Queen
Cramer Joseph P., shoes, Queen ab Crown (K)
Cramer John L., brushmr., Queen bel Marlborough (K)
Crammer Jonathan, Barker W of Sch 5th
Cramond Henry, atty. and coun., 149 Walnut, h 539 Chestnut
Cramp Alfred, fisherman, Dyott's ct (K)
Cramp Catharine, huckster, Queen bel Wood
Cramp George, ship carp., Marlborough below Bedford (K)
Cramp Jacob, fisherman, Queen n Wood (K)
Cramp John, fisherman, Cherry ab Queen (K)
Cramp Martin, ship carp., Vienna n Queen (K)
Cramp Martin, fisherman, Vienna ab Queen
Cramp Michael, lab., 8 Washington av
Cramp Peter, boat builder, rear Palmer above Queen (K)
Cramp William, boat builder, rear Palmer ab Queen (K)
Cramp Wm., grocer, Queen & Palmer (K)
Crandle Matthew B., trimmer, 17 Mary (S)
Crandol Elihu, tailor, 2 Peach
Crane Charles W. C., cabmr., 11th and Pine, h 151 Lombard
Crane Eleanor, 28 Queen
Crane Elias, grocery, 304 S 4th
Crane Wm., cabmr., 35 Lombard
Crane Wm. H., carder, Callowhill bel Sch 5th
Craner Jacob, machinist, Mary n F road (K)
Crangle Catharine Mrs., 17 P road
Crangle George, china ware, 336 S 2d
Crangles James, weaver, 11th ab Carpenter
Crankshaw Catharine, 5 Southampton pl
Cranmer Joseph S., cordw., 130 N 10th
Crans John S., collector, 167 Queen
Crans Peter, jr., atty. & coun., 300 S 5th
Crans Samuel, iron found., 167 Queen, h Christian ab 6th
Crans William J., clerk Moya. prison, h 331 S 5th
Cranston George, baker, rear 97 Noble
Cranston Robert, weaver, Fulton bel 13th
Crap George M., tin worker, 134 German
Crapper Henry, F road n Franklin (K)
Craven Aaron, blacksm., 5 St Joseph's av
Craven David S., capt., 26 Mulberry
Craven Ishi H., acct., 390 S 3d
CRAVEN JAS. C., tinplate worker, S E 9th & High, h 141 Locust
Craven Mrs. L., widow, 33 Laurel
CRAVEN THOS., agent, 14 Minor, h 77 Union
Craven Wm., lab., 21 Callowhill
Crawford A. L., grocer, Noble & Front
Crawford And. T., bookseller, 110 S 2d

Crawford Anna, shop, 120 German
Crawford Benjamin, boat builder, Hanover bel Queen
Crawford Benjamin, tailor, 230 and 240 High, h 169 N 7th
Crawford Charles, tailor, Lombard ab 12th
Crawford Christopher, cordw., 5 Washington
Crawford Hannah, 87 N 9th
Crawford Henry, engineer, 11th & Catharine
Crawford Henry M., leather dea'er, 204 N 3d
Crawford Henry M., mer., 40 High, h 13 Noble
Crawford Hugh, lime, 9th and Sp Garden
Crawford Samuel H., 10th bel Melon
Crawford Jacob, waterman, 2 Pratt's ct
Crawford James, lab., Lombard ab Sch 6th
Crawford James, constable, 211 Chestnut
Crawford James, carp., Christian ab 2d, h 187 Christian
Crawford Jannet, Thompson ab Charlotte
Crawford John, drayman, 9 S Sch 5th
Crawford John, whipmr., n Vienna ab Queen (K)
Crawford John, drayman, 181 Coates
Crawford John, weaver, Front bel Oxford
Crawford John, weaver, 2d ab Franklin
Crawford John, bookmr., 304 S 3d
Crawford John, weaver, cor Filbert & Sch 2d
Crawford Joseph, lab., Spinner's ct
Crawford Joseph, lab., Dorothy n Sch 4th
Crawford Mary, wid., 23 Garden
Crawford Matthew, combmr., Poplar n 4th
Crawford Peter M'C., furrier, 23 Noble
Crawford Richard, lab., rear Orchard
Crawford Robert, carp., 17 Cherry
Crawford Robert, carter, Spruce n Sch Front
Crawford Robert, carpet weaver, 431 R road
Crawford Samuel W. Rev., Mulberry n Sch 6th
Crawford Stephen R., gent., 9 Portico sq
Crawford S. W., tailor, Jefferson n G T road
Crawford Thomas, weaver, rear Fitler n 2d
Crawford Thomas, weaver, Howard bel Master (K)
Crawford Thomas, lab., Spruce n Sch 4th
Crawford Tobias, cordw., 4 Pleasant Retreat
Crawford Walter, weaver, Fitler n 2d
Crawford Wm., engineer, Joseph's al
Crawford Wm., grocer, Sch 6th n Locust
Crawford William H., tanner, 7th & Willow, h 270 N 7th
Crawley Abraham, card manuf., 3 Strawberry, h Noble ab 4th
Crawshaw James, weaver, 3 Hampton
Craycroft Benj. B., book keeper, 130 Catharine
Craycroft Joseph, cordw., M road ab Washington
Craythorn Wm., baker, Carpenter ab 9th
Crea Cath., b h, 14 Julianna
Creagmile Thomas, flour, 474 N 4th, h 5th ab Coates
Creagor Adolphus, mariner, Reckless' ct
Creamer Eleanor, 208 St John
Creamer Joseph, ropemr., Shackamaxon n Bedford (K)
Creamer Josiah, ropem., Shackamaxon n Franklin

Creamer Matthias, ship carp., Marlborough bel Bedford
Creamer Michael, carp., 104 Apple
Crean John, 12th bel Callowhill
Crease Wm. G., tailor, 117 N 3d
Creauthers Caroline, wid. of Peter V., dry goods, 379 S 2d
Creed Richard H., tobacconist, Preston
Creely John S., agent, 31 Dean
Creely Michael, lab., Marlboro' bel Bedford
Creery Watkins, hatter, 12 Brown (N L)
Creery Wm., distil., 200 N 5th, h 7 St Joseph's av
Crees M. E. C., lampmr., 11 S 6th, h 15 A road
Creesy Charles, moulder, Callowhill ab Sch 8th
Cregar P. A., teacher, 17 Madison
Cregar Samuel, cordw., 141 Vine
Creighton Garrett, shoes, Sch 7th & Bickham
Creighton Henry, lab., Oxford bel Front
Creighton John, carp., 2d ab Montgomery
Creighton John, manager Globe Mills, h St John ab George (K)
Creighton Robt., mer., 10 S Front, h Spruce ab Broad
Creirling John W. R., coachmr., Pennell's ct (K)
Crelier Maurice, b b, 20 Prune
Cress George, gent., 59 Buttonwood bel 8th
Cress Geo. J., clerk, Sp Garden bel 8th
Cress James, bricklayer, 175 Coates
Cress M. E. J. C., lampmr., 15 A road
Cress Rachel, Carlton bel Sch 5th
Cress Samuel, bricklayer, Nectarine bel 10th
Cressée George F., grocer, 33 Beck (S)
Cressman George, stone cutter, 9th bel Buttonwood
Cressman Isaac, tobacconist, 116 Marshall
Cressman Jacob, lab., 428 S 4th
Cressman Joachim, cooper, Sch 5th ab Spruce
Cressman Margaret, R road ab Wallace
Cressman Wm., military cap, &c. man., 96 N 3d
Cresson Caleb, druggist, 5 Commerce
CRESSON CALEB & CO., drug., 5 Commerce
Cresson Deborah, 236 Filbert
Cresson Elliott, Washington house
CRESSON, FISHER & CO., hardware, 18 Commerce
Cresson John C., superin. gas works, Filbert E Sch 6th
Cresson Joseph, 363 Sassafras
Cresson M. Mrs., gentw., 30 Sansom
Cresson Walter, mer., 18 Commerce, h 83 Marshall
Cresson Wm., mer., 18 Commerce, h 84 Marshall
Cresson William P., iron foundry, James ab 13th, h 191 N 5th
Cresswell Robt., mer., 207 High, h 383 Race
CRESWELL S. J., brass & iron founder and stove maker, 221 Mulberry
Creth Alexander, tailor, 6th and Small
Creth Daniel, clothing, 210 High, h 1 Quarry
Crew Henry, machinist, 27 Brandywine st
Crew Jas. H., apothecary, N W 5th & Callowhill
Crewsenmire Jas., engineer, F road ab Phoenix (K)
Criblier Peter, confectioner, 79 Queen (S)

Crider George, cordw., 101 Vine
Crider Geo., tobacconist, New Market bel Popl.,
Cridland John, morocco dress., 5 Townsend's a.
Cridland Leander, carp., 12th bel Parrish
Crilly Bridget, 15 Strawberry
Crilly Daniel, tavern, 2½ S 7th
Crilly Elias M., drayman, Sarah bel Bedford (K
Crilly Henry, grocer, N W 3d and Thompson
Crilly Marg., wid. of John, Phœnix bel G T roa
Crilly Michael, lab., Locust ab Juniper
Crilly Susan, b. h., 526 N 2d
Crim James, carp., 40 Carpenter (C)
Crim Mary, b. h., 108 Walnut
Crippen Abraham, tailor, Russell ab Fitzwater
Crippen Robert, shoemr., rear 517 N 3d
Cripps Richard M. L., cordw., 137 Buttonwood
Crips Joseph, chemist, Spruce ab Sch 4th
Crisp George, lab., St John bel George (K)
Crispenn D. D., dentist, N E 9th & Sassafras
Crispenn Robert, bricklayer, 8 St Joseph's av
Crissy Jacob, cordw., 119 Brown
Crissy James, printer and publisher, 4 Minor, h 58 Filbert
Crissy Wm., tailor, 28 Chester
Crist Christopher, vict., West bel Palmer (K)
Crist Geo., bill poster, Lily ab Green
Crist Henry, glassblower, Wood bel Duke (K
Crist Jane, washer, n Bedford bet Palmer an Cherry
Crist John, lab., Palmer ab West (K)
Crist Joseph, caulker, Franklin bel Palmer, (K
Crist Samuel, vict., West ab Hanover (K)
Crist Thos., lab., Hanover ab West
Cristiani Richard S., drug., Christian & Front
Criswell Isaac J., hardware, 299 High
Criswell John A., hardw., 86½ N 2d
Crittenden S. W., teacher of book-keeping, &c 140 Chestnut
Croasdale Eber, cordw., Clinton bel Poplar
Croasdale Mary, gentw., 461 S Front
Crock Geo., vict., rear 6th Poplar
Crock Peter, planemr., Rose n William (K)
Crocke John, porter, rear Olive bel Broad
Crocker Franklin, cordw., 8th bel Parrish
Crocker Lott, carpet weaver, Cadwalader be Oxford
Crocker Pascoe, tailor, 2 Winter's ct
Crocker Samuel, mariner, Reckless ct
Crockett David, blacksm., Jackson ct (N L)
Crockett Henry, cabman, rear 157 Coates
Crockett Joseph, blacksmith, 2 Mechanics' ct
Crockett & Noble, blacksms., Maiden bel Fror
Crocks Frederick, silver pl., 8 Liberty ct
Croft Henry, morocco dress., 4th ab George, h Perry bel Phoenix (K)
Croft John, carp., Bush-hill
CROFT SAMUEL, mer., 53 Commerce
Croghan Augustus, baker 13th ab Poplar
Croghan George, U. S. A., 29 Girard
Crokin Patrick, lab., R road ab Carpenter
Croll Christian, tailor, 149 Chestnut, h Frankl ab Buttonwood
Croll M. J. & Co., tailors, 149 Chestnut
Croll M. J., tailor, 149 Chestnut, h 99 Franklin
Crombarger Mary, 84 S 11th

Cromberger John, brushm., 266 Lombard
Cromelien & Brother, wines & liquors, 11 Walnut
Cromelien Geo., mer., 11 Walnut, h 41 N 11th ab Wood
Cromelien Washington, mer., 11 Walnut, h 15 City row
Cromey John, weaver, Mariner,
Cromlay John, shoemr., 9 Willing's al
Cromley Christopher, sad'r., Orchard ab George
Cromley Geo. M., baker, Front bel Phœnix (K)
Cromly Thomas, 31 N 7th
Crommie Andrew J., tailor, 334 Callowhill
Crommie Ed. H., cordw., 12 Richard
Crompton John, bandbox mr., 11 Gray's al
Cromwell Chas. S., cordw., rear 118 Brown
Cromwell Jas. S., bricklayer, Sch 7th n Cherry
Cromwell John, sailmaker, 111 S whfs
Cromwell John, jr., bricklayer, 64 N Juniper
Crone Hannah, Stoy's ct (K)
Cronen Marg., tavern, 294 S 7th
Cronhard Christian, shoemr., 3 Vernon
Cronmullar John, victualler, Front bel Master
Crook John, Monument Cemetery, h 10th and Poplar
Crooks Catharine, sewer., 147½ S 2d
Croome William, designer and engraver, S E 6th & Walnut, h 59 Buttonwood
Cropley & Sawyer, stoves, 75 Cedar
Cropper Daniel, porter, Emeline st
Cropper Edward, porter, Caroline pl
Cropper Henry, waiter, Fitzwater ab 12th
Cropper Lomax, baker, 83 W Callowhill
Cropper Samuel P., acct., 128 Catharine
Crosby Catharine, 422 N 9th ab Coates
Crosby David H., lab., rear 17 Barley
Crosby Elizabeth, 74 S 12th
Crosby George, clerk, 39 Madison
Crosby John, plasterer, Olive bel 12th
Crosby L. B., carp., Apple ab Culvert
Crosby Magnus, stonecutter, Prospect al bel Fayette
Crosby Thomas, clerk, 50 Filbert
Crosby William, carpenter, 3 Juniper lane
CROSKEY HENRY, lumber, Washington av Delaware ab Noble
Cross Benjamin, teacher music, 2 S 10th
Cross Benjamin C., teacher music, Sch 8th and Locust
Cross George W., dry goods, 30 S 2d, h 46 Lombard
Cross Wm., weaver, 7 M'Duffie
Crossin Elwood, drayman, 302 S 7th
Crossin Wm., hatter, 5 Howard pl
Crossin Wm., tailor, h 34 Bonsall
Crossman Elizabeth, milliner, 217 S 2d
Crossman J. M., mer., 123 High, h 364 Chestnut
Crosson James, shoemr., German ab 5th
Crothers John, cordw., 23 Julianna
Crothers Matilda, gentw., 389 Mulberry
Crothers William S., 389 Mulberry
Crotto E. Mrs., 32 Farmer
Crouch C. W., shoemr., 270 N 4th
Crouch Francis, furniture, 379 Race
Crouch Isaac, engineer, F road opp Allen
10

Crouch Richard, porter, Concord st
Crouder George, spinner, Lombard ab Sch 2d
Crouse Benj., 7 Western pl
Crouse Catharine, widow, Lemon ab 10th
Crouse Gotlieb, tavern, S W Penn and Cedar
Crouse Michael, painter, rear 392 Sassafras
Crouse Samuel, weaver, James's ct (K)
Crouse Thos., carman, Marshall ab Poplar
Crout Daniel, card manuf., 24 Lagrange, h 224 Green
Crout Joseph, cabinetmr., 88 S Front
Crout J. & A., cabinetmrs., 360 N 6th
Crout Mahlon, carp., 4 Lafayette pl
Crow James, vict., 12th ab Brown
Crowell David B., watchman, 220 S 9th
Crowell Elisha, alderman, office S W 6th & Pine, h 176 S 3d
Crowell Ellis B., 17 S 13th
Crowell Ellis B., jr., mer., 8 N 2d
Crowell James, store, Washington (W P)
Crowell James W., tobacco., N E 10th and Buttonwood
Crowell Smith, b. h., Front and Union
Crowell Smith, tailor, 175 Chestnut, h 8 Stamper's al
Crowell Thomas, painter, 145 Poplar
Crowell Thos. P., mer., 8 N whfs., h 98 Christian
Crowell Wm. G., Noble bel 8th
Crowers John, ropemr., 4th ab Thompson (K)
Crowley Chas., lab., 14 Lloyd's ct (K)
Crowley F. Doct., 8 Green
Crowley John, lab., 176 N Water
Crowley Michael, weaver, La Fayette ct
Crows George, lab., Dorothy n Sch 3d
Crows Jas., engineer, Filbert n Sch 3d
Crows Jas., lab., Filbert n Sch 4th
Crowther John, turner, New Market ab Laurel
Crowther Wm., lab., Sch Willow ab Spruce
Crox John, machinist, Sch 6th n Sassafras
Crozer James G., mer., 65 S Front, h 171 S 10th
Crozet Earnest, printing office, 151 S 6th & 32 S 3d
Crozier Andrew, teacher, 65 Christian
Crozier Benjamin, cordw., 124 S Front
Crozier Mary Ann, 14 John (S)
Crozier Robert, cordw., Perry ab Phœnix (K)
Crozier Robert, eating house, 244 High
Crozier Wm., carpet weaver, Cedar bel 13th
Cruikshank Robert J., dry goods, 73 Cedar
Cruikshanks John, watchman, Shackmaxon n Bedford
Crum John, blacksm., rear 121 O F road
Crumback Jacob, shoemr., Olivet pl
Crumback Peter, cordw., Union bel Franklin
Crumbar Charles, waiter, 1 Barley
Crumbley Geo., brickmr., George n Sch 2d
Crumbley Thos., brickmr., Beech ab Spruce
Crumbly Jacob, brickmr., Lombard ab Sch Front
Crumley John, oysters, 397½ High, h Parrish bel 10th
Crumley Martha, 7th bel Washington
Crumnel Elizabeth, rear 61 Garden
Crumwell Wm., carder, Apple bel Franklin
Crundwell Elizabeth, store, S W 13th & Green

Cruse Daniel, carter, George n Sch 4th
Cruse James, porter, 5 Lebanon row
Cruse John, shoemr., Deal's av
Cruse John, rigger, 121 Brown (N L)
Cruse John, waiter, rear Carpenter ab 8th
Cruse John, fisherman, 9 Poplar
Cruse Michael, huckster, 387 High
Cruse Peter, carter, George n Sch 2d
Crusemire Joseph, lab., 201 G T road
Crusemire Joseph, sr., lab., 4th bel Master
Crusemire Nicholas, machinist, Charlotte below Thompson
Crutcher Foster G., mer., 9 Merchant, h 26 Girard
Cruvillier Made., confec., S E 6th & Spruce
Crystal Sarah, tailoress, 181 Cedar
Cubberlay George, carp., Ogden ab Sch 8th
Cubberley Jas. H., cordw., Centre ab Brown
Cubbison Jas., carp., Lewis n Sch 7th
Cuddy Lawson, bootmr., 135 N Juniper
Cuesta Miss, 57 Pine
Cuff Ellen, 83 Locust
Cugan Patrick, lab , Fitler bel Harrison (K)
Culbert & Hunter, grocers, O Y road & Green
Culbert John, pedler, Shippen ab 12th
Culbert Joseph, cabman, 1 Buinton
Culbert Martha A., milliner, 34 N 10th
Culbertson Allen, lab., Sch 2d ab Vine
Culbertson James, weaver, Shippen la ab Fitzwater
Culbertson James, weaver, Fox's ct
Culbertson John, weaver, 8 Philip (K)
Culbertson John, weaver, Shippen ab 12th
Culbertson Robert, grocer, R. road ab Girard av
Culbertson Samuel, b. h., George ab Sch. 8th
Culbertson Wm., tavern, 2d and Cadwalader (K)
Culbertson Wm., drayman, Shippen ab 12th
Culbertson Wm., carter, 321 S 6th
Culin Eliza, 83 Vine
Culin George, bookbinder, 69 Noble
Culin Geo., tailor, S E 2d and High, h 31 New
Culin George, c Wood and Julianna
Culin George, saloon, 158 St. John
Culin John, tailor, 14 High
Culin John, wheelwright, Locust (W P)
Culin John jr., clerk, 133 G. T. road
Culin John N., cordw., 10th ab Coates, h 5 Franklin row (S G)
Culin V., druggist, N E 6th and Lombard
Culin Margaret, Harmstead n Sch. 2d
Culin Samuel, shoemaker, 45 Plum
Cullen George, grocer, 11 S 13th
Cullen Lawrence, drayman, 107 German
Cullen Peter, soap and candles, 289 Cedar
Cullen Thomas, shop, cor 7th and Wall
Cullen Wm., drayman, Perry bel Phœnix (K)
Cullin Edw., chandler, Shippen ab 7th
Cullman Jacob, b. h., 117 N 6th
Cully Thomas, gilder, 95 Dillwyn
Culp Charles, carp., Mechanic ab George
Culp Jacob, gent., 85 Vine
Culp John, brickmr., Sch. Front ab Spruce
Culp John, carter, Clinton ab Broad
CULP & SMITH, grocers, 226 N 2d
Culton George, victualler, 30 Perry

Culver Andrew, compositor, 308 Pine
Culver Daniel, atty. and coun., 89 S 3d
Cumback Thos., shoemr., 27 Beck
Cumins Jane, 183 Brown
Cumming & Brodie, copper and tin roofers, ? St. James
Cumming Charles, glue manuf., 6th bel Master and 1 S 3d, h 6th bel Poplar
Cumming Edward, 9 St. James
Cumming Jonathan, variety, N W 3d and High
Cumming Richard P., metallic roofer, 276 N 2? h 220 N 4th
Cumming Samuel M., carp., 305 N 7th
Cummings Alexander, publisher, N E 4th and Chestnut, h 321 N 6th
Cummings A. B., agent, 274 High
Cummings Bradley, blacksmith, Carleton below Sch. 2d
Cummings Chas. H., grain, 101 N Water, h 40? S Front
Cummings David, currier, 19 Melon
Cummings Henry, cordw., 33 Mechanic
Cummings Isaac, bricklayer, 88 Christian
Cummings Jacob, dealer, 128 S Water
Cummings James, weaver, 27 McDuffie
Cummings Jas., weaver, Benton n School (K)
Cummings Jane, shoe binder, 6 Lyndall's alley
Cummings John, jeweller, Rye ab Read
Cummings John S., clerk, Vine ab Sch. 4th
Cummings J. A., mer., 189 High, h 89 Wood
Cummings L., lab., Middleton ct
Cummings Mary, Chancellor n Sch. 7th
Cummings Mary Ann, gentw., rear 7 Maria
Cummings Matthew, blacksmith, 14 Elizabeth (N L)
Cummings Robt., weaver, Master n Howard (K
Cummings Samuel, weaver, Bedford bel Broad
Cummings Wm., weaver, Hope bel Master
Cummings Wm., jeweller, 7 Wall
Cummings Wm., grocer, 75 S whfs., h 21 Pine
Cummings Wm., gunsmith, 7 New Market
Cummings Wm. & Co., grocers, 75 S whfs.
Cummins Dan. B., mer., 103 High, h 282 Waln?
Cummins Edward, tavern, 29 Prune
Cummins Edward, Washington n 9th
Cummins John, tavern, Oxford and G. T. road (K)
Cummins John, wood, Shippen st. wharf, Sch h (W P)
Cummins John, ostler, Alice st
Cummins Margaret, 65 Mead
Cummins Patrick, iron dealer, 143 N Front
Cummins Rachel, 6 Howard's ct
Cummins Thos., blacksm., Ogden bel Sch. 8th
Cummiskey Eugene, publisher and bookseller 130 S 6th
Cunius Jacob, cordw., 13 Mark's lane
Cunningham Alexander, lab., 2 Parker
Cunningham Alex., shop, Callowhill n Sch. 3?
Cunningham & Crawley, card manuf., 3 Strawberry
Cunningham Elizabeth, 2 Loxley's ct
Cunningham Francis R., shoemr., Ogden's ct
CUNNINGHAM JAMES, lab., 181 N Front
Cunningham James, lab., 40 Garden

Cunningham James, lab., Sch. 2d ab High
Cunningham James, weaver, Shippen bel Broad
Cunningham James, painter, 205 N 9th
Cunningham James, cordw., 62 Perry
Cunningham James, moroc. dress., 187 N Front
Cunningham John, lab., F. road ab Phœnix (K)
Cunningham John, oyster house, 256 E Shippen
Cunningham John, lab., 39 Plum
Cunningham John, lab., Kinley's ct
Cunningham John, 179 Christian
Cunningham John, lab., 14 Quince
Cunningham John, lab., 188 Lombard
Cunningham Joseph, stone cut., Ann n Sch. 6th
Cunningham Joseph, porter, 38 Budd
Cunningham Martin, rear 40 George (S)
Cunningham Mary, widow, 18 Acorn alley
Cunningham Richard, engineer, Sch. 5th and Fairview
Cunningham Robert, shoemr., 307 S 6th
Cunningham Robert, engineer, 64 P. road
Cunningham Rosanna, widow, Small ab 5th
Cunningham Samuel, cordw., 436 N Front
Cunningham Samuel, lab., Senneff's ct
Cunningham Samuel H., carp., 62 Perry
Cunningham Susan, S E Sch. 3d and High
Cunningham Wm., card manuf., 3 Strawberry
Cunningham Wm., weaver, Philip ab Master (K)
Cunningham Wm., lab., Cedar E Sch. 2d
CUNNINGHAM WM. J., bookseller, 104 S 3d
Cunningham Winthrop, mer., 44 S Water, h 185 S 7th
Cunnington Wm., M. D., 46 Lebanon
Curby John S., cooper, 91 S Water, h 295 S Front
Curby Michael, cooper, 42 S Water, h 295 S Front
Curlet Hugh, cordwainer, 9th ab Ogden
Curnes John, carrier, 2 Pearl
Curran Jane, 305 Walnut
Curran Martin, com. mer., 119 S Front, h 20 German
Curran William, porter, Mintland's ct
Curran Wm., M. D., 29 Mulberry
Curren Margaret, Allen & Hanover (K)
Curren Martha, washer, 26 Portland la
Curren Wm., gent., 23 Prune
Curren Wm., blacksm., Hampton ct
Curren Wm., lab., Lily al
Currey Wm., importer, 71 Chestnut, h 154 N 3d
Currin D., constable, Cypress.
Currin Jas. W., jeweller, 6 Bank al, h 60 Catharine
Currin John, lab., Cherry ab Queen
Currin John, shop, 22 Elizabeth
Currin Thos., moulder, rear Washington ab 6th
Curry Daniel, cordw., Olive bel Broad
Curry Dorothy, shop, 480 Sassafras
Curry Enoch, wood turner, Elizabeth ab Poplar, h 5th bel Franklin
Curry Geo., lab., Barker n Sch 4th
Curry Geo. W., blacksm., Vienna bel Franklin (K)
Curry Hamilton, saddler, 253 S 6th
Curry Hugh, gent., 25 Dugan
Curry Jas., lab., Filbert n Sch 3d

Curry John, cordw., 160 Christian
Curry John, lab., Thompson n 3d (K)
Curry John, lampmr., rear 13 Poplar
Curry John, silversm., G T road bel Mud la
Curry John, lab., Spencer's ct
Curry John F., combmr., 443 N 4th
Curry Lewis V., bookbinder, Palmer bel Brown
Curry Marshall, weaver, 29 W Cedar
Curry Mary Ann, weaver, Harmony ct (K)
Curry N., lab., Sch 4th ab George (F V)
Curry Peter B., hat finisher, 38 Wood
Curry R. D. Mrs., dry goods, 131 Shippen
Curry Samuel, clerk, 13 Hampton
Curry Wm., paperhanging manuf., Sch Front n Vine, h c Callowhill and Sch Front
Curry Wm., cordw., 12 Boyd's av
Curry Wm., lab., Carpenter ab 13th
Curry Wm., bricklayer, Logan ab Wallace
Curry Wm., chairmr., 9 Baker's ct
Curten Daniel, weaver, Hanover ab Duke (K)
Curtis Ann, b. h., S E 4th and Walnut
Curtis Ann, teacher, 17 Elfreth's al
Curtis Anthony, waiter, 62 Gaskill
Curtis B. T., mer., 41 & 43 Commerce, h Filbert E Sch 6th
Curtis Cephas, combmr., 125 New Market
Curtis Charles C., barber, 269 Sassafras
Curtis Daniel, carpet weaver, rear Apple bel Franklin
CURTIS & HAND, hardware, 41 & 43 Commerce
Curtis Henry, carter, Fitler bel Harrison (K)
Curtis Henry W., trimmings, 386 N 4th
Curtis Jas., lab., Carbon pl.
Curtis John H., real est. agt. and collector, 121 Walnut, h 33 Marshall
Curtis J. D. Rev., 10th ab Poplar
Curtis Margaretta, 4 Chancery la
Curtis & Norcross, booksellers, S W 6th and Haines
Curtis Patrick, stable keeper, 3 Wagner's ct
Curtis Sarah J., rear 174 Marshall
Curtis Thomas, tailor, 54 N 8th
Curtis Thomas F., agt. and col., 105 Lombard
Curtis Wm., collector, 11 Brown (N L)
Curtiss John, brassfounder, 21 Marriott
Curtiss John M., blacksm., Greenwich ab 2d
CURTS JOSEPH L., refectory, 134 High
Curwen Wm., carpet weav., Fairmount
Curwen Wm., carp. weav., Dickson's ct (K)
Curwin John, shoemr., G T road ab 6th
Cusack John, lab., Ann n 12th
Cusack Wm., baker, High n Sch 3d
Cusack Wm., lab., Fleming's row
Cush Thomas, lab., 1 Lagrange
Cushart John, machinist, Beach ab Poplar (K)
Cushing Margaret Mrs., gentw., 421 S Front
Cushing Wm. F. stevedore, Front & Washington
Cushley Thomas, lab., G T road ab Thompson
Cushman G. H., min. paint., S W 7th & Sansom
Cushman Robt. W., mer., 189 High, h 4 Melrose pl
Cuskaden Elizab'h, wid of Geo., Cuskaden's ct
Csku Josephine, tailoress, Relief
Custelow Ann, 19 Prosperous al

Custer Albert, carp., Bledisloe pl
Custer Daniel, carp., Hutchinson ab Poplar
Custer Issacher, carp., 424 N 2d
Custer Nathan, black & whitesm., 159 Poplar, h 443 N 5th
Custins Wm., paint. & glaz., 108 Queen
Custis George, porter, Russel n Fitzwater
Custis George, waiter, 26 Bird's ct
Custis Lewis, shoemr., 10 Washington
Custis Moses, lab., Warren bel 12th
Custis Theodore W., 27 Sassafras
Cuthbert Allen, mer., 102 S whfs, h 355 Mulberry
Cuthbert Elizabeth, 137 S 9th
Cuthbert George, mer., 76 S 2d, h 355 Mulberry
Cuthbert John W., Marriott bel 9th
Cuthbert Mary, 355 Mulberry
Cuthbert Sarah, 205 S 9th
CUTHBERT & WETHERILL, druggists, 76 S 2d
Cuthbert Wm., clerk, 573 N Front
Cuthbertson John, machinist, Penn bel Broad
Cutherel Willis, tailor, 203 Shippen
Cutler Mary, teacher, Fitzwater ab 6th
Cutler Thomas, rigger, 9 Fitzwater
Cutter John, cordw., R road ab 13th
Cutter Saml. L., Prest. Buck Mt. Coal Co., 82 Walnut, h 48 N 13th
Cutter Wm. G., cordw., 11th & Coates
Cuyjet Stephen W., shoe., 1 Laurel (C)
Cuyler Cornelius C. Rev., 155 Walnut
CUYLER THEODORE, atty. & coun. 155 Walnut
Cyrus Anthony, cabman, 206 N 8th

Dainty James, morocco dress., rear 19 Maria
Daisy Aaron, mariner, 582 S 2d
Dalb John G., cordw., Lewellyn's ct
DALBY DANIEL, tavern, 234 N 3d
Dalby Moses S., stove finisher, Brinton bel 11th
Dale Edward C., Pres. Phil., Balt. & Wil. R. R. Co., 72 Walnut, h 383 Spruce
Dale Gerald F., mer., 74 High, h 146 S 4th
Dale James, butcher, 325 S 6th
Dale James, sailmr., N 11th ab Sassafras
Dale John M., U. S. Navy, 7 Dugan's row
Dale J., dry goods, 146 S 4th
Dale Peter, ropemr., Wharton ab 4th
Dale Richard C., mer., 74 High, h 75 Pine
Dale, Ross & Withers, mers., 74 High
Dale Wm. H., carter, Parker ab Washington
Dales Hiram, M. D., Front bel Master (K)
Dales Jas. H., 1 Howard
Dales John B. Rev., Juniper n Filbert
Daley Charles, drayman, 182 N Water
Daley David, drayman, 3 Duke st
Daley Francis, weaver, Phillip ab Jefferson (K
Daley James, baker, Christian bel 9th
Daley James, cabs, 28 Mintzer
Daley John, capt., 12 Beck pl
Daley John, lab., rear 463 N 4th
Daley John, shop, 22 Mayland
Daley Michael, lab., Jones n Sch 4th
Daley Peter, lab., Bedford bel Clifton
Dallam John, inspector, 55 S whfs
Dallas Edwin, cordw., Beaver ab 2d
Dallas George M., atty. & coun. and Vice Pres dent of the United States, 259 Walnut
Dallas Jacob, weaver, Gay's ct (K)

Dalzell Charles, baker, 15 Hampton
Dalzell James, conveyancer, 7 George, h Stanley bel 4th
Dalzell James, weaver, Milton ab 10th
Dalzell Wm., gent., Stanley bel 4th
Dalzell Wm., clerk, Catharine bel 4th
Damai Edward, hatter, 1 Strawberry, h 11 Vine
Damman Raymond, mer., 27 Church al
Dampman E., tailor, 391 N 3d
Dampman John, carp., Lybrand st
Danenhauer John, baker, 435 N 3d
Danenhower Chas. R., tobacconist, 27 N Water, h 38 New Market
Danenhower Charles R. & Co., tob. com. mer., 27 N Water & 14 N whfs
Danneberger Antoine, 2 Locust
Danfield & Beaver, grocers, 4th & Franklin
Danfield Conrad, tailor, 304 Cherry
Danfield John H., grocer, Franklin ab 4th (K)
Danguy Canelle, hair dr. & worker, 279 Chestnut
Daniel Aaron, clerk, 2 Buttonwood
Daniel James H., jeweller, 10 N 11th
Danielly Mrs. A., 45 Coates
Daniels A. Mrs., b. h., 8 Green
Daniels Eva, manuf., 189 Callowhill
Daniels H. Mrs., gentw., 409 S Front
Daniels Isaac, weaver, G T road & Mud la
Daniels Jane, 229 N 6th
Daniels John, bricklr., 10th n Washington
Daniels Joshua, jeweller, 350 S Front
Daniels Rachel, 12 Bread
Daniels Rachel, 51 Rose al
DANIELS & SMITH, books, N W 4th & Mulberry
Daniels Thomas, Cantrell's ct
Daniels Wm., tailor, 2 Dannaker's av
Daniels Wm., boat builder, Beach opp Warren, h Allen ab Shackamaxon (K)
Daniels Wm., books, N W 4th and Mulberry, h 244 St John
Daniels Wm., blacksm., 13th bel Brown
Daniley Wm., cordw., 95 Brown (N L)
Dankel Henry, coach trimmer, 6 Wharton
Dankworth John, saddler, 96 Willow
Danley Thomas, blacksm., Woodland (W P)
Dannaeker Mary, b h, 28 E North
Dannaher John, lab., Dorothy n Sch 4th
Dannaker Christian A., currier, 143 N 3d, h 97 New
Dannaker James G., cordw., rear 176 Poplar
Dantz Philip, turner & tavern, Willow & Dillwyn
Danzeiser Fredk., baker, Front ab Phœnix
Danzenbaker Horace, waterman, 49 Rose al
Darby Edward, wireworks, Marshall ab Poplar
Darby John, weaver, Camac ab G T road
Darcus Robert, weaver, Milton ab 10th
Dardis Francis, nailmr., Parker n Washington
Dare Collin, engineer, 5 Beck
Dare Conrad, brickmr., rear 176 Poplar
Dare & Cox, blacksms., 141 St John
Dare Edward, seaman, 6 Monmouth ct
Dare George, porter, 130 Marshall
Dare Isaac, hatter, 648 N 2d (K)

Dare Isabella, milliner, 225 N 6th
Dare James B., alderman, 655 N 2d (K)
Dare Julia, 225 N 6th
Dare Sarah, 1 Pt Pleasant ct
Darham Mary, 15 Parham
Darker Wm., jr., manuf., George n Juniper
Darker Wm., cotton cord manuf., Park (W P)
Darkies James, vict., George ab Apple
Darland Mary, 39 Chester
Darley F. O. C., designer, 417 High
DARLEY W. H. W. prof. of music, 184 Chestnut, h 417 High
Darlington F. M., dry goods, 8 S 8th
Darnell Henry, grain meas., 460 S 4th
Darnell Wm. S, measurer, 399 S 4th
Darney Wm., carter, rear 27 Morgan
Darr Jacob, baker, 32 Strawberry
Darr John C., baker, Sch 7th n George
Darrach Wm., M. D., 268 Mulberry
Darragh Daniel, bootmr., Lafayette ab 9th
Darragh Daniel, carp., Wood bel Sch 8th
Darragh Henry, dyer, Wood bel Sch 8th
Darragh John, lab., 9 Wood bel Sch 7th
Darragh John, lumber mer., 13th and Pine, h 165 Pine
Darragh John, carp., Clymer ab Mud la
Darragh John, lab., Perry bel Pine
Darragh John & Son, lumber mers., S W 13th and Pine
Darragh Patrick, shoemaker, N W 12th and Lombard
Darragh Thomas, potter, Wood bel Sch 8th
Darragh Tilghman, 151 Locust
Darrah Albert, shoemr., Coates ab Sch 7th
Darrah Wm., machinist, Phoenix bel G T road
Datz Mary, 21 Rittenhouse
Daudt Henry, sugar refiner, 12 Fetter lane
Daugherty Daniel, gent., 328 Pine
Daugherty Daniel A., acct., 328 Pine
DAUGHERTY MARTIN J., atty. & coun., S E 6th & Walnut, h 328 Pine
Daugherty M. J., M. D., 328 Pine
Daugherty Wm., messenger, 170 N 13th
Daughters John C., shoemr., 18 Mary
Davault John, carter, Cherry bel Franklin (K)
DAVENPORT & ELDRIDGE, hardware, 212 S 2d
Davenport James, boxmr., 368 S 5th
Davenport James, collect., 299 S 10th
Davenport Robert W., hardware, 212 S 2d
Daverix Robert, porter, 4 Esher's av
Davey John, carp., 7 Spragg's av
David E W., atty. & coun., 340 Sp Garden
David G., ropes and twine, 2 S Water, h 166 Swanson
David Jacob, gent., 100 N 7th
David John B., bookbinder, 4 Hudson's al
DAVID LOUIS, tavern, 20 Dock
David Lynch, 7 Morgan's ct
David, Springs & Co., dry goods, 167 High
David Wm. K., mer., 39 S 2d
David Wm. M., mer., 167 High, h 294 N 7th
Davids Benjamin, gent., 103 S 4th
Davidson Alex., watchm., 119 M road
Davidson Alex., currier, 314 E Vine

Davidson Ann, 143 N 13th
Davidson Edward, awningmr., 27 S Front, h 45 Apple
Davidson E. W., mer., 125 High
Davidson Joseph A., acct., 338 Sp. Garden
Davidson Julius, extractor of corns, 139 S 4th
Davidson N., gent., Girard College pl
Davidson Robt. B., brok., 79 Dock, h 101 S 12th
Davidson T., weaver, F road ab Oxford
Davidson Wm., confectioner, Callowhill n Wire Bridge
Davidson Wm., broker, 79 Dock, h 101 S 12th
Davidson Wm., dry goods, 188 S 2d
DAVIDSON W. & SON, stock brokers, 79 Dock
Davies Alex., groc., F road ab Montgomery
Davies & Bull, grocers, 348 High
Davies Edward S., grocery, 348 High
Davies Harriet, dressmr., 12 N 10th
Davies John, cider and vinegar, h Buttonwood bel 12th
Davies John & Co., cider and vinegar yard, 12th n Pleasant, and blacking manuf., Buttonwood 2d door bel 12th
Davies Rebecca, 133 S 4th
Davies Samuel N., auctioneer, 68 High, h 29 Spruce
DAVIES, STEVENSON & Co., auctioneers, 68 High
Davis Aaron, shoe store, Broad ab Coates
Davis Aaron, 7 Wood (K)
Davis Abraham, cabmr., 37 Apple
Davis Adam, constable, Beach bel Shackamaxon (K)
Davis Adam C., mer., 66½ N 3d, h 165 N 4th
Davis & Alexander, dry goods, 66½ N 3d
Davis Alexander G., mer., Almira pl
Davis Alfred, clerk, 176 Callowhill ab Sch 6th
Davis Allen, plasterer, 53 Chester
Davis Amelia, tavern, S E 7th & Coates
Davis Amos, machinist, 5 Lybrand
Davis Andrew, sea capt., 21 Catharine
Davis Ann, rear 15 John
Davis Ann, bookseller, 473 High
Davis Ann, 41 Union
Davis Ann, washer, Clifton & Cedar
Davis Ann, rear 41 Chester
Davis Ann, sempstress, 2 Willow ct
Davis Anna M., ladies' shoemr., 322 Sassafras
Davis Anthony, gent., 605 N Front
Davis Armon, alderman, 20 S 7th
Davis Ashton J., cordw., G T road n Phoenix
Davis Augustus, scalemr., 29 Melon
Davis A. G., brickmr., Marshall bel Parrish
Davis Benjamin, brickmr., Broad ab Poplar

Davis Charles, porter, 237 S 7th
Davis Charles, mer. 3 Church al, h 368 Walnut
Davis Charles, vict., Palmer ab Franklin (K)
Davis Chas. glass blower, Wood ab Queen (K)
Davis Charles, M. D., N W 8th & Chestnut
Davis Charles C., blacksmith, Green ab R road
DAVIS CHARLES H. & Co., hotel, High st for
Davis Charles T., blacksm., Hanover ab Franklin, h Palmer n Duke (K)
Davis Charlotte, 11 Elder
Davis & Chew, cabt. mrs., 276 S 2d
Davis Chloe, dressmr., 15 S 8th
Davis Collin K., ser capt., 80 Marshall
Davis Daniel, grave dig. Hanover n Duke (K)
Davis Daniel, coachman, Shippen la bel Bedford
Davis Daniel, potter, 539 N 2d
Davis David, carpenter, 9th bel Poplar
Davis David, blacksm., Oak (W P)
Davis David, agent Lehigh Coal and Nav. Co., Queen ab Shackamaxon
Davis David, sea capt., 269 S Front
Davis David A., collector, 4 Quince
Davis David L., sawmr., 4 Knight's ct
Davis David J., tobacc., Church bel Christian
Davis & Dolby, carps., Allen bel Shackamaxon
Davis Dorothy, 3 N 13th
Davis Edw. M., mer., 27 Church al, h 140 N 9th
Davis Eli, sea capt., 9 Mary ab Front
Davis Elias, waiter, Caroline pl
Davis Elijah B., porter, Giles' al
Davis Elijah M., trimmings, 131 Cedar
Davis Eliza, rear 117 Christian
Davis Elizabeth, Loud st
Davis Elizabeth, b h, 10 Sansom
Davis Elizabeth B., b h, 41 George
Davis Ellwood, mer., 39 Chestnut, h 176 Mulberry
Davis Eml., cordw., 12 N 2d, h rear 125 N 2d
Davis Esther, milliner, 71 Mulberry
Davis & Fitler, lumber mers. N E 4th & George (N L)
DAVIS, FAIRCHILD & Co., mers., 27 Church alley
Davis Francis, painter, Mifflin & 13th
Davis Francis B. bricklay. F road ab Phœnix (K)
Davis Gainer, b h, 1 Drinker's al
Davis George, shoemr., 48 George
Davis George, clothing, 115 N 2d
Davis George, carp., 7th ab Poplar
Davis Geo. P., coach painter, Davis' ct (S G)
Davis Hannah, cook, 12 Elizabeth
Davis Hannah, 7 Marion
Davis Harrison, tobacconist, 169 N 2d

Davis Isaac, lab., Apple ab Brown
Davis Isaac, grocer, N E 2d and Mary
Davis Isaac, mer., 12th and Cherry
Davis Isaac A., tailor, 12 Gray's al
Davis Isaac B., carp., Carroll ab 13th
Davis Isaac R., mer., 27 Church al, h 12th bel
     • George
Davis Isaac L., atty. & coun., 67 Pine
Davis Isabella, Black Horse al (S)
Davis Isaiah, combmr., 2d ab Laurel (K)
Davis James, lumber mer., 8th ab Green
Davis James, shoemr., 31 Prune
Davis James, chairmr., 4 Jenning's row
Davis James, cabmr., Preston bel Wallace
Davis James, blacksm., Elder
Davis James B., blindmr., 4 Quarry
Davis James M., custom house, Jones n Sch 5th
DAVIS JAMES M., mer., 249 & 251 High, h
     204 N 11th
Davis James M., Customhouse, h Jones W
     Sch 5th
Davis James M. & Co., forw. mers., 249 & 251
     High
Davis James P., stone cutter, Franklin ab Marl-
     borough (K)
Davis Jane, washer, 10 Middle al
Davis Jane H., Lombard ab Sch 8th
Davis Jesse W., ice dealer, 549 Chestnut
Davis John, engineer, Vienna bel Franklin (K)
Davis John, lead manufact., Beach ab Shacka-
     maxon (K)
Davis John, cordw., N E Fitzwater & 13th
Davis John, furs, 51 N 2d
Davis John, vict., 30 Apple
Davis John, paper hanger, 222 N 5th
Davis John, porter, George n Sch 7th
Davis John, sweep master, 52 Quince
Davis John, surveyor, Custom-house
Davis John, gent., 222 Cherry
Davis John, tavern 93 Plum
Davis John H. tailor, Washington (W P)
Davis John H., carp, 189 E Catharine
Davis John H. tailor, 553 Vine ab Sch. 8th
Davis John J., carpenter, Sch 8th ab Race
Davis John O. watchman, 1 Headman's pl
Davis John R., cordw., Moore's ct (S G)
Davis John S. carpenter, 8th bel Cedar, h Ca-
     tharine bel 10th
Davis Joseph, umbrellas, 6th and Chestnut, h
     3d ab Washington
Davis Joseph, b. h., 48 Penn. (C)
Davis Jos. C., cordw., Ann bel Sch 4th (F V)
Davis Julia, 345 Mulberry
Davis Julia A., gentw., 217 N 6th
Davis Lawrence, ropemr., G T road ab 5th
Davis Leonard, mariner, 6 Mary (S)
Davis Levin, lab., Shippen ab 8th
Davis Lewis Capt., 218 S 4th
Davis L. G., oyster house, 262 High
Davis Margaret, sempstress, rear 524 N 3d
Davis Margaret, confec. 202 S 5th
Davis Maria, washer, 6 Liberty
Davis Martha, gentw., 329 S 6th
Davis Mary, b. h., 160 Pine
Davis Mary, 482 N 3d

Davis Mary, 384 S 3d
Davis Mary, 3 Prune
Davis Matthew, carter, McDuffie E Sch 3d
Davis Michael, cabmr., 3d ab Federal
Davis Mordecai, carp., Ontario ab Poplar
Davis Mordecai, carp., 3d ab Franklin (K)
Davis Moses, clothier, 363 N 2d, h 24 Lily al
Davis Mrs. M. S., milliner, 210 N 6th
Davis Rebecca, b h, 355 N 3d
Davis Richard, huckster, Ten Feet al
Davis Robert, lab., 26 Paschall's al
Davis Robert, carter, 11 Dyott's ct (K)
Davis Robt. C., druggist, Vine and Sch 7th
Davis Saml., cordw., 458 S Front
Davis Saml., bricklayer, McBride's ct (K)
Davis Samuel, carp., Allen bel Palmer (K)
Davis Samuel, blacksmith, R road ab James
Davis Samuel, jeweller, Clark ab 3d
Davis Saml., gent., 256 Chestnut.
Davis Saml., corder, Whf. bel Noble, h 193
     Coates.
DAVIS SAMUEL, att'y & coun., 98 Walnut
Davis Samuel H., lab., 13th and Pearl
Davis Saml. H., lum. mer., 4th and George, h
     533 N 5th
Davis Saml. I., grocer, 111 N 3rd, h 232 N 6th
Davis Sarah, Sch 7th n Cherry
Davis Sidney, lab., Mariner ab 13th
Davis Stephen H., boot mr., 3 Hank's ct
Davis Susanna, Sch 7th n Vine
DAVIS & THATCHER, dry goods, 3 Church al
Davis Thomas, cabinetmaker, 40 Plum.
Davis Thomas, shoemaker, 3 Marion
Davis Thomas, weaver, Nectarine n 10th
Davis Thomas, bookseller, 171 High, h 14
     Marshall
Davis Thomas, tailor, 328 N 5th
Davis Thomas, gent., Oak, (W P)
Davis Thomas, carp., 40 Carpenter (C) h N W
     Sch 7th and Sassafras
Davis Thomas, cabinetmr., 234 S 3d
Davis Thomas, weaver, Master & Pink (K)
Davis Thos., oysterman, Mechanic
Davis Thos., carp., 153 Swanson
Davis Thos., hatter, 533 Vine
Davis Thos., stone cutter, 67 S 12th
Davis Thos. D., wheelwright, Melon
Davis Thomas J., Rev., 77 Lombard
Davis Thomas W., dry goods, 19 N 2d, h 52
     Marshall
Davis William, b. h., 278 Wood
Davis William, clerk, 55 Prime ab Church
Davis William, blacksmith, Pearl n Sch 8th
Davis William, carp., Queen ab F road (K)
Davis William, sexton, Lombard ab 13th
Davis William, carpenter, 7th n Brown.
Davis William, baker, 425 S Front
Davis William, 138 N 12th.
Davis William, M. D., 392 Coates
Davis William, driver, 7 Tiller's ct
Davis William, brushmr., 2 Marble pl
Davis Wm., carp., 1 Crockett's ct., h 8th below
     Catharine
Davis Wm., painter, 45 Mead
Davis Wm., tailor, Washington (W P)

Davis Wm., mariner, 231 Shippen
Davis Wm., brushmr., 274 High, h 37 R road
Davis Wm., plasterer, 12 Swanson
Davis Wm. H., shoemr., 96 N 5th
Davis Wm. J., tobacconist, 2 Bache
Davis Wm. M., sugar refiner, 9 Sergeant
Davis W. M., carp., 10th ab Christian
Davis W. M., machinist, Nectarine, & R road ab Wood
Davis Wm. P., lawyer, 14 Montgomery
Davis Z. A., mer., 270 Lombard
Davison Edw., awnmr., 27 S Front, h 45 Apple
Davison Robert, 59 Plum
Davison Wm., dry goods, 548 N 2d, h 354 N 3d
Davison William, carpenter 92 S 12th.
Davison Wm., carman, Apple & Jefferson (K)
Davisson Charles, acct., Catharine bel 6th
Davisson John, glassblr., Vienna ab Queen (K)
Davisson Robt., rear Barker E of Sch 4th
Davy John, instrumentmr., Rugan n Callowhill
Dawes J. C., druggist, N W 11th & Locust
DAWSON & AERTSEN, mers., 81 S Front
Dawson Charles, barber, Mers. Hotel, N 4th, h 188 Shippen
Dawson Catharine, rear 12 Shriver's ct
Dawson Elizabeth, Logan's ct (K)
Dawson George W., shoemr., 306 St John
Dawson Hannah, 240 High.
Dawson James, Broad & Paper al.
Dawson James, oyster house, 296 High
Dawson Job, dry goods, 208 S 2d
Dawson Josiah, 318 Mulberry
Dawson M. L., brewer, 10th & Filbert, h Spruce ab Broad
DAWSON M. L. & CO., brewers, N W 10th & Filbert
Dawson Robert B., furniture, 495 High
Dawson Wm., carp., 175 Cherry
Day Aaron R., 68 N 3rd
Day Adin, shop, 7th bel Cedar
Day Benj. F., ship carp., 3 Beck
Day Charles, tailor and clothier, 285 N 2d
Day Charles H., cordw., 178 G T road
Day Geo., tailor, Julianna, ab Callowhill
Day Isaac, coachman, 101 Burd's ct
Day Jacob H., carpenter, rear 5 Bread
Day James, capt., 3 Poplar
Day Jane Mrs., 282 S 2d
Day Joseph, shipcarpenter, 9 Queen (S)
Day Josiah, painter, Milton bel 11th
Day & Larer, bakers, 28 Carlton
Day Michael, gent., Marlborough ab Queen.(K)
Day Peter, lab., rear Olive bel Broad
Day Richard, gunsmith, 68 Maiden.
Day Robert, lab. 3 Farmer's row
Day Samuel, constable, 17 N 13th.
DAY S. M., comb & variety store, 10 N 4th
Day William, cordw., Brown bel Vienna. (K)
Dayman John, weaver, Jefferson ab 2d (K)
Days Elisha, grate mr. 57 Pratt
Dayton Joseph, segarmr., Bond ct (N L)
DEACON & BROGNARD. com. mers., 16 N Front
Deacon Edmund, publisher, 129 Chestnut, h 6th ab Green

Deacon Eph. T., hatter, 24 N 4th, h 59 Tammany
Deacon Israel K., conveyr., 5 Shackamaxon (K)
Deacon James, cabinetmaker, 331 S 4th.
Deacon John, porter, Diamond and Juniper
Deacon Joshua E., mer., 16 N Front
Deacon Mary, 237 Marshall
Deacon Robert, morocco manuf. rear 29 Coates
Deacon Mary, dressmr., Clinton ab Parrish
Deal Alexander, grocer, F road ab Phœnix, (K)
Deal Abraham, watchman, rear 97 O Y road
Deal Benj., lab., 11th bel Pine
Deal, Burt & Milligan, dry goods, S W 6th & High
Deal Catharine, shop, Marlboro' ab Franklin
Deal Charles, teller Manuf. & Mechanic's bank, h 22 Palmyra sq
Deal Charles, 520 N 5th
Deal Chas. C., carp., Penn bel Shackamaxon
Deal Christian, brass fitter, rear 529 N 4th.
Deal Daniel, mer., S W 6th & High, h 253 Pine
Deal Daniel, butcher, Garden bel Buttonwood
Deal David, cordwainer, 37 O Y road
Deal Elizabeth, Sch. 8th ab Sassafras
Deal Elizabeth, Queen and Hanover (K)
Deal Francis, vict., Trinity pl
Deal Jacob, butcher, G T road ab Camac (K)
Deal Jacob, potter, 4th n Creek
Deal Jane, milliner, Queen ab Shackamaxon
Deal John, victualler, Ann n R road (F V)
Deal John, gent., 19 S Penn sq
Deal John C., stone cutter, rear 97 O Y road
Deal John F., baker, 184 Sassafras
Deal John F., morocco fin., Elizabeth ab Poplar
Deal Joseph, oyster, Stout's al
Deal Michael, turner, 342 St John (K)
Deal Michael, carter, Rye ab Wharton
Deal Peter, carp., F road ab Franklin
Deal Reuben, cordw., 239 Wood
Deal Saml., baker, 14 Richard
Deal William, brass founder, Hope bel Phœnix
Deal W. H. C., dry goods, 3 S N 2d
Deal W. V., tailor, Brown bel 7th
Dealy James, shoe findings & tools, 292 S 4th
Deamer C., widow, China ab Front
Deamer Harriet, gentw., G T road n Master, (K)
Deamer Henry, saddler, 543 High, h 11 Howard
Deamer Joseph, mariner, 2d bel Marion
Dean Benj., weaver, Jackson bel Palmer (K)
Dean Charles, blacksmith, 82 Penn, h 21 Vernon
Dean James, grocer, 184 Vine
Dean Josh. A., carp., Buttonwood ab 13th
Dean Louisa, 2 Swatmore pl
Dean Thomas, weaver, 9th and Marriott
Dean Thomas, weaver, Fitler ab 2d (K)
Dean Wm., lab., rear Olive ab 12th
Dean Wm. F., att'y & coun., N W 3d & Chestnut, h 135 N 10th
Deaner Christian, carter, Hanover bel Duke (K)
Deans Euphemia, S E 8th and Wood
Deane Henry, stone cutter, Vienna ab Franklin
De Angeli J., tinsmith, 344 High, h 13th c. Budden's al
Deany Charles, carter, Marriott's la ab 4th
Deany J. A., tailor, 124 Walnut, h Marriott ab 4th

Dearie James, lab., 199 S Front
Dearie J. & J., manuf., Callowhill n Sch. (F M)
Dearie Sophia, white washer, 70 Union
De Armond Rich. C., manuf., 11th bel Parrish
Dearry James, carp., Quince
Deas James H., warm air furnaces, &c., 79 N 6th, h 8th and Coates
Deats Charles, clerk, 57 Coates
Deaves Edmond, painter, rear 55 Plum
Deaves Margaret, Centre bel 13th
Deaves, Susan, 5 Parker
De Barry John, mer. 16 N 2d, h 168 Spruce
De Bender Joseph, plasterer, Wood ab 8th
De Beust Chas. W., chairmaker, N W 10th and Walnut, h Perry bel Pine
De Beust & England, cabinetmrs., N W 10th & Walnut
De Beust Hannah, 6 S 12th.
De Beust Wm. R., blacksm., Filbert n Sch 7th
De Bitty John, waiter, 221 Lombard
De Boos James, dry goods, 10th ab Coates
Debow Mary, shop, 2d ab Edward (K)
Debozear Lewis, brass & bell founder, 9 Bread
De Bruin Morris J., dealer, 185 Cedar
Decan Peter A., ship master, 356 S 4th
De Castro Philip, gardener, 2 Lyndall's al
Decatur John, coach trimmer, Sch. 7th n Vine.
Decker Christopher, skin dresser, 596 N 3d
Decker P. I. Mrs., 175 Pine
Decker Solomon, clothes, 188 Shippen
Deckert Sarah, sempstress, 16 Little Pine
DECOT ROBT., clothing, 77 Chestnut, h Wallace bel 10th
De Coursey Jacob, cordwainer, 344 N 2nd.
De Coursey, Lafourcade & Co., mers., 77 High.
De Coursey Sam. W., mer., 77 High, h 43 Mulberry
Dedeker Catharine, Marlborough and Bedford (K)
Dedeker Cath., 200 Otter ab School (K)
Dedeker Valentine, bricklayer, Marlboro' and Bedford (K)
Deemer John, morocco dr., Alder ab Poplar
Deery Charles, shop, 62 Fitzwater
De Eslemauville F. H. acct. rear 20 Maria
Deeth Sylvester G., bookseller, 37 Arcade
Deever Saml., lab., Spruce n Sch Front
Deforest Samuel, capt., 118 Swanson
Deforia John, shoemr., 1 S 9th
Defrate Francis, cordw., rear 23 Castle
Defreitas John H., hair dress., S E Shippen and 2nd
egan John, cedar cooper, 218 S 2d, h P road n Carpenter
Degan Neal, lab., Cooper n Sch 3d
Degan Patrick, lab., Franklin bel Parrish
Deginther Michael, cabinet maker, 3 Assembly Buildings, h 82 S 11th
Degnan John, weaver, G T road ab Thompson
Degroose Ann, widow, Crawford's ct
Degroot Albert, grocer, Pine and Carbon
De Groot James, coach painter, 6 Lebanon.
De Haan Lewis, clothing 235 Cedar
Dehart John F., basketmr., 450 N 3rd.

11

D'Hauterive Le Baron Maurice, French Consul, 91 Locust
Dehaven Abram R., clerk, Coates ab 9th
Dehaven Ch. E., mer., 211 High, h 155 N 11th
Dehaven David, morocco manf., 424 Coates
Dehaven Eliza, 51 Apple
Dehaven George, vict., Montgomery & Front.
Dehaven Holstein, carp., 155 N 11th n Vine.
Dehaven H., carp., S Garden ab 12th
Dehaven H., teller Phila. Bank, h 31 O Y road
Dehaven Jacob, vict., Oxford ab F road
Dehaven Job I. Z., clerk, 62 Zane
Dehaven John W., cigarmr., Bush Hill
Dehaven J. R., carp., 11 School ab Rose (K)
Dehaven William, victualler, Vine bel Sch 6th
Dehaven Wm., cordw., Orchard bel Jackson
Dehuff Henry, engineer, Melon bel Broad
Deighan John, lab., Sch Front and Spruce
Deighton Thos., pianomr., Coates (Fairmount)
Deimling John C., 32 O Y road.
Deininger John H., cordw., 28 Beach (K)
Deiser John, lampmr., 1 Wall st
Deitz Geo., vict., 14 Magnolia
Deitz Geo., translator, Bickham n Sch 7th
Deitz Geo., turner, 9 Dillwyn
Deitz Henry, carp., 13 Harmony ct
Deitz Peter, comb mr. Rose al n Green
Deitz Peter, jr. oak cooper, 33 Union
Deitz Wm. cordw. Cox bel 2d
Deitz Wm., cordw., 16 Apple
Deklyne Theodore, pump & blockmaker, 164 N Water h 414 N Front.
Deklyne William, block and pumpmr., 242 N Water
Delacova Bictor, gent., 17 Scheetz st
Delacroix C. J., prof. of languages, 31 Filbert
Delagraw Joseph, tobacconist, 162 S 6th
Delamater John, bookbr., 112 N Juniper
Delancey Michael, cordw., Callowhill n Sch. William.
DELAND & GRANT, com. mers. 40 S whfs
Deland Thorndike, com. mer. 40 S wharves, h Walnut ab Broad
Delaney Jas., lab., rear Wood ab Broad
Delaney John, miller, Ulrich st
Delaney Patrick, tailor, 5 Diamond
Delanger Ann, washer, 20 Elizabeth
Delano James S., turner, 19 Nectarine.
Delano W., clerk, 139 Wood
Delany Ann, rear 2d ab Phoenix
Delany Charles, carp., F road ab Allen
Delany Daniel, 118 S Front
Delany Geo., bootmr., Pleasant ab 12th
Delany Henry, lampmr., 4 Hyde's ct
Delany H., blacksm., Penn ab Marsh, h Queen ab Shackamaxon
Delany James M., b h, 32 Julianna
Delany John, shop, Wharton ab 4th
Delany John, miller, 3d bel Franklin (K)
Delany Matt., lab., rear 2d ab Phoenix (K)
Delany Patrick, labourer, Sch 8th n Sassafras
Delany Patrick, lab., 576 S Front
Delany William, gilder, 324 S 6th.
Delany Wm., constable, 18 Barron
Delas T. P. printer, 74 Almond

Delasalle Lewis, distiller, 150 S 10th
Delavan Isaac, lab., 68 Swanson
Delavan Jas. L., chairmr., 150 N Front, h 3 Beaver
Delavan John, brushmr., 248 N 4th
Delavan Joseph, cordw., rear 116 German
Delavan J. W. S., druggist, Wood and 6th
Delight Saml, carp., Landall's ct
Delissa Samuel, shirt manuf., 78 N 3d
DELLEKER W. J., ship broker, 147 Chestnut, h 222 S 4th
Dellow Geo., hatter, 8 Dillwyn
Delmas Charles, carpenter, 29 Wood
Delp Joseph R., 2 Drinker's al
Delp Josiah M., carp., Hartshorne's ct
Delzell David, bootmr., 5 Linden
Demby Wm., lab., Orange ab Lemon
Demer Sol., bootmr., Front & Almond
Demery Wm., R road bel Buttonwood
Deminel Peter, tav., N W Brown & Charlotte
Demmè C. R. Rev., D. D., 41 N 4th.
Demmons Catharine, gentw., Marlboro' n F road
Demoyer Mary, 4 Stamper's al
Dempsey Edward, lab., Charlotte ab Thompson (K)
Dempsey James, cooper, 130 S Water
Dempsey Jeremiah, sawyer, 2 Sweed's ct
Dempsey John, brewer, 144 F road
Dempsey John, cordw., 66 Lombard, h Marriott ab 6th.
Dempsey Lydia, b h, S E 12th and Filbert
Dempsey Matthew, lab., Fothergill
Dempsey Stephen, vict., Charlotte bel Thompson (K)
Dempster Henry, Sch 8th ab Sassafras
Denan John P., caulker, 52 Mead
Denanhower Abram, paper stainer, 58 S 13th
Denby Edward, waiter, 4 Juniper al.
Denby James, spinner, M'Duffie
Denby John, weaver, Hone ab Phoenix (K)
Denby Mary, washer, M'Closkey's ct
Denckla A. H., mer, 34 Commerce, h Mulberry and Juniper
Denckla Mrs., wid. of A. H., Mulberry & Juniper
Denckla & Renken, cure N W 11th & High

Dennis Robert, engineer, R road opp Francis
Dennis Samuel, blacksm., Cedar ab 12th
Dennis Sarah, widow, Noble bel 9th
Dennis Stephen, porter, 5 Biddle's al
Dennis Stephen, porter, Currant al
Dennis Susan, 68 S 12th
Dennis Theodore H., shoemr., 56 Nectarine
Dennis Wash., huckster, Sweed's ct
Dennis Wm. H., oil factor, Christian bel 7th, h 27 Christian
Dennis W. P., waterman, 103 Swanson
Dennison Andrew, groc., N W 10th and Sassafras
Dennison Ruth Ann, R road ab Buttonwood
Dennisson Mason K. grocer, N E 6th and Buttonwood
Denny Elizabeth, 186 S 13th
Denny James, oysterman, Concord ab 2d
Denny James, tailor, Shippen ab 13th
Denny John, seaman, 6 Carpenter (S)
Denny John, lab., Oxford ab Front (K)
Denny Joseph, carter, Rose al
Denny Mary, Hanover ab West (K)
Denny Robt. harn. & trunkmaker, N W 5th & Prune
Dentler Lewis, driver, Barker n Sch 7th
Denton Francis, porter, Milton ab 10th
Denton Henry, lampmr., Sch 8th ab Race
Denworth Peter, tavern, Bread and Eetter la
Deny John, weaver, George n Beach (Sch)
Depagnier Jane, 129 New
Depau Francis A., gent., 30 Girard.
Depee Nathaniel W., tailor, 334 Cedar.
Deperven Catharine, widow, 38 Nectarine
Depoe David, Brown ab 10th
Depp Chas., baker, Wharton ab 4th
Deppel Henry, bootmr., 87 S 3d, h rear 115 Dillwyn
Deppell Henry, bootmr., 398 N 2d
De Putron John, bootmr. 426 S 2d
Deputy John, waiter, 221 Lombard
Deputy Sylvester J., shop, S W Swanson and Mead
Dupuy Jonathan V., dry goods, 25 N 8th.
Depuy J. Stewart, carpets, 353 N 2nd.
Derbyshire A. J., mer., 65 N Water, h 39 New.

Derr Sarah, Ogden bel 10th

Derr Wm., combmr., Brown & St John

Derrick Wm., ship joiner, Mead ab whf, h 544 S Front

Derrickson Daniel, Carleton ab Sch 8th

Derrickson Rebecca L., tailoress, rear 471 N 3d

Derrickson Samuel, 15 Dugan

Derrickson Samuel B., mer., 93 High, room S E 7th and Chestnut

Derrickson T. W. millwt. 39 Perry

Derrickson, William, mariner, 2d bel Marion

Derringer Henry, rifle manuf., Tamarind ab Green, h 370 N Front.

Derringer T. T., gunsmith, Green ab Front

De Sanno Frederick, jr., machinist, 12th ab Parrish

De Sanno Sarah, wid., engineer, 527 Coates

Desabaye Sarah, shop, 7 James st

DESAUQUE CHARLES L., wine mer., 289 High, h 139 N 9th

Desbordes John, silk cord, tassels, &c., 88 Sassafras.

Deschamps Francis, watchmaker, F road above Maiden

Desebey Lewis, painter, 266 N 5th

Desgranges S. A., mer., 165 High, h 140 S 9th.

Desher Abraham, drayman, Shackamaxon above Queen

Desher Abraham, morocco fin., Lee's ct (N L)

Desher Samuel, combmr., St John n Creek

Desher Wm., combmr., rear Schleisman's al

DESILVER & BROWN, mers., 43½ S Front

Desilver Chas., mer., 253 High, h N Penn sq

Desilver Frank, mer., 43½ S Front, h Chestnut W Sch 6th

DESILVER WILSON R., bookseller, 18 S 4th, h 50 S 4th.

Desilver Thos. Sr., Chestnut n Sch 6th

Desmond Daniel J., attorney at law, 99 Spruce st., Consul General of Pontifical States Vice Consul of Austria, Sardinia, Portugal, and Tuscany

Desmond Jas. T. mer. 210 Walnut, h 99 Spruce

Desmond John, lab., rear 112 N 8th

Dessalet Alexander, cordw., Front ab Green, h rear 21 Lily al

Dessalet John, grocer, Hanover and West (K)

Dessau Jacob H. mer. 96 N 3d, h 18 Chatham

Destenburg Henry, sug. refin., 18 Lily al

Destouet, Brothers, com. mers, 11 Church al

Destouet J. E., mer., 11 Church alley

Destouet S., mer., 11 Church al., h 385 Walnut

Detre Christian H., carp., Sch 7th n Vine.

Detterer Edward, tinman, 13 Tammany ct

Detterer Mary, 80 Sassafras

Detterer Samuel M., hardware, 126 N 2d

Detterline Henry, weaver, Hancock ab Norris (K)

Detterline Hen. weaver, Harriet bel P road (K)

Detwiler Abraham, segarmr., Beach ab Maiden (K)

Detwiler Benjamin, miller, Coates n F M.

Detwiler Henry, blacksm., 5 Railroad ct

Devault Philip, drayman, 6th ab Poplar

Develin Bernard, lab., Marlborough bel Duke.

Develin Catharine, wid., Thompson ab G T road

Develin Edwd., weaver, Cadwalader bel Master

Develin Hugh, weaver, Cadwalader ab Franklin

Develin Jas., moulder, Carlton ab Sch 7th

Develin Patrick, Small

Develin Patrick, clerk, 13 Mercer

Develin Peter, weaver, Cadwalader bel Master

Develin Peter, weaver, Rose & Shippen la

Develin Timothy, coachman, Currant al.

Deveney John, omnibus, Spruce ab Sch 7th

Devenney & McBride, hatters, 432 N 2d

Devenny Mahaliah, tavern, Front and Montgomery (K)

Devenny Patrick, lab. Sch 2d bel Lombard

Devenny Wm. lab. 30 M'Duffie

Dever Edward, tailor, 189 S 2d

Dever James, lab., M'Duffie ab Sch 3d

Dever Michael, shop, 264 Cedar.

Devereux Geo. F., engraver, S E 6th & Walnut, h N W Sch 6th & Mulberry

Devereux Geo. T., artist, Sch 5th & Mulberry

Devereux James, mer., 86 S whfs. h 89 Pine

Devereux John, mer., 79 S wharves, h 135 S 3d

Devereux John, tailor, 7 Logan

Devereux John James, atty. at law, & commissioner for Maine & Massachusetts, office 62 S 6th.

Devereux Michael, glass blower, Vienna ab Franklin (K)

Devereux Peter, maltster, 9th bel Poplar

Devine Edward, trimmings, 644 N 2d (K)

Devine Henry, lab., Spruce n Sch Front

Devine Hugh, lab., Middle al

Devine Hugh, painter, Juniper al

Devine James, tailor, Morris bel Catharine

Devine James, grocer, 125 S 8th

Devine John, bootmr. N W Shippen and George

Devine John, grocer, S W Sch. 8th and High, h Jones ab Sch 8th.

Devine Marg., dressm., 17 Fitzwater

DEVINE MARK, flour store, N E 2d & Green

Devine M. & B., grocers, S E 2d & Green

Devine Patrick, tavern, N E 4th and Stanley

Devine Patrick, shoemr. 323 S 4th

Devine Philip, drayman, 11th & Milton

Devine Quinton, tailor, 324 S 3d

Devine Rosanna, Jones n Sch 8th

Devine Thos., shop, 64 Vine

Devinger Jas., lab., Carpenter ab 12th

Devinney Arthur, blacksm., Jones W of Sch 5th

Devinney Asa, cordw., Roney's ct (K)

Devinney Hugh, shop, Parker & Clymer

Devinney Sarah, 12 Cresson's al

Devitt Charles, dry goods, 332 S 2d

Devitt Daniel D. Rev., Murray ab Sch 3d

Devitt John, 397 S 2d

Devitt Terence, baker, Fitzwater bel 8th

Devitt Wm. carp. Shepherd's ct

Devlin Andrew, lab. Cedar ab 12th

Devlin Archibald, weaver, 2d above Master (K)

Devlin Bernard, shoemr., 10th ab Buttonwood

Devlin Bernard, morocco dresser, Jefferson S. G T road

Devlin Edward, weaver, Jefferson ab Washington, (K)

Devlin Edwd., weaver, Cadwalader ab Phoenix (K)
Devlin Edward, tailor, 13th ab Catharine
Devlin Francis, weaver, Crown ab Franklin
Devlin Hugh, reed mr., Master ab Cadwalader (K)
Devlin Hugh, weaver, Crown bel Duke (K)
Devlin James, weaver, Harmony ct (K)
Devlin James, manuf. rear 4th bel Jefferson
Devlin John, blacksmith, Lombard n Sch 5th
Devlin John, weaver, Perry bel Phoenix
Devlin John, lab. Hancock & Master
Devlin John, weaver, Mariner ab 13th
Devlin John, lab., 300 S 7th
Devlin Marg., rear 72 Catharine
Devlin Michael, lab., Lombard's ct
Devlin Michael, weaver, Cadwalader ab Jefferson (K)
Devlin Patrick, weaver, Baker's ct
Devlin Patrick, salesman, 5 Watman's ct
Devlin Peter, Cadwalader ab Jefferson
Devlin Peter, weaver, Cadwalader ab. Phœnix (K)
Devlin Thomas, weaver, Crown bel Duke (K)
DEVOE & BURR, refectory, S. W. 6th and Haines
Devoe Isaac H., wine mer., 7 S 5th, h 16 Perry
Devoe James, captain, S W 6th and Haines, h S W 8th and Noble
Devoo Ann, Dunton bel Otter (K)
Devoux J., eating house, 169 Chestnut, h 69 Wood.
Dewald Frederick, tavern, 207 St John
Dewald S. C., mer., 62 N 3d, h 289 N 7th
Dewald Wm., waterman, Nelson's ct

Dialogue John, china ware, 292 N 2d, h Noble
Diamond Alexander, distiller, 205 Cedar
Diamond Edward, weaver, M'Mackin's ct
Diamond Francis, waiter, 6 Rose alley (C)
Diamond John, distiller, 172 Cedar
Diamond John, weaver, Jefferson ab 2d
Diamond Mrs. widow of John, gent., 56 Pine
Dick Alexander, machinist, 8 Hamilton pl
Dick Charles, tailor, 31 M road
Dick D. D., japanner, Wheeler's ct, h 55 Carpenter
Dick Francis B., dentist, 205 Spruce
Dick Frederick, Janitor at University, h S 11th and Locust.
Dick John, weaver, Sch. bank ab Lombard
Dick John, dealer, rear 387 N 3d
Dick John, lab., Brazier ab Broad
Dick John B., clothes dealer, 167 & h 581 S 2
Dick Louis, lampmr., 128 Dillwyn
Dick Matthias, cabman, 51 Apple
Dick Peter, gent., 4 Carpenter
Dick Peter, shoemr., Lancaster ab Reed
Dick Philip, japanner, Wheeler's ct., h 55 Carpenter
Dick S. A., dry goods, S W 11th & Locust
Dick Valentine, cordwainer, Kessler ab Coate
Dick Walter B., optician, 48 Chestnut, h 8 Mulberry
Dick William, clerk, Sch. 8th bel Locust.
Dick Wm., lab., Lombard ab 12th
Dick Wm. tailor, Carpenter ab 5th
Dickel Christian, weaver, Phœnix bel G T roa (K)
Dickel Mary, 470 N Front

Dickey R., M. D., 8 S 10th
Dickey Thomas, printer, 28 Federal
Dickheart Michael, Marion bel Corn
Dickinson & Hance, dry goods, 534 N Front
Dickinson Henry, printer, George n Sch 7th
Dickinson John, carp., 3d and Clark
Dickinson John, dry goods, 50 Wood ab 10th
Dickinson John, waterman, 4 Jones' ct
Dickinson John, seaman, 4th and Christian
Dickinson John J., tailor, 66 Brown
Dickinson John M., tailor, 28 Mintzer
Dickinson Margaret, N E 9th & Mulberry
Dickinson Martha, flour and feed, G T road & Front, h 534 N Front
Dickinson Mary, Ann ab Sch 6th
Dickinson Mary, 31 Wallace
Dickinson Morris, carp. 24 Logan
Dickinson Robert, lab., Sch 6th bel Pine
Dickinson Samuel, drayman, Duke bel Palmer (K)
Dickinson Sarah, dressmr., Spruce W Sch 5th
Dickinson Sarah N., gentw., 11 N 7th
Dickinson Thos. S., cooper, 40 Queen
Dickinson Wm. gent. 150 Christian
Dickson Benj., carter, Currant alley ab Spruce
DICKSON & CO., importers, 80 High
Dickson David, distiller, 2d and Phoenix
Dickson George, 578 N 3d.
Dickson Hannah, 72 N 9th.
Dickson Hugh, gent., Shippen n Broad
Dickson Isaac, brushmr., Rugan n Callowhill
Dickson James, weaver, Clinton ab Norris (K)
Dickson James, weaver, Nixon n F. M.
Dickson James N., merchant, 152 High, h 349 Spruce
Dickson Jas. N. & Co., dry goods, 152 High
Dickson John, lab., Sch. 7th bel Pine
Dickson John, druggist, N E 5th and Spruce
Dickson John, manuf. 572 N 3rd.
Dickson John, mer. Water & Chestnut, h 128 Pine
Dickson John, shoemr., F road & Duke
Dickson John & Co., mers., Chestnut and Water
Dickson John M., clerk, 89 Marshall
Dickson Jos., weaver, Shippen la ab Fitzwater
Dickson Jos. R., gent., Juniper n Filbert
Dickson Levi, mer., 152 High
Dickson Milford, waiter, 2 Prosperous alley
Dickson Richard, blacksmith, 10 Vaux's ct
Dickson Robert, clerk, Duke and F road
Dickson R. L., teacher, 4 Union
Dickson Samuel, gent., 424 N 5th.
Dickson Thomas, manuf. 6 Diamond
Dickson Thos. H. manuf. Broad bel Pine
Dickson Thomas J., brushmr., 493 N 4th
Dickson William, bricklayer, 13th bel Lombard
Dickson Wm. weaver, Fitler n 2d (K)
Dickson Wm., cordw., F road & Duke (K)
Dickson Wm., lab., West ab Walnut
Diedrichs Henry, machinist, 45, & h 86 Vine
Dieffenbacher Abraham, baker, 7 N Sch 7th
Diegel Martin, carpet weaver, 299 Callowhill
Diegel Martin, grocer, S E Franklin and Wood
Diehl & Co., mers. 86½ S Front
Diehl Daniel, lab., cab.mr., Charles and Willow

Diehl & Duff, com. mers., 35 N whfs.
Diehl George N., mer. 86½ S Front, h 182 S 3d
Diehl Jacob, tailor, Scott's ct
Diehl John, city commissioner, 224 Pine.
Diehl John, min. water, S W Front & Catharine
Diehl John H. mer. 86½ Front
Diehl Joseph, refectory, 234 N 3d
Diehl Thomas, mer., N E Front and Chestnut h 15 N 10th
Diehl William, mer. 27 N 5th, h 61 Pine
Diehr M. A., milliner, 10th ab Brown
Diehr Philp, silver plater, 10th ab Brown
Diely Henry, blacksmith, Maiden bel Front
Diely Philip P., blacksmith, 7 Maiden, h 561 N Front
Diemer Catharine, tavern, 418 N 4th
Diemer Geo., stone mason, Grape bel George (F V)
Diemer Jacob, lab. Palmer ab Duke
Diemer Michael, tavern, R road (F V)
Dierkes John, tailor, 6 Acorn alley
Dierkes Wm., tailor, 6 Acorn alley
Diesinger Joseph, bootmr., 93 S 5th
Diesinger Wendel, gunsmith, 7 Green
Dietrich Henry, M. D., 159 N 10th.
Dietrich Joseph, paper colourer, 27 O Y road
Dietrick John, baker, 268 R. road
Dietrick Louisa, 2 Peter's al
Dietz Charles, brushmaker, rear 337 N 3d
Dietz Joseph, artist, 118 Marshall
Dietz Michael C. carter, Wallace bel 13th
Dietzer John, tailor, 128 N 5th
Difer William, saw maker, 34 Sugar al.
Digit Daniel, tailor, 15 New Market
Diggins F. Marriott ab 5th
Dildine James, bricklayer, Stout's alley
Dildine Sarah, tailoress, 137 Green
Dilge Wm., framemr., Hummel's ct
Dilkes Jacob, cordw., 4 Abbott's ct
DILKS & BACON, lumber yard, 8th and Coates
Dilks George, carpenter, lumber yard, 8th and Coates, h 395 N 6th
Dilks Hannah, tailoress, 7 Relief
Dilks Jacob, sausage maker, 13th bel. Buttonwood
Dilks Joseph, shoemr., 7 Kirkpatrick's ct
Dilks Joseph, shoemr., 304 S 3d
Dilks Jos., fisherman, Wood ab Franklin (K)
Dilks Sukels, clerk, Freeston's pl
Dilks Wm., machinist, Carleton bel Sch. 2d
Dill Robert, lab., Bedford ab 13th
Dillahay Benj., waiter, Centre ab 12th
Dillan Danl., cordwr., Parker's pl
Dillard Geo. E., cooper, 24 Wash. Market pl
Dillard Thos., M. D., U. S. Navy, 493 Chestnut.
Diller Adam, real estate, 95 Garden, h 8th ab Green
Dillhorn, Wm., shoemr., Richard ab Sch 7th
Dillin A. C., boatmr., St. John ab George (K)
Dillin Charles, cordw., Front ab Poplar
Dillin Edward, clothing, 30 S 2d
Dillin Eli, dry goods, Green & R road
Dillin H. & M., 374 Vine
Dillin Sarah, 8 Gray's al.
Dillinger David, gent., 13 West.

Dillingham S., dentist, 192 Mulberry
DILLINGHAM W. H., atty. & coun., 385 Mulberry
Dillman Christopher, bleeder, 422 N 2nd
Dillman John, lab., rear 238 St John
Dillman Mary, 236 St John
Dillmore Andrew, lab., Prime ab Swanson
Dillmore Saml., cooper, Church & Reckless
Dillon Archibald C., cordw., St John n Globe Mill
Dillon Edward, clothes, Lisle bel Shippen
Dillon Enos, lab., Sch 4th n High
Dillon James, lab., 5th n Plum
Dillon James, lab., 4 Pleasant ct
Dillon L., clerk, 42 Shippen
Dillon Patrick, weaver, Crown ab Franklin (K)
Dillon Thos., blacksm., Christian ab 5th
Dillon Thos., morocco dress., rear 211 St John
Dillon Virginia, dressmr., 1 N Sch 7th
Dilts Sarah, rear 171 Green
DILWORTH, BRANSON, & CO., hardw., 59 High
Dilworth Charles, hardware, 8 Commerc, h 503 Chestnut
Dilworth John, turner, 10 Norris' al.
Dilworth John, weaver, Gabel's ct
Dilworth S. W., mer., 22 Pine
Dilworth Wm., mer., 59 High, h 141 Mulberry
Dimond Andrew, 317 S 6th
Dimond Andrew, jr., 317 S 6th
Dimond Francis, atty. at law, 317 S 6th
Dimond Joseph, 7 Swanson
Dimond Joseph, shoemr., 203 Cedar
Dimond J. & J., liquors, S wharves bel Cedar
Dinan James, lab., 1 John's ct
Dinan Timothy, grocer, Locust and Beach
Dine Sarah, gentw., rear 13th bel Brown
Dingee Charles, brickmr., Poplar bel Marshall
Dingee Danl., collector, Poplar ab 7th
Dingee Edmund, brickmaker, 7th ab Poplar
Dingee John, mer., Pine ab 10th
Dingee Lewis, brickmr., Poplar ab 7th
Dingee L., Cedar bel 12th
Dingee Wm., bricklayer, Poplar ab 7th
Dinglar Christopher, carter, 220 Vine.
Dingle Francis, Apple bel Master
Dingler George, plasterer, 597 N 2d
Dingler Wm., gunsmith, 3 Freed's av
Dingus Jacob, farmer, rear Charlotte ab Thompson (K)
Dinmore W. R., Washington ab 10th
Dinsman P. G., tobacconist, 471 N 4th
Dinsman Samuel K., carp., Penn ab 13th
Dinsman Thos. R., combmr., 1 Almyra sq
Dinnin David D., carp., 3 Sch av
Dinning Wm., omnibus, Bishop bel Queen (K)
D'Invilliers C., ex-broker, 11 S 3rd., h Walnut n Sch 7th
D'INVILLIERS C. & CO., ex. brokers, 11 S 3d
Dippell John, baker, 192 N 13th.

Dismant John, grocer, 116 Apple
Dison Christ., cooper, Allen ab Hanover (K)
Disston Henry, sawmr., Maiden bel Front, h 16. Poplar
Dithmar Charles, beer house, 99 Green.
Dithmar Fred'k., brewer, 520 & h 525 N 3d.
Dithmer Jacob, beer house, 453 N 3rd.
Ditmar John, upholsterer, 8th ab Mulberry
Dito Henry, grocer, Sch 8th ab Spruce
Dito Sherry, Sch 8th ab Spruce
Ditterline Charles, blacksm., Apple bel Franklin
Dittus John W., cordw., 19 New Market
Dittus Robert, comb mr., 2 Brown's ct (N L)
Ditzler F., stovemr., 27 Coates
Ditzler John, combmr., Elizabeth ab Poplar
Diver Edw., lab., Beach ab Locust
Diver John, tailor, rear Willow bel 8th
Diver John, huckster, 6th bel Little Poplar
Diver John, cordw., Sch 7th ab Chestnut
Diver Joseph, gent., 208 Mulberry.
Diver Joseph P., 185 Cherry
Divers J., tinsmith, High bet Sch 6th & 7th
Divin John, tavern, 83 S 5th.
Divin Mary, dry goods, Queen ab Shackamaxon (K)
Divine John, confect., Sch 5th and Filbert
Divine John, carter, 12 Juniper la
Divine-Mackey, manuf., M'Duffie n Sch 3rd
Divine Owen, lab., 13 Callowhill
Divine Wm., lab., Mulberry n Sch 2d
Divine Wm., wool manuf., M'Duffie st. Sch., h Spruce bel Sch 3rd
Divvers John F., 11th n Wood
Divvers John F., mer., 136 High, h 11th ab Vine
Dix Eliza, 7 Gebbard
Dix Isaac, watchmr., 104 Locust, h Washington ab 3d
Dixey Isaiah, pumpmr., Lombard n Sch. 6th
Dixcy Jacob, pumpmr., Mary (Sch)
Dixey Charles, carp., 439 N 5th
Dixey Chas, lab., Esher's av
Dixey Francis, tailor, 255 Sassafras
Dixey Jonathan, carp., Walnut (W P)
Dixey Mary, widow, Fitzwater ab 7th
Dixon Caleb J., house & sign painter, 46 N 8th
Dixon F. E., mer., 45 N whfs
Dixon H., brushmr., 124 N 2d
Dixon Isaac, clock & watchmr., 150 Cedar, h Washington bel 4th
Dixon James & Sons, agency, 2 Ranstead's pl.
Dixon John, b. h., 9 Morgan
Dixon John, cooper, 9th ab Parrish
Dixon Wm., gent., N E 6th and Spruce
Doak John, grocer, 614 S 2d
Doake David, blacksmith, Shippen bel 13th
Doan Crawford, currier, 281 N 2d, h 120 rear Dillwyn
Doan David, carp., Carpenter ab 6th
Doan George W., carpenter, 3 Union

Dobbins Elizabeth, Juniper ab Locust.
Dobbins H., tobacconist, 269 N 2d
Dobbins John, tailor, G T road & Jefferson (K)
Dobbins John, tobacconist, 231 S 2d
Dobbins Zebedee, carp., 15 Ogden h Poplar ab 10th
Dobbyn William A., gent., 193 Spruce
Dobelbower Elizabeth, wid. of John H., West n Hanover
Dobelbower John C., printer, Redwood (S)
Dobelbower Lewis, printer, 53 Perry
Dobelbower Lewis H. Jr., agent, 6 Concord
Dobleman J. C., fringe mr., 86 N 2nd and 144 N 3d
Dobler Jacob C., 11 Dean
Dobly Fred., susp. weav., Elm bel Franklin(K)
Dobson James, painter, Poplar ab 10th
Dobson Jonathan, cordw., rear brook bel Brown
Dobson Judah, gent., 475 Chestnut
Dobson Rich., blacksm., William and Benton(K)
Dobson Samuel, millw., 54 Laurel (N L)
Dobson Wm., ship carp., Rye ab Reed
Dock Jacob, 276 High, h 2 S Penn sq
Dockendorff Solomon, capt., 54 Mead al
Dodd Ann, tailoress, Parrish ab 13th
Dodd George, carriages, 34 & 50 Dock
Dodd Richard, grave digger, 527 High
Dodd S. H., cab. mr., 342 S 2nd
Dodd Wm., omnibus driv., R road ab Girard av
Dodge Danl. Rev., 462 N 4th
Dodge Henry S., ladies' shoemr., 8 M road
Dodge Nathan, carver, S E 5th & Walnut, h 240 Filbert
Dodge Samuel, glovemr., Schleisman's al
Dodson Richard W., engraver, 27 Minor, h 234 N 4th
Dodson R. B., atty., 40 S 6th, h 423 N 6th
Doerr Chas., grocer, Poplar and New Market
Doerr David, baker, 21 Lily al
Doerr Rosina, baker, 60 Union
Doessen Wm., lab., Brown ab Cherry (K)
Doflein Philip, chaser, 84 N 5th
Dohan Daniel, temperance grocer, N W 7th & Noble
Doherty Mary, dry goods, 540 High
Doherty William, mer. Chestnut and Front, h 65 N 11th
Doherty Wm., painter& glazier, 4 Sharpless' ct
Dohnert George W., wireworker, 104 N 6th, h Centre bel Parrish
Dohnert John H., county treas., & marb. paper manuf., Green ab Franklin and 21 St. James
Dohnert Maria C., shop, 6 Branch
DOHNERT WILLIAM, White Bear, c 5th & Sassafras
Dolan Jas., coal dealer, Ashton bel Walnut
Dolbow John, mariner, Perkenpine's ct
Dolby Abraham, tavern, 361 High
Dolby Harriet, Allen ab Shackamaxon (K)
Dolby John, acct., 394 Coates
Dolby Samuel, sea capt., 15 Powell
Dolda Christian, carpet weaver, 163 Coates
Dole Zacheus, tailor, 8 Wilson
Dolfes Henry, ropemr., Clinton ab Norris (K)
Doll Frederick, skin dresser, 385 N 3d

Doll George, turner & toy store, 106 N 2d
Doll George & John, toys & variety store, 106 N 2d
Doll John, toys, 106 N 2d, h 5 Harrison's ct
Dolby John, jr., clerk, 396 Coates
Dollard Richard, wigmr & hair cut. 177 Chestnut
Dollenburg Derrick H., shop, 5th & Jefferson(K)
Dolman John M., gent., Sch. 3rd & Mulberry.
Dolphin Geo. F., bonnet manuf., 273 S 2d
Dolphin Rebecca, Biddle's al
Doltan John, weaver, Hope ab Master
Dolton John, waiter, Pearl ab 12th
Doman J. M., carpenter, 133 Christian.
Doman Robt. K., carp., 133 Christian
Doman Thos., currier, Charlotte bel Franklin
Dominguezo Francis, waiter, 134 Locust
Dominique Charles, cabinet maker, S E Logan & Green
Domsler George, saddler, Domsler's ct (K)
Domsler Sarah, 195 G T road
Donaghoe Bernard, weaver, rear G T road bel Master
Donaghoe John, weaver, Jefferson bel Cadwalader
Donaghue James, weaver, Milton ab 11th
Donaghy James, coal agt., Spruce ab Sch 4th
Donaghy John, lab., Lombard ab Sch 2d
Donaghy Michael, lab., rear Fitler bel Harrison (K)
Donaghy Matthias, lab., Sch 4th and Locust
Donaghy Wm., lab., Sch 4th ab Spruce
Donahan Mich., lab., Carpenter ab 8th
Donahue Ann, Carpenter ab 8th
Donahue Bernard, dry goods, 28 N 13th
Donahue Daniel, lab., 5 Willow ct
Donahue Edw., variety, 191 Cedar
Donahue George, lab., 6 Lloyd's ct
Donahue James, manf., Carlton ab Sch 8th
Donahue James, fruit dealer, Cadwalader bel Master
Donahue James, stables, 6 O Y road
Donahue James, weav, Baker's ct (K)
Donahue James, stone cut., Sch 3d bel Chestnut
Donahue Jane, haird resser, and fancy store, 110 S 4th
Donahue John, cordw., Allen ab F road (K)
Donahue John, lab., Crans' ct
Donahue John, grocer, G T road bel Master
Donahue John S., cordw., 2d ab Laurel (K)
Donahue Michael, lab., Fitler n 2d (K)
Donahue Patrick, rear G T road bel Master (K)
Donahue Patrick, weaver, Pink ab Master
Donahue Patrick, dealer, G T road ab Master
Donahue Patrick, blacksm., Vine n Sch 8th
Donahue Philip, cooper, Carlton ab Sch 3d
Donahue R., atty. and coun., 60 S 6th
Donahue Thomas, lab., Division (F V)
Donahue Thomas, weaver, Cadwalader bel Master
Donahue Wm., 4th bel Carpenter
Donald David, cooper, 341 & 394 High
Donald John, painter, Morris bel Catharine
Donald Mary, Broad ab Spruce
Donalds Mary, dress mr., 84 N 5th
Donaldson & Bros., mast yard, 61 Swanson

Donaldson Jacob B., mast yard, 1st whf bel Almond, (S) and Penn ab Maiden (K)
Donaldson Eliza A., 193 Pine
Donaldson Isaac, porter, 160 S 11th
Donaldson Isaac, hatter, 11 Quarry
Donaldson Jacob, mason, 16 Ogden
Donaldson Jacob P., spar maker, Penn ab Maiden (K)
Donaldson John, agent, Lombard ab 12th
Donaldson John, Hope ab Phoenix (K)
Donaldson John, gent., Sch 8th & Spruce
Donaldson Lydia, widow, 163 Christian
Donaldson Mary, Penn ab Maiden (K)
Donaldson Mary, wid. of Wm. T., 25 German
Donaldson Sarah R., gentw., 9th ab Washington
Donaldson Thos., 9 S Sch 7th
Donaldson Joseph, hatter, 369 Callowhill
Donath James A., att'y & coun., 8 S 7th, h Broad ab Pine
Donath Mrs., 111 Spruce.
Donavan Cornelius, lab., 3 Grape ct
Donavan Daniel, lab., 1 Grape ct
Donavan Dennis, lab., ct ab William (F M)
Donavan Dennis, lab., 17 Clymer
Donavan John, boot store, German & 5th
Donavan Mary, 6 Franklin pl
Donavan Richard, weaver, rear 211 St John
Donavan Timothy, dealer, rear 125 Mulberry
Donegan James, sizer, G T road bel Phœnix
Donegan John, weaver, 422 N 4th (K)
Donegan J., weaver, 4th bel Master
Donehower Wm. H. sash mr., 388 High, h Centre n 13th
Donelan Edw., lab., Sch 2d n Filbert
Donelson Thos. J., 18½ Walnut, h 13 Sch 7th
Donlan Jas., lab., Barker E Sch 4th
Donlan Pat., lab., 3 Beaver's ct
Donlan Thos., perfumer, 12 Cresson's al.
Donley James, coal dealer, 14 Rittenhouse
Donley Joseph P., seaman, Prime ab 3 road
Donnagha E., nurse, 1 N 12th
Donnagha Thos. E., cabmr., Sch 8th bel Cherry
Donnahue Charles, blacksmith, 7th n Callowhill
Donnahue Patrick, carpet weav., Philip ab Jef-

Donnell Wm., carter, 1 Griswell's al
Donnell Wm. O., tailor, Callowhill ab Willin (Sch)
Donnelly & Boyle, tailors, 63 S 5th
Donnelly Catharine, 280 Cedar
Donnelly Chas., weaver, Cadwalader ab Mast.
Donnelly Charles, silversm., 25 John
Donnelly Daniel, hack, 10 Laurel ct
Donnelly Daniel, weaver, Shippen n Broad
Donnelly David, lab., Mariner st
Donnelly Edward, weaver, G T road bel Jeffe: son (K)
Donnelly Eliza, N E 4th & Tammany
Donnelly Francis, lab. Wood ab Franklin
Donnelly Frederick, vict., 6th ab Poplar
Donnelly James, lab. Ashton n Pine
Donnelly James, combmr., 62 Apple.
Donnelly James, weaver, Murray n Sch 2d.
Donnelly James, weav. rear G T road ab Mast.
Donnelly James, draym., F road ab Master (K
Donnelly Jane, rear Charlotte ab Thompson
Donnelly John, grocer, 70 Lombard
Donnelly John, lab., Christian ab 8th
Donnelly John, matches, 20 Bank
Donnelly John, stone cutter, Budd bel Juniper
Donnelly John, weaver, Murray near Sch 3d
Donnelly John, ostler, 20 Shriver's ct
Donnelly John, match manf., Linden bel Front
Donnelly John B., blacksmith, 20 Powell
Donnelly Jos. P., pawnbroker, 280 Cedar.
Donnelly Mary, milliner, 170 S 6th
Donnelly Michael, cabman, Barker n Sch 6th
Donnelly Michael, tailor, 63 S 5th, h 6th n Pir-
Donnelly & McManus, aucts., 161 N 3d
Donnelly Nicholas, teacher, 15 Willing's al
Donnelly Patrick, cabman, 4 Fisher's ct
Donnelly Philip, weaver, Jefferson ab Cadwal: der (K)
Donnelly Robt., lab., Marriott ab 5th
Donnelly Thomas, dealer, 6 Salem al.
Donnelly Thos., cutler, Woodlands (W P)
Donnelly Thos. R., cordw., Orchard bel Rawle
Donnelly Wm., agent, rear Wood ab Broad
Donnelly Wm., lab. 6 Kelly

Doran Alice, shop, 26 Strawberry
Doran Geo., morocco dress., Bedford & Shackamaxon (K)
Doran Henrietta, band boxes, 5 Sheaff's al.
Doran Hugh, storekr, S W Sch 8th & Sassafras
Doran James, weaver, 33 W Cedar
Doran John, lab., 29 Dyott's ct
Doran Joseph M., 245 S 3rd
Doran Mary, Shippen ab 12th
Doran Mary, R road ab Ann. (F V)
Doran Michael, lab., 33 W Cedar.
Doran Owen, grocer, 254 Shippen
Doran Patrick, Reed bel Church
Doran Stephen, stone cutt., Sch 5th bel Barker
Doran Wm., nail mr., 304 S 3d
Doran Wm. B., tailor, 337 Vine
Dore Robert N., carp., 6 Sommers' ct
Doredore Bernard, chand., Washington (W P)
Dorety Thomas, coachman, Crans' ct
Dorey Henrietta, 128 S 12th
Dorff Albert, tinsm., 77 W Callowhill
Dorff Patrick, tin smith, 10 S 6th, h Sassafras ab Broad.
Dorgan D., cabinetmr., 249 N 3rd
Doriot Louis, confect., 204 E Shippen
Doris St. John O., com mer., 27 Minor
Doriss James G., carpenter, 13th bel Callowhill, h Sp Garden bel 13th
Doriss Terence, lab., Filbert n Sch 3d
Dorlan John, carp., Shackamaxon bel Bedford, K
Dorman George, porter, 6 Library
Dorman Howell, clerk, P. T. Bank, 155 Marshall
Dorman John, weaver, rear G T road ab Master
Dorn C. W., chaser, 136 Sassafras
Dorn Philip, cordw., 509 N 3d
Dornan Robert, weaver, 11 Lebanon
Dornback Henry, weaver, F road bel Phœnix
Dornblasser Benj., lab., Beach ab Poplar (K)
Dorney D. J., dancing academy, N E Callowhill & Marshall
Dorney Eve, gentw., 8 Franklin
Doron Chas., tailor, 11 Queen (K.)
Dorr Benjamin Rev. D. D., S E 13th and Mulberry.
Dorr Christian, carter, Young's al
Dorr Henry, baker, Buttonwood bel 11th
Dorrance Mary, widow of David, Spruce ab Sch 8th
Dorsch John, b h, 54 Shippen
Dorschiemer George L., baker, 25 N 7th
Dorsey Augustus, clothes, 16½ S 2d, h 22 Barker
Dorsey Benedict & Son, crockery ware, 125 N 3d
Dorsey Diana, washer., Blackberry al
Dorsey Edward G., tailor, 207 Chestnut
Dorsey Hugh, 51 Sp Garden
Dorsey Jacob, lab., rear 49 Currant al
Dorsey John, waterman, 34 Mead al
Dorsey John, bottler, 8 Kelly
Dorsey Mary, 32 N 9th.
Dorsey Mary, 112 N Front
Dorsey Monington, morocco finisher, 4th above Beaver
Dorsey Nicholas, porter, 4 Pleasant av
Dorsey Peter, marble polisher, 13 Myers' ct.

Dorsey Robert, 27 Clinton
Dorsey Stanton, mer. 125 N 3d, h 112 N Front
Dorsey Thomas, waiter, 57 Currant al
Dorsey William, mer., 125 N 3d, h 112 N Front
Dorsey Wm. C., miller, Ann & Powell
Dorson Richd. carter, Filbert n Sch 3d
Dorton John, butcher, Montgomery bel 2nd (K)
Doster Michael, jew. & spec. manf., 155 St John
Dotger Casper, Poplar ab 8th
Dothard Cath. wid. 165 Christian
Dott Jacob, lab. Mary n F road (K)
Dotterer Charles, currier, Carpenter ab 9th
Dotterer James, currier, Carpenter ab 9th
Dottrow Maria, shop, G T road ab Camac (K)
Dotts Mary, b h, 193 Green
Doud Francis, weaver. 12th ab Cedar
Doud Henry, weav. Charlotte ab Thompson (K)
Dougherty Alex., brickmr., George n Sch 2d
Dougherty Alex., ostler, 5 Marshall's ct
Dougherty Alex. E. 439 Walnut
Dougherty Andrew, mason, Bedford ab 6th
Dougherty Charles, lab. Pearl n Sch
Dougherty Charles, spinner, Quarry row (F M)
Dougherty Charles, weaver, Sch 3d bel Locust
Dougherty Cornelius, weaver, 3 W Cedar
Dougherty Daniel, omnibus, Vine and Nixon
Dougherty Daniel, carp., 16 Vine
Dougherty Daniel, lab., 17 Perry (K)
Dougherty Daniel, b h, S W 6th & St. Mary.
Dougherty Daniel, currier, rear 195 Noble
Dougherty Daniel, lab. Pearl W Sch 7th
Dougherty Dominick, weaver, Spruce ab Sch. Front
Dougherty Edw., cordw., Pine bel Sch. Willow
Dougherty Elizabeth, milliner, 2 Filbert
Dougherty Elizabeth, gentw. rear 464 N 2d
Dougherty George, ostler, rear 198 Cedar
Dougherty Geo. W. steamboat capt. George n Beach
Dougherty Henry, confect. 10 Garden
Dougherty Henry, cabman, 2 Monroe ct
Dougherty Hugh, lab. 15 Griswold al
Dougherty Hugh, waterman, rear Marriott bel 5th
Dougherty Hugh, biscuit baker, rear 464 N 2d
Dougherty Hugh, tailor, 253 S 5th.
Dougherty Hugh, cordw. Brown bel 10th
Dougherty H., Willow bel 12th
Dougherty H. tailor, 23 Mayland
Dougherty Isaac, engin. George n Beach
Dougherty James, hat dyer, 9th bel Carpenter
Dougherty James, tobacconist, 46½ Walnut
Dougherty Jas., brickmr., Sch 5th bel Lombard
Dougherty James, labourer, 226 Shippen.
Dougherty James, tobacconist, German bel 4th
Dougherty James, carpet weaver, Baker's ct
Dougherty James, carp. Wistar's ct
Dougherty Jane, 8th & Carpenter
Dougherty John, lab., 8 Scott's ct
Dougherty John, lumber mer. Beach ab Poplar (K)
Dougherty John, lab. 5 Miller's ct
Dougherty John, weaver, Milton ab 11th
Dougherty John, turner, Beach bel Palmer.

Dougherty John, tavern, G T road n 3d
Dougherty John, shoemr., Wood n Sch. 2d
Dougherty John, labourer, 4 Vaux's ct
Dougherty John, grocer, 325 High, h 12 S 8th
Dougherty John, cordw. Green's ct (N L)
Dougherty John, grocer, 186 Lombard
Dougherty John, grave digger, Carpenter ab 9th
Dougherty John, iron founder, 31 Farmer
Dougherty John A., distiller, S W 2nd & Poplar.
Dougherty Joseph, messenger, 22 Wash. Market pl
Dougherty Joseph, lumber, 62 New Market
Dougherty Lewis, bricklayer, Brown ab 4th
Dougherty & McCall, iron founders, 31 Farmer
Dougherty Mary, grocer, 189 S Front
Dougherty Mary, shop, 22 Spafford
Dougherty Mich., lab., 5th n G T road (K)
Dougherty Mich., weav. Perry ab Phoenix (K)
Dougherty Michael, lab. St Mary
Dougherty Neal, cabman, rear 5 Quarry
Dougherty Neill, grocer, 3d & Franklin (K)
Dougherty Patrick, dealer, Dorothy n Sch 4th
Dougherty Patrick, lab., Willow n Lombard.
Dougherty Patrick, tavern, S W 5th & Small
Dougherty Patrick, lab. Shippen ab 13th
Dougherty Philip, Shippen ab 7th
Dougherty Rachel, shop, Mark's la
Dougherty Robert, lab., Small bel 6th
Dougherty Robert, clothes dealer, 272 Cedar.
Dougherty Robert, steamboat captain, George n Beach
Dougherty R & J. grocers, 388 N 2d
Dougherty Susan, gentw., 105 Filbert.
Dougherty Thomas, tavern, 139 Beach (K)
Dougherty Thomas, carter, 135 N Water
Dougherty Wm. blacksm., 32 Elizabeth
Dougherty Wm. brickmr., Sch 3d bel Chestnut
Dougherty Wm. brand cutter, rear 115 N 2d
Dougherty William, tavern, 289 Vine.
Dougherty Wm., c Vine and Nixon
Dougherty Wm., coachman, 269 Spruce
Dougherty Wm., grocer, 325 High
Dougherty Wm., umbrella, 129 Marlboro' bel Franklin (K)
Dougherty Wm., carp., 7th bel Carpenter
Dougherty W. & J. grocers, 325 High
Doughten Amanda, 200 Shippen
Doughty James H. & Co. publishers, 8 Minor
Doughty James H., publisher, 8 Minor, h 10th bel Cedar
Doughty John, pickl. & preserver, 72 Fitzwater
Douglass Aaron, lab., Apple bel George
Douglass Catharine, widow of James, confec., Marlboro' ab Bedford (K)
Douglass Henry G., R road and Wood
Douglass Jacob, capt., 64 New
Douglass Jacob M. Rev., 378 Coates
Douglass James, hotel, 46 N 6th.
Douglass James, blacksmith, 13th ab Willow
Douglass John, weaver, Mariner
Douglass John, tobacconist, 128 Sassafras
Douglass John, shop, Hanover ab Franklin (K)
Douglass John, cordwainer, 33 Perry.
Douglass John, weaver, Hope ab Master (K)
Douglass John B., cooper, 5 Swanson's ct

Douglass John C., cordwainer, 121 S 11th
Douglass John I., Washington H., Swanson and Washington
Douglass John J. N., dep. proth'y, Sch 5th bel Spruce
Douglass John R. cordw. 427 Chestnut, h 33 Perry
Douglass Josiah, waterm., 2 Lancaster
Douglass Lydia, 131 S 11th
Douglass Mary, 1 Hickory ct
Douglass Orson Rev., 33 Lombard
Douglass Peter, brushmr., Callowhill n Sch 8th.
Douglass Robert, sr. hair dresser, 54 Mulberry
Douglass Robert, jr., sign painter, 54 Mulberry.
Douglass Samuel C., sailmr., 16 Federal
Douglass Sarah, b. h., 43 Zane
Douglass Sarah M., teacher, rear 49 N 7th, h 54 Mulberry
Douglass Thomas, lab. rear 5th n G T road
Douglass William, lab., 2 Leyden's ct
Douglass Wm., Rev., 243 Spruce
Douglass Wm. M. lab. Pearl ab 12th
Douglass W. E., carp. Sch Water and Lombard
Doul James, watchmr., S E 4th and Spruce
Dounton James C., grocery, S W Juniper and Cherry
Douredoure B., chandler, 209 S 2d, h 255 S Front
Douty Morris, ship carp., Franklin ab Palmer (K)
Dove John S., tobacconist, N E Front & Cedar
Dover Eliza, dressmr. Queen n Crown
Dover Francis, tailor, 304 St John
Dow John, painter, 29 N 7th, h S E Sch 5th & High
Dow P., machinist, 9 George, h 14 Powell
Dowd Henry, weaver, Charlotte ab Thompson
Dowden Susan M., 125 Callowhill
Dowden Thos J., 125 Callowhill
Dowdle Samuel, turner, Union ab Bedford (K)
Dowell Catharine, Crown ab Duke (K)
Dowell Elizabeth, 300 Cherry
Dowell George G., silversmith, 112 Chestnut, h 14 Noble
Dowell Wm. wigmr. 215 Chestnut
Dowler Elizabeth, store, N W 11th and Coates
Dowler Jacob, pottery, 9th bel Coates
Dowling Edward, bricklayer, 12 Perry
Dowling Edward, plasterer, 14 Wagner's al
Dowling John, plasterer, 16 Wagner's al
Dowling John, gent. 286 S 6th.
Dowling Joseph, combmr., Parrish ab 6th
Dowling Matthew, Clay n Sch Willow
Down George, b h., 6 Penn
Downer Chas. weigh: 6½ N whfs. h 144 Sassafras
Downer George, clerk, 101 Catharine
Downey Alex. weaver, Fitler ab 2d (K)
Downey David D., barkeeper, Sch 4th bel Barker
Downey George, baker, G T road ab Phoenix
Downey George, potter, Sch 8th n Rail Road
Downey James, lab., Jones n Sch 5th
Downey John, shop, Rose ab School
Downey John, chandler, Shippen bel Broad
Downey John, glass blower, Duke ab Cherry (K)

Downey John A., gilder, Lane's ct
Downey Patrick, grocer, Shippen & Spafford
Downey Sarah, gentw., Clark and 4th
Downey Wilson, stevedore, Poplar st
Downie Sarah, 12 Rugan st
Downie Wm., millwright, School ab Rose
Downie Wm., conf., Vine ab 12th
Downing Catharine, grocer, 3 Elizabeth
Downing C. A., dressmr., 89 Charlotte above George
Downing Daniel, shop, Shippen ab Lisle
Downing Delia, dry goods, 129 S 8th
Downing Hugh, western telegraph office
Downing James, carp., Raspberry la
Downing Jas., carpet weaver, Marlbo. bel West (K)
Downing James, blacksmith, 269 Wood
Downing Jane C. 6 Freed's av
Downing John, dyer, 4th bel Franklin
Downing John, lab. rear 405 S 4th
Downing John W., coal, 21 Chestnut, h 251 Spruce
Downing J. W., com. mer., 6 Walnut, h 284 S 5th
Downing Levi, 37 Currant al
Downing Mrs., wid., Sch 8th n Cherry
Downing Richard H., mer., Sch 7th & High
Downing Thomas, porter, rear 196 Cherry
Downing Thomas, gent., Washington bel 4th
Downs Andrew, weaver, St Andrew's ct
Downs Elias, pedlar, 105 Swanson
Downs Furman, brushmr., 31 Margaretta, h 9 Wagner's ct
Downs H., lab., 8th bel Lombard
Downs Jackson, hatter, 324 Vine
Downs John, bottler, 89 Crown.
Downs John, carpenter, 448 N 4th
Downs Margaret, botanic store, 448 N 4th
Downs Thomas, boots and shoes, 499 Mulberry
Doyle Edwd., currier, George ab Broad
Doyle Eliza, milliner, 210 Walnut
Doyle George, bricklayer, 58 A road
Doyle Hugh, mer., 35 N 3d, h 137 N 10th.
Doyle James, furniture, 124 Cedar.
Doyle James, lab., 73 N Water
Doyle John C., clerk, 9 Prune
Doyle John C., moulder, Pearl ab Sch 8th
Doyle Joshua, weaver, 11th ab Carpenter
DOYLE & McNEELY, leather mers., 35 N 3d, factory 4th and Franklin.
Doyle Michael, hatter, 301 S Front
Doyle Michael, dealer, Dutch ct
Doyle Michael, lab., 7 Dilk's ct
Doyle Michael, dealer, 100 Plum'
Doyle Morgan, music store, 126 Cedar
Doyle Peter, 273 Wood ab 13th
Doyle Peter, seaman, Front ab Reed
Doyle Peter, weaver, Otter bel William (K)
Doyle Robert, lab., 2 John's ct
oyle Thomas, acct., George ab Broad
oyle Thomas, painter, Carpenter ab 9th, h 167 Poplar
oyle William, printer, 58 Moyamensing road
oyle Wm., clerk, 14 Benton
oyle Wm. T., stone mason, Lewis ab Poplar

Doylton John, weaver, Hope ab Master
Drain Patrick, lab. Sch Front & Chestnut
Drain Samuel, roof slater, rear 512 N Front
Drais Wm., brushmr., 71 N 6th
Drais Wm. P., brushmr., 291 High
Drake Isa., engraver, 212 Noble
Drake James, machinist, Sch 2d ab Lombard
Drake John, lab. Carlton n Sch 2d
Drake John C., dry goods, 235 N 3d, h 217 Coates
Drake Jno. C. & Co., dry goods, 235 N 3d
Drake John L., shoe manuf., 68 N 3d, h 97 St John
Drake Misses, teachers, Sch 8th ab Spruce
Drake Mrs. B., dressmr., 243 Wood
Drake Samuel, cordw., Jackson (N L)
Drake Thomas, manufacturer, M'Duffie n Sch 2d, h Sch 6th & Locust
Drake Thomas J., lab., Wood ab Nixon
Drane Arch., mariner, rear Church bel Christian
Drane Wm. L., printer, 115 Lombard
Draper A. C., M. D., 91 W Callowhill
Draper Charles, lab. 16 Apple
Draper Charles, lab., Pearl bel 13th.
DRAPER & Co., bank note engravers, 60 Walnut
Draper Elias, coachman, 18 Prosperous al
DRAPER E., math. & opt. instrument mr., 25 Pear n 3rd
Draper John, waiter, 1 Elizabeth
Draper Milby, lab., Pearl ab 12th
Draper Robert, engraver, 60 Walnut, h 100 S 3d
Draper Solomon, waiter, Barley n 11th
Draper Wm. engraver, 60 Walnut, h 100 S 3d
Draper Wm., barber, 175 S 2nd, h Barley n 11th
Draper Wm., carp., Vine n Crown, h Ogden bel 10th
Drayton Daniel, waterman, Washington av bel Brown
Drayton Joseph, 42 S 5th
Drayton W. H. att'y and coun., 152 Walnut, h 13 Portico sq
Dreby C., cooper, 233 High and 244 N 2nd
Dredger Christian, baker, 381 S Front
Dreer Ferdinand J., jeweller, rear 115 Chestnut, h Sch 7th ab Spruce
DREER & HAYES, jewellers, rear 115 Chestnut
DREER HENRY A., seedsman, 97 Chestnut
Dreger John, skin dresser, 9 Young's al
Dreher Michael, cordw., G T road ab 2d
Dreisbach Henry, stonecutter, 31 Crown.
Dreke Lewis, cab. mr., 152 S 4th
Dreser Wm., lithographer, 24 Pear
Dressler Frederick B., coach lace weaver, 540 2d ab Beaver (K)
Dressler F. J., hair plaiter, 47 S 2nd
Dressler John, weaver, Cadwalader ab Franklin
Drew Ann, 54 Queen.
Drew Catharine, conf., 13th & Pearl
Drew Henry, lab., 34 Plum
Drexel A. J., broker, 34 S 3d
Drexel & Co., ex. brokers, 34 S 3d

DREXEL FRANCIS M. broker, 34 S 3rd, h 506 Chestnut n Sch 6th
Drexel F. A., broker, 34 S 3d
Dreyfous Rebecca, 120 S 7th
Drinker Sandwith, sea capt., 31 Clinton
Drinkhouse Aaron, cabman, 20 Benton
Drinkhouse Geo. tinsmith, 265 S 5th, h 35 Paul
Drinkhouse Jacob, coal dealer, 1 N 6th, and Broad bel Lombard, h 106 N Juniper
Drinkhouse Wm., tinsm, 58 Cedar, h 480 S Front
Dripps Matthew, collector, Poplar ab 13th
Drips David, oil cloth manuf., 523 Coates
Drips Joseph, weaver, 678 N 2d
Driscoll Dennis, clerk, 6 Howard av
Driver Adam, 166 Locust
Driver Joshua, carpenter, 383 Sassafras
Driver Samuel, buttonmr., Sweeny's ct
Droge John, harness mr., 77 S 11th
Droge Wm., waiter, 20 Quince
Dromon Christian, farmer, Shackamaxon n Queen (K)
Dropsie Ann, 454 N 3d.
Dropsie M. A., watchmaker, 57 N 3d
Drouin Felix, ed. Gazette Francaise, 26 S 12th
Drown Thomas P., acct., 3d and Spruce
DROWN WM. A., umbrellas, 86 High, h 139 Mulberry
Droz Hannah, watchmaker, 118 Walnut.
DRUCHER LEVY, dry goods, 5 Bank
Druding Fran., jewelry, Young's ct
Drum Conrad, pork inspector, Nectarine above 10th
Drum David vict., 8th ab Noble
Drum Eliza, wid., Cherry bet Sch 7th and Gebhard
Drum Francis, weaver, Murray n Sch 3d
Drum John, victualler, 9th ab Noble
Drum John, victualler, Brown ab 13th
Drum William, victualler, 302 N 8th.
Drumel Philip, cordw., Hinckle's ct
Drummond Ann M., 10 Watson's alley
Drummond Fanny, wid., Hanover ab Queen (K)
Drummond H. B., Mrs., b h, 176 S 3d
Drummond James, weaver, Crown ab Duke (K)
Drummond Joseph, barber, 10 Watson's al
Drummond Lewis, shoemr., 17 S 2d, h Dean's alley
Drury Patrick, cordw., Marriott bel 6th
Dryburgh A., florist, S W Sch. 4th & Sassafras.
Dryden Wm. blacksmith, 2d bel Federal

Dubois Joseph A., confect., 306 N 2d
Dubois Maria, milliner, 159 S 2nd.
Dubois & Newkirk, confect., 306 N 2d
Dubois Samuel C., bootmr., 3 Jefferson
Dubois Thomas, 247 N Front
Dubois Wm., ass. assayer U. S. M., h 133 N 13th.
Dubois Wm., lab., rear 162 Carpenter
Dubois Wm. boarding, 186 N 5th
Dubois Zacheus, comb mr., Ogden bel 10th
Duborrow Parker, lab., Carlton bel Sch 8th
DUBOSQ, CARROW & Co., jewellers, 5 Bank alley
Dubosq Francis P., jeweller, 5 Bank alley, h 162 Catharine
Dubosq George, jeweller, 3d ab Catharine
Dubosq Henry, jeweller, 2½ Bank al., h 124 Catharine
DUBOSQ H. & W., silversms., 2½ Bank al
Dubosq Mary, gentw., 19 Lombard
Dubosq Peter, jeweller, 60 Christian
Dubosq Philip L. jeweller, 337 S 3d
Dubosq Theo., jeweller, 76 N 2d.
Dubosq Wm. A., pencilmr., 2½ Bank al., h Swanson bel Christian
Du Bouchette C. Auguste, French teacher, 58½ N 6th, h 216 S 4th
Dubourg John, trimming store, High bet Sch Front & Ashton
Dubree Alex. L., brassfounder, rear 21 Castle
Dubree John, carter, 321 N 3d
DUBS SAMUEL R., M.D., 354 Chestnut
Ducachet Henry W., D. D., 8 Girard.
Ducasse Francis, tobacconist, 12th bel Parrish
Ducher Thomas, gardener, 17 Pratt
Duchesne Louis C., port. painter, 113 Chestnut
Duckett A., acct., 5 Zane
Duckett & Bowman, paper and rags, 15 Commerce
Duckett Joseph H., mer., 15 Commerce, h 423 N 6th
Duckstein Wm. coachmr. 5 Hoffman's al
Duckworth Amos, oysters, Washington av, 11th
Ducommun H., clock & watchmr. h 127 N 3d
Dudding Esther, b h, 362 N Front
Duddy Bernard, type founder, Catharine bel 9th
Duddy John, coachman, St Mary ab 6th
Duddy Michael, shop, Lombard bel 12th
Duddy Wm., varnisher, Chatham ab 8th
Dudgeon John, cordw., 138 N 13th.
Dudichum Christ'n, cabinetmr. 309 St John (K

Duffee Eugene, bootmr., 247 S 2d
DUFFEE F. H., broker, 7 S 3d, h S W 6th & Mulberry
Duffee Wm., copper pl. pr., 4th and Christian
Duffee Wm., shoemr., F M
Duffee W. J., M. D., 307 S 8th
Duffel James, shoemr., Prime ab 2d
Duffel Luke W. shoemr., 4 Somer's ct
Duffield Chas., wheelwright, Hanover ab Franklin (K)
Duffield Joseph, cordw., Hanover ab Franklin
Duffield Robert, bottler, 46 Tammany
Duffield Thomas, carpenter, Union ab Franklin (K)
Duffin Joseph, weaver, Jefferson bel G T road
Duffins John, coachman, 355 Lombard.
Duffy Arthur, tailor, High W Sch 8th
Duffy Arthur, lab., M'Closkey's ct
Duffy Charles, dry goods, 77 S 11th
Duffy Edward, tallow chandler, 44 Filbert.
Duffy Edward, lab., Sch Front ab Filbert
Duffy Edward, lab., Mulberry n Sch 8th
DUFFY FRANCIS, stables, 180 Locust
Duffy George W., hatter, 147 Chestnut, h 135 O Y road
Duffy & Hickey, painters, 72 Chestnut
Duffy Hugh, glass blower, Vienna ab Franklin (K)
Duffy Hugh B., hat dyer, 110 New Market
Duffy James, oysters, 8 N 13th
Duffy James, weaver, 13th ab Catharine
Duffy James P., math. instruments, 91 S 8th
Duffy John, printer, Reef & Wheat
Duffy John, lab., 20 Vine
Duffy John, carter, Sassafras n Sch 3d
Duffy John, lab., Beach bel Chestnut
Duffy John, lab., Caldwell n Beach
Duffy John, tailor, S E Front & Sassafras, h 14 Mulberry
Duffy Michael, porter, 19 Jones' al.
Duffy Patrick, lab., 1 Melon pl
Duffy Patrick, grocer, 76 Locust
Duffy Patrick, 9 Dannaker's av
Duffy Roger, dyer, 43 Coates al
Duffy Wm., printer, 30 Lebanon
Duffy Wm., lab., Mechanic bel George
Duffy Wm., painter, 70 Chestnut, h 30 Lebanon
Duffy William, porter, Jones st W of Sch 6th
Duflon & Fassitt, mers., 53 High
Duflon P. V., mer., 53 High, h N E Sch 8th and Filbert
Dufour George, mer., 28 Walnut, h 63 S 7th
Dufrene T. W., artist, S W 10th & Chestnut
Dugan Edward, lab., Bedford bel 8th
Dugan Hugh, weaver, 9th bel Christian
Dugan James, bottler, Master ab Cadwalader
Dugan James, lab., Hope ab Phoenix
Dugan John, weaver, Fitler n 2d (K)
Dugan Joseph J., druggist, Cedar ab 12th
Dugan Margt., Jefferson ab Broad
Dugan Michael, rear Quigg's ct (S)
Dugan Mrs. Mary, 36 St John
Dugan Patrick, carter, 17 Baker st
Dugan Peter, gent., 345 Pine
Dugan Rosa, 11 Hampton

Dugan Sarah, Shippen ab 12th
Dugan Thomas, broker, 31 Jacoby
Dugan Timothy, weaver, 9 Ulrick's row (K)
Dugan Wm., carter, Pink ab Master (K)
Dugan Wm. W., painter, 175 Chestnut, h 282 Green
Dugee Rachel, wid. of John, 53 Apple
Duggin Patrick, cabman, 30 Strawberry
Duhamel Augustine J. L., druggist, N E 11th and Walnut
Duhamel A. G., clerk, 20 Prune
Duhring George, M. D., 134½ Mulberry.
Duhring Henry, coach lace, &c. 22 N 4th, h 167 N 6th
Duke Anthony G., cordw., 12th ab Vine
Duke Thomas, painter, 3 Sailor's ct
Dukeman Wm., tobacco, S E Penn & Cedar
Dukes Ann, trimmings, 67 Christian
Dull Anthony, manuf., 189 Brown
Dull Charles, paper warehouse, 8 Decatur, h Mantua village
Dull Christian, drayman, Front bel Master
Dull George, tavern, 440 N 2nd.
Dull Jacob, blacksm., Poplar & Elizabeth
Dull Jacob, blacksm., 30 Harmony ct
Dull James, drayman, Crown n West. (K)
Dull Valentine, cart., Thompson ab 4th (K)
DULLES & AERTSEN, commission mers., 8 S Front
Dulles Jos. H., mer., 8 S Front, h 159 S 9th
Dulles J. H., jr., mer., S E Water & Walnut
Duling Wm., tailor, 4 Spragg's av
Dulty & Johns, boots and bonnets, 98 High
Dulty Wm., mer., 98 High, h 9 City Row
Dumar Manuel, shop, 160 Shippen
Dumas G. B., mer., 138 High
Dumec John F., cabinetmaker, P road bel Fitzwater
Du Monlin Augustus, carver, rear 108 S 3d
Dumont Augustus, lab., 3 Marshall
Dumont A. J., book-keeper, 269 N 5th
Dumoutet Jane, gentw., 102 N 11th.
Dumphy Elizabeth, huckster, 1 Haffman's al
Dunan Geo., weaver, rear Locust n Beach
Dunbar Alexander, lab., Marriott bel 6th
Dunbar Elon, mer., 22 Chestnut, h 104 S 9th
Dunbar Morris, carpenter, 13th & Brown
Dunbar Wm., blacksmith, Prime ab Front
Duncan Alexander B., cabinetmr., 70 S 12th
Duncan C., warper, Hamilton n Fair Mount st
Duncan David, coal agent, Shackamaxon n Bedford (K)
Duncan Esther, P road bel Marriott's la
Duncan George, cabinetmr., St George's ct
Duncan George W., clerk, 5th bel Franklin
Duncan James J., & Co., hardware, 177½ High
Duncan James J., mer. 177½ High, h 20 N 7th
Duncan Joseph, drayman, Beach st
Duncan John, collector, 16 Filbert
Duncan J., sea stores, 93 S wharves
Duncan Louisa, Mrs., Chestnut n Broad
Duncan Mary, milliner, High ab Sch 5th
Duncan Moses, lab., Juniper and Pine
Duncan Noah, carp., 212 S 4th
Duncan T., carpenter, High n Sch. 5th.

Duncan Wm., dry goods, Front bet Chestnut & Market, h 479 Chestnut
Dundas James, paver, F road ab Phœnix
Dundas James, president commercial bank, h N E Broad and Walnut
Dunfee Saml., turner, rear 127 Noble
Dunfee Thos., shop, Callowhill ab Sch 3d
Dungan Ann, trimmings, 167 N 4th
Dungan Chas. L., druggist, N E 12th & Filbert
Dungan C. B., register and sec. N L Gas Works, h 330 N 6th
Dungan James, pedler, Orange bel Citron
Dungan Jesse, cordw., Marlboro' bel Duke (K)
Dungan John, real est. broker, 100 S Front
Dungan John, clerk, 80 Green
Dungan John, blacksm., rear 187 Coates
Dungan John A., clerk, Craig's ct (K)
Dungan Mahlon, gent., G T road ab Otter
Dungan Pugh, tavern, 181 O Y road
Dungan Robert W., druggist, 69 N Front, h 15 Penn
DUNGAN & SON, tavern, 237 N 3d
Dungan Thomas, cordw., 138 Buttonwood
Dungan Thomas M., carp., Phœnix bel G T road
Dungey Wm., shop, 167 N 12th
Dunglison Robley, M. D., 109 S 10th
Dungworth Samuel, cutter, Shackamaxon bel Franklin
Dunham Albert, clerk, Franklin ab Green
Dunham Charles, waterman, 6 Gilbert's ct
Dunham James, oyster house, 23 N whfs
Dunham Jno. ship master, 152 Queen
Dunham Thomas, tobacconist, 4 Orchard
Dunkerley Ann, dressmaker, 10th ab Willow
Dunkerley Geo. watch casemr. 10th ab Willow
Dunlap & Crossman, silk mers., 123 High
Dunlap James, mer., 14 S Front, h 70 N 11th
Dunlap James, lab., Wood bel Broad
Dunlap James, carp., James ab Charles
Dunlap Jas., weaver, 8 Little Green (K)
Dunlap James, carp., Dickerson's ct
Dunlap Jas., shop, S 9th bel South
Dunlap Jas., white smith, rear Apple ab George
Dunlap Jefferson, cabmr., 8 S 10th
Dunlap John, car driver, 29 Pratt
Dunlap J. & S. dry goods, 14 S Front
Dunlap John, tailor, 2d ab Phoenix (K)
Dunlap Mary, huckster, 201 Callowhill
Dunlap Mary, rear O Y road ab Tammany
Dunlap Misses, fancy milliners, 16 N 10th
Dunlap R., Filbert n Sch. 6th
Dunlap Sallows, mer., 14 S Front, h 154 N 5th
DUNLAP SARAH, City Hotel, 41 N 3d
DUNLAP THOMAS, atty. & coun., 88 S 4th
Dunlap Thomas, sexton, George ab Sch 7th
Dunlap William, coachmr. 169 N 5th, h N W

Dunn Cyrena, b. h., 91 New
Dunn Edward P., bookbinder, George bel Apple
Dunn Eleanor, 36 Chatham
Dunn Eliza, b h, 331 N 3d
Dunn Gottlieb, vict., Carroll ab 13th
Dunn Gotlieb, vict., 5th bel Camac (K)
Dunn James, carpet weaver, 6th ab Master
Dunn James, lab., Sch Beach ab Spruce
Dunn James, brickmr., Cedar n Sch 2d
Dunn James, weaver, Murray
Dunn James, lab., Milton ab 11th
Dunn Jas. W., printer, 4 Thorn's ct
Dunn Jeremiah, weaver, Philip ab Jefferson (K)
Dunn Jeremiah, weaver, School ab Rose (K)
Dunn John, blacksm., Perkenpine's ct
Dunn Margaret, 112 S 12th
Dunn Margaret, boots & shoes, 362 High
Dunn Mary, 121 Plum
Dunn Mary, 2 Swain's ct
Dunn Matthew, labourer, 315 S 6th.
Dunn Michael, clerk, 7 Elmslie's al.
Dunn Neal, lab., Senneff's ct
Dunn Patrick, shoemaker, 5 McKean's ct.
Dunn Robert, blacksmith, 10th bel Catharine
Dunn Sarah, 54 Almond
Dunn Thomas, laborer, Sch 6th and Ann
Dunn Thos., waterman, Lily al
Dunn Wm., weaver, Lombard ab Sch 2d
Dunn Wm., iron mould., Paul bel 7th
Dunn Wm. H., att'y, 75 S 6th
Dunnacliff Hugh, weaver, Jefferson ab 2d (K)
Dunnet John, carp., Parrish bel 10th
Dunnicliffe Abraham, weaver, Brinton.
Dunnot Chas., carp., 114 Dillwyn
Dunott Justus, M. D., 155 Pine
Dunphey Marg., gent., 100 Poplar
Dunsford Joseph, bookbinder, 5 Rugan
Dunsmoor Henry, lab., rear Barker E of Sch 4th
Dunsmoor Samuel, lab., 6 Richard
Dunston John, confectionary & b h, 150 Spruce
Dunton George, captain, 30 Green.
Dunton Jacob jr., 114 Lombard
Dunton Jacob, 58 Pine
Dunton John L., sea captain, 62 Tammany
Dunton Mary, wid. of Isaac, 130 S 8th
Dunton William, carp., 3 Myers' ct
Dunton Wilson, mer., 156 High
Dunwoody Ruth, 163 Sassafras.
Dupen Francis, shoemr., 5 S 13th
Duplaine R. C., mer., 2 Chestnut, h 202 N 4th
DUPLAINE, HOLLINGSHEAD & CO., commers., 2 Chestnut
Duplee Thos., Malseed's ct
Dupuy Bernard, gent., 45 Clinton
Dupuy Conrad, plast., Filbert n Sch Front
Dunn John, cap mak., Beaver bel Charlotte

Durang Jacob, umbrella mr., 1½ Locust
Durant Ann, Mrs., 292 S 10th
DURAR ENOCH, Exchange Coffee House, Merchant's Exchange, h 68 S 3rd
Durban John, cordw., Marshall ab Poplar
Durbin J. P. Rev., 9 N 7th
Durbin Wm. H., 460 Callowhill
Durbarrow A. C., mer., 18 N 4th, h 172 S 9th
Durborow Hugh, Alden ab Poplar
Durborow James H., prin., 4th ab Washington
Durborow Mary, 172 S 9th
Durbrow Townsend, shoemr., Race ab Sch 8th
Durdin John L., cordwainer, rear 128 Dillwyn
Durell Albert, sugar refiner, Nectarine ab 10th
Durell Kemsey, tavern, Front and Poplar
Durell Samuel, painter, 44 New Market
Durell Thomas, stove manuf., 59 & 61 N 6th, h 203 Noble
Durell William M., 8 Pleasant Retreat
Durfor E., 1 Pleasant Retreat
Durfor Geo., 180 R road
Durfor William, carpenter, 73 Buttonwood.
Durham Elijah, carter, rear Marriott bel 5th
Durham Elizabeth, 94½ N 8th
Durham Ezekiel, eating house, 7 S 3d, h 32 Harmony
Durham Jas., oysters, Marriott bel 5th
Durham N. L., barber, 377 N 3d
Durhan Samuel, oyster house, 260 High, rear Fifth bel Lombard
Durick Matthew, lab., Coates n Sch
Durk George, cordw., 213 St John
Durnell Henry, plasterer, 245 Christian
Durnell James, blacksmith, 156 Sassafras
Durnell Rosanna, Yhost bel Catharine
Durney Eliza, dry goods, 103 Catharine
Durney Tobias M., confectioner, 278 S 2nd.
Durning Thos., lab., 295 S 6th
Duross Jas., liquor mer., 172 N 5th
Duross Patrick, tavern, 600 S 2d
Duross Patrick, lab., 228 N Water
Duross William, bookseller, 131 N 2d
Durrah Hugh, plasterer, Smith's pl
Dusch Anthony, cordw., 2 Orchard
Dusch George, cordw., 27 Mayland
DUSENBERY W. C. & Co., mer., agts., 108 High
Du Solle John S. editor, 32 S 3d
Dutch Alexander, cordw., S E 10th & Sergeant
Duterle Francis A., carp., 235 Lombard, h 3 Washington ct
Dutilh Charles, Sec'ry Union Canal company, carpenter's ct., h Mulberry ab 13th
DUTILH EDMUND G., mer., rear 147 High, h Spruce ab 12th
Dutilh & Humphreys, forwd. & com. mers., rear 147 High.
Dutton Abraham, porter, 3 Miles' al
Dutton Absalom, carter, Smith's ct
Dutton C., Mrs. gentw., 48 Marshall
Dutton Isaac, carpenter, Washington ab 3d
Dutton John M., 48 George st
Dutton Joseph L., carp., 24 Union
Dutton Lewis T., shoes, 6th and Callowhill
Dutton Richard, porter, 1 Smiths' ct

DUTTON RICHARD R., boots and shoes, 132 High
Dutton Samuel, mer., 24 N Front
Dutton Samuel P., carp., 8th bel Washington
Dutton Sarah, dressmr., 13th bel Brown
Dutton Wm. currier, 49 Green
Duval Dayton, stockmr., 5 Arcade, h 8 Laurel (N L)
Duval Dayton, store keeper, 8 Laurel (N L)
Duval James, lab, Beach ab Maiden (K)
Duval P. S., lithogr., 7 Bank al
Duval Richard, moulder, Clair
Duvall Samuel, Dutton n Franklin
Dux S. M., dry goods, 36 Bank
DUY CHAS. A., mer., 108 High
Duy L., cloth mer., 108 High, h 37 Clinton
Dwaradomsky Joseph, mer., 42 Bank
Dwyer Daniel, fisherman, Wood & Franklin (K)
Dwyer Henry, fisherman, Franklin ab Wood (K)
Dwyer John, bootmr., 47 Prune
Dyball Caroline, gentw., 385 Callowhill
Dyball Robert, printer, 210 N 9th
Dych Frederick, ship carp., Duke bel Palmer
Dych John, coppersmith, Union ab Franklin (K)
Dych Michael, cordw., Schleisman's al
Dye John, plater, 366 N 4th
Dye Joseph R., tailor, 23 Queen, h Dean n Bedford (K)
Dye & Morris, tailors, Queen n F road. (K)
Dye Ralph, trader, Hope bel Phoenix
Dye Wm., beef curer, Poplar bel Broad
Dyer John, painter, Paul ab 6th
Dyer Nathan, tailor, Frazier's ct
Dyer Sarah, 97 Green (C)
Dyke, P. B., clerk, 435 2d
Dykes Cynthia, nurse, 113 Vine
Dykes Samuel, 324 Sp Garden
Dyott C. W., gent., Spruce & Sch 8th
Dyott J. B., M. D., 132 N 2d
DYOTT M. B., camphine lamps, 64 S 2d
Dyott T. W. & Sons, druggists & com. mers. 132 N 2d
Dyott T. W., M. D., 132 N 2d
Dyott T. W. Jr., druggist, 132 N 2d
Dyre James W., 46 Union
Dyre Michael, lab., 135 Carpenter
Dyre Milton, book binder, 52 Logan
Dyre Timothy I. jr., brass founder, Washington & Church, h Front ab Washington
Dyre T. I. Sr., Front ab Washington.
Dyson Christopher, oak cooper, Allen ab Hanover (K)
Dyson John, turner, rear 11½ Walnut ab 4th, h Lemon ab 10th
Dyson Thomas, cloth finisher, Carlton ab Sch Front
Dyson Wm., moulder, G T road ab 6th
Dyssinger Jacob P., watchman, Bacon's ct
Dyton John, type founder, 22 Lily al

———

Eache Wm. F., porter, 133 Locust
Eadie James, tavern, 417 S 2nd.
Eadline James, tailor, F road ab Maiden

Eagan John, lab., 15 Barker st
Eagan John, lab., 5 Beach n Walnut
Eager Mary, scouring, 135 Cherry
Eager Wm., ship carp., F road bel Bedford
Eagin James H., shoedealer, 6th ab Poplar
Eagin Morris, machinist, Clare st
Eagle Dominick, 107½ High, h 270 Pine
Eagle Jerome, mer. 26 N Front, h 302 Pine
Eagle Stephen F., mer., 161 High, h Vine bel Sch 3d
Eagle & Westcott, dry g'ds, 107½ High
Eakin C. M., civil engineer, Chestnut (W P)
Eakinpence Aug., lamp black manuf., Sch Front n Mulberry
Eakins Benj., teacher, 4 Carrolton sq
Eakins Cath., washer, 9 Parker's al
Eakins James, moulder, 8 York ct
Ealer Lewis W., gunsmith, 128 St John
Ealer Margaret, teacher, 9th ab Coates
Earl Hugh, hat presser, 5 Chancery la
Earl John, shoemr., 8th and P road
Earl Mary, 8 St John
Earle George, tailor, 175 Chestnut, h 95 N 10th
Earle Harrison, carver, 249 Pine.
Earle Henry, lab., Carlton bel Sch 8th
Earle James senr., carver, 169 Chestnut.
Earle James S., carver & gilder, 216 Chestnut.
Earle John H., tailor, 60 Walnut, h 369 Cedar
Earle Robert, mer., h 388 Walnut
EARLE THOMAS, atty. & coun., 44 N 5th
Earles Henry, plumber, Smith's ct
Earley & Abbott, cabinetmr., 311 S 2d
Earley Hugh, tinsmith, rear Dorothy n Sch 4th
Earley John H., pianomr., Washington (W P)
Earley Saml., shoemr., High n Sch Front
Early Jeptha, 8 Vernon
Early John, shop, N E 5th & German
Early William, mer., 12 High, h 227 N 6th.
Earnest David, tailor, 127 Spruce
Earnest Eli, wheelwr., Ogden bel R road
Earnest James, filemr., Cobb's ct
Earnhart Charles, guns, Charlotte ab Beaver
Earns A., sup. of highways, George ab Sch. 8th
EARP & BROTHERS, mers., 34 Commerce
Earp Edwin, mer. 41 S wharf. h 76 Marshall
Earp George, mer., 34 Commerce, h 302 Mul-

Eastlack Richard, Greenwood pl
Eastland Wm., rear 86 Locust
Eastman Benj., manuf. of spring beds, 410 High, h N E 7th and Cherry
Eastman Jonathan, shop, Hallowell
Easton David, tailor, rear 232 S 3d
Eastwick John W. plasterer, 40 Mead al
Eastwick, Steph., plasterer, Bedford ab Marlbo-rough (K)
Eastwood Eleanor, 63 New
Eastwood Mary, 15 S 13th
Eastwood Samuel, 5 Farmer
Eaton Aaron, waterman, Swanson bel Christian
Eaton Emily, stockm. 5th bel Washington
Eaton Francis, bleacher, 9 Cox.
Eaton Lewis, ship carp., rear Marlborough ab Bedford (K)
Eberbach J. C., baker, 3 Letitia ct
Eberle David, comedian, 128 Cherry.
Eberle Jesse, grocer, N E 13th & Lombard
Eberle Michael, baker, 13 Carter's al
Eberling Mrs., doctress, 17 Castle st
Eberly Daniel, currier, 56 St John
Ebert Fred'k, paint. & glaz., Front bel Otter(K)
Ebert James L., hair dresser, 107 Sassafras
Ebert Peter, dentist, 64 Coates
Ebert Saml., carp., 180 Coates
Ebling Angeline, 10th ab Poplar
Ebling M. L. Mrs. Gatchell's av
Ebling Robert, combm. Ross ab Queen
Eccles David, grocery, 10th & Coates
Eccles Wm., dry goods, 6th & Sassafras
Echeverria John, carp. Clair
Echtermyer John, weaver, Coates n Sch
Echternacht H. W., N E Spruce and Currant al
Echternoch Rudolph, shoem. 16 Franklin Place
Eckard F. S., M. D., 453 Chestnut
Eckard John, sawyer, rear Marshall ab Coates
Eckard Lewis, cordw., 12th bel Coates
Eckard Susan K., 68 S 8th
Eckhardt A. H., chandler, 326 N 2d, h 137 St John
Eckhardt C. H., chandler, 326 N 2d
Eckhardt William G., baker, 130 Callowhill
Eckhardt W. F. chandler, 326 N 2d
Eckel John, mer., 128 N 3rd, h 163 N 6th

Eckert John, coachmnr., Law's ct
Eckert Sarah, sempstress, 3 Perry ct
Eckert Sarah, 118 S 3d
Eckert W., 13 Dannaker's av
Eckert Wm., printer, St Joseph's av
Eckfeldt Adam, chief coiner U S Mint, h 156 N Juniper.
Eckfeldt Catharine, 130 N 13th
Eckfeldt George, machinist, 120 N Juniper.
Eckfeldt Jacob R., assayer U S Mint, h 154 N Juniper.
Eckfeldt Jacob S., machinist, U S Mint, h 142 N Juniper
Eckfeldt William, firehose manuf., 130 N 13th, h 125 Juniper
Eckhardt Hen. tin smith, Palmer bel Duke (K)
Eckhardt Henry, soap manuf., c Shackamaxon & Franklin (K)
Eckhardt Henry, lab., Benfer's ct (K)
Eckley John J., cooper, rear 386 S 2d
Eckley Wm., carter, Walter's ct ab Front
Ecklin Saml., type founder, 625 S 2d
Eekstein & Fiegl, dry goods, 28 N 2d
Eckstein Jacob, books & stationery, 118 N 4th.
Eckstein John & Co., marble saw mill, Ridge Road and Wallace
Eckstein John, brushes, 36 N 3rd.
Eckstein John H., marble saw mill, R road and Wallace, h 36 N 3d
Eckstein Lewis, currier, 35 Brown
Eckstein Mary, widow of Saml., 121 Callowhill
Eckstein Solomon, mer., 28 N 2d, h 182 Marshall
Ecky John H. druggist, 158 Lombard, h 10th ab Fitzwater
Ecles Robert, tavern, High n Sch. 3d
Eddier Robert, carter, 6 Union ct
Eddis Isaac, combmaker, Fontanell's ct
Eddis Samuel F., cordw. St John ab Beaver (K)
Eddis Wm., carp., Pleis' ct
Eddowes Mary, Green ab 9th
Eddowes Ralph, 101 Wood
Eddy Jason, lab., 9th bel Coates
Eddy Joshua P. B., hair dresser, 183 Cedar
Eddy Josiah, hair dresser, 460 Race.
Edel Ann, shop, 4th and Beaver
Edel Joseph, tavern, 375 N 3d
Edel Josiah, dry goods, 538 High
Edel Matthias, twister, Elm bel Franklin (K.)
Edel Wm. lab. 275 St John
Edelen Edw., planemr., Rachel ab Poplar
Edeline Joseph, machinist, Olive ab 13th
Edelman George W., bookkeeper U S Mint, h 22 Madison
Edelman Isaac, carpenter, 107 N 13th
Eden Robert, M'Duffie n 3d, Sch
Edenborn Benjamin, planemr, rear 27 N 7th, h 144 N 13th
Edenborn J., grocer, 155 & h 144 N 13th.
Edenborn J. A. & Co., tobacco, N E 3d and Sassafras, h Crown n Wood
Edenborn Mary, 144 N 13th
Edenborn Peter H., tobacconist, 99 N 4th
Eder Philip, drayman, 467 N 5th

13

Edes Wm., lab., 10th ab Catharine
Edgar James, hosier, 174 Poplar
Edgar Jas. senr., messenger, U S Mint, h 1 Kelly
Edgar John, bookbinder, 96 Cherry, h 40 Franklin.
Edgar John, printer, 375 Callowhill.
Edgar John, cabinetmr. Cherry ab 12th
Edgar John, lab., 13 Paschall's alley
Edgar John E., engineer, 42 Catharine
Edgar Samuel, book binder, N W Wallace and Franklin
Edgar Wm., coach trimmer, 44 N 13th
Edgar Wm. carp. 67½ Buttonwood
Edgar Wm. lab., rear 468 N 3d
Edge John, suspender weaver, Beach ab Hanover (K)
Edge Richard, weaver, Duke ab F. road (K)
Edixson Garrett, barber, Christian bel 4th and 2d & G T Road
Edler Anne, washer, 58 Queen
Edmonds Jos., painter, Carpenter ab 3d
Edmonds Nathaniel, 142 Sassafras
Edmondson John, painter, Ontario ab Poplar
Edmondson Wm. papermr. Logan ab Green
Edmonston Archibald, printer, Doman's place
Edmunds L. C., painter, 160 & h 365 S 3d
Edson S. D., 13 Commerce, h 286 N 7th
Edwards Augustine F. W., clerk, 95½ Walnut, h Sch. 5th bel Locust
EDWARDS & BROTHER, flour mers., 221 N Front and 214 N Water
Edwards Charles, cooper, 3 Parham
Edwards Charles, 270 N Front
Edwards Charles C., flour, 288 S 2d, h 427 S Front
Edwards Daniel, seaman, Biddle's alley
Edwards David, merchant, 23½ S 2d
Edwards David, tailor, 114 Sassafras
Edwards Edward, cooper, Union ab Franklin
Edwards Edward B., mer., 221 N Front, h 46 Brown (N L)
Edwards Eli, carp. 15 Freed's av
Edwards Elizabeth, 30 Stamper's al
Edwards Evans, oak cooper, Crown ab Bedford
Edwards George, cordw., rear 214 St. John
Edwards George, mer., 37 S 2d, h 213 Chestnut
Edwards Geo., cooper, 1 Bank
EDWARDS G. & SON, wholesale milliners, 37 S 2d
EDWARDS G. W., office 15 Mer. Exchange, h Sch. 5th bel Locust
Edwards Henry, cabinetmaker, Catharine ab 3d
Edwards Isacher, pianomr., 4 Decatur, h 295 Walnut
Edwards Jacob, clerk, Almira pl
Edwards James, grocer, Thompson ab Broad
Edwards James, chairmr. 90 Callowhill
Edwards James & S. R., chairmrs., 84 Callowhill
Edwards & Jenness, wool dealers and com. mers 27 N Front
Edwards John, cooper, 1 Bank
Edwards John & Son, coopers, 1 Bank.
Edwards Jonathan, saddler, Torr's al. n R. road
Edwards Joseph, mer., 184 N Front

Edwards Jos. C. coach painter, 160 Queen
Edwards Mary, dressmr., George ab 13th
Edwards Matthew, cutler, 15 Gray's al
Edwards Richd L., upholsterer, 102 S 12th
Edwards Robert, oak cooper, Gorrell's ct
Edwards Saml., 47 Quince
Edwards Saml., weaver, Edward ab School (K)
Edwards Saml., moulder, 2 Elizabeth (N L)
Edwards Samuel, lab. 8 Wagner's al
Edwards Samuel H., mer., High n Front, h 192 Spruce
Edwards Sarah, b h, 295 Walnut
Edwards Thomas A., Sch 5th bel Locust.
Edwards Wm. lab., 108 Washington av.
Edwards Wm. shoemr., 3 Spragg's av
Edwards Wm. jun. pilot, Swanson ab Queen
Edwards Wm. jun., Union ab Bedford (K)
Edwards Wm. sen., pilot, Swanson ab Queen
Edwards Wm., carp., 1 Washington (M)
Edwards Wm. B., book binder, 164 Queen
EDWARDS WM. CUNNINGHAM, cabinetmr. and upholsterer, 11 N 8th
Edwards Wm. P., mer., 37 S 2d
Edwards Wm. S. combmr. Parrish ab 10th
Edwards W. W., G T road and Phoenix
Edwin Mrs. C., 41 Madison
Eells Edward F., b h, 64 Penn
Egan Edward, lab. Allen's ct
Egan John, porter, 3 Ridgway's ct
Egan John D., book binder, 49 S 3d
Egbert Hannah, Wood ab Sch. 2d
Ege Jacob, shoemr., 4 Tiller's ct
Egee Martin, lab., 18 Clark
Eger Frederick, shoes, R road and Washington
Eggleson Jas., weaver, rear Amber ab Phoenix
Eggleston Geo., brushmr., Clinton ct
Eggleston Wm. H., wheelwright, Otter bel G. T. road (K)
Eggleton Albert, real est. agent, Queen ab Palmer (K)
Eggleton John, teamster, Franklin below Union (K)
Eggleton Jonathan, shipsm., Hanover bel Allen
Eggleton Wm., carter, Franklin bel Vienna (K)
Eglee Jacob L. printer, 365 S Front
Egner Chrs., wines & liq., 10 N 3d
Egner Jacob H., wine and liquors, 208 High
Egner Levi, brickmr., 7 Pleasant row
Egner Robert, brickmr., George n Sch 2d
Egner Robert, lab., Nixon ab Hamilton vil.
Egner Samuel, shoemr., Sch 2d ab Spruce
Ehret Michael, carp., Charlotte ab George
Ehret Michael, cordwainer, Apple ab Poplar.
Ehrhardt H., bootmr., 129 Vine
Ehrman Francis, boilermr., 7 Washington row
Ehrman Francis, blacksmith, 13th ab Willow
Eicheli Nathan, blacksmith, rear 210 St. John
Eichert Adam, baker, Marlborough bel Allen (K)
Eichhorn Fred., lab., 439 N 3d
Eichley John, lab. Broad ab Poplar
Eichoff Rosanna, Apple bel George

Eikelbarner D. skindress. N 3d bel Franklin (K
Eilers Rosanna, layer of dead, 13 Mulberry al
Einstein Joseph, b h, 269 N 2d
Einstein Lewis, mer., 182 N 9th
Einwechter Henry, bricklayer, rear G. T. road bel Master
Einwechter Maria, Apple bel Franklin
Einwechter Wm., bricklayer, Perry ab Franklin (K)
Einwechter Wm. jr., bricklr., Palmer n Frankford road (K)
Eisele Geo. P., baker, 16 Fitzwater
Eisen Daniel, soap & candle manufacturers, 9 Green
Eisenbraun F., cordw., 128 Buttonwood
Eisenbrey John jr., mer., Pear and Dock, h Pine ab 10th
Eisenbrey John jun. & Co. mahogany steam mill, Pear and Dock
Eisenbrey J. S., cordw., 259 N 9th
Eisenbrey Wm. tailor, N E 5th & Sassafras
Eisenbrice Christian, lab., 5 Brooke
Eisenhart Frederick, grocery, 482 N 6th
Eisenhour Elam, cordwainer, rear 107 New Market
Eisenhut John D., coppersmith, Cherry ab 4th, h 89 G T road
Eisenhut J. D., jr., tinsm., 611 N 2d
Eiserman D. & G. Jun. painters and glaz. 121 N 6th
Eiserman George, painter, 333 High
Eisley John, shoemr., rear 122 Swanson
Eisley John A. sugar boiler, 9 Wood
Eisley Philip, baker, rear 122 Swanson
Elberson Francis, pilot, 6 Powell's row
Elbert Wm. T., merchant, 42 S Water
Elder Elizabeth, wid., 71 Logan
Elder Henry L., mer., 493 High, and Green ab R. road, h Summer E. Sch. 6th
Elder John, drover, 28 Gaskill
Elder Robert, weaver, rear Hancock bel Phœnix (K)
Elder Walter, gardener, Lane's ct
Elder Wm., attorney, 16 Marshall
Elder Wm., tinman, 445 Vine
Elder Wm., S., oyster dealer, George ab 4th
Elder William T., genl., 8th bel Coates
Eldred Charles, printer, Sch. 6th bel Cherry
Eldred & Morris, hatters, 15 Minor
Eldred Wm., hatter, 3 Logan sq
Eldredge Stillwell, tailor, S E 7th and High, Franklin n Green
Eldridge & Brother, carpets, 41 Strawberry
Eldridge Daniel W., 7 N whfs., h 87 S 3d
Eldridge Guston, hardware, 212 S 2d
Eldridge Ephraim, bookbinder, Lemon bel 11th
Eldridge E. H., tailor, 65 Washington
Eldridge H. H. carpets, 41 Strawberry, h 39 N 2d
Eldridge Isaac B., last maker, 89 Callowhill
Eldridge Jas. W., grocer, N W 3d & Carpenter
Eldridge J. E. grocer, G T road ab 5th

Elldridge & Miller, tailors, S W 6th & Sassafras
Eldrige Mary, tailoress, rear 82 N 2d
Eleman Philip, tavern, 165 Shippen.
Elfelt Edwin 3. mer. 85 N 3d
Elfelt S., mer., 85 N 3d, h 173 O Y road
Elfelt S. & Son, dry goods, 85 N 3d
Elfreth Jacob R., acct., 84 Wood
Elfry George, bricklayer, 13 Olive
Elias Charles, waiter, 54 Quince
Elias Henry, gent., 143 N 10th
Eliason Andrew, brushmr., 317 High, h 373 N Front
Eling Henry, machinist, 14 Mary (S)
ELISON JOHN, tavern, S W 6th and Poplar
Elison Wm., shoe store, 33 N 3d, h S W 9th & Mulberry
ELISON WM. & Co., shoes, 33 N 3d
Eljeau Mrs., Smith's ct
Elkan Edward, mer. 157 N 3d
Elkin Abm., gent., 156 N 11th
Elkin Solomon, gent., 393 Callowhill.
Elkins Thomas, ladies' shoemaker, 114 S 8th.
Elkinton George M., soap and candle manuf., 12 Margaretta
ELKINTON JOHN A., M. D., alderman, 102 N 5th
Elkinton Joseph, soap & candle manuf. 377 S 2d
Ella John, mer., 42 Commerce, h 51 S 13th
Ella Rachel W., 514 Chestnut
Ellcock J., grocer, Maiden n Front
Ellender Wm., painter, Quince & Ohio
Ellet Charles junr., Pres. Sch. Nav. Co. 8 S 7th, & civil engineer, 33 Girard
Ellick Clement, hatter, Franklin ab Hanover (K)
ELLICOTT & ABBOTT, scale mrs., 9th and Melon
Ellicott Richard, mariner, Bethesda row
Elliman Andrew, tobacco, 217 S 6th
Ellinger Moses, turner, Schrader's ct
Elliot Catharine, E N 9th & Callowhill
Elliot Hugh, bookseller, 9 N 4th, h 35 S Penn square
Elliot John, lab., Senneff's ct
Elliott Adam, lab. cor Walnut & Ashton
Elliott Alexander, tavern, c 7th & Shippen.
Elliott Alexander jr., Christian ab 6th, h 7th & Shippen
Elliott Andrew, weaver, 2d & Phoenix (K)
Elliott Andrew C. mer. 58 S Front
Elliott Benjamin P., watchmr., 3 S 13th
Elliott Charles, coal dealer, Front and Dock, h 313 N 6th
Elliott Charles & Son, coal mers. Front & Dock & 62 Beach (K)
Elliott Charles A., printer, 51 Chestnut, h 5 Clover
Elliott Daniel M., collector, 126 Mulberry
Elliott Edward R., carp., c Juniper & George
Elliott Eli, 17 Melon
Elliott Elizabeth, tailoress, Wharton bel 2d
Elliott Francis, carp., Catharine bel 7th
Elliott Francis, 180 Mulberry
Elliott Geo., stonecut., rear Powell (F V)
Elliott George, tinplate worker, 471 High

Elliott George F., tavern, c Crabb & Shippen
Elliott Henry H. K. publisher, 85 Dock, h S E Tammany and Dillwyn
Elliott Isaac, conveyancer, 81 Chestnut, h W Penn sq.
Elliott James L., M. D., druggist, S E 10th and Mulberry, h 137 N 11th
Elliott Jane, trimmings, 196 N 5th
Elliott John, bottl., 97 Walnut, h Wharton ab 4th
Elliott John, gent., 242 Sassafras
Elliott John, mer., 6 Oak st (S Penn sq)
Elliott John, lab., Sch. 2d ab High
Elliott John, sashmr. rear High n Sch 2d
Elliott Joseph, carp., 369 S 3d
Elliott Louisa, dressmr., Catharine bel 8th
Elliott Margaret, b h, 45 Filbert
Elliott Margaret, 2 Kenworthy's ct
Elliott Mary, gentw., 33 Wallace
Elliott Mary, bootmr. Mifflin n 13th
Elliott Matthew, bootmr., 28 Castle
Elliott & Robinson, conveyancers, 81 Chestnut.
Elliott Robt., weaver, Mulberry n Sch 2d
Elliott Robt., lab., Sch 7th ab Sassafras
Elliott Robert, manuf., 609 N 2nd.
Elliott Robert, cordw., Broad ab Shippen
Elliott Saml. carp. George bel 3d
Elliott Sarah Mrs., M road bel Wharton
Elliott Thomas, shop, 240 Lombard
Elliott Thomas, cordw. Phoenix ab Front
Elliott Wm. carp. George n Sch 2d
Elliott William B., photographist, S E 5th and Chestnut, h S Garden bel 11th
Elliott Wm. B., machinist, 19 Quarry
Elliott Wm. B., Front & Dock, h 435 N Front
Ellis Amos, brickmr. Broad ab Poplar
Ellis Amos P., paper and rags, 5th & Coates
Ellis Ann, 236 High.
Ellis & Bancroft, dry goods, 32 Bank
Ellis Carey, lab., 11 Margaretta st
Ellis Chas., druggist, 56 Chestnut, h 95 S 8th
Ellis Chas., boat builder, 92 Washington av
Ellis Charles & Co., druggists, 56 Chestnut.
Ellis David, gent., Franklin ab Green
Ellis Edward, cordw., 6 Oliver's pl
Ellis Elizabeth, 3 Vaux's ct
Ellis Esther A., 159 S 3d
Ellis George, lab., rear 72 Catharine
Ellis Geo. D. inst. mr., Julianna ab Callowhill
Ellis H. G., flour mers., 73 and 75 Coates
Ellis Jacob, mer., 32 Bank, h 6 Montgomery
Ellis Jacob M., mer., 7 N 2nd, h 246 N 7th
Ellis James, morocco dr., rear 215 St John
Ellis James, lab., 3 Point Pleasant ct. (K)
Ellis James P., conveyancer, Green ab 7th, h Franklin ab Green
Ellis Jane, milliner, 45½ Sassafras
Ellis Jesse, coach lampmr., 42 Dock, h Oliver ab 13th
Ellis John, grocer, Allen & Shackamaxon (K)
Ellis John, livery stables, 13 Raspberry
Ellis Joseph, ladies' shoemaker, 156 S 5th
Ellis J. P., clerk, 103 Wood
Ellis Maria, 119 N Front
Ellis Mary Ann, Paul ab 6th

Ellis & Middleton, dry goods, 7 N 2d
Ellis Nathan W., carp., Parrish ab Marshall
Ellis P. H., mer., 35 Jones' al (C) h 7th ab Poplar
Ellis Robt. lab. Jones n Sch 5th
Ellis Sabina, plaster mill, Clinton ab Franklin
Ellis Sabina, jr., moulder, Hancock ab Franklin
Ellis Samuel O. jeweller, Catharine ab 9th
Ellis S. H., teacher, Cherry bel 9th
Ellis Thomas, salesman, Jones n Sch 4th
Ellis Thomas, grocer, Front bel Phœnix (K)
Ellis Thos. morocco dresser, Otter n School (K)
Ellis Thos. B., tailor, 19 S 3d, h 7th bel Parrish
Ellis Wm., druggist, 56 Chestnut, h Clinton ab 9th
Ellis William, lamp maker and crockery, 153 N 2d
Ellis Wm. porter, Perry's ct
Ellis William, shoemaker, 6 Mary's ct
Ellis Wm., shop, 9th bel Poplar
Ellis W. H. & N. W. plumbers & builders, Marshall & Parrish
Ellison John A., mer., 5 Morgan
Ellison John B., mer., 111 High, h 40 Mulberry
Ellison Robert, b h, 13 Lombard
Ellison S. & Peters, cloths, 111 High
Ellison Wm. C., mer., 111 High, h 248 Spruce
Ellison Wm. H., carp., 344 N 6th
ELLMAKER PETER C., grocer, 283 High, h 6 Sargeant
Elmes Abner, hatter, 196 High, h 248 Filbert
Elmes Charles, mariner, rear 11 Mead.
Elmes Edw. lumber deal. Spruce n Sch Front
Elmes H. S & E. H., batters, 198 High
Elmes H. S., hatter, 198 High
Elmes Lazell, hatter, Sch 5th and Barker, h 613 Chestnut
Elmes Thos., hatter, 104 High, h S E Broad & Poplar
Elmore Ann, 12 Mary (S)
Elmore Geo., Rihl's ct
Elmore Sarah, 9 Reckless (S)
Elmsley Henriette, 20 Pine
Elmslie Alex., gent., 232 S Front

Elvert Charles, segar box mr., rear Apple ab George
Elwanger Everhart, butcher, Charlotte n Creek
Elwell Ann, house cleaner, rear 29 Green
Elwell Eleazar, oysters, Lewis ab Sch 8th
Elwell Elizabeth, dressmr., 47 Mead
Elwell Evan, tavern, rear 58 High
Elwell Henry, blacksm., 8 Mead, h 380 S Front
Elwell Henry, jr., blacksmith, 384 S 3d
Elwell H. J., paper hanger, 4 Garden
Elwell Samuel, shipsmith, 124 Catharine.
Elwell Thomas, blacksmith, Steward ab Catharine, h 10th ab Catharine
Elwyn Alfred, M. D., Walnut E Sch 8th
Ely Ann, widow, 185 Green
Ely Britton, coachmr., George & Apple
Ely Clayton P., blacksmith, 18 Elizabeth (N L
Ely Eleazer S. capt., S 7th n Washington
Ely Elizabeth, b h, 297 Callowhill
Ely Ezra Stiles Rev., D. D., 351 N 7th
Ely Israel, waterman, 96 Carpenter
Ely John tailor, 35 N 6th, h 11 Filbert av
Ely John, mer., 108 N 3d, h 58 New
Ely John, gent. S E 10th & Spruce
Ely John jr., gent., S E 10th and Spruce
ELY, KENT, BROCK & Co., dry goods, 108 N 3d
Ely Sarah M., 190 Mulberry
Emach John, carter, 5 Rogers' ct
Emack John, suspend. weaver, Hope bel Master (K)
Emanuel Edward, painter & glazer, 106 N 6th, h 8th ab Coates
Emanuel Geo., shoemr., 1 Brown's ct
Embey Richard, dairy, Wood bel Sch Front
Embly John, carp., Quince
Embry Morris, chandler, 141 Buttonwood
Emerick Albert, silversm., Jackson bel Palmer
Emerick Ann, wid. of Peter K., 223 N 4th
Emerick Aug., hardware, 377 High, h 57 N 11th
Emerick Benjamin, bootmaker, 72 S 8th.
Emerick Daniel B., tinsmith, 72 S 8th.
Emerick David, constable, Palmer ab West(K
Emerick David, carpenter, West bel Palmer(K
Emerick Edgar, china, 210 N 2d, h 223 N 4th

Emery Henry, mer., 97 and 99 N 3d
Emery Henry, driver, GoodWill ct
Emery Jacob, tavern, 582 N 3d
Emery John, grocer, Edward n School (K)
Emery M. H., dealer, Poplar ab 8th
Emery Peter, whf builder, Swanson bel Christian
Emery Saml., lab., 6th bel G T road (K)
Emery William, waiter, 128 Locust.
Emery Wm., furniture car, 6 Roberts' ct
Emes Wm., shoemr., Lister's ct
Emick John, cordw., Cherry bel Franklin (K)
Emlen & Fisher, real est and stock brokers, 95 Walnut
EMLEN GEORGE, Jr., att'y & coun., 47 S 5th, h Walnut E Sch 6th
Emlen Geo., 255 Walnut
Emlen Joshua, pres. Phila. Mut. ins. co., 3 Mer. Exchange, h 79 S 12th.
Emlen Thos., lab., 11 Parker st
Emlen William F., real est. broker, 95 Walnut, h 307 Chestnut
Emley Gilbert, mer., 4 N 3d
Emley J. C. S., mer., 101 High
Emmerling Jacob, 306 Callowhill
Emmick Henry, cordw., 14 Pratt's ct
Emmit Enoch, lab., Vienna ab Franklin (K)
Emmit Solomon, spinner, Lawrence ct
Emmons Charles. shoemr., 3 Boyd's av
Emmons Edward, lumber, Swanson ab Washington
Emmons Geo., cordw., Poplar ab 12th
Emmot Thomas, cordw., rear 484 N 3d
Emory Ann, 187 S 7th
EMORY GEO. W., Monterey House, 457 N 3d
Emral Manuel L., cordw., Stackhouse ct
Enburg Andrew, tobacconist, 11 Ellet's av
Enburg Andrew, jr., wheelwr. Ross ab Queen
Enders Frederick, shoemr., Tammany ab 2d
Endress Catharine, Carpenter bel 6th
Endress Charles C., coachmr., 31 Chester.
Endriss John, currier, 330 St John
Eneu Elizabeth, nurse, Lily al ab Green
Eneu Geo. W., fruiterer, 10 Lily al
Eneu James, gent., Federal n P road
Eneu James Jr., 167 Shippen.
Eneu Joseph, 336 S 6th
Engard Abraham, painter, Brown bel 4th
Engard Adam, carp., 410 N 5th
Engard Benjamin, carp., Apple ab George
Engard Christopher, drayman, 35 Charlotte
Engard Edw. carp. Orchard ab Rawle
Engard John, tailor, 5 Barber's row
Engard Magdalena, gentw., Noble ab O Y road
Engard Saml., baker, Union ab Franklin (K)
Engard Samuel, agent, 8 Coates
Engard Thomas, carter, Washington av above Willow
Engard William, carter, Parish ab 10th
Engard Wm., combmr., Franklin ab Hanover (K)
Engard William H., grocer, Sch 7th & R road
Engel M. M., cap mr., 5½ S 3d, h 61 N 2d
Engelman John C., grocery, 214 R road
Enger Charles, bootmr., 4 Cresson's alley

England James B., att'y and coun., 61 S 4th, h 219 Spruce
England Lemuel D., shoemaker, 276 S Front
England Samuel, cabinet maker, N W 10th and Walnut,
Engle Aaron C., dry goods, 393 N 2nd.
Engle Albert, planemaker, Bedford bel Cherry (K)
Engle Edwin, flour & feed, High ab Sch. 6th, h 21 Barker
Engle Francis, lab., rear Locust, W Sch 3d
Engle John, drayman, rear 143 Coates
Englebert Amelia, 12 Powell
Englebert Cornelius, ladies' shoemaker, 87 S 8th
Englebert J., ladies shoemaker, 74 S 4th.
Englehart Charles M., jeweler, 52 Crown
Englehart Wm. F., tin plate wor., 5 Bacon's ct
Engleman Daniel W., machinist, Carroll ab 12th
Engler Christian, butcher, Otter n F road (K)
Engles Geo., trader, Walker's ct (K)
Engles Jane, nurse, 7th bel Fitzwater
Engles Joseph P., publisher, h 71 Filbert.
Engles Lewis B., dry goods, 78 High, h 212 N 6th
Engles William M. Rev., ed. Presb., 7th & George
Englesby Owen, weaver, 11th ab Carpenter
Englesby Thos., weaver, rear Carpenter ab 8th
English Abm., mer., 9 Bank, h 30 New Market
English Edward B., grocer, 3 Mulberry, h 110 N Front
English Elizabeth M., 121 S 8th
ENGLISH & ELLIS, tailors, 19 S 3rd
English Gustavus, mer., 10 Chestnut, h 121 S 8th
English G. B., mer., 39 Chestnut
English G. B. & J. B., importers, 39 Chestnut
English Henry, brass founder, rear 178½ Sassafras
English Hugh, blacksmith, 38 Cherry, h 42 N 6th
English H. N., tailor, S W 4th and Chestnut,
English James, blacksmith, 125 S 6th, h 25 Filbert.
English James C., paper, 495 N 2d, h 95 G T road
English Japhet, cordw., Pennell's ct
English John, commissioner, 388 N 6th.
English John B., 39 Chestnut, h 314 Walnut
English J. E., tailor, 19 S 3rd, h 7th bel Parrish
English Meyer, lab., Bedford ab Marlboro' (K)
English Mizeal, paper hanger, 165 S 3rd
English Monnington, carter, Fairview n F M
English Nathan, plasterer, 40 Sheaff
English Rachel, George bel 4th
English Robert, blacksm., Perry ct
English Robert S., 230 E South
English Sarah, 314 Walnut
English Stephen, teacher, 169 Locust, h 431 High
English Thos., drayman, rear George ab 3d (K)
English Wm., agent, Willow ab Broad, h Washington ab 13th
Engstrom A. B., academy, 2 N 9th

Ennis Chas., currier, Parrish ab 10th
Ennis Ellen Mrs., 62 Christian
Ennis John, carp. Parrish ab 10th
Ennis Joshua, bootmaker, 4 Hummell's ct.
Ennis J. J., paper hanger, Green n Broad
Ennis Robert H., combmr., Sch 8th ab Sassafras
Ennis Thomas L., 124 Pine
Enoch James, patternmr., Pleasant ab 12th
Enochs Elizabeth, Sch. 7th n Vine
Enochs Fredk., shoemr., 11 Turner
Ensor William, cordwainer, 10 Pleasant retreat.
Entriken Thomas, cooper, 9th bel Coates
Entwisel J., web manuf., Hermitage pl
Entwistle John, shuttlemr., Marlborough and Duke (K)
Enyard Charles, cordw., 520 N 2d
Enyard Jacob, mason, 520 N 2d
Epley Charles, refectory, Marshall & Callowhill, h Lewis ab Poplar
Epley Robert, cordw., 604 N 2d (K)
Eppeheimer Jonas, tailor, St John bel G T road (K)
Eppelsheimer, Daniel, tavern, 45 Callowhill
Eppelsheimer Edward, S E 5th & Vine
Eppelsheimer Lewis, sugar refiner, Coates ab Marshall
Eppelsheimer Wm., sug. refi., 384 N 4th
Eppinger John, blacksm., Irvine E of 13th
Eppwright Merit, mariner, 3d bel Queen
Eppwright Rudolph, oysters, Front bel Reed
Epstein Josias, tailor, 25 N 4th, h 264 N 5th
Erb George, grocer, George bel 3d
Erben Henry G., druggist, S W 12th & Vine
Erben Israel 15 Emlen's ct

ERSKINE JOSEPH, cordw., 2 Assembly building, h Flower bel Fitzwater
Erskine Martin, bootmr., 81 N 9th
Erskine Rufus M., boot & shoemr., 62 Zane
Ertel Philip, beer house, Poplar ab 9th
Erven Samuel, wheelwt., rear 403 S 4th
Ervin Alexander, manuf., 2d ab Master (K)
Ervin Frances, Green bel 13th
Ervin Henry, Sch 5th opp St Joseph's av
Erwin Casper, tavern, 227 Callowhill.
Erwin Deborah, milliner, 323 Vine.
Erwin James, lab. Sch 6th bel Lombard
Erwin John, waiter, 8 Raspberry
Erwin John, shoemr., 39½ Cedar
Erwin Joseph E., 6 S 10th
Erwin J. W., conveyancer, 5th and Library, h 108 Walnut
Erwin Marmaduke B., Beach ab Marsh (K)
Erwin Marg., wid., Penn ab Poplar (K)
Erwin Matthew, lab. Perry bel Master
Erwin Philip, confect. 482 Coates
Erwin Samuel, lab., Mintland's ct
Erwin Samuel, lab., Baird's ct
Erwin Samuel, lab., Shippen ab 8th
Erwin Sarah Ann, dry goods, 36 N 10th
Erwin Sarah Ann, b h, 110 Filbert
Erwin Stewart, lab., Sch 2d n Filbert
Erwin Susan Mrs., gentw., 340 Mulberry
Escher C. F., piano manuf., 54 Brown
Esdale Samuel, weaver, Steward & Catharine
Esenwein Mary, gentw., 55 Noble
Eshback Wm., lab., Orchard ab Rawle

Espy Mills B., broker, 51 S 3d, h Sch 6th bel Walnut
Espy Mrs., widow of George, Sch. 6th bel Walnut.
Essay John, lab., 435 S 2d
Essig Catharine, rear 317 N 3d
Essig Christian, bone turner, Poplar ab 6th
Essig Jacob, lab. Phoenix bel G T road (K)
Essig Jefferson, 11 Nectarine
Esterlan Ann, 244 Cedar
Estlack Clark, painter, 5 Mechanic
Estlack George, bricklayer, 37 S Sch 7th
Estlack Israel, blacksmith, Lewis E Sch 7th
Estlack John, blacksm. 60 N Juniper
ESTLACK THOMAS, jr., & Co., druggists, 25 N Front
Estlack Thos. jr. mer. 25 N Front
Estlack Thos. mer. 25 N Front, h 529 Chestnut
Estlin John, cooking stoves, 87 N 5th
Estlow Alfred, cigarmr., 20 John (S)
Estricker John, tailor, 122 Charlotte
Ethel John, painter, 8 E North
Ethell & Cuddy, painters, 11th ab High
Etris David, carp., O Y road bel Coates
Etris John M., stone mason, Front & Master (K)
Etris Robert, druggist, F road ab Master
Etris Samuel, cabinet maker, 44½, & h 416 S Front.
Etriss Joseph, bricklayer, 29 Reckless
Etriss Samuel Jr., cabinetmaker, 11 China
Etter David, painter, 159 Catharine
Etter James, tailor, 12 Harmony ct
Etter Peter, cab. mr., 302 Front
Etting Benj., mer., 46 N Whfs. and 93 N Water, h 525 Chestnut
Etting Edward J., iron mer., 46 N Whfs. & 93 N Water, h S W Sch. 8th and Spruce
Etting E. J. & Brother, com. mers., 46 N Whfs. and 93 N Water.
Etting Gratz, mer., 46 N Whfs. and 93 N Water, h 103 S 12th
Etting Henry, U. S. Navy, h 103 S 12th
Etting Horatio, mer., 17 Walnut, h 103 S 12th
Etting Reuben, gent., 103 S 12th
Ettinger & Gandier, dry goods, 252 S 2d
Ettinger George, builder, 2 Linden
Ettinger William, bricklayer, 26 Chatham
Ettinger Wolf, huckster, 304 N Front
Ettling Louis, fancy goods, 62 N 5th
Etzel Gotleib, carter, 5 Paschal's al
Eustis A. B., mer., 15 S Water, h Sch 8th ab Pine
Euston Jas. painter, 21 S 8th, h 192 N 11th
Euston & Weer, painters, 21 S 8th
Eva Lewis, blacksmith, 61 Mead
Evans Aaron, carp., h 30 Logan
Evans Albert, blacksm., 198 Queen
Evans & Allmendinger, mers., 34 N 2d
Evans Amy, rear 84 Walnut
Evans Andrew D., capt., 4 Beck pl
Evans Andrew W. carp. Centre bel 13th
Evans Ann, 4 Carlton pl
Evans Ann, baker, 13 S 10th.
Evans Anna, milliner, 289 S 2d
Evans Arthur, lab., William bel Edward, (K)

Evans Aurelia, dressmr., 189 N 10th
Evans A., grocer, Brown & Centre
Evans Benjamin, currier, 149 S Front, h Cox ab Front
Evans Benjamin M., grocer, 276 Cedar.
Evans Bishop, carp. Washington ab 13th
Evans Charles, photographist, 409 High
Evans Charles, machinist, Quarry near Bread, h 100 Vine
Evans Charles, boot & shoemr., 130 Green.
Evans Charles, M. D., 182 Mulberry.
Evans David, painter, 12 State st
Evans David, ropemr., Wood ab Franklin (K)
Evans David, lab., Salem al
Evans David, fire proof chest manuf., 76 S 3d, h 83 Walnut
Evans David R., lumber, 331 N 6th.
EVANS D., jr., hardware, 144 N 2d, h 74 Catharine
Evans Edward, baker, 75 N 8th
Evans Edward, tin plate worker, Flower al
Evans Edward, slater, Poplar ab 8th
Evans Edward R. druggist, 11 N 5th
Evans Elijah. waterman, Collins' ct
Evans Eliza, Benton's av
Evans Elizabeth, 186 Coates
Evans Elizabeth, b h, 89 S 5th
Evans Ellen, milliner, S W 11th and Mulberry
Evans Ellis, shoemaker, 290 S 6th.
Evans Esther, widow, 331 N 6th
Evans Evan, mer. 185 High
Evans E., coun. at law, 4 N Sch 6th
Evans Franklin, mer., 9 N 2d, h Union ab 2d
EVANS & GUILLON, dry goods, 214 Chestnut
Evans Hannah, 481 Vine.
Evans Hannah, Fayette
Evans Hannah J., 29 Wood.
Evans Harriet V., widow of Cadwalader, 417 Mulberry
Evans Henry, Wood ab Sch 4th
Evans Horace, M. D., 163 Walnut.
Evans Howell, printer, 35 S 4th
Evans Isaiah, engineer, 3 Reckless
Evans Jacob, currier, 88 Cherry.
Evans Jas. D. cordw. 7 Queen ab F road (K)
Evans Jane C., arti. flower maker, 5 S 4th
Evans John, bricklayer, Shippen ab Broad
Evans John, tailor, 4 White's ct
Evans John, inspector of lumber, 107 New Market
Evans John, teacher, 21 Perry
Evans John, moulder, rear 272 N 7th
Evans John C. 29 Palmyra sq
Evans John H. druggist, 198 Queen
Evans Jonathan, groc. Hanover & Franklin (K)
Evans Joseph, carp., Pearl ab 12th
Evans Joseph, cordw., Wood bel Duke (K)
Evans Joseph, watchman, Pearl bel Sch 7th
Evans Joseph, gunsmith, 10 Harmony ct
Evans Joseph, currier, 157 N 3d, h 94 Fitzwater
Evans Joseph, variety store, 233 S 2d.
Evans Joseph, clerk, S E 8th and Wallace
EVANS JOSEPH R., com. mer., 31 S whfs., h 103 Pine.

Evans Jos. R. Jr., mer., 31 S whar., h 101 Pine.
Evans Joshua D., 174 N Front
Evans Josiah, saddler, rear 60 Catharine
Evans Josiah, measurer, 5 S 4th
Evans J. Ogden, gent., 10th ab Buttonwood
Evans Lorenzo, seaman, 220 Lombard
Evans Maria, 9th & Wood
Evans Mary, b h, 11th and Mulberry
Evans Mary, 72 E German
EVANS M. G., 7 Girard
Evans Nathaniel K., carp., Melon n 10th
Evans Oliver, refrigerator, water filterer, & iron chest manufacturer, 61 S 2d, h 47 Almond
Evans Owen, queensware, 26 S 4th
Evans Owen B., lime, 9th & Sp Garden
Evans Powell, brickmr., Shippen ab Broad
Evans Rebecca Ann, b. h., Lily al ab Green
Evans Reese plasterer, Haas' ct
Evans Richard, William bel Edward
Evans Richard, 9 Jefferson
Evans Richard C. bricklayer, 144 S 13th
EVANS ROBERT, measurer, Wallace bel 10th
Evans Robert, slater, Parrish ab 8th
Evans Robert T., 178 N 9th.
Evans Rowland C., carp., 10th bel Sp Garden
Evans Rudulph H., conveyancer, 16 Filbert
Evans R. W., turpentine distiller, Poplar and Front
Evans Samuel, police officer, 9th ab Coates
Evans Saml. J. R., mer., 29 N 2d, h 331 N 6th
Evans Saml. S., carter, Mechanic's ct (N L)
Evans Sarah Mrs., 86½ N 9th:
Evans Sarah M., Mrs., Miller's ct
Evans Solomon, lab., rear Carpenter bel 9th
Evans Theodore, b. h., S W 3d and Cherry
Evans Theodore, stone mason, Brandywine ab 13th
Evans Thomas, gardener, Front bel Phoenix(K)
Evans Thomas, gent., 10th ab Washington
Evans Thomas, dry goods, 9 N 2nd.
Evans Thomas, lab. 17 Cresson's al
Evans Thomas C., tailor, 116 N 5th, h 331 N 6th
Evans Thomas L., boots & shoes, 35 S 3d, h 192 Pine
Evans T. & F., mers., 9 N 2d, h 55 Union
Evans T. Wallis, dry goods, 214 Chestnut
Evans W. Elbert, 9 Girard
Evans & Watson, iron chests and refrigerators, 76 S 2d

Everest Cornelius, engraver, 68 Sassafras
Everett Benjamin C., surgeon's bandages and instruments, 32 S 6th
Everett Charles, mer., 78 High,
Everett C. D., dentist, S W 9th & Mulberry
EVERETT & ENGLES, dry goods, 78 High
Everett Maria, 13 Morgan's ct.
Everett Newman, 47 Green, office 477 N 2d
Everham & Colsher, wheelwrights, R road and Vine, h R road & Sch 7th
Everham Saml., wheelwright, 67 St John
Everham Wm., wheelwright, Sch 7th ab Parrish
Everhart Geo., turner, Allen's ct
Everhart John, chairmr., 4th bel Poplar
Everhart Margaret, cake baker, 53 Brown
Everill John, stone mason, Buttonwood bel 9th
Everitt Jonathan, harnessmaker, 8 Torr's al., h 349 Callowhill
Everitt Mary, Green ab 13th
Everitt Samuel S., saddler, 14 R road
Everly George M., collector, 297 S Front
Everly M. N., button manuf., factory 5 Harmony, h 286 S 5th.
Everly W. A., merchant, 225 High, h 398 Mulberry
Everly W. H., painter & glazier, 2d bel Federal
Evers John A., shoemr., 11 Dannaker's av
Evers Thos., lab., Vienna ab Franklin (K)
Everson John W., tailor, rear 397 N 3d
Everson Wm. K., tailor, 157 Coates
Everswein Wm., carter, rear Jackson (S W)
Everwine Wm., lab., Melon bel 12th
Eves Charles, glass blower, Wood ab Frankl't
Evil Henry, carter, Chuch ab Washington
Evitt Jane, b. h., Franklin n School
Ewang Adam, weaver, rear Locust n Beach
Ewell Solomon, waterman, 56 Catharine
Ewen David, druggist, R road bel Green
Ewen Joseph, dry goods, 250 S 2d
Ewing Chas., shoemr., 81 S 8th
Ewing George H., bottler, 453 S Front.
Ewing James, lab., Sch. 2d ab Cedar
Ewing James K., barber, 388 S 2d
Ewing John, barber, Franklin ab Front (K)
Ewing J. O., gent., Spruce bel 12th
Ewing Robert com. mer., 27 Minor, h N W 8d

Eyre C. Cushing, capt., 421 S Front
Eyre Charles, shop, P road ab Federal
Eyre Edward E., mer., S W 4th & Mulberry
Eyre Franklin, shipwright, Queen bel Palmer, (K)
Eyre Franklin Mrs., gentw., Beach bel Palmer (K)
Eyre Jehu W., wharf builder, Beach ab Hanover (K)
Eyre John S., gent., S E 4th and George (N L)
Eyre Joseph K., com. mer., 61 S Front, h S E 13th & Spruce
Eyre J. Randolph, carp., Hutchinson ab Poplar
Eyre & Landell, dry goods, S W 4th & Mulberry.
Eyre Lewis, carp., 18 Logan
Eyre Lydia W., gentw., 264 Marshall
Eyre Mary Ann, 30 Bread
Eyre Mrs. Mary, Sch 8th ab Spruce
Eyre Richard W., alderman, office Queen n Palmer, h Beach ab Hanover (K)
Eyre Thomas, dry goods, 12th and Vine.
Eyre Wm., carp., Sch 8th n Arch
Eytinge Bernhardt, 99 N 2d
Eytinge D., sworn interpreter, 4 Quince
Ezekiel Isaac W., mer., 206 S 2d, h 22 Howard
Ezekiel Simon, clothing, 416 High

———

Faaham Patrick, Fitler (K)
Faany Mary Ann, dressmr., Lombard n 2d
Faas Anthony, accordian, 649 N 2d
Faas Francis S., confect., 649 N 2d (K)
Faber William, silversmith, 124 N 5th.
Fabian Charles, shoemr., 11 Linden.
Fable Barbara, widow, 9th ab Noble
Fable Wm., bookbinder, Lewis ab Poplar
Fabruius Samuel, cordw., 27 Noble
Fackler Frederick, baker, 37 New Market
Facney John, gent., 132 Spruce
Faddis Ezekiel, cordw., 358 N 3d
Fadely Jonathan, lab., Apple ab Brown
Fagan Alexander, ladies' shoemr., 134 S 10th
Fagan Danl., porter, rear 123 Plum
Fagan Edward, shop, Shippen lane bel Bedford
Fagan Hugh, grocer, S E 8th and Bedford.
Fagan John, stereotype foundry, 19 St. James, h W Penn sq
Fagan John, waterm., rear Penn bel Maiden (K)
Fagan John, 1 S 13th
Fagan Patrick, weaver, 50 Fitzwater
Fagan Peter, carpet weaver, 7th bel Baker
Fagan P. A., grocer, S E 8th and Lombard.
Fagioli Francis, cordw., 81 S 8th
Fagundus Jacob, brass founder, 161 N 4th
Fahy Patrick, lab., 246 N Water
Fair John, tailor, G T road bel 7th
Fair John, carpenter, Fries' ct, h 87 Fitzwater
Fair John, carp., 11th ab Buttonwood
FAIRBAIRN JOHN & CO., saddlery hardware, 11 N 4th.
Fairbairn John, saddler, 11 N 4th, h Mulberry n Sch. 7th

14

Fairbank Horatio, patent lamp, 9 N 8th
Fairbanks Drury, bandboxmr., 2 Thorn's ct
Fairbanks Sylvanus H., bootmr., Poplar and Ontario
Fairbrothers David, carter, 33 Mary (S)
Fairbrothers James, carter, 33 Mary (S)
Fairchild E. R. Rev., cor. sec., P. H. M. Society, 142 Chestnut. h 79 Locust
Fairchild Henry L., 192 N 8th
Fairchild John, buttonmr., Winters' ct
Faires J. W., seminary, George ab 11th, h Sch 7th bel Locust
Fairgrieve James, clerk, 82 S 2d
Fairlamb Geo. W., carp., Academy, h N E 13th and Budd
FAIRLAMB JONAS P., jr., att'y at law, 7 George, h 2 Clover
Fairman G. W., coal agent, Broad and Cherry, h Sch 6th and Emerald
Fairman Robt., ostler, 26 Prune
Fales George, mer., 6 S Front, h 131 Sassafras.
Fales, Lothrop & Co., mers., 6 S Front.
FALLON, C. & J., attys. & coun., 142 Walnut
Fallon James, lab., 246 N Front
Fallon Mary, Rugan ab Callowhill
Falls Francis, gratemaker, 83 N 6th
Falls John, chandler, 50 Union
Falls Michael, b h., 274 S Front
Falls Wm., lab., rear Fitler n 2d
Falweiler Saml., brushmr., 145 St John
Fannin John, ropemr., Cadwalader ab Phœnix
Fanning John, lab., 7 Bell's ct
Fanton Mary Anna, rear Broad ab Poplar
Faranger Margaret, grocer, Prime and M road
Fareira John, jr., hatter, 357 S 2d
Fareira Joseph, hatter, 284 High, h Pine ab 10th
Farhawk Henry, 2d ab Edward (K)
Faries James, coachmr, Carpenter ab 4th
Faries Wm., 366 Vine.
Farley Ann, tavern, 200 High.
Farley Edw., lab., Sch Front ab Mulberry
Farley Frederick, weaver, West n Vienna (K)
Farley James, lab., Pearl ab Sch 8th
Farley James, lab., Cedar bel 12th
Farley John, stone cut., Buist's ct
Farley John, weaver, Carpenter ab 13th
Farley Lewis, weaver, West ab Vienna (K)
Farley Michael, lab., 221 Shippen
Farley Robt., lab., rear Fitler n 2d
Farley Rosanna, 11th bel Carpenter
Farley Thomas, stone cutter, Pine bel 11th, h 3d ab Cedar
Farley Wilson J., drug., N W 4th & Catharine.
Farmer Felix, weaver, Cadwalader, ab Phoenix (K)
Farmer Patrick, weaver, Milton ab 11th
Farmer R., tailor, 28 Branch
Farndell George H., railroad curve layer, Lloyd bel Shippen
Farney James, carter, Carpenter ab 10th
Farnham B. A., mer, 36 S Front, h Broad below Spruce
Farnum Henry, mer., 12 Chestnut, h Walnut W Broad

ARNUM HENRY & CO., dry goods, 12 Chest-nut

ARNUM & IMBRIE, mers., 1 Church al

rnum James A., com. mer. 1 Church al., h Walnut W Broad

rnum John, mer., 26 S Front, h 257 Mulberry.

ARNUM, NEWHALL & CO., com. mers., 26 S Front

rnum Peter, mer. 26 S Front, h 477 Chestnut

ro Edw., blacksmith. 89 Apple

ARQUHAR & CARPENTER, conveyancers, 56 Walnut

rquhar Edward Y. conveyancer, 56 Walnut, h Sch 6th bel Walnut

rquhar Thos. W., tailor, 471 Vine

rr George, lab., 13 Brook

ARR GEORGE W., tailor, N W 5th & Chestnut, h 1 door ab Wood

rr John, chemist, N W 9th and Brown, h 151 N 6th.

ARR JOHN C., mer., 112 Chestnut, h 171 S 5th

rr John T., apoth., N E 13th & Callowhill

ARR, POWERS & WEIGHTMAN, chemists, N W 9th & Brown

rr Rebecca, Sch 8th bel Vine

rr T. T., druggist, N E 5th and Cedar, h 188 S 5th

rr Wm. A., druggist, N E 12th & Callowhill

rrady James, surg. inst. maker, 1 Cherry

rrady John, printer, 16 Mayland

rran John, carp., Curtis' ct

rran Michael, distiller, 471 N 3d

rran Michael, drayman, 19 Vernon

rran Thomas, lab., Sch Front n Chestnut

RRAND JAMES H., confec., 281 Chestnut

rell Barney, labourer, Sch 7th ab Wood.

rell Catharine, Jones n Sch 4th

rell Catharine, Goodwill ct

rell Daniel, lab., Sch Front bel Chestnut

rell Elizabeth, Palmer ab Duke (K)

rell Hugh, weaver, Hope ab Master (K)

rell James, weaver, Hancock ab Phœnix (K)

rell James, hat tip manuf., 309 Cherry

rell John, carp., 7 Harrison's ct (K)

rell Joseph, temp. tavern, 4 Zane

rell Joseph, captain, Chr.stian ab 3d

rell Patrick, ostler, 3 Pleasant ct

rell Rosina, teacher, 66 Gaskill

rell Walter, bootmr., 18 Howard

rolly James A., bon. presser, 119 Cedar

ren Ann, 250 Christian

ren Edward, 13 Adams' ct

ren Edward, carp., 8th ab Christian

ren Mary, 103 German

Farson Wm., carpenter, Catharine

Farthing John, victualle

Faser Christian, stone cu

Fassitt Alfred, mer., 48

Fassitt & Co. drygoods, 4

Fassitt E. C., atty. & cou

Fassitt Huson L., mer., 5

Fassitt Jas., gent., 329 M

Fassitt Jas. W., mer., 4 Broad

Fassitt, Mrs., widow of 7

Fassitt Robt. F., mer., 32

Fassitt T. S. R., gent., 4.

Farsold John, butcher, C

Farver Henry, lab., Rihl'

Fasy C. A., dressmr., Wo

Fasy Henry J., cordw. 4

Fasy John H. printer, 4t

Fater Jacob, shop, Mech:

Fatman Joseph, chemist,

Fatman L., mer., 41 N F:

Fatman L. & Co., match

Faulke George, capt., Pi

Faulkner J. H., painter, 1

Faulkner Robert, tailor, :

Faulkner Patrick, lab., 5

Faulkner Samuel, weave:

Faulkner Wm. H., carp.,

Faunce Christian, fisherm.

Faunce Conrad, fisherm.,

Faunce Daniel, fisherm., C

Faunce David, glassblowe

Faunce David, drayman, nix (K)

Faunce Geo., fisherman,

Faunce Geo., fisherm., Qu

Faunee Hannah, George

Faunce Henry, fisherm.,

Faunce Henry, glass blow

Faunce Henry, bookbind

Faunce Isaac Sen., fisherm

Faunce Isaac, fisherman, (

Faunce Isaac, fisherman,

Faunce Jacob, fisherman,

Faunce Jacob, fisherman,

Faunce Jacob, fisherman,

Faunce Jacob D., fisherm

Faunce Jacob H., fisherm

Faunce John, carter, Car

Faunce Jno. C., fisherman

Faunce Mary, wid., F roa

Faunce Michael, fisherm.,

Faussctt James, gent., 91 Crown.
Faust David, mer., 70 N 3d, h 189 N 7th
Faust Henry, cordw., Orchard
Faust Samuel, hatter, New Market bel Green
Faust & Winebrener, hardware, 70 N 3d
Fauver Casper, door keeper, Com Hall (N L)
Favour John B. mariner, 113 Queen
Fawcett Charles, wigmr., 174 Chestnut, h 180 Spruce
Fawcett Wm., 24 Logan's sq
FAY C. M., mer., 13 Commerce, h 68 Franklin
Fay Michael, weaver, 8 M'Duffie
Fay N., 121 N 6th
Fay Thomas, grocer, S E 6th & Powell.
FAYE & BELROSE, paper hangings, 100 Chestnut
Faye James, mer., 100 Chestnut, h 160 S 13th
Faye Thomas, mer., 100 Chestnut, h 431 Spruce
Fayle Wm., engraver, 9th bel Catharine
Fayette Lewis, cabinetmaker, 356 S 2d.
Feagley Joseph, tanner, 56 F road opp Queen
Feagley Simon, lab., 56 F road
Feagley Susanna, 31 Laurel
Fearon & Brother, mers., 15½ S. water
Fearon Hetty, b. h., 428 High
Fearon James, soapmaker, 49 Union, h 160 S 4th
Fearon Patrick, blacksmith, c Spruce & Pratt, h Vaughan bel Walnut.
Feass Henry, baker, 3d bel Franklin (K)
Feaster Maria, washer, Nectarine ab 10th
Feber Chas., tailor, 20 Mead al
Federschraid Gottleib, baker, 212 S 6th
Fee John, shoemr., Shippen & Lloyd
Fee Terence, clothes, 233 Cedar
Feeny James, shop, 5 Hurst
Feeny John, tailor, 46 Gaskill.
Feeny Michael, lab., 128 S Water
Fees Christiani, tavern, 85 Brown
Fees Christopher, cabinetmr., 91 Brown
Fees John L., piano mr., rear 83 Brown
Fegary Mr., wine mer., 220 E Spruce
Fegenbush Catharine, 386 N 6th
Fegenbush J., shoe store, 446 N 2d.
Fegley Ludwig, lab., Amber ab Phoenix (K)
Feherty Mrs., wid., 31 Union (S)
Fehlisen Christian, skin dresser, 27 Beaver st (K)
Feinack John, waiter, 2 Barclay
Feinour Catharine, gentw., 32 Plum st
Feinour Joseph, stove finisher & tin & iron pl. workers, 215 S Front
Feinour Mary, 188 Queen (S)
Feinour & Nixon, paper mrs., 231 N 3d
Feitig J. P., carp. 23 Jones' al, h 81 Brown (N L)
Feldman H. C., baker, 129 Sassafras
Felker Sarah, 273 Marshall
Felker Wm., cigar mr., rear 4th ab Brown
Fell Aaron, cordw., Poplar ab 10th
Fell Christian, currier, 12 Coates
Fell C. J., currier, Front and Coates, h 384 N Front
Fell C. J. & Brother, choc. manuf., 64 S Front.
Fell Franklin, mer., 64 S Front, h 12th ab Mulberry
Fell James G., Sec. Hazleton Coal Co., 58 Walnut

Fell Jesse A., printer, Bevan's ct
Fell Jonathan, M. D., 375 Mulberry
Fell Jos. G., 161 Sassafras
Fell & Kinsler, curriers, N W Front & Coates
Fell Penrose, tailor, 62 Chestnut
Fell Reese D., tailor, 62 Chestnut, h 464 Spruce
Fell R. D. & Brother, tailors, 62 Chestnut.
Fell Samuel, printer, 13 Marriott
Fellowes C., gent., Clinton ab 10th
Felt Elizabeth, 102 Prime
Felt George, boat builder, 107 Swanson
Felt Wm., tinsmith, 405 S Front
Feltham Joseph, lab., 273 S Front
Felthousen Henry, cordw., Hughes' ct
Felthousen Jacob, printer, 3 Hermitage pl
Felthousen Jacob, jr., printer, rear 115 Dillwyn
Felton Henry, frame mr., 7 St James, h Poplar bel 10th
Feltus Henry J., sugar refiner, Zane ab 7th
Feltus Mark, lab., Hutchinson ab Poplar
Feltus Thom., lab., rear Palm bel Parrish
FELTUS & ZIMMERLING, sug. refiners, Zane ab 7th
Feltwell Benjamin M., bricklr., and stove mr., 406 High, h 1 Dugan
Felty Charles, bricklr., 9 Orleans
Felty George, cordw., 91 W Callowhill
Felty John W., cordw., 3 Paschall's al
Felty Wm., blacksmith, Filbert n Sch. 4th.
Femington T. M., tax collector, N E 3d and Federal
Fender George W., dry goods, 44 N 4th
Fenderson Boston H., barber, 254 Chestnut, h Shippen bel Russell
Fenemore Valentine, wharf builder, Queen ab Wood (K)
Fenimore Jason L., 17 S Penn sq
Fenlin John, tavern, 120 N 3d
Fenn Titus, shoemr., 531 Chestnut
Fennell Mary Mrs., 390 N Front
Fennell Wm., register gas works, 11 S 7th, h 127 S 9th
Fenner Charles H., tobacconist, 10th ab James
Fenner Eliza, tobacconist, 93 N 4th.
Fenner H. P., tobacconist, 324 Callowhill
Fenner John F. Jun., tobacconist, Callowhill rear of 6th
Fenner John F., tobacconist, 213 N Front.
Fenner John R., saddler, rear 21 Chatham
Fenner Peter, tobacconist, R road and Wood
Fenner R., umbr. manuf., 126 High, h 118 Pine
Fennimore Benjamin, carp., 12th bel Coates
Fennimore Joseph, botanist, 6th ab Poplar
Fennimore Martha, b. h., 137 S 5th
Fennimore William, ladies' shoemr., 79 S 2d
Fenninger Rev. M., 282 N 3d
Fenton Abner, carp., Franklin bel Vienna (K)
Fenton Albert, sailmr., 361 N Front
Fenton Andrew, sailmr., 42 N Wharves, h 232 N Front
Fenton Eleazer, dry goods, 48 S 2d
Fenton Eliza, gentw., 48 German st
Fenton Elizabeth, book folder, 12th & Filbert
Fenton Randall T. P., collector, Charlotte ab George

Fenton Wm. C., mer., 16 Decatur, h 183 N 12th
Ferguson Alexander, cordw., h 33 N 4th
FERGUSON ALEXANDER S., cordw., 157 Cherry.
Ferguson Andrew, carp. 5 Pleasant Retreat
Ferguson Charles, blacksm, Watman's ct
Ferguson Corn, stovecnr., Smith's ct
Ferguson David, weaver, 47 Cedar
Ferguson Elizabeth, trimmings, 8th & Noble
Ferguson George, clerk, rear 12 Lawrence
Ferguson Henry, carp., Sassafras n Sch 2d
Ferguson Henry, weaver, Stewart's ct
Ferguson James, manuf., 122 High, h Crown bel Franklin (K)
Ferguson James, sailmr., U. S. Navy, 10 Wharton st
Ferguson Jas., grocer, N W 13th & Callowhill.
Ferguson Jesse R. printer, 23 Turner
Ferguson John, cottonmr., Cedar ab 13th
Ferguson John, tailor, 54 Apple
Ferguson John, weaver, 13th ab Fitzwater
Ferguson John, weaver, rear Perry, bel Phœnix
Ferguson John L., last mr., 121 S 6th
Ferguson John P., carp., 9th ab Parrish
Ferguson J. carp. rear Coates bel 12th
Ferguson P. L., 207 Chestnut
Ferguson Robert, supt. gas works, 66 Maiden (N L)
Ferguson Susan, wid. of Capt. J L., 304 S Front
Ferguson Wm., weaver, Hamilton n William
Ferguson Wm., weaver, 43 W Cedar
Ferguson William J., 13th ab Cedar
Ferkler Henry, baker, German ab 3d
Fernerer A. H., tobacconist, 9 Margaretta st
Fernan Francis, weaver, Centre and Dean
Fernberg Chas., coal dealer, Willow ab 13th
Fernberger Saml., clothier, 100 N 2d
Fernley J. E., bonnet manuf., 28 Margaretta st
Fernold Bennit, blacksm., Concord st
Fernon D. B., dry goods, 544 N 2nd.
Fernon James A., cabmr., rear 542 N 2d (K)
Fernon John, ship carpenter, Allen n Shackamaxon
Fernon John, collector, 544 N 2d
Fernon Peter, machinist, 12th bel Poplar
Fernon Thomas, painter, 544 N 2d
Fernon Wm. painter, 544 N 2d
Fernon Wm., lab., Coates n Fairmount
Fernsler John W., High W of Sch 6th
Ferrand Steph., carver, Filbert n Sch 4th
Ferree George, 39 N 2d
Ferree James B., mer., 172 High, h 13 Clinton
Ferree Philip, Madison House, 39 N 2d
Ferrell Ann, wid., Coates n Sch
Ferrell Benj., machinist, 249 S 6th
Ferrell Malachi, white washer, 33 Quince

Ferris Daniel, bonnets, 10 N 2nd., h M V
Ferris Edward B., watchmr., 84 N 3d
Ferris Ellen, gentw., 10 Powell
Ferris James, bricklayer, 556 S Front
Ferris Jas., weaver, P road bel Marriott
Ferris John, cordw., 12th ab Vine
Ferris Josiah, cordw. 35 Mechanic
Ferris William, coachsmith, Murray n Sch 2d
Ferry Geo., vineg. mr., 49 B road
Ferry Hugh, 137 Sp Garden
Ferry James, lab., Ann W Sch 4th
Ferry Wm., shoemr. 278 S 3d
Fessenden C. P., ink & black. manuf., 14 Quince
Fest Edwy, watchmr., 270 Sassafras
Fetherston H., b. h., 152 S 2nd.
FETTERS CHAS. S., tavern, N W Almond & Swanson
Fetters James, drayman, 183 Green
Fetters Jas., lab., rear Rose ab School (K)
Fetters John, carman, Stites' ct (K)
Fetters Rebecca, ice, N W Sch 6th & Chestnut
Fetters Wm., furniture car, Otter n F road
Fetters Wm., ladies' shoemaker, Hope below Phœnix
Fettinger Henry, plasterer, Pleasant ab 12th
Fewgate Oliver, carrier, 13th bel Spruce
Fickardt Frederick A., M. D., 85 S 11th
Fiechterer Fred., Garden ab Noble
Fiedler Jacob, morocco dr., Fraley's ct
Fiedler John, carp., New Market ab Brown
Fiedler John, butcher, Front bel Wharton
Fiegel Charles, Wood n Sch 8th
Fiegel Reviny, blacksmith, Van Buren pl, b Parrish ab 10th
Fiegl Levi, mer., 28 N 2d
Fichrer J., M. D., 414 N 5th
Fiekes John, tavern, 10th & Willow
Field Adeline, Jones' al (N L)
Field Benjamin, mer., 52 High, h 137 S 3d
Field Charles, plater, 80 N 2nd, h 8th ab Green
Field Charles, mer., 71 and h 200 S Front
Field Conrad, oyster house, 214 High
Field David, tailor, Ogden ab 10th
Field George, clothing, 238 S 3d
Field Isaac, carpenter, 83 Tammany
FIELD ISAAC C., com. mer., 34 High, h 204 Chestnut
Field James, mer., 83 High, h 21 Montg'y sq.
Field James, grocer, R road bel Ann (F V)
Field Joel, waterman, 30 Duke.
Field John, brickmr., 20 Garden
Field John, farmer, Parker's row
Field John W., mer., 81 S Front, h 18 Girard
FIELD & LANGSTROTH, hardware, 52 High
Field Mary, 483 S 2nd.
Field Mary, h 204 Chestnut

Field Thomas S. & Co., com. mers., 36 & h 112 N Front
Field W. Y., weigh master, 71 Pine, h 71 S Front
Fielding Ann, spooler, rear 23 F road
Fielding Esther, gentw., 97 Filbert
Fielding Jereh., milkman, 8th and Cherry
Fields Abraham, 80 S 3d
Fields Abraham, porter, 8 Acorn al
Fields Edmund, cordw., rear Poplar ab 9th
Fields George, basketmr., P road ab Federal
Fields Geo., carpet weaver, G T road ab Master
Fields Joseph, blacksm., Moser ct (K)
Fields Malcolm M'K., engineer, Sch Front ab Filbert
Fields Rudolph, constable, Loud ab 9th
Fields Samuel, cordw. Bedford ab Marlborough (K)
Fields Stuart, 19 Vernon
Fiering Christian, brass foundry, Hope bel Phoenix (K)
Fife James, reedmr. S E 10th & College av.
Fife Mat., boxmr., Biddle's al, h 7 Lagrange
Fife William, teacher, 98 Marshall
Fifield & Matthews, com. mers. and grocers, 60 Washington avenue
Fightly Fredk., cordw., rear 114 New Market
Fightly Lewis, stone cut., rear 114 New Market
Figley John, lab., Perry bel Master (K)
Figueira & Co., importers, 38 Walnut
Figueira F. J., mer., 38 Walnut, h 220 Spruce
File John, lab. 40 Charlotte
File Wm. A. machinist, Ontario ab Parrish
Filemyr Anthony, flour and feed, Otter and 2d (K)
Filemyr Henry, grocery, G T road ab Phoenix (K)
Filley Edward A., 436 High
FILLEY HARVEY, tin plate worker, 436 High
Filley Wm., agent, Brooklyn Glass Co., 12 N 5th
Fillot Alex., hair dresser, 79 S 8th
Filton Godfrey, brickmr., Coates ab Sch 5th
Fimple John, brushmr., 21 New Market
Finch A. D., 632 S 2d ab Reed
Finch George, carp., 65 New Market
Finch James, bootmr. 8th ab Mulberry
Finch Richard, coachmr., Lewis bel Girard av
Fine Henry M., gent., S W Lombard & Front
Fink Andreas, lab., 13th & R road
Fink Daniel, painter, 4th bel Jefferson (K)
Fink Geo., stocking weav., Phoenix n G T road
Fink Jacob, starchmr., Hope ab Master (K)
Fink Jacob, lab., 4 Melon pl
Fink Jacob, baker, 356 N 3rd.
Fink Jacob, blacksm., Cherry n Duke (K)
Fink Jacob, rope mr., G T road ab 6th
Fink John, founder, rear 287 St John
FINK JULIUS, cooking range manuf., 431 Chestnut
Fink Saml., machinist, George n 4th
Finkeni Frederick S. carp. Vernon bel 11th
Finlaw Low, 31 Cresson's al
Finletter Thos., manuf., 576 N 3rd.
Finletter Thos. K., attorney, 576 N 3d
Finley Andrew, conf., 220 Callowhill

Finley Chas., plasterer, G T road bel Jefferson
FINLEY & CO., upholsterers, S E 2d & Walnut
Finley Hugh, grocer, N E Shippen & Shipen la
Finley James, weaver, G T road bel Phoenix
Finley James, clerk, 357 S 5th
Finley James G., merchant, 63 N 2nd.
Finley John R., judge, 27 Palmyra sq
Finley Margaret, 144 Green
Finley Moses, weaver, Shippen bel Broad
Finley Richard, weaver, Lombard & Sch 2d
Finley Samuel, weaver, Weaver's row (K)
Finley Thomas, baker, 166 S 11th
Finley Thomas, carpet weaver, N W Broad and Fitzwater
Finley William, upholsterer, S E 2d & Walnut, 369 Callowhill
Finley Wm. lab. Lombard E Sch 6th
Finley Wm., painter, Marshall ab Brown
Finley Wm., weaver, 8 Gay's ct (K)
Finley Wm., weaver, Mariner
Finley Wm. A., tanner, rear 615 Front
Finn Ann, S E 7th and Mulberry
Finn & Burton, paper hangings, 142 Mulberry
Finn Edward, 8 Morgan's ct
Finn James C. paper hanger, 142 Mulberry
Finn John, cordw., rear 1 Paschal's al
Finneberger Benedict, sausagemr., George n 4th
Finnegan John, lab. Brazier ab Lloyd
Finnegan John, lab., 5 Ewing's ct
Finnegan Mrs. Ann, shop keeper, Filbert near Sch 7th
Finnegan Edward, weaver, Locust n Sch 2d
Finnessy John, stovemr., Higgins' ct
Finney Charles, hatter, 10th bel Poplar
Finney Christiana, 350 Chestnut
Finney Francis, 33 O Y road
Finney Henry, tailor, 144 High, h 25 Farmer
Finney John L., tailor, Nectarine ab 9th
Finney Wm., Baker n Sch 7th
Finnigan Francis, shop, Small ab 5th
Finnigan W. C., grocer, N W 7th & Baker
Finzi A., dry goods, S W 5th and Spruce
Fiot Augustus, importer of music, 196 Chestnut.
Fiot J. R., 243 High
Firing Sophia, variety store, 125 Green.
Firth Edw., mer., Sch 8th bel Walnut
Firth John, blacksm., rear Shackamaxon below Franklin (K)
Firth John, baker, High W of Sch 7th
Firth Joseph, baker, 112 N 4th
Firth J., milliner, 12th and Wood
Firth Mary Ann, tobacconist, 4 Arcade
Firth Samuel, cloth manuf., 492 Callowhill
Firth Thomas T., Brig. Insp., 66 S 8th
FISH ASA I., atty. and coun., 5th and Library
Fish Edward, cooper, Wheat and Keefe
Fish Hiram, lab., Wheat and Wharton
Fish Israel L., plasterer, 13th bel Buttonwood.
Fish Jacob S., plasterer, 10th bel Coates.
Fish James, b h, 1 Spring Garden
Fish Lemuel, hatter, Kline's ct
Fish Thomas, tailor, 142 Poplar
Fishblatt Louis, cap maker, 36 Bank, h 7 Callowhill ab Sch 6th

Fisher Abel, waterman, rear 156 Poplar
Fisher Andrew, baker, rear 297 Callowhill
Fisher Ann, widow, 277 Chestnut
Fisher Catharine, trader, Palmer bel F road
Fisher Charles, teamster, Sch 8th ab R road
Fisher Charles H. confectioner, 145 Poplar
Fisher Charles H. 264 Walnut
Fisher Charles N. mariner, back 75 Christian
Fisher Christopher, 280 S 4th
Fisher Coleman, broker, 94 Walnut, h 54 S 13th
Fisher David, waiter, 209 S 7th
Fisher David & Sons, paint. & glazs. 306 Chestnut
Fisher Deborah, Paschall's al
FISHER EDMUND N., collect., 306 Chestnut
Fisher Elizabeth, Church bel Christian
Fisher Elizabeth, Marlborough bel Franklin
Fisher Emanuel, printer, 65 New
Fisher Esther, 249 Mulberry
Fisher Ezekiel, mariner, Beck bel 2d
Fisher Francis A., mer., Locustn Sch 7th
Fisher Frederick, upholsterer, N E 8th & Zane
    and 297 N 2nd
Fisher Frederick, baker, 352 Callowhill
Fisher Fredk., jr., 352 Callowhill
Fisher F., morocco dresser, 79 & h 88 St John
Fisher George, brass worker, 149 S 6th
Fisher George, lab., 22 Brown
Fisher George R., tailor, 24 S 4th.
Fisher George S. 306 Chestnut
Fisher George W., clothing, 77 N 2d
Fisher Henry, wheelwright, Beach bel Maiden
Fisher Henry, cabinetmr. Coburn
Fisher Henry, butcher, Palmer bel Duke (K)
Fisher Henry, baker, Callowhill ab Sch 3d
Fisher Henry B., Willow bel 8th
Fisher Henry G., painter, 306 Chestnut, h 14
    Raspberry.
Fisher Henry M., carp., Samson's al
Fisher Jacob, vict. Shackamaxon bel Franklin
Fisher Jacob, carp., 22 Brown (N L)
Fisher Jacob, grocer, Apple bel George
Fisher Jacob, tavern, Broad and Wood
Fisher Jacob, coachsmith, 16 Webb's al
Fisher Jacob, lab., Franklin n Union
Fisher Jacob, vinegar store, Poplar ab 3d
Fisher Jacob M. blacksmith, 4 Irvine
Fisher James, collector, 5 Willow ab 3d
Fisher James, bookseller, 124 Green
Fisher James E., straw goods, 155 High
Fisher Joel, grocer, N W 5th and Cherry, h 25
    Appletree al
Fisher John, drayman, rear Front ab Franklin
Fisher John, cordw., 3 Ellett's av
Fisher John, cabinetmaker, 185 G T road.
Fisher John, victualler, Palmer n Duke (K)
Fisher John, butcher, Palmer bel F road
Fisher John, vict. 302 Callowhill
Fisher John, whf. builder, Front & Brown
Fisher John, tobacconist, Rugan ab Callowhill
Fisher John, cordw., 3 Linden st (K)
Fisher John D., painter, 306 Chestnut, h 173
    Buttonwood.
Fisher John G., cabmr., 189 Brown
Fisher John M., cutler, 216 S 5th
Fisher John N., gent., S W 7th & Buttonwood.

Fisher John & Philip, cabinetmrs., 496 N 2d
    185 G T road
Fisher John S., saddler, 101 Dillwyn
Fisher Jonathan, porter, 9 Washington
Fisher Joseph, thermometer mr., 58 Chestnut
Fisher Joseph, lab. 217 Locust
Fisher Joseph S., mer., 18 Commerce, h 357 N
    6th
Fisher J. F., att'y & coun. 170 Chestnut
Fisher Lewis, bottler, 6 Noble
Fisher Margaret, gentw., G T road ab Phoenix
Fisher Mary Ann, teacher, Palmer bel Frankl.
Fisher Mary P., gentw. 312 Chestnut.
Fisher Michael, fly net, Poplar ab 3d
Fisher Myers C. gilder, Lewis ab Poplar.
Fisher Patrick, weaver, Philip bel Oxford (K)
Fisher Peter, carter, Sch 8th bel Carlton
Fisher Peter, victualler, Crown and Bedford, h
    Shackamaxon bel Franklin
Fisher Peter, stone mason, Broad ab Poplar
Fisher P. S., saddler, Coates ab 9th
Fisher Richard, lab., Meredith's ct
Fisher Rodney, mer., 151 N 7th.
Fisher Samuel, bricklayer, Fisher's ct (N L)
Fisher Samuel, carter, Jones W Sch. 5th
Fisher Samuel, pearl worker, 10 St Joseph's av
Fisher Samuel, carter, 418 N 4th
Fisher Samuel A., baker, 239 S 6th.
Fisher Saml. H., Wallace ab 9th
Fisher Sarah R. 58 S 11th
Fisher Sarah W. 290 Chestnut.
Fisher Sidney G., att'y & coun., 57 S 7th.
FISHER, SONS & ROBINSON, agency, 43 High
FISHER S. F., atty. & coun., 76½ Walnut, h 457
    Chestnut
Fisher Thomas, dry goods, 42 N 4th
Fisher Thomas, seaman, 38 Blackberry al
Fisher Thos., mer., 110 S Front
Fisher Thomas R., hosier, 30 Church al
Fisher William, cooper, West ab Walnut
Fisher Wm., umbrellamr., Marshall n Willow
Fisher Wm., shipwrgt., Marlboro' ab Queen
    (K)
Fisher William, confectionery, Fisher's ct
    (N L)
Fisher William, atty. and coun., 218 Walnut, h
    480 Chestnut
Fisher William, tobacconist, Broad ab Sassafras
Fisher Wm. cooper, 409 High, h 3 Dorr's ct
Fisler C. H., ship broker, 40 Chatham
Fisler Daniel, tailor, rear 49 Brown (N L)
Fisler Jacob, clerk, 552 High
Fisler Jacob H., register Sch. Water Works, h
    363 N 6th
FISLER JACOB P., tavern, 2 N Front
Fiss Aaron W. carp., Robb's ct
Fiss Ann, Moore's ct (S G)
Fiss Catharine, Leopard ab Franklin (K)
Fiss Eliza Ann, 386 S 3d
Fiss Elizabeth, widow, 2 Gravel's ct
Fiss George, shoemr. 6 York ct
Fiss George, tobacconist, 18 Branner's al
Fiss John, carp. Coates ab Fairmount st
Fiss Rachael, Brinton ab R road
Fiss Samuel, cabinetmr., 20 Plum

Fiss Samuel, agent, Juniper ab Spruce
Fitchett John S., hardware, 47 High
Fite George, tobacconist, 5 Bonsall
Fite Henry, victualler, 7 Diligent av
Fite John B., tinsmith, 10 Gebhard
Fite Samuel, brewer, Sch. 8th n Vine
Fite Saml., stone cutter, 9th ab Coates (S G)
Fite Samuel, blacksmith, Sch. 3d n Locust
Fite Wm., tobacconist, 177½ S 3d
Fithian Aaron B., shoe store, 324 N 2d
Fithian Amable, dressmr., Shield's al
Fithian Chas., printer, Tyler st
Fithian Chas. B., mer., 38 N 2d, h 233 N 9th
Fithian Ephraim, carter, Court al
Fithian George, sexton, 46 P road
Fithian Geo., collect., 3 Knight's ct
Fithian Hannah, gentw., 13 Coates
Fithian, Jones & Co., dry goods, 38 N 2d
Fithian John, glassworks, Crown ab Bedford
Fithian Lemuel S., mer., 38 N 2d, h 175 S 7th
Fithian Matthias, printer & booksr., 82 S 3d
Fithian Wm. B., collector, 157 N 4th.
Fitler Alfred, conveyancer, 51 N 6th, h 2d and Otter.
Fitler Daniel, gent., G T road ab Camac
Fitler Elizabeth, 2d and Otter (K)
Fitler Henry, cordw., rear Schleisman's ct
Fitler & Hunter, morocco factory, Willow ab 3d
Fitler Joseph P., M. D., 2d & Beaver, (K)
Fitler J. P., conveyancer, 215 N 6th
Fittirnan Richard, lab., Sassafras ab 13th
Fitting Jacob, baker, 86 N 11th
Fitton John, baker, 479 N 2nd.
Fitzgerald Adam, farmer, 6th bel Christian
Fitzgerald David, jr. carter, 8½ Hurst
Fitzgerald Edward, baker, 181 N Front
Fitzgerald Hortiss N., mer., 23 S whfs, h 444 N Front
Fitzgerald Mrs. James, surg. inst. mr., 21 Franklin, h 5 Carberry
Fitzgerald John, cordw., rear 16 Wash. Market pl
Fitzgerald John, porter, 19 Eutaw
Fitzgerald John R., cooper, 5 Franklin pl, h 26 E North.
Fitzgerald K., 317 S 2nd.
Fitzgerald Morris, b h, 31 Jones' al
Fitzgerald Thomas, shoemr., 16 Elizabeth
Fitzgerald Thos., lab., 262 N Water
Fitzgerald Wilson, cooper, 4 Merchant
Fitzgerald Wm. L., boot & shoemr., 364 High, h 5 N 13th
Fitzgibbons James, dealer, 239 N Front & 244 N Water
Fitzhenry Francis A., wid., 32 Sch 8th n Cherry
Fitzinger John, carter, Stoy's ct
Fitzmorris Thos., lab., Locust n Sch 3d
Fitzone M. painter, 23 Prune
Fitzpatrick Bartholomew, 5 Dillwyn pl
Fitzpatrick & Burr, painters, High n Sch 7th
Fitzpatrick Bernard, dealer, 495 High
Fitzpatrick B., lab., Almira pl
Fitzpatrick Daniel, lab., 7 St. Mary
Fitzpatrick Bernard, shoemr., 229 Cedar

Fitzpatrick Dennis, cooper, Front ab Washington
Fitzpatrick Ellen, milliner, 138 S 11th
Fitzpatrick Ellen, tavern, 26 S Water
Fitzpatrick John, lab. Howard bel Master (K)
Fitzpatrick Joseph, engineer, 209 N Front
Fitzpatrick Joseph, marble polisher, Rugan bel Willow
Fitzpatrick Margaret, spooler, Higham's ct (K)
Fitzpatrick Matthew, weaver, Christian ab 11th
Fitzpatrick Michael, labourer, Beach ab Poplar (K)
Fitzpatrick Michael, weaver, George n Beach
Fitzpatrick M., hatter, 9 St Mary
Fitzpatrick Patrick, flour store, S W Front and Dock, h 81 Union.
Fitzpatrick Patrick, carp., Federal ab 7th
Fitzpatrick Peter, lab. 12 E Shippen
Fitzpatrick Philip, Middleton's ct
Fitzpatrick Thomas, weaver, Cadwalader below Phoenix (K)
Fitzpatrick Thomas, bricklayer, 30 St Mary
Fitzpatrick Thomas, lab., Factory bel Beach
Fitzpatrick Thomas, coachman, 12 Willing's al
Fitzpatrick William, drayman, Almira pl
Fitzsimmons Bernard, com. mer., 6th ab Washington
Fitzsimmons John, bootmaker, Vine ab 12th
Fitzsimmons John, lab., Small n 5th
Fitzsimmons Joseph, ladies' shoemr., Flower st
Fitzsimmons Thos., hardware, Jones n Sch 8th
Fitzsimmons Wm., carp., 8th n Carpenter
Fitzwalter Wm., cordw., 2 Hubble st
Fitzwater Mark, carp., Pearl ab 12th
Fitzwater Thomas, carpenter, 17 N Sch. 6th n Sassafras.
Fiz Moses, printer, Branch al
Fizell A., stove manuf., 414 High
Fizell Edward, stove manuf. 414 High, paper hanger, Chester & Maple
Fizell Thomas, ship carp., Allen bel Hanover, (K)
Fizone Ann, rear 19 Sterling's al.
Fizone Lewis, cordw., 5 Mayland
Flagg J. F. B., M. D., dentist, 216 Mulberry
Flagg Samuel G., mason, 504 Coates
Flagler Mary, widow, 27 E North
Flaherty Ann, silk dyer, 50 Lombard.
Flaherty Edward, lab., 185 N Front
Flaherty John, tailor, 303 S 5th
Flaherty Wm., 12 Coomb's al
Flaig Edward, dentist, 132 N 10th
Flake Samuel, ship carp., Crown bel Bedford (K)
Flake Thos. cordw. Warren & Queen (K)
Flake Wm., currier, 198 Mulberry
Flanagan Edward, carter, Wood ab 13th.
Flanagan Francis, weaver, 4 Sch Beach
Flanagan George W., bottler, Beach ab Hanover (K)
Flanagan Jas. lab. 9th bel Marriott
Flanagan James, Monument House, Beach ab Hanover. (K)
Flanagan James, lab., Fitzwater ab Broad

Flanagan John, carter, Shippen ab Broad
Flanagan Luke, carpenter, rear 70 S 2nd, h Broad ab Sassafras
Flanagan Pat. lab. Dorothy n Sch 3d
Flanagan Philip, lab., 13th and Centre
Flanagan Robert L , plumber, 318 S 2nd
Flanagan Robt., tavern, 112 N 6th
Flanagan Stephen, clerk, 477 S 2d
Flanagan Thomas, carp. 9th and Christian
Flanagan Wm. G., plumber, 45 Walnut, h 39 Almond
Flanagin George H., mer., 5 S Water, h 71 Marshall
Flanagin James S., mer., 5 S Water
Flanagin John, mer., 5 S Water, h 347 N 6th.
FLANAGIN JOHN & SONS, mers., 5 S Water
Flanders Andrew, lab. Queen ab Marlboro' (K)
Flanigan Jones Mrs., Jones n Sch 4th
Flanigan Mary, dry goods, Broad ab Sassafras
Flanigan Rodney, lab., Ogden ab Sch 8th
FLANIGIN JOSEPH R. mer, Walnut and Sch Beach, coal office, Walnut st. whf. Sch.
Flanigin William C., dry goods, 190 S 2d
Flannery John F., combmr., 419 N 4th
Flavell Ann, wid., Master and Howard (K)
Fleck Benj., moulder, Sassafras n Sch 8th
Fleck Geo., porter, Carlton bel 13th
Fleischman Conrad A. Rev. rear 5 Ogden
Fleisher M., mer. 61 N 2d, h 20 New
Fleeman Saml., weaver, Howard bel Master (K)
Fleet Reuben, wheelwr., Poplar and Marshall, h Lewis ab Poplar
Flegel John G., dry goods, 437 N 2nd.
Flchr Carl, weaver, rear 552 N 2d
Fleming Aaron, cabinetmr., Marlborough below Allen (K)
Fleming Andrew, weaver, 13th ab Fitzwater
Fleming & Buzby, com. mer., 19 S Water
Fleming Chas. carter, Prosperous al
Fleming Elizabeth, Phoenix bel 2d
Fleming Geo., mer., 603 Spruce
Fleming George M., mer., 19 S Water, h 603

Flemming Joseph, com. mer. N W Front an Walnut, h Spruce bel 12th
Flemming Wm., weaver, Carpenter ab 8th
Flenard William, tailor, Magnolia ab Noble
Flenner Lewis, tailor, h 180 St John
Fleshour Catharine, wid., tailoress, 408 N 4th
Fletcher Ann, 6 Little Pine.
Fletcher Ann, c Perry & Lambert.
Fletcher Anthony, drayman, Harmony bel 4th
Fletcher Benjamin, engraver, 9 Mechanic
Fletcher Catharine, baker, 190 Sassafras
Fletcher Eleanor, widow, Buttonwood W 13t
Fletcher Eliza, book folder, 213 Lombard.
Fletcher George, engraver, 15 Merchant, Wood n 8th
Fletcher James, vict., Washington (W P)
Fletcher James W., Alderman, 248 Shippen, Lebanon ab Christian
Fletcher John, upholsterer, 10 North.
Fletcher Joshua S., coach trimmer, 16 George h 11th bel Cedar
Fletcher Lucy, shop keeper, 38 Cherry.
Fletcher Milford, porter, Osborn's ct
Fletcher Rebecca E., Filbert n Sch 7th
FLETCHER THOMAS, silversmith, Morris House, 188 Chestnut
Fleu Albert, cordw., 5 Washington row
Fleu Charles, printer, 85 Apple.
Flew Charles, cordw. Marshall ab Poplar
Flich Geo. L., store, 84 N 2d
Flick Andrew, currier, 136 N 3rd, h 51 Wood.
Flick Charles, chairm. Beach bel Shackamaxon (K)
Flick Jacob, fisherm. Cornelius' ct n Bishop (K
Flick Lewis, baker, 46 Filbert
Flick Sarah, b h, 147 N Front.
Flick & Smith, shoe find. 136 N 3d
Flick Thomas, cordw. Brown bel Vienna (K)
Flick Wm., fisherm., Cornelius' ct n Bishop (K
Flickinger Isaac, 355 N 6th
Flickwir D. Henry, carpenter, 163 S 3rd.
Flickwir Jeremiah W. druggist, 34 Lombard.

FLINT A., tract depository, 4 Hart's Buildings, h 24 Sansom
Flint Hannah, trimmings, 596 N 2d (K)
Flint James, machinist, Franklin bel Front, h F road opp Franklin (K)
Flint Thomas, cordwainer, 14 Providence ct.
Flint W. A., bookseller, 4 Hart's Buildings
Flomerfelt Armstrong I., sailmr., Lombard st whf. h Sutherland
Flood Edward, harness mr., 3 Gaskill
Flood Eliza, 18 Cresson's al
Flood Henry, laborer, rear 24 Duke
Flood Isaac, shoemaker, Carpenter ab 5th
Flood James, jeweller, 123 Prime
Flood John, weaver, Front bel Oxford (K)
Flood Lawrence, 356 N Front
Flood Lawrence, currier, 33 Dillwyn, h 20 Vine
Flood Peter, carpet weaver, F road bel Bedford
Flood Thos., drayman, 560 N 2d
Flood Wm., stone cut. 39 New Market
Flood William, blacksmith, 234 N Water
Florance J. L., gent., 11th and Walnut
Florance Wm. 339 Chestnut
Florence Sarah, artificial flowermr. and variety store, 81 Buttonwood
Florence Thomas B., Sec'ry. Comptrollers public schools, Atheneum buildings, h 48 Lombard
Flory Wm. b h, Broad & Paper al
Flounders Wm. B., shoemr., 256 S 5th
Flower Reese Wall, office S 8th bel Fitzwater
Flowers Aaron, shoemr., 27 N 9th
Flowers Catharine, S E 8th and Sassafras
Flowers Robert, printer, Beaver bel Charlotte
Flowers Thomas, chairmr., Parrish ab 5th
Flowers Wm., brushmr., Wood ab 13th
Floyd Elijah, packer, rear 4 Perry's ct.
Floyd Geo., hostler, P road bel Marriott
Floyd Henry, grocer, 12th & Lombard
Floyd James, grocer, S W 9th and Catharine
Floyd Jas., manuf., 2d bel Jefferson (K)
Floyd John, 265 S 3rd.
Floyd John, grocer, 4th and German
Floyd Saml., book keeper, 191 Catharine
Fluck Jacob, shoes, 172 High, h 158 Marshall
Fluck Samuel, cordw., 70 Coates
Flum B., coachmaker, R road ab S Garden, h S Garden ab 12th
Flumacher Christian, machinist, 2 Madison av
Flure Frederick, butcher, Greenwich ab Front
Flure Fred'k jr., vict., Front bel Greenwich
Flynn Catharine, sempstress, Murphy's ct
Flynn John, cooper, Lombard ab 12th
Flynn Patrick, ostler, 3 Mineral pl
Fobes G. W., mer., 83 High, h 23 Montgomery sq.
Fobes & Gibbons, dry goods, 83 High
Fodell John, carp. rear 268 N 5th
Fodernsham Saml., combmr., 11 Mechanic
Fuehl Frederick, baker, 1 Chancery lane.
Foering Abraham, 16 Centre
Foering Albert R., clerk, 231 Marshall
Foering Elizabeth, tailoress, 1 Loxley's ct
Foering Frederick, stove mer., 87 N 2nd, h 1 Crown.

Foering Saml., clerk, 10 Wagner's ct
Foering Susan, 9th ab Poplar
Poering & Thudium, stoves and castings, 87 N 2d
Foering Wm., coal mer., 65 N 5th, h 529 N 4th
Foertsch H., bootmr., Poplar n 6th
Fogg Aaron, bricklayer, 5 W North n 10th.
Fogg Samuel, ropemr., Corn bel Wharton
Fogg Sam'l., bricklayer, 6 Benezet
Foley James, Miller's al
Foley John, weaver, Lombard n Sch 2d
Foley John, cordw., 10 Cypress
Foley John F., tailor, 46 Walnut, h Marriott bel 3d
Foley Michael, dealer, 228 Shippen
Foley Rebecca, 109 Filbert
Foley & Thomas, tailors, 46 Walnut
Folkrod Elizabeth, 296 Vine.
Foll Henry, cordw. 33 Charlotte
Follin George, Prest. Bk. Commerce, h 57 Pine
Follrir Thos. lab. Poplar ab 3d
Folm Frederick, boot crimper, 167 St John
Foloney Jas., weaver, 13th bel Catharine
Folwell C. F., tailor, 95 N 5th.
Folwell C. S., Bank U. S., h 37 Marshall.
Folwell Edward, Bank N. America, h Spring Garden ab 10th
Folwell James, N. A. Bank, h 19 Montgomery
Folwell John G., Philada. Bank, h 260 N 7th
Folwell John T., jeweller, 285 Vine
Folwell Joseph, turner, 4th bel Poplar
Folwell Joseph D., mer., 14 S 2d h 310 Coates
Folwell J. W., cordwainer, 183 Callowhill
Folwell & Pitfield, cloth store, 14 S 2d
Folwell Robt., 217 Chestnut
Folwell Thomas J., mer., h 5 Carlton sq
Folwell Wm., cordw., Bedford bet Cherry and Palmer
Folyer Arthur, lab., rear 210 St.John
Fontaine C., ladies' shoemr., 204 Walnut
Fontaine Lewis, shoemr., 6 Sheldon row
Fontanell Maria, blindmr., 499 N 3d
Fontanges P. F., broker, 8 Bank al, h Spruce ab Sch 4th
Foote Charles, seaman, Hutton's ct
Foote Elizabeth, 27 Mead.
Foote Henry C., mer., 34 Church al, h 79 Marshall
Foote John, brickmr., 43 W Cedar
Foote Margaret, Cherry & Brown
Foote Skelton, shoemr., c Marriott & 6th.
Foote Wilhelmina, Vine bel 13th
Fopless Adam, chairmr. Apple ab Brown
Fopless Andrew, watchman, 3 Harmony ct
Foquet Charles, butcher, 294 S 10th
Foran Paul, painter, 170 S 5th
Forbes Charles, lab. Parker's pl
Forbes Henry, weaver, rear George ab 2d (K)
Forbes Hugh, shoemaker, 49 W Cedar.
Forbes James, watchman, Lombard n Sch 7th
Forbes John, weaver, Fitler bel Harrison (K)
Forbes John, cordw., Cadwalader ab Franklin (K)
Forbes Joseph, clerk, S Garden bel 11th
Forbes Margaret, Otter ab School (K)

15

Forbes Sarah, tailoress, 8 Clair
Forbes Thomas, printer, 24 Clark
Forbes Wm., lab. Jones W Sch 8th
Force Geo. ship carp. Wharton ab ½ road
Force Henry, blacksm., 6 Morris
Force James R., clerk, 305 Callowhill
Force John, ladies' shoemaker, Greenwich ab Front
Forcer Franklin, carp. 52 Laurel
Forcum Hester, 60 Corn
Ford Athanasius, dep. marshall, State House, h 6th bel Little Poplar
Ford Chas. lab. Jefferson's pl
Ford David, ivory turner, 83 Sassafras, h 260 N 5th
Ford Edwin, turner, 83 Sassafras, h 260 N 5th
Ford Eliza, shop, 37 N 12th
Ford Elmer C., machinist, Filbert W Sch 5th
Ford E. & D. turners, 83 Sassafras
Ford Isaac, mer., 36 N Front, h 439 Chestnut
Ford Jacob, lab., Locust bel 13th
Ford Jas. carp. Crown bel Franklin (K)
Ford Jas. plasterer, Cherry W Sch 8th
Ford Jas. B. teacher, 24 Barker
Ford John, blksm. 59 Carlton
Ford John, machinist, 523 High
Ford John, mer. Rittenhouse
Ford John, waiter, Gale's ct
Ford John, lab. Path st
Ford John, corder, Vine st whf., h 13 Vine.
Ford John M., plated saddlery, 32 N 3rd, h 12 Franklin
Ford Joseph, bricklayer, Lewis ab Poplar
Ford Margaret, 12 College pl
Ford Maria, sempstress, 39 Currant alley
Ford Mary, 3 Fayette

Forepaugh Solomon, tobacconist, 8 Sansom al
Forepaugh W. F., currier, Strawberry & Chestnut, h 17 Vine
Forgrave John, carpet weaver, Howard bel Master (K)
Forker John W. ladies' shoemr. 131 Charlotte
Forker Samuel, tailor, 121 Charlotte
Forley Francis, weaver, Front ab Phœnix (K)
Forley Owen, lab., Wiley's ct
Forman Eliza, dressmr., 2d and Federal
Forman Francis, shoemr., 87 S 2d, h O. Y. road ab Noble
Formoses George, rear Jay bel Coates
Forney John W., custom-house, h 272 N 6th
Forrest George, boot crimp., Marshall ab Poplar
Forrest Jacob, copper smith, 459 N 4th
Forrest J. D., Ann (F V)
Forrest Rebecca, 144 N 10th
Forrest Robert, lab., Mulberry n Sch. 2d
Forrest Samuel, cordw., Rye ab Reed
Forrestal Dominick, Rev. 116 S 4th
Forrester Ann, b. h., 63 Chestnut.
Forrester John, tailor, rear 2d op Laurel
Forst Frederick, upholsterer, 147 S 11th, h 16 Raspberry
Forst & Wright, upholsterers, 147 S 11th
Forsyth David, moroc. dresser, 14 Franklin (K)
Forsyth John, vict., G. T. road bel Master (K)
Forsyth Joseph W., plumber, 15 S 7th, h 64 S 6th
Forsyth Presley B., plumber, 15 S 7th, h Pine bel Broad
Forsyth P. B. & Brother, plumbers, 15 S 7th
Forsyth Samuel, lab., 4 Barker
Forsyth Thomas H., carpenter, 11th bel Brown
Forsyth W. T.

Foster C. B., dentist, 237 Mulberry
Foster D. H., cordw., 372 S 2d
Foster Edward F., tailor, 59 Cherry
Foster Elizabeth, Monroe ab Palmer
Foster Elizabeth, nurse, 1 West st
Foster E. B., stencil engraver, 256 h 268 N 3rd.
Foster E. M., shoemr., 441 Vine
Foster Frederick, farmer, Duke and Cherry (K)
Foster Geo., fancy dyer, rear Hope bel Phœnix (K)
Foster & Gebhard, batters, 49 S 3d
Foster G. W., ship carp., Cantrell's ct
Foster Hetty, widow of William, 304 Mulberry
Foster Hezekiah, farmer, Crown bel Duke (K)
Foster Jacob, printer, Callowhill n Sch 5th
Foster James, watchman, 24 Dugan
Foster James, paper stain., G T road ab Thompson
Foster James M., Reed ab Front
Foster John, lab., 5 Loxley's ct
Foster John, ship carp., Franklin ab. Hanover (K)
Foster John, carp., Marlborough ab Duke (K)
Foster John E., hatter, 49 S 3d
Foster John G., tobacconist, Allen ab Marlboro' (K)
Foster Joseph, artist, George n Sch. 7th
FOSTER J. H., awning maker, 259 N 3d
Foster Leonard, brass founder, rear 292 St. John
Foster Mahlon, messenger, 7th & Zane
Foster Mary, F. road and Franklin (K)
Foster Margaret, William ab Hamilton
Foster Nathaniel C., blacksmith, Sch. 6th n Barker, h St. Joseph's av
Foster N. L., book agt., Franklin ab Crown (K)
Foster Pool, cooper, Pegg n New Market
Foster Robert, acct., Sch. 7th bel Walnut
Foster Robert, M. D., 532 Vine
Foster Saml., shipw., Hanover ab Franklin (K)
Foster Saml. N., printer, 20 S 4th, h 207 S 7th
Foster Sarah, Crown ab Bedford, (K)
Foster Solomon, mer., 266 High
Foster Summers, saddler, Brown and St John
Foster Thos., engineer, Poplar ab 12th
Foster Thomas, weaver, Elk st (K)
Foster Thomas, weaver, Fairmount
Foster Thomas, weaver, 4 Gay's ct (K)
Foster Thomas S., mer., 163 High, h 21 Clinton
Foster Walter, moroc. finisher, Paschall's al.
Foster Wm., ladies' shoemr., 120 S 10th
Foster Wm., ship carp., rear 502 S 2d
Foster Wm., carp., Vienna bel Franklin (K)
Foster Wm. lab, 4 Farmer's row
Foster Wm. H., exchange office, 1 Library
Fotterall S. G., gent., 2 Portico Square
Fotterall William F., gentleman, N W 13th and Chestnut.
Fouche Wm. W., dentist, 79 N 6th
Fougeray Augustus P., stoves, Callowhill and O Y road
Fougeray H. J., U. S. insp., 14 Sassafras
Fougeray R. J., stoves, 107½ N 2d, h 101 New

Foulke Eleanor P., S E 12th and Mulberry
Foulke Eliza M., b. h. 49 George
Foulke Everart, pumpmr., 3 Conkle's ct
Foulke Frederick, watchman, 6 Shaffer's ct
Foulke George, sea capt., Pine bel 11th
Foulke Isaac, cordwainer, 302 S Front
Foulke John P., seaman, 3 Mint ct.
Foulke Richard P., 34 Sansom
Foulke Richard & Son, tailors, 154 Callowhill
Foulke William, agent P. G. & N. R. R. Co., 9th and Green, h 293 Green
FOULKE WM. P., att'y & coun., 34 Sansom
Foulkrod Emanuel, cordw., 478 N 4th
Foulkrod John, cordw., Phoenix bel Front (K)
Foulks Charles, sea capt., 50 Mead
Foulon Robert, plasterer, Ann (F V)
Fountain A., ship carp., Palmer bel Franklin (K)
Fouse B., widow, Coates n Fairmount
Fouse Daniel, porter, 212 New Market
Fouser H., brickmr., Elizabeth ab Poplar
Foust George N., stone cutter, 306 Vine
Foust Jacob, lab., G. T. road ab 6th (K)
Foust Jas. B., tinsmith, S E 4th & Franklin (K)
Foust John, lab., rear 5th n G T road
Foust R. M., teacher, 141 Franklin
Foust Samuel, lab., G T road bel 7th
Foust Wm. stonecutter, rear Apple bel George
Foust Wm., box maker, Westford av
Fow David, vict., Cherry bel West (K)
Fow George, brickmr., Sch 3d ab Spruce
Fow George, butch., Marlborough bel Franklin.
Fow Henry, vict., Palmer n F road
Fow Jacob, vict., Duke and Marlborough
Fow John, vict., Crown ab Duke (K)
Fow Joseph, vict., Jefferson ab Front (K)
Fow Lewis, victualler, Hanover ab Bedford (K)
Fow Peter, brickmr., Locust n Sch 3d
Fow Wm., brickmr., Spruce n Sch 3d
Fowler Ann, sewer, 2 Cresson's al
Fowler Francis, mail carrier, rear 410 Coates
Fowler George, painter, 154 Carpenter
Fowler Henry, potter, Hay's ct (K)
Fowler Isabel, b. h., Pine and Sch. Beach
Fowler Jacob P., hardware, 282 N 2d, h 542 N 2d
Fowler James, hardware, 542 N 2d
Fowler Jesse, lab., Monroe and Cherry (K)
Fowler John, painter and glaz. 8 S 10th
Fowler John A., druggist, S W 13th and Wood
Fowler Jos. C., shoemr., rear Nectarine ab 10th
Fowler Lewis, cooper, 4 Sheetz
Fowler Mahlon, tailor, 367 N 2d
Fowler Manlove C., machinist, Brown ab 9th
Fowler Mary, milliner, 80 Sassafras
Fowler Matthew, confect., 2 Tammany
Fowler Rennels, tailor, 152 Coates
Fowler Saml. tobacconist, Rose n William
Fowler Sarah, rear 116 Brown
Fowler Wm., carp., Parrish ab 11th
Fowler Wm., skin dresser, Clinton ab Poplar
Fowler William, plasterer, Lewis ab Sch 6th

Fowler Wm. H., glass blower, Queen bel Palmer (K)

Fowles Rev. James H., Filbert n Sch. 7th

Powls Willis, waiter, 160 S 5th

Fox Ann, shop, Baker and 7th

Fox Benjamin K., clerk, Cherry ab Jacoby

Fox Charles, brickmaker, 464 Sassafras.

Fox Charles, surveyor, Juniper bel Spruce

Fox Christian, cordwainer, 138 Brown (N L)

Fox Christian, cordw., R road n 10th

Fox Mrs. C., widow, 113 Green

Fox Daniel, gardener, Hanover ab Duke (K)

Fox Daniel M., conveyancer, 339 N 3d

Fox Edward J., Police Office, 14 Jacoby

Fox Elijah J., bricklayer, 195 Christian

Fox Elizabeth, Montgomery bel Front, (K)

Fox Evan, carp., Olive bel 10th

Fox E. J., dress maker, 1 St John

Fox Francis, carver, 7 Dock, h 14 Pine

Fox Frederick, grocer, Marlborough bel Duke.

Fox George, sailmr., 3 N 7th, h 10 James

Fox George, M. D., 491 Chestnut.

Fox George, tobacconist, N W 6th & Poplar

Fox George, lab., Brown bel Vienna (K)

Fox George, weaver, Harrison

Fox Geo. W. flour, S E Front and Otter, (K)

Fox Hannah, Broad bel Chestnut

Fox Henry J., coach maker, 49 Prune, h rear 390 Sassafras

Fox Horace, recruit. serg. U. S. A., High bet. Sch. Front and Ashton

Fox Jacob, cordwainer, 102 New Market

Fox James, weaver, 2d bel Oxford (K)

Fox James, blacksmith, Marlboro' ab Bedford

Fox Jas., printer, 25 North

Fox John, grocer, Sch. 3d & Dorothy

Fox John, flour & feed, 673 N 2d (K)

Fox John, mer., Marshall bel Poplar

Fox John, gent., 105 New Market

Fox John, dry goods mer. N E Sch. 7th and High

Fox John D., cooper, 196 N 3d, h N E 9th and Callowhill

FOX JOHN E., ex. brok., 5 S 3d, h N E 10th & Wallace

Fox John G., hatter, Pearl bel William

Fox John J., chairmr., Rachel & Poplar

Fox Jonas, beer house, 350 N Front

Fox Jos., basket maker, Hallowell

Fox Joseph L., 10th bel Green

Fox L., lab., Palm ab Brown

Fox Margaret, 42 Beck st

Fox Mary, sempstress, Bedford bel Broad

Fox Michael, brushmr., 1 St. John

Fox M. & C., millinery & dressmrs., Sch 5th n Wood

Fox Nicholas, dealer, Lombard bel 12th

Fox Patrick, lab. Brazier ab Lloyd

Fox Patrick, carp., Jones n Sch 4th

Fox Peter, lab., High n Sch 2d

Fox Peter, rigger, 8 Queen

Fox Peter, carp., 8 Queen

Fox Samuel A., cab. mr. Harmony & Hudson's al, h 270 S Front

Fox Samuel M., atty. & coun., 47 S 5th

Fox S. M., brickmaker, 3 Park pl

Fox & Wagner, awningmr. 3 N 7th

Fox William, tailor, 196 N 2nd.

Fox Wm., carp., 177 Catharine st

Fox Wm. P., brickmr., 3 Park pl

Fox W. A. police off. 143 N Juniper

Foy Anthony, lab. 12th bel Lombard

Foy Hugh, dealer, Wharton ab 2d

Foy James, flour & feed st., 1 Kelly

Foy Joseph, cordw., 13th & Green

Foy Margaret, Pine ab 13th

Foy Wm. tailor, 375 S 2d

Foyle Edward, groc., Sassafras al & Mulberry al

Frailey J. Madison, U S N, Sch 6th bel Walnut

Fraley Chas., chandler, School bel Franklin (K)

Fraley Charles W., lampmr., Vienna opp Brown

Fraley D., bonnets and shoes, 3½ S 2d

Fraley Edward L., mer., 333 Sassafras

Fraley Enoch, ship carp., Barker's ct (K)

Fraley Frederick, Sec'y. Am. Fire Ins. Co., 72 Walnut, h 365 Sassafras.

Fraley Geo. W. shoemr. Beaver ab St John (K)

Fraley Henry, drum mr., Hope bel Phoenix (K)

Fraley Hester, Beach ab Poplar (K)

Fraley John U., 79 N 10th

Fraley Peter, shoe store, Beach bel Maiden

Fraley Peter, machinist, Clinton ab Franklin (K)

Fraley R. W., gentw., 137 S 3d

Fraley Wm. K., bricklr, Callowhill ab Sch 6th

Fraley W. W., cordw., Beach bel Maiden, (K)

Frame Festus, lab., 10 Acorn alley

Frame George, waterman, Franklin Sch

Frame John, baker, Bledisloe pl

France Abm., grocer, 114 Frankford road (K)

France Betsey, Frankford road opp Queen (K)

France Jacob, 4 Short ct.

Francis Ann, 98 S 4th.

Francis Benj., cigar mr., Sch Front ab Mulberry

Francis Charles, waiter, Russell ab Fitzwater

Francis Charles, waiter, 23 Green (C)

Francis Charles, tinsmith, 440 Sassafras.

Francis Dolly, gentw., Spruce ab 12th

Francis Edward, chairmr. Vernon ab 10th

Francis Elizabeth, Bickham W Sch 8th

FRANCIS, FIELD & FRANCIS, tinmen & saddlery hardware, 80 N 2nd

Francis George, bookbinder, 15 Franklin pl

Francis Henry, tinman, 80 N 2d, h 37 Jacoby

Francis James W., potter, Jones E Sch. 5th.

Francis Joseph, black & white smith, 26 Dock, h 62 Union.

Francis L. C. math. inst. mr. 13 Dock

Francis Margaret, Melon ab 9th

Francis Maria, washer, George n Sch 7th

Francis Thomas, plater, 80 N 2d, h 98 Dillwyn

Franck Elizabeth, widow, Sarah n Bedford (K)

Franck Wm. auctioneer, N W 2d & Tammany, h G T road & 2d

Francks John, tobacconist, Washington (W P)

Frank Asher, dry goods, 170 N 2d

Frank Christian, gent., 479 Race

Frank Henry, tailor, N E 4th and Walnut

Frank Henry, carp. Wallace & Preston

Frank Isaac, pedler, Tammany ct

Frank Jacob, coachmr., rear 39 N 4th

Frank Jacob, watchmr., 137 Cedar
Frank John, cordw., Duke n Marlborough
Frank Lindenberger, coachmr., 14 Green's ct
Frank Lydia A. 301 N 7th
Frank Moses, gent. 170 N 2d
Frank Sebastian, baker, 165 Catharine
Franklin Andrew, Coates ab Sch 7th
Franklin Benj., carp., 2 Park pl
Franklin Benj. wheelwright, 24 & h 16 Dock
Franklin Edward, shoes & bonnets, S E 10th & High
Franklin Henry, plaisterer, Barker E of Sch 4th
Franklin James, plasterer, George ab Sch 6th
Franklin James E., M. D., 1 N 13th
Franklin John G., painter, 246 Catharine
Franklin Joseph, plasterer, rear 107 N Market
Franklin Margaret R., 11 Wallace
Franklin Richard, lab Bedford ab 6th
Franklin Ruth, Poplar bel New Market
Franklin Wm. H. organ builder, Sch 8th ab Chestnut
Franks Charles, tobacconist, rear 143 Green
Franks George, moulder, 31 Sarah (K)
Franks Henry, tobacco, 372 N 4th, h 52 Coates
Franks Herman, moulder, Otter & Dunton (K)
Franks John, brush maker, Brown ab Cherry
Franks Philip, boot & shoemr. 311 N 2d
Franks William D., 31 Charlotte
Frans P. S. 1 Seneca ct
Frantz Jacob, carp., Orchard ab Rawle
Frantz Mary A. milliner, 27 Filbert
Frantz Zachariah, carter, Pleis' ct (K)
Frantzman John, cordw. 174 Coates
Fraser Frederick G. upholsterer, 415 High
Fraser James P. jr., stone cutter, Wallace ab R road
Fraser Robert, smithery, O Y road & Wood, h Wood n West (K)
Frashier Elizabeth, baker, rear 462 N 2d
Frasier G. Mrs., dress mr., 21 Green's ct
Frasier Mary, 145 Poplar
Frazer Benjamin T., dry goods, 302 S 2d
Frazer James, b h, 80 S 2d
Frazer John F., profess. Walnut ab Sch 8th
FRAZER ROBERT, att'y & coun., 93 S 3d
Frazier Anthony, carp. Wheat bel Wharton
Frazier Anthony, carpenter, Pine ab 13th.
FRAZIER & ASPINWALL, forward'g. mers., Dock st whf
Frazier Benjamin W., mer., Dock st whf., h 2 Linden pl
Frazier Gurney, blacksmith, Parrish bel 12th
Frazier James, plasterer, Carpenter ab 6th
Frazier John, grocer, Broad ab Shippen
Frazier John, carp., 12 Washington market
Frazier Joseph, stevedore, 75 Christian
Frazier Nalbro, mer., 5 Walnut, h Spruce ab 11th
Frazier Robert, trunkmr., Carpenter n P road.
Frazier William, weaver, Shippen ab 12th.

Freas Jacob, grocer, N E 5th & Sassafras
Freas John, lab., rear 495 N 3d
Freas John W., blacksmith, Prime bel Front
Freas Solomon, grocer, Washington (W P)
Frecase Isaac, S W Branch & Wood
Frederick Elizabeth, Wood bel Duke (K)
Frederick Dan'l, silver plater, rear 196 Cherry
Frederick Geo., fisherman, Wood ab Queen (K)
Frederick Isaac, shoemaker, 96 S 2d, h 6 Carter's al
Frederick Jacob, fisherman, Wood bel Duke (K)
Frederick John, baker, Moyamensing av
Frederick John, lab., 121 G T road (K)
Frederick John, pedler, West n Vienna (K)
Frederick John, fisherman, Wood ab Franklin (K)
Frederick John H., jeweller, 6 Hoffman's al
Frederick John L., engr., 53 S 4th, h 5 City row.
Frederick Margaret, tailoress, 256 Catharine
Frederick Wm., fisherman, Wood bel Duke
Frederick Wm. S., grocer, 348 Callowhill
Fredericks Samuel, printer, Turner bel 4th
Frederickson Henry, lab., Gorrell's ct
Frederickson Wm. tobacconist, Parrish bel 11th
Frederitze Joseph, ladies' shoes, 59 New
Fredline John L., jeweller, 374 S 4th
Free Elijah, carp. 276 Wood
Free George, stables, 11 & h 21 Cherry
Free James, lab., rear 116 Brown
Free Joseph, sailmr., 3 Dock, h 17 Turner
Free Martin, blindmr., 518 N 3d (K)
Freeborn Mrs. Christiana, High n Sch 5th
Freeborn Mary, milliner, High n Sch 5th
Freeborn Noble, labourer, Say.
Freed Anthony, supt. M. prison
Freed David, mer., 448 High, h 308 N 6th.
Freed Jacob, grocer, Green & Linden
Freed John, baker, 532 N 3d
Freed Joseph M., mer., 448 High, h 308 N 6th
Freed J. L., cork cutter, 138 Callowhill
Freed Philip, carp., Myrtle ab 11th
Freed, Ward & Freed, flour and for. mers. 448 High
FREEDLEY JOHN, marble depot, Chestnut st whf. Sch
Freedley J., miller, Chestnut st whf. Sch
Freedly John, G T road bel Jefferson (K)
Freedly Samuel, M. D., S E Green & Marshall.
Freeland David S., hats, 22 and 56 High, h 26 Sassafras.
Freeland John, cordwainer, 369 S 6th
Freeland Nathan S., hatter, 58 Garden
Freeland O. S., piano tuner, 56 Vine
FREELAND & SON, hatters, 22 and 56 High
Freeland Wm. N., hatter, 56 High
Freeman Alex. H., clerk, 35 S Sch 6th st
Freeman Amanda, feather manuf., 35 N 4th.
Freeman Amelia, 4 Prosperous al
Freeman A. & E. W., milliners, 70 Mulberry.
Freeman A. H., mer. 92 High, h 70 Mulberry

Freeman Charles M., cordw., 86 S 3d, h 303 Walnut
Freeman George, port. painter, 167 Spruce
Freeman George, furniture car, 9 Prosperous al
Freeman G., waiter, 21 Currant al.
Freeman Hiram, porter, Juniper al
Freeman H. G., atty., 72 S 5th, h Locust and William (W P)
Freeman James, wood sawyer, 115 Christian
FREEMAN JAMES A., auctioneer, 106 Walnut, h 382 Vine
FREEMAN JAMES B., atty. & coun., 115 S 6th, h 203 Mulberry
Freeman John, porter, Essex st
Freeman Mary A., trimmings, 146 S 2d
Freeman Nathan, Ross & Queen sts (K)
Freeman Richard, lab., rear 529 N 2d (K)
Freeman T. W. L., real estate brok., 115 S 6th
Freeman Wm., waiter, 4 Little Pine
Freeman Wm., pedler, Penn bel 12th
Freeman Wm., cabinetmr., Centre ab Brown
Freeman Wm. G., steward, 5 Barley
Freeman Wm. Henry, U. S. Consul at Curacoa, Filbert W of Sch 8th
FREEMAN WM. S. agt. Union Transport. Line, 45 S whfs.
Freese Jacob R., mer. 64 N 3d
Freeston Wm., keeper M. prison, h 498 S 2d.
Freitas J., wines and liquors, 338 N 3d
Frenaye Mark A., St. John's 13th
Frenaye P., professor, 59 S 11th.
French Anastasia, Maria and Ulrich's al
French & Baker, riggers, S wharves ab Cedar
French Clayton, druggist, 10th and High
French Eliza, School st
French Elizabeth, 8 Wiley's ct.
French George, rigger, S Whfs. n Cedar, h 30

Frick Edwin P., real est. brok. & conv. 119 S 6th bel Walnut
Frick Jacob, brass foundry, 364 N 3d.
Frick Jacob, cordw., 37 Garden
Frick John H. editor Amer. Sentinel, 73½ Dock, h 118 Crown
Fricke Albert, M. D. 37 N 4th
Fricke Elizabeth, gentw. 272 Coates
Fricke George, mer., 14 N 3d
Fricke Henry, mer., 14 N 3d, h 160 N 8th
Fricke Henry, tavern, 26 Spruce
Fricke H. & G., saddlery hardware, 14 N 3d
Fricke Susanna, 209-St. John
Fricker George, vict., Apple ab George (N L)
Fricker Mary, wid. of Richard, Rose al rear of Green
Fridenburg Pharez, 133 Dillwyn
Fried John, cork cutter, 113 Buttonwood
Friedauf Louis, dentist, 63 N 7th
Friedline Sarah, b h., Washington bel 10th (S G)
Friel Edward, grocer, 9th Sp Garden
Friel John, conf., High between Ashton & Sch Front
Friend Andrew B., blacksmith, 6 Juniper al, h 73 George
Friend John, corder, Coates st. wharf, h 426 N Front
Frient Philip, cordw., rear 200 Christian
Fries John, umbrella mr., 414 Vine
Fries Hugh, porter, Sch 3d ab Walnut
Fries John, watchmaker, 160 N 2d.
Fries John, lab., Cooper n Sch 3d
Fries Wm. cordw. rear Orchard bel Rawle
Fries P., watchmaker, 353 N 2d
Friesz Samuel H., labourer, 112 Wood.
Frieze Maria, dressmr., 61 S 11th
Frisby Charles, cabinetmaker, 191 Lombard

Fritz Jacob, cabinetmaker, 267 Mulberry, h 124 N Juniper
Fritz Jacob, comb & variety store, 196 N 3d
Fritz James, brickmr. rear 609 n 6th
Fritz John, blacksmith, Brown and Kesler
Fritz John, baker, 153 S 6th
Fritz John, dyer, 27 Duke
Fritz John, combmr., Brook bel Brown
Fritz J. M., bootmr., 47 Callowhill
Fritz John S., cabmr., 15 Schriver's ct
Fritz Lewis, bookbinder, 6 Rose al
Fritz Peter, marble mason, yard 226 Sassafras, h 214 Sassafras
Fritz Peter, dealer, rear 198 Sassafras, h 181 St John
Fritz Wm. tin smith, rear 6 Lawrence
FRITZ & WILLIAMS, morocco drs., 15 Margaretta
Fritzinger John, carter, Allen bel Hanover
Froggatt Wm. gun smith, 392 N Front
Fromberger M., rear 30 St John
Fromerger Margaret, Buttonwood ab 10th
Fronefield Jos. carp., George & Mechanic (N L)
Fronton Emma, mantua mr., 93 P road
Frost Augustus, 61 Washington (S G)
Frost Elizabeth, Wood ab 11th
Frost & Isnard, mers., 3 Church al
Frost John, publisher, S E 6th and Walnut, h Sch 8th bel Walnut
Frost John H. P., teacher, rear 35 Mulberry
Frost M. A., importer, 3 Church al, h 92 Locust
Frost Silas, brass found., 40 N 7th, h 90 S Front
Frost Wm., dealer, 3 Monmouth ct
Frowert C. E., bricklayer, 207 N 9th
Frowert Daniel, 78 Sassafras
Frowert Isaac, boot & shoemaker, 64 N 5th.
Frowert John B., painter, 2 N 7th, h 20 Cresson's al
Frowert John K., book bind., 4 Kenworthy's ct
Frowert J., gent., Wood bel 9th.
Frowert Lewis H., superinten., 262 Catharine
Frowert Samuel W., cordw., 511 S 2d
Fry Christian, lab., Lewellen's av
Fry Edmond, cooper, 10 Filbert, h Prospect al.
Fry George, wheelwright, 30 Castle
Fry Geo., carp., 12 Whitehall
Fry Jacob, dry goods, 58 N 3d
Fry Jacob, tobacco., 265 N 3d, h 39 Coates' al
Fry Jacob S., mer., 45 N 2d, h 14 Chatham
Fry Jacob W., clerk, 463 5th ab Poplar
Fry John, pattern maker, 158 Sassafras, h 270 N 8th
Fry John, cabinetmr., 270 N 8th
Fry John A., dry goods, Washington ab 9th
Fry John J., baker, Elizabeth ab Poplar
Fry Joseph G., tailor, 19 Green
Fry Lucian, Wood ab Sch 6th
Fry Mary L., 306 Pine
Fry N. L. silversmith, rear 71 S 2d, h 306 Pine
Fry Samuel B., mer., 385 Sassafras
Fry Thomas & William, confectioners, 191 N 3d.
Fry Wm. C., confect., 191 N 3d, h 99 Dillwyn
Fry Wm. C., engraver, 270 N 8th
Fry Wm. W. planemr. Henderson's ct
Fryer George, cordw., 1 Ellet's av

Fryer John, tailor, 206 Sassafras, h 8 Nicholson.
Fryer Kirk, 98 Wood
Fryer Wm., dry goods, 38 S 2d.
Fryhardt Fred., skin dress., Charlotte bel Poplar
Fuccarci J., pict. fr., rear Carpenter ab 9th
Fuguet S., mer., h 83 Lombard
Fuhr Henry, basket mr., rear 26 Charlotte
Fulce Fredk., Robb's ct
Full Adam, lab., Pleis' ct (K)
Full Francis, eating house, M'Avoy's ct
Fullaway Charles, trunkmaker, 23 Shippen
Fullen Henry, painter, Poplar ab 10th
Fullen Jas., S 2d bel Wood
Fullen J., coachmr., 20 Quince
Fuller Archibald, cart., N E ½ road & Wharton.
Fuller Daniel, real estate broker, h 26 Sansom
Fuller E., shop, Cedar ab 9th
Fuller John, pilot, 479 S Front
Fuller Oliver, mer., h 16 Clinton
Fuller Peter, shop, St Mary ab 6th
Fuller Zelotes Rev., editor, Spring Garden bel R road
Fullerton Aaron, Hanover ab Bedford (K)
Fullerton Alexander, druggist, 174 High, h 264 Spruce
Fullerton Edward, bootmr., 490 Sassafras
Fullerton Henry, weaver, Master bel Hancock (K)
Fullerton Hugh, weaver, Lemon
Fullerton Jacob B., coachmr., Broad & Carlton, h Sch 3d bel Callowhill
Fullerton Jas. lab., Lewis n Sch 6th
Fullerton James, 442 Vine
Fullerton John R. bricklayer, Franklin bel Cherry (K)
Fullerton Matthew, grocer, 39 Pratt
Fullerton Stephen B., plasterer, 485 Vine
Fullman Ann, shop, 12 Bonsall
Fulmer Ann, tailoress, Beckett st
Fulmer Bennet, clerk, 83 Brandywine
Fulmer Caspar, carp., Otter bel G T road (K)
Fulmer Chas., 213 N 9th
Fulmer F. cooper, 19 Maria
Fulmer Henry, Cobb
Fulmer Jacob, combmr., Union ab Franklin (K)
Fulmer Jas., sawyer, Wilson's ct
Fulmer John, carp., Butler bel West (K)
Fulmer John, vict., rear Poplar ab 6th
Fulmer John J., carp., 9th and Nectarine
Fulmer Mary, rear O Y road ab Tammany
Fulmer Michael, butcher, 29 Franklin pl
Fulmer Wm. lab. School ab Rose (K)
Fulton Alex'r., weaver, 7 Brinton
Fulton Ann, Randall's ct
Fulton James, lab., Gulielma
Fulton John, weaver, Miller's row (K)
Fulton John, paint. & glaz., N W 5th & Prune, h 322 S 4th
Fulton John, lab., S 7th bel Catharine
Fulton John L., coachmr., rear 14 Filbert, h 11 Pratt
Fulton Mahlon, wheelwr., 5 Hunter
Fulton Saml., lab., Beech and Spruce
Fulton Samuel, warper, Jackson ab Adams
Fulton Sarah, 251 Cedar

Fulton Wm., weaver, Hanover ab West (K)
Fulton William, manuf., Sch 4th ab Cedar
Fulton Wm. H., carpenter, 14 S Sch 8th bel High, h 53 S Juniper.
Funck Charles F., cabinetmaker, 587 N 3d
Funck Henry, lab. Coates n Fairmount
Funk Godfrey, tailor, Garden & Willow
Funk James M., victualler, rear 4 Chatham
Funk John S. mach., Hancock bel Phoenix (K)
Funk Jno. T. chemist, Hancock bel Phoenix (K)
Funk Mary, 9 Cresson's al
Funk Wm. carp. rear 5th ab George (N L)
Funk Wm. carter, Coates n Sch
Funston Mr., carter, Amber ab Phoenix (K)
Funston John, grocer, Poplar & Hutchinson
Funston Oliver, weaver, 7 Derringer's av
Furbee Edward, porter, Giles' al
Furbee Jonathan, waterman, Collins' al
Furber Thos., agricultural warehouse, 291 High
Furey And., cordw., rear Washington bel 3d
Furey John S., teacher, 101 Spruce
Furey Thomas, shoemr., High ab Sch. 6th
Furlong Elizabeth, grocer, N W 7th & Cherry
Furlong John W. coach painter, 34 Dock, h 108 Cherry
Furlong Lawrence, salesman, 333 Lombard
Furlong Richd., Sch Pine and Ball al
Furman & Appleton, tailor, 43 N 6th
Furman David, tailor, 43 N 6th, h 179 Mulberry
Furman Elizabeth, c Sch. 8th & Filbert
Furman Elizabeth, 451 Vine
Furman Jonathan, waiter, rear 305 Walnut
Furman Richard P., cooper, rear 30 Commerce
Furman Saml., trimmings, 179 Mulberry
FURNESS, BRINLEE & CO., com. mers. and auctioneers, 22 & 24 N 2d
Furness James T., auctioneer, 22 N 2d, h Spruce n Sch. 8th
Furness John, carp. 9 State
Furness Samuel, iron moulder, Hope bel Jefferson (K)
Furness Wm. H. Rev., Pine bel Sch 8th
Furphy Thomas, weaver, Mariner st
Furrow Joseph, lab. 8 Lombard row
Furter Ann, Buttonwood ab 10th
Fury John, cordw., Hanover & Duke (K)
Fury Michael, grocer, Lombard & 7th
Fury Michael, lab., Fitzwater ab 13th
Fury Saml., lab., Coates ab Sch 5th
Fury Thomas, Walnut n Sch Beach
Furze John F, machinist, Rugan n Willow
Fussell Henry B., umbrellas, 2 N 4th, h 128 Mar-

Gabel Peter, bricklayer, 563 N Front (K)
Gabel Peter, carp., rear 575 N Front
Gabel Rachel, layer out of dead, 3 Brown
Gabel Thomas, tobac'st., G T road ab 2d (K)
Gabell & Co., plumbers, 17 S 8th
Gabell G. T., plumber, 17 S 8th
Gable Joseph, painter, 420 N Front.
Gabriel John, lab., Mulberry n Sch Front
Gadeken Henry L. jeweler, 25 Library, h 6 Acorn al
Gadsby Henry, weaver, 12 Jones' al
Gadsby John, manuf., shoemaker's ct
Gaffin Peter, weaver, 10th bel Prime
Gaffney Eliza, 34 N Sch 8th
Gaffney James, porter, 13 S 8th
Gaffney John, bottler, 15 Mercer.
Gaffney Mary, Vaughan bel Walnut
Gaffney Thomas, stone cutter, Grape bel George (F V)
Gagen James, lab. Filbert E Sch 3d
Gaillard E., baker, 18 Mulberry
Gaily Wm., lab., M'Duffie n Sch 2nd
Gaines Henry, lab., rear 8th ab Carpenter
Gaines Richard, lab., 30 Blackberry al
Gakeler Jacob, butcher, Hanover bel F road (K)
Galberny Thomas, 112 N Water
Galbraith & Binder, wood, Vine st whf.
Galbraith Edward, carp., 7 Sailor's ct
Galbraith H. lab., 20 W Cedar
GALBRAITH JAMES, wood wharf, Callowhill, h 116 New Market
Galbraith James, weaver, Filbert n Sch 3d
Galbraith John, marble paper mr. 27 N 7th, h Rugan ab Callowhill
Galbraith Margery, Dorothy n Sch Front
Galbraith Robert, lab. 7 Gabell's ct
Gale James, barber, 1 Decatur, h Russell
Gale Jane, wid., Penn bel Maiden (K)
Gale Malachi, 83 P road.
Gale Sarah, dressmr., 79 Filbert
Gale Thomas S., acct., 225 Wood.
Galen William, clerk, Marriott & Christian
Gales Lewis, lab., Stevenson's ct
Gales Wm., seaman, Ball al
Galindo John, cab. mr., 314 N 4th
Gallager Ann, 22 Rittenhouse
Gallagher Andrew, drayman, Federal bel M road
Gallagher Ann, shop, Mifflin & Orleans
Gallagher Anthony I., dry goods, 20 Wallace
Gallagher A. F. X., bootmr., 77 George
Gallagher A. M. milliner, 158 S 5th

Gallagher James, agent, rear Beach bel Maiden (K)
Gallagher James, grocery, S E Fitzwater & 7th
Gallagher Jane, Patton's ct
Gallagher John, drayman, S 8th ab Christian
Gallagher John, lab. 328 S 6th
Gallagher John, carp., Front bel Greenwich
Gallagher John, lab., 2 Farmer's row
Gallagher John, waiter, Juniper bel Walnut
Gallagher John, tailor, Carpenter ab 3 road
Gallagher John, capt., 357 S Front
Gallagher John, driver, 3 Tiller's ct
Gallagher John, watchman, Chestnut n Beach
Gallagher Margaret, shop, Spruce n Sch Front
Gallagher Nealis, lab., Coates n Fair Mount
Gallagher & Nix, perfumers, 7 N 9th
Gallagher Patrick, sawyer, 10th n Milton
Gallagher Peter, tailor, 2 S 13th
Gallagher Richard, labourer, Vine n Sch 3d
Gallagher Robert, carter, 9 Marshall's ct
Gallagher Saml. corder, 3 Sansom
Gallagher Susan, Penn ab Maiden (K)
Gallagher Thomas, lab., Mulberry n Sch 3d
Gallagher Thomas, clerk, Pine ab Sch 6th
Gallagher Timothy, ostler, Sycamore ab Locust
Gallagher Wm., saddler, Perry & Mifflin
Gallagher Wm., morocco dresser, Kessler's ct
Gallagher Wm. M., shoemr., 2 Filbert av.
GALLAWAY WM., alderman, 11 Sp. Garden, h Sp. Garden ab 8th
GALLEN CHARLES, tavern, 46 Prune.
Gallen Isabella, tavern, 111 Shippen
Gallen James, Small ab 5th
Gallen John, coachman, Brown ab Cherry
Gallesee Michael, lab., 14 Dilk's ct
Gallett August, wig maker, 38 S 4th.
Galliard James, painter, Sch. 7th ab Chestnut, h Ann ab Sch. 4th.
Gallins Ralph, S W S whfs. and Cedar
Galloney Charles, mer., 387½ High, h 242 Callowhill
Galloney S. A., dressmr., 176 Marshall
Galloway Benj., dyer, 10 Bonsall
Galloway Isaac, coachman, 22 Watson's al
Galloway James, seaman, Scott's ct
Galloway James, sailmr., Sassafras bel Water, h 33 Elfreth's al
Galloway James, weaver, Carpenter ab 8th
Galloway John, hatter, 52 Sassafras
Galloway John L., hatter, rear 211 Christian
Galloway Wm., dealer, rear 36 Sassafras
Galloway Wm., alderman, Sp Garden and 7th, h Sp. Garden & 8th
Galusha I. I., livery stables, Green ab 5th
Galvray Andrew, boxmr., Filbert n Sch 4th
Gamble Alexander, plasterer, 9th ab Coates
Gamble Asa C., currier, 3d & Noble
Gamble Charles, jeweller, 265 N Front
Gamble Charles S., shoemaker, 3d & Marriott
Gamble Eleanor, shop, 104 Plum
Gamble Ellis, cooper, Crawford's ct
Gamble George W., morocco manuf., 5 Margaretta, h 41 Noble
Gamble Hugh, grocer, Fitzwater ab 13th
Gamble Hugh, porter, Fitzwater n 13th

16

Gamble James, waterman, 265 N Front
Gamble John, weaver, Shippen ab 11th
Gamble John, weaver, Shippen bel Broad.
Gamble John, morocco manuf. 32 Callowhill
Gamble John, constable, 15 Orleans
Gamble John V., polisher, Culvert bel 4th
Gamble J. & Sons, morocco manufact. 5 Margaretta
Gamble K. J., morocco manuf., 5 Margaretta, h 7 Noble
Gamble Lucretia, b h, 98 S Front
Gamble Philanah, G T road n Rose
Gamble Robert, morocco dress., Warner's ct
Gamble Samuel, weaver, Ashton n Sassafras
Gamble Samuel. stonecut., Pine ab Sch 6th.
Gamble Saml., coachman, 3 Centre
Gamble Susanna, Beach ab Maiden
Gamble Warren, waterman, 265 N Front
Gamble Wm., morocco finisher, Marlborough ab Duke (K)
Gamble William, cordwainer, 265 Green
Gambling William, cabinet maker, Callowhill n Rugan
Games Rufus, barber, 184 N 8th, h 226 S 7th
Gamister David, lab., 27 Crabb
Gampher Geo. W., cooper, P road ab 6th
Gampher John, cooper, S 5th bel Queen.
Gampher Michael, cooper, 230 S 2nd, h 274 S 5th
Gandy E. S., mer., 79 S Front, h 318 S 4th
Gandy Sheppard, gent. 79 S Front, h 318 S 4th
Ganer Michael, lab., Sch Willow
Ganges Rachel, washer, Russell ab Fitzwater
Gangheimer Philip, glovemr., Rihl's ct
Gano Martha, Noble bel 8th
Ganon John, carp., Adams
Gans, Leberman & Co., tailors, High & N W 3d
Gans Mary Ann, shop, Sch 5th ab Spruce
Gans Solomon, mer., 3d & High
Ganser John, shoe store, 469 N 2d
Ganser John M., shoemr., 2d ab Edward
Ganstert Joseph, shoemaker, 80 N 9th
Gant Jane, 385 S 6th
Gantz John, machinist, Pleasant bel 13th
Ganzhorn John Godfrey, carter, Palmer ab Duke (K)
Gapel Anthony, stocking weaver, 439 N 3d
Garber Benedict, carp., 7th ab Poplar
Garber Christian, carp., 7th ab Poplar
Gardel Bertrand, teacher, 275 Chestnut
GARDEN & BROWN, hatters, 196 High
Garden Christopher H., hatters, 196 High, h 85 Tammany
Garden Martha, O Y road and Tammany
Garden Wm., printer, 5 Hyde's ct
Gardener Serena, nurse, rear 6 Locust
Gardener Wm., M. D., R road n Girard av
Gardette F. B., M. D., dentist, 246 Walnut
Gardiner H. S., cooper, 131 S Front.
Gardiner R. M. D., 85 Catharine
Gardiner Thomas W., tailor, rear 452 Callowhill
Gardiner Thomas W. mer. 59 S Water
Gardiner W. W., tailor, 91 N 9th
Gardner Abraham, lab., 36 Burd's ct
Gardner Alex., carp., Nectarine bel 10th

Gardner Alexander, bricklayer, rear 177 S 3d
Gardner Archibald, dealer, c 11th & Sassafras
Gardner Catharine, 17 Coates' al
Gardner Charles, machinist, G T road bel 2d
Gardner Charles W. Rev., 8th ab Catharine
Gardner Daniel W., cordw., 6th bel Washington
Gardner Edward, brush maker, 4 Torr's ct.
Gardner Geo. H., coach maker, 13th bel Brown
Gardner George W., reporter of fashions, 116 Chestnut, h 21 Logan
Gardner Gransom, lab., Culvert bel 5th
Gardner Isabella, rear Beck bel 2d
Gardner Jacob, 293 Vine
Gardner Jacob H., skin dresser, 311, & h 312 Vine.
Gardner Jacob L. carp., 293 Vine
Gardner John, lab., Sch 6th bel Lombard
Gardner John, ship carp., John & Front
Gardner John, bootmr., Herrige's ct
Gardner John, collarmr., rear School above Rose (K)
Gardner John, mer., 181 N 8th
Gardner John K. caulker, Cadwalader bel Phœnix
Gardner Jonathan, seaman, 30 Elizabeth, (N L)
Gardner Joseph, barber, 213 Walnut, h 4th and Christian
Gardner Joseph R. barber, G T road ab Phœnix
Gardner M. M. shoemaker, 12th bel Bedford
Gardner Resolved W., Carlton n Sch 3d
Gardner Richard, furniture, 406 High
Gardner Robt., lab., Robeson's ct
Gardner Sarah, wid. of John, 47 Franklin
Gardner Sarah M., dry goods, 82 N 2nd.
Gardner Wm., cordw., 12th ab Pine
Gardner Wm., carp., Sch 6th bel Lombard
Gardner William, skin dresser, 29 Logan.
Gardom George, drugs & colours, 13 S 7th.
Gardom Wm. stovemr., 9 Cresson's al
Gardy Jos., carpenter, Hanover ab Franklin (K)
Caraccha C. 205 Walnut

Garrett Ann, Depot bel 9th
Garrett Cornelius, ostler, 10 Knight's ct
Garrett Ezra T., tailor, S E 5th & Sassafras
Garrett George, porter, 8 Burd's ct
Garrett G. H., 128 S Front, h 8 Washington
Garrett Henry, mer. 125 High, h 19 Logan sq
Garrett Henry & Co., dry goods, 125 High (up stairs
Garrett Hugh, coachman, Juniper bel Walnut
Garrett James, currier, 102 N 13th
Garrett John, grocer, 186 High, h 143 N 12th
Garrett John, lab. Mayland & Mulberry al
GARRETT LEVI & SONS, tobacconists, 128 Front.
Garrett Margaret, 258 Spruce
Garrett Samuel, currier, 11 Steinmetz's ct
GARRETT THOMAS C. mer., 122 Chestnut, h 6 Palmyra sq
Garrett Thomas C. & Co., dealers in watches & jewelry, 122 Chestnut
Garrett William, U S mint, h 136 N Juniper.
Garrett W. E., tobacconist, 128 S Front, h 19 Spruce.
Garrettson Edmund, mer., 62 N whfs
Garrigen Patrick, grocer, Wood and Sch. 2nd
Garrigues E. B., druggist, N E 10th & Coates
Garrigues Isaac B., marble mason, c 5th an Buttonwood, h 181 N 7th.
Garrigues James, clerk N. L. Bank, h Wallace bel 10th
Garrigues M. 28 Rittenhouse
Garrigues S. M., milliner, 235 Mulberry
Garrigues Wm. constable, 17 N 6th, h 30 E Nor-
Garrison Edwin H., Jefferson pl
Garrison Firman, baker, 3d and Clark
Garrison Israel, biscuit baker, 11 Madison
Garrison James, potter, Hummell's row
Garrison Jas. driver, Warner's ct
Garrison Jno. mer., 6 Lætitia ct., h 366 Mulberry

Garver Thos., tailor, 10 Griswold's al
Garvey James, tavern, 10 S 8th.
Garvey Michael, lab. 3 Coates
Garvin Alex. C. vict. Oak (W P)
Garvin Archibald, lab. rear West bel Hanover
Garvin Dennis, weaver, 10th bel Christian
Garvin John, carter, Lombard n Sch 6th
Garvin Sarah, Lombard n Sch. 8th.
Garvin Thomas, lab. 18 Vernon
Garwood Benjamin, tavern, 416 N 2nd.
Garwood Frederica, huckster, rear 524 N 3d
Garwood R., dry goods, 66 S 2nd.
Garwood Wm. lab. rear Marshall ab Poplar
Gash Frederick, butcher, 36 George (S)
Gaskill Aaron W., plasterer, 10th bel Melon
Gaskill Abner, lab., Locust n Beach
Gaskill Benjamin, bookbinder, 42 S 5th, h 348 Vine
Gaskill Benj., engraver, 18 Minor, h Cherry n Sch. 7th.
Gaskill Charles, Marlborough bel Duke (K) .
Gaskill Charles T. 4 Wood ab 11th
Gaskill & Copper, book binders' tool cutters and engravers, 18 Minor.
Gaskill Edmund, ladies shoemaker, 28 N 11th
Gaskill Edward, book binder, 42 S 5th, h 348 Vine
Gaskill John, shoes, 10th ab Ogden
Gaskill John, stone cutter, Elder
Gaskill Joseph W., 4 Poplar
Gaskill Thomas, tailor, 4 Mary (S)
Gaskill Thos., driver, rear 107 N Market
Gaskill Peter Penn, mer., 97 N Water, h Sch 5th n Cherry
Gasner Fred. porter, rear 31 S 2d
Gassler Marg., Carlton ab Sch 7th
Gassman M., 226 N Front
Gaston Simeon, watchman, Lewis ab Sch 6th
Gatchel Edmund K., carp., G.rad av bel 11th
Gatchell John, builder, N W 5th & Lombard
Gatchell Joseph, messenger, city treasurer's office, h 117 S 5th
Gatchell Joseph, Jun., County Auditor, State House
Gates & Baird, granite yard, Sch Front and Chestnut
Gates John, carter, Ann ab Sch 5th
Gates Nathaniel, carp., N W 4th & Marshall
Gates Stephen, ship carp. Front bel Greenwich
Gatter Wm. cooper, 26 Rose al
Gatzmer Alex. C., clerk, Camd. & Amboy R road office, 45 S wharves, h 227 S 9th
Gatzmer Wm. H., agent Camd. & Amboy R road, office 45 S wharves
Gaubert Lewis T., upholsterer, 136 S 2d
Gaughran Michael, tavern, 87 S wharves
GAUL FREDK. brewer, New Market and Callowhill, h 358 Mulberry
Gaul Jacob, gent. 64 Franklin
Gaul John, carp. Johnson's la bel 4th
Gaul John F., carp., 130 Coates
Gaul Philip, brewer, 97 New Market.
Gaul Susan, rear 371 S 3d
Gaul Wm. sugar refiner, Sassafras and Crown, h 248 N 5th

Gault Elizabeth, 132 Callowhill
Gault Francis, bonnet presser, Yhost
Gaun Henry, lab., 440 N Front
Gaun Margaret, 440 N Front
Gaunn John, carp., Marlborough ab Queen (K)
Gauntt Chas. S., M. D. 194 Locust
Gauss Gottlieb, lampmr., 114 Wood
Gauss Jacob F., baker, Vine ab 12th.
Gaut Wm. painter & glazier, 8th ab Carpenter
Gautier Anthony, upholsterer, 7 Sheldon row
Gavett Nelson, machinist, Broad ab Filbert, h 9 N Sch 7th
Gavett Robert S., cordwainer, Clark bel 4th
Gavett Samuel, Filbert n Broad
Gavin Michael, brass-founder, 238 S 5th.
Gavit Saml., machinist, 127 W Sassafras
Gavit Sanders, oysterh. F road & Otter (K)
Gaw Alex. G. clerk, 145 Marshall
Gaw Henry L. clerk, 50 S 3d
Gaw James, dry goods, 234 S 2nd.
Gaw Jason, dry goods, 232 S 2nd.
Gaw Robert, ornamenter, 280 S 2nd
Gaw Robert M. engraver, 15 Pratt
Gaw Wm., engineer, 1 Harmony st
Gaw William, mer., N W Front & Spruce, h 395 S 2nd.
Gaw William P., acct., Washington bet 10th & 11th
Gay Edward F. super. motive power Col. R. R. Lancaster pike ab Washington (W P)
Gay James, real est. of. 632 N 3d (K)
Gay John, grocer, 4th & Brown
Gay Richard, porter, Osborn's ct
Gayley James, box mr., Adelphi al ab Pegg
Gaylord H. V., carp., Juniper al
Gear Ephraim, lab. Olive bel Broad
Gearheart Abraham, mor. dresser, 2 Wheelock's pl
Geary Benjamin, shop, 126 N Front
Geary Edw. hatter, 2d bel Poplar
Geary George N. tanner, 12 Franklin ab 3d (K)
Geary Lydia A., milliner, 366 Vine
Geary Thos. lab. Queen ab Shackamaxon (K)
Gebhard James, hatter, 49 S 3d
Gebhard Lewis, tavern, Wood & 4th
Gebhard Lewis P., M. D., 216 Sassafras.
Gebhart Adam, baker, Cox bel 2nd.
Gebhart Samuel, carp., Cox bel 2d
Gebler Charles F., conveyancer, Parrish bel 8th
Geddes John S. meat shop, rear Parrish ab 10th
Geddes Wm. F., printer, 112 Chestnut, h 152 Christian
Gee John, rope maker, 2nd n Master (K)
Gee Joseph, cordwainer, 4th bel Tammany, h Smith's al
Gee Noah, cabinetmr., Lafayette pl
Gee S. C. Mrs. milliner, 179 Pine
Geeler Charles T. tobac. 412 N 2d
Geer George, trader, Wallace bel 10th
Gegan John, M. D., druggist, S E Front & Cedar
Gegan Michael, shop, Juniper and Norman's al
GEGAN THOS., druggist, S E 9th & Cedar.

Gegenheimer Conrad, cordw., Rihl's ct
Gegenheimer John, cooper, 420 N 4th
Gegenheimer John, bootfitter, George ab R r'd (F V)
Gegenheimer Lewis, cooper, St John ab Beaver (K)
Gehen Patrick, shop, 19 Strawberry
Gehring Christian, shoemr., 43 N 4th
Geib Wm., M. D., 271 N 7th
Geiger Jos., capmaker, 31 Carter's al
Geiger Lewis, tobacconists, 324 N 3d
Geiger Lewis, lab. rear 467 N 4th
Geisenberg Isaac, clothing, Poplar bel 2nd
Geisenberger Joseph, clothing, Brown and New Market
Geisil John, tailor, 305 N 10th
Geisinger George, carp., 178 Coates
Geiss John, waterman, 43 Mead al
Geisse, Brothers & Co., chemists, 111 N Front
Geisse Christian H., drug., 111 N Front
Geisse Edward C. mer., 60 S Front
Geisse George W. jr., druggist, 111 N Front
Geisse Joseph, dry goods, 198 S 6th
Geisse Lewis, mer., 111 N Front
Geisse Peter, tailor, 7 Nectarine
Geisse William, merchant, 60 S Front.
GEISSE WM. & SONS, import. looking glass plates, 60 S Front.
Geissert Henry, currier, 22 Green
Geissinger Eliza S. milliner, 70 Coates
Geitt John, tanner, rear 13 Lily al
Gelbech George, brass founder, Hope bel Phœnix (K)
Gemeny A. R., dry goods, S E 9th & Lombard
Gemmill James R., mer., 75 High, h 106 S 3rd
GEMMILL, SINNICKSON, STORMS & CO., dry goods, 75 High
Gemmill Zachariah, mer., 207 High, h 153 N 10th
Gemmill Z. & Co, mers., 207 High.
GEMRIG JACOB H., surg. inst. mr., 43 S 8th
Gendell John A., carpenter, 103 N 7th, h 6 Nicholson.
Gennings John C., dry goods, 509 N 2d
Gensbey Henry, plasterer, Parrish ab 5th
Genter Fred. cordw., Poplar ab Beach (K)
Gentle Wm. blacksm. Duke & Wood (K)
Gentner Frederick, teacher, 118 Brown
Gentry Mary, 65 New Market
Gentry Robert, tobacconist, Beach bel Maiden (K)
Gentz John, cordw., rear 86 N Market
George Anthony jun., pewterer, 607 S 2d

George Margaret, Wistar n 11th
George Margaret M., Sch 8th n Cherry
George Moore R. shoemaker, Thompson ab Sch 7th
George Nathan P., painter and glazier, 577 S 2d
George Richard S. H., bookseller, 26 S 5th, h 356 S 3d
George Thos. sashmr. Broad & Paper al
George Thos. & Edmund, iron mers. N E 12th & High.
George William, waterman, Mead n Front
George Wm., lab., Schrader's ct
George Wm. Henry, huckster, Jefferson opp Hope (K)
Gercke Helfrich, baker, Sassafras n Sch 7th.
GERHARD BENJAMIN, atty. & coun., 100½ S 4th
Gerhard W. W., M. D., 301 Walnut
Gerhart A. L., mer., 365 High, h 11 Lybrand
Gerhart A. L. & Co., com. mers., 365 High
Gerhart Jacob, lab., 38 Callowhill
Gerker Henry, glue manuf., 1½ N 3d and 5th and Camac
Gerlach George A., 1 Lawrence ct
German David, cooper, F road below Master.
German John, lab., Thompson bel Sch 7th
German W., chemist, Marlborough & Allen
Germon W. L., engraver, 80½ Walnut
Gerrish Elizabeth, 92 Poplar
Gerrish John C., 368 N Front
Gerry Rev. Robert, Callowhill ab 12th
Gersher John, spinner, Montgomery bel Front (K)
Gerst Fred., tailor, rear 210 St John
Gerstley Morritz, clothier, 217 N 2d
Gesper Louis, barber, 6 S 8th
Gessler Bainhart, tailor, rear Marshall bel Poplar
Gessler Christian, jeweller, 93 Green
Gessler Elizabeth, tailoress, Clinton bel Parrish
Gest John, land agent, h 174 S 11th.
Gest John B., atty. & coun. 174 S 11th
GEST JOSEPH, clerk, 81 S 11th
Gest Nich. gard. Vienna & West (K)
Gest Valentine, lab. Madison av
Getler, Andrew, cordw. 41 Mechanic
Getman Jacob, carp., 15 Rachel (N L)
Getman Michael, tobacco'st, rear Palmer below Queen (K)
Getman Nicholas, tobacconist, Stiltz' ct
Getter John, stone cutter, 21 Beaver (K)
Getty Charles, carp. 203 S 4th
Getty Hugh, porter, Traquair's ct
Getty M. Mrs., Sch 5th bel Spruce

Geselott Margaret, gentw., 396 N 4th
Geverd Henry, dealer, 156 Carpenter
Geyer George, clerk, 139 Dillwyn
Geyer George C., collector, 290 N 8th
Geyer George, sen., carp., 9th bel Buttonwood
Geyer Isaac, vict., rear Nectarine ab 10th
Geyer Simon, 3 Carlton sq
Geyer Wm. B., leather dealer, c 3rd & Lombard, h 74 Lombard.
Gfroerer Chas. confectioner, 46 N 8th
Gheen John R., drove yard, R road bel Coates
Ghegan Bartholomew, stoves, Sarah n Queen (K)
Ghegan Alice, gentw., 151 Pine
Ghegan George, stove manuf. 111 N 2d, h 298 N Front
Ghriskey L., b h, 265 High
Gibb David, jr., painter, 209 Sassafras.
Gibb David, refectory, under Arcade, h 170 S 11th
Gibb John, carpet weaver, 147 Carpenter
Gibboney Wm., manuf., 17 M'Duffie
Gibbons Ann, shop, Lombard ab Sch 2d
Gibbons Bernard, lab., Chestnut n Sch Beach
GIBBONS CHARLES, attorney & coun., 116 S 3rd
Gibbons George W., conveyancer, 51 Wood
Gibbons George W. Jr., mer., 83 High h 51 Wood
Gibbons Henry, M. D., 167 S 3rd
Gibbons James, carpenter, 163 Pine.
Gibbons James, cordw., 5 Lemon
Gibbons John, dealer, R road & Buttonwood
Gibbons John, carp., Middle al
Gibbons Theresa, teacher Lombard ab Sch 2d
Gibbons Thomas, blacksm., 2 Lodge pl
Gibbs Aaron, blacksmith, 41 Apple
Gibbs Ann, corsetmr., 125 N 5th
Gibbs A. V., mer., 25 S 2d
Gibbs C., N W Front & Mulberry, h 43 New
Gibbs Eulogius, shoemr., 312 Sassafras
Gibbs Geo., grocer, Crown and Bedford (K)
Gibbs Harriet, washer, 11 Mayland
Gibbs Isaac, carp. rear 58 Zane, h 521 N 5th
Gibbs James, watchmr., Spruce and Green's ct
Gibbs James L., ostler, Sch 4th ab George (F V)
Gibbs Job R. jr., carp. Parrish ab 9th
Gibbs Job R., carp., 249 N 7th
Gibbs John M. grocer, Marlboro' & Franklin(K)
Gibbs John W., mer., 25 S 2d h 20 Buttonwood
Gibbs Joseph, porter, Caroline pl
Gibbs Joshua, coachman, 78 George
GIBBS J. W., cloths, 25 S 2d, h 140 S 4th
Gibbs J. W., Mayor's Office, h 215 Pine
Gibbs Maria, Eagle ct
Gibbs M. W., carp., Middle al
Gibbs Peter C., carpenter, rear 58 Zane, h 5th n George.
Gibbs Richard, carp., 57 Chestnut, h 125 N 5th
Gibbs Shephard, sexton, 259 Lombard.

Gibesson Joseph, carter, Haydock bel Front
Gibson Alfred, grocer, New Market & Brown
Gibson Archibald J., salesman, Hughes' ct
Gibson E. J., Wood ab Julianna
Gibson Henrietta, 10th ab Lombard
Gibson Henry, bookbinder, 33 Castle.
Gibson Jacob, periodicals, 3d and Dock, h New Crown bel Green
Gibson James, city watch, Centre bel 13th.
Gibson James, S E 8th & Spruce
Gibson James, oil cloth manufr., G T road n 4th
Gibson James, mariner, 603 S Front
Gibson James G., conveyancer, 212 N 6th, h 6 North
Gibson James M., tinsmith, 310 S 6th
Gibson John, plain & decorative house painter, 79 S 11th.
Gibson John, shoemr., Sutherland
Gibson John, shoemaker, 259 Cherry.
Gibson John weaver, Ann n 12th.
Gibson John, distiller, 31 Chestnut, h 331 Sassafras.
Gibson John, weaver, Gulielma
Gibson John, 104 N 4th, h Wood ab Juliana
Gibson Mary Ann, shop, 274 N 5th
Gibson Mary Ann, 98 St John
Gibson Matthew, painter, Maiden n Beach (K)
Gibson Merrit, cordw., 500 S 2nd
Gibson M., dress mr., Vine ab 12th
Gibson Nathaniel, agent, 68 N 9th
Gibson Robert, tinplate worker, 220 S 5th
Gibson Robert C., clerk, 29 Franklin
Gibson Sarah, dry goods, 157 Cedar
Gibson Thomas, plumber, 34 Carter's al., h 5 M'Leod pl
Gibson Thomas, gun smith, 2 Nicholson
Gibson Thomas., clerk, 21 N Sch 8th
Gibson Wm., cordw., N E 5th and Catharine
Gibson Wm., jeweller, 119 G T road (K)
Gibson Wm., lab., 3 Elizabeth (N L)
Gibson Wm., barber, 10th ab Lombard
Gibson Wm., M. D., N W Sch 7th & Chestnut.
Gibson Wm. H., tinsmith, Carpenter st
Gicker Wm. B., flour, 138 F road
Gideon Andrew, butcher, rear 135 Wood
Gideon Casper P., mariner, 15 Federal
Gideon George, insp. office, Pennsylvania av n William
Gideon Henry S., bootmr., 130 Sassafras
Giebler Ludwig, tailor, Beach ab Poplar (K)
Giffear Peter, brickmr., Sch 3d and Ann
Gifford Alfred, carp., 354 S 5th
Gifford A. B., shipmaster, Carpenter ab 5th
Gifford Bethuel, cabinetmaker, Rose al ab Green
Gifford Deborah, mantua mr., Shippen ab 9th
Gifford James, cordw., Trinity pl
Gifford James, seaman, 407 S Front
Gifford John, shoemr., 5 Stanley
Gifford Wm., paper stainer, 50 Washington av
Giggen Jos., tanner, Bedford opp Elm (K)

Gihon David W., bookbinder, 98 Chestnut, h 189 Queen

Gihon James, book binder, 2 Sergeant

Gihon James L., acct., 130 High, h 22 Powell

Gihon John C., gold beater, 2 N 5th

Gihon John H., printer, N E 6th and Chestnut, h 22 Powell

Gihon Wm. B., engraver, N E 6th and Chesnut

Gilberry Dennis, carter, 8 Pearl

Gilbert Adelaide, trimmings, 63 N 10th

Gilbert Alexander, shoemaker, 117 Brown

Gilbert Benj., lab., Sch Beach n Walnut

Gilbert Benjamin S., cordw., 103 New Market

Gilbert Charles, porter, 50 Mechanic

Gilbert Charles, lab., Locust bel 13th

Gilbert Charles, stove manuf., 249 N 2d, h 4th and Green

Gilbert Chas. M., grocer, 11th and Parrish

Gilbert Christiana, washer, Perry ct

Gilbert Christopher, shoemaker, 156 S 11th.

Gilbert Daniel, cooper, rear 114 German

Gilbert George, grocer, 52 Union

Gilbert & Gihon, engravers, N E 6th & Chesnut

Gilbert Hart, twister, Clay av (K)

Gilbert Henry, shoemr., rear 10 Barclay

Gilbert Henry W., potter, 107 Melon ab 13th

Gilbert Jas., lab., Union bel West (K)

Gilbert Jacob, Gilbert ab 9th

Gilbert John, druggist, 179 N 3d, h 69 Vine.

Gilbert John, bricklayer, rear 340 Coates

Gilbert Joseph, blacksmith, 1 Lodge al, h N W Chester and Maple

Gilbert Joseph, carp., 466 Callowhill

Gilbert Joseph, tailor, 1 Loxley's ct., Mulberry.

Giles Edward, mathematical instrument maker, 257 Catharine

Giles Ezra G., clerk, Filbert E Sch 3d

Giles John, blacksm., Mechanic ab George

Giles Lewis, porter, Dugan

Gilfillan Robert, grocer, S E 3d and Poplar

Gilfillin John, carter, Sch 3d and Vine

Gilfoyle Martin, lab., Cooper n Sch 3d

Gilfrey Catharine, widow, 129 New Market

Gilkey James, lab., 21 Helmuth

Gilkin Henry, tailor, 35 Strawberry

Gill George, watchman, 129 S 10th

Gill Henry, carp., 49 Charlotte

Gill Hugh, lab., Filbert ab Sch Front

Gill James, lab., 14 Quarry

Gill John drayman, 131½ N 2nd

Gill John C., chair paint., 7th bel Carpenter

Gill John L., bootmr., 310

Gill John S., carp., F road ab Otter

Gill Lawrence E., saddler, 299 Walnut

Gill Patrick, dealer, 5 Boyles' ct

Gill Robert, gent., Sch 8th bel George.

Gill Sydney P. 421 Spruce

Gill Thomas, bricklayer, Wood ab Sch 6th

Gill Thos. H., manuf. plast. Paris, 76 Charlotte

Gill William, gent., 55 S 12th.

Gillam Jesse, Simmons' ct.

Gillam John, printer, Crawford's ct

Gillam R., waiter, Emeline

Gillam Thomas, waterman, Crawford's ct

Gillan Anthony, weaver, William & Benton

Gillan Jas., weaver, Wagner's al

Gillan Jas., lab., 20 Griswold al

Gillan Mary, Lewis bel Sch 6th

Gillet Joseph & Co., mers., 75 S Front
Gillet Wm., 120 Prime
Gillett Abraham D. Rev., 69 N 12th
Gilliam Margaret, tailoress, 4 Hause's ct
Gilliam Wesley, waiter, 11 Wagner's alley
Gilliams Jacob, dentist, 35 Mulberry.
GILLIAMS JAMES L., M. D., 35 Mulberry
Gillies Adrian, trunk mr., 110 Chestnut, h 7th opp Brown
Gillies James, salesman, 29 Julianna
Gillies James, baker, Elizabeth ab Poplar
Gillies & Ruggles, trunk makers, 110 and 181 Chestnut
Gillig J. W., baker, 144 Coates.
Gilligan Thomas, dry goods, 69 Cedar
Gillilan A. H., mer., 10 Church al, h 128 S 3d
Gillilan & Co., mers., 10 Church al
Gillilan James M., mer., 10 Church al
Gillin Alex., watchman, 13th ab Catharine
Gillin Daniel, weaver, 10th ab Federal
Gillin James, lab., Small bel 6th
Gillin John, stone mason, Pearl bel Sch 8th
Gillin Patrick, watchm., Factory ab Sch Willow
Gillin Patrick, soap boiler, 3 Charles
Gillin Robert H., Pearl ab Sch 8th
Gillingham Ann, rear Sch. 3d ab Walnut
Gillingham Charles, cordw., Oran's ct
Gillingham Christian, teacher, 537 N Front
Gillingham G. W., hatter, 200 S 2nd.
Gillingham Henry B., hatter, 65 Cedar
Gillingham Henry W., druggist, S E 9th and Sassafras
Gillingham Jonathan, iron mer., 535 N Front, h 537 N Front
Gillingham Jonathan & Son, iron mers., 535 N Front
Gillingham Joseph, 12th bel Sp. Garden
Gillingham Joseph J., iron mer., 537 N Front
Gillingham Lewis, hatter, Paul bel 7th
Gillingham Mahlon, mer., 24 Bank, h 141 N 7th ab Willow
Gillingham M. H. & S. R., seminary, 56 O Y road, h 180 Sassafras
Gillingham Samuel, grocer, Marshall and Poplar
Gillingham Samuel H., lumber mer., Beach n Shackamaxon.
Gillingham Thomas, coal mer., 74 N 6th
Gillingham Thomas, coal mer., 17 Ellen
Gillingham T., coal yard, Beach above Poplar (K)
Gillingham William H., M. D., 352 Chestnut
Gillingham W. J., bricklayer, Willow and 2d
Gillingham Yeaman's C., agt., Hazleton Coal Yd., Front ab Poplar, h Front bel Otter
Gillingham Yeamans M., mer., 359 Mulberry
Gillis Bartholomew, driver, George ab Sch 7th
Gillis Charles J., bookseller, 46½ Walnut
Gillis James, drayman, rear 16 Wagner's al
Gillis Joseph, weaver, c Sch. 3d and George
Gillis Peter, cordw., 504 S 2nd
Gillis Robert cordw., Vienna ab Queen (K)
Gillis Robert F., cordw., Prime bel Front
Gilmore James C., mer., 109 High, h 47 Union
Gillum Robert A., cordw., Hallowell (S)
Gilman Ambrose, lab., Mechanic bel Culbert

Gilman Daniel, blacksmith, Penn ab Maiden h Shackamaxon bel Bedford (K)
Gilmer John, tavern, 7 N 12th
Gilmor Thomas C., 108 S 4th
Gilmore Isaac, grocer, 13th and Coates
Gilmore James, grocer, S E 13th and Wood
Gilmore John, gas works, Chesnut bel Sch 3rd
Gilmore Maria, wid. groc. N W Sch 8th & Vine
Gilmore Mary, Brand's ct
Gilmore Mary, Say ab Sch 8th
Gilmore Robert, carp., Christian bel 7th
Gilmore Thos., fruiterer, 14 Carter's alley
Gilmore Thos., tea store, 418 N 2d
Gilmore Wm., weaver, 43 W Cedar
Gilmore W., grocer, 13th and Fitzwater
GILPIN CHARLES, atty. & coun., 171 Walnut
Gilpin H. D., atty. & coun., 24 Washington sq
Gilpin John F., brok., 67 Dock, h Spruce ab 12th
Gilpin Mary, 4 Monroe pl
Gilpin Nathaniel, lab., rear Rose ab School (K)
Gilpin Vincent, broker, 67 Dock, h 138 Pine.
Gilpin V. & J. F., brokers, 67 Dock.
Gilpin Wm., cabinet mr., 303 S 10th
Gilpin Wm., carter, Perry ab Franklin (K)
Gilroy Charles, cordw. Tyler st
Gilroy Henry, findings, 449 High
Gilroy H., ladies' shoemr., 76 S 2d
Gilroy H. E. Rev., 9 Ellen (N L)
Gimson Henry, hosier, Howard & Master
Ginder Charles, blacksmith, 33 Wistar
Ginder Edward, blacksmith, 33 Wistar
Ginder Elizabeth, widow, 33 Wistar
Ginder Henry, hosemr., 33 Wistar
Ginder Peter, shoemr., 33 Wistar
Ginder Valentine, hosemr., 33 Wistar
GINDER WM., gent., 12 Lombard
Ginder W. A., collector, 46 S. Wharves, h 135 Catharine
Ginenback Frederick, saddler, 247 S 2d
Ginhart John, glass blower, Cherry ab Queen(K)
Ginnigs David, potter, Franklin and Front (K)
Ginnings H. Mrs., 118 Beach (K)
Ginnis Peter, cordw., 2d ab Washington
Ginnity Bernard, coachman, 19 S 7th
Ginnodo John Q., carp., 10 Madison
Ginnodo Wm. B., carp., Callowhill ab 13th, h 229 Wood,
Ginsly Saml. F., hair dresser, 183 Coates
Ginther E., milliner, 269 N 2d
Ginther Geo., engineer, Bishop & Queen (K)
Ginther George, victualler, Beaver ab 3d
Ginther Margaret C., wid of David, 1 Baker's ct
Giovanni & Oliver, fruiterers, S E 5th & High, and 248 High
Gipson Wm. S., barber, 83 S 3d
Girard Levy, cabmr., 291 S 10th
Girdon Catharine, widow, 53 Franklin
Gisert Charles, currier, 189 Poplar
Githens Charles, cooper, 134 Coates.
Githens Clement, blacksmith, 12th ab Parrish
Githens G. W., bootmr., 4th and O. Y. road, h Brown ab 10th
Githens Joel B., wheelwrt., 3 Brown (N L)
Githens Joseph, confectioner, Marriott bel 6th
Githens Rebecca, dress mr., 27 Powell
Githens William M., gent., 134 Queen

Given John, tailor, Reed ct
Given John, Rev., 7 Lebanon
Given Rebecca, William n Sch. 3d
Given Robert, grocer, 7th and Carpenter, h 152 Carpenter
Given Samuel J., grocer, Atherton & Marriott
Given Wm., stone mason, Shippen ab Broad
Giverson Elizabeth, 28 Jacoby
Givin Hester, Sassafras ab Sch 8th
Givin Joseph, broker, 176 Marshall
Givin Robert, 217 Locust
Glackin Daniel, hatter, 10th bel Poplar
Glackin Sarah, widow, 17 Christian
Glackens Daniel, printer, Lewis ab Sch. 6th
Gladding Chas., victualler, Mechanic n Creek (N L)
Gladding John, books & stationery, 341 High.
Glading David, blacksmith, Callowhill ab Crown, h 152 Poplar
Glading Elizabeth, 39 Wood
Glading Frederick, clerk, Peach bel Coates
Glading George, hair dresser, 504 N 2d
Glading James, clerk of High st. Market, S W Little Water and Lombard
Glading Joseph, tinsmith, 275 and 498 N 2d.
Glading Wm., cooper, 151 S Water, h 145 S 4th
Gladney David, oysterman, 118 Carpenter
Glanden James, chairmr., 10 Poplar
Glanding John W. coachmr. Ogden ab 10th
Glasby Felix, turpent. dist., Perry bel. Phœnix, (K)
Glasgow Augustus, lab., 8 Blackberry alley
Glasgow Jesse, waiter, 25 Washington ab 11th
Glasgow Peter, plasterer, Fitzwater ab Flower
Glasgow Samuel, lab., Carpenter ab 8th
Glasgow Wm., carp., Jones n Sch. 4th
Glaspell John, 8th ab Buttonwood
Glass Alexander, dealer, 541 N Front
GLASS A. F., Merchant's Hotel, N 4th ab High
Glass Matthew, box maker, 4 Crockett's ct h Lagrange pl
Glassen Richard, weav., St. John bel George(K)
Glassmire Jacob, cordw. Henk's ct
Glasz Francis, cordw., 173 St John
Glause Samuel, gent, 300 S 10th
Glaystine B. sugar refiner, 162 Vine
Glaze John, cordwainer, 5 Tammany ct
Glazier Elizabeth, b. h., 6 Wallace
Glazier Henry, cordw., F road ab Otter
Glazier John R., brickmr., Dunton ab Otter (K)
Gleason Anna, shop, 4 Webb's al.
Gleason Dennis, labourer, Carpenter ab 10th.
Gleason James, cabman, 7 Grape ct
Gleason Jonas, stove manuf., 9 St. James & 23 N 5th, h 463 High
Gleason Jonas P. 412 High, h 238 Filbert
Gleason Patrick, dealer, 72 N 5th
Gleason Wm., lab., Shippen la bel Bedford
Gleaves Rosanna, rear 72 Christian
Gledhill Henry, machinist, Sch 3d ab Lombard
Gleeson John, brassmr., 54 Federal
Gleeson Rosanna, Sch 4th n Ann (F V)
Gleisner John, cordw., 11½ Quarry
Glenat Joseph, omnibus proprietor, 12 Phila. Exchange, h Beach bel Maiden

Glendenning R., oat meal & pearl barley manf, h Pleasant ab 12th
Glenn Benj. F., acct., 13th bel Green
Glenn Elizabeth, shoe binder, 13 Maria
Glenn Geo., druggist, 293 S 6th
Glenn Henry, ship carp., Duke ab Vienna (K)
Glenn James, perfumer, 117 Melon
Glenn John, ship carp., rear Noble ab 8th
Glenn Joseph, cordwainer, 2 Goldsmith's ct
Glenn Lewis, saddler, Murry's ct
Glenn L. W., perfumer, 20 S 4th, h 115 S 9th.
Glenn L. W. & Son, perfumers, 20 S 4th
Glenn Margaret, 4 Littleboy's ct
Glenn Mary, gentw., Elizabeth n Poplar
Glenn Michael, stone mason, Barker and Sch 3d
Glenn Ralph, carp., Catharine ab Lebanon
Glenn Robt., weaver, 604 N 2d
Glenn Wm., trunkmr., Queen bel Marlboro' (K)
Glenn Wm., lab., 36 P. road
Glenn Wm., mariner, 382 S Front
Glenn Wm., cabinet maker, 404 S 2d
Glenn Wm. D., mer., 20 S 4th
Glennox Patrick, Milton bel 11th
Glentworth George, druggist, 287 Sassafras.
Glentworth G. P., acct., 232 N 11th
Glentworth Jas., broker, 55½ Walnut, h 91 S 3d
Gleser John, dealer, 2d ab Phoenix
Glessner Oliver P., printer, 334 S 4th
Gloninger George, druggist, 22 Lagrange
Gloucester Stephen H. Rev., Lombard ab 5th
Glover Ann A., 369 High
Glover Joseph, machine mr., h Court alley
Glover Saml., 7 Zane
Gluck John, cordw., Crown ab Callowhill
Gluyas Geo. K., machinist, Christian and Swanson, h 5th bel Queen
Gmelin Charles, doctor, 131 Poplar
Gnavel Christ., cabtmr., Hanover bel Duke (K)
Gobrite George, saddler, rear Wood ab Sch 6th
Gocklen Bernard, flour and feed, 2d and Otter
Godbon John, house painter, 242 Callowhill
Goddard J. L., acct., 352 Walnut
GODDARD & PARKER, grocers, 180 High
GODDARD PAUL B., M. D., 241 Walnut
Goddard Wm. B. mer. 180 High, h 447 Sassafras
Goddard W. C., broker, 31 S 3d, h N E 10th and Lombard
GODEY LOUIS A., publisher Lady's Book, 101 Chestnut, h 489 Chestnut
Godfrey Andrew, carp. 4 Beldin's row
GODFREY B. G., silk goods, 6 Bank
Godfrey Darius W., cordw., Mint ct
Godfrey Dennis, lab., 4 Sch Water
Godfrey Robt. tailor, Kirkpatrick's ct
Godfrey Thomas, plast., Palmer n F road, (K)
Godley Jesse, mer., 84 High, h 199 Mulberry
Godley, Spry & Co., dry goods, 84 High
Godon R. V. Mrs., gentw., 23 Sansom.
Godon Victor L., M. D., 206 Walnut, h 23 Sansom
Godshall Andrew B., tinman, 340 S 2nd.
Godshall Frederick, clerk, h M road bel Prime
Godshall Wm., rope mr., P road bel Christian
Godwin Wm. M., com. mer., 73 S whfs., h 157 Pine

Goebel George, hair dresser, 304 Chestnut
Goehler P., tailor, 367 N 3d
Goekeler Christian, sexton, rear 47 Brown
Goekeler Frederick, grocer, S W 4th & Culvert.
Goekeler Godfrey, baker, 96 Crown.
Goff Henry, carter, 18 Wharton
Goff Henry, jr., butcher, Greenwich ab 2d
Goff Jacob W., mer., 12 N 4th, h 7th n Green
Goff John, butcher, 2d bel Greenwich
Goff Michael, victualler, Greenwich ab 2d
Goff & Peterson, hardware, 12 N 4th.
Goger Martin, beer house, Lewis ab Poplar
Gogula G. W., oysterman, Loud
Goheen John, coachmr., 85 S 8th
Gohl Dorothy, baker, 109 S 5th.
Goines G. W., hair dresser, 8 Exchange pl, h 305 Lombard
Goines Luke J., hairdress., 1 Assembly Building, h 193 Lombard
Goines Wm., barber, 489 High, h George n Sch 7th
Golcher James, gunsmith, G T road ab 2d
Golcher William, blacksmith, 124 N Front
Gold James, bricklayer, Nectarine bel 11th
Gold Thomas, baker, Queen bel Wood (K)
Gold Wm., baker, Queen ab Wood (K)
Golden Alex., weaver, Front bel Phœnix (K)
Golden Ann, washer, Tenfoot al
Golden Benj. W., barber, 481 N Front
Golden David, cordw., 492 N 4th (N L)
Golden Elizabeth, 8 Gray's al
Golder Jeremiah, cordw., 494 S 2d
Golder Robert, M. D., Bedford bel Broad
Golder Robert, paper hangings, 126 Chestnut.
Goldey Abraham, boot crimper, 171 N 12th
Goldey Catharine, 139 New Market
Goldey Jacob, Kensington Exchange, Beach ab Shackamaxon
Goldey Jacob, coachmr., 173 S 11th
Goldey James, porter, 2 Richardson's ct
Goldey James, shoemr., 402 N 2nd.
Goldey Joseph, boots & shoes, S E 10th & Sassafras, h Wood ab Sch 8th
Goldey Thomas, cordw., Elizabeth ab Parrish
Goldman Dav., shoes, 18 S 4th, h 10th ab Parrish
Goldsberry Solomon, clothing, 32 Apple
Goldsmith Clark, 10th ab Poplar
Goldsmith Elijah, fisherman, Cherry ab Queen (K)
Goldsmith George, lab. rear 44 Pegg
Goldsmith George, planemaker, 38 Laurel
Goldsmith H. S., paper hanger, Laurel & Rachel
Goldsmith John S., machinist, 38 Laurel
Goldsmith Napoleon, mer., 44 N 8th, h 272 Sassafras
Goldsmith & Rosenthal, tobacc.. 285 N 3d
Goldsmith Thos. O., M.D., Marlboro' ab Beach
Goldsmith Vestina, 24 Sassafras
Goldsmith Wm., planemaker, New Market and Green, h 50 Green
Goll Englehart, lab., 13th ab Poplar
Goll F. C. tavern, S W 12th & Pine
Gollocker James, sign painter, 67 S Front
Golton Maria S., 180 Christian
Golz Chas., weaver, Poplar ab 2d
17

Gomersall Benjamin D., manuf. Hanover below Duke (K)
Gominger Catharine, 83 Callowhill
Gominger Geo., whf. build., Marlborough bel Franklin (K)
Gominger Joseph, Crown bel Bedford (K)
Gominger Wm., carp., Crown ab Queen (C)
Gonter W. D., broker, 35 S 4th, h 10th ab Pine
Good Caleb J., Rev. 25 S 13th
Good Chalkley, carp., Ulrich al
Good Cyrus J., mer., 138 High, h 52 N 13th
Good James, gent., 194 S 9th
Good John, furnishing undertaker, 174 Spruce
Good John S., wines & liq., 224 N Front, h 43 New Market
Good Saml. T. waterman, Tamarind bel Coates
Good Wm., lab., Mulberry n Sch 3d
Good Wm., confect., 240 Callowhill
Goodall & Co. com. mers., 21 Chestnut
Goodall Isaac, mcr. 21 Chestnut
Goodall Sarah, nurse, 96 N Juniper
Goodall Wm., painter, 112 Chestnut, h 10th ab Buttonwood
Goodbred David, grocer, Dillwyn & Tammany
Goodbred F. grocer, Vernon ab 10th
Goodburn Joseph, Wood bel 12th
Goodchild Thos., victualler, Washington ab 6th
Goodeir John, manuf., Edward n School (K)
Goodfellow & Coane, confectioners, 71 S 6th
Goodfellow James, teacher, 133 Lombard
Goodfellow Mrs., Wood ab 11th.
Goodhart Fredk., weaver, Carroll bel 13th
Goodhart John, hatter, 595 N 3d
Goodiear John, vict. Queen ab F road, h Hanover bel Franklin
Goodin Henry, lab., Harmony bel 4th
Goodin John, porter, 320 Cedar
Goodin Wm., tailor, Middle al
Goodman James, paper stainer, 354 N Front
Goodman James, cordw., Apple ab George.
Goodman James, atty. & coun., 277 N 6th.
Goodman John, gent., 87 Callowhill.
Goodman John, tailor, 601 G T road (K)
Goodman John, carman, Howard bel Franklin (K)
Goodman Julia Ann, gentw., Dickerson ct
Goodman Mary Ann, Hammell's row (K)
Goodman Steph. cordw. rear Crown bel Franklin (K)
Goodman Wm., boot fitter, Poplar bel Broad
Goodrich Ann, b h, 289 High
Goodrich John, printer, 26 It road.
Goodrich Joseph, dealer, 273 Callowhill
Goodrich Wm., butcher, 44 Green's ct
Goodrich Wm. mer., 116 High, h 451 Chestnut
GOODRICH WM. & Co., com. agents, 116 High
Goodrick Eliza, 466 S 4th
Goods George, biscuit baker, F road n Bedford (K)
Goods Wm. J. tailor, 98 Sassafras
Goodwin Algernon M., collector, 474 Vine
Goodwin Benj., cordw. 127 G T road (K)
Goodwin Charles T. dentist, 5½ S 11th
Goodwin Cornelius, oysterman, 59 Locust, h Lyndall al bel 13th

Goodwin James, cordw. Marshall ab Poplar
Goodwin James, cooper, rear 115 Brown
Goodwin John, cordw., rear 605 N 6th
Goodwin John, seaman, 34 Harmony
Goodwin John S., cabinetmr., 8 Hyde's ct
Goodwin Jonathan, carpenter, Orange, h 7 Randall's ct
Goodwin Michael, oysters, Williamson's ct
Goodwin Oliver W., 115 Callowhill
Goodwin Sam. bootmr., Hope bel Phœnix (K)
Goodwin Susan, Maria bel 5th
Goodwin Susan, Parrish ab 9th
Goodwin Thomas, cooper, 102 Cedar
Goodwin Thomas F., letter carrier, 174 S 9th.
Goodwin William, hatter, 305 N 2nd
Goodwin Wm., tailor, 210 High, h Wood bel Garden
GOODYEAR JOHN, druggist, S E Pine and Sch 6th
Gool Fred., cordw., Bledisloe's pl
Gool Mary Ann, Pearl ab 13th
Goorley Robert, dry goods, Lombard & Schuylkill 3rd.
Gorbut Robert, carver, P road opp Plum
Gorder David, carter, Barker n Sch 4th
Gordon Alex., weaver, 125 G T road
Gordon Charles, porter, 6 Eagle's ct.
Gordon David, carpenter, 108 German.
Gordon Elizabeth, 3 College av
Gordon George, plasterer, Lombard n Sch. 4th.
Gordon George, stone cutter, 166 Callowhill ab Sch 6th
Gordon George, watchmr., 238 N 2d
Gordon George R. carp. 196 Christian
Gordon Henry, Smith's ct
Gordon Henry, clothes, 69 S 2d, h 194 Shippen
Gordon James, marble polisher, Sch 4th and Lombard
Gordon James, porter, 12 Washington ab 11th
Gordon James, 153 Marshall
Gordon James & Berger, com. mer., 53 N whfs
Gordon James R., hair dresser, 239 N 2nd, h 123 S 6th
Gordon John, weaver, S E 13th & Brinton.
Gordon Joseph, shop, Lombard E Sch 6th
Gordon Joseph, teacher, 6 Burd's ct
Gordon Joseph A., mer., 183 N 4th, h 86 N 7th
Gordon M. K., dressmaker, 96 N 4th
Gordon Nathaniel, manuf., Lombard ab Sch 4th
Gordon Robert C., ladies' shoemr., 4th & Union
Gordon Samuel, whitewasher, 6 Burd's ct
Gordon Sarah Ann, cake baker, 53 Pine

Gorgas E. W., woodwhf., Beach ab Palmer (K) h Allen bel Shackamaxon
Gorgas George, jr., coal merchant, h 6th above Brown
GORGAS G. & H., jr., coal mers., Washington av ab Willow.
Gorgas Henry, coal mer. 216 N Front
Gorgas Mrs. wid. of George, 216 N Front
Gorgas Peter K., lumber, mcr., h 310 N 6th.
Gorgas Samuel jr., broker, 4 S 3rd.
Gorgas Wm., barber, 65 N 3rd.
Gorgos Joseph, mer., 67 N 2d
Gorley John, weaver, 11th ab Carpenter
Gorllier Philip, baker, 322 S 2d
Gorman Ann, washer, 3 Kelly's ct.
Gorman Anthony, tailor, Randall's ct
Gorman Archibald, bootmr., Marriott ab 5th
Gorman & Dillon, blacksmiths, O Y road ab Noble
Gorman Felix, weaver, William ab Otter, (K)
Gorman Jacob, brickmr. 5th n G T road
Gorman Jacob, lab., Hancock above Norris (K
Gorman James. maltster, Vaughan ab Locust
Gorman James, stone cut., Linden bel Sch 6th
Gorman James, tailor, 2 Clymer
Gorman Jane, 57 Gaskill
Gorman John, cooper, 12 Mercer
Gorman John, weaver, 10th bel Master
Gorman John, dyer, rear F road ab Phœnix
Gorman John, shoemr., Marble ct.
Gorman John L., tavern, High and Juniper
Gorman Margaret, 62 German
Gorman Mary, widow, Garrigue's ct
Gorman Michael, cooper, 17 Farmer
Gorman Michael, cordw., Marriott bel 9th
Gorman Michael, cordw. 20 Flower
Gorman Michael, blacksmith, 95 O Y road
Gorman Patrick, lab., Adams bel 13th
Gorman Stephen, lab., Small ab 5th
Gorman Stephen, driver, Shippen ab 8th
Gorman Thomas weaver, William & Hamilton
Gorman Wm. baker, 105 Spruce
Gorman Wm C., turner, 264 Lombard
Gorman William T., mer. S W 2d and Sassafras h 131 N Front
Gormley Edward, lab., Bedford ab 6th
Gormley James, weaver, Catharine bel 13th
Gormley James, weaver, Mariner ab 13th
Gormley James, carter, 6 Margaretta
Gormley John, grocer, N E Shippen & 6th
Gormley Manus, grocery, Sch 5th & Cedar
Gormley Mary. shop. 134 Locust

Goss M., trunkmr., Emeline st
Goss Robert, lab., 4 Hickory ct
Gossen Nicholas, gardener, Palmer n P road
Gosser Jacob, fisherman, Wood ab Franklin (K)
Gosser Mary, wid. of Jacob, Wood ab Queen (K)
Gosser Philip, fisherman, Wood bel Duke
Gossman B., shop, 9th ab Willow
Gossman John, broker, 291 N 10th
Gossner Joseph, pottery, 189 Coates
Gosthalf Myer, lab., 310 St John
Gosthol Michael, cigar mr., rear Rose al
Gotier Raymond, gent., rear 232 S 3d
Gott John, driver, 18 Barker st bel Sch 6th
Goucher David, carp., 13th bel Brown
Goudy Charles, grocer, S W Fitzwater & Adam
Goujon Lewis, screw maker, 6th ab Poplar.
Gould Edward, lab., Allen bel Hanover (K)
Gould George W., coach painter, 51 Prune, h Paul ab 6th
Gould John H., pothographist, 179 Chestnut, h Mechanic
Gould John S., printer, 292 High
Gould Susannah, 17 Prosperous al
Gould Theodore, reedmr., 84 Brown
Gould Walter, port. & min. painter, 194 Chestnut
Gouldy Henry, brickmaker, Locust n Broad
Gouldy Jacob, lampmr., Lombard E Sch 6th
Gouldy Jacob, brickmr., Richard & Alton
Gouldy Samuel, police officer, Sassafras n Sch 7th
Gouldey Henry, lampmr., George n Sch 2d
Gouldey Samuel, brickmr., George n Sch 2d
Gourley Susan, gentw., 28 Union
Gousha Joseph, victualler, Dunton ab Otter (K)
Govett George, watchmr., 49 S 10th, house 244 Filbert.
Govett Joseph, carpenter, 367 Cedar
Govett R. A., carpenter, 355 Cedar.
Govett Sarah, b h., 130 Mulberry
Govett Wm., 3 Carpenter's ct.
Gow George, bonnet presser, 161 S 11th
Gowen, Jacobs & Co., wine mers., 81 Dock.
Gowen James, wine mer., 81 Dock.
Gowen Margaret, 31 North
Graben John, weaver, Philip ab Jefferson (K)
Grabenstatter Michael, baker, 220 Coates
Grabenstine Jacob, tailor, 29 John (S)
Grace Edward R., printer, Shields' alley
Grace James, machinist, Prime ab Swanson
Grace John, victualler, Brown bel 12th
Grace Samuel, vict., Ogden bel 11th
Grace Thomas A., cordw., 156 Coates
Grace Walter, lab., 11 Swanson st
Gracey John, 228 Noble
Gracey L. Mrs., cook, 173 Lombard
Gracey Sarah, b h, 56 Filbert.
Grady James, umbrella maker, Washington av ab Brown
Graeff Charles E., mer., 148 High
Graeff Geo. W., dry goods, 467 N 2d
Graeff H. & Co., stamp cutters, N E 8th & High
Graeff J., looking glass framer, Apple ab Brown
Graeff Joseph, tavern, S E Water & Callowhill.
Graeff Wm. D., mer., 143 High, h 79 New
Graff Ann, 14 Mechanic

Graff Charles, jr. 498 Chestnut
Graff Charles, gent, 265 Mulberry.
Graff Charles M., cordw. 3 Greble's ct
Graff Frederick superintend. water works, 200 Cherry, h N W 10th & Cherry.
Graff George W., bricklayer, Myrtle
Graff John, lab., rear 319 Shippen
Graff John M., shoemr., 136 New Market
Graff Joseph, tin & coppersm., 370 S 3d
Graff Lawrence, muff mr., Front ab Franklin (K)
Graff Samuel, attendant, 182 Poplar
Graffin Robert, variety store, 5th bel Shippen
Graft Rosanna, Charlotte ab Poplar
Grafton Nathan M., printer, Lombard ab Sch 5th
Gragg Wm., weaver, Sch Front & Spruce
Graham Abigail, George W Sch 7th
Graham Abraham, watchman, Perry and Mifflin
Graham Ann, teacher, rear 124 Catharine
Graham Anna, James st bel R road
Graham Augustus, carp., 2 Lætitia ct
Graham A. H., M. D., Lombard & Orleans
Graham Daniel, lab., Ogden ab R road
Graham David, weaver, rear Bedford bel Broad
Graham David, importer, 14 Church alley, h 364 Vine
Graham Edward J., carp., Concord bel 3d, h P road bel Washington
Graham Eliza, trimmings, c 7th & Wallace.
Graham Elizabeth, 40 Quince
Graham Frances, nurse, Dean ab Locust
Graham Francis, tailor, 77 P road.
Graham George R., publisher North American, N E 4th & Chestnut, h 191 Mulberry
Graham Geo. R. & Co., pub. Graham's Magazine, 129 Chestnut
Graham & Gilmore, tea store, 418 N 2d
Graham Hugh, lab., Bedford opp Elm (K)
Graham James, clerk, 18 Jefferson row
Graham James, tailor, 352 & h 358 High
Graham James, grocer, Cedar ab 12th.
Graham James, grocer, Callowhill ab William
Graham James, grocer, 403 High
Graham James, weaver, Hanover ab West (K)
Graham Jane, 5 Plum
Graham John, lab., Reed's ct
Graham John, lab., rear Front ab Phœnix (K)
Graham John, weaver, Hanover ab West (K)
Graham John, driver, Spruce n Sch 5th
Graham John, lab, Clay bel Sch Beach
Graham John, seaman, 47 Penn
Graham John K. mer., 1 Franklin row
Graham Margaretta, teacher, rear 124 Catharine
Graham Margaret, b. h., 1 S 9th
Graham Margaret, gentw., 280 S Front
Graham & M'Michael, pubs., N American, N E 4th & Chestnut
Graham Mitchell, State n Sch 7th
Graham Noah, carp., Wall & Grubb
Graham Noble, police officer, Lombard ab 12th
Graham N. H. & Co., provisions, 3 N Water
Graham N. H., mer., 3 N Water, h 1 Franklin row
Graham Raymond, furniture, 136 Cedar
Graham Richard, lab., Carleton ab Sch 2d
Graham Robert, mariner, Beck st bel 2d

Graham Robert, mariner, 54 Christian
Graham Robt., weaver, Master & Hope
Graham Robert, labourer, Vine ab 12th.
Graham R., chandler, Pearl ab Sch 8th
Graham Thomas, blacksm., 365 S 6th
Graham Thomas, grocer, N E 6th & Cherry
Graham Thomas, gent., 38 Girard
Graham Thomas, pump & blockmaker, 99 S Wharves, h 79 Christian
Graham Thomas, printer, Morris ab Catharine
Graham Thos., limeburner, Carlton bel Sch 2d
Graham Thos, bricklayer, 65 Queen
Graham Thos., carp., P road ab Federal
Graham Westley, tailor, 5 Plum st
Graham Wm., cordw., Pearl bel Nixon
Graham Wm., chairmr., 4 Jefferson ct
Graham Wm., agent. 148 Sassafras
Graham Wm., slater, Poplar ab 10th
Graham Wm., lab., 18 Helmuth
Grain Peter, artist, 198 Locust
Grake Henry W., carter, 2 Reckless
Grambo Henry, mer., 9 N 4th, h 6th n Poplar
Grandfield Wm. shop, 18 Elfreth's al
Grandgent Francis, oyster shop, Coates bel 9th, h 419 N 9th
Granello Francis, grocer, S E Front and Pine
Granett Xavier, shoemr., 86 N 4th
Grange Wm., china store, 429 N 2d
Granger John, shoemr., Poplar bel 10th
Granite Henry, tailor, Oran's ct
Gransback George, bootmaker, 33 Coates.
Grant Daniel, b h., 9 Chestnut
Grant Dennis, weav., Hamilton n William (FM)
Grant Edith, S E Pegg & 2d
Grant Edward H., carpenter, Willow n 12th h Poplar bel 10th
Grant George, mer., 39 N 3rd, h 29 Union
Grant John, baker, Clay bel Sch Willow
Grant John L. Rev., 390 Vine.
Grant Jonathan, bootmr., Rose ab School (K)
Grant Maria, dressmr., 51 New Market
Grant Ralph, dealer, 213 Shippen
Grant Robert, 112 Chestnut
Grant & Ruddach, carp., Willow bel 12th
Grant Samuel, mer., 12 S Whfs., h 44 Pine.
Grant Samuel, jr., 40 S wharves, h 205 8th
Grant & Stone, com. mers., 12 S Whfs.
Grant Wm., oysterman, Marriott bel 5th
Grant Wm. R., M. D., Oak and High
Grantlin Samuel, lab., rear 458 S Front
Granville B., 42 Chester
Grasby Hannah, 51 S 13th.
Grass Anthony, box mr., beer house, 453 Coates
Grass Jacob, brickmr., rear 174 Poplar
Grass Lawrence, tailor, 234 S 4th .
Grattan E., printer, 48 S 3d
Gratz David, mer., 2 S 7th, h Green la n College
Gratz Ed. mer., 2 S 7th, h Green la n College.
Gratz Edward & D., mers., 2 S 7th.
Gratz Hyman, President Penna. Life In. co., 66 Walnut, h 2 Boston row
Gratz H., gent., 310 Shippen
Gratz Jacob, mer., 2 Boston row.
Gratz Jos., mer., 125½ S Front, h 2 Boston row.
Grauel Catharine, sewing, Thomas' al

Gravat Charles, carp., Shackamaxon ab Queen
Gravat Geo. W., b. h., 218 S 4th
Gravat Johnson, carp., Fraley's al (K)
Gravat Ralph, stevedore, Mead ab Swanson
Gravel George, grocer, N W R road and Callow hill, h 373 Callowhill
Gravel Henry, carpenter, 373 Callowhill
Gravel Henry, jr., grocer, 6 High, h 373 Callowhill
Gravel John, carpenter, 377 Callowhill.
Gravel John, lab., 29 Laurel
Gravel Matthew, carp., 2 Brooks' ct
Gravel Wm., carp., Penn bel R road
Gravell John, shoemr., Ogden ab Sch 8th
Gravenstine John, baker, Miller's ct (N L)
Graver Mary A., gentw., F road bel Franklin
Graver Nicholas, tailor, 15 Kessler's al
Graves Bartholomew, 132 S 3d
Graves James, turner, Atherton
Graves James, wheelwright, 6 E North
Graves John, turner, Wheat bel Marion
Graves Joseph R. soap & candles, 190 Vine
Graves Wm., tavern, 15 Queen (K)
Graves Wm., lab., Carter st
Gray Andrew, cordw., 257 S 6th
Gray Ann, shop, R road ab Broad
Gray Anson, mer., 34 Walnut, h 39 Scheetz st
Gray Benjamin, planemr., 14 School (K)
GRAY & BROTHER, scales & coal, 34 Walnut
Gray Catharine, artificial flower maker, 73 Mulberry.
Gray Charles, lab., Fraley's al (K)
Gray Elizabeth, rear 489 N 3d
Gray Esther, milliner, 15 Poplar
Gray Esther, Callowhill n Nixon
Gray Fithian combmr., Crown ab Franklin
Gray George W., brewer, 24 & h 46 S 6th
Gray Henry M., seaman, 390 N 3d
Gray Isaac, cordw., rear 450 N 4th
Gray Jas., cordw., Carpenter ab 8th
Gray Jarvis, waiter, 34 Prosperous al
Gray John, blacksm., Philip ab Jefferson (K)
Gray John, butcher, rear 514 N Front
Gray John, tavern, N W 13th & Wood.
Gray John, moulder, Franklin ab Front (K)
Gray Joseph, blacksmith, c James & R road.
Gray Joseph, grocer, N E 4th and Plum
Gray Lewis, lab., 201 S 7th
Gray Lucy, washer, 14 Burd's ct
Gray Mary, washer, 1 Loxley's ct
Gray Orlando, coal mer., N E Callowhill & Broad, h Sch 8th ab Cherry
Gray Peter, weaver, Crown ab Duke (K)
Gray Richard, 210 St John
Gray Robert, weaver, William n Edward (K)
Gray Robert A., machinist, Poplar bel Broad
Gray Robert E., N W 9th & Mulberry
Gray Samuel, cordwainer, Shackamaxon bel Franklin (K)
Gray Samuel W., grocer, S W 8th & Zane
GRAY & STEEL, stovemrs., 72 N 6th
Gray Stivens, saw., 30 Duke, h 5th bel Federal
Gray Terence, lab. S E Catharine & Flower
Gray & White, brewers, 24 S 6th
Gray William, chairmaker, 177 S 2d, h 1 Shippen

Gray Wm., stovemr., 72 N 6th, h Christian bel 6th
Gray Wm. H., mer., 34 Walnut, h 64 Union
Gray Zachariah R., cordw., Vine bel 13th
Grayson F. W. att'y and coun. 36 Walnut
Grear David, vict. 12th ab Brown
Grear Geo., vict., rear Brown bel 12th
Grear Henry, vict. Jackson (S G)
Grear Jacob, jr., vict., Parrish ab 10th
Grear Jacob, victualler, 234 N 8th
Grear John, vict., Alder ab Poplar
Grear Samuel, jr., vict., 10th bel Poplar
Grear Samuel, vict., 10th bel Wallace
Greason Michael, lab., Milton ab 10th
Great Geo. W., saddler, 104 Elizabeth
Greatbach Susan, 10th ab Christian
Greaves Alexander Jr., plumber, 63 N 5th, h 354 S 4th.
Greaves Charles, mer., 39 Christian, h 264 S 2d
Greaves Jonathan, weaver, Monroe ab Palmer (K)
Greaves & Sons, agency, 2 Ranstead pl.
Greaves William, acct. 3 Montgomery
Grebe Henry, carpet weav., 83 N 3d
Greble Edwin, marble mason, N W P road and Christian, steam saw mill Willow n 13th, h 235 S 5th bel Gaskill
Greble Matthias, cordw., Wood bel West (K)
Greble Sarah, 130 Brown
Greble Susan, wid of Lewis, rear 117 Christian
Green Aaron, carp. 20 High & 10 Jones' al
Green Alex. B., mer., 2 N 3d, h 26 Buttonwood
Green Alpheus, ropemaker, Shackamaxon ab Bedford (K)
Green Andrew, lab. Hope ab Phoenix (K)
Green Ann, washer, 12 Elizabeth
Green Anthony, mer., 41 High, h 63 Marshall.
Green Ashbel, D. D., 150 Pine.
Green Ashbel Jr., att'y & counsellor, 4 George
Green A., widow, 97 Noble
Green Benjamin, waiter, 32 Eagle ct
Green Chas. mariner, Moore's ct
Green Chas. conf. rear 121 Queen
Green Chas. baker, Little Pine
GREEN & CLARK, dry goods, 2 N 3d
Green Conrad, candy sto., 444 N 4th
Green Branch, Coates and Kessler
Green Caleb, agent, Vine n Sch. 7th
Green Charles, mer., 21 N 6th, h 16 Chester
Green Charles B., capt., 285 St. John.
Green Cyrus D. plumb., 346 N 3d, h 243 Green
Green David, mer. 364 Vine
Green David, plast., 25 Parker
Green Dennis, barber, N E 7th & Sp Garden
Green Eben., brickmr., Green Hill
Green Edward, grocer, S W Fitzwater & 6th
Green Edward, grocer, Shippen bel 8th
Green Edward, machinist, Perry ab Phoenix (K)
Green Edward, dealer, Callowhill ab 12th
Green Edward E., boat builder, Mulberry n Sch Front
Green Eliza, b h, 77 Chestnut
Green Eliza, washer, Boyle's ct
Green Elizabeth, gentw., 42 S 13th

Green Elizabeth, washer, Lombard ab Sch 7th
Green Francis, cordw. 4 Walters' ct
Green George, waiter, Warren bel 12th
Green George, porter, 4 St Mary
Green George S. carp. 30 Hazel
Green Glover P. baker, Coates bel 12th
Green Henry, moulder, rear Palmer bel Queen
Green Henry, carp. 106 German
Green Henry, carp., 14 Plum
Green Henry M., capt., 30 Stamper's al
Green Hester, 235 Christian
Green Hugh, lab. 9 Richard
Green Isaac, carp. Mechanic bel George
Green Jabez, lab., 15 Coombe's al
Green Jacob, machinist, 13th ab Poplar
Green Jacob, paper stainer, Sch Front ab Mulberry
Green James, waterman, rear 135 Green
Green James M., M. D., 5 S 9th
Green Jedediah S. furniture store, 274 S 2d
Green Jesse, lab. 4 Eutaw
Green John, weaver, Murray n Sch 3d
Green John, oysterman, Callowhill ab 12th
Green John, sea captain, 392 S 3d
Green John, lab., 2 Warren's ct
Green John, tobacconist, Shippen ab Shippen la
Green John, saddler, 12 Jones st
Green John, drayman, 280 S 6th.
Green John, lab. 445 S Front
Green John, cabmr., 4 Bell's ct
Green John B., carp., 197 Buttonwood
Green Jonas, coachtrimmer, 12th bel Poplar
Green Joseph, collector, 96½ S 3d, h George ab Sch 8th
Green Joseph, barber, Flower ab Christian
Green Joseph, waiter, Washington ab 11th
Green Joseph, moulder, Federal ab 5th
Green Joseph, cordwainer, 29 Swanson.
Green Joseph, cordwainer, 179 Callowhill
Green Joseph, dry goods, 37 N 2nd, h 99 Noble
Green Jos. B., carp., 13 Brandywine
Green Julia, 7 Wood
Green Leva Mrs., rear Benton bel William
Green Lewis, cordwainer, 119 G T road (K)
Green Lewis, tinsmith, 70 Maiden
Green Lydia, b h, 250 High
Green Lydia 1 Faries' ct
Green Lydia, Wallace ab R road
Green Marion, 20 Morgan
Green Margaret, tobacco, S W 6th & Porland la
Green Marshall, paper hanger, Fraley's ct (K)
Green Martha, Carlisle ct
Green Mary, 12 Adams
Green Mary, wid. of Joseph, 120 Dillwyn
Green Mary Ann, rear 9 Lily al
Green Patrick, drayman, 2 Norris' al.
Green Peter, baker, 490 Coates
Green Peter, druggist, Christian ab 7th
Green Philip, lab. Callowhill ab Nixon
Green Philip P., mer., 109 S Front
Green Rachel, Leyden's ct
Green Rhoda, widow, 22 Bird's ct
Green Robert, cordw. Carpenter ab 6th
Green Samuel, porter, 38 Currant al
Green Sarah, huckster, Crown ab Franklin (K)

Green Solomon, porter, 169 Carpenter
Green Stephen, tavern, O Y road and Coates
Green Stephen, cordwainer, rear 465 N 4th
Green Thomas, waiter, 3 Prosperous al
Green Wm. carp. Sch 2d bel Pine
Green Wm., pawnbroker, 243 S 3d.
Green Wm., plasterer, 32 Apple.
Green Wm., labourer, Bickham n Sch. 7th.
Green Wm., porter, 39 Currant al
Green William, weaver, Marlborough above Franklin
Green Wm. hair-cloth manuf. Dock & Pear, h Bedford ab 12th
Green Wm., cordw., Perry bel Phoenix (K)
Green Wm. L., carver & gilder, 65 S 8th, h 91 N 5th
Green Wm. M., carp., 166 N 8th
Greenawald B., dry goods, 152 N 2d, h 29 Vine
Greene Daniel, tavern c Water & Walnut.
Greene Francis, M. D., druggist, 49 S 2d
Greenfield James, lab. 12 Nectarine
Greenfield Jerred J., boilermr., 421 S 6th
Greenhalgh Adam, weaver, Shackamaxon above Franklin
Greenhart L., shop, 40 Bonsall
Greenig John, grocer, Front & Montgomery
Greenleaf Hudson, blacksmith, Master ab Hancock (K)
Greenleaf John, trader, Ann (F V)
Greenman H. H., paper hanger, 287 N 7th
Greenman James, paper hanger, 374 N 2nd.
Greenman Wm., paper hanger, 306 Green
Greenough S. W., cordw., Poplar ab 7th
Greentree E. J., dealer, 220½ E Cedar
Greenvall Jacob, lab. 24 Pegg st
Greenwood John, combmr., 341 N 3d
Greenwood Robert T., cabmr., Marlborough n Duke (K)
Greer Abraham, manuf. 13th ab Pine
Greer Alexander, gold beater, 357 N 3d
Greer And. carp. Cuskaden ct
Greer James, cordw., rear 137 Green
Greer James, dentist, 21 S Sch 6th
Greer James, carver, 2 Jenning's row
Greer James, drayman, 452 Sassafras
Greer John, weaver, Shippen bel Broad
Greer Johnson, warper, Orleans
Greer Josh. constable, George n Sch 8th
Greer Mary, 23 E North
Greer Peter, Bedford bel 8th
Greer Robert, manuf., 57 S 12th
Greer Thomas, machinist, 50 N 6th
Greer Wm. manuf. Callowhill n F M, h 13th bel Pine
Greeves Alexander, grocer, Sassafras n Sch. 8th.
Greeves Jas. manuf. Lawrence ct (K)
Greeves James R. gent., 510 Chestnut
Greeves Thos., mer., 10 Beck pl
Greeves Abraham, agent, ...

Gregg Wm., nailer, rear Carpenter ab 7th
Gregory A. L., M. D., Washington (W P)
Gregory Cornelius, weaver, Sch 8th and Wagner's ct
Gregory Cornelius, oysterman, 124 Queen
Gregory David, painter, rear 100 Carpenter
Gregory Gotlieb, baker, Prime bel 2d
Gregory Henry D., teacher, 382 High, h 147 Sp Garden
Gregory James, lab., rear Carlton bel Sch 6th
Gregory Jonathan, N W 3d & Chestnut, ab stairs
Gregory Joseph II., mer. 34 N 2d
Gregory Margaret, 21 N 12th
Gregory Nathaniel, turner, 22 Hazel
GREGORY, PRICE & CO., dry goods, 34 N 2d
Gregory Thomas, manuf., F road ab West
Gregory William, cordw., New Crown
Gregory Wm., currier, 277 Callowhill
Gregory Wm. carman, Mechanic's ct
Gregory Wm., porter, 3 Relief pl
Gregory Wm. H. clerk, 11 Knight's ct
Gregory Wilson, boot and shoe manuf., 16 Bank, h 260 Marshall
Greiner Christ'r. M., portrait painter, 43 N 4th
Greiner F., teethmr., 129 Race
Greiner George, treas. Phil. saving fund soc'y, h 206 N 6th.
Greiner Isaac, plasterer, 48 Perry
Greiner Lewis, toymaker, 223 Callowhill.
Greiner Stephen, varnisher, 112 S 10th
Greiner Wm. M., mer., 33 N 3d, h 1 Sergeant
Greiner Wm. S. mer. 42 N Whar., h 119 N 9th
Greinpart John, baker, 210 N 8th
Greis Wm. R., mer., 16 N 3d, h 42 Mulberry
Grelaud D., female seminary, 120 S 3rd.
Greshaw Andrew, drayman, 9 Monroe ct
Gresimer Jonah, tailor, 284 N 2nd.
Greswold Augustus, gent., S W 5th & Pine
Gretzinger Jacob, skin dress., Hummel's ct
Gretzinger Leonard, vict., Palmer ab Franklin (K)
Greul G. lace and fringe mr. 104 N 6th, h 10th ab Poplar
Greul J. G., lace and fringe mr., Hinckle's ct
Greussier Joseph, bootmr., 6 Charles
Greveland Jos., weaver, Carpenter bel 11th
Grew Henry Rev., 11 S 4th
Grew Wm. C. shoemr., 473 N 3d
Grice Francis, machinist, Beach ab Hanover, h 71 Queen
Grice John E., tailor, 4 Myers' ct
Grice Samuel, lumber mer., Beach ab Hanover, h Beach bel Shackamaxon
Grice S. B. & F. & Co., steam engine makers, Beach bet Hanover and Palmer
Grieb Sarah, tailoress, Shippen ab 10th
Grier James, grocer, 387 High
Grier Jane, dry goods, Pine and Perry
Grier John D., mer., 272 High

Griesemer Peter S., grocer, 499 N 2d, h 124 N Market
Griesen Harman, tobacconist, 394 N Front
Grieson James, carp., Olive ab 12th
Grieves John, marble mason, Sch 5th & Spruce
Griffee Wm., chair mr., 65 St John's
Griffee Peter, bookbinder, 72 N 6th, h 50 Duke
Griffenberg Thos M., saddler, Church ab Washington
Griffenburg David, boilermr. Stoy's ct & Allen (K)
Griffenburg Thomas, saddler, 2d bel Queen, h 2 Reckless
Griffin Ann, b h., 7 Chancery lane.
Griffin B., lab., Lloyd bel Shippen
Griffin Edward, cordw., rear 3 Wall st
Griffin Eliza, rear Carpenter bel 7th
Griffin E., M. D., 286 Green
Griffin Henry, lab., Rose al
Griffin Matthew, carter, 48 Quince
Griffin Patrick, lab., Locust n Sch 2d
Griffin Peter, lab., Bickham n Sch 7th
Griffin Seth, lab. Queen n F road (K)
Griffin Thomas, slater, 13th ab R road, h 13th ab Green
Griffin William, mer., 241 Pine.
GRIFFIS JOHN L., coal mer., 74 S 3d (C) and whf bel Christian
Griffith Aaron, lab., 5th ab Poplar
Griffith Abel, whip mr. 4th bel Franklin (K)
Griffith Amos, stove manuf., S W 2d & Vine.
Griffith A. E., shop, 463 N 4th
Griffith C. & Co., dry goods, 447 N 2d
Griffith Dorothy, books, 384 N 2d
Griffith Ely, dry goods, 283 Chestnut.
Griffith Geo. F. jeweler, Apple ab George
Griffith Harvey, books, 114 N 3d, h 384 N 2d
Griffith Isaac, gent, 138 Dillwyn.
Griffith Isaac, dentist, N W Sch. 7th & Filbert
Griffith James, carter, Willow ab Front
Griffith John, plasterer, Mechanic ab George
Griffith John, bandbox maker, 6½ S 3d, h 51 Spruce
Griffith John, cooper, 4 Lodge pl
Griffith John T., cooper, 20 St James, h 4 Lodge pl
Griffith Joseph, whipmr., rear Poplar bel 10th
Griffith Lewis, carpenter, 70 N Juniper
Griffith Maria, shop, Orchard
Griffith Matthew, gent., Franklin ab Green.
Griffith Michael, shoemr., 89 Gaskill
Griffith Philip, porter, 12 Burd's ct
Griffith Robt., M. D., 6 Monroe pl
Griffith Saml. flour and feed, Vienna ab Queen (K)
Griffith Saml., watchmaker, Vicker's ct N of Barker
Griffith & Simon; booksellers, 114 N 3d, & 50 N 6th
Griffith Thomas, plasterer, Alden ab Poplar
Griffith William, engraver, 35 N 4th
Griffith Wm., upholsterer, 55 N 6th
Griffith Wm., coal mer., Sch 3rd ab Filbert.
Griffith Wm., segar mr., 3d and Culvert
Griffith Wm., piano manuf., 7 Pleasant Retreat

Griffith Wm. S., carp., Penn bel R road
Griffith W. C., grocer, 13th and Marion
Griffiths A. W. M. D., 188 Coates.
Griffiths Charles, M., M. D., 293 Coates
Griffiths Eliza, 283 N 6th
Griffiths Elizabeth, dressmr., 89 Locust
Griffiths Mary, 200 Locust
Griffiths S., Sp. Garden tube works, Vine bet Sch 2d & 3d, h Sch 3d n Vine
Griffiths Thomas, mer, 185 Chestnut
Griffiths Thomas, teacher, rear 12 Schiver's al
Griffiths Wm., broker, 2 York, h 200 Locust
Griffiths Wm., machinist, Wharton ab 4th
Griffitts S. P. Jr., clerk, George ab 9th
Griffitts Wm. F., mer., 7 minor, h 33 Clinton
Grigg Anthony, printer, 19 St. James, h 2 Carlton sq.
GRIGG, ELLIOT & CO., booksellers, 9 N 4th
Grigg George, salesman, 117 N 5th
Grigg John, bookmr., 9 N 4th, h 298 Mulberry.
Grigg Mark, 7 Marriott
Grigg Mark, tailor, 170 S 9th
Grigg Robt., mer., 31 Castle
Griggs & Brother, boots & shoes, 181 N 3d
Griggs John, bricklr., rear 385 S Front
Griggs Wm., chairmr., rear 332 S 2d
Grim Benj., brickmr., Elizabeth ab Poplar
Grim Daniel K., dry goods, 171 N 3d
Grim Geo., brickmr., Elizabeth n Franklin
Grim Jacob, brickmr., Charlotte ab Poplar
Grim John, brickmaker, Charlotte c Poplar.
Grim Jos., baker, 262 S Front
Grim Jos., brickmr., Elizabeth n Wager
Grim J. & N., brickyard, 6th & Master (K)
Grim Martin, weaver, 2d bel Master (K)
Grim Mattis, drayman, Green's ct
Grim Nicholas, brickmr., 5th ab George
Grim Peter, brickmaker, 480 N 3d.
Grim Saml, brickmr., Elizabeth ab Franklin
Grim Sarah, dry goods, 478 N 3d
Grimes James, weaver, 24 W Cedar
Grimes Jos., weav., rear Hope bel Phoenix (K)
Grimes Richard, lab., Ann n Sch 4th
Grimes Wm., tinsmith, 4 S 5th, h Union above West
Grimshaw R., carp. 8th & Shippen, h 50 Lebanon
Grimston John, Mariner, 3 Mead
Griner J., coach painter, 16 Acorn al
GRISCOM GEO., att'y & coun., 223 Walnut
Griscom John D., M. D., 325½ Mulberry
Grissim Adam, ship carp. Vienna & Duke (K)
Grissim Caspar, ship. carp., West ab Cherry (K)
Grissim Daniel, West ab Cherry (K)
Grittan Samuel, cordw., Wood bel 3d
Gritzinger Christian, tailor, rear 435 N 4th
Grives Thos., lab., Hope ab Otter (K)
Grodel Frederick, 228 N 9th
Groff Jonas, morocco dr., 340 St John (K)
Groff J. R., watchmr., 58 High, h 75 New
Groff Wm. C., blacksm., Wood n Sch 2d, h 182 Poplar
Grogan James, weaver, 4th bel G T road
Grogan Wm., chaise driver, Christian ab 6th
Groman Wm., stone mason, Hartshorn's ct

Groom Benj., cordw., Ogden bel 10th
Gropengiesser J. L., chronometer & watchmr., 100 S 3d
Grosholtz L. & P., importers, 38 Church al
Grosholz Louis, Schiller Hotel and wine mer., 86 Sassafras.
Gross Adam, vict., 12th ab Brown
Gross Andrew, printer, 8 New Crown
Gross Christian, butcher, Front ab Otter (K)
Gross Christian, rear 146 St John
Gross Christian, morocco dress., rear 7 Brooke
Gross & Co., printers, N E 3d & Sassafras
Gross G. W., coachm., Beach st
Gross John, lab., Carpenter ab 12th
Gross John, cordw., 124 Apple
Gross J. F., vict., 12th ab Brown
Gross Lewis, victualer, Willow bel Broad
Gross Mary Ann, 51 S 12th
Gross Wm., cabinetmr., 3 Drinker's al
Grossman E. N., printer, rear 130 Sassafras, h 13 Crown
Groul George, lab., 6th bel G T road
Groul John, blacksm., G T road ab 6th
Grouse Fred., cordw., 118 New Market
Grouse Maria, Mechanic ab Culvert
Grout H. T., attorney, 14 Sansom, h Green bel 12th
Grove & Brother, grocers, 142½ N 3d
Grove Conrad S., grocer, 142½ N 3d, h 89 N 4th
Grove D. B., piano forte manuf., 34 N 7th
Grove Elizabeth, widow, James ab 10th
Grove Henry, grocer, 142½ N 3d, h 96 New
Grove John, tobacconist, 147 Poplar.
Grover Abigail, 5 Lombard
Grover Charles, 18 Coates
Grover Lorenzo H., oil cloths, rear 36 N 2d
Grover Priscilla, wid of Hugh, 21 Christian.
Grover Thomas D., County Com., h 12 Federal.
Groves Anthony, gent., Pine ab Broad
GROVES ANTHONY, jr., transportation agency, 19 S Whfs
Groves Daniel, bricklayer, 156 N 9th.
Groves Eliza, tailoress, 57 Shippen
Groves Elizabeth, b h, N W 9th and Chestnut
Groves Jacob, tailor, 19 Mulberry
Groves Jas., tailor, 10 Kelly's av
Groves Michael F., M. D., 200 S 5th
Groves Thomas D., watchman, 291 St John
Groves Wm., shoemr., Clinton ab Parrish
Groves Wm. H. & Co., publishers, 65 S 3d
Growley Mich., tailor, Wirtz's ct
Grubb Chas., cab mr., Wyler's ct
Grubb Christiana, Wood bel Franklin (K)
Grubb Curtis, 89 Race

Grubb Wm. M., blacksmith, 144 Franklin
Gruber Geo., car-man, 32 Pegg st
Gruber John C., blacksmith, 176 St John
Grugan Charles C., mer., 134 Chestnut, h Library 1st house ab Custom House.
Grugan Florence, tailor, 23 Dean
Grugan Michael, drayman, Marriott bel 6th
Grum John H., potter, 87 W High
Grumholz Conrad, tailor, Charlotte & Thompson (K)
Grumshield John, tailor, 297 N 2nd
Grund Charles, cordw., 82 Apple ab Poplar
Grund Francis J., 370 Chestnut
Grundlock Henry, cabinetmr., Burchell's ct
Grundlock Wm., bricklayer, Orchard ab George
Grundy Edmund, merchant, 16 Church alley, h 27 Branch
Grunewald & Kolberg, dry goods, 152 N 2d
Gruninger J., cordwr., St John and Callowhill
Grussmire Nicholas, baker, 17 Quince
Gubert L. C., grocer, N W 8th & Mulberry, h 301 Mulberry
Gubert T. E., 301 Mulberry
Guckas Matthias, lab., rear 123 Green
Gudknecht John, harness mr., 120 New Market
Gueckler Adam, cab maker, 4th and Jefferson (K)
Guenat Margaret, gentw., 230 Walnut
Guenter Gottlieb, baker, 108 New Market
Guenther Philip, lab., Melon bel 12th
Guentman & Plumar, confec., 352 S 2d
Guest Albin, lab., Church ab Washington
Guest Charles, cordw., Prime bel 3d
Guest Mordecai, blacksmith, Brown bel 6th, h Parrish ab 5th
Gugler Robert, glovemr., 15 N 4th
Guhring John, razor grinder, 116 Crown
Guier Elizabeth C., rear 5th bel Christian
Guier George, notary public, 8 Library, h Poplar and Green Hill
GUIER & ROBERTS, ship and ins. brokers, & government claim agents, 8 Library
Guier William, stone cutter, rear Lemon bel 11th
Guilberry J. B., tailor, Lysle
Guilbert Nicholas, printer, 56 N 3d, h 254 Marshall
Guilbert N., carp., Sch 6th bel Callowhill
Guilkey M. M., milliner, 197 S 2d
Guillou Acelie, ladies' seminary, N W Penn sq and Filbert
GUILLOU CONSTANT, att'y. & coun., 39 S 4th
Guillou Rene, mer. 214 Chestnut, h Penn ab 6

Gummey John M., coal, Broad n Mulberry, dry goods, N E 8th & Vine
Gumpel J., mer., 101 N 3d, h 1 West
Gumpert B. Barton, druggist, 120 N 2d.
Gumppert Jacob J., dentist, 316 N 2d, h 11 Emlen's ct
Gunn John, laces, 415 N 2d
Gunn Wm., weaver, 10th and Washington
Gunnell Charles W., capt., 79 S 6th
Gunnis Wm., chemist, Sch 6th and Lombard
Gunsalus Robert H., baker, Pike
Gunther David, baker, 10th and Washington (S G)
Gunther Erhard, baker, Franklin ab Union (K)
Gunton Thomas, hosier, 250 S 5th
Gunzer Frederick, baker, 50 P road
Gurney Mary, 6 Union
Gustin John S., foreman, Beach ab Marlboro'(K)
Gustine Prentice P., chairmr., 114 N Front, h 104 Vine
Gutgesell's John B., mathematician, 25 Plum
Guth Anthony F., tailor, 17 Exchange place, h rear 31 S 2d
Guthrie Adam, blacksm., Cadwalader ab Franklin (K)
Gutzell Christa., wid., Union ab Bedford (K)
Guy Alexander, labourer, 33 Quince.
Guy Amos, lab., 28 Burd's ct
Guy Ann, dressmr., 12 Mead al
Guy David, grocer, Sch. Front bel Spruce
Guy John, tavern, 23 S 7th
Guy Robert, manuf., Spruce n Sch Front
Guy Saml., car driver, rear 39 P road
Guyant John, waterman, 359 N Front
Guyant J. H., clerk, 10 Lybrand
Guyant Susan, 24 Duke
Guyent David, glass cutter, Queen ab Shackamaxon (K)
Guyer Benjamin, watchman, 29 Jones' al (C)
Guyer Godfrey H., carp., Carlton ab Sch 8th
Guyer Wm., grocer, R road and Sp Garden
Guyger George, tobacconist, Callowhill n Sch 5th
Guyger George W., hatter, 300 Vine
Guyger Mary, tobacconist, 8 N 13th
Guyint David, glass cutter, rear 16 Mulberry, h Queen n Crown (K)
Guyn Chas., cordw., Perry ab Franklin (K)
Guyn Daniel, chandler, 2d bel Wharton
Gwilliam John, bootmr., 14 Lebanon
Gwin Francis, lab., 5 Leiper
Gwin George, mer., 204 High
Gwin William, carter, 162 Christian.
Gwinn Ann, b. h., 37 Garden
Gwins Wm., tavern, 6 Little Pine
Gwynn Chas, weaver, Union bel West
Gwynn Robert, printer, Lister's pl
Gysi Theo., inst. mr., 262 N 3d, h rear 19 Lily al

———

Haag Daniel, tavern, 93 New Market
Haag Godfrey, bootmr., 25 Tammany
Haas Andrew F., chemist, 51 Duke
Haas Anna Maria, 361 N 3d
18

Haas Charles, painter, 13 Emlen's ct
Haas Chas. J., carp'r, 15 Emlen's ct.
Haas Edward, lab., Franklin ab Hanover (K)
Haas Ernest, chemist, 318 N 3d
Haas Frederick, Green ab 12th
Haas Fred'k, jr., grocer, 2d & Noble, h Greenwood pl
Haas George, tobacconist, 537 High
Haas George, 625 Coates
Haas Henry A., painter, Perry bel Phoenix (K)
HAAS & HOLLINGSWORTH, dry goods, 18 N 2nd
Haas Jacob, lab., Queen and Crown (K)
Haas Jacob S., victualler, 531 N 4th
Haas John, lab., 13th ab R Road
Haas John, cooper, 389 N 3rd.
Haas John, grocer, c 2d & Noble, h 361 N 3d
Haas John lab., Washington (W P)
Haas John K., painter, Parrish bel Broad
HAAS JOHN & CO., grocers, 2d & Noble
Haas Joseph, dry goods, 18 & h 278 N 2d
Haas Maria, b. h., 4 N 11th
Haas Michael, baker, Brown n 8th
Haas Michael B., framemr., rear 404 N 3d
Haas Nicholas, gunsmith, 152 Wood
Haas N., watchmr., rear 402 N 2d
Haas William, dry goods, 278 N 2nd, h 361 N 3d
Haasmiller Lorenty, hatter, 439 N 3d
Haber John, shoes, S E Noble & Franklin.
Habermehl Henry, case maker, 131 S 6th.
Haberstick Jacob J., suspender manf., 579 N 3d
Haberstick Rudolph, tobacconist, 407 N 2nd.
Habisreitinger J. G., brewer, 84 Apple
Hachrelin J. F., hatter, 113 Race
Hackenburg J. L., mer., 166 Sassafras
Hacker, Brother & Co., mers., 101 High
Hacker George W., China, 62 N 2d, h 133 N 10th
Hacker Henry M. mer. 101 High, h 8th bel Pine
Hacker Isaac, mer., 32 Chestnut, h 11th below Lombard
Hacker Isaac, jr., 11th bel Lombard
Hacker Isaiah, mer., 32 Chestnut, h 112 S 3rd
Hacker Jeremiah, merchant, 32 Chestnut, h 144 S 4th
Hacker Joseph, silverplater, 89 Mulberry
HACKER, LEA & CO., mers. 32 Chestnut
Hacker Rachel, tavern, Front and Pegg
Hacker William E., mer., 32 Chestnut, h S E 8th and Pine
HACKER WILLIAM P., china ware, 62 N 2d, h 57 O Y road
Hacker W. Alfred, mer., 101 High, h 8th bel Pine
Hackett Catharine, widow, 5 Jefferson row
Hackett H. Mrs. 2 Whitaker's ct
Hackett John, grain & feed, 124 Plum
Hackett John, lab., G T road and 6th (K)
Hackett Matthew, carter, Carpenter bel 9th.
Hackett Philip, coachman, 13 Paschal's al
Hackett Rich., teach., Dyott's ct & Franklin(K)
Hackett Robt. E., broker, 5 Jefferson row
Hackney & Burton, clothing, 119 S 2d
Hackney Joseph, tailor, 119 S 2d

Hackney John, store, 223 S 6th

Hadden John, lab., Sch 8th bel Vine

Hadder F., clerk, 42 Jacoby

Haddock Daniel, jr., mer. 10 S whfs, h 139 S 3rd

Haddock, Haseltine & Reed, shoes, bonnets and caps, 10 S wharves

Haddock Hazen, mer., 10 S whfs

Haddock James, stone cut., F road ab Franklin (K)

Haddock Jos., carp. weaver, Sycamore

Haddon James, clerk, 13th ab Coates

Hadfield John, presser, 152 Cedar

Hadnot Thos., confec., High bet Sch Front and Ashton

Hadry H. P., 11 Powell

Haedrich Henry, musician, 8 Randall's ct

Haeffer Andrew, tailor, 1 Moore's ct (S G)

Haffelfinger Martin, acct., 79 Franklin

Haffey Bernard, carp., Carpenter n 10th

Haffey Henry, clerk, 24 Wallace

Haffey Mary, 48 Washington av

Haffey Rosanna, b h, 44 Oak, (N L)

Hafner Martha, gentw., 97 Brown

Hafran Christian, weaver, Mariner

Hagaman Washington G., fur blower, Sterling al, h 62 Laurel.

Hagan Arthur, stonecutter, 259 S 6th

Hagan Barnard, shop, 225 G T road

Hagan Charles, bookseller, S E 6th and High, h 12 Quince

Hagan George, carp. 10th ab Walnut

Hagan Henry, cordw., 216 N 8th

Hagan John, lab., White's ct

Hagan Michael, lab., rear 296 S 7th

Hagan Michael, carter, Walnut W Sch 2d

Hagan Michael, shoemr. 112 Cherry

Hagan Patrick, bootmr., Logan's ct

Hagan Wm. paper stainer, 55 Perry

Hagany Joseph, 2 Myers' pl

Hagar P. F., stoves, 69 N 2d, h 36 Wood

Hager Daniel, cordwainer, 52 Oak, (N L)

Hagely Gottlieb, beer-house, 92 Green

Hager George, weaver, Carlton ab Sch 3d

Hager John, boots & shoes, 72 S 3d, h 29 Wallace

Hagerbricker G., 102 Spruce

Hagerdorn C. F., Bavarian Consul, 72 S, 5th

Hagert J. E., brushmaker, 8 N 3rd, h 350 Vine

Hagerty Bernard, morocco shaver, 11 William (F M)

Hagner & Co., dry goods, 314 High

Hagner Charles V., drug mill, Beaver ct., h Broad bel Chestnut

Hagner Jefferson, mer., 314 High

Hagner John F., mer., 314 High

Hagner Saml. A., saddler, 39 S 8th, h 356 E Cedar

Hagner Wm., Rutter's ct

Hague Andrew, bricklr. Hanover ab Bedford

Hague Christiana, Franklin and Elm (K)

Hague Henry, caulker, Hanover n Bedford.

Hague Henry, fisherman, Chandler's ct (K)

Hague Jacob, tavern, 22 Swanson.

Hague Jane, rear Pearl ab Sch 6th

Hague John, ship carp., Hanover ab Queen (K)

Hague Michael, blacksmith, Hanover bel Franklin (K)

Hague Thomas, astrologer, Francis & Powell (F V)

Hagy William, dry goods, 274 N 2d.

Hahn Adam, lab., 20 Rachel

Hahn Christian, baker, 148 N 5th.

Hahn G., M. D., 95 Noble st

Hahn Joseph F., baker, 165 Vine

Hahn Mary, 10th ab Buttonwood

Hahn Jacob, baker, 85 New

Hahn John, hotel, F road opp. West

Hahn John Henry, grocer, N W St John and George

Haig Jacob, St John bel Beaver (K)

Haig James, potter, Charlotte ab Poplar

Haig James & Thomas, fire brick manuf., 545 N 2d bel Beaver, (K)

Haig Robt. potter, R road ab 13th

Haig Thomas, potter, 456 N 4th

Haigh John, moroc. dres., Shackamaxon n Bedford (K)

Haight Cornelius, painter, 13th ab Locust, h Cedar ab 13th

Haight Mary, Winter ab Sch 3d

Hailer Geo., shoem., 1 Sailor's ct

Hailstock Charles S., barber, 16 S 5th, h rear 27 Bonsall

Haines Aaron N., mer. 59 N Water

Haines Abraham W. carp. 281 Coates

Haines Abraham, carpenter, 1 St James

Haines Abraham, mer., 367 High, h 194 N 12th

Haines Ann, Poplar bel 11th

Haines Aquila, carp. rear 448 N 3d, h Willow ab Broad

Haines Elton, bricklayer, Washington bel 11th
Haines Elwood, carp. George E Sch 5th
Haines Ephraim, mer., 6 Commerce, 170 N Front
Haines Franklin B., painter, George bel 3d (K)
Haines Fred. oyster house, N E 6th & Spruce
Haines Geo., cop. plate print. 141 New Market
Haines George, painter, Cedar n Sch 2d
Haines Girard, clerk
Haines G. W., cordw., 10 Jackson (N L)
Haines Henry, surveyor and convey., 10th and Thompson, h Girard av
Haines Henry, fisherman, Wood bel Duke (K)
Haines James, waterman, 4th ab George
Haines James, butcher, 4th and Marriott's la
Haines James B., painter, 23 Union (S)
Haines John, huckster, 5 Poplar
Haines John, shoemr., 63 Mead
Haines John, collector, 620 N 2d.
Haines John, saddler, William ab Otter (K)
Haines John jr., saddler, 2d bel Franklin (K)
Haines Joseph, saddler, Edward & William (K)
Haines Joseph B., keeper M. Prison, 386 S 5th
Haines Joseph C., cordw., Rex's ct
Haines Joshua, combmr., Apple bel Franklin
Haines Josiah, carp., 10th ab Coates.
Haines Lindley, mer. 13 S 2d, h 76 N 10th
Haines Mary, widow, Crown ab Queen (K)
Haines Mary, 2d bel Franklin (K)
Haines Mary, tailoress, 79 W Callowhill
Haines Matthias, lab. 6th bel G T road
Haines Michael, potter, Brown ab 13th
Haines Michael, carp. 8 Adams
Haines Mordecai W., brickl. Sch 8th ab Spruce
Haines Peter, fisherman, Wood ab Queen (K)
Haines Rachel, 35 Currant alley
Haines Reuben, carp., 9th bel Poplar
Haines Reuben W. moulder, Corn bel Wharton
Haines Samuel, hatter, 266 N 2d, h 398 N 3d
Haines Samuel, butcher, Perry ab Franklin (K)
Haines Samuel, whip-thong maker, Crown ab Queen (K)
Haines Thompson, tailor, George n Juniper
Haines William, carp., 531 Coates
Haines William S., M. D. 6th & Green
Hains Jacob, baker, 123 Filbert.
Hains Samuel, city surveyor, 9 S 5th, h 317 Mulberry
Haire Rebecca, shop, Queen ab Shackamaxon
Haith Anna M., Brown bel 13th
Haldeman Elizabeth, Duke ab Vienna (K)
Haldeman Michael, wheelwr't, Ash bel Duke (K)
Haldorn Thos. butcher, 9th bel Carpenter
Haldt Lewis, grocer, Shackamaxon and Franklin (K)
Hale Charles W., waterman, 46 Penn
Hale Almy S., 21 S Sch 7th
Hale Isaac, bootmr., 278 E Cedar
Hale Jacob, butcher, Carpenter ab 9th
Hale James, mer. 2 Ranstead pl
Hale Joseph, lab., Alden ab Poplar
Hale Ruth, 36 Coates' al
Hale Thos., paper hanger, 15 Jacoby
Hale Thomas S., acct., 133 Buttonwood

Hale William, tailor, 378 High, h 5 Castle.
Hale Wm., shop, 21 Little Pine
Hales Wm., bricklay'r. Front ab Reed.
Haley Edward, boxmaker, 106 Cherry
Haley John, weaver, G T road ab 4th .
Haley John, dealer, 87 Shippen
Haley John, moroc. dress. 6 Franklin (K)
Haley Jos. plasterer, 10 S Broad
Halfman Ethelbert, tailor, 7th and High, h 4 Magnolia
Halfman Gerhard, coal dealer, rear 48 Brown
Halfman G., spade & shovelmr., Willow, bel 3d. h Olive ab 10th
Halfman Herbert, gent. 68 Gaskill
Halfman Wm., blacksmith, 12 Farmer
Halfman Wm., cordw., R road ab Vine, h 329 Vine
Halfpenny Catharine, 4 Marion.
Halfpenny John, machinist, Cadwalader above Franklin
Hall Albert H., porter, 1 Cresson's al
Hall Alexander, mariner, 31 Beck (S)
Hall Alexander W., mer. 104 N 3d, h 82 Tammany
Hall Alice, washer, 71 George.
Hall Augustus, stonecutter, 9th & Coates
Hall, Boardman & Co., britannia ware, 104 N 3d
Hall, Brothers, dry goods, 26 Chestnut
Hall Catharine, Franklin bel Palmer (K)
Hall Catharine, gentw. Broad bel Pine
Hall Charles, 7 Garden
Hall Charles, porter, Paschall al
Hall Charles, mer., 23 Church alley, h 4 Dugan row
Hall Charles, livery stable, George ab Sch 6th
Hall Charles B. mer. 34 Church al, h 81 Marshall
Hall Christiana, 318 S Front
Hall Clement, currier, 38 Lombard
Hall Cornelius, chairmr., 94 N 13th
Hall Daniel, waiter, 10 Acorn al
Hall Daniel A., carp., Charles & Noble, h 117 Buttonwood
Hall David, lab. 251 S 7th
Hall David, lab., rear 527 N 2d (K)
Hall Ebenezer, waiter, Gulielma
Hall Edward A., M. D., 119 S 8th
Hall Edwin, mer. 7 S 2d
Hall Elizabeth, gentw., 236 S Front
Hall Ellen F., dressmr., 118 S 10th
Hall Emmor, cordw., Carlton ab 12th
Hall Enos, lab., Barley
Hall E. C., ornamental painter, 218 Noble
Hall Francis, carp. Swede's ct
Hall Fredk. book binder, 82 N 6th
Hall F. D. mer., 101 N 3d, h Division ab 11th
Hall F. T. waiter, 2 Pearl
Hall Geo., tobacconist & variety store, 23 N 9th
Hall Geo., blacksm., Shackamaxon bel Franklin
Hall Geo., barb., 19 Carpenter, h 2 Bulkley (C)
Hall Geo. T. cordw., 10th ab Parrish
Hall Harrison, surveyor & publisher, 22½ Walnut, h 6 Sansom
Hall Henrietta, washer, 6th ab Poplar
Hall Henry M., machinist, Brandywine ab 13th.
Hall Isaac, wood eng., 31 Paschall's al

Hall Isaac & Son, dry goods, 357 High
Hall James, printer, Carpenter bel 5th
Hall James, furniture, 250 Sassafras
Hall James, weaver, 13th bel Cedar
Hall James, baker, 5 Poplar
Hall James E. tavern, 101 Swanson
Hall Jane, shop, Pearl ab 13th
HALL JOHN, tavern, 42 N 2d
Hall John B., cordw., 297 Callowhill
Hall John G., architect, 51 N 6th
Hall Joseph, 42 N 2d
Hall Joseph, basketmr., 11th bel Callowhill
Hall Joseph, salesman, Callowhill n Sch Front
Hall Joseph A., carp., Mechanic ab George
Hall Joseph S., 199 Walnut
Hall Jos. W., dealer, G T road ab Phoenix (K)
Hall Margaret, 85 Locust
Hall Martha, Pearl ab Sch 6th
Hall Mary Ann, 119 S 8th
Hall Mary Ann, shop, Madison & Sheaff's al
Hall Morris, coachman, 129 Cherry
Hall Nathan, shoes, 238 S 2d
Hall N. H., mer., 40 N 2nd, h 233 Marshall
Hall N. P. Mrs., mer., 53 N 2d, h 285 Sassafras
Hall Oscar D., saddler, 25 S 4th, h 52 Duke
Hall Patrick, engineer, Otter bel G T road (K)
Hall Peleg, dry goods, 3 S 2nd, h 236 S Front
Hall Robert A., oyster house, N W 5th and Spruce
Hall Samuel, carp., Vienna bel Franklin (K)
Hall Sarah, Pearl bel 13th
Hall Sarah, Wharton ab Front
Hall Susan, wid. of Lewis, Beach ab Marlboro'
Hall Thos., 186 N 13th
Hall Thomas, machinist, rear 493 N 3d
Hall Thos., cordw., Ann n Sch 4th (F V)
Hall Thomas, weaver, Rose n Shippen la
Hall Washington, lace goods, 40 N 2nd
Hall Wilfred, agt. Phila. Bible Soc. 144 Chestnut, h 3 Sch Rittenhouse
Hall Wm., blacksm., 118 Duke
Hall Wm., carp., Brown bel Vienna (K)
Hall William, captain, 27 Queen
Hall Wm., waiter, 48 Quince
Hall Wm. O., collector, Poplar bel Broad
Hall Wm. R., dentist, Noble bel 8th
Hall W. & Co. lace goods, 40 N 2d
Halliday Abigail, gentw., 69 Pine
Halliday Elias, trunkmr., 17 Lagrange pl
Halliday E. C., dry goods, 65 N 2d
Halliday Samuel L., saddler, 26 High
Halliday Wm. J., grocer, S W 2d and Mulberry
Halliwell Edw. T. machinist, Barker n Sch 6th
Halliwell Sarah A., milliner, High ab Sch 4th
Hallman Anthony, mariner, rear 135 Christian
Hallman Jacob, b h, 165 Race
Hallman Mary, 227 S Front
Hallman Wm., painter, Coates bel 10th
Halloway John S., clerk East. Penitentiary, h Sch. 2d ab Vine

Hallowell Caleb W., mer., 143 High, h 125 N 9th
Hallowell Charles, mer., 173 High
Hallowell D. Albert, mer., 143 High, h 240 N 11th
Hallowell Ed. Dr. Broad & S Penn sq
Hallowell Eli, coachmr., R road n Willow.
Hallowell Elizabeth, 197 N 3d
Hallowell Hannah, 499 N 4th
Hallowell Hiram L., tailor, 11 Coates
Hallowell Jesse, bricklayer, Oliver's pl
Hallowell Joel, carp., Kessler's ct
Hallowell John, brickmr., 170 Coates.
Hallowell Jonah, leather, 227 N 2nd.
Hallowell Joseph T., Logan n Green
Hallowell Joshua L. mer., 143 High, h 13 Montgomery sq
Hallowell Morris L. & Co. silk and fancy goods, 143 High
Hallowell M. L., mer. 143 High, h 240 N 6th
Hallowell Rifford R., builder, 10 Pleasant
HALLOWELL & SELLERS, trimmings, 143 High
Hallowell Thomas, currier, rear 9 Rose al
Hallowell Wm. S., merchant, 168 N 2nd, h 305 N 6th
Hallowell W. S. & Co., hardware, 168 N 2nd.
Hally Peter, dry goods, 524 N 2d.
Halpin John, lab., 4 Harmony ct
Halpin William, tinsmith, Phoenix below G T road (K)
Halsall James J., 142 Catharine
Halsey James, trimmings, 23 S 4th, h 366 E Cedar
Halsted Geo. W., coal mer., 69 S 6th
Halsted John, 28 N 9th
Halt Richard, 13 Morgan's ct
Halton Sarah, Catharine ab 8th
HALY WM. W., atty. and coun., 72 S 6th
Halzel Mary Ann, milliner, 159 Green
Halzel Philip, chairmaker, 515 N Front
Halzell John, shoe dealer, 100 Elizabeth
Halzell Samuel, 253 N Front
Ham Jos., dentist, Swede's ct
Hama Godfrey, grocer, c St. John and Green
Hama James D., grocer, St. John and Green
Hambaker Christopher, tailor, 27 Mayland
Hambly John, millwright, 4 Fetter's la
Hambly William, millwright, 13 Wiley's ct
Hambright Wm. A., 280 Callowhill
Hamel Jacob, porter, G T road ab Franklin (K)
Hamel J. C., 83 Garden
Hamelin Joseph P. clerk, 161 Catharine
Hamell Hugh, bookseller, 3½ S 10th, h 4 Filber avenue
Hamell Mary, milliner, 56 Chester
Hamer Eli, tailor, 38 N 6th
Hamer Jacob jr. tailor, 65 Zane
Hamer Jacob & Son, tailors, 38 N 6th.
Hamer Thomas, weaver, 9th n Christian

Hamill James, carp., Hope ab Master (K)
Hamill James, farrier, 194 S 4th
Hamill Patrick, weaver, Middleton's ct
Hamilton Alex., broker, 246 S Front
Hamilton And., weaver, Front ab Phœnix, (K)
Hamilton Andw., 220 N 4th
Hamilton Arthur, cordw., St. John bel George (K)
Hamilton A. Boyd, publisher, 72 Dock
Hamilton Chas., turner, 441 Lombard
Hamilton David, cordwainer, N W Cedar and Penn
Hamilton Elijah, cordw., Willow bel Garden
Hamilton Eliza, Lisle bel Shippen
Hamilton Elizabeth, 56 Mulberry
Hamilton & Forney, pubs. Pennsylvanian, 72 Dock
Hamilton Francis J., printer, 30 Rittenhouse
Hamilton Geo., janitor, Franklin Institute, Parrish ab 7th
Hamilton George, teller K. Bank, h Marlboro' ab Queen.
Hamilton George, M. D., Sch 7th and Summer
Hamilton George, grocer, S E 12th & Coates.
Hamilton Geo., seaman, 327 S 10th
Hamilton Geo., printer, Gorrell's ct
Hamilton Hanse, drayman, 419 S 4th
Hamilton Jacob C., hatter, 255 N 2d
Hamilton James, landscape painter, S E 9th and Walnut, h 336 S 4th
Hamilton James, morocco dress., Hancock bel Phœnix (K)
Hamilton James, shop, 499 Vine
Hamilton James, lab., 7 St Joseph's av
Hamilton James, lab., Perry ab Phœnix (K)
Hamilton James, lab., Shippen la bel Shippen
Hamilton Jas., shoemr., Lewis ab Sch 6th
Hamilton Jas., carman, 28 Charlotte
Hamilton Jas., drover, 519 Callowhill
Hamilton Jas., lab., Pollock's av
Hamilton Jane, 102 George
Hamilton John, 7 Quigg's ct
Hamilton John, stove finisher, West and Union (K)
Hamilton John, jr., atty. and coun., 12 George
Hamilton John, sailmr., rear 463 N 4th
Hamilton John, dry goods, 249 S 2d
Hamilton John, lab., Crabb ab Plum
Hamilton John M., acct., S. School Union, h 169 Catharine
Hamilton Joseph, drayman, 421 S 4th
Hamilton Joseph, carpet weaver, Otter bel G T road
Hamilton J. B. W., builder, 4 Crockett's ct., h 12 Swanwick
Hamilton Lydia, rear Mulberry bet Sch 7th & 8th
Hamilton Margaret, 10th bel Wallace
Hamilton Mary, gentw., 316 Chestnut.
Hamilton Mary Ann, shop, 8 Assembly buildings
Hamilton Mary & R., trim'gs, R road & Melon
Hamilton Morris, att'y., Beach ab Maiden (K)
Hamilton Owen, Bedford bel 8th
Hamilton Philip, cooper, 4 Smith's pl
Hamilton Robt., weaver, Philip ab Jefferson(K)

Hamilton Robert, bootmr., N E 8th & Mulberry, h Park n Locust (W P)
Hamilton Robert S., Secretary Col. Ins. Co., h 102 George ab 12th
Hamilton R. J., clerk, 593 N Front (K)
Hamilton Samuel, cordw., rear 200 Christian
Hamilton Samuel, carriage trimmer, Juniper bel Walnut
Hamilton Samuel G., gas pipe welder, Franklin ab 4th
Hamilton Sarah, 153 S 11th
Hamilton Sarah, tailoress, Elk st
Hamilton Sarah, tailoress, 33 Apple
Hamilton Stephen, cordw., 11 Parker
Hamilton William, actuary Franklin Institute, h 169 Catharine
Hamilton William, chandler, 4 Plum.
Hamilton Wm., bootmr., N E 8th & Mulberry, h 34 Garden
Hamilton Wm., distiller, Pearl ab Nixon
Hamilton Wm., carver, 22 Magnolia
Hamilton Wm. H., boiler mr., F road opp West
Hamilton William H., dry goods, 20 S 2d.
Hamilton William T., clerk, Sch 6th below Chestnut.
Hamlin Margaret, sempstress, rear 103 Dillwyn
Hamlin Richard, lab., Shippen ab 7th
Hamlin William E., mer., 58 Chestnut, h 70 Walnut
Hamlin Wm. K., mer., 110 N 3rd, h 10 Dillwyn
Hamm Daniel, vict., Apple ab George
Hamm Hoffman, 55 Spruce
Hamm James A., combmr., 272 S 5th
Hamm John P., rear Wood ab Broad
Hamm P. E., asst. city treas., c 5th & Chestnut, h 50 Clinton
Hamm Wm. A., ropemr., G T road bel 7th
Hamm Wm. P., agent, 11 Perry
Hamman John, mer., 96½ High, h Buttonwood ab 9th.
Hamman, Snyder & Co., dry goods, 96½ High
Hammar Catharine Mrs., 37 Dock
Hammar Charles, tinsmith, 37 Dock
Hammar Barb. Ann, 99 G T road (K)
Hammar Joseph, grocer, 152 S 6th
Hammar Maria, rear G T road above Phœnix
Hammar Wm. combmr., James' ct (K)
Hammar Wm., tailor, 100 S Front
Hammar Wm., cigar mak., 511 N 3d
Hammell Francis J., shoes, 200 High, h Lawrence (C) ab 12th
Hammell H. M., bootmr., 4th ab Shippen
Hammell John, engineer, Wood ab Sch 2d
Hammell Mary Ann, shoebr., Brown bel 7th
Hammer Charles, combmr., Davis' ct
Hammer Deborah, 5 Rachell's row.
Hammer Gotlieb, baker, Christian and 8th
Hammer Issacher, confect., 241 N 2d
Hammersley George, mer., 85 S Front.
Hammersley George, turner, Logan's ct (K)
Hammett Elizabeth, b. h., rear 254 S 2d
HAMMETT & HILES, coppersmiths, 128 Vine
Hammett John K., shipwright, Maiden st whf., h Penn ab Maiden (K)
Hammett Thomas, coppersmith, 296 Coates

Hammill Barnard, 166 Queen
Hammill Chas., carman, Brown bel Vienna (K)
Hammill Thos., drayman, Marlboro' ab Franklin (K)
Hammitt John, lab., Wood ab Queen (K)
Hammitt Thos., ship carp., Marlboro' ab Bedford (K)
Hammon Barbary, washer, 13 Lybrand
Hammond Christ., lab., Murray n Sch 3d
Hammond E. Mrs., 31 Logan
Hammond John, lab., Hancock ab Phoenix (K)
Hammond John, lab., Fitler n Harrison (K)
Hammond John, tailor, 3 Parker st
Hammond Moses W., Buttonwood ab 10th
Hammond Richard, tavern, High ab Sch. 5th
HAMMOND SAMUEL, refectory, 210 High & 1 Decatur
Hammond Vincent P., Pine Ward Hotel, 138 S 4th
Hammond Wm., b. h., 80 Swanson
Hampsay Francis, hatter, Spruce n Sch 5th
Hampton Benjamin, tobacconist, 11 N 10th
Hampton David, tailor, 372 N 2d
Hampton Elizabeth, gentw., 3 Kelly's ct
Hampton Jacob, carter, 72 Christian
Hampton John J. coach and wheelwright, Callowhill n Sch, h Wood bel Nixon
Hampton Rudolph, paper hanger, 6 Scott's ct
Hampton Thomas S., lampmr., 9 Prospect al
Hampton T. Eber, cooper, Olive bel Broad
Hamrick Adam D., carp., 72 F road
Hamrick John, painter, Elm bel Franklin (K)
Hamrick John A., painter, 72 F road (K)
Hamrick Paul, packer, Duke ab Hanover (K)
Hamrickhouse John, lab., Palmer n Duke (K)
Hamshire Adam, pumpmr. G T road ab 5th
Hamshire Antrim, cigar mr., G T road ab 6th (K)
Hamshire Isaac, turner, rear Marshall ab Brown
Hamson Joseph, artisan, Reefe ab Front
Hanan Dennis, lab., Seller's ct
Hanberg John, lab., Jefferson ab 5th (K)
Hanbest T. Passmore, att'y., 28 Spruce
Hanbest Wm., dealer, Shippen bel 4th
HANCE DAVID E., coal mer., High Bridge, h 450 N 4th
Hance Jeremiah, grocer, 90 New Market, h N W 7th and Poplar
Hance John, teacher, 96 Union
Hance John, clerk, 6th bel Christian
Hance Joseph S., lime, Rachel and Poplar
Hance Samuel, weaver, Mulberry n Sch 3d
Hance T. H., clerk, Duke & Vienna (K)
Hancock Biddle, bricklayer, 11th bel S Garden
Hancock Hewbitt, tobacconist, Nectarine n 10th
Hancock James B. clerk, 144 Catharine
Hancock John, att'y and coun. 46½ Walnut
Hancock John, lab., 31 Cresson's al
Hancock Joseph, brass founder, 46 Bread
Hancock Joseph M., carp., Cherry n Sch 8th, h 6 Jacoby
Hancock Samuel P., corder, High st wharf Sch, h N W Sch 7th & Mulberry
Hancock Wm., silk dyer, 93 Vine
Hancock Wm. C., carpr., 444 Callowhill

Hancock Wm. C., bricklayer, Washington ab 12th
Hand Caleb, gent., 7th bel Poplar
Hand & Eagle, mers., 161 High
Hand Harvey, collector, 15 York ct.
Hand Jacob F., clerk, 3d ab Washington
Hand Jas. C. mer. 41 Commerce, h 237 Vine
Hand Jeremiah, gent., 32 Almond
Hand John K., clerk, Com. Bank, Hanover ab West (K)
Hand Jonathan, fisherman, Franklin ab Wood (K)
Hand Joseph, goldbeater, 21 M road
Hand Joseph S. K., jeweller, 10 Minor, h 263 N 7th
Hand Jotham, cordw., Harvey's ct (K)
Hand Smith, cordw. Elizabeth ab Parrish
Hand Thomas, sea capt., 26 Union (S)
Hand Thomas, grocer, Washington (W P)
Hand Thomas, waterman, Penn bel Maiden (K)
Hand Thos., waterman, 13 Poplar
Hand Thomas C., mer., 161 High, h 88 Marshall
Hand Wm., cordwainer, Prime bel 2d
Handlan John, cutler, Plum bel 4th, h 268 S 4th
Handy Edward S., mer., 98 High
Handy Edward S., & Co., hardware, 98 High
Handy George, mer., 17 N whfs
Handy Isaac S., mer. 98 High
Handy James, waiter, Prosperous al
Handy John, shoemr., Grover
Handy John H., M. D., 488 N 5th ab Poplar
Handy Somersett, porter, rear Milton bel 11th
Handy Susan E. milliner, 131 S 8th
Haney Alex., baker, 11th & Milton
Haney Elizabeth, Meredith's ct
Haney Elizabeth A., milliner, 152½ S 2d
Haney James, lab., Clay bel Beach
Haney John, lab., N Sch Front
Haney John, baker, 40 George (S)
Haney John, dealer, 11 Franklin place.
Haney Thomas, turner, 152 S 2d
Haney Thomas, blacksm., 666 N 2d (K)
Haney Wm., clerk, Washington ab 10th (S G)
Haney Wm., turner, 81 German
Hanford Peter, tailor, Evans
HANFORD W. S., com. mer., 38 Chestnut, h 118 S 4th
Hangary Gabriel, cordw., Crown bel Franklin (K)
Hangary Susan, Marlboro' bel Franklin
Hanhauser Anthony, cork maker, 95 S 5th.
Hanhauser John, shop, 142 F road.
Hank Lewis, stone cutter, 12th & Cherry
Hanker Abraham, dry goods, 100 W High
Hankins Charles, 496 Callowhill
Hankins William, carp., Wallace bel 9th
Hankins Wm. H., coal mer., Broad bel Vine h 522 Vine
Hankinson Isaiah, waiter, 11 Little Oak
Hankinson Thomas A., grocer, 3d & Beaver
Hankinson Thomas, bricklayer, 5th ab Poplar
Hankinson Wm. W., hatter, 4 Townsend av
HANLEY DAVID, clerk O. C., 3 S House, h 22 Laurel (N L)

Hanley George, hatter, 6 Butler's av
Hanley Jeremiah, blacksm., 11 Jones' al., h Gray's al
Hanley John, waterman, 15 Poplar
Hanley John, lab., Milton ab 11th
Hanley Margaret, 3 Pratt's ct
Hanley Sarah, dressmr., 100 S 5th
Hanlin Thomas, carter, Lombard n Sch Bank st
Hanline Alfred, mer., 3 Bank, h 469 N Front
Hanline & Ostheimer, importers, 3 Bank
Hanlon Patrick, lab., Franklin bel Cherry (K)
Hanly James, lab., 3 Leiper
Hanly John, dry goods, S W P road & Wall.
Hanly Wm., drug store, S E 7th and Lombard, h 39 Lombard
Hanna Andrew, lab., 4th bel Wharton
Hanna Elizabeth, Bedford bel Broad
Hanna George, carp. 12th ab Parrish
HANNA JAMES, atty. & coun., 11 Prune
Hanna James, blacksmith, St Mary
Hanna James, lab. Sch 4th & Lombard
Hanna John, lab., Wood bel Franklin (K)
Hanna John, lab. Sch 3d n Pine
HANNA JOHN, atty. and coun., S E 6th & Walnut, h N W 11th and Green
Hanna Joseph, lab., Rye ab Reed
Hanna Mary, 114 Catharine
Hanna Richard, weaver, Hanover bel Duke (K)
Hanna Robert, weaver, 3 Fairmount av
Hanna Samuel, carpet weaver, Sch 6th & Jones
Hanna Samuel, weaver, Perry ab Franklin (K)
Hanna Sarah, washer, rear 178 Coates
Hanna Thomas, grocer, 2d ab Montgomery (K)
Hannabery George P. hair dresser, 6th bel G T road (K)
Hannan Mary, washer, 7 Hampton
Hannan Thomas, Carpenter ab 12th
Hannay A. grocer, N W 4th & Wharton
Hannigan Hugh, Shippen ab 12th
Hannings Henry, combmr., 9 Torr's al
Hannings William, clerk, 380 Coates
Hannis Andrew, grocer, 139 M road
Hannis Wm., oak cooper, 120 St. John
Hannold George Sen. tailor, 23 Coates' al
Hannold George Jun. tailor, 23 Coates' al
Hannold John S. blacksmith, Lemon ab 10th
Hannold Mrs. M. C., 559 S Front
Hannum Wm., engineer, Coates n Fairmount
Hannum Wm. E., East. Penit., h Ann ab Powell
Hansberry Jane, 87 Locust
Hansberry Josiah, carter, George bel 4th
Hansberry Margaret, shop, 147 Buttonwood
Hansberry Samuel, lab. Franklin bel Crown (K)
Hansberry Wm., paper hanger, 10th & Lemon
Hansbury John, shingle shaver, 2 Gebhard
Hanse Reuben, 32 St John
Hansell Ann, Dorothy n Sch 4th
Hansell, Charles G., Sch 7th ab Parrish
Hansell Edmund M., 191 High, h Sch 8th n Mulberry
Hansell Geo. W., grocer, Washington. (W P)
Hansell H. H. & Brother, saddlers and saddlery hardware, 28 High
Hansell H. H. mer., 28 High

Hansell Issachar, 100 S 12th
Hansell Jacob, coach smith, Broad ab Vine, h Carlton ab Sch 8th
Hansell James, watch maker, 236 High, h 76 N 11th.
Hansell James S., turner, Barley ab 10th, h Pine ab 10th
Hansell Jesse, coachsm., Callowhill ab Sch 8th
Hansell John R. marketman, Ogden ab Sch 7th
Hansell Mary H., dry goods, 8 N 9th
Hansell Standish F. mer., 28 High, h 164 N Front
Hansell Thos., turner, N W 13th & Budden's al.
Hansell Wm., shop, Lombard ab Sch 3d
Hansell Wm., U. S. Mint, h 34 N 8th
Hansell Wm. F., silk dyer, 24 Merchant
Hansell Wm. S., mer., 28 High, h 109 S 3d.
Hansell W. A. & G. dry goods, 34 N 8th
Hanson Albert F. mer., 23 Chestnut
Hanson & Elliott, tobacco com. mers. 58 S. Front
Hanson Jacob, blacksm., Carleton bel Sch 7th
Hanson James C. b h, 77 S Water
Hanson Johanna, 12 Poplar
Hanson J. B., mer., 58 S Front, h 153 N 9th
Hanson William, baker, Simmon's ct
Hanson Wm. R. mer., 23 Chestnut, h S E 12th and George
HANSON WM. R. & Brother, com. dry goods, 23 Chestnut
Hanthorne Rachel, shop, Shippen la
Hapolsheimer John, shop, Rose bel G T R (K)
Harbach Eliza, confectioner, 48 N 8th
Harback A. J., clerk, 9 Gebhard
Harber Wm., lab., Brooks' ct
Harberger Henry, machinist, 16 Howard
Harberger Henry, tin sm., Sch 6th W of High
Harbert Charles, lumber mer., 10th & Callowhill, h 177 N 11th.
Harbert & Davis, lumber mers., c 10th and Callowhill,
Harbert Elizabeth, cupper, 177 S 11th
Harbert Isaac, gent., 146 N 10th.
Harbert Isaac, 28 Madison
Harbert Isaac J., clerk, 13th & Coates
Harbert Jacob, tailor, Sch 8th ab Sassafras
Harbert John B., bricklayer, 15 Short ct
Harbert Wm., bricklayer, Sch 8th n Vine.
Harbeson Jane, Perry bel Master (K)
Harbeson John, weaver, Cadwalader ab Master
Harbeson John, weaver, Hancock bel Master
Harbeson Wm., grocer, Jefferson row
HARBORD RICHARD, refectory, S E 8th and Walnut, h 20 Sansom
Hardcastle Henry, blacksm., 2 Moffitt's ct
Harden Wm. whitesmith, G T road bet 6th & 7th
HARDER HENRY A. druggist, 4th & Carpenter
Harder J. L., druggist, N. W. 4th & Queen
Hardicker Elizabeth, 6 Juniper la
Hardie James G., clerk, 166 Spruce
Hardin John, oak cooper, Palmer bel West (K)
Hardin Wm., tobacconist, 21 Chester

Harding Alex., weaver, rear Benton n William (K)
Harding Eli, chemist, 30 Charlotte
Harding H., ship master, 85 Pine.
Harding Isaac, trimmings, 13th bel Callowhill
Harding Isaac, ladies shoemr., S W 12th & Locust
Harding James, undertaker, 184 S 6th.
Harding Jesper, prop. Penn. Inquirer, office 57 S 3rd, h Pine ab 9th
Harding John, jr., mer., 28 & 30 S Water, & 29 & 31 S Front, h 98 S Front
Harding Joseph, carter, 110 Apple
Harding Wm., porter, 56 Currant al
Hardman Jas. H., brass manuf., 139 N Juniper
Hardrich Anthony, glass blower, Orchard
Hardt Henry, cordw. Phœnix bel G T road (K)
Hardwick Daniel, M D., 17 Mulberry
Hardwick Wm., acct., 33 Powell
Hardy Charles, hatter, Marriott ab N road
Hardy Craford, porter, 42 Bread
Hardy Ellis, teacher, Beach ab Palmer (K)
Hardy Francis A., grocer, 27 N road.
Hardy Hugh, teacher, 14 Plum
Hardy Jacob, waiter, 2 Burd's ct
Hardy John, hatter, Catharine bel 5th
Hardy John D., druggist, N W 4th and Plum.
Hardy Mary, gentw., 1 Relief
Hardy Mary, b. h., Front ab Reed
Hardy Thomas, clerk, 297 Plum st
Hardy Wm., engineer, Union ab West (K)
Hardy Wm., saddler, Harmony st
Hare Charles B., U. S. mint, h 34 Perry.
Hare Charles W., Mrs., gentw., Clinton ab 10th
Hare Elizabeth, Lindall & Dean
Hare George E. Rev., Girard av
Hare Jacob, piano mr., Haines ab 6th
Hare Jane, 34 Chester.
Hare John, weaver, Brinton ab 12th
Hare John, sawyer, rear 75 German
Hare John, laborer, Sch 5th ab Spruce
Hare John, stone cutter, N E Broad & Locust
Hare John J. tobacconist, 76 New
HARE J. I. CLARKE, atty & coun., 133 S 6th
Hare Martha, S. W. 9th & George
Hare Nicholas, carp. manuf. G T road bel Phoenix (K)
Hare Robert, M. D., 291 Chestnut.
Hare Robert H., att'y & coun., 133 S 6th
Hare Thomas, tobacconist, 260 Coates
Hargadon Timothy, baker, S E 5th & Gaskill.
Hargan Corn., lab., Murray n Sch 3d
Hargan Jane, 17 Duke
Hargesheimer Wm., cabinetmr., Carpenter's al
Hargis Benjamin, lab. 137 S 11th
Hargis Hester, tailoress, Conkle's ct
Hargrave Thomas, stone cutter, R road & 13th, & 43 Dock, h Washington ab 13th

Harker Samuel, plasterer, Vienna ab Franklin
Harker Wm., lab., Mechanic ab Poplar
Harkins Ambrose, printer, 34 S 4th
Harkins Daniel, cabman, Deal's av
Harkins Edward, grocer, S W 11th & Milton
Harkins George, carp., Clark ab 3d
Harkins Hugh, stovemr., Shippen bel P road
Harkins James, lab. Sch 4th and Barker
Harkins Jas., jeweller, 208 Queen
Harkins John, lab., rear High n Sch 2d
Harkins Neal, 4th ab Shippen
Harkins Thos., shoemr., 10 Branner's al
Harkness Chas., wholesale clothing store, S. E. 4th & High, h 1 Quarry
Harkness Daniel, manuf., 6th ab Master, h Elizabeth bel Franklin
Harkness John, lab. Master and Hancock (K)
Harkness Wm., carp., Carpenter bel 8th
Harlan Chas., conveyancer, 107 S 6th, h 380 Walnut
Harlan Ellis, matron, widow & single womens' asylum
Harlan Hannah, gentw., Filbert E Sch 7th
Harlan Michael, tailor, rear Carpenter ab 4th
Harland John, gent., 140 Mulberry.
Harley Connell, lab., Sch Water n Cedar
Harley Fena, weaver, Jackson bel Palmer (K)
Harley George, coppersmith, 95 S Front; h 169 S 3d
Harley Isaac, cordw., rear 180 Poplar
Harley James, shoemr., Sch 7th n Lombard
Harley Jas., lab., Jones n Sch 4th
Harley Jessie, grocer, N W Marshall & Wood
Harley John, skin dresser, 25 St John
Harley John, clerk, N W Marshall & Wood
Harley John J., skin dr., McAvoy's ct
Harley Mary Ann, shop, 132 Brown (N L)
Harley Mrs. Francis, 112 S Front
Harley Walter, coppersmith, Littleboy's ct
Harman Christian, glassbl., 18 Dyott's ct (K)
Harman Issachar, lab., rear Penn ab Poplar (K)
Harman Jacob, varnisher, Brunner's ct (K)
Harman Jacob, shop, Coates' & Sch 5th
Harman John, lab., Duke ab Cherry (K)
Harman John, blacksmith, rear 20 P road
Harman John M., collector, 523 Coates
Harman Painter, lab., Marriott ab 6th
Harman Sarah, market, Gray's ct (N L)
Harman Sarah, dressmaker, 220 Cherry.
Harman Wm., preacher, Baker ab 7th
Harmen Jas., cordw., rear 180 Poplar
Harmer Chas., tailor, Washington & Brown
Harmer Charles P., lab., rear 28 Duke
Harmer David, ship carp. Franklin ab Union (K)
Harmer Gideon D., shoemr., G T road ab 6th
Harmer James, jr., collector and house agent, 199 Spruce
Harmer Jesse, ship carpenter, Union ab Frank-

armon Timothy, porter, 7 Poplar ct
armoning Henry, baker, Carpenter ab 5th
arnsden Wm., carter, Sch 5th bel High
armstad Edwin, bricklr., Sch 7th bel Walnut
armstad George R., carp., 13th n Lombard
armstead Charles, carp., 54 Perry
armstead Charles, carp , Chancellor bel 6th
armstead Harvey, bricklr., 148 S 13th
armstead Henry, stone cutter, 148 S 13th
armstead James, bookseller, 40 N 4th, h 151 N 10th
armstead Joseph, carp., 148 S 13th
armstead Lawrence, carp., 148 S 13th
armstead Martin, gent , 21 Wood.
Lrmstead, Oliver P., bricklr., 148 S 13th
armstead Samuel, carp., S Juniper bel Spruce
armstead Susan, rear 87 N Juniper
arned Henry, carver, 4 Hudson's al
arned John, tin smith, 390 High, h Wood ab 10th.
arned J. E., M. D., 13th bel Citron
arned Lewis M., blind mr., 386 N 2d, h 7th ab Poplar
arner John, tailor, rear 468 N 3d
arnett Wm., shoemr., Cherry n Juniper
arney Nathaniel, carpenter, Hutchinson ab Poplar
arnicsh Julius, cabinetmr., S 8th ab Christian
arpel David, tailor, 300 Sassafras.
arpel Jacob, tailor, 300 Sassafras
arpel John, sexton, Sterling ab School-house
arpel Jonah, cordw., 265 Coates.
arper Alex., druggist, 451 High.
arper Ann D., 29 S 13th.
arper A. J., mer., 13 S Front
arper Catharine, N E Sch 7th and Cherry
arper Charles, carter, 23 Washington av
ARPER CHRISTOPHER, tavern, 28 Carter's al.
ARPER CLAUDIUS, Sec. & Treas. Sch. Nav. Co., 8 S 7th, h Sch 6th bel Locust
arper George, lab., 340 Sassafras
arper James, hatter, 5 Shaffer's ct
arper Hannah, Cedar bel Shippen la
arper Henry, sailor, Almira pl
arper James, brickmaker, Lombard bel Broad
arper James, gent., Walnut n Seh 5th
arper John, brushmr. Cedar ab 11th
arper John M., importer of watches, 3 Bank al, h 43 Union
arper Joseph L., auditor P. O., 422 Poplar
arper Lucien, cordw., Hazel bel 12th
arper Nathan, com. mer., 6½ N whfs, h 28 Buttonwood
ARPER ROBERT, tavern, 434 High
arper Robt., drayman, S E 13th & Sassafras
arper Samuel, gilder, 160 Lombard
arper Sarah, gentw., 7th ab Brown

Harpur John, clerk, 179 Catharine
Harpur Wm. E., chronometer & watchmaker, 136 Chestnut, h 172 Christian
Harraden J., for. & com. mer., Vine st whf, Sch., h Vine ab Sch. 2nd.
Harrar Benjamin T., stone mason, Poplar bel 7th
Harrar David, wheelwright, Walters' ct
Harrar Edmund, rulemr , R road ab Broad
Harrar George, rulemr., Apple ab Brown
Harrar John, provisions, Dean and Locust
Harrar John, carpenter, China ab Front.
Harred Clement, carter, Marriott ab 5th
Harrer John, cordw., Roney ct (K)
Harres Gebhard, cabinetmr., 3d bel Catharine, h 353 S 3d
Harrigan Julianna, shop, Orchard
Harrigan Patrick, lab., Sch 5th and Chestnut
Harrington Dennis, provisions, 145 Lombard
Harrington Dennis, labourer, Hallowell n 7th
Harrington D., dentist, 311½ Chestnut
Harrington Esther, 2 Christian
Harrington Robert, coachman, 3 Loxley's ct
Harrington Saml., publisher, 3 Jacoby
Harrington Saml. G., grocer, 2d ab Greenwich
Harris Andrew, stove mr. 65 N 7th
Harris Ann, rear Elizabeth ab Parrish
Harris Ann, milliner, 129 Spruce
Harris Augustus, surg. inst. mr., 36 Farmer
Harris Benjamin, pumpmr., Powell bel Sch 4th
HARRIS & CO., stock & ex. brok., 50 Walnut
Harris Conner, mer., 27 Scheetz st
Harris & Dungan, druggists, 69 North Front
Harris Eliza, 7th and Christian
Harris F. B., saddler, 8 Benton av
Harris F. M. painter, R road bel Callowhill, h 182 W Callowhill
Harris George W., for. mer., 13 and 15 S 3d, h Locust ab Sch 8th
Harris Geo. W., atty. & coun., 4 George
Harris Gilbert, tobacconist, 23 Duke st
Harris G., porter, 113 N 10th
Harris G. S., printer, 119 N 4th
Harris Harriet, 7th and Christian
Harris Harvey, lab., 118 Washington av
Harris Henry, porter, 3 Emeline
Harris Jacob, lab., rear, 26 Charlotte
Harris James M., dentist, 158 S 10th
Harris John, cordw., F road ab Phœnix (K)
Harris John, carp., Bishop bel Queen (K)
Harris John, farmer, 28 Duke st
Harris John M. D., mer., 201 High, h 110 Mulberry
Harris John W., Vernon ab 10th
Harris John W., carp., 9th bel Green, h 357 N 6th
HARRIS JOHN W., Mulberry E Sch 5th
Harris Joseph, carp., Catharine bel 10th
Harris Jos. jr., bricklr., Catharine bel 10th
Harris J. A., tobacconist, 24 S whf

Harris Maria, Cherry ab Sch 7th
Harris Maria, widow, Carpenter ab 12th
Harris Mary, 6 Chester
Harris Maiy, 9th bel Lombard
Harris Mary, gentw., 475 Sassafras
Harris & Mason, combs. &c., 149 High
Harris Michael, brass founder, Lewis ab Poplar
Harris Moses, porter, 23 Mayland
Harris M. E., manuf., 49 N Front
Harris Nicholas, livery stable, 20 Merchant
Harris N. Sayre Rev., Washington ab 11th
Harris & Owens, stovemr., 65 N 7th
Harris Richard, bootmaker, rear 117 Christian
Harris Richard, tailor, 296 S 8th
Harris Richard, printer, 113 Chestnut
Harris Robt., lab., 16 Duke
Harris Robert P., M. D., S E 12th and Walnut
Harris Rosina, St. John bel Beaver (K)
Harris Ruth, 23 Duke
Harris R. W., millinery 4 N 7th.
Harris Sarah, colourer, 6 Trotter's al
Harris Sarah, milliner, 148 S 10th
Harris Sarah Ann, widow, Clinton ct
Harris Theophilus Mrs., 162 N 9th
Harris Thomas, merchant, 149 High, h 163 Sassafras
Harris Thos., bonnetmr., 5 Reid's av
Harris Thos., carp., 51 Currant al
Harris Thomas, plasterer, Sch 5th n Chestnut
Harris Thomas C., wh. washer, 5 Acorn al
HARRIS, TURNER & IRVIN, druggists, 201 High
Harris Washington, stove manuf., 3 N 9th, h 29 Filbert
HARRIS WM., M. D., S. E. 12th and Walnut
Harris William, grocer, 50 Spruce
Harris Wm., mer., 69 N Front
Harris Wm., printer, Cherry n 10th
Harris Wm., lab. Spruce and Ashton
Harris Wm., broker, 50 Walnut
HARRIS WM. D., paper and rags, 1 Strawberry, h 357 N 6th
Harris William P., plumber, N W 6th & Mulberry, h Wood ab 9th.
Harrison Alexander, agent & publisher, 8½ S 7th, h 431 Walnut
Harrison Ann, 13th ab Poplar
HARRISON APOLLOS W., books, maps and ink, 8½ S 7th, h 431 Walnut
HARRISON BROTHERS & CO., white lead manuf., cor. 2d and Harrison, office 19 S. Front
Harrison Catharine, Hamilton n Fairmount
Harrison Charles, machinist, 3 De Witt's av (K)
Harrison George L., mer., Pine ab 9th
Harrison Hugh, painter, 37 Sheaff alley
Harrison James, weaver, Ann n 13th
Harrison James. weaver. 5 Lyndall's al

Harrison Mary, rear 112 Carpenter
Harrison M. F. engraver, 27 S 8th, h 155 Buttonwood ab 10th
Harrison M. Leib, chemist, 19 S Front, h 3d bel Pine
Harrison Peter, lab., Haydock bel Front (K)
Harrison Rebecca Mrs., gentw., 11 Girard
Harrison Richard G., bank note engraver, 154 Wood.
Harrison Samuel, shoemr., 123 S 2d, h Hallowell ab 6th
Harrison Samuel, tobacco, 10th bel Ogden
HARRISON SAMUEL A., mer., 204 Chestnut
Harrison Sarah, 195 Spruce
Harrison Sarah, Sch. 7th ab Mulberry
Harrison Simeon G., stovemr., 390 High
Harrison Sophia, 156 Chestnut
Harrison Virgil F., engraver, 27 S 8th, h 137 Buttonwood
Harrison V. F. & M. F., engravers, 27 S 8th.
Harrison Wm., mer., 12 S whfs, h 7th ab Brown
Harrison Wm., waterman, 28 Parham
Harrison Wm. F., tobacconist, 35 Franklin
Harrison Wm. F., tobacconist, Parrish ab 13th
Harrison William H., brushmaker, Queen above Hanover (K)
Harrold F. W., mer., 9 N 5th
Harrold Geo. S. mer. 656 N 2d, ab Franklin (K)
Harrold Geo. S. & Co., variety store, 246 N 2d
Harron John, carp., 274 S 6th
Harron Robert, grocer, S W 9th and Cedar
Harron Wm., carp., Dutch ct
Harrop Eliza, b. h., 72 S 3d
Harrup Philip, mariner, 109 Queen
Harst John, framemr., 588 N 3d
Hart A., bookseller, S E 4th & Chestnut, h 126 S 4th.
Hart A. & S., quilting, Ogden ab 9th
HART, CUMMINGS & CUSHMAN, dry goods 189 High
Hart Daniel, cordw., Brown bel Cherry
Hart Esther, 87 S 5th
Hart & Flanagan, plumbers & manuf. of lead pipe, 45 Walnut
Hart Francis, 219 Vine
Hart George H., U S Gazette office, 66 Dock
Hart James, lab., Pearl ab 12th
Hart James H., mer., 229 N 3rd, h 221 Vine
HART JAMES H. & WM. B., wholesale grocers, 229 N 3d
Hart John, shoemr., 13 Small
Hart John, ropemr. Crown ab Duke (K)
Hart John, mariner, 30 Union
Hart John E. eating house, 84 S 2d
Hart John H., chair painter, rear 2 Rose alley
Hart John H., 219 Vine
Hart John L. carp. 4 Bauersach's ct (K)
Hart John L., porter, Taylor's ct

:ary, lab., 1 John's ct
LOUIS, tavern, 26 Franklin place
ydia Mrs. 7th bel Green
irgaret, 45 Spruce
arks, tailor, 422 N Front
ary, rear Crown ab Duke (K)
ordecai, grocer, Sp. Garden bel 8th, h 21
allace
ichael C., printer, Allen bel Marlbo' (K)
iineas, mer., h 315 S 5th
.muel, stationer, 27 S 4th, h 26 Clinton
.muel C., druggist, 18 S 2nd.
imuel & Co., impts. stationery, 27 S 4th
irab, 145 Pine
:lah, agent, 10 Bank
olomon, cap manuf., 138 High, h 207
)th
iphia, dry goods, 18 and h 158 N 9th
isanna, 37 Quince.
iomas, 7th bel Green
'illiam, mer., Pine ab 10th
'm., mer., Cherry ab 12th
'm., weigher, Parrish bel 9th
'm., rope maker, Crown bel West (K)
'm., lithogr. printer, 21 Bank, h 4th ab
anklin (K)
'm. scale beam mr. Shippen ab 11th
'illiam B., grocer, 229 N 3rd, h 169 N 6th
'illiam H., gent., 106 Mulberry.
'm. H. blacksmith, Harper's pl
'illiam H., plumber, 45 Walnut, h 40 Pine
'm. S. dry goods, 379 N 3d
Asher D., cordw., 5 Pearl
ine John, spinner, 5 Cadwalader (K)
Josepb, coal dealer, 13 Green
Deborah, 290 Vine
Jacob jr., grocer, G T road bel 6th (K)
James, carter, Gravel's ct
Jeremiah, watchmaker, 135 Cedar
John, lab. School
John M., tailor, Vine and 8th
Jonathan, cordw., Clinton ab Poplar
Joseph, bedding warehouse, 148 S 2nd.
J. D., upholst., S E 2d & Walnut, h 65
:ust
& Knight, upholsterers, 148 S 2d.
Lewis M., enginr., Duke ab Vienna (K)
Matthias A., wheelwr., G T road & Jef-
on, h 4th bel Jefferson (K)
Robert, lab. Front ab Franklin (K)
Samuel, silversmith, 73 Coates
Thomas, mer., 27 & h 48 N 5th.
Wm., sashmaker, 2 R road, h 13 Castle
T. & Co. wines and liquors, 27 N 5th.
Charles, 268 N 5th
Henry, biscuit baker, Sch. 7th bel
afras
Henry, segarmr. George ab St John (K)
Jacob, bricknr., Hope ab Phœnix (K)
John, blieder, 277 S 2nd.
John, biscuit baker, 90 S Wharves, h
'enn (C)
AN JOHN B., tavern, 110 Sassafras
Matthias, baker, 390 S 2d.

Hartman Wencel, glass blower, Sch Beech and
Locust
Hartman Wm., baker, 34 John (S)
Hartnack Ann Mrs. 507 N 3rd
Hartnack Charles, combmr. 12 Logan
Hartness David, weaver, Benton & School (K)
Hartnett Jeremiah, weaver, Philip bel Jefferson
(K)
Hartnett William H., collector, 266 Cedar.
Hartranfft Geo., cordw., Mechanic
Hartranfft Wm. cordw. Carpenter ab 5th
Hartsgrove James, oysterman, 8 Paynter's ct
Hartshorne James L., cabinetmr., 303 N 6th
Hartshorne Joseph, M. D., 272 Mulberry
Hartshorne Lawrence, mer., 38 N Front, h 96
S 5th.
Hartsough Benj., machinist, R. road ab Button-
wood
HARTWELL H. J., Washington House, Chest-
nut ab 7th
Harvey Alexander, shoemr., College av
Harvey Anthony, cordw., Carpenter ab 6th
Harvey Arthur, lab. Steammill al
Harvey Bernard M. Greenwich ab Front
Harvey Charles L., mer, 14 Merch. exchange
Harvey David, manuf. 2d ab Oxford (K)
Harvey Gabriel, tailor, 7 Stampers' alley
Harvey George, vict., G T road ab 6th (K)
Harvey George lab., Franklin ab 3d (K)
Harvey Geo. N., broker, 13 Philada. Exchange,
h 67 Spruce
Harvey Geo. W. messenger, h 41 N 8th
Harvey Hannah S., shop, 54 F road (K)
Harvey Henry, lab., Swanson bel Queen
Harvey Isaac, gent., 320 Chestnut.
Harvey Isaac, clothing, 234 E Cedar
HARVEY JAMES, bootmaker, 50 N 8th
Harvey James, refectory, S E 2d and Lombard
Harvey James, morocco dress., 3 Margaretta pl
Harvey James, weaver, Clay and Sch. Beach
Harvey James W., druggist, 235 High
Harvey John, brass finisher, 7 Charles pl
Harvey John, shoemr., 3 Paynter's ct
Harvey John, combmr., Monroe n Cherry (K)
Harvey John, shoemr., Depot bel 9th
Harvey John C., grocer, F road and Master (K)
Harvey Joseph, tailor, 297 N 3d
Harvey Joseph, moulder, 141 M road
Harvey Joseph, office 139 High, h 10 Union sq
Harvey Joseph, dealer, 262 E Cedar
Harvey Lovely, tailoress, rear 23 Beck
Harvey Luke, chairmr., Juniper ab High
Harvey Mary, 182 S 9th
Harvey Mary, shop, Marlboro' ab Queen (K)
Harvey Mary Ann, N E Linden & Benton
Harvey M. K., lampmr., rear 111 Dillwyn
Harvey Philip J., dealer, 265 S 7th
Harvey Richard, moulder, Buttonwood W 13th
Harvey Rich'd, wheelwr., Lombard bel Sch. 7th
Harvey Robert, stone cutter, 3d and Brown, h
Brown ab 3d
Harvey Samuel, stone cutter, Gabel's ct
Harvey Samuel, lampmr., rear 111 Dillwyn
Harvey Samuel, office, 52 Commerce

Terrence, porter, Marble ab 10th
Thos., shipwright, Little Pine
William, dry goods, 542 N 2nd.
Wm. M., clerk, Parrish ab 11th
Wm. T., waterman, rear 494 N 3d
y W. J. broker, 10 Carter's al, h 147 Pine
od Ezekiel B., carter, Spruce ab Sch 5th
od L., mer., 7 Bank, h 481 Chestnut
od William, visiter of the poor, h R road
Callowhill
ine John, merchant, 10 S Wharves, h 260
pruce
ine Ward B., merchant, 10 S Wharves, h
th and Pine
pat C., hatter, 334 N 3d
ELL EBENEZER, coachmr, 16 George
b 6th, h 38 Prune
ell J.M., M. D., 419 Coates
ns Wm. lab. Paschal's al
n Abraham, machin., Duke bel Palmer
K)
m Geo. weaver, rear 125 Charlotte
m Isaac, enginr., Marlboro' bel Duke (K)
m Joseph, corder, 12 Duke
m R. H., corder, 221 N Water, h 14 Duke
m Sarah, 1 Noble
m Thomas, bonnet wire maker, 150 St.
ohn
m Thomas, tavern, c Front & Montgome-
y (K)
m Thos. A., carp., Montgomery bel Front
K)
m T. G. corder, 197 N Water
m W., 468 Callowhill
n Wm T., carp., F road bel Oxford (K)
Isaac, optician, rear 114 New Market
James, cabman, 15 Monroe ct
Wm., weaver, 654 N 2d
tt Alex., miller, Hanover bel West (K)
tt William D., high constable, Brown bel
ront
ll John, cordw., 181 N 2d
ll John Jr., cordwainer, 181 N 2d.
a George S., harness mr., 60 Dock, h 6
owell
Charles, chemist, G T road bel 5th (K)

Hastings Robert, goldbeater, 56 N 5th
Hastings S. P., lumber mor., 411 High
Haswell G. D., printer, 293 High, h Locust n
    Sch 6th
Hatch Edward, real estate broker, 125 Vine, h
    51 Tammany
Hatcher Jac. J., pencilmr., 10 Christian
Hatcher Thomas, cordwainer, 6 Loxley's ct.
Hatcher Wm. saddler, 53 New
Hatfield Ann, Hope ab Otter (K)
Hatfield Catharine, 327 N 8th
Hatfield Ezra, cordw., Green n 7th
Hatfield John, watchman, 35 Sassafras
Hatfield Nathan L., M. D., Franklin & Button-
    wood
HATHAWAY E. A. & CO., com. & coal mers.,
    23 N Wharves
Hathaway Ephraim A., mer., 23 N wharves,
    h Locust n Sch 7th
Hathwell Susan, 7 George
Hatkins Thomas, skindresser, 512 N Front.
Hattrick James R., silverplater, 54 N 6th, h
    448 S 4th
Hatz Wm., tobacconist, 1 Lytle's ct.
Hatzmann Wm., tailor, G T road bel 5th (K)
HAUEL JULES, import. & perfum., 46 S 3rd
Haug Wm. L. music teacher, 76 Pine
Haughey Bernard, clerk, 9 Marshall
Haughey James, ostler, 7 John's ct
Haughin Henry, weaver, G T road ab Jefferson
    (K)
Haughin Lewis, manuf., G T road bel Master (K)
Haun Alfred, machinist, 16 Christian
Haun John, 16 Christian
Hauptman George, butcher, 2d bel Greenwich
Hauptman Henry, plaster., 10th ab Buttonwood
Hauptman John, gent. P road ab Federal
Hauptman John, tavern, 105 E Shippen
Haury George, huckster, 5 Lagrange
Haus J. W., oysters, Juniper and High
Hause C. W., tavern, 8th and S Garden
Hause George, machinist, Teas' ct
Hause John, carp., 176 Coates
Hause Wm., gent., Filbert E Sch. 6th.
Hauss Benjamin, lab. George ab Apple
Haven Chas. E., mer., 41 S whs., h 400 Mulberry

HAVILAND JOHN, architect, 196 Spruce
Haviland John, shoemr., 6th bel Catharine
Haviland Mary, Lombard bel Juniper
Havilland Edward, 196 Spruce
Haw Thomas, tailor, Prospect al
Hawes C. R., agent, 108 High, h 433 Chestnut
Hawk John, cordw., Apple ab George
Hawke Rachel, ready made linen, 67 S 8th
Hawkes George, copperplate printer, 6 Howard's ct.
Hawkes Robt., lab., Pine n Sch Willow
Hawkey Chas., weaver, Carpenter ab 13th
Hawkins Chas., dealer, 110 Plum
Hawkins Edw., ingrain carp, weaver, 555 N 3d
Hawkins Edward P., shoemr., Loud bel 10th
Hawkins E. L., cake baker, Coates ab 8th.
Hawkins George, lab., Barley
Hawkins John, blacksmith, Paul bel 7th
Hawkins Jos., carp., rear 332 S 3d
Hawkins Luke, fisherman, Beach ab Warren (K)
Hawkins Mark, fisherman, Bishop bel Queen (K)
Hawkins Matt., fisherman, Bishop bel Queen (K)
Hawkins Philip, tavern, 91 Plum
Hawkins Sarah, wh. washer, 36 Prosperous al
Hawkins Wm., secretry & treasurer of Lykens
    Valley R. R. & Coal Co., 46½ Walnut
Hawkins Wm., kid glove mr., 238 N Front
Hawkins Wm., saddler, 184 N 11th.
Hawkins Wm., tailor, 91 N 3d,
Hawkins Wm., cordwainer, 93 Shippen
Hawkins Wm., carp., Lewis ab Poplar
Hawkins Wm., boot fitter, 10 Orchard
Hawkins Zachariah, cordw., 13th ab Coates
Hawks Adam, carp., Say st
Hawksley James, flag dress. rear Broad ab 13th
Hawley Andrew, 6th ab Parrish
Hawn Wm., lab., Front bel Greenwich
Haworth Stephen, chairmr, 93 N Front, h 105
    N 9th
Haworth Susannah, 9 Vine.
Hawthorn Mary, rear 397 N 3d
Hawthorne Mich., lab., Jones n Sch 4th
Hay Chas., clerk, Cadwalader bel Phoenix (K)
Hay David G., painter, 350 N 2d, h 63 G T road
Hay Francis, lab., Ontario bel Poplar
Hay Henry, conveyancer, 385 N Front
Hay Jane, b h., 100 S 3d.
Hay John, cooper, Beach bel Maiden (K)
Hay Maria G., 135 Franklin
Hay Peter, 202 S 4th
Haydock Eden, watches & jewel., 122 Chestnut
Haydock Mary Ann, 4 Lodge
Haydock James B., jeweller, 59 Carpenter (S)
Hayes Daniel, lab., 178 N Water
Hayes George, jeweller, rear 115 and h 108
    Chestnut
Hayes James, b h., 92 N Water
Hayes James, bootmr., S E 3d and Catharine
Hayes John, weaver, 13th ab Catharine
Hayes Michael, labourer, 153 N Water.
Hayes Morris, lab., 178 N Water
Hayes Owen, shoemr., Division bel 12th
Hayes Patrick, master warden, 33 Walnut, h 10
    Franklin row
Hayes Robert, mer., 67 N 3d, h 352 N 6th

Hayes Robt., painter, 13th n Sassafras, h 4 Elder
HAYES SAMUEL, grocer, N W 11th & Walnut
Hayes Sarah, wid., Shackamaxon n F road (K)
Hayes Thomas, mer., 34 Walnut, h 78 S 12th.
Hayes Wm., vict., Shippen ab 13th
Hayes Wm., weaver, Shackamaxon bel F road
Hayhurst A., trimmings, 227 N 10th
Haymaker Jacob, shoemr., G T road ab 4th
Hayman James R., tobacconist, Elizabeth ab
    Poplar
Haynes Charles Y., embosser, 10 Pear
Haynes Godfrey, saddler, 278 N Front
Haynes Moses W., tinsmith, 7 Benton
Haynes Williams, 4 Lombard ct
Hays Ann, gentw., 3d and Lombard
Hays A., carp., 15 James
Hays A., vict., James ab 10th
Hays Caleb, waiter, 8 Washington ab 11th
Hays David, lab., Aspen ab Spruce
Hays Elijah B., potter, rear F road n Queen (K)
Hays Henry, vict., 10th ab James
Hays Henry, dealer, Broad n Shippen
Hays Hugh, carter, 37 W Cedar
Hays Isaac, M. D., 3 Boston row.
Hays James, weaver, rear Milton bel 11th
HAYS JOHN, stoves, N E 4th and Branch
Hays John, lab., rear 552 N 2d (K)
Hays John, vict., Hay's ct
Hays Martha, rear 164 Swanson
Hays Michael, lab., 8th bel Catharine
Hays Richeal, 210 Locust
Hays Robert, carpenter, 132 N 13th
Hays Robt., turner, Elder
Hays Samuel, pattern maker, Queen ab Palmer
Hays Saml., watchman, Sch 5th ab Fairview
Hays Samuel C., mer., 193 High, h 106 N 5th
Hays Wm., butcher, Shippen ab 13th
Hayter Ann, shop, Front ab Franklin (K)
Hayward E. H., dry goods, 31 N 9th
Hayward Frances, confectioner, 39 Green
Hayward Joel W., teacher music, 43 Prune.
Hayward Joseph, chinaware, 54 N 4th
Hayward Martin, boots and shoes, 14½ S 4th
Hayward Thomas, hatter, 96 Christian
Hayworth A., widow, George n Sch 2d
Hazard A. Fullerton, mer., 174 High
Hazard Catharine, 136 S 10th
Hazard Erskine, mer., 142 S 2d
Hazard John, cigar mr., rear Perry bel Franklin
Hazard Joseph, cabinetmr., 8 Parham
Hazard Madame, teacher of dancing, Assembly
    buildings, h 319 Walnut
Hazard Samuel, editor of the U. S. Commer. &
    Stat. Register, 28 Walnut, h 256 Filbert
Hazard Wm. P., barber, Lisle
Hazel David, tailor, 127 S 11th.
Hazel John, cordw., 246 S 6th
Hazel Joseph, shoemr., 123 S 11th
Hazel Philip, painter, 40 Quince
Hazelton Isaac, hatter, rear Peach
Hazelton Isaiah, trunkmr., Tomlin's ct
Hazen Miner S., hatter, 19 Sassafras
HAZLEHURST ISAAC, attorney & coun, 26
    Washington square
Hazlehurst Julianna, N E 10th & Shippen.

Hazlehurst Samuel, gent., Spruce ab Broad.
Hazlet Samuel, bootmr., N E 10th & Sassafras
Hazlet Wm., manuf., William bel Edward (K)
Hazlet Wm., lab.,, Marriott's la n 6th
Hazleton Cynthia, Plynlimmon pl
Hazleton Henry, trunk mr., Laurel & Rachel
Hazleton Richard, liv. sta., rear Madison House
Hazleton Robert, weaver, Hanover ab Duke(K)
Hazleton Charles, dealer, Callowhill bel Sch Front
Hazlett Edgar, cook, Washington bel 11th
Hazlett Isaac, musician, Goldsmith's ct
Hazlett John, weaver, 13th bel Cedar
Hazlett Samuel, stone cutter, 1 Somer's ct
Hazley Wm., weaver, Shippen ab 13th
Hazzard Daniel, lab., 194 S Front
Hazzard David, cabinetmr., 10 Olive
Hazzard E., watchman, 465 S 2d
Hazzard Israel, waterman, 8 Parham
Hazzard Jacob, lab., 10 Foot al
Hazzard John, cabinetmr., 465 S 2d
Hazzard John, cigar mr., 6th & Marriott's la.
Hazzard John L., engraver, 92 Christian
Hazzard J. P., paper hanger, rear 110 Catharine
Hazzard L., paper hanger, 313 S 2d
Hazzard L. & W. H., paper hangers, 313 S 2d
Hazzard Maria, dressmr., 386 N 3d
Hazzard Theo., carp., Fraley's ct (K)
Hazzard Thos., lab., Dorothy n Sch 4th
Hazzard Wm., tobacconist, Marriott ab 6th
Hazzard Wm. H., paper hanger, 313 S 2d
Heacock Geo., grocer, N W 4th & Christian
Head Joseph, 122½ S 3rd
Heade M. J., port. painter, S W 8th & Mulberry
Headlam Wm., 65 Plum st
HEADLY CHARLES B., dry goods, N W 5th and Mulberry
Headman David, potter, 19 & h 17 S 8th.
Headman Francis W., machinist, 8 Lodge al, h 226 N 9th
Headman George, potter, 19 S 8th
Headman G. & D., potters, 19 S 8th
Headman Jacob, coachmr., 119 Buttonwood
Headman William, watchmr., 39 S 8th, h 54 N Sch 7th
Headman William, potter, 78 George.
Heal William, locksmith, 177 Cedar
HEALD, BUCKNOR & COMPANY, merchants, 16 N wharves and 41 N Water
Heald Newton, bookbinder, 12 S 4th
Heald Peter, tavern, 14 Strawberry
Heald & Price, bookbinders, 12 S 4th
Healy James, tinsmith, 303 Pine
Healy John, lab., 14 Dilk's ct
Healy John, weaver, G T road bel Oxford (K)
Heaney Patrick, stovemr., 66 N 6th
Heaney Peter, Mechanics' Hotel, 48 Spruce
Heap John, suspender manuf., 26 Bread.
Hearn Michael, agent, 5 Lodge pl
Heartley Isaac S., engineer, Race ab Queen (K)

Heaton Adelaide, b. h., 110 Chestnut
Heaton A., mer., 34 commerce, h S E Sch 5th and Cherry
Heaton & Denckla, com. mers., 34 Commerce
Heaton Joseph, carter, 142 Marshall.
Heaton Wm., Elizabeth bel Franklin
Heaton Wm., mer., 135 and h 110 Chestnut
Heazlitt James, dry goods, 236 S 2d.
Heberton Ann, widow of Doctor, 77 N 9th.
Heberton G. Craig, M. D., 77 N 9th
Heberton Henry F., mer., 179 High, h 342 Mulberry
HEBERTON & MILES, dry goods, 179 High
Heberton Robt., collector, Mulberry W Sch 7th
Heberton Robt., mer., 179 High
Hebrews Lemuel, lab., White's ct
Heck Amos, machinist, 600 N 2d
Heck Sarah, gentw., 40 Vine
Heckman Archimedes, tobacconist, 79 N 2d.
Heckman Jas., ship carp., Sch 5th bel High
Heckman John, rear 18 Cherry
Hedderly Henry, cordw., 97 Prime.
Heddleson Alex., shop, P road & Christian
Heddleson Thos., distiller, P road & Marriott
Hedelt Leopold, tailor, 6 Exchange pl, h 43 N 4th
Hedges Benjamin F., broker, 95½ Walnut, h 8th n Poplar
Hedges Eunice, venetian blind mr., 111 S 2d
Heerman J. F., tailor, 209 Green
Heff John, lampmr., 8 Franklin (K)
Hefferman James, waiter, rear 27 Quince
Heffernan John, shop, Vine bel 12th, h 5 Middle al
Hegamin John, porter, 168 Locust
Heichheimer Hyneman, peddler, Justice's ct
Heidenrich Jacob, beer house, Apple bel Franklin
Height Adam, 221 Wood
Heighton Caleb, bell hanger, Perry ct
Heileg John, watchmaker, 5 R road.
Heiler Christian, 7 Madison av
Heilman Wm., mer., Front & Willow, h 353 N 6th
Heim Frederick, tailor, 597 N 3rd.
Helm Fred'k, jr., tailor, 507 N 2d.
Heim Henry, blacksm., Mechanics' ct
Heim John C., tailor, 283 St John
Heim Joseph, tailor, 2 Eutaw
Heim Valentine, blacksmith, 9 Jackson (N L)
Heiman Leopold, pedler, Justice's ct
Heimberger Washington, gauger, 47 O Y road, and 65 Callowhill
Heims Mary, 310 Callowhill
Heineman Geo., watchmr., 84 Mulberry
Heinman John C., clerk, Gatchell's av
Heimer Joshua, carp., 13 Nectarine
Heinick John C., baker, 161 St John st
Heinitsh Elizabeth, Wood ab 10th
Heinker Henry, 348 S Front
Heinold Samuel,

Heins John W., tobacconist, Sassafras ab Broad
Heins Simon, 318 N 3d
HEINS & THOMAS, mers., 11 Church al
Heins Wm., carp., Hanover bel Bedford (K)
Heins William F., mer., 11 Church al
Heins William G., mer., 11 Church al
Heintzelman John J., M.D., druggist, Callowhill and Sch 5th
Heintzelman R. B., druggist, Callowhill & 10th, h 273 N 7th
Heintzelman Samuel, atty., 273 N 7th
Heinzenknecht Andw., cordw., 10th bel Pleasant
Heisley Wm., tailor, 61 Garden
Heisligh Geo., Stearly ct
Heiss E. L., painter & glazier, 3 Lemon
Heiss James, grocer, Front and Phoenix (K)
Heiss John S., dentist, 493 N 3d
Heiss John T., 3 Lemon
Heiss Joseph, cordw., 604 N Front (K)
Heiss Matthias, cordw., Front and Phœnix (K)
Heiss Timothy, shoemr., rear 604 N Front (K)
Heiss Wm., gent., 206 N 4th.
Heiss Wm. Jr., coppersmith, 213 N 2d.
Heiss Wm., cordwainer, Front bel Phoenix (K)
Heiss Wm. L., druggist, 3 Lemon
Heite Chas., clerk, Alder ab Poplar
Heitz Fred'k, potter, Melon ab 13th
Helffenstein Abm., M. D., Queen bel Shackamaxon
Helffenstein E., att'y & convey., 114 Mulberry
Helffricht C F., math. inst. mr., 25 S Front
Helffricht Wm., 60 Vine.
Helin John, shoemr., S W 9th & Locust
Heller Alexander, tobacconist, 600 N 2d (K)
Heller Charles, salesman, 96 Franklin
Heller Gotlieb, baker, Shippen bel 2d
Heller Hen., cop. sm., Marlborough ab Franklin
Heller Jacob, silv. pla., Marlboro' above Franklin (K)
Heller Jacob, rear 441 Vine
Heller Joseph, gent., Franklin ab Union (K)
Hellerman John, carp., 364 N 4th
Hellerman William, shoes, 332 Coates
Hellings Edward, hatter, rear 9th ab Coates
Hellings Isaac P., painter, 8th ab Brown
Hellings Wm., combmr., 184 Coates
Helm Thomas, watch case mr., 4 Hudson's al, h 143 Sp Garden st
Helman Joseph, bedstead mr., 89 St John
Helmbold Alfred, paper warehouse, 183 S Front, h 35 Queen
Helmbold Eliza, 314 Cedar.
Helmbold Frederick, livery stables, 132 Filbert, h 431 High
Helmbold George, paper dealer, 456 S Front
Helmbold George, West. Bank, h 157 N 11th
Helmbold George W., paper dealer, 91 S Front
Helmbold Wm., livery stables, Filbert n Sch 4th
Helmboldt Earnest, shop, 72 Catharine
Helme Hugh, hosier, Crown bel Duke (K)
Helmolt Lewis, cutter, 36 Lebanon st
Helmolt O., cutler, 7 Assem. Buildings, h 12 Lebanon
Helms Aaron, ship joiner, Plynlimmon pl
Helms John, bricklayer, 402 Coates

Helms Leonard, carp., Nectarine n 10th
Helms Thomas, tailor, Magnolia ab Noble
Helmsley Elizabeth A., 284 Walnut
Helmstadt A., trimmings, 257 S 2d
Helmuth George, mer., 35 S Water, h Spruce bel Sch 8th
Helmuth George, clerk, 357 Lombard
Helmuth George, lab., rear 75 Beach
Helmuth Henry, atty. & coun., 218 Walnut, h Spruce E Sch 8th
Helmuth John H., mer., 5 Commerce
Helmuth Wm. S., M. D., 235 Pine.
Helstab Jacob, cabinetmr., 4 Washington row
Helser Philip, lab., Brown ab Cherry (K)
Helt Lewis, cordw., rear 464 N 2d
Helt Mary, Wood ab 12th
Helverson Alex., tailor, rear Marshall ab Brown
Helverson Elizabeth, St John, ab George (K)
Helverson Jacob, stone finisher, 9 Jackson's ct
Helverson Nicholas, coffin warehouse, 93 and h 91 Coates
Hembel William, gent., 17 N Front.
Hemmenway James, barber, 51 Pine.
Hemmetsbough Wm., weaver, Gray's ct
Hempel Thomas, weaver, West bel Hanover (K)
Hemphill Ann, b. h., Callowhill ab 13th
Hemphill Mary A., drygoods, Callowhill bel 13th
Hemphill John, provisions, S E 13th & Sassafras
Hemphill R. C., gent., Poplar & Sch 8th
Hemphill Thomas, cordwainer, 58 Zane.
Hemphill Thomas J., secty. Phil. Loan Co., 6 Minor, h 145 S 6th
Hemphill Thos. W., cordw., Torr's al
Hemple Charles, tobacconist, 5 Pennsylvania av
Hemple Samuel, tobacconist, 47 N 4th.
Hemple Samuel, painter, Wood ab Sch 6th
Hemsher, Frederick, cooper, N W 7th & S Garden, h Palm bel Parrish
Hemsher Mary Ann, sempstress, Miller's ct
Hemsing William H., 14 Dannaker's av
Hendel Peter M., carp., Hanover bel West (K)
Henderson Barton F., mer., 53 High
Henderson Charles, carp., 2 Schuylkill av
Henderson Charles, hatter, 6 S 4th, h 85 Mulberry
Henderson Clayton W., printer, 4 Clare
Henderson David, carter, F road bel Otter
Henderson David, sexton, 5 Magnolia
Henderson Davis, 496 Chestnut
Henderson Edward, hatter, 144 High, h 504 N 5th
Henderson Edward, Lawrence ct
Henderson Elizabeth, 87 N Juniper
Henderson Ezekiel, lab., Flower ab Christian
Henderson George, shoemr., 155 Swanson
Henderson Geo., hatter, 19 N 3rd., h 467 Mulberry
Henderson George R., grocer, 22 Gaskill
Henderson Guy, gent., 99 Cherry
Henderson Henry H., carp., N W Poplar and Lewis
Henderson Jacob, porter, Juniper al
Henderson James, drayman, George W Sch 4th
Henderson James, weaver, Bedford ab 13th
Henderson James, lab., Davis' ct

Henderson John, barber, U. S. Hotel
Henderson John, wool spin., Marlborough near Bedford
Henderson John, weaver, McDuffie n Sch 2d
HENDERSON JOHN, grocer, 90 & 92 W High
Henderson John brickmr., Lombard ab Sch 8th
Henderson John, saw mr., 4 Danaker's av
Henderson John, 328 Pine
Henderson John, carter, Johnson's la n 5th
Henderson John L., printer, 476 S 4th
Henderson John N., tailor, R road ab Spring Garden
Henderson Joseph, gent., 8th n Wallace
Henderson Joseph, rear 13 Wagner's al
Henderson Joseph, cordwr., Gray's ct.
HENDERSON & LEVICK, hatters, 144 High
Henderson Maria B. Mrs., gentw., 18 N 7th.
Henderson Mary Ann, 5 Osborn's ct
Henderson Mary, spooler, rear Philip ab Master (K)
Henderson Robert, brickmr., 51 W Cedar
Henderson Robt., coal dealer, Penn bel Maiden (K) h 163 N 5th.
Henderson Robert H., cigarmr., 366 N 6th
Henderson Robert H., dentist, 381 Sassafras
HENDERSON SAMUEL J., atty. & coun., 16 N 7th, h 268 Walnut
Henderson Susan, 2 Sch av
Henderson Thomas, weaver, Brazier ab Broad
Henderson Thomas, lab., Milton ab 10th
Henderson Thos., carp., New Market ab Laurel
Henderson Wm., cabt. mr., rear 200 Christian
Henderson Wm., lab., Water ab Callowhill
Hendle Gottleib, tailor, Benton n School (K)
Hendley Clarissa, wid., Carpenter bel 10th
Hendley John, boots & shoes, 369 N 2d.
Hendrick Felix, weaver, Mariner
Hendricks Isaac, tailor, S W 11th & Sassafras
Hendricks John, b h, 46 Cherry
Hendricks John, carp., Church bel Christian
Hendricks Joseph, lab., rear 152 Poplar
Hendricks Joseph M., com. mer., 99 Water, h 90 Vine
Hendricks Randolph, driver, 2 Williams' ct
Hendricks Samuel, carter, rear 410 N 3d
Hendricks Wm., mason, Lombard bel Juniper
Hendrickson Ann, tailoress, 482 Coates
Hendrickson Charles J., carpets, 87 Chestnut, h Mantua Village
Hendrickson Francis W., barber, Sassafras n Broad, h Pearl ab 13th
Hendrickson Joshua F., bricklr, 227 Marshall
Hendrickson Wm., spectaclemr., 3 Short ct
Hendry John A., leather, 6 S 3d, h 325 N 6th
HENDRY & OVERMAN, leather, 6 S 3d
Hendry Rhoda, b h, 11th n Wood
Hendry Theodore A., furniture, 7 N 8th, h 52 Chester
Henheiffer Albanus, suspender maker, Palmer

Henion Wm., waterman, rear Swanson below Queen
Henkel & Reigle, dry goods, 316 N 2d
Henkels Chas. W., mer., 316 N 2d, h Dillwyn ab Tammany
Henkels Daniel H., chairmr., 132 Dillwyn
Henkels George J., chairmr., 173 Pine
Henkels Thomas J., cabinetmr., 132 Dillwyn
HENKLE ANDREW, Social Hall, 38 Carter's al
Henley Elizabeth, 20 Washington sq
Henley Robt., weaver, 17 Gay's ct (K)
Henne William, boot maker, 82 S 4th.
Henneck Jacob, bricklayer, 611 N 3d
Hennessey George, Callowhill ab Nixon
Hennessy James, mer., 12 S Front, h 23 Sassafras
Hennessy Jeremiah, carp., Small n 6th
Hennessy M., blacksmith, Sch 8th bel Willow
Henning Hannah, b h, 188 N 5th
Henning Wm., tailor, rear 30 Pascal
Henniss Charles J., 13th & Sp Garden
Henny John, lab., High n Sch 4th
Henop & Co., mer., 17 Walnut
Henrich John C., baker, 161 St. John.
HENRION & CHAUVEAU, importers of confectionery, 242 High
Henrion C., mer., 242 High
Henry Alexander, merchant, 8th above Fitzwater
HENRY ALEX., jr., att'y & coun., Walnut ab 6th, h 15 Clinton
Henry Alex., mer., 27 Minor, h 254 Mulberry
Henry Ann, shop, Small
Hehry Arthur, shoemr., 23 Lombard
Henry Ann, 434 N 3d
Henry Claudien, 24 Bread
Henry Bernard, 35 Girard
Henry Dennis, weaver, 13th bel Fitzwater
Henry Francis, blacksmith, Wilson's ct
Henry Gabriel, carp., Thompson ab 4th (K)
Henry George, coach painter, 6 Lombard ct
Henry George, dealer, Dean c Lyndall's al
Henry George W., 139 S 5th
Henry George W., dealer, 8 Acorn al
Henry George W., hardware, N W 9th & High, h 7 N 13th
Henry Henry, coachman, Apple bel George
Henry Henry C., mariner, Washington ab 5th
Henry H., captain U. S. N., 33 S 13th.
Henry Isaac, mer., 152 High h 251 Pine
Henry James, plasterer, Sch 8th bel Callowhill
Henry James, saddler, 41 Filbert
Henry James, painter, 13th n Buttonwood
Henry James, 202 Lombard.
Henry Jane, wid., 7 N 13th
Henry John, lab., 291 S 6th
Henry John, waiter, 23 Blackberry
Henry John, innkeeper, Coates ab Broad

Henry Mary Ann, confect., Shippen bel 9th
Henry Michael, coachmr., Dock below 2d, h Mechanic
Henry Morton P., atty & coun., 35 Girard
Henry Nancy, 134 Apple
Henry Patrick, quill manuf., 119 S 6th
Henry Paul, lab., 4 Dillwyn pl
Henry Peter, lab., 9 Wheeler's ct
Henry Robt., weaver, S 11th ab Carpenter
Henry Saml., clerk, Philadelphia Bank, h 19 Filbert
Henry Samuel, coach mr., 25 Dock
Henry Samuel C., collee., 103 O Y road
Henry S & M., coach mrs., 25 Dock
Henry Wm., baker, 10 Paschall's al
Henry William, M. D., 321 S 2d
Henry Wm. paper stainer, 6th ab Poplar
Henry Wm., lab., rear Centre bel Parrish
Henry Wm. K., paper hanger, 103 O Y road
Henry Wm. W., potter, Sch 8th ab Callowhill
Henschen E., mer. 4 Chestnut
Hensey Samuel, real est. br., 8 Marshall
Hensman Mary, gentw., Cedar bel 12th
Hensel John, carp., Sassafras bel Sch 7th
Hensel J. G., baker, 2nd ab Franklin (K)
Hensler Jacob, lab., Olive bel 13th
Henson Ann, cook, 3 Elizabeth
Henson George, clerk, 21 Magnolia
Henson Hannah, rear 24 Nectarine
Henson Maria, cook, 24 St Mary
Henszey C. & E., stocks and ready made linen, 121 Chestnut
Henszey C. Mrs., 4 Library
Henszey Joseph, bootmaker, 31 N 4th, h 4 Library
Henszey Marshall, bricklayer, 46 Sassafras
Henszey W. C. mer. 301 High, h 28 Palmyra row
Hent Valentine, dentist, 27 Castle.
Hent Wm. brass founder, 119 Callowhill
Henty Philip, mail carrier, 34 Sheaff
Henty Richard, carp., 27 Castle
Hentz Jacob, inspector, 342 N 5th
Hentz John, h 10th bel Spring Garden
Henwood Abraham, corder, 66 Plum.
Henwood & Rickards, corders, Almond st whf
Henwood William corder, Almond street whf, h Sheetz
Hepburn Charles, hatter, Carpenter ab 4th.
Hepburn Chas. W., ex. broker, 28 S 3d, h Catharine ab 6th.
Hepburn Eliza, Morgan's ct
Hepburn Elizabeth, 1 Lodge pl
HEPPBURN JAMES, atty. & coun., 109 S 6th, h Sch 8th bel Spruce
Heppard Charles, painter, rear 10 Queen
Heppard John, painter, 124 S Front
Heppard Samuel, painter, 281 S Front
Heppard Thomas, lab. 6 Relief pl
Herbell Ann, wid. of Caspar, gardener, Mary bel F road
Herbert Albert, wheelwright, Frances. (F V)
Herbert Chas., cordw., rear Beaver bel 3d (K)
Herbert Charles C., refectory, N E Marshall & Callowhill

Herbert Eliza, hair worker, 48 Mulberry
Herbert Elizabeth, 112 Christian
Herbert Henry, huckster, Washington ab 8th
Herbert Jacob, waterman, 7th bel Federal
Herbert John B., carp., 321 S 5th
Herbert Lawrence, tobacconist, 74 N 2d
Herbert William, stables, 136 Cherry
Hergesheimer Elizabeth, huckster, Culvert ab 4th
Hergesheimer Sam. carp. Queen ab Warren (K)
HERING CONSTANTINE, M. D., 98 S 11th
Heringer Charles, jeweller, 3 St John
Heritage Samuel P. M., shoemr., 6th bel Carpenter
Heritage Wm., shoemr., 294 S 5th
Herkness Alfred M., auc., Carpenter's ct., h Vine bel Sch 6th
Herkness Mary, milliner, Sch 8th & Wood
Herman Chas., tailor, Washington av ab Brown
Herman Charles, printer, Tyler
Herman Jacob, fringe mr., 132 N 4th
Herman John, druggist, S W 4th and Vine
Herman J. & G., wheelwrights, 283 Callowhill, h 264 N 8th
Herman T. H., prof. of music, 273 Coates
Hermstead Joseph, book binder, 89 New
Heron Alexander jr., mer., 35½ N whfs., & lumber, Beach & Marlboro', h 7 St John
Heron Archd., weaver, 4 Brinton
Heron John, gent., 5 Wood
Heron John, Kensington planing mill, Beach ab Marlboro', h 7 St John
Heron Matthias, Locust n Sch 3d
Heron Wm. R., bookkeeper, 99 P road
Herr H., machinist, R road ab S Garden
Herr H., machinist, Ontario ab Parrish
Herr John, saddler, Green's ct
Herrick Edward, lab. 174 N Water
Herrigel John G., tailor, 550 N 2d
Herriges John G., 471 N 2d
Herriges Jos., tobacconist, N E 4th & Lombard.
Herring Adam, lab., rear 83 G T road (K)
Herring & Brothers, confectioners, N W 3d & Mulberry
Herring George C., cabinetmr., 123 Cedar
HERRING THOS. J., mer., N W 3d & Mulberry, h 8th bel Coates
Herring W. N., mer., N W 3d & Mulberry, h 135 Vine
Herrington John, carter, Vaughn ab Locust
Herrington Mary, Garden & Willow
Herrod Charles, victualler, Cedar ab 13th
Herrod Richard, cordw., 9th ab Carpenter
Herron James, civil engineer, h 277 S 10th
Herron John B., cordw., 55 Shippen
Herse Geo. P., mer. 64 High, h Cedar bel 9th
Hersey Anderson, bricklayer, 1 Lemon
Hershberger George, shoemr. N W Poplar and Apple
Hershey D., M. D., 529 N 5th
HERTH HENRY, bootmr., 49 S 4th
Hertig Frederick, baker, 27 Laurel
Hertzog Mrs. widow of Peter, gentw. Sassafras and Crown
Hervey Robt., clerk, 28 Cherry

20

Herzer John G., store, 83 New Market
Hess Ann Eliza, b. h., 78 Vine
Hess Benjamin, carp., 281 High.
Hess Caroline, rear 2d & Laurel (K)
Hess Cath., Moyamensing av
Hess Christian, conf., 2d & Catharine
Hess Conrad, morocco dresser, rear 2d ab Laurel (K)
Hess David, lab., 139 New Market
Hess Elisha M., tinsmith, 7 Bosler's row (K)
Hess Elizabeth, 4th ab Franklin (K)
Hess Frederick, blacksmith, Benton's ct
Hess Godfrey, baker, 9th and Poplar
Hess Henry, cabinetmr., Bedford & 7th
Hess Jacob, tinsmith, 34 Dillwyn
Hess Jacob, blacksmith, Robb's ct
Hess Jacob, sailmr., Painter's ct
Hess James, mariner, 4 North Court ●
Hess John, baker, 403 S Front.
Hess John, coachmaker, Coates bel Broad
Hess Jno., glass blow., Vienna bel Franklin (K)
Hess John, capt., 8 John (S)
Hess John A, stove finisher, rear 2d ab Edward (K)
Hess John C., toys, 122 O Y road
Hess John I., gent., 179 Green
Hess Joseph, cordwainer, 5 Jackson's ct
Hess Joseph, oak cooper, Rose n William (K)
Hess & Knapp, bakers, 27 N 6th
Hess Louis, baker, 27 N 6th
Hess Maurice, clothing, 276 N 2d
Hess Peter, tobacconist, 189 N 3d, h 27 Wood
Hess Peter, cabinetmr., 258 St John
Hess Philip, tinsmith, Sp Garden ab 7th, h Poplar ab 10th
Hess Pierce, hairdresser, 482 N 4th
Hess Samuel M., grocer, S E Sch. 8th & Vine.
Hess Susanna, shop, 258 St. John
Hess William, cooper, Rose and William (K)
Hessel William F., furrier, 103 N 3d
Hesselpoth John, carpenter, School bel Franklin (K)
Hesselpoth Rachel, tavern, N E 3d & Poplar
HESSENBRUCH THEOPHILUS, importer, 1 N 5th, h 45 New
Hessenbruch T. & Co. importers hardware, 1 N 5th.
Hesser Charles, stone cut., 14 Fayette
Hesser John, blacksmith, 13 Union (S)
Hesser John, stone cutter, 2 M'Knight's ct
Hesser R. M. 107 Buttonwood
Hesser William, tailor, 309 Lombard

Hettrick Margaret, Jackson's ct (N L)
Hettrick Robert, cordw., 112 Dillwyn
Hetzel Adam, lab., Clymer ab Montgomery (K)
Hetzel John, cooper, N E Melon and 10th
Hetzel John, baker, 102 Apple
Hetzel Joseph, manuf. 48 George (S)
Hetzell And., bricklr., Clay's av (K)
Heugh & Stewart, stonecutters, High ab Sch 5th
Heuman John, bootmr., 5 N 7th
Heumann Nicholas, pill-box mr. rear 484 N 3d
Heusman John, glassbl., Queen ab Palmer (K)
Hewes Nathan, carp. Apple bel Franklin
Hewett Eliza, 315 Pine
Hewitt Andrew C., cordw., Queen bel Marlborough (K)
Hewitt Charles, moroc. dress., Allen bel Palmer (K)
Hewitt Ephraim, waterman, 1 Walter's ct
Hewitt Henry, tanner, Brown bel Front.
Hewitt John, 22 Jones' al (C)
Hewitt S. B., book binder, 27 S 4th
Hewitt Mrs. Thomas, S W 10th & Shippen
Hewitt Thos. T., lab., Stoy's ct (K)
Hewitt Wm. blacksm. Janney's ct
Hewitt Wm., weaver, Hanover ab Duke (K)
Hewitt Wm. K., port. painter, 207 N 6th
Hews Edward, 142 S 4th
Hews George F., bootmr., 24 N 12th
Hews James E., ladies' shoem., 36 Reed
Hews Jane, washer, 186 S 4th
Hews John, waiter, Middle al
Hews T., stevedore, 14 Middle al
Hewson Thos., weaver, 11th bel Carpenter
Hewson Thomas T., M. D., 243 Walnut.
Hewss Rebecca, tavern, 52 St Mary
Hewston John, gent., 6 Perry
Hey M. & E., manufs., 53 N 3d
Heyberger Frances, 50 Coates
Heyberger George W., German and French goods, 68 N 3d
Heyer Charles, furrier, 82 Sassafras
Heyer Laurence, morocco dresser, George bel 4th
Heyl, Blanchard & Co. dry goods, 31 N 2d
Heyl D. S., mer., 40 S Front, h 49 S 13th
Heyl Francis, mer., 139 High, h 130 N 9th
Heyl John, 9 Marshall
Heyl John, jr., brushmr., 273 N 6th.
Heyl John B. mer., h 9 Marshall
Heyl John S., dry goods, 188 N 2d
Heyl Robert, carpenter, St John ab Beaver (K
Heyl T. C. mer. 139 High, h 260 S 4th

Hibberd Geo., seaman, 42 Queen st
Hibberd Susan, gentw., 10th & Brown
Hibberd J. R., livery stable, Goodwill ct
Hibberd Mary, gentw., 128 N 10th
Hibberd Wm., 157 N 12th
Hibbert Henry, carp., Sch 3d n Lombard
Hibbert Mary, dry goods, 4 Cedar ab 11th
Hibbert Robert, weaver, rear G T road ab 5th
Hibbert Septimus, cutler, Front ab Otter (K)
Hibbits Wm., weaver, Carpenter ab 13th
Hibbler, Freese & Son, boots, shoes & caps, 64 N 3d
Hibbler Stuart, mer., 64 N 3d, h 91 Vine
Hibbs Abdon B., carp., Bickham W of Sch 8th
Hibbs Danl. carp. Washington n 2d
Hibbs John, carp., 12th bel Sp. Garden.
Hibbs Joseph G., hardware, 102 N 2nd.
Hibbs S. L. painter, 7 N 8th, h Callowhill ab Sch 8th
Hibbs Wm., grocer, Wood ab 12th
Hibler John, grocer, 56 N 3rd, h 96 N 9th
Hickey Alexander L. trunkmr. 150 Chestnut, h 298 N 7th
Hickey Barthw., stone cut., Barker bel Sch 6th
Hickey Daniel, manuf. 2d ab Jefferson (K)
Hickey James, painter, 72 Chestnut, h 9 Lagrange pl
Hickey James, grocer, 124, & h 126 Locust.
Hickey John, printer, Harmony ab 4th
Hickey John, stone cutter, Vaughan ab Locust
Hickey John, ropema., Crown n Bedford (K)
Hickey Michael, blacksmith, 5 Faries' ct
Hickey Peter, manuf. 2d ab Master (K)
Hickey Thos., tailor, 3 St Stephen's pl
Hickling C., brok., 12 Bank al., h 138 N 10th.
Hickling Geo. M., Pres. City & Co. Ins. Co., h 209 Pine
Hickman & Brother, hardware, 48 High
Hickman Elizabeth, tailoress, 29 Coombe's al
Hickman Fredk., Vicker's ct N of Barker
Hickman George, blacksm., Ashton n Walnut, h 28 Rittenhouse
Hickman Geo. W., & Co., tobacco's., 48½ High
Hickman Harbeson, mer., 48 High
Hickman Isaac, lab. Lancaster bel Wharton
Hickman James, acct., N E Cherry & 12th, h Cherry n Sch 8th.
Hickman John, plasterer, 195 Catharine
Hickman John W., grocer, New Market and Laurel
Hickman Joshua, seaman, 16 Keefe
Hickman N. W., mer., 48 High
Hickman Samuel, shop, hay and feed, R road ab James, h Noble bel Garden
Hickman Wm., chairmr., Jefferson n Sch 6th
Hickman Wm. H., tavern, 2 Decatur
Hickman Wm. J., bricklayer, Marion bel 2d
Hicks Charles, measurer, Green ab 11th
Hicks Cooper, carp., 9th ab Parrish
Hicks Gilbert, carp., Chancellor ab Sch 7th
Hicks Isaac, carp., Front bel Otter (K)
Hicks Isaac, carp. Washington av bel Brown
Hicks John, carpenter, Centre, h 17 Dean.
Hicks John, waiter, 216 S 7th
Hicks John W., boilermr., 2d ab Reed

Hicks Joseph, bricklr., rear 167 Coates
Hicks Phebe, gentw. 189 N 9th
Hicks Phebe, 17 Garden
Hicks Seth S., carpenter, 24 Rittenhouse.
Hicks Wm., tailor, 286 High
Hicks Wm., tailor, 53 Buttonwood
Hicks Wm. D. mer. Montgomery pl
Hicks Willit, carp., 293 N. 7th
Hicks & Worman, fancy goods, 229 Mulberry
Hider John, collector, 17 & h rear 366 N 6th
Hider Samuel, carter, 1 Drinker's al
Hierholzer Jacob, shovelmr., 81 St John
Hieskell Colson, mer. N W 5th & High, h 13 Franklin sq
Hieskell Ferdinand, mer. N W 5th & High, h N W 7th & Pine.
HIESKELL & HOSKINS, drygoods, N W 5th and High
HIESKELL WM. B., att'y & coun. 46 S 6th, h 426 Sassafras
Higbee Charles, waterman, Wood bel Franklin
Higbee Chas., carp., rear 129 Walnut
Higbee Elizabeth, Wood ab Queen (K)
Higbee H., drayman, Goldsmith's ct
Higbee Mary Ann, teacher, Dugan's ct
Higbee Matthias, fisher., Wood ab Queen (K)
Higgens T. W., atty. & coun., 115 S 6th
Higginbottom Mrs. S., Seybold's ct
Higgins Caroline, twister, Crown bel Duke (K)
Higgins Edw., M. D., 238 Callowhill
Higgins Edward J. goldbeater, 95 Christian
Higgins Francis, cordw., 58 P road
Higgins George, Rev., 144 Queen
Higgins John, lab., 10th n Milton
Higgins John, dyer, Raspberry ab Spruce
Higgins John, labourer, Front ab Otter (K)
Higgins Patrick, lab., 106 Plum
Higgins Sarah, Lydia n William
Higgins S. Hale Rev., 150 S Juniper
Higgins Solomon Rev., 592 N 3d
Higgins Stephen F., carver, rear 129 Walnut, h Lombard ab 13th
Higgins Thomas, gent., 26 John, (S)
Higgins Wm. waiter, Eagle ct
Higginson Mary, 507 S 2d (S)
Higginson Wm. blacksmith, Ruddach's ct
Higgs Mahlon, capmr., 6 N 5th, h 9th bel Poplar
Higgs Richard, blacksm., Sch. 3d ab High
Higgs Wm. printer, 513 N 2d
High Abraham G., 399 N 3d
High Margaret, tavern, 121 Vine.
Higham Daniel, machinist, Front ab Greenwich
Higham Henry, blacksmith, 7 Mechanics' ct
Higham Isaac, lab. Brown bel 11th
Higham Wm., drygoods, G. T. road ab Phœnix.
Highgate T. D. barber, 2 N 11th
Highgate Wm., grocer, 42 Currant alley
Highill Adolph, cabinetmr. 251 Cedar
Highland James, brass founder, 6 Howard's ct
Highlands Findley, marble mason, 12th ab Sassafras.
Highlands Findley & Co., marble masons, 12th ab Sassafras
Hight Aaron, brick moulder, 6th bel G T road
Hight Adam Jr., victualler, 221 N 8th.

Hight Amelia, Paschall's al
Hight David, lab., Wilson's ct
Hight Esther, 23 Washington bel 12th
Hight Frederick, victualler, Brown bel Broad
Hight Hen. A., coachmr., 27 Nectarine bel 10th
Hildebrand John, shoemr. 15 Eutaw
Hildebrandt A., baskets, 142 High, h 103 Buttonwood.
Hildeburn John M., mer., 17 N Whfs., h Spruce bel 12th
Hildeburn Joseph H., mer., 72 High, h Spruce ab 11th
HILDEBURN SAMUEL, SON & CO., commers. 17 N Whfs. & 39 N Water
Hildeburn Saml. merch., 17 N Whfs., h Spruce ab 11th
Hildeburn Wm. L. Spruce ab 11th
Hildreth Daniel, dry goods, 229 S 2d
Hile John, hatter, N E 8th and Chestnut, h 41 S 8th
Hiles A. L., coppersmith, 206 Noble
Hiles Martha, sempstress, Oneida place
Hilferty Felix, lab., rear 10th ab Carpenter
Hilge George, artist, Traquair's ct
Hill Abraham, waiter, Centre bel 13th
Hill Adam, distiller, Sch 4th ab Cedar
Hill Adam, shipwright, Bedford n Elm (K)
Hill Adam, fisherman, Cherry ab Queen (K)
Hill Adam, fisherman, Queen ab Warren (K)
Hill Alexander, distiller, Lombard n Sch 6th.
Hill Catharine, washer, 8th bel Lombard
Hill Champion, shoemr., 42 N 2d, h rear 115 Queen (S)
Hill Charles, boat builder, Washington ab 3d
Hill Charles, dyer, Jefferson bel 2d (K)
Hill Charles, bricklayer, 6 Knight's ct.
Hill Charles J., bricklayer, 151 N 5th
Hill & Cline, stoves, 233 N 2d
Hill Daniel, glassblower, Brown ab Cherry (K)
Hill David, Filbert E Sch 8th
Hill Edwin J., painter, 9 Nicholson
Hill Eliza, teacher, Buttonwood ab 12th
Hill Ellen, Cherry ab Queen (K)
Hill Felix, hatter, 18 Catharine.
Hill George, acct., 242 S 11th
Hill George, machinist, 173 Coates
Hill Geo. M., fisherman, Queen ab Cherry (K)
Hill Henry, bootmr. 211 Walnut
Hill Henry, lab., 8 Blackberry al
Hill Henry, lastmr., 180 Callowhill ab Sch. 6th
Hill Jacob, ship carp., Cherry bel Duke (K)
Hill Jacob, caulker, Cherry bel West (K)
Hill James, hatter, 207 Callowhill.
Hill James, cordwainer, 43 N 13th
Hill James, ship carp., Marlborough bel Franklin (K)
Hill James B., cordw., rear 362 N 3d
Hill Jane, 98 N. Front
Hill John, distiller, 129 S 12th.
Hill John, weaver, Phoenix bel Front.
Hill John, ship carp., Marlborough bel Franklin.
Hill John, tavern, 91 S Water
Hill John, brushmr. 5 S 7th, h 45½ N 5th
Hill John, fisherman, Cherry ab Queen (K)
Hill John, barber, Callowhill ab Nixon

Hill John S., tailor, rear Ontario ab Poplar
Hill John T., blacksmith, James & R. road, h 555 Vine
Hill Joseph, buttonmr., Wood bel Sch. 5th
Hill Joseph, bootmaker, 61 S 5th.
Hill Joseph, sea captain, 107 Catharine
Hill Lawrence, carp., Brown ab Cherry (K)
Hill Margaret, 2 Morgan
Hill Marshall, mer., 32 High, h 10 Palmyra sq
Hill Martin, glassbl., Mechanic ct (N L)
Hill Mary, milliner, 151 N 5th.
Hill Mary, rear Bedford bel Broad
Hill Nathan, white washer, 6 Eagle ct
Hill Patrick, shop, 32 St. Mary
Hill Richard, sexton, Ann (F V)
Hill Robert F., undertaker, 144 S 8th
Hill Rowland, chairmr., Parrish ab 8th
Hill R. W., Wallace bel 10th
Hill Samuel, stovemr., 233 N 2d, h 10 West
Hill Samuel, 35 S 10th
Hill Samuel, button cutter, Vine ab Sch 8th
Hill Samuel, shoemr., 6 Knight's ct
Hill Shadrack, trimmings, 136½ S 2d
Hill Thomas, machinist, 419 S Front
Hill Thomas, weaver, Milton ab 10th, (S)
Hill Thomas, mer., 27 S Water, h 31 Pine
Hill Thomas, tavern, S E 9th & Green.
Hill Thompson, brickmr., Fox's ct
Hill Vincent, porter, Caroline place
Hill William, lab., Crown ab Duke (K)
Hill William, victualler, Apple bel George
Hill William, importer needles, 176 S 2d
Hill Wm., fisherman, Dyott's ct (K)
Hill Wm., printer, 16 Olive
Hill Wm., carter, Say
Hill William B., actuary Pa. Co. Ins. on lives, 66 Walnut, h 178 S 9th.
Hill Wm. F. bootmr, 22 Washington av
Hill Wm. H., gent., 362 N 10th
Hill Wm. H., gent., 68 Coates
Hill Wm. T., chairmr., Coates ab 2d, h 219 Marshall
Hillary & Abbot, druggists, 533 High
Hillary Wm., druggist, 533 High
Hillborn Cyrus, mer., 15 Church al, h 339 N 6th
Hillborn & Co., com. mers., 15 Church alley
Hillburn Mary, widow, 513 N 3d
Hillburn Samuel, parchmentmr. Schleisman's al
Hillegas Adam, carp., 4th & Maria
Hillegas Adam, clerk, 66 Apple
Hillegas Chas., segar maker, Jackson ct (N L)
Hillegas Lewis, carp., 13th ab Poplar
Hillegass Wm., mer. 109 Sassafras
Hillen Christian, lab., 6 Branner's al
Hiller Henry, pianomr. 10 Raspberry la
Hilley Bridget, Broad bel Cedar
Hilliard T., carp., 9th bel Ogden
Hillier Joseph, gilder, 82 Mulberry, h 78 Noble
Hillis Robert, moulder, Front ab Reed
Hillman Allen S. carp., Currant al, h 262 S 3d
Hillman Ann M., Haines ab 6th
Hillman Eliakim, cordw., Fraley's alley (K)
Hillman Martha, matron 13th & Willow
Hillman Peter, blacksmith, Green's ct
Hillman Wm. G., turner, Perry bel Phœnix (K)

Hillsee Edward, baker, rear Rose bel William (K)

Hilsee Charles, tailor, 314 N Front

Hilsee George, carp., Nonnater's ct

Hilsee Joel C., tailor, 471 S 2d

Hilsee Joseph, tailor, 141 S Front.

Hilsee William, tailor, 314 N Front.

Hilsman Thomas L., shoemr., Budden's al.

Hilson Francis, rigger, Church ab Prime

Hilt Catharine, 6 Torr's alley

Hilt Geo. G., carter, Front ab Master

Hilt Isaac, cordw. Dungan's av (K)

Hilt John, bricklayer, 5 Madison

Hilt Joseph D., cordw., Pleasant bel 10th

Hilt Lewis, shoemaker, 277 N 7th

Hilt Martin, dealer, R road and Callowhill

Hilt Mattson, book binder, 8 Lodge pl

Hiltman Henry, segarmr., Elizabeth n Wager

Hiltner Sarah, Parrish ab Sch. 7th

Hilton Abraham, polisher, Mackey ab 2d

Hilton G. W., barber, 246 S 3d

Hilton Sarah, Helmuth n Sch 7th

Hilyard Hollingshead, shoemr., 77 N 7the

Himas Saml., umbrellamr, Palmer & Duke (K)

Himas Wm., chairmr., Palmer bel Duke (K)

Himeback Charity, 114 Washington av

Himes Charles, cabinetmr., 5 Garrigues' ct

Himes Mark, lime kilns, Sassafras st. Sch.

Himes Martin, waterman, Lombard W Ashton

Himmelwright C. S., tailor, 126 N 4th

Himmelwright F. W., tailor, 266 N 12th

Himmelwright Philip, drayman, Elizabeth ab Poplar

Himmelwright Rebecca, Seh. 7th bel Vine

Hinchman B. M. sec. Reliance Mutual Ins. Co. S W 5th and Walnut, h 212 Chestnut

Hinchman Charles, tailor, rear 198 Christian

Hinchman Eliza W., teacher, Wood bel 11th

Hinchman Howard, mer., 156 N 9th

Hinchman Isaac, clerk, 9 Scott's ct

Hinchman James jr., grocery, N E 11th and Callowhill

Hinck John, confectioner, 166 Shippen

Hinckle William, teller Western Bank, h Callowhill ab Franklin

Hinckley Robert H., umbrellamr. 321 Vine

Hindermeyer Jos., brass found., 3 Headman's pl

Hindermeyer Michael, shop, 4th bel Franklin

Hindermeyer Michael, carpenter, rear Wood ab Broad

Hindle Edmund, machinist, 28 Chatham, h 15 Tammany ct

Hindle James, machinist, 28 Chatham, h 14 Tammany ct

Hindle & Son, machinists, 28 Chatham

Hindley Joseph, tavern, Front and Laurel

Hindman Edward, saw grinder, 83 Sassafras

Hindman Elizabeth, 91 Buttonwood.

Hindman James, moulder, Sarah bel Bedford

Hindman Steward, 2d ab Jefferson (K)

Hinds Meeker, carp. 16 Hubbel

Hinds Wm. P., gent., 4 Belmont place

Hinecle John, blacksmith, 146 N 13th

Hinecle George, machinist, 5 Rittenhouse

Hines Addison, grocer, Brown and Mintzer

Hines Albert, clerk, 22 Mulberry

Hines And., fisherman, Allen bel Palmer

Hines Chas., oyster house, Maiden ab Beach

Hines Christian, ice, Front ab Greenwich

Hines James C., blacksmith, Church av., h 13th ab R. road

Hines Jas. W., cordw., Washington av bel Brown

Hines John, waiter, Butler's av.

Hines John M., carver, N W 2d and Dock, h 34 Christian

Hines Stephen, glass bl., Allen bel Palmer (K)

Hines William, ship carp., 9 Shield's ct

Hinesley Risdon S., biscuit baker, 36 Bonsall

Hink Peter, confec., 527 N 2d (K)

HINKEL ADAM H., ship chandler, 38 S whfs., h 32 New Market

Hinkle Aaron, saddletree mr., 10 China

Hinkle Adam, sr., victualler, N E Callowhill & Franklin

Hinkle Ann, 151 St. John.

Hinkle Benjamin, jeweller, 44 German

Hinkle Charles, capt., 285 N 6th

Hinkle Charles, collar mr., Melon bel 10th

Hinkle Chas., tobac., Mechanic ab George

Hinkle Henry, coffee roaster, 350 Callowhill

Hinkle Henry, vict., Cherry n Duke (K)

Hinkle Henry, brickmr., Locust, W of Sch 3d

Hinkle Henry, jr., blacksm., 172 N 4th, h Rugan bel Willow

Hinkle Henry W., carp., Wiley's ct

Hinkle John, brickmr., George bel Sch 3d

Hinkle John, vict., 12th and Coates

Hinkle Mary, Mrs., James bel 10th

Hinkle Peter, Elizabeth ab Parrish

HINKLE P. Jr. & CO., grocers, N W Julianna and Callowhill

Hinkle Sarah, rear 161 Christian

Hinkle Sarah, doctress, 26 N 11th

Hinkle Wm., hatter, George W Sch 3d

Hinkle Wm., Torr's al n R road

Hinman D. B., mer., 24 N Front, h S W Pine and 9th

Hinman D. B. & CO., com. mers., 24 N Front

Hinton F. A., hair dresser, 148 Chestnut, h 18 Powell.

Hinton N. B., variety store, 343 High, h 411 Sassafras

Hinzel John, butcher, 9 Kesler's ct

Hiorth Geo., rigger, 38 Union

Hippert John, cordw., 7th ab Poplar

Hipple Anna, milliner, Christian bel 9th

Hipple Anna, milliner, 350 Sassafras.

Hipps Mahlon, stone cutter, rear Ontario above Poplar

Hirschberg Jacob, fruiterer, 145 S 5th

Hirchbirg Ann, 2 Centre

Hirneisen Susan, 46 S 13th

Hirogoyen M., 7 Whittecar ct

Hirsch Isadore, hatter, Apple ab George

Hirschman John, coachmr., Charlotte ab Brown

Hirshfeld & Gumpel, shirt manuf., 101 N 3d

Hirshfeld Louis, mer. 101 N 3d; h 54 George

Hirst Andrew, salesman, 14 North

Hirst Henry B., att'y, 40 S 6th

Hirst John, cooper, 71 St John, h 21½ Duke

Hirst Leon B., atty. at law, 57 Prune, h 4th bel Federal
Hirst Lucas, atty. at law, 64 S 7th
Hirst Mortimer R., atty. at law, 57 Prune, h 4th bel Federal
Hirst Robert R., hatter, h 10 N 13th
Hirst Sarah S., N W Sp Garden and Marshall
Hirst Stephen, cordw., 102 Poplar
Hirst William L., tailor, 63 Mulberry
HIRST WILLIAM L., att'y & coun., 63 S 7th, h Chestnut E Sch 7th
Hirtzel Philip, 30 Dillwyn
Hirzog And., susp. weaver, Cherry n Duke (K)
Hiscuk Mary, 35 Federal
Hislop Eben., tailor, Fisher
Hitchcock Chas., tailor, Queen and Crown (K)
Hite Martha, Bond's ct
Hites Benj., harnessmr., rear Sutherland bel Queen
Hitner George, printer, 49 S Juniper.
Hitzelburger Jacob, cordw., Fisher bel Marriott
Hoag Cornelius, carter, 97 New Market
Hoagland Samuel, coachsmith, Filbert bel 12th, h 126 Filbert
Hoar Wm., shop, 22 Currant al
Hobbs Elwood, stone mason, George & Sch 2d
Hobbs John, seaman, Catharine ab Front
Hobbs Joseph, stone cutter, rear of Sch 3d bel High
Hobensack John N., drugg., N E 2d and Coates
HOBENSACK JOHN N. & G. S., druggists, S E 8th & Coates
Hobson E. Mrs., stationery and fancy goods, 194 Chestnut.
Hobson Francis, carp., R road ab 9th
Hobson George W., mer., 45 High
Hobson James, tobacconist, Callowhill ab Broad
Hobson Jeremiah, shoemr., 141 S 11th
Hobson Sarah, 43 O Y road.
Hobson Thos., M. D., 244 Green
Hobsworth Lewis, shop, 28 Apple
Hocker George, tavern, 1 Franklin pl
Hocker John, jr., druggist, N W 11th & Poplar
Hocker John, sen., stone cutter, 11th & Poplar
Hocker Willis, jeweller, 36 George (S)
Hockerseimer Thos., cabinetmr., 1 Harper's pl
Hockey Hugh, weaver, Mariner
Hockley John, cashier B. N. A., h Sch 8th n Chestnut.
Hockstrasser H., bell hanger, 49 S 8th
Hocter James, lab., 90 George
Hodgdon Mary, widow, 321 Spruce
Hodge H. L., M. D., N W 9th & Walnut.
Hodge John L., mer., 102 S 8th
Hodge Lydia, cook, 22 Portland la
Hodge Richard, ship carpenter, 108 F road.
Hodge Washington, carp., Sarah n Bedford (K)
Hodge Wm., chairmr., Shackamaxon ab Bedford
Hodges Edward, shoemr., rear 14 German
Hodges Henry, carp., Robinson's ct (K)
Hodges John, bosoms & collars, 110 N 2d
Hodges John, moroc. dress., Union ab F road(K)
Hodge John C., carpenter, Adams ab Perry.

Hodges Robert, clerk, 148 Christian
Hodges Wm., machinist, Bickham W of Sch 8th
Hodgkinson Mary, Crown n West
Hodgkinson Robert, blacking manuf., 2 Quarry
Hodgson F. Rev., 162 N 8th
Hodgson Joseph, clerk, Penn ab Maiden
Hodgson William, tailor, Maiden bel Front.
Hodgson William Jr., druggist, N E 6th & Mulberry, h 172 Mulberry.
Hœckley B. F., druggist, Cherry ab 12th
Hœckley Fred. S., mer., 45 N Front h 64 New
Hœckley Jacob F., scrivener, 248 N 3d, h 232 Sassafras
Hœflich Catharine Mrs., 26 Ellen (N L)
Hœflich George, segarmr., 26 Ellen (N L)
Hœfsich John, baker, 112 Dillwyn
Hœffliger Vanentine, b. h., 199 Buttonwood
Hœhling Adolphus A., cabinetmaker, 196 Pine,
Hoenes Philip H., cooper, 17 Dock
Hoesch John, shoemr., 47 New Market
Hœth Charles, mer., 10th ab Brown
Hoff George, bricklay., Francis ab Powell (F V)
Hoff Geo. & Co., capmrs., 20 N 4th
Hoff George, furrier, 20 N 4th, h Crown below Bedford
Hoff John, gent., 340 N 6th.
Hoff John G., shoemr., c Noble & New Market
Hoff Lewis, cooper, Perry bel Master (K)
Hoff M. M., 8th n Wallace
Hoffman Adam, 3 Crown
Hoffman Adam, glassblow., Wood ab Franklin
Hoffman Ann C., Willow ab Franklin
Hoffman Anthony, drayman, 5 Linden ct
Hoffman Baltus, cordw. Rachel bel Laurel
Hoffman Barbara, variety, 98 Coates
Hoffman Caspar, dealer, 18 Parham
Hoffman Charles, shoemr., Duke bel Wood (K)
Hoffman Chas., Globe Mill, Vienna bel Duke(K)
Hoffman C. J. clerk, Washington ab 9th
Hoffman David, att'y & coun., 117 S 5th, h 15 Girard
Hoffman D., Mrs., Wood ab Queen (K)
Hoffman Edward, sparmr., Swanson bel Christian.
Hoffman Francis Rev., Beaver ab 2d (K)
Hoffman Frederick, shop, 30 Paschal's al
Hoffman Frederick, silversmith, 16 Castle
Hoffman & Gaul, sugar refiners, Sassafras and Crown
Hoffman George, lab., Monroe bel Cherry (K)
Hoffman Geo., fisherman, Queen ab Wood (K)
Hoffman Geo. W., brushmr., Ogden ab Sch 8th
Hoffman Jacob, fisherman, Cherry ab Queen(K)
Hoffman Jacob, shoemr., Clinton bel Poplar
Hoffman James, china packer, 34 Julianna
Hoffman James N. spar mr. 4 Powell row
Hoffman John, brushmr., Culvert ab 4th
Hoffman John, stocking manuf., Bridge st, M. Village
Hoffman John, moulder, 12 Jackson's ct
Hoffman John, cordw. rear 41 Duke
Hoffman John, ship carp. Marlboro' bel Bedford
Hoffman John, beer-house, Paschal's al
Hoffman John B., gas fitter, 11 S 6th, h 8 Parket

Hoffman John C. cabinetmr. West & Union
Hoffman John C., tailor, 7 Magnolia
Hoffman John S., lab., Raspberry la
Hoffman John D., china, Elder
Hoffman Joseph, capt., Clay av (K)
Hoffman Margaret, shoe binder, Hanover above Queen
Hoffman Norris J., clerk, Franklin ab Green
Hoffman Philip, dyer, 389 N Front
Hoffman Philip, mariner, 232 Catharine
Hoffman P., beer-house, 200 N 8th
Hoffman Philip J., brewer, 528 N 2d (K)
Hoffman Robert, lab., rear 180 R road
Hoffman Samuel T., mast maker, Whf. below Christian, h 15 Christian.
Hoffman Sebastian, turner, rear 20 Lily al
Hoffman Wilhemine, ready made linen, 38 S 6th
Hoffmaster Mary, gentw., Hoffmaster's ct
Hoffmeister Hannah, hair dresser, 142 N 8th
Hoffnagle Jacob, carp., Otter n F road (K)
Hoffner Charles B., manuf., Powell and Vineyard (F V)
HOFFNER FREDERICK, inn-keeper, Coates and N Market
Hoffner George, pilot, 82 Christian
Hoffner Henry, machinist, 2d ab Edward (K)
Hoffner John D., alderman, office 221½, and h 229 S 6th
Hoffstadt Lewis, barber, 72 Brown
Hoffy A., artist & lithographer, 88 Walnut
Hofheimer Abm., peddler, 3 Northampton ct
Hogan Barcos, porter, 50 Little Oak
Hogan David M., clerk, 108 Chestnut, h 181 S 9th
Hogan James, stationer, 30 N 4th, h 309 Chestnut
Hogan John, lab., Western pl
Hogan J. G., 15 Rittenhouse
Hogan Mary, dressmr., 41 N 12th
Hogan Mary, b. h., 264 High
Hogan M., shoemr., 37 S 8th, h 2 Vaux's ct
Hogan Philip, porter, 2 Allen's ct
Hogan Philip, coachman, John's ct.
HOGAN & THOMPSON, booksellers and stationers, 30 N 4th
HOGAN & THOMPSON, stat'rs., 108 Chestnut
Hogarth Joseph, blacksmith, 14 Dyott's ct (K)
Hogbin John, tailor, 16 High, h 31 Wood
Hoge Thomas H., gent., N E 10th and Pine
Hogeland Eleanor, tailoress, Sp Garden ab 12th
Hogeland E. M., b h, 33 Chester
Hogeland George L., lab., Perry ab Franklin
Hogeland & Myers, planing mill, Christian st wharf
Hogg Alexander, grocer, N E 5th & Christian
Hogg Christ., lab., Mary n Beach
Hogg James, lab. Marlborough and West (K)
Hogg Michael, confectioner, 64 Dock
Hogg Peter, gas fitter, 63 S 13th
Hogg William, manuf. Hanover bel West (K)
Hoguet Francis, cabinetmr. 41 Plum
Hoguet Mary, Buttonwood n 13th
Hohenfels S., dry goods, 272 N 2d.
Holahan Amos, 45 S 10th.

Holahan Jacob, tavern, N W 10th and Locust.
Holahan James, porter, 19 Walnut
Holahan John, blacksmith & coachmr., Shoemaker st, h c 8th & Zane.
Holbert John, brickmr., 186 Marshall
Holbrook Benjamin, 33 Walnut, h 362 S Front
Holbrook Charles N., ex-broker, 47 Chestnut, h 231 S 9th
Holbrook Jacob, lab., 4 Washington pl
Holbrook Wm., bootmr., 47 Callowhill
Holby A. bootmr. 86 N 6th
Holby Jas., stone cutter, rear 123 Race
Holby John, porter, Mark's la
Holby Wm., shoemr., rear 123 Race
Holby Wm. V., paper ruler, 1 Mark's la
Holcomb B. D., printer, 5 Shields' al
Holcomb Martha, Jones' al
Holcombe Charles H., cordw., Mary n F road
Holden Almira, widow of Ezra, 100 N 11th
Holden Ann, washer, Caroline pl
Holden Eli, watchmr., 238 High
Holden Henry, dealer, rear Carpenter ab 8th
Holden Isaac, grocer, West and Marlboro' (K)
Holden Thomas, 139 N 7th n Willow.
Holderman Lewis, butcher, 4th ab George
Holeman Matt., shoes, Marlboro' ab Duke (K)
Holgate Samuel, shoes, 389 S Front
Holiday Diana, spooler, G T road ab 2d
Holladay James, 75 Catharine
Holladay John, 75 Catharine
Holladay Samuel, 75 Catharine
Holland B., carter, Maitland's ct
Holland Charles, coachman, George E Sch 7th
Holland Charles F., paper ruler, 8 Pennsyla. av
Holland Harriet, 328 Walnut
Holland Isaac, lab. 8 Wagner's al
Holland John, lab., Dorothy n Sch 4th
Holland John, weaver, M'Duffie
Holland Martha H., 129 S 9th
HOLLAND NATHANIEL atty. and coun., 10 S 7th
Holland Patrick, lab., 197 N Front
Holland Rachel, Steel's ct
Holland Robert, broker, 79 Dock, h 19 S 13th
Holland Terrence, gardener, 6 Kelly
Holland Thomas, waiter, 6 Lewis' ct
Holland Thomas, lab., Johnston's la ab 4th
Hollaway John T., capmaker, 6th bel G T road
Hollenback B. U., painter, 267 Mulberry, h 9th bel Melon
Hollick Frederick, M. D., 36 Sansom & 105 Chestnut
Hollick John, blacksm., Rose ab Sch 8th
Holliday Jas., weav., Hancock bel Phoenix (K)
Hollifield W. L., dentist, 140 Pine
Hollinger Andrew, capt., 511 S Front
HOLLINGSHEAD B. M., dry goods, 14 N 6th
Hollingshead Chas. F. 505 N 2d, h 291 N 6th
Hollingshead H. H. mer. 2 Chestnut, h 293 N 6th
Hollingshead Joseph M. mer. 43 N Water, h 112 S 3d
Hollingshead Mary & Sarah, bonnets, 14 N 6th
Hollingshead & Zelley, grocers, 505 N 2d

Hollingsworth George, boot black, 90 Gaskill
Hollingsworth Hamilton, weaver, Fitler n 2d
HOLLINGSWORTH HENRY, tavern, Sch 4th & Cedar
Hollingsworth Henry, h Spruce F. Sch. 7th
Hollingsworth James, weaver, Higham's ct
Hollingsworth Matthew, weav., Fetter bel Harrison (K)
Hollingsworth Matthew, weav., 2 Philip st (K)
Hollingsworth Robt. ship carp. Amber ab Phœnix
Hollingsworth R. J. machinist, 70 Tammany
Hollingsworth Samuel L., M. D., 199 Locust
Hollingsworth Thomas C., mer. 18 N 2d, h 143 Dillwyn
Hollingsworth T. G., stock and exchange broker, 53 Walnut, h 336 Chestnut
Hollingsworth Wm. P. dry goods, 120 W High
Hollins James B., chinaware, 346 High.
Hollins John, china ware, 371 High.
Hollinshead Chs. E. mer. 23 N Front, h 56 S 2d
Hollinshead Jas. S. 23 N Front, h 56 S 2d
Hollinshead Wm. atty., 207 N 6th, h Marshall & Green
Hollinshead, Sherrerd & Co. com. mers. 23 N Front
HOLLLINSHEAD & SHERRERD, dry goods, 56 S 2d
Hollis Ann, milliner, 6 S 13th
Hollis Catharine L., 2 Belmont row
Hollis, Caudrae & Co., perfumers, 222 Chestnut
Hollis Chs. J., engraver, 57 S 3d
Hollis Cordelia, Nonnater's ct
Hollis James, waiter, Eagle ct
Hollis John, grocer, S W 7th & Pine
Hollis Pelham L. perfumery, 222 Chestnut
Hollis Peter, lithograph., 43 Spruce
Hollis P. L., mer., 2 Belmont row
Hollis William, 11 Green's ct
Holloway A. mariner, 14 Mead
Holloway Charles, clerk, Catharine ab 3d
Holloway George, lab. Ann (F. V)
Holloway Geo. W. machinist, Front ab Haydock
Holloway Geo. W., confec., 117 G T road (K)
Holloway Thomas, gent. New Market & Ellen
Holloway Wm. machinist, Front ab Haydock
Hollowbush Jacob, books & paper, 23 N Front, h N E 7th & Willow
Hollowbush Wm., baker, Carroll ab 13th
Hollowell James, lab. 8 Rawle
Holly Aaron, lab. Pearl ab 12th
Holman Andrew J. engineer, School bel Franklin (K)
Holme Jas. C., flour & feed, F road & Bedford (K)
Holmes Alex. V., clerk, Marriott ab 5th
Holmes Anna, dry goods, Sassafras n Sch 7th
Holmes Archibald, weav., Benton bel William (K)
Holmes Benjamin F., hair dresser, Queen ab Palmer (K)
Holmes Caroline M. dressmr. Poplar & Rachel
Holmes Charles, weaver, Jackson ct (N L)
Holmes Chas., weaver, Charlotte bel Master (K)

Holmes Edm'd. A., mer., 4 Church al, h Spruce W Sch 8th
Holmes Elizabeth, rear 23 F road
Holmes E. M. Mrs., teacher, 50 S 5th
Holmes George, lab. rear 9 James' st
Holmes George, tailor, Perry bel Phœnix (K)
Holmes Geo. H., lapidist, 5 Burke's al, h 72 S 2d
Holmes Geo. W., teacher of drawg., N W 12th & Filbert
Holmes Glasgow, importer, 6 Chestnut
Holmes Henry, shoemr. 181 S 6th.
Holmes Henry, pa.bro., 87 Shippen.
Holmes & Hubbard, mers., 4 Church al
Holmes James, chandler, 43 Plum.
Holmes James, waiter, 5 Prosperous al
Holmes Jas., boatman, George n Ashton
Holmes Jas., porter, 5 Prosperous
Holmes Jane, dressmr. 646 N 2d
Holmes John, tavern, c Front & Phoenix (K)
Holmes John, mer., h Logan's sq n Sch 5th
Holmes John, weaver, Perry ab Franklin (K)
Holmes John, weaver, F road opp West
Holmes John, jr., bookkeeper, Front and Phoenix (K)
Holmes John, machinist, School ab Rose (K)
Holmes John, M. D. Sch 7th bel Locust
Holmes John C. cordw. 273 S 5th
Holmes Jos., engineer, Coates, (F M)
Holmes Leonard, baker, rear 136 S 9th
Holmes Levi, carter, Milton ab 10th
Holmes Mary, gentw., 14 Franklin
Holmes Philip, waiter, 23 Quince
Holmes Robert, drayman, Dunton ab Otter
Holmes Robert, mariner, 442 S Front.
Holmes Robert, lab., Gebhard & Sassafras
Holmes Robert H., porter, Sch 8th ab Sassafras
Holmes & Rowan, lapidists, 5 Burk al
Holmes Samuel S. carp. 3 Rittenhouse
Holmes Seth C., mer., 13 S Water, h Logan's sq n Sch 5th
Holmes Thos., 456 Callowhill
Holmes Wm., iron founder, Elizabeth ab Poplar
Holmes Wm., waiter, 8 Juniper la
Holmes Wm. cordwainer, Sassafras n Sch 7th
Holser Jacob, rear 217 St John
Holst Charles A., cabt. mr., 11 Parker.
Holstein Ann, tailoress, Ogden ab 10th
Holston Wm. trader, Corn ab Reed
Holt John, cott. spin., Shackamaxon bel F road (K)
Holt Rich., clerk, Mechanic ab George
Holt Richard, grocer, Sch 3d and Harmstead
Holt Saml., machinist, Beach bel Shackamaxon (K)
Holt Samuel, cooper, 5 Shippen
Holt Seth, grocer, 361 N 2d, h Franklin & Green
Holt Stephen, lab., 35 Quince
Holzinger Fredk., baker, Sch 8th & Carlton
Homan & Hughes, undertakers, 332 Sassafras & 126 N 10th
Homan John, undertaker, 332 Sassafras
Home Thomas, carp. 1 Hermitage pl
Homemiller Michl, vict., F road & Marlborough (K)

Homer Benjamin, 406 Coates
Homer B. A. P., dry goods, 146 E Spruce
Homer Henry, brassfounder, 77 Sassafras
Homer James, 92 Callowhill.
Homer Matthias, variety store, 58 S 2d
Homer Timothy, pokt. book manuf. & variety store, 189 Chestnut
Homer Wm., brassfounder, 77 & h 31 Sassafras
Homestead S. tailor, Prime bel 3d
Hone Catharine, 2d ab Edward
Honeywell Elliott, capt., 7th n Washington
Hong Elizabeth, shop, 67 Sassafras
Hood Benjamin, polisher, Sutherland
Hood Eliza A, gentw., 12 Sansom.
Hood James, cordw., Callowhill bel Sch 7th
Hood James, weaver, Lombard ab Sch 4th
Hood John, lab., Sch 7th & Richard
Hood Joseph, cordw., Washington (W P)
Hood Lambert, cordw. Washington (W P)
Hood Matthew, gent., 79 Filbert
Hood Nathaniel, 139 Franklin
Hood Rebecca, milliner, Washington (W P)
Hood Samuel, bootmr. Willow bel 10th
Hood Samuel, mer., N E 5th & High, h 150 N 12th
HOOD SAMUEL, atty. & coun., S E 6th and Walnut
HOOD SAMUEL & CO., mers., N E 5th and High
Hood Saml. H., carter, rear 28 Duke
Hood Thomas, cordwainer, 12 Castle
Hood Wm., painter & glazier, 75 W Callowhill
Hood Wm., cordw., Cherry ab 11th
Hood Wm. P., labourer, 11th ab R road.
Hoodless Thomas, carpenter, S W 10th and Marble
Hook Christ., bricklr., 593 N 3d
Hook Daniel, carp. 648 S 2d
Hook Martha, 288 S 5th
Hook Peter, sawyer, Marriott bel 6th
Hooke Francis, cabinetmaker, 28 N 10th
Hooke Jane, milliner & dress mr., 28 N 10th.
Hooker Benjamin, painter, Flower bel Fitzwater
Hooker C. S., dentist, 330 Vine
Hooker Herman, bookseller and stationer, 16 S 7th
Hookey A. & Son, undertakers, 637 N 2d (K)
Hooley Abm., manuf., 16 Hudson's al, h Stamper's al
Hooley Benjamin, silk spinner, 2 Hudson's al
Hooley B. & A., silk manuf., 16 Hudson's al
Hooley Wm., carp. & cabinetmr., 315 N Front
Hoomsworth Wm., spinner, 205 G T road (K)
Hoone Ellen, Locust n Sch 3d
Hoop John, sugar ref., 4th n George
Hooper Abraham, cordw. Duke ab Cherry (K)
Hooper Emanuel, glover, Maria ab 4th
Hooper Hezekiah, sawyer, rear 7 Lisle
Hooper John, merchant 27 Chestnut, h 313 Mulberry
Hooper John, tailor, 351 N 3d
Hooper Jos., lab., Carpenter ab 8th
Hooper John, porter, 2 Washington ab 11th
Hooper, Larned & Co. com. mers., 27 Chestnut

21

Hoopes Alfred, wheelwright, High n Sch 4th, h M Village
Hoopes Bernard, com. mer., 33 N Front, h Sch 7th ab Spruce
Hoopes David, gent., Washington and Mansion (W P)
Hoopes John, saddler, Sassafras ab Broad
Hoopes John, iron store, Washington (W P)
Hoopes J. R. mer. 411 High, h Coates bel 13th
Hoopes M., saddler, Vine n Sch
Hoopes Penrose R., mer., Crammond (W P)
Hoopes Pierce, lum. mer., 10th and Cedar, h 292 Pine.
Hoopes Thomas P., mer., S W 5th & High.
Hoopes Wm. M., carp., S W Sch 8th & Cherry
HOOPES, WOLFE & BAKER, hardware, S W 5th & High
Hoot Henry, carp. Hutchinson ab Poplar
Hooven Albert, bricklayer, Pearl ab Sch. 8th.
Hooven James, blacksmith, Wood bel Sch 2d
Hooven William, wheelwright, 446 N 4th,
Hoover Adrian, lab. Roney's ct (K)
Hoover Andrew, brickmr., 346 N 5th.
Hoover Anthony, brickmr., Apple ab George
Hoover Anthony, brickmr., Orchard ab George
Hoover Benj., bricklayer, Sch 4th ab Vine
Hoover Catharine, Carlton ab Sch 6th
Hoover Eli, carp., Ellis ab Washington
Hoover Henry, ship carp. 62 M road
Hoover Henry, spinner, Sch Front n Filbert
Hoover Henry F. upholsterer, 44 Commerce, h 7 Chatham
HOOVER JACOB, drover's tavern, Callowhill bel Broad
Hoover Jacob, brickmaker, Gabell's ct
Hoover Jas, waterman, New Market & York ct
Hoover John, lampmr. 16 Poplar
Hoover John, brickmr. Lemon ab 12th
Hoover Samuel, painter, F road bel Oxford, h Oxford bel Front
Hoover Wm., brickmaker, George ab Apple.
Hoovers Wm., shoemr., rear 123 N 5th
Hope Dominick, stone cut., Chestnut n Beach
Hope Jacob, weaver, Hope ab School (K)
Hope John, weaver, Stewart & Catharine
Hope Joseph D., tobacconist, 4th & Walnut
Hope Patrick, lab., High S Sch 2d
Hope Thomas, portrait painter, 345 N 3d
Hopewell G W., clothing, 90 S 2d, h 146 Locust.
Hopkins Allen M. & Co., U. S. refectory, 18 & 20 S 5th
Hopkins Benjamin, coachman, 20 Raspberry
Hopkins David C., mer., Sch 7th ab Locust
Hopkins Edward, cork mer., 35 & h 47 Prune
Hopkins Enoch, carp., Sch 5th ab Mulberry
Hopkins Francis, 6 Sander's ct (K)
Hopkins George, 31 Prosperous al
Hopkins, Gilbert & Co., mers., 64 N 3d
Hopkins Hetty E., milliner, 85 S 8th
Hopkins Howell, atty. & coun., 12 Prune.
Hopkins Jacob, cordwainer, 306 S 10th
HOPKINS JAMES, druggist, N E Broad and Chestnut
Hopkins John, manuf. hosiery, 70 N 4th.

Hopkins John, gent., Chestnut n Broad
Hopkins John C., clerk, 207 Green
Hopkins Joseph, shoes, 67 Buttonwood
Hopkins Joseph, stocking mer. 392 N 4th
Hopkins Joseph, gent., Sch 6th bel Wood
Hopkins Margaret, Hummel's ct
Hopkins Mary C., 48 Dillwyn
Hopkins M., carp., Sch 5th & Wood
Hopkins N., mer., 103 S Front, h Spruce ab Broad
Hopkins Robt., wheelwright, Elizabeth below Poplar
Hopkins Samuel, carp., Washington & Mary (W P)
Hopkins S. Mrs., N E Broad & Chestnut.
Hopkins S. U., clerk, Custom house
Hopkins Thomas, cabinet maker, Emlin's ct & Pegg
Hopkins Thomas, carpenter, Melon ab 13th.
Hopkins Wm., sail mr., 2 Emlen's ct
Hopkinson Francis, clerk Dist. Court U. S., h Chestnut opp. mint.
Hopkinson Oliver, atty. & coun., 65 S 7th, h 159 S 5th
Hopmar John, cordw., Poplar bel 10th
Hoppel John, combmr., Coates bel Broad
Hoppel Kesiah, Poplar ab 8th
Hoppel Sarah, b. h., 17 Linden st (K)
Hopper B. C. watchmr. 60 Dillwyn
Hopper D. G., undertaker, 107 N 5th
Hopper Edward, att'y & coun., 22 N 7th
Hopper James M., carter, Parrish bel 11th
Hopper Jeremiah, carpenter, 12th ab Spruce, h Locust ab Broad
Hopper Joshua, stone cutter, 10th below S Garden
Hopper Levi, sexton, 84 Mulberry
Hopper Mary, gentw., Mint ct
Hopper Offaly, undertaker, Sch 7th n Sassafras
HOPPER SAMUEL M., jeweller, 65 Chestnut
Hopper Wm., dry goods, 289 N 2d
Hoppin Hen., mer., Filbret ab Broad
Hopple John, cordw., P road bel Christian
Hopple William, shoes, M road bel Christian
Hopson Wm. brickmr. Richard
Hopton Lewis, mason, Sch 6th ab Vine
Horan Daniel, 13 Union
Horan Morris, tailor, Ewing's ct
Hore Wm., carp., N W 12th & Tidmarsh.
Hore Wm., carp., Marriott ab 4th
Horey Elizabeth, sewer, M'Bride's ct (K)
Horn Alex. E., acct., 16 S Broad
Horn Alfred Fentham, clerk, 16 Broad n Chestnut
Horn Catharine, 349 Pine
Horn Chas. S., acct., 16 S Broad
Horn David, dry goods, 4th & Poplar
Horn Eliza, huckster, Carroll ab 13th
Horn & Ellis, shoer, tools, rear 71 Race
Horn Henry, S W 10th & Clinton
Horn Henry, weaver, Beach ab Spruce
Horn Henry J. acct. 16 S Broad
Horn Jacob, blacksm., Sch 8th bel Vine

Horn James H., atty. & counsellor, S E 6th & Walnut
Horn Jane, Ellis ab Washington (S G)
Horn Johanna, shop, 30 Small st
Horn John, 16 S Broad
Horn John, druggist, N E 3d and Brown.
Horn Joseph, stonecutter, 410 Poplar
Horn Philip H., druggist, S W 4th and Poplar
Horn Richard J., coachmaker, 16 George
Horn, the Misses, 321 Sassafras
Horn Wm. Henry, instrument mr., Julianna a Callowhill.
Horn W & H., mers., N W 8th and Locust, h S W 10th & Clinton
Hornberger Henry L., hatter, 394 S 5th
Hornberger, Lewis, hatter, Sch 2d ab South
Hornberger Wm., tailor, 315 S 2d.
Hornby Wm. leather & shoe findings, 192 Sassafras
Horne Caroline, Nectarine ab 10th
Horne Cyrus, wax flowers, 81 Tammany
Horne Henry H., gent., 285 Sassafras
Horne I. R. tavern, Washington (W P)
Horne Pearson, hatter, Olive ab 11th
Horne Salome W., Elizabeth ab Poplar
Horne Sermon, stables, 12th & Vine, h 11th & Pearl
Horner Alfred, mer., 145 High, h 287 Spruce
Horner David S., dry goods, S E 12th & Sassafras
Horner Gustavus R. B., M. D., 297 Spruce
Horner H. B., wheelwright, Beaver ab Charlotte
Horner John, cooper, 31 Church al
Horner John, mer., 97 High, h Sch 7th ab Filbert
Horner John, lab., Sch 3d ab Walnut
Horner Joseph, printer, 8 Elfreth al
Horner Joseph, cordw., Freestone pl
Horner Michael, shoemr., 18 Lagrange pl
Horner Richard, drayman, 7 Drinker's al
Horner Richard D., varnisher, 3 Weccacoe
Horner Roger, capt., 66 N road
Horner Samuel, weaver, 137 G T road (K)
Horner Samuel M., grocer, N W 2d & Cedar
Horner Wm. E., M. D., 263 Chestnut.
Hornish Jas., sail mr., Marriott ab 5th
Hornketh Jeremiah, brickmr. School
Hornketh Nicholas, brickmr., Say
Hornor Benjamin, hardware, 6 Commerce, h W Penn sq
Hornor B. C., druggist, 8 Lagrange, h 316 Mulberry
Hornor S. S. dentist, 247 Walnut
Horrocks Henry, engineer, Queen n Vienna (K)
Horsey Jos., bookbind., S E 7th & High, h 23 Green.
Horsfall John, barber, 131 Queen (S)
Horst Diedrich, lab., 4 Lagrange pl
Horstman F., wool dealer, 69 German
Horstmann Sigmund H. mer. 51 N 3d
Horstmann Wm. H., military store, 51 N 3d, h 68 Mulberry.
HORSTMANN WM. H. & SONS, military store. 51 N 3d
Horstmann Wm. J. mer. 51 N 3d, h 166 N 5th

Hort Benjamin S., Allen bel Marlboro' (K)
Hort Herman, susp. weav., Franklin ab 4th (K)
Horter George, dry goods, 288 N 2d
Horter John, jr., provisions, N E 11th & Callowhill, h S E 12th & Graff
Horter J. W., real estate office, 133 Vine.
HORTON DAVIS, Forrest House, High n Sch 6th
Horton Jas., carver, 155 S 9th
Horton James, saw filer, 4 Little Dock.
Horton John, bricklayer, 148 S 4th
Horton Mary, corset mr., 155 S 9th.
Hortor George, 280 High
Hortor John & Son, Allegheny house, 280 High
Hortter Abm. R., druggist, Broad and Coates
Hortz Charles, grain measurer, 103 Queen
Hortz Peter, gent., 270 S 5th.
Horwitz T. B., M. D., 41 S 10th, h 293 Chestnut
Hory Henry, printer, 24 Mintzer
Hosey George, Carleton ab Sch 3d
Hosfield George, bootmr., 343 Callowhill
Hoskin Wm., wheelwt. and blacksm., G T road ab Maiden.
Hoskins Anson, drugs, 122 N 5th
Hoskins A. M., artificial flowers, 7 S 4th, and 48 Mulberry
Hoskins Draper, 7 S 4th
Hoskins E. A. druggist, 412 High, h 135 Filbert
Hoskins Francis, mer., N W 5th & High, h 294 Mulberry
Hoskins & Gleason, druggists, 412 High
Hoskins John, 238 Filbert
Hoskins John, glue mr., 484 N 3d
Hoster George C., carp., Lemon ab 10th
Hot Jacob, tanner, 1 Miller's ct
Hottman Fred., shoemr., Hanover bel Duke (K)
Hotz Charles, vict. Garden bel Buttonwood
Hotz Daniel, gent., 11th and Sp Garden
Hotz Daniel, jr., vict. 11th and Sp Garden
Hotz Peter, vict., S W 11th and Sp Garden
Houck Christian, porter, 274 High
Houck Isaac, cabinetmr., Haas ct
Houck Joseph, machinist, 13th ab Coates
Houck Nathan, carp., 91 G T road
Houck Wm., stone cutter, Rachel ab Poplar
Hougendobler J., b. h., 295 High
Hough Catharine, 17 Coates' al
Hough Eliza, 14 Madison
Hough George, baker, Vienna ab Queen (K)
Hough John, flour, 441 High.
Hough John L., flour, 7 Sargent
Hough Oliver, conveyancer, 91 Walnut, h 8 Union sq
Hough Thos., cab maker, rear 81 Tammany st
Houghton George R., brass founder, 4th above George (N L)
Houghton Luther, brass nailmr., 159 Shippen, h 5th ab Christian
Houghton Michael, lab., Prospect pl
Houlding Maria, 4 Beck (S)
House Samuel, carter, Scott's ct
House Wm., mariner, 5 Burd
House Wm., lampmr., Mulberry n Sch. 7th
Householder A., cabinetmr., 6 Hermitage place

Householder Wm., carp., 2 Gebhard
Housekeeper Benjamin, M. D. Queen ab Cherry (K)
Housekeeper C. H., att'y & coun., 114 S 4th, h Spruce ab 2d
Housekeeper John, tobacconist, 179 Poplar.
Houseman Daniel, butcher, 25 Mary (S)
Houseman James, cordwainer, c Perry & Pine.
Houseman James, ship carp., 37 Clark
Houseman John, butcher, 25 Mary (S)
Houseman John S., carp., Apple bel Franklin
Houseman Richard, shoemr., 487 S Front
Houser Catharine, 5 Fitzwater.
Houser Joseph, paper carrier, 439 N 3d
Houston John, shoemr., Lombard ab Sch. 2d
Houston J. M., Franklin and Wallace
Houston Richard, weaver, 204 Queen
HOUSTON ROBT., boots and shoes, 79 High
HOUSTON & ROBINSON, wool, 66 S Front
Houston W. C., mer., 66 S Front, N E 11th and Pine
HOUSUM P., tavern, 241½ N 3d
Houzelot Daniel, grocer, Marlboro' & Allen (K)
Hovell Richard, cordw., Loud st
Hover John, plasterer, 3d bel Wharton
Hover Joseph E., ink manufactory, 87 N Third
Hovey Eliza, milliner, Sch. 7th ab Sassafras
Hovey Ira, cordw., Olive bel 12th
How Benjamin, lab., Lyden's ct
How George, shoemaker, 132 N 13th.
How Jacob, boat build., Sch. Front ab Mulberry
How Jane, b. h., N W Callowhill and Dillwyn
How John, cordw., Filbert W Sch 4th
How Joseph, 5 Flower
How Margaretta F., Noble ab Franklin
How Robert, tanner, Sch. Front ab Mulberry
Howard Ann, 206 Locust
Howard A. & E., stockmrs., 18 S 8th
Howard Benj., lab., Bedford ab 7th
Howard Daniel, classical teacher, 20 Jacoby.
Howard Daniel, blacksm., Carleton ab Sch 6th
Howard David, rigger, 21 Union (S)
Howard & Davis, blacksmiths, Broad and Vine
Howard Edward, lab., Bedford ab 6th
Howard Edward, sea capt., Federal ab 5th
Howard Eliza, 534½ Chestnut
Howard & Fulton, wheelwr. and blackksmiths, 5 Hunter
Howard George, brushmr., N W Catharine and Morris
Howard George, machinist, Broad & Paper al
Howard James, livery stable, 5 Raspberry
Howard Jas. T., blksm. 5 Mary's ct, h 5 Hunter
Howard James W. bricklayer, 9 S 5th
Howard John, shot manuf. 27 Union (S)
Howard John, finding store, 78 S 4th
Howard John G., oak coopers, 6 Rogers' ct
Howard Matilda, T., teacher, 106 Union.
Howard O. G., agent, 183 Callowhill ab Sch 6th
Howard Patrick, lab., Beach bel Chestnut
Howard Peter, lab., Eagle ct.
HOWARD P. R. & CO., stock and exchange brokers, N W 3d and Walnut
Howard Robert, 7 Middle alley
Howard Sarah, High W. of Sch. 7th

Howard Susan, dressmr., Rutter's ct
Howard Walter, 364 E. Cedar
Howard Wm., 30 John, (S)
Howard Wm., porter, Broad and Paper alley
Howard Wm. H., machinist, Broad and Paper alley, h 353 Cherry.
Howard Wm. H & Son, machinist, Broad and Paper al
Howcraft Henry, plasterer, 2 Whitaker's ct.
Howe De Wolfe M. A., Rev., Broad ab Spruce
Howe Frances, 8th bel Coates
Howe Henrietta, b. h., 96 N 5th
Howe John, grocer, N W 2d & Lombard, h 236 S Front
Howe Wm., bootmaker, 27 N 9th
Howell Albert G., seaman, 16 Filbert
Howell Arthur H., mer., 88 Chestnut
Howell Bertimus, 465 Chestnut
HOWELL & BROTHERS, paper hangings, 116 Chestnut
Howell Caleb, mer., 99 High, h 300 N 3d
Howell Charles, carp., Dunton ab Otter (K)
Howell Daniel, roller, Reed ab Front
Howell David, roller, Reed ab Front
Howell Deborah, 150 S 9th.
Howell Eleanor, 20 Cherry.
Howell Eli, omn. driv., Llweyln's ct (K)
Howell Eli, moulder, Reakirt's ct (K)
Howell Eliza, b. h., 29 Mulberry.
Howell Eliza H., confectioner, 147 N 2d.
Howell Elizabeth, b. h., 9th ab Washington
Howell Elizabeth, shop, Wood ab Sch 6th
Howell Elizabeth, washer, Liberty ct
Howell E. B., milliner & dressmr., 387 Sassafras
Howell Frances, Wood ab 10th.
Howell George, lab., 160 Queen
Howell George, mer., 116 Chestnut, h 51 Pine
Howell George G., collector, S W Rugan and Willow
Howell George M., hatter, 4th ab Green
Howell Henry C., mer., 165 High, h Noble bel 8th
Howell Isaac, lab., rear 23 Tammany
Howell James, gent., 302 N 3d.
Howell John A., mer., 116 Chestnut, h Sch. 5th bel George.
Howell John C., blacksmith, 8 Juniper alley
Howell John C., painter, 12 Lagrange.
Howell Jonas, moulder, Buttonwood ab 13th
Howell Joseph, mer. 88 Chestnut, h 217 Spruce
Howell J. & Co., hides & leather, 88 Chestnut,
Howell Lemuel, cordw., 123 New Market
Howell Lewis, blacksm., 13th ab Wallace
Howell Louisa, furnishing store, 93 Chestnut
Howell Mary P., Blackhorse alley
Howell Matilda, washer, 5 Providence ct
Howell Matthias, blacksmith, Melon bel 13th
Howell Phebe, Mrs. 121 Noble
Howell Richard, oysters, 6 Locust.
Howell Richard, cordwainer, 19 Charlotte
Howell Richard G., carp., Dunton bel Franklin
Howell Richard L., deputy collector, custom-house, h Filbert & Sch 7th.
Howell Robert, hatter, 78 S 3rd, h 10th bel Cedar

Howell R., mer, 88 Chestnut
Howell Sarah, 10 Lagrange pl
Howell & Smith, blacksmiths, 8 Juniper alley
Howell S. Mrs., b h, 293 Chestnut
Howell Wm., rear Hanover bel Franklin (K)
Howell Wm. H., mer., 207 S 9th
Howell Wm. H., mer., 20 N 4th, h 8th bel Pine
Howell Wm. T., mer., 181 High, h 319 Sassafras
Howell William T. & Co., hardware, 181 High.
Howell Zachariah, carpenter, 522 N Front
Howell Z. C., mer., 116 Chestnut, h Sch 5th bel George
Howett Danl., blacksm., 6 Pearl bel Sch 7th
Howey Benj., blacksm., 18 Catharine
Howey Isaac, tobacconist, 375 S Front, h 14 Beck pl
Howey Hillman, seaman, S W Almond & Swanson
Howley Patrick, iron store, South bel Pine
Howorth Gershom, furn., 172 Sassafras
Howshall James, gent., 4 Cypress
Howshall John, porter, 4 Cypress
Hoxsie S. K., stone cutter, Sch. 2d & Chestnut, h Chestnut n Sch 2d
Hoy Francis, botanic Dr., 9th ab Ogden
Hoy James Jr., mer., 11 S Water, h 4 Clinton sq
Hoy John, painter, Beach bel Chestnut
Hoy Mrs. R., milliner, F. road ab Bedford (K)
Hoy Thomas, spooler, Wistar's ct
HOY & WHITE, grocers, 11 S Water
Hoyland Wm., gent., 172 Shippen
Hoyle Michael, lab., Pearl ab Sch. 8th
Hoyt Daniel, engineer, 13th ab Poplar
HOYT F. A., boys' clothing, 264 Chestnut, h 7 Jefferson row
Hoyt John, gent., 523 Chestnut
Hoyt P. J., carp., Olive bel 13th
Hubbard Charles, painter, 62 N 10th, h 11th bel Green.
Hubbard John, plasterer, Wood ab Sch 6th.
Hubbard J. F., tailor, Ann ab Sch. 6th
Hubbard Wm., bricklayer, Carlton n Sch 3d
Hubbard Wm., grave digger, Wood ab Sch 6th
Hubbard Willis, mer., 4 Church al, h 31 Mulberry
Hubeli Jacob, hotel, N W O. Y. road and Green
Hubbell Caroline, dressmr. 315 S 2d
Hubbell F. W., att'y & coun., 92 S 4th
Hubbell H., att'y & coun., 115 S 6th, h 10th ab Shippen.
Hubbell Saml., carpenter, 79 M road.
Hubbell Wm. W., atty. and coun., 73 S 4th
Hubbert Benjamin, cordw., 56 Laurel
Hubbert Elizabeth, matron, 2d ab Phœnix (K)
Hubbert John, drayman, Hanover ab West
Hubbert John, starch manuf., 2d ab Oxford (K)
Hubbert John A., starch manufr. F road bel Norris
Hubbert Wm. H., collector, 12 York ct.
Hubbert Wm. T., starch manuf., Phoenix below Hancock
Hubens Andrew, distiller, 617 N 3d
Huber David F., boot crimper, 405 S 2d
Huber H. Jr., cutlery manf., 2 N 5th and R road & Sch 8th, h 7 Morgan.

Huber Jacob, grocer, F road bel Bedford
HUBER JAMES S., conveyancer, 145 Walnut
Huber John, baker, Barker W. of Sch. 6th
Huber John, tailor, 10 Scott's ct
Huber Rudolph, driver, 9th bel Coates
Huber Tobias, refectory, 16 S 6th, h 182 Vine
Hubert Richard, lab., Fox ct
Hubert Solomon, lab., 75 George
HUBLEY JOHN A., Indian Queen, 15 S 4th
Hublitz Francis, shoemr., rear 116 Dillwyn
Huchins Edwin, carp., Centre ab Brown
Huckel Benj., druggist, S E 5th and Lombard
Huckel F. & Sons, chair makers, S E 5th and Lombard.
Huckel Jacob, dentist, 16 Lombard.
Huckel Joseph J. dry goods, S E O Y road and Green
Huckerby George,.provison store, S E 6th and Pine
HUDDELL GEORGE.H., rail road agent, S E 11th & High, h 7 N 11th
Huddell Martha, wid. of Joseph, 316 S Front
Huddell Robert, commis. mercht., 5 Dock, h 19 Penn
Huddell Washington A. mer., 80 Christian
Hudders John R., carpenter, 22 Franklin place, h 34 Wood.
Huddleston Caroline A., milliner, 172 Chestnut
Huddy Benjamin F., distiller, N E Willow and O Y road, h 55 O Y road
HUDDY BENJ. F. & BROTHER, wines, &c., N E O. Y. road and Willow
Huddy Henry, distiller, N E Willow and O Y road
Huddy William M. artist, N E 9th & Wallace
Hudson George, painter, 13 M road
Hudson James, alderman, Woodland (W P)
Hudson John, grocer, Jones W Sch. 5th.
Hudson John, carpet manuf. Marlborough ab Franklin
Hudson John, printer, 294 S 5th
Hudson John, 10th bel Sp. Garden
Hudson Joseph, lab. rear Jackson (S G)
Hudson Joseph, weaver, Jefferson ab Front (K)
Hudson Matthias, lab., rear 380 S 2d
Hudson Philip, dyer, Jones W Sch 6th
Hudson Robert, S E Green and Franklin
Hudson Robert M., carpenter, Sch. 8th ab Parrish, h Poplar ab 13th
Hudson Saml., hatter, 57 N 6th, h Noble ab 8th
Hudson Thomas, agent, Cherry n Sch. 6th
Hudson Thos., carp., Poplar bel 9th
Hudson Wm. paper carrier, Lewis E Sch 6th
Hudson Wm. B., segarmr., Jefferson ab Sch 6th
Hudspeth Wm., cordw., Culvert ab 3d
Huesman Augustus, tailor, Penn av
Huestis Joseph, brushmr., 16 Mayland
Huet Flavian, carp., 5 Herriges' ct
Huet Langolf, doctor, 74 Spruce
Huey Henry, Front bel Greenwich
Huey James, tailor, 492 Coates
Huey John, shoemr., Jones W Sch 5th
Huey Samuel C. salesman, 13th bel Melon
Huey Spencer, morocco dress., 60 New Market

Huff David, lab., 11 W Cedar
Huff & Husted, boot & shoemanuf., 137 High
Huff Job, cordw., St. John bel George
Huff John, shoe manuf., 137 High, h 155 N 13th.
Huff Joseph, bricklayer, 14 Helmuth st
Huff Michael, cordw. rear Mechanic ab George
Huff Solomon, carp., 12th bel Coates
Huffman Wm., carter, Jefferson n Sch 6th
Huffnagle Adam, baker, 1 Washington ct
Huffnagle Casper, sugar boiler, rear Kessler's al
Huffsey Samuel, glass blow., Wood ab Franklin (K)
Huffsinger Elias, cordw., 39 Green
Hufnal Adam, paper & rags, High ab Atherton
Hufnal Benjamin, paper manuf., 201 N 3d
Hufty Geo. M., machinist, Green ab 11th
Hufty Joseph, engraver, 23 S 4th, h 13th ab Wallace
Hufty Saml., engraver, 95½ Walnut, h 203 S 9th
Hugg Charles, cordw., 332 S 2d
Hugg Isaac, tailor, rear 324 S 5th
Hugg Mary, shop, 70 Almond
Hugg Wm., rigger, Franklin ab Shackamaxon
Huggs Brazillai, porter, 95 Bedford
Huggs Isaiah, lab., Carpenter bel 9th
Huggs Wm., waiter, 4 Flytax al
Hughes Albert, plumber, 32 N 12th, h 17 Montgomery
Hughes Alexander, paper boxmr., 44 Prune, h Swarthmore pl
Hughes Amer, gent., 69 Christian
Hughes Amos P., piano fortemr., 13 E North
Hughes Ann, gentw., 8 M road
Hughes Ann, washer, 30 Burd's ct.
Hughes Ann, gentw., 25 M road
Hughes Ann, rear 277 Callowhill
Hughes Arthur, carp., Loud ab 9th
Hughes Bernard, lab., 2 Ulrich's row n 2d (K)
Hughes Catharine, shop, 215 Shippen
Hughes Charles, lab., Drinker's ct.
Hughes Charles D. 101 N 13th
Hughes Chas. L., grocer, S E 2d and Mulberry, h 260 S Front
Hughes Clement, grazier, 469 S 2d
Hughes Danl. painter, Shackamaxon bel Franklin
Hughes Deborah A., milliner 446 Vine
Hughes Edward, dyer, Chestnut n Beach
Hughes Edward, dealer, 25 Walnut
Hughes Edward, waterman, 5 Flickwir's ct
Hughes Edward Al undertaker, 102 N 8th
Hughes Edward D., grazier, 464 S 2d
Hughes Felix, weaver, Fitler bel Harrison (K)
Hughes Francis, weaver, 10th bel Christian
Hughes Francis, machin., Sch 7th ab Sassafras
Hughes George, carter, rear 3 Gray's al
Hughes George, tailor, 162 Shippen
Hughes Hannah, shop, Allen and Fraley's al
Hughes Henry, tavern, 233 S 6th
Hughes Jas. carp. Ontario ab Poplar
Hughes Jas., plumber, 177 N 4th, h 56 Dillwyn
Hughes James, 152 S 10th
Hughes James, teacher, 89 N 9th
Hughes John, rag dealer, 412 High

Hughes John, cordw., Brown ab Cherry
Hughes John, grocer, 172 Locust
Hughes John, 158 Wood.
Hughes John, leather manuf., 240 S 4th.
Hughes John, weaver, Franklin ab Front (K)
Hughes John, lab., Filbert ab Sch 4th
Hughes John, tailor, 88 S 5th, h Callowhill bel 10th
Hughes John, baker, 3 Blunston's av
Hughes John C., oyster house, F road ab Maiden
Hughes John M., nautical store, 130 S Front
Hughes Jos., captain, 20 Prime
HUGHES JOSEPH B., mer., 6 N 5th, h Vine E Sch 8th
Hughes Josiah, cordw., Brown bel 10th
Hughes Matthew, waiter, Juniper bel Walnut
Hughes Michael, labourer, rear Carlton bel Sch 6th
Hughes Owen, lab., Jones n Sch 4th
Hughes Owen, lab., Carpenter ab 7th
Hughes Patrick, lab., Brinton bel 13th
Hughes Patrick, lab., Fitzwater ab Broad
Hughes Richard, weav., Palmer ab Duke (K)
Hughes S. B. Mrs., b h, N W 5th & Prune
Hughes Terrence, lab., Glenats' ct (K)
Hughes Thomas, lab., Nixon bel Callowhill
Hughes Wm. barber, 58 N 6th
Hughes Wm., undertaker & ven. blind manuf., 102 N 8th, h 93 N 10th
Hughes William, weaver, Shippen bel Broad.
Hughes William, tavern, Lancaster turnpike, (W P)
Hughes William F. flour and feed, N road & 2d, h 479 S 2d.
Hughes W. W. coppersm., 712 F. Lombard
Huhn Charles, brickmaker, cor 10th & Melon (S G)
Huhn Daniel, grocer, N W 7th & Lombard
Huhn George, M. D., 182 R road
Huhn Henry, tailor, 59 N 2d
Huhn John D., brickmaker, 533 High
Huhn John R., brickmr., Bedford ab 13th
Huhn Julianna, trimmings, 471 Chestnut
Huley John, lab., 70 Christian
Hulfish David, bootmaker, rear Brooke bel Brown
Hulfish David, bootmr., Hazel ab 11th
Hulfish Ewen E. tailor, 81 N 6th
Hulfish George W., tobacconist, 33 Brown
Hulings Joel, wheelwright, 4 Clark (S)
Hulings John, bookbinder, 4th ab Wharton
Hulings Michael, paper stainer, 44 Pegg
Hull Anna, wid. of Commodore, 537 Chestnut
Hull Elias, hair cutter, 47 Chestnut
Hull George, waiter, Eagle ct
Hull John, baker, Spruce ab Sch. Front.
Hull Thos., clerk, 473 N 5th
Hulme Thomas, 325 Walnut.
Hulseman B. H., leather dealer, 34 Queen

Humburg Peter, druggist, S W 9th & Callowhill
Hume Wm. lab. Walnut E Sch 3d
Hume Wm., brass founder, 2 Wilson
Humelback Philip, pedler, 5 Fetter la
Humes George, blockmaker, Penn ab Marsh, h Maiden bel Beach
Humes Harriet, 48 S 6th
Humes James, labourer, Sycamore ab Spruce.
Humes Jane, Lewis E Sch 6th
Humes Murtha, moroc. dress., 8 Northampton ct
Humes Robert, weaver, 42 W Cedar
Humes Sarah Jane, 25 N road
Humes Thos., morocco dresser, 19 W Cedar
Humes Thomas, cordw., Callowhill bel Sch 2d
Humes Thomas, lab. Korndaffer's ct
Humes William M., paints & varnish, N W New Market & Brown.
Hummel Christopher, carp., Clinton ab Franklin
HUMMEL JACOB, moroc. & leather, S S 3d, h 529 N 3d
Hummel Jacob, brassfounder, 102 Coates
Hummel Matthias, cordw., 118 New Market
Hummell Wendel, leather dresser, 5 Beaver
Humphrey Daniel, mastmr., Queen bel Marlborough
Humphrey Wm., butcher, Carlton & 13th
Humphreys Charles, forw. & com. mer., rear 147 High, h 369 Walnut
Humphreys Charles, hatter, 220 N 3d
Humphreys Daniel, tailor, Buist ct
Humphreys Elizabeth, Cherry ab Duke (K)
Humphreys Francis, engraver, 71 Chestnut
Humphreys Jacob, ship carp. Cherry ab Queen (K)
Humphreys James, ship carp. Vienna ab Queen (K)
Humphreys James, ropemr. Washington ab 13th
Humphreys John, bricklayer, 280 Wood
Humphreys Mary, 71 Franklin
Humphreys Solomon, clerk, Park ab Walnut (W P)
Humphreys S., mer., 5 Walnut, h 222 Mulberry
Humphreys Thos., Bedford bel Broad
Humphreys William, boot maker, 57 S 5th
Humphreys Wm. S. collector, Park ab Walnut (W P)
Humphreys Wm. W., clerk, 292 Green
Humphries John T., distiller, Vine n 13th
Humphries Joseph, tailor, 166 S 3d
Humphries Mary, dressmr., 166 S 3d
Hundreth, Eakins & Co., People's Works, Front & Franklin (K)
Huneker Elizabeth, b h, Brown & Jones' al
Huneker Francis waterman, 10 Mechanic's ct
Huneker Francis, gardener, rear 3 Wall st
Huneker John, house & sign painter, 77 Mulberry, h 56 Brown

Hunneker & Brant, painters, 77 Mulberry
Hunsberger Christian S., tailor, rear 11 Mark's la
Hunsberger John, trader, 9th bel Coates
Hunsecker Abraham, mer. Brown bel Broad
Hunssbery John, gent., 69 Noble
Hunsworth John, mould. Front ab Franklin (K)
Hunt Benjamin, dry goods, 304 Green
Hunt Caleb, 252 N 5th
Hunt Caleb S., bookseller, 44 N 4th, h 252 N 5th
Hunt Caroline, tailoress, 7 Sch av
Hunt Charles, shoemr., 11th bel Cedar
Hunt C. J., boots & shoes, 107 W High
Hunt George, lab., G T road opp 5th
Hunt Humphrey, cabinetmr., 36 Perry
Hunt Israel, tailor, Higgins's ct
Hunt James, vict., S E 6th & Buttonwood
Hunt James, hats and caps, 346 N 2d, h 286 N 7th
Hunt John, oysterman, P road ab Carpenter
Hunt John, hatter, 11 M road
Hunt John, vict., Craig's ct (K)
Hunt John, ropemr., 7 Hamilton pl
Hunt Joseph, gent., 107 W High
Hunt M., clothing, 185 Shippen
Hunt Philip, stone cutter, Sch. 3rd & High, h George ab Sch. 3d
Hunt Robt., pianofortemanuf., Brown bel Broad
Hunt Samuel, clothing, 246 Cedar
Hunt Sarah, gentw., Sumner ab Sch 7th
Hunt Sarah, gentw., 121 Walnut
Hunt Thomas, manuf. of iron, Sch 6th below George
Hunt Thomas, cabinet maker, 109 N Front,
Hunt Uriah, stationer, 44 N 4th, h 129 O Y road
Hunt Uriah & Son, booksellers, 44 N 4th
HUNT W. P., Mansion house, 122½ S 3d
Hunter Abm., grocer, N E 5th and Green, h 181 Coates
Hunter Ahab, carp., Duke ab Cherry (K)
Hunter Albert G., organ builder, 41 Chester
Hunter Amelia, 8th ab Christian
Hunter Andrew, grocer, Shippen la & Shippen
Hunter Benj., fisherman, 3d bel Poplar
Hunter Brown, blacksm., Amber ab Phœnix (K)
Hunter Cath., 10 Lebanon
Hunter Charles, livery stable, George ab 8th
Hunter David, lab., Helmuth n Sch. 6th
Hunter David, tailor, 27 Farmer
Hunter David, stone cutter, 5 Demery's ct
Hunter David, lab., 11 Quince
Hunter Eliza C., milliner, Sch 3d & Spruce
Hunter Eliza E. dressmr., 97 N 9th
Hunter Esther, widow, 12 North
Hunter Frederick S., mer., 193 High
Hunter George, lab., 263 N Front
Hunter George, lab., Bedford bel Union (K)
Hunter Geo W., moulder, G T road bel 6th (K)
Hunter George W., Mulberry n Sch 7th
Hunter Isaac, cabmr., 5 Allen (K)
Hunter James, watchman, 53 Perry
Hunter James, carter, Richard
Hunter James, gent., 478 S 4th
Hunter James, 345 Walnut
Hunter James W., cabinetmr., 135 S 2d

Hunter John, plasterer, 334 Pine.
Hunter John, ropemr., rear Queen ab Palmer (K)
Hunter John C., gasfitter, 14 S 8th, h Pine ab Juniper
Hunter John C., grocer, N E 8th & Shippen
Hunter John R., gent., 386 Vine
Hunter Mary, Lewis ab Poplar
Hunter Mary, shop, Bedford ab 6th
Hunter Mary Ann, Rush's ct
Hunter Rebecca, dressmaker, State n Sch. 8th
Hunter Samuel, manuf., Pine n Sch.
Hunter Samuel, dentist, Green and 8th
Hunter Samuel, lab., Kinley's ct
Hunter Samuel, lab., Lombard n Sch Front and William (K)
Hunter S. V. R., dry goods, 28 S 2d
Hunter Wm., M. D., 27 S Sch 6th
Hunter William, cordw., Callowhill ab Sch 8th
Hunter William, lab., Lombard n Sch 7th.
Hunter Wm., lab., Walnut n Sch 3d
Hunter Wm., morocco dresser, 33 N 3d, h Edward n William (K)
Hunter William A., tailor, 75 N 6th.
Hunter Wm. C., 150 S 6th
Hunter Wm. C., tailor, Clymer ab 6th
Hunter Wm. M., Capt. U. S. N., Mulberry n Sch 7th
Hunterson Adam, ropemr., 2 S 9th
Hunterson Henry, tavern, S W 11th & Cedar
Hunterson John, shoemr., 195 N 10th
Hunterson John, jr., 195 N 10th
Huntington Thomas, broker, 10th bel Cedar
Huntley John, book binder, 12½ Minor, h Brown ab 10th
Huntley Susan, rear 27 Cresson's al
Huntly Robert, blacksmith, 10th bel Fitzwater.
Huntsworth Anne, b h, Front bel Franklin
Huntzigker Danl., tobac., Poplar ab 10th
Hupfeld C. F., prof. music, 12 S 9th, h 49 Filbert.
Hupfeld C. F. jr., music store, 12 S 9th
Hupfeld C. F. & Son, music store, 12 S 9th
Huplet Henry, cabinetmr., Franklin ab Hanover (K)
Huplits Wm., cordw., 23 Charlotte
Huquenell Elizabeth, 29 Filbert
Hurbut Frances, Korndaffer's ct
Hurlbut Wm., 22 Logan's sq
Hurlburt Ebenezer, carter, China bel 2d
Hurley Aaron A., agent, 218 Spruce
Hurley George, confect., 608 S 2d
Hurley Margaret, b. h., 154 N Water
Hurley Michael, weaver, 5 Pratt's ct.
Hurley Patrick, bootmr., 100 Apple
Hurley Timothy, manf., McDuffy n Sch 2d
Hurley Wm., coachman, rear 122 N 4th
Hurlick William, collector, 3 Short ct.
Hurlock Wm., blacksmith, rear Elk (K)
Hurst Charles, tailor, 74 George
HURST EDW., att'y & notary public, 6 Library, h S E 6th and Prune
Hurst Eli, com. mer., 26 Lombard
Hurst Hannah, 210 Shippen.
Hurst Jacob, cordwr., G T road bel Jefferson

Hurst John, carp., Loud bel 10th
Hurst Joseph G., tailor, 60 Garden
Hurst Wm., shoemr., 26 Lombard
Hurst Wm., carp., Cedar ab 11th
Hurst Wm., shoemr., Queen bet 4th & 5th
Hurstman Wm., gunsm., Mechanic bel George
Hurtmeyer Jos., weaver, Duke bel Wood (K)
Hurtt James H., ven. blind mr., Queen & Ross' court (K)
Husbach Richd., cloth weav., Front bel Franklin (K)
Husband George, carpenter, Sch 5th below Spruce
Husband J. J., jr., architect, 128 Mulberry
HUSBAND THOMAS, J., druggist, N E 3d & Spruce
Husbands Clement M., 6 N Sch 6th
Husbands J. L., conveyancer, 141 Walnut, h 34 S Sch 8th
Husbands V., lab., Hank's ct
Huss John, seaman, 239 S Front
Husselbock John, tinsmith, Charlotte ab Culvert
Hussey Margaret, shop, 20 Almond
Husted Dayton, shoc mer., 137 High, h 206 N Front
Husted Henry, waterman, Paul bel 7th
Husted Jonathan, 6 Rogers' ct
Husted Samuel, shoemr., West ab Cherry (K)
Husted Webster, bootmr., Perkenpine's ct
Husted Wm., mariner, Front ab Washington
Huston Alexander, carpenter, 7 Marion.
Huston Charles, M. D., 27 S 10th
Huston Edmond, cab. mr., 109 Melon
Huston Eliza, gentw., 122 N 9th.
Huston Elizabeth, 108 Chestnut
Huston Elizabeth, Sav ab Sch 8th
Huston John, dyer, Front bel Phoenix (K)
Huston Joshua, waiter, 24 Currant al
Huston Robt., blacksmith, Prospect al
HUSTON R. M., M. D., 1 Girard.
Huston Samuel, mer., 33 Church al
Huston Seth C., M. D., Sch 5th n Cherry
Hutchings Samuel, umbrella mr., 5 Jenning's row
Hutchings Wm., cordw., 4 Clair
Hutchins Daniel, waiter, Rose al (C)
Hutchins James, waiter, 4 Little Pine
Hutchins John, stove fin., Poplar bel 6th
Hutchins Jos., spinner, Cadwalader ab Franklin
Hutchins Rebecca, 300 St John
Hutchinson Ann, 9 Providence ct
Hutchinson Benjamin, atty. and qoun., 648 N 2d
Hutchinson Ben. P., stock broker, 2 Merchants' Exchange, h S W Spruce and Quince
Hutchinson Charles, coffee roaster, 61 Sassafras
Hutchinson Charlotte, 6th ab Poplar
Hutchinson Darius, carter, 3 Washington
Hutchinson D. L., broker, 5 S 3d, h 388 Mulberry ab 15th
Hutchinson Elijah, waiter, 71 George
Hutchinson Enoch R., mer., 143 High
Hutchinson George, lab., 9 Mechanic (F M)
Hutchinson Hugh, carp., 170 Spruce

Hutchinson I. Pemberton, gent., 366 Spruce
Hutchinson Jacob, varnisher, 12th bel Green
Hutchinson James, measurer, 58 S 12th.
Hutchinson James, blacksm., Queen bel Palmer (K)
Hutchinson James H., inspector, 52 S 12th
Hutchinson John, milkman, (M V.)
Hutchinson John, carter, 6 Juniper la.
Hutchinson John, shoemr., 12 Little Water
Hutchinson John, dyer, 2 Mechanic (F M)
Hutchinson Joseph, saddler, Front ab Phœnix
Hutchinson Joseph, carpenter, rear 10th n Shippen, h 225 S 9th
Hutchinson J. Pemberton, jr., mer., 10th below Fitzwater
Hutchinson Margaret, 7th and Orange.
Hutchinson Mary, 110½ Filbert
Hutchinson M. P., M. D., 423 Sassafras
Hutchinson Pearson, grocer, Linden and Green
Hutchinson Randal, atty., 10th bel Fitzwater.
Hutchinson Robert, currier, 7 N 5th, h 146 S Juniper
Hutchinson Samuel H., gent., 5th & Haverford, M Village
Hutchinson Sarah, confect., Lombard bel 13th
Hutchinson Thos., carp., Sycamore, h 146 S 7th
Hutchinson Thos., agt., Washington bel 10th
Hutchinson William, mason, 237 Wood.
Hutchinson William, cabinet maker, Marshall & Brown
Hutchinson Wm., mariner, 397 S 4th
Hutchinson Wm., carter, Woodland (W P)
Hutchison John, drayman, 6 Washington pl
Hute Catharine, shop, 330 N Front.
Hute John, 330 N Front
Hutson John, cordw., Front & Federal
Huttelson Peleg, sea capt., 102 Catharine
Huttenloch G., lab., Palmer & West (K)
Huttenloch Michael, lab., Coates bel Broad
Hutton A. B., Principal Deaf and Dumb Inst., Pine & Broad
Hutton Edwin, painter, George bel 5th
Hutton George, clerk, Garden and Buttonwood
Hutton John, carter, Penn bel 12th
Hutton Moses, clerk, N. L. Bank, h 212 Green
Hutton Samuel, clerk, 5 Jenning's row
Hutton Thomas H., mer., 94 High
Hutton William, coppersmith, 49 German.
Hyatt James G., cordw., Thompson ab 4th (K)
Hyatt James G., cordw., Walker's ct (K)
Hyatt William E., corder, 55 N wharves, h Camden
Hyde Francis, baker, 314 N 5th
Hyde Joseph, machinist, 1 Fetter la, h 8 Creson's al
Hyde Lawson, flour inspec., 367 Cedar
Hyer Alexander C., mer., h 202 Callowhill.
Hylind John, block & pumpmr., rear 43 Coates
Hyland Patrick, lab., 226 N Water
Hyndman Stuart, weaver, rear 2d ab Master
Hyndman Wm., carpet weaver, 2d above Jeferson (K)
HYNEMAN CHAS. F. hotel, N W 6th and Carpenter (C)

Hyneman John, Franklin ab Green
Hyneman Joseph, tailor, Poplar ab 3d
Hyneman Leon, cigars & tobacco, 149 N 3d, h 222 N 2d
Hyneman Moses, dry goods and trimmings, 223 N 2d
Hynson Matthew, tailor, rear 117 Christian
Hyser Samuel, gun smith, rear 461 N 3d
Hyser & Stover, milliner, 65 W. Sassafras
Hyzer James, currier, Palmer ab West (K)

———

Ibbotson H J., mer., 18 Commerce
Ibbotson Jane, rear 1 Clark
Iddings R. J.; mer., 35 Chestnut, h S W Franklin and Vine
IDDINGS, WELLS & TROTTER, com. dry goods, 35 Chestnut
Ide Geo. B., Rev., 345 Mulberry
Iden Thomas, carp., Poplar bel Broad
Idler Charles, band box mr., 309 High
Idolet John, pilot, c Front and Almond
Iehle John G., tailor, 337 N 6th
Ifill Samuel, Sch 8th ab Cherry
Iler Folbert S., pilot, 21 Swanson
Ilgee Wm., machinist, 10 Pearl bel Sch 7th
Illman Henry, music printer, 194 High, h 21 Sassafras
Illman & Sons, engrav. & printers, 194 High
Illman Thos, engraver, 194 High, h 26 Morgan
Illman W., cop. pl. printer, 194 High, h Locust n Broad
Imbrie James jr., mer., 1 Church al, h 64 S 13th
Imkenberg Henry S., cabinetmr. 395 S Front
Immel Catharine, gentw., c 3rd & Cherry
Incledon John, bricklayer, Lombard n Sch 4th
Indinbrock Henry, moulder, Orange bel Melon
Ingersoll Benjamin, carp., 36 Christian
Ingersoll Benj., waterman, M road bel Washington
Ingersoll Catharine, gentw., Sch 7th ab Spruce
Ingersoll Charles, atty. & coun., 136 Walnut
Ingersoll Charles J., atty. & coun., 130 Walnut
Ingersoll Edward, att'y & coun., 34 S 5th
Ingersoll H., lieutenant U. S. Navy, 250 Chestnut
Ingersoll Jane, gentw., Bank ab Lombard
INGERSOLL JARED, atty. and coun., Walnut ab 6th
Ingersoll Joseph R., atty. & coun., 77 S 4th.
Ingerson John, watchman, Locust and Sch 3d
Ingham Hen. cabinetmr., Julianna ab Callowhill
Inghram Saml., agricultural instruments, High, h Sch 6th bel Mulberry
Ingleman Jos., confec., 6 Jones W of Sch 8th
Ingraham E. D., atty. & coun., 6 York Buildings.
Ingraham George, carp., rear 1 Bread
Ingraham James, carp., Callowhill ab 13th, h 284 Wood
Ingram A., Brinton bel 11th
Ingram Charles, b. h., 143 N 2d
Ingram C. L., confect., 67 N 8th
Ingram Jane, wid. of Archibald, Dorothy W Sch 4th

Ingram John, weaver, 583 N 3d
Ingram John, cordw., Hagg's ct (S)
Ingram John H. bookbinder, 372 Vine
Ingram Mary, washer, 28 Prosperous al
Ingram Robert, bookbinder, 42 Jacoby
Ingram Thomas, dentist, 72 Sassafras.
Ingram Thomas, watchman, 372 Vine.
Ingram William, weav., Cadwalader ab Franklin
Ingram Wm. clerk, 77 Mulberry
Ingram Zadoc, carp., 13th bel Buttonwood, h 514 Vine
Innes Samuel P., potter, F road n Queen.
Innes Wm., block cutter, Swanson ct
INSKEEP, MOLTON & WOODRUFF, silk goods, 116 High
Inskeep Sarah S., b h, N E 4th & Mulberry
Inskeep Wm. H., mer., 116 High
INSLEE J. A. real est. brok., 64½ Walnut ab 3d, h S Sch 8th ab Pine
Iorgenson I. P. tailor, 5 Exchange pl, h 63 Dock
IREDELL THOMAS, farmers' hay market, 6th ab Brown
Irelan John W. wood wharf, S E Shippen and wharf, h n Almond st wharf
Ireland Deborah, 6 Duke
Ireland Edward P., cordw., Elizabeth ab Poplar
Ireland Elizabeth J. 11 Providence ct
Ireland Francis, machinist, Wharton bel 5th
Ireland George, 50 Brown, h 413 N Front
Ireland George & Son, vinegar, 50 Brown.
Ireland James P., officer, Shield's ct
Ireland Wm., moroc. dresser, Marlboro' & Bedford (K)
Ireland Wm., lab., 19 Queen
Ireland Wm., boxmaker, 37 New
Ireland Wm., blacksmith, Korndaffer's ct
IRELAND WILLIAM F., Ald., 48 Brown, h 413 N Front
Irons Samuel, carp., Front ab Reed
Irvin Ellen, rear 535 Vine
Irvin John, grain measurer, 20 Federal
Irvin Thomas, brickmr., 210 Green
Irvin Wm., M. D., druggist, 201 High, h 180 Mulberry
Irvine Gerrard, carp., Shippen ab Broad
Irvine James, turner, 51 Coates
Irvine Robert W., 111 Wood
Irving Hester, Mrs., 5 Sommers' ct
Irving Mary, milliner, 272 Callowhill
Irwin Andrew, printer, 3d ab Clark
Irwin Ann, trimmings, 230 S 2d
Irwin Arthur, weaver, Shippen bel Broad
Irwin Deborah, milliner, 323 Vine
Irwin Edward, carp., n George Sch 8th
Irwin Henry W., dentist, 277 S 2d
Irwin James, carter, Coates ab 13th
Irwin James, weaver, Perry bel Phoenix (K)
Irwin James, manuf. 580 N 3d
Irwin John, waterman, 5 Coates
Irwin John H., mer., S W Front and Walnut, h 258 Walnut
Irwin Robert, weaver, 12 Bauersach's ct (K)
Irwin Robert, weaver, 11 Philip (K)
Irwin Robert, miller, M'Manemy's ct
Irwin Robt., city watch, Ann n 12th

22

Irwin Robt., shoemr., 172 Vine
Irwin Samuel, combmr. 60 Almond
Irwin Samuel, tobacconist, Fraley's al
Irwin Samuel, grocer, N W 10th and Coates
Irwin & Stinson, carders, 30 Dock
Irwin Wm., weaver, Cedar ab 12th
Irwin Wm., carp., Hamilton's ct
Isaacs Eleazer, clothing, 260 Cedar
Isaacs Henry, whip and cane mr., Newton bel Carpenter
Isaacs Jane, 203 Catharine
Isaacs Mark, optician, 309 S 6th
Isaacs Solomon, clothing, 336 N 2d
Isard Charles, alderman, 3d and Catharine
Isard Eleazer, seaman, 3d ab Catharine
Isard Michael, shoemr., 411 S 2d
Isard Mrs. E., 3d and Catharine
Isbell Alonzo, manuf., Sch 8th ab Mulberry
Isby John, cooper, Swanson bel Queen
Iseminger George, butcher, Turner
Iseminger Sarah, shop, 2d ab Reed
Iseminger Shubert, painter, 380 S 5th
Isphordeng Anthony, grocer, S E Coates & St John.
Israel Abraham, clothier, 202 Cedar
Israel Abraham E., sexton, rear 1 Cherry
Israell Joseph H.. clerk bd. brokers, 55½ Walnut, h 91 S 3d
Iungerich Louis, grocer, 12 Decatur, h 20 Castle
IUNGERICH & SMITH, grocers, 12 Decatur
Ivans Mary, 28 N Sch 8th
Ives John, shop, 11th & Olive
Ivins Aaron B., teacher, Marlboro' ab Duke (K)
Ivins Ann, Chancery la
Ivins Job, carp., 336 Coates
Ivins Rebecca, wid., 7th ab Parrish
Ivins Wm. C., teacher, 168 Cherry, h 27 Melon
Izard James, engineer, 76 Catharine
Izner Daniel, cordw., Wood ab Sch 8th

———

Jack Ann Eliza, dressmr., N W 9th and Filbert
JACK C. J., atty. & coun., 12 N 7th.
Jack John, compositor, 325 Vine.
Jack Robert, grocer, Cedar ab 12th
Jack William, coachmaker, 29 Prune, h Noble ab Franklin
Jackson Alexr., manufacturer, Amber ab Phoenix. (K)
Jackson Alexr., constable, 5 Hauses' ct
Jackson Amelia, 17 Elizabeth (N L)
Jackson Andrew, ladies' shoemr., 510 Coates
Jackson Anna, washer, Apple ab Brown
Jackson Bartley, blacksmith, Franklin ab Wood
Jackson Benjamin, carp., 557 Vine
JACKSON CHARLES C., tailor, N E 5th and Mulberry, h 218 Cherry
Jackson Charles W. mer. 4 N 3d, h 8 Crown (C)
JACKSON CHARLES W. & CO., dry goods, 4 N 3d
Jackson Danl., baker, Barker n Sch 5th
Jackson Danl., carman, 4 Poplar ct
Jackson David, coachman, 3 White's ct
Jackson David, boot and shoemr., Kelly's ct

Jackson David, coachman, George ab Sch 7th
Jackson Edward F., mer., N E 3d and High, h 118 Christian.
Jackson Eli, lab., Steel's ct
Jackson Ellis, shuttlemr., 100 Charlotte
Jackson Elizabeth, shop, Beach n Maiden (K)
Jackson Elizabeth, 29 Paschall's alley
Jackson Enoch, pilot, 19 Clark (S)
Jackson Ezekiel, carp., Pleasant bel 13th
Jackson Ephraim, lab., Washington ct
Jackson Eveline, washer, Ten Foot al
Jackson E. B., trimmingmr., 7th and Callowhill
Jackson Francis, Bedford ab 7th
Jackson Franklin, printer, Nectarine n 10th
Jackson George, nailmr., 39 Lily al
Jackson Geo., plasterer, 21 Hubble ct
Jackson George W., constable, 18 Garden
Jackson Henrietta, Pearl ab Sch 8th
Jackson Isaac, gent., 70 Marshall
Jackson Isaiah, lab., Bedford bel Clifton
Jackson Jacob, stevedore, 23 Christian.
Jackson Jacob jr., mate, 23 Christian
Jackson Jacob B. rear 9 Crown
Jackson James, wool sorter, Gay's ct (K)
Jackson Jas., tavern, Washington av ab Green
Jackson James, hosier, Queen ab Vienna
Jackson James M. rigger, 22 Little Water
Jackson John, dry goods, N E 13th & Filbert
Jackson John, bootmaker, Willow ab Marshall
Jackson John, machinist, William n Rose, h 619 N 2d
Jackson John, porter, Caledonia ct
Jackson John, Poplar bel Broad
Jackson John A., Harper's pl
Jackson John D., loan office, 55 Pine
Jackson John S., turner, Washington ab N road
Jackson Joseph, collector, 2 Hermitage pl
Jackson Joseph, well digger, La Fayette bel 16th
Jackson Jos., carp., 17 S Sch 6th
Jackson Levi, lab., Van Buren pl
Jackson Louisa, gentw. Spruce ab Broad
Jackson Phœbe Ann, Ball al
Jackson Rachel, 19 Schriver's ct
Jackson Randolph, waiter, 20 Eagle ct
Jackson Reb., sempstress, Davis' ct
Jackson Rebecca H., 35 Garden
Jackson Richard, clerk, Union ab Franklin
JACKSON & ROSS, dry goods, N E 3d & High
Jackson Samuel, M. D., professor, 108 S 8th.
Jackson Saml., pyrotechnist, Carpenter bel 5th
Jackson Samuel, M. D., 30 N 9th
Jackson Saml., currier, 526 N 2d
Jackson Samuel, druggist, c 10th and Button wood
Jackson Samuel, machinist, 622 N 2d
Jackson Saml., shop, Sch 4th ab Cedar
Jackson Sarah, S W 5th and Mulberry
Jackson Thomas, Caledonia ct
Jackson Thomas, broker, 9 Green
Jackson Thos., weaver, rear Carpenter ab 8th
Jackson Thomas, grocer, Perry & Phœnix (K)
Jackson Thomas, die sinker, 271 N 5th
Jackson Thomas S., stovemr., 131 N 6th
Jackson T., boot & shoemaker, 364 N 6th

Jackson Walter, 6th bel Carpenter
Jackson Washington, machinist, 31 Parker
Jackson Wilford, Paschall's al
Jackson William, broker, 61 Dock
Jackson Wm. Rev. 205 S 2d
Jackson Wm., mer., N W High & 2d, h 43 Vine
Jackson Wm., carp., 12 Jackson's ct
Jackson Wm. A., confect., M'Devitt's av (K)
Jackson Wm. H., stove finisher, 419 N 6th
Jackson W. H., grocer, Marshall and Parrish
Jackway John, plasterer, G T road ab Laurel
Jackway Samuel, plasterer, Apple ab Thompson (K)
Jacob Seaman, weaver, 10th ab Poplar
Jacobs Ann, dealer, 9 Hickory ct
Jacobs Benjamin, bartender, Washington (W P)
Jacobs Benj., huckster, 2 St Joseph's av
Jacobs Brinton, steam saw mill, Cherry st whrf., Sch, h 520 Chestnut
Jacobs Charles, U. States mint, h Sch 8th and Cherry
Jacobs Daniel, stone cutter, rear 9th ab Coates
Jacobs Elizabeth, 31 Franklin
Jacobs Frederick, tailor, James ab 10th
Jacobs George, plasterer, Parrish bel 12th
Jacobs G., 9th bel Washington
Jacobs Henry, gardner, 3d ab Jefferson (K)
Jacobs Henry, lab., New Market ab Laurel
Jacobs Isaac, furniture, 254 Cedar
Jacobs Israel, furniture, 225 Cedar
Jacobs James, lab., Webb's al
Jacobs John, last mr., 322 N 3d
Jacobs John, Sr., innkeeper, Washington (W P)
Jacobs John, plasterer, Lydia bel William
Jacobs Joseph, mer., 215½ High, h 50 Vine
Jacobs Julius, mer., 16 Strawberry, h 314 N 3d
JACOBS & KERSEY, steam saw mill, Cherry st whf., Sch
Jacobs Lucretia, shop, 26 Elizabeth
Jacobs Mary Ann, widow, Ball al
JACOBS, MAYER & CO., mers., 215½ High
Jacobs Philip, teacher, 22 Cherry
Jacobs Samuel, dry goods, 15 S 2d, h 12th and Washington
JACOBS S. W., carriage manuf., 12 Library
Jacobs Thos., plasterer, 18 School
Jacobs Thomas H., mer., 81 Dock, h 179 S 3d
Jacobs Wm., carp., 428 N 5th
Jacobs Wm. B., Callowhill ab 11th
Jacobson Letitia, tailoress, 25 Harmony ct
Jacobus Edwd., cordw., rear 21 Charlotte
Jacobus Jacob, blacksmith, 6 Lindle ct
Jacobus Peter, turner, 6 Lagrange
Jacoby Charles, cabinetmaker, 176 Sassafras.
Jacoby Edwd., M. D., 149 G T road (K)
Jacoby George L., mer., 109 Sassafras, h 163 N 4th
JACOBY, HARRIS & HILLEGASS, dry goods, 109 Sassafras
Jacoby Wm., lab., G T road & 6th (K)
Jacoby Henry, porter, 2 Acorn al
Jacoby John F., mer., 90 N 3d, h 60 O Y road
Jacoby Samuel, potter, 6th ab Poplar
Jacoby Solomon, cooper, rear 462 N 3d
Jacot Celestin, casemr., 65 S 2d

Jacot H. W., jeweller, 7 Weccacoe
Jacot Wm., mer., 34 Commerce
Jacquin James, chemist, Chestnut (W P)
Jaffers Wm., lab., rear Denton bel William (K)
Jaggers John, machinist, 7th ab Poplar
Jaggers Margaret, 8 Kenworthy's ct
Jaggers Wm. collector, 52 Green
Jahns Christian, 92 N 9th
Jahraus Adolph & Jacob, bakers, 18 Christian
Jahraus Adolph, baker, rear 416 S Front
James Abel M., cordwainer, O Y road ab Brown
James Albert, cordw., Front and Catharine
James Ann, 11 Lombard row
James Charles, boat builder, Union n F road
James Chas., bootmr., Front and Catharine
James Chas. H., cooper, 8 Christian
James Ebenezer, boot & shoemaker, High, bel Sch Front
James Edward, porter, 172 Pine
James Edwd., lab., Orange ab Lemon
James Francis, bookbinder, 19 Jefferson row
James George, carter, Bickham n Sch. 7th.
James Israel E., collector, 182 S 10th
James Jer., tailor, 39 George
James Jesse, carp., 468 N 3d
James John F., actuary Girard Life Ins. & Trust Co., 159 Chestnut
James John M. ladies' shoemr., 172 Poplar
James John O., mer., 146 N 3d, h 135 Dillwyn
James John R., combmaker, 27 Merchant
James John T., post office, 163 Poplar
James Joseph, mason, 14 Brandywine st
James Joseph, cordw., 19 Jefferson row
James Jos., whip mr., Marlboro ab Franklin (K)
James Judy, 236 Lombard
JAMES, KENT & SANTEE, mers., 146 N 3d
James Levi, waiter, George ab Sch 7th
James Lewis T. blacksmith, Queen (K)
James Lewis T., blacksm., Odd Fellows' Hall (K)
James Marshall, mer., 83 N Water, h 294 Cherry
James Mary, 201 Pine.
James Martin, 181 Vine
James Mason, stone ma., Poplar ab 4th
James Mrs., wid of Isaac W., tavern, 140 N 2d
James Peter, carp., 219 Shippen
James Peter, mer., 79 High
James Richard, lab., Wood bel Sch. 6th & 7th.
James R. P., tax collector, 75 Cherry
James Samuel M. bricklayer, 13th bel Lombard
James Samuel N. & Co. druggists, O Y road & Wood
James Simon, boxmr. G T road n Jefferson
James Steph. tin plate & sheet iron, 218 Callowhill
James Thomas, cordw., 111 Brown
James Thomas, N W 5th & Parrish
James Thomas C. wheelwright, Beach below Shackamaxon
James Thomas C., mer., 135 S Front
James Thomas D., teacher, S W 11th & High, h 60 N 11th
JAMES THOMAS P., druggist, 212 High, h 4th & Wood
James Westley, brickmr., Shippen ab 12th

James Wm., lab., Walnut n Beech
James Wm. carter, Bickham W Sch 8th
James Wm. H., com. mer., Broad ab Mulberry, h 4 Library
James Wm., shoemr., George n Sch 7th, h High E of Sch 2d
Jamison A., musician, Rugan n Willow
Jamison G. W., Dr., 357 E Pine
Jamison John, cabmr., 25 Library
Jamison Pryor P., cordw., Mechanic ab Culvert
Jamison Robt., drayman, Cherry and Sch 3d
Jamison Thos., cabinetmr., 2d and Queen
Janeau Margaret, matron, 42 Prune
Janes Abel, tavern, 211 N Front
Janeway Thomas L. Rev., 104 Marshall
Janke John N., teacher, 17 N 12th
Janney Ann, 89 Wood
Janney Benjamin S., M. D., 334 N 6th.
Janney Benj. S. Jr. mer., 239 High, h 121 Wood
Janney Israel, gent., 7th ab Noble.
Janney Jas., lum. mer., 273 Green
Janney O. S., drug broker, S E Front & Chestnut, h 72 N 11th
Janton John, bootmr., 86 N 4th
Janvier Francis, clerk, 126 Catharine
Janvier Samuel W., sea capt., 442 S Front
Jaques James, engineer, 76 S 2d
Jaquett Azell, Crown bel Bedford (K)
Jaquett Catharine, 438 N 4th
Jaquett Nathan, carp., Shackamaxon bel Bedford (K)
Jarbo Jos., coal deal., Brown bel Front
Jarden Catharine, 54 S 11th
Jarden Charles, cordwainer, 157 S 9th
Jarlen Jacob, brickmaker, 206 N 11th
Jarden John, marble yard, 226 S Front, h Cherry n Sch 6th
Jarden M., trimmings, 385 Sassafras
Jarden Robert, Sr., gent., Callowhill ab 12th
Jarden Samuel, gent., 11 City row.
Jarden William, brickmaker, S Garden above 12th
Jardine James, tailor, Poplar ab 7th
Jardine John, hatter, 317 N 3d
Jardine Wm., weaver, Fulton ab 12th
Jarman Ezekiel, bricklayer, 99 Poplar
Jarman E. Samuel, capt., 9th ab Coates
Jarman Jona., lab., 163 N Front
Jarman Reuben, b. h., 31 Coates
Jaroslawski Leopold & Brother, tailors, 188 Cedar
Jarrett-Rebecca, b h, Green ab 9th
Jarvis Benj., bricklayer, 290 Coates
Jarvis C., teacher of music, Pine ab 10th
Jarvis John, lab. Budden's al
Jarvis Robert, plasterer, 11 Dugan
Jarvis Wm. H., shoemr., rear 7 Elfreth's al
Jasney Isaac, clothing, 153 South
Jatho Ferdinand, cabinetmr., 83 N 5th
Jaudons & Mason, nail warehouse, 9 N 5th
Jauffert C. G., baker, Callowhill n Sch William
Jauretche Peter, mer., 261 S Front, h Spruce

Jeanes Amos, coal mer., High st whf., h Filbert & Sch 6th
Jeanes Charles, carp., Francis (F V)
Jeanes Isaac, fruiterer, 6 Chestnut
Jeanes Isaiah, gent., 208 N Front
Jeanes Jacob, M. D., 175 Vine
Jeanes Joseph, h 208 N Front
Jeanes Joseph, mer., 9 S Front
Jeanes Joshua T. mer. 85 High, h 208 N Front
Jeanes & Morris, fruiterers, 9 S Front
JEANES S. & CO., dry goods, 85 High
Jeanes S., mer., 85 High, h 208 N Front.
Jeanes & Scattergood, fruiterers, 28 S whfs
Jeanes Thomas, fruiterer, 28 S whfs
Jeans Ann, teacher, F road ab Otter
Jefferies David, jeweller, 495 S 2d
Jefferies M., fancy goods, 19 S 9th
Jefferies Wm. W., carp., 13 Perry
Jefferis Edw. G., fancy goods, 55½ N 8th
Jeffers Alexander, watchman, 119 N Juniper.
Jeffers Jane, sewer, Jones E of Sch 5th
Jeffers John H., carp. Logan bel Wallace
Jeffers Perry, moulder, 7 Mary's ct
Jefferson Edmund A., clerk, 3 Wagner's ct
Jefferson John, baker, 6 Swanson ct
Jeffery Ann, corset maker, 5 S 6th.
Jeffery John C., vict., Brown bel 12th
Jeffery Mary, 458 S Front
Jeffras Daniel, gentleman, 486 N 4th.
Jeffras Sarah Mrs., Elizabeth ab Poplar
Jeffrey Daniel, carter, Poplar bel 8th
Jeffrey John, waiter, 176 Locust
Jeffrey John, supt., Sch 7th ab Cherry
Jeffrey Robert, stone mason, Lombard n Sch 7th
Jeffries Benj. M. coachmr. 7 Green (C) h 188 Spruce
Jeffries Daniel, stables, 19 Bread
Jeffries Emmor D., ornamental painter, 3 Federal
Jeffries George, coach maker, 31 Spruce
Jeffries Hester, whitewasher, 35 Bonsall
Jeffries James, coach spring maker, Lodge ab 8th, h 8th bel Coates
Jeffries John, victualler, Buttonwood bel 10th
Jeffries Joseph, brickmr., G T road ab 5th
Jeffries J., & Son, coach spg. makers, Lodge ab 8th
Jeffries Robert, ropemr. Rye ab Reed
Jeffries Samuel, flour dealer, Catharine ab 6th
Jeffries Thos., oak cooper, Cadwalader ab Phœnix (K)
Jeffries Thomas J., spring mr., Lodge ab 8th, h 293 N 8th
Jeffries Wm. ropemr. Washington ab 13th
Jeffries Wm., porter, 98 Gaskill
Jeffris Thomas, cordwainer, 22 Callowhill
Jeffry Wm., car driver, rear Rose ab School (K)
Jellett Thos., blacking mr., rear 92 St John
Jemison S. A., dentist, 116 N 9th
Jenkins Benj. fruiterer, N W 6th & Spruce, h Callowhill n Sch 2d
Jenkins Caldwell C.,

Jenkins Edw. J., jeweller, 7 N 9th, h 3 Bonsall
Jenkins Henry, 69 Franklin
Jenkins Hunn, mer., 150 High, h 17 Branch
Jenkins Israel, carp., Wood bel West (K)
Jenkins Jacob, plasterer, Morris ab Christian.
Jenkins Jacob, tanner, rear Paschall's al
Jenkins Jabez, 244 High, h 7 Palmyra sq
Jenkins James, tailor, Woodland (W P)
Jenkins James B., barber, 4 N 13th
Jenkins John, chair store, Penn ab 13th
Jenkins John, carp., 25 Franklin pl
Jenkins John, mason, Edward bel 2d (K)
Jenkins John G., bookbinder, 11 Sergeant.
JENKINS JOHN P., Great Western, 485 High
Jenkins J. C., grocer, 244 High, h 63 Spruce
JENKINS J. & J. C., grocers, 244 High
Jenkins Margaret, 13th bel Cedar
Jenkins Mary, b h, 160 Vine
Jenkins Nicholas, carman, Rachel bel Laurel
Jenkins R. W., nurse, 318 Cedar.
Jenkins Samuel, hosemr., 29 Castle
Jenkins Sarah, 2 Eagle ct
Jenkins Wallis W. tailor, 7 Hause's ct
Jenkins Wm., harness mr., 268 N 8th
Jenkins Wm. P. cordw., Marshall ab Poplar
Jenks Abraham S. mer. 26 N 8th
Jenks Daniel T., dry goods, 26 N 8th
Jenks Edwin, blacksmith, 2 Gaskill
Jenks John, engineer, Harrison pl
Jenks Jonathan, ship joiner, Beach and Hanover, h Beach ab Palmer (K)
Jenks Joseph R., gent., 188 Mulberry
Jenks & Ogden, druggists, 106 N 3d
Jenks Watson, mer. 65 N Water, h 11 Franklin
Jenks W. J., druggist, 106 N 3d
Jennens Thomas, brass founder, 173 S 5th
Jenner Geo., Gray's ct
Jenni Abraham, wheelwright, Jay bel Coates
Jenni Michael, boot mr., 91 N Front
Jenning Benj. F., saddler, Ogden bel R road
Jennings John, weaver, Vine ab Nixon
Jennings Napoleon, Sch 7th bel Chestnut
Jennings Rachel, Wheat & Wharton
Jennings Richard, gent., Washington ab 6th
Jennis Lewis, b h, 11 Little Water
Jenny Mathias, carp., Hope bel Phoenix (K)
Jentz Fred'k Dr., 41 Shippen
Jeppeson John, cabinet mr., Kelly's ct
Jerman David, cooper, F road bel Master (K)
Jerman Geo. W., missionary, 458 S Front
Jerman James, waterman, 30 Reed
Jermon James, grocer, 2d ab Greenwich
Jermon Joseph W., grocer, 6 South 7th
Jerrar S., shop, Carpenter bel 9th
Jerread Anna, 5 Elizabeth ct
Jerrett Francis, stovemr., Hughes' ct
Jerter John, blacksm., 7 Marion
Jervis George F., actor, 9 Filbert av.
Jervis Daniel, boxmr., Filbert n Sch 4th
Jess Ruth Mrs., 30 N 5th
Jester Elizabeth, milliner, 63 S 13th
Jester Susannah, Carpenter ab 3d
Jessup A. mer., 21 Commerce
Jessup A. D., mer.; 21 Commerce, h Washington ab 9th

Jessup & Moore, com. paper warehouse, 21 Commerce
Jewell George, bootmaker, 14 Flower
Jewell Henry, cordw., Marriott ab 6th
Jewell Jacob, lab., 31 Palmer
Jewell J. B., paint. & glaz., 4 S 5th, h 328 Vine.
Jewell Leonard, mer., 3 Strawberry, h 124 N 9th
Jewell Wilson, M. D., 238 N 6th.
Jinnings John, weaver, Vine n Sch
Job Aaron, trader, 50 W Cedar
Jobes Isaac H., brass nail maker, Carpenter n P road
Jobes Thomas B. mer. 19 Sergeant
Jobson Joseph, rolling mill, Penn, (K) h 151 Franklin ab Wallace S G
Jobson Joseph & Co. rolling mill, Penn ab Poplar (K)
Johann Matthew, soap and candle manf., Olive bel 13th
John Charles A., port. painter, S W 8th & Mulberry
JOHN FREDERICK L., druggist, 118 Sassafras
Johnes George W., mer., 153 High
Johnes Peter, baker, 73 Lombard
Johns Daniel, painter, 13th bel Melon
Johns John J., bricklayer, Callowhill ab Sch 2d
Johns Jos., measurer, N W 11th & S Garden
Johns Joseph S., mer., N E 4th and Mulberry
Johns Mary, 6th & Christian
Johns Michael S., boots & shoes, 4 S 4th, h Wood bel 8th
Johns & Payne, dry goods, N E 4th & Mulberry
Johns Thomas A., mer., 98 High, h Wood bel 8th
Johns William, measurer, Pine W Broad.
Johns William T., tobacconist, 8 S 5th, h 40 Jacoby
Johnsen Edward, lab., 3 Callowhill
Johnsen Elizabeth, 131 N Juniper
Johnsen Isaac, plumber, 103 N Juniper
Johnsen Jonathan, carp., 3 Drinker's al
Johnson Abraham, carp., Linden n Sch 6th
Johnson Adam, brickmr., Sch 2d & Walnut
Johnson Alex., lab., Carlton bel Sch 6th
Johnson Alex., blindmr., George bel 3d
Johnson Alexander R., dentist, 231 Mulberry
Johnson Alex., W., gent., 7 Clinton sq
Johnson Amos, lab., Goodwill ct
Johnson Andrew, tailor, Dean ab Locust
Johnson Andrew, lab., Lombard ab Sch 6th
Johnson Alex., tallow chand., Wood ab Sch 8th
Johnson Anna, 48 Currant al
Johnson Aug., musician. rear 202 Lombard
Johnson A., sea capt., 59 Prime
Johnson Barbara, huckster, 4 Sanders' ct (K)
Johnson Benjamin, tailor, 123 New Market
Johnson Benj. F., clerk, 122 S 4th
Johnson & Branch, com. mers., 30 S whfs
Johnson Caleb, Broad bel Walnut
Johnson Caroline, 7 Hyde's ct
Johnson Catharine, rear Carpenter ab 4th
Johnson Cecilia, washer, Eagle ct
Johnson Charles, lab., 6th bel G T road (K)
Johnson Charles, saw manuf., 24 & h 67 Cherry
Johnson Charles, ink manuf., 10th bel Lombard, h 21 Jefferson row

Johnson Chas., engineer, 365 S 6th
Johnson Charles S., grocer, 25 N 11th
Johnson Charles W., cooper, Olive ab 13th
Johnson Charity, sempstress, Sch 8th ab Sassafras
Johnson & Conaway, saw manf., 24 Cherry
Johnson & Crowell, provisions, 8 N whfs
Johnson Daniel, waiter, 14 Hurst
Johnson Daniel, porter, 25 Giles' al
Johnson Daniel, cooper, Paul ab 6th
Johnson David, morocco dresser, Mechanic ab Culvert
Johnson David, 202 S Water.
Johnson David, skin dresser, Marlboro' bel West
Johnson David, cordw., rear Dean ab Bedford
Johnson Diana, washer, rear 335 S 2d
Johnson Edward, moulder, Brown bel Front
Johnson Edward, porter, 16 Washington ab 11th
Johnson Edward, Rev., 21 Hurst
Johnson Edward, turner, 8 St George's ct
Johnson Edward, lab., Pearl ab 13th
Johnson Edward, 34 New Market
Johnson Edward D., tobacconist, 195 Callowhill
Johnson Edward H., capt., 94 Carpenter
Johnson Edwin, lab., Crown n Bedford (K)
Johnson Edwin, lab., Pearl ab 13th
Johnson Eliza, nurse, 23 Merchant
Johnson Elizabeth, gentw., Harmstead st
Johnson Elizabeth, 2 Schriver's ct
Johnson Ellaya, tailor, Lombard ab Sch 2d
Johnson Esther, washer, Bedford bel 12th
Johnson & Evans, druggist, 11 N 5th
Johnson Frederick F., carp., 13 Coombs' al, h rear 15 Noble
Johnson Gab'l, rigger, Swanson ab Washington
Johnson George, waiter, 23 Currant al.
Johnson George, plasterer, 275 Wood
Johnson George, Callowhill ab Sch 2d
Johnson George, waiter, rear 89 S 6th
Johnson George, cordw., Boyd's av
Johnson George M., dyer, 132 S 11th.
Johnson George P. dry goods, NW 2d & Prime
Johnson George R., tinsmith, S W 7th & High, h Buttonwood ab 12th
Johnson Grace, washer, 8 Fothergill st
Johnson & Green, att'ys. & couns., 4 George
Johnson Hannah, b h., 20 Carter's al
Johnson Hannah, 221 Wood ab 12th
Johnson Hannah, Mrs., 10 Flower
Johnson Harvey, ivory turner, 4 Hamilton's ct
Johnson Helen, milliner, 195 S 7th
Johnson Henrietta, 218 Shippen
JOHNSON HENRY, oyster house, 109 Shippen
Johnson Henry, mariner, Bedford bel 8th
Johnson Henry, lab., Carpenter ab 12th
Johnson Henry, lab., 304 S 7th
Johnson Henry, conveyancer, 353 N 3d
Johnson Isaac, lab. Carlton bel Sch 6th
Johnson Israel H. mer. 36 & h 112 N Front
Johnson Jacob, barber, 361 E Lombard.
Johnson Jacob, barber, R road bel Ann (F V)
Johnson Jacob, dyer, 10 Sterling al
Johnson Jacob, musician, Dean's al
Johnson Jacob M., mer., 30 S whfs., h Washington ab 9th

Johnson James, lab., rear 6 Locust
Johnson James, carp., 16 Blackberry al
Johnson James, cordw., 5 Mechanic
Johnson James, china store, G T road ab Master
Johnson James, painter, 265 Spruce
Johnson James, carter, rear Wood ab Sch 6th
Johnson James, baker, 208 Buttonwood
Johnson James, lab., High W of Sch 3d
Johnson James, porter, Lewis n Sch 6th
Johnson James, cordw., rear 109 Queen
Johnson James P., eating-house, 179 S 6th
Johnson Jane, S W 12th & Cherry
Johnson Jane S., 26 Plum st
Johnson Jesse, moulder, Buttonwood W of 13th
Johnson Jesse, cabmr., 43 Carpenter (S)
Johnson Jesse H. carp. Master & Hope (K)
Johnson John, lab., Parrish ab 7th
Johnson John, wheelwright, Fitzwater ab 6th, h P road ab Catharine
Johnson John, fisherman, Bishop bel Queen (K)
Johnson John, shoemr., 95 R road
Johnson John, carp., William opp Benton (K)
Johnson John, lab., Sch 8th ab Callowhill
Johnson John, weav., rear Charlotte ab Thompson (K)
Johnson John, coachman, 155 Locust
Johnson John, wheelwright, Lemon and 10th
Johnson John, cordw., Marriott ab 5th
Johnson John, druggist, New Market & Laurel
Johnson John A., cordw. rear 116 Brown
Johnson John D., chairmr., S E Dillwyn & Wood
Johnson John G., huckster, 460 S Front
Johnson John H., blacksmith, 12th bel Coates
Johnson John H., cordw., 112 Brown
Johnson John H., grocer, Lysle & Fitzwater
Johnson John J., carp., Church ab Washington
Johnson John M., shoemr., 51 S 11th
Johnson John N., grocer, 63 S 2d
Johnson John S., brushmr., 80 Green
Johnson John T., carpt., 8 Lodge alley, h 7 Castle
Johnson Jonathan, carter, 16 Helmuth.
Johnson Joseph, lab. 2 Relief pl
Johnson Joseph, mer. 77 S whfs. h 282 Filbert
Johnson Joseph, confect. Pearl ab 13th
Johnson Jos., real estate broker, 410 Vine
Johnson Joseph, moulder, Carlton ab 13th
Johnson Joseph, carp. rear Carlton ab Sch 6th
Johnson Joseph, manuf., Chestnut ab William, (W P)
Johnson Josephine, Vaughan ab Locust
Johnson Josiah, 55 S 11th
Johnson J. Warner, law bookseller, 197 Chestnut
Johnson Lavinia, sempstress, 8 Pryor's ct
Johnson Lawrence, clerk, Poplar ab 8th
Johnson Levi, capt. Sch 7th n Vine
Johnson Limas, clothing, 74 S 2d, h 201 S 8th
Johnson Lydia, Swede's ct
Johnson L., stereotype founder, 6 George, h 275 Pine
Johnson L. & Co., stereotype found., 6 George
Johnson Margaret, rear Wood ab Sch 6th
Johnson Maria, cupr. and leech. 11th ab Coates
Johnson Maria, dressmr., 15 Coates

Johnson Martin, shop, S W 3d & Queen
Johnson Mary, wid., Phoenix ab G T road (K)
Johnson Mary Ann, Pearl ab 13th
Johnson Matt., lab. 2d ab Montgomery (K)
Johnson Misses, milliners, 206 Chestnut.
Johnson Moses, 220 Mulberry
Johnson & Neal, mers., 30 S whfs, and 53 S Water
Johnson Nelson J., blacksmith, 163 N 7th
Johnson Ovid F., atty. & coun., office 4 George, h 25 N 10th
Johnson O. H. dry goods, 22 S 2d
Johnson Patrick, waiter, 34 Quince
Johnson Peter, doctor, Bedford ab 13th
Johnson Peter, seaman, 52 George
Johnson Peter, carp., Dillwyn ab Willow, h 67 Logan
Johnson Peter, clothes, 103 S 2nd, h Raspberry ab Spruce
Johnson Peter, 269 Cherry.
Johnson Peter, porter, German ab 3d
Johnson Peter A., 32 Quince
Johnson Philip, flour, 13th & Melon
Johnson Rachel, Marriott ab 4th
Johnson Reuben, carp., Sch 4th ab Chestnut
Johnson Reuben, Fraley's ct (K)
Johnson Richard, lab., Pleasant av
Johnson Richard B., turner, 63 Walnut.
Johnson Richard H., druggist, 11 N 5th, h 100 High
Johnson Robert, carp., 132 S 9th
Johnson Robt., spinner, 5th bel Marriott
Johnson Robert, sailmr. Gilles' al
Johnson Rob., police officer, Sycamore n Spruce
Johnson Robert, cook, 16 Little Pine
Johnson Robert, waiter, 32 Burd's ct
Johnson Robert S., ironmer., 50 & 52 N Front, h 383 Mulberry
Johnson Rowland, grocer, 8 N wharves, h 6 Comptroller.
Johnson Samuel, dealer, 21 Prosperous al
Johnson Samuel, wire worker, 79 Catharine bel 2d
Johnson Samuel, flour mer., 446 Sassafras.
Johnson Samuel, shoemr., 70 2d, h 64 N road
JOHNSON SAMUEL P. C., mer., 30 S whfs
Johnson Sarah, 178 Mulberry.
Johnson Stacy D., Front bel Phœnix (K)
Johnson Stansberry, lab., Lawrence ct (K)
Johnson Stephen, mariner, 22 Union st
Johnson & Sterrett, chairmrs., 179 N Front
Johnson Susan, washer, Eagle ct
Johnson Susanna, Sch 8th bel Callowhill
Johnson Theodore T. com. mer. 61 N whfs, & 127 N Water, h 76 N 5th
Johnson Thos., blacksm., 16 Gebhard
Johnson Thos., watchman, High n Sch 3d
Johnson Thomas, weaver, Pleasant bel 13th
Johnson Thomas, weav. Lydia bel William (K)
Johnson Thomas, baker, 182 N 13th.
Johnson Thomas, shop, 5th ab Buttonwood
Johnson Thomas R., mer., 26 N 2d
Johnson Thomas M. packer, Aydelott's ct
Johnson Topliff, law bookseller, 197 Chestnut, h 144 S 2d

JOHNSON T. & J. W., law booksrs., 197 Chestnut
Johnson & Trimble, mers., 61 N whfs.
Johnson Walter, brickmr. 13 Helmuth
Johnson Walter R., prof'r., Broad bel Chestnut
Johnson Wm., confec., 262 S 4th
Johnson Wm., trunkmr., 175 N 10th
Johnson Wm., cordw., 17 Charlotte
Johnson Wm., lab. 66 E Lombard
Johnson Wm., ship caulker, Hanover ab Franklin (K)
Johnson William, blacksmith, Sheaff's al.
Johnson William, shoemr., 60 N 5th.
Johnson William, manuf., G T road & Master
Johnson William, b. h., 9 Lombard.
Johnson Wm., lab., Apple ab Brown
Johnson Wm., tobacconist, 3 N 7th
Johnson Wm., waiter, 10 Currant al
Johnson Wm., lab., 41 Quince
Johnson Wm., tanner, 4 Apple
Johnson Wm., gunsmith, 2 Rose al
Johnson Wm., carter, Marriott la ab 6th
Johnson Wm., carter, 1 Carberry ct
Johnson Wm. bricklayer, Brandywine ab 13th
Johnson Wm. lab. Front ab Phoenix
Johnson Wm. lab. 10 Warren
Johnson Wm. coachman, Mercer
Johnson Wm. drayman, Sch 6th n Sassafras
Johnson Wm. T., tailor, 5 Nonnater's ct
Johnston Adam, curb setter, 467 Sassafras
Johnston A. W., gent., 7 Clinton sq. Chestnut ab Broad
JOHNSTON, BURK & CO., dry goods, 77½ High.
Johnston Charles W. carp. Cobb's ct
Johnston Elizabeth, 268 S 5th
Johnston E. R., merchant, 77½ High, h N W 6th & Willow
Johnston E. R., teacher of music, 293 N 10th
Johnston Francis S., cabt. mkr., 343 S Front, h 26 Almond
Johnston James, brewer, 197 Locust
Johnston James, printer, 32 N 13th
Johnston James, cordwr., 77 Crabb st
Johnston James cigarmr, Cobb's ct (N L)
Johnston James, chandler, 117 N Juniper
Johnston James E., planing mills, South below Broad, h Buttonwood ab 12th
Johnston Jeremiah, curb setter, Hazel
Johnston John, dry goods, 205 S 2d
Johnston John, weaver, Hope ab Master (K)
Johnston John, lab., 4 St Joseph's av
Johnston Jos., 10 F road (K)
Johnston Margaret, dressmr., Wood bel Sch 7th
Johnston Maria, dry goods, S W 9th & Sassafras
Johnston Martha, wid., rear Nectarine bel 11th
Johnston Mattw. carpet weaver, rear 27 Quince
Johnston Peter, cloths, 103 S 2d, h Raspberry al n Spruce
Johnston Robt., tobacconist, Mulberry al
Johnston Robt., lab., Cedar ab 12th
JOHNSTON ROBT., stock & ex. brok., 24 S 3d, h 110 N 7th.
Johnston Robert, watchmr., 132 S Front, h 120 Catharine

Johnston Robert, currier, Swanson bel Almond
Johnston Robert E., alderman, 238 S 7th, h 13th bel Pine
Johnston Samuel, lab., McCloskey's
Johnston Samuel, weaver, Fulton ab 12th
Johnston Susan, 154 S 9th
Johnston Thomas, blacksmith, 280 S Front
Johnston Thomas, grocer, 326 S 5th
Johnston Thos. lab. R road ab Ann (F V)
Johnston Thos. P., mcr., 21 S 3d, h 154 S 9th
Johnston Wm., lab., rear F road ab Phœnix
Johnston William, bootmr., 7 S 13th.
Johnston William, grocer, S W 11th & Lombard
Johnston Wm., shoemr., High n Sch 5th
Johnston Wm., milkman, Queen and Palmer(K)
Johnston Wm. B., mcr., 165 High, h Washington ab 9th
Johnston W., architect, 101 S 5th
Joiner Henry, cordw., Wood bel Sch 3d
Joline Wm., captain, 618 S 2d
Jolivet John, jeweller, Carpenter n P road
Jolly Mary Ann, rear 253 Cedar
Jones Aaron, painter, rear 221 St. John
Jones Abner, plasterer, Apple bel George
Jones Abraham, turner, 88 Callowhill, h 313 N 2d
Jones Alban, coal dealer, 7 Pratt's ct
Jones Albert, whitewasher, 12th ab Pine
Jones Alfred C., engineer, 186 Queen
Jones Alfred T., clerk, 25 N 3d, h 42 Prune
Jones Alice, Currant ab Locust
Jones Andrew M., mer., 17 S wharves, h 500 Chestnut.
Jones Ann, dry goods, 112 W High.
Jones Ann, wid., 34 Paschall's al
Jones Ann, trader, 9th ab Ogden
Jones Anna C., gentw., 116 N 12th
Jones A. & E. & Co., milliners, 9 N 2d
Jones A. M. & B. W., iron mers., 17 S Whfs.
Jones Bachel, hatter, 3d ab Washington
Jones Benjamin, 267 Chestnut.
Jones Benjamin, jr., gent., 234 S Front.
Jones Benjamin, carter, Crown ab Franklin (K)
Jones Benjamin W., mer., 17 S whfs, h 267 Chestnut
Jones B. M., grocer, 178 High, h 401 Walnut
Jones Caleb, mer., 7 Church al., h Walnut W Sch 6th
Jones Catharine, b h, 141 N 6th
Jones Catharine, shop, c Queen & Marlborough.
Jones Catharine, 176 S 11th
Jones Charles, porter, 6 S 8th
Jones Charles, 26 Logan sq
Jones Charles D., grocer, N E 6th & Callowhill
Jones Charles, barber, 95 N 2d
Jones Charles, distiller, Catharine & P road
Jones Charles, waiter, 39 Quince
Jones Charles, gent., Julianna ab Vine
Jones Charles F., cordw., Orchard bel Rawle
Jones Charles T., att'y. and coun., 478 5th
Jones Christopher, lab. 42 Bread
JONES CORNELIUS, tavern, Exchange pl & Carter's al
Jones Daniel, carp. rear 102 Christian
Jones David, chairmr. 85 W Callowhill

Jones David, lab., 47 Franklin
Jones David, sup., 6th bel Washington
Jones David, bootmr., 343 N 6th
Jones David, hatter, 3 Lagrange pl
Jones David, carp., 163 Christian.
Jones Douglass, vict., 6 Wallace
Jones Edward, currier, rear 2d opp Laurel (K)
Jones Edward, porter, 4 Benton
Jones Edw., wheelwright, Shippen n P road
Jones Edward, stair rodmr., 1 Swanwick, h 132 Catharine
Jones Edward E., printer, Brown ab 10th
Jones Edward P., slater, 116 Catharine.
Jones Edward R. conveyancer, Walnut ab 6th
Jones Edw. S., clerk, 204 Noble
Jones Elijah, bricklayer, 120 Lombard.
Jones Elijah, carp., Richard ab Sch 7th
Jones Elisha, bricklayer, 9 Madison
Jones Eliza, gentw., 225 S Front.
Jones Eliza, b h, Wood ab 11th
Jones Elizabeth, dressmr., 45 N 4th
Jones Elizabeth, 17 Linden (K)
Jones Elizabeth, rear 7 Pegg st
Jones Elizabeth, 2 Quigg's ct
Jones Elizabeth, trimmings, 583 S 2d
Jones Ellen, Sch 8th ab Cherry
Jones Ellen, 42 S 13th
Jones Emery, coachman, 18 Acorn al
Jones Ephraim, chairmr., 95 N Market
Jones Evan, paper hanger, 151 Swanson.
Jones Evan W., paper carrier, 7th & Hallowell
Jones E. Hicks, varieties, 18 N 2d
Jones Frances, b h, 400 N Front
Jones Franklin C., mer., 29 Chestnut
Jones F. L., painter, 307 S 2d
Jones George, lab., Lewellen's av (K)
Jones George B., auctioneer, 34 S Front, h N W 8th and Chestnut
JONES GEO. D., cabinetmaker, 62 S 4th
Jones George F., merchant, 19 S Sch 7th.
Jones George F. T., gent., 12 Portico sq
Jones George W., blacksm., 108 Broad
Jones George W., merchant, N E Franklin and Green
Jones George W., clerk, Green ab 14th
Jones George W., burnisher, 13 Chatham
Jones Gideon F. mer. 38 N 2d
Jones Grace E., 20 Strawberry
Jones Griffith, ice cream, 7 S Garden and 180 Chestnut
Jones Hannah, 379 Spruce
Jones Harriet, 46 Marshall
Jones Henderson M. tobacconist, 129 Callowhill
Jones Henry, lab., 3 Sp. Garden Retreat
Jones Henry, waiter, 79 S 2d, 18 Currant al
Jones Henry W., glassblower, 196 S Front.
Jones Horatio, carp., 531 N 5th
Jones Humphrey, lab., Ogden bel 11th
Jones Isaac, cabinetmaker, 75 & h 77 N Front.
Jones Isaac, cordw., Pearl ab 12th
Jones Isaac, pumpmr., 100 Carpenter (S)
Jones Isaac B., lab., rear Orchard ab Rawle
JONES ISAAC C. mer., 29 Chestnut, h 230 Sassafras
Jones Isaac C. Jr., mer., 20 N 4th, h 36 N. 9th.

Jones Isaac L... liquor store, High n Sch 5th
Jones Isaac T., mer., 11 N 2nd, h 83 Marshall
Jones Isaac T. waterman, rear 45 N road
Jones Isabella, confect., 121 Spruce
Jones Isaiah, provisions, R road ab Wallace
Jones Ishmael, blacksm., Sch 6th ab Pine
Jones Israel, cordw., Craig's ct (K)
Jones Israel, carpenter, Sch 6th & Cox
Jones Jabez, carp., 8 Jackson (N L)
Jones Jacob, clerk, 5th n George
Jones Jacob, carp., Queen ab Hanover, (K)
JONES JACOB H., Red Lion Hotel, 200 High
Jones Jacob P., mer., S W Sch 7th & High, h 215 Filbert
Jones Jacob T. oysterman, Swanson bel Christian
Jones James, brass founder, 93 Mulberry.
Jones James, carp. Clinton ab Brown
Jones James, clerk, 25 Howard st
Jones James L. grocer, 257 Callowhill
Jones James M. shipwt. Wood bel Franklin (K)
Jones James M., chairmr., Marriott bel 6th
Jones Jehu, cordw., 13 Pine al.
Jones Jehu, tailor, Lebanon ab Catharine
Jones Jesse, porter, 2 Pray's ct
Jones Joel, judge Dist. Court, h 429 High
Jones Joel, carp. Beaver ab 3d
Jones John, sen., skindresser, 2 Townsend's av
Jones John, tailor, 2d & Washington
Jones John, finding store, High W of Sch 5th
Jones John, ruler, Lombard ab Schuylkill
Jones John, waiter, 305 E Pine
Jones John, brickmr., Cedar n Sch 2d
Jones John, messenger, 53 Catharine
Jones John; dyer & scourer, 28 N 5th
Jones John, hosiery, Coates & Franklin
Jones John, 12 Somers' ct
Jones John, carter, 580 S Front
JONES JOHN A., Union Hotel, 152 Chestnut
Jones John D. harnessmr. 2d & Dock
Jones John D., carp., Chancellor W Sch 7th
Jones John H., printer, 34 Carter's al, h 112 S Front
Jones John M. wheelwt. 48 W Cedar
Jones John M., cordwainer, Pearl n Sch 6th
Jones John M. upholsterer, Callowhill & Dillwyn, h Witmer's al
Jones John M. com. mer. 1 Boyles' ct
Jones John M'Kenzie, 51 Chestnut
Jones John P., dry goods, S E. 8th & Sansom
JONES JOHN SIDNEY, carpet hall, 18 & 20 N 2d c Church al., h 2d ab Reading R road
JONES JOHN S., broker, 43 N 6th.
Jones John T., plane maker, 28 N 8th
Jones John W., 7 Penn
Jones John W., cordw., S W 5th & Vine
Jones John W., M. D., 579 S 2d
Jones Joseph, clerk, Vine bel 13th
Jones Joseph, lab., rear Wood ab Broad
Jones Joseph, dealer, 149 Sp. Garden
Jones Joseph, cabinetmr. 72 S 2d
Jones Joseph, gardener, Vine bel 13th
Jones Joseph, mer., h 22 N 11th
Jones Joseph, mer., 6 N Front

23

Jones Joseph, plasterer, Mechanic bel George (N L)
Jones Joseph H., Rev., 162 S 4th
Jones Joseph S., turner, rear 110 Walnut, h 53 Gaskill
Jones Joseph W., variety store, 18 N 4th, h 149 Sp Garden
Jones Josiah, lab. Gorrell's ct
Jones Josiah, waiter, South ab 12th
Jones Josiah, lab., Union ab Franklin (K)
Jones Justus P., mer., 11 N 2d.
Jones J. Hillborn, mer., 82 High
JONES J. SHIPLEY, printer, 3 Lagrange, h 10th bel Callowhill
Jones J. D. & C., mers. office 7 Church al
JONES J. & H. brass cockmrs. 93 Mulberry
Jones Lætitia, eating house, 525 High
Jones Lemuel, steward, 58 Middle al
Jones Lewis, waterman, 25 Washington av
Jones Lloyd, gent. 299 Race
Jones Margaret, dressmr. 326 Sassafras
Jones Margaret, shop, Queen ab Warren (K)
Jones Mark T., tailor, 136 N 8th
Jones Martha, b h, 319 Callowhill
Jones Martha D., b h, 49 N 8th
Jones Martin, waiter, Davis' ct.
Jones Mary, 19 Federal
Jones Mary, 18 N 5th
Jones Mary, 63 Union
Jones Mary, gentw., Liberty al.
Jones Mary, Ogden n 10th
Jones Mrs. Mary H., gentw., Spruce n Sch 8th
Jones Meredith, bricklayer, Queen bel Marlborough (K)
Jones M. & Garrett E. milliners, 57 Mulberry
Jones M. H., mer., 41 High, h 195 Spruce
Jones Nathan, hosier, 45 Chestnut, h 83 Union.
Jones Owen, tailor, 200 High
Jones Pennington, mer., 6 N Front, h 320 Mulberry
Jones Phineas, clerk, 2 Warder pl
Jones Purnell V., shoemr. 109 Christian
Jones Rachael, b'h, 363 N Front
Jones Redding, lab., 8 Flytax al
Jones Rees, packer, 6 Southampton ct
Jones Richard, coal, 9 York ct
Jones Richard B., 77 Dock
Jones Richd., coal dealer, 28 Walnut
Jones Richard & Co., coal mers., 22½ Walnut
Jones Robert, ship master, 186 Queen.
Jones Robert, hair dresser 104 Spruce.
Jones Robert E., gent., Bridge M. village
Jones Samuel, saddler, rear 212 St John
Jones Saml. teacher, N E 7th & Carpenter (C), h 162 S 4th
Jones Samuel B. cordw. 3 Linden
Jones Saml. P., bookbinder, 493 High
Jones Samuel S., acct. 516 N 8th.
Jones Samuel W., mer., 103 N Front, h 154 N Front.
Jones Sarah, 62 S 4th
Jones Sarah, shop, 9 Hubble
Jones Simeon, Otter ab F road (K)
Jones Susan, widow, 86 Apple
Jones Thomas, painter, 25 Richard

Jones Thos., stevedore, Morrell's ct
Jones Thomas, waterman, Sarah n Bedford (K)
Jones Thos., tailor, 408 High, h Vine n Sch 7th
Jones Thomas, lampwickmr., 123 M road
Jones Thomas, cord. 7 Poplar
Jones Thomas, oysters, 324 High.
Jones Thomas, carp., Beaver bel Charlotte
Jones Thomas C., collector, 43 Noble
Jones Thomas, lab., Orange ab Lemon
Jones Thomas R., artist, Bread & Quarry
Jones Thomas W., saddler, 29 Cresson's al
Jones Timothy, b h, 13 Filbert
Jones Tustin, plasterer, 7 Poplar
Jones T. W., dentist, 309 N 3rd
Jones Venire, watchman, 15 Mary (S)
Jones Warner C., mer., 34 N 2d, h 24 Chester
Jones Wilkinson, tailor, 19 Lebanon
Jones Wm., ship carp., 8 Pt Pleasant ct (K)
Jones Wm., carman, Marlboro' ab F road (K)
Jones Wm., patternmr., Marlboro' ab Bedford (K)
Jones Wm., butcher, Kline's ct
Jones Wm. acct. 174 Pine
Jones Wm., lab., 23 Beck (S)
Jones Wm. tobacconist, N E Brown and 5th
Jones William, cabinet maker, 351 S 6th
Jones William, mer., 6 N Front, h 320 Mulberry
Jones William, dry goods, 8 and h 40 N 5th
Jones William, barber, 107 N 7th
Jones Wm., lampmr. 209 N 9th
Jones Wm., cabinetmr., Mifflin bel Perry
Jones Wm., machinist, 39 Brandywine
Jones Wm. & Sons, com. mers., 6 N Front
Jones William B., brickmr., 2 Apple
Jones Wm. D., painter, 20 & h 13 N 2d
Jones Wm. D. & Co., dry goods, 11 N 2d
Jones William D., mer., 11 N 2d.
Jones William F. & Brother, mers., 29 Chestnut, h 230 Sassafras
Jones William H., printer, 11 Chatham
Jones Wm. H., mer., 139 Walnut
Jones Wm. H., carpenter, 184 Locust.
Jones Wm. J. shoemr. Queen ab F road
Jones Wm. M., groc., S E 12th & Poplar
Jones W. F. port. painter, Walnut ab 6th, h 105 Filbert
Jones W. H. mason, Washington bel 7th
JORDAN & BROTHER, grocers, 121 N 3d.
Jordan Charles, weaver, Mariner
Jordan Charles, bricklayer, 4 Gebhard
Jordan Charles, waterman, Landing ab Coates
Jordan Francis, grocer, 121 N 3d, h 87 Race
Jordan Frederick, baker, 67 Prune
Jordan Frederick, baker, 507 N 4th.
Jordan George, brussel carp. weav., Charlotte bel Beaver
Jordan Hannah, washer, 20 Prosperous al
Jordan Henry, currier, Lewis ab Poplar
Jordan Henry, cotton spin'r., Mariner
Jordan James, waiter, 4 Barley.
Jordan Jesse, cordw., Higgins' pl
Jordan John, clerk, 244 Filbert
Jordan John, jr., mer., 121 N 3d, h 91 S 3d
Jordan Jonathan, cordw. R road bel 13th
Jordan Levi, lab., M'Devitt's av. (K)

Jordan Margaret, gentw., 119 New
Jordan Matthew, labourer, 1 Dorothy
Jordan Moses, lab. rear 25 Ogden
Jordan Nicholas, weaver, 5 Helmuth.
Jordan Patrick, lab., 3 Pearl
Jordan Pennington, porter, Lombard bel 11th
Jordan Peter R. shoemr. Allen ab F road
Jordan Richard, coal dealer, 5th & Queen
Jordan Sam. wheelwright, h rear 102 Christian
Jordan Samuel, stone cutter, rear 285 St John
Jordan Susanna, 144 S Front
Jordan Thos., carter, 239 7th
Jordan William, shoe mer., 232 High, h Wood ab 9th.
Jordan Wm. shoemr., 24 Gebhard
Jordan Wm., coachman, George n Sch 6th
Jorden John, ship carver, 122 S Front
Jordon Samuel, labourer, 198 Cherry.
Joseph Harmon, cordw., 2d ab Edward (K)
Joseph Jane, Paschall's al.
Joseph John, tailor, rear 288 N Front
Joseph Salmon, pedler, St John bel Beaver(K)
Josephine Mary, teacher, 13th and Clover
Jostlen Ambr., bootmr. 436 Sassafras, h 154 N 8th
Joy Cyrus, R road bel Green.
Joy Maurice, shoemr., Juniper ab High
Joyce Ettweine, blacksm., 97 Cherry, h 120 N 9th
Joyce E., moulder, Willow ab 5th
Joyce John J., blacksmith, 90 Cherry, h 5 Haines
Joynes Dr., 454 E Spruce
Joynis Charles, carp., 13 Scott's ct
Judson Mary B., widow of Rev. Albert, 38 Sansom
Juel Joseph, feather and artificial flower manufactory, 156 N 3d
Juel Wm., hosier, rear 174 Poplar
Juel Wm. H., druggist, Mead and 2d
Juery John, copper plate planisher, 90 S 8th
Juhan Lewis, clerk, 139 G T road
Julian A. H., merchant, 156 High, h 221 Filbert
Julian, Mason & Co. dry goods, 156 High
Julian Edmund, cabmr., 42 Dock
Julius Theodore, sea captain, 18 German.
Jump Henry, printer, 8 Hall's av
Junelle Frederick, tobacconist, Bedford & Shippen la
Jungandreas C., 110 Wood
Junior George, lab., Orchard ab Rawle
Junior Thomas, lab., rear 132 Apple
Juppenlatz Frederick, baker, 68 Christian
Justice Alfred B., mer., 149 High, h Wood 2 doors ab Franklin.
Justice Charles, bookbinder, Carlton bel Sch 3d
Justice C. M., tailor, 102 Chestnut, h 32 Marshall
Justice Emeline, 474 Sassafras
Justice George, gent., rear 443 N 2d
Justice Geo. M., mer., 149 High, h 260 N 4th.
Justice George R., mer., 149 High, h 249 Vine
JUSTICE G. M. & G. R. & CO., hardware, 148 High.
Justice G. W., clerk, 27 Chatham
Justice Jacob, 243 Vine
Justice James P., clerk, 343 S 3d

Justice John, carp., 197 Locust
Justice Joseph, plasterer, 141 Green.
Justice Joseph, distiller, 314 N 2d
Justice Jos., clock & watchmr., 443 N 2d
Justice Philip S., mer., N W 5th & Commerce, h 117 Marshall.
Justice Samuel, baker, 285 N 7th.
Justice Warner, carp., 8th & Parrish.
Justins Wm., whip mr., 189 Green.
Justus Philip, 24 Wood
Juvenal A. W. gent., Coates bel 11th
Juvenal Jacob, gent., Coates bel 11th.
Juvenal Wm. W. att'y, Coates bel 11th

————

Kachele Gotlieb, shop, Apple ab Brown
Kady Isabel, S 7th ab Catharine
Kagle Christian, victualler, 108 New Market
Kahmer Wm., silver plater, Elm bel Franklin
Kahnweiler Benedict, b. h., 30 Margaretta
Kaib John, brewer, 319 St John (K)
Kaighn H., gentw., 199 Pine
Kaighn James E., mer., 9 S 2d.
Kain Dennis, ladies' shoemaker, Clinton ab Brown
Kain John, vict., S E 8th & Shippen
Kain Mennis, lab., 191 N Front
Kain Robt., bottler, Sch 3d and High
Kain Thos., lead worker, 5 Marion
Kain Wm., shoemr., 17 N 3d, h 21 Madison
Kalaher John, lab., Locust n Sch 2d
Kalb John L., tailor, 263 St John
Kalbach Daniel, potter, Ogden bel 12th
Kalbach M., stone cutter, Ann (F V)
Kale Jacob, cigarmaker, Lewis ab Poplar
Kale Jacob, brass founder, Jackson pl
Kale John, cordw., Howard bel Franklin (K)
Kale Joseph, tobacconist, Charlotte below George
Kale Wm., cigarmr., N E Charlotte & Culvert.
Kalehoff Henry, segarmr., 1 Beck
Kalehoff Jacob, lab., 1 Beck
Kall Christ., lab., rear Broad ab Poplar
Kallenberg E. L., mustard, 95 Callowhill
Kalpin Peter, baker, Jones al
Kaltenbach James, bak., New Market ab Coates
Kame Francis, weaver, Conrad's ct
Kame Francis, lab., 196 Shippen
Kames George S., printer, 17 Benton
Kames John, cordwainer, 1 Fairies' ct.
Kames Thos., printer, 17 Benton
Kampen Theodore, tailor, 1 Beaver ct
Kampmann Catharine, variety store, S E 6th & Noble
Kanada Josh., bootmr., 196 E Lombard
Kane Andrew, lab., 230 Shippen
Kane Andrew, dry goods, 155 Cedar
Kane Barney, rear 6 Carpenter
Kane Charles, carp., rear 62 Catharine
Kane Daniel, tobacconist, 53 Queen
Kane David, blacksm., Beach ab Poplar (K)
Kane Dennis, shoemr., Drinker's ct
Kane Dennis, bottler, Linden bel Howard
Kane Elizabeth, 3 Poplar ct

Kane Ellen, Adams n 13th
Kane George, tobacco inspector, city store, h S W 4th and Gaskill
Kane George, tobacconist, rear 100 Christian
Kane George, cordw., 3d bel Thompson (K)
Kane Henry, chimist, S 10th ab Bonsall
Kane James, fat gatherer, 296 S 7th
Kane John, lab., 10th bel Christian
Kane John, porter, 5 Deal's av
Kane John, baker, 9th & Washington
Kane John, lab., lab., Broad ab Poplar
Kane John, lab., 298 S 7th
Kane John, blacksmith Green's ct
Kane John, mariner, 33 Christian
Kane John K., Judge District Court U. S., h Sch 7th & Locust
Kane Joseph C. M., M D., 402 S 2d
Kane Lawrence, lab., Broad ab Mulberry
Kane Matthew, stone cut., Jones W of Sch 6th
Kane Michael, coachman, 7 Elliott's av
Kane Morris, mariner, 33 Christian
Kane Owen, trader, Carroll ct
Kane Owen, shop, 233 Shippen
Kane Owen, lab., 5 Adams
Kane Patrick, lab., 7th ab Fitzwater
Kane Patrick, Filbert ab 13th
Kannyatt Henry, skin dress., Haydock bel Front
Kany Patrick, lab., Palmer ab Beach (K)
Kappes Gotlieb, musician, 5 Randall's ct
Kappler Frederick, hotel, 442 N 2d.
Karcher Philip, cordwainer, George bel 3d
Karney Michael, clothing, 201 E South
Karns Edward, cabman, 14 Crabb
Karpes Henry, baker, 156 N 13th
Karr Matthew, vinegar, Shippen ab 13th
Karrigan Wm., plumber, Lewis bel Sch 6th
Karsten H. W., confectioner, 352 N Front
Kartsher John C., ropemaker & ship chandler, 78 S wharves, h 38 Lombard.
Kasinger Jos., oyster house, 362 High
Kassehnan Edw., turner, Orchard ab Culvert
Kast George, oak cooper, Otter n F road (K)
Kast Joseph, Locust n Broad
Kater James, weaver, S E 10th & Sergeant
Kater John, 13th and Cherry
Kates Henry, shoemr., Gabell's ct
Kates John, weaver, Christian and 8th
Kates M., bell hanger, 28 N 7th, h 305 Mulberry
Kates Samuel, chairmr., R road ab Wood
Kates William, locksmith, Mulberry W Sch 7th
Katon Jesse, waterman, Maiden bel Beach (K)
Katts Isaac, peddler, 3 Galbraith's ct
Katz Caroline, 7 Duke
Katz Daniel, pedler, rear 100 St John
Katz Geo. D., confec., 171 Race
Katz Levi, Samson's al
Katzman Margaret, wid., 78 Green
Kauffman Abram B., shoemr., 98 German
Kauffman Joseph, dealer, 57 Gaskill
Kaufman Michael, beer house, 219 St John
Kaupp Jacob, Jones' al
Kautzman John, shoemr., Franklin ab Union (K)
Kavnaugh Mary Ann, dress maker, 4 Castle
Kay & Brother, booksellers, 183½ High, printers, rear 50 N 6th

Justice John, carp., 197 Locust
Justice Joseph, plasterer, 141 Green.
Justice Joseph, distiller, 314 N 2d
Justice Jos., clock & watchmr., 443 N 2d
Justice Philip S., mer., N W 5th & Commerce, h 117 Marshall.
Justice Samuel, baker, 285 N 7th.
Justice Warner, carp., 8th & Parrish.
Justins Wm., whip mr., 189 Green.
Justus Philip, 24 Wood
Juvenal A. W. gent., Coates bel 11th
Juvenal Jacob, gent., Coates bel 11th.
Juvenal Wm. W. att'y, Coates bel 11th

———

Kachele Gotlieb, shop, Apple ab Brown
Kady Isabel, S 7th ab Catharine
Kagle Christian, victualler, 108 New Market
Kahmer Wm., silver plater, Elm bel Franklin
Kahnweiler Benedict, b. h., 30 Margaretta
Kaib John, brewer, 319 St John (K)
Kaighn H., gentw., 199 Pine
Kaighn James E., mer., 9 S 2d.
Kain Dennis, ladies' shoemaker, Clinton ab Brown
Kain John, vict., S E 8th & Shippen
Kain Mennis, lab., 191 N Front
Kain Robt., bottler, Sch 3d and High
Kain Thos., lead worker, 5 Marion
Kain Wm., shoemr., 17 N 3d, h 21 Madison
Kalaher John, lab., Locust n Sch 2d
Kalb John L., tailor, 263 St John
Kalbach Daniel, potter, Ogden bel 12th
Kalbach M., stone cutter, Ann (F V)
Kale Jacob, cigarmaker, Lewis ab Poplar
Kale Jacob, brass founder, Jackson pl
Kale John, cordw., Howard bel Franklin (K)
Kale Joseph, tobacconist, Charlotte below George
Kale Wm., cigarmr., N E Charlotte & Culvert.
Kalehoff Henry, segarmr., 1 Beck
Kalehoff Jacob, lab, 1 Beck
Kall Christ., lab., rear Broad ab Poplar
Kallenberg E. L., mustard, 95 Callowhill
Kalpin Peter, baker, Jones al
Kaltenbach James, bak., New Market ab Coates
Kame Francis, weaver, Conrad's ct
Kame Francis, lab., 196 Shippen
Kames George S., printer, 17 Benton
Kames John, cordwainer, 1 Fairies' ct.
Kames Thos., printer, 17 Benton
Kampen Theodore, tailor, 1 Beaver ct
Kampmann Catharine, variety store, S E 6th & Noble
Kanada Josh., bootmr., 196 E Lombard
Kane Andrew, lab., 230 Shippen
Kane Andrew, dry goods, 155 Cedar
Kane Barney, rear 6 Carpenter
Kane Charles, carp., rear 62 Catharine
Kane Daniel, tobacconist, 53 Queen
Kane David, blacksm., Beach ab Poplar (K)
Kane Dennis, shoemr., Drinker's ct
Kane Dennis, bottler, Linden bel Howard
Kane Elizabeth, 3 Poplar ct

Kane Ellen, Adams n 13th
Kane George, tobacco inspector, city store, h S W 4th and Gaskill
Kane George, tobacconist, rear 100 Christian
Kane George, cordw., 3d bel Thompson (K)
Kane Henry, chimist, S 10th ab Bonsall
Kane James, fat gatherer, 296 S 7th
Kane John, lab., 10th bel Christian
Kane John, porter, 5 Deal's av
Kane John, baker, 9th & Washington
Kane John, lab., lab., Broad ab Poplar
Kane John, lab., 298 S 7th
Kane John, blacksmith Green's ct
Kane John, mariner, 33 Christian
Kane John K., Judge District Court U. S., h Sch 7th & Locust
Kane Joseph C. M., M D., 402 S 2d
Kane Lawrence, lab., Broad ab Mulberry
Kane Matthew, stone cut., Jones W of Sch 6th
Kane Michael, coachman, 7 Elliott's av
Kane Morris, mariner, 33 Christian
Kane Owen, trader, Carroll ct
Kane Owen, shop, 233 Shippen
Kane Owen, lab., 5 Adams
Kane Patrick, lab., 7th ab Fitzwater
Kane Patrick, Filbert ab 13th
Kannyatt Henry, skin dress., Haydock bel Front
Kany Patrick, lab., Palmer ab Beach (K)
Kappes Gotlieb, musician, 5 Randall's ct
Kappler Frederick, hotel, 442 N 2d.
Karcher Philip, cordwainer, George bel 3d
Karney Michael, clothing, 201 E South
Karns Edward, cabman, 14 Crabb
Karpes Henry, baker, 156 N 13th
Karr Matthew, vinegar, Shippen ab 13th
Karrigan Wm., plumber, Lewis bel Sch 6th
Karsten H. W., confectioner, 352 N Front
Kartsher John C., ropemaker & ship chandler, 78 S wharves, h 38 Lombard.
Kasinger Jos., oyster house, 362 High
Kassehnan Edw., turner, Orchard ab Culvert
Kast George, oak cooper, Otter n F road (K)
Kast Joseph, Locust n Broad
Kater James, weaver, S E 10th & Sergeant
Kater John, 13th and Cherry
Kates Henry, shoemr., Gabell's ct
Kates John, weaver, Christian and 8th
Kates M., bell hanger, 28 N 7th, h 305 Mulberry
Kates Samuel, chairmr., R road ab Wood
Kates William, locksmith, Mulberry W Sch 7th
Katon Jesse, waterman, Maiden bel Beach (K)
Katts Isaac, peddler, 3 Galbraith's ct
Katz Caroline, 7 Duke
Katz Daniel, pedler, rear 100 St John
Katz Geo. D., confec., 171 Race
Katz Levi, Samson's al
Katzman Margaret, wid., 78 Green
Kauffman Abram B., shoemr., 8th German
Kauffman Joseph, dealer, 57 Gaskill
Kaufman Michael, beer house, 219 St John
Kaupp Jacob, Jones' al
Kautzman John, shoemr., Franklin ab Union (K)
Kavnaugh Mary Ann, dress maker, 4 Castle
Kay & Brother, booksellers, 183½ High, printers, rear 50 N 6th

Kay & De Haven, hardware, 211 High
Kay Edward, weaver, Mariner
Kay Elizabeth, shop, Callowhill bel Sch. 7th.
Kay James Jr., bookseller, 183½ High
Kay Jas. Hutchinson, mer., 211 High, h 253 Spruce
Kay John, carp., rear 17 Farmer
Kay John I., bookseller, 183½ High, h Chestnut E Sch 8th
Kay Joseph E. dry goods, Sp Garden bel 10th
Kay Sarah H. 135 O Y road
KAY & TROUTMAN, booksellers, 183½ High
Kayser Charles, tailor, 68 Cedar
Kayser Solomon, tailor, 73 S 2d
Keach Abner, stone mason, Jones W of Sch 5th
Kean Henry, undertaker and sexton, Bache
Kean John, blacksm., Green's ct., h 4th bel Lombard
Kean John W., jeweller, 108 S 10th
Kearnes Jos., drayman, Sch 3d bel Chestnut
Kearney A. teacher, S E 8th and Walnut, h 150 S 2d
Kearney Christopher, cordwainers, 156 Lombard
Kearney Henry, waiter, Carlton bel Sch 6th
Kearney John C., lampmr., 13 S 6th, h 4 Juniper
Kearns John, carter, 6 Elmslie's al
Keates William, ship joiner, Catharine st. whf., h 19 Beck (S)
Keating Edwd., morocco dr., Dean ab Bedford
Keating John, gent., 111 S 4th
Keating Lambert, b h, 60 Zane
Keating Michael, lab. c Sch 2d and Filbert
Keating William, painter and glaz., Plum ab 3rd
Keating Mrs. W. H., Sch 8th bel Spruce
Keating Wm. V., M. D., 111 S 4th
Keaton Jesse, lab., 3 R road ct
Keaton Wm., tobacconist, rear 8th bel Parrish
Keats Samuel, carp., 7 Mary (S)
Keay Wm., stone cutter, George n Sch 6th
Keck Charles H., plast., 30 Charlotte
KECK JACOB, mer., 293 High, b 63 Filbert
Keck Samuel, book binder, Beaver ab 3d
Kee Geo. W., printer, Olive bel Broad
Kee James, carp., R road ab Broad
Kee John J., tailor, 78 Callowhill
Kee Wm., coppersmith, Federal ab 2d
Kee J., coppersmiths, 318 S 3d
Keech Baldwin, engineer, 127 New Market
Keech John, stone cutter, Woodland (W P)
Keech John, stone mason, Locust (W P)
Keech Wm., dealer, 305 S 6th
Keefe Anthony, vict., Mary n F road
Keefe Bartholomew, eating house, 194 High, h Warner's ct
Keefe Edw., lab., 5 Elder
Keefe James, manuf., 13 City Stores, h 7 Federal.
Keefe Jeremiah, weaver, 4 Lloyd's ct
Keefe John, 9 Federal
Keefe John, watchman. 23 Strawberry
Keefe Michael, weaver, 20 Lloyd's ct (K)
Keefer Henry, bootmr., rear 130 F. road (K)
Keefer Philip, lab., Perkenpine ct
Keefer Valentine, lab., G. T. road bel 7th (K)

Keegan Edward, tailor, 233 Christian
Keel David, lab., 3 Little Oak
Keel George, paper stainer, 17 Emlen's ct
Keel John, tailor, Mint ct.
Keel John, cordw., 8 Diligent av
Keel Mary, gentw., 195 Green.
Keeler Jacob, carter, rear 302 N 10th
Keeler J. N., M.D., N W 3d & Cedar
Keeley Jacob B., bar tender, Harrison place
Keeley Joseph, carp., Lewis ab Poplar
Keely Frederick, agent, Green ab 13th
Keely Frederick, paper stainer, Front and Vine, h 28 Beaver (K)
Keely Jacob, tailor, 9th and Poplar
Keely Patrick, ostler, Dean ab Spruce
Keely Wm., builder, 13th bel Green
Keemlè Isaac A., scrivener, 3 Carpente'rs ct., h 10th ab Parrish
Keemlè Margaret, shop, 79 N 3d
Keemlè Samuel, atty. and coun., N E 4th and Cherry
Keemlè Saml. R., mer., 37 N Whfs., h N E 4th and Cherry
Keen Adam, fisherman, Vienna ab Queen. (K)
Keen Charles, carter, 4 Goldsmith's ct
Keen Charles, bootmaker, 54 Mulberry.
Keen Charles, cashier Kensington Bank, h N W Front & Ellen.
Keen Chas., cordw. 229 St John
Keen Charles L., bricklayer, 331 Pine
Keen Clement, ship joiner, Penn ab Maiden, h Queen n Crown. (K)
Keen & Coats, tannery, 509 N Front.
Keen Eli, cordw., 229 St John
Keen Geo. B., mer., 5 and 6 S Whfs., h Chestnut (W P)
Keen Jacob, ship carp., Crown below Franklin (K)
Keen Jas., U S steamboat insp., Shackamaxon ab Queen
Keen James & Bros., ship joiners, Penn bel Shackamaxon (K)
Keen James B., ship joiner, Bedford bel Crown
Keen James C., cordwainer, 58 Vine.
Keen Jesse, shop, 551 S 2d
Keen John C., cordw., Beaver bel 3d
Keen John E., tanner, 509 N Front
Keen John F., mer., 78 High, h 368 Mulberry
Keen Joseph, currier, 61 Chestnut, h 27 New Market.
Keen Joseph S., coal mer., Bridgewater, (W P)
Keen Jos. S. & Son, coal mer. Bridgewater (W P)
Keen Mary Ann, milliner, 39 N 12th
Keen Moses, labourer, Palmer ab West. (K)
Keen Morris L. & Bro. machinists, Washington (W P)
Keen Morris L. machinist, Chestnut (W P)
Keen Rebecca, West ab Palmer (K)
Keen Sarah, gentw., 147 S 9th.
Keen Wm., shipwright, Palmer ab West (K)
Keen Wm. E. G., mer., 6 N Wharves
Keen William W. & Co., curriers, 61 Chestnut.
Keen W. L., glass cutter, 6 Lagrange pl., h 2 Pemberton al

Keen W. W., currier, 61 Chestnut, h Chestnut E Park (W P)

Keenan Edward., manuf., G T road ab Master.

Keenan Edw. J., manuf., Cadwalader bel Jefferson

Keenan Ellen, 230 Water ab Vine

Keenan Hugh, weaver, 239 N Front

Keenan John, carp., 2d bel Master (K)

Keenan Michael, manuf., 700 G T road ab Master

Keenan Peter, lab., 236 Water

Keene Sarah, gentw., N W 10th and Chestnut

Keeney C. R., druggist, Sch. 7th and Mulberry

Keever George, hatter, 204 St John

Keffer Anthony, caulker, Vienna bel Duke (K)

Keffer Catharine, McClung's ct

Keffer George, cordw., S W 2d & Sassafras, h 248 N Front

Keffer & Gorman, boots and shoes, S W 2d and Sassafras

Keffer John, lithographer, 12 Bank

Kehoe Catharine, 9 Dean

Kehœ Dominick, grocer, 337 High, h 16 N 9th

Kehr Samuel, cabmr., 440 N 3d

Keichline C. P., M. D., 4th ab Tammany

Keichline David, vict., Brown bel 12th

Keichline Elizabeth, gentw. 187 Green

Keichline George, vict., R road (F V)

Keichline Jacob, vict., 12th ab Brown

Keichline Wm., vict., Brown bel 12th

Keifaber Bernard, suspend. weav., Monroe and Cherry (K)

Keifer Michael, lab., Lily al

Keighler Margaret, 8 Castle

Keighler Thomas, cordw., Swanson bel Queen.

Keighler Thomas, 46 St. John

Keighley T. W., paper and rags, Front and Vine

Keil John, shop, 162 Brown

Keim Alex., silversmith, S 8th ab Christian

Keim Bernard S., suspend. weav., rear 246 N 2d

KEIM & BROWN, turners, 123 N 4th

Keim & Brown, turners, 127 N 4th.

Keim & Co., plumbers, 125 N 4th

Keim George, turner, Ogden ab 10th

Keim Geo. M., mar. East. Dist. Pa., office State House, h 18 S 6th

Keim Jacob, steel and copperplate maker, 2 Hause's ct, h 187 Cherry.

Keim Mrs. John M., dry goods, S W 6th & Sp Garden

Keim Joseph, turner, 8th bel Coates

Keim Josiah, copperplate maker, 6 Gebhard

Keim Rebecca, shop, Buttonwood bel 6th

Keim Samuel, tailor, Pleasant bel 11th

Keim Wm., printer, 15 Well's row

Keisen Elias, cordw., Clinton bel Poplar

Keiser Martin, tailor, N W 5th and Spruce

Keisewetter E., tailor, 367 N Front

Keith Ann, 21 Currant al

Keith Ann, 2 Richardson's ct

Keith Ann, 4 Durham, oyster house, 260 High

Keith Elizabeth Mrs., Tammany & St John

Keith Matthew J., oyster house, 260 High, h 14 Bonsall

Keith Michael, lab., Wistar ct (K)

Keith Saml., gent., 231 S Front.

Keith S. A., dressmr., Phoenix ab Cadwaladar.

Keith Washington, 231 S Front

Keith Wm., M. D., 141 Spruce, h 231 S Front

Kelch James, saddler, S W 5th and Prune

Kelch Joseph P., machinist, 94 German

Kelch Lydia, trimmings, 86 N 5th

Kelchner Peter, tinsmith, Grubb

Kelefer Henry, sugar refiner, 9 Emlen's ct

Kell John, lab., Ashton bel Walnut

Kellar Thomas, painter, 102 Fitzwater

Keller Adam, bottler, 204 Water

Keller Adam, cordw., 8 New Crown

Keller Adam, undertaker, 197 Sassafras

Keller A., bootmr., 44 Callowhill

KELLER CHRISTIAN, tailor, 160 Sassafras

Keller Conrad, tin and sheet iron worker, 10th and Callowhill

Keller George, Miller's ct (N L)

Keller George, shoemr., 30 Sheaff

Keller George L. shoemr., 37 Perry

Keller Henry, baker, rear 382 S Front

Keller H., painter, Pleasant bel 10th

Keller Isaac, cordw., Harmony st

Keller John, Rev., Sch 5th n Barker

Keller John, bottler, 204 N Water & 209 N Front

Keller John, combmr. 111 N Juniper

Keller Joseph, tailor, Palmer ab Duke

Keller Mary, shop, 119 Poplar

Keller Michael, baker, 433 S Front

Keller Peter, painter, 116 Cherry

Keller Philip, lab., G T road bel 4th

Keller Wm. carp. weav., Charlotte bel Franklin

Keller Wm., mer., 21 Branch

Keller Wm., M. D., 52 O. Y. road

Kelley John, lumber, Catharine bel 8th, h Christian ab 9th

KELLEY WM. D., att'y and coun., 14 Sansom

Kellinger John V. brass worker, G T road opp 5th

Kellinger Maurice, bricklayer, 94 New Market

Kellner D., grocer, S E 3d & Coates

Kellogg Geo. R., mer., 17 S Front

Kellogg Henry C., mer., 17 S Front

Kellogg Hosea, mer., 17 S Front, h 151 N 9th

Kellogg H. & Sons, mers., 17 S Front

Kellogg Joseph, confectioner, 228 Vine

Kellogg Martin A., livery stable, 11 & h 5 Filbert

Kellum Eli, rear Wood ab Sch. 4th

Kelly Alexander, china store, 108 W High

Kelly Andrew, labourer, 8 Dorothy.

Kelly Andrew, carp. Penn bel Broad

Kelly Ann, widow, Olivet place

Kelly Ann, widow, rear 118 W. High

Kelly Ann, 2 Elliott av

Kelly Ann Eliza, 1 Skerrett's ct

Kelly Bernard, carp., Mulberry n Sch. 2d

Kelly Bridget, widow, Steam Mill alley

KELLY & BROTHER, tailors, 165 Chestnut

Kelly & Brothers, tinsmiths, 444 High

Kelly Caroline, Bacon's ct

Kelly Charles, brushmr., Carpenter bel 7th

Kelly Chas., shoemr., 7th bel Carpenter

Kelly Closon, cordw. Beaver ab 3d
Kelly Daniel, tailor, 5th and Walnut
Kelly Daniel, weaver, Front ab Jefferson (K)
Kelly Daniel, grocer, 87 P. road
Kelly Danl. A., harness mr., 5th and Prune
Kelly David J., shoemr., Dorothy n Sch 4th
Kelly Edward, carpenter, Little Pine bel 7th, h 189 Christian.
Kelly Edward, gent., 168 S 6th.
Kelly Edward, tailor, High W Sch 3d
Kelly Edward, blksmith, Carlton ab Sch. 6th
Kelly Edward, moulder, Fraley's alley (K)
Kelly Edw. P., tailor, 165 Chestnut, h 173 S 3d
Kelly Elizabeth, b h, 349 High
Kelly Ellen, store, Sch 7th ab Filbert
Kelly Elliott, waterman, 9 Duke
Kelly Elwood, huckster, 2 Vernon pl
Kelly Erasmus, plasterer, Ross ab Queen (K)
Kelly Erasmus, plasterer, Master n Charlotte(K)
Kelly E. J., dressmr., 42 Julianna
Kelly Francis A., carp., Lemon ab 10th
Kelly Francis X., currier, 141 Lombard, h 9 Morgan
Kelly George, bricklayer, Stackhouse ct
Kelly Geo., paper hanger, 297 S 5th
Kelly Griffith, stonemason, Olive bel Broad
Kelly Hannah, rear 252 Christian
Kelly Henry, ship carp., Church bel Christian
Kelly Henry, watchman, Swanson ab Washington
Kelly Hugh, cordw., Carpenter bel 7th
Kelly Hugh, lab., 9 Little Oak
Kelly Isaac, cordw., 3 Paynter's ct
Kelly Isaiah, cordw., Van Buren pl
Kelly James, 71 Plum.
Kelly James, teacher, 12 Ann W Sch 4th
Kelly James, tailor, 14 S 12th
Kelly James, weaver, Middleton's ct
Kelly James, lab., Rutter's ct
Kelly James, weaver, Shippen bel Broad
Kelly James, carp., rear High n Sch 2d
Kelly James, tailor, George n Sch 6th
Kelly James, barber, 70 N Front
Kelly James, tailor, 3 Randall's ct
Kelly Jas., stationer, 90 Walnut, h 2 Baxter's ct
Kelly James, bootmr., Wale's ct
Kelly Jas., blacksmith, 289 E South
Kelly Jas. brick maker, 227 E Lombard
Kelly James, tailor, 5 Randall's ct
Kelly James, lab., rear Pleasant ab 12th
Kelly James, lab., Eyre's ct (K)
Kelly James M., tailor, 33 N 6th.
Kelly James R., pilot, 55 Carpenter (S)
Kelly James S., 84 N 7th
Kelly Jeremiah, cordw., Franklin and Shackamaxon
Kelly John, collector, 136 German
Kelly John, tailor, 7 Kelly's ct
Kelly John, boilermr., Front and Jefferson (K)
Kelly John, farrier, 4 College av
Kelly John, cordw., 2 De Witt's av (K)
Kelly John, tailor, 175 S 3d
Kelly John, lab., rear 109 Dillwyn
Kelly John, 2 Dilk's ct
Kelly John, weaver, Crown ab Franklin (K)

Kelly John, cordw., Rose ab School (K)
Kelly John, lab., Lemon ab 12th
Kelly John, jr., tailor, 102 Chestnut
Kelly John, cordw. 336 High
Kelly John, mariner, 10 Beck (S)
Kelly John, weaver, Harmony ct (K)
Kelly John, cordw., Haydock bel Front
Kelly John, pilot, 477 S Front
Kelly John, tobacconist, 9th bel Carpenter
Kelly John W., blacksm., G T road & Franklin
KELLY JOHNSON, tavern, 13th & Cedar
Kelly J. W., mer., 60 High, h 133 O Y road.
Kelly Lawrence, trunkmr., 157 N Front
Kelly Malachi, fruiterer, N E 4th & High
Kelly Margaret, shop, 288 S 3d
Kelly Mary, 75 P road.
Kelly Mary, Paynter's ct
Kelly Mary, washer, rear 281 High
Kelly Matthew, coachman, 144 Locust
Kelly Michael, mariner, Sansom's al
Kelly Michael, P road ab Carpenter
Kelly Michael, weaver, rear Cadwalader below Master
Kelly Michael, livery stable, 1 New Market h 19 Vine
Kelly Michael, tailor, S E 9th and Buttonwood
Kelly Neal, drover, Mantua vil
Kelly Neil, lab., Mifflin
Kelly Owen, grocer, N W 4th & Lombard
Kelly Patrick, drayman, P road ab German
Kelly Patrick, weaver, Jones n Sch 4th
Kelly Patrick, M. D., 144 Vine
Kelly Patrick, carter, 456 S 4th
Kelly Patrick, Coates bet Sch Front & William
Kelly Patrick, lab. 319 Spruce
Kelly Patrick H. tailor, 165 Chestnut, h 175 S 3d
Kelly Peter, lab. Dorothy n Sch 4th
Kelly Peter, 25 Filbert
Kelly Peter, lab., Thompson ab 3d (K)
Kelly Peter, marble imitator, 45 Zane, h 3 Filbert avenue
Kelly Peter, 1 College pl
Kelly Peter, lab., Paul bel 7th
Kelly Philip, 100 N 13th
Kelly Philip, tinman, High n Sch 5th
Kelly Philip, blacksm., Ball al
Kelly Rich, bootmr., Gray's ct (K)
Kelly Robert, tailor, 199 N Water
Kelly Samuel S., tailor, 59½ S 4th
Kelly Thos., stonemason, rear 2 Wash. Market
Kelly Thomas, tailor, Atherton
Kelly Thomas, cordw. rear 121 Queen (S)
Kelly Thomas, gent., 303 Chestnut.
Kelly Thomas, tailor, 112 N 8th
Kelly Thomas, fruiterer, 21 S 9th
Kelly Timothy dealer, N W 11th and Carpenter
Kelly Timothy, mariner, Geddes' ct
Kelly Uriah, coachman, 121 Pearl
Kelly Wallace, seaman, Baxter's ct
Kelly William, cordwainer, Redford bel Broad
Kelly William, ostler, Vaughan ab Locust
Kelly William, architect, 79 S 3d, h 12 Christian
Kelly Wm. weaver, 9th ab Carpenter
Kelly Wm. ropemr, Hallowell ab 6th
Kelly Wm., currier, 31 Perry

Kelly Wm. porter, Pike
Kelly Wm., lab., 6 Twelve foot al
Kelly Wm., clerk, 2 Letitia ct
Kelly Wm., sailmr., 3 Dock, h Rose al ab Green
Kelly Wm. B., caulk., Marlborough ab Franklin
Kelly Wm. B., weaver, 1 Gay's ct (K)
Kelly Wm. C., printer, Washington bel 3d
Kelly Wm. H., 109 Wood
Kelsall Peter, hatter, rear 20 Green
Kelsh Patrick, 5 St Mary's ct
Kelsh Thomas M. harnessmr. 10 George
Kelso Thomas, weaver. 8 Myers' ct
Kelter David, combmaker, 140 Cedar.
Kelter Elizabeth, dressmr., Vernon ab 10th
Kemble Charles, surg. inst. mr., Dean ab Bed-
    ford (K)
Kemble Charles, bookbinder, 64 Noble.
Kemble Charles, 41 N 6th
Kemble Edward, cordw., 7th ab Brown
Kemble George, saddler, 11 Crown.
Kemble John J., hatter, 9 Stanley st
Kemble J. B., bricklayer, Lewis ab Poplar
Kemble Rebecca, Brown bel Cherry
Kemble Samuel, rear 17 Eutaw
Kemble Susan M., milli., Crown n Bedford (K)
Kemp George, bootmr., 82 Locust
Kemp John, music, 102 Christian
Kemp Wm. L., cordw., Marriott la bel 5th
Kemper S., clerk, 276 Green
Kempf Henry, lab., 7th bel Carpenter
Kemps James, lab., Lewis ab Poplar
Kemps John, stone mason, Wood n Sch Front
Kempton & Coppuck, mers., 30 N Front
Kempton George, Rev., 269 S 10th
Kempton Moses, mer., 30 N Front, h 228 N 5th
Kemrey Wilson, scalemr., Carroll ab 12th
Kendal Charles, tailor, 100 Catharine
Kendall Caroline, P road bel Marriott
Kendall George, provisions, 6th and Parrish
Kendall John, weaver, 2 W South
Kendall Otis, professor in High School, h Sch
    7th & Chestnut
Kendall R. G., tinsmith, &c., 135 N 2d, h 200
    N 4th
Kendall William, tailor, 21 N 12th
Kendel Geo., carp., rear 525 N 4th
Kenderdine Charles, hardware, 200 Callowhill,
    h 27 Sp Garden
Kenderdine E., wid. of Jacob, 96 Dillwyn
Kenderdine J. R., hardware, S W 7th and Sp
    Garden
Kendig John, lab., Haydock n Canal
Kendrick Geo. W., b h, 8 S 10th.
Kendrick Sarah Ann, 253 Catharine
Kendrick Wm. S., painter, 73 R road
Kennady Ellen, dressmr., rear 202 Lombard
Kennady Mary, shop, Mantua v
Kennard Cyrus, waiter, 18 Acorn alley
Kennard Geo. W., waterman, Beach bel War-
    ren (K)

Kennedy Alfred L., teacher, 52 N 6th, h 181 S
    5th
Kennedy Andrew, carter, 4 Callowhill
Kennedy Andrew J., upholsterer, 364 S 5th
Kennedy Ann M. milliner, 346 Sassafras
Kennedy Charles, mason, Carlton ab Sch 2d
Kennedy Charles C. machinist, 442 S 6th
Kennedy Chs. E. purser's cl. Washington ab 6th
Kennedy Christopher, weaver, G T road below
    Master (K)
Kennedy Cornelius, stone mason, Murray n Sch
    2nd
Kennedy David, cordw., 117 Callowhill
Kennedy David J., R. R. agt., Broad ab Cherry,
    h Sch 7th and Cherry
Kennedy Dennis, mason, Callowhill ab Sch 2d
Kennedy Elizabeth, rear Schleisman's al
Kennedy Elizabeth, b h., 117 N 11th
Kennedy Elizabeth, wid. of Jas. shop, 12th and
    Buttonwood
Kennedy Elizabeth, Webb's al
Kennedy Elias D., mer., 125 High
Kennedy Henry B. printer, Garden ab Callow-
    hill
Kennedy Henry P., clerk, 327 S 5th
Kennedy Hugh, watchmaker, 105 St John
Kennedy H., tailor, 3 Exchange pl
Kennedy James, weaver, rear Crown bel Frank-
    lin (K)
Kennedy Jas., weaver, Filbert n Sch 3d
Kennedy Jas., shoemr., Filbert n Sch 3d
Kennedy Jas. F., clerk, Queen ab Palmer (K)
Kennedy James M., mer., 125 High, h Mulberry
    W Sch 7th
Kennedy James M. & Co., dry goods, 125 High
Kennedy John, weaver, Perry ab Phoenix
Kennedy John, weaver, Hanover bel Duke
Kennedy John, lab., 12 Lawrence
Kennedy John M., tailor, 88 Walnut
Kennedy John M., mer., 40 N wfs., h 211 N 4th
Kennedy John M., & Co., com. mers., 40 N
    Wharves
Kennedy John Q. plasterer, G T road bel Jef-
    ferson
Kennedy Joseph, lab., 3 Myers's ct
Kennedy Joseph, teacher of flute, 17½ S 5th
Kennedy Joseph, stevedore, Baker bel 8th
Kennedy Josh., weaver, Pine n Sch
Kennedy Michael, coachmr., Nonnater's ct
Kennedy & McGaurk, tavern, 306 Sassafras
Kennedy Mos., weaver, Dunton bel Franklin (K)
Kennedy Nathaniel, carp. weav., 555 N 3d
Kennedy Rachel, 453 N 6th
Kennedy Robert, musician, 7 Gulielma
Kennedy Robert, weaver, 31 M'Duffie
Kennedy Robert, naval store-kr., 476 S Front, h
    468 S 4th
Kennedy Robert, weaver, Perry bel Phoenix
Kennedy Robt. weav. rear Master bel Hancock
Kennedy Samuel, carter, Ann n 12th

Kennedy Wm., lab., Front ab Phœnix (K)
Kennedy William, weaver, Mariner
Kennedy Wm., weaver, 2d ab Montgomery
Kennedy Wm. chairmr. Vernon ab 11th
Kennedy Wm., stone mason, 105 Dillwyn
Kennedy Wm., blacksmith, rear 116 Brown
Kennedy Wm., shoes, 195 S 2d
Kennedy Wm. M., atty. at law, 49 Vine
Kennedy Wm. T., shoes, 252 N 2d
Kenney C. T., trunkmr., Sarah ab Queen (K)
Kenney Edw., bricklayer, Hallowell
Kenney Edwd. J., tailor, 183 S 2d
Kenney George, clerk, 10 Magnolia
Kenney Jas., pedler, High W Sch 3d
Kenney John, carp., Hallowell ab 7th
Kenney John B. ald. 119 S 6th, h 10 Comptroller
Kenney Letitia, 4 Wiley's ct
Kenney Maria, Amber ab Phoenix (K)
Kenney Mary, gentw., 58 Catharine
Kenney Richard, driver, rear 12 Bickham
Kenney Roger, lab., 3 Braceland's ct
Kenney Wm., shop, 30 Plum
Kennief B., dentist, 181 S 3d
Kennief Jeremiah, lab. 31 Stamper's al
Kennington John, cutler, Perkenpine's ct
KENNY & NUGENT, manufs., 31 N Front
Kenny Patrick G., mer., 31 N Front, h 10 Magnolia
Kenrick Francis Patrick D. D., St. John's, 13th.
Kensil Benjamin J., silk dyer, 125 S 11th
Kensil Charles, ship joiner, 25 Emlen's ct.
Kensil Elizabeth, shop, Crown ab Franklin (K)
Kensil George, plasterer, William bel Edward (K)
Kensil George, machin., Perry bel Phoenix (K)
Kensil H. H. tobacconist, 385 Race ab 11th
Kensil John, shipjoiner, Allen ab F road
Kensil Lewis, jr., spinner, N E Poplar and St John
Kensil Robert W., blindmr. 347 Sassafras
Kensil William, cordwainer, 16 Rachel
Kensil Wm. A., carp., Henk's ct
Kensill Lewis, carter, 270 St. John
Kent Frederick, button maker, 9 Flower
Kent John, bootmr., 7 Myers' ct
Kent P. & W., tailors, Thompson ab 3d
Kent Rodolphus, mer., 108 N 3d, h 156 N Front
Kent Wm. C., mer., 146 N 3rd, h 51 Marshall
Kenton Augustus, white washer, 188 S 4th.
Kenton Eliza C., Garden & Willow
Kenton George W., blacksmith, R road bel Melon
Kenton Joseph, distiller, Sp Garden bel R road
Kenton Catharine, wid. of Levi, 310 S Front
Kentzel John, cordw., Parrish bel 11th
Kentzel Wm., 42 Cherry
Kenyon John, lab. Teas' ct
Kepler Charles, morocco dresser, 41 Lily al
Kepler Wm., vict., Callowhill ab Sch 2d
Keplinger Christian, lab. 13 Dilk's ct
Kepner Isaac, weaver, Monroe bel Cherry (K)
Kepner John, weaver, Wood bel Duke
Keppel Samuel B., carp., shop 25 Margaretta, h 305 N Front
Keppele Catharine, 262 Walnut.

Kepper Samuel, stovemr., G T road ab Laurel
Keppler Louisa, Higgins' pl
Ker Joseph, 119 Mulberry
Kerbaugh Jacob, lime burner, Sch Beach above Spruce
Kerbaugh Opman, lime burner, Lombard s: wharf Sch, h Ashton & Lombard
Kerbaugh Wm., stone mason, Phœnix bel G T road (K)
Kerchoff Christian, combmr., 173 Coates
Kereven Patrick, gardener, Sch 5th & Chestnut
Kerk Charles H., machinist, 5 Appletree alley, h 69 N 8th.
Kerk John K., wire worker, 48 N 4th
Kerl Samuel, huckster, rear 552 N 2d (K)
Kerlin John, b h, 78 Walnut
Kern Aaron, tavern, 150 N 4th
Kern Benj. F. hardware, Sch 6th & W High, h 35 Dean
Kern Daniel, carp. 615 N 3d
Kern Enos S., tavern, 38 Pine
Kern George, U. S. Mint, h 149 N 10th
Kern George, clerk, 40 St John
Kern George P., clerk, Locust n Sch 3d
Kern H. G., surgical inst. mr., 5 N 8th.
Kern John, 62 Filbert, h 1 Olive
Kern John, teacher of drawing, 1 Olive
Kern John B. A., tobacconist, 31 N 4th
Kern R. H. & E. M., teachers of drawing, 62 Filbert
Kern Wm. H., ice dealer, N W 3rd & Walnut, h Sch 7th ab Filbert
Korman Michael, lab. Carlton bel Sch 7th
Kernbean Jacob, tailor, Lemon ab 10th
Kerney Wm., weaver, Front ab Phoenix
Kerns B., plasterer, Poplar bel 9th
Kerns Charles T., brush manuf., 42 N 2nd, h 4 Chatham
Kerns George, plasterer, 392 N 6th.
Kerns James, tavern, Broad and Sassafras
Kerns John, lab., 66 George
Kerns Stephen, plasterer, Parrish ab Broad
Keron Sarah, Smith's ct
Kerper Edward, cooper, Mechanic ab George
Kerper Joseph, cedar cooper, N W Front and High, h Front & Noble
Kerr George, watchman, 15 New Market
Kerr James, dry goods, 121 Buttonwood.
Kerr James, gent., 252 Walnut.
Kerr John J. Rev., 340 Coates
Kerr Joseph, mer., 191 Chestnut, h 6 Franklin row
Kerr Sarah, gentw., 4 Perry st
KERR & SON, china hall, 191 Chestnut.
Kerr Thomas, cabinet mr., 174 S 2d.
Kerr Thomas, brickmaker, near Sch Bank
Kerr William, saddler, 57 Chestnut
Kerr Wm., shoemr., Sch 5th ab Spruce
Kerr Wm. Joseph, mer, 191 Chestnut
Kerrans John, hatter, 250 Christian
Kerregan Danl., lab., rear Barker E of Sch 4th
Kerrer Martin, baker, 6th bel Carpenter
Kerrick George, brickmr., Lafayette bel 10th
Kerrison Robert M., watchmr., 161 S 10th

Kerrison T. E. J. bathing house, Arcade
Kershaw John, tinsmith, 428 High
Kershow & Co. D. B. ice dealers, Broad ab Mulberry
Kershow D. B. ice dealer, 312 Cherry ab Broad
Kershow Jacob, ice mer., 441 Race
Kesler Henry, starch manuf., Jefferson & Hancock, h Master and Hope
Kesler Samuel, brickmr., Juniper n Locust.
Kesler Theodore, cordw., G T road ab 6th
Kesler Wm., farmer, rear Carpenter bel 8th
Kessler Bartholomew, beer house, G T road ab Master
Kessler Bartholomew, lab. Jefferson bel G T rd
Kessler C. R., Rev., 183 St John
Kessler Daniel, combmr. 371 N 4th
Kessler Elizabeth, rear Charlotte ab Poplar
Kessler George, lab., Cherry ab Duke, (K)
Kessler John, jr., grocer, 166 Coates
Kessler John jr., grocer, S W 4th & Coates.
Kessler Wm. butcher, 4 Jones' al (N L)
Kester J. W., mer., 24 Bank
Ketcham Frederick Rev., 607 N 2d (K)
Ketcham Samuel, ladies' shoemaker, 156 S 6th
Ketcham W. H., att'y & coun., 10th bel Ogden
Ketchum Jno., carp., Coates ab 8th, h 314 Coates
Ketler Chas., tobacconist, 3d ab Plum, h 53 Carpenter
Ketler Daniel, harness mr., 48 Rose al
Ketler Geo. W., plast., Paul ab 6th
Ketler John, plasterer, 7 S 7th
Ketler Margaret, 270 & h 272 S 3rd.
Ketterlinus E., printer, 40 N 4th, h 34 O Y road
Ketterlinus Paul, printer, 40 N 4th, h 34 O Y road
Kettring Elizabeth, Palmer ab West (K)
Kettring Geo., turner, Palmer ab West (K)
Key Robert, rear Washington ab 6th
Keyes Chas. B., Rev., 589 N Front
Keys Ann, b. h., 186 S 11th
Keys Edw., grocer, 11th & Carpenter
Keys Robt., blacksmith, Filbert ab Sch. 5th.
Keys Wm., stone mason, Sch 2d ab Spruce
Keys Wm., clerk, 11 Union st (S)
Keyser Aaron, hatter, 519 N 2d.
Keyser Adeline, 110 Vine
Keyser Andrew, dry goods, 154 S 2d.
Keyser Charles, tailor, 12 Well's row
Keyser Charles, butcher shop, 222 S 6th
Keyser Christopher W. tavern, 5th & Poplar
Keyser Conrad, blacksm., 69 Poplar
Keyser E. W., lumber mer., Green & 10th, h 144 N 9th.
Keyser & Fox, saw mill, 21 Crown
Keyser George, lab., Queen bel Palmer (K)
Keyser Geo., baker, Buttonwood ab 13th
Keyser Henry, baker, Mintzer
Keyser Jacob, saw mill, 19 Crown
Keyser Jacob, 19 S Sch 6th
Keyser John, cabmr. Poplar ab 9th
Keyser John, Willow ab Dillwyn
Keyser John, carp., Stewart's pl
Keyser John F., printer, 3 Burd, (S)
Keyser John S., 9th & Nectarine
Keyser, Joseph, blacksm., 330 N Front
24

Keyser Jos., grocer, S W 2d & German
Keyser Jos., oyster house, Broad and Wood
Keyser Louisa, rear 529 N 4th
Keyser Magdalen, rear 3 Paschall's al
Keyser Margaret, 524 N 5th
Keyser Mary Ann, 2 Rudolph's ct
Keyser Michael, hair dresser, 26 N 6th
Keyser N. L., lumber mer., 323 N Front, h 16 Margaretta.
Keyser Paul, mer., 52 High, h 212 N 4th
Keyser Peter A., lumber mer., 225 N Water, h 35 Callowhill.
Keyser Susan, 34 Vine.
Keyser & Warner, lumber mers., 225 N Water
Keyser William, cooper, Haydock n G T road.
Keyser Wm. G., lumber mer., 16 Margaretta st
Keyser William W., gun smith, 377 N 2nd
Kiar Jonathan, cordw., rear Paul ab 6th
Kiarman J., bootmr., G T road ab Master (K)
Kibler John, baker, 88 N 7th
Kibler John, oyster house, 90 N 4th
Kibler Joseph, 25 Callowhill.
Kidd John, dyer, Jackson ab Adams
Kidd John C., Parrish & Elizabeth
Kidd Samuel, cordw., 14 Wells' Row
Kiddy Joseph, weaver, Morris n William
Kiderlen W. L. J., editor, 9 S 4th
Kiehl Joseph, mer., 161 Chestnut
Kiefer Henry, baker, 6th bel Poplar
Kiefer Jacob, baker, 82 S 11th
KIEHL JOHN, dry goods, 50 S 2d.
Kiel Barbary, Paschall's al
Kienzel G. baker, 46 Green
Kienzle John, baker, 50 Apple
Kiernan Ellen, Camac ab G T road
Kiersted Chas., ropemr., Clare st
Kiesley John, watchman, O Y road & 5th
Kiggins Peter, lab., Marlborough ab Beach (K)
Kiipfent A., boot and shoe mr., 73 Poplar
Kiker Saml., butcher, George n Sch 2d
Kiker Wm., tobacconist, Wood ab Sch 4th
Kilburn Uriah, stone cut., Queen ab Palmer, (K)
Kildea Catharine, M'Mackin's ct
Kilduffe Robert M. D., S E 6th and Shippen.
Kile Ann, capmr., 1 Orchard
Kilhower Saml., gardener, Washington bel 2d
Kille Aaron F., clerk, 452 S 4th
Kille Eliza E., 228 N 5th.
Killean Francis, boot mr., 16 Little Water
Killeene Francis, shoemr. S 7th ab Catharine
Killen George, tailor, 457 S 2d (S)
Killen John, stone cutter, S 7th bel Catharine
Killen Joseph, weaver, 2 Wagner's ct
Killen Mark, tobacco, 2d ab Catharine
Killgore & Hudders, carpenters, 22 Franklin pl
Killgore John, carpenter, 22 Franklin place, h 36 Wood.
Killhour Michael, lab. Dutton's ct
Killhower Jeremiah, farmer, 6th bel G T road
Killian Jacob, rags, St John ab George
Killingsworth E., painter, 5 S 7th, h 64 Mulberry.
Killion Henry, groc., 327½ High, h 8 Filbert av
Killion H. & D., grocers, 327½ High
Killion Wm., drayman, 102 Coates

Kilpatrick And., collector, P road ab Christian
Kilpatrick Archibald, porter, Drinker's ct
Kilpatrick Francis, chandler, 322 Callowhill
Kilpatrick Francis, M prison, 10th bel Washington.
Kilpatrick George, blacksmith, Kennedy's ct
Kilpatrick Hugh, machinist, 365 S 5th
Kilpatrick James, Fulton ab 12th
Kilpatrick James, watchman, 7 Myers' ct
Kilpatrick Jane, 11th & Washington
Kilpatrick John, Cochran bel Brinton
Kilpatrick John, carter, Wood bel 13th.
Kilpatrick Robert, lab., Spruce n Sch Front
Kilpatrick Wm., blacksm., 7th bel Washington
Kimball Chas., mer., 5th ab Poplar
Kimball F. S., book-keeper, Pine ab 10th
Kimball Samuel, cordw. Union bel Franklin
Kimball Stephen, merchant, 10 S whfs, h 36 S 13th
Kimber Caleb, paper stainer, 107 Coates
Kimber Emmor, jr., hatter, 34 N 4th h 97 O Y road.
Kimber Samuel, com. mer., foot of E Willow st, h 347 N 7th
KIMBER SAMUEL & CO., com. mers., Willow st wharves
Kimber & Sharpless, booksellers, 50 N 4th.
Kimber Thomas, bookseller, 50 N 4th, h 374 Mulberry.
Kimberry Liscomb, waiter, 36 Currant al
Kimberry Ruben, waiter, 36 Currant al
Kimble Blanchard, drayman, Hanover ab West (K)
Kimble George, carman, Hanover ab West (K)
Kimble Nathan, machi., Shackamaxon ab Bedford
Kime Jacob, stone cutter, 16 Short ct
Kimley John, carter, 120 Swanson st
Kimley Mary, gentw., 117 Swanson
Kimmey Henry M., clerk, 171 Mulberry
Kimmey Mrs., b. h., 144 N 8th
Kimsey Job, grocer, Penn ab Maiden
Kincade Eliza, widow, Wood ab Sch 6th
Kincade John, lab., Morgan's ct
Kincaid Andrew, shoemr., Boyd's av
Kincaid Wm., moulder, G T road bel 7th
Kindick Samuel S., tavern, Front & Noble
Kindle Robert, waterman, Jones' al
King Alexander, weaver, 10 M'Duffie
King Alex., hatter, 24 Queen (K)
King Anderson, lab., Amber ab Phoenix (K)
King Ann Mrs., Warner's ct
King Catharine, 47 Laurel
King & Baird, printers, 9 George.
King Catharine, Beach ab Shackamaxon.
King Charles, carter, Union ab Bedford. (K)
King Charles R., M. D., S E 13th and Chestnut
King Darius, 3 Liberty ct
King Edmund, cordw., Nectarine ab 10th.
King Edward, President Judge Court Common

King Francis, gent., 332 Mulberry
King George, oil mer., H. Village
King Geo. W., carter, Dean ab Bedford
King Henry, carp, Otter bel G T road (K)
King Henry, shop, Pine st whf.
King Henry G., 287 N 8th
King Henry H. tailor, Dock & 2d, h 70 German
KING HERMANUS, bookseller & tailor, 10th bel Buttonwood
King Hermeon, tailor, Poplar ab 9th
King H., capt., 4th & Redwood
King Jackson, lab. rear Benton n School (K)
King James, shop, Master bel 2d (K)
King James, bricklayer, 4th ab Jefferson. (K)
King James, tavern, 3d & George (N L)
King James A. carp. Poplar bel 7th
King Jane, 105 Christian
King John, sailmr., rear 382 S Front
King John, shoemr., Bedford ab 12th
King John, pedler, Crown ab Franklin (K)
King John, cordw., 3 Smith's al (N L)
King John, carpet weaver, 318 S 6th.
King John, chair manuf., 539 N Front
King John, waterman, Laurel & Rachel
King Joseph, book binder, 14 Centre
King J. & Abram, innkeepers, Fairmount
King Levi, lab. Little Pine ab 7th
King Levi R., carp., 8 Watson's al., h 13th bel Catharine.
King Margaret, sewing, Reakirt's ct
King Mary, corsets and variety, 66 S 12th
King M. A., spooler, Perry ab Phoenix
King Richard, carman, Johnson's la ab 4th
King Robert E., potter, Haig's ct
King Robt. S., blacksm., 23 Parker
King R. P., printer, 9 George, h 6 Prune
King Saml., House of Refuge, h Poplar ab 10th
King Samuel, porter, rear 121 Noble
King Samuel G. brushmr. 266 N 2nd, h 62 Dillwyn
King Sarah, rear 30 Bread
King Sarah, 330 S Front.
King Thomas, carpenter, Jones ab Sch. 7th
King Thomas, 117 N 7th
King Thomas, confect. rear 9 Crown
King Westley, coal, 11 Beck (S)
King Wm., druggist, Franklin & Marlboro' (K)
King Wm., gold beater, 23 Union
King William, carpenter, William bel Edward (K)
King Wm., carp., 5th bel Federal
King Wm., Filbert W Sch 7th
King Wm., livery stable, N W 3d and Wood
King Wm., labourer, rear 193 Christian
King Wm. waiter, Watson's al
King Wm. House of Refuge, h Poplar ab 10th
King Wm., ship carp., Fraley's al
King Wm. E., brushmr., rear 15 Noble
King Wm. H., mer., 21 S 2d
King Wm. H.

Kingsland Jacob, ship joiner, bel Prime bet 6th & 7th
Kingsmore Charles, cordw., rear 2 Carpenter
Kingston Harriet, gentw., 183 Spruce
Kingston John, book binder, Thompson ab Sch 8th
Kingston John, collector, 3rd & Washington
Kingston Stephen B., acct., 288 N 6th
Kingston Stephen B. jr., conveyancer, 129 Mulberry
Kingston S. B. & Sons, conveyancers, 129 Mulberry
Kinkade Andrew, weaver, White's ct
Kinkade James, carter, Mifflin and 12th
Kinkade Jane, Jackson's ct (N L)
Kinkade Samuel, seaman, 29 Prosperous al
Kinkelin A., M. D., 83 Union.
Kinkner John, bricklayer, 350 Brown
Kinnard J., tavern, Callowhill ab 12th
Kinnard Thomas, waiter, 43 Mechanic
Kinnear James, ladies' shoemr., 282 S 4th
Kinsell Benjamin, 18 Morgan
Kinsell Hannah, 7 Elder
Kinsey Anthony, 31 Dugan
Kinsey John, compositor, 17 Nectarine
Kinsey John, wharf builder, Fraley's al
Kinsey J. M., carpenter, 120 S Front
Kinsey Mary, b h, 213 Spruce
KINSEY WM. & SON, morocco manuf., 251 N 3d and Willow
Kinsinger Charles, cordw., rear 450 N 4th
Kinsinger Frederick, morocco dresser, Charlotte ab Culvert
Kinsler George M., 276 N Front
Kinsler John, cordwainer, 127 N 5th.
Kinsler Joseph, lab., Lombard and Ashton
Kinsley Charles H., wheelwright, 12th bel Locust, h Sch. 6th bel Lombard
Kinsley Christian, butcher, 17 Crown
Kinsley Daniel, brickmr., Juniper ab Locust.
Kinsley Elizabeth, Lombard ab Sch 7th
Kinsley Ellen wid. of John, grocer, 388 N Front
Kinsley George, brickmr., Harmstead
Kinsley Henry, wheelwt., Barker n Sch 3d
Kinsley James, shoemr., Coombs' ct
Kinsley John H., cordw., 474 Sassafras
Kinsloe Wm. A., perfumer, 36 N 7th, h 39 S 10th
Kinslow Michael, fireman, 14 Barker
Kinsman Eliza, gentw., S 10th ab Shippen
Kintzing Abraham W., mer., 449 Chestnut
Kintzing Wm., 31 Logan sq
Kintzle Christian, merchant, 66 N 3d
Kinzer George, mer., Broad, h 139 N 13th
Kiple Jacob, clerk, 323 N 2d
Kipp Peter, shoemr., rear 191 N 2d
Kippen Mary, Wallace ab 8th
Kipple Margaret, b h, 7 Vine
Kirbey Samuel, stove finisher, 181 S 2d.
Kirby Ann, milliner, 343 N 2d.
Kirby James, sawmr., 4th & Franklin (K)
Kirby James, sawmr., 25 Elfreth's al
Kirby James, seaman, 21 Benton
Kirby John, lab. Carpenter ab 3d
Kirby Richard, painter, P road n Fitzwater
Kirby Robt., seaman, 21 Benton

Kirby Wm. K., 4 & 6 S Sch 8th bel High
Kirchner Andrew, grinder, 66 Vine
Kirchof Jos., cabinet mr., 7th ab Poplar
Kirchoff Henry, turner, Miller's ct (N L)
Kirk Ann, 5 St. Mary
Kirk Christian, engine builder, Crown n Franklin (K)
Kirk Edward, lab., 2 Hoffman's al
Kirk George, boat builder, Beach ab Maiden
Kirk George W., weigh master, 55 N Water, h 10th ab Buttonwood
Kirk James, boat builder, Beach bel Maiden (K)
Kirk James, tavern, 25 S Garden
Kirk James, cordw., rear G T road, ab 5th
Kirk John, shoemr., Yhost bet Catharine and Queen
Kirk John, coachmr., Broad ab Filbert, h 12 Barker
Kirk John, painter, 470 N Front
Kirk John, chandler, 353 Callowhill
Kirk J. W., Filbert E of Sch 6th
Kirk Mary, spooler, Fitler bel Harrison (K)
Kirk Stephen, coal mer., Penn bel Maiden, h 78 Penn (K)
Kirk Susan, nurse, rear 15 Eutaw
Kirk S., 13 Carlton
KIRK S. L., grocer, 146 N 4th, h 149 Dillwyn
Kirk Thomas, waterman, Beach bel Maiden (K)
Kirk William, blacksmith, F road and Shackamaxon (K)
Kirk William, brickmaker, yard Sch 3d & Walnut, h 2 Colonnade row.
Kirk Wm., weaver, 2d ab Jefferson (K)
Kirk Wm., weaver, Fitler n 2d (K)
Kirkbride Thos. S., physician to the Penna. Hospital for the Insane
Kirkham Charles, att'y and coun., S E 3rd & Pear
Kirkham George H., mer., 36 S Front, h 127 Filbert
Kirkham Wm., 127 Filbert
Kirkland Charles, milkman, Bedford ab 13th
Kirkland Wm. R., mer., 47 N Whfs. & 95 N Water, h S E 10th & Clinton
Kirkner Leonard, lime burner, Sch 3d ab Callowhill
Kirkpatrick Andrew, ship carp., Penn above Maiden (K)
Kirkpatrick Ann, widow of Robert B., 252 N 4th
Kirkpatrick Benj., weaver, Poplar
Kirkpatrick D., leather dealer, 21 S 3d, h 193 Mulberry.
KIRKPATRICK D. & SON, hides and leather, 21 S 3d
Kirkpatrick E., mer., 21 S 3d, h 193 Mulberry
Kirkpatrick George, dep. keeper County Prison, h 6th bel Shippen
Kirkpatrick James, barber, N W 7th & Zane
Kirkpatrick James, carter, Lewis ab Sch 6th.
Kirkpatrick James, carp., 29 Rittenhouse
Kirkpatrick James, distiller, 2 S 7th, h t Fayette
Kirkpatrick John, carp., 308 Shippen

Kirkpatrick J. T. & Co., hides & leather, 213 N 3d, h 193 Mulberry
Kirkpatrick Rachel A., 94 Crown.
Kirkpatrick Robert, carter, Spruce W Sch 5th
Kirkpatrick Robert B., mer., 52 High, h 193 Mulberry.
Kirkpatrick Rowland, mer., 137 N Water
Kirkpatrick Samuel, shoemr., 224 Vine
Kirkpatrick Wm., blacksmith, bel Prime n 6th
Kirnan James, cordw., 273 N 3d
Kirrigan Wm., grocer, S E Christian & 2d
Kirscheman Godfred, tailor, Palm ab Brown
Kirschenman J. M., tavern, Coates bel 5th
Kirscherman Christian, lab., Brown ab 9th
Kirshner Henry, tavern, R road ab Poplar. (F V)
Kirtland George, com. mer., 34 Church al
KIRTLAND, MANSFIELD & HALL, com. mers., 34 Church al
Kisselman Mrs., gentw., 166 S 2d
Kissick J. W., tailor, Pleasant ab 12th
Kisterbock J., stoves & warm air furnace manuf., 467 High.
Kitchen A. B., 407 Chestnut
Kitchen James, M. D., 39 Spruce.
Kitchen James, carp., Carlton ab Sch 4th
Kitchen Rebecca, b h, 450 Vine
Kitchen Uriah, teacher, Weaver
Kitcherman Richard, weav., Callowhill n Sch 3d
Kitchinman Jas., carpet weaver, 76 Maiden
Kite Edith, 32 N 5th
Kite Edmund A., tailor, 220 Wood ab 12th
Kite George, cordw., Beach ab Maiden (K)
Kite James, cabinetmaker, 129 Walnut, h 26 Powell
Kite John L., M. D., 262 N 5th.
Kite Jonathan, potter, 122 Beach (K)
Kite Jonathan, cordw., Lancaster & Rule
Kite Joseph, printer, 4th & Appletree al., h 265 N 5th.
Kite Joseph & Co., printers, 4th & Appletree al
Kite Joseph J., book store, 9th & Sp Garden
Kite Joseph S., 32 Palmyra sq
Kite Nathan, bookseller, 32 N 5th
Kite Paschal, carpenter, 13th ab Carroll
Kithcart David, weaver, G T road opp 4th
Kittell Mary, nurse, 29 Dyott's ct (K)
Kitterson John, brickmaker, Spruce W Sch 5th
Kitterson Wm., weaver, Crown bel Duke (K)
Kittinger Leonard, 154 Sassafras
Kitts Hannah P., gentw., 188 Coates.
Kitts Henry, cordw., Beach ab Poplar (K)
Kitts Jacob, tobac., Stearly's ct

Kleigbrink John, lab., rear Melon bel 12th
Klein Fredk., nailer, Wood bel Franklin (K)
Klein Fredk., nailer, 5 Bauersach's ct
Klein Jacob, carter, Palmer ab Duke (K)
Klein John, watchmaker, 197 N 3d, h, 72 Noble
Kleinfelder Gottleib, butcher, rear Brown below 13th
Kleinz Christ., La Fayette ct
Kleiz Henry, blacksmith, 11th ab Willow
Klem Bernhardt, shoemr., 20 Green
Klem Jacob, butcher, F road ab Maiden
Klemm & Brother, imp. of musical inst.'s, 275 High.
Klemm F. A., importer, 275 High, h 3 City Row.
Klemmer Henry, carter, 3 Moore's ct
Klett Andrew, druggist, 246 St John & 226 N 3d
Klett Fred., N E 2d & Callowhill, h 53 Callowhill
Klett Frederick, & Co., druggist, N E 2d & Callowhill
Klett Mary, Rachel & Brown
Klett Rachel, Front & Lombard
Klewell Abrm., turner, 6th bel G T road
Klewell Daniel, turner, 7th ab Weaver's Rope Walk
Kline Adam, brickmr., State n Sch 7th
Kline Bartholomew, jeweller, rear 38 Charlotte
Kline Demarius, rear Charlotte ab Poplar
Kline Daniel, bootmr., George ab Apple
Kline Francis, combmr., 7 Stearly's ct
Kline Frederick, cane manuf., 126 New
Kline Geo., wheelwt., Hanover bel West (K)
Kline Geo., cordw., rear Apple ab George
Kline Geo., cordw., Elizabeth ab Poplar
Kline Hannah, shop, 129 Poplar
Kline Isaac, cordwainer, 231 Cedar
Kline Isaac, M. D., 183 G. T. road
Kline Jacob, buttonmr., Vienna bel Duke (K)
Kline Jacob R., wood mer., Green st. wharf, h 492 N 3rd.
Kline James, cordw., Gatchell's av
Kline John, gent., 18 St Mary
Kline John, shoemr., 98 Apple
Kline Mary, wid. of Peter, 374 N 3d
Kline Michael, Melon bel 10th
Kline Michael, shoemr., 408 N 4th
Kline Michael, lab., Mary bel F road
Kline Peter, machinist, Brown ab 13th
Kline Peter, collector, 107 Noble
Kline Philip, lab., Wood bel Sch 5th
Kline Rachel, trader, Vienna ___ ___ (K)

Klotz John C., tailor, rear 2d ab Edward (K)
Klotz John M., tailor, 103 Poplar
Klufkee George, blacksm., Union ab Franklin
Klufkee John A., whitesmith, Marlborough ab Franklin. (K)
Klump Frederick, machinist, Coates ab 9th
Klump John, framemr., 1 Jackson (N L)
Knapp George, twine & cords, N road ab Marker, h Marion ab Front
Knapp Sarah, rear 109 Christian
Knapp Solomon, baker, 27 N 6th
Knauff Henry, organ builder, 212 N 5th, h 167 Vine.
Knause Ephraim, tobacconist, School bel William
Kneap Thos., lab., Hope ab Otter (K)
Kneass Ann, toys, 28 Tammany
Kneass Charles, carp., Poplar ab 7th
Kneass C. F., 154 Cedar
Kneass D. A., hatter, 87 Cedar
KNEASS HORN R., att'y & coun., 61 S 7th
Kneass Jane, b. h., 139 Chestnut
Kneass John, gent., 228 S 7th
Kneass Napoleon B., mer., 172½ High
Kneass Samuel, 393 Spruce
Kneass Sarah, 81 S 6th
Knecht Catharine, gentw., Wirtz ct
Knecht Gabriel, drover, 263 N 8th.
Knecht George Jr., vict., Franklin ab Noble
Knecht John G., butcher, c Willow & Julianna
Knecht John J., carter, 7th ab Master
Kneck Henry, butcher, 11 Magnolia st
Kneedler Chas. J., coal mer., Broad & Sassafras
Kneedler Jacob, 205 Green
Kneedler Jacob E., harness mr., Coates ab 6th
Kneedler J. S., mer., Sassafras & 3d, h 28 Washington sq
Kneedler Magdalen, 4 N 9th
Kneedler Simon, carter, 7th ab Brown
Kneeland Amelia J., stock maker, 96 Green.
Kneeland Edward, 6 Bank al
Knepley Thos. J., tobacconist, rear Noble ab 5th
Knettle Wm., bricklayer, rear 202 N 10th
Knickerbocker Rebecca S., trimmings, 407 N 3d
Knight A. L. paper machine, rail road & Sch 8th, h 12th bel Coates
Knight Bushrod W., bricklayer, 87 Fitzwater.
Knight C. D., agent, 45 N Front
Knight Daniel R., carp., 166 N 9th, h Wood n Sch 8th
Knight David, butcher, 197 S 7th
Knight Edward, tailor, rear Elizabeth above Poplar
Knight Elizabeth, Johnson's lane n 5th
Knight Esther, gentw., Green ab Marshall
KNIGHT E. C., grocer, S E Water & Chestnut, h 267 S Front
Knight George, carpet manuf., S W 4th & Callowhill
Knight Jacob, carpenter, 241 Marshall
Knight James, weaver, rear Pleasant ab 12th
Knight James, waiter, 49 Curraut al
Knight Jesse J., coach painter, 143 Queen
Knight John, lab., 9 Nonnater's ct

Knight Joseph & Son, iron & coal mer., 203 N 2d
Knight Joseph, carp., Sch 8th & State
Knight Mary, washr., 11 Stamper's al
Knight & Parry, trimmings, 6 Sp Garden
Knight Phœbe, trimmings, 6 Sp Garden
Knight Reeve L, upholsterer, 148 S 2nd.
Knight Robt., porter, rear 50 P road
KNIGHT ROBERT B., att'y & coun., 113 Sassafras
Knight Robt. T., carp., 196 Cherry
Knight Saml., clerk, Queen ab 3d
Knight Sarah, Morris bel Catharine
Knight Wm., engineer, Francis (F V)
Knight William, machinist, 13th bel Green
Knight Wm. H., hardware, 255 High, h 127 N 9th
Knight William L., M. D., N W Vine & Sch 5th
Knight Wm. S., carp., Bread, h 72 New
KNIGHT W. W., hardware, 229 High
Knipe Christian, shoemaker, St John ab Beaver (K)
Knipe Conrad, grocer, N 5th ab Noble
KNIPE C. & SONS, grocers, S E 3d & New
Knipe Fred. A. O., 155 S 12th
Knipe John R., furniture, 79 Sassafras
Knipe Thos., brickmr., Thompson ab Sch 8th
Knizel Lydia, nurse, rear 280 S 2d
Knochel John, cordw., 3 Carlisle ct
Knock Julius, die sinker & chaser, 8 Samson al
Knoell F., frame mr., Buttonwood ab 5th
Knoffloch P., tavern, John and Callowhill
Knoll John, carter, Cherry bel Duke (K)
Knopp Harman, sugar Boiler, 238 St John
Knorr Francis, 3 Logan's sq. ab Sch 5th
Knorr George, gent, Poplar ab 13th
Knorr George, sen., printer, 159½ S 11th.
Knorr George, shoemr., 4 Swanson ct
Knorr G. Fredk., teacher of langs, 119 Filbert
Knorr G. T., printer, 329 Lombard
Knorr James, printer, 327 W Pine
Knorr John K., M. D., Front ab Poplar
Knorr Joseph, sign painter, 89 S 2nd.
Knorr J. F., mer., 11 N 4th, h 3 Logan sq
Knorr Nath. K. druggist, N W Front and Brown
Knorr Peter, tobacconist, Corn bel Wharton
Knorr Polly, 87 N 9th
Knorr Wm., baker, Pleasant ab 11th
Knot John, Jackson & Adams
Knouse Geo., wheelwright, Otter ab Front
Knouse Harman, lab., Beach ab Maiden (K)
Knouse Mary, 3 Wood
Knouse Peter, lab. Thompson bel Sch 6th
Knouse William, gun smith, Marlboro' n West
Knowles Austin, coach maker, 288 Sassafras, h 143 Wood
Knowles David, carp., 74 Coates
Knowles Henry, bootmr., Lane's ct
Knowles James A. shoemaker, 319 Shippen
Knowles Levi, mer., 428 High, h Sch 5th and Cherry
Knowles Marmaduke, carp. Sch 2d & Lombard
Knowles M., carp., Sch 2d ab South
Knowles Nathaniel, acct., Western Bank, h 258 N 7th

Knowles Ralph H., 247 N 7th
Knowles Wm. hatter, 73 N 8th
Knowles Wm., weaver, Crown ab Duke (K)
Knowles Wm. H., carp., 4 Keefe
Knows Jacob, 369 N 4th
Knox Ann, b. h., 4 Howard's ct
Knox Charles, lab. F road opp Master
Knox Deborah, shoebinder, Melon bel 12th
Knox Elizabeth, dressmr., 2 Lyndall's al
Knox Ezekiel, weaver, Amber ab Phoenix (K)
Knox Geo., fisherman, Allen ab Hanover (K)
Knox Jacob, copper pl. printer, 2 Hubbell
Knox James, fisherman, Cherry ab Queen (K)
Knox James, blacksmith, Wood ab Broad
Knox John, cordw., Gay's ct (N L)
Knox John, printer, Wharton ab 3d
Knox John N. shoemr., R road & Wallace
Knox Lewis, cordwainer, 557 S 2d.
Knox Samuel, bricklayer, 6th bel G T road
Knox Sarah, Crown bel Franklin (K)
Knox Sarah, dry goods, 11 S 9th
Knox Sarah, Franklin ab Palmer (K)
Knox Susan, 7th n Washington
Knox Wm., carp., Allen ab Hanover (K)
Knox Wm. L., millwright, rear 297 Callowhill
Kobel Christian, barber, 294 Front st
Koch Carl, jeweller, 23 N 2d
Koch M. & T., tailors, 158 Vine
Koch Otto, tailor, 153 Vine
Koch Philip, cordw., 16 Assembly Buildings
Koch Philip, 4 Northampton ct
Kochenspicer Isa., butcher, Queen ab Palmer(K)
Kocher John, whitesm., Palmer n F road (K)
Kochersperger Almira G., tavern, 483 High
Kochersperger Daniel, grocer, R road & Melon, h Brown ab 13th
Kochersperger Geo., shoemr., Sch 4th bel Locust
Kochersperger Jane, grocer, 13th and Poplar
Kochersperger John, sexton, rear 37 N 4th
Kochersperger Saml. A. C., tailor, High ab Sch 5th, h 472 Callowhill
Koechlein Geo. H., turner, 129 Coates
Koecker Joseph D., architect, 104 S 4th
Koecker Leonard R., M. D. dentist, 208 Walnut
Koehl Geo. W., barber, Front bel Phœnix
Koehler Charles A., 394 S 3d
Koehler Conrad, stovenr., 51 Elfreth's al
Koehler Danl., wheelwright, 24 Clark
Koehler Maria, sewing, 4 Friendship ct
Koehler Sarah, S W Marriott & Atherton
Kohl George, lab., Cadwalader bel Phœnix
Kohlenkamp N., tinman, 78 N 2nd
Kohler & Co., hardware, 328 N 2d
Kohler Fredk. W., hardware, 328 N 2d, h 175 O Y road
Kohler Geo. A., hardw., 328 N 2d, h 266 Coates
Kohler John, gent., 138 Franklin
Kohler John F. & Co., hardware, Shackamaxon & Queen (K)
Kohler J. B., stove manuf., 154 N 2d
Kohler J. J., hat., 159 N 3d
Kohler M., lab., 101 Swanson
Kohlhas Peter, tailor, 410 N 2d
Kohn Israel, currier, 245 N 3d, h 54 Duke

Kohne E. Mrs., Chestnut ab 10th.
Kohns John, butcher, Wharton ab 3d
Kolb John, baker, 135 Buttonwood
Kolb Louis, shoemr. 7 Elfreth's al
Kolb Peter, silver plater, Poplar bel 9th
Kolesnomy Bayar, S E 9th and George
Kollock Burton J., cabinetmr., Atherton
Kollock David H., cabinetmaker, 304 S 2d.
Kolm Ferdinand, baker, 191 N 4th
Kolsterman Herman, tinman, 196 S 2d
Konn Sarah, 17 Linden
Koockegey Wm., sign painter, 299 Mulberry, h 13 Logan
Koockegy George, whipmr. 5 Penn. av
Kookin Geo. C., tailor, Mantua vil
Koons Chas., dry goods, 172 N 3d, h 314 N 6th
Koons F., iron founder, Bush Hill, h 100 Wood
Koons & Heilman, dry goods, 172 N 3d
Koons Isaac, sugar refiner, O Y road & Willow, h 54 O Y road
Koons Michael & Co., grocer, 239 & 241 N 3d, h 230 N 4th
Koons Philip, boots and shoes, 430 N 2d
Koplin Justice, umbrellas, 188 E Lombard
Koplin Nathaniel, dep. flour ins., 81 Franklin.
Kopp John, baker, Marriott and 5th
Kopp Michael, ostler, 271 N 2d
Koppelberger, Isaiah, cordw., Schlessinger's ct
Korb John, shoemr., 52 New
Kore Rebecca, Chestnut n Sch 3d
Korn Deborah, b. h., 70 Brown
KORN HENRY, manuf. coach lace fringe and milit. goods, 22 N 3d.
Korn Isa., 15 Coombe's al
Korndaffer G. W., trunkmr., 324½ High, h Rogan bel Willow
KORNDAFFER JACOB, grocer, 453 S 2d
Korndaffer Nicholas, farmer, Brown bel Cherry (Kensington)
Korndaffer Parker, boots and shoes, 324½ High
Kornman Henry, beer house, Franklin bel 6th
Koscritz Mary Ann, trimmings, 125 Spruce
Koul Christ., lab., Sanders' ct
Koy Valentine, botanic doctor, 9th ab Ogden
Kraeger Christ., shoemr., 424 S Front
Kraft August, b. h., 121 Sassafras.
KRAFT C. H., tavern, 149 Race
Kraft George, cabinetmaker, 94 N 7th.
Kraft Geo. W., patternmr., Carlton bel Sch 2d
Kraft Henry, shoemaker, 110 S 2d.
Kraft Henry A., shoemaker, 6 N 12th.
Kraft Jacob, cordw., Orchard and Green's ct
Kraft Jercy, tailor, 49 Duke
Kraft M., cordw., Mayland
Krall Geo., brickmr., M'Duffey ab 3d
Krall P., brickmr., M'Duffie ab 3d
Kram Jacob, carp., Poplar bel Broad
Kramer Andrew, machinist, 599 N 3d
Kramer Francis, turner, 9th bel Ogden
Kramer Francis, turner, 10th ab Parrish
Kramer Henry, painter, Palmer bel West (K)
Kramer Henry, coachmr., Budden's al
Kramer John, bl ndmr., Hope ab Phoenix (K)
Kramer John, chairmr., Mercer and Warren
Kramer John E., cracker baker, 93 R road

Kramer L. S boot & shoemr. Vienna ab Queen (Kensington)
Kramer Philip, carp. Wood n Sch 8th
Kramer Richard A., printer, Budden's al
Kramer T., tailor, 106 New Market
Kramer Wm. shop, 540 N Front
Kramm Gustavus, lithographer, 1 Elmslie's al
Krauch M., pie baker, 115 N 6th
Krause Casper, brewer, 140 Coates
Krauss & Emanuel, painter, 106 N 6th
Krauss Godfrey, lab., Washington ab Willow
Krauss Joseph P. painter, 106 N 6th, h 14 Hallowell
Krautz John, brewer, 169 N 4th
Kreamer Charles, salesman, 15 Nectarine
Kreamer Jno. butcher, Fitler bel Harrison (K)
Kreamer Mary, Hope bel Phoenix (K)
Krecker Margt., G T road bel 2d
Kreeger Gustavus H. M. D. 188 S 8th
Kreer Henry, engineer, Beach ab Marlboro'(K)
Kreichebaum John, engraver & mouldmr. 318 N 3d
Kreider Fred. C., atty., 309 N 3d
Kreider Henry, grocer, Vine & R road, h 292 S Garden bel R road
Kreiner Henry, wharf builder, Allen bel Palmer (K)
Kreiss Chas., tailor, 22 Branner's al
Kreklah Lewis, machinist, Ontario bel Poplar
Kreller George, cooper, Coates n Sch
Kremer Fredk., chairmr., 20 Hazel
Kremer Fredk., baker, Queen ab Marlboro'(K)
Kremhan Alex., shoe finder, 394 N 3d
Kreplin Sarah, widow of John F., 7 Union (S)
Krepp Frederick, baker, Locust ab 12th
Kresler George R., carp., 239 Marshall
Kretschau A. & Gildea, artif. limb mrs. 61 Dock
Kretschmar Peter, 61 Dock
Kreuser Christian F., baker, 443 S 6th
Krewson Mordecai, carpenter, Callowhill and Sch. 7th.
Kridel John, wheelwright, Leopard (K)
Krider Geo. shipcarp., Union ab Franklin (K)
Krider Geo., baker, Carpenter ab 8th
Krider Harriet, 129 Spruce
Krider Henry, grocer, R road and Vine
Krider H., distill. & rectifier, 46 Washington av
Krider John, gunsm., 101 & 103 S 2d ab Walnut
Krider John J., baker, 70 Swanson.
Kridler Thomas, tailor, 2 Richards
Krier Henry, engineer, Wood n West
Krim H., widow, Washington bel 2d
Krin Adam, weaver, 100 Tammany
Krips Margaret, gentw., rear 464 N 2d
Krips Philip, dyer, 247 St John
Kritser Jacob, cordw., Beaver ab 3d
Kritser Sophia, rear 443 N 3d
Kroll Catharine, Willow bel 4th
Kroll Earnest, acct., 343 Vine.
Kroman Henry, 47 Filbert
Kromer E. G., tailor, 151 N 3d
Kromer & Flenner, tailors, 151 N 3d
Kromm Henry, drover, James ab Charles.
Kromschield Chas., tailor, 40 Exchange
Krop John, cab mr., 215 St John

Krotel F., baker, 264 N 8th
KROUSE CHARLES, tavern, 100 New
Krouse Christian, weaver, R road bel S Garden
Krouse Jacob, ostler, 30 Branch
Krouse Wm., bricklayer, rear Noble ab 8th
Krug Edwd. C., mer., 151 High
Krug F. V., mer., 151 High, h 308 Mulberry
Krug F. V. & Co., com. mers., 151 High, ab stairs
Krull George, collector, 53 P road
Krumbhaar Lewis, Sec. Spring Garden Ins. Co., N W 6th and Wood.
Krupp Eli, grocer, 4th and Thompson (K)
Krupp John, spigot turner, S W 4th & Tammany
Kubblier John, Wood bel Sch 2d
Kucher Wm. W., shoes, 391 N 2d
Kucker John, planemr., 6th bel G T road
Kucker John L., brass frounder, 7th ab Weaver's rope walk (K)
Kuemmerle Christ., conf., R road ab Vine
Kuemmerlen John, baker, G T road n 3d
Kuen Joseph, combmr., 48 Apple
Kuen Samuel, combmr., 7th ab Weaver's rope walk (K)
Kuermmerle Martin, syringemr., 45 S 8th
Kugler Benj., M. D., 116 Franklin
Kugler Elizabeth, 45 P road.
Kugler George, carter, Vine ab Sch 2d
Kugler Lewis, grocer, h 377 S Front
Kuhl Frederick, 46½ Walnut, h rear 120 S 2d
Kuhl F. & C., lithographers, 46½ Walnut
Kuhl George, lithographer, 46½ Walnut, h 4 Courtlin pl
Kuhl James, lab., Orange ab Lemon
Kuhl John G., tailor, 31 Elfreth's al
Kuhlmann Gerhard, cordwainer, N W 6th and Lombard
Kuhn Charles jr., atty. and coun., 167 Spruce
Kuhn Eliza, gentw., 253 Walnut
Kuhn Hartman, jr. 240 Walnut
Kuhn Hartman, gent., 314 Chestnut.
Kuhn Henry, lab., rear 252 S Front
Kuhn John, hatter, 190 N 2d.
KUHN JOHN, tailor, 45 S 4th
Kuhn P. H., baker, rear 276 N 3d
Kuhn Wm., varnisher, rear 298 Sassafras
Kulp John, lab., R road ab Broad
Kulp Joshua, brickmr., Watt
Kummer Mark, susp. weav., Cherry and Monroe (K)
Kundell George, tailor, 2 Garrigues ct
Kunitz Lewis, dentist, 129 Plum
Kunitz Lewis, blindmr., Tyler
Kunkle Christian, vict. Nectarine bel 11th
Kunkle George, R road ab Francis (F V)
Kunkle Jacob, cordw., rear 116 Brown
Kunkle John, vict. R road bel Girard, av (F V)
Kunkle John B. & Co., dealer in leather, Garden and Willow, h 10th ab Brown
Kunkle P. vict. R road ab Wood
Kunts Wm, blindmr., 129 S 2d, h Spruce ab 13th
Kuntz Caspar, cordw., 4 New Market
Kuntz John, clothing, 380 N 2d
Kuntz Joseph, dealer, 7 Shepherd's al
Kuntz Mich., dealer, 126 Swanson

Kunz Jacob, gun smith, G T road ab Phoenix.
Kunzmann F. P., baker, 26 Jones' al.
Kupp Rachel, Beaver bel Charlotte
Kurlbaum Chas., chemist, h Oxford & Front (K)
Kurlbaum & Co., chemists, 190 Coates
Kurtz Catharine, rear 2d ab Edward (K)
Kurtz Christian, cordwainer, 389 N Front.
Kurtz Christopher, brickmr., 6th and G T road
Kurtz Henry, cabinetmr., Cherry n Franklin(K)
Kurtz Henry E., brushmr., Poplar and Kurtz
Kurtz Jos., lampmr., 13th bel Brown
Kurtz John, wood sawyer, 14 New Market
Kurtz John, cabmr., Apple bel George
Kurtz John, shoemr. 236 High, h rear 25 N 6th
Kurtz Richard M. copper pl. printer, 18 Bonsall
Kurtz William, cabinetmr., 118 Apple
Kushmer Lawrence jr.,weav.,Palmer n West(K)
Kutchen Miles, porter, 15 Gaskill
Kutchin Parson, carp., Walter's ct
Kutter John A., painter, rear Perry bel Phœnix
Kyle Catharine, St John bel G T road
Kyle Hugh, engineer, Lancaster ab Reed
Kyle Robert, lab., Pine bel Sch Beech

———

Labbree John H., cabinetmr., Queen ab Sarah (K)
La Boulee Louis, tailor, 2 York ct
Lace & Hanley, blacksm., 11 Jones' al
Lace Wm., blacksm., 11 Jones' al
Lacey Geo. Rev., 124 Catharine
Lacey Mary, huckster, St Joseph's av
Lacey Paul, tailor, 24 Shippen
LACEY & PHILLIPS, saddlers, 12 S 5th
Lacey Return, oyster-house, High E Sch 7th
Lacey Wm., lab., Sch 8th ab Race
Lacey William N., saddler, 12 S 5th
Lachenmayer John, M. D., 106 Callowhill
Lackey David, tailor, Shippen bel Broad
Lackey James, ladies' shoemr. 202 Mulberry
Lackey Wm., lab., Mifflin n 13th
Lacman Jacob, cabinetmr., 7 Nicholson
Lacy Edward, brewer, 6 Leiper
Lacy John, drayman, Richard n Sch 7th
Lacy Patrick, porter, 3 Branch
Ladd Hannah, b h, N E 8th and Sansom
Ladd L. D., widow of Samuel, Filbert ab Sch 8th
Ladd Saml. G., dentist, 282 Chestnut
Ladomus J., watchmaker, 33 S 4th
LADOMUS LEWIS, watchmr., 413½ High, h 103 N 13th
Lafaver Philip, shop, 615 S 2d
Lafferty Charles, pedler, 338 N Front
Lafferty Charles, carter, Sch 2d ab Lombard
Lafferty George, vict., Olive bel 12th
Lafferty James, grocer, 144 Cherry
Lafferty Jas. weav.,rear G T road bel Master(K)
Lafferty John, manuf., G T road ab Master (K)
Lafferty Joseph, pedlier, 338 N Front
Lafferty Messmar, butcher, Fisher ab Marriot
Lafferty Patrick, lab, 6 Flickwir's ct

Lafore A., ornamental hair manuf., 28 S 4th.
Laforgue L., mer., 138 High h 12 S 12th.
Lafourcade Edward, mer., 77 High, h 153 Mulberry
Lafourcade James, stock broker, 74 S 3d,
Lafourcade Marcelin, mer., 77 High, h 49 Wood bel 8th
Lafourcade Peter M., gent., 100 Crown.
Lagrave Augustus, art. flowers, 66½ S 4th
Laguerenne E., mer., 39 S Front,
Laguerenne P. L., importer, 59 S Front
Laher Joseph, baker, 51 N 6th
Lahman George, cordw. Coates bel 12th
Laib G. cabinetmr. 110 Walnut
Laidlaw Alexander, lab., Ann n 12th
LAING ALVE E., hatters' goods, 24 N 3d, h 2 Logan sq
Laing C. W., engraver, Lewis ab Poplar
Laing Henry M., shoe findings, 24 N 3d
Lainhoff Godfrey, police, Rose al
Lainhoff Joshua, carp., Olive bel 12th
Lair John, brickmr., George n Sch 2d
Lair Philip, plasterer, Thomas' al
Laird Alex., weaver, Crown ab Duke (K)
Laird Francis, dep. keeper N Prison, Carpenter bel 5th
Laird Hugh, weaver, Crown ab Duke (K)
Laird John L., tobacconist, 102 N 3d, h 17 New
Laird Wm., segarmr., 3d & Coates
Laird Wm., tallow chandler, Harrison av
Lajus, D. P., M. D., 99 S 4th
Lajus Paul, mer., 39 S whfs. h 99 S 4th.
Lajus Paul & Co.-com. mers. 39 S whfs.
Lake Ann, gentw., 47 George (S)
Lake Azarjah, waterman, 400 N Front
Lake Edward, carter, Brinton bel 11th
Lake Thos., mariner, 150 Dead al
Lake Wm., vict., 6th ab Poplar
Lakey Lewis, carp., George n Juniper
Lalanne A., trimmings, 95 S 6th
Lalanne J. P., furniture, 75 Lombard.
Lalande John, jeweller, Christian ab 7th
Lallow Eugene, paper hanger, Justice's ct
Lamar John, boot & shoemr., 5 Hickory ct
Lamasure James, tailor, 117 Chestnut
Lamax John, Wood ab Sch 8th
Lamb Chas., malster, rear Vaughan ab Locust
Lamb Isaac, flour and feed, 404 N Front, h 273 Marshall
Lamb Jacob, cordw. Charlotte ab Poplar
Lamb James, coachman. Pearl ab Sch 8th
Lamb James, grocer, S E Crabb & Cedar
Lamb James, manf., 3 Brinton.
Lamb James, lab., Washington (W P)
Lamb John C. vict. rear O Y road ab Tammany
Lamb Joseph, cordw., Orchard
Lamb Lemuel, 386 Mulberry
Lamb Owen, tailor, 165 S Front
Lamb Peter, waterman, 24 Catharine
Lamb Peter, jr., chairmr., 24 Catharine
Lamb Thomas, coachman, 6 Monroe

Lambert E. C., atty and coun., 68 S 6th
LAMBERT JOHN, atty. & coun., 5 S 7th, h N
   E R road & Turner's la
Lambert John, ship joiner, 2 Powell's row
Lambert John, cabinetmr. Rutter's ct
Lambert John, printer, Alder ab Poplar
Lambert Joseph H. capmr. 38 Chester
Lambert Matilda, b h, 12th ab Bedford
Lambert Peter, gent., 185 Noble
Lambert Stephen, draym., Front bel Oxford (K)
Lambert Thos., machinist, Fairview ab Sch 5th
Lambert Wm. P., dentist, 5 N 9th
Lamberti Joseph, capmr., 62 Dock,
Lamberton Robt., grocer, Front bel Master (K)
Lamby Jane, spooler, Hanover ab West (K)
Lame Charles, wheelwrt., G T road & 7th
Lame Joseph, cabinet mr., 28 Marion.
Lamen Robert, carpet weaver, Duke n F road
Lammel Lewis, chaser, rear 33 Cherry
Lammey F., cordw., 12 Fitzwater
Lamon George, carpets, 60 Beach bel Maiden
   (K)
Lamon Philip, boilermr., Monroe n Cherry
Lamont John, tobacconist, 354 High
Lamont Margaret, 2 Dugan row
Lamorelle Augustus, gent., h 61 Lombard
Lamorelle Elizabeth, 61 Lombard
LAMPARTER HENRY, tavern, 327 N 3d
Lamparter Lewis, baker, R road & Ann (F V)
Lamping Margaret, 4 Biddle's al
Lamplugh Isaac, dentist, 353 S 2nd.
Lamplugh Samuel, capt., 2d bel Christian
Lamsin Michael, coachmr., Palm bel Brown
Lanagin Thos., lab., 254 N Water
Lanahan Lucy, Church bel Christian
LANCASTER JACOB B., grain and feed,
   Spruce st. wharf, h 116 Lombard.
Lancaster John, carter, rear Poplar ab 6th
Lancaster John, weaver & dealer, 385 S 2nd
Lancaster Joseph, porter, 100 Gaskill.
Lancaster Joseph, gents. furnishing store, 204½
   Chestnut
Lancaster Mary R. wid of Joseph, Brown ab 10th
Lancaster Merious, jeweller, Race ab 13th
Lancaster Rachel, rear 129 Walnut
Lancaster Richard, waiter, Shippen la bel 13th
Lancaster Thos., driver, George n Sch 6th
Lancaster Thomas, grain mer., 110 Lombard.
Lancaster Wm., carpet weaver, 171 & h 132
   Cedar
Lance James, morocco dresser, Elizabeth below
   Franklin (K)
Land Samuel, painter, O Y road bel Coates, h 8
   Marble pl
Landell George, lumber mer., Beach ab Ken-
   sington Market.
Landell George, & Sons, lumber mers., 2d ab
   Oxford & Beach ab Maiden (K)
Landell G. A., mer., 22 N Water, h Beach. (K)
Landell John, lumber mer., Penn ab Maiden, h
   Shackamaxon ab Queen (K)
Landell Washington I., mer., S W 4th and Mul-
   berry, h 340 O Y road
Landenberger Andrew, stockingmr., Piper's ct
Landenberger Martin, stockingmr., 653 N 2d (K)

Landerberger Matthias, stock weav., rear Perry
   ab Franklin (K)
Landis Abby, Marlborough bel Duke
Landis Amos, painter, Crown bel Franklin
Landis Catharine, 191 Cherry
Landis & Co., mers., 40 N 2d
Landis Henry D., mer., 59 High
Landis Michael, contractor, Green E of Broad
Landon John, silk dyer, 17 Lebanon
Landress Garett, lab., Goldsmith's ct
Landreth D., seedsman, 65 Chestnut, h 69
   Spruce
Landrey M. A., doctor, 249 Christian
Landsinberg Geo., cooper, 337 N Front
Landy James, groc., 2d & Brown, h 58 Coates
Landy John, carpenter, 59 Coates.
Lansdown Jas., sailmr., Cedar ab 10th
Lansdown James P., sr., tailor, 318 E Pine
Lane Abraham V., coachman, Prospect al
Lane Anthony, lab., Sch 3d bel Chestnut
Lane E. & Co., coachmrs., Washington (W P)
Lane Henry, lab., Eyre's ct (K)
Lane Henry, driver, Mechanic bel Culvert
Lane Hugh, Rev., 375 S 3d
Lane James, stonemason, 201 N 3d
Lane James S., bookbinder, 24 Mulberry
Lane Jeremiah, weaver, rear Fitler ab 2d
Lane John, Inspector in Custom House, h 3
   Howard
Lane Joseph blacksmith, Reeve bel Sch 2d
Lane Lemuel, lab., rear Sutherland & Queen
Lane Mary, tailoress, 99 German
Lane P., captain, 6 Flower st
Lane Wm. B., police officer, 1 Union sq
Lane Wm. L., editor, 367 S 3d
Lane William M., tobacconist, 236 N Front
Lang Ben., lab., 8 Elizabeth
Lang Francis, dyer, rear 466 N 3d
Lang E., M. D., 150 S 7th
Lang George S., 37 N 8th
Lang Jane, dry goods, 37 N 8th
Lang John, saddler, rear Parrish bel 10th
Lang John C., consul, 67 S 4th
Lang Leopold, pedler, 298 N 10th
Lang Rebecca, Carpenter ab 6th
Lang William, suger refiner, 39 Shippen
Lang William, sugar refiner, 28 Scheetz
Langabartel Augustine, tinsm., 495 N 4th
Langabartel Elizabeth, 495 N 4th
Langbartel Isaac, shoes, 427 N 3d.
Langdon Walter, hair seating, 59 Dock
Lange Frederick, cabinet mr., 70 N 5th
Lange Joachim, clerk, 22 N 12th
Lange M., 502 Callowhill
Langenheim W. & F., daguerreotype establish.,
   25 & 27 Exchange
Langenstein John, hair manuf., 598 N 3d
Langer A. B. Mrs., rear Shackamaxon n Bedford
Langer Joseph, baker, R road ab Buttonwood
Langer Joseph S., suspender manufac., Shacka-
   maxon ab Bedford.
Langert Geo., coachmaker, George bel 10th, h
   Garden n Callowhill
Langguth C. A., baker, 51 Duke
Langham Sarah, shop, Front bel Phoenix (K)

Langher Theodore, type founder, Federal ab Front
Langley Isaac, coal dealer, 17 Queen
Langon Thos., grocer, Sch. 5th and Wood
Langsdorf Jacob, mer., 274 N 3d
Langstaff Wm., pilot, Court alley
Langstroth C. S., lum. mer., 142 N 9th, yard c 10th & Green.
Langstroth T. F., mer., 52 High
Laning Aaron. engineer, 10th ab Poplar
Laning & Baldwin, painters, 169 Callowhill
Laning Joshua, clerk, 177 Catharine
Laning R. G., house and sign painter, 206 N 2d
Laning Wm. M., painter, 169 Callowhill
Lankenau John D., mer., 28 Chestnut, h 174 Chestnut
Lankford Susan, washerw, 30 Mechanic
Lanky Cath., widow, Hanover ab West (K)
Lannahan Dennis, lab., Sch. 3d ab Spruce
Lannegan Jacob, tailor, Beach ab Poplar (K)
Lanning Joseph, carp., Parrish bel 12th
Lansdown James P., sailmr., 3 Dock, h Cedar n 11th
Lansdown James P. & Co., sailmrs., 3 Dock
Lantz Christian, carp., 41 New Market
Lantz Louisa, widow, Marshall ab Poplar
Lantz Wm., book binder, Kean's ct
Lapine James, tailor, 315 Walnut
Lapp Abraham, comb maker, 523 N 3d
Lapp D. C., brass founder, 178 Marshall
Lapp John, flour & feed store, S W Julianna & Willow
Lappin James, carder, M'Duffy n Sch 2d
Lapsley Catharine, 260 Lombard
Lapsley David, treas. Harrisbg. & Lan. R. Road Co., 16 Merch. Exchange, h 1 Portico sq
Lapsley John, 64½ Walnut, h 271 Pine ab 9th.
Lapsley J. B., gent., 64½ Walnut, h 268 Spruce
Larason Jacob, shoes, 98 Sp Garden
Larason Wm. B., currier, 280 St. John
Larcombe Thomas Rev., S Garden bel Logan
Lardner Alex., broker, 93½ Walnut, h Broad ab Locust
Lardner J. L., U S Navy, Spruce E Sch 8th
Lardner Richard P., 607 Spruce
Lare Dorothy, widow, George n Sch. 2d
Lare George A., cordw., Newton bel Carpenter
Lare Henry, brickmaker, Walnut ab Sch. 3d.
Lare John, cordw., James bel 10th
Lare John, brickmr., Sch 3d bel George
Lare Joseph, shipwright, 51 Green
Lare Margaret, widow, Walnut n Sch 3d
Larer Alex., jeweller, 25 P road
Larer Wm., umbrella maker, 4 George ab 2d
Large Christopher, machinist, 630 N 3d
Large David K., cabinetmaker, 27 Walnut

Larkin Patrick, coachman, rear 11 Mercer
Larkin Thomas, rear 15 Lilly alley
Larned Wm. Henry, mer., 27 Chestnut, h 147 N 13th
La Roche Peter F., seaman, 115 Swanson
La Roche Renie, M. D., 2 Monroe pl
Laroue Ann, confectioner, 129 S 4th
Laroux Ives, dyer, Drinker's ct
Larrentree Augustus, broker, 43 S 3d, h 2d bel Prune
Larringer John, weigher, Loud st
Larsen Jacob, waterman, 7 German
Larue Moses, carp., 8th ab Wallace
La Rue Nicholas, tailor, Maiden bel Front
La Rue Wm., silver plater, Shoemaker's ct
Larzelere William, clerk, Green and R road
La Serre Susan, 4 Garrell's ct
Lasher Francis, jr., mer., 44 N 2d, h 54 Wood
Lasher Francis sen., cop. and tin smith, Beach ab Marlborough, (K)
Laskey Edward W., quill manuf., 194 S 4th
Laskey John, Buttonwood & Charles
Latham Betty, shop, Callowhill ab Broad
Latham William C., confect., Callowhill above Broad
Lathbury James, baker, 163 Shippen.
Lathmore Sophia, widow, 501 Chestnut
Latimer E. & Parker J. A., seminary, 222 Sassafras
Latimer Misses, gentw., 6 Dugan's Row.
Latimer Thomas, atty and coun., S E 5th and Library, h 23 German
Latour Amada, capt., 55 Lombard
Latour John, mer., 261 S Front
Latta & Hamlin, com. mers., 38 Chestnut
Latta John E., mer., 38 Chestnut, h 229 N 13th.
Latting Wm., agent, 101 Chestnut
Lauderdale Edward, bootmaker, 11 S 8th.
Lauek Catharine, widow of Wm., Green ab 9th
Lauenger Frederick, lab., Sheppard ct
Lauer John, tavern, Front and Washington
Lauer John, carp., 27 Federal
Lauer John C., M. D., 68 Coates
Lauer Joseph, carp., 3d bel Wharton
Lauffee Harman, beer house, 214 St. John
Laughlin John, weaver, Hanover ab West (K)
Laughlin Martha, widow, 431 S 6th
Laughlin Mary, dressmr., 132 S 10th
Laughran Jas., weaver, Hope bel Master (K)
Laugrs Anthony, 6 Cox
Laukney James, boatman, Beach ab Walnut
Launay Augustus, store keeper, 184 R. road
Lausser Henry, lab., Palm ab Brown
Lausterer Peter, carp., Coates n Fairmount
Laval John, Mrs., 210 Pine.

Law E. E., att'y. & coun., 49 S 5th, h 326 Walnut.

Law John, bootmr., Lombard ab Sch. 3d

Law Robert, cabinetmaker, 301 Vine.

Law Smith, cap manuf., 118 N 3d, 10th n Parrish

Law Wm., jeweller, 13th ab Cedar

Lawgon Matt., weaver, Perry bel Master (K)

Lawless I. J., bootmr., Morris n Fitzwater

Lawn Francis, engineer, Cedar n Sch 2d

Lawn Michael, lab., Beach bel Walnut.

Lawn Patrick, lab., George n Beach

Lawrence Alfred, lab., 227 Lombard

Lawrence Alfred jr., vict., Pleasant ab 10th

Lawrence Ann, 83 N 9th

Lawrence Beulah, rear 9 John (S)

Lawrence Charles B., plumber, 298 Sassafras

Lawrence David, lab., 66 German

Lawrence Diana, 32 Prosperous alley

Lawrence Eliza, 289 Spruce

Lawrence E. & Co., trimmings, 88 N 2d

Lawrence George W., U S Mint, h 93 N 13th.

Lawrence Hamilton, comb maker, 8 Stamper's alley

Lawrence Isaac, coachman, Lewis n Sch. 7th

Lawrence Jacob, corder, h 527 S 2d

LAWRENCE JACOB & SON, corders, 3d whf. bel Almond

Lawrence James, collector, 468 N 4th

Lawrence John, tavern, c Penn & Maiden (K)

Lawrence John, corder, 3d whf. bel Almond, h 29 Federal

Lawrence John A., carp., Van Buren place

Lawrence Joseph, silver plater, 466 Sassafras, h 174 N 12th

Lawrence J. R., bricklayer, 576 S Front

Lawrence Lawrence, skin dresser, 118 Charlotte

Lawrence Lucinda, washer, 19 Acorn alley

Lawrence Margaret, widow, 135 E. Shippen

Lawrence Mary, crockery, P road bel Christian

Lawrence Mary, Cantrell's ct

Lawrence Michael, capt. of watch, 37 R road

Lawrence M. E., 4 Virginia Row

Lawrence N. S., Agent Southworth Manuf. Co., 3 Minor

Lawrence Richard, boot black, 37 S 3d

Lawrence Samuel, baker, 44 Sassafras

Lawrence Samuel, lab., 63 N 5th

Lawrence Sarah, widow, 10th bel Pleasant

Lawrence Sarah, 168 N 8th

Lawrence Sarah Ann, variety store, 154 N 3d

Lawrence Thos., blacksm., Johnson's la bel 4th

Lawrence Thomas, butcher, Sch 3d and Lombard

Lawrence & Westcott, plumbers, 298 Sassafras

Lawrence Wm., cabinetmr., Olive ab 10th

Lawrence Wm., pumpmr., Lombard ab Sch 3d

Lawrence W. P., Camden Bank agency, 12 Church al

Lawrie Robert D., silversm., 25 Library, h N E Franklin & Noble

Laws Ann, washer, 14 Russell

Laws Daniel, druggist, 206 N 9th

Laws Elisha, waterman, 9 Rose alley (C)

Laws George, 149 N 7th

LAWS ISAAC Jn., soap boiler, 641 N 2d

Laws James, 157 N 7th

Laws James, mariner, Front and Hazel's ct

Laws John, tanner, Thomas' al

LAWS JOHN, alderman, 74 Green

Laws J. D., coachmr., 32 Dock, h 56½ Gaskill

Laws Mary Ann, milliner, 431½ N 2d

Laws Outten, grocer, N E 7th and Callowhill

Laws Peter, porter, 256 Lombard

Laws Peter E. chinaware, 403 N 2d

Laws Stephen, lab., Cedar ab 10th

Laws Wm., coachman, Carolina pl

Laws Wm., seaman, 13 St. Mary

Laws Wm. L. mer. 138 High

Laws Wm. L. & Co., straw goods, 138 High

Lawson David, tobacconist, Bedford ab 12th

Lawson Elizabeth, Cherry bel Franklin (K)

Lawson Jacob, saddler, 45 Noble, h 40 Coates

Lawson James, weaver, Linn ab Willow

Lawson John, weaver, Camac ab G T road

Lawson Matthias, cooper, Aspen ab Spruce

Lawson Thomas, grocer, 461 N 4th

Lawson Wm., F road bel Master (K)

Lawson Wm. carp. Queen bel Palmer

Lawton Daniel, bricklayer, 370 S 4th

Lawton Geo. R., real estate agent, 183 Queen

Lawton John, tavern, 11 Walnut

Lawton John, clerk, 12 York ct

Lawville Cornick, cordw., Beach bel Chestnut

Lay Thomas, gent., N E 10th and Callowhill

Laycock John, book binder, 2 Roger's ct

Laycock John Jr., bookbinder, 2 Fries' ct

Laycock J. C., atty. and coun., 6th and Locust

Laycock Mary, fancy goods, 59 Chestnut

Laycock Mich., tailor, William st.

Layman F., capt. 14 Beck (S)

Layton Elias, shoemr., 17 Elizabeth (N L)

Layton Francis, drover, Wood bel Sch 8th

Layton Geo., lab., 5th bel Christian

Layton Susanna, 4 Lancaster

Layton Wm., stevedore, 19 Emlen's ct

Lazarus Abraham, clothing, 231 N 2d

Lazarus Henry, stationery, 117 Coates

Lazarus Mordecai, speculator, 1 Mechanic

Lazell Mary, shop, 151 Poplar

Lazellier Saml., Carlton bel Sch 2d

LEA, BUNKER & CO., com. mers., 71 S whfs.

Lea & Blanchard, book publishers, 4th below Chestnut

Lea Isaac, bookseller & publisher, c 4th and Chestnut, h 360 Walnut

Lea Joseph Jr., mer., 52 Chestnut, h 183 Vine

Lea Joseph, carpet weaver, Hancock bel Master (K)

Lea Jos., gent., Sch 7th ab Spruce

Lea M. Carey, atty. and coun., 114 Walnut

Lea Robeson, com. mer., 71 S whfs., h 70 Spruce.

Lea Thomas T. com. mer. 32 Chestnut, h Spruce n Sch 7th

Leach Andrew, porter, 9 New Market

Leach Sarah, 85 N 9th

LEACH WILLIAM, tavern, 14 Cherry bet 3d and 4th.

Leacock & Fravel, cabmr., 15 Crown
Leacock Wm., tinsmith, Jones n Sch 4th
Leadbeater John, Spruce ab 13th
Leadbeater Joseph, machinist, rear 658 N 3d
Leadbeater Jos., machinist, rear 26 N 6th, h 3d ab Brown
Leadbeater Mary Ann, trimmings, 120 S 5th
Leaf William, 8 Jay
Leahy Dennis, b. h., 169 S Front
Leahy Jas., tailor, 11 Benton st
Leak Thomas, painter, 28 Lombard.
Leakner Henry, lab., G T road opp 5th (K)
Leamer Eliza, 7 German
Leaming Cath., Queen ab Bishop (K)
Leaming J. F., mer., 28 S Front, h 288 Chestnut
Leamy Ann, 5 York buildings
Leamy Thomas, shoemr., 9 Chancery la .
Leaney Thomas, William & Biddle (F M)
Leans Martin, graver, N E 3d and Dock, h 163 Catharine
Lear Ann, 110 Green
Lear Wm., shoemr., Higgin's ct
Leary G. S., printer, 143½ N 2d
Leary John, carter, St John bel George (K)
Leary John, lab. Washington (W P)
Leary William A., bookseller, 158 N 2d c New
Leathem James, cordw., 8 Skerret's ct.
Leatherberry Abel, cordwainer, 286 St. John.
Leatherberry Ed., cordw., rear Front bel Phœnix
Leatherberry John, cordw., Allen ab Shackamaxon
Leatherberry Wm., cordw., Queen ab Shackamaxon.
Leatherby Joseph, grocer, S W Front & Master (K)
Leatherman Henry, brass founder, Hope bel Phoenix (K)
Leatherman John, wheelw., Locust n Beach
Leatherman John, brickl., Sch. 7th ab Cherry.
Leavitt Hart A., mer., Juniper n Filbert
Lebo Daniel, tanner, c Orchard & Green ct.
Lebon Anth. stonecut. Franklin & Front (K)
Le Boutillier, Brothers, fancy dry goods, 218 Chestnut
Le Boutillier Charles, mer., 218 Chestnut, h 133 N 9th
Le Brun N., architect, 59 N 7th
Leberman Henry, cordw., 32 Garden
Leberman J. L., 42 Coates
Lechevallier M. A. R., trimmings, 427 S 2d
Lechler Adam, lab. Coates bel 9th
Lechler George, vict., rear 6th ab Poplar
Lechler Henry, morocco dresser, M'Ginley's ct bel Swanson
Lechler Henry Jr., gunsmith, 133 N Front.
Lechler Joseph, dep. bark inspector, Church ab Prime
Lechler Wm., victualler, 6th ab Poplar.

Lecount Josh., lab., 30 Bonsall st
Lecount Samuel, carter, Cherry bel Duke (K)
Lecroy C., conf., 520 High
Lecture Wm., shoemaker, 382 S 3d
Leday Andrew, lab., Jones n Sch 6th
Ledder Richd., car. driv., rear 462 N 2d
Leddon Perriman, combmaker, Cadwalader n Franklin (K)
Leddy Jos., gardener, 142 Queen
Leddy Michael, lab., Barker ab Sch 7th
Ledent John, painter, 16 Gray's al
Ledford Wm., currier, rear 103 Dillwyn st
Ledger Nath., clerk, Marlboro' & Queen (K)
Ledlum Abm., lab., Liberty ct
Ledyard Edwd. S., Sp Garden and 11th
Lee Andrew, lab., 7 Lombard row
Lee Benjamin, grocer, 11th & Coates
Lee Benj., chairmr., 547 High
Lee & Brady, dentists, Franklin ab Marlborough (K)
Lee Caroline, chairmr., 547 High & N E Montgomery and 13th
Lee David, carpet manuf., 34 Crown
Lee Dennis, soapmaker, 323 S 5th.
Lee Francis, mer., 46 N 2d
Lee Francis, mer., 53 Franklin
Lee Franklin, bricklayer, N W 3d and Tammany
Lee George, jeweller, Prime ab Front
Lee Geo., rigger, Marlboro' bel Queen (K)
Lee Hiram W., tailor, 120 G T road
Lee James, weaver, 518 N Front
Lee Jas., mer., Queen bel Shackamaxon (K)
Lee James A., coachman, Parrish bel 10th
Lee James F. & Co., flour & feed, Beach & Marlboro' (K)
Lee John, tobacco., N W Duke & New Market
Lee John, tobacco., N W 3d & Walnut
Lee Joseph, mer., 183 Vine
Lee Joseph, tailor, 49 N 6th, h 126 N 7th
Lee Julius, library, 120 Walnut
Lee Lydia, shop, 4th ab Master
Lee Mary, washer, 12 Elizabeth st
Lee Matthias H., tailor, 17 Wallace.
Lee M. & E., dry goods, 22 N 8th.
Lee Nicholas, weaver, 4 Orchard
Lee Osborn, 63 Currant al
Lee Ralph, manager Richmond Coal Co., h Queen bel Palmer (K)
Lee Richard, skindresser, 622 N 3d
Lee Richard, skin dresser, James bel 10th.
Lee Richard, weaver, M'Duffie n Sch 2d
Lee Robert, carter, Front and Marion
Lee Robt., lab., rear Marriott bel 6th
Lee Robert, glove mr., 293 N 3d
Lee Robert M., atty. & coun., 49 N 6th.
Lee Sebastian, lab., Sarah n Queen (K)
Lee T. M. K., sailmaker, 8 N wharves, h 16 Cherry
Lee & Walker, library and musi—

Lee Wm., lab., rear 266 S 4th
Lee Wm. A., teacher, G T road ab Otter
Lee William L., bleeder, Franklin ab Marlborough (K)
Leech Abm., engineer, Franklin above Howard
Leech Charles, tailor. 370 N 2d.
Leech Charles W., auction, 4 Shaffer's ct
LEECH D. & CO., fordw. mers., 13 & 15 S 3d
Leech Henry, alderman, Washington, (W P)
Leech Isaac E., shoemr., 338 Coates
Leech John, blacksmith, 114 New Market
Leech John, shoemr., School n Edward (K)
Leech John, moulder, Allen ab F road (K)
Leech Malcolm, weaver, Rose bel Broad
Leech M., blacksmith, Nectarine ab 10th
Leech Samuel, machinist, rear 575 N Front
Leech Sarah Ann, 55 Chester
Leech Wm. watchman, Carlton bel Sch Front
Leech Wm., weaver, Hope ab Otter (K)
Leech Wm., carp., 9 Roberts' ct
Leedom Benj., acct., 70 N 9th
Leedom Jacob H., tailor, Division bel 12th
Leedom Jacob H., druggist, 44 Tammany
Leedom Jonathan, iron mer., 211 S Front and 210 S Water, h 29 Pine.
Leedom Jonathan Jr. 211 S Front, h 176 S 3d
Leedom Jonathan & Son, iron merchants, 211 S Front & 210 S Water
Leedom Wm., weaver, 506 N 2d (K)
Leeds Ann, 5 Duke.
LEEDS & BAGGS, tailors, S W 4th & Chestnut
Leeds Benjamin S. shoes, 186 N 2d
Leeds Charles F., tailor, S W 4th & Chestnut, h 235 Marshall
Leeds Ezra C., coal mer., 46 Walnut, h 133 S 10th
Leeds Gideon, gent., 174 N 9th
Leeds Gurdon, com. mer. 16 Walnut, h 213 N 6th
Leeds Japheth, shoes, 204 N 2d.
Leeds Joseph, h Spring Garden ab 11th
Leeds Joseph, tailor, 3 & h 55½ N 8th
Leeds Josiah, carp., 8th bel Coates
Leeds & Maddock, milliners, 310 N 2d
Leeds Mahlon, carp., 245 N 3d & 156 Sassafras
Leeds Nathan, lumber, 8th bel Wallace
Leeds Nathan & Co., lumber, 11th & R road
Leek John, cordw., h Washington ab 4th
Leemen James, waterman, Lancaster & Reed
Lees Ann, b. h., 363 N 3d
Lees Henry, vict. 6th bel Little Poplar (K)
Lees Henry, victualler, 5th ab Poplar
Lees James, carp., Washington (W P)
Lees John, vict., 6th bel G T road
Lees Peter, tailor, 107 Vine.
Lees William, stone cutter, Clifton bel Cedar
Leeser Geo., carter, rear 124 Apple
Leeser Isaac, reader Jewish Congregation, Cherry, h 118 S 4th
Leeser John, carp., 2d ab Franklin (K)
Leeser Jos., harness mr., Vernon ab 10th
Leet James T. capmr. 118 N 3d, h 118 O Y road
Leeti Amos, blacksmith, F road ab Otter (K)

Le Fever James, Jun., mer. Bank & High, b 276 N 7th
Le Fevre James, gent., 38 Sassafras.
Leffman H., hatter, 40 Strawberry
Lefler J. George, coachmr. Elizabeth & Franklin
Leger Ann, washer, 34 Mayland
Leger, Brothers, importers, 127 S Front
Leger Ferdinand, mer., S W Front & Walnut
Leger Mary Jane, 2 Butler's av
Legg Daniel B., straw bonnets, 42 Chestnut
Legg George, lab., Franklin & Vienna (K)
Leggett Geo., tailor, 142 Christian
Leggett John, weaver, Union ab West (K)
Leggett Wm., dealer, Barker W of Sch 6th
Legrand Henry, lab. 118 New Market
Leguin John, carp., Vienna bel Brown (K)
Lehman A., trimmings, 209 N 2d
Lehman Charles, clerk G. B., 46½ Walnut, h 263 Coates
Lehman Edwin W. mer. 3 N 3d, h 408 Vine
Lehman Elizabeth B., b h, 286 Sassafras
Lehman Fred., druggist, rear Cadwalader ab Phoenix
Lehman G. F., M. D. & Postmaster, h Spruce ab 13th
Lehman Henry, cordw., Vine bel 13th.
Lehman Jacob, carter, 279 N 5th
Lehman Jacob S., tailor, 9th bel Coates
Lehman James, shop, Lombard ab Sch 3d
Lehman John C., M. D., 19 S 10th
Lehman Leopold, pedler, 13 Mechanic
Lehman Mary, widow, 3 Montgomery sq
Lehman Mary, 172 Cherry
Lehman Saml., locksmith, 158 St John
Lehman Wilhelmina, 25 Elizabeth (N L)
Lehman Wm. E. jr., att'y and coun. 106 S 4th, h 85 Lombard
LEHR PHILIP, wood wharf, Washington and Brown h 397 Front
Lehr Samuel, dry goods, 286 N 2d
Lehr William, dry goods, 248 N 2d
Le Huray George, 28 Wood
Le Huray Theodore, jeweller, 72 N 2d
Leib Henry F., M. D., Filbert W Sch 7th, 141 N 12th
Leib Jacob, lab. rear 219 St John
Leib Thomas J., capt. U. S. Navy, 228 Pine
Leibert John S., Poplar ab 11th
Leibert & Wainwright, rolling mill, foot Marlborough (K)
Leibert Wm. lumber mer. h Shackamaxon ab Queen (K)
Leibert W. W., rolling mill, foot of Marlboro' (K).
Leibrandt John, stove finisher, Marshall's ct
LEIBRANDT FRED., stove manuf., h 31 Vine
Leibrandt Susan, rear 3 Rose al
Leich Richard, senr., tailor, 437 S 2d.
Leich Richard, jr., tinman, 2d & Christian
Leidigh Jonathan, grocer, 185 N 3rd, h 380 N 4th
Leidigh L. N., clerk, Callowhill ab Broad
Leidy Conrad, bootmr., 160 N 3d.

Leidy George C. shoemr. rear 367 N 3d
Leidy & Hauberger, grocers, N E 5th & Poplar
Leidy Henry, grocer, N E 5th and Poplar
Leidy Jacob, sexton, 27 Centre
Leidy Mary, 255 St John
Leidy N. B., M. D., drug. & coroner, S E 2d & Vine
Leidy & Peters, tailors, 3d & Chestnut
Leidy Philip, hatter, 180 N 3d.
Leidy Snyder, clerk N. L. Dist., h 199 N 6th
Leidy Thos., druggist, N W 4th and Noble
Leidy William B., tailor, 3d & Chestnut, h 11th below Cedar.
Leigh Robert, seaman, 3 Lytle's ct
Leight Nicholas, porter, 5 Union (S)
Leighton James, printer, Catharine ab Lebanon
Leighton John, chair mr., 551 Chestnut, h Barker n 6th
Leinau George A., com. mer., 159 Mulberry
Leinau Hannah, gentw. 6th ab Parrish
Leinhardt Elizabeth, 11th bel Green
Leiper James W., M. D., 1 Carlton sq
Leiper Saml. M., lumber, Laurel (C) h Locust E Sch 8th
Leisenring Daniel M., 509 N 4th.
Leister Abraham, carp., School n Edward (K)
Leister Jesse, carter, rear 9th ab Coates
Leister Peter, blacksmith, 9th bel Ogden
Leister Saml., cabinetmr., Franklin n School (K)
Leitch John, mariner, 41 Penn
Leitch Thomas, bookbinder, 51 S 3rd, h 280 Coates
Leitman Henry mer. 271 Coates
Le Jambre A, upholsteress, 301 Chestnut.
Le Jee Wm. R. 284 Filbert
Leland Amos, mer., 84 High, h Spruce W Sch 8th
Leland Benjamin L. hatter, 7 Pennsyla. av, h 12th ab Wood
Leland Charles, 306 Walnut
Leland & Guion, Leghorn & straw goods, 84 High
Lelar Charles, Morris bel Catharine
Lelar Edwin, coal mer., 87 S Front, h 11 German
LELAR HENRY, High Sheriff, State House, h 131 Lombard
Lelarge Henry, tobacconist, 4 St George's al
Leman Walter M. comedian, Jefferson n Sch 5th
Lemark John, lab., Crown bel Bedford (K)
Lemark John B. morocco dresser, Crown ab Bedford (K)
Lemberger Wm. lab. 10 Dilk's ct
Lembert Gustavus, draughtsman, 218 N 4th
Lemitre John, toys, High bel Sch 5th
Lemmens Leopold, tinsmith, 168 S 3rd
Lemmon Elizabeth, dressmr., Barker ab Sch 7th
Lemon Francis, Simmons' ct
Lemon Hugh, gent., Front bel Master (K)
Lemon John, 9th and Locust
Lemon John, shoemr., 324 High
Lemon John, oak cooper, Collins' ct
Lemon John B., loom mr., F road ab Phoenix (K)
Lemon Robert, watchman, G T road ab Franklin

Lemon Stephen, segarmr., 3 Townsend's av
Lemon Thomas, lab., Spruce n Sch Front
Lemon Thomas, lab., Hall's av
Lemont Dennis, tavern, Queen & Wood (K)
Lenci Augustus, statuary, 122 Walnut, h 37 Union
Lendawer Lewis, buttonmr. rear Hanover bel Duke
Lendower John, porter, 79 German
Lendrem Geo., tailor, Denning's row
Leneghan John, lab., 376 Vine
Leneker Sarah, Atherton
Lenen Edward, lab., Walters' ct
Lennard Michael, stevedore, 443 S Front
Lennig Harriet, 9th & Wood
LENNIG N. & Co., drug. importers, 56 S Front
Lennig Charles, druggist, 56 S Front, h N W Juniper & Filbert
Lennig F., mer., 56 S Front, h Broad & Walnut
Lennox Thos., lab., 4th ab Carpenter
Lenoir James, tobacconist 492 S 2nd
Lenoir John G. wheelwright, George bel Apple
Lenoir Mary, 22 John (S)
Lenoir Samuel J., blacksmith, Clark ab 3d
Lenoir Wm., jeweller, 25 John (S)
Lenon A., tavern, S E 6th & Cherry
Lenox Ann, Harmony ct (K)
Lenox Charles, weaver, G T road ab Jefferson, (K)
Lenox John, carter, Budden's al
Lenox Samuel, shoemr., Gray's ct (K)
Lenox Thomas, weaver, G T road ab Phoenix
Lenthall John, naval constructor, 352 S 4th
Lentner Mrs. Uree, 78 S 8th
Lentz Catharine, 178 Sassafras
Lentz Christiana, wid., Phoenix bel G T road (K)
Lentz Eliza, gentw., 95 P road
Lentz George, blacksmith, School ab Rose (K)
Lentz George, weaver, Cherry n West
Lentz Jacob, soap boiler, Willow bel 8th
Lentz Jacob, tailor, Collins' al
Lentz Jacob, vict., Hanover n F road (K)
Lentz John, looking glass manuf., 500 & h 437 N 3d
Lentz Margaret, Garden & Willow
Lentz Martin, tobacconist, 341 N 6th
Lentz Michael, lab. Cherry bel West (K)
Lentz M. B., widow, 8th & Brown
Lentz Samuel, cordw., 415 N 4th
Lentz Samuel, grocer, P road & Christian, h 388 S 5th
Lentz Wm., vict., Palmer n F road (K)
Lentz William D., grocer, S E P road and Christian, h 388 S 5th
Lentz Wm. D. & S., grocers, S E P road & Christian
Lenze A., tinsmith, 2 Shaffer's ct (S G)
Leo Joseph, sen., Sch 7th bel Locust
Leo Patrick, driver, Jefferson ab Broad
Leon A., M. D., 280 N 6th
Leon Joseph, M. D., 338 Sassafras
Leonard A., die sinker, 12th ab Washington
Leonard Daniel, huckster, Palmer & Duke (K)
Leonard Edward, tobacconist, 25 Laurel

Leonard Edward, segarmr., Culvert ab Mechanic
Leonard Ellen, shop, 162 S 5th
Leonard George, cabinetmr. 318 S 5th
Leonard Jacob, carp., Queen n Crown, (K)
Leonard James, William ab Morris F M.
Leonard John, 1 Bell's ct
Leonard John, cabtmr., 318 S 5th
Leonard John S., oak cooper, Lewis ab Poplar
Leonard Margaret, nurse, 62 Garden
Leonard Mary, gentw., 13th ab Lombard
Leonard Michael, millright, Trinity pl
Leonard Patrick, cordw., 142 N Front
Leonard Peter, machinist, Harrison pl
Leonard Robert, bricklayer, 4 Howard pl
Leonard Solomon, lab., rear 147 Cherry
Leonard Thomas, tavern, 427 High
Leonard Wm., cordw. 196 Callowhill ab Sch 6th
Leonard William A., painter, Federal ab 2d
Leonard & Wilson, silversm., 18th & R road
Leonhard Frederick, tailor, Fisher st
Leonhardt Frederick, cordw. 18 Mintzer
Leopold Peter, cordw., Ogden bel 10th
Leot Jos., cook, 7 Franklin pl
Lepage James, cordw., 120 Carpenter
Lepage Peter, hair dresser, 311 Chestnut
Lepper John, framemr., Poplar ab 8th
Leppien J., mer., 29 Church al, h S E 7th and Wood
Lerch Wm , moulder, Crown bel West (K)
Le Sage Thomas H., oil cloth manuf. 177 S 3rd
Lescure Edward P., jeweller, 12 Noble
Lesher Catharine, 241 Christian
Lesher Christian, carp., 7 Clark
Lesher Francis, farmer, 252 Christian
Lesher John, stone mason, Shackamaxon ab Bedford
Leshey Frederick, tailor, Lewis ab Poplar
Liesk George, seaman, 22 Cedar
Lesley Jacob, cordwr., Ribl's ct
Lesley Joseph, mer., 103 S Front, h 22 Wood
Lesley Peter, Sec. Chesapeake and Delaware Canal Co., 80½ Walnut, h 185 Vine.
Lesley Robert, hardware, 243 High, h 22 Wood
Leslie Andrew, grocer, S W 6th & Cedar & 7th & Shippen
Leslie Jacob, tallow chandler, 241 S 3d
Leslie James, carp., c Sch 4th & Spruce, h 262 W Locust
Lesser Christian, tobacconist, 139 Cedar
Lesstrange, Thomas, dealer, rear 22 Raspberry
Lester Peter, bootmaker, 76 N 7th
LETCHWORTH ALBERT S., druggist, N W 12th & Spruce
Letchworth Elizabeth, N W 12th & Spruce
Letford John H., confec., 285½ N 2d
Letford William, bootmr., 12 St John and 255 Sassafras
Letourneau Lewis, tinman, 14 Knight's ct
Letterle George, jr., 154 Poplar
Letterle G., tobacconist, 158 Poplar
Levan Harvey, butcher, 246 N 2d
Levan Isaac, hatter, Depot ab 8th
Levan Jacob, varnisher, 281 Coates
Levan William, grocer, 195 N 3d, h 171 N 7th
Levans Wm., lab., Hope ab Jefferson

Levely Mary, b. h., 342 Chestnut
Levering Charles, currier, 3 Fetter la
Levering Charles, morocco dresser, 4th and Franklin
Levering Francis R., stonecut., 19 Brandywine
Levering George A., carp. Walnut al, h Washington ab 12th
Levering Jacob, mer., h 7th below Poplar
Levering L. S. com. mer. 63 S Front
Levering Michael, tobacconist, 491 N 3d
Levering Nathan, cabinetmr., 216 Noble
Levering Rebecca, 7 Providence ct
Levering Wm., paper hanger, 119 Queen
Levi Joseph, hosiery, 136½ S 2d
Levi Solomon, shoemr., 209 S 6th
Levick Ebenezer, 240, & h 230 N 4th
LEVICK EBENEZER & Co, leather dealers, 240 N 3d
Levick E. D. Mrs., b. h., 32 Mulberry
LEVICK, JENKINS & Co., shoes and leather, 150 High
Levick Peter S. hatter, 144 High, h 84 New
Levick Richard, mer., 150 High
Levick Robert R., mer., 150 High, h 156 N 5th
Levick Wm. M. & Co. curriers, N E St John & Callowhill
Levick William M., currier, 37 Dillwyn
Leviestein H. E., mer., 10 George, h 191 Pine
Levine David, fur. & skin dealer, 79 Chestnut
Levine Simon, suspender and moccason manuf., 112 Sassafras
Levingstein Moses S. cordw. 71 Coates
Levis Elizabeth, Sch 6th ab Cherry
Levis H. J., gent., 95 Locust
Levis Mahlon M., M. D., 236 N 6th
Levis & Taylor, paper & rags, 33 Carter's al
Levis William, boots & shoes, 141 High, h 236 Mulberry
Levis Wm., mer., 33 Carter's al
Levison David, lab., Elizabeth ct
Levy Aaron, mer., 90 N 2d
Levy Benj. Washington (W P)
Levy Benjamin, dry goods, 4th ab Brown
Levy B. W., 237 N Front
Levy Eliza, 325 S 5th
Levy E. P., mer., 28 N 4th, h 324 E Pine
Levy H. A., watchmr., 381 S 2d
Levy Isaac, mer. 27 S 4th
Levy Jacob I., 25 Powell
Levy John P. machinist, Beach bel Palmer, h Queen ab Hanover (K)
Levy Joseph, mer., N E 4th & Pine
Levy L. J., mer. 134 Chestnut, h 276 Spruce
LEVY L. J. & Co., fancy dry goods, 134 Chestnut
LEVY PATRICK, wines & liquors, 453 High
Lewallen David, wheelw., G T road ab 2d (K)
Lewallen Wm. drayman, Liberty al
LEWARS CHS., grocer, S W c 2d & Tammany
Lewars Jas. E., mer., 177 High, h 313 Sassafras
Lewellen A., blacksm., Shackamaxon ab Franklin
Lewellen Thomas, U. S. Mint, 30 Perry
Lewellen Wm., carter, Beach ab Poplar (K)
Lewin Wm., frame mr., Olive & 11th

Lewink John, weaver, 302 St John.
Lewis Albin H., flour & feed, High n Sch 2d, h Hamilton vil
Lewis Amelia, clothing, 169 S 6th
Lewis Anna Maria Miss, 72 S 12th
Lewis Ann M., drug store, S W 10th and Sp Garden
Lewis Augustus, fisherman, Queen near Vienna
Lewis A. J., mer., 20 N Front, h 292 Walnut
Lewis Benjamin N., teacher, 359 S 2d
Lewis Charles, printer, Carlton ab 12th
Lewis Charles, coachman, 2 Poplar ct
Lewis Charles, saddler, 96 Wood
Lewis Charles S., mer., 53 S whfs.
LEWIS & Co., mers., 20 N Front
Lewis Daniel, brushmr., Baker ab 7th
Lewis Daniel D., dry goods, 208 S 2d
Lewis David, coachman, 54 Quince
Lewis David, Sec. Phœnix Ins. Co., 52 Walnut, h 6 Belmont pl
Lewis David P., carpenter, Vernon ab 10th
Lewis David P., carp., Wistar bel Franklin, h 29 Vernon
Lewis Edwd., seaman, 387 S Front
LEWIS EDWD., mer., 11 Commerce, h 21 Vine
Lewis Edward C., tailor, 207 Cherry
Lewis Edwin M., mer., S E Front and Walnut, h 7 Logan's sq
Lewis Edwin M. & Co., mers., S E Front and Walnut
Lewis Elizabeth, 190 Noble
Lewis Elizabeth, 98 Locust
Lewis Ellis, attorney, 128 S 4th.
Lewis E. J., M. D., 3 Girard
Lewis Francis, car driver, Oneida pl
Lewis Francis, hatter, Browne bel Broad
Lewis Frederick, cabinet mr., 388 N 3d
Lewis George, shop, Winter
Lewis George, secty. Mutual Union Insurance Co., 6 Exchange
Lewis George, moulder, 3 Marion
Lewis George, cordw., Beach ab Maiden
Lewis George, porter, Lisle bel Shippen
Lewis George, carp., Western pl
Lewis George, carp., Linden ab Sch 7th
Lewis George A., clerk, Barker bet Sch 5th and 6th
LEWIS GEO. F., copperplate printer, 10 S 5th, h 6 Carrollton sq
Lewis George R., cordw., rear 41 Chester
Lewis George T. mer., 135 S Front, h 40 Girard
Lewis Hector, tailor, 194 Christian
Lewis Henry, mariner, 103 Christian
Lewis Henry, carp., 505 Mulberry
Lewis Henry, 11 Bonsall
Lewis Henry, agent, 148 S 3d
Lewis Henry jr., mer., 29 Church al
Lewis Henry R., machinist, Broad and Paper al, h Cherry n Sch 6th
Lewis Hetty L., Union ab 3d.
Lewis Hezekiah, vict., Jackson (S G)
Lewis Jacob, mer., 52 S 4th, h 10th bel Brown
Lewis James, brickmr., Smith's ct
Lewis James, hatter, 47 Duke.

Lewis James, lab., 20 Mary (S)
Lewis James, lab., rear 4 Burd
Lewis, James, & Co., mers., 135 S Front
Lewis James E., mer., 313 Sassafras
Lewis Jason, slater, Franklin bel Front
Lewis Jefferson, broker, S W 10th & Spring Garden
Lewis Jefferson, gent., Poplar ab 8th
Lewis Job, fisherman, 197 Christian
Lewis John, brickmr., 6 Gabell's ct
Lewis John, watchmr. 144 S Front, h 19 Scheetz
Lewis John, porter, 35 Quince
Lewis John, drayman, Cherry n Duke (K)
Lewis John, janitor, Philosoph. Hall
Lewis John, teamster, rear Wood ab Sch 8th
Lewis John, tavern, 9th and Vine
Lewis John A., mer., S E Front and Walnut, h S W Walnut & Sch. 7th
Lewis John A. J., dep. clerk, Orphan's ct., h Wood n 9th
Lewis John B., waterman, rear 10 Margaretta.
Lewis John B., blacksmith, P road bel Carpenter, h Washington bel 7th
Lewis John F., mer., h Walnut & Sch 7th
Lewis John L., stove mr., Cedar ab 8th
Lewis John T., mer., 135 S Front, h 270 Walnut
Lewis Joseph, waterman, Crown ab Bedford(K)
Lewis Joseph, brickmr., Lombard bel Sch. 2d
Lewis Jos., skin dresser, 587 N 3d
Lewis Joseph S., coal mer., Broad & Vine, h Spruce E Sch. 6th
Lewis J. S., manuf., S W Pine & Sch 8th, h Locust ab Sch 8th
Lewis Lawrence, Sec'y. Mutual Assurance Co., 54 Walnut, h 345 Chestnut
Lewis Lawrence Jr., mer., 37 S whfs., h 266 Walnut
Lewis Lewis, tobacconist, Sch 3d n Vine
Lewis Lucinda, 26 Watson's al
Lewis Marg., 13 Washington sq
Lewis Mary, 550 N 3d
Lewis Mary, 10 Perry
Lewis Mary, tavern, 354 High
Lewis Michael, 53 Mead alley
Lewis Mordecai, white lead manuf., 135 S Front, h 497 Chestnut
Lewis Mordecai D., gent., 328 Chestnut
Lewis M. & Co., wh. lead manuf., 135 S Front and S W Pine and Sch. 8th
LEWIS M. & S. N., mers., 135 S Front
Lewis N. C., oak cooper, 17 Beck pl
Lewis Oliver P., shoe dealer, Hutchinson above Poplar
Lewis Peter, dealer, 281 & 327 Cedar
Lewis Rebecca, gentw., Juniper ab Pine
Lewis Rebecca, Adams n Perry
Lewis Richard Rev., 184 Marshall
Lewis Robert M., mer., 266 Walnut
Lewis Samuel, M. D., 3d & Spruce, h 4 Belmont pl
Lewis Samuel, ven. blinds, O Y road ab Buttonwood, h Kessler n Coates
Lewis Samuel A., mer., 58 S whfs., h 179 Walnut
Lewis Saml. A. & Brother, ship. mers. 58 S whfs

Lewis Samuel N., broker, 50 Walnut
Lewis Sarah, dressmr., S W 10th & Locust
Lewis Sarah, gentw., 180 Vine
LEWIS SAUNDERS, atty. & coun., 98 S 4th
Lewis Sidney Ann, h N W Vine and N Market.
LEWIS & STERLING, com. mers., 37 S whfs.
Lewis S. A., cotton yarn, 200 N 3d, h 294 N 6th
Lewis S. B., provisions, 12th and Spruce
Lewis, S. N., jr., mer., 270 Walnut
Lewis Theodore C., mer., S E Front & Walnut, h Walnut and Sch 7th
Lewis Thomas, mariner, 15 Union (S)
Lewis Wharton, mer., 296 Mulberry
Lewis Wm., carter, rear Apple ab Broad
Lewis Wm., weaver, 3 Beaver ct
Lewis Wm., blacksmith, Meredith ct
Lewis William, waterman, Rye ab Reed
Lewis Wm., waterman, 389 S 6th
Lewis Wm., tavern, 159 S Front
Lewis William D., stock broker, 2 York ct, h 360 Spruce
Lewis William G., mer., 140 Sassafras
Lewis Wm. J., teacher, 4th bel Chestnut.
Lewis Wm. S., mer., 20 N Front, h 292 Walnut
Lewis Wm. T., grocer, S E Plum & 5th
Lewis William W., lab., 10 Coombe's alley
Lewry Joseph, dry goods, 339 N 2d
Lewry Stephen, brass founder, New Market ab Green
Lex Adam, porter, Shackamaxon ab Franklin
Lex Andrew, vict., Lemon ab 12th
LEX CHAS. E., atty. & coun., 51 N 6th, h 352 Mulberry
Lex C. F., gent, 471 Mulberry
Lex George, victualler, 16 Logan.
Lex Henry, vict., Ann (F V)
Lex Henry, sugar refiner, 12 Quarry
Lex Jacob, grocer, 213 High, house 352 Mulberry
Lex Jacob H., mer., 213 High, h 2 City row
Lex Jacob & Son, grocers, 213 High
Lex John D., sugar refiner, 29 Elfreth's al
Lex Lucy, vict., 93 New Market
Lex Sarah, 4 Diligent av
Ley A. B. Mrs., F road opp Bedford (K)
Ley Mary, F road opp Bedford (K)
Lhulier Cassimer, jeweler, Christian ab 7th
Lhulier John, musician, Christian ab 7th
Lhulier Lewis, jewell., Taylor's al, h 5th and Buckley
Liautier Thomas, tailor, 384 S 2d
Libe Henry, carpenter, 211 N 10th.
Libezey John, carter, 360 Vine
Libhart Jacob, agt., S W 8th and High
Lichtel Jacob, gent., 133 Coates
Lichtem M., tailor, 241 S 5th
Lichtenstein Jacob, clothing, 14 High, h 497 N 2d
Lichtenstein J., tailor, 239½ N 2d
Lichtenuer Ludwick, cabinet mr., 198 Pine
Liddle Geo. C., mariner 280 Lombard
Liddle Hester, rear 39 Mary (S)
Lieautier John, carp., rear Lemon bel 11th

26

Lieb Jacob, tailor, 3 Bryan's ct
LIEBER B., wines and liquors, 121 N 4th, h 159 N 4th
Liebfort John, butcher, Front below Franklin (K)
Liebig Geo., tavern, 5th bel Franklin
Liebing John, beer house, Charlotte & Poplar
LIEBRICH CONRAD, lock and white smith & bell hanger, 46 S 8th
Liebrich John, butcher, 191 St John
Liggett Samuel, weaver, Hope ab Phoenix (K)
Liggett Robert, furniture, 420 High
Liggins T., sinker maker, 2d & George
Light Charles, blacksmith, Union ab Bedford
Lightcap Henry, porter, 150 Poplar
Lightfoot F., conveyancer, 2 Brown
Likes Jacob, tavern, 337 N Front
Lilley John M., stationer, 324 S 4th
Lilley W. G., cordwainer, 216 S 6th
Lillibridge Charlotte, 121 New
Lilly Bernard, lab., Charlotte ab Thompson(K)
Lilly Henry, weaver, F road n Cherry
Lilly Jacob, wine mer., 2 Noble
Lilly John, moulder, Wiles row
Lilly John, carp., F road n Cherry (K)
Lilly Martha, shop, F road ab Palmer (K)
Lilly Rebecca, b. h., 114 Walnut
Limber Henry, lab., 10 Dannaker's av
Limburgh Theo., cordw., Hallowell (S)
Limeburner Alexis P., 294 Coates
Limeburner A. P., trunkmr., N W Willow & New Market
Limeburner John, b. h., F road opp Queen
Limeburner John, tobacconist, Poplar bel 9th
Liming W., sea capt., 582 S Front
Linard Joseph B., mast mr., Washington av n Noble, h 26 Green
Linbarger Wm., chairmr., Jones E of Sch 5th
Linberg Jesse, cordw., 3 Linden st (K)
Linck Christian, fringe manuf., 408 N 2d
Linck E. H. & Co., stove mrs., 311 High, h 92 N 6th
Linck George, carp., c Buttonwood and 11th, h S W 10th and Cherry
Linck Jacob, cordw., 76 Dillwyn
Linck Jacob, cordw., 9th ab Parrish
Linck John, boot mr., 106 N 8th
Lincoln Abel, grocer, 196 and 198 Callowhill
Lincoln Charles, blacksmith, 12 Madison
LINCOLN ELNA., leather dealer, 157 N 3d, h 175 Catharine
Lincoln E., mer., 33 S wharves, h Pine ab 9th, S side
LINCOLN E. & CO., com. mers., 33 S wharves
Lind & Brother, dry goods, 10 S 4th
Linde Lewis F., musician, Orchard ab Rawle
Linden James, lab., 7 William (F M)
Linder C. A., fancy boxmr., 350 N 3d
Linderman John, cordw., Poplar ab St John
Lindley George, blacksmith, G T road bel Phœnix
Lindner Adam, soap & candle mr., 11 Poplar
Lindner Fred'k., bootmr., 3 Zane
Lindower Gottlieb, tailor, 483 N 3d
Lindsay Andw., oysters, 3 Seiser's ct

LINDSAY & BLAKISTON, booksellers & stationers, N W 4th and Chestnut, and book binders 253 High
Lindsay Catharine, 13th bel Pine
Lindsay David, painter, 269 Sassafras, h 337 N 7th
Lindsay Geo., shop, Mariner & 13th
Lindsay G. F., capt & asst qr master U S marine corps, 36 Walnut
Lindsay G. Robert, tailor, 4 Myers ct
Lindsay Mary Ann, widow, 269 Green
Lindsay John, comb mr., 87 Gaskill
Lindsay John, weaver, F road bel Master (K)
Lindsay John, carpenter, 8 Belmont pl
Lindsay John, lab., 3 Harrison's ct
Lindsay John, wheelwright, 343 N 6th
Lindsay John F., lampmr., rear 339 Callowhill
Lindsay J. M., bookbinder, 7 Chatham
Lindsay Margaret, eating house, S E 6th and Minor, h Mechanic and Culvert
Lindsay Oliver A., bookbinder, 3 Miller's ct
Lindsay Robert, bookbr., 253 High, h Franklin ab S Garden
Lindsay Samuel, grocer, N W 5th & Cedar
Lindsay Samuel, lab., Bedford ab 12th
Lindsay Susanna, dealer, 4 Smith's ct
Lindsay William, house painter, rear Mint ct
Lindsey Ann, 43 Cherry
Lindsey Edwin G., fruiterer, rear 31 S 2d
Lindsey Jeremiah, tavern, c Callowhill and Sch 2nd
Lindsey Joseph, mer., 13 S 2d, h 45 Cherry
Lindsey Wm., tailor, Catharine ab 6th
Lindsey W., lab., 299 S 7th
Lineberger Geo., Carpenter's ct in Peach st
Linemeyer Augustus, tailor, Brown's ct
Liners Chas., lab., Hancock bel Master (K)
Ling Joseph, chocolate manf., Shippen ab 12th
Lingle Hannah, b h., 152 Marshall
Lingle John, tailor, Parrish ab 6th
Lingerman Henry, blacksm., Dean & Bedford (K)
LINGO LEVI, corder, Queen street wharf, h 363 S 3d
Lings Douglass, druggist, 2d & Christian
Link Geo., carp., 4 Little Green
Link George, waterman, Pratt's ct
Link Peter, farmer, Weaver's row (K)

Linn W. H., bartender, rear 205 S 2d
Linn W. H., weaver, rear Shippen la
LINNARD & BROTHER, hardware, 443 H
Linnard James, mer., 443 High
Linnard Jas. M., Washington (W P)
Linnard John R., confec., 210 Chestnut
Linnard J. T., hardware, 443 High, h 401 Spruce
Linnard S. B., lumber yd., 11th & Pine, h 355 Chestnut
LINNARD & CO., lumber mers., S W 11th and Pine
Linnard T. M., mer., 401 Spruce
Linnard Wm. J., lumb. mer., S W 11th & Pine, h 401 Spruce
Linse Elias, dealer, 120 Cedar
Linton Benjn., shop, 56 Apple
Linton Elizabeth, gentw., 34 Mead
Linton James, cordw., Elizabeth ab Poplar
Linton James, carter, Lemon st
Linton John, tobacconist, 17 S 4th, h 299 N 3d
Linton John L., Sec. Harris. & Lan. R. R. Co. 16 Exchange, h N W 9th & Chestnut
Linton Lewis, gent., 396 N 10th
Linton Robert, lab., 20 Vaux's ct
Linton Saml., city watch, Lombard bel Juniper
Linton Sarah, shoes, N W 11th and Cedar
Linton & Woodward, tobacco, 17 S 4th
Linville George W., mer., 224 N 6th
Linville James, carp., 61 S 11th
Lion John, baker, 10th bel Poplar
Lion Wendell, cordw., Ogden ab 9th
Lipman Hymen L. stationer, 139 Chestnut, h 10 Montgomery sq
Lipman Jacob, umbrella mr., 235 Cedar
Lipman Martha, clothing, 224 Cedar
Lipp Christian, baker, 115 N 9th
Lippard George, 10th bel Buttonwood
Lippard Mary, gentw., 7th ab Poplar
Lippard Mary, dry goods, 73 S 11th
Lippincott Aaron S., mer., 18 S Front, h 36 Mulberry.
Lippincott Achsa, milliner, 10 N 13th
Lippincott Agnes S. milliner, 369 N 3d
Lippincott Barclay, tailor, 200 High, h 112 N Front
Lippincott Ecurious, rear 388 N Front
Lippincott Elizabeth, dressmr., 160 Coates

Lippincott Joshua, jr., S W 2d & High, h 210 N 4th

Lippincott Joshua, sen., gent., 9 Clinton sq

Lippincott Joshua B., bookseller, S W 4th and Sassafras, h 364 Mulberry

Lippincott J. B. & Co. booksellers, S W 4th & Sassafras

Lippincott Lewis, tailor, 35 N 6th

Lippincott Mary, Hubbell ab Catharine

Lippincott Nathan, bricklayer, Walker's ct

Lippincott Noah E., cordwainer, Chatham n Green

Lippincott & Parry, cloth, cassimeres, &c., S W 2nd and High

Lippincott Sarah, huckster, rear 116 Christian

Lippincott S. W., com. mer., 72 S Front, h 9 Clinton square

Lippincott Thos., bricklayer, 141 Sp Garden

LIPPINCOTT, TAYLOR & CO., clothing, 200 High

Lippincott Tyler, shop, 4 Harmony court and Hudson's alley, h 386 S Front

Lippincott & Way, mers., 18 S Front

Lippincott Wm., weaver, Brinton ab 12th

Lippincott Wm. V. mer., 27 N 3d

Lipps John, varnish mr., Maiden bel Front

Lips Jacob, beer house, 70 Vine

Lips John, brewer, 2d & G T road

Lipsey, Anthony, weaver, Bedford ab 12th

Lipsey Thomas, manuf., 330 Pine

Lipsey Thomas, watchman, Lombard and Juniper

Lisby Isaac, porter, 23 Prosperous al

Lish Henry, cordwainer, 188 Cherry

Lisle Elizabeth, 127 S 2d

Lisle Ellen, Sch 8th bel Locust

Lisle James, M. D., 160 Mulberry

Lisle John, stonecut., Reakirt's ct (K)

Lisle John M., broker, S E Dock & Walnut, h Sch 8th n Pine

Lisle Wm., tailor, Ball & Little Pine

Lispel Henry, tailor, 299 Callowhill

List John, jeweller, Taylor's al, h 355 S 6th

List & Smith, jewellers, Taylor's al

Lister James, brickmr., Locust and Sch Front

Lister James S., M. D., 209 S 2d

Lister Robert, carp., St John bel Willow, h 293 N 3d

Lister Thomas S. livery stables, 300 S 4th

Lister Wm., carp., George n Sch 2d

Litchfield Samuel, cordw., 4th bel Tammany

Lithan Richard, 12 Morgan's ct

Litherland Wm., weaver, 5th ab Master (K)

Lithgow James, engineer, Pleasant row

Lithgow Robert, lab., rear 25 Garden

Lithgow Samuel P., lampmr., Green bel R road

Litle Thomas, sugar refiner, 12th ab Pine

Littell Squire M. D., 117 N 9th

Little Aaron, barber, 325 Spruce

Little Ann C., German ab 3d

Little Arthur W., mer., 143 High, h 21 Logan square

Little Barth., tailor, Sch Front n Mulberry

Little Catharine, rear 495 N 3d

Little Chas., brassfound., Ann (F V)

Little Charles, grocer, 573 S 2d

Little Charles, cooper, Swanson bel Cedar, h 87 Prime

Little Charles, weaver, Barker n Sch 4th

Little David, barber, 282 S 6th

Little David M., clerk, Winter ab Sch 3d

Little G. P. keeper Moy. Prison

Little Ellen, sempstress, 2 Perry

Little Francis, drover, High E Sch 2d

Little George, suspender mr., 145 G T road

Little George F. carpet weaver, 618 N 3d

Little Henry, carpenter, Filbert E Sch. 6th

Little Hubbard, tailor, 72 N 7th

Little Jemima, dressmr., 151 Green

Little John, carp., Miller's al

Little John C., weaver, 124 New Market

Little John L., saddler, 10th bel Ogden

Little Joseph, cordw., 4 Pratt s ct

Little Lindsey, weaver, Fitler bel Harrison (K)

Little Mary, 3 Jenning's row

Little Robert, lab., Ashton n Sassafras

Little Robert, dyer, Adams n 13th

Little Samuel, trader, 143 G T road

Little Stacy, George n Sch 2d

Little Stephen, bootmr., Cox ab Sch 6th

Little Susan, 84 Noble

Little Thos., blacksm., Juniper ab Cherry

Little Thomas R., worker in metal, 32 Green

Little Wm., lab., Ann ab R road (F V)

Little Wm., weaver, Otter n G T road (K)

Little Wm., metal worker, 345 N 6th

Littlefield & Shannon, lock smiths, 54 N 6th

Littlefield Theodore L. lock manuf., 54 N 6th, h Wallace bel 13th

Litzenberg George, brassfounder, 6 Madison

Litzenberg Jos., lab., Mulberry n Sch Front

Litzenberg Perry, grocer, Washington (W P)

Litzenberg Samuel, shoemaker, Jones W Sch 5th

Lively Catharine, washer, 20 Morris st

Livensetter John, collector, 10 O Y road

Livensetter M. D., conveyancer, 88 Mulberry, h 10 O Y road

Livezey John, agent, 3 Somers' ct

Livezey Saml., shoes, 310 High

Livezey Wm., furniture, 225 S 3d

Livingood Rebecca, dressmr., 6 Coates

LIVINGSTON & CO., package expr., 43 S 3d

Livingston Mary, gentw., 289 S 10th

Livingston Walter C., mer., 23 Commerce, h 2 Girard

Livingston Wm., lampmr., Parrish bel 11th

Livingston William, machinist, 23 Farmer

Llewellyn Samuel, pianomr., 12 Jefferson row

Lloyd Anna Maria, stovemr. 406 High, h 384 Vine

Lloyd Christiana, milliner, Spruce n Sch Front

Lloyd & Co., grates, fenders & stoves, S E 7th & Cherry

Lloyd Edith, b. h., 9th & Spruce

LLOYD & FELTWELL, Olmsted stove manf., 406 High

Lloyd Gibbons, shop, 45 Green

Lloyd Horatio, grocer, Wallace and Ellis

Lloyd Isaac, mer., 53 S wharves, h 88 Union

Lloyd Isaac jr., mer., 53 S wharves, h 199 S 7th

Lloyd Isaac & Son, mer., 53 S wharves

Lloyd James, manuf., 668 N 2d bel Master
Lloyd John, tobacconist, 95 S 2d
Lloyd John, broker, 84 S 3d, h 195 N 9th
Lloyd John, granite cutter, Chestnut n Sch 6th, h George bet Sch 7th & 8th
Lloyd John, carp., Sch 6th ab Lombard
Lloyd John D., stovemaker, 406 High, h 384 Vine
Lloyd & Keany, granitecut, Chestnut n Sch 6th
Lloyd Margaret, widow, 153 St John
Lloyd Maria, 1 Beck pl
Lloyd Marshall, acct., 2 Shriver's ct
Lloyd Richard L., machinist, Penn ab Poplar, h 359 N 6th
Lloyd Robert, rear 457 N 4th
Lloyd Robert, carp., 7 Brandywine
Lloyd Robert, mariner, Church bel Washington
Lloyd Thos., stovemr., S E 7th and Cherry
Lloyd Thos., ship carp., rear 461 S 2d
Lloyd Wood, real estate, 58 Walnut
Loag David, saddler, S E 4th and Queen
Loag E. M., milliner, 35 S 10th
Loan James, shoemr., Fitzwater bel 6th
Loan Michael, weaver, Cedar ab 12th
Loan Mrs. wid. of John, Harmony bel 4th
Loan Rosanna Mrs., Cedar ab 12th
Loane Paul, Rugan ab Callowhill
Lobb Benjamin, 8th bel Catharine
Lobar Jacob, lab. 11 Sander's ct (K)
Lobdell Stetson, gent., N W 8th and Cherry
Lobe Isaac, furniture, 115 S 2d, h 138 Pine
Lober John B. S., painter, 366 N 3d
Lober Wm., Sanders' ct (K)
Lochary Daniel, bottler, Chestnut ab 2d, h 11 Hubbell
Lochran Mary, 150 S Front
Lock Samuel, tavern, Beach n Hanover (K)
Lockart John, weaver, Amber ab Phœnix
Locke Z., alcohol dist., 5 Marble & h 352 High
Locke Z. & Co., alcohol distillers, 5 Marble
Locken James, bookbind., Schriver's ct & Shepherd's al, h 17 Chester
Locken John, bookbinder, 311 High
Locken Wm., bookbinder, 42 N 4th, h 10th n Buttonwood
Locker Enoch, cordwr., Queen bel Palmer (K)
Locker Geo., cordw., 29 Laurel
Lockhard Lewis, dentist, R road ab Wallace
Lockhart Amelia, 44 Catharine
Lockhart Charles, sea capt., Carpenter ab 4th
Lockhart John, cabinetmr., rear 512 N Front
Lockhart Mary Ann, washer, 12 Marks' la
Lockhart Wm., lab., St Joseph's av bel Sch 5th
Lockhart Wm. H. saddler, Hallowell
Lockmon H., hod carrier, Wilson's ct
Lockwood Danl. C. collector, Cherry W Sch 7th
Lockwood G. F., 504 Chestnut
Lockwood Wm., bootfitter, 10 Hubbell
Lockworth Catharine, 89 Buttonwood
Lodge John S., machinist, 13 Christian
Lodge J., machinist, 57 Dock, h 88 Lombard
Lodine Wm., porter, 10 Hunter
Lodor Benjamin, turner, 315 Sassafras
Lodor Jacob A., hatter, 536 High
Lodor Maria, matron

Locb Charles, weaver, 2 Pegg's al
Locb Henry, cooper, rear 529 N 4th
LOESER CHAS., tavern, N E 6th & Willow
Loeser Jacob, bricklayer, 364 Coates
Loeser John, 364 Coates
Loew John J., watchmaker, 272 N 4th
Lofland Danl., carp., Marriott ab 5th
Lofland James, sea capt., Prime ab M road
Lofland Nutter, cabtmr., 291 S Front
Loflin Smith, cabtmr., 33 Almond st
Loflin Wm. J. carp., rear 7 N 9th, h 22 Benton
Lofman Thos., shipwright, Crown ab Queen
Lofton Eli, harnessmr. 446 N Front
Logan Bridget, shop, Jones n Sch 4th
Logan David, carter, R road ab Francis (F V)
Logan & Fuguet, mers., 83 S Front
Logan Hannah, Stoy's ct (K)
Logan Henry, flour and feed, 204 Shippen
Logan James, Sch 5th n Locust
Logan Jas. W., collector, Mechanic st
Logan J. D., M. D., 27 Logan sq
Logan John, carter, Walnut & Ashton
Logan John, weaver, Shippen la
Logan John, lab., Orange ab Washington
Logan John, carter, Budd bel Juniper
Logan John, watchman, Filbert W Sch 4th
Logan John, coffee roaster, rear Front below Phœnix
Logan John W., stone cutter, 8th & Coates, h 7th ab Parrish
Logan Joseph, carter, Sch 4th ab George
Logan Luke, stone mason, 8 Shoemaker
Logan Margaret, 286 N 3d
Logan Mary, rear 126 S 6th
Logan Patrick, grocer, S W 3d & Gaskill
Logan Patrick, dealer, 3 Scott's alley
Logan Peter, mer., 198 S 4th
Logan Robert M., atty. and coun., 286 N 3d
Logan Sarah W., 115 S 4th
Logan Spencer, porter, 4 Bonsall
Logan Thos., mer., 326 Pine
Logan William, silk printer and dyer, 17 Filbert
Logo John, gold beater, 9 Pear, h 12 Charlotte
Logo Joseph, tailor, 12 Charlotte
LOGO & NELMS, gold beaters, 9 Pear
Logue Charles, livery stable, Quarry st, and tavern, 481 High
Logue Daniel, shoemr., Sch 4th bel Barker
Logue Daniel H., batter, Spruce n Sch 5th
Logue Eliza, dressmr., rear 448 Sassafras
Logue Hugh, driver, Filbert & Sch 8th
Logue John, lab., St Mary ab 7th
Logue John C. tailor, 8 Hubbell
Logue John J., gent., 7 Lybrand
Logue Wm., tailor, Murray n Sch 2d
Logue William, Sassafras n Sch 7th
Loque Wm., jr., lab., Pearl ab Sch 6th
Loller George, cordw. M'Bride's ct (K)
Loller Hannah, dry goods, 332 N Front
Lollor Alex., boat builder, Sarah n Queen (K)
LOMAN W. N. hairdress., 54 New, h 13 Sassafras al
Lomas Henry, stonecut., h 6 Marble pl
Lomax Eliza, baker, 90 Locust

Lomax James, tailor, 11 N 13th
Lonabach Elizabeth, 16 Well's row
Lonabach Jacob, vict., 16 Well's row
London & Booth, Mansion House, 11th & High
LONDON JAMES, 11th & High
Lone Patrick, coachman, Dean ab Centre
Lone Patrick, cordw., Crans' ct
Long Abraham, varnisher, Flickwir's ct ·
Long Alice, Dunton n Franklin (K)
Long Andrew, carter, 15 Helmuth
Long Andrew K. gas fitter, 2 S 5th, h 10th ab
    Catharine
Long Andrew, weaver, Gulielma
Long Anthony, lab. Dutch ct
Long Benj., 6th & Wood
Long Catharine, 10 Sterling al
Long Charles, cooper, 324 High
Long Charles, 6th & Wood
Long Christian, biscuit baker, 198 N Front, h
    Parrish ab 8th
Long David, carpenter, 11 Fitzwater
Long David, waterman, Front n Prime
Long Elizabeth, 414 Coates
Long Elizab., tailoress, Steam Mill al bel St John
Long Elizabeth, 4th ab George
Long George, rear Brown ab 13th
Long Geo., lab., 4 Howard's pl
Long George W., jeweller, 3 Fitzwater
Long Geo. W., clerk, Brown & Marshall
Long Henderson, carter, Jefferson & Hope (K)
Long Henry, cordwainer, 405 Sassafras
Long Henry, police off., 54 Penn
Long Henry, carter, Marriott n 5th
Long Isaac, cordw., rear 319 Shippen
Long Jacob, cordw., Buttonwood ab 13th
Long Jacob, carpenter, 203 Marshall ab Brown
Long Jacob, ropemr., Hanover bel F road (K)
Long James, bonnet presser, S 5th ab Christian
Long Jas., clerk, Charlotte ab George
Long John weaver, Cedar ab 13th
Long John, carter, 6 Robinson's ct
Long John, weaver, 487 N 3d
Long John, lab. rear Parrish bel 10th
Long John N., gilder, Raspberry la
Long Kersey W. artisan, Wood bel Duke (K)
Long Lydia, 1 Hampton
Long Mary, b. h., Sch 3d n Vine
Long Mary, shopkeeper, 7 Raspberry
Long Mary, Ann n Powell (Francisville)
Long Michael, locksmith, 477 N 4th
Long Peter B., tobacconist, 132 Locust
Long Robert, cabinetmr., 19 P road
Long Robert, weaver, Filbert n Sch 4th
Long Sarah Ann, wid., Howard bel Master (K)
Long Sarah, Wood bel 6th
Long Thomas, carp., 13th bel Shippen
Long Thos. A., collector, 202 Noble
Long William, carpenter, 141 S 9th
Long Wm., carp., Carberry ct
Long Wm., U. S. Mint, h 26 Perry ab Race
Long Wm., painter, 327 Vine
Long Wm., carter, Ball's ct
Long Wm., carp., 16 Western av
Long Wm., runner Phil. Bank, 135 Lombard
Long Wm., cabinetmr., Dunton bel Franklin (K)

Long Wm., tobacco, 314 S 3d
Long Wm., carp., Shippen bel 11th
Long Wm., 132 W High
Long Wm., cordw., rear 338 S 5th
LONG WILLIAM L., tobacconist, 47 Cedar
Long Wm. T., drayman, 198 S Water, h How-
    ard & Master
Longa Wm. bootmr. 18 Mayland
LONGACRE JAMES B., publish. Nat. Portrait
    Gallery, 27 Minor, and engraver, h S Garden
    3rd door ab 12th
Longan William, morocco dresser, 262 St John ƨ
Longbine George, carpenter, 11th ab Coates
Longcake Thos., carp. weaver, Gay's ct (K)
Longcope, Wm. H., mer., 23 Bank, h 251 N 7th
Longmire Emanuel, 77 P road
Longmire Francis B., 112 Queen
LONGMIRE N. mer. 30 Bank st, h Scheetz bel
    2d
Longstreet John, cordw., Van Buren pl
Longstreth Buzby, hardware, 137 High
Longstreth Charles, paper hanging manuf., 7
    N 3d, factory Hartung's al, h 70 N 10th
LONGSTRETH CHARLES & SON, paper
    hangings, 7 N 3d
Longstreth Daniel, agent, 7th ab Parrish
Longstreth Deborah M., 86 Mulberry
Longstreth Henry, bookseller, 347 High
Longstreth John R., 5th n Franklin
Longstreth John R., 17 Brandywine
Longstreth Joshua, mer., 12 Church al, h 185
    Mulberry ·
Longstreth J. H. mer. 7 N 3d, h Callowhill ab 11th
Longstreth M. A. & S., teachers, 3 N 11th
Longstreth M. F., mer., 64 S 8th
Longstreth Sarah, b. h., 92 S 8th
Longstreth Thomas B. bricklayer, 272 N 3d
Longstreth Wm. W., 8 Colonnade row
Longthorn John, variety store, 49 S 9th
Looby Edward, lab. Spruce & Auston
Lookinbill I. S., 124 Callowhill
Loomis G. N., bookseller, 3d and Mulberry, h
    124 Mulberry
Loomis & Peck, booksellers, 3d and Mulberry
Loomis S., phrenologist, 64 S 8th
Looney Robert, plumber, 9 S 7th
Loorcher Henry, butcher, 7th bel Lombard
Loos Christian, baker, 2d ab Franklin (K)
Loos Christian jun. carp. 653 N 2d
Loos Mary, milliner, 2d bel Phoenix (K)
LOPER & BAIRD, com. mers., 46 S wharves
Loper David, carter, 23 Linden (K)
Loper R. F., 46 S wharves, h 19 Pine
Loper Sarah, Benton n William
Loperman Jonathan, waiter, Washington ab 11th
Lopez A., mer., Filbert bet Sch 6th & 7th.
Loraine Jas. Wm. trader, 591 N Front
Lorch Herman G., cabmr., rear 96 Cherry
Lord Chas., shoemr., 17 Schriver's ct
Lord Daniel, dry goods, 17 Merchant
Lord Deborah, Eagle ct
LORD G. W., auc. & com. mer., 208 & 210 High,
    h 5 Oak (W Penn sq)
Lord John, cordw., Montgomery bel Front
Lord Phebe, tailoress, 7 S 7th

Lord Wm. cordw. Franklin n Union (K)
Lord Wm. H. House of Refuge
Lord Willis, Rev., Filbert W of Sch 6th
Lore George W., Woodland (W P)
Lorentz Christopher, tanner, Young's al
Lorentz Gotleib, tavern, 500 Coates.
Loreny Jacob, baker, Marshall ab Poplar
Lorrilliere Julius, cabi mr., Morris bel Catharine
Lorton Margaret, 121 N Juniper·
Lortz Mrs. M., dressmr., 341 S Front
Lot Henry, carp. weav., F road ab Palmer (K)
Lothrop Z., mer., 6 S Front, h 139 S 9th
Lotier Benj. C., silversm., Alder ab Poplar
Lott George W., carpenter, 377 E Pine
Lott Henry, carp., 13th ab Shippen
Lott Jacob, tailor, Nectarine ab 11th
Lott Mary, 13th ab Cedar
Lott Wm. L., bricklayer, Union ab Bedford(K)
Loud John, pianomr., 9th bel Parrish
Loud Thomas, pianomr., 19 Minor, h Sp Garden
    ab 11th
Loud Thomas C., pianomr., 19 Minor, h 8th ab
    Green
Loud Wm. H., piano forte, 131 Franklin
Louden Andrew, carp. 35 Washington
Louden John, vict., Palmer bel Duke
Louden Thomas, shoemr., 262 S 5th
Loudenslager Adam, vict., Buttonwood ab 9th
Loudenslager Christopher H., butcher, S E
    Garden and Noble.
Loudenslager George, prov., 336 Sassafras
Loudenslager Henry, butcher, Charles below
    Buttonwood
Loudenslager Jacob, saddler, 39 Cherry
Loudenslager James, clerk, 93 Callowhill
Loudenslager John L. distiller, 62 Dillwyn
Loudenslager John U., carp., rear Hanover ab
    Queen (K)
Loudenslayer Thomas J., tobacco't., 11 Clinton
Loudenstine Wm., blacksmith, Ogden ab 9th
Louderback Augustus, upholsterer, 2 Cherry
Louderback Davis, tobacconist, 329 N 3d
Louderback Elijah H. collarmr. Ogden bel 11th
Louderback Elizabeth, Rose ab School (K)
Louderback Henry, ship joiner, 16 Parham
Louderback Isabella, 6th bel Christian
Louderback John, ship carp., 13 Parham
Louderback Joseph, bricklr., Catharine & 9th
Louderback Margaret, widow, Harper's pl
Louderback Matthias, tobacconist, 20 Rose al.
Louderback Mrs., sempstress, 20 Rose al
Louderback M. A., b h., 18 Sansom
Louderback M. J., milliner, 142 S 5th
Louderback Peter, printer, 273 S 5th
Louderback Robert W. shipjoiner, 467 S 2d
Louderback Samuel, bricklayer, Locust ab 12th
Louderback S. A. milliner, 31 N 7th
Lough Jos., dry goods, 13 S 9th
Loughead Jas, cooper, 24 S Water, h 23 New
Loughead James, blacksmith, Hallowell
Loughead James H., agent, 144 Franklin
Loughead John, lab. Lombard n Sch 5th
Loughead Matthew, weaver, West bel Hanover
Loughead Thomas, blacksmith, Shippen ab 8th,
    h 349 Cedar

Loughead Thomas, gent., 54 Green
Loughead Wm., lab., Sch 7th bel Pine
Loughlin John, carp., 127 E Shippen
Loughlin Mary, dressmr., George ab Sch 8th
Loughlin Sarah, tailoress, Barker E of Sch 4th
Loughlin William, Health Office, 6th & George,
    h 215 S 6th
Loughran Patk., weaver, Philip ab Jefferson(K)
Loughran James, carter, Shippen bel Russell
Loughran Mary, sewer, Smith's ct
Loughran Wm. Rev., 2d ab Master (K)
Loughridge Abram, lab., Sch 3d ab Callowhill
Loughridge Andrew, lab., Benton n School (K)
Loughridge Samuel, Front and Catharine
Loughry Margaret, Locust n Beach
Louis Samuel, furrier, 80 Mulberry
Louiset A. D. & Co., dyers, 463 N 3d
Lounsberry Christ., tavern, Noble & Washington
Lounsberry Francis, sailmr. 3 Dock, h 7 College
    place
Lounsbery Geo., waterman, 31 Duke
Lounsbery John, boat builder, 33 Duke
Lourd John, plasterer, Morris bel Fitzwater
Lourd Michael, M. D., Cedar ab 11th.
Louty Thomas, carp., rear 254 S Front
Lovatt George, carp., 103 Cedar
Lovatt Wm., tavern, 316 N 3d
Lore Alexander, grocer, Franklin & Crown (K)
Love Ann, Edward n School
Love Benj., atty. & coun., 26 George, h Green
    ab 13th
Love George, lab. Federal ab 2d
Love Giles, conveyancer, 26 George h Green
    ab 13th
Love James, cooper, Allen ab Marlboro' (K)
Love Jane, Green ab 13th
Love John, gent., 294 Fitzwater
Love John, cooper, Jefferson pl
Love John, cordw., Culvert ab Mechanic
Love Robert, weaver, rear 2d ab Edward
Love Robert, shoemr., 6th bel G T road
LOVE, SMITH & Co., cloths, 147 High
Love Thomas, weaver, 12th ab Cedar
Love Thos. C., tailor, 124 and h 150 Catharine
Love William, cordwainer, 486 N 3d
Love William H. cloths, 147 High, h 348 N 6th
Love Wm. J., carp., Paul bel 7th
Loveaire Jeremiah, confectioner, 469 Chestnut
Loveaire John, plasterer, 4 Park av
Lovedy Charlotte, washer, 367 E Lombard
Lovell A. E. clocks, 183 N 3d, h 176 N 3d
Loveridge Mary Ann, 81 S 11th
Lovering J. S., steam sugar refiner, 27 Church
    al, h 340 Chestnut
LOVERING J. S. & CO., steam sugar refiners,
    27 Church al
Lovett Catharine, tobacconist, 389 N 2d
Lovett D., Charlotte bel Poplar
Lovett Elisha, carp., 2nd bel Phœnix
Lovett Jane E., Hay's ct
Lovett John, lab., Pine c Sch Front
Lovett John R., coachmr., Dillwyn ab Tammany,
    h 18 Maiden (K)
Lovett Patrick, capt., Spruce ab Sch. Front
Lovett Richard O. R., tavern, 222 Walnut

Lovett Robert jr., seal engraver, 32 S 5th
Lovett Rodman, carp., rear 523 N 3d
Lovett Thomas, teacher, 329 S 3d
Low Bennet, hatter, Rye ab Reed
Low James H., sink cleaner, Wood ab Sch. 7th
Low Joseph J., jeweller, 5 Exchange pl
Low Mark, watch case maker, 8 Somer's ct
Low Peter, lab., G T road and 6th
Low Robert, lab., rear 24 Queen (K)
Low Thomas, hatter, Newton bel Carpenter
Low Wm., carter, Clinton ab Brown
Lowber Bowers, shoes, 233 N 3d, h 219 N 4th
Lowber Caleb D., doctor, Rose ab School (K)
Lowber Daniel, tanner & currier, Willow below 2d, h 294 N 3d
Lowber Edward, gent., 104 S 8th
Lowber John H., pearlmr., 11 George, h 305 S 10th
Lowber Wm., M. D., 104 Walnut
Lowber & Wilmer, dye stuffs, 20 S Front
Lowber W. T., merch., 20 S Front, h Walnut bet Sch. 6th and 7th
Lowder Thomas, sailmr. Shackamaxon below Franklin
Lowe Edward A., agent, Paul ab 6th
Lowe Lewis, pilot, 511 S Front
Lowe Richard, gent., Montgomery place
Lowe Samuel, engraver, 23 N 2d
Lowenberg Louis, capmr. 25 N 4th
Lowengrund Moses, peddler, Beaver bel St John
Lowengrund Samuel, tailor, 3 Noble
Lower Abraham, collector, 44 St John
Lower & Barron, hardware, 174 N 3d
Lower Eliz. A., stockmr., G. T. road and Rose
Lower George, carp., 4th ab Carpenter
Lower George G., carp., 18 Bank, h Charlotte ab Poplar
Lower Harriet, washer, Malseed's ct
Lower Henry, brickmr., Hancock ab Norris
Lower Jacob, silversmith, 1 Lawrence ct
Lower John, wheelwright, 321 N Front, h 1 Rogers' ct
Lower John J., blacksm., rear Irvine
Lower Joseph, lab., 4th bel Jefferson (K)
Lower Joseph, cooper, College av
Lower Joseph, rear 4th bel Carpenter
Lower Rachel, widow, 167 N 2d
Lower Susanna, 137 Dillwyn
Lower Wm., silversmith, Marriott ab 6th
Lower Wm. S., 174 N 3d, h 7th and Sp. Garden
Lowery Andrew, butcher, Parrish ab Sch 8th
Lowery B. Mrs., 24 Queen
Lowery Elizabeth, dressmr. Rose n William (K)
Lowery Francis, provision, 9th bel South
LOWERY & FULLER, wood whf., Christian
Lowery James, cordw., 6th bel Christian
Lowery James, cordw., 6 J. Baker's ct (N L)
Lowery Joseph, furniture, Beach ab Poplar (K)
Lowery Joseph, butcher, Mantua vil
Lowery Lewis, gardener, William's ct
Lowery W. H., wood mer., 14 Christian
LOWNDS J. J., pencilmr., 7 Bank al
Lowrey Geo., carp., rear Lemon bel 11th
Lowrie R. B., silver smith, Franklin and Noble
Lowry Abigail, 29 Callowhill

Lowry Ann, 27 Filbert
Lowry & Baker, clothing, S W Water & Walnut
Lowry Benjamin, mer., 61 Almond
Lowry Comfort, lab., 32 Portland lane
Lowry Emanuel P., vict., Willow ab 8th
Lowry E., dressmr., Marriott ab 4th
Lowry George, provision, 165 Locust
Lowry George W., millwright, Charlotte and Culvert
Lowry Isabella, Hanover ab Duke
Lowry John, tailor, S W Walnut & Water, h 19 Gaskill
Lowry John S., mer., Pine st. wharf, Sch., h 2 Sch. 5th
Lowry Juliana, R. road ab Francis (F V)
Lowry Lewis, clerk, Ruddack's ct
Lowry Mary, rear 4 Burd
Lowry Mary, Pink bel Jefferson, (K)
Lowry Philip jr., victualler, Washington (W P)
Lowry & Stuckert, provision, 165 Locust
Lowry Thomas J., bricklayer, Parrish ab 9th
Lowry Wm. C., ship master, 486. S 2d
Lowry Wm., carp. 110 Christian
Lowther John, lab. Lombard n Sch 2d
Loxley Benj. R. Rev., 31 N 6th
Loxley G. W., 31 N 6th
Loxley Richard, gent., 117 Mulberry
Loyd Joseph, carp., Wallace ab 9th
Loyd Joshua, cordw. 36 Juliana
Loyd Mary Ann, 153 Filbert
Loyd Nathaniel, dealer, Aspen ab Spruce
Loyle John, ladies' shoemr., 356 Coates
Luberg Christiana, dry goods, 358 S Front
Lucas Eleanor, 18 Lombard
Lucas Francis, waterman, 384 S Front
Lucas Henry, weaver, 54 W Cedar
Lucas James, trader, 203 G T road
Lucas John, watchman, 395 S Front
Lucas John, shoemr., 62 N 6th
Lucas Joseph V., grocer, 37 & h 196 N Front
Lucas & Sharp, grocers, 37 N Front
Lucas Thomas, weaver, Hope bel Jefferson
Lucas Thomas, collar maker, 9th ab Poplar
Luce Joseph, dealer, 18 Vernon
Luchsinger H. carpet weaver, h 533 N 4th
Luckerbach George, cabmr., 124 S 5th
Ludenburg Wm. founder, Vienna ab Queen
Ludenburgh John, carp., Lewis ab Girard av
Ludie Jacob, carp., Culvert ab 4th
Ludlam John, tailor, 101 Poplar
Ludlam Wm. cordw. 2d and G T road
LUDLOW, BEEBEE & CO., exch. brokrs., 17 S 3d
Ludlow Jas. R., atty. and coun., Walnut ab 6th
Ludlow John, D. D., Provost of Pa. University, 25 Montgomery sq Sassafras n 11th
Ludlow J. I., M. D., 25 Montgomery sq
Ludlow Primus, sawyer, Emeline st
Ludlow Robert M., broker, 17 S 3d
Ludman John, stone mason, N E 12th & Green
Ludon Saml., paper stainer, Barker below Sch. 6th
Ludwick Adam, grocery, 118 E. Lombard
Ludwick Jacob, cordw., Orchard bel Jackson

Ludwick Vin., weaver, Bedford n Elm (K)
Ludwig J. H., tailor, 83 N 2d
LUDWIG, KNEEDLER & CO., dry goods, 110 N 3d
Ludwig Wm. C., mer., Sassafras & 3d, h 223 Vine
Ludy Adam, baker, 57 Federal
Ludy Christian, baker, 16 S 10th
Ludy Christian, glue boiler, 2d ab Jefferson (K)
Ludy Geo., baker, 104 N 13th
Ludy Jacob, sugar boiler, rear 18 Lilly al
Luederitz Wm., baker, 58 Dillwyn
Luff Ann, cook, Eagle ct
Luffberry Andrew, boat build., Wood ab Queen
Luffberry John, shipwright, Queen ab Shackamaxon
Luffberry John, boat builder, Dyott's ct (K)
Luffberry John B. carp. Franklin ab Union
Luffberry Michael, boat builder, Wood below Franklin (K)
Lugar George, dyer, 521 N 3d
Lugar John, combmaker, 528 N 2d. (K)
Lugar Sophia, 546 N 2d
Lugar Wm. combmr. 546 N 2d
Lukemire Charles, lab., Queen opp Cherry (K)
Luken Lewis, h 267 Green
Lukenbill R. ostler, rear 97 Noble
LUKENS ABEL, tavern, 242 N 2d
Lukens Abner, dealer, rear 109 Dillwyn
Lukens Amos, confect., 49 N 4th
Lukens Andrew, flour mer., 448 N 2d
Lukens Benjamin, drayman, Poplar bel 7th
Lukens Charles, lab., rear 480 N 4th
Lukens Charles, M. D., N E 11th and Chestnut
Lukens Chilion, cabinetmr., 140 Brown
Lukens Comly S., carp., George bel Apple
Lukens Edith, confect., 83 S 8th
Lukens Edward, merchant, 105 High, h 37 Mulberry
Lukens Elizabeth, shop, 10th ab Parrish
Lukens Emeline S. 235 Wood
Lukens Ephraim, pat. wash. machine, 114 N 6th
Lukens Francis, stone mason, 13th bel Wallace
Lukens Geo., lab., 2 Taylor's ct
Lukens Hannah Ann, Lemon ab 12th
Lukens Isaac, stonemason, 231 Wood
Lukens Jacob, lab. 16 Lily al
Lukens James, dry goods, 156 N 8th
Lukens John, shoemr, Cadwalader bel Oxford (K)
Lukens Jonathan, gent., 113 S 3d
Lukens Joseph, carp., Beaver ab 2d (K)
Lukens Lewis A., iron store,
Lukens Mahlon, Apple and Culvert, h 144 Poplar
Lukens M. J., saddlery, 102 High, h 113 S 3d
Lukens Nathan, constable, Maria ab 4th
Lukens Seneca, watchman, 86 New Market
Lukens Silas, stone mason, 358 N 10th
Lukens Thomas, saddler, Callowhill ab 5th
Lukens Thomas, saddler, 203 N 5th
Lukens Wm. carp. Dean ab Bedford (K)
Lukens Wm., jeweller, St. Joseph's av., h 238 N 3d
Lukins Reuben, flour, N W 3d and Noble, h 207 N 4th

Lumbrey James, turner, 110 Prime
Lumsden John, brick layer, William's ct
Lund Charity, 248 N 7th
Lund Letitia, rear 380 S 2d
Lundbeck Silas, lumber dealer, Hallowell
Lundburg John, seaman, Reed bel Church
Lungren Jane D., b. h., S E 8th and High
Lungren John S., teacher, 83 S 3d, h 161 N 7th
Luning Augustus, cabtmr., La Fayette ct
Lunn Mrs. Leah, b. h., 8th bel Green
Lunny Hugh, lab., rear Charlotte bel Thompson (K)
Lunny John, lab., George bel 4th
Lunny Joseph, shop, Sch 6th bel Wood
Lunny Patrick, lab., Sch. 6th bel Wood.
Lunsfelder Sol., dealer 38 N 10th
Lupold Samuel, miller, Washington bel 13th
Lush John, printer, 10 Marion
Lush John Henry, blacksmith, 128 N 5th
Luther Robt., bricklayer, 20 Rittenhouse
Lutton John, carter, 32 Pascal alley
Lutts Henry, lab. Lemon ab 12th
Lutz Armand, carp., rear 84 N 2d
Lutz Charles, cordw., Court al.
Lutz Christopher, boot crimper, rear 21 Charlotte
Lutz David, painter, Hope ab Franklin
Lutz Francis, piano maker, Crown & O Y road
Lutz Frederick, vict., Parrish ab 10th.
Lutz F., tobacconist, G T road ab Master
Lutz George, Jr., fisherman, Brown bel Vienna (K)
Lutz Geo., shipwr. Shackamaxon bel Franklin
Lutz George, cordw. Thompson ab Sch 8th
Lutz Henry, vict. Thompson bel Sch 7th
Lutz Henry, cooper, St. John ab George (K)
Lutz Ignatius, cabinetmr., 292 Chestnut, h Juniper ab Pine
Lutz Jacob, vict., rear James bel R. road
Lutz Jacob D., blacksmith, 1 Rachel's ct
Lutz James, vict., Duke ab Cherry (K)
Lutz John, vict. Pleasant bel 10th
Lutz John P., wheelwright, rear 404 N 3d
Lutz John P., vict., Pleasant ab Charles
Lutz Martin, alderman, 443 Vine
Lutz Samuel, lab., 6th bel G T road
Lutz Samuel, salesman, 267 N 7th
Lutz Sarah, Brown and Vienna (K)
Lutz Stimmel, Moyamensing av
Luzenberg Edwd. C. apothecary, 3d & Beaver
Lybrand C. D., druggist, h 38 Filbert
Lybrand Henry J., trunk & harness maker, Crown bel Bedford, (K)
Lybrand Isabella, wid. of Joseph, 10th ab Wallace
Lybrand Margaret, gentw., 135 N 9th.
Lybrand W. C. clerk, 10th bel Wallace
Lye E. Mrs., medicines, 385 High
Lye Henry, surveyor, 385 High
Lylburn John, clerk, 58 Sassafras
Lyle James M., printer, 4 Harrison's pl
Lyle James P., clerk, h 147 Queen
Lyle Jane R. trimmings, 263 S 4th
Lyle John, carp., Thompson ab Broad

Lyle Mary, 46 Almond
Lyle Thomas, shipmaster, 448 S Front
Lyman N. P., hardware, 23 Commerce
Lynch Bartholomew, Christian bel 12th
Lynch Daniel, chaise driver, George ab Sch 7th
Lynch Dennis, b. h. 73 N Water
Lynch Edward, carter, Sch Beech ab Locust
Lynch James, 169 N 4th
Lynch Jas., carter, Mulberry n Sch 2d
Lynch Jas., lab., 7 Pearl
Lynch John, grocer, 2d & Master, (K)
Lynch John, morocco tanner, 8 Hickory ct
Lynch John, lab. Lloyd ab Fitzwater
Lynch John, lab., Mulberry and Sch 2d
Lynch Jonas, bootmr., Moon's ct
Lynch Mary, grocer, 195 S 4th
Lynch Mary, milliner, 18 S 12th
Lynch Matthew, coachmr., Pleasant ab 10th
Lynch Patrick, shoemr., Juniper ab High
Lynch Thomas, weaver, Shippen ab 12th
Lynch Thomas, clerk, Mechanics' Bank, h 90 Buttonwood.
Lynch Timothy, bookseller, 9 S 8th
Lynch Urban, cabinetmr, 4 Prune
Lynch Wm. blacksmith, 60 Plum
Lynch Wm., gent., 4 Porter
Lynd James, senr., 85 Marshall
Lyndall Benjamin, blindmr., 129 S 2d, h Front bel Christian
Lyndall Catharine, wid. of Robert, 45 Christian
Lyndall Mary, 345 S 2d
Lyndall Mary, gentw. 10th bel Pleasant
Lyndall Wm. B., carp. 508 Coates
Lynes Thomas, weaver, Sch 7th bel Pine
Lynmire Ellison B., sea captain, 58 New Market
Lynn John F., ship joiner, F road opp Otter (K)
Lynn Marg., shop, 3 Middle al
Lynn Matthew, ship carp., Shackamaxon whf, h Hanover ab Bedford (K)
Lynn Robt., ship carp., Beach ab Palmer (K)
Lynn Samuel M., conveyancer, 3 Carpenter's ct h 315 N 6th
Lynn Wm., weaver, Hope ab Otter (K)
Lyon Abraham, gent. 121 N 7th
Lyon Philip, tailor, Randall's ct
Lyons Adam, weaver, rear Howard ab Phœnix
Lyons Catharine, shop, 24 Carter's al
Lyons Chas., shoemr., 3 Howard's ct
Lyons Edmund W., shoemr., 233 E Lombard
Lyons Edward, bricklayer, 12 Willing's al
Lyons Edwd., cabinetmr., 209 9th
Lyons Ellis, fruiterer, 9 Assembly Build.
Lyons Hiram, baker, rear 8th bel Christian
Lyons Hiram, weaver, Perry ab Franklin
Lyons James, weaver, Philip ab Master
Lyons James, lab., 11 Carter's al
Lyons John, drayman, 18 Parker
Lyons John, lab., George and Juniper la
Lyons John, stovemr., 41 R road
Lyons John C. Rev., 659 N 2d (K)
Lyons John H., tailor, 140 Chestnut, h Sch 8th ab Vine
Lyons Moses, cordw., 114 Carpenter
Lyons Patrick, dealer, 1 Pleasant ct
Lyons Samuel, lab. 22 Jones' al (C)
27

Lyons Saml., gent., 98 Union
Lyons Sarah, Hubbell ab Catharine
Lyons Thomas, cordw. Levy's ct
Lyons Wm. weaver, 47 W Cedar
Lyons Wm. O., chairmr., Newton st
Lysinger Joseph S. blacksmith, S W 9th and James
Lyttle James, lab., 28 Pratt st

M'Adam James, tavern, S E Vernon and Cedar
M'Adam Jas., weaver, G T road bel Jefferson
M'Adam Robert, weaver, Linn ct n Fair Mount
M'Adam Thomas, teacher, George ab 11th, h 12 City Row
M'Adams Thos., weaver, Phoenix ab 2d (K)
M'Adams Thos., shoemr., Clinton ab Franklin (K)
M'Adams Wm., silver plater, 193 N Sch 7th
M'Adoo Daniel, lab., Montgomery bel 2d
M'Adoo James C., paper hanger, 143 N 10th
M'Adoo Sarah, 25 N 13th.
M'Afee John, weaver, Shippen ab 13th
M'Afee John, lab., Filbert n Sch Front
M'Afee Michael, shoes, 207 Cedar
M'Afee Mr., 516 High
M'Afee Wm., cordw., 333 S 5th
M'Affee Robt., tailor, Benton and William
M'Aleer Charles, lab. Lombard W Sch 7th
M'Aleer Daniel, weaver, rear Fitler n 2d
M'Aleer Hugh, lab., 194 E Lombard
M'Aleer John, grocery, 10th & Willow
M'Aleer John, manuf., 2d bel Master
M'Aleer Matthew, grocer, 6 Little Dock.
M'Aleer Michael, weaver, Hancock ab Jefferson (K)
M'Aleer Patrick, weaver, Higham's ct (K)
M'Aleer Patrick, lab., 15 Turner
M'Aleer Patrick, lab., Adelphi al
M'Aleer Patrick, shop, Bedford bel Broad
M'Aleer Wm., lab., Sch 2d bel Lombard
M'Allister Alex., lab., Washington av bel Brown
M'Allister Charles, weaver, Cadwalader bel Montgomery
M'ALLISTER & CO., opticians and cane manuf. 48 Chestnut
M'Allister Danl., machinist, Philip and Jefferson
M'Allister Hector, grocer, Sch 2d and High
M'Allister James, jeweller, 33 Concord
M'Allister Jas., lab., rear 296 S 7th
M'Allister John, grocer, S W 8th and Sassafras
M'Allister John, jr. mer. 48 Chestnut, h W Penn sq
M'Allister Margaret, dry goods, 105 N 9th
M'Allister Marg., dealer, Crabb st
M'Allister Randle, painter, 19 Mercer
M'Allister Thos., lab., Hope bel Master
M'Allister W. Y., optician, 48 Chestnut, h 4 S 13th
M'Allmont Mary, Mulberry n Sch 7th
M'Alonan John, cordwr., Vine bel 12th
M'Alpin Jas., gent., Hamilton vil.
M'Anall James, lab. 274 S 3d
M'Anall James, Spruce n Sch Front

M'Anall Jas., weaver, Smith's ct
M'Anally James, lab., Pearl ab William
M'Anally Jerry, weaver, Hope ab Master (K)
M'Anally John, weaver, Milton ab 11th
M'Anally Michael, grocer, S W 4th & German
M'Anally Robt., cabinetmr., 13th bel Cedar
M'Anally Wm., lab., Lombard n Sch Front
M'Anar Thos., baker, Richard n Sch 6th
M'Anany Edwd., lab., 18 Farmer
M'Anany Francis, lab., 13 Lloyd's ct (K)
M'Anany Henry, lab., Brazier ab Lloyd
M'Anany John, carter, Carpenter bel 8th
M'Anany Wm. weaver, 7th ab Fitzwater
M'Anaspy Dennis, weaver, 19 Lloyd's ct (K)
M'Anizland James, cordw., Carlton ab Sch 6th
M'Arlane Francis, weaver, Hancock bel Master (K)
M'Arpine Geo., carp. weav., West bel Hanover (K)
M'Arran Wm., lab., Cherry ab 11th
M'Arthur John, sawmr., Lebanon ab Christian
M'Atee Thomas, grocer, G T road N 4th
M'Attimore Elmer, cabmr., 83 Green
M'Auliffe Patrick, grocer, S W 3d & Christian
M'Avinna Michael, lab., Fitler n Harrison
M'Avoy Edward, shoemr. 324 High
M'Avoy Edwd., weaver, Milton bel 11th
M'Avoy Francis, bottler, N W 6th & Fitzwater
M'Avoy Jas., weaver, 18 Lloyd's ct (K)
M'Avoy James, weaver, Pine ab Sch Front
M'Avoy John, weaver, Milton bel 10th
M'Avoy John, M. D., G T road bel Phœnix
M'Avoy John, plasterer, rear Nectarine ab 9th
M'Avoy Mich., wool comb, 4th n Creek
M'Avoy Richard, grocer, 36 Brown
M'Avoy William, weaver, 3 Mechanic (F M)
M'Berney And., gent., Lombard ab Sch 2d
M'Beth John, weaver, Bedford ab 12th
M'Blane Jas., weaver, Union ab Franklin (K)
M'Brandle John, lab., Chestnut bet Sch 3d & 4th
M'Bride Andrew, distiller, G T road and 2d
M'Bride Benj., porter, Wiley's ct
M'Bride Daniel, tailor, 1 N 12th
M'Bride Edwd., lab., Murray n Sch 2d
M'Bride Francis, distiller, S W 12th & Cedar
M'Bride Henry, weaver, 13th ab Poplar
M'Bride James, lab., Hamilton & Fairmount
M'Bride John, lab., Murray ab Sch 3d
M'Bride John, weaver, Marlboro' ab Duke
M'Bride John, ship smith, Church ab Reed
M'Bride John, stone cut., Hope bel Phœnix (K)
M'Bride John, weaver, 6 S Garden Retreat
M'Bride John, stone cutter, 1 Harrison
M'Bride Joseph, weaver, Camac ab G T road
M'Bride Marg., shop., Cherry ab 11th
M'Bride Matthew, trimmings, S W 5th and Queen
M'Bride Matthew, tavern, S W Almond & Swanson
M'Bride Matthew, weaver, Howard bel Franklin (K)
M'Bride Michael, lab., Beach bel Chestnut
M'Bride P. & Co., grocers, 251 N 2d
M'Bride Robert, weav., Amber ab Phoenix
M'Bride Robert, manuf., 601 N Front (K)

M'Bride Samuel, manuf., Hamilton n Ju., (F M)
M'Bride Thos., manuf., Front bel Franklin (K
M'Bride T., weaver, Perry's ct
M'Bride Wm., weaver, Hope ab Oxford (K)
M'Bride Wm., furniture car, rear 202 N 10th
M'Bride Wm. T., manuf., Marlborough ab Duk (K)
M'Burney John, gardener, Fulton bel 13th
M'Burney S. P., confect., 89 N 6th
M'Cabe Catharine, spooler, rear G T road be Jefferson
M'Cabe Geo., stone cut., Carlton ab Sch 6th
M'Cabe Hugh, grocer, S E 6th and Lombard
M'Cabe John, bootmr., rear G T road ab Master (F)
M'Cabe John, lab., Carlton ab Sch 6th (K)
M'Cabe Michael, lab. Franklin bel Cherry (K)
M'Cabe Michael, lab., Shippen ab 13th
M'Cabe Patrick, shop, Christian & Essex
M'Cabe Paul, paper hanger, Cedar ab 11th
M'Cabe P. M., weaver, Wood ab Sch 7th
M'Cabe Richd., dealer, 268 Cedar
M'Cabe Wm., lab., Vine ab Nixon
M'Cafferty Barney, oysters, 229 S 5th
M'Cafferty B., Small ab 5th
M'Cafferty Daniel, lab., Spruce n Sch 2d
M'Cafferty Edward, weaver, Cedar bel 13th
M'Cafferty Wm., ostler, 20 Quince
M'Caffrey Cecilia, Front ab Master (K)
M'Caffrey Hugh, victualler, N W 6th and Marriott
M'Caffrey James, lab., 149 Poplar
M'Caffrey James, lab., 16 Barker bel Sch 6th
M'Caffrey Patrick, drover, 178 Shippen
M'Caffrey Patrick, weaver, 6 Gay's ct (K)
M'Cahan W. G., 36 Franklin
M'Cahen John J. 398 N 6th
M'Cahey Jas., coachman, 6 Peach
M'Cahey John, weaver, Howard bel Master
M'Cahey Patrick, coal office, 78 N 3d, yard Willow ab Broad
M'Cahey Samuel, weaver, 606 N 2d (K)
M'Cain James, weaver, G T road bel Phœnix
M'Cain John, weaver, Hancock ab Norris
M'Cain Thos., G T road ab Thompson (K)
M'Cain Wm., weav., Fitler bel Harrison (K)
M'Cale John, lab., Sch Beach n Walnut
M'Call Alex., paper mr., Rose bel William(K)
M'Call Andrew, iron founder, 31 Farmer
M'Call Archibald, printer, 17 N road
M'Call Dennis, lab., 10 Farmer
M'Call Eleanor, 12 John (S)
M'Call Elizabeth, grocer, S E Front and Catharine
M'CALL HENRY, atty. and coun., 102 S 3d bel Willing's al
M'Call Hugh, 5 Gilbert's ct
M'Call John, drayman, Jefferson bel Sch 8th
M'Call John C., 10th n Pine
M'Call Jones, atty., 255 S 6th
M'Call Joseph, carpenter, 12th n Lombard
M'Call Lewis, carp., Vine bel 13th
M'Call Maria, lemon sirup, 6th bel Christian
M'Call Matt., tailor, G T road bel 2d

M'Call Patrick, carter, Carpenter bel 11th
M'CALL PETER, att'y & coun., 100 S 4th
M'Call Robert, grocer, Broad and Locust
M'Call Robert, gent., 323 Chestnut
M'Call Sarah Ann, shoebinder, Price's ct
M'Calla Alexander, lab., Lewis ab Sch 6th
M'Calla Alex., 119 N 9th
M'Calla Andrew, hatter, 252 High, h 177 N 7th
M'Calla A. H., com. mer., 7 Walnut
M'Calla Charles, clerk, 44 Madison
M'Calla Edwin, mer., 64 High, h N W 6th and Green
M'Calla Jas., manuf., William bel Edward (K)
M'Calla James S., printer, 12 Pear, h 6 Jefferson row
M'Calla John, paper hanger, 66 N 10th, h 430 Vine
M'Calla John, 5 N 11th ab High
M'Calla Robert P., 18 Dean
M'Calla Sanford, com. mer., 175 N 13th
M'Calla William, collector, 5 N 13th
M'Calla Wm., lab., Pearl bel Sch 5th
M'Calla W. L. Rev., Mantua vil
M'Calley John, lab., Carlton bet Sch 2d and 3d
M'Calley Robert, carp. 2 Smith's pl
M'Calley Robert, senr., 3 Wells' Row
M'Callister Alex., lab., 23 Bonsall
M'Callister Charles, cordw., 2 Clare
M'Callister James, bookseller, Lombard near Quince
M'Callister Richard, shoemr., rear 74 Catharine
M'Callister Robt. bookseller, George ab Sch 8th
M'Callister Robt., lab., 40 W South
M'Callister Saml., clerk, 8th ab Carpenter
M'Callister Wm., blacksm., rear 103½ Christian
M'Callmont & Bond, mers., 35 N Front
M'CALLMONT GEORGE F., mer. 35 N Front, h 303 Spruce
M'Calmont George & Co., office 2 Ranstead ct
M'CALLUM ANDREW & CO., carpets, 87 Chestnut
M'Calvey George, shoemr., 2 Sheppard's al
M'Calvey James, weaver, 11th ab Carpenter
M'Calvey James, pattern maker, 90 Cherry, h Sch. 7th n Vine
M'Calvy Edward, trader, Fraley's al (K)
M'Calvy James, trader, Fraley's ct (K)
M'Cambridge Richard R., 26 Elfreth's al
M'Cammen S., George, (F V)
M'Cammon David C., gent., 123 Lombard
M'Cammon Wm., clerk, 17 Catharine
M'Can John, cabtmr., 125 Catharine
M'Candless Thos., grocery, Sch 3d bel Pine
M'Cane Wm. lab. Lombard n Sch 4th
M'Canles John, grocer, 72 S Front, h 106 Sassafras
M'Canless David, shop, Sch 6th and Lombard
M'Cann Aaron, tanner, St. John ab Beaver (K)
M'Cann & Co., provisions, 119 S Front
M'Cann Bernard J. printer, 12 Small
M'Cann Bernard, jr., com. mer., 119 S Front
M'Cann Bridget 22 Garden
M'Cann B., weaver, 145 Locust
M'Cann Chas., weaver, Hope ab Phœnix
M'Cann Edward, lab. M'Bride's ct

M'Cann Edward, gent., 198 Christian
M'Cann Edward, weav., 652 N 2d
M'Cann Edward, weaver, Perry ab Phoenix
M'Cann Eleanor, confectioner, 241½ S 2d
M'Cann Felix, lab., 20 Mary
M'Cann Francis, lab., 8 Clark ab 3d
M'Cann George, upholsterer, Dugan below Spruce
M'Cann Henry, porter, Little Pine
M'Cann Henry, weaver, 13th ab Fulton
M'Cann James, lab. 6 Warner's ct
M'Cann James, lab., rear 11 Blackberry alley
M'Cann James, collector, 161 Shippen
M'Cann James, lab., Bedford ab 13th
M'Cann Jas., agent, S E Spruce & Comptroller
M'Cann John, lab., Lombard n Sch 7th
M'Cann John, carter, Milton ab 10th
M'Cann John, lab., 33 Garden
M'Cann John, blacksm., 6 Warner's ct
M'Cann Margaret, spooler, rear Charlotte above Thompson
M'Cann Mary, shop, 29 Crabb
M'Cann Thos., fruit st., 169 E South
M'Cann Thomas, packer, 4 Grape ct
M'Cann Wm., blacksmith, 8th ab Baker
M'Canna Isabella, 37 S Juniper
M'Canna James, tailor, 7 Howard's ct
M'Canna John, baker, 316 S 3d
M'Canna Patrick, lab., 2 Kelly
M'Caraher Elizabeth, widow of Alexander, 206 Noble
M'Caraher James, custom-house, h 206 Noble
M'Caraher Timothy, lab., Sch 5th bel Barker
M'Carney Edward, lab., Sch 5th n Cedar
M'Carney John, lab., Reed bel Church
M'Carney Marg., 10 Lagrange pl
M'Carren Elizabeth, 150 N 13th
M'Carren Isaac, overseer, Carpenter ab 13th
M'Carren John, lab. Callowhill ab Sch 6th
M'Carren J. S., clerk, 182 Carpenter
M'Carren Thomas, blacksmith, rear 25 Ogden
M'Carren Wm. driver, 5 Tiller's ct
M'Carroll Hugh, lab., 14 Shippen
M'Carroll Joseph, carter, Chestnut bel Sch 3d
M'Carroll Peter, grocer, 108 Plum
M'Carroll Robert, police officer, Jefferson ab Sch 6th
M'CARRY JAS., tavern, Beach n Chestnut
M'Carter Alexander, carp., 13th ab Shippen
M'Carter James, lab., Pearl ab William
M'Carter John, jeweller, Jones W Sch 3d
M'Carter Park, weaver, Philip ab Master (K)
M'Carter Richard, miller, Charles' place
M'Carthy Daniel, lab., Philip ab Jefferson
M'Carthy Thos., watchman, 14 Fitzwater
M'Carthy Wm., stonecut., R road ab Girard av
M'Cartney Daniel, lab., Hope ab Otter (K)
M'Cartney Francis, weaver, 10 Philip
M'Cartney Henry, gent., Lombard ab Sch 2d
M'Cartney James, weaver, Brinton and 13th
M'Cartney James, carp., Jefferson ab Front (K)
M'Cartney James, lab., Bedford ab 6th
M'Cartney John, cooper, Prime ab 2d

M'Cartney Mary, rear Hope ab Master
M'Cartney Patrick, Sch Front and Spruce
M'Cartney Wm., milkman, 21 Fitzwater
M'Cartney Wm., camphine oil, 5th bel Shippen
M'Carty Aaron, tavern, Beach ab Maiden (K)
M'Carty Charles, carpet weaver, Justices' ct
M'Carty Chas., lab., Clinton ab Poplar
M'Carty Danl., shop, 92 Swanson
M'Carty Daniel, baker, Farries' ct.
M'Carty Daniel, lab., 1 Grape ct
M'Carty Dennis, lab., 2 Grape ct
M'Carty Dennis, lab., 2 Grape ct
M'Carty Edward, lab., Smith's ct
M'Carty Edward, silversmith, 105 N 3d
M'Carty Edward, lab., Washington (W P)
M'Carty Elizabeth, tailoress, Juniper ab Locust
M'Carty Geo., weaver, 2d ab Master
M'Carty Harmin, cordw., rear 337 N 3d
M'Carty James, lab., Dorothy n Sch 4th
M'Carty James, lab., 26 Richard
M'Carty Jane, shop, 321 Spruce
M'Carty Jeremiah, tailor, Pratt's ct
M'Carty John, lapidist, Dorothy n Sch 4th
M'Carty John, carp., Washington bel 7th
M'Carty John, cooper, Wheat ab Wharton
M'Carty John, bricklayer, Rose bel Broad
M'Carty John, iron dealer, 189 N Front
M'Carty Mary, Centre bel 13th
M'Carty Mary, 616 N 3d
M'Carty Patrick, lab., Sch Front & Filbert
M'Carty Patrick, lab., 2 Grape ct
M'Carty Patrick, weaver, Baker's ct (K)
M'Carty Patrick, lab. Prospect al
M'Carty Rachel, 80 N 6th
M'Carty Thos., lab., 14 Fitzwater
M'Carty Thomas, lab., 1 Grape
M'Carty Timothy, lab., 5 Northampton ct
M'Carty Timothy, weaver, rear G T road above
  Phoenix
M'Carty Wm., carp., 81 Gaskill
M'Carvell Wm., weaver, 666 N 2d (K)
M'Caslin Margt., S 4th opp Barker
M'Caughen Henderson, wire worker, Cadwala-
  der bel Jefferson
M'Caughen Samuel, weaver, Front bel Master(K)
M'Cauley Archibald, blacksmith, Sch 6th below
  Market, h Jones W Sch 5th
M'Cauley Arthur, dry goods, 566 N 2d (K)
M'Cauley Cornelius, morocco dress., 174 Cedar,
  h 213 S 4th
M'Cauley Cornelius, bootmr., 252 S 4th, h 174
  E Cedar
M'Cauley Dennis, wood dealer, Chestnut st whf
  Sch
M'Cauley Francis G., 17 Girard
M'Cauley James, brickmr., George n Sch 2d
M'Cauley James, weaver, Graham's ct
M'Cauley James, bricklr., Leopard bel Phœnix
M'Cauley John, cordw., 3 Steinmetz's ct
M'Cauley John, weaver, Sch 6th ab Lombard
M'Cauley John, lab., Fulton ab 12th
M'Cauley John, lab., Irvine n R road
M'Cauley Jos., brickmr., George n Sch 2d
M'Cauley Lawrence, lab., Hope ab Phoenix(K)
M'Cauley Margaret, Lombard W Sch 8th

M'Cauley Michael, trunkmr., 29 Dillwyn, h Front
  bel Green
M'Cauley Neal, lab., 327 S 6th
M'Cauley Neal, manuf. 610 N 2d
M'Cauley Robert, plasterer, rear Crown below
  Bedford (K)
M'Cauley Robert, brickmr., George n Sch 3d
M'Cauley Samuel, brickmr., George W Sch 3d
M'Cauley Thomas, shoemr., Kinley's ct
M'Cauley Wm., alderman, Federal and P road
M'Causland Alice, 217 Locust
M'Caw John, shoe store, 41 P road
M'Caw Matthew, clothes dealer, 108 Cedar
M'Cawl And., ropemr., 6th bel G T road
M'Cay Alex., real est. brok., Sch 7th n Filbert
M'Chay James, lab., 6 Peach
M'Chesney Mary, Supert. Female Hos. Soc. 5
  Appletree al
M'Chesney Wm. J., photographist, 142 Chest-
  nut, h S E 6th & Washington
M'Clain, grocer, 12 Howard
M'Clain Alexander, lab., Washington av above
  Willow
M'Clain Andrew, machinist, Phoenix bel 2d
M'Clain Edward, chairmr., Franklin bel Coates
M'Clain Henry, weaver, Milton ab 10th
M'Clain Hugh, carpenter, 8 Juniper lane
M'Clain James, spinner, 3 Cadwalader
M'Clain John, weaver, 652 N 2d
M'Clain Julia, shop, 221 Callowhill
M'Clain Richard, wire worker, 76 Locust
M'Clain Robt., 10 N 12th
M'Clain Sarah, George n Sch 6th
M'Clain S. W., shop, Front & Keefe
M'Clain Timothy, lab., 259 Catharine
M'Clane Alexander, grocer, Front bel Master
M'Clane Andrew, tavern, 237 S 2d
M'Clane Archibald, grocer, Noble & O Y road
M'Clane Danl., agt., Wood ab Sch 8th
M'Clane George, seaman, 154 Pine
M'Clane George F., morocco dresser, Centre
  bel Parrish
M'Clane John, stone cutter, P road ab Carpen-
  ter
M'Clane Joseph, grocer, High W Sch 7th, h
  Barker n Sch 5th
M'Clane Michael, weaver, Cadwalader above
  Jefferson
M'Clane Robert, spin., Cadwalader ab Phoenix
M'Clane Thomas, weaver, 4th bel Jefferson (K)
M'Clanning Mich., grocer, 10th & Ogden
M'Claranan James, marble mason, Sassafras n
  Juniper, h 116 N Juniper
M'Claren Lawrence, cabmr., 32 Pratt
M'Clarey Robert, weaver, Hope ab Phœnix (K)
M'Clarnen John, clerk, rear 291 St John
M'Clary John, chairmr., 5 J. Baker's ct
M'Clary Joseph, bricklr., Franklin n Union(K)
M'Clary Joseph, weaver, 2d n Montgomery (K)
M'Clary Wm., weaver, Philip ab Master (K)
M'Clary Wm., 67 Tammany
M'Claskey Ann, shop, Wharton ab Front
M'Claskey Catharine, 57 M road
M'Claskey Charles, butcher, 32 Reed
M'Claskey George, weaver, 2d ab Master (K)

M'Claskey Hugh, carter, Wheat bel Wharton
M'Claskey James, innkr., P road bel Christian
M'Claskey John, carter, Ashton ab Spruce
M'Claskey Margt., shop 4th n Carpenter
M'Claskey Mary, shop, 513 S 2d
M'Claskey Matt., dealer, 513 S 2d
M'Claskey Patrick, weaver, Linn n Nixon
M'Claskey Richard, shoemaker, Front bel Phœnix, (K)
M'Claskey Thomas, lab., S 7th bel Shippen
M'Clawner Felix, lab., 6 Little Green (K)
M'Clay Aaron K., carp., Irvine E of 13th
M'Clay James, lab., Murray n Sch 2d
M'Clay John, cordw., 580 S 2d
M'Clay, weaver, Hanover ab West (K)
M'Cleallan Wm., paper carrier, Christian ab 3d
M'Clean Charles, weaver, rear G T road below Master
M'Clean David, alderman, office Shippen and 11th, h 11th ab Shippen
M'Clean Elizabeth, wid., 4 Emlen's ct
M'Clean John J., blacksm., 15 Short ct
M'Clean Joseph, chair paint., Dutton n Franklin (K)
M'Clean Stephen, shop, Front and Greenwich
M'Clean Thomas, blacksmith, 236 S 4th, h 16 W. Market pl
M'Cleary And., sheet iron work., Beckett
M'Cleary Daniel, locksmith & bellhanger, Marshall bel Parrish
M'Cleary Joseph, lab. Lombard n Sch 7th
M'Cleery Hugh, weav., Philip bel Jefferson,(K)
M'Cleery James, lab., Brooks' ct
M'Clees & Germon, photographists, 80½ Walnut
M'Clees James, cordw., Apple ab Poplar
M'Clees James, cordw., 50 Laurel
M'Clees James E., photographist, 80½ Walnut, h Beaver ab 3d
M'Cleester Alex., machinist, 4th ab Wharton.
M'Clellan George, M. D., 248 Walnut
M'Clellan Hugh carp. 8th ab Brown
M'Clellan John, dry goods, 212 E Spruce
M'CLELLAN J. H. B., M. D., 255½ Walnut
M'Clellan Matthew, morocco dr., 684 N 2d
M'Clellan Robt., weaver, rear 2d ab Master
M'Clellan Robert, carp., West bel George
M'Clellan Samuel, M. D., 181 Walnut.
M'Clellan Wm., weaver, Jefferson ab 2d (K)
M'Clellan Wm., bootmr., 63 Locust
M'Clelland G. W., gent., 214 Mulberry.
M'Clelland Wm., capmr., 76 S 3d, h Sch 3d n Filbert
M'Clement John, saddler, 9 Spragg's av
M'Clennah Amelia, shop, 521 N 4th
M'Clennan John, printer, 9th bel Carpenter
M'Clinchy Patrick, lab., Jones n Sch 4th
M'Clintick Alex., brickmr., George n Sch 2d
M'Clintock Arthur, lab., Front bel Master
M'Clintock James, M. D., 1 N 11th
M'Clintock James, mer., 39 N 3d, h 99 Pine
M'Clintock Jane, Lombard ab Sch 7th
M'Clintock John, weaver, Lombard n Sch 2d
M'Clintock John, trea. Beaver Mead. Coal Co., 84 Walnut, h 8 Sergeant
M'Clintock J. & Co., 526 High

M'Clintock Robt., variety store, 414 High
M'Clintock Thomas, Elder st
M'Clintock Wm., saddler, 6 Jefferson row
M'Clintock Wm., lab., Dean ab Centre
M'Clintock Wm., weaver, Union ab West (K)
M'Closkey Edward, dealer, 7th bel Cedar
M'Closkey Francis, weaver, 11th bel Christian
M'Closkey James, carp., 8th ab Catharine, h 332 Cedar
M'Closkey James, curb setter, Broad ab Parrish
M'Closkey James, lab., Small bel 5th
M'Closkey James, oysterhouse, 9th bel Cedar
M'Closkey Jas. F. K., M. D., Broad ab Parrish
M'Closkey John, drover, Parrish n Broad
M'Closkey Martha, milliners, 50 Zane
M'Closkey Peter, weaver, Fitler bel Harrison (K)
M'Closkey Thomas, weaver, Fitler n 2d
M'Closkey Wm., tailor, George n Sch 6th
M'Closky Patrick, lab., Carpenter ab 5th
M'Clossen Charles, weav., 11 Bauersach ct (K)
M'Cloud Daniel, grocer, P road bel Fitzwater
M'Cloud Elizabeth, rear 311 Cherry
M'Cloud John, hatter, 46 High, h 488 Coates
M'Cloud John & Son, batters, 46 High
M'Cloud Malcolm, batter, 46 High
M'Cloud Margaret, 25 Crabb
M'Cloy James, lab., Ann n 13th
M'Clune George, boot and shoemaker, 579 S 2d
M'Clune James, teacher, Hanover bel West
M'Clung John, lab., Gulielma st
M'Clung John, stove finisher & pattern maker, 76 N 6th, h 13th ab Washington
M'Clung Mary, shop, Gulielma st
M'Clung Thos., carp., Prospect al
M'Clung William, grocer, S W 2d and Pine, h 66 Spruce
M'Clure Ann, sempstress, 112 Filbert
M'Clure Anna M., milliner, 54 Palmyra sq
M'Clure Archibald, shop, Beach ab Poplar (K)
M'Clure Eliza Mrs., Clare
M'Clure G. W., hatter, Providence ct
M'Clure James, acct., 111 N Water, h 134 N 9th
M'Clure James, shoemr., Lombard n Sch 7th
M'Clure John, carpenter, Vine & Sch. 8th, h S W Spruce and Perry
M'Clure John, carter, Gulielma
M'Clure Robert, 2d ab Willow, h Callowhill n Sch 8th
M'Clure Robert, 5th ab Camac (K)
M'Clure Samuel, carp. Lombard & Juniper
M'Clure Wm. M., mer., 287 High, h 5 Sergeant
M'Clurg Elizabeth, 111 Noble
M'Cluskey Patrick, weaver, Cadwalader above Jefferson
M'Colgan Barney, lab., rear 15 Strawberry
M'Colgan Dennis, lab., White ct
M'Colgan H., tailor, 280 E Cedar
M'Colgan Michael, harnessmr., 30½ S 6th, h 7 Kelly
M'Colgen Mark, tanner, New Market n Laurel
M'Collin Allan, tailor, 203 Cherry
M'Collin John, collector & general agent, 58 Mulberry
M'Collin Susannah, milliner, 58 Mulberry

M'Collin Thomas, acct., 13th bel Green
M'Collim James, lab., Bedford ab 12th
M'Collogh John, shoemr., Callowhill ab Nixon
M'Collon Charles, waiter, rear 126 S 6th
M'Collom John, Sec'y City & County Mutual Ins
  Co. 74 Walnut, h 191 Spruce
M'Collom Mary Ann, Atherton ab Carpenter
M'Collum Danl. weaver, F road ab Phoenix (K)
M'Comb Alexander, lab., Lombard W Sch 7th
M'Comb David, lab., rear Carlton ab 13th
M'Comb John, grocer, 146 F road (K)
M'Comb Wm., lab. Miles' ct (K)
M'Comb Wm., weaver, 23 W Cedar
M'Combs John, weaver, Shippen ab 13th
M'Conaghy Charles, lab., Linn's ct n F M
M'Conaghy John, weaver, Brazier ab Lloyd
M'Conn John, blacksmith, 353 S 5th
M'Connell Fredk. A., tobacconist, 11 Callowhill
M'Connell Henry, tailor, rear Bedford ab 12th
M'Connell Hugh, teamster, Christian ab P road
M'Connell James, cordw., 2 Gabel's ct
M'Connell James, ostler, rear 246 Christian
M'Connell James, storekeeper, 160 Swanson
M'Connell John, saddler, Lombard bel 12th
M'Connell John, porter, 192 N 10th
M'Connell John L., grocer, 392 Sassafras.
M'Connell Matthew, spectaclemr., 6 Chatham
M'Connell Mary, milliner, 289 Chestnut
M'Connell Patrick, temperer, Linden ab Sch 7th
M'Connell Rebecca, wid. of Jas., Ruddack's ct
M'Connell Robert, furnit. car, 12th bel Lombard
M'Connell Samuel, white lead manuf, Lombard
  n Sch 4th
M'Connell Thos., buttonmr., Little Green above
  Cadwalader (K)
M'Connell Wm., porter, 194 N 10th
M'Convill Edward, weaver, 4th ab Jefferson
  (K)
M'Cool Adam, bricklayer, 8 Orchard
M'Cool Daniel, combmr., 34 Charlotte
M'Cool Samuel, boot & shoemaker, 485 N 2d
M'Cool Walter, vict., Palmer ab Franklin
M'Cool Wm. lab. 469 N 4th
M'Cool Wm. brickmr. 5th above Camac (K)
M'Cord David, tin smith, 12 Schriver's ct
M'Cord George A., hatter, 143 N 10th
M'Cord George W., printer, 3 Flickwir's ct.
M'Cord Grace, rear of 118 W High
M'Cord James, porter, Jones W of Sch 6th
M'Cord Joseph, tobacconist, 13th & Sassafras
M'Corkell Alex. plasterer, Wood n Sch Front
M'Corkhill John, cordw., Van Buren pl
M'Corkle Andrew, carp., Charlotte bel Poplar
M'Corkle J., teacher, Sch 7th ab Ogden
M'Corkle Maria Mrs., Locust & Sch 6th
M'Corkle Thomas, moulder, 290 Wood below
  Broad
M'Cormack H. C., atty. & coun., Locust and
  Washington, h 45 Almond sq
M'Cormack Patrick, coachman, Carlisle's ct
M'Cormack Robert, grocer, N W 12th & Cedar
M'Cormack Stewart, lab., rear Cadwalader bel
  Phœnix (K)
M'Cormick Ann, wid., 33 Pine
M'Cormick Arthur, Budden's al

M'Cormick Benjamin, ropemaker, Mary ab F
  road
M'Cormick Bernard, jeweller, 254 Catharine
M'Cormick Daniel, tailor, Curtis' ct
M'Cormick David, cordw., 285 S 5th.
M'Cormick Elizabeth C., trim st., 136 E Spruce
M'Cormick Francis, weaver, Murray n Sch 3d
M'Cormick Francis, tobacconist, R road ab c
  Broad
M'Cormick Francis, farmer, Dorothy E Sch 3d
M'Cormick George, weaver, Fraley's ct (K)
M'Cormick Geo., lab., Mary n F road (K)
M'Cormick Henry, bricklayer, Crown below
  West (K)
M'Cormick Henry, shoemr., Washington ab 5th
M'Cormick Hugh, tailor, 38 S 3d.
M'Cormick Isabella, wid., George n Sch 2d
M'Cormick James, painter, 4th ab Washington
M'Cormick James, weav., Otter bel Front (K)
M'Cormick James, bricklayer, Perry below
  Phoenix (K)
M'Cormick James, lab., Juniper & Lombard
M'Cormick James, printer, Lombard bel 12th
M'Cormick James H., Broad st Exchange
M'Cormick James H., Sch 6th ab Chestnut
M'Cormick John, stone cutter, 38 Coat's al
M'Cormick John, shoemr., Mary n F road (K)
M'Cormick John, tavern, Wire Bridge
M'Cormick John, weaver, Mariner ab 13th
M'Cormick John, boots & shoes, 65 S 2d
M'Cormick John C., sailmr., 3d ab Washington
M'Cormick Levi, drover, 3 Kelly's av
M'Cormick Maria, 45 Almond
M'Cormick Maria, washer, 124 Apple
M'Cormick Mary, Washington ab 10th
M'Cormick Mary, Cadwalader ab Franklin
M'Cormick Patrick, cordw. 217 S 6th
M'Cormick Patrick, weaver, 4th ab Master
M'Cormick Phillips, watchman, Crans' ct
M'Cormick Saml., 31 New Market
M'Cormick Sarah, b. h., 203 N 9th
M'Cormick Sarah, Perry bel Phoenix (K)
M'CORMICK & SHINN, Broad St. Exchange,
  n Chestnut
M'Cormick Stewart, 155 S 6th
M'Cormick Thomas, tinsmith, 14th bel Jefferson
  (K)
M'Cormick Thomas B. undertaker, 133 S 6th
M'Cormick Wm. lab. Reid's av
M'Cormick Wm. cooper, 56 N Water, h rear 5
  Elfreth's al
M'Cormick Wm. mer. 5½ N 2d, h 33 Pine
M'Cormick Wm. weaver, rear G T. road below
  Master
M'Cormick Wm. lab., Senneff's ct
M'Cort John, carpet weaver, G T road above
  Phoenix
M'Cort Peter, weaver, G T road ab Master
M'Cosker Bridget, wid. of Thomas, 283 Cedar
M'Cosker Francis, dealer, 198 Shippen
M'Cosker John, grocer, 7th & Shippen
M'Cosker Michael, dealer, 239 Cedar
M'Couch John, weaver, Sch 2d & Lombard
M'Couch John, mer., Broad and Pine
M'Couch Wm., lab., Beach n Spruce

M'Court Patrick, lab., Barker bel Sch 6th
M'Court Robert, coachman, 7 Western av
M'Court William, tavern, 23 N 8th
M'Cover Henry, shoemr., 18 Cresson's al
M'Cowen Charles, dry goods, 2 N 6th
M'Coy Alex. carp. Pearl ab Sch 8th
M'Coy Alex. vict. 5th ab Camac (K)
M'Coy Andrew R., weaver, Freytag's al
M'Coy Benj., lab., Pearl ab 12th
M'Coy Cain, dealer, 1 Traquair's ct
M'Coy Daniel, cordw., Haig's ct (K)
M'Coy Dennis, lab., Sch 3d bel George
M'Coy Edw., constable, St John ab George (K)
M'Coy Elijah V. hat finisher, 7 Green
M'Coy Ephraim, carp. Marriott's la ab 4th
M'Coy George, cordw., 5 Marble pl
M'Coy Geo. W. watchmr. 206 St John
M'Coy James, lab., Marriott ab 4th
M'Coy James, ropemr. George ab 2d (K)
M'Coy James, carter, 24 O Y road
M'Coy James, ostler, 1 St Stephen's pl
M'Coy James, grocer, 308 S 6th
M'Coy James, carp. Sch 6th bel Pine
M'Coy Jane, crockery, 509 High
M'Coy John, city watch, Lombard ab 13th
M'Coy John, cordw., 220 Shippen.
M'Coy John, tavern, 181 S Front
M'Coy John, ostler, 1 Hyde's ct
M'Coy John, grocer, 2d & Brown
M'Coy John C., store, 509 High
M'Coy Manassus, tailor, Carpenter bel 8th
M'Coy Robert, porter, rear 8th ab Carpenter
M'Coy Sarah, dry goods, 30 N 8th
M'Coy Thos., carter, Roger's ct
M'Coy Thos., carp., 7 Lagrange
M'Coy T., grocer, S W 4th & Catharine
M'Coy Wm., shop, 20 Currant al
M'Coy Wm. carpenter, Queen bel 5th
M'Coy Wm. A., stone cutter, Powell (F V), h Chancellor n Sch 7th
M'Cracken Alex., weaver, F road ab Norris (K)
M'Cracken Colwell, weaver, Weaver's row (K)
M'Cracken James, lab., Carlton n Sch 3d
M'Cracken James, cordw., Wheat bel Wharton
M'Cracken James, weaver, Cadwalader bel Oxford
M'Cracken John, weaver, 28 M'Duffie
M'Cracken John, lab., Jones n Sch 5th
M'Craith Wm., engraver, 74 Chestnut
M'Cray Jas., hatter, 1 St George's al
M'Crea Alex., clerk, Queen & Swanson
M'Crea Ann, 3 N 12th
M'Crea John, 2 Norris al., h Locust W Broad
M'Crea John, blacksm., Coates bel 12th
M'Crea Thos., capmr., Olive bel Broad
M'Crea Thomas, starchmr., 602 N Front
M'Crea William, gilder, 21 Montgomery
M'Crea Wm., trader, G T road ab Camac
M'Cready Thomas, glassblower, Franklin below Vienna (K)
M'Creden Edw., plaster., rear Carpenter ab 8th
M'Credy Bernard, mer., 63 S Front, h 411 Chestnut
M'Credy Bridget, Elizabeth ct

M'Credy Dennis A. mer. 7 N Water, h 39 Mulberry
M'Credy Francis, tavern, S E Pine & Penn
M'Credy Henry, waterman, Callowhill n Nixon
M'Credy Jeremiah, M. D., 110 S 8th
M'Credy Joseph, wire cloth manuf., 3 Hyde's ct
M'Credy Robt., morocco dr., rear 7 Pegg
M'Crellish A., 265 N 3d
M'Creery Benj., weaver, Shippen bel Broad
M'Creight Robt., manuf., School & Rose (K)
M'Cristel Francis, weaver, Cadwalader n Phoenix.
M'Cristel John, weaver, Fitler n 2d
M'Cristol Edward, 7th bel Federal
M'Crodden Wm., weaver, Sch 2d & Lombard
M'Crory & Divvers, dry goods, 136 High
M'Crory James, chairmr. Parrish ab 5th
M'Crory Robert, mer. 136 High
M'Crossan Charles, hay dealer, Schrader's ct
M'Crossan Chas., hay dealer, 7 Bauersach's ct
M'Crossan Robert, grocer, 3d and Green
M'Crossin Jas., weaver, M'Carty st
M'Crudden Hugh, carter, rear 16 Noble
M'Crudden James, lab. 8 William (F M)
M'Crudden Wm., reedmr., Linden ab Sch 7th
M'Crummill C., hair work, 264½ N 3d
M'Crummill James, dentist, 266 N 3d
M'Crystal Dennis, grocer, S E Master and Apple (K)
M'Crystal Michael, weaver, G T road ab Thompson
M'Cue Bernard, lab., Division (F V)
M'Cue Chas., lab., Mariner st
M'Cue Joseph, lab., Nixon (F M)
M'Cuen Michael, lab. 322 S 3d
M'Cuen Wm., dyer, Wood ab Sch 6th
M'Cullagh Robert P., mer., 42 S Front, h 105 Locust
M'Cullagh Sarah, 308 Walnut
M'Cullaugh Owen, manuf. Cadwalader bel Jefferson
M'Cullen Jas., constable, Shippen ab 13th
M'Cullen John, watchman, Quince & Lombard
M'Cullen Wm., lithographer, 12 Harmony ct
M'Culley Andrew, blacksm., Pleasant bel 13th
M'Culley Ann, gentw., Lombard ab 11th
M'Culley George H., watch mr., 216 S 2d
M'Culley Thomas, carpenter, 361 S Front
M'Culloch R., bootmr., 4th bel Carpenter
M'Culloh Ann, gentwo., 214 Spruce
M'Cullough Andrew, Bedford ab 6th
M'Cullough Barney, porter, Allen's ct
M'Cullough James, h. h., 11 Chestnut
M'Cullough James, lab. 15 Prosperous al
M'Cullough James, brushmr., 4 Tiller's ct
M'Cullough John, paper carrier, Lombard ab 12th
M'Cullough John, oyster house, 154 S 6th
M'Cullough John, chairmr., 101 N Front, h 501 Coates
M'Cullough Peter, lab., Mulberry n Sch 2d
M'Cullough Robert, lab., Filbert n Sch 3d
M'Cullough Thos., weaver, Hope ab Phoenix
M'Cullough William, grocer, 21 Farme

M'Cully Francis, morocco dresser, 4 Hallowell
M'Cully James, boat builder, Mulberry n Sch Front
M'Cully James, inspector, 359 S 6th
M'Cully John, lab. Filbert W Sch 4th
M'Cully John, dry goods, Locust ab Dean
M'Cully John, manuf., Locust ab 12th
M'Cully John, cordw., 1 Gebhard
M'Cully Nathaniel, agent, 217 Coates
M'Cully Patrick, lab., High n Sch 2d
M'Cully Robt., cordw., 73 Queen
M'Cully Selina, Dungan's av (K)
M'Cully Wm., Providence ct
M'Cully Wm., butcher, 2d & Marion
M'Cully Wm. W., matchmr., 52 Chestnut, h 267 S 3d
M'Cune Chas., porter, rear 13 Strawberry
M'Cune Clement, manuf., 13th bel Callowhill
M'Cune George, grocer, c Sch. 6th & George.
M'Cune John, carter, Callowhill bel Sch 4th
M'Cune Margaret, 19 Chester
M'Cune Saml., painter, Pearl bel 13th
M'Cunny R. T., clerk, George ab Sch 7th
M'Curdy & Co., dry goods, 542 High
M'Curdy Jacob W. conveyancer, 20 S 13th
M'Curdy James R., mer., High bet Sch 7th and 8th, h 13 Howard
M'Curdy John, printer, 1 Hight's ct
M'Curdy John K., M. D., druggist, 320 High, h 60 Filbert
M'Curdy J., boot and shoemr., 111 Walnut
M'Curdy J. K., bootmaker, 111 Walnut
M'Curdy J. W., ladies' shoemr., 7 Ranstead pl
M'Curdy Robert, mer. 10 North
M'CURDY & STRATTAN, ladies' shoe manufs. 7 Ranstead pl
M'Curdy Wm. mariner, 238 Callowhill
M'CURDY WILLIAM H., bootmr., 111 Walnut
M'Curran James, weaver, Murray n Sch 3d
M'Cusker James, block maker, 57 & h 59 Swanson
M'Cusker Thos., Barker n Sch 6th
M'CUTCHEON & COLLINS, com. mers., Chestnut st whf. S side
M'Cutcheon James, mer. S whfs. & Chestnut
M'Cutcheon John, variety store, 505 N 2d
M'Cutchin John, plasterer, 6 Dorothy
M'Cutchin John, Barker E of Sch 6th
M'Cutchion Wm., blacksm., 24 Mifflin
M'Dade Arthur, weaver, 5 Lloyd's ct (K)
M'Dade Daniel, weaver, 2d ab Master
M'Dade David, lab., 132 Lombard
M'Dade James, weaver, Cadwalader bel Master
M'Dade Robt., drayman, rear Amber ab Phoenix (K)
M'Dade Thos., paper stainer, 4th ab Carpenter
M'Dade Wm., lab., 397 S 4th
M'Daniel Benj., lab., Pearl bel Sch 7th
M'Daniel John M. jr., stone cutter, 141 N Juniper
M'Daniel Joseph A. bonnet presser, Culvert ab Charlotte
M'Daniel Wm. clerk, Ogden bel 11th
M'Daniel Wm., planemr., 20 Mintzer
M'Daniels Benj., waterman, Sander's ct (K)
M'Dermond Geo., cab mr., 6 Harmony ct

M'Dermott Patrick, tinner, 7th ab Cedar
M'Dermot Cornelius, lab., Plum ab 2d
M'Dermot Jas., shoemr., Crown ab Franklin (K)
M'Dermott Catharine, Marriott n 5th
M'Dermott Michael, paver, 247 Shippen.
M'Dermott Edward, gent., 186 Spruce
M'Dermott Edward, stevedore, 69 Union
M'Dermott Ellen, 131 Plum st
M'Dermott Henry, tavern, G T road ab Master
M'Dermott Hugh, lab., George n Sch Beach
M'Dermott James, cordwainer, 156 N Water
M'Dermott James, lab. Lombard E Sch 6th
M'Dermott Jas., oyster house, 483 High
M'Dermott Lawrence, tin smith, 85 P road
M'Dermott Martin, tinsmith, 185 Shippen
M'Dermott Matthew, carp., Biddle's al
M'Dermott Michael, dry goods, G T road below Jefferson (K)
M'Dermott Michael, paver, 247 Shippen.
M'Dermott Patrick, coal dealer, Harrison av
M'Dermott Sarah, 32 Beck st
M'Dermott William, tavern, c 13th and Centre
M'Devitt Catharine, 141 Plum st
M'Devitt Chas., driver, Filbert & Sch 3d
M'Devitt Daniel, acct., 196 Noble
M'Devitt Hugh, grocer, 23 M'Duffie
M'Devitt Hugh, susp. weaver, 275 N Front
M'Devitt James, carpet weaver, Front below Master (K)
M'Devitt John, copper smith, Front bel Reed
M'Devitt John, blacksmith, 9 N 13th
M'Devitt John, lab., Filbert E Sch 3d
M'Devitt John, curb setter, N W 5th and Catharine
M'Devitt John, weaver, Harmstead n Sch 4th
M'Devitt John, stovemr. 4 Galbraith's ct
M'Devitt John, carp. Carlton ab Sch 7th
M'Devitt John, moulder, Carberry ct
M'Devitt John, clothing, High bet Sch 4th & 5th
M'Devitt Mary, shop, vineyard (F V)
M'Devitt Patrick, lab., Hamilton n William
M'Devitt Patrick, plumber, rear 33 Marriott's la bel 6th
M'Devitt Patrick, lab., High n Sch 4th
M'Devitt Richard, omnibusses, Palmer above Queen
M'Devitt Thomas, blacksmith, Marble ab 10th, h 12 Juniper la
M'Devitt William, weaver, 275 N Front
M'Devitt Wm. shoemr. 63 Walnut
M'Devitt Wm., yeoman, Callowhill ab 13th
M'Devitt William, tavern, 273 N Front
M'Donald Aaron, hardwr., S E Beach & Maiden (K)
M'Donald Abigail, 6th n Washington (S)
M'Donald Alexander, shop, 60 New Market
M'Donald Alex., shop, High and Sch Front
M'Donald Andrew, tobacconist, 7 Blunston's av
M'Donald Andrew lab., Camac ab G T road
M'Donald Arch'd., blacksm., Dorothy n Sch 3d
M'Donald Barney, engineer, Fitler n 2d
M'Donald Bernard, grocer, 146 Lombard
M'Donald Catharine, 7th ab Little Poplar
M'Donald Daniel, brickmr., Carpenter ab 12th
M'Donald Daniel, cabman, 22 Sergeant
M'Donald David, vict., New Crown bel Green

M'Donald Edmund, tobacconist, Callowhill n Sch 3d
M'Donald Elizabeth, Clinton & Oxford (K)
M'Donald Esther, shop, 3 Cresson's al
M'Donald George, weaver, Perry bel Master
M'Donald George, W., locksmith, 71½ N 6th, h Lewis ab Poplar
M'Donald Hester, shop, S E Church & Prime
M'Donald Hugh, tavern, 162 N Water
M'Donald James, hatter, Korndaffer's ct
M'Donald James, coachman, 11 Prosperous al
M'Donald James, dealer, N E 7th & High
M'Donald James, weavr., Cadwalader bel Phœnix
M'Donald Jas., lab., Marlboro' ab Beach (K)
M'Donald Jas., cooper, Jefferson ab Broad
M'Donald Jas., cooper, 15 Jones' al, h Lewis ab Broad
M'Donald Jeremiah, lab. 15 Reckless
M'Donald John, teacher, 211½ S 2d
M'Donald John, cooper, 39 N 2d, h St John bel Beaver (K)
M'Donald Mariner, Olive ab 11th
M'Donald Mary, shop, 31 Bonsall
M'Donald Mary Ann, b h, 86 Union
M'Donald Mary Ann, M'Namany's ct
M'Donald Patrick, weaver, 54 Fitzwater
M'Donald Patrick, lab., Biddle's al
M'Donald Randall, weaver, Phoenix ab 3d
M'Donald R., grocery, Caldwell & Sch Beach
M'Donald Samuel, wheelwright, 6th & Parrish
M'Donald Sarah Ann, Emerald
M'Donald Terrence, weaver, 616 N 3d
M'Donald Wm., tavern, 87 E Plum
M'Donald Wm., wheelwright, 2d and Wharton, h 2d bel Wharton
M'Donald Wright, machinist, Clare
M'Donnell Ann, wid., 2 Middleton's ct
M'Donnell Charles, tinman, 348 N 2d
M'Donnell Hugh, shop, 39 W North
M'Donnell Hugh, lab. Camac ab G T road
M'Donnell Jas., druggist, S W 4th & Lombard
M'Donnell James, carp., 206 S Front
M'Donnell Jas. M. grocer, 24 New
M'Donnell Margaret, Carlton ab Sch 3d
M'Donnell Mordecai, Wood bel Sch 3d
M'Donnell Nicholas, lab., Fitler bel Harrison(K)
M'Donough Abraham, chairmaker, 113 S 2d, h 96 S 2d
M'Donough Charles, clothing store, 216 Cedar, h 201 Shippen
M'Donough James, tailor, 32 N 8th
M'Donough James, trader, Carpenter ab 4th
M'Donough John, weaver, Jefferson bel G T road
M'Donough Margaret, b. h., 145 N Front
M'Donough Michael, gilder, 34 Cadwalader (K)
M'Donough Patrick, cars, 3 Nectarine
M'Dougal John, manuf. William bel Edward (K)
M'Dowell Andrew, weaver, 7th bel Baker
M'DOWELL & DAY, dry goods, 68 N 3d
M'Dowell James, stevedore, 190 Christian
M'Dowell James, carp., Lombard W Sch 6th
M'Dowell James, iron roller, Fralcy's al (K)
M'Dowell John, lab., Sch 3d bel Market
M'Dowell John, carp. Centre ab Brown

M'Dowell John, spinner, Sch 5th & Spruce
M'Dowell John, Jr., mer., 68 N 3d
M'Dowell John, D. D., 175 Sp Garden
M'Dowell Jos., stationer, 37 High, h 234 Mulberry
M'Dowell Lydia, dry goods, S W 6th & Locust
M'Dowell Martha, 11th bel Cedar
M'DOWELL RICHARD W., coal, 117 S 3d, h S W 6th and Locust
M'Dowell Saml., shoemr. R road ab Buttonwood
M'Dowell Thomas, S W Poplar & Charlotte
M'Dowell Wm., lab. 296 Front
M'Dowell William A., D. D., cor secty and agt Board of Missions, 29 Sansom, h S W 11th & Wood
M'Dowell Wm. H. engraver, N E 5th & Chestnut, h 163 N 11th
M'Duff James, weaver, 7 Lloyd's ct
M'Elmecl James, cordw., 25 Flower
M'Elroy Adam, carp., S W 4th & Brown, h 416 N 5th
M'Elroy Archibald, publisher of the Philadelphia Directory, h 127 N 12th
M'Elroy Eliza, gentw., Washington ab 9th
M'Elroy Geo., weaver, 2d n Fitler (K)
M'Elroy Geo., marble dresser, 234 Wood
M'Elroy Hugh, lab. Vernon bel 11th
M'Elroy James F. M. carp. 491 S Front
M'Elroy Jane, 43 Currant al
M'Elroy Martha Miss, 193 Christian
M'Elroy Patrick, tobacconist, Scriver's ct
M'Elroy Patrick, shop, 6 St Mary
M'Elroy Paul, weaver, China row (K)
M'Elroy Peter, tailor, 12 Plum
M'Elroy Richard D., dry goods, 463 High, h Filbert E of Sch 7th
M'Elroy Robert, weaver, 11 Vernon
M'Elroy Robert, weaver, 19 Perry
M'Elroy Wash., watchman, Jones n Sch 5th
M'Elwee Alexander, weaver, M'Duffie n Sch 3d
M'Elwee Bernard, weaver, Mariner ab 13th
M'Elwee John W. book keeper, 249 S 10th
M'Elwee Patrick, lab., Beach bel Chestnut
M'Elwee Wm, farmer, Murray n Sch 2d
M'Euen Alexander, printer, Carlisle's ct
M'Euen John, Callowhill ab Sch 3d
M'Euen Thomas, M. D. 298 Walnut
M'Ewen Alexander, weaver, Pearl bel William
M'Ewen Andrew, weaver, Front bel Oxford
M'Ewen James, stables, O Y road ab Noble, h 269 N 5th
M'Ewen Jane, spooler, Hope bel Master
M'Ewen John, brassfounder, Hughes' ct
M'Ewen John, tailor, 20 Perry
M'Ewen John, lab., Sch 7th ab Locust
M'Ewen John, N E 3d and Shippen
M'Ewen Matthew H., grocery, 235 N 6th
M'Ewen Robt., carp., Filbert n Sch 4th
M'Ewen Rachel, Robinson's ct
M'Ewen Robert, cordw., 12th and Whitehall
M'EWEN & SCHEETZ, grocers, 235 N 6th
M'Ewen Wm. engineer, 6 Hause's ct
M'Ewen Wm., ladies' shoemr., 33 Perry
M'Fadden Douglass, carp. Amber n Phoenix (K)

M'Fadden D., stone cut, 1 William (F M)
M'Fadden James, lab., Bedford bel Clifton
M'Fadden James, acct., 36 S Front, h 199 N 7th
M'Fadden John, carp., 28 Jones, h Amber n Phœnix (K)
M'Fadden John, lab. Marriott ab 5th
M'Fadden Michael, nailer, Penn ab Maiden (K)
M'Fadden Robert, grocery, Milton ab 10th
M'Fadden Saml., weav., rear Amber ab Phœnix
M'Fadden Samuel H., mer., 36 Bank, h 4th ab Wharton
M'FADDEN & WATKINS, mers, 36 Bank
M'FADDEN WILLIAM, mahog'y sawmill, 5½ Sterling alley, h 9 Cherry
M'Faden Sarah, George ab 13th
M'Fall Henry, tavern, 287 Cedar
M'Fall John, carp., 3 Hubbell
M'Fall John, carter, Callowhill ab Sch 2d
M'Fall Thomas, driver, Dugan
M'Falls John, grocer, c Sch 3d and Cedar
M'Falls Mich., oyster h., 481 High
M'Farland Alex., lab., Franklin bel Cherry (K)
M'Farland Andrew, grocer, High E Sch 2d
M'Farland And., flour & feed store, High ab 7th
M'FARLAND JAMES, coal, Cedar and Broad
M'Farland James, bootmr. 100 Swanson
M'Farland James, Carlton n Sch 2d
M'Farland James, gent., 212 Shippen
M'Farland Jas , coachman, 5 Randall
M'Farland Jane, 13th bel Cedar
M'Farland John, weaver, Fitler bel Harrison (K)
M'Farland John, drayman, Carlton bel Sch 2d
M'Farland John, printer, rear Parker's al
M'Farland John, weaver, Hope bel Master
M'Farland John, 13th bel Catherine
M'Farland Joseph, weaver, Nixon ab Wood
M'Farland J. B., mer., 105 High h 145 N 4th
M'Farland Park H., printer, 3d bel Prime
M'Farland Robt., cordw., 130 S 12th
M'Farland Saml., machinist, Carbon pl
M'Farland Thomas, bootmr., Sch 5th ab High
M'Farland Walter, tobacconist, 73 Green
M'Farland William, Chestnut W Sch 3rd
M'Farland Wm., shoemr., Sycamore ab 11th
M'Farr Wm., bottler, Wood bel Sch 2d
M'Farren Robert, carpenter, Front bel Reed, h Prime ab Front
M'Fate Samuel, dep sheriff, 37 Coates
M'Fee John, carpet manuf., Hamilton & Sch 6th, h 516 High
M'Feeters Robert, lab. Lombard E Sch 6th
M'Ferren John, shoemr., 3rd bel Prime
M'Feters Andrew, coachman, Dean ab Centre
M'Feters David, dyer, Centre n 13th
M'Fetrich Robert, cordw., 168 S 11th
M'Fetrich Samuel, weaver, 19 Lebanon
M'Fetrich Wm., gilder, rear Poplar ab 6th
M'Fetteridge James, Lawrence ab 12th
M'Fetteridge Matthew, drayman, Garrett's ct
M'Fetteridge Samuel, grocer, 13th & Shippen
M'Fettrich John, lab., N. E 12th and High
M'Fillin James, tailor, 214 Cedar
M'Gahan Thos., porter, 5 Brooks' ct
M'Gahey, James, printer, 5th ab German
M, Gahey Wm., tobacconist, 174 S 5th

M'Gann John, lab., Hay's ct
M'Gann Mary, 52 St John
M'Garragh Alexander, teacher, Sch 8th & M : ler's al
M'Garrigle Wm., weaver, F road bel Master
M'Garrity Peter, lab., Beach ab Locust
M'Garry Abraham, grocer, 213 S 6th
M'Garry Alex., carter, Wood n Sch Front
M'Garry John, 2 Linn (F M)
M'Garry Michael, labourer, rear 15 N 13th
M'Garry Sarah, grocer, S E 11th & Cedar
M'Garvey Anthony, boot mr., 37 S 8th
M'GARVEY EDWARD, collector, Sch 4th a Cedar,
M'Garvey Edward, lab., Sch 6th bel Lombard
M'Garvey Geo., lab., Mechanic ab Franklin
M'Garvey & Hogan, boot mrs., 37 S 8th
M'Garvey James, weaver, Hancock bel Phoenix
M'Garvey Jas., Barker ab Sch 7th
M'Garvey John, lab., Lewis n Sch 7th
M'Gaughey Alexander, labourer, Sch 8th abov: Sassafras
M'Gaughey Charles, lab., Pine n Ashton
M'Gaughey Samuel, cordw., Sch 8th bel Vine
M'Gaughy Moses, porter, Sch 8th n Vine
M'Gaw Ann, huckster, Hope bel Master (K)
M'Gaw Robt., weaver, 6th bel Little Poplar
M'Gee Ann, shop, 30 Brown
M'Gee Andrew, weaver, Wood ab Sch 6th
M'Gee Angeline, grocer, 321 Shippen
M'Gee Barnard, drayman, 23 Flower
M'Gee Henry, tailor, Lombard bel Sch 7th
M'Gee Henry, lab., 63 Bedford
M'Gee James, weaver, White's ct bel 13th
M'Gee James, weaver, Union bel West (K)
M'Gee John, cordw., 123 Plum
M'Gee John, weaver, Perry bel Master (K)
M'Gee John, lab., Hamilton and Fairmount
M'Gee Julianna, Church and Christian
M'Gee Nicholas, lab., Flower ab Christian
M'Gee Patrick, lab., William ab Hamilton
M'Gee Patrick painter, Flower ab Christian
M'Gee Richard, shoemr., 6 Lawrence
M'Gee Richard, bookstore, 55 Gaskill
M'Gee Thos., lab., George n Beach
M'Gee William, grocer, Shippen & Shippen l
M'Gee Wm., butcher, Poplar ab Lewis
M'Geehan Chas., lab., Sassafras n Sch 8th
M'Geehan John, weaver, 7th bel Christian
M'Geehan Peter, cordw., Shippen bel Broad
M'GEOY MICHAEL, tavern, 9 Walnut
M'Gerrah James, carp., 7 Lodge al., h 28 Per:
M'Gerrill Hugh, weaver, Fitler ab 2d (K)
M'Gettigan John, baker, Shippen and Broad
M'Gettigen Patrick, bootmr., 59 Fitzwater
M'Gill Andw., weaver, Penn bel Shackamaxo:
M'Gill Chas., ropemr., Duke ab Vienna (K)
M'Gill David, weaver, Stewart ct
M'Gill Isabella, Pine ab Sch 7th
M'Gill James, cooper, h 258 S Front
M'Gill James, tailor, 71 Union
M'Gill Matthias, sexton St. Paul's ch, h 6 Pear
M'Gill Mary, widow, Spruce bel Sch 4th
M'Gill Michael, corder, Coates st wharf, h 1: Green

M'Gill Patrick, cordw., rear Mechanic below George
M'Gill Saml., cooper, 45 S Front, h 6 Christian
M'Gillon P., blacksmith, New Market & Duke
M'Gin Owen, lab., 246 Christian
M'Ginity Mary, nurse, 25 N 7th
M'Ginity Owens, Powell ab Francis (F V)
M'Ginley Barney, lab., 7 Spafford st
M'Ginley Daniel, paper maker, Kessler's al n 4th
M'Ginley Edward, grocer, Murray & Sch 3rd
M'Ginley James, engineer, 9th ab Coates
M'Ginley James, tanner, N W 7th and Willow
M'Ginley James, lab., Fairmount
M'Ginley John, lab., William ab Hamilton F M
M'Ginley John, packer, 147 Cherry
M'Ginley Townsend, rear 140 Brown
M'Ginn James, lab., 258 Shippen
M'Ginnis Conrad, butcher, Pleasant ab 12th
M'Ginnis David, plast., rear 153 G T road (K)
M'Ginnis Henry, porter, Ann ab 12th
M'Ginnis James, tailor, Harmony bel 4th
M'Ginnis James, blacksmith, Robinson's ct (K)
M'Ginnis John, tailor, 13 Relief st
M'Ginnis John, lab., Carpenter ab 8th
M'Ginnis John, grocery, 13th & Adams
M'Ginnis Michael, baker, 148 S Front
M'Ginnis Michael, stevedore, 284 N Front
M'Ginnis Richard, weaver, G T road ab Master
M'Ginnis Robert, grocer, 7 N 10th
M'Ginnis R. Mrs. 197 N Front
M'Ginnis Timothy, gent., 87 Apple
M'Ginnis Vessey, weaver, rear Fitler n 2d (K)
M'Ginnis Wm. coachman. George ab 11th
M'Ginnis Wm. cordw. Sch 6th bel Chestnut
M'Ginty Jas., lab., rear Christian bel 10th
M'Ginty Jas., rear 108 Plum
M'Girr Felix, carter, 6 Hubbell
M'Girr Owen, 16 Strawberry
M'Girr Patrick, cabman, 12 Benton
M'Githan John, lab., Vine ab Nixon
M'Gittigan Daniel, 7th bel Fitzwater
M'Gittigan Edwd. lab. 59 Fitzwater
M'Gittigan James, baker, Lombard ab Sch Front
M'Gittigan John, 18 Small
McGittigan John, Baker & Shippen
M'Gittigan Patrick, 4 Boyle's ct
M'Gittigan Thomas, dry goods, 69 Cedar, h 106 S 3d
M'Gittigan Thos., lab., Sch 8th ab Sassafras
M'Given Thomas, malster, West & Cherry (K)
M'Givney John, shoemr., P road bel Christian
M'Glathery Elizabeth, rear 408 N 3d
M'Glathery Isaac, store, 67 N 5th
M'Glathery James, carp., 344 S 5th
M'Glathery John, currier, 321 S 4th
M'Glathery Levi, carp., 13th bel Callowhill
M'Glathery Sarah, 494 S 2d
M'Glaughlin Hugh, cordw., Barker E Sch 4th
M'Glaughlin Jas., carp., 2 Brooks' ct
M'Glaughlin John, lab., Caldwell n Beach
M'Glaughlin John, shoemr., 13th & Walnut al
M'Glaughlin Michael, grocer, Shippen & Shippen l
M'Glaughlin Owen, shop, Marriott bel 5th
M'Glaughlin Saml., driver, Linden ab Sch 7th

M'Glaughlin Sarah, Emerald n Sch 6th
M'Glaughlin T., dealer, Pearl ab 12th
M'Glaughtin James, machinist, Carlton ab 13th
M'Glenn James, tavern, Lombard & Sch 5th
M'Glennon Henry, blacksmith, 7th bel Wash'on
M'Glennon Robert, grocer, Sch Willow ab Pine
M'Glensey John, grocer, N E 13th & High
M'Glensey John, tavern, 4th & Shippen, h 103 Shippen
M'Glensey John, jeweler, Catharine bel 2d
M'Glensey Patrick, lab., Milton ab 11th
M'Glensey Patrick, 264 S 6th
M'Glensey Wm., grocer, S E 13th & Fitzwater
M'Glinn John, lab., 180 N Water
M'Gloin Mich., machinist, Stiles' ct (K)
M'Glue Luke, coach trimmer, 174 Lombard
M'Glue Luke, saddler, 476 S 4th
M'Goarty Francis, shoemr., 12 Juniper al
M'Goldrick Edward, lab., 6 Diamond
M'Goldrick Hugh, carp., 2 Mechanic's av
M'Goldrick James, 30 Barker
M'Goldrick Jas., lab., 5 Baker st
M'Goldrick John, tailor, 240 Christian
M'Goldrick, John, lab., Jones n Sch 4th
M'Gonegal Catharine, 16 Juniper la
M'Gonegal Catharine, Mrs. 8 St Joseph's av
M'Gonegal Daniel, stone cutter, 1 Mechanic's av
M'Gonegal Daniel, lab., 175 N Front
M'Gonegal George, carp., 6th ab Fitzwater
M'Gonegal James, weaver, Clay bel Beech
M'Gonegal James, type caster, 12 Centre
M'Gonegal John, driver, Fitzwater W 7th
M'Gonegal John, type caster, 165 S 11th
M'Gonegal John, type caster, 15 College av
M'Gonegal John, painter, Benton n William (K)
M'Gonegal John, carter, P road ab Carpenter
M'Gonegal Samuel, type caster, 15 College av
M'Gonegal Thos., shop, 7th bel Carpenter
M'Gonegal Wm., bootmr., M'Kean's ct
M'Gonigle Patrick, bootmr., 147 S 10th
M'Gonnall Jas., lab., Walnut n Beach
M'Gonnall Thomas, buttonmr. Little Green (K)
M'Gonnigal James, tavern, Callowhill n William
M'Gork Francis, weaver, rear G T road below Phoenix
M'Gork Margaret, Keenan's ct (K)
M'Gouldrick Thomas, lab. 2 William (F M)
M'Govern Bridget, shop, 440 High
M'Govern Edward, china mer., 321 High
M'Govern James, lab., Carpenter ab 8th
M'Govern Thomas, 23 Blackberry al
M'Govern Thomas, tavern, 198 N Water
M'Gowan Ann, 5 Marshall ct
M'Gowan Daniel, lab., Lewis n Sch 5th
M'Gowan Edward, police officer, 288 S 6th
M'Gowan Eliza, gentw., Floyd's ct
M'Gowan Elizabeth, Plum ab 4th
M'Gowan Hugh, boilermr. G T road ab Thompson (K)
M'Gowan James, fire proof chest & stove manuf., S E Front & Mead, h 35 Beck (S)
M'Gowan John, grocer, 142 N 2d
M'Gowan Mich., bricklayer, Loud ab 9th
M'Gowan Patrick, gent., 91 Walnut
M'Gowan Peter, teacher, 27 Perry

M'Gowan Samuel, umbrella mr., 266½ N 2d
M'Gowan Wm., blacksmith, 2 Southampton ct
M'GOWAN WILLIAM, iron founder, N W Broad and Fairview, h 91 Walnut
M'Gowen Hugh, lab., Sch 3d n Lombard
M'Gowen James, tailor, 172 S 9th
M'Gowen James, lab., Poplar bel Broad
M'Gowen John, drayman, 4 Fetter la
M'Gowen John, tailor, Dannaker's ct
M'Gowen Joseph, 3 Salem al
M'Gowen Mary Ann, agent, 403 Chestnut
M'Gowen Roger, lab., Sch 2nd ab High
M'Gowen Wm., shop, Crabb ab Shippen
M'Gowen Wm. blacksmith, Pleasant ab 12th
M'Grain Patrick, lab., rear 14 Quarry
M'Granagan Susanna, Locust n Broad
M'Grann Patrick, grocer, 6th & Shippen
M'Grann Philip, drayman, 8 Mary's ct
M'Grann Rosetta, Carlton bel Sch 2d
M'Grannigan Patrick, lab., 8th bel South
M'Grath Andrew, 248 S 6th
M'Grath Charles, plasterer, 15 Stamper's al
M'Grath Charles, dealer, 13 College av
M'Grath Edward, ostler, 5 Quarry
M'Grath Hannah, dealer, 442 High
M'Grath Henry, bookseller, 1 S 8th
M'Grath Hiram, cordw. 45 Crabb
M'Grath John, dry goods, 207 S 2d
M'Grath John, grate mr., 32 N 6th
M'Grath John, tailor, 207 Chestnut
M'Grath John, lab. rear 123 Plum
M'Grath John W., mer.,78 High, h 52 Coates
M'Grath Lawrence, b h, 79 S Water
M'Grath Michael, labourer, 142 N Water
M'Grath Michael, porter, 12th bel Coates
M'Grath Michael, shop, Bedford & 7th
M'Grath Michael, shop, S W Coates & St John
M'Grath Patrick, lab., 1 Moffitt's ct
M'Grath Philip, lab., 194 N Water
M'Grath R. M. D., dentist, 328 Mulberry
M'Grath Samuel, tailor, 179 Chestnut, h 164 N 8th
M'Grath & Sarmiento, tailors, 211 Chestnut
M'Grath Thomas, tailor, 211 Chestnut, h 173 Callowhill
M'Grath Thomas, weaver, Milton ab 11th
M'Grath Wm., bartender, High ab Sch 8th
M'Grath William, watchman, 191 Christian
M'Graw Hugh, lab., Cadwalader bel Oxford (K)
M'Graw Hugh, Jr., morocco dresser, Cadwalader bel Oxford (K)
M'Gregor John, flax dress., Carpenter ab 13th
M'Gregor Robert, carp. Perry bel Phoenix
M'Gregor Robert, dry goods, 234 Chestnut
M'Grouty Henry, weaver, 30 W Cedar
M'Guckey Wm., weaver, Amber ab Phoenix
M'Guckin Andrew, lab., rear 2d ab Master (K)
M'Guckin Hugh, lab., rear 343 S 5th
M'Guckin James, weaver, 2nd bel Harrison (K)
M'Guckin John, weaver, 11th ab Carpenter
M'Guffin Barnard, lab., Cherry n Sch 8th
M'Guigan Ann, fancy store, 146 S 11th
M'Guigan Ann, Philadelphia Museum Building
M'Guigan Arthur, fruiterer, 410 High
M'Guigan Charles, weaver, 2d bel Master

M'Guigan Charles, weaver, Crown bel Duke (K)
M'Guigan Hugh, weaver, rear G T road below Master
M'Guigan Hugh, lab. rear 117 Callowhill
M'Guigan James, lab., Orange & Lemon
M'Guigan James, lithographer, 116 Chestnut, 57 Plum
M'Guigan James, weaver, China row (K)
M'Guigan James, weaver, 8th ab Catharine
M'Guigan Jas., weav., rear G T road ab Master
M'Guigan John, collector, 19 Powell
M'Guigan Patrick, groc., Crown ab Franklin (K
M'Guigan Thomas, importer, 2 Strawberry
M'Guigan William, naturalist, Philad. Museum, 9th bel Chestnut
M'Guin Margaret, 127 S 4th
M'Guin Thomas, cabinetmr., 135 S 2d
M'Guire Bernard, tailor, 4 Grape ct
M'Guire Hugh, weaver, 2d bel Master
M'Guire Hugh, shop, 255 E Cedar
M'Guire Isaac L., blacksm., Wood ab Sch 8th
M'Guire James, tailor, 7 Grape ct
M'Guire James, manuf., G T road ab Master
M'Guire James, G T road bel Jefferson
M'Guire John, tailor, 18 Barker E Sch 6th
M'Guire John, dyer, Jefferson ab 5th (K)
M'Guire John, lab. rear Charlotte ab Thompson
M'Guire Michael, lab. rear 445 N 4th
M'Guire Noble, tailor, 55 Fitzwater
M'Guire Patrick, lab., 285 S 7th
M'Guire Patrick, sawyer, Charlotte n Master (K
M'Guire Patrick, tavern, Sch Front & High
M'Guire Patrick, weaver, Cadwalader ab Jefferson (K)
M'Guire Patrick, lab. Brown's ct
M'Guire Philip, ostler, rear 89 S 6th
M'Guire Thos., lab., Carlton ab 13th
M'Gurk Alexander, carter, Hancock bel Master
M'Gurk Ann, 91 P road
M'Gurk Francis, weaver, G T road ab Phoenix (K)
M'Gurk John, weaver, Milton bel 11th
M'Gurk Patrick, leather dresser, 74 Locust
M'Gurk Patrick, weaver, 2d above Montgomery (K)
M'Henry Dennis, weaver, Sch 3d ab Spruce
M'Henry George, rear 25 S whfs.
M'Henry James, com. mer., 25 S wharves bel Chestnut,
M'Henry James, weaver, rear G. T. road ab Thompson (K)
M'Henry James, tailor, Barker W of Sch. 5th
M'Henry Margaret, 242 Catharine
M'Henry Mark, manuf., Catharine bel 7th
M'Henry Ruth, Sch 5th ab Cedar
M'Henry Samuel, Sch 5th & Lombard
M'Hugh Dominick, lab., Peach
M'Hugh John, tavern, 133 Shippen
M'Hugh John, shop, Mariner
M'Hugh Margaret, shop, 24 N 13th
M'Hugh Michael, weaver, Milton ab 10th
M'Hugh Patrick, distiller, 399 Sassafras
M'Hugh Patrick, baker, 1 Pascal av
M'Ilhenney Andrew, lab., Cherry ab Queen (K)

M'Ilhenney A., lab., Kinley's ct
M'Ilhenney Daniel, lab., 57 Pegg
M'Ilhenney James, lab., Beach ab Poplar (K)
M'Ilhenney John, blacksmith, Gravel's ct
M'Ilhenney John, dry goods, Poplar ab 13th
M'Ilhenney Joseph E., dentist, 223 Mulberry
M'Ilhenney Thomas, carter, 7th bel Fitzwater
M'Ilhenney William, sec'y. Philad'a. Atheneum and consul for Venezuela, office S W 5th & Chestnut, h 139 Walnut
M'Ilhenney Wm. S., M. D., dentist, 223 Mulberry
M'Ilhenney W. H., mer., 12 S Water, h Parrish bel 8th
M'Ilhone Charles, lab., Perry ab Franklin (K)
M'Ilhone James, carpet weaver, 5 Philip (K)
M'Ilhone Patrick, weav., Crown ab Franklin (K)
M'Illace Francis, weav., Front ab Jefferson (K)
M'Ilree Samuel, 152 S 13th
M'Ilroy Archd., shoemr., Lombard bel Sch. 6th
M'Ilroy Archibald, manuf., S E Broad & Rose
M'Ilroy R., grocer, Shippen la bel Bedford
M'Ilvain Francis, stoves, 12 and h 275 S 8th
M'Ilvain Hiram, blacksm., M road bel Carpenter
M'Ilvain Horatio, printer, 387 S 6th
M'Ilvain Hugh, Lancaster pike (W P)
M'Ilvain Hugh, shoemr., 119 German
M'Ilvain Humphrey, Chestnut (W P)
M'Ilvain James, mer., Woodland (W P)
M'Ilvain James & Co., lum. mers., Washington (W P)
M'Ilvain John H., lumber mer., h Bridge (M Village)
M'Ilvain John S., coal mer., Broad n Locust, h Sch 8th ab Spruce
M'Ilvain J. A., lumb. yard, 8th and Washington
M'Ilvain Neal, lab., rear High n Sch. 2d
M'Ilvain Richard, gent., Washington (W P)
M'Ilvain Robt. L., 11th bel Spruce
M'Ilvain Wm., stovemr., 25 Elfreth's al
M'Ilvaine A., cabinetmr., 353 E Lombard
M'Ilvaine George, printer, Nectarine bel 10th
M'Ilvaine Henry, att'y. and coun., 48 S 4th
M'Ilvaine J. B., mer., 3 Monroe pl
M'Ilvaine Wm., jr., artist, S E 9th and Walnut
M'Ilvanna David, weav., Philip ab Jefferson (K)
M'Ilvany Matthew, weaver, Otter n Front (K)
M'Ilvany Terrence, lab., Gray's ct
M'Ilwain Geo., trimmings, 152 Mulberry
M'Ilwain J. K. & Son, trimmings, 44 S 2d & 208 Chestnut
M'Ilwain Robert, clothier, 316 Cedar
M'Ilwain Robert, weaver, M'Duffie n Sch 3d
M'Ilwain Thomas, shoemr., M'Duffie n Sch 2nd
M'Intier Eliza, 12 Clark
M'Intire Ann, widow, Murray n Sch. 3d
M'Intire Ann, shop, Rachel & Poplar
M'Intire Charles, carp., George ab Plum
M'Intire Edwin, brushmr., Cox bel 2d
M'Intire Elizabeth, gentw., 160 S Front
M'Intire George, manuf., 30 Pratt
M'Intire Henry, weaver, Richard n Sch 6th
M'Intire Hugh, tailor, 3 Clifton
M'Intire Isaiah, shoemaker, 133 S Front
M'Intire James pedler, Lombard n Sch 6th
M'Intire James, lab., Cedar bel Clifton

M'Intire John, lab., Madison av
M'Intire John, carter, Garden bel Willow
M'Intire John S., George W of Broad
M'Intire J. F., blacksm., Beach bel Hanover (K)
M'Intire Mary, Crown ab Duke
M'Intire Mary Mrs., 34 Chester
M'Intire Patrick, paper carrier, 235 Christian
M'Intire Patrick, shop, 193 S 6th
M'Intire Peter, lab., Charlotte ab Thompson (K)
M'Intire Richard, bootmr., 406 Cedar
M'Intire Sarah, gentw., Marlborough bel Allen
M'Intire Thos., lab., Philip ab Jefferson (K)
M'Intire Wm., carp., 60 George
M'Intosh Benjamin, lab., Allen bel Shackamaxon
M'Intosh Charles, stonecut., 12th bel Poplar
M'Intosh James, shoemr., 14 Harmony
M'Intosh John, cordw., 28 Parker
M'Intosh Mary Ann, dry goods, N E 10th & High
M'Intosh Wm., ladies shoemr., S E 3d & Church al, h 165 Green
M'Intosh Wm., grocer, 136 Locust
M'Intosh Wm. C., distiller, c 4th & Carpenter, h 75 Carpenter
M'Intyre Andrew, 8 Dean
M'Intyre Archibald, gent., Walnut ab Broad
M'Intyre Bernard, lab., 3 Robinson's ct
M'Intyre John, att'y at law, Walnut ab 6th,
M'Intyre John, weaver, Nixon ab Callowhill
M'Intyre Peter, tailor, 159 S 11th
M'Kain Esther, Cedar bel Broad
M'Kain John, lab., Shippen ab Broad
M'Kane Saml., lab., McDuffie & Sch 4th
M'Kanna Arthur, dealer, 438 High
M'Kanna Bridget, 8 Dilk's ct
M'Kanna Francis, bottler, Bedford ab 7th
M'Kanna Mary, shop, 287 S 7th
M'Kanna Patrick, grocer, 182 Shippen
M'Kanna Thomas, porter, Budden's alley
M'Karaher C., fancy store, 27 N 2d
M'Karney Patrick, weaver, Atherton
M'Kay Elizabeth, widow of Jeremiah, tavern, c G T road and Rose
M'Kay Geo., printer, 358 S 4th
M'Kay John, cordwainer, 358 S 4th
M'Kay John, jr., printer, Walnut n Sch 3d
M'Kay Thos., cabtmr., 358 S 4th
M'Keague Danl., lab., Sch 6th bel Pine
M'Kean, Boric & Co., importers, 45 Dock
M'Kean Elizabeth, 11th bel Buttonwood
M'Kean H. Pratt, mer., 45 Dock, h Spruce ab 10th
M'Kean Mary F., gentw., 222 N 9th
M'Kean Patrick, shoemr., Griswold alley
M'Kean Thos., seaman, 198 Lombard
M'Kean Wm., capt. U. S. N., 198 S 9th
M'Kean Wm. V., type caster, 117 Christian
M'Kearny James, lab., 11 Marshall's ct
M'Kechnie Robert, driver, rear of 118 W High
M'Kee Ann, washer, Bedford bel 8th
M'Kee Edmund, bookbinder, Sch 3d ab Walnut
M'Kee James, weaver, 154 S 13th
M'Kee John, weaver, Cadwalader bel Jefferson
M'Kee John, lab., rear Christian bel 9th
M'Kee John H., 13 S Sch 7th

M'Kee Joseph, manuf., 19 Brinton
M'Kee Lawrence, sailmr., 188 N Water
M'Kee Patrick, manuf., G T road ab Master
M'Kee Peter, tanner, 252 Sassafras
M'Kee Robert, furniture, 424 High
M'Kee Robert, weaver, Shippen ab 13th
M'Kee, Robert, shoemr., Shippen bel 13th
M'Kee Samuel, manuf., Howard bel Master
M'Kee Sarah, S W Cherry and Brown
M'Kee Thomas, engineer, Crown bel West (K)
M'Kee Thomas, bootmr., 168 N Water
M'Kee Thomas, mer., 19 Church al
M'Kee Wm., mer., 19 Church al, h 386 Walnut
M'Kee Wm., weaver, Hope ab Master (K)
M'Kee Wm., manuf., G T road bel Phoenix
M'Kee Wm. A., com. mer. & agent for Norfolk
    & Petersburg packets, 24 N whfs, h 9 Coates
M'KEE WM. & CO., importers. 19 Church al
M'Keen Henry, watchmaker, 142 High, h 11
    Merchant
M'Keever Bernard, shop, 235 Shippen
M'Keever Elizabeth, Winter (N L)
M'Keever Elizabeth, gentw., 120 E Pine
M'Keever H. B., teacher, Locust ab 8th
M'Keever Isaac, stone cutter, 349 S 5th
M'Keever James, jeweller, Queen n 4th
M'Keever James, cordw. Queen ab Shackamaxon
M'Keever John, 207 Spruce
M'Keever John B., mer., 39 N wharves, h 120
    Pine
M'Keever Peter, ropemaker, Newton (S)
M'Keever Thos. M., painter, N W Decatur and
    Carpenter, h 248 Shippen
M'Keever Wm., lab., 24 Gaskill
M'Kelvy Alex., gent, Lombard ab Sch. 2d
M'Kelvy James, boatman, Sch Beach ab Spruce
M'Kendrick Joseph, lab., Sch. 4th and Barker
M'Kenna Alex., weaver, Master and Hope (K)
M'Kenna Anthony, suspender & girth mr., 44
    Shippen
M'Kenna Charles, lab., Reiff's ct (K)
M'Kenna Edward, carp., Christian bel 5th
M'Kenna James, dealer, St Mary bel 7th
M'Kenna James, lab., Milton ab 11th
M'Kenna James, lab., Marriott's la bel 6th
M'Kenna John, baker, 86 Fitzwater
M'Kenna John, trader, Federal ab 7th
M'Kenna Mary Ann, Juniper bel Walnut
M'Kenna Patrick, ostler, Spruce E Sch 4th
M'Kenna Patrick, lab., 21 Crabb
M'Kenna Ross, weaver, 9 William (F M)
M'Kenney James, lab., G. T. road bel 4th
M'Kenney John, sashmr., Lewis ab Poplar
M'Kenney John, chandler, 118 German
M'Kenney Matilda, shop, 77 New Market
M'Kenny James, stone mason, 117 G T road (K)
M'Kensrey John, weaver, rear 2d ab Master (K)
M'Kenty Samuel, weaver, Otter ab Front (K)
M'Kenzie Janette, Front bel Greenwich
M'Keogh James, grocer, N E 2d and Spruce
M'Keon John, dry goods, 203 Cedar, h 148 S 5th
M'Keon John, bookseller, 241 S 6th
M'Keon Mrs., milliner, 148 S 5th
M'Keown Benj., shoemr., 325 S 2d
M'Keown George, tavern and refect., 227 S 2d

M'Keown Jane, corsetmr., 654 N 2d (K)
M'Keown John, weaver, Harmstead st
M'Keown Thomas, weaver, Harmstead st
M'Kern Edw., weaver, Cadwalader ab Jefferso;
M'Kernan Edward, Sch. 3d ab High
M'Kernan Hugh, lab., Sch. 5th bel High
M'Kernan James, mechanic, 12 Cedar
M'Kernan James, whf. builder, Sch Beach and
    Spruce
M'Kernan James, weaver, 6 Ulrich's row (K)
M'Kernan Michael, blacksmith, rear 1 Paschall's
    al
M'Kernan Michael, lab., Spruce n Sch Front
M'Kernan Owen, weaver, 2 Ulrich's row (K)
M'Kernan Pat., lab., Lombard ab Sch. Front
M'Kernan Patrick, tavern, G T road ab Thomp-
    son
M'Kernan Robert, weaver, Pine n Beach
M'Kewen Peter, gas fitter, 42 Carpenter, h 7
    Lodge al
M'Kibbin John, porter, Cedar & Hurst
M'Kibbin John, vinegar, Sch 4th ab Spruce
M'Kibbin John, grocery, 199 E Cedar
M'Kibbin William, ice, Sch 5th ab Chestnut.
M'Kibbin Wm., shoe mr., Cedar ab 12th
M'Killips Charles, mer., 365 High
M'Kim J. M., Anti-Slavery office, 31 N 5th, h
    97 N 10th
M'Kinley Alexander, coachman, Academy
M'Kinley Alexander, att'y at law, 187 Walnut
M'Kinley Archibald, Dunton bel Otter (K)
M'Kinley & Bradley, coopers, 52 New
M'Kinley B. B., teacher of deaf & dumb, Juniper
    ab Pine
M'Kinley Elizabeth, 115 N Juniper
M'Kinley Hugh, 184 N 13th
M'Kinley James, grocer, 285½ High, h 9 Dugan
M'KINLEY JAMES & CO., grocers, 285½ High
M'Kinley John, grocer, N W 12th & High
M'Kinley John, cooper, 52 New, h 8 Branner's al
M'Kinley John S., carp., 3 Lawrence's ct
M'Kinley Mary, Tiller's ct
M'KINLEY NATHAN, alderman, 6th ab Queen
M'Kinley Robt., conveyancer, 5th & Library
M'Kinley Stephen, spinner, 9 Mechanic
M'Kinley Thomas, carter, 339 S 5th
M'Kinley William, grocer, 5 S 5th, h 4 Sansom
M'Kinley William Jr., grocer, 307 High
M'Kinley Wm., carter, Sch 4th bel High
M'Kinney Alexander, weaver, West n Marlboro'
M'Kinney Felix, lab., Sch 6th bel High
M'Kinney Francis, lab., rear 112 Cherry
M'Kinney James, weaver, West n Marlboro'
M'Kinney James, lab., Cedar E Sch 4th
M'Kinney John, weaver, Fitler n 2d
M'Kinney Jno., jr. cordw., rear 6th ab Franklin
M'Kinney John, weaver, 27 Otter st (K)
M'Kinney Joseph, warper, Watts
M'Kinney Owen, soap & cand., Apple & Frank-
    lin (K)
M'Kinney Owen, stone mason, 13 Crabb st
M'Kinney Saml., butcher, Ogden ab Sch 8th
M'Kinney Samuel, cordw., 6 Friendship ct
M'Kinney Thomas, lab., rear Hanover ab Frank-
    lin (K)

M'Kinney Wm., blacksm., Sch. 4th & High
M'Kinsey Ann, 28 Beck (S)
M'Kinsey Jas., weaver, Jefferson bel Philip
M'Kinsey Sidney, rear 2d bel Oxford (K)
M'Kinzey Henry, barber, 303 Walnut
M'Kinzie Alex. D., gold printer, 90 Cherry, h 132 N Juniper
M'KISSACK DAVID, grocer, Sch 7th & State
M'Kissick & Brother, bootms., 33 S 8th
M'Kissick Hannah, Fitzwater ab Hubbell
M'Knight David, grocer, St John & Green
M'Knight John, weaver, Bedford ab 12th
M'Knight John, weaver, Christian bel 12th
M'Knight Rachel, shop, Sch. 6th & George
M'Knight Robt., tinsm., Howard ab Phoenix (K)
M'Knight Robert, weaver, Howard bel Master
M'Knight Samuel, lab. F road bel Otter
M'Knight Wm., bootmr., 427 Chestnut, h 12th and Salem al
M'Knight Wm., watchman, Vine ab 12th
M'Koy Robert, stamp cutter, 5 Tammany
M'Lae, Roderic, lab. 23 Gaskill
M'Lain Thos., weaver, 4th bel Jefferson
M'Lanagan Jane, 10 Centre
M'Lanahan J., mer., 14 Chestnut, h 138 Walnut
M'LANAHAN J. & CO., mers., 14 Chestnut
M'Lane A., painter, 303 Shippen
M'Lane Bernard, carter, Powell (F V)
M'Lane John, tailor, 6 Randall's ct
M'Lane Matthias, ladies' shoemr., Crown n Vine
M'Lane Nathan, lab., rear Brown bel 12th
M'Laran James, contractor, 47 Coates
M'Laren Alex., dealer, Traquair's ct
M'Laughlin And., Western pl
M'Laughlin Bernard, tailor, 180 Lombard
M'Laughlin Bernard, cordw., Front n Almond
M'Laughlin Bridget, rear 94 N 11th
M'Laughlin Caleb, bookbinder, rear 209 Cherry
M'Laughlin Cornelius, lab., Walnut ab Sch 2d
M'Laughlin Daniel, lab. 2d ab Master (K)
M'Laughlin Daniel, att'y. & coun., 32 Prune
M'Laughlin Daniel, lab., Murray
M'Laughlin Douglass, iron roller, Townsend's av
M'Laughlin Edw, boatman, Mulberry & Ashton
M'Laughlin Geo., carter, Sch 6th n Lombard
M'Laughlin George, cordw., Sheppard's ct
M'Laughlin George, weaver, F road bel Master
M'Laughlin George, drayman, Elizabeth ab Polpar (N L)
M'Laughlin George, weaver, Cedar ab 7th
M'Laughlin Hugh, manuf., 623 N 2d
M'Laughlin James, steward Navy Yard, h 13 Federal
M'Laughlin James, shop, 34 P road
M'Laughlin James, carter, N E 10th & Morgan
M'Laughlin James, shoemr. Sch 8th ab Wood
M'Laughlin Jas., lab., Mulberry n Sch 2d
M'Laughlin Jas., porter, 416 Sassafras
M'LAUGHLIN JOHN, livery stable, 14 and h 16 Prune
M'Laughlin John, clothes, N W 7th & Bedford
M'Laughlin John, lab., Sch 7th n Vine
M'Laughlin John, lab., 131½ N 2nd
M'Laughlin John, iron roller, 13 Ellen (N L)
M'Laughlin John, carp. rear G T road ab 5th

M'Laughlin John, lab., Bedford ab 6th
M'Laughlin John, dealer, 5 Eutaw
M Laughlin Jno., manuf., Shackamaxon n Franklin (K)
M'Laughlin John, coachman, rear 260 Sassafras
M'Laughlin John, lab., 2 Robinson's ct
M'Laughlin John, lab., 130 German
M'Laughlin John, cordw., Court al
M'Laughlin Margaret Mrs., 3d ab Federal
M'Maughlin Michael, carp., Gabell's ct
M'Laughlin Michael, blacksmith, 7 Juniper al
M'Laughlin Patrick, cordw., High nb Sch 4th
M'Laughlin Rachel, 323 S 6th
M'Laughlin Reuben, milkman, G T road ab 5th
M'Laughlin Robt., stove finisher, Court al
M'Laughlin Robt., shoemr., 147 S 10th
M'Laughlin Saml., chandler, Steam Mill al
M'Laughlin Terence, weaver, 2d above Master
M'Laughlin Thomas, fruiterer, Carpenter ab 8th
M'Laughlin Thomas, paver, Cedar bel 8th
M'Laughlin Wm., grocer, Cedar bel Broad
M'Laurin G. S. painter, Green E of Broad
M'Lean Archibald, cordw., Grubb
M'Lean James, camphine oil, R road ab 13th
M'Lean James, paper carrier, rear 73 Poplar
M'Lean James V., tailor, N W 2d & Queen (S)
M'Lean John D., bootmr., 371 S 3d
M'Lean Samuel, weaver, 3 Otter n School (K)
M'Lean Thos., painter, 34 N 10th, h R road ab 13th
M'Leary Clark, lab., Allen ab Hanover (K)
M'Lees John, tailor, Benton ab School (K)
M'Leese Francis, weav., Front above Jefferson
M'Leod Henry, lampmr., 143 St John
M'Leod Mary, shop, 18 Cypress
M'Leod Thos., cordw., Carpenter ab 8th
M'Leod Wm., clerk, 153 St John, h 80 Buttonwood
M'Leran James B., book keeper M B, h N W 10th and Wood.
M'Mackin Edwd., weaver, Brinton ab 13th
M'Mackin James, tailor, 36 S 4th
M'Mackin James, tailor, Lombard ab Sch 8th
M'Mackin John, lab., 12 Lybrand
M'Mackin Michael, manufactory, N W Dugan and Pine
M'Mackin William, tailor, S W 2d and Chestnut, h 226 N 5th
M'Mahan Ever, lab., Front & Phoenix
M'Mahan Hugh, dealer, 124 Cherry
M'Mahan Jas., weaver, Christian ab 8th
M'Mahan Saml., cordw., Morris bel Catharine
M'Mahan Wm., lab., rear F road ab Phoenix
M'Mahen Conrad, cabinet maker, G T road and Franklin
M'Mahon Ann, 7 Clover
M'Mahon James, ostler, rear 58 Zane
M'Mahon James, grocer, Vine n Sch
M'Mahon John, surg. Inst. mr., Sch 3d & George
M'Mahon John W. carp., 181 N 10th
M'Mahon Moses, polisher, 167 Cedar
M'Mahon Owen, cordw., Broad n Cherry
M'Mahon Patrick, lab. Ann W Sch 4th
M'Mahon Peter, bricklr., High W of Sch 4th
M'Mahon Saml., dyer, 11 Wagner's al

M'Mahon Thos., watchman, Bedford ab 6th
M'Mahon Wm., gardener, Thompson ab 6th
M'Main Thos., machinist, Oat st
M'Maken Susan, trimmings, 204 Sassafras
M'Makin Andw., publisher S. Courier, 97 Chestnut
M'Makin Benjamin, 32 S whfs, h Franklin ab Buttonwood
M'MAKIN J. & B., Bath Coffee House, 32 S Wharves
M'Makin Miss, dressmr., 155 Vine
M'Manaman Andrew, moroc. dress., Perry ab Franklin (K)
M'Manaman James, tailor, Shippen ab 13th
M'Manaman Patrick, skin dress., Fisher st
M'Manamy Edward, morocco dr., Concord st
M'Manamy Patrick, skin dress., Mayland
M'Manamy Thos., tailor, Hallowell n 7th
M'Manamy Wm., cordw., Hallowell ab 6th
M'Maneman Jas., bootmr., 180 South
M'Manemy Samuel, grocer, 226 S 5th
M'Manus Barney, painter, 4th ab Master
M'Manus Bernard, oyster house, Spruce st whf.
M'Manus Bernard, tailor, Barker E Sch 6th
M'Manus Catharine, 172 N Water
M'Manus Chas. B., mer., 3 N 4th, h 8 Comptroller
M'MANUS FRANCIS, oysters, 9th & Depot, bel Green
M'Manus George, tavern, 9 N 6th
M'Manus Hen., watchm., Bickham E of Sch 7th
M'Manus John, bookbind., Carpenter bel 7th
M'Manus John, tailor, bet 6th & 7th bel Washington
M'Manus John, cabinetmr. & undertaker, Kensington Com. Hall
M'Manus John, bill poster, rear 19 N 8th
M'Manus John, cordw., Sch 4th & High
M'Manus Oliver, weaver, 16 Gray's al
M'Manus Owen, carter, 8 Cypress ct
M'Manus Philip, auctioneer, 161 N 3d, h 80 Buttonwood
M'Manus Thomas, tailor, 125 S 2d
M'Manus Wm., brickmr., Sch 5th n Lombard
M'Masters Hugh A., watchmr., 334 S 2d
M'Masters John jr., collector, 80 Union
M'MATH JAMES, tavern, 334 High
M'Meneman Edward, tailor, Brinton ab 13th
M'Meneman John, cordw., 61 S 13th
M'Meneman Mich., saddler, High E of Sch Front
M'Meneman Patrick, tailor, 8 Haines
M'Menneman Patrick, painter, 8 Howard pl
M'Meney Samuel, collector, 159 S 11th
M'Mennomy Henry, tailor, 8th bel Shippen
M'Menomy Chas., tailor, rear 242 Christian
M'Menomy Edward, tailor, 6 Moyamensing av
M'Michael Hannah, widow, h 55 Wood
M'Michael Jas., cordw., 646 N 2d (K)
M'Michael John, plasterer, 10th ab Federal
M'Michael Morton, Ed. North American, 4th & Chestnut, h Filbert 2d door ab Broad
M'Michael Samuel, stone cut., Sch 4th n High
M'Michael Wm., cordw., 1 James' ct (K)
M'Millin E. F., milliner, 379 N 2d

M'Millin Mary, milliner, 41 S 13th
M'Millin William, grocer, N W 2d and Union
M'Millin Wm., bootmr., Malseed ct
M'Minn Henry, lastmr., Clinton ab Parrish
M'Minn Jas., tobacconist, 21 S 10th
M'Minn Jane, 114 N 12th
M'Minn Mary, 18 Perry
M'Minn Rebecca, dress mr., 114 N 12th
M'Minn Robt., agent, 101 N 5th
M'Minn Samuel, shoe findings, 96 N 7th
M'Minneme H., tavern, 10th and Pleasant
M'Morris James, stonecutter, Cedar ab 12th
M'Morris Mary, shop, Cedar & Clifton
M'Mullen Alexander, grocer, 180 Swanson
M'Mullen Anthony, carp., rear 347 S 5th
M'Mullen B., Mrs., Benton & William
M'Mullen Daniel, lab., Robeson's ct.
M'Mullen Francis, lab., Locust E of Sch 3d
M'Mullen James, wood wharf, Spruce st. whf. h 62 Spruce
M'Mullen James, blacksm., rear 135 Carpenter
M'Mullen John, glue boiler, Phoenix below Front (K)
M'Mullen John, shoemr. Rose n G T road
M'Mullen John, cordw. Cadwalader bel Phoenix
M'Mullen John, blacksm., Orange & Citron
M'Mullen Lydia, gentwo., 62 Swanson
M'Mullen Margaret, wid., 242 St John
M'Mullen Martha, spooler, rear Hope below Master (K)
M'Mullen Patrick, lab., Sch 5th bel Chestnut
M'Mullin, Alex., bricklayer, Melon bel 13th
M'Mullin Arch., gent., 130 Christian
M'Mullin A. Rev., St Joseph's church
M'Mullin David, weaver, 612 N 2d (K)
M'Mullin David, blacksm., Palmer bel Queen
M'Mullin Edw., clockmr., Smith's al bel Coates
M'Mullin Jas. corder, Spruce st whf. h 62 Spruce
M'Mullin James, currier, Carlton ab 12th
M'Mullin John, weaver, Otter ab Front (K)
M'Mullin John, clerk, Leaper's al
M'Mullin Joseph, Vineyard ab Powell (F V)
M'Mullin Joseph, grocer, 15 N Water, h 8 Lombard
M'Mullin Joseph jr., mer., 15 N Water, h 24 Ellen
M'Mullin Joseph & Sons, grocers, 15 N Water
M'Mullin Joseph T. ladies' shoe manuf., 10 N 4th, h 127 N 6th
M'Mullin J. A., com. mer., Church alley, h 103 S 8th
M'Mullin J. S. collector, Juniper n Filbert
M'Mullin Martha, gentw., Mantua vil.
M'Mullin Patrick, carter, Carlton ab Sch 6th
M'Mullin Robert, mer., 15 N Water, h 89 Lombard
M'Mullin R., broker, 2 Exchange, h 115 Pine
M'Mullin Samuel, grocer, 173 Queen
M'Mullin Sarah, 104 George
M'Mullin Sutton H., bricklayer, R road below Broad
M'Mullin Thomas, bootmr., 9 S 4th
M'Mullin Thos., Torr's al n R road
M'Mullin Wm., cabman, 13 Benton
M'Mullin Wm., blacksm., Beach bel Palmer (K

M'Mullin Wm., coachman, 2 Marshall's ct
M'Mullin Wm., weaver, Cedar ab 12th
M'Mullin Wm., carp., McDuffie & 3d
M'Mullin Wm., blacksmith, 32 Duke
M'Munn Hugh C., spinner, Lombard ab Sch 4th
M'Murray Andrew, M. D., 325 Pine
M'Murray Robt., lab., Lancaster bel Reed
M'Murray Robert, 12 Philip (K)
M'Murry David T., brushmr., 23½ Lagrange, h 40 Castle
M'Murtrie Elizabeth, 276 Chestnut
M'Murtrie Henry, M. D., 9 Palmyra Row
M'Murtrie James, mer., 11 Girard
M'Murtrie Richard C., atty. & coun., 48 S 4th, h 276 Chestnut
M'Nabb James, weaver, Amber ab Phoenix (K)
M'Nabb John, weaver, Bickham E Sch 7th
M'Nabb Mary, tavern, N E 11th & Filbert
M'Nair A. H., M. D., 260 Mulberry
M'Nair Wm., gent., Washington bel R road
M'Nally A. Mrs., dressmaker, 21 Prune.
M'Nally B., tobacco, 184 S 2d
M'Nally Danl., warper, McDuffie n Sch 2d
M'Nally Edw'd., grocery, Sassafras & Sch 8th
M'Nally Edward, cordw. G T road ab Phoenix
M'Nally James, tinsmith, St John ab Beaver
M'Nally Patrick, weaver, rear Perry below Master
M'Nally Patrick, coachman, 5 Boyle's ct
M'Nally Wm., weaver, Spruce ab Sch Front.
M'Nalty Patrick, lab., 83 St John
M'Namara Henry, sawyer, 585 S 2d
M'Namara Matthew, cart., rear Pleasant ab 12th
M'Namara Michael, lab., Filbert E Sch 3d
M'Namara Thomas, shoemr., Dorothy n Sch 4th
M'Name Bernard, Mariner
M'Namee Ann, shop, 24 Farmer
M'Namee Catharine, wid of John, tavern, Broad ab Cedar
M'Namee Charles, blacksm., 42 Lily al
M'Namee Hugh, shoemr., Filbert W of Sch 8th
M'Namee Jas., oysters, 4 Zane, h 1 Randall's ct
M'Namee James, cordw., Front & Phoenix (K)
M'Namee James, boots & shoes, 336 High
M'Namee John, blacksmith, Front ab Jefferson
M'Namee John, 7 Turner
M'Namee John, carp., Buttonwood W of 13th
M'Namee John, cabman, rear 11 Blackberry al
M'Namee Mary, 260 N Water
M'Namee Morris, smith, Shippen bel 4th, h 173 Pine
M'Namee Neallans, cordw., 10th ab Melon
M'Namee Patrick, founder, Howard n Franklin (K)
M'Namee Red. S., bootmr., 80½ S 5th
M'Namee Samuel, millwright, Sch 8th & Rittenhouse
M'Namee Wm., Small bel 6th
M'Naney Francis, weaver, 13 Lloyd's ct (K)
M'Naney Patrick, lab., Baker bel 8th
M'Nanney Patrick, hostler, 124 Locust
M'Nanny Mary, wid., 5 Poplar ct
M'Neal Charles, tinplateworker, 405 High
M'Neal James, weaver, Philip bel Jefferson (K)
M'Neal Thos., lab., Stewart's pl
29

M'Nearnon Felix, weaver, Crown bel Duke (K)
M'Nearnon Robt., weaver, Crown bel Duke (K)
M'Nearny John, lab. 91 O Y road
M'Neelis Thos., grocer, 10 Eutaw
M'Neely John, drayman, Crown ab Franklin (K)
M'Neely W. T., leather mer., 35 N 3d, h G T road n Franklin
M'Neil Ann, 410 N 4th
M'Neil Archibald, grocer, S W 5th & Carpenter (S)
M'Neil B., M. D., 136 S 4th
M'Neil Arch., groc., Hope bel Phoenix (K)
M'Neil Cornelius, machinist, Phœnix ab F road
M'Neil James, weaver, Harmstead
M'Neil John, shoemr. Marion bel 2d
M'Neil Joseph, paper hanger, rear 29 Green
M'Neil Margaret, 16 Coopers' ct
M'Neil Thomas, lab., 263 S 7th
M'Neil Wm., grocer, N W 12th and Pine.
M'Neil Wm., lab., Quince n Lombard
M'Neil and Thomas, lab., Washington bel Orange
M'Neill Archibald, grocer, c Swanson and Washington
M'Neill Catharine, shop, 81 Plum
M'Neill Hugh, lab. 80 N 7th
M'Neill Kennedy, weaver, Dickson's ct
M'Neill Malcom, dry goods, N W 4th & Cedar
M'Neill Michael, 6 Grape ct
M'Neille P. C., milliner, 103 Mulberry
M'NEILLE P. R. clothing, 105 Chestnut, h 247 N 7th
M'NEIR Wm. watchcase mr., rear 26 N 2d, h 4 New Market
M'Nelly Edward, brass founder, Hanover and West (K)
M'Nelly John, printer, 39 Gaskill
M'Nelly John, stone mason, Ogden bel 11th
M'Nelly Wm., saddler, Marriott ab Fisher
M'Nelly Wm., saddler, 386 S 3d
M'NENNY MICHAEL, real estate broker, 58 Walnut, h 203 Pine
M'Nevin E., boarding house, 111 S 6th
M'Nichol Alex., shoemr., 1 Abbott's ct
M'Nichol Charles, bootmr., 54 S 4th
M'Nichol Charles Jr. painter, 1 and 2 Bank al
M'Nichol E., carpenter, 1 Crockett's ct, h 16 Swanwick
M'Nichol James, collector, 331 S 6th
M'Nichol Wm., lab., 46 W Cedar
M'Nichol Wm. weaver, rear Crown bel Franklin (K)
M'Night Robert, clerk, Barker n Sch 6th
M'Night Robt., agent, High W Sch 5th
M'Nutt Archibald, lab., Irvine
M'Nutt Elsy, lab.. Stevens' ct
M'Nutt Henry, lab. Lombard n Sch Front
M'Nutt Hugh, lab. Shippen ab 13th
M'Nutt Mary, 136 S 10th
M'Nutt Samuel, weaver, Shippen ab 12th
M'Nutt Samuel, weaver, Shippen bel Broad
M'Nutt Valentine, lab. Lombard W Sch 7th
M'Phail Maria, asst. matron, House of Refuge, h 47 Plum
M'Pherson Anna, Prime ab 2d
M'Pherson John, die sinker, 62 Walnut

M'Pherson Joseph, bricklayer, Pleasant bel 10th
M'Pherson Robert, Horstman's ct
M'Pherson Robert, weaver, Charlotte n George
M'Pherson Saml., weaver 2d ab Master
M'Pherson Thomas, brickmr., 16 Poplar ct
M'Philemy Eliza, 5 Juniper alley
M'Philemy John, machinist, Sch 3d ab Callowhill
M'Quaid Danl., weaver, Jefferson bel Cadwalader
M'Quaid Felix, soap & candle manuf., N E Noble and O Y road
M'Quaid Felix, soap & candles, O Y road below Coates
M'Quaid Hugh, lab., 116 N Water
M'Quaid James, ostler, 3 Bell's ct
M'Quaid James, tailor, Spafford
M'Quaid, stonecut., Sch 8th & Filbert
M'Quaid Patrick, soap manuf., 317 St John (K)
M'Quaid Patrick, shoes and bonnets, 506 N 2d
M'Quale Owen, livery stab., Blackberry al, h Park
M'Queen Archi., rigger, Penn ab Poplar, h Fraley's al (K)
M'Question Robert, carpet weaver, 346½ High, h Jackson
M'Quiestan Hugh, weaver, rear Amber above Phoenix
M'Quiggen Henry, shop, 143 Coates
M'Quiggin John, lab., Vine ab Broad
M'Quiggin Joseph, lab., Carlton ab Sch 6th
M'Quilkin Wm. manuf. brittania ware, 91 N 2d
M'Quillan Thomas, coffee roaster, Perry above Jefferson (K)
M'Quillin Charles, weaver, 2d ab Master (K)
M'Quillin James, cordw., 10th bel Christian
M'Quillin Patrick, clothier, 775 Cedar
M'Quillin Thomas, weaver, Hancock bel Master
M'Quillin Thos., lab., Bedford ab 6th
M'Quillin Wm., weaver, 2d ab Master (K)
M'Quin Martha, dry goods, 338 S 2d
M'Raith Wm. tailor, 137 N 6th
M'Renney Patrick, weaver, 4th bel G T road
M'Reynolds A., chemist, Pine ab Sch. 7th
M'Roy Catharine, shop, 622 N 3d
M'Shane Daniel, baker, 13th ab Catharine
M'Shane John, tailor, 74 George
M'Shane John, shoemr., 127 N 11th
M'Shea John, weaver, 11th & Milton
M'Shea William, cordw., 231 S 6th
M'Sordley James, tavern, 226 S 6th
M'Sorley John, dealer, 36 Quince
M'Sorley John, lab., Small n 5th
M'Sorley Mary, Centre ab 12th
M'Sorley Philip, weaver, Ulrick row n 2d (K)
M'Sorley William, weaver, Shippen la bel Bedford
M'Sparrow Arch., teacher, Sch 6th n Callowhill
M'Stay John, lab., Sch. 8th n Sassafras
M'Stocker Francis, watch mr., 144 Christian
M'Stocker John, carp., Front bel Oxford (K)
M'Swiggin John, dealer, 11th & Shippen
M'Taggart Matt., weaver, Spruce n Sch Front
M'Tague James, shoemr., Pine n Sch Willow
M'Vaugh Benj., Orchard bel Rawle

M'Vaugh Jesse, bricklayer, St John bel Poplar
M'Vay Danl., lab., Hutton ct
M'Vay Frederick, cordw. Sch 7th & Wood
M'Vay, George, machinist, Orange ab Wallace
M'Vay Hugh, weaver, O'Neal (K)
M'Vay Hugh, lab., 5 Esher's av
M'Vay James, weaver, rear G T road ab Master
M'Vay John, weaver, Fitler n 2d (K)
M'Vay John, lab. Washington ab Jefferson (K)
M'Vay Livinia, 258 Christian
M'Vay Neill, clerk, Richard n Sch 7th
M'Vay Patrick, weaver, Master ab Cadwalader
M'Vay Thomas, weaver, 7 White's ct
M'Veety Arthur, saddler, 2 Shield's al
M'Vey James, weaver, G T road ab Thompson
M'Vey John, weaver, Charlotte bel Master (K)
M'Vey Michael, grocer, Water & Spruce
M'Wharter Christian, bootmr. 1 Catharine
M'William Edw., porter, 235 Christian
M'William Mary Mrs., 4 Lebanon.
M'Williams Charles, weaver, rear G T road ab Phoenix (K)
M'Williams Charles, coachman, rear 11 Blackberry al
M'Williams D., printer, 229 Christian
M'Williams Mary, china, 75 Buttonwood
M'Williams Thomas, weaver, Pink bel Jefferson (K)
Maag Adam, butcher, 8 G T road (K)
Maag Adam, lab., 7th bel Carpenter
Maag Adam, tavern and bottler, S E 8th and Callowhill, and stocking weav. 174 St John
Maag Frederick, bottler, St John ab George (K)
Maas Jacob, engraver, 23 Perry
Macalaster J. W. C. shoemr., 5 Freed's av
Macalester Ann, 29 Clinton
Macalester Charles, stock and ex. bro., 50 Walnut, h 364 Spruce
Macauley Isaac, jr., oil cloth manuf., 6 N 5th, factory, Bush hill
Macauley James F., att'y and coun., & com. for New York and South Carolina, 55 S 7th
Macfarren Wm. gent., 401 N 5th
Macferran Hannah, 41 Charlotte
Machette Edwin V. mer., 124 N 3d, h Buttonwood ab 12th
Machette & Raiguel, hardware, 124 N 3d
Machette Saml. T., importer, 38 Walnut
Machette Susan, S W 11th & James
Machge John, shoemr., George ab Apple
Machin George, filemr., 50 N 2d
Mack Christian, gardener, West op Wood (K)
Mack Geo., shoemr., rear 5 Quarry
Mack Jacob, 18 Helmuth
Mack Judy, dressmr., Taylor's al
Mack Washington, lab., Charlotte bel Franklin
Macafess Randolph, grocery, 12 Lombard row
Mackason Hannah, rear 22 Duke
Mackason Mary, 25 Sassafras
Mackay John, grocer, S W 8th & Coates
Mackenzie Henry C., 207 Chestnut
Mackenzie Peter, florist, Spruce n Sch 5th
MACKEY C. C., auctioneer, 31 N 3d, h 90 N Front
Mackey James, shop, Callowhill bel Sch 2d

Mackey Mary, washer, 3 Gay's ct (K)
Mackey Robert, shoemr., 9 W Cedar
Mackey W. J., cab mr., 204 N 8th
Mackie Matthew, clerk, Callowhill n Sch 2d
Mackin James, lab., rear Carpenter bel 8th
Mackintosh Alex., china, 117 E Front
Macklin Alexander Rev., 10 Clinton.
Macklin Isaac, 4 Portland la
Macklin Moses, lab., Harmony bel 4th
Macknet G., dentist, 21 N 8th
Mackrey Henry, waiter, 32 Powel
Mackrey James, lab., 7 Lombard row
Macpherson Alex. M., mer. 39 S Front
Macready Wm., shoemr., 38 Mary (S)
Mactague George W., painter, 5th & Prune, h Washington ab 5th
Macurdy Hugh, gent., 128 N 12th
Madara Henry F., lab., Phoenix and Hope (K)
Madden Charles, saddler, 219 Cherry
Madden David, shop, G T road bel Master
Madden John, driver, Jefferson n Sch 6th
Madden John, carp., 90 Union
Madden John, moroc. finisher, 109 Dillwyn
Madden Mary & Sarah, milliners, 78 Mulberry
Madden Miss M., dry goods, 359 N 2d
Madden Nathaniel, lab. rear 394 Sassafras
Maddock D. R., clerk Penn. Bank, h 4 Carlton square
Maddock Edward F., printer, German ab 3d
Maddock Saml. B., lab., Pearl ab Sch 8th
Maddock Thomas, carpenter, 226 Noble
Maddock William A. shoemr., Mackey ab 2d
MADDOCK WILLIAM L., grocer, 55 & h 134 S 3d
Madeira Gilbert, lab., 37 Christian
Madeira Isaac H., carpenter, 13th bel Pine
Madeira Mark, cordw., rear 75 Beach (K)
Madeira Pugh, surg. inst. mr., 37 S 8th, h 283 N 6th
Maechtle C. C., baker, 433 N 5th
Maennel C. F., mer., 24 Church al
Maffett Caroline Mrs., S 8th bel Shippen
Magan John F., lab., Beach ab Marlboro' (K)
Magan Mary, variety store, 71 S 5th
Magarge Charles, paper warehouse, 52 Commerce
MAGARGE C. & COPE E. R., pap. warehouse 52 Commerce
Magarge Danl., car driv., Mechanic bel George
Magarge Jonathan, miller, 22 Logan
Magargil Allen, currier, Poplar ab 5th
Magarham James, patternmr., Carroll and 12th
Magee Anthony, painter, 240 Catharine
Magee Eliza, 148 N 8th
Magee George, gas fitter, 1 Jackson's ct
Magee Hugh S., cooper, 146, and h 132 Vine
Magee Isaiah, hatter, Garden and Willow
Magee James, bookbinder, 3 Magnolia
Magee James, saddler, 18 Decatur, h 465 Mulberry
Magee James H., bottler, 118 Vine, h 47 Buttonwood
Magee Mary, rear Poplar bel 6th
Magee Michael, saddler, 18 Decatur, h 26 Palmyra row

Magee Patrick, lab. Apple bel Master (K)
Magee Richard, bookseller, 45 Chestnut, h 55 Gaskill
Magee Robt., carp., rear Poplar bel 10th
Magee Stewart, gauger, 8th and Brown
Magee, Taber & Co., saddlers, 18 Decatur and 172 High
Magee Thomas, lab., Cadwalader ab Jefferson
Magee Wm. S., gauger, 119 N 6th
Mager Anthony, brickmr., Duke ab Hanover (K)
Mager Catharine, shop, 40 Zane
Mager Nicholas, ship carp., Hanover ab Queen (K)
Mager Philip, bricklayer, Franklin & Union (K)
Mager William, shipcarpenter, Hanover bel Queen (K)
Magill David, 41 Marshall
Magill Louisa C., b h., 226 Walnut
Magill Morris, bricklr., 25 N 10th
Magill Robert M., currier, 529 N Front
Magill William H., merchant, 4 S Front, h 75 N 9th
Maginnes James, police off., Tyler
Maglone Jos., tailor, George ab 10th
Magoffin John, engraver, Sch 5th ab Spruce
Magrady Charles, hair dresser, 97 Coates
Magrath Michael, gent., 489 Mulberry
Magruder Geo. A., U. States Navy, Walnut E Sch 6th
Maguire Ann, 29 Union (S)
Maguire Bernard, tavern, S W Front and Laurel
Maguire Charles F., postman, Noble ab 7th
Maguire Daniel, stone cutter, Essex
Maguire Edward, 2 Myers' ct
Maguire Ezekiel, shoemr., rear Queen bet 3rd and 4th
Maguire Geo., brickmr., 6th bel G T road (K)
Maguire Henry, lab., 2 Sharpless' ct
Maguire Hugh, weaver, 642 N 2d (K)
Maguire James, moulder, 257 S 7th
MAGUIRE JAMES, conveyancer, 126 Walnut
Maguire James, tailor, 386 High, h 88 N 11th
Maguire James A., boots and shoes, 4th and Callowhill
Maguire Jas., 5 Morgan's ct
Maguire Jas., ironmonger, 8 Benton
Maguire Jno. moulder, near Washington ab 6th
Maguire John, dairyman, Oxford n Front (K)
Maguire John, grocer, S E 4th and Callowhill
Maguire John, tavern, N W 6th and Elizabeth
Maguire John, Lombard bel 12th
Maguire John, bricklr., 20 Logan
Maguire Jos. E., dancing master, 9 Magnolia
Maguire Mary, 4 Baxter's av
Maguire Nicholas, teacher, 11th ab Washington
Maguire Peter, porter, 12 Baker's ct
Maguire Robt., driver, Beach ab Poplar (K)
Maguire Stephen, shoe store, 294 & 342 N 2d
Maguire Wm., tailor, 380 High
Mahaffey John, cordw., La Fayette ab 9th
Mahaffy Edw., gardener, P road bel Marriott
Mahan A. B., publisher, N E 7th and Mulberry h 197 S 9th
MAHAN F., publisher Philadela. fashions, 211 Chestnut

Mahan Hannah, shop, Mulberry n Sch 3d
Mahan John, cordw., Olive ab 10th
Mahan Jos., lab., Philip ab Jefferson (K)
Mahan Patrick, tallowchandler, Buttonwood ab 10th
Mahan Thomas T., printer, rear 191 Cedar
Mahon Wm., tailor, Mariner ab 5th
Maharg Jas., mor. finish., St John ab George(K)
Mahauffey James, tailor, High n Ashton
Mabaun Thomas, rigger, 31 Beck (S)
Maher John, clerk, 81 Lombard
Maher Patrick, lab., Marriott ab 4th
Maher Stephen, lab., Parrish bel Sch 8th
MAHLKE LUDWIG, bootmr., 44 S 8th
Mahn John, printer, 8 Cox
Mahon Morris, acct., 277 S Front
Mahon Peter, bootmr., Lombard ab Sch 2d
Mahoney Daniel, tavern, S W 13th and Vine
Mahoney Daniel, lab., 3 Grape ct
Mahoney Dennis, carp., 5 Little Green
Mahoney James, weaver, Phoenix ab 2d
Mahoney Jeremiah, weaver, Benton n William
Mahoney John, weaver, 2d bel Master (K)
Mahoney Patrick, lab., 16 Jones' al
Mahoney Pat., lab., rear Benton bel William(K)
Mahoney Wm., tailor, 5 Ridgway's ct
Mahony M. B., mer., 20 S Front, h 178 S 3d
MAHONY M. B. & CO., iron mers., 20 S Front
Mahony Susanna, gentw., 480 S 2d
Mahourn Frances, shop, Wheat ab Wharton
Mahr Conrad, tavern, 28 Washington av
Mail Thos., weaver, Philip and Jefferson (K)
Main Alexander, cordw., Wharton ab 4th (S)
Main Thos., dealer, 63 Callowhill & 17 Julianna
Main Thos., grocer, 17 Julianna
Mains Robert, weaver, Shippen ab Shippen la
Mair George, G T road ab Franklin (K)
Mair & Higgins, carvers, rear 122 Walnut
Mair John, G T road ab Franklin (K)
Mair Thomas, shoemr., 560 N 2d
Mair Wm. H., carver, rear 129 Walnut, h 122 S 2d
Maires Walter F., carp., Apple ab George
Maison Peter, biscuit baker, 134 N Front, h 132 N Front
Maitland John, gent., 153 Pine
Major Benjamin F., carp., 12th ab Vine
Major Emily, fancy goods, 173 Mulberry
Major Henry Rev., Mulberry n Sch 5th
Major Henry, shoemr., 9 Cresson's al
Major Isaac, carp., 12th bel Green
Major Louisa P., dressmr., 213 Cherry
Major Thos., lab., Harrison
Makeinson Henry, vict., Olive ab 12th
Maker Joseph, cordw., Marriott bel 4th
Makin Elizabeth G., bonnetmr, 148 Sassafras
Makinson Edward, carpet weav., G T road ab 5th
Malcom Thos. S. Rev., see'ry. A. B. P. S., 31 N 6th, h 251 S 9th
Malcolmb Hugh, carpet weaver, 14 Perry
Malcomson Joseph, carpet weaver, 268 Sassafras
Male William, tailor, 349 N Front
Malech Gustavus, barber, S W St John & Beaver (K)

Maley Julianna, gentw., 140 N Juniper
Maley Susan, Pearl N Broad
Malin David, Rev., agent Am. Board Com. For Miss., office 142 Chestnut, h 494 Chestnut
Mall Frederick, lab., Duke n Vienna (K)
Maller Mariano, Rev., seminary, Sch 5th & Sassafras
Mallery Daniel, collector, 9th bel Catharine
MALLERY EDWARD G., atty. and coun., h S 4th
MALLERY GARRICK, att'y. & coun., 48 S 4th, h Library bel 5th
Malloch Wm., stone cut., Chestnut W Sch 2d
Malloch William H., stone cutter, Barker W Sch 4th
Mallock Elizabeth, Barker W of Sch 6th
Mallon Ann, tavern, 10th bel Fitzwater
Mallon Arthur, lab., 173 N Front
Mallon Francis, weav., rear Charlotte ab Thompson (K)
Mallon James, lead pipe, 3 Turner
Mallon Jas., carp. weaver, Perry ab Phoenix(K)
Mallon John, weaver, 4th bel G T road
Mallon Michael, lab., Spruce n Sch 5th
Mallon Patrick, lab., Hancock ab Phoenix
Malone Annie F. Mrs., 14 Chester
Malone Francis, lab., Christian bel 9th
Malone Michael, lab., 6 Rail road ct
Malone Nich., dealer, 55 Duke
Malone Terrene, blacksm., Spruce n Sch 5th
Maloney Catharine, trimmings, 372 S 3d
Maloney Charles, morocco dr., 52 Fitzwater
Maloney James, shoemaker, 220 Cedar
Maloney James, 245 Vine
Maloney Solomon, lab., Pearl ab 12th
Maloy Alex., weaver, Thompson ab 3d
Maloy Edw., sailmr., 4 China
Malseed John, boots and shoes, High n Sch 6th
Malthamer Frederick, tavern, 16 N Water
Malthous G., Sp Garden ab 11th
Maltman John, butcher, Moore bel Church
Maltman Wm., ship carp., Rye bel Marion
Man Daniel, gent., 43 Sassafras
Managh Hugh, lab., Filbert n Sch 4th
Manahan Daniel, lab., 74 N Water
Manderfield Henry, drug., 137 Christian
Manderfield Thomas, carp., 78 Christian
Manderson Andrew, gent., Beach bel Shackamaxon (K)
Manderson Andrew, jr., lumbermer., Beach bel Shackamaxon (K)
Manderson Andrew, jr. & Co., lumber mers. Beach n Marlborough (K)
Manderson James, mer., Beach n Marlborough
Manderson John, tailor, 369 N Front
Manderson Margaret, Beach ab K market
Manderson Wm., 63 Washington (S G)
Mandry John, livery stable, 306 & h 308 Sassafras.
Mancely David weav., rear Hope ab Phoenix(K)
Manes Robert, weaver, Shippen ab 13th
Manese Edward, weaver, Hope bel Phoenix (K)
Manese Thomas, lab., Hope ab Otter
Mangan George C., upholsterer, 365 N 4th
Mangan John J., coach smith, 15 Quince

Manger John, painter, 58 German
Manger J. G., brewer, 56 New
Maning J. H., N L news rooms, 213 N 3d
Mankim P., artist, 69 S 2d
Manley David, iron dealer, Broad ab Cherry
Manley George, ex-brok., 41 S 3d, h 239 S 10th
Manley R., ex. broker, N W 3d and Chestnut, h 490 Chestnut
Manley Sarah, dress mr., 8 Bread
Manley Thomas, weaver, Shippen la ab Shippen
Manlinson Philip, waterman, 60 Queen
Manluff Alexander, lab., rear 83 New Market
Manluff John, lab., Orchard bel Rawle
Manly Ann, Sassafras ab Sch 7th
Mann Benj. G., attorney, 284 N 3d
Mann Charles tailor, 339 Callowhill
Mann David, waiter, 22 Webb's al
Mann Francis S., carp., Callowhill ab Sch 6th
Mann Henry, baker, Bedford ab 13th
Mann Isabella Mrs., 78 Marshall
Mann John, collector, 263 S 3d
Mann John machinist, Tea's ct
Mann John E., plasterer, Wood ab Sch 8th
Mann J. M., dry goods, 155 High
Mann Peter G., carp., School n Edward (K)
Mann Theodore, bootmr., 41 S 4th
Mann Thomas, dry goods, 146 Sassafras
Mann T. F., mer., 142 Green
Mann William, saw sharpener, Washington av ab Green
Mann Wm. B., atty & coun., 284 N 3d
Mann Wm. S., 15 Dock, h 78 Marshall
Mannal Andrew, baker, 87 Brown
Mannal Michael, mason, 13th ab Poplar
Mannery Richard, waterman, Front ab Reed
Manning Charles, cabinetmr. Washington ab 2d
Manning Joseph S., cordwainer, 58 Queen
Manning Joseph S., carpenter, S E 11th and Brown
Manning J. H., oysters, 7 S 3rd, h 5 Danna-ker's av
Manning Napoleon B., broker, 20 Minor, h Marshall ab Parrish
Manning T. S., printer, 7 S 6th
Mansfield Charles F., paper hanger, 275 S 2d
Mansfield Edward W., clerk, 163 Apple
Mansfield E. A., gentw., 163 Apple
Mansfield Isaac K., mer., 34 Church al, h 79 Marshall
Mansfield John, ship carpenter, 2 Callowhill
Mansfield John, dealer, 241 N Front
Mansfield Mary, rear 13 Poplar
Mansfield Thomas, curb setter, 477 Race
Mansfield Thomas, tailor, 35 New Market
Mansfield Thomas W., paper hanger, 2 Clark (S.)
Manson George W., druggist, S E 10th and Coates
Manson Thos., lumber mer., 513 N Front
Manson Wm., waterman, 114 N Water
Mansur Moses, blacksmith, 9 Benton
Mansure John, jeweller, Bank al, h Clark ab 3d
Mansz George, cordw., 44 Garden
Mantell Conrad, barber, Beach bel Maiden (K)
Manthorp Geo., lab., 9 Swanson

Manton Peter, watchman, Clymer st
Manuel & Bro., gas fitters, Fetter la
Manuel E., painter, 4 Clinton av
Manuel Jacob A., lab., Orchard ab Rawle
Manuel John, gas fitter, Fetter la
Manuel Joseph, gas fitter, Fetter la
Manuel Joseph E., carp., Fetter la
Manypenny Henry, combmr., 79 Cedar
Manypenny James, warper, Wood ab Sch Front
Maples Joseph, marble mason, Broad ab Mulberry, h S W Sch 7th & Vine
Mapus Wm., blacksm., St John and Poplar
Mara John, lab., 15 Clymer st
Marbaeker, John, brass found., Beach ab Shackamaxon, h Race n Sch 5th
Marce Henry, 66 S 6th
Marcer Isaac, carp., Elizabeth bel Poplar
March Elizabeth, shop, G T road n Jefferson
March George, tavern, 101 Coates
March James, cordw., 96 St John
March Joseph, hosier, 3d ab Franklin
March Robt. G. morocco dresser, 359 N 3d
Marche Eliza, milliner, 125 Morgan
Marchment Stephen, ladies shoemaker, 368 N 2d
Marconnier A. P., cook, 9th bel Catharine
Marcus H., barber, 180 Shippen
MARGETTS JOHN, refectory, S W 10th and Chestnut, h 20 Sansom
Margrum Eliza, 122 Cherry
Margrum Samuel, carter, Hope bel Phoenix
Mariner And., 1st h ab High bridge (K)
Mariner Andrew, oysterman, 40 Coates
Mariner Andrew, waterman, Brown st wharf
Mariner Henry, waterman, 75 New Market
Mariner John, watchman, 14 Brown
Mariner Mary Ann, dressms, 40 Coates
Marion Terrence, lab., 10 Prosperous al
Mariott John, lab., 13 Eutaw
Maris John M., druggist, 9 S 3d, h Wood bel 8th
MARIS JOHN M. & CO., druggists, 9 S 3d
Maris Rachel R., 107 S 8th
Maris Richard, M. D., 107 S 8th
Maris Sarah N., 108 S 3d
Maris Thomas R., mer., 145 High, h 107 S 8th
Maris Wm. Jr., lumber mer., 13th and Locust, h Juniper bel Locust
Mark & Co., coal dealers, 14 Exchange
Mark Edward, clerk, rear, 63 Franklin
Mark John, coal mer., 14 Mere. Exchange, h 78 Lombard
Marker J. D., merchant, 16 Commerce, h 367 Callowhill
Marker Mary, 2d bel Greenwich
Markland James, brass founder, 9th bel Washington (S)
Markland John H., att'y and coun., 51 S 5th, h Sch 7th ab Spruce
Markland Thomas T., pearl button maker, 8th bel Shippen
Markle C., printer, 75 W Callowhill
Markle Jacob, carpenter, 96 Tammany
Markle John, wire manuf., 1 Lodge
Markley Benj., coach trimmer, rear 124 Apple

Markley Edward C., bookbinder, 4 Minor, h 19 Madison
Markley Isaac, carter, 124 Apple
Markley Jacob, bookstore, 124 Coates
Markley John, baker, 2d bel Wharton
Markley John, machinist, 9th bet Coates and Brown
Markley Joseph, blacksmith, 93 Apple
Markley Mrs. S., rear Mechanic ab Poplar
Markoe H. Mrs. Walnut W Sch 7th
Markoe James, Locust W Sch 8th
Marks Charles S., baker, 87 N Water, h 104 N Front
Marks Christopher, lab. 3 Poplar ab Front
Marks D., tailor, S E 6th and Cedar
Marks Henry, lab., Hanover ab Bedford (K)
Marks Henry R., bricklayer, Charles bel James
Marks James, ship master, 36 E Lombard
Marks John, 104 N Front
Marks John, weaver, Shippen la ab Fitzwater
Marks John, painter, rear 127 Noble
Marks John, carp., Jones N Sch 4th
Marks John, shoemr., Queen bel 5th
Marks John, glue manuf., F road ab Palmer
Marks John F., cordwr., 9th ab Willow
Marks Mary Ann, rear Jackson (S G)
Marks Moses, dealer, 189 Shippen
Marks M., pedler, 328 St John
Marks Nathaniel, tailor, 544 N 2d (K)
Marks Peter, carter, Queen ab 2d
Marks Samuel, blacksmith, rear 512 N Front
MARKS SAML. P., clerk, Health Office, h 376 S 5th
Marks Simon, tailor, Poplar ab 3d
Marks Stephen, machinist, Coates ab 13th
Marks Thomas, weaver, Duke ab Cherry (K)
Markward Samuel A., saw maker, 8 Fayette
Marley James, weaver, Locust n Sch 3d
Marley Rosanna, 110 Union
Marlin John, carter, 23 Allen (K)
Marlin John, carp. Poplar ab St John
Marlin Jos., drayman, Union bel Franklin (K)
Marlin William, drayman, Sarah bel Bedford (K)
Marlow Edward, buttonmr., Wood bel Sch 3d
Marlow John, weaver, 8th ab Catharine
Marlow John, grocer, G T road and Master
Marlow Patrick, weaver, St John & George (K)
Marmion John, carp. Jefferson ab Front (K)
Marot William, bookbinder, 4th & Appletree al, h 173 Vine
Marotte L., dentist, 99 S 5th
Marple Enoch, upholsterer, 8 Whitticar's ct
Marple Jacob, cabinetmr., F road ab Queen, h Sarah bel Bedford (K)
Marple Jane, F road n Bedford, (K)
Marple John, plasterer, Pleasant ab 12th
Marple Joseph, watchman, 6 Whitecar's ct
Marple Morris M., dry goods, 15 N 3d, h 122 Green
Marple Robert L. bookbinder, 7 Spring Garden
Marple Samuel, lime mer., 15th ab Coates
MARPLE & SEISER, dry goods, 15 N 3d
Marple Wm. M. tanner, rear 4th ab Beaver
Marput Jacob, lab., G T road opp 5th (K)
Marr John J., morocco dresser, rear 7 Pegg

Marrah Jas., lab., 120 Plum
Marron Richard, lab., 18 Fitzwater
Marry Patrick, weaver, Milton ab 11th
Marsdan Joseph, sailmr., Little Water ab Cedar
Marsden John, carp. manf., 2d ab Jefferson (K)
Marseilles Peter, mer., 153 High, h Pine ab 9th
Marselis Isaac N., M. D., 341 S 2d
Marselis Warren, ladies' shoemr., Broad and It road
Marsh Abraham, teacher of music, 450 Sassafras
Marsh Benjamin, book keeper, 13 Montgomery
Marsh Elisha, saddler, 450 Sassafras
Marsh James, mer., 46 N 5th h 290 N 6th,
Marsh John, vict., G T road ab Jefferson (K)
Marsh John, stone cutter Johnson's la (S)
Marsh Joseph, printer, Federal ab 5th
Marsh Pamelia, tailoress, 1 Knight's ct
Marsh Peter, lab., Paschall's al
Marsh Thomas, carp., Filbert bel 12th, h 22 State
Marshall Abraham, frame maker, 375 Sassafras
Marshall Abraham, carter, 6th ab Franklin
Marshall Alex. D., jeweller, rear 97 Chestnut
Marshall Alexander, labourer, 214 Shippen
Marshall A. H., carp., 9 Christian
Marshall Benj., mer., 151 High, h 12th & Spruce
MARSHALL & BROCK, mach. and calico engravers, 6 Lagrange place
Marshall Charles, cooper, 117 G T road (K)
Marshall Charles, boatman, High E Sch 2d
Marshall Christopher, gent., 421½ Mulberry
Marshall Davis, carp., 2 Park av
Marshall Elizabeth, shop, Beach ab Pine
Marshall Elijah D., calico printer, Sch 8th ab Mulberry
Marshall Ethelbert A., Sch 7th ab Cherry
Marshall E. D., machinist, 6 Lagrange pl, h Sch 8th ab Mulberry
Marshall George, porter, 20 Pratt
Marshall Henry, miller, Washington (W P)
Marshall Henry, manuf., Vine ab Nixon
Marshall Isaac, carp., 10th bel Coates
Marshall Isaac, morocco dresser, 3d bel Phoenix
Marshall James, bleeder, Front ab Master (K)
Marshall James, grocer, 169 Locust
Marshall James, frame maker, 1 W North
Marshall James, labourer, Salem al ab 12th
Marshall James, grocer, 46 P road
Marshall Jephtha, carp., 23 N 11th, h Jones' ab Sch 8th
Marshall Jeremiah, capt., 4 Carberry
Marshall John, cordwr., 6 Pearl
Marshall John, gilder, Wood bel 12th
Marshall John, teacher, 605 S 2d
Marshall John, Linn
Marshall John, porter, Cedar n 11th
Marshall John, feed store, P road ab Fitzwater
Marshall Joseph, jeweller, 87 S 2d
Marshall Leas, upholsterer, 295 High
Marshall & M'Calla, paper hangers, 66 N 10th
Marshall Mary, 249 Spruce
Marshall Mary Ann, 481 Mulberry
Marshall Moses D., cordwainer, Ann ab Sch. 4th
Marshall M. & J. Y., wafer manuf., 59 Walnut
Marshall M. Mrs., wafer manuf., 59 Walnut

Marshall Preston, wool dealer, c Front and Poplar, h 542 N Front
Marshall Robert, grocer, c 13th and Cedar
Marshall Samuel, waterman, Ann n Sch. 3d
Marshall Saml. R., machinist, 1 Filbert av
Marshall Solomon, lab., 178 Locust
Marshall & Tempest, jewellers, 87 S 2d
Marshall Thomas, brick layer, Marshall's ct (K)
Marshall Thomas, lab., rear 302 St. John
Marshall Thomas, cedar cooper, High n Sch 4th
Marshall Thos., machinist, Callowhill ab Sch 8th
Marshall Wallace, druggist, 270 Mulberry
Marshall Wm., Front bel Oxford (K)
Marshall Wm., shoemr., Willis' ct
Marshall Wm., tailor, Wayne ab Washington
Marshall Wm., grocer, 628 N 3d (K)
Marshall Wm., coachman, 273 Cherry
Marshall Wm., lab., 7 Richard
Marshall Wm., spinner, Callowhill and William
Marshall Wm., grocer, Allen and F road (K)
Marshall Wm. A., mer., N W Walnut & Front, h Sch 8th bel Spruce
Marshall W. G., bricklayer, Wallace bel 13th
Marshes & Shepherd, manufs. and mers., 12 N 5th
Marshman Charles P., mariner, capt., 4th bel Christian
Marston Catharine, Olive bel 11th
Marston David, plasterer, Green bel Broad
Marston John, jr., commander, U. S. navy, 5 Summer
Marston John, coachmr., 6th & Brown, h 7th ab Poplar
Marston T. H. painter, Linden ab Sp Garden
Martel Charles, hair dresser and whig maker, 137 Chestnut
Martel J. B., sashmr., Apple ab Poplar
Marter E. M., mer, 15 N 2d
Marter Isaac, mer. 15 N 2d, h 131 Dillwyn
Marter Isaac & Son, dry goods, 15 N 2d
Martien J. W., com. mer., 65 S Front, h Mulberry n Sch. 5th
Martien William S., printer and publisher of Presbyterian, 37 S 7th, h 106 N 11th
Martin Ann, Pearl ab 12th
Martin Aaron S. copal var. manuf. 37 Strawberry
Martin Adam, tavern, 6th & G T road
Martin Alexander V., Union ct.
Martin Ambrose, jeweller, 190 Sassafras
Martin Benjamin, gent., 463 S 2d
Martin Benjamin, jr. hay press and scales, Greenwich ab Front, h 137 Christian
Martin Cath., spooler, Hanover ab West (K)
Martin Chas. F., tailor, Charlotte ab George
Martin Clarissa P., b h, 168 Chestnut
Martin & Crothers, grocers, N W 2d and Washington
Martin Daniel, distiller, N W 7th & Cedar
Martin Danl. C., blindmr., rear 454 S Front
Martin David, weaver, Rose al ab 13th
Martin Edward, machinist, 49 Coates' al
Martin Edward D., brickmr., New Market bel Coates
Martin Eliza, readymade linen, 35 S 8th
Martin Eliza, b h, 41 Coates' al

Martin Eliza, Higgin's ct
Martin Ezra, cordw., 1 Hight ct
Martin F. A., M. D., 292 N 3d
Martin George, hosier, G T road bel Mud la
Martin George, weaver, 6 Gay's ct (N L)
Martin George, mer. 10 N Front
Martin George, M. D., 175 N 4th
Martin George, cordw., 56 M road
Martin Geo., machinist, Carlton ab Sch 8th
Martin G. H., mer., 113 High, h 132 S 8th
Martin Hannah, 107 Shippen
Martin Harriet, 516 S 2d
Martin Henry, tavern, 102 Plum
Martin Henry, lab., Brown's ct
Martin Hugh, carter, Vine bel Sch 8th
Martin Isaac, bonnet presser, 134 N 4th
Martin Isaiah, clerk, 189 G T road
Martin James, tobacconist, 2d and Franklin
Martin James, porter, N W 2d & Wharton
Martin James, cordwainer, Wood ab 13th
Martin James, com. mer., 10 N Front, h 181 Vine
Martin James, chandler, Noble bel Garden
Martin James, grocer, 274 S 7th
Martin James, tailor, rear 135 S 9th
Martin James K., attorney & coun., Lily al and Green.
Martin James S., hat and cap manuf., 118 High
Martin James W., umbrella mr., 7 and h 4 Bread
Martin Jane, S W 2d & Washington
Martin Jane, Pearl ab 12th
Martin John, collector, 19 Duke
Martin John, waiter, rear 3 Gray's al
Martin John, Capt., 222 S Front
Martin John, carp., 96 N 13th
Martin John, clerk, 529 N 5th
Martin John, weaver, Union bel West (K)
Martin John, blacksm., 39½ Cedar
Martin John, sexton, Cedar ab 12th
Martin John, weaver, Union bel West (K)
Martin John, weaver, Front ab Phoenix (K)
Martin John, cordw., Noble and Garden
Martin John, weaver, Rose ab Shippen la
Martin John, cabtmr., 13th ab Poplar
Martin John, lab., 5 Monmouth's ct
Martin John, coffee roaster, rear 122 N 4th
Martin John, provision, Nixon and Vine
Martin John, dancing teacher, Pine ab 10th
MARTIN JOHN C., superintendent Philadel. Exchange, h 319 Spruce
Martin John H., mer., 94 High
Martin John H. weav., Jefferson and Cadwalader
Martin John H., atty., 141 Walnut, h Pine ab Juniper
Martin John J., clockmr., 189 G T road
Martin John L., grocer, N E 13th & Fulton
Martin Joseph, pattern mr., Ogden n R road
Martin Joseph W., clerk, 12th and Division
Martin Joshua, porter, 2 Ball's ct
Martin Jules, dancing school, Assembly build., h Pine ab 10th
Martin J. G., wine and liquor, 2d and New
Martin J. Willis, mer., 28 N Front
Martin Letitia, Carpenter ab 8th
Martin Luther, clerk, 139 Buttonwood

Martin Marshall, lab. Cadwalader bel Phœnix (K)
Martin Mary, washer, Dean ab Locust
Martin Mary, milliner, G T road ab Franklin (K)
Martin Mary, 5 Monroe pl
Martin Michael, 190 S 6th
Martin Michael, bricklayer, Jones W Sch. 8th.
Martin Oliver, variety store, 24 N 4th, h 61 Marshall
Martin Owen, tailor, 178 N Front
Martin Patrick, watchmr., 52 P road
Martin Patrick, waiter, Pine n Sch 7th
MARTIN & PATTON, hats and caps, 118 High
MARTIN PETER, chairmaker, 87 and 89 N. Front, h 287 N 3d
Martin Peter, tailor, 101 O Y road
Martin Prosper D., mer., 75 High, h 6th ab Vine
Martin P. C., grocer, 30 Elizabeth
Martin Robt, whip mr., Elizabeth bel Franklin
Martin Robert, collector, 310 S 4th
Martin Robert, weaver, Union ab F. road (K)
Martin Robert B., umbrella mr., 128½ S 6th
Martin Robert C., cabmr., 10 Bread
Martin Robert C., Juniper n Filbert
Martin Saml. W., mer., 80 S 2d, h 25 Schectz
Martin & Smith, hardware, 113 High
Martin Susan, Harmstead
Martin Sylvester, carp., 10th ab Carpenter
Martin S. A., bonnet manuf., 25 Wood
Martin Thomas, hatter, 117 S 2d
Martin Thomas, house and sign painter, 124 S 10th, h Wharton ab 4th
Martin Thos., porter, rear 16 Little Pine
Martin Thos., lab., Linn n Nixon
Martin Thomas, lab., 57 Fitzwater
Martin Thomas G., dry goods, 80 S 2d, h 139 Lombard
Martin William, Pres. Del. Mut. Safety Insurance Co., S E 3d and Dock, h Pine ab Juniper
Martin Wm., tailor, 250 E Cedar
Martin Wm., dyer, Harmstead n Sch 2d
Martin Wm., weaver, Cedar ab Sch 5th
Martin Wm., moulder, Franklin bel Vienna (K)
Martin Wm., clerk, 17 Relief
Martin Wm., carter, 7 Barber's row
Martin Wm., lab., Sch. 2d and Filbert
Martin Wm. A., variety store, 67 S 2d
Martindale John, mason, 133 Vine
Martindale John B., gent., 413 Sassafras
Martindale Samuel L., b. h., 13 Branch
Martine G. Augustus S., 104 S 4th
Marts Susan, washing, 8 Mark's la
Marvel Alfred, tailor, rear 450 S Front
Marvel Thos., waterman, Hughes' ct
Marx Philip, cordw., Conrad's ct (N L)
Marx Stephen, machinist, rear Olive bel Broad
Mascher John F., watchmr., 64 Brown, h 2 Rachel
Mash Sarah, Wood bel Franklin (K)
Maslin M. M., hardware, Locust n Sch 8th
Mason Ann, 5 Wood
Mason A., philosophical instrument maker, 89 S 5th, h 69 Cherry
Mason Charles, tailor, N W Front and Almond
Mason Chas. H., conveyancer, 212 N 6th, h 96 Wood

Mason Christopher, regulator of weights, N W 13th and Filbert, h 12th bel Wood
Mason C. A., wines and liquors, N E 6th and Coates
Mason George R. mer., 149 High, h 78 Dillwyn
Mason George W., philoso. inst. mr., 5 Benton
Mason & Huhn, milliners, 59 N 2d
Mason Isaac, gent., 135 S 11th
Mason Jacob, oysters, 23 Madison
Mason Jacob, lab., 23 Beck (S)
Mason Jacob, oysters, Spruce st. wharf
Mason James, cooper, St. James, h 9 Lybrand
Mason James, mariner, Washington ab Swanson
Mason James, hatter, 20 Barron
Mason James, glass bender and painter, 105 Queen (K)
Mason James, carp., 490 N 4th
Mason James A., baker, 108 S 12th
MASON JAMES S., blacking manuf. & writing ink, 192 N 3rd & 16 Willow
Mason John, cordw., rear 81 N 5th
Mason John, mer., 47 N wharves and 95 N Water, h 128 Spruce
Mason John, shoemr., Culvert bel Apple
Mason John, weaver, 35 S Juniper
Mason John C., supt., Christian ab 9th
Mason John K., M. D., Sch. 8th bel Spruce
Mason John M. G., tailor, 8 China (S)
Mason J. H., grocer, 248 S Front, h 47 Catharine
MASON & KIRKLAND, mers., 47 N wharves and 95 N Water
Mason Mary, shop, 3 Chatham
Mason Mary Ann, 14 Freed's av
Mason Mary A., dressmr., Charles bel Buttonwood
Mason Mrs., gentw., 78 Union
Mason Parthenia, b. h., 106 N 5th
Mason Richard M., clerk, 154 N 13th
Mason Robert, lab., Vernon bel 11th
Mason Robert A., wine and liquor, N E 6th and Coates
Mason Samuel, Sec. and Treas. M. H. and Sch. H. R. R. Co., 11 S 7th, h 68 N 7th
Mason & Smith, tailors, 333 S 2d
Mason Tantom, baker, 7 Tammany ct
Mason Thos., machinist, 17 Maria
Mason Thomas T., mer., 156 High, h N W 5th and North
Mason Wm., cabinetmr., S E 2d & Master (K)
Mason Wm., eating-house, 67 Dock, h 2d n Master
Mason William, cooper, 158 Cherry
Mason Wm. M., shingle shaver, Crown ab Queen (K)
Mason Wm. jr., gauger, St. James, h 59 N 2d
Mason Wm. E., wire worker, 24 N 6th
MASON WILLIAM G., engraver, 46 Chestnut h Filbert ab Sch 7th
Mason W. R., fancy store, 5 High, h 424 N Front
Mason Wm. W., philos. inst. mr., 89 S 5th
Mass Sarah, 300 S 6th
Massey Charles, Jr., mer., 28 S wharves, h 170 Mulberry

Massey Charles B., brushmr., 68 Noble
Massey James, 6 Phoenix (K)
Massey John, waterman, rear 106 Christian
Massey John W., tobacconist, 8 Tammany ct
Massey John W., dentist, N 8th bel Coates
Massey Joseph R., mer., 26 Church al, h 47 N 11th
Massey J. A., Rev., 10th bel Ogden
Massey Lemuel, grocer, 414 S 4th
Massey L. E., trimmings, 102 S 3rd
Massey L. R., mer., 28 S Whfs
Massey Mary, tailoress, rear 3 Eutaw
Massey R. V., leather store, 244 N 3d, h 205 N 4th.
Massey Thomas, tailor, 320 Sassafras
Massey Wm., lab., rear 78 Brown
Masson A., carp., 268 N 7th
Masson Charles A., jeweller, 52½ N 8th
Masson James, carp., 179 Brown
Master Elizabeth, dry goods, 68 Spruce
Master Joseph, mer, Mulberry E Sch 6th
Masters George, shingle shaver, Penn bel Maiden (K)
Masterson John, blacksm., Filbert n Sch 4th
Masterson Terence, lab., Alder ab Poplar
Mastin James, porter, Harmony bel 4th
Matchett John, carpenter, Thompson bel Sch 6th
Mateer James, bricklayer, Irvine
Mather Edwin M., gardener, 111 M road
Mather & Hallowell, dry goods, 143 High
Mather Joseph H. painter, Janney's ct
Mather Joseph T., merchant, 143 High, h 473 Chestnut ab Broad
Mather Patrick, lab., Allen's ct
Mather Susan, tailoress, rear 139 Green
Mather Thomas, moulder, Dunton below Franklin (K)
Mathers James, clerk, 5 Carlisle's ct., h 199 Marshall
Mathers Peter, baker, 201 S 9th
Mathers Richard, cordw., Hazel ab 11th
Mathes Joseph, boot maker, 85 S 3d
Matheson Andrew, dyer, Bedford ab 12th
MATHEYS R. E., bathing house, rear 124 S 2d
Mathieu Dauphin M., carver, bel Washington ab 8th
Mathieu & Doiseau, stove manufacs. 187 S 2d
MATHIEU E., vinegar manuf., 12 Lombard
Matlack Ann, 38 Marshall
Matlack C. F., M. D., 148 Mulberry
Matlack Elizabeth Ann, rear 16 Ogden
MATLACK ELLWOOD, tailor, 306 High, h 129 N 10th
Matlack Francis F., cordw., 228 Green
Matlack I. R., M. D., 289 Marshall
Matlack James, waiter, 20 Burd's ct
Matlack James, combmr., West bel Vienna (K)
Matlack John G., shoemaker, 186 Sassafras
Matlack Joseph, machinist, rear 128 Beach bel Shackamoxon
Matlack Joseph, 33 S 10th
Matlack Joseph B., bricklayer, 146 Marshall.
Matlack Louisa, 161 Marshall
Matlack Mahlon, N E Filbert and Sch 6th
Matlack Mason, carpenter, 18 Gebhard
30

Matlack Thomas, lime burner, N E Sch 6th and Filbert
Matlack William, tobacconist, R road & 12th
Matlock Aaron G., cordw., Ontario bel Parrish
Matsinger Adam, blacksmith, 448 Sassafras, h 15 Montgomery.
Matson James, carter, 9 Marion
Matson John, seaman, 8 Queen
Matthes Henry W., turner, Beaver ab 2d
Matthews Alpheus, salesman, 274 N 2d
Matthews Amy, 11th bel Sp Garden
Matthews Andrew, lab., Sycamore ab Locust
Matthews Ann, Centre ab 12th
Matthews Ann, widow, Sp Garden ab 7th
Matthews Austin, 19 Pleasant st
Matthews Caleb, M. D., 138 N Front
Matthews Charles, carter, Crown ab Queen
Matthews Charles, cordw., Palmer above Franklin (K)
Matthews Daniel, porter, Hurst's st
Matthews David, carp., 11 Orleans
Matthews David, grocer, Perry and Pine
Matthews Edward, carp., 630 S 2nd
Matthews Ellen A., confectioner, S E 11th and Locust
Matthews Enoch J., medicines, S E Front and Sassafras
Matthews Esther, gentw., 279 S Front
Matthews George, 548 N 2d
Matthews George W., cordw., Marlborough ab Queen
Matthews Hannah, 39 Middle alley.
Matthews Harrison, tailor, Queen st n Shackamaxon (K)
Matthews Henry, clerk, 41 Duke
Matthews Henry, carter, Sherborn's ct
Matthews Heppy, widow, Queen and Shackamaxon (K)
Matthews H., blacksmith, 42 N 7th, h 3 Clover
Matthews Isaac, captain, 5 Brown
Matthews Jane, 16 Filbert
Matthews James, blacksm., 6th and G T road
Matthews James, livery stable, 11th bel High, h 2 N 11th
Matthews James, cordwainer, 5 Goldsmith's ct
Mathews James, tailor, Sycamore
Matthews John, fruiterer, S W 9th & High, h Sassafras W of Sch 8th
Matthews John, piano finisher, Parrish n Broad
Matthews John, lab., Francis ab Powell (F V)
Matthews John, tinsmith, Sassafras ab Sch 8th
Matthews John H., oysterman, 24 Beck st
Matthews Lawrence, morocco dresser, G T road bel Master
Matthews Ludlam, mer., 19 Brown (N L)
Matthews Marg., widow, Duke ab Palmer (K)
Matthews Mary, Wheat ab Wharton
Matthews Mary, paper maker, 391 High.
Matthews Nathaniel, porter, Warren bel 12th
Matthews Patrick, lab., G T road ab Master
Matthews Peter V. painter, 33 Carleton
Matthews Samuel, shoemr. 7 Bank, h 218 Green
Matthews Samuel, carter, Lemon bel 11th
Matthews S. & Sons, boots and shoes, 7 Bank
Matthews Thomas, weaver, Sch 3d & Barker

Matthews Uriah, jr., clerk, 150 High, h 230 Green

Matthews William, boxmaker, Cadwalader ab Phœnix.

Matthews Wm. iron moulder, Callowhill ab Sch 5th

Matthews Wm. printer, 2 Carpenter (S)

Matthews Wm. cordw. 120 N 9th, h Spring Garden ab 8th

Matthews Wm., furniture, George & South

Matthews William H. broker, h 40 George (S)

Matthews Wm. W. carp. 154 Locust

Matthews W. M., mer., 7 Bank

Matthews W. Z., 11 Carlton

Matthewson Fan., washer, rear 142 S 4th

Matthewson Isabella, Fulton n 13th

Mattheys Charles T. salesman, 4 Jefferson row

Matthias Abel, carp., 94 St John

Matthias Benj., gent., 352 Vine

Matthias Isaiah, cordw., Brown and Charlotte

Matthias Joseph I., umbrella maker, 373 N 2d

Matthias Margaret, G T road n 4th

Matthias William M., moulder, 1 Rachel (N L)

Matthist James, waiter, 24 Elizabeth

Mattingly Lewis, shoemr. Catharine & Lebanon

Mattis Geo., carp., Ross n Queen (K)

Mattson Mary, milliner, 475 N 3d

Mattson Mary, sempstress, 11 Fayette

Mattson Noah S., tailor, 5th bel Franklin

Mattson Samuel H., tailor, 287 Chestnut

Mattson Thomas W., trunkmr., 198 & 299 High, h 12 N 3d

Mauck J. H., mer., 163 High, h 232 N 4th

Mauger Frederick, lime burner, Sch 2d above Vine

Mauger Martin, wheelwright, rear 3 Pascal al

MAULE & BROTHERS., lumber, Sch 6th bel Spruce

Maule Daniel, gent. 148 Mulberry

Maule Edward, lumber, Sch 6th bel Spruce, h Pine ab 10th

Maule Elisha P. steam flour & dye wood, Chestnut (W P) h Park and Chestnut

Maule Israel, lumber mer. Sch 6th bel Spruce, h Sch 6th bel Chestnut

Maule Joseph E., leather manuf., Margaretta bel 2d, h 436 N 5th

Maule Livinia, wid. of Caleb, Pine ab 10th

Maule Rachel, teacher, 531 Chestnut

Maule Wm., real est. broker, 46 Walnut, h 425 Mulberry

Maule Wm. 425 Mulberry

Maull Catharine, b h, 315 Cherry

Maull Elisha, cabinetmr., 4th bel Federal

Maull James, sail maker, Spruce st wharf, h 83 Pine

Maull James, jr., com. mer., 9 N Whfs., h 273 S 8th

Maull John, tobacconist, 63 N 6th

Maull John, tailor, 3 road bel Washington

Maull John T., atty. & coun., 35 Dock

Maull Joseph, ship carpenter, 25 Federal

Maull Joseph E., mer., 30 N 2d, h 132 Queen

Maull Joshua, lab., Carpenter ab 8th

Maull Mary, 19 Christian

Maull Robert F., hatter, 23½ N 2d, h 17 Lagrange place

Maull Robert W., sailmr., 18 Quarry

Maull Samuel, blacksmith, Pratt

Maull Wm. M., mer., 30 N 2d, h 49 Carpenter ab 3d

Maull Wm. M. & Joseph E., manufs. of straw goods, 30 N 2d

Maull Wm. N., sailmr., Spruce & S wharves, h 35 George (S)

Maully Thos., morocco dress., Mechanic above George

Maurer Andrew, cabinetmr. Hight's ct

Maurice William H. dry goods, 10th and Spring Garden

Mauty John, match mr., Clinton bel Parrish

Mawdsley John, chronometer mr., S E 5th and Siberg

Mawley Samuel, ostler, 16 Watson's alley

Maxem Wm., weaver, Carleton ab Sch 8th

Maxfield Alexander, porter, 4 Burd's ct

Maxfield Elizabeth, Fitzwater & Flower

Maxwell Andrew, carp., 3 Rittenhouse

Maxwell Andrew R., carp., Christian bel 3d, h Marriott bel 3d

Maxwell Catharine, Beach bel Maiden (K)

Maxwell David, tinsmith, 449 S 2d

Maxwell E. Mrs., 21 Coates

Maxwell Geo., carter, 127 G T road (K)

Maxwell Henry, lab. China bel 2d

Maxwell Hiram, carp. 12 Ogden

Maxwell Jac. G., coop., 196 S Water, h 170 S 2d

Maxwell James, manuf., Cedar ab 12th

Maxwell John, Sr., carp. 116 Christian

Maxwell John, tinsmith, Washington ab M road

Maxwell John, saddler, Kessler's al

Maxwell John, 171 Cherry

Maxwell John, boiler maker, rear Hanover ab Franklin (K)

Maxwell John, jr., carp., 27 Marriott

MAXWELL JOHN C., American House, 18 S 6th

Maxwell J. G. Rev., Beach ab Palmer (K)

Maxwell Marg., Sch 3d ab Walnut

Maxwell Maria, b h, 12th & Walnut

Maxwell & Mitchell, manuf. 13th bel Lombard

Maxwell Sarah, gentw. 8 Magnolia

Maxwell Sarah, teacher, 33 Plum

Maxwell Teresa, 195 S 9th

Maxwell Theodore, bootmr., 301 S 3d

Maxwell Thomas, gardener, Wagner's alley ab Fitzwater

Maxwell Wm., lab., Hanover bel Duke (K)

Maxwell Wm. R. Rev., Poplar & Rachel

May Elizabeth, gentw. 7 Coates

May Esther, 24 Parham

May Frederick, huckster, rear 402 N 2d

May George E., sea capt., 436 S Front

May Henry, brass founder, 8 Reun's av

May Henry, corder, Christian st whf, h Chrstian bel Front

May H. cabinetmr. 16 Beck

May Isaac, dry goods, 10 Rachel

May John, gent., 18 Apple

May John, piano mr. 128 N 5th

May John, drayman, Miller's ct
May Jonathan, capt., 3 Beck pl
May Lewis, carp. Smith's ct, Pearl ab 12th
May Mary, 85 N 10th
May Philip, machinist, 13th ab Coates
May Peter, dealer, 248 S 3d
May Samuel, lab., 4 Elmslie's al
May William, tailor, Rose alley n Green
Mayben James, manuf., 608 N 2d
Mayben John, carp. weaver, Hancock bel Master (K)
Mayberry Rebecca, Callowhill ab Sch 2d
Mayberry William, hatter, 21 Queen, h Hanover ab West
Maybury Wm., M. D., Wood & 8th
Mayer And., house and sign painter, 11th bel Callowhill
Mayer Chas., 205 N 6th
Mayer Charles, vict. G T road ab Jefferson
Mayer E. R., M. D., 138 Mulberry
Mayer Frederick P., Kesler ab Coates, h 174 Parrish
Mayer Henry S., M. D., S E 10th and Lombard
MAYER JACOB F., Globe Hotel, 42 S 6th
Mayer Jas., blacksm., 2d and Franklin (K)
Mayer John, broker, Sch 8th n Mulberry
Mayer John, baker, 100 St John
Mayer John, cordw. G T road ab 5th
Mayer John, lab. Clymer ab Mud la (K)
Mayer Lazarus, mer., 215½ High, h Crown and Vine
Mayer P. F. Rev., D. D., 20 Montgomery sq
Mayer Saml., store, 263 N 3d
Mayer Saml., 8 West st
Mayes Jos. buckskin finisher, Alder ab Poplar
Mayes Wm. brickmr. rear Alder ab Poplar
Mayger Henry, mer., 137 S 10th
Mayhew David, flour store, 6th bel Parrish, 64 Apple
Mayhew Gamaliel C., Orchard bel Jackson
Mayhew H., comb maker, 193 G T Road
Mayhew Mark, waiter, Raspberry ab Spruce
Mayhew Mary, rear 158 Brown
Mayhew Mrs., 189 S 5th
Mayhew Stanford, last maker, 81 Apple
Mayland Francis, lab., 7 Shippen
Mayland Henry, lab., Barker n Sch 6th
MAYLAND JACOB, ice mer. 129 Chestnut, h 153 N 6th
Mayland Jacob Jr. tobacconist, 111 Sassafras
MAYLAND J. jr. & CO., tobacconists, 111 Sassafras
Maynard Henry J. manuf. of fancy trimmings, 58 N 4th
Maynard & Hutton, com. mers., 94 High, h U S Hotel
Maynard John, com. mer. 94 High
Mayne Alexander, lab., Elm bel Franklin
Mayne Thomas, shoemaker, 15 Poplar
Maynes James, constable, Baker ab 7th
Maynes John, cordw., 130 Plum st
Maypole Tobias, beer house, G T road bel 4th (K)
Mays Ann, 16 Bonsall
Maze Benj., carp., 23 Mary (S)

Mazurie James V., gent., 60 Union
Mead Albert, 1 Norris' ct
Mead Alva C., 1 Norris' ct
Mead Eliza J., b. h., 75 Locust
Mead Elizabeth, gentw., 291 S 3d
Mead George, U S N, Sch 7th & Spruce
Mead John, porter, 5 Skerrett's ct
Mead Lewis, hair dresser, 4 N 13th
Mead Patrick, lab. 5 John's ct
Mead Richard H., coachman, 6 Acorn alley
Mead Thos., barber, 480 N 4th
Meade Edwd., druggist, 13 Sassafras
Meade Francis, port. painter, 13 Sassafras
Meader Edwd. M. printer, 287 S 3d
Meads Lucy, rear Carpenter ab 8th
Mealy Cath., provision store, 5 Perry st
Mealy Dennis, La Fayette ab 9th
Mealy John, clothier, 200 Shippen
Mealy Wm., brickmr., 13th bel Walnut
Means Elizabeth, 392 S 5th
Meany Thomas, brickmr., N E 12th & Shippen
Mearns Andrew, weaver, Marion and Corn
Mears Henry H., mer., Broad ab Cherry, h 25 Madison
Mears Jas., stone sawyer, Barker ab Sch 7th
Mears Jas., tobacco, 88 E Cedar
Mears John, lab. 24 Union (S)
Mears Jonathan W. waterman, 476 S Front (S)
Mears, Raynor & Co., fordw. and com. mers., Broad ab Cherry
Mears Jos., driver, Haydock bel Front
Mears Samuel, hatter, 401 High, h 30 N 10th
Mease Isabella, Sch 7th bel Spruce
Measles Jeremiah, waterm., 122 Washington av
Mecaskey Charlotte, 66 M road
Mecauley Thomas J., tin smith, 21 High, h 12th ab Brown
Mechesney John, lab. Harmstead n Sch 2d
Mecke George, cabinetmaker, 355 N 2d, h 171 Coates
Mecke Geo. H., saddler, Rose bel G T road (K)
Mecke George H., mer., 29 Church al, h 10th bel Spruce
Mecke Henry, cabinetmaker, 371 N 2d
Mecke Jacob, cabinetmr., 60 Coates
Mecke John, clock & watchmr., 359 N 2d, h 58 Duke
MECKE, PLATE & CO., mers., 29 Church al
Mecluer John P., carp., Lemon bel 11th
Meconch, James, weaver, Sch 2d bel Lombard
Meconch John, coal, Spruce n Sch
Meconnahey Joseph, carp. 10th ab Ogden
Mecutcheon Samuel M., millwr., Haydock bel Front, h 536 N Front
Medad George, shoemr. 41 Quince
Medara Joseph S., mer., 12 N 3d, h 58 Franklin
Medara Joseph S. & Co., mers., 12 N 3d
Medara Paschel H. mer., 12 N 3d
Medary Charles, blacksm. Front ab Otter (K)
Medary Margaret, Front bel Poplar
Mee John, mustard manuf., 30 Dock, h 93 Buttonwood
Mee John C., 93 Buttonwood
Meehan John, dealer, 7 Filbert av
Meehan Patrick, 20 Farmer

Meeker C. H., cordw., 507 N 3d
Meeker John, cordw., rear 30 Charlotte
Meeker Stephen, cordw., Coates ab 13th
Meeks Oliver P., shoemr., Mechanic
Meenan Francis, weaver, 3 Lloyd's ct
Meenen Mary, milliner, 93 S 6th
Mecser Christian, upholsterer, 17 Logan
Meeser & Coyle, japanners, 27 St John
Meeser Fred., gardener, West ab Wood (K)
Meeser Philip, japanner, 396 N 5th
Meeteer George B., livery stables, 340 N 3d, h 6 West
Megargee Samuel, lum. mer., Beach ab Marsh, h 430 N Front
Megargee Sarah, Rose ab School (K)
MEGARGEE S. J. & CO., paper ware house, 29 Commerce
Megargy Tacy, 4 Rittenhouse
Megear T. J., watch maker, 20 N 2d, h 49 Mulberry
Megee George, coppersmith, 11 Branch, h 39 Dillwyn
Megee John, bookbinder, 58 Wood
Megee Mary, b. h. 360 S Front
MEGEE & ROBERTS, coppersms., 11 Branch
Meggit John S., painter and glazier, 1 Boyd's av
Meggs John G., bootmaker, 17 S 5th, h 5th & Prime
Meggs Rachel, b h, 238 High
Megill Chas., machinist, 271 Wood
Megines Jas., plasterer, rear Beach bel Maiden (K)
Meginnis John, carter, 38 Fitzwater
Meginnis Wm. F., rope mr., 8th ab Carpenter
Megirkey Thos., weaver, 559 N 2d (K)
Megonegal James, stonecutter, Ann (F V)
Megonegal Michael, sign painter, 5 N 9th, h 11th ab S Garden
Megonegal Saml., cotton spin., 13th ab Christian
Megonegal Wm., shop, Poplar ab 5th
Megrew Sarah, shoe binder, Ogden's ct
Meguire James D., clerk, 25 Coombe's al
Meguire John, manuf., 2 Kelly's ct
Mehaffey Thomas, h George ab Sch Beech
Meholand Wm., baker, 561 N Front ab Otter
Meholland Robt., weaver, rear 561 N 2d (K)
Mehtens John, baker, 12th bel Poplar
Meichel Geo., hair dresser, Beach bel Marlboro'
Meigs Charles D. jr., mer., 177½ High
MEIGS C. D., M. D., 284 Chestnut
Meigs J. F., M. D., 317 Walnut
Meiley Jas., porter, rear of Barker W of Sch 5th
Mein Harriet Mrs., 10th & Brown
Mein Isaac P., clerk Philadelphia Bank, Brown bel 10th
Melbeck John H., Franklin ab Hanover (K)
Melcher Charles, brickmaker, 6th ab Poplar
Melcher John, cooper, 4th ab Culvert
Melcher John Jr., c 4th and Culvert
Melcher Wm., cooper, 13 Farmer
Meley Wm., tailor, 303 S 8th
Melius Wm., ladies' shoemr., Otter n School
Melizet John M., mer., 112 S whfs, h 95 Spruce
Mellon John, carp., M'Clung's ct ab Orange
Mellon John, hatter, 103 S 5th

Mellon Mary, Washington bel 2d
Mellon Mary, Church bel Christian
Mellon Nathaniel, blacksmith, 22 Catharine
Mellon Thomas, gent., 270 Spruce
Mellon Thos., paper stain., 186 Carpenter
Mellon Thos., druggist, 127 Spruce
Mellor Austin, veterinary surg., Hunter ab 10th, h 14 College av
Mellor Charles, machinist, 11th bel Sp Garden, shop Pleasant ab 12th
Mellor George, druggist, 113 Walnut
Mellor Joseph, porter, Vaux's ct
Mellor Thomas, druggist, 127 Spruce
Mellor Thomas, importer, 99 Mulberry, h R road ab G. College
Melloy John M., tinsmith, 303 High, h 5 Clinton
Melsh Wm. F., stove fin., 370 S 5th
Meltler Wm. lab., Perry ab Franklin (K)
Melvin Mary, stone cutter, Callowhill bel 10th
Mench Chas. B., upholsterer, 121 S 2d
Mench George C., cabinetmaker, 282 R road
Mench Mary Ann Mrs. feather manuf. 310 N 2d
Mendenhall Albert, teacher, Parrish bel Broad
Mendenhall Eli, Melon ab 9th
Mendenhall Milton, machinist, 169 Mulberry
Mendenhall James, machinist, Melon ab 9th
Mendenhall Philip, acct., 76 N Front
Mendes Antoin, barber, Penn & Cedar
Meneely Wm., carpet weav., Franklin ab Shackamaxon
Menige Dominick, plas., 2 P road
Menk Anthony, lab., 2 Fisher's ct
Menns John, victualler, James ab Charles
Menns Joseph H., vict., Charles & Pleasant
Menough Wm., tailor, 7 Baker's ct. (N L)
Mensing Wm. D., ladies' shoemr., 2 Oldham's ct
Mentz Charles, painter, 202 N Front, h 18 New Market
Mentz Edward, carp., 422 N 5th
Mentz James, waterman, 6 Burd st
Mentz & Rovoudt, booksellers and stationers, 53 N 3d
Mentz Wm. G., stationer, 53 N 3d, h 7 City row
Menzies John, watchmr., Carpenter ab 6th
Menzies John, watch maker, S W Front and Spruce, h 142 S Front
Mercer Alex. G. Rev., 1 Boston row
MERCER, BROTHERS & CO., com. mers, 21 S whfs. and 31 S Water
Mercer David, car. weav. Queen & Palmer K
Mercer George P., corder, 1st whf ab Catharine, h 60 Queen
Mercer Hall W., mer., 21 S whfs. and 31 S Water, h 1 Boston row
Mercer Henry, ship carp., Warren ab Beach (K)
Mercer Jane H., 1 Boston row
Mercer John A. corder, 1st wharf ab Catharine h 36 Catharine
Mercer J. C., mer., 21 S whfs., h 4 Colonnade row
Mercer Maria, washer, 20 Burd's ct
Mercer Robert, blacksmith, Say & Sch 7th
Mercer Robert, 27 Spruce
Mercer Robert J., mer., 1st whf bel Swedes' church, h Washington ab 3d, (S)

Mercer Singleton, h 457 S Front
Mercer Singleton A., mer., 21 S whfs., h Sch. 7th ab Spruce
Mercer Thomas, gent., 457 S Front
Mercer & Pechin, steam saw mills, Wharf above Washington
Mercer William, glass cutter, Palmer bel Queen (K)
Merchant Elihu B., Chestnut, h 183 N 10th
Merchant Robert, stone cutter, Ann n Powell
Mercier Charles, confectioner, 111 S 3d
Meredith Edwin, druggist, 184 High
Meredith Edwin & Co. druggists, 184 High
Meredith Geo., dealer, 13th & Coates
Meredith Henry, 93 Catharine
Meredith James, lab., Marriott ab 5th
Meredith John, coppersm., Allen's ct
Meredith Levin, coachmr., 72 Queen
Meredith Robt., shoemr., 3 Lodge al
Meredith Samuel, drayman, 132 F road
Meredith Wm., tobacconist, 108 F road
MEREDITH WM. M., att'y & coun., 9 York buildings
Mereto Joseph, fruiterer, 424 High
Merker James, weaver, 15th & Catharine
Merkle Aug. C. prov., Beach bel Hanover (K)
Merkle Ben., moulder, Monroe n Palmer (K)
Merkle Conrad, bootmaker, 404 Coates
Merkle John, keeper M. prison, P road bel Carpenter
Merkle John, moulder, Queen ab Hanover (K)
Merkle Josh., agent, Little Dock
Merkle Perry, silver plater, Front and Green
Merkle S. B., engineer, Marlborough ab Beach
Merrefield John G., dry goods, 459 N 2d, h 266 N 4th.
Merrefield Joseph, mer., 13 N 2d h 116 Mulberry
Merrick Ann, gentw., 254 S Front
Merrick Charles, gent., Queen bel Ross (K)
Merrick Charles B., druggist, 313 E Pine
Merrick & Co., com.mers, 19 N 4th
Merrick Elizabeth, Washington ab Front
Merrick George, carpenter, 1 Elfreth's al
Merrick Henry, baker, Fitzwater n 13th
Merrick James, carp., 4 Mineral pl
Merrick Robert, weaver, Walnut & Ashton
Merrick Saml., driver, George ab R road (F V)
Merrick Saml., mer., 19 N 4th, h 9th ab Coates
Merrick Samuel, pattern mr., Ogden ab 12th
Merrick Saml. V., steam engine manuf., Prime bel 5th, h W Penn square
Merrick & Towne, steam engine builders and engineers, Prime bel 5th, office 32 Walnut
Merrihew S. E., printer, 7 Carter's alley, h 246 Christian
Merrihew & Thompson, printers, 7 Carter's al
Merrill John, bonnet presser, 15 Pear
Merrill John P., port. painter, 92 N 7th
Merrill Wm., O.B. keeper, Parrish ab Sch 8th
Merritt Elizabeth, milliner, 67 Mulberry
Merritt Geo., blacksmith, Beach ab Maiden (K)
Merritt John, ship carp., Marlborough below Allen
Merritt Thomas, glass cutter, Allen & Palmer (K)

Merritt Wm., ship carp., Marlborough bel Allen (K)
Merritt Williamson R., carter, Crown ab Queen (K)
Merron Wm., cordw., Perry bel Master (K)
Merry Felix, weaver, 225 Shippen
Merry John, box mr., Moore's ct (S G)
Merry Michael, gent., 127 S 6th
Merryman John, tailor, rear 68 Catharine
Merryweather A. M., bookbinder, 3d and Mulberry, h 131 N 10th
Merser George, weav., rear Otter bel G T road (K)
Mershom James, waterman, Queen ab Hanover (K)
Mershon Daniel, locksm., 21 N 7th, h Division bel 12th
Mersinjer Jacob, brewer, 261 St John
Mertz John G., fly net mr., 36 N 6th
Mervin Ferdinand, cordw., 8 Shield's ct
Mervine Geo., carrier, 7 Nectarine ab 10th
Mervine Isaac, blacksm. 8 Dunkers, h 18 Barron
Mervine Joseph, skin dresser, School
Mervine Mary, Orchard, bel Rawle
Mervine Reuben, vict., Powell bel Sch 4th
Mervine Samuel, machinist, 6 Hickory ct
Mervine Thomas, farmer, 149 Buttonwood
Mervine Thos., stone cutter, 2 Smith's pl
Mervine Washington, butcher, Sch 8th below Coates
Mervine Wm., plasterer, Vinyard ab Powell (F V)
Merwin Mary, 409 Chestnut
Meserve Wm., lab., Grover
Mesker George, butcher, rear 116 Brown
Mesquita A. J., tailor, 254 S 4th
Messchert H., 15 N 8th
Messeck Eliza, 41 Union (S)
Messele Jacob, gardener, West bel Cherry
Messick John, shoemr., 10 Harmony st
Messinger John, baker, 92 Cherry
Metcalf Joseph, painter, 202 Sassafras
Metcalf Thomas, watchman, 34 Pratt
Metcalf Wm., printer, 3d ab Franklin (K)
Metcalfe James, lab., Jones n Sch 4th
Metcalfe Mary A., 61 New
Meter Calvin, mariner, 32 Union (S)
METLAR G. W., currier, 102 N 4th, h Clinton ab Brown
Mette G. W., blacksmith, 15 Dyott's ct (K)
Mettenheimer Henry, tailor, 143 Vine
Metter William, coachmr., Marriott ab 4th
Mettern Samuel, machinist, 2d bel Jefferson (K)
Mettler Lydia, 48 Green
Mettler I., cake br, S W New Market & Green
Mettler Samuel, New Market & Geeen
Mettler Wm. baker, S W New Market & Green
Metts Adam, bricklayer, 10 Chatham
Metts Thomas, waterman, 58 M road
Metts George, carp., 10 Chatham
Metz Adam, Pearl bel Sch 7th
Metz Geo., shipsmith, Lancaster ab Reed
Metz George, locksmith, Nixon ab Callowhill
METZ GEORGE W., brushmr., 317 High, h 166 Cherry

Metz Hannah, Marriott and 5th
Metz Henry, turner, Wood ab R road
Metz John, cabtmr., 45 Lombard
Metz Jonas, clerk, 71 German
Metz Robert, brush maker, 267 S 4th
Metz Samuel, stone mason, 31 John (S)
Metzger Christian, twister, 123 Brown
Metzger George, grocer, G T road & Master
Metzger Godfrey, brassfound., Elm bel Franklin
Metzger Jacob, ship carpenter, Allen ab Marlborough
Metzger John F., cordw., 180 Poplar
Metzger Mary, 5th bel George (N L)
Metzker John, high constable, 23 Montgomery
Metzler George, lab., Hanover bel Franklin
Meurer Frederick W., dyer, Crown & Queen(K)
MEYER & BATTIN, grocers, 302 N 2d
MEYER CONRAD, piano fortemr., 52 S 4th
Meyer C. H., teacher, Sch 3d ab Sassafras
Meyer Enos, grocer, 74 Noble
Meyer Fred. scale manuf. 196 High, house George bel 3d,
MEYER FREDERICK & CO., scale manufacturers, 196 High
Meyer Geo. O., cooper, 71 St Johns
Meyer Henry, tailor, 6 Laurel (C)
Meyer Henry C., capt. watch, Broad ab Locust
Meyer Herman, bootmr., 4 Wagner's ct
Meyer John, lab., 2d ab Edward (K)
Meyer John H., blacksmith and stove finisher, 58 F road
Meyer Joseph, bootmr. 1 Zane
Meyer Martin, carpenter, 81 New
Myers Charles W., lampmr., 7th ab Poplar
Meyers Catharine, Mechanic & George (N L)
Meyers George, carp. Wallace bel 10th
Meyers Henry, lamp mr., 3 Logan
Meyers Joseph, dealer, 201 Shippen
Meyer Mart., carp., 24 Franklin pl, h Rogers' ct
Meyer Michael, pianomr., 4 Raspberry la
Meyers Lewis, cabinetmr. 24 Dyott's ct (K)
Meyers Wm., cigarmr., 9 Charlotte
Meyers & Wise, candymrs., 7th & Sp Garden
Meyring John G., confectionery, 107 Cherry
Michael Peter Mifflin & Orleans
Michael Philip, carter, Mechanic bel Green
Michaels Anthony, capt., 253 S Front
Michaels John, paper stainer, State ab 8th
Michaels Louisa, wid. of John, Hanover above Franklin
Michener Frances, b h, 57 N 4th
Michener Geo. W., tailor, 372 N 2d
Michener Israel, mer., 17 S Water
Michener J. H. & Co. provisions, 17 S Water
Michin John, turner, 237 S 5th
Mickle Jas., stirrup filer, Franklin bel Cherry (K)
Mickle James, cooper, 52 Allen
Mickle Wm. H., cordw., Queen ab Shackamaxon
Mickley Joseph J., pianomr., 359 High
Middleton Aaron, oak cooper, 26 Union (S)
Middleton Anna, 5 Combes' al
Middleton & Co., morocco and leather, Willow n 2d

Middleton Edward P. grocer, 9 High
Middleton Elizabeth, 22 Union (S)
Middleton Francis, porter, Stevenson's ct
Middleton Francis, St John ab Beaver (K)
Middleton Frederick M., dealer, 344 N 3d
Middleton George W. mer. 11 High, h 19 Ellen (N L)
Middleton Hendon, b h, 375 Mulberry
Middleton Jedediah, carp., 279 Coates
Middleton John Jr., 12 George
MIDDLETON JOHN B., scourer, 16 N 8th
Middleton John L., wharf builder, Beach bel Marlborough (K)
Middleton John W., iron & coal mer., 279 N 2d, h 222 N 4th.
Middleton Josiah, mer., Pleasant bel 13th
Middleton Martha, Church bel Christian
Middleton Nathan, bricklayer, 7th & Parrish
Middleton Nathan, iron & coal mer., R road ab Callowhill, h Wallace bel 8th
Middleton Rebecca, 3 Say's ct
Middleton Samuel, bricklayer, Prime bel 3d
Middleton Samuel, machinist, Whitehall
Middleton Spencer, mer., 7 N 2d
Middleton Thomas K., bootmaker, Sch 7th bel Pine
Middleton Wm. drayman, Dunton bel Franklin (Kensington)
Middleton William, shoemaker, Pike
Middleton Wm., plumber, 311 Shippen
Middleton Wm. H., dealer, 4th bel Poplar
Midlen Wm. tobacconist, 17 Mead
Midwinter Mrs., milliner, 148½ Cedar
Mier Samuel, brewer, 140 Swanson
Miercken Henry F., captain, Spruce ab 12th
Miercken John W., captain, 84 Lombard
Mierly Jacob, cordw., rear 48 Brown
Miesell Isaiah, cabmr., R road bel Broad
Mifflin Ann, washer, Tenfoot al
Mifflin Ann, gentw., 226 Spruce
Mifflin Benjamin, 144 S 10th
Mifflin Eliza, 25 Dock
Mifflin Elizabeth, 324 Walnut
Mifflin Henry J. attorney and coun. 12 Prune
Mifflin James D., brush maker, 524 N 2d
Mifflin James L., mer., 338 Chestnut
Mifflin John L., mer., 91 S Front, h 338 Chestnut
Mifflin Sarah, 338 Chestnut.
Migeod John M., saddler, 9th bel Poplar
Mihlbauer John, upholsterer, 13 New Market
Milburn Geo., rear Carpenter ab 8th
Milburn Thomas, currier, 154 Cherry
Milby George, drayman, 6 Prosperous al
Milby John, Customhouse off., 236 S 3d
Miles Abraham, watchman, 26 Gebbard
Miles Catharine, dry goods, 429 N 3d
Miles Edward W., mer., 179 High, h 291 N 8th
Miles George W., bookbinder, 431 N 3d
Miles Henry, carp., Torr's al ab 9th
Miles Isaac L., cabmr., 66 Queen
Miles Jacob, bootmaker, 25 S 4th, h 176 N 9th
Miles John, carp., Richard n 7th
MILES JOHN, att'y & coun., 2 York Building.
Miles John T., turner, Sun ct

Miles J. & Son, bootmrs., 25 S 4th.
Miles Mary, eating house, 26 High
Miles Mich., spinner, rear 487 N 3d
Miles Richard L., cordw., Loud bel 10th
Miles Robert, stonecutter, 3d & Tammany
Miles Robert, plater, 102 S 10th
Miles Thos., bootmr., 25 S 4th, h 48 Franklin
Miles Wm., tinsmith, Van Buren pl
Miles Wm. G., carp., 5 Linden (K)
Miles W. H., machinist, 9 Maiden
Miley Barbara, 91 N Juniper
Miley Catharine, shop, Cherry & Gebhard
Miley Fred., Callowhill ab Sch 6th
Miley George, lab., 10 Bickham
Miley Hannah, Queen ab Schack (K)
Miley John, silver plater, Hallowell's ct (S G)
Miley Samuel, wheelwt., 18 W Cedar
Milford Ann, teacher, Sch 7th n Vin
Milford Mary, milliner, 116 N 4th
Millar Thomas, collector, 41 Race
Millard James, ship carver, Palmer bel Duke (K)
Millard Wm. clerk, Concord ab 2d
Millburn James, barber, 197 E Lombard
Millechop Matilda, trimmings, 393 Sassafras
Miller Aaron H., engineer, rear 114 Cherry
Miller Abraham, potter, Willow n Broad, h
   Spruce and Sycamore
Miller Adam, planemr. Sassafras ab Broad
Miller Adam, lab., rear 607 N 6th
Miller Alexander, cab. mr., 153 S 2d, h 3d bel
   Washington
Miller Allen B. broker, Sch 8th n Cherry
MILLER ANDREW, rec. of deeds, State House,
   h Catharine bel 7th
Miller Andrew H., com. mer., 152 N 3d, h 93
   New
Miller Ann, 27 Turner
Miller Anthony, baker, 13th ab Coates
Miller Anthony, carter, 49 New Market
Miller Anthony H., provisions, 302 Vine, h 143
   S 6th
Miller Augustus, fly netmr. R road ab 13th
Miller Benedict, umbrella mr., 116 N 6th
Miller Benjamin, coachman, Salem al
Miller Benjamin, lab. Pearl ab Nixon
Miller Benjamin, shop, 230 S 7th
Miller Benjamin F., cigarmr., 3 New Market
Miller Benjamin R., grocer, Hamilton & Cedar
Miller & Brother, com. mers., 152 N 3d.
Miller Caleb, pianomr. S W 6th & Sassafras
Miller Caspar, weaver, Perry ab Phoenix
Miller Catharine, Green ab 6th
Miller Catharine, rear Olive bel 13th
Miller Catharine M., Sch 8th ab Wood
Miller Charles, cordwr., Rose ab School (K)
Miller Charles, ship carp., 145 Beach (K)
Miller Charles, printer, Duke bel Palmer (K)
Miller Chas., machinist, Spruce ab Sch Front
Miller Charles, coal dealer, Exch. Buuildings, h
   98 Marshall
Miller Charles, varnish boiler, 90 Poplar
Miller Chas., carter, Gray's ct (N L)
Miller Chas., waiter, Pearl ab 13th
Miller Charles F., baker, 156 S Front
Miller Chas. G. bookbinder, 368 N 6th

Miller Charles G., 36 S 8th
Miller Charles M. clerk, 7th bel Parrish
Miller Charles P., mer., 95 High, h 4 Montgo-
   mery sq
Miller Christian, skin dresser, 5 Young's al
Miller Christian, baker, 601 N 2d
Miller Christian, brewer, Bryan's ct
Miller Christian, baker, 176 Pine
MILLER CHRISTIAN A., tavern, 69 Sassafras
Miller Christiana, shop, Coates ab Sch 7th
Miller Clayton, clothes, 34 S 2d, h 14 Currant al
MILLER, COOPER & Co. dry goods, 95 High
Miller Cyrus B., hair dresser, 44 N 4th
Miller Daniel, shoemr. Wharton ab 4th
Miller Daniel, combmaker, Front ab Oxford (K)
Miller Daniel, porter, 27 Quince
Miller Daniel K., 310 N 2d
Miller Daniel L. jr. merchant, 56 S Front, h 139
   N 10th
Miller David, lab., Raspberry ab Spruce
Miller David, 16 Quince
Miller David, waterm., Palmer bel Franklin (K)
Miller David, blacksm., Crown ab Queen (K)
Miller David, 210 N 13th n Callowhill
Miller D. L. & Co., druggists, 56 S Front
Miller D. L., mer., 95 High, h 250 Mulberry
Miller D. Sutter, mer., 95 New.
Miller Ebenezer, tooth brushmr. Crown above
   Duke (K)
Miller Edward, shoemr., Western pl
Miller Edward, tailor, Vail's ct
Miller Edward, civil engineer, 7 Sansom, h 64
   S 13th
Miller Edward, ladies' shoes, 13th and Pearl
Miller Edward, waiter, 27 Currant al
Miller Edward J., carp., 75 Queen (S)
Miller Edward W., bookbinder, George ab 6th,
   h 7th bel Parrish
Miller Elizabeth, cake baker, 348 N 3d
Miller Elizabeth, 71 Green
Miller Elizabeth, washer, West bel Hanover (K)
Miller Elizabeth, wid. of Jas. 8th bel Carpenter
Miller Elizabeth, 7 Harmony ct
Miller Enoch, waiter, 90 Gaskill
Miller Esther, milliner, 10th bel James
Miller E. Spencer, atty. & coun., 45½ S 5th
Miller Francis, carp. Lewis E Sch 5th
Miller Francis, tavern, 54 Callowhill
Miller Francis, cordwr. School bel Franklin (K)
Miller Francis X., shop store, Poplar ab 3d
Miller Frederick, rigger, 35 Marion ab 2d
Miller Frederick W. music store, 35 N 4th
Miller Frederick W., planemr., Maria n 5th
Miller George, gunsmith, 30 Queen
Miller George, whitewasher, Eagle's ct
Miller George, butcher, 262 N 8th
Miller George, tailor, Beach ab Poplar, (K)
Miller George, confectioner, 214 High, h 35 Filbert
Miller George, blacksmith, G T road & 6th
   (K)
Miller George, drayman, 356 S Front
Miller George, Son & Co., dry goods, 112 N 3d,
   h 51 Callowhill
Miller George, carp., 16 Mary (S)
Miller George, bootmr. 264 St John

Miller George, gunsmith, 203 Queen
Miller Geo. B., clerk, M road bel Washington
Miller George G., combmr. 55 Apple
Miller George H., hardware, 79 N 3d, h 187 N 7th
Miller Geo. K., dry goods, 182 N 2d
Miller George W., moroc. finisher, 189 St John
Miller George W., tailor, N E 13th & Locust
Miller Georgianna, milliner, G T road ab Phœnix (K)
Miller Hannah, teacher, 158 Wood
Miller Hego, boot fitter, rear Noble ab 5th
Miller Henrietta, tavern, 5th and Queen
Miller Henry, fisherman, Vienna bel Franklin (K)
Miller Henry; cordw., 13 Maria
Miller Henry, butcher, Square bel Corn
Miller Henry, machinist, G T road ab Phœnix
Miller Henry, dyer, 291 Sassafras
Miller Henry, tailor, Atherton
Miller Henry, bricklay. Vienna ab Franklin (K)
Miller Henry, broker, 9 Exchange pl
Miller Henry G. combmr. 12 Bread
Miller H. Henry, vict., 61 Garden
Miller Hiram, carp., Green ab 13th
Miller Horace, weaver, Crown bel Duke (K)
Miller Hosea, broker, 9 Exchange pl. h 8th ab Cedar
Miller Hugh, lab. 4 Truxton
Miller Isaac, iron, 125 N Water or 60 N whfs., h 211 N 6th
Miller Jacob, sashmr., Melon bel R. rd., h Penn bel Broad
Miller Jacob, sail maker, 33 & 34 S Whfs, h 9 Queen
Miller Jacob, carp., 3 Franks' ct
Miller Jacob, ship carp., Hanover n Bedford (K)
Miller Jacob, combmaker, 563 N 5th
Miller Jacob, butcher, Hanover ab Franklin (K)
Miller Jacob, tailor, 292 Coates
Miller Jacob, carp. 252 Marshall
Miller Jacob, ropemr., Washington ab 13th
Miller Jacob S., mer. h 308 Coates
Miller James, lab., Reed bel Front
Miller James, baker, 27 Prune
Miller James, shoemaker, Little Green ab Cadwalader (K)
Miller James, weaver, court Front bel Master
Miller James, planemr., 241 St John
Miller James, carter, Filbert E. of Sch. 5th
Miller James jr., cooper, Mulberry bet Sch. 7th and 8th
Miller James F., carp, York place
Miller James F., sea captain, 11 German
Miller James H. painter, 137 N Juniper
Miller James J., porter, 2 Osborn's ct
Miller James W., turner, 48 S 5th
Miller Jane, gentw., Sch. 4th bel Lombard
Miller Jane, fancy store, 260 Sassafras
Miller Jane, huckster, 15 Farmer
Miller Jane, milliner, 89 N 2d
Miller John jr., clerk, 182 N 2d
Miller John, bleeder, Bedford bel 8th
Miller John, waterman, Newton (S)
Miller John, lab., 42 Bread
Miller John, seaman, 56 Blackberry al

Miller John, weaver, court Front bel Master
Miller John, carpet weaver, 225 St John
Miller John, tailor, 31 N 6th
Miller John, lab., Greenwich ab 2d
Miller John, carter, Jones E Sch. 4th
Miller John, measurer, 182 N 2d
Miller John, clerk County Comrs., h 470 N 4th
Miller John, blacksmith, 153 S 5th
Miller John, stevedore, 118 Swanson
Miller John, bricklayer, Hanover ab West (K)
Miller John, drayman, Lewellen's av (K)
Miller John, lab., Sch. 8th bel Walnut
Miller John, baker, School n Franklin (K)
Miller John, bootmr. 9 Quarry
Miller John, carter, Green ab R road
Miller John, weaver, 9 Bauersach's ct (K)
Miller John, farmer, (W P)
Miller John, lab., 100 Apple
Miller John, weaver, F. road ab Master (K)
Miller John, lab., Jackson ct (N L)
Miller John, shop, G T road ab Thompson (K)
Miller John, salesman, 81 Juniper
Miller John B., carp., 49 New Market
Miller John C., baker, R. rd & Vineyard (F V)
Miller John C., mariner, rear 1 Wall
Miller John C., saddler, 471 N 4th
Miller John D., lab., School ab Otter (K)
Miller John F., baker, 474 N 2d
Miller John G., book bind., Elizabeth ab Poplar
Miller John G., music and pianos, 35 N 4th h 141 Wood
Miller John L., turner, 259 St. John
Miller John P., carp., Elizabeth ab Poplar
Miller John S., hatter, 31 Sp. Garden
Miller John T., M. D., 278 N 8th
Miller Jonah, blacksmith, 155 Shippen, h 58 Federal
Miller Joseph, tailor, 247 Christian
Miller Joseph, gent., 93 New
Miller Joseph, cooper, 201 O Y road
Miller Joseph, real estate, 3 Sp. Garden, h 8th bel Wallace
Miller Joseph A., grocery, 210 Noble
Miller Joseph D., tailor, 6 Filbert av
Miller Joseph H., tavern, W Wood and Broad
Miller Joseph S., harnessmr., 110 Chestnut, h 460 Callowhill
Miller Jos. W., com. mer., 152 N 3d, h 93 New
Miller Jupiter, lab., 28 Mayland
Miller Justice Henry, gent., Washington ab 13th
Miller J. Craig, gent. 194 Spruce
Miller Lewis, lab., 5th bel G T road (K)
Miller Lewis, bill poster, rear 47 Commerce
Miller L., cordw., 352 N 3d
Miller Manilla, miller, 157 S 11th
Miller Margaret, Elizabeth ab Poplar
Miller Margaret, huckster, rear 402 N 2d
Miller Mark, cabtmr., rear 23 John
Miller Mark W. wheelwright, Vine ab 13th, h 13th ab Callowhill
Miller Mary Mrs., tailoress, 36 S 5th
Miller Mary, gentw., 177 Green
Miller Mary, tailoress, 450 N Front
Miller Mary, washer, rear 11 Eutaw
Miller Mary, washer, 444 Sassafras

Miller Mary Ann, dry goods, Poplar ab 13th
Miller Mary Ann, nurse, Garretson's row
Miller Mary Ann, tailoress, Pearl ab 13th
MILLER MATTHEW jr., coal deal., 32 N 7th
MILLER MATTHEW T., exchange broker, 20 S 3d, h Spruce bel 11th
Miller Michael, lab. 4 Moore's ct (S G)
Miller M. Mrs., gentw., N W 7th & Walnut
Miller M. A., milliner, 161 Green
Miller Nicholas, blacksm., Centre bel Parrish
Miller Paul N., plasterer, Bedford n Elm (K)
Miller Perry, clothing, 499 High
Miller Peter, M. D., 101 N 5th
Miller Peter, grocer, 3d & Vine. h 78 Franklin
Miller Peter, carp., Green ab 6th
Miller Peter H., carp., Loxley's ct, h rear 148 Sassafras
Miller Philip, tavern, c F road and Hanover
Miller Philip H., barber, Poplar ab Charlotte
Miller Philip J., boiler mr., Franklin bel Front (K)
Miller Ralph, carter, Pearl ab 13th
Miller Reading, wheelwt., Kennedy's ct (N L)
Miller Reuben B., mer. 112 N 3d, h 144 Marshall
Miller & Rinehart, carps., Loxley's ct
Miller Robert, porter, Pearl bel 13th
Miller Robert, porter, Levy's ct
Miller Robert, carp., Shippen ab 12th
Miller Robert L. flour & feed, High & Ashton
Miller Robert T. grocer, High ab Sch 4th
Miller Samuel, teamster, Coates bel Broad
Miller Samuel, ship carp., 487 S 2d
Miller Samuel, vict. Bedford bel Crown (K)
Miller Samuel, drayman, Chandler's ct (K)
MILLER SAMUEL, Chestnut st. House, 121 Chestnut
Miller Samuel, oak cooper, George ab 4th
Miller Samuel, carp., 420 N 9th
Miller Samuel, lab., 59 Apple
Miller Samuel, saddler, rear 210 Cherry
Miller Samuel A., carp., 13th bel Green
Miller Samuel B., confectioner, 202 N 6th
Miller Samuel C. teacher, Elizabeth ab Poplar
Miller Samuel P. blacksmith, 172 Spruce
Miller Sarah, shop, Vienna bel Franklin (K)
Miller Sarah, 97 G. T. road
Miller, Son & Erringer, grocers, 3d & Vine
Miller Stephen, waiter, Juniper ab High
Miller Susannah, gentw., Franklin n Spring Garden
Miller Thomas, reed mr., N W 12th & Shippen
Miller Thomas, lab., 25 Prosperous al
Miller Thomas, lab. Charles ab William
Miller Thomas, cabinetmr., 15 John
Miller Thompson, rear 55 Mulberry
Miller Valentine, baker, 29 Powell
Miller William Mrs., 258 N 7th
Miller William, master Navy Yard, 18 Federal
Miller William, drayman, 245 S 7th
Miller William, drayman, 2 Rittenhouse
Miller William, grocer N E 6th and Carpenter
Miller Wm., watchman, Loxley's ct
Miller Wm., shoemr., Perry ct
Miller Wm. stonecutter, Filbert bel Sch 4th
Miller Wm., bricklayer, Hanover ab West (K)

Miller Wm., clockmr., 12th bel Callowhill
Miller Wm., tinsmith, Sch. 8th bel Cherry
Miller Wm., lab., Coates ab Broad
Miller Wm. H., dep. marshall, State House, h 18 S 6th
Miller Wm. R., carp, 106 Prime
Miller Wm. S., clockmr., 270 Cedar
Miller William T., tavern, N E Broad & Coates
Millet John, coffee roaster, 600 N 4th
Millette Thomas, book agent, 26 Cherry
Millham William C., vinegar, Pleasant ab 11th
Millick John, vict., 12th and Parrish
Millick Wm., butcher, 7th bel Washington
Milliette Joseph, type founder, 36 P. road
Milliette Mrs. Margaret, Wheat ab Wharton
Milligan Francis, mer., S W 6th and High, h 133 Pine
Milligan George A., clerk, Lombard bel 13th
Milligan George W., tailor, rear 136 Swanson
Milligan John, weaver, Philip ab Master (K)
Milligan Patrick, shop, S 7th ab Fitzwater
Milligan P. W., oysters, 524 High
Milligan Robert, gent. 10th bel Cedar
Milligan Thomas, lab., Brown ab Cherry
Milligan Wm., tailor, Gulielma
Milligan William, tailor, 163 and h 461 S 2d
Milligan Wm., confect., rear 20 Rose alley
Milligan Wm., lab., rear Mintzer
Milligan Wm. locksmith, 91 S Water
Milligan Wm. C., mer., S W 6th & High, h 133 Pine
Milliken James, tavern, 460 N 2d
Millikin Samuel, furniture, 90 N 6th
Millikin Samuel, linens, 70 Chestnut
Milliman Francis, tailor, M. road bel Washington
Milliman Sarah, 3 Lemon
Millington Mathias, printer, 270 N 2d
Millis A., umbrella mr., 91 Franklin
Millis James, lab., rear 5 Quarry
Millis John H., umbrella mr., 42 Tammany
Millis Wm., furniture, 506 High
Millman James K. carp. 13th bel Wallace
Millman M., 98 N 6th
Millman Wm., cordw., 284 St John
Milloy Peter, tavern, 62 E Cedar
Mills Edward, lab. Bickham W Sch 8th
Mills Elizabeth, 9 Tamarind
Mills George, cordw., Vine ab Broad
Lills Jacob, carter, Thompson bel Sch 6th
Mills John, weaver, Marlboro' ab Bedford (K)
Mills John, tavern, 13 Norris' al
Mills John D., cordw. Edward bel 2d
Mills John L. 12 Pratt
Mills Joseph D. shoemr. Davis' ct
Mills Martha, 3 Wiley's ct
Mills Samuel, shoemr., 61 N 8th
Mills Sarah, 12 Pratt
Mills Stephen, shoemr. 451 Vine
Mills William, weaver, F road & Otter
Mills Wm. C., saddler, Olive bel Broad
Mills William F., hair dresser, 468 N 3d
Mills William H. hair dresser, 212 N 9th
Millwood Sarah, Fraley's al (K)
Milne David, mer. 21 Church alley, h S E 10th & Shippen

31

Milne David & Son, com. mers., 21 Church al
Milne James, mer., 21 Church al, h 10 Jefferson row
Milner John, 44 Marshall
Milner Wm B., clerk, rear 46 N 7th
Milnor Beulah, b. h., 10 N 7th
Milnor Geo., cabinetmr., Mechanics' bel George (N L)
Milnor Jas. C., grocer, Franklin ab Cherry (K)
Milnor L., cabinetmr., 342 S Front
Milnor Nathan, blacksmith, 23 Sergeant
Milnor R. L. Mrs., b h, 103 N 5th
Milward John, mer., 52 S whfs., h 131 Wood
Minagh James, weaver, Pink ab Master
Minch Adam, tavern, Washington ab Noble
Minch & Barbier, tailors, 154½ Sassafras
Minch Henry, tailor, 154½ Sassafras
Miner Elizabeth, Steel's ct (S)
Miners Corn., cabinetmr., Sch 7th n Cherry
Minford John, grocer, Callowhill ab Sch 6th
MINFORD THOMAS, grocer & tea dealer, S W 2d and Walnut
Ming Maria, trimmings, 12 N 2d
Mingen Samuel, shop, 573 S Front
Mingey Lewis, carp., Crown ab Franklin (K)
Mingle Anna C., Poplar ab Sch 7th
Mingle Henry, vict., rear Hanover ab Queen
Mingle John, stirrup filer, Oxford n Front
Mingle John, machinist, Poplar bel Sch 6th
Mingle John, machinist, 65 N 8th
Mingle Philip B. mer. Front & High, h 73 N 7th
MINGLE P. B. & CO., seeds, &c., S E High & Front
Mingle Sophia, huckster, Elm bel Franklin (K)
Mingus P. P., blacksm., Cherry and Juniper,
Mingus Robert W., baker, 139 S 10th
MINHINNICK WILLIAM, gas fitt. & plumber, 32 N 7th, h 83 Franklin
Mini John, varnish mr., 6th ab Poplar
Minichini G. T., teacher, 348 Sassafras
Minier Chas., harness mr., 5 Thorn's ct
Mink Michael, brickmr., Sch 3d ab Walnut
Minnepenny Thos., carp., High W of Sch 6th
Minnett John, cordw., Brown bel 10th
Minnick George, gunsm., rear 287 St John
Minnick Jacob, cordw., 554 N 3d
Minnis Hiram, lab. 2 Dorothy
Minnis James, lab., Hallowell ab 6th
Minor Anthony lab. Pearl bel Broad
MINOR D. K., Franklin House, 105 Chestnut
Minor Wm. P., dry goods, 236 N 2d
Minshall Mary, b. h., 102 Chestnut
Minster Lydia S., 37 S 10th
Minster N. D., agent, 274 High, h 466 Sassafras
Mintess Elizabeth, 1 Gray's al
Mintess James S., currier, 22 Raspberry
Minton Henry, refectory, 4th & Chestnut, h 25 Washington ab 14th
Minton John, carter, 6 Hurst
Minton Robert, barber, 47 N 5th, h Wiley's ct
Mintzer Adam, collector, 501 N 4th
Mintzer Andrew, butcher, 12 Pegg
Mintzer Charles, stove finisher, Rex's ct

Mintzer Englebert, Sch 4th ab Callowhill
Mintzer Francis, cordw., rear 51 Mead
Mintzer George M., hatter, 11 Gaskill
Mintzer Jacob S., treas. dist. N. L., Hall N 3d
Mintzer John, variety store, 138 N 3d
Mintzer John, vict. 603 N 6th
Mintzer John P., senr., vict., Centre bel Parrish
Mintzer Joseph, butcher, 11 Gaskill
Mintzer Joseph, basket mr., 431 N 2d, h 182 Marshall
Mintzer Joseph, stove finisher, 393 S 2d
Mintzer Maria, Gray's ct (N L)
Mintzer S. L., dentist, 339 S 3d
Mintzer William, victualler, 113 Brown
Mintzer Wm., vict., Orchard ab George
Mintzer Wm. G., fly nets & coach lace, 83 N 3d, h 3d ab Washington
Mintzer Wm. L., cedar coop., 177, N 3d
Mintzor Charles A., teach. music, 537 N 5th
Miskell Thos., brushmr., 11 Tammany ct
Miskey Anthony, 6th bel Poplar
Miskey Wm. F., clerk, Coates ab 13th.
Missing Charles, jeweller, Charles ab Noble
Mitchell Alexander, lab. Centre bel 13th
Mitchell Ann, washer, 20 Elizabeth
Mitchell Ann, 2 Washington row
Mitchell Anthony, clerk, 57 Catharine
Mitchell Archibald, grocer, N W 13th and Vine
Mitchell A. Mrs., 491 S Front
Mitchell, Brognard & Co., com. mers., 22 Church alley
MITCHELL & BROTHER, lumber mers, 146 N 2d, & 143 N 3d
Mitchell B. G., conveyancer, 50 S 4th h 197 Walnut
MITCHELL CHARLES, ladies' shoemr., 12 N 3d, h 19 Franklin
Mitchell Charles W., clerk, 17 N 6th
Mitchell Daniel, shipcarp., 12 Marion
Mitchell & De Barry, dry goods, 16 N 2d
Mitchell Edward, chairmr., rear 7 N 7th
Mitchell Edward P. 219 Chestnut, h 18 S 7th
Mitchell Edwin, mer., 22 Church al., h 11 Montgomery square
Mitchell Elijah, dry goods, 16 N 2d, h 316 N 6th
Mitchell Elijah, shop, Sch 7th and Railroad
Mitchell Evan, brickmr., Duke n Hanover (K)
Mitchell Francis, Wood bel 12th
Mitchell George, U S mint, h 204 Wood
Mitchell George, shipwright, S W Keefe & Front
Mitchell George, shoe mr., 260 S 7th
Mitchell George J. lumber mer. 146 N 2d & 143 N 3d, h 24 Buttonwood
Mitchell George W., conveyancer & draftsman, 47 S 4th, h 8 O Y road
Mitchell Gideon, lab., Jones' al
Mitchell Hannah, 262 Coates
Mitchell Henry, silversmith, 3 Pleasant Retreat
Mitchell Henry K., tailor, 100 Walnut
Mitchell H. P., tavern, S E 5th & German
Mitchell Jacob, gent., Mantua vil
Mitchell James, chair manuf., Montgomery pl
Mitchell James, manufacturer, 649 N 2nd ab

Mitchell James, M D., 157 S 5th
Mitchell James H., mer., 23 N whfs., h 6 Colonnade Row
MITCHELL JAMES & SON, burr-mill grindstones &c. 12 and h 8 O Y road
Mitchell John, butcher, 238 Christian
Mitchell John, waiter, rear 160 Queen
Mitchell John, baker, 472 N 4th
Mitchell John, baker, Washington (W P)
Mitchell John, tailor, rear 5 Ogden
Mitchell John, carp., Lombard ct
Mitchell John, mariner, 487 S Front
MITCHELL JOHN C., att'y and coun., 173 Walnut
MITCHELL JOHN K., M. D., S W 11th and Walnut
Mitchell John M. lumber mer. 146 N 2d, & 143 N 3d, h 5 Vine
Mitchell Jonathan B., bookbinder, Beaver ct, h 17 N 6th
Mitchell Joseph, lab., Lombard E Sch 6th
Mitchell Joseph B., president Mech's Bank, h S E 10th and Morgan
Mitchell Joseph G., teller Mechanics' Bank, h 5½ S 11th
MITCHELL JOSHUA, alderman, 17 N 6th
Mitchell Lavinia, St John ab George (K)
Mitchell Margt., wid., rear 110 Catharine
Mitchell Margt., washer, rear 94 N 11th
Mitchell Mary, washer, 222 S 7th
Mitchell Mine, rear Ohio
Mitchell M. & H., milliners, 60 Mulberry
Mitchell M. P., U. S. Hotel, 151 Chestnut
Mitchell Obed, tea dealer, 89 Chestnut & 337 High, h 10 Filbert av
Mitchell Robert, lab., 21 Parham
Mitchell Robert, shop, Carlton bel Sch 6th
Mitchell Robert, draymen, rear Brown bel 12th
Mitchell Rachel, 12 Chancery la
MITCHELL S. AUGUSTUS, map publisher, 7th and High, h 362 Chestnut
Mitchell Theodore, pres. Lehigh Crane Iron Co., 44 N whfs, h Mulberry n Sch 6th
Mitchell Thomas, brickmr., Fitler bel Harrison (K)
Mitchell Thomas, conveyancer, 50 S 4th, h 197 Walnut
Mitchell Thos. S., conveyancer, 90 S 4th
Mitchell T. M., conveyancer, 93 S 3d
Mitchell William, tailor, 27 Appletree alley
Mitchell Wm., cake baker, 179 Cedar
Mitchell Wm., boilermr., Jefferson & Hope (K)
Mitchell Wm., lab., Fox's ct
Mitchell Wm., whip mr., Poplar ab Marshall
Mitchell Wm., dentist, Dugan
Mitchell Wm., 4 S Sch 8th bel High
Mitchell Wm., weaver, Fulton ab 12th
Mitchell Wm. A., hardw., 148 N 2d, h 72 S 3d
Mitchell William H., clerk, 29 Sansom, h 296 Cherry
Mitchell W. Fisher, real est. br., 93 S 3d, h 200 Marshall
Mitchenor A. C., 159 Wood
Mitcheson Jane, Little Green n Cadwalader (K)
Mitcheson Robert, Coates bet 11th & 12th

Mitchner Frances, b h, Allen ab F road
Mitten Daniel, carp., Carberry ct
Mivclaz Henry, dry goods, 132 S 2d
Mock Catharine, 524 N 3d
Mock John, machinist, 524 N 3d
Mock Mary, rear 134 St John
Mock Robert, tailor 524 N 3d
Mockason Margt., rear 402 N 2d
Mode Henry, oyster house, 384 High, h 8 Poplar ct
Moeer Isaac, shop, 173 Brown
Mochring G., M. D., 126 S 11th
Moench Godfred, cabinctmr., 1 Kelly's ct
Moffat Arch., plasterer, Watt
Moffat Eliza, tailoress, rear 43 Coates
Moffit David, carpet weaver, Baker's ct
Moffit Elizabeth, milliner, 8 S Sch 8th
Moffit George, shoemr., 5 Wale's av
Moffit John, weaver, Sch 2d ab High
Moffit Richard, grocer, Marlboro' & Queen (K)
Moffitt Adam, grocer, Beach and Manderson (K)
Moffitt Adam, potter, La Fayette ab 9th
Moffitt Caspar M., police officer, Sch 2d below High
Moffitt David, weaver, rear 2d bel Master
Moffitt John, stone cut., Jones E of Sch 6th
Moffitt James, weaver, West bel Hanover (K)
Moffitt James, weaver, 2d ab Master (K)
Moffitt John, weaver, Jefferson ab 2d (K)
Moffitt John, oysters, Brown st whf
Moffitt Martin, lab., Washington (W P)
Moffitt Richard, grocer, 138 N 2d
Moffitt Robert 13 Magnolia
Moffitt Robert, weaver, Sch 4th ab Chestnut
Moffitt Wm., weaver, Hope ab Phoenix (K)
Mogridge Joseph, Morris n Lombard
Mogridge Mary, teacher, Filbert ab 8th
Mogridge Richard P., stereotyper, rear 95 Walnut
Mogridge Thomas, currier, 198 N 3d, h 15 Dillwyn
Molan James, mer., 178 Chestnut, h 10th bel Wallace
Molan Peter, tobacconist, 8th bel High
Moland Wm., engraver, 23 S 5th, h Callowhill n 12th
Molherin George, baker, 117 Plum
Molineaux E. J. tailor, 168 S 5th
Molineaux E. P. shoemr., 281 S 2d
Moll Henry, druggist, 8 Butz's ct
Mollock John, stove finisher, 47 Rose al
Molone Thos., weaver, Mariner st
Molloy Daniel, carp., 11 Prosperous al
Molloy Joseph C., clerk, Grubb
Molloy Michael, trader, 111 S Water
Molloy Michael, pilot, rear 92 Christian
Molony Barry, waiter, 178 Locust
Molony James, gent., N W 7th and Vine
Molony Matthew, fruiterer, S E 8th & Walnut
Molt Henry, clerk, 57 Carpenter
Molten Albert, mer., 116 High, h 388 Vine
Molyneux Giles, tavern, 2d & Oxford
Monachesi N., portrait painter, 156 Pine
Monaghan John, hatter, 85 S 5th
Monaghan Patrick, lab., Reckless ct

Monaghan Peter, lab., Christian bel 9th
Monaghan Terrence, lab., Christian bel 9th
Monahan Edward, lab., 21 Dyott's ct (K)
Monahan Henry, lab., 9 Baker st
Monahan James, shoemr., 352 N 5th
Monahan John, lab., 21 Dyott's ct (K)
Moncravie James, blacksmith, Atherton
Monell John I., U S mint, h 7 Carrolton sq
Monell Peter, cordw., rear Marshall ab Coates
Monell Wm., cordw., 106 Apple
Money John T., 333 S 5th
Monheimer Jacob, reflectors, 192 St John
Monier Joseph, bookbinder, 16 Decatur, h 10 Wagner's ct
Moninger, John, shoemr., 10 College pl
Moninger Stephen, cabman, 99 Crown
Monnier Daniel, watch mr., 240 S 2d
Monnier Philip, watchmr., 240 S 2d
Monroe Ann, Thompson ab 3d (K)
Monroe Franklin, bricklayer, 258 Green
Monroe James, brickmr., 661 N 2d
Monroe John, brickmr., 2 Harrison's ct
Monroe Michael, boots & shoes, 481 High
Monroe Susan, rear Carpenter bel 7th
Monroe Thomas G., sea capt., 149 Queen
Monroe Wm. F., shoemr, 55 S 5th
Monrose A. F. Ott, importer, 1 Commerce
Monsey James G., shoemr., 9th ab Parrish
Montague James, shoemr., Pine ab Willow
Monteith Chas., clockmr., 525 High
Monteith Eliza, Juniper bel Walnut
Monteith John, drayman, Cherry bet Sch 6th and 5th
Monteith Samuel, lab., Ann n 13th
Monteith Saml., weaver, rear Philip ab Jefferson
Montelius Wm., mer., h 9 S 9th
Montgomery Andrew D., painter, 4 Decatur, h 129 Cedar
Montgomery Ann, widow, Phoenix below G T road (K)
Montgomery Archibald, weav., Fulton ab 12th
Montgomery A. J. clerk, Brandywine bel Broad
Montgomery Edward, manuf. hosiery, 593 N 2d ab Otter (K)
Montgomery Elizabeth, Hanover ab Bedford (K)
MONTGOMERY GEORGE W., grocer, S W Sch 7th & Spruce
Montgomery G., weaver, 13th ab Shippen
Montgomery Hugh, watchman, Sch 3rd ab Filbert
Montgomery James, sexton, Lombard ab 12th
Montgomery James, wharf builder, Crown bel Bedford (K)
Montgomery James, printer, 4th n Washington
Montgomery Jane, 370 Coates
Montgomery Jane, 305 Spruce
Montgomery John, brickl., Lombard n Sch. 4th
Montgomery John, bricklayer, 252 S 6th
Montgomery John, carp. Jackson bel Palmer(K)
Montgomery John C., Prest. Little Schuylkill & Susq. R. R. Co., 34 Walnut, h 233 Pine
MONTGOMERY JOHN P., att'y. & coun., & commiss. for Del., Tenn. & Lou., 47 S 5th, h 233 Pine
Montgomery John T., att'y & coun., 62 S 6th

Montgomery Joseph, mer., 121 S Front, h 344 Mulberry
Montgomery Jos., carp., Callowhill ab Sch 5th
Montgomery Neill, carpet weav., 1 Walker's ct
Montgomery Robert, 316 Cedar
Montgomery Robt., cab mr., Melon bel 10th
Montgomery Robt., miller, Pine ab Sch Front
Montgomery Robert W., stone cutter, 178 Callowhill ab Sch 6th
Montgomery & Ryan, com. mers., 121 S Front
Montgomery Sarah M., corsets, 12 Chester st
Montgomery Wm., manuf., Front bel Otter (K)
Montgomery Wm., weaver, Union and West (K)
Montgomery Wm., carp., Thompson ab Sch 7th
Montgomery Wm., shoemr., Jones W of Sch 4th
Montier Hiram, 201 E Lombard
Montier Solomon, cordwainer, 9 N 10th, h 24 Portland la
Montre H., cabinetmr., S E 11th & Chestnut, h 355 High
Monyer Christian, gent., 4th bel Master
Monyer Christian, jr., vict., 4th n Master
Monyer Jacob, vict., G T road ab Jefferson (K)
Monyer John, vict., Shackamaxon below Franklin (K)
Moock Valentine, cordw., Jackson & Orchard
Mood George, fisherman, Queen ab Wood (K)
Mood Jacob, fisherman, Dyott's ct (K)
Mood Jacob, fisherman, Wood bel Duke (K)
Mood John, fisherman, Wood ab Franklin (K)
Mood Wm., fisherman, Wood bel Franklin (K)
Moody Lydia K. 14 Lagrange pl
Moon Edward, lab., Elk st (K)
Moon John, grocer, Shippen la & Bedford
Mooney Ann, 24 Fitzwater
Mooney Dennis, blacksmith, 305 N 3d, h 92 Dillwyn
Mooney Felix, weaver, Harrison ab Fitler (K)
Mooney Hugh, cordw. Fitzwater n 13th
Mooney Hugh, weaver, 16 Lloyd's ct (K)
Mooney Hugh, tavern, S E 11th & George
Mooney Jacob, butcher, 252 St John
Mooney James, tailor, Carpenter ab 10th
Mooney John, weaver, Charlotte ab Thompson (K)
Mooney John, teacher, 36 Vine, h Edward and School (K)
Mooney John, looking-glass manuf., 16 N 6th
Mooney John B. boots and shoes, 116 Cedar
Mooney Patrick, tailor, Kelly's ct.
Mooney Patrick, weaver, 2d bel Harrison (K)
Mooney Richard, printer, Turner bel 4th
Mooney Thomas, blacksm., Sch 5th bel High, h Emerald ab Sch. 7th
Mooney Timothy, lab., 13th ab Poplar
Mooney Wm, weaver, Higham's ct (K)
Mooney Wm. lab. Carpenter ab 7th
Mooney Wm. moulder, 10th bel Buttonwood
Moore Abednego, wire manuf., 126 New Market
Moore Alexander, weaver, Richard n Sch 6th
Moore Alfred, painter, Allen ab Hanover
Moore Amasa W., 8 N 12th
Moore Andrew, weaver, White's ct
Moore Andrew, brushmr. 46 N 4th
Moore Andrew M., distiller, 308 St John

Moore Anthony, cordw., 67 New Market
Moore Ann, Christian ab P road
Moore Asher Rev., 110 Lombard
Moore Benjamin, surveyor, 545 N 2d (K)
Moore Benjamin, agent, 165 Queen
Moore Benjamin F., tailor, 70 S 3d, h S Garden bel 11th
Moore Bethuel A. builder, Carlton bel 12th, h 17 Carlton sq
Moore B. H. mer., 23 Commerce, h 8 Carlton sq
Moore & Campion, cabinet makers, 161 S 2d
MOORE CARLETON R., cotton yarn, 116 N 3d, h Sp Garden ab 11th
Moore Caroline S., trimmings, 114 N 10th
Moore Catharine, milliner, 113 N 2d
Moore Charles, port. painter, 129 Wood
Moore Charles, waiter, 231 Lombard
Moore Charles, drayman, 4th & George (N L)
Moore Charles, carp., 259 Green
Moore Charles, undertaker, 4 Lawrence's ct
Moore Charles, victualler, James ab 10th
Moore Charles, carp. 3 Naglee's ct
Moore Christian, tailor, Otter bel G T road (K)
Moore Cornelius, cab mr., 8 Knight's ct
Moore Cornelius, cupper and bleeder, 28 S 13th
Moore Cyrus C. druggist, F road & Phoenix
Moore C. M., dry goods, 36 S 8th
Moore Daniel, lumber counter, Penn bel Shackamaxon (K)
Moore David, lab., Bush Hill
Moore David, bricklayer, 27 Logan
Moore David B. capt. 441 S Front
MOORE DAVID P., undertaker, 181 Mulberry
Moore David W., tailor, 149 N 3d
Moore D., fancy store, 40 N 6th.
Moore Eber, lab., Tailor's ct
Moore Edward, lab., Fitzwater ab Broad
Moore Edward, cordw., 7 Linden (K)
Moore Eli, machinist, Sch. 8th bel Willow
Moore Elizabeth, clothes, 15 Spruce
Moore Elizabeth, 26 Elizabeth st
Moore Elizabeth trimmings, 28 Chester
Moore Emily, grocery, Middle al
Moore Esther, wid. of Robert, M. D., 123 S 9th
Moore Esther, b. h., N E 11th & Callowhill
Moore Francis C., tailor, 150 Locust
Moore Francis W., cabmr., Jacoby ab Cherry
Moore Gabriel, paper manufacturer, Edward n School (K)
Moore George, ship carp., 273 S 4th
Moore George, morocco dresser, N E St John & Willow, h 324 Coates
Moore George, china, Thompson ab 4th (K)
Moore George, common 300 Coates
Moore Geo., flour & feed, 520 Callowhill
Moore Geo., refec., 193 S 7th
Moore Gideon F., carp., 223 N 9th
Moore Green., confectioner, 139 Locust
Moore G. B. painter, 31 S 3d, h 99 N 5th
Moore G. & H., morocco manufacturers, N E St. John and Willow
Moore Henry, morocco dresser, Willow and St. John, h 485 N 4th

Moore Henry, weaver, Fordham's ct (K)
Moore Henry, pedler, rear Jones' al
Moore Henry B., provisions, 12th & Graff
Moore Henry D., marble saw mill, R road and Wallace, h 15 Franklin
MOORE, HEYL & CO., hardware, 139 High
Moore Isaac Rev., 13th and Lombard
Moore Isaac, lab., Jones n Sch 5th
Moore James, brewer, Shippen ab 13th
Moore James Rev., 72 Wood
Moore James, cordw., 27 Beck
Moore James, lab. rear 129 Walnut
Moore James, mer., 64 N 2d
Moore James, printer, 3d ab Clark
Moore James, blacksm., 1 Clymer st
Moore James, Carleton ab Sch 7th
Moore James, dry goods, 7th ab Vine
Moore James, lab., 156 S 12th
Moore James H., carp., Washington n 6th
Moore James L., brewer, Shippen ab 13th
Moore James M. agent, 470 S Front
Moore James M., clerk, N E 4th and Tammany
Moore James S., baker, 25 N 9th
Moore James T., mer., 108 Sassafras
Moore James W., saddler, 262 Cherry
Moore Jeptha, machinist, Gravel's ct
Moore Jesse, constable, 292 Lombard
Moore Joel A., tailor, 14 Green
Moore John, drayman, 4 Greble's ct
Moore John, carp., Wood ab Sch 6th
Moore John, cordw., Pearl ab 13th
Moore John, lab., R road ab Girard av (F V)
Moore John, lab., Goodwill ct
Moore John, dry goods and trimm., 256 N 2d
Moore John, weaver, Vail's ct
Moore John, lab., rear 2d ab Montgomery
Moore John, blacksm., Lafayette ab 9th
Moore John, carp., 11 St. James, h 53 Filbert
Moore John, carpenter, 118 Dillwyn
Moore John, machinist, Sch 8th ab Vine
Moore John, tailor, 242 Wood
Moore John, 7 Rittenhouse
Moore John, jr., carp., rear 110 Dillwyn
Moore John D., M. D., dentist, 133 Spruce
Moore John G., bricklayer, Parrish n Broad
Moore John J. Rev., 18 Watson's al
Moore John W. bookseller, 158 Chestnut, h 367 N 6th
Moore John W., M. D., 63 Spruce
Moore John W. tailor, 76 N 4th
Moore Joseph, carpenter, c Truxton and Budd
Moore Joseph, gent., 322 N 6th
Moore Joseph, carp., Columbia row n F M
Moore Joseph, lab., Hallowell's ct (S G)
Moore Jos., waterman, Wood bel Sch 3d
Moore Joseph D. gratemr., 20 Parker (S)
Moore J. & Co., provisions, 99 N Water
Moore Leopold, tailor, Torr's ct ab 9th
Moore L. S., periodicals, 224 Chestnut, h 229 S 9th
Moore Maria M. 29 Union
Moore Marmaduke, merchant, 139 High, h 153 N 13th
Moore Martha, trimmings, 223 Marshal

Moore Mary, wid., 467 Vine
Moore Mary Ann, Sch West ab Walnut
Moore Mary A. washer, Leopard bel Phoenix (K)
Moore Matthew, carter, Sch West ab Walnut
Moore Mordecai, lab., rear Browne bel 12th
Moore Mordecai, hotel, N W 9th & High
Moore Patrick, brushmr. New Market bel Brown
Moore Patrick, grocer, 5th & George
Moore Philip, cordw., 9 Mechanic (N L)
Moore Phœbe, b h, 31 Cherry
Moore Rachel, 10 Carlton sq
Moore Rebecca, 85 N 9th
Moore Richd. M., acct., 143 High, h 138 Walnut
Moore Richard S., collector, 36 Jacoby
Moore Robert, cordw., Lombard ab 13th
Moore Robert, meat curer, 597 N Front (K)
Moore Robert, carter, Sch bank bel Pine
Moore Robt., weav., rear Fitler bel Harrison (K)
Moore Robert M. merchant, 231 Coates
Moore Rosanna, rear 6 Locust
Moore Saml, finisher, 28 Benton st
Moore Saml., shop, Hallowell & 7th
Moore Samuel, pres. Hazleton Coal Co., office 58 Walnut
Moore Samuel, book binder, 34 Palmyra sq
Moore Samuel Jr.. mer., 20 Marshall
Moore Samuel, book binder, N E 4th & Chestnut, h 10th bel Wood
Moore Samuel, weaver, Shippen n Broad
Moore Samuel J., dentist, 105 S 9th
Moore Sarah, gentw., Spruce bel Broad
Moore & Sexton, grocers, 6th and Parrish
Moore Thomas, lead worker, Kinley's ct
Moore Thomas, hosier, 330 S 3d
Moore Thomas, baker, 193 N Front
Moore Thomas, carp., rear 128 Dillwyn st
Moore Thomas C. carp. 211 St John
Moore T. H., cabinetmr., 161 S 2d, h Lombard ab 3d
Moore William, carp., Bedford bel Broad
Moore William, lab., Sch 2d n Lombard
Moore William, labourer, 18 Stamper's al
Moore William, morocco dresser, 100 Green
Moore Wm., dyer, Allen ab Shackamaxon (K)
Moore Wm. manuf., William bel Edward (K)
Moore Wm., weaver, Benton n William (K)
Moore Wm., lab., 20 Middle al
Moore Wm., carp., 6th and Christian
Moore Wm., watchman, Cherry n Sch 7th
Moore Wm., shoemr., 66 Chester
Moore Wm. A., cordw., Willow ab 8th
Moore Wm. C. oak cooper, Coates ab 13th
Moore Wm. E., printer, Carpenter ab 4th
Moore Wm. G. bricklayer, 347 N 6th
Moore Wm. H. student, 319 Vine
Moore Wm. H., carp., rear 118 Dillwyn
Moore William H., furnishing undertaker, 181 Mulberry, h Mulberry ab Sch 7th
Moore William W., druggist, N W 2nd and Spruce.
Moorehouse Charles H., mer., 76 High
Moorhead Hugh S., acct., 9 Noble
Moorhouse Samuel T. Rev., Catharine bel 7th

Moothart Henry, lab. 46 Rose al
Moran Edward, labourer, 7 Linden
Moran Edward jr., lab., 7 Linden st
Moran James D., musician, 8 College pl
Moran John P. weaver, Harmstead
Moran R. H., painter, Pleasant ab 10th
Moran Peter, com. mer. Harmony ab 4th
Moran Thomas, weaver, rear G T road ab 5th
Moran Wm. C. manuf., cotton goods, 9th be. Washington
Moran Wm. F., moulder, 7 Linden st
Morange L., com. mer., 123 S Front, h 102 Mulberry
More E. B., blacksmith, State
Morehead Turner, h 3 Morgan
Morehead T. G., mer., 397 N 6th
Morehouse Margaret, nurse, 9 Juniper la
Moren Peter, lab., 4 Lagrange
Moreland Jabez, lab. Vine ab Broad
Morfan Geo., machinist, 536 N 2d
Morgan Alex., druggist, 213½ High, h 181 N 6th
Morgan Arthur, Doman's pl '
Morgan Barbara, shopkeeper, G T road be 2d
Morgan, Buck & Co., mers., 57 High.
Morgan Charles E., dry goods, 13 N 3d, h Cherry bel 11th
Morgan Chas. P., stone cut., Jefferson n Sch 6th
Morgan Chas. Waln, com. mers., 9 S whfs
Morgan Daniel, sailmr., Spruce st whf
Morgan Danl. refectory, Middle al n 7th
Morgan Delilah, 12 German
Morgan Edmund, fireman, Marlboro' ab Beach
Morgan Elizabeth, Logan ab Green
Morgan Elizabeth, gentw., 181 S 5th.
Morgan, Gardner & Co., mers., 9 Merchant
Morgan George W., shoemr., Front bel Prime
Morgan Gilbert, machinist, 2 Baker's ct
Morgan G. W., potter, Callowhill ab Sch 3d
Morgan James, upholsterer, 100 N 3d
Morgan James C., druggist, 1 N 5th
Morgan Jane P., milliner, 92 Cedar
Morgan John, bookbinder, Ontario ab Poplar
Morgan John, weaver, F road ab Mary
Morgan John, gardener, Bush hill
Morgan John, lab., Beach ab Poplar (K)
Morgan John C., stovemr., 145 N Juniper
Morgan John W., corder, Snowden's whf (S)
Morgan Joseph, dentist, Ogden bel 10th
Morgan Joseph, mer. 349 High, h 8th ab Green
Morgan Joseph, tailor, 258 High, h 2 Providence ct
Morgan Joseph & Co., upholsterer, 207 N 2d
Morgan Lewis R., carp., 4 St Joseph's av
Morgan Maria, shop, 397 N 3d
Morgan Mary, 55 Queen
Morgan Mary Ann, sewing, Hope ab Jefferson (Kensington)
Morgan Mordecai T. clerk, 165 N 12th
Morgan Nathan E., spectacle mr. 20 Strawberry
Morgan Nathaniel, lab., Pryor's ct
Morgan Nicholas, sailmr., Freeston pl
Morgan Peter, barber, 294 E Pine
Morgan Racy Ann, 21 Tammany
Morgan Saml, upholsterer, 200 N 6th

Morgan Saml., carp., rear 45 M road
Morgan Sarah, cook, 5 Acorn alley
Morgan Thos., agent, Pearl ab Sch 4th
Morgan Thos., tailor, Sch 5th bel Barker
Morgan Thos., dry goods, 108 N 9th
Morgan Thomas A. mer., 42 Pine
Morgan T. W. & Co., mers., 10 S wharves
Morgan T. W. merchant, 10 S whfs, h Spruce n Sch 6th
Morgan Ward, copperplate print., 18 Beck st
Morgan Wm., barber, N E 2d & Walnut, h 128 Locust
Morgan Wm., skindresser, 9th ab Callowhill, h 11th ab Callowhill
Morgan William C., mer., 57 High, h 329 N 6th
Morgan Wm. H., gilder, Queen ab 3d
Morgan W. H., gilder, 303 Callowhill
Morgenthaler Hen , brewer, Warner's ct (N L)
Morin Alexander C., die sinker and chaser, 86 Walnut.
Morley Ann, shop, 251 Catharine
Morley Daniel, hatter, Boyd's av
Morley Eliza, shop, 164 Shippen
Morley Timothy, bootmr., 6th bel Hallowell
Morley William, stocking framemr., Wistar's ct, Phoenix bel G T road (K)
Morley Wm. A., stocking weaver, Spruce W Sch 3d
Mornen Lar., bootmr., 227 E Cedar
Mornen Thomas, shoemr. 271 S 5th
Morningdollar Philip, tailor, 1 Parham st
Moroney William, tavern, 57 Dock
Morrell Ann, Mrs., 56 S 11th
Morrell Catharine, nurse, 399 S 6th
Morrell Charles R. clerk, 109 N 9th
Morrell Danl., mer., 147 Marshall
Morrell David B., patternmr., Jacoby & Cherry, h 181 N 13th
Morrell Elizabeth, Spruce ab 11th
Morrell James, sec'ry Phila. and Trenton R. Co., 46 S Whfs. (ab stairs) h 96 Marshall.
Morrell Jas., Callowhill ab 12th
Morrell John, machinist, Thompson ab 3d (K)
Morrell Mary Ann, 57 New
Morrell Robert, lab. rear Front ab Otter (K)
Morrell Robert E. & Son, carpenters, Crockett's ct
Morrell Robt. F., carp., Crockett's ct
Morrell R. H., gent., 5 Lombard
Morrell Wm. B., 441 S 6th
Morrell W. A., clerk, 45 S whfs
Morrell W. C., acct., 127 N 10th
Morrell W. H. G., cordw., 135 S 6th
Morris Abigail, Mulberry n Sch 6th
Morris Amelia, Hamilton vil
Morris Andrew, mason, Coombs' ct (S)
Morris Ann, gentw., 93 S 8th
Morris Ann, shop, 139 Cherry
Morris Anna, dry goods 361 N 2d

Morris Benjamin, brushmr., 21 S 7th
Morris Cameron, combmr., 1 Maria st
Morris Caspar, M. D., Chestnut ab Broad
Morris Catharine, 247 Spruce
Morris, Catharine W., 56 N 4th
Morris Chas. M. mer., 39 N Front, h 250 Spruce
Morris & Dallas, wheelwri'ts, 6th bel Catharine
Morris David, lab., Lawrence ct (K)
Morris David, lab., George ab 3d
Morris De Witt C. att'y & coun. S E 6th and Walnut
Morris D., carp., Sansom al
Morris Edward, ship carp., 6 Beck st (S)
Morris Edward, waiter, Lisle ct
Morris Edward, oil cloth, Clymer ab Mud la (K)
Morris Elias, blindmr., rear Sutherland below Queen
Morris Eliza, b h, 125 N 9th
Morris Elizabeth, widow, Mechanic bel Culvert
Morris Ellwood, civil engineer, 22 Prune
Morris Emanuel W., barber, rear 57 S 3d, h Middle al n 7th
Morris Enos, printer, 6 Weccacoe
Morris Evans, hatter, 15 Minor
MORRIS E. JOY, att. and coun., 20 Washington square
Morris, Ford & Melloy, stove mrs., 303 High
Morris Francis, grocer, 319 Lombard
Morris George, button mr., rear 362 N 3d
Morris George, painter, 380 S 3d
Morris Geo. B., tinsmith, rear 467 N 3d
Morris G. W., brushmr., 18 N 3d, h 125 N 12th
Morris G. W, jr. druggist, O Y road & Tammany
MORRIS G. W. & SON, brushmrs., 18 N 3d
Morris Harry W., mer., 18 N 3d
Morris Henry, weaver, G T road bel Phoenix
Morris Henry, coal grate manuf., S E 3d & Walnut, h 5th bel Franklin (S)
Morris Hiram, bricklayer, 5 Diligent av
Morris Isaac, lab. 4th bel Wharton
Morris Isaac, oysterman, Lisle
Morris Isaac, cordw., 44 Coates
Morris Isaac P., iron founder, Sch 7th and High h 381 Spruce
Morris Israel, iron mer., S W Sch 7th and High, h 280 Filbert
MORRIS I. P. & Co., iron f'drs, Sch 7th and High
Morris James, moulder, Beckett st
Morris James, porter, 58 Mechanic (C)
Morris James, cordw., 42 German
Morris Jehu, cordw., 101 Poplar
Morris John, blksm., Hanover bel Franklin (K)
Morris John, Far. & Mec. Bank, h 192 Locust
Morris John, painter, 76 Noble
Morris John, lab., 60 Fitzwater
Morris John, grocer, N E 7th & Green
Morris John, carp. Franklin ab Hanover (K)

Morris & Jones, iron mers., S W Sch. 7th and High
Morris Joseph, lab. 98 Prime
Morris Joseph, vict. Montgomery bel Front (K)
Morris Jos., measurer, 444 Callowhill
Morris Joseph M., black and whitesmith, 121 N 10th, h 11th ab Washington
Morris Joseph S., cordw. Allen ab F road
Morris Joshua H., real estate broker, 23 Filbert
Morris Josiah, mer., 313 High
Morris Julianna, washer, 29 Barron
Morris J. & William M., furniture, 313 High
Morris Michael, carter, 9 Pegg st
Morris Morris, painter, 284 Mulberry
Morris Patrick, lab., Sch 4th n Dorothy
Morris Perry, lab., Lombard row
Morris Phebe, Warren bel 12th
Morris P. J., carp., Wood ab Sch 3d
Morris P. Pemberton, att'y & coun., 2 Prune
Morris Reese, printer, Wayne ab Washington
Morris Richard, weaver, 2 Gay's ct (K)
Morris Robert, M. D., 327 Spruce
Morris Robert, editor Pennsylvania Inquirer, h 354 Vine
Morris Robert, lab. S W Shippen & Swanson
Morris Robt., whitewash., Raspberry ab Spruce
Morris Samuel, drayman, 157 N Front
Morris Samuel, tailor, 9th bel Coates
Morris Samuel B., wheelwright, P road bel Carpenter, h Washington bel 7th
Morris Sarah, 68 Catharine
Morris Sarah, rear 13 German
Morris Sarah, weaver, Fox's ct
Morris Simeon, bricklayer, Federal bel 2d
Morris Simon, dealer, 89 N 2d, h 236 Christian
MORRIS, TASKER & MORRIS, man. coal gra's & welded iron pipes, & iron founders, 5th bel Franklin (S), store S E 3d and Walnut
Morris Thomas, carp., Dillwyn ab Tammany, h 26 Tammany
Morris Thos., confect., rear Carpenter ab 6th
Morris Thomas E., grocer, N E 6th and Callowhill, h Marshall bel Poplar
Morris Thos. Y. tin smith, 303 High, h 41 Carlton
Morris Thompson, George n Sch 7th
Morris Warder, druggist, 45 N 3d
Morris William, watchmaker, High W Sch 5th, h 2 Benezet
Morris William, turner, 228 Catharine
Morris William, silk mer., 31 S 2d
Morris Wm., blind painter, Wiley's ct
Morris William, insp. of mahogany, Harmony, h 368 E Cedar
Morris Wm., watchman, 8 New Market
Morris Wm., clerk, 42 Marshall
Morris Wm. E. prest. Phila. Ger. & Norris. R. R. Co. 70 Franklin
Morris Wm. H., 291 Vine
Morris Wm. J., mer., 9 S Front
Morris William M., mer., 513 High
Morris Wistar, S E 3d and Walnut
Morrison Abraham, cabinetmr. 2d bel Reed, h Rye ab Wharton
Morrison Andrew, keeper County Prison, h P road ab Federal

Morrison Andrew, jr., tailor, bel Washington bet 7th & 8th
Morrison Ann, 2 Loxley's ct
Morrison Ann M., Allen's ct
Morrison Anthony, lab. Sch Beech ab Spruce
Morrison Arch., blacksm., 378 S 3d
Morrison Benj., carp., 390 High, h George n Sch 6th
Morrison Charles S., tailor, 4 Providence ct
Morrison Elizabeth, teacher, 142 S 9th
Morrison James, shoemr., Oliver's pl
Morrison James, carter, 1 Mifflin
Morrison James M., hatter, 91 N 6th
Morrison James H., carp., 104 Crown
Morrison John, carp., Ross ab Queen (K)
Morrison John, weaver, Milton n 11th
Morrison John, blacksmith, Walker's ct (K)
Morrison John H., capt., Elm bel Franklin (K)
Morrison John N., cabmrs., George n Juniper
Morrison John W., carpenter, Olive ab 12th
Morrison Jos., tailor, 209 Wood
Morrison Joseph, oak cooper, rear Brooke bel Browne
Morrison Thos., lab., Sch 3d bel Callowhill
Morrison Thomas, weaver, Wood ab Sch 6th
Morrison William, brewer, N W 10th and Filbert, h 300 Mulberry
Morrison William, tailor, 24 S 6th
Morrison Wm., weaver, Benton ct n William
Morrissey John, tavern, N W Water and Sassafras
Morrow James, weaver, Shippen ab Shippen la
Morrow June, wid. of John, Shippen bel Broad
Morrow John, weaver, Howard bel Franklin (K)
Morrow John G., paperhan., 220 E Cedar
Morrow Mahala, 14 Knight's ct
Morrow Robt., lab., rear Beaver bel 3d (K)
Morrow Mary, c Cherry & Juniper
Morrow Samuel, weaver, Howard bel Franklin (K)
Morse Geo. W., card manuf., Marshall and Willow, h 224 Noble
Morss Sarah, b h, 23 Elfreth's al
Morss Thomas L., carpenter, 75 Sassafras
Mort Joseph, clerk, 172 Marshall
Mortimer Samuel, agt. Queen bel Palmer (K)
Morton Abraham, lab., Russell bel Shippen
Morton Anna, 39 Jacoby
Morton Benjamin, carpenter, 328 S 2d
Morton & Berstler, paper manuf., 17 Commerce
Morton Charles, acct., Lewis n Sch. 7th
Morton Charles, blacksmith, rear G T road ab 2d, h De Witt's av (K)
Morton D. W., mer., 17 Commerce, h 1 Courtlin place
Morton Elliott, mariner, 19 Union (S)
Morton Francis K., M. D., 366 N Front
Morton George, furniture, Division bel 12th
Morton George, bookbinder, 66 Coates
Morton Hannah, Master ab Howard (K)
Morton Henry J. Rev., 9 Clinton
Morton Isaac H., cordw., 6 Wilson
Morton James, clerk, Sch 8th ab Pine
Morton John H., wheelwright, 244 N 10th
Morton Joshua, boat builder, F road & Franklin

Morton Joshua, lab., Carpenter & Atherton
Morton Mark, cabinetmaker, 161 Cedar
Morton Mary, gentw., 8th bel Poplar
Morton Robert, M. D., 99 N 10th
Morton Ruth, gentw., 187 Coates
Morton Samuel, tavern, Washington (W P)
Morton Samuel C., mer., 70 S Wharves
Morton Samuel C. & Co., mers., 70 S wharves
Morton Samuel G., M. D., 387 Mulberry
Morton Thomas, bar-tender, Washington (W P)
Morton Thos., shoemr., 31 Sheaff st
Morton Wm., ship carp., Ross ab Queen (K)
Morton Wm. C., cordw., 6th bel Carpenter
Mosely Samuel, blacksm., Moser's ct (K)
Moser Elizabeth, milliner, 192 Chestnut
Moserf Frederick, carter, Moser's ct (K)
Moses Ezekiel, steward, Cobb
Moses Henry, currier, Poplar bel 10th
Moses John, lab., Carpenter n Broad
Moses John B., mahogany sawyer, 174 Cherry
Moses Solomon, wool mer., 103 S Front
Moseley Samuel, bricklr. 4th & Franklin (S)
Mosier Amos, oysterman, 24 Strawberry
Mosley Charles, waiter, 8 Barley
Mosley George H., carp., 55 S Juniper
Mosley George L., Fisher ab Carpenter
Mosley Isaac, waiter, 37 Bonsall
Mosley Nathaniel B., wines and liquors, 97 S
  Front, h 22 Jacoby
Mosley Samuel, cabinet maker, 134 S 5th
Mosley Teresa, wid. of William, 7 Wale's av
Moss Ann Maria, washer, rear 115 Brown
Moss Charles L., lab., 1 De Witt's av (K)
Moss Edward, labourer, 6 Wiley's ct
Moss E. L., mer., 64½ Walnut, h 22 Washington
  square
Moss Henry, mariner, 3 Jones' ct
Moss Isaac M., quill manuf. bookseller and sta-
  tioner, 12 S 4th
Moss James P., upholsterer, 70 S 4th
Moss John, gent., 64½ Walnut, h 189 Spruce
Moss John D., lab., rear 52 Christian
Moss Joseph L., broker, 64½ and h 370 Walnut
Moss Michael, stove finisher, Wiley's ct
Moss Misses, Sch 8th ab Spruce
Moss Patrick, Shippen ab 13th
Moss Thomas G., mer., 140½ High
Moss William, broker, 225 Callowhill
Mossop John, bootmaker, 254 Callowhill
Most Frederick W., stovemr., 78 N 6th, h 8th ab
  Coates
MOST & STICHTER, stove makers, 78 N 6th
Mosta Frederick, tailor, 19 Sterling al
Mott Aaron, dyer, 129 N 12th
Mott Edward T., mer., 47 N 3d, h 151 Vine
Mott James, wool mer., 27 Church alley, h 138
  N 9th
MOTT JAS. & CO., wool mers., 27 Church al
MOTT, SCHOBER & CO., china and glass, 47
  N 3d
Mott Thomas, mer., 27 Church al, h 61 N 11th
Mott William B., manuf. copp. print. ink, Front
  bel Franklin (K)
Mottram Thomas & Sons, importers agency, N E
  5th & Commerce
32

Motz A. H., mer., 64 N Front, h 110 Chestnut
Mouat James, lab., Crane's ct
Mouat Jane, 35 Penn
Moughan Mich., dealer, George n Sch. 7th
Mouille Charles, bottler, 4 Acorn alley
Mouille George, lampmr., Paul ab 6th
Mouille Stephen, lampmr., Wood ab Sch. 4th
Moulder Esther S., b h., 75 S 4th
Moulder Joseph, ship carp., Front n Federal
Moulder William D., clerk, 11 Sassafras
Moullié Mathurin, mer., 203 High
Moullié M. & Co., boots and shoes, 203 High
Moulson John, photographist, S E 8th & Chest-
  nut
Moult Wm., gent., 360 S 5th
Moulton Samuel, carp., 4th bel Franklin (K)
Mount Barney, lab., 3 White's ct
Mount E., cabinetmr., 153 S 2d
Mount James A., baker, 7th and Christian
Mount Sarah, whitewasher, 247 S 7th
Mountain Joseph, oysters, 19 Plum
Mountain Joseph, carp., rear 9th ab Coates
Mountain Matthew, gent., Parker n Washington
Mountain Wm., plasterer, S E Washington and
  P road, h 162 Carpenter
Mourer John, gunsmith, G T road bel 5th
Mousley Joseph, cordw., G T road opp 4th
Mower Saml., blksmith, Marlboro' ab Queen (K)
Mowery H., bookbinder, 13th ab Brown
Mowery Jacob, bookbinder, 35 Vernon
Mowery Philip, stonecutter, 33 Vernon
Mowrer Frederick, carpet weaver, Rose above
  School (K)
Mowrer Lewis, carp., Bedford and 7th
Mowry & Heitrech, lamp manuf., 70 Coates
Moxey John G., baker, R road ab 13th
Moyer Adam, cordw., Grim's ct
Moyer Charles, mer., 174 High, h 205 N 6th
Moyer Charles, saddler Otter ab F road
Moyer Edward P., saddler and harness mr., 38
  and 250 High, h 137 N 9th
MOYER & HAZARD, druggists, 174 High
Moyer Isaac, currier, 55 Brown
Moyer Jacob, trunk and collar maker, 150 Chest-
  nut, h Shackamaxon ab Queen
Moyer Michael, dry goods, 118 N 3d
Moyer Michael, cabinetmr., rear 141 Green
Moyes Mary, gentw., 119 Pine
Moyn William, bootmaker, 116 S 3d
Much Adam, shipwright, 37 Marion ab 2d
Muckfus Henry, lab. Charlotte bel Franklin
Muckler M., 45 Pegg
Mudge Simon, collector, 246 High
Mueller John, St. John bel G. T. road (K)
Muendler Adolphus, tobacconist, 367 N 3d
Muhlenberg D., iron founder, office N E 9th &
  Vine, h 295 Sassafras
Muir Alex. F., blindmr. trimmings, 431½ N 2d
Muir Esther, 53 N 9th
Muir William, polisher, Dorothy E Sch 3d
Muirhead John, grocer, Front and John
Mulcahy Thos F., manuf., Perry ab Franklin
Muldoon Edward, tavern, Beach and Palmer(K)
Muldoon Hugh, shoemr., Murray n Sch. 3d
Muldoon James, porter, 12 Vaux's ct

Muldoon Wm. cordw. Spruce n Sch Front
Mulency James, rear 260 Sassafras
Mulford & Alter, grocers, 247 High
Mulford Catharine, rear 109 Christian
Mulford Chas., confect., c Tamarind and Deringer ct
Mulford G. W., tailor, h Washington bel 6th
Mulford John, 6 Logan's sq
Mulford Julia, 34 New Market
Mulford John, Jr., grocer, 247 High, h Vine bet. Sch. 4th and 5th
Mulford Jonathan, mer., S W Water and High, h 30 Buttonwood
Mulgraw Patrick, grocer, Clay & Beach
Mulhall Henry, 10 Prosperous al
Mulholland Arthur, weaver, Murray n Sch 3d
Mulholland David, waiter, 5 Abbott's ct
Mulholland Gilbert, machinist, Jackson bel Orchard
Mulholland Jas., skin dress., rear 98 Carpenter
Mulholland John, tailor, 5 Lyndall's alley
Mulholland Joseph, gilder, 5 Charlotte
Mulholland Michael, lab., Cooper n Sch. 3d
Mulholland Samuel, weaver, 298 St John
Mull Michael, stovemr., rear 45 Duke
Mullen Ambrose, merchant, 52 S Front, h S E 8th and Lombard
Mullen Ann, Milton ab 10th
MULLEN A. & SON, tobacco, 52 S Front
Mullen Bernard, tavern, 23 S 9th
Mullen Catharine, rear 1 Mechanic
Mullen Catharine, 8th bel Catharine
Mullen Dominick, dealer, Spruce W Sch 5th
Mullen David, lab., 7 John's ct
Mullen Edward, Sch 6th and Helmuth
Mullen Fred., grocery, 185 S 6th
Mullen Hugh, shoemr., 8th bel Catharine
Mullen Hugh, b h, 13 Chestnut
Mullen Isaac, grocer, G. T. road and Master (K)
Mullen James, lab., rear William bel Benton (K)
Mullen Jas., segarmr., rear Church bel Christian
Mullen James, tailor, Christian ab 7th
Mullen James, carp., Pleasant ab 12th
Mullen James, tailor, 45 Shippen
Mullen John, coachman, George bel Cedar
Mullen John, bottler, N E 9th and Filbert
Mullen John, milkman, Bushhill
Mullen John, lab., 11th bel Carpenter
Mullen John, lab., Shippen ab 7th
Mullen John, weaver, 15 Lloyd's ct (K)
Mullen Jos., engineer, Marlboro' and Franklin
Mullen Mary, rear 390 Sassafras
Mullen Mary A., dressmr., 129 N 6th
Mullen Michael, 36 Strawberry
Mullen Michael, coachman, Eagle ct
Mullen Neal, machinist, William ab Otter (K)
Mullen Patrick, grocer, N E 13th and Locust

Mullen Thomas, wheelwright, Mansion (W P)
Mullen Thomas, dentist, Washington (W P)
Mullen Wm. morocco dresser, 12 Ellott's av
Mullen Wm., lab., Mansion (W P)
Mullen Wm., shoemr., 5th & Washington
Mullen William C., bricklayer, 10th ab Washington
Mullen Wm. G., mer., 13 Marshall
Mullen Wm. J., surgeon dentist, 278 Catharine
Muller Charles, machinist, Walnut (W P)
Muller Charles C. carp. Queen bel Ross (K)
Muller Mary S., b h., 133 Walnut
Mullica Benj., lab., West ab Hanover (K)
Mullica Wm. corder, rear Queen ab Marlboro'
Mullica Mary, Vienna bel Franklin (K)
Mulligan John, blacksmith, Wood ab Sch. 8th
Mulliken Charles P., saddler, 157 Marshall
Mulliken Magdaline, b. h., 182 Sassafras
Mullikin Hillary, broker, 12 Arcade, h Marshall bel Poplar.
Mullin Charles, drayman, 20 Montgomery
Mullin Isaac, grocer, 2d and Master (K)
Mullin James, waterman, 260 N Water
Mullin Patrick, tailor, 200 Shippen
Mullin Wm., lab., Cooper n Sch. 3d
Mullins Dennis, skindresser, rear 9 Rugan
Mullins Edward, mer., 10 Commerce, h 173 Sp. Garden ab 10th.
Mullison Emeline, Noble bel O. Y. road
Mullison Mary, Sherborn's ct
Mullison William, bricklayer, 418 Coates
Mulock Ann, 63 Franklin
Mulock Geo., currier, G T road ab Thompson
Mulock L., b. h., 645 N 2d
Mulock Sarah, 3 Beldin's row
Mulvany James, lab., 7 Bell's ct
Mulvany Matthew, lab., 9 Marshall's ct
Mulvay Andrew, lab., Juniper and Lawrence
Mumbower Abraham, 3d ab Franklin (K)
Mumford Edward, teacher of drawing, Franklin Marlborough (K)
Mumford Thos. H., engraver, 43 S 5th, h Chestnut W of Sch. 2d
Munce Sylvester, refectory, S E 3d and Vine
Mundall Deborah, 72 S 5th
Mundy George, 282 Mulberry
Munn James, lab., 114 Plum
Munn Mary G., dress mr., 4 Sheldon row
Munns L. C., dentist, 200 E Spruce
Munroe W. H., mer. 19 Commerce
Munsey Christian, tailor, 6 Demery ct
Munson Joseph, lab., Bedford ab 13th
Munyon George, machinist, 12 Perry
Murchison John, shoemr., 3 Southampton ct
Murdock Edward, bookbinder, Federal ab 5th
Murdock Ely, cordw., Atherton
Murdock George, tailor, 12 Wagner's ct

Murphy Alexander, soap boiler, 10 Providence court
Murphy Alexander V., Poplar bel Broad
Murphy Andrew, lab., 68 Swanson
Murphy Anthony, lab., Bird bel Catharine
Murphy Arthur, cabinetmr., 3 Fisher's ct
Murphy Arthur, bricklayer, Poplar ab 13th
Murphy Barney, carp., Crown bel Duke (K)
Murphy Bernard, lamps, 191 N 2d
Murphy Bernard, dealer, 304 N Front
Murphy Charles, grocer, 2d & Reed
Murphy Christiana, Passmore's place
Murphy, Cooper & Co. dry goods, 27 N 3d
Murphy Daniel, lab., 15 Laurel ab Front
Murphy Daniel, dry goods, 27 N 3d, h 68 New
Murphy Dennis, lab., 1 Elmslie's alley
Murphy Dinnis, lab. 170 N Water
Murphy Dominick, carpet weaver, Perry bel Master (K)
Murphy D., coal grate maker, 34 N 6th
Murphy Edward, city watch, 11 Dugan
Murphy Edward, sailmr., 341 High
Murphy Edward, porter, 27 Blackberry alley
Murphy Edward H., cooper, 128 Cedar
Murphy Eliza, wid. of Patrick, Cadwalader bel Phoenix (K)
Murphy Elizabeth, shop, Shippen ab 12th
Murphy Francis, grocer, Pine & Beach
Murphy George, weav., Shippen la bel Shippen
Murphy George, grocer, High & Sch. 3d
Murphy Guy, machinist, 5 Spragg's av
Murphy Harriet, tailoress, 9 Juniper al
Murphy Jacob, carp., Wood bel West (K)
Murphy James, clerk, 158 S 5th
Murphy James, coachman, 1 Lyndall's al
Murphy James, book binder, 37 Commerce
Murphy James, blacksm., 2d bel Mester (K)
Murphy James, carp. M'Mackin's ct
Murphy James, cabt mr., 30 and h 32 S 5th
Murphy James, weav., 97 High, h 107 N 2d
Murphy James, carp. manuf., Hancock ab Phoenix (K)
Murphy James, paver, Buttonwood ab 9th
Murphy James, chairmr, 2 Howard's ct
Murphy Jane, widow of John, grocer, S W 6th & Fitzwater
Murphy Jeremiah, lab., 144 N Water
Murphy John, bootmr., Sch 3d ab Lombard
Murphy John, lab., Locust n Sch 2d
Murphy John, lab., Miles's ct (K)
Murphy John, machinist, 238 Wood
Murphy John, dealer, 8 Monroe ct
Murphy John, cordwainer, Broad ab Vine
Murphy John, manuf., Pine bel Broad
Murphy John, watchman, rear 15 N 13th
Murphy John, blacksmith, Broad ab Vine, h Vine ab Broad
Murphy John, drayman, Marble ab 10th
Murphy John, cabman, Small ab 5th
Murphy John, weaver, 11th ab Milton
Murphy John, manf., Hancock bel Phoenix (K)
Murphy John, carp., 12th n Washington (S)
Murphy John, lab., Sch 3d ab Spruce
Murphy John, hatter, M'Afee's ct
Murphy John, carp., 250 N Front

Murphy John A., 250 Filbert
Murphy John K., 21 Dean
Murphy John P., collector, Wood ab Sch 8th
Murphy John W. 12 Library
Murphy Jos., lab., Corn ab Wharton
Murphy Jose, weaver, 24 M'Duffie
Murphy Lawrence, porter, 5 Miner pl
Murphy Martin, 185 Queen
Murphy Mary, rear 5 Quarry
Murphy Mary, gentw., 7th and Gaskill
Murphy Mary, shop, F road ab West (K)
Murphy Matthew, weaver, Marriott's la bel 6th
Murphy Matthew, lab., 11 Juniper al
Murphy Maurice, cordw. Crown bel Franklin(K)
Murphy Michael, cooper, rear 62 Catharine
Murphy Michael, paver, Lynn n Nixon
Murphy Michael, segars, Brown and Washington
Murphy Michael, lab., 1 Elmslie's al
Murphy Mich., bricklr., rear 452 Callowhill
Murphy Miles, tailor, 208 N 9th
Murphy Patrick G., b. h., 90 N Water
Murphy Philip J., lab., rear 121 Noble
Murphy Robert, dental filemr., 110 N 4th
Murphy Samuel, waterman, Fraley's al (K)
Murphy Sarah, wid., 384 S Front
Murphy Sarah, Queen n Vienna (K)
Murphy Sarah, washer, 151 Locust
Murphy Susan E., 114 Cherry.
Murphy S., M. D., N W 12th and Mulberry
Murphy S. & A., milliners, 50 Mulberry
Murphy Thos., porter, 2 Beaver ct
Murphy Thomas, lab., Federal ab 7th
Murphy Thomas, lab., Pearl ab 13th
Murphy Thomas, surg. inst. maker, 60 N 6th.
Murphy Thos., lab., Pearl bel Broad
Murphy Thos., bricklayer, Sch 7th ab Wood
Murphy Thomas D., machinist, 158 Sassafras, h 11th ab Washington
Murphy Thomas P., 49 Walnut
Murphy Timothy, dealer, 48 Gaskill
Murphy Timothy, cordw., 6 M'Duffie
Murphy Wm., carp., Crown bel Franklin (K)
Murphy Wm., ship joiner, Hanover opp Bedford (K)
Murphy Wm., teacher, 11th and Milton
Murphy Wm. C., shoes, 247 Cedar
Murphy Wm. C., painter, 47 Chestnut, h 82 Spruce
Murphy Wm. F., stationer, 27, & h 19 N 7th
Murphy Wm. N., awningmr., 5 S Front, h Cherry n Sch 7th
Murphy William P., grocer, 20 P road.
Murray Alex., combmr., rear 82 F road
Murray Beauchamp, weaver, 9th bel Christian
Murray Catharine, 17 Noble.
Murray Dennis fireman, Sch 3d ab Spruce
Murray Daniel, weav., 2d ab Master (K)
Murray David, stevedore, 1 Osborn's ct
Murray Edward, coachman, Budden's al.
Murray Edward, manuf., 682 N 2d
Murray E. variety store, 549 S 2d
Murray E. H., sign painter, 135 Sassafras, h 17 Noble
Murray Francis, carter, Carpenter bel 11th

Murray George, watchman, Ann n 12th
Murray George E., dentist, 60 S 11th, h Christian ab 9th
Murray Henry, clothing, 100 S 2d
Murray Henry, confectioner, 137 Locust
Murray Jacob, cordw., Pearl bel Broad
Murray James, coal, Callowhill n Sch
Murray James, waiter, rear 5 Coombes' alley
Murray Jas., bookbr., 37 Commerce
Murray Jas., engineer, 10 Spragg's av
Murray Jeremiah, porter, Pearl bel Broad
Murray Jeremiah, eating house, 16 High, h 10 Buckley
Murray Jeremiah, cabinet mr., Prospect al
Murray John, weaver, Poplar
Murray John, shoemr., 195 Locust
Murray John, waiter, 78 George
Murray John, manuf., 3d bel Thompson (K)
Murray John, blacksmith, 42 Spruce
Murray John, tavern, S W Penn and Pine
Murray John, cordw., Maple & Mechanic
Murray John, bootmr., 218 S 3d
Murray John, lab., Seller's ct
Murray John, atty. & coun., 11 Prune
Murray John, jr., atty., 49 Morris bel Caow tharine
Murray John D., lab., 3 Kelley
Murray John E., currier, 209 Callowhill
Murray Joseph, boot manuf., 53 S 3d
Murray Julianna, 12½ Pearl
Murray Levi, cordw., 9th & Maple, h R road (F V)
Murray Michael, cordw., 1 Sharpless' ct
Murray Michael, cooper, 140 N Water
Murray Owen, lab., 210 N Water
Murray Patrick, grocer, G T road and Jefferson
Murray Patrick, weaver, 11th ab Carpenter
Murray Patrick M., 170 S Front
Murray Peter, lab., Hancock bel Master
Murray Robert, tailor, 11 Whitehall
Murray Samuel, waiter, 25 Currant al
Murray Samuel, porter,, rear 3 Gray's al
Murray Thomas, grocery, 184 Lombard
Murray Thomas, carp., Robinson's ct.
Murray Thomas, ostler, 9 Dean
Murray Wm., lab., Drinker's ct
Murray Wm., lab., 26 Gaskill
Murray Wm., boat build., Sch 3d and R road
Murray Wm. A., combmr., 298 Pine
Murrell James, mer., 43 High, h 138 Walnut
Murren Caroline, rear 13th bel Brown
Murrow Jos., crockery, 576 S 2d
Murta John P., clerk gas works, 11 S 7th, h 110 S 4th
Murtagh James C., teacher, 222 S Juniper
Murtagh Patrick, weaver, rear G T road above Master
Murtha Thomas, skin dresser, Apple ab George
Murtha Thomas, clerk, 42 N 4th
Murtha William, merchant, 34 S 2d
Murtland John, carter, 112 German
Murtland Wm., grocer, 120 Swanson
Murvine Charles, carp , Race ab 13th
Muschart Charles J., tobacconist, 342½ N 2d.
Muschart George, bricklayer, 4 Kniesel's ct

Muschart Joseph, cigar mr., Haydock n Canal
Musgrave Edw., atty., rear Federal ab 5th
Musgrave James, stock and ex. bro., S E 3d and Chestnut, h 234 Spruce
Musgrave J. P., M. D., 142 Pine
Musgrave William, 175 High, h Mantua Village
Musgrave, Wurts & Co., dry goods, 175 High
Musgrove M., looking glass store, 147 S 2d.
Mush C., moulder, 625 S 2d
Music Josiah, printer, Paschal's al
Musick Reuben, printer, 10 Wheeler's ct.
Musnuff C., bootmr., G T road bel 6th (K)
Musselman David, 346 N Front
MUSSELMAN & HERTZLER, forwd. & com mers., Front and Willow st R road
Musser William, mer., 263 High, h 315 Mulberry
MUSSER WILLIAM & CO., hides and leather, 263 High
Mussintine James, cordw., rear 15 Maria
Mustin A., clerk, George ab 9th
Mustin Ebenezer, 171 N 2nd
Mustin George, 171 N 2d
MUSTIN JOHN & CO., trimmings, S E 7th & Mulberry
Mustin John Jr., mer., S E 9th & Chestnut & S E 7th and Mulberry, h Mulberry W Sch 6th
Mustin Robt. F., trimmings, P N 11th
Mutson Isaac, lab., Mulberry n Sch 8th
Mütter Thomas D., M. D., 244 Walnut
Mutz John, eating house, 346 N 3d
Muzzey Benj. A., mer., 47 High
Muzzey & Monroe, New Eng. Glass Co. and other agencies, 19 Commerce
Muzzey Wm. M., glassware, 19 Commerce, h 104 N 9th
Myer Fred., scalemr., George bel 3d (K)
Myer Fred., lab., Hay's ct (K)
Myer Isaac, agent Girard Estate, 7th n Pine
Myer L. F., clerk, 11 S 7th, h 196 S 7th
Myerle Frederick, dry goods, 192 S 2d
Myers Abraham, lab., 21 Mayland
Myers Abraham, paper warehouse, 143 N 3d, h 96 Callowhill
Myers Abraham, grocer, Poplar & Charlotte
Myers Abrm., gas fitter, Maiden bel Front
Myers Abrm., plumber, Laurel bel Front, h y¹ G T road
Myers & Afflick, milliners, 49 N 2d
Myers Alex., weaver, Hope ab Otter (K)
Myers Ann, confectioner, 130 Sassafras
Myers Ann, Beckett,
Myers Ann, wid., 14 Orchard
Myers Bartholomew, drayman, Orchard above Culvert
Myers Bennett, grocer, 178 Lombard
Myers Caspar, cabinet mr., Fraley's ct (K)
Myers Catharine, gentw., Cox
Myers Catharine, rear 15 Cresson's al
Myers Charles, cahm., La Fayette
Myers Charlotte, b. h., 292 Vine
Myers Christian, bootmr., 60 N 8th
Myers Christian C., shoes, 92 N 9th
Myers Christopher, carp., 44 Commerce, h 64 N 8th

MYERS, CLAGHORN & CO., aucti. and com. mers., S W Bank & High
Myers Cornelius F., block and pump mr., 47 Swanson, h 58 Queen
Myers C. & F., ladies' shoes, 92 N 9th
Myers Daniel, shoemr., F road ab Jefferson (K)
Myers Eleanor 83 N 9th
Myers Elizabeth, Graffin's ct
Myers Ferdinand, moulder, Green bel R Road
Myers Frederick, baker, Green n Broad
Myers Fred., actor, Front and Wharton
Myers Frederick, shoemr., 92 N 9th
Myers Frederick, bricklayer, 371 Callowhill
Myers Gracie, wid., 3 James
Myers George, cabinetmr., 536 N 4th
Myers George O., cooper, Penn ab Maiden (K)
Myers George W., paper stainer, 3 Lagrange
Myers G. H., mouldmr., 15 Crown, h 105 Noble
Myers Henry, baker, Sch 3d n Spruce
Myers Henry, alderman, Callowhill ab Sch 2d
Myers Henry, warp frame knit., Vernon bel 11th
Myers Henry, carp., Gay's ct
Myers Henry, dry goods, 108 N 7th
Myers Hen., machinist, Howard bel Phoenix (K)
Myers Henry, conveyancer, Coates & Nixon
Myers Jacob, vict., Lemon ab 10th
Myers Jacob, baker, 37 Pine
Myers Jacob, mead garden, Front bel Wharton
Myers Jacob R., earp., 3 Shield's al
Myers James, painter, Lombard W Ashton
Myers John, oysterman, Relief ct
Myers John, cordw., rear 6th ab Poplar
Myers John, carp., 195 Noble
Myers John, cordw., Scott's ct (N L)
Myers John, printer, Baker n 8th
Myers John, mariner, 25 Cox
Myers John, paper & rags, 299 Vine
Myers John, blacksmith, F road n Master
Myers John, sexton, rear First Presbyterian Ch., (K)
Myers John, vict., 151 Buttonwood
Myers John, cabinetmr., Orchard ab George
Myers John B., auct., S W Bank & High, h 368 Mulberry
Myers John D. moulder, Washington ab 10th
Myers John H., hatter, 40 Christian
Myers John H., tavern, N E Chestnut & Water
Myers John M. moulder, 10 Wells' row
Myers John R., tanner, Warren n Beach (K)
Myers Jonas, saddler. Rose bel William (K)
Myers Joseph B., merchant, 88 Chestnut, h 368 Mulberry
Myers Joseph G. scourer, 200 Cedar
Myers Joseph S. & Son, block and pump mrs., 47 Swanson
Myers Lawrence, brass & iron founders, Broad ab Sassafras.
Myers Marmaduke, lab., rear Sutherland below Queen
Myers Martha, rear 130 Sassafras
Myers Martha, widow of Benjamin, 399 Pine
Myers Martin, carp., 24 Franklin pl, h Rogers' et
Myers Mary Mrs., 3 Shriver's ct
Myers Mary Mrs., 498 Vine

Myers Mary, wid. of Henry, Charles below Buttonwood
Myers Matthias, blindmr., Beaver bel 4th
Myers Melchor, carter, Shepherd's ct
Myers Michael, cooper, 99 New Market
Myers Michael, stone mason, 3 Butz's ct
Myers Moses, mariner, Lancaster bel Wharton
Myers Nathan, machinist, Penn ab Maiden (K)
Myers Peter, broker, Filbert W. of Sch 5th
Myers P. D., acct., 276 N 6th
Myers Rachael, shop, 212 S 7th
Myers Robert S, cooper, Marshall ab Poplar
Myers Samuel, grocer, 5th and Poplar
Myers Samuel, cabinetmr., 20 Laurel (C)
Myers Samuel S., blacksmith, 525 N 5th
Myers Simon, blindmr. 21 Rachel
Myers Stephen, carp., Baker bel 8th
Myers S. & M., blindmrs. 160 N 4th
Myers Thomas, seaman, Doman's pl
Myers Thomas A., mer., 165 High, h Spring Garden n 13th
Myers Washington, 8 Laurel (C)
Myers, Wm., baker, 197 Callowhill
Myers Wm., skin dresser, Marshall ab Poplar
Myers Wm., equestrian, N E Queen & Front
Myers Wm., pedler, Fraley's al (K)
Myers William, carter, 353 Coates
Myers William, lab., Charlotte n Creek
Myers Wm., last mr., 30 Cherry
Myers Wm., manuf., 6th ab Camac, h G T road and Montgomery
Myers Wm. G., barber, Sp Garden bel 9th, h 493 Poplar
Myers William H., carp., 11 Logan
Myhover Jacob, lab., Front ab Poplar
Mylor Wm., 145 St John
Myrick Benjamin, oil manuf. 10 Christian, h 348 S 4th
Myrtetus Benjamin, ship carp., 186 Swanson
Myrtetus Charles, ship carp. 446 S Front
Myrtetus Christopher, cooper, 43 Christian
Myrtetus Salome, gentw., 23 Catharine
Mytinger F. A., clerk, 502 Coates
Mynick Barbara, 89 N 5th

———

Nace Jacob jr., nail manuf., 163 St John
Nace James, nailer, 22 Lily al
Nace Joseph, 10th bel Willow
Nace Saml., combmr., Poplar ab 5th
Nace Tobias, dealer, rear 167 St John
Nacey John, shop, St Mary bel 8th
Nagel G. P., silversmith, 8 Nectarine
Nagel Samuel, machinist, 3 Caroline
Nagle & Boyer, tobacconists, 1 S 3d
Nagle Bridget, milliner, 186½ S 4th
Nagle Catharine, Shippen ab 9th
Nagle Frederick, carp., Mechanic
Nagle F. G. tobacconist, Green ab 13th
Nagle F. J., mer., 1 S 3d, h Green ab 13th
Nagle Geo., stonecutter, Catharine & Lebanon
Nagle George, 45 Cherry
Nagle George, lab. Dugan n Pine

Nagle George L., dentist, 280 N 7th
Nagle Henry L. gauger, rear 6 S wharves, h 80 Vine
Nagle John, grocery, 12th and Pine
Nagle John, tailor, Cedar bel 10th
Nagle John, cabmr., Noble & Garden
Nagle John, ostler, 11 Marshall's ct.
Nagle John F., tailor, Locust W Sch 4th
Nagle Margaret E. 6 Carlton sq
Nagle Mary, teacher, 123 Catharine
Nagle Patrick, lab., Prospect al
Naglee Caroline, millinery, 367 N 2d
Naglee Hannah R., 140 Green
Naglee Henry A. dry goods, 366 N 10th
Naglee John, lumber mer. High Bridge, h Front and Brown
Naglee John jr., lumb. mer., High Bridge, h Front and Brown
NAGLEE JOHN & SON, lumb. mers., High Bridge
Naglee Martha, Marion bel Corn
Naisby J. D., tailor, 181 Callowhill
Naisby J. G. carpet weaver, 220 N 5th
Naismith James, lab., Steward
Nancrede Joseph G., M. D., S E 10th & Walnut
Nancrede Nicholas, M. D., 100 Spruce
Nancrede Thos. D., mer., 24 Church al, h 12 Clinton
Nangle Mary, 43 Cedar
Nangle Walter, carp., 209 S 6th
Nanzel Fredk., baker, 28 Garden
Naphas Danl., lab., Franklin ab Hanover
Napheys Abraham, carpenter, Brandywine bel Broad, shop Brinton bel 11th
Napheys George C., mer., 4 Chestnut, h Wood ab 10th
Napheys George H. carp. Division bel 12th
Napheys Sarah, Wood ab 10th
Napier Alex., turner, 4 Parker
Napier Hannah, nurse, Marriott's la ab 5th
Napier John, chairmaker, 68 Tammany
Napier John N , painter, 85 Dock, house 22 Coombe's al
Napier Wm., stevedore, Carpenter ab 6th
Nariston Joseph, dentist, 25 Turner
Nary Edwd., stonecutter, Lewis n Sch 6th
Nash Wm. tinsmith, 109 Cedar
Nassau Eliza, gentw., 15 N 11th
Nassau William jr., tobacconist, 231 High, h 22 Buttonwood
Nathans David, clerk, Ogden bel 10th
Nathans Isaac, auctioneer, 162 N 3d
Nathans Jacob, broker, 259 S 3rd
Nathans Moses, clerk, Carlton & Brown's ct
Nathans Moses, auctioneer, 84 S 2nd, h 7th bel Parrish
NATHANS PHILIP, loan office, N E Marshall & Callowhill, h 97 Franklin
Natt John, engineer, Mel bel R road
Natt Joseph S., mer., 192 Chestnut,
Natt Mary, 451 Mulberry
Natt Thomas J., looking glasses, 134 High, h Vine n Sch 4th
Nau Valentine, barber, 393 N 4th
Naudain Arnold, M. D., Broad n Poplar .

Naudain Isaac, lab., Carpenter ab 12th
Naulty James, currier, 215 Lombard
Naulty J., shoemr., Pine bel Willow
Naulty Thomas, currier, 51 Walnut
Naves Benjamin H. mariner, 409 S Front
Naves Walter, waterman, 409 S Front
Naylor Charlotte, tailoress, N W Green and Marshall
Naylor & Co., agency, 11 Commerce
Naylor Eliza, dressmr., 313 N 5th
Naylor Francis E., tailor, 213 Queen
Naylor George J., brushes, 319½ High, h 123 Christian
Naylor Jacob, plasterer, Duke bel Vienna (K)
Naylor Jeremiah, tanner, Mulberry n Sch 2d
Naylor John G., shoemaker, Parrish ab 10th
Naylor Joseph, cordw., 225 N 10th
Naylor Mason, constable, 18 Carter's alley
Naylor Mrs., b h, Broad ab Cherry
Naylor Sampson, carp., Jefferson ab Sch. 6th
Naylor Thos. plasterer, Union ab Franklin (K)
Nead James, watchman, Wood ab Sch 2d
Nead Wm. contractor, 162 Callowhill n Sch 6th
Neafie Jacob, machinist, Beach bel Palmer, h Queen ab Palmer (K)
Neagle John, portrait painter, 9 Sansom
Neagle J. B., engraver, Filbert E Sch. 6th
Neal Charles, lab., rear Hope ab Otter (K)
Neal Ebenezer, M. D., 82 Crown
Neal Jacob, lab., Goodwill ct
Neal James, tailor, 4 Furlong's ct
Neal James, waterman, 50 Washington av
Neal James, cordwainer, Barber's row
Neal James, tavern, 333 N Front
Neal James A., mer., 30 S whfs., h 8th n Buttonwood
Neal James A., collector, 293 N 8th
Neal Jane, shop, 10 Maiden (K)
Neal John, lab., Cooper n Sch 3d
Neal John, carp., 7th bel Carpenter (S)
Neal Joseph C. editor, N E 4th and Chestnut, h 16 S 7th
Neal Joseph C. & Co. pubs. of Neal's Saturday Gazette, N E 4th and Chestnut
Neal Robt., lab., rear Edward bel 2d (K)
Neal Samuel, carp., Prime bel Front
Neal Susan, Edward bel G T road (K)
Neal Thomas B. carp. 7 Railroad ct
Neal William, mer., 7th n Green
Neal William, sailmr., N wharves & Sassafras, h Budd ab Poplar
Neale James, plumber, P road bel Christian
Nealis James, pawnbroker, 412 E Cedar
Nealis James, lab., Cooper n Sch 3d
Nealis Tim., blacksm., rear Vaughan ab Locust
Neall & Barrett, mers., 85 S Wharves, and 5 Penn
Neall Daniel Jr. dentist, 325 Mulberry
Neall E. M., dentist, 12th ab Mulberry opposite Grace church
NEALL JAS., iron founder, Bushhill, h 492 Sassafras
Neall James E., insp., 153 Queen
Neall Samuel, mer., 86 S Wharves, h 208 S 3d
Neall Samuel W., dentist, 187 N 6th

Neath George, mariner, 382 S 3d
Nebinger Andrew, dentist, 482 S 2d
Nebinger Andrew jr., druggist, c 2d and Mary
Nebinger Geo. W., druggist, P road and Washington
Nece Jesse, saddler, Brown ab 10th
Nece Barbara, widow, 206 Sassafras
Nece Henry, grocer, S E 4th & Poplar
Nece Reuben, coal, 155 N 3d, h 206 Sassafras
Nece Ruth, tailoress, Paschall's al bel 5th
Needham James, hair dresser, 1 N 6th, h 25 Elizabeth
NEEDLES CALEB H., druggist, S W 12th and Sassafras
Needles Deborah, gentw., 130 N Front
Needles Edward, druggist, N W Broad & Vine
Needles Jos. A. Jr. wire worker, 54 N Front
Needles Jos. A. & Co,, sieve mrs., & wire workers, 54 N Front
Needles Tristram, druggist, 492 Sassafras
Needles Wm., druggist, N W Broad and Vine, h 12th bel Sassafras
Neel John W., Barker E of Sch 5th
Neel Thos., watchman, 3 Vicker's ct
Neel Robert, carpenter, Ogden bel 10th
Neeld James, carp., 430 Poplar
Neeley Jas., lab., Sch 4th bel High
Neely Francis, manuf. Fulton ab 12th
Neely James J., cabinet maker, Shippen below Broad
Neely John, grocer, S E Cedar & Shippen la
Neely John, engineer, Sch 6th bel high
Neely Josiah, clerk, 1 Jacoby
Neely Margaret, shop, Lombard n Sch 7th
Neely Martha, 133 N Juniper
Neely Matthew, weaver, Lloyd ab Fitzwater
Neely Philip, gardener, Duke ab Hanover
Neely Thomas, lab., Fulton ab 12th
Neenhold Frederick, cabinetmaker, 18 Concord
Neff Charles, vict., 6 Carter's al
Neff Charles, grocer, N E 11th and Locust
Neff Christiana, 217 N 8th
Neff Daniel W., grocer, 3d and Tammany, h 113 Dillwyn st
Neff Frederick, bootmr., 4th and Brown
Neff Geo. Rev., Washington bel 7th
Neff Henry, engraver, 141 Buttonwood
Neff Jacob, cordw., Henderson's ct
Neff John, superintendent Railroad, N E Broad & High, h 10 Howard
Neff John, porter, 22 Dock
Neff John, broker, N E Lombard and 3d
Neff John D., baker, 207 S 6th
Neff John J., 213 N 8th
Neff John R., mer., 6 N wharves, h 124 Spruce
Neff Mary, widow, 24 Rose alley
Neff Robert K., com. mer., 25 S Wharves, h 77 Pine
NEFF RUDOLPH, grocer, N W 8th and Vine
Neff R., dry goods, 42 S 2d
Neff Samuel, brushmr., Northampton ct
Neff Wm. C., 3½ S 7th
Negley Elizabeth, 5 Cox
Negley James R., tailor, 5 Cox
Negus J. Engle, Mulberry n Sch 6th

Negus J. Rea, com. mer., 30 Walnut
Negus J. Rea & Co., mers., 30 Walnut
Neher Charles, rear 123 Mulberry
Nehlig John P. stove finisher, Brook ab Coates
Neidhard C., M. D., 100 S 9th
Neihans Bernard, grocery, Mulberry al
Neil Geo., blacksm., Cherry n Sch 8th
Neil Jane, Tammany ab 4th
Neil John, painter, 51 Mead
NEIL WILLIAM, tavern, 84 S 2d
Neild Luke, cotton carder, 319 St John
Neiles George, tavern, 20 S wharves
Neiles Patrick, shoemr., 6 N 13th
Neill Archibald, tailor, 572 N 2d (K)
Neill Geo. W., piano mr., 12 Pleasant Retreat
Neill John, M. D., 295 Spruce
Neill John, ladies' shoemr., 6 N 8th & 309 High
Neill John L., shipwright, Marine Railway, h 20 Christian
NEILL J. P. W. druggist, N E 7th & Chestnut, h 375 Pine
Neill Lewis, shoemr., 608 S 2d
Neill Robert, tailor, 121 Mulberry
Neill William, Rev., D. D., 206 Pine
Neill William, shoes, 192 S 5th
Neill William, tailor, 4 S 9th
Neille Ann, 392 S 5th
Neilson Elizabeth, dressmr., 3 N 10th
Neilson Jane, 71 N 5th
Neilson Robt., 13th and Spruce
Neilson Wm. S., mer., 93 S Front, h Walnut ab Sch 8th
Neily Mary Ann, 43 Franklin
Neiser Joseph, segarmr., Perry bel Phoenix
Neisser Augustus, combmr., 7th and Parrish
Neisser William, blacksmith, 125 Charlotte
Nekervis Wm., mer., 20 Bank
Nelius Jacob, manuf., Swanson bel Catharine
Nell Jesse, carp. Wall opp. Queen, h 206 Fitzwater
Nellis John, Jones west Sch 8th
Nellis Patrick, lab., Jones W Sch 8th
Nelms Henry, gold beater, 9 Pear
Nelms Richard, cabinetmr., 125 Queen
Nelms Thos., tobacconist, 125 Queen
Nelson Ann, 391 S 6th
Nelson Elizabeth, 272 St John
Nelson Elizabeth, Christians' ct
Nelson George, mariner, 473 S Front
Nelson Geo., weaver, Front bel Jefferson (K)
Nelson G. S., barber, 30 S 7th
Nelson James, shingle shaver, 6th bel Christian
Nelson James, oyster house, 50 N 2d
Nelson John, cordwainer, St Mary bel 7th
Nelson Mary, 106 Carpenter
Nelson Mary I., Locust n Sch 3d
Nelson Philip, 8th bel Catharine
Nelson Robt., distiller, Vine n Sch
Nelson Susanna, 3 School
Nelson Thomas, glass and china, 273 N 2d
Nelson Thomas, engraver, Sch Front bel Vine
Nelson Wm., vict., Garden ab Noble
Nelson Wm., blacksm., 10th ab Catharine
Nepp Fidell, rear 9 Lily al
Nesbit A., com. mer., 58 O Y road

Nesbit James, weaver, 13th n Fitzwater
Nesbit John, collector, 23 Emlin's ct
Nesbit Thomas, printer, 414 S 4th
Neslier Wm., lab., Faries' ct
Nessle Christian, lab., Van Buren pl
Nesswenger Edgar, lab., Brandywine ab 13th
Netter Joseph, gunsmith, 12 Rachel
Neubauer Wm. locksmith, Nectarine bel 11th
Neuber Christ., hostler, F road ab Palmer (K)
Neuber John G., shoemr., 7 Butz's ct
Neuber Valentine, cordw., 16 New Market
Neuhart Michael, lab. 78 New
Neuman Lewis, shoemr., 82 S 8th
Nevall Ephraim, lab., rear 146 Poplar
Nevell Geo., lab., 7 Young's al
Nevers James, oysterman, rear 264 S 5th
Neriel Joseph, morroc. dresser, Poplar ab 5th
Neville Edward Rev., rector St Philip's Church, Franklin and Vine, h Wood bel 8th
NEVILLE JOHN, Washington Inn, 3 George
Neville Wm. II., mer., 15 N 4th
Nevinger George, blacksmith, rear Swanson bel Queen
Nevins John, lab., rear 121 Noble
Nevins James, broker, 68 S 3d, h Broad bel Spruce
NEVINS J. W., stock broker, 80 S 3d, h Sch 6th bel Mulberry
Nevins Morris, carp., 50 Zane
Nevins Patrick, porter, 24 Mifflin st
Nevins Samuel, broker, 80 S 3d, h Penn sq & Filbert
Nevins & Whelen, ex. broks., 68 S 3d
Nerling Henry, wharf builder, Warren ab Beach
Nevling John, wharf builder, Beach n Warren (K)
New Conrad, lab. Fontanell's ct
New Wm., tinsmith, Hanover bel Franklin (K)
Newall Robt., mer., Sch 6th and Bickham's ct
Newall Robt., engin., Cherry bet Sch 5th & 6th
Newbern Wm., lab., 63 Orchard,
Newberry James W., dentist & watchmaker, 18 F road
Newberry J. B., painter and glazier, 23 S 8th, h 18 Castle
Newberry Robt K., bootmr., 277 Green
Newell Eliza, teacher, 218 E Lombard
Newell Geo., moulder, 6 Federal st
Newell Maria Mrs., widow, n Sch 4th
Newbold Caleb, Prest. Ches. and Del. Canal Co., h 309 Spruce
Newbold Charles, mer., 51 S whfs., h Spruce bel Broad
Newbold George L., M. D., 121 N 12th
Newbold James S., ed. & pub. of Banner of the Cross, 89 S 5th, h 115 S 4th
NEWBOLD JOHN L., att'y & coun. 115 S 6th, h 215 N 4th
Newbold Josiah H., hides, skins, sumach, &c. 242 N 3d, h 145 Franklin
Newbold Richd. S., Secy. Del. Ins. Co., 3d and Dock, h 102 Chestnut
Newbold Saml., 18 Pine
Newbold Wm. A., att'y & coun., 100 Walnut

Newbold William H., broker, S W Dock & Walnut, h 132 N 9th
Newbold Wm. L., real estate office, 58 Walnut
Newburn Phebe, sempstress, 89 O Y road
Newcomb B., atty. and coun., 38 S 5th
Newcomb Hezekiah, currier, N E 4th and Sassafras, h 55 Vine
Newcomb Sarah, rear 512 N Front
Newcomb Wm., waterman, Court al
Newcomb William, 8th ab Christian
Newell Ann D., Pine ab Sch 7th
Newell Elizabeth, 100 Wood
Newell Saml., broker, 75 Dock, h S W 7th and Locust
Newell Simon, shipwright, Crown below Bedford (K)
Newell Wm., mer., 3 S Water, h 8th bel Pine
Newhall H. P., shoes, S Garden bel 8th
Newhall P. W., merchant, 26 S Front, h 202 Spruce
Newhall T. A., mer., 62 S Front, h Pine ab 9th
Newhouse Charles, dyer, Sch 3d ab Lombard
Newhouse Jacob W., dentist, 51 N 8th
Newhouse John, cordwainer, 8 Jackson's ct
Newhouser Mary, wid. of Jacob, Sch Beach n George
Newitt A., tailor, 22 Plum
Newkirk Andrew J., confect., 306 N 2d
Newkirk Cath., 507 Chestnut
Newkirk Matthew, gent., 80½ Walnut, h S W 13th and Mulberry
Newkirk T., tavern, 1 Mulberry
Newkirk Victor M., tailor, Callowhill bel 11th
Newland E. & Co., looking glasses, 218 N 2nd
Newland Francis, paper hanger, 227 Mulberry
Newland Wm. A., musician, 22 S 13th
NEWLIN & ALLIBONE, mers., 17 S whfs
Newlin James W., acct., 103 Filbert
Newlin John S., mer., N E 2d and High, h 21? Mulberry
Newlin & Price, coal dealers, N E 12th and Willow
Newlin Robert, brewer, 86 N 2d, h 28 Sassafras
Newlin Thomas S., merchant, 151 High, h 15th ab Spruce
Newlin Wm. Parker, mer., 17 S whfs, h 5 West Locust
Newman And., carter, 39 Ogden
NEWMAN & BEALE, com. mer. 70 S Front
Newman Charles, grocer, Washington bel 13th
Newman Charles W., feed, R road ab James, h 39 Ogden
Newman Conrad, ostler, 5 Butz's ct
Newman Daniel, grocer, 261 N 8th
Newman Edgar P., plasterer, Loud st
Newman Edw., carp., N W Noble and 6th
Newman Fred., rear 23 N 6th
Newman G. painter, Cedar n 13th
Newman Henry, Eagle hotel, 331 High
Newman Henry, cordw., Haight's ct
Newman Henry, mariner, Prime ab Front
Newman Henry K., clerk, Noble & 6th
Newman James, white washer, 12 Currant alley
Newman Jas. L., mer., 70 S Front, h 312 Walnut
Newman James W., clerk, Noble & 6th

Newman John B. jr., mer., 89 S Front, h 18 Washington sq

Newman Joshua, tavern, 83 Plum st

Newman J. A., jeweller, 3 Franklin place, h 181 Green

Newman Sarah, grocery, Franklin & Wallace

Newman Wm. dyer, Hummel's ct

Newnam Henry, printer, 11 Jefferson

Newnam Rebecca, Jefferson ab Sch. 6th

Newnan Charles G., plasterer, Dean ab Centre

Newport Ann, Sch 6th & Cherry

Newport James, clerk, Boyd's av

Newport Thos., skin dresser, Franklin below School (K)

Newport Thos. J. dent., S E Sch 6th & Cherry

Newsam Nathan, lab., 136 Apple

Newsham Henry, pattern mr. 390 S 5th

Newsham John, machinist, 372 S 5th

Newsham John, jr. blacksmith, Shackamaxon ab Bedford (K)

Newsley John, agent, N W 3d & Washington

Newton Andrew, machinist, Hope ab Otter (K)

Newton Daniel, tinsmith, 410 N 4th

Newton Elizabeth, dry goods, F road opp Marlborough

Newton Hannah, nurse, 155 S 11th

NEWTON ISAAC, confectionary, 187 Chestnut

Newton Peter, weaver, Howard bel Franklin (K)

Newton Ralph, druggist, Beach & George Sch

Newton Richard Rev., 92 Union

Newton R. & B., stock & ready made linen, 75 Chestnut

Newton William, tavern, S W 8th and Buttonwood

Newton Wm., Irvine st

Nibblock Wm., lab., Lewis n Sch 7th

Niblick James, bricklayer, Filbert W Sch 4th

Nice Abraham, grocery, N E 4th & Noble

Nice Adam, blacksm., rear Marshall ab Poplar

Nice Andrew, shoemr., Shackamaxon n Franklin (K)

Nice Charles, 13 Mead

Nice George P., teacher, N E 8th and Chestnut, 129 N 9th

Nice John, cabinet & chair maker, New Crown bel Green

Nice John, lab., rear of Amber ab Phoenix

Nice Levi, machinist, 88 Noble

Nice Margaret, 2 Goodwill ct

Nice Stephen, shoemr. Shackamaxon below Franklin

Nice William, currier, 386 N 3d

Nice Wm., cordw., Otter bel G T road (K)

Nichol Alexander, weaver, Adams bel 13th

Nichol James, carp., 45 W Cedar

Nichol Jeremiah, carp., Adams & 13th

Nicholas Charles, blacksm., Orchard ab Rawle

Nicholas Etienne, saddler, High W of Sch 7th

Nicholas Geo., tobacconist, Sch 8th ab Race

Nicholas Samuel, gent., 185 Walnut

Nicholas Wm. H., carp., Beaver ab Charlotte

Nicholl & Burkhard, cistern builders, 31 Dillwyn

Nicholls Ebenezer, painter, 2 S 8th

33

Nichols Albert G., tailor, 8 S 3d, h 16 Ellen st (N L)

Nichols Archibald, watchman, Juniper bel Pine

Nichols George, 104 German

Nichols James, clerk, 7 Ellen

Nichols Jas. R., D. D., Chestnut n Sch 2d

Nichols Joseph, saw maker, 28 Norris' alley, h 26 Walnut

NICHOLS L. F., tavern, Broad ab Cherry

Nichols Margaret, 87 Penn (S)

Nichols Margaret, Front bel Marion

Nichols Mary, washer, 365 Lombard

Nichols O. C., 36 S 8th

Nichols Reuben, organ builder, 12 Wallace

Nichols Robt., spinner, Perry ab Franklin (K)

Nichols Samuel, waiter, 187 Catharine

Nichols Samuel, clothier, 192 Shippen

Nichols Wm., cordw., 9 Wilson st

Nichols Wm., cabinetmr., 342 Callowhill

Nicholson Emma, dry goods, 188 S 3d

Nicholson Geo. B., carp., Mifflin n 13th

Nicholson James B., bookbinder, 5 Mint ct

Nicholson L., gent., 24 S 12th

Nicholson Mary, gentw., Parrish ab 9th

Nicholson Saml. B., carp., 13th bel Coates

Nicholson Thomas, carp., Sch 7th n Vine

Nicholson Thomas, cotton spinner, Otter ab F road

Nicholson Wm., carp., 17 Orleans

Nicholson Wm., atty. & coun., 161 Coates

Nichuals Andrew J., carp., 23 Elizabeth (N L)

Nichuals Robert, tailor, 152 N 13th

Nichuals William, carp., 66 O Y road

Nickel Jane, Say street

Nickel John, weaver, William n Edward (K)

Nickerson & Bishop, hatters, 41 N 2d

Nickerson Charles, hatter, 51 Mulberry h 408 N 5th

Nickerson James S., hatter, 41 N 2d

Nickerson Joshua, keeper of penitentiary, R road & Sp Garden

Nickert Daniel & Baker John M., tailors, 315 N 2nd

Nickins William C., barber, 15 Chestnut, h 219 E Lombard

Nickles Samuel, oak cooper, Marriott & 6th

Nickless Samuel, clothing, 87½ S 2d, h Shippen bel Russell

Nickum Caroline, widow, Hanover above Franklin (K)

Nickum Elizabeth, umbrella mr., High n Sch 6th

Nickum Hannah, widow, 53 Duke

Nicolai Christian, tailor, 24 Vine

Nicoll Alexander, carp., 41 Dillwyn, h 29 Elfreth's al

Nieland A. H. & C. Burrichter, clothing, 145 S 2nd

Nielson George W., clerk, 300 S 3d

Nightingale James, sailmr., Duke n Bedford (K)

Nightingale Richard, tavern, F road opp Bedford (K)

Nightingale Rich'd, spinner, Washington (W P)

Nightlinger Adam, vict., Powell (F V)

Niles Daniel, shoe findings, 97 Mulberry

Nill John, shoemr., 19 Quince

Ninesteel John D., victualler, 11th bel Buttonwood
Nippard David, potter, rear Poplar ab 3d
Nippes Abraham, gunsmith, 111 Dillwyn
Nippes Anna C., wid of Wm., 127 Dillwyn
Nippes Anna M., widow, 130 Dillwyn
Nippes Henry, grocer, 163 Green
Nippes John C., atty. and coun., 6th & Coates
Nipps Wm., baker, Lombard n Sch 7th
Nishman Fredk., sugar refiner, 53 Rose al
Niskey Maria, 7 West
Nispel Henry, tailor, 452 Sassafras
Nix Arthur, perfumer, 20 N 8th
Nixon Alex., chair paint., Dean ab Bedford (K)
Nixon Catharine, spooler, rear Phillip ab Master (K)
Nixon Charles C., painter, 170 S 13th ab Pine
Nixon Francis, lab., 372 S Front
Nixon Geo., pedler, Clay & Beach
Nixon Jacob, barber, rear 303 Walnut
Nixon James, printer, Carpenter bel 6th
Nixon Jane, Centre ab 12th
Nixon John, lab., Essex st
Nixon Maria, Monroe pl
Nixon Mary, huckster, Shield's ct
Nixon Mary, 13 Well's row
Nixon Robert, drayman, Brown ab Cherry
Noble Alexander, bottler, 2d & Chestnut, h Allen's ct
Noble Andrew, tanner, Charlotte and Culvert
Noble Catharine, trimmings, Catharine bel 2d
Noble Chas., lab., rear 66 P road
Noble Charles, M. D., 270 N 3d
Noble Ellen, dry goods, 381 S 2d
Noble Geo., grocer, High and Ashton
Noble Isaac, lab., Ann n 12th
Noble James, weaver, Marlboro' bel Duke (K)
Noble James, coiner, 28 Logan
Noble James, weaver, Sch 6th bel Lombard
Noble James A., bookbr., 13 Pennsylvania av
Noble John, carter, Sch 8th & Parrish
Noble Joseph, locksmith, High bel Sch 5th
Noble Jos., weaver, Alton ct
Noble Maria, shop, 58 Apple
Noble Samuel, cordw., rear 139 Green
Noble Sarah, wid. of Samuel, 263 N 3d
Noble & Stuntevants, mers., 21) Exchange
Noble Thomas H., bookbinder, 5th ab German
Noble Webber, blacksmith, Washington av below Brown
Noble William, wood merchant, 12 Green
Noble Wm., keeper E. Penitentiary, h Sch 2d bel Callowhill
Noble Wm., lab., Mulberry n Sch 8th
NOBLE WILLIAM & CO., com. mers., Broad ab Sassafras
Noble Wm. H., grocer, N W Vine & Sch 8th
Noblit Stephen, cabmr., 11th ab Poplar
Nock Joseph, lock manuf., 13th ab Poplar
Noe Amos, blacksm., 5 Dilk's ct
Noe W. C., cabmr., 6th bel Carpenter
Noeleng Ludwig, Mary n F road
Nolan John, weaver, Murray
Nole John H., tailor, 2 Filbert
Nolen Alfred, lab., 6 Biddle's al

Nolen Bridget, sempstress, Robinson's ct
Nolen Catharine, shop, Small bel 6th
Nolen Daniel, stone mason, Ontario bel Poplar
Nolen Elizabeth, 56 Filbert
Nolen Henry, auctioneer, 76 Coates, h 384 N 10th
Nolen Henry, senr., 384 N 10th
Nolen James, gilder, 10th & Brown
Nolen John, lumb. mer., 515 S Front
Nolen John, carman, 7 Howard pl
Nolen Margaret, shop, Small
Nolen Martin, ostler, Peach ab Green
Nolen Spencer, looking glasses, 78 Chestnut.
Nolen Wm., mason, Shippen la ab Cedar
Nolen W. C., tailor, 3d ab Catharine
Noll Jacob, lab., 5 Ellet's av
Noll Jacob, huckster, 99 St John
Noll Michael, beer house, Poplar ab 3d
Noll Peter, brewer, 548 N 3d
Nones J. B. Dr., 201 S 4th
Noon Thomas, cordw., Phoenix ab 2d (K)
Noonan B., porter, 4 College pl
Noonan Timothy, tailor, 27 Jones' al (C)
Nooney Thomas, machinist, 143 Buttonwood
Norbury Susan, 91 N 5th
Norcross Daniel, collector, Wallace bel 9th
Norcross Isaac, cordwainer, Parrish ab 9th
Norcross Samuel, type founder, 122 Beach (K)
Norcross Thos., painter, Orchard ab Rawle
Nordman L. E., druggist, Sch 6th & George
Norgrave Jeremiah, capt., 48 Almond
Norden Lawrence, seaman, Swarthmore pl
Norman Catharine, b. h., 343 High
Norman Henry, cordw., School
Norman Henry R., bricklayer, 10 Pratt
Norman John, coachman, 52 Currant al
Norman John, pilot, Federal ab Front
Norman Joshua L., boatman 93 Prime
Noronha Maria L., teacher, 153 S 10th
Norr G. R., 14 New Market
Norrett John, stone cutter, 125 Melon
Norris A., painter, 6 Marion
NORRIS, BROTHERS, loc. eng. builders, Sch 6th on Bush Hill
Norris Edward S., locomotive eng. builder, Sch 6th on Bush Hill
Norris Elizabeth H., gentw., 307 Chestnut
Norris George, timber sawyer, Corn ab Mackey
Norris G. W., M. D., 443 Chestnut
NORRIS ISAAC, att'y and coun., 147 and h 24 Walnut
Norris Isaac W. Mrs., 218 N Front
Norris James shoes, 10th & Parrish
Norris John, seaman, Collins' ct
Norris John, shop, Poplar ab 10th
Norris Joseph, shipwright, Queen ab Palmer (K)
Norris Joseph J., shipwright, Beach bel Marlborough
Norris J. P. att'y. and couns., 147 Walnut, h Broad ab Filbert
Norris Martha, Beach bel Warren (K)
Norris Matthew, tailor, 318 High
Norris O. A. 24 Girard st

Norris Richard, founder, Sch. 6th on Bush Hill, h Locust W Sch 8th
Norris R. & M., milliners and trimmings, S W Marshall & Coates
Norris R. W., 210 N Front
Norris Samuel, sea captain, 21 Plum
Norris Samuel, 307 Chestnut
Norris Thaddeus, merchant, 3 Minor, h 61 N 12th
Norris T. & Co., clothiers, 3 Minor
Norris William, locomotive engine builder, office and works Sch. 6th on Bush Hill, h Turner's lane ab R road
North Caleb, 208 Locust
North George, clerk, 5 Belmont pl
North Gibson, stovemr., 390 High
NORTH & HARRISON, stove dealers, 390 High
North John, dyer, Willow n Pine
North Richard, 33 Farmer
North Thomas R., carp., Hudson's al, h 13th bel Spruce
North Wm. buttonmr. P road bel Washington
North Wm. F., capt., 25 New Market
Northrop Ann, 68 S 4th
Northrop George, att'y & coun., 116 Walnut
Northrop Jeremiah, shop, R road bel Broad
Northrop John, conveyancer, 79 S 3rd, h Walnut n Sch 6th
Northrop Samuel, constable, R road bel Broad
Norton Charles, tinsmith, S W 6th and Cherry
Norton George, atty. at law, 40 S 6th, h S E 3d and Christian
Norton James, brushmr., 460 Vine
Norton Joseph F. mariner, 12 Reckless
Norton Margaret, washer, back 130 Sassafras
Norton Patrick, carter, Christian ab 8th
Norton Wm. G. tailor, 6 S 3d
Norvell C. C., agent, 7 S 3d
Nothwang Christian, lab., Parrish bel 10th
Notman John, architect, Spruce bel Sch 8th
Notman Peter, clerk, Broad ab Locust
Notson John, printer, Washington ab 5th
Notson Wm., teacher, rear 177 S 2d, h 74 German
NOTTER J. J., tavern, N E 3d & Green
Nottingham Clark, clerk, 5 Coates
Noud Wm., shop, 245 S 6th
Nowlane Joseph S, cordw., Cherry n Franklin (K)
Noyes Charles W. waterman, 530 S Front
Noyes Melville, printer, Christian ab 3d
Nugent Arthur, weaver, 2d bel Harrison (K)
Nugent Emma G., b h, 255 High
Nugent George, jr., com. mer., 6 N 5th, h 48 Wood
Nugent James, weaver, Beach ab Pine
Nugent John, cabman, Sch 6th & Chestnut
Nugent John, lab., Reed ab Church
Nugent John, tailor, 349 N 2d
Nugent Patrick, manuf., 31 N Front, h 2 Fayette
Nugent Peter, grocer, 246 Shippen
Nugent Richard, labourer, 14 Washington Market place
Nugent Thomas, shop, Sch. 3d & Callowhill
Nugent Wm., shoemr 645 High

Nngent Wm., pattern mr. Penn bel Broad
Null Anthony, shoes, S W 7th and Callowhill
Nullet Jacob, New Market ab Willow
Nulty E., profes. of mathematics, Sch 8th ab Walnut
Nunes Amelia, trimmings, 168 S 6th
Nunes Esther, 381 High
Nunes James A., attorney and counsellor, 381 High
Nunez Aaron, rear 4 John (S)
Nunnemaker John, confect., Wood ab 13th
Nunnemaker John, butcher, 2d bel Reed
Nuskey John, F road ab Bedford
Nuskey Lewis, rope mr., Marlboro' ab Duke
Nuskey Samuel, ropemr., Amber ab Phoenix
Nuskey Wm., ropemr., rear Hanover ab Franklin (K)
Nutt A. M., broker, 7 Exchange place, h 180 N 9th
Nutt John, tailor, 35 New
Nutt Richard G., agent, 25 Lily al
Nutt William, grocer, 9th & Parrish
Nutt Wm. L., tobacconist, Magnolia ab Noble
Nuttall Wm., tailor, 61 S 8th, h Cherry n Sch 7th
Nutter Hen., gasfit., 38 N 10th, h 3 Hinckle's ct
Nutter Margaret, 54 Centre
Nuttle Robert E., coach and harness maker, 197 S 5th, h 123 Currant
Nutts Edward, lab., 63 Currant al
Nutz Elizabeth, 50 Mulberry
Nutz Geo. N., 34 Almond
Nutz Henry K., dentist, 9th and Filbert
Nutz Leonard, spinner, McDuffie n Sch. 3d
Nye Wm., seaman, 12 Stamper's al

O'Brian Michael, tavern, Bush hill
O'Brien Albert, mer., 128 N 3d
O'Brien Andrew, mer., 86 Cedar
O'Brien Chas., weaver, Barker W Sch 4th
O'Brien Dennis, lab., 1 Ridgway's ct
O'Brien James, weaver, Bickham n Sch. 7th
O'Brien James, dealer, St Mary ab 7th
O'Brien James, biscuit baker, 171 N Front
O'Brien James P. carp. Sch 7th bel Vine
O'Brien John, fruiterer, 4 John's ct (K)
O'Brien John, shop, South bel Broad
O'Brien John, weaver, 5 Gay's ct (K)
O'Brien John, lab. 14 Jones' al (C)
O'Brien John, dealer, 232 S 4th
O'Brien J. G., publisher, 1 Hoffman's alley
O'Brien Mary, shop, Mulberry n Sch Front
O'Brien Mary Jane, 145 St John
O'Brien Matthew, fruiterer, 8th & Chestnut, h 3 John's ct
O'Brien Michael, lab., Sch. 8th ab Race
O'Brien Neil, dry goods, G T road below 4th (K)
O'Brien Patrick, lab., Mulberry n Sch 3d
O'Brien Patrick, baker, Spruce n Sch 5th
O'Brien P. M., M. D., 204 S 4th
O'Brien Richard, weaver, 13th ab Cedar

O'Brien Thomas, chairpainter, 467 S Front
O'Brien Thomas, lab., Jefferson ab 5th
O'Brien Wm., lab., 2d ab Master
O'Brien Wm., fruiterer,, S W 7th & High.
O'Brien Wm., lab., 14 Franklin pl
O'Bryan L. & A. Rose, tinsmiths, 299 Mulberry
O'Bryan Mary, milliner, 80 S 4th
O'Bryan Matt., lab., 1 Juniper al
O'Bryon Benjamin F., coppersmith, Cherry ab 4th, h 634 N 3d
O'Callaghan Corns., clerk, 8th ab Cedar
O'Connell Charles, shop, Bedford ab 7th
O'Connell Dermott, shop, Shippen ab 12th
O'Connell John, umbrella mr. 223 Cedar
O'Connell Matthew, china, 19 G T road (K)
O'Connell Michael, lab., rear 38 George
O'Connell Thomas, lab., 6 Ewing's ct
O'Connell Wm., 8 Mayland
O'Connell Wm., baker, 2 Crabb st
O'Conner Alexander, store, 331 S 5th
O'Conner Ann, rear Beck bel 2d
O'Conner Elizabeth, 32 Dillwyn
O'Conner Elizabeth, wid. of Richard, hotel, R road, (F V)
O'Conner Jeremiah, chemist, 11 Perry
O'Conner Jeremiah, lab., 2 Bell's ct
O'Conner John, 6 Sansom's al
O'Conner Michael, tailor, Lombard ab 12th
O'Conner Michael T., tailor, 6 St Stephen's pl
O'Conner Thomas, lab., 5 Drinker's ct
O'Conner Thomas, bootmaker, 2 Baxter's av.
O'Connor James, weaver, Crown ab Franklin (K)
O'Connor Margaret, shop, 179 S 3d
O'Connor Michael, dentist, 190 S 5th
O'Connor Thomas, lab., 4 Bell's ct
O'Connor Thos., cordw., Gabell's ct
O'Connor Thomas D., tavern, 17 Chestnut
O'Connor W. Mrs. 15 Mead
O'Daniel Cyrus, bootmr., Sch 3d bel Lombard
O'Daniel George, tailor, 2 North
O'Daniel Perry, watchmr., 226 High
O'Daniel Peter, tailor, 226 High
O'Daniel Thos., overseer, Chestnut W Sch 2d
O'Donnell Bartholomew, carter, S E Shippen and Lloyd
O'Donnell Bernard, tailor, Dean ab Centre.
O'Donnell Charles, weaver, Murray
O'Donnell E., carter, Bedford ab 13th
O'Donnell Felix, pedler, Dean n Franklin (K)
O'Donnell George, gratemr., Melon ab 10th
O'Donnell George, carp. Vaughn ab Locust
O'Donnell Henry, lab., 5 Kelly's ct
O'Donnell Hugh, lab., Charlotte bel Poplar
O'Donnell Hugh, distiller, 392 S 2d
O'Donnell Hugh, shop, 210 Cedar
O'Donnell James, tailor, 236 Cedar

O'Donnell Mary, wid. of Henry, 41 Apple
O'Donnell Mary, milliner, 33 Prune
O'Donnell Michael, paver, 26 Pegg
O'Donnell M., carpet weaver, Lombard bel... Sch 7th
O'Donnell Peter P. atty. & coun., 64 S 6th, h is Powell
O'Donnell Rogers, lab., 193 N Front
O'Donnell Thomas, lab. Sch Front & Filbert
O'Doris St. John, com. mer., 25 Minor
O'Driscoll C. F., printer, 4 Franks' ct
O'DWEYER JOHN P., Pastor St Augustine's. N 4th opp New
O'Farrell Philip Rev., 2d ab Master
O'Hanlon Felix, tailor, 218 Cedar
O'Hanlon Michael, lab, 7th ab Fitzwater
O'Hara Edward, lab., Sch 2d and Cedar
O'Hara Henry, butcher, Crans' ct
O'Hara James, tailor, 229 N 9th
O'Hara John, blacksm., 292 S 7th
O'Hara John, die cutter, Pine bel Broad
O'Hara John, lab. Sch Beach n Walnut
O'Hara Joseph, lab., Sch 3d bel Lombard
O'Hara Patrick, b. h., 412 High
O'Hara Thomas, carpenter, 24 Hurst
O'Hara Wm., lab., High ab Sch 4th
O'Hare Patrick, bell hanger, 90 Cherry
O'Harra Isaac Harrison, tailor, 26 S 3d, h 229 N 9th ab Willow
O'Harra James, weaver, 2d ab Master (K)
O'Hine Wm., att. & coun., 183 G T road (K)
O'Kane David, tavern, 246 S 4th
O'Kane James, lab., 297 S 7th
O'Kane Manassah, tailor, Baker, bel 8th
O'Kane Roderick, tea mer., 163 E Cedar
O'Keefe Ann, china ware, 199 Sassafras
O'Keefe Thomas, lab., 37 Plum
O'Keefe Wm., lab., 110 Cherry
O'Keeffe Amelia, 468 S 2d
O'Keeffe Robert M., painter, 468 S 2d
O'Keilly Eliza, teacher, S S 12th
O'Maddin Isabella, 112 N 7th
O'Meara James, beamer, Allen's ct
O'Meara James, shoemr., 9th ab Willow
O'Meara Mary, teacher, 1 Howard
O'Neal Arthur, lab., 3 Marble pl
O'Neal Hugh, weaver, Shippen la bel Shippen
O'Neal James, lab., Sch 8th ab Race
O'Neal James, furniture, 93 Lombard
O'Neil Ann, gentw., 3d n Washington
O'Neil Catharine, tavern, Pine n Sch
O'Neil Daniel, pedler, Jefferson ab 2d (K)
O'Neil Edward, shop, 19 Hurst
O'Neil Henry, lab., Filbert bel Sch. 5th
O'Neil Hugh, weaver, Christian bel 12th
O'Neil James, shop, 148 N Front
O'Neil Louisa, 317 Pine

O'Neill Arthur, labourer, 241 S 4th
O'Neill Catharine, 302 S 6th
O'Neill Charles, engineer, 11 College pl
O'Neill Charles, shoemr., Division bel 12th
O'Neill Charles, att'y & coun., 5 S Penn sq
O'Neill Charlotte, 10th ab Buttonwood
O'Neill Constantine, chemist, Shackamaxon n Bedford (K)
O'Neill C. B. F., att'y & coun., 4th bel Master(K)
O'Neill Daniel, weaver, Benton n William (K)
O'Neill Daniel, weaver, 2d ab Franklin, (K)
O'Neill Edward, cordw., 6 N 13th
O'Neill Edward, feed, Maiden ab Beach (K)
O'Neill Henry, tavern, Hancock & Phoenix (K)
O'Neill Hugh, lab., rear Pleasant bel 13th
O'Neill Hugh, drayman, Gaskill & Barron
O'Neill James, carter, Lombard n Sch 6th
O'Neill James, lab., G. T. road bel Jefferson
O'Neill James, weaver, Perry bel Master (K)
O'Neill James, distiller, 13 W Lombard
O'Neill James, lab., 122 Plum
O'Neill John, clerk, Washington ab 3d
O'Neill John, weaver, G T road ab Master (K)
O'Neill John, carter, Hancock ab Norris (K)
O'Neill John, collector, 7 Powell
O'Neill J S., dentist, 121 S 5th
O'Neill Kennedy, weaver, Shippen la & Bedford
O'Neill Mary, tavern, Brown and High Bridge
O'Neill Owen, manuf., rear G T road bel Jefferson (K)
O'Neill Robert, surveyor Pa. Fire Ins. Co. 134 Walnut, h 6 S Penn sq
O'Neill Susan, shop, Sch Front & Pine
O'Reilly Edward, shop, 25 Laurel (C)
O'Reilly John, grocer, S W 4th & Spruce
O'Reilly Thos., lab., Marriott bel 3d
O'Rourke Peter, cordw., 10 Monroe ct
O'Rourke Patrick, tailor, 166 Queen
O'Rourke Thomas, carp., 31 Farmer, h 2 Nonnater's ct
OAKFORD CHAS., hatter, 104 Chestnut
Oakford Isaac, hatter, 210 S 2d, h Scheetz bel 2nd
Oakford John, clerk, 359 S Front
Oakford Parsey, att'y & coun., Athenæum, h 126 Marshall
Oakford Richard, mer., 95½ Walnut, h Filbert E Sch 6th
Oaks Michael, driver, High n Sch Front
Oat Charles, 30 R road
Oat Charles, C., clerk, Parrish ab Franklin
Oat Geo. H., acct., Washington bel 11th
Oat George R., coppersmith, 12 Quarry h 4 Sergeant
Oat Joseph, bookbinder, rear 13 Castle
Oat Joseph, coppersmith, 12 Quarry, h Callowhill ab 12th
OAT JOSEPH & SON, coppersm., 12 Quarry
Oat Joseph C. carp., 13th ab Brown
Oat Julia, 289 Walnut
Obdyke Wm., tinsmith, 15 Whitehall
Oberteuffer J. C., Vine bel Sch

Oberteuffer J. H., merchant, 41 High, h 218 N 4th
Odenatt Wm. machinist, Marlboro' bel Bedford
Odenheimer Mary E., 267 Catharine
Odenheimer John M., mer., 93 High, h 397 Walnut
ODENHEIMER & TENNENT, dry goods, 93 High, & 22 Church al
Odenheimer Wm. H. Rev., 180 S 3d
Odenwelder Elisha L. mer., 29 N 2d
Odiorne Abigail, 83 N 7th
Oehlman Henry, cordw., Gray's ct (N L)
Oehlschlager Jas. C., teacher, 36 Sansom
Oelhaf Xavier, tailor, 3 Washington row (N L)
Oellers James S., grain & feed, n Pine st. whf., h 89 Catharine
Oelsner Samuel, capmr., 85 N 3d
Oertelt Charles E., watchmr., 401 N 2d
Oertelt Charles G., jeweller, Pegg and New Market
Off Bernard, grocer, N E Sch 3d and Ann
Off George, baker, Duke & Cherry (K)
Off Gotleib, dentist, 554 N 3d
Off John, baker, Sch 3d & M'Duffie
Offerman Wm. A., dentist, 309 S 8th
Ogborn Aaron, frame maker, rear 609 N 6th
Ogden Abraham, carp. Sch 8th ab Race
Ogden & Brother, tailors, 110 Chestnut
Ogden Charles S. druggist, 106 N 3d, h 68 Marshall
Ogden Elizabeth, Sheaff's alley
Ogden Henry S., tailor, 110 Chestnut
Ogden Jesse, mer., N W 4th and Sassafras
Ogden John, seaman, Hughes' ct
Ogden John, cabinetmr., rear 441 Vine
Ogden John M., surveyor, 68 Marshall
Ogden Jonathan, tailor, 110 Chestnut, h 214 Cherry
Ogden Lewis, carp. George bel 3d
Ogden Michael, carp., Vernon ab 10th
Ogden Robert, segarmr., 466 N 3d
Ogden Ruth, Hughes' ct
Ogden R. W. gent. Catharine ab 6th
Ogden Samuel, tinsmith, 424 High, h R road ab Buttonwood
Ogilby Fred. Rev., 267 S 10th
Ogilby Joshua, machinist, 529 Coates
Ogle James F., lace store, 291½ N 2d
Ogle Maria, milliner, 14 S 6th
OGLE WILLIAMS, coachmr., 280 Chestnut, h N W 7th and Sansom
Ohl Elizabeth, 13 Perry
Ohl Henry S, 101 S wharves, h 349 S 3d
Ohl John F., merchant, 102 S wharves, h 259 S Front
Ohl John F. & Son, mers., 102 S whfs.
Ohmes Gotlieb, lab., 104 New Market
Oker Bradloe, 5 Logan's sq
Okie J. B., mer., 70 High, h 5 Logan sq
Okill Wm. tailor, Bevans' ct
Oks John, chaise driver, N E Vine and 10th
Oldden Burling, bookbinder, rear 81 N 5th
Oldden Esther, gentw., 30 Crown
Olden H., coach trimmer, Stoys' ct (K)

Olden James, coach trimmer, Stoy's ct (K)
Oldenbergh C. W. variety goods, 6 N 4th, h 41 O Y road
Oldham Alexander, confectioner, 378 N 3d
Oldry Michael, gent., 3 Jefferson row
Oler John, lab., Parrish bel 12th
Oliphant Benj., whf. build., rear 121 Queen (S)
Oliphant Mary, 25 Jones' al (C)
Oliver Charles, porter, 16 Mercer
Oliver Ebenezer, wire worker, 36 N 6th, h 211 N 9th
Oliver George H., mer., N W 2d & Chestnut, h 200 Spruce
Oliver George L., mer., 131 High, h 90 Wood
Oliver Henry C., mer., 178 Chestnut, h 20 Madison
Oliver John, segarmr., Sassafras ab 13th
Oliver John D., oysters, 12 Wagner's al.
Oliver John M. hatter, Perry bel Phoenix (K)
Oliver Jordon H. hatter, 5 Magnolia
Oliver Joseph, box maker, 145 Carpenter
Oliver Joshua B., inspector of lumb., 3d ab Carpenter
Oliver J. C., 246 N 5th
OLIVER & MOLAN, trimmings, 178 Chestnut
Oliver Paul G., druggist, S W 10th and Sassafras
Oliver Thomas, druggist, N E 10th and Walnut
Oliver Wm., printer, 9 Wheeler's ct.
Oliver Wm., broker, 58½ Walnut
Ollis Anthony, turner, 39 Strawberry, h 4 Drinker's al
Ollis Thomas, turner, 14 Freed's av
Ollis Wm. turner, 4 Drinker's al
Ollis Wm. H., turner, 4 Roberts' ct
Olmstead Sarah, 143 Spruce
Olmstead Anthony I. 47 George
Olmsted Edward, atty. and coun., office 53 S 5th, h Sch 8th bel Spruce
Olmsted William, cordwainer, 266 S 6th
Olwine Jacob K. Sch 7th ab Pine
Olwine Henry, watchmr. R road ab 11th
Omensetter John, cordw., rear 10th ab Coates
Omensetter Winnard, coach lacemr. 2 Star al
Omer Peter, blacksmith, Madison av
Onderdonk H. U., Pine bel Broad
Onger Henry, variety store, 55 P road
Onimus M., Carlton bel Sch. 7th
Opdyke Martha, b. h., 91 New
Opie P. V., salesman, 94½ High
OPP & BEIDEMAN, coal dealers, 53 Chestnut and Green st whf. Delaware
Opp Morgan, coal mer., 53 Chestnut & Green st whf. h 125 Dillwyn
Opp Peter, hardware, 204 R. road
Oppell John, whipmr. and alderman, 289 Coates
Oppenheimer Abraham, dry goods, 166 N 2d,
Opperman Jacob, harnessmr. 357 Coates
Oram James, carp., 476 Callowhill
Oram G. Rev., Carpenter ab 3d
Oram John F., ladies' shoemaker, 70 Sassafras
Oram Zachariah, bookbinder, 23 Minor, h 20 Rittenhouse
Ord George, gent., 354 S Front

Ord John, teacher, 57 Tammany
Ord John F., sign painter, 5 S 7th
Ore Matt., lab., Marriott bel 5th
Orem James, lab., 517 N 3d
Orme George R., U. S. agent, U. S. Arsenal of Sch, h Pine ab Juniper
Orme James, umbrella mr., Sch. 5th bel High
Ormsby Henry, watchmr. & jeweller, 366 N
Ormsby Wm. cooper, 30 Stamper's al
Orne Benjamin, mer., 183 Chestnut, h 132 Pine
Orne Herman, clerk, 298 Green
Orne James, mer., 183 Chestnut, h 132 Pine
Orne James H., mer., 183 Chestnut, h 117 Pine
Orne J. & B. & Co., carpet warehouse, 183 Chestnut
Orne Samuel, teacher, Wood bel Sch 2d
Orne Wm., teacher, Wood bel Sch 2d
Orr And., dyer, Benton ab School (K)
Orr Ann, Sch. 8th ab Cherry
Orr David, shop, Bedford bel Broad
Orr Eliza, washer, 9 Baker's ct
Orr Elizabeth, gentw., 53 Spruce
Orr George, cabman, Park alley
Orr Hector, printer, 45 Chestnut, h 53 Spruce
Orr James, trimmings, 362 N 2d
Orr James, weaver, Richard
Orr James, weaver, 4 Wagner's al
Orr James W., drayman, 4 Norris' al
Orr John, dealer, 1 Vernon pl
Orr John, lab., Richard
Orr John, weaver, Brinton
Orr John B. weaver, Bedford bel 13th
Orr John R., tobacconist, S E 2d and Almond
Orr Margaret, rear Charlotte ab Thompson (K)
Orr Mary, 9 Castle
Orr Robert, waiter, 17 Mercer
Orr Robert, gent., Francis n Sch. 5th. (F V)
Orr Robert M. H., currier, 82 Gaskill
Orr Samuel, stone cutter, Chestnut n Sch. 2d
Orr Samuel, Lombard ab 13th
Orr Samuel, weaver, Shippen lane
Orr Thomas, acct., 9 North
Orr Wm, cordw., 64 N 10th
Orr Wm. manuf. 2d ab Jefferson (K)
Orrell And., wid. of Wm., 603 Front bel Otter
Orrell Robert, reed mr., 89 New Market
Orrell Thomas I., carp., Poplar ab 13th
ORRICK & CAMPBELL, iron mers., 109 N Water and 54 N Wharves
Orrick Samuel D., mer., 109 N Water h 217 Walnut
Orth Alex., hatter, rear Paul bel 7th
Orth Christiana, 1 Ewing's ct
Orth John, turner, N E 4th & German
Orth W. C. paper hanger, 44 Vine
Orthwein Lewis, liquors, 444 N 3d
Orum & Brother, dry goods, 52 N 4th
Orum C. L., mer., 52 N 4th, h 40 Crown
Orum Rachel W., 52 N 4th
Orum Wm. lab. rear Lemon bel 11th
Osborn Anthony, waiter, 20 Acorn alley
Osborn B. F., tailor, Gilbert bel 10th
Osborn Edward, ostler, Kelly's ct
Osborn Emily, teacher of music, 110 N 8th

Osborn Lydia, washer, rear 390 Sassafras
Osborn Peter, upholsterer, 81 N 2d
Osborn Thos., carp., 14 Allen (K)
Osborne Charles, cabtmr., Marshall ab Poplar
Osborne Charles C., clerk, 47 S Juniper
Osborne Geo. W., manuf., 368 Coates
Osborne Jeremiah, 294 S Front
Osborne Peter, tavern, Broad & Race
Osbourn Alexander, mer., 6 Franklin sq
Osbourn Ebenezer, carp., 29 N 10th
Osbourn Franklin, carder, Hamilton ab Sch. 6th
Osbourn J. G., music saloon, 112 S 3d
Osbourn Lewis G., mer., N W 2d and Mulberry, h 29 N 10th
Osbourn Samuel B., mer., 235 Chestnut
Osgood —— port. painter, 204 Walnut
Osler Hugh, mer., 335 S 2d
Osler Martha, 8 Nicholson
Osman James, tinman, 9 Boyd's av
Osmond M. A., dressmr., Coates bel 6th
Osterberg John, porter, 19 Coates
Osterheldt Elizabeth, vict., Charles ab Noble
Osterheldt Fred., jr., vict., Garden above Noble
Osterheldt Peter, vict., 9th and Willow
Osterloh A. F. dry goods, 64 N 3d, h 80 Wood
Ostertag J., bootmr., 25 Parham
Ostheimer Maurice, mer., 3 Bank, h S E 8th & Noble
Otherholt Christian, bricklr., 6th bel G. T. road
Otherholt Christopher, lab., 6th bel G. T. road
Otherholt Isaac, brickmr., 6th bel G. T road (K)
Otis James, shoemr., 31 Beaver (K)
Otley Deborah, Sassafras n Path
Ott Catharine, tailoress, 8 Linden (K)
Ott Catharine, 48 Shippen
Ott Chas., tobacconist, rear St. John ab George
Ott C. B., clerk, 48 Shippen
Ott Francis J. brushmr. 336 Callowhill
Ott George, hosier, 13th bel Shippen
Ott Henry, tobacconist, Maiden ab Beach (K)
Ott Jesse, tobacconist, 476 N 2d
Ott Thos. tobacconist, St John bel George
Ott Martha, sempstress, Middleton's ct
Otter & Gihon, gold beaters, 2 N 5th
Otter Robert, cabinetmr., 331 N 3d
Otter Wm. gold beater, 2 N 5th
Ottinger Eliza, Poplar ab 5th
Ottinger Elizabeth M., b. h., 14 E North
Ottinger Erasmus, painter, 8 Norris' ct
Ottinger Oliver, stone cutter, 5th ab Coates, h Maria bel 5th
Ottinger Robert, chairmr., 16 John (S)
Otto Charles, cabinetmr., 146 Vine, h Willow bel 8th
Otto Chas. W. dry goods, W Penn sq & High
Otto David M., cabtmr., 6 Charles place
Otto Eliza, gentw., Spruce E Sch. 8th
Otto John W., combmr., 12 Harrison
Otton J. Hare, carver, 82 S 5th
Ottway Catharine, wid., 22 Queen
Otty Thomas, grocer, M road & Marion
Ouram Wm. H., blacksmith, 310 Pine
Ourocker Joseph, oysterman, 30 Farmer
Ourt Charles, combmr., Jones alley
Ourt Lewis, blacksmith, 102 N Juniper

Ourt Lewis, jr., bridle-bit mr., Sassafras ab Broad
Outerbridge Alex. E., mer., 23 N Wharves
Oalt James, lab., Caldwell n Beach
Ovens Thos., grocer, Spruce E Sch 4th
Ovenshine E., grocer, h 551 Vine
Ovenshine Henry, clerk, Sch 8th ab Vine
Ovenshine Samuel, 12th ab Callowhill
Overdorf Isaac, pedler, Marlboro' bel Bedford
Overholzer Elam, dry goods, 46 N 8th, h 8th bel Poplar
OVERHOLZER ISAAC B., coal, 5th & Willow
Overman Henry W., mer., 6 S 3d
Overman William W., mer., 106 High, h 124 N 10th
Overy Mary, washer, Catharine n Lebanon
Ovington Phebe, Franklin ab Hanover (K)
Ovington Wm., tanner, 316 N 6th
Owen Ann, 167 N 2d
Owen, Cox & Budd, grocers, 23 N Water
Owen Eugene, 11 N 12th
Owen Evan J., stone cut., 10th bel Washington
Owen & Fithian, printers, 21 S 3d
Owen Hugh, lab., cooper, n Sch 3d
Owen Jesse, 167 N 2d
Owen Jesse, tinsmith, 149 Poplar
Owen Joseph, plough mr., 50 Crown
Owen Parker, mer. 23 N Water
Owen William, tinsmith, 536 N 2d
Owen William Y., printer, 21 S 3d, h 8 Wharton
Owens Ann, b h, 10 Branch
Owens Bernard, millinery, 3 Cypress
Owens Catharine, 136 Buttonwood
Owens & Currin, jewellers, 6 Bank al
Owens Edward, wharf builder, Eyre's ct (K)
Owens Edward, shoemr., 87 P road
Owens Eller, shop, St Mary ab 7th
Owens Peter, potter, Bedford n Hanover (K)
Owens Reed, broom mr., 2d ab Jefferson (K)
Owens Jacob, Culvert ab Mechanic
Owens James, stovemr. 65 N 7th
Owens John, coachman, 7 Watson's al
Owens John, carp., N road bel Wharton
Owens John P. att'y & coun. 62 S 7th, h Locust and Mary (W P)
Owens Jonas, coachman, rear 303 Walnut
Owens Mary, gentw., S E 4th & Harmony
Owens Mary, Pine bel Juniper
Owens O. G., shoes, 450 High
Owens Reuben, bricklayer, 23 Nectarine
Owens Samuel W., jeweller, 6 Bank al
Owens Sarah, Vine ab Broad
Owens Thomas, lampstore, 269 N 2d
Owens Thomas, lab. rear 7 Elfreth's al
Oxley Geo. weaver, Vine n Sch
Ozard Robt., shoemr., 19 N 9th
Ozeas E., gentw., 41 Zane

Packer Amos, carp., 197 N 4th
Packer Asa, coal mer., 74 S 3d
Packer Eliza, nurse, 22 Queen
Packard Frederick A., Am. S. S. U., 146 Chestnut, h 9th n Pine
Packer Hannah, 17 Webb's al

Packer James E., engineer, 2 Webb's al
Packer Joel, hotel, 72 Shippen
Packer John, lumber mer. Almond & Front, h 22 Scheetz
Packer John & Co. lumber yard, Almond and Front, & S E Front & Shippen
Packer Robt. W., forwd. mer., 74 S 3d
Padan Thos., lab., 275 S 4th
Paddack D. M., teacher, 30½ S 7th, h N E Lombard n 11th
Paddan Wm., malster, Pearl ab Nixon
Padelford E., Clinton ab 7th
Padmore Chas., clerk, Race & Sch 8th
Paeff Margt., 484 N 3d
Page Ambrose, 24 Stamper's al
Page Charles, clerk, Green bel 10th
Page Chas. F., mer., 57 High
Page Christian J. Rev., 452 N Front
Page Emanuel, furrier, 119 Green
Page George W., cashier Custom House, h 101 Walnut
Page James, collector customs, h 101 Walnut
Page John, leather dresser, 3d ab Franklin(K)
Page John, tinsm., 3d ab Franklin (K)
Page John Jun. farmer, R road ab George (F V)
Page John A., modeller, 24 N 5th
Page Jos., lab., Carpenter ab 12th
Page Joseph F., mer., 57 High, h 190 E Spruce
Page Randolph, cordwainer, 13 Lagrange pl
Page William Byrd, M. D., 297 & 256 Chestnut
Pagel Samuel, tailor, 118 E Cedar
Paget Thomas A., distiller, 53 Tammany
Paine Robert, book store, 180 N 2d
Paine Washington, silver plater, 3 Meredith's ct
Painter Abm. bookbinder, 42 Garden
Painter Adam, cooper, Willow ab 8th
Painter Catharine, b. h., 9th bel Noble
Painter Charles, bookbinder, 256 R road
Painter Edward, bricklayer, 4 Culvert
Painter Eliza, shop, Brown n Washington av
Painter George, lab., rear 300 St John
Painter Geo., caulker, Marlboro' bel Queen (K)
Painter George W., brewer, 106 Filbert
Painter Isaac, collector, 27 Nectarine
Painter Isaac, jr., silver plater, 2 Sailor's ct
Painter Jacob, harness maker, Broad ab Cherry
Painter Jacob, tailor, 123 G T Road
Painter Jacob, tailor, 260 High, h 11th and Lemon
Painter Jacob, bricklayer, Mechanic ab George
Painter John, bricklayer, h Poplar n St. John
Painter John M., pumpmr., 89 Prime
Painter John S., silver smith, 125 G T road
Painter Joseph, cooper, Swanson ab Cedar, h Prime ab Front
Painter Jos., moroc. fin'r., Charlotte ab George
Painter Julia, gentw., 31 Washington n 12th
Painter Mary, 488 N 3d
Painter Nich., carp., Hanover bel Franklin(K)
Painter Rachel, Franklin bel Palmer (K)
Painter Rebecca, 127 Wood
Painter & Rugan, dry goods, Logan & Sp Garden
Painter Samuel, carp., Hanover bel Franklin
Painter Sarah, huckster, 144 Poplar
Painter Susan, Franklin bel Palmer

Paisley Elizabeth, b h., 19 Prune
Paisley John, 7th & Catharine
Paisley Joseph, moulder, 6th bel G T road
Paisley Robert, moulder, G T road bel 7th
Paiste Mercy, gent., Chatham bel Green
Paleske Lewis, capt., Sch. 5th and Walnut
Palethorp Abigal K., 381 N 4th
Palethorp John H., 133 Sassafras
Paley Thos., presser, 22 N 5th
Palm C. H., shop, Manderson ab Beach
Palm Michael, lab., 157 Poplar
Palmatray James T., agent, Yhost bet Catharine
Palmer Amos, gent., George ab Sch 6th
Palmer Ann, b. h., Callowhill n Nixon
Palmer David, gardener, 49 Franklin
Palmer Edw., ropemr., rear Queen ab Palmer(K)
Palmer Edwin A., mer., 16 S whfs., h Sch 8th bel Spruce
Palmer Ephraim, printer, 242 Christian
Palmer Francis, machinist Green ab 11th
Palmer Frederick V., cabinetmr., 126 Coates
Palmer Henry, weaver, rear Perry ab Phoenix
Palmer George W. cordwainer, 318 N 8th
Palmer George W., gunsmith, 109 Shippen, h Fitzwater ab 8th
Palmer Henry, shoemakers' tools, 2d ab G T road (K)
Palmer Jacob, cordw. Franklin ab Hanover (K)
Palmer James, baker, 240 Cedar
Palmer James P. turpentine distiller, 15 Pratt h 2d ab Greenwich
Palmer John, tailor, 350 High, h 114 N 9th
Palmer John, carp., Lafayette ab 9th
Palmer John, bookbinder, 15 Minor, h 30 Perry
Palmer Jonathan, mer., High st wharf, h 171 S 10th
Palmer Jonathan, jr., conveyancer, 107 Mulberry, h 29 N 5th
Palmer Joseph, pencil maker, 7 Bank al, h 27 Wood
PALMER J. & Co., com. & shipping mers., High st Wharf
Palmer La Fayette, machinist, 5 Scott's ct
Palmer Lewis, smith, 279 S 5th
Palmer Margaret, dealer, Queen above Palmer
Palmer Mary, b h, 289 Sassafras
Palmer Michael, bootmr., Otter bel G T road(K)
Palmer Michael, bootmr., Mechanic ab George
Palmer N. B., mer., 97 High
Palmer Richard, alderman, 64 Shippen
Palmer Robert, shoes, 182 S 2d
Palmer Samuel, gent., office 21 Bank, h Walnut ab Broad
Palmer Samuel C. teller Com. Bank, 346 S 4th (K)
Palmer Thos., cordw., Phœnix ab Cadwalader (K)
Palmer Thos. Hope, oyster house, Beach above Maiden (K)
Palmer Thos. H., turner, 55 Union
PALMER V. B., coal office, 29 Pine
PALMER V. B., newspap. advertising & collecting agency, & coal office, N W 3d & Chestnut
Palmer William, carp., Shippen ab 8th, h 161 Queen

Palmer Wm. wheelwrt., Leopard & Phoenix (K)

Pancast R. M. Dr., 10 Morgan

PANCOAST Aaron, tailor, 206 Chestnut, h Pine ab Quince

Pancoast Chas. S., atty & coun., 48 S 4th

Pancoast James, bricklayer. Olive bel 12th

Pancoast Joseph, M. D., 300 Chestnut

Pancoast Joseph, bookseller and stationer, 268 N 2d, h 10th ab Wallace

Pancoast Robert T., apothecary, S W 7th and Buttonwood

Pancoast Samuel S., carp., 25 Melon

Pancoast Seth, Cedar n 13th

Pancoast Stephen, starch manuf., 13th & Carpenter, h Cedar n 13th

Pancoast Tacy R., 10th bel Coates

Pandrich Geo., machinist, Callowhill bel 13th

Pantillon John, M. D., 202 N 6th

Pape G. Rev., 50 George (S)

Paramore Jas., grinder, rear 83 Sassafras, h rear 19 Farmer

Parcels Saml., fisherman, Beach ab Hanover (K)

Pardee A. & Co., coal yard, Front & Poplar, off. 56 Walnut

Pardee James, trader, Callowhill bel Sch 2d

Pardee M. Mrs., milliner, 31 S 8th

Parent Joseph A. painter, 10th ab Poplar

Parham John, carp., Sch 8th George

Parham John, jr., Sch 8th bel George

Parham Joseph C., plasterer, 49 Tammany

Parham Robert, cabinetmaker, 39 Noble

Parham Samuel P., George and Sch 8th

Parham William M., merchant, 32½ N 3d, h 39 Noble

Park Andrew, porter, 68 Union

Park Arthur, weaver, 28 W Cedar

Park Geo., weaver, Wagner's al

Park Ingram, grocer and brickmr. 465 High

Park Isaac, tavern, Swanson & Almond

Park James, dealer, 2d bel Federal

Park Jane, Barley n 11th

Park Mary, 9 Comb's al

Park Robert J. bowling saloon, N W 6th & Chestnut, h 217 Cedar

Parke A. M., shoes, 286 High

Parke C., b h, 178 Chestnut

Parke James D., shoes, 248 Callowhill

Parke James P., 99 Locust

Parke John P., gent., S Garden ab 10th

Parke Richard, livery stable, Union

Parke Richard, weaver, Fulton ab 12th

Parker Adam, waiter, 10th ab Catharine

Parker Alexander, gardener, 1 Parker's row

Parker Ann, 542 High

Parker Catharine, shop, 262 Shippen

Parker Charles, 51 Buttonwood

Parker Chas., Pearl bel Broad

Parker Chas. & Co., dry goods, N W 4th & Callowhill

Parker Chas. C., M. D., 74 S 6th

Parker Clarkson, barber, 28 N 2d

Parker Edwd., clothing, 171 S 6th

PARKER EDWD., broker, 48½ N 3d, h 458 Callowhill

Parker Edward, segars, 131 Lombard

Parker Edward, clerk, 29 N 9th

Parker Edward L. mer. 399 High

Parker Eliphalet, huckster, 61 Currant al

Parker Elisha, Traquair's ct

Parker Eliza, b h, 127 Mulberry

Parker Elizabeth A., N W 4th & Callowhill

Parker Elizabeth E., 384 S 3d

Parker E., washer, 11th ab Lombard

Parker George, cutler, 37 R road

Parker George, carp., 10th & Vernon

Parker Geo. E., rear 365 S 5th

Parker Hannah, washer, 34 Paschal's al

Parker Isaac, watchmr., 81 N 3d

Parker James, lab., 23 Tammany

Parker James, fisherman, Winter

Parker James, porter, Lombard ab 9th

Parker Jane, 12 Elder

Parker Joel Rev., 29 Clinton

Parker John, shoemr., 190 Callowhill

Parker John, carp. weav., Otter near Front (K)

Parker John, lab., 89 N 3d

Parker John, carp., Nectarine ab 9th, h 19 Ogden

Parker John, gent., 121 N 9th

Parker John, cordw., 8 Harrison's ct (K)

Parker John B., mer., 180 High, h Sch 4th bel Wood

Parker John H., hatter, rear 140 Brown

Parker John H., grocer, N W 11th and High, h 542 High

Parker John S., Wood bel 6th

Parker John W., grocer, 112 F road (K)

Parker Joseph, ropemr. Brown ab Cherry

Parker Joseph, clothes dealer, 92 S 2d, h Harmony bel 4th

Parker Joseph, 86 Wood

Parker Joseph Jr., mer., 3 N 3d, h 86 Wood

Parker Joseph D., hatter, New Crown below Green (K)

Parker Joseph E., dentist, S E 11th & Mulberry,

Parker & Lehman, dry goods, 3 N 3d

Parker Mary, whitewasher, 28 Burd's ct

Parker Mary, 98 S 5th

Parker Mary, rear 160 Queen

Parker Mary, lab., 29 Paschal's al

Parker Nancy, lab., 29 Paschal's al

Parker Peter, coachman, Juniper al

Parker Peter, hatter, Wallace ab Franklin

Parker Richard, stone cutter, Watt

Parker Richd., gilder, 26 Morris

Parker Robert, porter, rear 186 Lombard

Parker Robert, weav. Howard below Franklin (K)

Parker Robert, cordw., 13th ab Vine

Parker Robert, carp., 6 Winter's ct

Parker Samuel, weaver, Ulrich's row (K)

Parker Samuel, grocer, 41 S Front

Parker Samuel W., bootmr., 324½ High

Parker Sarah, library, Beach ab Maiden (K)

Parker Sarah, rear 9 Maria

Parker Sarah T., b h, 236 Spruce

Parker Stephen, lab., 10 Lombard row

Parker S. E., 63 New

Parker Thos., bricklayer, Hyde's ct

Parker Thomas, perfumer, 59 S 3d

Parker Thomas, carter, P road & Washington
Parker Thomas B., carbuilder, Broad bel Vine, h 8 Lybrand
Parker Thos. G., tavern, 43 S Front
Parker Wm., painter, 18 S 10th
Parker Wm. lab. Acorn al
Parker Wm., boot and shoe manf., 122 High, h Julianna ab Wood
Parker Wm., collee., rear Mulberry bel Sch 6th
Parker William C., ladies' shoes, 87 N 6th
PARKER WM. T., refectory, N E & N W 6th & Chestnut, h 163 Pine
Parkerson Hester, Marriott ab 5th
Parkhill James, drayman, Irvine ab R road
Parkhill John, weaver, 3d ab Franklin (K)
Parkhill Joseph, 11 Marks' lane.
Parkin Richard, cabinetmaker, 134 S 2d
Parkins Joseph, weaver, 13th bel Catharine
PARKINSON & Co., ice dealer, N W 3d and Walnut
Parkinson Eleanor, Sch 7th ab Filbert
Parkinson Joseph, tobacconist, 4 North
Parkinson J. W., confectioner, 38 S 8th
Parkinson Robert, wheelwt., 343 S 5th
Parkinson Robert B., mer., 9 S 3d
Parkinton Wm., brewer, 516 N Front
Parks James, clothing, 133 S 2d
Parkson Harma, sawyer, Carpenter ab 8th
Parmallee J. C., broker, 45 N 5th, h 185 Catharine
Parmelee Charles N wood engraver, Sassafras ab 5th, h 237 S 9th
Parmenter Charles G., teacher, 6 Trotter's al
Parmentier Charles T., agent, 189 Chestnut, h 14 Parker
Parmentier Julia, 17 N 12th
Parr Wm., umbrella mr., Duke bel Palmer (K)
Parris Benjamin, turner, 150 N Front, h Brooks' ct
Parris Mary Mrs., 42 Vine
Parris Nathan B., 102 N Front
Parris Rosanna, shop, 243 Shippen
Parris Samuel C., tailor, 344 High, h 226 S 5th
PARRISH DILLWYN, druggist, S W 8th and Mulberry, h Cherry ab 10th
Parrish Edward, druggist, N W 9th & Chestnut h 93 Filbert
Parrish George D., mer., 12 N Front, h 5 Montgomery sq
Parrish Isaac, M. D., 165 Mulberry
Parrish & Price, com. mers., 12 N Front
Parrish Robt. A., jr., atty. & coun., 66 S 6th
Parrish William D., paper warehouse, 4 N 5th, 339 Sassafras
Parrott Henry, wine mer., 107 High
Parrott John, weaver, Shippen la ab Rose
Parrott Robert, carp. 85 New Market
Parry Chas., dentist, Sp Garden ab 11th
Parry Chas., machinist, 21 Brandywine
Parry Edwin, machinist, 250 Sassafras
Parry Geo., clerk, 352 Coates
Parry Gustavus A., clerk, R road bel Sp. Garden
Parry Isaac, sup of com., 214 Green
Parry M. Mrs., 10th bel Cedar
Parry M. C., Sp Garden ab 11th

Parry Oliver, lumber mer., S E 5th and Brown, h 3 Marshall
Parry & Randolph, lum. mers., S E 5th & Brown
Parry Samuel, cloth store, S W 2d and High, h 325 N 6th
Parry Samuel, lab., 10th bel Pleasant
Parry Thomas, lab., Carpenter ab 10th
Parry Thomas F., lea. dealer, 229 N 2d, h 149 Dillwyn.
Parry W. F., coal mer., 11 George, h Sp Garden ab 11th
Parsels Hannah, 5 Charlotte
Parsons Alonzo W., druggist, 112 N 12th
Parsons A. V. judge, Spruce E Sch 8th
Parsons Benjamin F., grocer, Marlboro' below Duke
Parsons Chas., cordw., 258 N 8th
Parsons Charles R., cordw., 4 Tammany ct
Parsons Christopher, ship carp., 2d bel Prime
Parsons Elijah, lab. Gill's al
Parsons George, cordw., 6 Chatham
Parsons George, hosier, 137 Cedar
Parsons Leonora, Ann W Sch 4th
Parsons Roswell, shoes, 431 N 2d, h 6th and Parrish
Parsons Thomas, carp., Brown ab 12th
Parsons Wm., chairmr., rear 6 Carpenter
Part A. F., cabmr., 51 Queen
Partenheimer Jacob, beerhouse, 112 Apple
Partenheimer Martin, grocer, N W 12th and Parrish
Partenheimer Philip, manf., 100 N 3d
Partridge John W., bonnets, 234 Callowhill, h 15 Melon
Partridge Maria, 34 Castle
Partridge O. H., M. D., 83 Chestnut and 195 Spruce
Parvin Hannah, rear 8 Bread
Parvin William, shingle dresser, Shackamaxon ab Franklin
Parvis Isaac, Madison ct
Pascal Charles, hatter, 6 S 6th
PASCAL JOHN, tavern, S W 10th and Carpenter
Paschall Albert, carp., Division (F V)
Paschall Elwood J., bonnet presser, 21 O Y road
Paschall Robt. S. conveyancer, S E 3d & Walnut
Paschall Thomas, clerk, Washington ab 3d
Pasco Henry, plasterer, Sch 8th n Sassafras
Passey Jane, geutw., 123 N road
Passmore Emma, sempstress, Lemon
Passmore R., bookmr., 36 Castle
Passmore Thos., M. D., office G T road below Master (K)
Paster John, cabt mr., rear 68 S 2d
Paster Matthew, cabt mr., rear 68 S 2d
Pastorius Daniel, grocer, 35 Marshall
Pastorius John, sea cap. 273 N 5th
Pastorius Washington, dry goods, 47 N 8th
Patchell George, printer, Linden ab Sch 7th
Patchell Thomas, weaver, 19 Pratt
Patrick John, mer., 146 S 11th
Patrick L. H., printer, 332 S 4th
Patrick Nimrod, stove mr., 236 N 5th
Patrick Ruben, Broad St House

Patrick William A., conveyancer, 95½ Walnut, h 572 S Front
Patridge Thomas, machinist, 10 Sheaff al
Patrullo P. N., mer., 190 E Pine
Patten Ann, corset mr., S E 6th and Mulberry
Patten George, weaver, Fitler bel Harrison (K)
Patten John W., leather and hides, S W 3d and Vine
Patten William, optician, S E 6th and Mulberry
Patterson & Brooks, grocers, 21 N 2d
Patterson Callender, painter, 25 Hubble
Patterson Daniel, lab., St Joseph's av
Patterson David, blacksmith, 3 Furlong's ct
Patterson Edward, tobac., 140 Chestnut ab 6th
Patterson George, weaver, Wood n Sch Front
Patterson Henry S., M. D., 94 Mulberry
Patterson Hiram, grocer, 136 N 12th
Patterson Jacob, carp., Dunton ab Otter (K)
Patterson James, silverplater, 7th bel Hallowell
Patterson James, mer., 2d and Church al, h Locust n Sch 8th
Patterson James, carp., Master ab Front
Patterson James, boatman, Sch 3d ab Walnut
Patterson James, brickmr., Lombard n Sch 3d
Patterson James, V., M. D., 282 N 6th
Patterson Jane, shop, High E Sch. 2d.
Patterson Jane, Benton n School (K)
Patterson Jeremiah, shoemr. Poplar bel 6th·
Patterson John, boatman, Filbert n Sch Front
Patterson John, shoemr., High W of Sch 6th
Patterson John, boatman, George n Sch 6th
Patterson John, pedler, Cedar ab 11th
Patterson John, watchman, George ab Sch 7th
Patterson John, mer., S E 4th and Sassafras, h 61 N 4th
Patterson John B., carp., Shackamaxon ab Bedford.
Patterson John C., watchman, rear Lombard & Juniper
Patterson Jonathan, jr., grocer, 21 N 2d, h 78 N Front
Patterson Jonathan, 5 S 11th
Patterson Joseph, carter, Bacon's ct
Patterson Joseph, President West. Bank, h Walnut bet Sch 6th & 7th
Patterson Joseph, waiter, 5th bel Christian
Patterson Joseph M., carp., Washington below Church
PATTERSON J. T., grocer, S E 4th and Sassafras,
Patterson Lewis Amer, scale mr., Robb's ct
Patterson Martha, shop, Race ab Broad
Patterson Mary, Christian and Church
Patterson Mary, gentw, 465 S Front
Patterson Mary, 254 Lombard
Patterson Mary, Bickham, ab Sch 8th
PATTERSON MORRIS & CO., grocers, 239 High
Patterson M., mer., 239 High, h Spruce below Broad
Patterson Rachel, 16 Madison
Patterson Robert & Sons, grocers, S W 10th and Milton
Patterson Robert, lab., George ab Sch. 6th

Patterson Robert, Genl., 182 High, h S W 13th and Locust
Patterson Robert, weaver, Wood ab Sch Front
Patterson Robert, weaver, Nixon ab Vine
Patterson Robt., lab., Nixon bel Wood
Patterson Robert & Co., grocers, 182 High
Patterson Robert G., paper & rags, 274 S 7th
Patterson Robert M., Pres. U. S. Mint, h N W Locust and Vaughan
PATTERSON ROBERT M., druggist, Sch 7th and Chestnut
Patterson Samuel, weaver, Lombard ab Sch 6th
Patterson Samuel, grocery, Sch 3d and Pine
Patterson Samuel, umbrellas, 342 S 2d
Patterson Saml., carter, Wood ab Sch 8th
Patterson Saml., lab., rear Brown ab 13th
Patterson Sarah, 282 N 6th
Patterson S. D., Navy agent, 98 Chestnut, h 84 Marshall
PATTERSON S. D. & CO., publishers U. S. Saturday Post, 98 Chestnut
Patterson Thackara, lab., Edward n William (K)
Patterson Thos., teacher, 65½ N 2d ab Phoenix
Patterson Thos. tavern, c Callowhill and Sch 3d
Patterson Thomas B., carp., Marshall ab Brown, h 7th ab Brown
PATTERSON WALTER, grocer, S W 12th & High, h 2 S 12th
Patterson Walter, seeds, N E Water & Mulberry
Patterson Wm., 408 N 6th
Patterson Wm., lab., Walnut n Sch 3d
Patterson Wm., weaver, Hope ab Otter (K)
Patterson Wm., grocer, Sch 3d & Cedar
Patterson Wm. watchman, Lombard E Sch 6th
Patterson Wm., weaver, Cedar n Sch 5th
Patterson Wm., lab., Wood bel Sch Front
Patterson Wm., grocery, 12th and Cedar
Patterson Wm. B., tailor, 45 N 5th, h 4 Weaver
Patterson Wm. C., mer., 182 High, h Mulberry E Sch 6th
Patterson Wm. F., M. D., 8th & Baker
Patteson Edward, grocer, 62 S Front, h 8th ab Green
PATTISON JAMES, dry goods, 5 Church al, h Locust n Broad
Patton Ann, Higgin's ct (S)
Patton David, sexton, 2 Howard pl
Patton David M., drayman, Front ab Reed
Patton Edward, lab. Elme's ct.
Patton Ellen, 13 Morgan
Patton Elinor, dressmr., 51 E Lombard
Patton & Harper, distillers, 13th & Rose
Patton Henry, baker, Cedar ab 7th
Patton James, jr., mer., 3d wharf ab Sassafras, h 293 Sassafras
Patton Jas. M., planing machine, 3d whf. above Coates, & mer. 9 N whfs., Broad & Cedar
Patton Jennet, dressmr. 144 S 10th
Patton John, mariner, 41 Catharine
Patton John, mer., 92 Gaskill
Patton John, waiter, Juniper bel Walnut
Patton Mary, trimmings, G T road bel Master
Patton Mary, milliner, 75 Mulberry
Patton Matthew, lab. Helmuth n Sch 6th
Patton Matthew, carp., 158 S 11th

Patton Michael, baker, 164 Locust
Patton Price hatter, Buckley ab 5th, h 23 Powell
Patton Price J., mer., 118 High, h 23 Powell
Patton Robert, grocer, 6 Union sq
Patton Samuel, 139 S Front
Patton Samuel, engineer, 2 Humphrey's ct
Patton Susan, 9 Howard's pl
Patton Thomas, harnessmr., 23 Benton
Patton Thomas, weaver, Lombard n Sch 6th
Patton Thomas W., mer., h Sch 7th bel Walnut
Patton Wm. grocer, 12th & High
Patton Wm., dealer, 6th and Washington
Patton William, Jr., cashier Farmers' and Mechanics' bank, h 179 S 5th
Patton Wm. S., blacksm., rear Church below Christian
Patton W H., paper hanger, 93 N 6th
Paul Aaron, turner, 104 N 6th
Paul Abraham H., victualler, Ann ab R road (F V)
Paul Abraham R., vict., 5th ab Poplar
Paul A., weaver, Fulton ab 12th
Paul Benj. R., biscuit baker, 41 Brown (N L)
Paul Bettle, mer., 25 High, h 155 O Y road
Paul C., gent., 3 Portico sqr
Paul Daniel H. vict. 5th ab Poplar
Paul Daniel V. grain measurer, 13th & Parrish
Paul David B., victualler, Mantua Village
Paul David S., bricklayer, 489 S 2d
Paul George W., carp., 2d n Montgomery (K)
Paul Hannah, gent., 162 N 5th
Paul Henry, vict., 260 N 8th
Paul & Hicks, saw manufs., Carlisle ab Girard av
Paul Jacob, tailor, 452 S Front
Paul Jacob A., bookbinder, 30 Laurel (N L)
PAUL JAMES W., atty. and coun., 101 S 4th
Paul John, cabtmr., Federal bel M road
Paul John, tailor, 1 Myers' pl
Paul John T., framemr., 438 N 3d
Paul Jonathan, sawmr., Carlisle ab Girard av
Paul Joseph, victualler, Palmer & Franklin (K)
Paul Joseph C., blacksmith, 524 N Front
Paul Joseph R., 400 O Y road
PAUL JOSEPH S., mer., S E Sassafras and Water, h 148 Spruce
Paul J. Marshall, M. D., 335 Spruce
Paul J. R., M. D., Spruce ab 10th
Paul Marg., Prosperous al
Paul Mary, huckster, 3 Boyle's ct
Paul Perry, 7 Liberty ct
Paul Reinhart, lab., Perkenpine's ct
Paul & Reynolds, turners, 104 N 6th
Paul Samuel, hatter, 487 N 2d
Paul Samuel W., conveyancer, 52 N 6th, h 8 Montgomery sq
Paul Sidney, 331 Spruce
Paul Simon P., 8 Laurel (C)
Paul Theodore, vict., George bel 5th
Paul Wm. L. broker, 23 Carter's al, h 70 Gaskill
Paul Wm. R., hatter, 487 N 2d, h 398 N 5th
Paul Wm., W., mer., 203 High, h 8 Montgomery square
Paulding T., mer., 96 High, h 19 Palmyra row
Pauli Lewis J., dealer, Callowhill ab 13th

Paullin Benjamin, tailor, 13 Flower, h 11 Carleton sq
Paullin B. H., blacksmith, Barker n Sch 5th
Paullin Joel, tailor, 251 S 6th
Paullin John, tailor, 5 Cresson's al
Paullin S. F. & D., tobacconists, 216 N 2d
PAULSON & CANFIELD, brokers, 51 Chesnut
Paulson Joseph R., broker, 51 Chestnut
Pauly Louis L., clerk, 114 Green
Pavonarius C. & J., wire workers, 21 N 6th
Pavonarius Maria, 2 Farmer
Pawley Robert, distiller, 19 Hunter
Pawling Abraham, whitesmith, 17 N 9th
Pawling Benj., blacksm., 69 S 12th, h Barker bel Sch 4th & 5th
Pawson James, bookbinder, Cherry n Sch 6th
Paxson Benjamin, stonecutter, Duke bel Palmer (K)
Paxson Edwd., attorney at law, 153 N Front
Paxson H. K., b. h., 56 Marshall
Paxson John, cabinetmr. High W Sch 6th
Paxson Jno., sawyer, Beach bel Shackamaxon (K)
Paxson Joseph, bricklayer, Shackamaxon below Bedford (K)
Paxson Joseph, carp., Palmer ab Duke (K)
Paxson Joseph B., clerk, 32 Chatham
Paxson Joseph S., mer., 209 High
Paxson Margaret, Palmer & Duke (K)
Paxson Richard, mer., 209 High
Paxson Richard, jr., mer., 209 High, h 13 City row
PAXSON RICHARD & SONS, hardware, 209 High
Paxson Samuel, blindmr. Beach ab Poplar (K)
Paxson Samuel W., 32 Beach (K)
Paxson Sarah, 33 Dean
Paxson S. W., blindmr., 124 N 2d
Payne Edwin W., mer., N E 4th & Mulberry
Payne George, weaver, 13th ab Fitzwater
Payne George, weaver, Union bel West (K)
Payne Hester, 71 Union
Payne Hannah S., Catharine ab 8th
Payne James, seaman, 19 Cedar
Payne John, capt., Quince
Payne Mary, 164 S 5th
Payne Mary Ann, 10 Jacoby
Payne Wm. R. cordw. 10 Short ct
Paynter John C., dry goods, 156 Mulberry
Paynter Jos., cooper, Christian ab Swanson
Paynter Lemuel, gent., 117 German
Paynter Lemuel Jr., carp., 235 Christian
Paynter Mary, milliner, 65 N 10th
Payot J. M., mer., 132 Chestnut
Payran Joseph, tailor, 302 N 10th
Payran Richard, saddler, S W 8th & Green
Paysont Rebecca, 42 Lebanon
Payton E. J., R road bel Sp Garden
Peabody Edwd. G., com. mer., 58 Filbert
Peabody George F., mer., 38 S Front, h 5-S 13th
PEACE EDWARD, M. D., S W 9th & Walnut
Peace Washington, atty. & coun., N W 6th and Walnut, h S W 9th & Walnut
Peach Anna M., teacher, 172 Marshall
Peach Wm., printer, 172 Marshall

Peaco Georgiana, b h, 485 Chestnut
Peacock David B., com. mer., S W cor. Broad & Cherry, h 11 Carleton sq
Peacock Eber, shoemr., Sarah ab Queen (K)
Peacock James, patternmr., Shackamaxon ab Queen (K)
Peacock Joel, shoemr. Warren ab Beach (K)
Peacock Martha, widow, Ann E Sch 4th
Peacock Sarah, 10 Carleton
Peak Daniel, silverplater, Crown ab Queen
Peak Edward, shipwright, Sarah ab Queen (K)
Peak Edward, silver plater, Queen bel Shackamaxon (K)
Peak Elias, tavern, N W ³ road and Federal
Peak John M., bricklayer, 4 Perry ct
Peak Samuel, shipwt., Shackamaxon ab Queen
Peak Thomas, cordw., Sarah ab Queen (K)
Peake Henry, baker, Piper's ct
Peal George, mariner, rear 10 Concord st
Peal Jas., clerk, 613 S 2d
Peal Robert, blacksm., Broad and Paper al
Peale Augustin R., County Auditor, State House, h 278 Lombard
Peale Edmund, museum, Masonic Hall
Peale Franklin, U. S. Mint, h 31 Girard
Peale James, daguerreotyper, N W 6th & Walnut, h 278 Lombard
Peale Maria, b h, 27 Sansom
Peale Rembrandt, portrait painter, 502 Vine
Peale Washington, Washington ab 13th
Pearce Ann, Cedar ab 11th
Pearce E. W., saddler, 171 N 5th
Pearce G. & Co. importers, 9 Church al
Pearce Henry W. cooper, 70 German
Pearce John, carp. weaver, Stile's ct (K)
Pearce John, mer., 50 N 3d, h Noble ab Franklin
Pearce Mary, b h, 33 Filbert.
Pearce M. & E., dress and millinery, 84 Crown
Pearce Rebecca, b h, 124 Mulberry
Pearce Thomas H., clk. Collector's off. Col. R. R., Sch 3d ab Sassafras
Pearce Wm., cordw., 3 Linden st (K)
Pearl John, carp. Hallowell's ct (S G)
Pearsall Elizabeth, 12th bel Cherry
Pearsall Robt., merchant, 46 N Front, h 483 Mulberry
PEARSE & ELBERT, com. mers., 42 S Water
Pearse O. P., mer., 42 S Water, h N W Walnut & Sch 7th
PEARSON DAVIS, coal mer., Mulberry and Broad, h 23 Branch
Pearson Elizabeth, widow of Samuel, 8 Marion
Pearson Elizabeth, gentw., 56 Swanson
Pearson George, carp., 399 S 2d
Pearson Hamlet, carp., Queen n 3d, h 3rd and Queen
Pearson Henry, carp., Wharton ab 2d
Pearson James S., ship joiner, N E Queen and Swanson, h 138 Swanson
Pearson Jane, shop, 34 Marion.
Pearson John, drayman, Rachel bel Laurel
Pearson John, tavern, 133 N 4th
Pearson John, whip mr., 1 N 4th, h 396 N 6th
Pearson John, brushmr., Poplar bel 9th

Pearson John, 33 New
Pearson John M., wheelwright, 166 Queen
Pearson Margaret, 2 Crown
Pearson Martha B., gentw., 79 Wood ab Marshall
Pearson Morris, grocer, O Y road & Parrish
PEARSON & SALLADA, whip mrs., 1 N 4th
Pearson Samuel J., custom house, 135 Wood
Peart & Bailey, carps., 7 Quarry
Peart Eugene, carp., 7 Quarry, h Dunton and Otter (K)
Peart Thos. J., umbrella mr., Hyde's ct
Pease Charlotte, b. h., 72 S 4th
Pease David, grocer, S W 6th & Mulberry
Pease & Foster, com. mer., 20 Chestnut
Pease Julius A., teacher, 48 S 3d, h 161 N Front
Pease J. I., engraver, 7th and Sansom, h Morris bel Pine
Pease J. Oliver, merchant, 20 Chestnut, h Sch 8th bel Spruce
Pease Margaret, 396 Vine
Peaslee Charles S., mer., 38 S Front
Peberdy Ann, Dyott's ct (K)
Pechin John, gent., 157 S 10th
Pechin Lewis, machinist, 6 Plum st
Pechin Robert W., currier, 37 Lombard, h 157 S 10th
Pechin Wm., tanner, Mulberry & Ashton
Peck Benjamin G. bookbinder, 27 S 4th, h 120 New Market
Peck David, porter, 170 Pine
Peck Hannah, 8th ab Christian
Peck Horace C., bookseller, N E 3d & Mulberry, h Marshall and Buttonwood
Peck John, cordw., 29 Duke
Peck Joseph, lab., 29 Duke
Peck Joseph E., baker, 29 Duke
Peck Maria, dressmr., 3 Stanley's ct
Pecken Rebecca, teacher, 4 Salem al
Peckera F., gent., 9th bel Pine
Peckersgill John, bottler, 121 N 6th
Peckworth Chas. W., coalyd., Broad ab Sassafras
Peden Wm., carter, P road and Federal
Pedrick Geo., machinist, Miller ab 13th
Pedrick John, baker, Miller ab 13th
Peddle George R., 44 Maria
Peddle Richard A., capt., 47 Carpenter (S)
Peddle William A., 126 Green
Peddrick Michael, tailor, 28 Stamper's al
Peddrick Washington F., varnish and paints, 98 N 4th
Pedrick & Allison, tailors, 270 and 316 High
Pedrick George L., plasterer, Parrish bel 11th
Pedrick John, paper stainer, Mechanic n Creek (N L)
Pedrick Joseph, tailor, 318 High
Pedrick Jos. D., tailor, 316 High, h 164 Wood
Pedrick Silas, captain, 22½ Walnut, h 65 N 8th
Pedrick Thomas, dentist, 500 Green
Peeble Alex., lab., Hope ab Otter (K)
Pecker Edward, 37 Elizabeth
Peel Cornelius, carp., Johnson's la bel 5th
Peel Eliza, 531 S Front
Peel Joseph, sail mr., 33 & 34 S Whfs, h 142 Swanson
Peepard Jacob, lab., 195 N Front

Peet Francis, carter, 115 Queen
Pehrson J. G., M. D., 311 E Lombard
Peiffer Henry, drayman, Apple bel George
Peiffer Henry, painter, 119 Poplar
Peiffer John, lab., 9 Brown's ct (N L.)
Peile John, teacher of music, rear 196 Cherry
Peirce Caleb, conveyancer, 374 S Front
Peirce Caleb, 75 N 7th
Peirce Charles, gent., 366 Chestnut
Peirce Chas., cordw., Parrish ab 7th
Peirce Henry, bricklr., Brinton bel 11th
Peirce Jane, sempstress, 10 Brown's ct
Peirce Maria, 8 Logan
Peirce Samuel, ship carp., Swanson bel Washington
Peirce Timothy, bricklr., Rose al n Green
Peirce Wm. S., atty. and coun., 73 S 4th
Peirsol Joseph, Bank N. L., h 10th ab Vernon
Peirsol Mrs. M., 134 N 10th
Peirsol William, 201 N 9th
Peirson Elizabeth, gentw., 254 N 5th
Peixotto A. C., clerk, 92 Spruce
Pelen Abrm., grocer, S W Sch 7th and Cherry
Pelger Peter, cordw., 54 Charlotte
Pell Wm., 11th and Carlton
Pelletier W., cook, 1 Nicholson
Pelling, E., carp. weaver, 5th & O Y Road
Pellon Matthias, stockingweaver, 122 St John
Peloux P., gun maker, 60 Cedar
Pelouze Edwd. jr., type founder, N E St John and Wood
Pelouze Lewis, type founder, 40 S 3d, h 17 St John
Pelton C., map publisher, 7th & Callowhill, h 12 Marshall
Peltz Richd., grazier, 320 S Front
Peltz Samuel, farmer, Washington ab 8th
Pembers Christian, cordw., Marshall ab Poplar
Pemberton Henry, 204 N 6th
Pemberton John, Spruce bel Broad
Pembroke Margaret, Webb's al
Pence Wm., sawyer, Cherry n Sch 8th
Pendergass Elizabeth, shop, Mulberry bel Broad
Pendelberry Robt., dyer, 7 Harrison's ct (K)
Pendleton Wm. S., mer., 169 High
Peneveyre Charles, gent., 59 Spruce
Penhaeffer Jos., carp. weav., Apple ab Franklin
Penicks James B., cordw., Beach ab Maiden
Penicks Mary, washer, rear Washington n
Penicks Wm., cordw., Shackamaxon bel Allen (K)
Penington Edward, Locust n Sch 5th
Penington Helena, 391 Spruce
Penington H., att'y & coun., 36 S 5th, h Spruce ab 12th.
Penington John, bookseller, 169 Chestnut, h 13th bel Locust
Penington Wm., grocer, Sch 4th & Callowhill
Penn Eleanor, rear 487 N 3d
Penn-Gaskell E., 535 Chestnut
Penn Jesse, lab., Front bel Oxford (K)
Penn John B., mer., 112 High
Penn Wm., waterman, Harriet bel Ross (K)
Pennebaker Amos, M. D., 91 N 4th
Pennell Edw., planemr., 115 Dillwyn

Pennell Jonathan, carp., 7 Hunter, h Barker Sch 5th
Pennell Joseph P., mer., Marshall bel Poplar
Pennell Robert, carp, 4th bel Wharton
Pennewill David, blacksm., Cedar ab 13th, Bedford bel Broad
Penniman Edward A., N E 11th & Vine
Penniman Edward A. & Co., publishers of Spirit of the Times, 32 S 3d
Penning Daniel, cedar cooper, 489 N 2d
Pennington Eliza S., trimmings, 622 S 2d
Pennington Jacob, porter, 16 Mercer
Pennington J. W., refec., 168 High, h 30 Appletree al
Pennington Margaret, milliner, 20 N 9th
Pennington Mary, Lily al
Pennington Samuel, cabinetmaker, Franklin a' Hanover
Pennington Thomas, 20 N 9th
Pennington William, printer, Christian ab 7th
Pennington Wm., machinist, Bridge N Village
Pennock Abraham L., 231 High
Pennock Caspar W., M. D., 484 Chestnut
Pennock David, shoemr., Crown ab Duke (K)
Pennock Horatio B., mer., 157 N 6th
Pennock Isabella N., 336 Mulberry
Pennybaker Henry, Depot bel 9th
Pennypacker Harman, mer., 19 N 6th
Pennypacker Henry, lab., 6th ab Franklin
Pennypacker James, tavern, R road & 13th
PENROSE & BURTON, ship. mers., 34 S whs
Penrose Charles, gent., Penn and Shippen
Penrose Charles Jun. mer. 15 S Water, h Penn and Shippen
Penrose James, carp., Apple ab Brown
Penrose John, carpenter, State st
Penrose J. R., merchant, 34 S whs., h 52 Pine
Penrose Margaretta A., 132 S 9th
Penrose Wm., cooper, 5 N 12th
Pentland Margaret, dry goods, 32 Laurel
Pentland Robert F., grocer, Cadwalader and Phoenix
Penwell Elizabeth, tailoress, Sch 8th & Filbert
Peoples David, grocer, S E 10th and Spring Garden
Peoples David, shoemr., Boyd's ct
Peoples James, cordw., h High n Sch. 4th
Peoples John, lab. Vine n Sch
Peplow John, butcher, 159 M road
Pepper Amos, nail cutter, 55 M road
Pepper Christopher G., printer, 240 S 5th
Pepper Edward, gent. Walnut E Sch 6th
Pepper Francis, painter, 121 N 11th
Pepper George Mrs., gentw., 225 Chestnut
Pepper George J., broker, N W 3rd & Walnut
Pepper Henry, carp., 53 M road
Pepper Henry, 381 Walnut
Pepper Henry B., 167 Chestnut, h 232 N 5th
PEPPER HENRY J. & SON, watches, jewellery & silver ware, 167 Chestnut
Pepper H. J. watches, &c., 167 Chestnut, h 232 N 5th
Pepper James, fancy store, 164 Callowhill
Pepper John, ship carp., 53 M road
Pepper Joseph, printer, S E 5th & Harmony

Pepper Michael, carp., Mechanic ab George
Pepper Margaret Miss, 50 S 13th
Pepper Napoleon, cabinetmr., 70 Almond
Pepper Richard, painter, 14 Quarry
Pepper Sarah, 4 Madison's av
PEPPER WILLIAM, M. D., 361 Walnut
Pepper Wm. C. printer, 257 S 3d
Pepperdy Wm., chemist, rear Vienna ab Queen (K)
Perce Jacob, lab., 108 Green
Perch Michael, soap manuf., F road ab Franklin (K)
Percival Benj., engraver, 9th bel Catharine
Percival Benj., confectioner, 89 S 6th
Percival Benj., printer, 110 Crown
Percival Phœbe, confect., 156 N 5th
Percival Hannah, stockmr., 304 N 5th
Percival Joseph G., lab., Swanson bel Christian
Percival J. & Son, mers., 82 S Front
Percival Thomas C., mer., 82 S Front, h Broad and Locust.
Percival Thomas C., designer, 5 Swarthmore pl
Percival Wm., carp., 152 Carpenter
Perdreaux Mary, dressmr., 139 S 6th
Perdriaux Peter, mer. 7 Dock st whf.
Pereyra Henry, segars, 88 N 6th
Pereyra Peter, mer. George's al
Perfect Geo., vict., Apple bel George
Peries A., mer., 33 Walnut
Perine Daniel, bricklayer, 101 N Juniper
Perine Wm. turner, 22 New Market
Perit John W., mer., 445 Chestnut
Perkes Peter, shoes, 2 Eutaw
Perkinpine David, skin dr., Haydock bel Front
Perkinpine George, cooper, 275 High, h 447 N 4th
Perkinpine Henry, cooper, rear 308 St John
Perkinpine James, cedar cooper, rear 467 N 3d
Perkinpine John, skindresser, 9th ab Coates
Perkins Abraham R., dry goods, 1 S 9th, h 102 S 9th
Perkins Amelia, washer, 138 Cherry
Perkins Anna, b. h., 25 Brandywine st
Perkins Caleb S., waterm., Queen & F road (K)
Perkins Edward, waterman, Sch. 4th & Ann
Perkins Geo., dry goods, 253 N 2d
Perkins Henry, bookseller, 142 Chestnut, h 169 Pine
Perkins Isaac S., cooper, 1 Bread
Perkins Jeremiah C., 27 German
Perkins John, carp., 10th bel Poplar.
Perkins John, weaver, Carpenter ab 10th
Perkins John, boot & shoemr., 6 Pleasant row
Perkins John, lab., 75 Beach (K)
Perkins Paul, cordw., 119 German
PERKINS SAMUEL H., att'y and coun., office 141½ and h 143 Walnut, 4 doors E of 5th
Perkins Thomas, lab., Marriott's la bel P road
Perkins T. J. mer. 1 S 9th, h 13 N 11th
PERKINS & VAN HARLINGEN, dry goods, 1 S 9th
Perkins Wm., cordw., 32 German
Perkins Wm., carp., 292 Wood
Perkins William B., keeper M prison, h Fitzwater bel 8th

Perkins William L., ivory turner, Olive ab 10th
Perlasca James, lampmr., 8 Laurel (C), h 2 Miller's ct
Perlaska Ellen, 2 Miller's ct.
Permar Elizabeth, rear 35 Plum
Perney Mary, shop, West bel F road (K)
Pernier Francis, bricklr., rear 121 Queen (S)
Pernier John, bottler, rear 125 Plum
Perot Charles, mer., S E 3d and Walnut, h 297 High
Perot C. & J., com. mers., S E 3d & Walnut
Perot Elliston, mer., 29 Church al, h 29 Morgan
Perot Francis, brewer, 120 Vine, h 101 New
Perot F. & W. S., brewers, 120 Vine to 107 New
Perot Joseph, mer., S E 3d & Walnut, h 111 S 8th
Perot Mary, 297 High
Perot William S., brewer, 120 Vine, h 247 Pine
Perpignan Stephen, tailor, Queen n 4th
Perreau Jno., brass found., G T road bel Master
Perrine G. W. & Co., oil manuf., 41 Dock, h 492 N 5th
Perrine Nicholas Rev., 181 Spruce
Perrine Penrose, bootmr., 28 S 7th
Perrine Wm., weaver, Sch 2d bel Callowhill
Perrine William W., M. D., N E 7th and Noble
Perrins John carp. par., Apple bel Franklin
Perrott Fred., watchmr., Washington (W P)
Perry Alfred H., carp., 11 Rose alley
Perry David, refectory, 2d and Cedar
Perry James, painter, 23 Quince
Perry Jas., agent, Hanover ab Bedford (K)
Perry James, blacksmith, rear 25 F road
Perry James C. weaver, 9 Mary's ct
Perry Jane, dressmaker, N E 5th & Spruce
Perry John, manuf., Lombard & Perry
Perry John, clerk, Co-com., h Sch 7th ab Pine
Perry John B., bookbinder & stat., 198 High, h 37 Vine
Perry Julianna, Little Pine n 6th
Perry Mary, 2 Mercer
Perry Robert, carter, Francis bel Sch 5th (F V)
Perry Robert painter, 159½ S 11th
Perry Robt. C., piano mr., 7th bel Fitzwater
Perry Sarah, dyer, 143 Locust
Perry Thomas, 6 Mercer
Perry William, gent., Cedar n 13th
Perryjohn Isaac, lab., Carpenter ab 12th
Pervard Phillas, washer, 20 Gaskill
Peso Phila, Noble bel 9th
Pesoa David, dry goods, 160 S 2nd
Peter Fredk., cordw., rear 68 Shippen
Peter Wm., British Consul, 152 S 3d
Peterman Abraham, gun smith, 3d ab Washington
Peterman Ezekiah, carp., Montgomery bel Front
Peterman Geo., carter, Barker bel Sch 6th
Peterman Geo. F. & Co., chairmrs., 432 N 5th
Peterman Henry, stone cutter, White Hall ab 12th
Peterman Jacob, lumber inspr., 6 Laurel (N L)
Peterman John, drayman, Fraley's al (K)
Peterman Joseph, bricklayer, Hope bel Master (K)
Peterman Lewis C. gunsmith, 1 Hartshorne's ct

Peters Abraham, printer, 50 N 6th, h 35 Apple
Peters A. Mrs., doctress, N E N Market & Green
Peters Charles, book binder, 26 S 4th, h 133 N 12th
Peters Charles, cordw., Rumel's ct
Peters Charles, mariner, 395 S Front
Peters Christian, carp., 11th bel Brown
Peters Christiana, rear 319 St John
Peters Dell P., mer., 111 High, h 151 N 12th
Peters Edw., cordw., Howard bel Franklin) K)
Peters Elizabeth, huckster, Harper's pl
Peters Franklin, mer., 105 N 2d, h Sassafras
Peters George S. stove and pattern maker, 76 N 6th
Peters Henry, barber, Beach bel Maiden (K)
Peters Jacob, stage office, 106 and 108 Sassafras
Peters Jacob, manager, G T road & Franklin
Peters Jacob, jr., hotel, R road and Girard av (F V)
Peters James, confec., 96 N 11th
Peters James, spectacle maker, 105 N 2d, Poplar W Broad
PETERS JAMES & CO., spectacle and thimble manuf., 105 N 2d
Peters James H., barber, 10th ab Ogden
Peters John, lumb. mer., Queen bel Ross
Peters John, book binder, Callowhill bel 13th
Peters Joseph A., baker, 148 Locust
Peters L. R., White Swan, 108 Sassafras
Peters Nicholas, huckster, rear 1 Rachel (N L)
Peters N. L. hatter, Charles & Pleasant
Peters Peter, sailmr., 17 Beck st
Peters Phoebe, washer, 340 Sassafras
Peters Randolph, tailor, 3d & Chestnut
Peters Richard, att'y and coun., 18 Girard
Peters Theodore H., mer., rear 7 N 7th
Peters William S., silver plater, 152 N 8th
Peterson Alex. tanner, Front ab Brown
Peterson Ann M., gentw., Division (F V)
Peterson Benj., grocer, Catharine & Swanson, h 246 Sp Garden
Peterson C. J., att'y at law, & pub. Lady's Nat. Magazine, 98 Chestnut, h 246 Sassafras
Peterson Daniel, clothier, 218 and h 179 S 6th
Peterson Geo., gent., 342 N 6th
Peterson George, waterman, 296 S Front
Peterson Geo. lab. rear 9 Maria
Peterson Harriet, 18 Watson's al
Peterson Henry, editor, 98 Chestnut
Peterson Henry, clerk Elizabeth ab Poplar
Peterson Horace L., clerk, Locust n Sch 6th
Peterson Isaac, mariner, 232 Christian
Peterson Israel, gent., 221 N 4th
Peterson Jacob, waterman, 17 Union (S)

Peterson Peters combmr., 8 Emlen's ct
Peterson Philip, morocco dresser, Franklin 3d (K)
Peterson P. M., piano manuf., George n Sch 7
Peterson Reuben, rear St John ab George (K)
Peterson Robert, 11 Logan sq
Peterson Robert, coachman, 30 Prosperous al
Peterson R. E., att'y at law, 10 N 7th, h 11 Legan sq
Peterson Theophilus B. bookseller, 98 Chestnut, h 28 R road
Peterson Thomas, 28 R road
Peterson Thomas K., mer., 12 N 4th, h 280 Sassafras
Peterson Wm., carp., Ross ab Queen (K)
Peterson William, boot mr., Washington ab 3d
Peterson Wm., carter, 34 Mulberry
Peterson Wm., porter, 130 Locust
Petit Edgar A., atty. & coun., S W 6th & Pine, h Sassafras ab Broad
Petrey John, blacksmith, Apple ab Poplar
Petrey Nicholas, blacksm., Apple ab Poplar
Petrey Philip, shoemr. Apple ab Poplar
Pettibone Daniel, lamp mr., 32 R road
Pettit Alex., carp., 194 Queen
Pettit Benj. Cadwalader & Jefferson (K)
Pettit Charles, clerk, Washington ab 3d
Pettit James, machinist, Fraley's al (K)
Pettit Martin, enginemr., Pearl bel Sch 7th
Pettit Mary Ann, shop, 54 Dillwyn
Pettit Richard, mer., 45 N Front, h 2 Lodge
Pettit Robert, purser, U. S. N. Asylum, h Spruce
Pettit Rebecca M., b. h., 206 Cherry
Pettit Sarah, Sch 5th n Chestnut
Pettit Thomas M., atty. & coun., 5th & Library, h 41 Clinton
Pettit Wm., engineer, 13th ab Wallace
Pettit Wm. R. J., tobacconist, G T road & Jefferson
Pettit Wm. V., 10 Colonnade row
Pew Ezekiel, agent, 71 Shippen
Peyton Julius, waiter, 10 Miles' al
Peyton J. E. mer. 89 High, h 331 Mulberry
Peyton Thos., coachman, 4 Miles' al
Pfaff Augustin, clockmr., 505 N 3d
Pfander Christopher, baker, 295 S 5th
Pfander John, baker, 57 Lombard
Pfeiffer Adam, lab., Wheat ab Wharton
Pfeiffer Carl, dyer & scourer, R road ab Washington
Pfeiffer G. T., M D, 3 Palmyra row
Pfeiffer G. S. F., M. D., 78 Wood
Pfeil Ann, dressmaker, 302 Green
Pfeil Chas., dry goods, S E 8th & Sp Garden
Pfeil Wm, machinist, rear Irvine st

Phares Joseph, drayman, Front ab Franklin (K)
Phares Thomas, Howard bel Master
Pharo A R. mer. 191 High, h 31 Palmyra row
Phelan Edward, hatter, 239 Christian
Phelps W. C., cordw., 3 Clinton av
Phile Charles, ropemr., Penn bel William (K)
Phile Peter, lab., rear 527 N 4th
Philes John, lab., Berks' ct
Philibert F., dyer, 323 S 2d
Philips David A., shop, 216 Shippen
Philler Andrew, trimmings, 269 S 2d
Philler George, cashier Bank of Penn., h 11th bel Lombard
Phillippe Henry, carp., 33 Queen
Phillips Amos, dep. sheriff, h 120 Marshall
Phillips Ann, 37 N Sch 8th
Phillips Ann L., milliner, 279 Walnut
Phillips Asa, tailor, 478 Callowhill
Phillips Catharine, 15 Lombard
Phillips Charles, cordwainer, 37 Cherry
Phillips Clement S., mer., h Spruce ab 12th
Phillips Edw., lastmr., 341 N 3d
Phillips Elizabeth, dressmr., 156 S 3d
Phillips George, dealer, 256 Cedar
Phillips George G., refectory, N W 3rd & Chestnut, h 12 Filbert av
PHILLIPS GEO. L., Mers. Coffee House, 1 & 3 Merchant
Phillips Goody, 5 Lemon
Phillips & Henderson, dry goods, 96 Sp Garden
PHILLIPS H. M., attorney and counsellor, 58 S 6th
Phillips Isaac, gent., Broad bel Walnut.
Phillips Jacob, 178 S 11th
Phillips Jacob, lab., 37 Currant al
Phillips James, shop, 249 S 4th
Phillips James, lab. Lombard E Sch 5th
Phillips John, drayman, 4 Kesler's ct
Phillips John, merchant, 13½ S Front, h 327 N 6th
Phillips John, cordw. G T road opp 5th
Phillips John, sad. treemr., Reed bel Church
Phillips John W., carp., 6 Washington
Phillips John W., jeweller, 201 Spruce
Phillips Jonas, cooper, Brown bel 9th
Phillips Jonathan, gentleman, Marlborough and West (K)
Phillips Joseph, cakebaker, 1 Gilles' al
Phillips Joseph, lab., rear Vienna bel Franklin (K)
Phillips J. A., atty. and coun., 56 S 6th.
PHILLIPS J. D., real estate broker, 75 Dock, h 120 Marshall
Phillips Lydia, 30 S 13th
Phillips Mary, rear 67 Queen
Phillips Mary, tailoress, 113 Swanson
Phillips Mary, glov., 55 Sassafras
Phillips Mary, nurse, Centre bel 13th
Phillips Mary Ann, gents. furnishing st. 82 N 4th
Phillips Patrick, lab. Clay bel Beech
Phillips Robt., teacher, Sch 7th bel Spruce
Phillips Robt., plumber, Washington bel 6th
Phillips Robert, cabinet mr., 231 S 4th
Phillips R., confectioner, 196 Shippen
35

Phillips R. O'N., printer, 5 Steward
Phillips Samuel, coachmaker, 24 Perry
Phillips Samuel R., sadd., 12 S 5th, h Hyde's court
Phillips Samuel T, carp., Dilligent av & Pleasant st
Phillips Sarah, 7 Northampton ct
Phillips Sarah, 137 Mulberry
Phillips Slater C., salesman, 37 N Sch 8th
Phillips & Sooey, coach mrs., 94 N 13th
Phillips S. Mrs., trimmings, 431 N 5th
Phillips S. Mrs., b h, 104 S Front
Phillips Thos., carp. weaver, 2 M'Devitt's av (K)
Phillips T. T., merchant, 190 Chestnut, h 69 N 10th
Phillips Wm., carp., Catharine & Steward
Phillips Wm., 3 Rogers' ct
Phillips William, lastmaker, 55 Walnut
Phillips William, shoemaker, 214 S 6th
Phillips Wm., coachmr., 94 N 13th, h 55 Sassafras
Phillips Wm. H., tailor, 246 Wood
Phillips Wm. S., real est. broker, 46½ Walnut, h S E 11th & Spruce
Philpot Francis, collector, 58½ N 6th
Philpot F. C., lawyer, 97 Catharine
Philpot William, stone mas., Clinton ab Poplar
Philpot Wm. H. C., silversm., 56 Mulberry
Philson M., Farmers and Mechanics' Bank, h Juniper bel Spruce
Philson R. A. druggist, 9th bel Parrish
Phipps Chas., hardware, S W 3d and Mulberry
Phipps Manuel M., mer., 34½ N 2d
Phipps Stephen, hardware, 236 N 3d, h 77 Marshal
Phister Benjamin, flour mer., 164 Vine, h 239 N 7th
Phraes & Hacketts, leather store, 285 N 3d
Phy Rudolph, lab., Lemon ab 10th
Phyfe Robert, dry goods, 13½ N 8th
Phyney Joseph S., brickla., Allen ab Marlboro'
Physic Emlin, gent., 204 Spruce
Pichetti Andrew, 4 Boyd's ct
Pickands Samuel J., acct., 34 S 7th, h Townsend's pl
Pickel Caspar, Sch 4th and Chestnut
Pickell Henry, segarmr., rear 119 Queen
Picken Robert, drayman, R road ab Ogden
Pickens Robt., weaver, 6 Bauersach's ct (K)
Pickering Elihu, scrivener, 270 N 6th
Pickering George, tailor, George ab 9th
Pickering Samuel, oysters, 36 Mead
Pickering T. F., stone mason, rear Harriet bel Ross (K)
Pickett John C., japanner, 13 S 6th, h 7th ab Poplar
Pickford John, grocer, G T road ab Franklin (K)
Pickman James, wigmr., 1 N 8th
Pickton John, lab., 4 Skerreth's ct
Picot Cha's., French seminary for young ladies, 15 Washington sq
Picot Xiver, cabmr, 4 Willow's ct
Pidgeon David, collector, 411 Sassafras
Pidgeon James, tavern, 5th ab Cedar
Pidgeon James C., saddler, 6th bel Washington

Pidgeon John, brassfounder, Nectarine bel 11th
Pidgeon John W., brickla., West ab Cherry (K)
Pidgeon Samuel, ladies' shoemr., Hallowell
Pidgeon Wm. R., plumber, rear 116 Christian
Pidgeon Wm. W., mast maker, 95 Catharine
Pieffer Mary Ann, b h, 78 N 9th
Pierce David, sailmr., Pegg and Emlen's ct
Pierce David, mer., 5 Dock
Pierce E. J., umbrella maker, 86 High, h 139 Mulberry
Pierce Geo., waiter, Pearl ab 13th
Pierce James, shoemr, 26 Harmony
Pierce John, bricklayer, Baker n 8th
Pierce John, carpenter, Weaver
Pierce Joseph, whf. builder, Wheat ab Reed
Pierce Lewis, carp., 13th bel Parrish
Pierce Lewis, boot and shoemr., Franklin ab Union (K)
Pierce Peter, ivory turner, 299 S 4th
Pierce Richard, waiter, Catharine ab Lebanon
Pierce Samuel, carter, 488 N 4th
Pierce Thomas, painter, Sun ct
Pierce Thomas M., blacksmith, Carpenter ab 6th
Pierce Timothy, cordwainer, 37 Noble
Piercy William C., baker, Crown bel West
Pierie Charles, coachmaker, 37 Dean
Pierie John G., mer., 5 Dock, h 119 Lombard
Pierie W. H., 384 N Front
Pierce W. H., dealer, Charles & Cedar
Pierie Wm. S., N E Wallace & Franklin
Pierpont Mary Ann, Sch 7th ab Locust
Pierpont Robert, silk dyer, 69 Filbert
Piers Joseph, mer., 2 Montgomery
Pierson Ann Mrs., Reed ab Church
Pierson F., atty and coun., 109 Vine
Pierson George W., hatter, 59½ N 2d, h 7 Wood
Pierson Hiram B., books, 349 S 2d
Pierson Lucius C., 6 Torr's al
Pierson Richd., cordw., Higgin's pl
Pierson Thos., bookseller, 88½ N 2d
Pierson Wm., book binder, 66 N 4th
Piggott John T., merchant, 9 Bank, h 155 N Front
Piggott & Richards, dry goods, 9 Bank
Pigott Isabella, gentw., Wharton ab 4th
Pike Ellen, 25 Perry
Pike Henry, 212 Cherry
Pike M. W., gent., c 6th and E North
Pike Samuel, cedar cooper, rear 13 Charlotte
Pike Thornton, mer., 29 N 3d
Pile Thos., carp., 32 John (S)
Pile Wilson H., druggist, 73 P road
Pilkington Aston, upholst., 512 Vine
Pilling Ellis, auctioneer, 63 N Front, h Poplar E of Sch 6th
Pilling John, bleacher, West n Vienna (K)
Pilling Joseph, shoe findings, 95 Mulberry
Pilling Ralph, calico printer, Beach ab Warren
Pilling Samuel, dry goods, 15 Bank, h 87 New
PINCHIN WILLIAM, manuf. military & fancy art., Jacoby, h Filbert ab Sch 7th
Pincot Samuel, pianomr., Lewis ab Poplar
Pincus Theodore, mer., 100 High, h 146 S 2d
Pinder Perry, carp., 50 Charlotte
Pindett Robt., chairmr., Baker's ct

Pine Charles, jeweller, 4 Rule's ct
Pine Samuel, back 45 Cherry
Piner Isaac, lab., Stevenson's ct
Pinkerton James, painter, 83 R road
Pinkerton Matthew, weaver, George E Sch 6th
Pinkerton Samuel, lab., Pearl ab Sch 8th
Pinknard Wm., cabmr., 3 Union ct
Pinney George, coal agt., 10th ab Christian
Pintard C. Mad., milliner, 74 S 5th
Pintard James H., mer., 74 S 5th
Pinto Thos. J., cigar mr., N W Front & Green
Pinyard Ann, rear 38 St John
Piolet George, umbrellamr., 458 N 4th
Piper Augustus, carp., Pike
Piper Charles, mer., 28 New Market
Piper Elizabeth, c Diamond & Juniper
Piper Elizabeth, wid., 23 Green
Piper George J., tailor, Beach ab Maiden (K)
Piper Jas., lab., 6 Harrison's ct (K)
Piper John, vict., 9th bel Poplar
Piper John, jr., vict., 135 Locust, h Powell ab Vineyard
Piper Wm. trader, 328 N Front
Pippitt Mary, confectioner, 164 S 3d
Piquet Joseph, jeweller, 29 Beck (S)
Pisanell Francis, barber, 243 S 4th
Pister John, ship carp., Dean ab Bedford
Pitfield Benjamin H., mer., 14 S 2nd
Pitfield Robert L., President N L Bank, h 317 N 6th
Pitfield Wm. F., clerk, 18 New
Pitman Barzilla, blacksmith, Elizabeth above Poplar
Pitman James, spinner, Harmstead n Sch 2d
Pitman Wm. D., plasterer, 52 Christian
Pitt Elizabeth, wid., Clinton ab Brown (S G)
Pitt Samuel, Steel's ct
Pitt Thomas H., watchman, Budden's al
Pitt Wm., capt. 510 N Front
Pittinos Ann Maria, shop, Christian & Flower
Pittman A M., machinist, 5 Sp Garden Retreat
Pittman Jacob, bricklayer, Parrish bel 7th
Pitts Mark, clothes, 108 N 2d h Linden near Sch 6th
Place John A., dry goods, 42 S 8th
Planck George, cooper, 277 N Front
Planck John, cooper, 277 N Front
Plankinton Joseph, h Franklin bel Green
Plankinton Robbins, mer. 36 N 2nd, h 250 N 7th
Plant John B. engineer, Church ab Prime
Planton John S. cabinetmr. N E Plum & George
Plantou Gustavus A., dentist, 142 Spruce
Plate C. F., merchant, 29 Church al
Platt Catharine, 20 Sergeant
Platt Clayton T. mer. 17 N Whfs. h 343 Chestnut
Platt Franklin, mer., 43 N Water, h 126 Spruce
Platt George, weaver, Olive bel Broad
Platt Henry, stone cut., Vineyard (F V)
Platt Henry, dry goods, N W 7th and Green
PLATT, HOLLINGSHEAD & CO., grocers, 43 N Water
Platt John, weaver, Hanover bel West (K)
Platt Sarah, 28 Girard

Platt Theophilus, cordw. Vienna bel Franklin (Kensington)

Platt William, merchant, 17 N Wharves, h 343 Chestnut

Platt William, mariner, 1 Plynlimmon pl

Platt Wm. & Son, mers., 17 N wharves

Platz Philip, lab., 4 Linden ct

Pleasants Charles G. Rev. Sch 6th bel Walnut

Pleasants Henry, M. D., Washington (W P)

Pleasants I. P., stock & exchange broker, 46½ Walnut, h Walnut ab Broad

Pleasants Joseph, mer. 14 Chestnut, h 31 S 13th

Pleasants M. T. Mrs., widow of Joseph, 31 S 13th

Pleasants Peter, cordw., Pearl ab 13th

Pleasants Samuel, gent., Washington (W P)

Pleasants Samuel, com. mer., 13 Walnut, h 31 S 13th

Pleasants Wm., broker, 75 Dock

Pleasonton A. J., att'y and coun., 10 Portico sq

Pleis Catharine wid. of Matthias, dry goods, 530 N 2d

Pleis C. tailor, Almira pl

Pleis Frederick L. baker, 343 S 4th

Pleis Jacob F. stovemr., 97 N 2d

Pleis John M., druggist, S W 3d and Poplar

Plews John, tinsmith, Littleboy's ct

Plish Andrew, cordw., Poplar ab 5th

Plitt Catharine, b. h., Cherry bel 11th

Plitt Geo., clerk U S Circuit Court, State House

Plotts George, blacksm., Federal ab Front

Plowman Thomas L., publisher, 184 N 9th

Pluck Charles, hay dealer, Elizabeth bel Poplar

Pluck Peter, hay dealer, Elizabeth ab Parrish

Plucker Jacob J., wheelwright, 13th ab Poplar

Plum Jacob B. chair maker, 11 Tamarind

Plum Peter, brickmr., 39 W Cedar

Plum Susanna, Elizabeth ab Poplar

Plumbe, photographist, 136 and 142 Chestnut

Plumby G. W. & Co., paper boxmrs., 54 Chestnut

Plumer Nath'l D., boot and shoe manuf., 172½ High, h 179 Wood

Plumley John, 126 Callowhill

Plumley Nathan, blacksm. Rugan ab Callowhill

Plummer Charles H. boot and shoe manuf. 6 N 5th, h Marshall bel Brown

Plummer Everett H., boots and shoes, 77½ High, 92 S Front

Plummer Frederick Elder, Shippen bel Vernon

Plummer John, 177 N Front

Plummer Mary, 4 Comptroller

Plumstead Mary, 24 Girard

Plunket Alex., shoemaker, 281 S 3d

Plunket Thomas, carp., Poplar bel Broad

Plunket William, stone mason, Ann ab Powell (F V)

Plunkett Mary, Sch 6th bel High

Plunkett Mary, starcher, 18 S 10th

Plunkett Mary, conf., 21 F. road (K)

Plunkett Patrick, weaver, 7th bel Christian

Plunkett Thomas, weaver, Christian and 8th

Plympton Charles, mer., 177½ High

Plympton Shepherd, mer., 177½ High

Plympton S. & Co., straw goods, 177½ High

Podesta John, conf., 8 Chancery lane

Poe Geo. H., cordw., Locust n Sch 3rd

Pogue & Trevor jr., cotton spinners, 10 Branch

Pogue William, grocer, 6th & Fitzwater

POH LUDWIG, tavern, 3d and Coates

Pohl Henry, confect. and fruiterer, 8 Sch. av

Pohl Paul, com. mer., 39 S Wharves, h 86 S 5th

Poiner Thos. F., chair ornamenter, Wharton ab 4th

Point Joshua M., chairmr., Poplar and Marshall

Pointe V. Mrs., b. h., 73 S 6th

Pointer Nathan, clothier, 95 S 2d, h 13 Elizabeth

Pointer Wm., cordw., 6 Swanson

Pointer Wm. porter, Russell n Fitzwater

Pole Edward, machinist, 26 Hazel

Pole I. F. V., carp., 32 Lebanon

Polis George S., chair manuf., 127 Cedar

Polis Rachel, 178 Queen

Polk Aaron, teacher, 23 Rose alley

Polk Ann L., gentw., 40 S 13th

Polk Levin, lab., 11th ab Lombard

Polk Margaret, Parrish ab 11th

Polk Robert, laborer, Melon & 13th

Polk Tamer, washer, Brown bel 10th

Pollard John, cordw., h Carpenter bel 5th

Pollard Joseph, clerk, 106 E Spruce

Pollett David, grocer, 293 S 10th

Pollett James, hatter, 6 Lodge pl

Polley John, skindresser, Duke bel F road

Pollin Margaret, gentw., 215 S 9th

Pollitt James, spinner, 127 G T road

Pollock Chas., dealer, 417 N 4th

Pollock David, collier, Filbert E of Sch. 7th

Pollock David H., ladies' shoem., 232 Callowhill

Pollock Edward, weaver, Sch 5th n Cedar

Pollock George, weaver, 69 F. road (K)

Pollock Hyman, jeweller, e 7th & Buttonwood

Pollock James, weav., 4 N 7th, h 121 N Juniper

Pollock James, porter, Adams bel 13th

Pollock John, carp., Sch 8th & Vine

Pollock John, watchman, 36 W Cedar

Pollock John, carrier, 10th ab Washington

Pollock Joseph, drayman, Sch. 8th bel Sassafras.

Pollock Joseph, carpt. weaver, Coates n 9th

Pollock J. R., publisher, 205 Chestnut, h George ab Broad

Pollock Robert, lab., 6 Myers' ct

POLLOCK ROBERT & CO., dry goods, 10 S 2d

Pollock Sarah, Sch. 5th and Chestnut

Pollock Thomas lab., Lombard ab Sch 8th

Pollock Wm., tailor, 24 Tammany

Pollock Wm., lab., Penn ab Poplar (K)

Polly Andrew, ostler, Lewis n Sch. 5th

Poltz F. W., clerk, 521 S Front

Pomeroy & Co., bookbinders, 21 St. James

Pomeroy Elizabeth, 7 Franklin row (S G)

Pomeroy George, lab., ab Sch. 8th

Pomeroy Geo. W., mer., 12 N Water

Pomeroy James Y., bookbinder, 21 St. James, h 24 Chatham

Pomeroy John H., bonnet presser, 137 S 6th

Pomeroy Wm., plasterer, Clay av (K)

Pomeroy Wm., tinman, Orchard ab Rrawle
Pomroy Israel T., cordwainer, N 4th n George
Pomroy Valentine, tinsm., 27 High, h Lagrange place
Pond Daniel, 12 Franklin pl
Pond Jos., fancy goods, 10 Commerce, h 341 N 6th
Ponder John, mer., 7 N 2d
Ponder Thomas, printer, 232 Wood
Pontius Andrew, tailor, Greenwood pl
Pontzler Lewis S. lab. rear 398 N 4th
Pool Hiram, machinist, Carroll bel 13th
Pool James, brass founder, Catharine ab 10th
Poole Caroline, 35 Almond
Poole John, grocer, S W 2d and Dock
Poole Loudon, skindresser, Mechanic ab George
Poole Thomas, suspender mr., N E 11th and Shippen
Poole Thomas, silver plater, 9 Mineral pl
Poole Wm. E. dry goods, 13th bel Spruce
Pope Betsy, tavern, S W Swanson & Cedar
Pope George, cooper, Pleasant bel 11th
Pope Mora, spice factor, 481 S Front
Pope Saml., shoemr., Shackamaxon n Bedford
Poppal Chas., provision, S W 8th and Cherry
Porter Alfred, stage driver, 42 Strawberry
Porter Archibald, U. S. mint, h 114 N Juniper
Porter Benj., boot fitter, rear 143 Franklin
Porter Brewster H., Shackamaxon n Bedford
Porter Charles E., clerk, 25 Pratt
Porter Charles H., bricklayer, 3 Hansell's ct
Porter Daniel, gauger and cooper, 12 Pine, h 163 S Front
Porter Eleanor, 3 Mentzer's ct
Porter Ellen, 15 N Willow
Porter Elizabeth, 225 N 10th
PORTER & ENGLISH, grocers, 3 Mulberry
Porter Frederick W., sec'y Am. S. S. Union, 146 & h 309 Chestnut
Porter Geo. W., carp., 13 Bank, h 87 Coates.
Porter Henry, lab., rear 128 N 5th
Porter Henry S., dent., 159 Queen, h 200 S 10th
Porter Herschel S. Rev., 139 N 7th
Porter Hester, rear 374 S Front
Porter Isaac, tinner, 375 N 2d
Porter James, tailor, 94 N 11th
Porter James, cedar cooper, 114 Washington av
Porter James, music printer, Crockett's ct, h 76 Lombard
Porter James, lab., Bedford ab 12th
Porter James, porter, rear 112 Cherry
Porter Jane, 87 N 9th
Porter Jesse R., oysterman, 1 Monmouth ct
Porter John, blacksmith, 263 Catharine.
Porter John, shoemr., 12 Magnolia
Porter John, dry goods, 55 N 8th, h 5 Fayette
Porter Letitia, b. h., 120 S 4th
Porter Matthew, lab., R road ab George (F V)
Porter M. A., Mrs., dealer, 10 Fayette
Porter, Nicholas, lab., Budd n Juniper
Porter Robt., blacksmith, 318 S 3d
Porter Robt., tailor, Lisle and Shippen
Porter Robt. G., saddler, Jefferson n Sch. 8th
Porter Robt. R., U S Mint, h Spring street

Porter R. C., tinsmith, 198 N 2d
Porter R. G., grocer, 3 Mulberry, h 406 N 6th
Porter Samuel, 437 Walnut
Porter Saml., blacksm., 13 Fayette, h 27 N 10th
Porter Samuel H. druggist, 30 N 12th
Porter Susan, rear Olive bel 13th
Porter Wm., watchman, R road bel Ann (F V)
Porter Wm., tavern, N E 5th and Plum
PORTER WILLIAM A., att'y and coun., 151 Walnut ab 6th
Porter Wm. G., commission mer, 43 S Water, h Lombard n 12th
Porter W. G., mer., 508 Chestnut
Porterfield Wm., cordw., Lebanon ab Christian
Porteus Jas. A., chemical works, 581 N Front, h 308 Mulberry
Posey Eleanor R., milliner, 48 Mulberry
Posnett Leonard, painter, 226 N 6th
Post Ann, dry goods, 372 S 3d
Post Henry, gas works, Sp. Garden ab 10th
Post Isaac M., hatter, Elizabeth ab Poplar
Post John, combmr. Otter bel G T road
Post & Miller, hats & caps, 202 N 2d
Post Wm. F., bookbinder, 42 N 4th
Postly Charles, 53 N 8th
Pote Charles, fisherman, Wood bel Duke (K)
Pote Christian, glass blower, Wood ab Queen
Pote Fanny, gentw., Wood ab Queen
Pote George, tavern, Queen ab Wood (K)
Pote Henry M. fisherman, Wood ab Queen (K)
Pote Henry P., fisherman, Vienna above Queen,
Pote Jacob C. fisherm., Wood bel Franklin (K)
Pote John P., fisherman, Queen n Wood (K)
Pote Mary, Wood ab Queen (K)
Pote Matthias M., fisherman, Wood ab Queen
Pote Matthias M., shipwright, Wood ab Queen
Pote Peter M. fisherman, Wood ab Queen (K)
Pote Saml., fisherman, Franklin bel Palmer (K)
Pote Wm., fisherman, Vienna bel Duke (K)
Potsdamer & Rosenbaum, caps & furs, 24 N 3d
Potsdamer T., cap mr., 24 N 3d, h 40 Prune
Potter Alonzo, Bishop of Pa., Broad bel Spruce
Potter Andrew R., tailor, Perry ab Sassafras
Potter & Carmichael, oilcloth manuf., 568 N 3d
Potter Edmund, chair painter, rear 129 Green
Potter George, waiter, 255 Walnut
Potter Harriet, gentw., 156 S 9th
Potter Harris, porter, 237 Lombard
Potter Jacob, 18 John (S)
Potter James, lab., Philip ab Jefferson (K)
Potter John, tobacconist, 398 S 2d
Potter John, mer., 16 S Front, h 156 S 9th
Potter John H. dentist, 109 S 9th
Potter Joseph, carp., 3 Blackberry alley
Potter Matthias R., furniture car, M. road bel Carpenter
Potter Matthias S., Western place
Potter, McKeever & Co., mers., 39 N Wharves
Potter Phineas, Ven. blind maker, 77 N 6th
Potter Robt., chandler, Lombard ab 12th
Potter Robert S. painter and glaz., Pine n 12th, h Lombard n Juniper
Potter R. B., mer., 116 High, h 19 Montgomery square
Potter Sarah, 267 Cherry

Potter Thomas, oil cloth manuf., 3d bel George h 558 N 3d

Potter Thomas E., broker, 25 Bank, h Sch 6th bel Mulberry

Potter Thomas G., spinner, Callowhill n Nxion

Potter Wm., oysterman, 76 George.

Potter Wm. shoemr. 3 Williamson's ct

Potter Wm. A., mer., 39 N wharves

Potts Benjamin B., bricklayer, 15 Perry

Potts Daniel, wheelwr., 85 Dillwyn

Potts David, weaver, Jefferson ab 2d

Potts D. & H. & Co., dry goods, 35 N 2d.

Potts Edward D., merchant, 67 N Water, h 161 N 4th

Potts George, drayman, Perry ab Franklin (K)

Potts Howard N., atty. & coun., N E 7th and S Garden, h 6th ab Parrish

Potts Ignatius, clerk, 85 Dillwyn

Potts Isaac, wheelwright, 85 Dillwyn (K)

Potts Isaac W., mer., 21 S Front, h Locust ab Broad

Potts James, gauger and cooper, 99 N Front & 96 N. Water, h 107 N Front

Potts James H., vict., Vernon and 11th

Potts John, segarmr., Garden bel Willow

Potts John, butcher, Greenwich bel 2d

Potts John, baker, rear 52 Christian

Potts Joseph, grocer, S W 6th and Spruce

Potts Joseph, mer., 35, and h 517 N 2d

Potts & Lewis, fancy goods, 132 S 10th

Potts, Linn, & Harris, druggists, 213½ High

Potts L. M., white and blacksmith, 9th & Vine, h Poplar bel Broad

Potts Mary, gentw., rear 43 Coates

Potts Moses, lab., 20 M'Duffie

Potts Nathaniel, mer., 30 N Water, h 26 N 7th

Potts Nathan R., atty & coun., N E 7th & Spring Garden, h 304 N 6th

Potts Philip, tailor, 10th & Coates

Potts Richard J., bricklayer, Sch 8th bel Callowhill

Potts Robt. B. mer., 213½ High, h Spruce n Broad

Potts Samuel, acct., 57 S 11th

Potts Thomas J. mer., 151 N 2d, h 73 Race

Potts Wm., vict., Wharton ab 2d

Potts William B., flour mer., 67 N Water, h 189 N 6th

Potts Wm. B. & Co. flour and grain, 67 N Water & 34 N wharves

Potts William F., iron, 457 & 461 High, h S3 Palmyra sq

Potts William L. & Son, iron, 151 N 2nd, h 18 Sassafras

Potts & Yocom, iron, N E 2d & Sassafras

Poulson Charles A., 172 S Front

Poulson Chas. A., jr., atty & coun., 93 S 3d, h 172 S Front

Poulson E., tailor, 475 S 2d

Poulson James, baker, 581 Race

Poulson John C., S E 2d and Union

Poulson John, 37 S 4th

Poulson John K. lab., 14 Kesler's al

Poulson Richard A., dry goods, 552 High

POULSON W. S., coal and real est. off., 4 Carpenter's ct, h 37 S 4th

Poulterer Saml., cordw., 199½ Callowhill

Poulterer Samuel, cordw., S 7th ab Catharine

Poulterer Stephen, 9 N 12th

Poultney Charles W. brewer, 10th & Filbert, h 249 Pine

Poulton Ambrose, salesman, Washington av bel Brown

Poulton Charles, cordw., Allen ab Shackamaxon (K)

Poulton James, carter, Front bel Phœnix (K)

Pouson Erastus, dry goods, N W 2d and Pine

Poutser Lewis, mason, 3 Thorn's ct

Pow Christian, tanner, Elk st

Powell Abraham, carpenter, 3 Wharton

Powell Anna, 38 Jacoby

Powell Catharine, 323 Walnut

Powell Chas., carp., 28 Queen

Powell Elizabeth I., shop, 43 Green

Powell George, seaman, rear 129 Walnut

Powell George, tailor, 36 Nectarine

Powell George, wheelwr., Dean ab Bedford (K)

Powell George, cooper, 196 Front, h 250 S 5th

Powell George S., carp., 11 Wharton

Powell Henry, seaman, 38 Quince

Powell Howell, grocer, 14 Hamilton pl

Powell Isaac, 285 High

Powell Jacob, blacksmith, 6 Almond

Powell James, porter, 2 Lombard ct

Powell Jesse, oysterman, 155 Swanson

Powell John, bootmr., 81 S 5th

Powell John, lab., 46 Currant al

Powell John, tailor, 3 Mary st

Powell John A., cabinetmr., 274 Shippen

Powell John W., livery stable, 86 S 11th, h 323 Walnut

Powell Joseph, mahog. sawyer, Shield's ct

Powell Julia, 3 Farries' ct

Powell Margaret, rear 301 S 3d

Powell M. S., seeds, 23 High, h 39 Sassafras

Powell O. S. Rev., gen'l agent Philad. Sabbath Asso., 20 Pine

Powell Philip, clerk, 7 Diamond

Powell, Renshaw & Co., dry goods, 48 High

Powell Rhoda, nurse, 221 S Front

Powell Richard, carp., 1 Powell row

Powell Samuel, tinsmith, 8 High, h 206 S 2d

Powell Susan, 56 Currant al

Powell S. & Co., tinsmith, 8 High

Powell Thomas, waiter, Russell ab Fitzwater

Powell Thomas, biscuit baker, F road above Allen

Powell Thos., tailor, 199 Christian

Powell Wm., cordw., Pennell's ct (K)

Powell Wm., mer., 32 High

Powell Wm. H., mer., 48 High, h 165 N 9th

Powell Wm. M., druggist, 258 S 2d

Power Edwd., cabinetmr., 2 Boyle's ct

Power John F., shoemaker, 96 Spruce.

Power Wm., clerk, Queen bel Hanover (K)

Powers Ann, 8 Madison av

Powers John, omnibus proprietor Elm's ct

Powers Martin, porter, 20 Cypress

Powers Michael, carp., 2 Ewing's ct

Powers Thomas, plumber, 500 N 2d

Powers Thomas, lab., Little Pine

Powers Thomas H., manuf. chemist, Parrish and 9th, h 101 Franklin (S G)
Powers Wm., driver, Pearl ab Nixon
Poynter Manlove H., tailor, 2 Beck pl
Prader Anthony, gardener, P road bel Catharine
Prader Jos., blacksm., 6th bel Catharine
Pragheimer Samuel, grocer, 146 N Front
Prahl Samuel, carp., 177 G T road (K)
Prakett Samuel B., painter, 159 N 3d, h New Crown bel Green
Prall Edwd., 278 Sassafras
Prat Louisa, dry goods, 296 Chestnut
Pratt David, carp., 290 Sassafras, h Brown bel 10th
Pratt D T., mer., 80 High, h 128 Pine
Pratt Erasmus C. importer, 28 Bank, h 10th n Cedar
Pratt George, grocer, S W Buttonwood and R road
Pratt Henry, lab., 85 German
Pratt Thomas, gent., 147 N 10th
Prattis Belinda, Webb's al
Prattis Hannah, 9 Lombard row
Praul Jonathan, varnisher, Federal ab 5th
Pray Chas., tavern, Logan & Sp Garden
Prayer Lewis, machinist, Bond's ct (N L)
Preall Andw., printer, rear 156 Queen
Preall Jas., bootmr., 8 Little Pine
Prendavill Maurice, tailor, Baker ab 7th
Prenot Chas., watch sp. mr., Elmslie's al
Prentice Geo. G., 230 Noble
Prentice George W., ornamental painter, 18 Lagrange, h 4 Whitaker's ct.
Prentiss A. B. mer., Barker n Sch 8th
Prentiss A. B., mer., N E Front and Chestnut, h Sch 5th n High
Prentiss & Brother, drugs & dye stuffs, N E Front & Chestnut
Prentiss E. F. mer., N E Front & Chestnut, h 17 S Sch 7th
Prentiss John, broker, 246 S 3d
Prentiss John, Jr., broker, S E 4th & Cedar
Prentzell Samuel D., com. mer., 402 High
Prentzell S. D. & Co., flour and grain, 402 High
Preole Geo., cordw., Bickham's ct
Preole John, bootmr., M'Closkey's ct
Prescott David W., mer., 57 N whfs., h 8th ab Cedar
Prescott Thos., lab., Cherry n Franklin (K)
Presho Isaac, feed store, Nectarine ab 10th
Press George, labourer, 45 Currant al
Press Wm., blind cutler, Olive bel 10th
Presser Jacob, baker, N E 7th and Lombard
Presser Philip, clothes, Maiden and F road
Presser V., brass turner, 3 Seneca ct
Pressler Henry, cooper, Hanover bel F road (K)
Pressler Jos., oak cooper, Apple bel Franklin
Prester Joseph, painter, Hanover ab Bedford(K)
Preston Eliza, Sch 2d bel Wood
Preston James, weaver, Smith's ct
Preston Jane, 2 S Penn sq
Preston Jefferson, tobacconist, 137 Carpenter
Preston John, shoemr., 18 Greswold's al
Preston J., eating-house, 311 E Pine
Preston Mary, Carlton bel Sch 2d

Preston Wm. B., refectory, 216 R road
Preston Wm. R., gent., 372 Mulberry
Preston Wm. T. & Co., publishers, 98 N 6th
Preswick Mary, 74 S 3d
Prettyman Jacob, shoemr., Horstman's ct
Prettyman Mary, Crabb & Shippen
Prettyman Robert, carp., 2 Hamilton's ct
PREUSS & MAENNEL, import's, 24 Church al
Prevost A. M., broker, 75 Dock, h 357 Spruce
Prevost Francis M., 148 Catharine
Prevost S. M., M. D., 357 Spruce
Price Alicea, teacher, 306 Mulberry
Price Benj., cordw., rear 142 St John
Price Benj., gent., 9th bel Catharine
Price Benj. C., cordwr., Church bel Christian
Price Callender, mer., 151 High
PRICE ELI K., att'y & coun., 309 Mulberry
Price Ellen, gentw., Ham. Vil.
Price Ferris, gent., 96 S 12th
Price George R., plasterer, 6 Hydes' ct
Price & Green, dry goods, 42 Bank
Price Henry, bricklr., George bet Sch 2d & 3d
Price Henry, machinist, 80 Locust
Price Hubert, clerk, 388 S 3d
Price Isaac, 161 S 9th
Price Isaac C., coal, 12th & Willow, h R road ab Spring Garden
Price Jacob, carp., 11th ab Shippen
Price James, brickmr., Poplar n Broad (M)
Price James, vict., Palmer n F road
Price James E., oyster house, Front & Dock
Price John, paper hanger, 4 Maiden (K)
Price John, mariner, Simmon's ct
Price John, mariner, 15 Beck (S)
Price John B., 10th bel Poplar
Price John H., blacksm., rear Olive bel Broad
Price John P., ship smith, 176 Swanson, h S Union
Price Joseph, mer., 133 High, h 14 N 11th
Price Joseph, 1 Tammany ab 4th
Price Joseph, seaman, 119 E Calhoun
Price Joshua L. mer., 12 N Front, h 41 N 5th
Price Josiah, waterman, Reed bel Front
Price Kirk J., shoes, 108 N 3d, h 216 N 7th
Price Leander, painter, 57 Charlotte
Price Lewis, chairmr., 264 St John
Price Marg., gentw., 388 S 3d
Price Margery, 140 N 10th
Price Mary, dry goods, 5 N 2d
Price Nathan, porter, Carpenter ab 6th
PRICE, NEWLIN & CO., hardware, 151 High
Price Philip, printer, 66 and h 68 Lombard
Price Philip M. & Co., surveyors & con., Sp Garden ab 11th
Price Philip M., survr, Spring Garden ab 11th
Price P. & Co., booksellers, 152 Chestnut
Price Rebecca, milliner, 30 Lombard
Price Reynolds, lab., Pearl ab 13th
Price Richard, merchant, 133 High, h 185 Mulberry
Price Robt., printer, York pl
Price Samuel, confectioner, 266 Mulberry
Price Samuel, pilot, Bevan's ct
Price Samuel, ship joiner, 11 Allen st
Price Saml., bricklr., 11th ab Shippen

Price Sarah, Sch 6th c St Joseph's av
Price & Shaw, oyster house, S E 3d & Chestnut
Price Susan, Alice ct
Price S. A., gentw., 145 S 9th
Price Thos, chairmaker, 267 St John, h 40 New Market
Price Thos. B., mer., 34 N 2d
Price Thos. W., book bind., 12 S 4th, h 10 St John
Price Timothy, stone mason, Front n Montgomery (K)
Price Wm., lastmaker, 417 N Front
Price Wm., ship joiner, 19 Allen (K)
Price Wm., pilot, 34 John
Price Wm., carp., 275 S Front
Price Wm., bootmr., 189 S 6th
Price Wm., cordw., Carpenter bel 9th
Price Wm., M. D., 276 Mulberry
Price Wm. H., waterman, 76 Catharine
Price Wm. S., atty. & coun., S E 5th & Library, h Pine n 7th
Price Wilson, inspector, Almira pl
Prichard Alex., carp., 24 Strawberry
Prichett Edith, gentw., 9th & Spruce
Prichett Foster, salesman, 24 Magnolia
Prichett Gideon, shop, 8th & Nectarine
Prichett Jas., stovemr., 227 S 3d
Prichett John, chairmr., Garretson's row
Prichett John, gent., 98 S 8th
Prichett John S. blacksmith, 495 Vine
Prichett Joshua, lab., 2 Elizabeth (N L)
Prichett Thomas, hides and leather, 85 S 2d, h 100 S 8th
Prichett William, carter, N E 2d and Wharton
Prichett Wm. P., bricklayer, N W Wheat and Wharton
Priddee Thomas, ropemr., 351 S 5th
Priest Benjamin, blacksmith, 1 Fries' ct
Priest Charles, engineer, 4 Fries' ct
Priest George, tailor, 37 N 4th ab Cherry
Priest Isaac, blacksmith, Jackson ab Adams
Priest John, bootbinder, Baker ab 7th
Priest Sarah, 1 Braceland's ct
Priester Henry C., tailor, Clinton ab Franklin
Priestly Alexander, mer. 33 Commerce
Priestly Robert, weav. rear Master bel Hancock
Priestly Samuel, paper mer., 62 O Y road
Prifold John P. jr., drayman, 346 N 5th
Prifold John P., drayman, 348 O Y road
Priman Frederick, lab., Amber ab Phoenix (K)
Primrose J. S., clothing st., 163 S 2d, h Queen bel 4th
Primrose Violet, S W 10th and Cedar
PRIMROSE WM., real est. broker, 48 S 6th, h 15 Logan sq
Primrose Wm. F. & Co., trunkmr., 92 High ab 3rd
Prince Abm., porter, Biddle's al
Prince H., salesman, 379 Callowhill
Prince Isaac, Arch n Sch 8th
Prince Jacob, carpenter, Trinity pl
Prine Charles, sparmr. Marion bel 2d
Pringle J. S., mer., 6 Commerce, h Filbert W Sch 7th
Pringle Mary, 212 Pine

Pringle Wm., 212 Pine
Prior John, cabinet mr., 2 Wells' row
Pritchett A. H., bootmr., Garden and Callowhill
Pritchett Jas., wharf builder, Beach ab Shackamaxon (K)
Pritchett Lorenzo, blacksmith, Hanover below Franklin (K)
Pritchett Wm. H. L., Noble bel Garden
Pritner Mary, widow, 111 St John
Prizer Enos, furniture car, R road ab 13th
Prizer Francis G. feed, 13th bel Wallace
Prizer & Hum.cel, flour & feed, R road above Green
PRIZER JEHU B., tavern, R road bel Broad
Prizer Peter, mason, 13th bel Wallace
Probasco John, carp., Freeman's ct
Probasco William G., carpenter, 316 High
Procter Wm., druggist, S W 9th and Lombard
Proctor James H., U. S. N., Shippen ab 13th
Proctor John, porter, 13th bel Brinton
Proctor Joseph, lab. Sch 4th n High
Proctor L. B., machinist, 2 Kelly's av
Proctor Walter, shoe mr., 17 Elizabeth
Proctor Wm., ice cream 38 N 7th
Prodler Margaret, Queen ab Cherry (K)
Prosser James, oysterhouse, 274 High
Prosser Wm., shoes, 224 S 2d
Proud Joseph, lab. rear Carpenter ab 8th
PROUTY DAVID O., seed store, 194½ High h 276 N 8th
Provins Andrew, sup. pow. looms, 5 M'Duffie
Provost Andrew, carter, G T road ab 6th (K)
Prowattain E., brushes, 155 High, h 121 Chestnut
Pruitt Walter, carter, 40 Currant al
Prutzman August, locksmith, 31 & 33 Strawberry
Pryor Amelia, Brown ab 8th
Pryor D. B. 3 Pemberton al
Pryor Edmund, druggist, 371 N Front
Pryor Elijah, broker, 123 O Y road
Pryor George, tinsmith, 10 Boyd's av
Pryor Gilbert, acct. 13 Wallace
Pryor John, cabtmr., 8th bel Green
Pryor Patrick, porter, rear 115 Sassafras
Pryor Patrick, tavern, 157 S Front
Pryor Richard, real est. brok., 132 Buttonwood
Pryor Thomas E., druggist, N E 2d and Poplar
Psotta Charles, brewery, 56 New
Psotta Christian, shop, Wood & Garden
Psotta Wm., tavern, 104 Callowhill
Pue Hugh, gent., 304 S 6th
Pue Hugh A, dry goods, 116 W High
Pue Thomas, soap boiler, Stanley ab 3d
Pugh Benj., auger mr., Washington (W P)
Pugh Charles, machinist, Rihl's ct (N L)
Pugh Charles J., vict., Powell bel Vineyard (F V)
Pugh Isaac, paper hangings, 118 Chestnut, h 70 Marshall
Pugh Isaac & Co., paper hang., 118 Chestnut
Pugh James, lab., Bache
Pugh John M., M. D., Lancaster Pike (W P)
Pugh Jonathan, silverplater, 71½ N 6th, h Lewis ab Poplar

Pugh Jonathan, tailor, Parrish bel Elizabeth
Pugh Margaret, 20 Gebbard
Pugh Samuel, paper hanger, 6th & Willow
Pugh Samuel, bar-tender, Mechanic
Pugh William, morocco dresser, 6 Rihl's ct
Pugh Wm., shoemr., Locust W Sch 4th
Pughe Hugh, white leather and skiver manuf., Willow bel 2d
Pugsley Susannah, 2 Sansom
Pullin Elisha, wheelwright, N road bel Christian
Pullinger Collin W., shop, George ab 10th
Pulte C. A., atty and coun., 119 Race
Purdon Alexander, lab., 7 Bickham ab Sch. 8th
Purdon Charles, paver, 29 Quince
Purdon Harriet, 74 Christian
Purdy Emma, 204 Green
Purdy George, victualler, Greenwich ab 2d
Purkit Julia, Carroll ab 12th
Purllz John, clerk, 15 Dock, h 37 Almond
Purnell Charles, coachman, Salem al
Purnell Daniel, sawyer, Carpenter ab 8th
Purnell Edward, Bedford ab 7th
Purnell Hiram, manuf., Wood bel Sch 2d
Purnell Joshua, carter, 8 Twelve foot al
Purnell Josiah, waiter, 226 E Lombard
Purnell Roda, washer, Smith's ct
Purnell Stephen, lab. Taylor's ct
Purnell Thos., porter, Currant al ab Locust
Purnell William M., tailor, 92 German
Purnell Z. J., barber, 52½ Carpenter (C) h 9th bel Christian
Purple Isabella, tavern, 355 N Front
Purple Susan, 23 Beaver (K)
Pursell John, shoemr., 22 Hurst
Pursley George, tailor, 5 Howard's ct
PURVES ALEX., iron dealer, N W Front & Cedar, h 57 Mead
Purves Hugh, stove manuf., S E 2d and Shippen, h 21 German
Purves Jacob, porter, Portland la
Purves Lydia, 177 S 7th
Purves Mary, Washington ct
Purvis Wm. cordw. rear 21 Castle
Purves Wm., 179 S 7th
Pusey Alex., coachman, 7 Emeline
Pusey Elwood T. mer. 154 High
Pusey Joshua, oyster house, S W 6th & Cherry
Pusey Susan, dry goods, 93 N 5th
Putnam Saml. P., N W 3d & Chestnut, ab stairs
Pye Joseph, blacksmith, 176 S 11th
Pyfer Wm. carver, 18 Library, h 3 Willow ct
Pyle Adley, Hay's ct (K)
Pyle Ann, baker, 15 Mulberry
Pyle Emma, trimmings, 208 Green
Pyle Jacob, ladies' shoemr., Hutchinson ab Poplar
Pyle Joseph, cordw., Washington av below Brown
Pyle Mary A., b h., 76 S 4th
Pyle Robert C. tailor, Washington ab 4th

Quaas John M., cabinetmr., 46 Plum
Quail John H., daguerreotype, 89 N 5th
Quan Wm., lab., Callowhill ab Sch 6th
Quandrill William., tobacco spinner, 133 Green
Quantin Alphonzo, upholsterer, 292 Chestnut
Quantin Henry, police of., 21 Pratt st
QUANTIN B & & LUTZ, upholsters., 292 Chestnut
Quantrell William, grocer, c Vineyard and Division (F V)
Quarrne F., engraver, 198 S 3d
Quayle Ann, dressmr., 16 S 12th
Quear Saml., cordw., rear 464 N 2d
Queen Jas., lab., rear 10th ab Carpenter
Queen James, lithographer, 3rd ab Federal
Queen Jane, Steel's ct
Queen John A. printer, 142 Catharine
Queen J. W., optician, 48 Chestnut
Queen Wm., blacksm., 252
Quein George, grocer, N E 13th and Vine h 27 Montgomery
Quereau Margaret, shop, Charles & Willow
Quervelle Anthony G., cabinet mr., 126 S 2d
Quick Charles, capmr., 19 Beck pl
Quick George, butcher, Palmer n F Road
Quick Peter S., bricklayer, Rex's ct
Quicksall Hannah, gentw., 35 German
Quicksall Henry, cordw'r., rear 14 Mechanic (N L)
Quicksall Jacob H., oysters, 532 N 2d
Quicksall John R., painter, rear 35 German
Quicksall Jos., 532 N 2d (K)
Quicksall Joseph, clerk, Eyre's ct (K)
Quig Henry, copper plate printer, 9 George, h 17 S Garden
Quig James, hatter, 9 Coombs' al
Quig Margaret, Duke n Palmer (K)
Quigg Henry, bricklayer, Sch 7th ab Race
Quigg Hugh, clothes, 37 Swanson
Quigg Isaiah, shoe store, 457 N 2d
Quigg Robert, currier, 11th & Olive
Quigg Robert, weaver, 3d ab Franklin (K)
Quigg Thomas, tailor, 205 N Front & 200 N. Water, h N E 7th & Vine
Quigg Thos., 243 Vine
Quigley Barney, lab. 202 Shippen
Quigley Bernard, carter, 66 N 6th
Quigley Dominick, tavern, 455 High
Quigley Edward, storekeeper, 29 S Sch 6th
Quigley Isabella, shop, 6th bel Cedar
Quigley James, grocer, 6th and Shippen
Quigley Josiah, Rev., 3d ab Federal
Quigley Patrick, lab., James n Sch 4th
Quigley Sarah, Barron
Quin John, lab., 305 N 5th
Quin Thos., wire worker, 16 N 6th
Quinan Thomas H. Rev., Catharine bel 7th
Quinbey Wm. P. carp., 16 Pleasant
Quinby Josiah, ice dealer, 312 N 2d
Quine Robert, grocer, S W Front and Paine

Quinn Charles B., tailor, S E Front and Dock, h 208 S 2d
Quinn Davis, b n, 118 N 9th
Quinn Edward, lab., Vaughn bel Walnut
Quinn Elizabeth, Sch 7th n Washington
Quinn Emily, 154 N 10th
Quinn Francis, shop, Perry & Phoenix (K)
Quinn Hannah, P road bel Washington
Quinn James, coachmr., 158 Sassafras h Noble ab O Y road
Quinn James, gardener, 110 N 13th
Quinn James, weaver, Murray W Sch 3d
Quinn John, porter, 10 Vaux's ct
Quinn John, lab., Locust n Sch 3d
Quinn John, pump mr., Church bel Christian
Quinn John, waiter, 6 Kenworthy's ct
Quinn John A., variety, 114 N 5th
Quinn John T., tailor, 11 Concord
Quinn Joseph, plasterer, 7th n Hallowell
Quinn Kennedy, carter, Federal ab 7th
Quinn Marg., Hammill's row (K)
Quinn Mary, spooler, rear 2d ab Master (K)
Quinn Matthew, gent., Cedar bel 12th
Quinn Michael, warper, Union ab Franklin (K)
Quinn Michael, dyer, 10 Cadwalader (K)
Quinn Michael, porter, 16 Vernon
Quinn Michael, turner, G T road ab Phoenix
Quinn Owen, 80 F road (K)
Quinn Patrick, weaver, 7 Philip
Quinn Patrick, tavern, c 10th and Pryor's ct
Quinn Rosanna, Phœnix ab 2d (K)
Quinn Terrence, lab., La Fayette ab 9th
Quinn Thomas, black and white smith, 34 Lebanon
Quinn Thomas, soap boiler, Brown bel 11th
Quinn William, tailor, S E Dock and Front, h 58 Penn
Quintin David S. tavern, F road & Manderson
Quinton Alexander, milkman, 133 Plum
Quinton Thomas, house painter, 266 S 6th
Quiot L. Eugene, upholsterer, 160 S 4th
Quire Peter cordw., Bedford & 12th
Quirk John, blacksmith, John's ct
Quirk Patrick, blacksmith, 7 John's ct
Quirk Wm. H., patternmr., 3 Madison

———

Raabe Peter, florist, 7th & Parrish
Rabe Justin, cabmr., 110 Walnut, h 61 Gaskill
Rabe & Laib, cabinet mrs. 110 Walnut
Race James, weaver, G T road ab 4th
Racine Frederick, 435 S 6th
Radbourne Elizabeth, dressmr., High n Sch 5th
Radcliff James, tavern, Shippen bel 11th
RADEMACHER C. L., bookseller and homœo-pathic druggist, 39 N 4th, opp Appletree al
Radford Benj., painter, 362 Vine
Radford Julia J., milliner, 33½ N 10th
Radford Thomas, Military Hall, Library
Raetzer C. G., chocolate, 288 St John
Rafferty Bernard, weaver, Baker's ct (K)
Rafferty Bernard, gratemr., 116 Cherry
Rafferty Elizabeth, rear 86 Locust
Rafferty James, weaver, Master bel 2d (K)
36

Rafferty James, tavern, 145 Cedar
Rafferty Patrick, lab. Beech & Spruce
Rafferty Patrick, coachman, Prospect al
Rafferty Patrick, blacksmith, 642 N 2d
Rafferty Peter, lab., Franklin ab 3d (K)
Rafferty Sarah, sempstress, rear 343 S 2d
Rafield Wm. W., tailor, 11th bel S Garden
Rafsnyder John, plasterer, George E Sch 6th
Ragan Daniel, fruiterer, 440 High
Ragan Dennis, lab. 4 Harmony
Ragan James, weaver, G T road bel Master (K)
Ragan John, lab. 145 Cherry
Ragan John, weaver, G T road bel Master (K)
Ragan Thomas, 10 Morgan's ct
Ragan Wm. cabinetmr. 17 S 7th
Ragen Charles, weaver, Mariner
Ragen Charles, weaver, Cadwalader ab Phoenix
Ragen Patrick, weaver, Philip ab Jefferson (K)
Ragen Timothy, warper, Philip ab Jefferson
Rager Maria, Brown's ct
Rahim John, cordw., rear 448 N 3d
Raiguel Abraham H., mer., 219 Coates
Raiguel Augustus H. mer., 177 High, h 49 Marshall
Raiguel Wm., mer., 128 N 3d, h 224 Mulberry
Raihl James, carter, Mechanic bel George
Raily John, lab., Ashton bel Walnut
Raimond F. X., baskets, 142 High, h Elizabeth ab Poplar
Rain Geo., engineer, 14 Mary
Rain Samuel, carp., 8 Carrolton sq
Rainbolt Catharine, Prospect pl
Rainbow Wm. weaver, rear Front bel Master
Rainer Mary, art. flowrmr. Callowhill ab Franklin
Rainier Wm., moroc. dress., Parrish ab 8th
Rains John, carp., Week's ct
Rainsburger Godfrey, shoemr. Adams n 13th
Raivley Edward, lab., Vine n Sch 5th
Rakert Andrew, cordw., Apple bel Franklin
Rakestraw Joseph, printer, 4th and Appletree al h 22 Chatham
Ralph Martin, lab., 1 Beach n Walnut
Ralston A. G., mer., 4 S Front
RALSTON A. & G. & Co., mers., 4 S Front
Ralston Gerard, mer., 4 S Front
Ralston Henry, 5 Boston Row
Ralston James, carpet weaver, Fairview B. Hill
Ralston James & Co., carpet weavers, Fairview B. Hill
Ralston Jane, weaver, Quince
Ralston John, lab., Carpenter ab 10th
Ralston Joseph, brickmr. Cedar ab Sch 5th
Ralston Mrs. Matthew C., 8 Clinton
Ralston Robt., stonecutter, 2 Boyd's av.
Ralston Robert, mer., 4 S Front, h n Laurel Hill Cem.
Ralston Robert, Church bel Christian
Ralston Thomas, watchman, 17 Jefferson
Ramage Adam, press maker, 18 Library, h 94 Lombard
Ramage John, shoemaker, 14 N 12th
Ramager Amer, plasterer, 2 Poplar pl
Rambler Peter, carp., Cherry & Gebhard
Rambo Danl., hatter, Carroll
Rambo David, painter, Catharine ab 7th

Rambo Israel, carter, Bedford n Elm (K)
Rambo Jacob, cooper, Hanover & Bedford (K)
Rambo Margaret, deal. Hanover ab Bedford (K)
Rambo M., 145 N 5th
Rambo Peter, post office, h Queen ab F rd (K)
Rambo Wm., blacksm. Hanover & Bedford (K)
Ramborger John J., sea capt., 311 Mulberry
Rammo Sarah, washer, Middle al
Ramsay James B., upholsterer, 253 Green
Ramsay John, weaver, 13th ab Fulton
Ramsay Joseph, carver, 196 N 10th
Ramsey Alex., book keep., Hamilton vil
Ramsey Ant., grocer, Cherry & Duke (K)
Ramsey Charles, grocer, Queen ab Shackamaxon
    h Cherry & Duke (K)
Ramsey Charles, upholsterer, Parrish ab 9th
Ramsey Hannah A., dressmr., rear 153 Green
Ramsey Henry, conf., rear 7 Sheppard's al
Ramsey Henry, cabinetmr., Pleasant bel 10th
Ramsey John, lab., 49 Quince
Ramsey John, carp., Parrish bel 6th
RAMSEY SAML. M., tavern, 218 High
Ramsey Thomas, shop., 238 Shippen
Ramsey Wm., shoemr., 3 Kenworthy ct
Ramsey Wm. Rev., Broad ab Cedar
Ramson John, stone mason, Hutchinson ab Poplar
Rand B. H., writing academy, 106 S 9th
Randall Ann, dry goods, 146 S 2d
Randall Benjamin, upholsterer, 379 High h 50
    Marshall
Randall Daniel, coachman, 55 Mechanic
Randall George, blacksmith, 10th bel Walnut, h
    12th ab Sp Garden
Randall Hannah, Sch 2d ab Vine
Randall Harriet, 182 S 13th
Randall Henry, mer., Washington sq. & Walnut
Randall Jacob, blacksm., 2d ab Reed
Randall John, painter, Leaper's al
Randall Joseph, gent., 103 S 9th
Randall Joseph C., mer., 9 N 5th, h 158 S 13th
Randall Joseph S., clerk West. Bank, h 10th
    bel Shippen
Randall Josiah, att'y and coun., office Washing-
    ton sq n Walnut, h c Walnut and Washing-
    ton sq
Randall Margaret, 115 Melon
Randall Susan, wid. of judge, 76 N 12th
Randall Samuel, teacher, 321 Walnut
Randall Sugden, waterman, 24 Almond
Randall W. S., mer., Washington sq & Walnut
Randolph Ann, 95 Franklin
Randolph Evan, com. mer., 21 S Front, h 93
    Franklin
Randolph E. T. & Co., iron foundry, 13 N Front
Randolph Garret, dry goods, 355 Coates
Randolph Geo., lumber mer., Sch 7th and High,
    h 491 Arch
Randolph Jacob, M. D., 123 S 4th
Randolph James, carp. Juniper bel Spruce
Randolph John, cabinetmr. Madison ct
Randolph John F., carp., Sch 8th ab Locust, h
    Perry and Lambert
Randolph Joseph, hatter, 4 Nonnater's al
Randolph Josiah, inst. mr., Rugan & Willow
Randolph Margaret, b h., 415 Mulberry

Randolph Nathaniel, lum. mer., S E 5th and
    Brown, h 241 Vine
Randolph Richard, 33 S 12th
Randolph William, chairmr., 7 Dock, h 41 Car-
    penter (S)
Randolph Wm., tanner, Mechanic n Culvert
Raney Henry, weaver, Perry bel Master (K)
Raney James, engineer, Fetter bel Harrison (K
Raney John, carter, Front bel Franklin (K)
Raney John, blacksm., Hope bel Master
Ranguett Sarah, confectioner, 108 S 3d
RANK, BROOKE & REPPLIER, dry goods,
    72 N 3d
Rank Joseph, mer., 72 N 3d, h 255 N 6th
RANKEN DAVID, tea warehouse, 73 Chestnut
Ranken George, cordwainer, 7 St. James
Ranken George W., jr. bookbinder, 7 Fayette
Ranken William, cabinetmaker, N E Callowhill
    & Sch 8th
Rankin Alexander, block maker, 61 N Water n
    Mulberry, h 10 New Market
Rankin John, lab., 40 Mechanic
Rankin Geo. H., cordw., Alden ab Poplar
Rankin John, carp. 18 Lagrange
Rankin William, painter, 494 Callowhill
Rankins Thomas, cordw., 6 Elizabeth (N L)
Ransley Ann, Federal ab 2d
Ransley Robt. H., gold beater, 62 Dock, h Fe-
    deral ab 2d
Ranthler David, baker, 435 N 4th
Ranton Sarah Ann, 149 N Juniper
RAPHAEL WM., importer, 26 Chestnut
Raphun Christopher C., hatter, 205 N 2nd
Rapin Eliza, Melon bel 10th
Rapp Gotlieb, baker, Shackamaxon ab Bedford
Rapp Joseph, young ladies' institute, 202 But-
    tonwood
Rapp Philip, fringemr., Culvert ab 3d
Rapp S., bone and brass turner, 175 St John
Rapp Wm. D., watchmaker, 258 Sassafras
Rapson Henry, 21 S 7th
Rapson John, oar maker, 20 Ellen (N L)
Rarbough Mary E., 149 N 5th
Raser Ann, b. h., 156 Cherry
Raser Thos. M., printer, 420 S 4th
Rasp George, lab., 34 W Cedar
Rasp Robt., brickmr., 54 W Cedar
Rass Christian, steel manuf., Franklin bel Pal-
    mer (K)
Ratcliffe Joseph, lab., Hanover ab West (K)
Rath Henry, weaver, R road bel Wallace
Rathfon Jacob, 341 Sp. Garden
Ratliff James, carman, Hanover bel F road (K)
Ratliff John, trunkmr., 7 Dannaker's av
Ratyel John, shop, R road ab Broad
Rau Edward N., bookbinder, 85 Dock, h 153
    N 12th
Rau Frederick, varnish mr. 82 N 4th
Rau John, butcher, 609 N 3d
Rau Moses, vict., Poplar bel 2d
Rau Peter, tailor, rear 31 Green
Rauber John, lab., Winter st
Rauch Mary B., nurse, Baker bel 8th
Raule Jacob, baker, S E 7th & Noble
Rausenberger Jacob, baker, 269 S 5th

Rautenberg E. A., mer., 20 Church al, h 101 Spruce

Ravesius J. G. gent. 132 S 5th

RAWLE WILLIAM, attorney and coun., 131 Walnut

Rawle Wm. Henry, att'y & coun. 131 Walnut

Rawlings James S., printer, 3 Harmony

Rawlings Joseph C., tailor, 350 S 2d

Rawlings Thos., jr., painter, 285 N 2d, h Coates and St John

Rawlins Catharine, N W Vernon & Shippen

Rawlins Geo. E., mer., 36 Commerce, h 540 O Y road

Ray Charles, lab., Crabb ab Shippen

Ray David & Son, tailors, 356 High

Ray Geo., clerk, 28 Apple Tree al

Ray Henry, weaver, Amber ab Pheonix (K)

Ray Jacob, lab., Warren bel 12th

Ray James, manf., 2d ab Master

Ray John, drayman, Sassafras n Sch 7th

Ray John. W., agt. Central Education Society, 142 Chestnut, h 138 Walnut

Ray Jos., 94 N 5th

Ray Joseph J., wheelwright, 3 Paschall's al

Ray Margaret, 11th ab Coates

Ray Sarah, milliner, 94 E Cedar

Ray Wm. J., carp., Wistar ab 11th

RAYBOLD FREDERICK A., att'y and coun., Washington sq & Locust

Raybold John, paper stainer, Carlton n Sch 8th

Raybold Joshua M., scrivener, 13 State House, h Catharine ab 6th

Raymond Israel, 57 Wood

Raymond Jas, mer., 23 N whfs, h 25 Sassafras

Raymond John M., cordw., 389 S 2d

Raymond & Brother, grain & flour, 23 N whfs.

Raymond Timothy C., grain & flour, 23 N whfs h 3 Elfreth's al

Raymond Wm., lab., 9 Mechanics' ct

Raynor Chas., com. mer., Broad ab Cherry

Rayns Robert, tailor, 21 Garden

Rayson Thos., glove mr., 3 Baker's ct

Rea Elizabeth, 551 N 3d

Rea James, weaver, 2d ab Master (K)

Rea James, shoemr., 163 S Front

Rea John, carpets, 145 Chestnut

Rea Thomas, nailer, 15 Parker

Rea Thos. D., carp., Green st, h 22 Clark (S)

Read Alex., china mer., 205 High

Read Ambrose, cordw., 9th bel Brown

Read Catharine, 83 Green

Read Chas., brickmr., Cadwalader bel Oxford

Read Christian, 48 New Market

Read B. T., cordw., 4th and Marriott

Read Elihu, oyster house, 261 N Front

Read Elizabeth, shoes, 283 Coates

Read F. M. clerk, G T road ab Laurel

Read George, brickmr. 498 N 3d

Read George C. commodore, U. S. N. Yard, h Clinton bel 11th

Read Jacob, waiter, Essex st

Read James, stevedore, Harper's pl

Read James, lab. 4 Sch Water

Read James, bottler, Scott's ct

Read Jeremiah, baker, 261 N Front

READ JOHN M., att'y and coun., 85 S 6th

Read John S., paper hanger, 221 S 2d

Read Joseph, tailor, Boyd's av

Read Joseph A., carver, Queen & Hanover (K)

Read Joseph S., gent., 106 Poplar

Read J. J., oak cooper, 11 Penn

Read Mary Ann D., Leopard (K)

Read Peter, brickmr., Harmstead n Sch 3d

Read Samuel, weaver, 8 Dauersach's ct

Read Samuel, wharf builder, Franklin ab Palmer

Read Samuel, lab., Carpenter ab 6th

Read Theodore F., cordw., 9th ab Coates

Read Thos. B., artist, 36 Sansom

Read Wm., bricklayer, 175 Brown

Read William H. J., watch and clk mr., 44 Chestnut

Read Wm. W. shoemr. 126 Cherry

Reader Mary, 2 Pegg

Reading Daniel, shoemr., Swanson bel Washington

Reading Danl., lab., 2 Monmouth ct

READING JOHN G., mer., 109 S Front

Reading Michael, 2 Beaver ct

Reakirt Conrad, 599 N 2d

Reakirt John, gent., 444 N 5th

Reakirt Joseph & John, druggists, S E 3rd and Callowhill

Reall James, drayman, Hanover bel Duke (K)

Ream Francis, capmr., St John bel Beaver

Reamer John, butcher, Duke ab Palmer

Reamer Mrs., 42 Madison

Reaney, Neafie & Co., machinists, Beach bel Palmer (K)

Reaney Thomas, machinist, Beach bel Palmer, h Palmer bel Franklin

Reany Robert, watchman, Elm bel Franklin (K)

Reap John, cordw., Crown ab Duke (K)

Reap John C., shoemr., Crown ab Duke (K)

Reap Philip, carp., 100 New Market

Reap Samuel, cordw., Marlborough ab Duke

Reardon Wm., marble pol., Carroll's ct

Rease John, whitesmith, Sch 3d & Pine

Rease Wm., brickmr., Mariner

Rease Wm. H. lithographer, 17 S 5th, h Green ab Marshall

Reath Benj. B., mer., 14 N 4th

REATH & COWPLAND, looking glasses, &c., 14 N 4th

Reath Thomas, Broad ab Locust

Reathmiller Jacob, carpet weaver, Marlboro' bel Duke

Reathmiller Samuel, brushmr., Marlborough bel Duke

Reaver Charles, grocer, c 6th and Wood

Reber John L., findings, 76 Green

Reber Jos., tailor, Hummell's row (K)

Reber Samuel L., pianomaker, Parrish bel 6th

Rebille Jos., tobacconist, rear 73 G T road (K)

Rebman John, cabinetmaker, 152 St John st

Reburn Mary Ann, 1 Hunter

Reckefus Edwin A., clerk, 149 S 10th

Reckitt George, tailor, rear 141 Green

Reckitt Joseph, lumb. ins., rear 141 Green

Reckless Anthony, waterman, 2d below Wharton

Reckless Samuel, grocer and baker, S E Front and Christian
Recktenwald John M. lab. West bel Cherry (K)
Reddon George L., mariner, 18 Gaskill
REDFIELD WILLIAM, Head Quarters, Franklin pl, h 401 S 6th
Redheffer Andrew, hatter, 65 G T road (K)
Redheffer Benj. machinist, Clinton bel Poplar
Redheffer Jas., tinsmith, rear Orchard ab Rawle
Redheffer Jesse, drayman, Kessler ab Coates
Redheffer Wm. combmr. rear 174 Marshall
Redifer Andrew P., cordw., Charlotte & Beaver
Redifer Jacob, jeweller, 267 N 2d
Redifer Peter, cordw., Parrish & Elizabeth
Redles A., turner, 23 Strawberry
Redles John, mer., h 18 Plum
Redman Benj., gent., 263 S 6th
Redman James, weaver, 187 E Pine
Redner L., grocer, N W Laurel and Spruce
Rednott Peter, Baker's ct (K),
Redstreke John, cabinet maker, 390 S 3d
Reed Abel, sash maker and glazier, rear 127 N 3d, h 191 Coates
Reed Andrew, shoemr., 18 Scott's ct
Reed Ann, huckster, Hope bel Master (K)
Reed A., 5 Miller's ct
Reed Bernard, stone mason, High n Sch 2d
REED & BROTHER, dry goods, 177 High
Reed Catharine, tavern, 119 S Water
Reed & Cecil, porter house, 13 Swanson
Reed Charles, grocer, 421 High
Reed Charles D., mer., 10 S Whfs, h 37 Crown
Reed Charles L., lab., rear Penn bel Shackamaxon (K)
Reed D. H. baker, 220 Green
Reed Edward, carter, Crier's ct
Reed Edward J., mer., 177 High
Reed Elias, cabmr., 6 Sansom
Reed Elizabeth, shop, 502 S 2d
Reed Elizabeth, b. h , 34 Quarry
Reed Elizabeth, b. h., 107 N 13th
Reed E. S., hatter, 177 Coates
Reed E. S., 73 Wood
Reed Francis S. baker, 216 N 6th
Reed George, weaver, Howard and O'Neal (K)
Reed Geo., printer, Vale's av
Reed G. Washington, watchmaker, N W 2nd & Vine h 57 Vine
Reed Hannah, Green bel Front
Reed Harriet, b. h. 76 Vine
Reed Henry, professor, h 48 S 13th
Reed Hiram, printer, 84 Tammany
Reed Hosea, lab., Prime ab Swanson
Reed H. H., mer., 177 High, h 124 N 9th
Reed Isaac, lab. Mariner

Reed John, printer, 45 Brandywine st
Reed John F. cordw. 10 Chester
Reed John R., gasman, 45 Chester
Reed John W., clockmr., Travis' ct
Reed Margaret, S E St John and Beaver (K)
Reed Maria, 13th bel Locust
Reed Martin, confec., Freytag's al
Reed Mary, shop, 656 N 2d (K)
Reed Mary, washer, 19 Currant al
Reed Mary, trimmings, 110 S 10th
Reed Mary, 11 Laurel st
Reed Mary Ann, Apple ab George
Reed Michael, mer., 177 High, h 7 Franklin
Reed Miller J., coach trimmer, Stiles' ct
Reed Osmon, watches and jewellery, 74 High, h 2 Franklin
Reed Priscilla, 2 Swede's ct
Reed Robert, grocer, 482 Sassafras
Reed Robert, lab., 15 Fitzwater
Reed Robert, cordw., 88 German
Reed Saml., grocer, Brown and Washington av, h 117 New Market
Reed Saml., mariner, rear Marriott bel 6th
Reed Samuel, gunsm., Bledisloe pl
Reed Samuel F., wheelwright, Lancaster pike (W P)
Reed Samuel F., att'y & coun., 115, and h 234 S 6th
Reed Samuel R., wheelwright, Ashton n Walnut Sch.
Reed Saml. S., clerk, 256 Cherry
Reed Sarah, 8 S 13th
Reed Sarah, Benton bel William (K)
Reed Stacy, 39 Clinton st
Reed Thomas, dealer, 61 Fitzwater
Reed Thomas S., carman, rear 463 N 4th
Reed T. S., M. D., Christian ab 3d
Reed William, gent., 10th bel Shippen
Reed Wm., weaver, Phoenix ab F road (K)
Reed William B., att'y & coun., 187 Walnut
Reed Willoughby H., mer., 177 High, h 126 N 9th.
Reeder David L., cordw., rear 30 St John
Reeder Wm. P., accountant, 11 Commerce, h 261 Coates
Reedy Wm., cordw., 5 Wilson (S)
Reef John, lab. F road ab Mary
Reel Frederick, shoes, 507 & 516 N 2d
Reel Henry, ship carp., Sarah and Bedford
Reel Jacob S., shoemr., 7 Allen (K)
Reel John, blacksmith, William bel Rose (K)
Reel Michael, carp. Duke bel Palmer (K)
Rees Charles B., provision store, S W Wood an Sch. 4th

Rees Rebecca, 85 N 7th
Rees Samuel J., frame maker, 4 Exchange pl, h Raspberry la
Rees William, combmr., 8 Pratt's ct
Reese Andrew, boot & shoemr. 256 N 3d, h 432 N 5th
Reese Geo. B., mer., 8 N Front, h 256 Walnut
Reese George G., oak cooper, 2 Fetter la
Reese Henry, paper stainer, Ann W Sch 4th
Reese & Heylin, dry goods, 185 High
Reese Jacob, cooper, Wood bet Sch 2d & 3d
Reese Jacob & Sons, mers., 8 N Front
Reese James A. bootmr. 13 Eutaw
Reese James M., tailor, 21 Quince
Reese Jane, rear 394 Sassafras
Reese J. J., M. D., Sch 7th & Chestnut
Reese Maria, Locust n Sch. 3d
Reese Mary, Sassafras ab Sch. 2d
Reese Peter W., boot fitter, Apple ab George
Reese Sarah, shop, 137 Cherry
Reese Sarah, wid. of Jacob, 399 Mulberry
Reese Sylvester, engineer, 7th bel G T road (K)
Reese Wm J. mer. 185 High, h Mulberry W Sch 7th
Reese Wm. Z., instrument mr., 56 Tammany
Reeside Ann, Carlton ab 12th
Reess Samuel, bricklayer, 1 Mercer
Reeve Hosea, oysterman, Penn ab Poplar (K)
Reeve John, teacher, 263 N 5th
Reeve M. M., M. D., 133 N 12th
Reeves Aaron, blacksmith, Benton n School
Reeves Abigail, 327 Chestnut
Reeves Allen R. & Co., hardware, 177½ High
Reeves Andrew, carp., Sch. 6th bel Buttonwood
Reeves Biddle, gent. 8th ab Green
REEVES, BUCK & CO., nails, &c. 45 N Water
Reeves B. bedstead manuf. 93 St John, h 8th ab Green
Reeves David, mer., 45 N Water, h 4 S 12th
Reeves Edward, plasterer, Poplar bel 11th
Reeves Elwood, plasterer, Centre bel Parrish
Reeves & Gaskill, flour and grain, Brown st whf. h Washington ab Brown
Reeves George, wood dealer, 1 Ellen (N L)
Reeves Hannah, 28 Ellen (N L)
Reeves Mrs. Hannah, 5 Clinton sq
Reeves Henry, plasterer, 61 Locust
Reeves Isaac, farmer, 225 Filbert
Reeves Isaac, engineer, 28 St. John
Reeves I. C. & Co. grocers, N E High & Water
Reeves Jacob, 20 Elfreth's alley
Reeves Jesse, cordw., Carpenter ab 9th
Reeves Joel, plasterer, 8th ab Green
Reeves Joel M. carp. Washington ab 11th
Reeves John, collector & agt. 288 Wood
Reeves John, cordw., Sch. 6th bel Callowhill
Reeves John A. printer, 23 Laurel (N L)
Reeves John W. carp. Union ab Franklin
Reeves Joseph, waterman, Scott's ct
Reeves Julianna, 253 Christian
Reeves Mark, grocer, Washington (W P)
Reeves Mark S. dealer, S W Brown and Front
Reeves N., cordw., Atherton
Reeves O., baker, Wood & St John

Reeves Robert D., carp., 10th ab Washington
Reeves Saml., tailor, Orange bel Melon
Reeves Saml. J., mer., 45 N Water, h 5 Virginia row
Reeves Thomas, Brown ab Front
Reeves Thos., lab., 24 Spooner's ct
Reeves Wm., bricklayer, Orange bel Melon
Reeves Wm., plasterer, Hutchinson ab Poplar
Refile Joseph, tobacconist, Moore's ct
Regan Andrew, weaver, 11 Bauersach's ct K))
Regan Wm., weaver, 26 New Market
Reger Isaiah, dry goods, 239 Green
Regester Lydia, 54 St. John
Regins Elizabeth, Korndaffer's ct
Register Wm. carp. George ab Sch 8th
Regnault Francis, paper hanger, George below Sch 5th
Rehfuess Ulrich, vict., 5th ab Jefferson
Rehn Casper, mer., 145 N 12th
Rehn Isaac, painter, 242 Green
Rehn Thomas J., combmr., 39 Brown
Rehn W. L., mer., 140 High, h 145 N 12th
Rehr John, bootmr., 10 Exchange pl, h 63 Dock
Rehse M. B., M. D., G. T. r. ad bel 5th (K)
Reich Samuel, lab., rear 487 N 3d
Reichenbach Fredk. C. piano maker, 12 S 7th
Reichert Frederick, bootmr., 25 Tammany
Reichert George, baker, Poplar bel 6th
Reid Alex. J., mer., 149 S 9th
Reid Isaac E., gent., Christian and 5th
Reid Jas. D., supt. Magn. Tel. Co., 31 Mer. Exc. h 191 S 7th
Reid John & Co., importers, 40 Chestnut, h Mantua V.
Reid Neville C., M. D., Christian bel 5th
Reid Robt., watchman, 10 Blunston's av
Reiff Daniel, coal mer., Kesler ab Coates
Reiff Deborah, Pearson's ct (K)
Reiff Garret, lab., Allen bel Shackamaxon
Reiff Jacob B., grocery, N W 3d and Callowhill
Reiff John, boot crimper, Almira place
Reiff Martin, lab., 205 G. T. road (K)
Reiff Wm. grocer, 8th & Cherry, h 260 Green
Reiff Wm. K., grocer, N E 8th and Cherry
Reifsnyder John, lab., Ontario bel Parrish
Reigard Richard, cabinetmr., 42 Dock
Reighner Wm. weaver, 38 Charlotte
Reilly Christopher, lab., Sch. 7th ab Wood
Reilly Edward, cordw., 5 Humphrey's ct
Reilly James, porter, 13 Quarry
Reilly John, b. h., Filbert ab Sch. 8th
Reilly John J., clerk, 578 S Front
Reilly Matt, grocer, Marriott and 6th
Reilly Michael, blacksm., P road bel Christian, h Christian ab P road
Reilly Patrick, grocer, 9th and Carpenter
Reilly Paul, upstore, Chatham and Sch 6th
Reilly Philip, grocer, 7 N Water, h 122 Spruce
Reilly & Smith, grocers, 7 N Water
Reilly Terrence, tailor, 4 Laurel (N L)
Reilly Thomas, soap boiler, 13 James
Reilly Thomas A., M. D., Coates bel 13th
Reilly Wm. M., druggist, 2d and Wharton
Reinel Nicholas, shoemr., 6 Myers' ct

Reimger Thos., carter, Say st
Reimold Jacob, baker, 546 N 3d
Reinan Patrick, milkman, Bushhill
Reinboth John C., agent, 13th ab Coates
REINBOTH JOSEPH D., real est. agt., 4 Filbert, h Spring Garden bel R. road
Reineck Henry, carp., Seh. 7th bel Cherry
Reineck Lewis, carp., Vernon bel 11th
Reineck Lewis, brickmr. George & Sch 2d, h Wood bel Sch 7th
Reinecks Jacob, brickmr., High n Sch. 3d
Reinfried Joseph, lab., 319 N Front
Reinfreid Lawrence J., tavern, 67 G T road
Reinfreid L., cordw., 316 N Front
Reinfreid L., cordw., 67 G. T. road (K)
Reinhamer Jacob, lab., 58 Almond
Reinhard Michael, dry goods, 134 S 4th
Reinhart Benedict, fringewr., 42 New Market
Reinhart John, blacksmith, 75 G T road (K)
Reinhart John, skin dresser, Orchard
Reinhart John E., sen., shipsmith, 54 Oak, h New Market ab Coates
Reinhart Mary, 32 New Market
Reinhart M., music teacher, 140 N 11th
Reinhart Wm. H., shipsmith, Washington av n Noble, h 23 Brown (N L)
Reininghaus Frederick W., cabinet mr., rear 18 Mechanic
Reinseimer Christ., carp., Palmer ab Franklin
Reinsimer Christian, gardener, Hanover bel Duke (K)
REINSTEIN FREDERICK, dentist, 221 Walnut
Reir Christian, cooper, Haydock bel Front
REISKY JAMES, furrier, 93 N 3d, h 96 N 8th
Reiss, Brothers & Co., importers, 16 S Front
Reistter John, tailor, 27 Garden
Reitz Wm., b. h., 2 Blackhorse alley
Relf Charles P., mer., 14 N wharves & 25 N Water
Relfck John, shoemr., 119 Queen
Remak Gustavus, atty & translator, 208 N 6th
Remels T., shoes, 407 N 4th
Rementer & Beam, painters, S E 5th & Walnut
Rementer Edw., tavern, 8th & Lisle
Rementer James, carp., 245 S 4th
Rementer Lewis W. painter, S E 5th & Walnut
Rementer Peter, carp., Washington bel 7th
Remer Henry, blacksmith, 4 Ogden
Remer Matt., ship carp., Franklin bel Union (K)
Remick Daniel, clothing, 185 S 2d, h N E Pine and 2d
Remick Enoch, tailor, 206 High, h 64 Franklin
Remick James, hatter, 304 N 2d, h 595 N 2d
Remier Ann, 117 Poplar
Remington Charles, lumber mer., Sch 5th and Spruce, h 8 Dugan row
Remington Edward, mer., 80 High, h 105 S 4th
Remington Isaac, M. D., 192 N 6th
Remington James, lum. mer., c Sch. 5th and Spruce, h 8 Dugan row
Remington John S., shipmaster, 350 S 4th
Remington J. B., gent., 105 S 4th
Remington Richd. P. mer. 92 High, h 105 S 4th
Remington Sarah, 308 S 2d

Remington T. P., merchant, 22 S Front, h 359 Walnut
Remington Wm., mer. 92 High, h 492 W Spruce
REMINGTON W. & R. P., silk goods, 92 High
Remmey Henry, stoneware manuf., Marshall ab Poplar, h 7th ab Poplar
Remmey John, shoemr., rear 473 N 3d
Remsen Ann Mrs., 234 Filbert
Remsen G., 9 N 4th, h 75 Marshall
Rennels Elizabeth, 85 N 9th
Rennels Silas S., mer., 267 High
Renner John, blacksmith, 477 N 4th, h Charlotte ab Poplar
Renney David, seaman, 64 Vine
Renouf Joshua, carp., Elizabeth ab Poplar
Renouf Nicholas, tailor, rear 6th ab Poplar
Renshaw A. B., mer., 48 High
Renshaw Lewis, clerk, 119 7th
Renshaw Martha, Wallace bel 9th
Renshaw Richard, attorney, 13 Sansom
Renton Wm., shoemr., 3 Roberts' ct
Rentz Frederick, baker, Hutchinson ab Poplar
Renz Christian, baker, 125 Brown
Reppert Josephine, b. h., 128 Filbert
Repplier C. A., mer., N W Broad and Mulberry, h 439 Sassafras
REPPLIER & CO., coal dealers, office N W Broad and Mulberry
Repplier John G., mer., 72 N 3d, h 167 Spruce
Repplier Joseph M., coal dealer, N W Broad & Mulberry, h 439 Sassafras
Repsher Ann, shop, Otter ab F road
Repsher Leonard, turner, 35 Coate's alley
Rest John, cabinetmr., Howard ab Master (K)
Retzback Windell, cordw., 323 S 6th
Retze J. Z., boot and shoemaker, 436 N 2d
Reuben Patrick, Broad st house, Broad ab Vine
Reves Sarah Ann, gentw., Relief ct
Rever David, Poplar ab 11th
Reville Henry, 5 Madison
Rew Thomas, harnessmr., Filbert n Sch Front
Rex Abraham, mer. 77 N 3d
Rex Berry, clothing, 88 S 2d, h 2 Juniper la
REX, BROOKE & BROWN, dry goods, 77 N 3d
Rex Enoch G., carp., 9th and Brown
Rex Hannah, gentw., St John n Beaver (K)
Rex Jesse, flour and feed, 2d & Montgomery
Rex Mary, b h, 121 Mulberry
Rex Millon lab., rear 129 Walnut
Rex Moses, porter, 38 Blackberry al
Rex Samuel, gent., 8th bel Coates
Rex Saml. S., broker, 5 S 3d, h 12 Branch
Rex Sarah, innkeeper, 2d & Montgomery (K)
Rex Wm., lab., Coates n Fairmount
Rex William M., bottler, 211 Green
Rex Willoughby M., 363 N Front
Rexrath Henry, vict., F road ab Otter
Reyle Andrew, tailor, 603 N 2d
Reynegom John, capt., 459 S Front
Reynolds Ann E., 128 Green
REYNOLDS & ARMSTRONG, grocers, 11 N Water
Reynolds Benjamin, grocer, 11 N Water, h 138 Walnut

Reynolds Bernard, turner, 104 N 6th
Reynolds Britton C., shoes F road n Master
Reynolds Caleb, coal mer., Pine ab Sch 7th
Reynolds Charles M., mer., 204 High, h 73 S 12th
Reynolds C. G., painter, 202 Queen
Reynolds Eli, wharf builder, Vienna ab Queen
Reynolds & Gwin, grocers, 204 High
Reynolds Hannah H., b h, 138 Walnut
Reynolds James, queen's ware, 352 N 2d
Reynolds James, carter, F road and Duke (K)
Reynolds James, tailor, rear 60 Catharine
Reynolds Jesse, stovemr., 31 Perry
Reynolds Joel, agent, 22 Arcade, h Chesnut n Sch 2d
Reynolds John, tailor, 66 S 4th
REYNOLDS JOHN & CO., bottlers, 14 & h 16 Pear
REYNOLDS, McFARLAND & CO., dry goods, 105 High
Reynolds Michael, shop, 21 Nectarine
Reynolds Peter, baker, Doman's pl
Reynolds Rachel, 11 Pear
Reynolds Richard, lab., 25 Dyott's ct
Reynolds Dr. R. T., dentist, 6th & Noble
Reynolds R. F., artist, 20 Gaskill
Reynolds Samuel W., mer., 33 S whfs
Reynolds Theodore, cordwainer, 4 Washington court
Reynolds Thomas, wheelwright, Lewis below Sch 6th
Reynolds Thos. livery keep. h Jones W Sch 8th
Reynolds, Thomas, basket fnr., 120½ Coates
Reynolds Thos. H., tailor, 3 Centre
Reynolds Thomas M., Jones n Sch 4th
Reynolds Wm., carter, 67 George (S)
Reynolds Wm. merchant, 105 High, h 495 Chestnut
Reynthaler John, vict., 461 N 5th ab Poplar
Rezer Benjamin, wheelwr., 5 Wheelock's pl
Rhea James, shoemaker, S E 2d and Cedar, h Church bel R road
Rhees J. Loxley, teacher, Camden, h 12 S Sch 8th
Rhein John M. D., Spring Garden ab 10th
Rhein Rachel conf., S E Callowhill & Sch 5th
Rheinstrome Isaac, baker, 32 Margaret
Rhinheart Joseph, bootmaker, 8 Union st
Rhoads Alex., bricklayer, 191 Callowhill ab Sch 6th
Rhoads Andrew, dry goods, Sch 3d & Carlton
Rhoads Charles, carp., Carlton bel Sch 2d
Rhoads James, moulder, Penn bel R road
Rhoads Jeremiah, lab., rear 50 Charlotte
Rhoads John, lab., Bedford ab 6th
Rhoads John, tailor, Clinton bel Parrish
Rhoads John, brickmr., Hanover n F road
Rhoads John P., mer., 42 Bank
Rhoads Joseph, gent, N E 2d & Poplar
Rhoads Levi P., brushmr., 72 N 3d, h 8th ab Noble
Rhoads Rachel M., wid. of Thomas, dry goods, 186 S 2d
Rhoads Samuel, tinsmith, rear 264 St John
Rhoads Saml., waiter, 7 Rose al (C)

Rhoads Wm., teller Farmer's & Mechan. Bank, h Vine n Sch 4th
Rhode Geo., 26 Garden
Rhodes Geo., weaver, Crown ab Duke (K)
Rhodes Hannah, George n Sch 2d
Rhodes Jos., manuf., n Fairmount
Rhodes Joshua, M D, Sch 4th bel Callowhill
Rhodes Mary, Mrs., 6 Virginia row
Rhodes Mary, 13 Madison
Rhodes Samuel, com. mer., Green ab 13th
Rhynear Wm., stone mason, 4 Franklin row
Rial James, tinsmith, 321 E Cedar, h 7th ab Carpenter
Rial Jos., lab., rear 514 N Front
Rianhard John, mer., N E 11th and Cherry
Rianhard John, boot & shoe mr., 231 N 6th
Ripple Andrew, plast., rear Orchard ab Rawle
Ribble Chas., carp., 459 N 4th
Ribble John, fisherman, Apple bel George
Ribble Wm., planemr., rear 22 Charlotte
Riblett Joseph, baker, 145 N 10th
Riblett Peter, carrier, G T road ab Phoenix
Rice Alfred H., ladies' shoemr., 285 Chestnut
Rice Ann, 53 Almond
Rice Arthur, coachmr., Broad & Filbert, h Filbert ab Sch 8th
Rice Bernard, lab., 2d bel Master (K)
Rice Charles, weaver, Milton ab 11th
Rice Daniel, 130 Mulberry
Rice David, trimming store, 10 Pine
Rice Geo., lab., China st
Rice George, porter, 324 Cedar
Rice Francis, malster, rear Cadwalader ab Master, (K)
Rice Jacob, fisherman, Queen n Wood (K)
Rice Jacob, carp., Flower al
Rice James, brewer, 1 Raspberry al
Rice James, millwright, N E 10th & Cherry
Rice James, carter, Filbert ab Sch. 8th
Rice James, lab., 298 S 10th
Rice James, weaver, Shippen la ab Fitzwater
Rice Jane, b h, 65 N 5th
Rice John, builder & lumber yard, 6th & Coates
Rice John, clothes, 149 N 2d, h 12th ab Shippen
Rice John P., fisherman, Queen below Wood (K)
Rice Joseph S., carp., 67 Carpenter (S)
Rice Lewis J., machinist, 64 Carpenter
Rice Martin, fisherman, Queen n Bishop (K)
Rice Martin, baker, 482 Callowhill
Rice Mary, 43 Brown
Rice Mary, 169 Queen
Rice Michael, cabtmr., Wagner's al
Rice Owen, lab., Lombard ab Sch 2d
Rice Peter, fisherman, Queen n Wood (K)
Rice Philip, carp., 537 Vine
Rice Samuel, fisherman, Queen n Wood (K)
Rice Thomas, bootmr., 2 Leiper
Rice Thomas, lab., Bickham's ct
Rice Vitus, musician, McAvoy's ct
Rice Willard, broker, 95½ Walnut, h 280 N 7th
Rice Willard M., teacher, S E 8th and Cherry, h 11th ab Sp Garden

Rice William, cordwainer, 570 S 2d
Rice Wm., paint manuf., Maiden bel Front, h 12th ab Buttonwood
Rice Wm., weaver, Master bel 2d (K)
Rice Wm. C., watchmaker, and jeweller, 394 N 2d
Rich Alfred H., grocer, 605 N 2d
Rich Charles, coachman, 8 Little Pine
Rich Charles C., grocer, Sch 7th and High, and dry goods, 479 High
Rich Chas. C., grocer, George and Sch 7th
Rich Edward, coachman, 8 Little Pine
Rich Hannah, dry goods, 479 High
Rich Jeremiah, cedar cooper, rear 402 N 2d
Rich John, grocer, George & Sch 7th
Rich Naomi, 71 S 8th
Richard John, painter, 216 Callowhill
Richard Saml., carp.,Harrison st
Richardet James B., saddler, High above Sch. 6th
Richardett Samuel, carp., Poplar bel 11th
Richards Ann, washer, 8 Gray's al
Richards Ann M., 347 Mulberry
RICHARDS & BISPHAM, auctioneers, 34 S Front
Richards B. W., mer., 34 S Front, h Walnut n Sch 7th
Richards Catharine, gentw., 33 Pratt
Richards Catharine, wid. of George, Pearson's ct (K)
Richards Charles W., lab., Sheaff
Richards Deborah, tailoress, 155 S 11th
Richards Edward, painter & glazier, Marriott & Fisher
Richards Edwin S., mer., 9 Bank
Richards Elizabeth, 106 Carpenter
Richards Frances, 62 S 12th
Richards Geo. W., 7 George
Richards G. W., mer., 21 S Front, h S E Broad & Spruce
Richards Hannah, whitewasher, Vernon above 10th
Richards Hannah, sempstress, Smith's ct
Richards Henry, carman, Ann n Sch 6th
Richards H. S., eat. house, 13th & Washington
Richards James, 297 Vine
Richards John, spade and shovel manuf., San-som's al, h 271 N 3d
Richards John, printer, 299 High, h 285 N 8th
Richards John, carp., Callowill n Broad
Richards John, jeweller, 2d ab Federal
Richards John, tailor, 1 Beaver ct
Richards John C., tailor, 14 S 10th
Richards John R., combmr., 5th bel German, h 393 S Front
Richards Joseph, grocer, 432 High
Richards Joseph, gent., Filbert E Sch. 6th.
Richards Joseph, carp., 15 Jefferson st
Richards Mary, Wallace ab R road
Richards Mary, 41 N 11th
Richards M. Mrs., b. h., 139 Walnu
Richards Sarah, trimmings, 213 N 10th
Richards Sarah, cook, Ten foot al
Richards Thos., porter, rear 3 Gray's al

Richards Thomas, glass manf., S W Front & Mul-berry, h S W Mulberry al. and 5th.
Richards Thos. J., bootmr., 525 N 2d ab Otter (K)
Richards Thos. M., carp., Sp Garden bel 11th
Richards T. S., 609 Spruce
Richards Wm., carp., Duke bel Palmer (K)
Richards Wm. H., gent., 422 Sassafras
Richards Wm. H. jr., N W 10th & High
Richards Wm. S., bricklayer, 122 Filbert
Richards W. H., druggist, Vine ab Broad
Richards W. W. & J. J., spade and shovel manf. Sansom al
Richardson Anna, cook, rear 7 Richard
Richardson Benj., gaspipe layer, Johnson la and 5th
Richardson B., cutler, 77 S 2d, h 14 Cypress al
Richardson B. & Son, cutlers, 77 S 2d
Richardson Caspar, cordw., Union ab Franklin
Richardson David, Union ab Franklin (K)
Richardson D. C., carp., 10th bel Poplar
Richardson Edmund, printer, 71 Gaskill
Richardson Franklin, door spring manuf., 394 High
Richardson George, carp., Wall, h 148 Queen
Richardson Geo., clerk, Newton
Richardson Hannah, 520 S Front
Richardson Henry, capt., Sch 3d ab Cedar
Richardson Isaac, machinist, Dean ab Bedford (K)
Richardson James, weaver, Cedar bel 13th
Richardson James, confect., 42 High, h 3 New Market
Richardson James, weaver, rear Hanover below Duke (K)
Richardson John, Pres't. Bank North America, h Spruce W of Broad
Richardson John, coal mer., 37 S 5th, h 252 Spruce
Richardson John J., confectioner, 42 High, h 3 New Market
Richardson Joseph, lab., 126 German
Richardson J. E., mer., 9 Church al, h 32 Wood
Richardson Leander, actor, Thompson ab 4th(K)
Richardson Lemuel, carp., Wood bel Sch 2d
Richardson Mark, carp., 113 N Juniper
Richardson Mary R., b h, 216 High
Richardson Nathan, carp., 4 Blunston av
Richardson Nathaniel, hydraulic engines, 394 High, h 298 Cherry
Richardson Oliver, b. h., 262 S 5th
Richardson Ralph, weaver, 8 Brinton
Richardson Robt., lab., Cherry n Sch 8th
Richardson Samuel, oysterman, Shippen bel 8th
Richardson Sarah, 72 N 10th
Richardson Stephen B., 11 Walnut
Richardson Thomas, copperplate printer, S 9th bel Fitzwater
Richardson Thomas, lab., Shippen bel 13th
Richardson Thos., painter, Providence ct
Richardson T. P., merchant, 82 S Wharves, h 115 Pine
Richardson & Watson, importers, 8 Chestnut
Richardson William, umbrella maker, 106 High, h Spruce ab Broad

Richardson Wm., carp., S E 7th and Pine
Richardson Wm., cutler, 75 S 2d, h Baker bel 8th
Richardson Wm., tanner, M'Devitt's av (K)
Richardson Wm., porter, Times ct
Richardson Wm., mariner, rear 467 Christian
Richardson Wm. & Co., umbrella manufs., 106 High
Richardson Wm. C., mer., 27 Chestnut, h 85 Wood
Richardson Wm. H., umbrella maker, 104 High, h 264 N 6th
Richardson Wm. T., brass spigot mr., 5 John (S)
Riché Charles S., prest. Washington Mutual Ins. Co., 48 Walnut, h 24 Clinton
Richee William, morocco dresser, 542 N 3d
Richers Danl., lab., Winter
Richie Alexander, stone cut., 4 Southampton ct
RICHIE EDWARD, currier, 245 N 3d
Richie John, cabman, Alice ct
Richie Joseph S., vinegar dealer, 3d & Noble
Richie Robt., vinegar dealer, 3d & Noble, h 54 Marshall
Richie Robert, vinegar dealer, 251 N 3d, h 54 Marshall
Richings Peter, actor, Pine ab 10th
Richman Charles, tinsmith, 13 Cherry
Richman Christian, tinsmith, 13 Cherry
Richman Francis, carpt., Willow above 5th
Richman John, machinist, Buttonwood ab 13th
Richman Richard, lab., rear 6 Rose al
Richmond Geo. A., ornamental painter, Maiden & Penn
Richmond James, b. h., 18 Branch
Richmond James, porter, 19 Little Pine
Richmond John, wharf builder, Beach ab Warren (K)
Richmond Wm., seaman, rear 7 Elfreth's al
Richmond Wm., silver plater, 20 Coates
Richstine Fred., cabmr., Williams' ct
Rick Philipena, b. h., 34 Strawberry
Rickards Nutter, jeweller, 71 Christian
Rickards Wm. ropemr. Lancaster ab Reed
Rickards Wm. D., jeweller, 250 Christian
Ricker George W., shoe. manuf., 1 Strawberry, h 2 Baker's ct
Ricketts J. T., biscuit baker, 192 N Front, h 192 Vine
Rickman Mary, wid. of Frederick, cooper, 246 N Front
Ricks Henry, whitewasher, 210 S 7th
Rickson John, carp., 69 Queen (S)
Ricords Elisha, pilot, 446 S Front
Ridabock Maria, gentw., 349 Pine
Riday Charles S., brickmr., G T road op 5th (K)
Riday John, jr., brickmr., G T road op 5th (K)
Riday John, brickmr., G T road op 5th (K)
RIDDELL CRAWFORD, cabinetmaker, 173 Chestnut, h 54 Gaskill
Riddell John, architect, 65½ S 3d
Riddell Richard, drayman, 6 Hunter
Riddell Samuel, cabinetmr. 4 Montgomery pl
Rider Henrich, 209 F road (K)
Ridey Wm., butcher, Mechanic ab Poplar
Riddle Alexander, clerk, 2 Montgomery pl
Riddle I. M. & W. curriers, 93 Sassafras

Riddle James, crier, 24 Almond
Riddle John, cabinetmr., 55 N 8th
Riddle John, blacksmith Gulielma
Riddle John M., currier, 93 and h 17 Race
Riddle John S., com. mer., 76½ Walnut, h 7 Portico sq
Riddle Robert, biscuit baker, 11 Ellen (N L)
Riddle Wm., currier, 93 & h 17 Sassafras
Rider Andrew, tailor, Van Buren pl
Rider Ann, washer, 6 Rose alley
Rider Christian, shop, 71 Queen
Rider Joseph, grocer, Front ab Otter (K)
Rider Thomas, grocer, 93 Christian
Ridge Danl., shoemr., Marriott bel 6th
Ridge Mary, china, 53 N 8th
Ridge Thomas, 20 Laurel (N L)
Ridgely Otho B., carp., h 19 Magnolia
Ridgway Ann, b. h., 30 S 2d
Ridgway Asa, wharf builder, Lombard n Sch Front
RIDGWAY, BUDD & CO., flour mers., 77 N whfs & 157 N Water
Ridgway Charles, 227 N 13th
Ridgway Charles W., hatter, 128 N 2d
Ridgway Daniel P., merchant, house 2d below Reed
Ridgway Esther, 217 Chestnut
Ridgway George W., drug mill, S W Sch 6th & Hamilton, h Sch 6th bel Mulberry
Ridgway Jacob, blacksm., rear Pleasant ab 12th
Ridgway Job, carp. 16 Farmer, h 10th ab Poplar
Ridgway John J., off. 14½ Minor
RIDGWAY & KEEMLE, com. mers., 37 N whfs
Ridgway Moses C., tailor, 149 Buttonwood
Ridgway Richard S., agent, 238 N 2d
Ridgway Samuel H., chairmr., 157½ S 2d
Ridgway Thomas, bricklayer, 25 Sergeant
Ridgway Thomas, flour mer., 137 N Water, h 353 Mulberry
Ridgway Wm., flour, wood and lumber factor, Brown st whf, h 7th bel Parrish
Ridgway Wm. P., druggist, 45 Mulberry
Ridings Caleb, shuttlemr., Marlboro' & Duke
Ridings James, shuttlemr. Cedar ab 13th
Ridpath Moses, manuf., Shackamaxon bel F road
Ridy Wm., paper stainer, rear 13th bel Brown
Riebel Wm., framemr., rear 22 Charlotte
Riechber & Co., tailors, 24 Vine
Riechers Peter J., stone cutter, Elizabeth and Poplar
Riechman Jacob F., baker, Parrish ab 6th
Riedt Jacob, lab., F road n Marlboro' (K)
Riegel Jesse, lumber, Front & Maiden, h 501 N 2d
Riehl Frederick, brushmr., Mechanic bel George
Riehl Geo., cooper, 4th bel George
Riehl John, brass founder, 4th bel George
Riehle H. J., tanner, 249 N 6th
Riehle J. & H. J., tanners 4th n Willow
Riehle William jr., 53 N 4th
Riehle Wm. senr, 53 N 4th
Ricker Jacob, baker, Hanover ab Franklin
Rickie Wm. shipwright, 440 S Front
Rienar Henry, cordw., 589 N Front
Riesenberger C., bootmr., 292 S 4th

37

Riess John, wine mer., 71 P road
Riesz John, boatmr., Dunton bel Otter (K)
Rifford Henry, drover, 12th and Brown
Rifford Joseph, ship carpenter, Allen bel Marlborough
Rigby Harriet, silk dyer and printer, 95 N 13th
Rigby Israel, waiter, 13 Elizabeth
Rigg Thomas, dyer, Clinton ab Poplar
Rigg Wm., bricklr., Shackamaxon n Bedford (K)
Riggins John, waterman, 7 Duke
Riggins Wm., capt., 29 Queen
Riggs Isaac, brickmr., Duke n Crown (K)
Riggs Isaac, brickmr., Apple bel George
Riggs Romulus, Mrs., 262 Spruce
RIGGS W. H. C., watch & chronometer maker, 126 S Front and 13 Dock
Righter Henry G., bookbinder, 275 N 3d
Righter Hugh, carp., 16 Tammany ct
Righter Jacob, trunkmr., Mechanic
Righter Jesse, tavern, 468 Sassafras
Righter John, sand paper manuf., Brandywine ab 13th
Righter John C., shipping master, U. S. N., 162 S Front
Rightley Charles, baker, Shackamaxon bel Franklin
Rigler Charles, vict. West ab Marlboro' (K)
Rigler Henry, carp., F road bel Franklin (K)
Rigley Joseph, oysters, 355 N 3d
Rigoulet Fred., waiter, rear 300 S 3d
Rihl Catharine, Cadwalader ab Phoenix
Rihl Emeline, St John bel George (K)
Rihl Henry, blindmaker, 497 N 3d & 450 N 2d,
Rihl John, fisherman, Allen and Hanover (K)
Rihl John, blindmr., 497½ N 3d
Rihl Thomas, fisherman, Hanover bel Queen (K)
Rihle Mary A., 126 Brown
Rikards John, 139 N 5th
Rile Jonathan, brickmr. G T road opp 6th
Rile Wm., drayman, Logan n Green
Riley Alexander, weaver, 7th bel Christian
Riley Amos, porter, Marshall's ct
Riley Ann, washer, rear 108 Filbert
Riley Ann, shop, 7 Jones' al
Riley Benj. S., clerk, Elizabeth ab Poplar
Riley Bernard, silversmith, 2 Mineral pl
Riley Chas., waterman, Vienna bel Franklin (K)
Riley David, tanner, Hummel's ct
Riley Emily, milliner, 548 N 2d (K)
Riley Francis, machinist, Ogden bel 10th
Riley Hugh, lab., 2 Warner's ct
Riley Hugh, cabman, 7 Knight's ct
Riley James, lab., Factory
Riley James, cabman, G T road ab Master
Riley James, weaver, Sch 5th & Lombard
Riley James, lab., Fitler n 2d
Riley James M., clerk, Sch 8th ab Race
Riley John, lab. Eyre's ct (K)
Riley John M. dry goods, 363 N 2d
Riley Joseph S., dry goods, 363 N 2d
Riley Joseph S., jr, acct., Elizabeth ab Poplar
Riley Julia, shop, 291 S Front
Riley Maria, Wilson's ct
Riley Mary Ann, cupper & leecher, G T road ab Master

Riley Matthew, chandler, Shippen la
Riley Michael, weaver, 7th bel Christian
Riley Michael, lab. Sch Water n Cedar
Riley Michael, lab., Pine bel Beach
Riley Owen, Pearl bel William
Riley Owen, stovemr., 4 Shield's al
Riley Patrick, cabman, 10 Knight's ct
Riley Patrick, lab., Factory ab Willow
Riley Patrick, 5 Mineral pl
Riley Patrick, lab., 6 Hampton ct
Riley Peter, waiter, 13 Barley
Riley Philip, carter, 9th & Christian
Riley Rudolph, bricklr., Pine ab Sch 7th
Riley Samuel, baker, 9 Letitia ct
Riley Sarah, West ab Palmer (K)
Riley Sarah, 15 Relief
Riley Thos., carman, Sch 3d and Spruce
Riley Thos., agent, 12 Carpenter
Riley Tobias, baker, 391 & h 396 Sassafras
Riley Wm., cabinet mr., 25 Montgomery
Riley Wm., carman, 13 P road
Riley Wm. D., hatter, 11 Scheetz
Riley Wm. H., shoemr., 129 S 4th
Riling Thomas, basket mr., Allen ab Hanover (K)
Rimby Joseph, paper, 88 N 3d, h 66 New
Rine Henry, oysterhouse, 339 N Front
Rinear James, plasterer, Ogden bel 10th
Rinedollar Samuel, ship carp., Washington n Front
Rinehart Geo., carp., Loxley's ct
Rinehart Michael, carman, 64 Garden
Rinehart Thomas, boxmr. Buttonwood ab 13th
Ring Jacob G. H. carp. 31 Commerce, h 216 Noble
Ringe Conrad, confect., 483 N 3d
Ringe Harman, confect. 154 N 4th
Ringgold Saml., waiter, rear 305 Walnut
Ringland John, boots and shoes, 206 High, h 130 Christian
Rink Francis, musician, 264 N 12th
Rink Jacob, 212 St John
Rink Jacob, tobacconist, 64 Coates
Rink John, carter, 8 Passmore's pl
Rink John, bone sawyer, Carlton ab Sch. 2d
Rink John V., tobacconist, 406 N 3d
Rink Joseph, fancy goods, 230 Chestnut
Ripka Joseph, mer. and manuf., 32 S Front
Rinkver Catharine, Paul ab 6th
Ripley Christian, shoemaker, 310 Vine
Ripley John L., india rubber goods, 40 S 2d
Ripperger Benj., dentist, 226 Walnut
Ripperger C., cupper and bleeder, N W 6th and George
Ripperger Henry J., tobacconist, 201 Chestnut
Ripperger Mary Ann, 4 Richardson's ct
Ripperger William, dentist, N W 4th & Pine
Rippy Samuel, huckster, Filbert n Sch 3d
Risbrough Henry, mer., 10 Church al
Risbrough John, dry goods, S W 2d & Union
Risler Wm. T. attor'y & coun. 141 Walnut
Risley Ann, milliner, 119 N 2d
Rissel Daniel, lath mr., Harrison st
Rissing Hannah, 6 O Y road
Ristine Frederick, printer, 463 S Front

Ristine Geo., pumpmr. Sarah bel Bedford (K)
Ristine Henry, trader, Howard ab Oxford (K)
Ristine Jacob, tailor, 540 N 2d
Ristine John, tavern, Master & Front (K)
Ristine John, hotel, Coates and Fairmount
Ristine John, boxmr., 3 Swain's ct
Ristine Jos., comb mr., Union bel Franklin (K)
Ristine Matilda Mrs., rear 134 Brown
Ristine Wm., tailor, rear Jones' al
Riston George, broker, 75 Dock, h Sch 8th bel Chestnut
Ritch Leister, tailor, 6 Lawrence ct
Ritchie Ann, Paul ab 6th
Ritchie Arthur, mer. 232 N 3d, h 11th ab Callowhill
Ritchie A. C. Mrs. 216 Pine
Ritchie Henrietta, widow of James S., 222 Pine
Ritchie Jacob, engineer, 6 Reckless
Ritchie Robt., carp., Ogden bel 12th
Ritchie Robert, lab., Rose ab 13th
Ritchie Thos., grocer, 8th & P road (S)
Riter Augustus, machine mr., 127 Race
Riter John A., carp., Brown bel 11th
Riter Matilda, widow of George W. 141 N 9th
Riter Michael M. mer. 22 N 9th
Riter Susan, Pink ab Master
Ritner Wm., drayman, Otter & Dunton (K)
Ritschman Jacob, grocer, N. Market & York ct
Rittenhour Elias, carp., Front ab Jefferson (K)
Rittenhour Nathan, carp., Front ab Jefferson (K)
Rittenhouse Abm., machinist, Scott's ct
Rittenhouse Charles, vict. G T road ab 6th
Rittenhouse Christopher, 167 Coates
Rittenhouse David, Caledonia ct
Rittenhouse Eliza, 19 N 8th
Rittenhouse Godfrey, vict., G T road bel 7th
Rittenhouse Hannah, 10th bel Coates
Rittenhouse Henry, combmr., 590 N 3d
Rittenhouse Joseph, tobacconist, 197 Green
Rittenhouse Peter, vict. G T road ab 6th
Rittenhouse William, carp., 17 Magnolia
Ritter Abraham, real estate agent, 114½ Mulberry, h 12th ab Cherry
Ritter B. J., druggist, N W 3d & Branch, h 4th & Mulberry
Ritter Catharine, Rose alley (C)
Ritter Daniel, gent., 49 Franklin
Ritter Edward, varnish & turp. mr., 82 & h 80 Maiden
Ritter Eliza, dry goods, 129½ S 4th
Ritter George, coffin maker and undertaker, 72 N 4th
Ritter Geo. R, blacksmith, Van Buren pl
Ritter Henry, machine, Washington (W P)
RITTER ISAAC L. & BENJ. J., druggists, N W 3d & Branch
Ritter Isaac L. druggist, N W 3d & Branch, h 13th n Coates
Ritter Jacob K., tailor, 127 New
Ritter John, painter, Margaretta (W P)
Ritter John G., bookseller, 263 N 2d
Ritter J. B., importer, 58 N 3d, h 121 S 9th
Ritter J. D., accountant, 253 N 6th
Ritter J. H., painter, Washington (W P)

Ritter L. A. & Co., trimmings, 25 N 6th
Ritter Mary Ann, trimmings, 12th ab Race
Ritter Sarah, tailoress, Myrtle ab 11th
Ritter Susan, widow of J. jr., 253 N 6th
Ritterson Adam, ropemr. Marlboro' ab Franklin
Ritterson John, carman, Palmer ab Franklin (K)
Ritterson Joseph M., collec., water rents, Marlboro' ab Franklin
Ritterson Susan, widow, Marlborough ab Franklin
Rittmayer Peter, cabinetmr. 131 S 2d
Ritzel Geo., stonemason, Bledisloe pl
Rival Wm. tobacconist, M road & Washington
Rivel Adam, trader, School bel Franklin (K)
Rivel Joseph, oysterman, 59 S 13th
Rively Andrew, grocer, Sch 8th & Filbert
Rix Mingo, porter, Washington ab 14th
Rizer Charles, druggist, S W 5th and Shippen
Roach Benjamin S., wheelwright, Marlboro' ab Bedford
Roach Ellen, Wistar ab 11th
Roach Henry, lab. Steam Mill al
Roach Isaac, Treasurer of the Mint, 245 Spruce
Roach John, bookbinder, rear 347 S 3d
Roach Jos. H. merchant, 18 Church al, h 245 Spruce
Roach Martha, tavern, Beach & Poplar (K)
Roach Mary, rear 164 Swanson
Roach Patrick, lab., Pine and Beach
Roach Thomas, lab., rear 260 Sassafras
Roach Thomas, lab , Jones W Sch 7th
Roach Wm., carp., Higgin's ct
Roan John, stone mason, Sch 3d ab Spruce
Roat Andrew, acct. Robb's ct
Roat Jacob, shoe findings, 153 N 4th
Roat John, carter, Yernon ab 10th
Roatch James P. tailor, 395 S 6th
ROBARTS & WALTON, coal dealers, 59 S 2d, & Willow st. wharf & Broad & Willow
Robarts W. S. coal dealer, 59 S 2d, h Sch 5th bel Cherry
Robb Alex., type founder, 8 Pear, h 84 S 5th
Robb Ann, Carlton ab Sch 2d
Robb Charles, gent., 155 S 5th
Robb Christian, saddler, Pearl bel Sch 5th
Robb Hannah, 372 S 4th
Robb Isabella Mrs., 3 Benezet
Robb Isabella Mrs., 7 Christian
Robb James, lumber, Swanson bel Christian, h 151 Queen
Robb James, gent., 125 Pine
Robb James, turner, 6 Margaretta
Robb James A. type founder, 3 Powell
Robb John, watchman, 28 Quince
Robb John, bootmr., 6 Mary's ct
Robb John, saddler, Carlton ab Sch 7th
Robb John H., atty. & coun., 21 Prune
Robb Peter, cabinetmr., 34 Parker
Robb Saml., lab., rear 109 Queen
Robb Thos., oysterman, Shippen ab 7th
ROBB THOMAS, lumb., mer., N W 7th and Catharine, h 211 S 4th
ROBB, WINEBRENNER & CO., mer. tailors 102 Chestnut
Robbins Amos, silver plater, rear 450 N 4th

Robbins Ann, gentw. 137 N 13th
Robbins Caleb S., baker, 447 S Front
Robbins Charles N. bricklayer, Park st
Robbins George, watchmaker, 315 High
Robbins Isaiah, waterman, 124 Queen (S)
Robbins Jas. J., atty. at law, 177 Sassafras
Robbins John, Jr. steel manuf., F road ab Queen, h 118 Beach (K)
Robbins John A., baker, 138 S 9th
Robbins Samuel J., sec'ry. Guardians Poor, 19 S 7th, h 97 N 5th
Robbins Stephen, clerk. 88 F road
Robbins Susan, gentw., N W 8th and Green
Robbins Thomas, whitesmith, Monroe bel Cherry (K)
Robbins & Verree, rolling mill, Penn bel Maiden
Robbins Zachariah, 23 S 2d
Robeno Andrew, tailor, S W Front and Cedar, h 87 Catharine
Robeno F. H. mer. 84 High, h 87 Catharine
Roberton John, classical teacher, 119 S 9th
Roberts Aaron, porter, 11 Willing's al
Roberts Albert N., grocer, Master & Howard
Roberts Anna Maria, 174 Mulberry
Roberts Ashton, feed store, Bread & Pleasant, h Wallace bel 10th
Roberts Ashton & Co., feed store, R road and Pleasant
Roberts A. S., mer., 76 S 2d, h Sch 5th opp Logan sq.
Roberts A. S. & E. & Co., druggists, 76 S 2d
Roberts Bathsheba, 10th and Sp Garden
Roberts Caroline C., M road bel Christian
Roberts & Carver, manufs. cotton laps, Arch st whf Sch
Roberts Catharine, wid. of Jas. Union ab Bedford (K)
Roberts Charles, sparmr. Sarah ab Queen
Roberts Charles H., constable, 40 Tammany
Roberts Chas. H., potter, Mechanic ab Poplar
Roberts Christiana, 82 Noble
Roberts & Conrad, com. mers. 35 High
Roberts C. B., M. D., 610 N 3d
Roberts C. T. & J. A., carps., 5th ab Franklin
Roberts C. W. & Co., drug mill, 115 N Water, h N E Wood & Crown
Roberts Daniel, saddler. 33 Crown
Roberts Daniel, bar tender, 12 Laurel (N L)
Roberts David, blacksmith, rear 321 St John
Roberts David, pipe caster, 1-a Fayette st
Roberts D. F., watchmr., 116 Chestnut and 104 Locust
Roberts Edward, confect., 137 S 6th
Roberts Edward, druggist 76 S 2d, h N E 11th and Spruce
Roberts Edward, gas fitter, Boyd's av
Roberts Edward W., ship broker, 8 Library
Roberts Eleanor W. milliner, 46 German
Roberts Elihu, mer., 35 High, h 67 N 9th
Roberts Eliphalet, teacher, S E 8th & Mulberry, h 5 S Rittenhouse
Roberts Eliza, washer, 18 E Lombard st
Roberts Elizabeth, 6th n Poplar
Roberts Elizabeth, 258 Chestnut
Roberts Elizabeth, nurse, 128 Filbert

Roberts Ellen, b. h., 45 George
Roberts Ellett, collector, 96 New Market
Roberts Ellis, blacksmith, 6 Feinour's ct
Roberts Evans, blacksm., 22 Beck (S)
Roberts Francis, cordw., 165 Christian
Roberts Geo., painter, 486 Coates
Roberts George, gent., 157 St John (N L)
Roberts George, waiter, 20 Prosperous al.
Roberts Geo. H. mer. 187 High
Roberts George H., mer., 127 N 3d, h 100 Callowhill
Roberts & Green, carpets, N E 2d & New
Roberts Hannah, 105 N 7th
Roberts Henry, constable, 9 Crown
Roberts Henry, cordw., Hughes' ct
Roberts Henry, tailor, 12th ab Pearl
Roberts Henry, slater, rear Vienna ab Franklin (K)
Roberts H. B., tailor, 140 Brown
Roberts Isaac, cutler, 169 S 3d, h rear 575 N Front
Roberts Isaiah, blacksmith, William's ct
Roberts Jac. S., hatter, 76 S 3d, h 452 S 4th
Roberts James, coal dealer, George W Sch 3d
Roberts James, carp., Sch 5th bel Wood
Roberts James W. coppersmith, 11 Branch, h 11th ab Callowhill
Roberts Jesse, lamp mr., 130 Sassafras
Roberts Jesse, 232 N Front
Roberts Johanna, 380 Walnut
Roberts John, blacksmith, 58 Laurel (N L)
Roberts John, bookbinder, 269 S 3d
Roberts John, jeweller, Winter ab Sch 3d
Roberts John, lab., 56 Washington av
Roberts John, lab., Tamarind bel Coates
Roberts John, cordw., M road bel Christian
Roberts John, bookbinder, 12 Rittenhouse
Roberts John, silver pl., 31 Apple
Roberts John A. lab. 21 Mary (S)
Roberts John P., messenger Girard trust, h 9 S 5th
Roberts John R., sail mr., S W 4th & Lombard
Roberts John T., plumber, 143 Chestnut, h 167 S 11th
Roberts Joseph, gent., 66 S 3d
Roberts Joseph, shoemr. Barker's ct (K)
Roberts Joseph, rear 72 Christian
Roberts Letitia, corsetmr. 399 S 2d
Roberts Lewis, porter, 29 Currant al
Roberts Lewis, mer., 322 S Front
Roberts Lucy, Swede's ct
Roberts Lydia, 123 N 9th
Roberts Margaret, silk fringe manuf., 176 N 8th
Roberts Margaret S. milliner, 50 Mulberry
Roberts Maria, 4 St Stephen's pl
Roberts Martha, cab mr., 59 S 8th
Roberts Martin, box mr., 7 Roldolph's ct
Roberts Mary, 220 Cherry
Roberts Mary & Isabella, milliner, 93 Noble
Roberts Matthias B., druggist, 9 Merchant, h Sch 8th ab Vine
Roberts Nelson L., waiter, 13 Lisle
Roberts Nichols, lab., 601 S Front
Roberts Nick., shoemr., Marlboro' ab West (K)

Roberts Owen, blacksmith, 3 Ton al, h 14 Lombard
Roberts Richard, seaman's b h, 38 Penn.
Roberts Robert, porter, 9 Sterling al
Roberts Robert, waiter, Barker n Sch 6th
Roberts Robert D., blacksmith, 144 Swanson
Roberts Samuel, waiter, 20 Watson's al
Roberts Saml., machinist, Crans' ct
Roberts Samuel, book-keeper, 93 Noble
Roberts Samuel A., bookseller, 9 Acorn al, h Hutchinson ab Poplar
Roberts Sarah, Apple ab Culvert
Roberts Solomon W., civil engineer, 174 Mulberry
Roberts Spencer, dentist, 266 N 6th
Roberts & Walker, plumbers, 143 Chestnut
Roberts Wm. cooper, 31 Commerce, h 4 North
Roberts William, teacher, 247 S 9th
Roberts William, cordw., 92 St John st
Roberts Wm., cordw. 282 St John
Roberts Wm., engraver, rear 82 N 2nd
Roberts Wm. G., china store, 127 S 4th
Roberts Wm. R. & Co., manufs., Mulberry whf., Sch
Roberts William S., carp. 104 Locust
Roberts Wm. S., dealer, 125 Cedar
Roberts W. F., engineer, 74 S 3d
Robertson Archibald, Spruce ab 11th
Robertson James, gent., Spruce bel Sch. 7th.
Robertson Jas., tarpaulin manuf., 136 Swanson
Robertson Jane, rear 2d ab Edward (K)
Robertson John, toy and book store, 151 Cedar
Robertson Thomas, cabinetmaker, 24 Morgan
ROBERTSON WILLIAM, gunsmith, 90 S 2d, h 8 Norris' al
Robertson Wm. B., agent, Spruce and Aspen
Robertson William H., cordw., 673 N 2d
Robeson Jane, dressmr., 258 Mulberry
Robeson Mary, milliner, 252 Chestnut
Robinett A., mer., 64 High, h Mulberry ab Sch 7th
Robinett, M'Calla & Herse, cloths, 64 High
Robins Edward, mer., 32 High
ROBINS, HILL & CO., com. mers., 32 High
Robins Jeremiah, jeweller, Catharine ab 6th
Robins John, hod carrier, St Mary ab 7th
Robins Oliver, baker, Sch 7th bel Vine
Robins Tho's., mer., 32 High, h Spruce ab 11th
Robinson Abraham, mer. 399 High, h Sch 8th & Mulberry
Robinson Alexander, tailor, 4th ab Washington
Robinson Alfred, barber, 39 S 8th, h 16 S 5th
Robinson Amour, car driver, Winter st
Robinson Andrew, clerk, Lombard n Sch 7th
Robinson Ann, 293 S 5th
Robinson Anthony W., mason, Brown bel Broad
Robinson Benjamin, carpenter, 188 N 13th
Robinson Benj., carp., Taylor's ct (K)
Robinson Benj. H., mariner, 7 Penn
Robinson Byer, bricklayer, 219 N 8th
Robinson Charles, printer, 162 S 3d
Robinson Charles, brickmr., rear 22 Lilly al
Robinson Charles B. sail maker, 7 Beck pl
Robinson Charlotte, tailoress, 9 Burd
ROBINSON, COLLINS & CO., druggists, 87 High

Robinson Comfort, washer, 10 Foot al
Robinson C. N., look. glass manuf., 86 Chestnut, h Pine ab 10th
Robinson C. W., conveyancer, 81 Chestnut
Robinson Daniel M., stock and exc. broker, 72 S 3d, h S W Broad and Spruce
Robinson David, waiter, 12 Liberty ct
Robinson David, tailor, 10 John st (S)
Robinson D., moulder, 7th and Christian
Robinson Edward J., broker, 72 S 3d
Robinson Edward W., 322 Walnut
Robinson Eliza, dry goods, 524 High
Robinson Elizabeth, 59 Mead
Robinson Elizabeth, washer, Marble ct
Robinson Francis, combmr., F road n Queen (K)
Robinson George, carp., 41 Christian
Robinson George Capt., 15 Catharine
Robinson Geo., grain measurer, Parrish ab 13th
Robinson George, tavern, 55 N Broad
Robinson George, carp. 7 Roberts' ct
Robinson Geo., porter, rear Marriott bel 6th
Robinson Geo., seaman, Prime ab Swanson
Robinson Hanson, merchant, 66 S Front, h Locust n Sch 6th
Robinson Henry, waiter, 4 Mercer
Robinson Hosea, cordw. Apple bel Franklin
Robinson Henry, morocco finisher, Otter ab F road
Robinson Henry B., copperplate print., 4 Tamarind
Robinson Isaac J. cordw. 4 Little Willow
Robinson Isaac W., hatter, 40 High
Robinson Israel, carp., Federal ab 5th
Robinson Israel, shoes, 107 High, h 147 Franklin
ROBINSON I. & CO., ladies' shoe manufs., 107 High
Robinson Jacob, stone ma., 254 N 13th
Robinson Jacob, whipmr., Franklin ab Marlboro'
Robinson James, cabman, Marble ct
Robinson James, baker, Lombard ab Sch 6th
Robinson James, lab., Juniper ab High
Robinson James C., carp., 20 James
Robinson Jehu, gent., 117 Vernon st
Robinson Joel, porter, 11 Willing's al
Robinson John, coach trimmer, Carpenter ab 4th
Robinson John, druggist, 87 High, h 33 Mulberry
Robinson John, 207 Cedar
Robinson John, cabinetmaker, N E 4th & Queen
Robinson John, watchman, 19 M road
Robinson John, stonecutter, Washington ab 5th
Robinson John, carp., Ann ab Powell (F V)
Robinson John, printer, 41 Christian
Robinson John, tailor, 5 Budd
Robinson John, Sch wharf, Vine
Robinson John, tinsm., N W St John & Poplar
Robinson John J. carp. 26 E North, h 308 N 8th
Robinson John P. Lynn (F M)
Robinson Joseph, capt., 48 Union
Robinson Julia, washer, Mayland & Mulberry al
Robinson Levy, lab., 17 Barley st
Robinson Lewis, waterman, Burchell's ct
Robinson Lydia, 10 Pearl ab 12th
Robinson Margaret, gentw., Federal ab 2d
Robinson Marg., teacher, Franklin & Sassafras

Robinson Margaret, shop, 153 N Water
Robinson Major, furniture car, 242 Lombard
Robinson Martha, Juniper ab Pine
Robinson Mary, Ann ab Sch 6th
Robinson Mary, Marriott's la ab 5th
Robinson Mary, nurse, Willow and Charles
Robinson Mary, rear Poplar ab St John
Robinson Mary, sempstress, 5 Rose al (C)
Robinson Mary A., 80 F road
Robinson Mary D., N E 5th & Mulberry
Robinson Mary F., Brown ab 10th
Robinson Matthew, shoemaker, 415 N Front
Robinson Moncure, Spruce W Sch 8th
Robinson Paris, lab.; Carpenter bel 10th
Robinson Philip, lab., Emeline
Robinson Richard, clerk, 10 S Broad
Robinson Robt., blacksm., 8 Thorn's ct
Robinson Robt. W., carp., Parrish bel Broad
Robinson Samuel, shoemr., 98 Plum
Robinson Sam'l, blacksm., Sycamore ab Locust
Robinson Saml., book-keeper, N E 4th & Chestnut, h 31 Filbert
Robinson Sarah, huckster, 8 Black horse al
Robinson Sarah, Apple ab Brown
Robinson Sarah, shop, 42 Quince
Robinson Thomas, gent., 17 Palmyra square.
Robinson Thomas, labourer, 198 Cherry
Robinson Thomas, ven. blind mr. 55 N 8th
Robinson Thomas, tailor, 248 Lombard
Robinson Thomas W., barber, 16 S 5th
Robinson William, weaver, Rose bel Broad
Robinson William, jr., Sec. Del. Coal Co., 78½ Walnut, h 10th bel Catharine
Robinson William, weaver, Warren ab Beach (K)
Robinson William, oyster house, Queen opp Wood (K)
Robinson Wm., stone cutter, 142 S 12th
Robinson Wm. potter, 9 Abbott's ct
Robinson Wm. segarmr. 243 S 5th
Robinson Wm. plasterer, Sycamore ab Spruce
Robinson Wm. sawyer, Wharton bel 2d
Robinson Wm. S., tinsmith, 5th bel Marriott
Robinson W. C., printer, 519 Coates
Robinson W. D., jeweller, Catharine bel 7th
Robison Joseph, printer, 1 Swarthmore pl
Robson Charles, cabinetmr., Pleasant bel 10th
Robson Dorothy, 301 Callowhill
Robson James, rigger, Marlboro' bel Franklin
Robson Louisa, Lisle bel Shippen
Robson Wm., carp., rear Marlboro' bel Franklin (K)
Roby Hannah, doctress, 110 N 12th
Roby Thomas, druggist, 110 N 12th
Rocap Adam, hatter, S E 4th & High
Rocap Jacob, corder, Washington av & Noble, h 600 N 3d
Rocap James, corder, Whf. bel Almond, h 105 Swanson
Roch George C., carp., Traquair's ct, h Wood bet Sch. 7th & 8th
Roche John, gardener, Filbert ab 13th
Roche Martin, teacher, S E 8th & Walnut, h Sch 7th bel Pine
Rockford Richard, lumber mer., h Sch 8th ab Race

Rock James, printer, 100 George
Rock John, bootmr., 13th ab Fitzwater
Rockenburg George, painter, 299 Mulberry, h 200 N 6th
Roeker Carson, shop, 451 S Front
Rockey A. B., portrait painter, S W 7th and Sansom
Rockhill Abraham C. mer., 160 High
Rockhill Amos, grocer, 33 Chatham
Rockhill Daniel H., tailor, 109 Chestnut, h 217 N 2d
Rockhill Joseph B., tailor, 117 Chestnut
Rockhill & Lamasure, tailors, 117 Chestnut
Rockhill Thomas C. com. mer., 160 High, h 217 Chestnut
Rockhill T. C. jun., atty., office 152 Walnut
Rockhill T. C. & W. P. & Co., dry goods, 105 High
Rockhill Wm. P., mer., 160 High, h 93 Locust
Rockhill & Wilson, clothing, 109 Chestnut
Rockwell John, lab., Fraley's al (K)
Rockwell Thomas H., 8 Lodge al, h 122 Buttonwood
Roda Mr., tavern, 13 E Pine
Rodamel Peter, plasterer, 2 La Fayette pl
Rodarmel Hannah, 13th & Olive
Roddon Charlotte, sempstress, rear 128 S 6th
Roddon Danl., lab., Filbert n Sch 3d
Roddy John, lab., 15 S Sch 6th
Roderick, Sarah, Stevenson's ct
Rodermel Henry, marble worker, 1 Wile's row
Rodes Joseph, cabinetmaker, Marshall ab Brown
Rodgers Alex. bricklayer, 7 Madison
Rodgers Dennis, weaver, Cadwalader bel Jefferson
Rodgers Eliza, 245 St John
Rodgers Elizabeth, china, High ab Broad
Rodgers Harriet, dressmr., 224 N 13th
Rodgers Henry, carp., Sch 8th ab Callowhill
Rodgers Hugh, stone cut., 4 Southampton ct
Rodgers Hugh, bricklayer, 105 N 13th
Rodgers Hugh, lab. 31 Lebanon
Rodgers Isaac, confectioner, 34 Powell
Rodgers James, shoemr., West ab Walnut
Rodgers James, weaver, 8 Lloyd's ct (K)
Rodgers James, cordw. 56 Shippen
Rodgers James, jr., weaver, 10 Lloyd's ct
Rodgers John, weaver, 1 Lloyd's ct
Rodgers John, rear 109 Christian
Rodgers John, keep. prison, Bush hill
Rodgers John B., carp., Markle bel Ontario
Rodgers Martha, 78 S 11th
Rodgers Mary C., gentw., Sch 6th bel Cherry
Rodgers Patrick, carter, G T road ab Thompson
Rodgers Patrick, lab., Pink ab Master (K)
Rodgers Peter, locksmith, 42 N 7th, h 3 Schriver's ct.
Rodgers Phebe Ann, rear Carpenter ab 8th
Rodgers Robert, tobacconist, S W A road ab Christian
Rodgers Thomas, carp, R road bel Coates
Rodgers Thomas, lab., rear 22 Fitzwater
Rodgers Wm., ropemr., Thompson ab Sch 5th
Rodgers Wm. R., tinsmith, 338 Vine
Rodman Benj., cordw., 7 Tammany

Rodman Margaret, Jefferson bel G T road
Rodman L., M. D., 431 Mulberry
Rodney C., lab., Mulberry al n 6th
Rodney Henry F., mer., 17 N 3d, h 9 Montgomery sq.
Rodney H. F. & W., shoes & bonnets, 17 N 3d
Rodney Simon, tanner, Willow ab Front
Rodney William, merchant, 17 N 3rd, h 94 Union
Roe James, weaver, James ab Nixon
Roe Thos., shoemr., Wharton ab 4th
Roe Wm., carp., Washington ab 3rd
Roedel C., varnisher, St John bel Beaver (K)
Roeder Ernst, tinsmith, 141 N 4th
Roehm Adam, pianomr., 322 High, h 7 St. Stephen's pl
Roehm Edward, piano maker, 60 St John
Roemech Jacob, drayman, 477 N 6th
Roesch Gottlob, baker, c 9th and Maple
Roesch G. L., baker, S E 11th and Filbert
Roesler Christopher, scalemr., 109 Poplar
Roesler Christopher, tavern N E 4th & Poplar
Rogers Ann, Raspberry ab Spruce
Rogers Ann C., milliner, 211 S 2nd
Rogers Arthur, weav., Phoenix ab Cadwalader
Rogers Benj., tailor, 30 N 10th
Rogers Benjamin, copperplate printer, 4 S 5th, h 23 Castle
Rogers & Caldwell, coal deal dealers, 441 N 3d & N W 12th & Callowhill
Rogers Charles, waterman, Rogers' ct
Rogers C. H., broker, 60 Walnut, h 133 S 3d.
Rogers David, seaman, 411 S Front
Rogers Edward, huckster, Penn ab 13th
Rogers Elizabeth, day school, 8 Virginia row
Rogers Elton J., 47 N 8th
Rogers Ephraim, weaver, West bel Hanover
Rogers Evans, gent., c Locust & Washington square
Rogers Francis, weaver, 11 Lloyd's ct (K)
Rogers Francis, mason, Marriott's la ab 4th
Rogers Francis, widow, 6 Moffit's ct
Rogers George, stone cut., R road ab Ann
Rogers George, carpenter, 104 Poplar
Rogers Hannah, 76 S 8th
Rogers Henry C., 2 Clover
Rogers H. G., 5 St John
Rogers James, weaver, Harmstead
Rogers James, weaver, Hancock bel Master (K)
Rogers James B., M. D., 90 S 12th
Rogers James J., moroc. dr., Apple & Culvert
Rogers James K., merchant, 140 Marshall
Rogers Jane, milliner, 68 N 8th
Rogers Jane, b. h., 107 N 2d
Rogers John, lab., Bedford bel 12th
Rogers John, grocer, 9th bel Cedar
Rogers John, shoemr., P road n Carpenter
Rogers John L., bootmr., 4 Nicholson
Rogers Joseph, coal mer., N W 12th and Callowhill, h 441 N 3d
Rogers J. M., grocery, Callowhill bel Sch 5th
Rogers Mary, 122 S 12th
Rogers Matthew M., carp., 322 S 6th
Rogers Michael, 266 S 5th

Rogers Orrin, publisher Christian Repository, 64 Spruce
Rogers Owen, dealer, Shippen bel 8th
Rogers Patrick, shop, Shippen & 7th
Rogers Patrick, carter, G T road above Franklin (K)
Rogers Samuel, 1 Little Oak
Rogers Samuel, mer., 11 N Front, h Sch 6th bel High
ROGERS, SINNICKSON & Co., coal mers., 44 Walnut
Rogers Thos., provision store, Lombard above Sch 3d
Rogers Thomas, plaster, Rittenhouse ab Sch 6th
Rogers Thos., carpenter, Sassafras & Sch Front
Rogers Thomas, carpenter, 2 Lebanon
Rogers Thomas J., sea capt., 32 Almond
Rogers Wm., clerk, 103 Noble
Rogers William, mason, 5 Harmony ct
Rogers Wm., lab., Dorothy n Sch 4th
Rogers William B., printer, Pemberton's al
Rogers Wm. D., coachmr., 6th & Brown
Rogers Wm. E., colourman, 16 Arcade, h Morris ab Christian
Rogers Wm. M., coal mer., 44 Walnut, h 88 Chestnut
Rogers W. D. carp., 226 Sassafras, h M'Clung's nut
Roget Edward, prof. languages, 73 New
Roggenbergger Marcus, mer., 185 Coates
Rohde William, bootmaker, 7 Exchange pl
Rohe Michael, tavern, 84 Green
Rohman I. H., 7th bel Poplar
Rohner Jacob, b h, 29 Carter's al
Rohr Louisa A., 8th bel Wallace
Rohrbacher Peter, cordw., G T road n Phoenix
Rohrer John S., M. D., 529 Chestnut.
Rohrman Henry, tinsmith, 441 N 2d, h Broad ab Poplar
Rohrman H. & Son, tinsmith, 441 N 2d
Rohrman Wm. C., tobacco, rear 6th ab Poplar
Roland Catharine Mrs., 14 N 7th
Roland Edward D., musician, 39 Quince
Roland John, engineer, 242 Christian
Roland Thos., engineer, Coates n Sch
Rolfe Henry, coachman, 9 Mercer
Rolin B. R., collector, Fitzwater ab 12th
Rolins Thomas, weaver, 38 W Cedar
Roll David, tailor, 27 Julianna
Rolley Abner, hair dresser, 112 N 5th
Rolph Thos., painter, 3d ab Catharine
Roman Andrew, barber, Front & Catharine
Romich Leonard, mason, 182 St John
Rommel Jacob F., lab., 8 Orchard
Rommell John, mer., 387 High, h 444 N Front
Ronaldson David, sailor, 83 Swanson
Ronaldson Isabel, shop, 255 Catharine
Ronaldson Richard, gent., 200 S 9th
Ronckendorff Mary, George n Sch 8th
Rondthaler Emanuel Rev., 74 Sassafras
Rone Michael, lab., 12th ab Washington
Ronert Charles, 6 Northampton ct
Roney Archibald, wea., Benton n School
Roney Charles J., printer, 1 Howard's ct
Roney Edward, lab., 105 Bedford

Roney James, lah., Kneass' ct
Roney James, printer, 184 S 11th
Roney James M., lab., Washington (W P)
Roney John, gent., 2d bel Beaver
Roney Margaret, wid., rear 6 Emlen's ct
Roney Patrick, lab., Vine ab Broad
Roney Thomas, leather, 81 S 2d, h 177 S 5th
Roney Thomas, weaver, George n Sch 3d
Roney Thomas B., weav., P road bel Fitzwater
Roney Wm., weaver, Sch 3d ab Walnut
Roney Wm., weaver, Benton n William
RONEY WM. Jr., grocer, S W 3rd & Branch
Rood Anson Rev., 335 N 6th
Roofner Michael, brickmr., Jefferson n Sch 6th
Rooke F. M., bootmaker, 9th and Nectarine
Rookstool Abm., vict., Kessler's al
Rookstool Catharine, rear 143 Coates
Rookstool George, vict., Phœnix bel G T road
Rookstool Samuel, carpenter, 377 N 4th.
Room Barzillai, stevedore, 45 Swanson
Room Benjamin, stevedore, 8 Lombard
Room Nathan D., cabtmr., 411 S 2d
Room Samuel L., Sailors' Home, 10 Lombard
Room Wm., stevedore, 29 Beck (S)
Rooney Ellen, grocer, 4th & German
Roop H., ven. blindmr., S E 7th and High, h 35 Wallace
Roop Jacob, lab., Parrish bel 10th
Roop Saml. W., clerk, 240 N 4th
Roop Wm., carp., Noble ab Franklin
Roorke Charles, pedler, 6 Brook's ct
Roorke Edw., cabman, 6 Brook's ct
Root G., grocery, R road ab Broad
Root Marcus A., teacher of writing and photographist, 140 Chestnut, h Sch 8th bel George
Root Orlow, shoemr., 230 S 3rd
Root William, morocco dresser, 21 P road
Rop John, teamster, Wood ab Sch 6th
Roper L., M. D., dentist, 381 Mulberry
Roper William, stone cutter, Ann, Francisville
Rorebaugher J., tailor, G T road ab Jefferson
Rorer Albert, mer., 148 High
Rorer & Graeff, shoes & bonnets, 148 High
Rorer James, oak cooper, 10 Charles pl
Rorer James B., surgical instrument maker, 28 N 6th, h 70 Wood
Rorer John, surgical instrument maker, 28 N 6th
Rorer John & Sons, surgical instrument makers, 28 N 6th
Rorer Saml., farmer, 540 N 2d (K)
Rorer Samuel jr., moroc. fin., 540 N 2d (K)
Rorer Wm., surgical instrument maker, 28 N 6th, h 42 Franklin.
Rorke James, carp., Carlton ab Sch 4th
Roscoe Martha, gentw., rear 24 Brown
Rose Abraham, provisions, Coates ab 9th
Rose Atkinson, tinsmith, 299 Mulberry
Rose Andrew, shoemr, 21 Cedar, h 64 Swanson
Rose Benjamin A., 17 Keefe
Rose Charles, Walnut W Sch. 3d
Rose Charles F., cabinetmr., 195 Locust
Rose Charles, ship carp., 64 Swanson
Rose Conrad, piano maker, 11th bel Sp Garden
Rose David, tavern, 213 S 2d

Rose Elias, hatter, 12 Pegg
Rose E., huckster, 393 N 3rd
Rose Francis B., missionary, Sch 8th ab Cherry
Rose H. L., beer house, 150 Coates
Rose Jacob, tanner, 29 Charlotte
Rose Jacob, Dr., Hamilton vil
Rose Jacob L., M. D., 18 S 8th
Rose John, brickmr., F road n Franklin
Rose John, Sch. 6th ab Cherry
Rose John, shoe dealer, 482 N 4th
Rose Joseph, lab., Sch 8th bel Vine
Rose R., tailor, 222 N 4th
Rose Thomas, 3 Orleans
Rose Watson, carp., 437 N 5th
Rose William, combmr., rear 291 St John
Rose Wm., vict., N W 13th & Pine, h 3 Orleans
Rose William, cutler, Washington (W P)
Rose Wm., grocer, R. road and George (F V)
Rose Wm., jr., cutler, Oak (W P)
Rose William & Son, cutlers, Washington. (W P)
Roseberry Joseph, cordw., 11 Rachel
Rosell Mahlon M., shoemaker, 392 S 2d
Roseman John, pearl turner, Hubbell ab Catharine
Rosenbaum Joseph, capmr., 24 N 3d, h 210 S 2d
Rosenberg Jacob, Front & Coates
Rosenberg E., Sansom's alley
Rosenberger Christ., vict., 20 Ogden
Rosenberger & Lewis, grocers, Poplar & Sch 8th
Rosenberry Christian, grocer, G. T. road ab 5th
Rosencrantz John, carpet manufac., Apple and Franklin, store 32 S Front, h 122 S 8th
Rosenfelt Harman, weaver, 125 O. Y. road
Rosenfelt Moyer, 31 Apple
Rosengarten G. D., chemical laboratory, c Sch 7th and Vine, h 13 Palmyra sq
Rosenheim A. H., mer., 42 N 2d, h 5th & Wood
Rosenheim Samuel M., trader, 178 Poplar
Rosenthal & Cotti, mers., 28 Bank
Rosenthal H., lab., rear 174 Marshall
Rosenthal Levi, tobacconist, 272 Sassafras
Rosenthal F. A., dry goods, 36 N 8th
Roser Frederick, shoemr., Perry bel Master (K)
Roser Philip, tailor, 3 Sheetz
Roset John, mer., 120 High, h Spruce ab Sch 8th
Roset, Troutman & Thomas, dry goods, 120 High
Roskamp Joseph, tailor, 34 Pegg
Ross Aaron, saddler, 15 Filbert
Ross Alexander, milliner, 176 S 5th
Ross Ann, Black Horse alley
Ross Anna, confectioner, 481 Sassafras
Ross Bertrand, hatter, 120 Chestnut, h 29 Noble
Ross Christian K., mer., 115 High
Ross Cornelius, carp., Sch. 4th ab Spruce
Ross David, rigger, 495 S 2d
Ross Diana, washer., 30 Gray's alley
Ross Elizabeth, 22 Chester
Ross George, hatter, Jones' pl, h 59 Coate's al
Ross Harriet, 19 Barclay
Ross James, brickmr., Cedar n Sch 5th
Ross James, clothing, Ogden bel 11th
Ross James, ham curer, 275 Cherry
Ross James B., 283 Spruce

Ross Jane, Sch 4th n Ann
Ross Jane, 276 S 6th
Ross John, mer., 74 High, h 435 Sassafras
Ross John, shoemr, 255 Cedar
Ross John, grocer, S W Brown and 2d, h 411 N Front
Ross John, weaver, 10 Gay's ct (K)
Ross John, ropemr., High W. of Sch. 7th
Ross John L., cooper, 35 Mead al
Ross John M., tailor, 30½ N 11th h 33 North
Ross Joseph R., barber, High W Sch 7th
Ross J. & S. H., grocers, S W 2d and Brown, and F road ab Maiden
Ross Minus, lab., Steam Mill alley
Ross Richard, Pearl ab 13th
Ross Robert, lab., Sch. 5th opp St. Joseph's av.
Ross Samuel, hair seating and curled hair manufactory, 63 Dock & 33 Dillwyn
Ross Samuel, painter, 28 Powell
Ross Samuel, brickmr., Sch. 4th ab Spruce
Ross Wm., grocer, 13th and Buttonwood
Ross Wm. coachman, 12 Burd's ct
Ross Wm. P. M., writ. master, S E 5th & Library
Rossell Jacob, cork manuf. 271 Callowhill
Rosseter N., drayman, 184 Lombard
Rotan Fredk. ship carp., Palmer bel Duke (K)
Rotan Wm., ship carp., Queen n Hanover (K)
Rotch Martha, tavern, N W Poplar & Beach (K)
Roth Chas., tailor, 124 Chestnut, h 194½ Spruce
Roth Charles & Co., tailors, 124 Chestnut
Roth Christian, bootmr., 203 Callowhill
Roth John, shoemr., 34 Catharine
Roth John, baker, 249 S 3d.
Roth Michael, vict., 505 N 4th
Roth Wm., baker, 208 S Front.
Rothengass Conrad, labourer, 30 Strawberry
Rothermel P. F. portrait painter, 16 Sansom
Rothschild Solomon, bootmr., 94 N 4th
Rotrong Michael, weaver, Poplar bel 2d
Rottenbury James, shoe maker, 45 Gaskill
Rottenbury John, shoemr., 19 Stamper's al
Rottenbury Wm., tailor, 98 Cherry
ROUDET, CAUET & CO., sugar refiners, 37 St John
Roudet John B. sugar refiner, 37 St John, h 95 Spruce
Roudet Mary, 95 Spruce
Roumford John C., clerk, 22 Pratt
Round Wm., shop, 153 E Lombard
Rourke Bernard, lab., 7 Brooke's ct
Rourke Jas., weaver, Caldwell n Beach
Rouscher John, cordw., Gray's ct (N L)
Rouse & Kennedy, tailors, 88 Walnut
Rouse Richard W., tailor, 88 Walnut
Roush Peter, driver, rear 527 N 4th
ROUSSEL EUGENE, perfumer, 114 Chestnut
Rouvoudt Ellen, b h, 303 Mulberry
Rovoudt Andrew, mer., 164 N 3d, h S E 5th and Noble.
Rovoudt Peter, mer., 164 N 3d, h Dillwyn n Wood
ROVOUDT P. & A., China mers., 164 N 3d
Rovoudt William, mer., 53 N 3d, h 11 Dillwyn
Rowan Adam, 93 Cedar
38

Rowan Phineas, U S Mint, h George ab Sch 8th
Rowan Wm. G., lapidist, 5 Bank alley, h S W 2d and Wharton
Rowand A. H., bookbinder, 188 Callowhill
ROWAND JOS. T., druggist, 376 High, h 260 Filbert
Rowand Josiah S., druggist, 2 Mark's lane
Rowand Samuel, varnisher, 21 Nectarine
Rowbotham Wm., weaver, 574 N 3d
Rowe James D., shoemr., Yhost ab Queen
Rowe John A., M. D., G T road and Phœnix
Rowe Manley, brooms & wooden ware, 63 N 3d, h 594 N 3d
Rowe Spencer, 200 Mulberry
Rowe Wm. H., cordw., 422 S 4th
Rowell Dr. C. T., S W Front and Shippen
Rowen Christopher, ship wright, Marlboro' ab Queen
Rowen Henry, brickmr., Palmer n F. road (K)
Rowen Henry, ship carp., Duke below Vienna (K)
Rowen James, ship carp., Queen bel Palmer (K)
Rowen John, carp., Cherry ab Queen. (K)
Rowen Michael, ship carp., Vienna & Duke (K)
Rowen Peter, ship carp. West bel Crown (K)
Rowen Wm. granite cutter, Bedford ab Crown (K)
Rowen Wm. G., stone cutter, M. road & Wharton
Rowland Albert G., Kensington iron works, h 492 N 4th
Rowland A. G., tract missionary, 454 Callowhill
Rowland Charles, machinist, Barber's row
Rowland David, carter, Pearl ab Sch. 6th
Rowland George, carter, Pearl ab 12th
Rowland Hugh, dealer, Pearl bel Sch 7th
Rowland Isaac P., machinist, Franklin ab Front
Rowland James, Kensington Iron Works, h 243 Marshall
Rowland James, pres. Beaver Coal Co. 84 Walnut, h 28 Mulberry
Rowland James & Co., Kensington Iron Works Beach bel Maiden
Rowland John, cabinetmr., 6 Mary
Rowland John, scaman, M. road bel Carpenter
Rowland Mary L. 297 Sassafras
Rowland Nathan, rolling mill, h 7 Brown
Rowland N., Kensington Iron Works, h 7 Brown
Rowland Peter S., blacksmith, 2 Wood
Rowland P. S., importer of wines & liqs. 28 Walnut, h 113 Spruce
Rowland Wm., machinest, 224 N 13th
ROWLAND WM., saw manuf., Zane n 7th, h 24 N 9th
Rowland Wm, cordw., 6th and Christian
Rowland Wm., manuf., 311 N 6th
Rowland William Jr., saw manuf., S E 9th and Filbert
Rowlett M. M., b. h., 4 Crown
Rowley, Ashburner, & Co. mers., 5 & 6 S wharves
Rowley Edward H., mer., h 7 whfs, h Sch 6th bel Walnut
Rowley James, dentist, Clinton ab Parrish
Rowley Jane, Sch 6th bel Walnut
Rowley Latitia, washer, 204 Lombard

Rowley Nathan W., grocer, N E 3d and Shippen
Rowntree Thomas, blacking manf., Benton's av
Rox Edward, weaver, G T rd bel Jefferson (K)
Rox John, dyer, 2d ab Master
Roxberry Alex., engraver, 7 Edward (K)
Roxberry Wm., brickmaker, F road bel Oxford
Roy George, butcher, rear 6th ab Poplar
Roy James, hatter, 10 Culvert
Roy John, tavern, 434 N 3d
Roy John, shoemr., 5 Clymer
Royal Wm., manf., Apple bel Franklin
Royer Alfred I., carp., Ogden ab 9th
Royer George, carpenter, 126 Dillwyn
Royer John, clerk, 305 Callowhill
Royer Philip, carp. Myrtle
Royer Sarah, Ogden ab 9th
Royl Charles A. bricklayer, rear 33 Charlotte
Royston Sarah, 33 Laurel
Rozell Isaac, carp., Sch. 7th and Poplar
Rozell Peter, manuf., 129 E Shippen
Ruan Heyliger, clerk, 12 Hamilton pl
Rubicam Charles, carpenter, 179 N 11th
Rubicam Daniel, 122 N 7th
Rubicam George, carp., 30 Carlton
Rubin John, lab., Carpenter ab 12th
Rubincam Caleb, tailor, 125 Mulberry
Rubincam Jonathan, carp. 13th & Wallace
Rubincam Joseph, gent., 96 Sassafras
Rubincam Richard, fruiterer, 113 N 3rd, h 208 Noble
Rubincam & Sellers, confect. and fruits, 113 N 3d
Ruby Mrs. C., milliner, 150 S 4th
Ruby Philip S., chair painter, rear 9 Rose al
Ruby Robert, carp., Palmer bel Queen (K)
Ruck Joseph, coachmr., Laurel and Yorke, h 47 Spruce
Ruckman & Price, boots and shoes, 108 N 3d
Ruckman Wm. D., mer., 108 N 3d, h Franklin ab Wood
Ruckstool John, saddler, 111 Apple
Rudd Michael, sawmr., rear 8 Broad
Ruddach Dav. J. & Son, mers., 35 S Water
Ruddach David J., mer., 35 S Water, h 107 S 4th
Ruddach & Eiserman cabtmrs., Coates bel 11th
Ruddach Geo. J., carp., 5 Bread, h 150 Marshall
Ruddach Wm. H., mer., 35 S Water
Rudderow Anna, 8th and Wallace
Ruddles James, wines and liquors, Broad ab Vine
Ruddock Andrew, pearl ornament mr., 48 Filbert
Ruddock Mary, Perry ct
Rudduck Wm., tailor, rear 57 S 3d
Ruddy Wm. Rev., Ann (F V)
Rudiman Wm., cordwainer, 59 Federal
Rudloff John, tailor, 285 Callowhill
Rudman William C., brewer, 121 Green
Rudolph Barbara, Palmer n F road
Rudolph Christian, turner, 297 St. John
Rudolph Elizabeth, Wagner's ct
Rudolph E. C., tailor, 464 Vine
Rudolph George, carp., Harmony ct, h 26 Marion
Rudolph Henry, papermr., School bel Edward (K)

Rudolph Henry C., watchman, 289 N 10th
Rudolph John, carp., Dorothy E of Sch. 3d
Rudolph John, bootmr., Marriott la ab 5th
Rudolph Joseph, cooper, 5th ab Jefferson (K)
Rudolph J. F., druggist, 10th & Ogden
Rudolph Martin, shoemr., 30 Castle
Rudolph Samuel, tailor, 325 S 4th
Rudolph Samuel, rear 338 S 5th
Rudolph Sarah, Lemon ab 10th
Rudolph Wm., tailor, 236 N 13th
Rudolphus F., engraver, 360 Vine
Rudrauff Godfrey, Willow bel 8th
Rudrauff H., tailor, 315 Callowhill
Rudy David J., cabinetma., Hoover's ct
Rudy Henry, turner, Winter (N L)
Rudy Jacob, combmr., 460 N 4th
Rudy Jacob L. combmr. Elizabeth ab Poplar
Rue Elijah, cabinetmaker, 15 Cox
Rue Francis J., dry goods, 292 S 2d
Rue Harvey, bonnet st., N E Union & 3d
Rue Joseph, carpenter, 9th and Parrish
Rue Joseph, machinest, Green bel 10th
Rue Lewis S., saddler, Brown bel 13th
Rue Samuel, cabinetmaker, 20 Sassafras
Rue William, steam sawyer, Marlborough ab Queen
Rue Wm., mariner, 4 John (S)
Ruelius Joseph, printer, 15 Cherry
Ruhe Joseph, grocer, S W Catharine & Lebanon
Rufer Elizabeth, rear Jones' al
Ruff William Jr., tavern, 264 Sassafras
Ruffel Chas. B., bleeder, Queen opp Crown
Ruffel George, trader, F road op Master
Ruffin Daniel, lab. Lawrence's ct
Ruffin Robert, carp., 26 Blackberry alley
Rugan Charles, mer., N wharves & Sassafras, h 100 N 8th
Rugan George, acct., 248 Sassafras
Rugg James, b h, Penn & Lombard
Ruggles James, distiller, Broad & Vine, h Poplar bel Broad
Ruggles Samuel, saddler, 110 Chestnut, h 105 Cherry
Ruhl George, coachmaker, c Wood and O Y road, h Smith's ct
Ruhl John E., bow mr., N W 8th and Wood
Ruhlman Samuel, trunkmaker, 18 Franklin pl
Ruhmann F. C., N E 13th & Callowhill
Rule John, chandler, 291 S 5th
Ruley John G., cordw., 1 Clare
Ruley Jos., cordw., Burchell's ct
Rulon Ephraim, copper smith, Trinity pl
Rulon James, blacksmith, Cherry ab Queen (K)
Rulon Marg., 29 Mary, (S)
Rulon John W., mer., 36 N Front, h 7th ab Buttonwood
Rumberger Henry, segarmr., rear 493 N 3d
Rumble Elizabeth, 129 S 8th
Rumbol John, tin smith, 5 Robert's ct
Runnel Geo., plast., 3 John (S)
Rumel Jacob, plasterer, 25 Wharton
Rumel Mich., plasterer, Wharton & Corn
Rumer Henry, b. h., 298 Sp Garden

Rumer John, mason, Olive bel Broad
Rumford Samuel, brickmaker, Walnut W Sch 3rd
Rummel Charles, vict. Coates bel 12th
Rump John, cooper, 213 N 2d, h 177 Brown
Rump Philip, cordw. 10th ab Poplar
Rumsey William, M. D., 225 Coates
Rumtherford Robt., drover, Cox n 5th
Rundle George, stock & ex. broker, 2 York, h 101 Locust
Runner Geo. J., victualler, 241 N 5th
Runner Martin, vict., 2 Frank's ct
Runner S., Mrs., 5th ab Noble
Runnigan John, weaver, G T road bel Master
Runt Christian, tailor, Jefferson ab 5th (K)
Runyan Geratus B. clerk, rear 443 N 3d
Runyan John, crackers, 30 Catharine
Ruoff Charles, locksmith, 31 Green
Ruoff John, shoemr., 107 Poplar
Ruoff John, baker, 340 S Front
Rupp Thomas, baker, 262 Mulberry
Rush Ann, 12 Palmyra sq
Rush Ann, gentw., 335 Sassafras
Rush Benjamin, att'y & coun., 98 S 4th
Rush Benj. H., blacksm., Elizabeth bel Franklin
Rush Daniel, lab., rear 4 Seybold's ct
Rush F. W., confectioner, 244 Sassafras
Rush George, carpenter, 211 Cherry
Rush John, carp. Ogden ab 10th
Rush John, ship carver, Penn ab Maiden, h Penn ab Poplar (K)
Rush John, blacksmith, 13th bel Brown
RUSH J. MURRAY, attorney & counsellor, 98 S 4th
Rush Lawrence, waterman, Mary bel 2d (S)
Rush Mary Mrs. 125 Race
Rush Samuel W., collector of water rents, h 371 Mulberry
Rush Stephen, jr., carp., Broad bel Coates
Rush Stephen, Green ab 13th
Rush Thomas M., clerk, Sp Garden n 10th
Rush Wm. acct. 59 N 10th
Rush William, M. D., Sch. 7th ab Spruce
Rush William, acct., 165 N 5th
Rushton Abraham W., bookseller, 22 Sp Garden
Rushton James, importer, 49 Chestnut, h 429 N 3d
Rushton J. Y., mer., 245 High, h 149 N 12th
Rushton William, cotton spinner, Beach below Shackamaxon, h Beach ab Maiden (K)
Rushworth William, tavern, 87 S Water
Rusk Charles, shop, Brown bel 12th
Rusk Elizabeth, rear 525 N 2d
Rusk James, waterman, Collins' ct
Rusk Matthias, brickmr. George ab Apple
Rusk Peter, cordwainer, Franklin ab Howard (K)
Rusk Robt., grocery, 11th and Mellon
Rusk Samuel, carp., 11 Somer's ct
Russ Wm., glovemr., rear 521 N 3d
Rusling Sarah G., wid. of Rev. Jos., Marshall ab Parrish
Russell Alex., weaver, 44 W Cedar
Russell Arthur, lab., Clare st
Russell Benj., watchman, Jones W Sch. 5th

RUSSELL & BLAIR, tea dealers, 33 S Front
Russell Cath., milliner, 144 S Juniper
Russell Cæsar, lab., 21 Middle al
Russell Edwd., manuf., 178 Swanson
Russell D. C., confectioner, Charles bel Button-wood
Russell Ebenezer D., cordw., Union ab Franklin (K)
Russell Elizabeth, 327 Spruce
Russell Evans E., biscuit dealer, High n Sch 5th
Russell Francis, mer., 33 S Front, h 166 S 4th
Russell George, brickmr., 5 St James
Russell George, watchmaker, 18 N 6th
Russell George, clerk, Wood bel 11th
Russell Geo., machinist, 24 Hazel
Russell George P., druggist, 87 High, h 297 Chestnut
Russell Henry H. cordw., 187 Brown
Russell Henry R., cordw., rear 48 Charlotte
Russell Isaac, seaman, 14 Gaskill
Russell Jas. cashr. Bank Penn Township, h Sp Garden bel 12th
Russell James, lab., Ann E Sch. 3d
Russell James B, lab., High n Sch 2d
Russell John, blacksm., 151 N Juniper
Russell Jonathan, boot tree and last maker, 3 Cherry, h 2d ab Sassafras
Russell Joseph, carter, Sch 2d & Lombard
Russell Joseph, cordw., 102 Elizabeth
Russell Jos., com. mer., Hamilton Village
Russell Joseph B., chairmr. 5th bel Franklin
Russell Lucy, 53 S Juniper
Russell Lydia, 18 Green st
Russell M. M., att'y & convey., Cedar ab 11th
Russell Richard, porter, c 4th and Christian
Russell Richard, basket mr., Griffith's ct
Russell Rinah, widow, b h, 2½ S 8th
Russell Robert, lastmr., 3 Cherry
Russell Samuel, lab., 7 Clair
Russell Samuel, lab., Rugan bel Willow
Russell Thelwell, iron moulder, rear Coates ab 13th
Russell Wm, police officer, Lombard E Sch 7th
Russell William, merchant, George ab St John (K)
Russell Wm , sailmr., Corn ab Reed
Russell Wm. G., carp., 1 Jones' ct (S)
Russum Thos. B., dry goods, S W 2d & Union
Rust Luther C., dry goods, 24 Bank
Ruth Abm., grocery, 6th and Poplar
Ruth Absalom, hatter, 62 High, h 345 S 5th
Ruth Adam, mer. 263 High
Ruth Andrew, lab., 12 Culvert bel 4th
Ruth Christian, blacksm., Catharine ab 3d
Ruth David, collar mr., 20 Elizabeth (N L)
Ruth David, shoemr., G T road ab 5th
Ruth David jr., weaver, G T road ab 5th
Ruth Elizabeth, 1 Clawges' ct
Ruth Henry, blacksmith, Culvert bel 4th
Ruth Jacob, shoemr., Tammany and St John
Ruth Jacob, machinist, Alden ab Poplar
Ruth Jacob, carpenter, Sch. 2d bel Callowhill
Ruth Jacob, shoemr., Charlotte ab Thompson (K)
Ruth Joseph, bricklayer, G T road ab 5th
Ruth Wm., weaver, rear G T road ab 4th (K)

Ruth Wm. clerk, Millers's ct
Ruth Wm. lab. Vine n Sch
Rutherford Allen, court aud., Juniper ab Locust
Rutherford Hugh, carter, Lombard n Bank
Rutherford James, carp., Centre, h Locust ab Juniper
Rutherford John Jr., 202 Locust
Rutherford John Senr., Walnut ab Juniper
Rutherford Joseph, pilot, N W 2d and Federal
Rutherford Robt. weaver, Lombard n Sch Bank
Rutherford Wm. bookbr., Locust ab Juniper
Ruths Garret, collector, 10th n Catharine
Rutter Alice, shop, 50 New
Rutter C. S., mer., 62 S Front, h 191 Spruce
Rutter David, M. D., 370 S 2d
Rutter John, carp., Wheat bel Wharton
Rutter Lydia, tailoress, 572 S 2d bel Marion
Rutter, Patteson & Newhall, mers., 62 S Front
Rutter Peter, jeweller, Rye bel Marion
Rutter Robert, victualler, Federal ab 2d
Rutter S. P., clerk, 80 George (S)
Rutty John, lab., Sch 4th ab George (F V)
Ryall George C., bricklayer, Carpenter bel 9th
Ryan Amelia, 6 Clair
Ryan Charles, weaver, 7th ab Poplar
Ryan Charles, mer., 121 S Front, h 14 Montgomery square
Ryan Cornelius, shop, 10 Hurst st
Ryan Daniel, shoemr., 5th ab Plum
Ryan Edmund, shop, 209 Shippen
Ryan Edward, weaver, Cadwalader ab Master
Ryan Francis A., acct., 14 Montgomery sq
Ryan Hannah, widow, New Market and Laurel
Ryan James, lab., Cypress n 3d
Ryan James, bootmr., 5 Charles
Ryan Jane T., Ogden bel 10th
Ryan John, cordwainer, 90 N 9th, h 205 Cherry
Ryan John, blacksmith, G T road and 4th (K)
Ryan John W., manuf., 112 Queen, h 513 S Front
Ryan John W., mer., 47 N 3d, h 28 Mellon
Ryan Jos., carp., 131 Locust
Ryan Lewis, gent., 373 Walnut
Ryan Martin, morocco dress., Justice's ct
Ryan Mary, dry goods, 172 S 6th
Ryan M. A. dry goods & milliner, 66 N 8th
Ryan Patrick, cabinetmr., 6 Bell's ct
Ryan Richard, clerk, 127 Buttonwood st
Ryan Thos., bootmr., 198 S 5th
Ryan Thos., grocer, 22 Barron's ct
Ryan Thomas, bootmr., George ab Sch 8th
Ryan Wm. blacksmith, Jackson ct (N L)
Ryan Wm., mer., 47 N 3d, h 28 Mellon
Ryan William, currier, 128 N 4th
Ryan William, ladies' shoemr, 16 S 4th, ab stairs, h 8th ab Wallace
Ryan Wm., tavern, 76 N Water
RYAN WM. & CO., Ladies' shoemr., 16 S 4th
Ryder Jos., weaver, William and Benton (K)
Ryder Rebecca, 4 rear Green st
Ryder J. R., painter, Washington bel R road
Ryland, Wm. blacksmith, Torr's al
Rymer Chas., moulder, rear Carpenter bel 8th
Rynard Henry, stonemason, Marshall ab Poplar
Ryno Ephraim, hair dresser 33 S 3d

Ryrce Simon, glass blow., Vienna ab Queen (K
Rysinger Hyneman, peddler, 32 Margaret st

———

Saabye Hannah, Workman's ct
Saben Rhoda, Cherry bel Franklin (K)
Sabins Saml. glassblow., Cherry ab Duke
Saboy Adelaide, washer, 104 Gaskill
Sackriter Daniel P., cabinetmr., 259 S 7th at.
76 Bedford
Sadharnd John G., shovelmr., 47 Lily al
Saddler Emery, 9 Pryor's ct.
Sadler C. C. mer., 9 N Water
Sadler C. C. & Co. mer., 9 N Water
Sadler James, lab., 258 N Water
Saffin Wm., butcher, bel Washington bet 7th & 8th
Safford E., mer., 81 Dock, h 6 Montgomery sq
SAFFORD E. & CO., coal mers., 81 Dock
Safford Henry, coal dealer, 419 N 6th
Safford H. W., coal dealer, 81 Dock, h Mulberry n Sch 6th
Safried John, cordw., rear Schleisman's al
Sage Benjamin, saddler, Washington (W P)
Sage S. Mortimer, capt., 440 S Front
Sagee Andrew, furrier, 16 Brown
Sagee Wm., clerk, 176 S 9th
Sager Amos D., cabinetmr., 21 Duke
Sager Michael, baker, 274 Mulberry
Sagers James W., mer., 435 N 5th
Sagers Thomas R., looking glass manuf., 560 N 3d.
Sagers Wm., coachmr., rear G T road ab 2d (K)
Sague John, cordw., Hazel bel 12th
Sailer John, gent., 332 Vine
Sailer Peter, framemr., rear 83 G T road (K)
Sailor George M., marble yd., James n 10th
Sailor Henry, tobacconist, 13 N 5th, h 165 N 6th
Sailor James, grocer, 2d & Greenwich
Sailor John, barber, G T road ab Master
Sailor John M. mer., Buttonwood bel 13th
Sailor Joseph, editor, 146 Catharine
Sailor Saml., lab., Queen opp Cherry (K)
Sailor Thos., painter, rear 63 New Market
Sailor William, lab., R road ab 13th
Sailor Wm., painter, rear 123 Plum
Sale Thos., Barker n Sch 6th
Salkeld Mary, 62 S 11th
Sallada Martin, tobacconist, rear 291 Coates
Sallada Reuben A., whipmr., 1 N 4th, h 42 Mulberry
Salman John W., shipsmith, Swanson and Shippen, h Sheetz n Front
Salmon Jas., 14 Somers' ct
Salmon James, clerk, 47 Apple
Salmon John, tinman, Front bel Phoenix (K)
Salomon Paul, gent., Sch. 7th n Locust
Salsburg Andrew, paper stainer, N E Mackey & Corn
Salsburg Cassell, painter, 135 S 10th
Salsbury Elizabeth, rear 390 Sassafras
Salsbury John, carter, George ab R road
Salter Caspar, carp., Orchard ab Rawle

Salter Catharine, Queen ab Hanover (K)
Salter F. A., grocer, F road ab Stone bridge
Salter Heliakil A., convey., Queen ab Hanover
Salters Robert B., carp., Hudson's al, h Wharton bel 5th
Saltzman Cath., 303 Vine
Saltzman Jacob, 303 Vine
Samanos A. A., tobacconist, 85 Chestnut
Sammons Elizabeth, 9th bel Christian
Sammons Thomas, lab., 34 Blackberry al
Sammons Wm., coachman, 28 Prosperous alley
Sample Archibald, George ab 11th
Sample James, Rugan bel Willow
Sample James G., engineer, 19 Jefferson
Sample John, weaver, Shippen la ab Rose
Sample Thomas C., cabinet mr., 4 Grubb
Sampson Benjamin, carter 6 Maiden (K)
Sampson Maria, Mulberry n Sch 7th
Sampson M., milliner, 9th and Walnut
Sampson Samuel, 21 Swanson
Sampson Saml., waiter, Caroline pl
Samuel A., tailor, N E Water and Spruce
SAMUEL D., mer., 78 High, h 329 Walnut
Samuels John, lab., Penn bel Shackamaxon
Samuels John, glass blower, Vienna bel Franklin
Sanborn Charles, carp., rear 58 Zane, h Pine ab 2d
Sanborn Mary Mrs., 57 Pine
Sanborn Wm., cabtmr., Oneida pl
Sanders A., teacher, 73 N 7th
Sanders George, carp., Hutchinson ab Poplar
Sanders Geo. J. H., teacher, Sch 8th ab Cherry
Sanders James, alderman, 252 S 4th, h S W 5th & German
Sanders Jas., waterman, 7 Little Oak st
Sanders John, carp., Yhost st
Sanders Jeremiah, clerk, 5 Marion
Sanders Robert, porter, 8 Little Pine
Sanders Sarah, Paul ab 6th
Sanders Solomon, porter, Apple bel George
Sanders Thomas L., constable, 153 Cherry
Sanders William W., carp., Yhost
Sanderson, Brothers & Co., agents, 42 Commerce
Sanderson Charles, blacksmith, Carlton ab 13th
Sanderson John, atty. & coun., 34 S 5th
Sanderson J. M., 105 Chestnut
Sanderson Mary, gentw., Mary bel 2d
Sanderson Wm., chairmr., 107 Walnut, h 414 N 5th
Sandford A., driver, 3 Holmes' pl
Sandgram Mitchell, plumber, 355 S 2d
Sandland Thomas, silk button manuf., 94 N 6th
Sandman Charles, tobacconist, Palmer op Allen (K)
Sandman Phoebe, Perry ab Franklin
Sands Aaron, cabinetmr., 226 Catharine
Sands Jane, shop, Shippen la
Sands John, lab., 12 Gabell's ct
Sands Mary, Mary n Beach
Sands Mary, shop, 6th and Marriott
Sands Nathan, cordw., Davis' ct.
Sands Nicholas, cordw., Davis' ct
Sands Samuel, driver, 17 Beck
Sandy John, blacksm., Lewis ab Poplar

Sandy Wm. G., tailor, 13th & Olive
SANFORD E. S., package exp., 80 Chestnut
Sanford G. F., 80 Chestnut
Sanford Jas., pap. hang., Cobb's ct
Sanford J. J., teacher, Elizabeth ab Poplar
Sanford Richard, shoemr., Lane's ct
Sanford Thomas, oyster house, 202 N 2d
Sangerly Jos., carp., Crown & Franklin (K)
Sangram Charles M., ship plumber, S whfs bel Walnut, h 13 Beck pl
Sank J. Rinaldo, mer., 15 N whfs, h 95 N 2d
Sanna Hugh, weaver, Phillip ab Jefferson (K)
Sansom Hannah, 96 Mulberry
Sansom Isaac, mezzotinto printer, 28½ Sansom, h 311 S 4th
Santee Charles, mer., 146 N 3d, h 30 St John
Santman Jesse, carp., 8 Jackson
Santos A. F., 161 Pine
Sanvills John, cordw., Dean bel Bedford (K)
Sanvill Wm., cordw., Vienna n Queen (K)
Saphore Daniel A., coach lacemr., rear Jackson (S G)
Saphore John N., barber, 5th bel Poplar
Saphrey Edward, skindress., Harvey's ct (K)
Sapp Isaac, carter, West bel Hanover (K)
Sappington Saml., clerk S G Dist., h Sp Garden bel 8th
Sappington Thos., agent, 135 S 4th
Sarbacher, Anthony, shop, St John bel Beaver
Sarch Sam., blacksmith, 63 N 6th, h 23 Sheaff
Sarchet Joseph T., merchant, 10th below Parrish
Sarchet Margaret, vest mr., 8th ab Noble
Sargent F. W., M. D., Sch 7th & Filbert
Sargent George W., gent., 344 Chestnut
SARGENT & GUSTINE, chairmrs., 114 North Front
Sargent James L., broker, 314 N 5th
Sargent R. W. chairmr., 114 N Front, h Wallace n 9th
Saring Nicholas, wheelwright, 13th bel Green
Sarmiento Ferdinand, tailor, 211 Chestnut, h 183 S 9th
Sartain John, engraver, 28 Sansom
Sartain & Sansom, mezt. paint., 28½ Sansom
Sartori Charles, M D, 49 Wood ab 10th
Sartori Charles W., dry goods, 305½ Callowhill
Sartori Victor A., mer., 86 S Front, h 11th ab Clinton
Sartorius George, teacher 130 Vine
Sass John P. watchman, 25 Catharine
Sassa Charles W., tailor, 26 Vine
Sasseman Henry, 5 Madison av
Satterthwait Wm., carp., 7th bel Poplar
Satterthwaite Jas., 197 N 3d
Sattler Augustus, chairmr., 413 N 4th
Sauer Fredk., cordw., 4 Lagrange
Sauerbier John, hatter, 62 High, h 328 Sassafras
Sauerbier & Roth, hats, &c., 62 High
Sauerbier Wm. hatter, 62 High
Saul Martha, 4 Mayland
Saulner Henry E., engraver, 76½ Walnut, h 11th ab South
Saulnier Rachel, S W Jacoby & Sassafras

Saun John, shop, 349 Coates
Saunders & Brantin, window shades, 161 N 2d
Saunders Edward, shoemr., 261 Spruce
Saunders Elizabeth, b h., 116 Mulberry
Saunders G. waiter, 31 Quince
Saunders Jacob, sawyer, Gilles' al
Saunders James, blindmr., Willow ab 8th
Saunders Jas., barber, 192 Callowhill
Saunders James, pilot, 164 Swanson
Saunders James M., Willow ab 8th
Saunders John, pilot, 164 Swanson
Saunders John, Simmon's ct.
Saunders John, mer., 21 & h 295 N 6th
Saunders John, Bedford n Elm (K)
Saunders John L., chairmr., 71 Noble
Saunders John W., pilot, 3d bel Christian
SAUNDERS J. & M., bonnet warehouse, 21 N 4th
Saunders M'Pherson, merchant, 21 N 4th, h 213 N 4th
Saunderson Jonathan, prof. of music, 303 Mulberry
Saunderson, Wood & Co. mers., 42 S Front
Saunderson Z. W., mer., 42 S Front, h 322 E Pine
Saurman Jonathan, pumpmr., R road bel Coates
Saurman Yerkes, collector, Sp Garden bel 9th
Sauscline Andrew, cordw., Apple bel George
Sauser Charles, lamp mr., 172 Buttonwood
Sausman Martin, victualler, 12th ab Parrish
Sausman Wm., biscuit baker, N Market & Green
SAUTER CHARLES F., dry goods, 74 S 8th
Savage Charles, carpenter, Reeve bel Sch 2d
Savage C., tailor, rear 380 S 3d
Savage Foster W., carp., Carlton bel Sch 2d
SAVAGE & JAMES, dry goods, 79 High
Savage Jane, widow of John, Franklin ab Spring Garden
Savage John, gent., N W 11th & Spruce
Savage John R., 10th ab Fitzwater
Savage John R., gent., N E 3d & Pine
Savage Richard, lab., 84 George (S)
Savage Sarah, dressmr., Carberry ct
Savage Wm., carpenter, 165 N 4th, shop, Nectarine ab 10th
Savage Wm., carp., rear 471 N 3d
Savage William J., merchant, 79 High, h 190 S Front
Savery & Co., manuf. iron castings, 41 & 43 Commerce, foundry S Front bel Navy Yard
Savery P. B., manuf., S Front bel Navy Yard, h Catharine bel 3d
Savery Rebecca, 20 N 5th
Savery Thomas, lumb. mer., 289 N 6th
Savery Wm., lumb. mer., 269 N 7th
Savidge Enos, bricklayer, Coates ab 12th
Savill Samuel, waiter, 241 S 7th
Savin Deborah, 13 Duke (N L)
Savin George D. clerk, 13 Duke
Savin Samuel B., 231 S Front
Savington Fred., hatter, 6 St. Stephen's pl
Savoy John R., sheet iron worker, 107 N Juniper
Sawtell Henry, painter, 20 N 2d
Sawyer Chas., plumber, 24 Almond
Sawyer H., 136 S 5th

Sawyer J. R. livery stable, 17 Green (C)
Sawyer Martha, wid. of Robert L., N E Mash. u and 7th
Saxer Adam, lampmr., Thompson ab Sch 7th
Saxton Charles, coachmr., Gabel's ct
Saxton Chas. jr., sheet iron worker, 69 Rose
Saxton Edwd., blacksmith, Green bel 13th
Saxton Hannah, wid., 69 Beach (K)
Saxton William, hatter, Perry above Franklin (K)
Saybold John, huckster, 6 Butz's ct
Sayen George, merchant, 68 S Front, h 273 Spruce
Sayers Edward, seaman, Jefferson pl
Sayers James, stone cut., Shippen bel Broad
Saynor Samuel, cordw. North n 11th .
Sayre John P. cordw. 70 F road
Sayre Peter, tailor, Jay bel Coates
Sayre Wesley, combmr. 16 Franklin (K)
Sayres Edward S., mer. and Vice Consul of Brazil, 17 Walnut
Sayres Ethan, tailor, 45 Wood
Sayres Sarah, 3 Marks' la
Sayres Thomas, b. h., 4 Powell
Scales C. pumpmr. Carlton bel Sch 2d
Scallon John, dealer, 4 Franklin pl
Scank Alfred Wm., chairmr., rear 111 Brown
Scandel Anthony, tobacconist, 71 Shippen
Scanlan Ebenezer, shoemr. 355 S 2d, h 6th bel Christian
Scanlan Edw., Shippen la and Rose
Scanlan John, marble polisher, 7th bel Christian
Scanlan R., cordw., 270 S 4th
Scanlin & Fulton, coachmrs., rear 14 Filbert
Scanlin Robert T., coachmr., rear 14 Filbert
Scanlon Timothy, carp., Lewis ab Sch 7th
Scarf Thos., tavern, G T road ab 4th (K)
Scarlet John, carter, Shackamaxon ab Franklin
Scarlett Samuel, artist, 446 S 4th
Scattergood Ann, 60 Franklin
Scattergood & Bousted, tanners & curriers, 8th and Willow,
Scattergood Charles, coachmr., 103 New Market h Linden bel Front
Scattergood C., bricklayer, Lebanon row
Scattergood David, chemist, 60 Franklin
Scattergood James, weaver, Pink ab Master
Scattergood Joel M., carp., Ogden bel 11th
Scattergood John, shoemr., Morris bel Catharine
Scattergood John, coachmr., Union ab Franklin (K)
Scattergood Jos., chemist, 70 N 3d, h 97 Spruce
Scattergood Joseph S., chairmr., 175 Queen
Scattergood Joshua, tailor, S W 6th and Haines, h 314 Pine
Scattergood Samuel, coach painter, Schleisman's al
Scattergood Samuel S., fruiterer, 28 S whfs
Scattergood S. Miss, dry goods, 1 S 10th
Scattergood Thomas, blacksmith, Queen and Crown (K)
Scattergood Thomas F., carpenter, 79 N 5th
Scattergood Wm., carter, Parrish ab 10th
Scattergood Wm., gent., 244 N 5th
Schadel Jacob, Apple ab Poplar

Schaechterle Paul, baker, 56 Apple
Schaeffer Casper, M. D., 135 Sassafras
Schaeffer Charles, cooper, 4th bel Brown
Schaeffer John C., cordw., 5 Ellet's av
Schaeffer John M., weaver, 3 Warner's ct
Schafer George, teamster, 7th bel Federal
Schafer John, teamster, 7th bel Federal
Schaffer Charles, druggist, 227 High, h 485 Mulberry
Schaffer Christ., cabinetmr., Crown ab Queen (K)
Schaffer Christopher, cabinetmr., 13 Freed's av
Schaffer Conrad, brewer, rear 42 New Market
Schaffer Enoch, lab., Jackson
Schaffer Fredk., vict., 4th n Master (K)
Schaffer George, mer., 187 High, h 8th ab Green
Schaffer Gotlieb, baker, 25 Apple tree al
Schaffer Henry, wheelwt., Maiden bel Beach (K)
Schaffer John B., baker, 315 S 3d
Schaffer Margaret, shop, 5th ab Poplar
Schaffer Philip, lab., 30 Pegg
Schaffer & Roberts, variety store, 187 High, ab stairs
Schaffer V., lab., 116 Brown
Schaffer William L. cashier Girard Bank, h 459 Mulberry
Schanbel Fredk., blacksm., rear G T road bel 2d
Schanden Jacob, tailor, 76 Sassafras
Schanfler John, tavern, Front and Callowhill
Schank George, tobacconist, Poplar bel 9th
Schanninger Leopold, locksm., rear 236 High, h 5 Levering's ct
Schantz Adam, cordw., 72 Coates
Scharbach Joseph, cabinet maker, 85 S 12th
Scharp Thomas, combmr., Elizabeth, bel Poplar
Scheel John D., clerk, 5 Carrolton sq
Scheeley Wm. painter, rear 33 Cherry
Scheer John C. jeweler, 72½ High, h 376 S 3d
Scheerer Christian, b h., 45 Prune
Scherer Christian, cordw., Vienna bel Franklin (K)
Scheerer Gottlieb, boot maker, 20 N 6th
Scheetz Christian, 80 Noble
Scheetz Jacob, 18 Scheetz
Scheetz Wm. A., grocery, 235 N 6th
Scheffel C. S., baker, N E Queen and 5th
Scheide C. baker, 9 Callowhill
Scheide Samuel, cabinetmr., 12 German
Scheidel Frederick, tailor, 42 New Market
Scheirenbrand John, shop, 26 Apple
Schell Andrew, baker, 444 N 4th
Schell Benjamin, marble yard, 10th and Vine, h Division bel 12th
Schell Henry, gent., 19 Branch
Schell Henry Jr., collector, 45 Chatham
Schell John F., stone cutter, James bel 10th
Schell John J., broker, 118 Catharine
Schell Joseph, stone cutter, 10th and Vine, h 10th bel Spring Garden
Schell Lawrence, bootmr. Franklin ab 3d
Schell Margaret, N W 4th and New
Schell Michael, lab., G T road ab Laurel
Schellenberg F., hatter, 353 N 3d
Schellenger George W., grocer, 2d & German

Schellenger John, waterman, 113 Catharine
Schellinger Aaron, saddle tree mr., Washington ab 5th
Schellinger Daniel M., tavern, 155 Swanson
Schellinger Franklin, shoemr., Vail's ct
Schellinger Henry, shoemr., 529 S Front
Schellinger J., pilot, Front bel Greenwich
Schellinger Samuel M., pilot, 142 Swanson
Schellinger William, pilot, 62 Queen
Schenck Christian, cordwainer, 408 N 3d
Schenck Frederick, boots and shoes, S E 6th & Parrish
Schenck Jos. H., pulmonic sirup, off. 32 S 6th, h S E Marshall and Coates
Schenck William F., cordwainer, 553 N 3d
Scherer Louis, pianomr., 45 Prune
Scherf Christopher, tailor, School
Scherhammer Joseph, bottler, 48 N 6th
Scherle John, cordw., rear brook bel Brown
Scherr Caroline, 153 S 9th
Scherr Lewis, clocks, 49 Brown
Scherr E. N., piano forte manufacturer, 266 Chestnut
Schetky G., Mrs., Juniper bel Spruce
Schey John, tallow chandler, Callowhill bel Sch 5th
Schick John, matchmr., St John ab Poplar
Schiedel F., baker, 6 Cherry
Schiedel Jacob, baker, R road ab Francis
Schiedt Frederick, baker, 203 Locust
Schiedt Jacob, victualler, Bedford bel Hanover (K)
Schiedt Jacob, baker, 152 N 4th
Schieferdecker Charles Christian, hydropathist, Beach and Chestnut
Schienle John, baker, 208 Noble
Schiffel Edward, bell hanger, Raspberry la
Schill Chas., upholsterer, 50 Fitzwater
Schill Fred., store, 391 N Front
Schiller Chas., tinsmith, 29 Apple
Schilling Christian, stove finisher, 31 Coates
Schilling Henry, furrier, 125 Coates
Schilling John, baker, 601 S 2d
Schilling John, skindress., Mechanic ab George
Schilling Jonathan A. baker, 473 Sassafras
Schimpff August, engineer, 9 Harmony ct
Schirck Peter, tavern, Washington & B road
Schiveley Jacob F., machinist, 3 Ogden
Schively Chas., surg. inst. mr., 64 S 8th
Schively George P. surg. inst. mr. h 65 Cherry
Schively H., surg. instr. maker, 64 S 8th, h 397 Spruce
Schively Julianna, 79 N 11th
Schively Maria, 79 N 11th
Schively Wm. H., mer., 43 N Front
Schlabeck J., tailor, 46 Vine
Schlafer Harmer, bootmr. 46 Vine
Schlater Benjamin, high constable Philadelphia county, h 274 Coates
Schlater Jacob, weaver, Lemon ab 12th
Schleanes Charles C., manuf., 39 S 3d
Schlecht John M., tavern, F road and West
Schlecht Matthias, oyster house, F road above Maiden
Schleffer John B., tailor, 419 N Front

Schleich Michael, lab., 439 N 4th
Schlegelmilch John, bootmr., 261 N 8th
Schlesinger & Henschen, mers., 4 Chestnut
Schlesinger P., mer., 4 Chestnut
Schlesserman John, chairmr., 1 Hudson's al
Schlemm & Greer, collectors, 96½ S 2d
Schley John, skindresser, 121 G T road (K)
Schlicherman John, baker, 410 N Front
Schlicherman John, 39 N 4th
Schlosser, Wm., cordw. 8 Kessler's ct
Schmauk Benjamin F., hair dresser, 358 N 2d
Schmelzer John, Queen & Bishop (K)
Schmick Henry, boot and shoemr., N W Noble and 8th
Schmidt Henry, druggist, N W George & 4th
Schmieding Frederick, math. instr. maker, Sch. 8th c Lewis
Schmitt Francis, tailor, 44 Prune
Schmitt Henry, 22 S Rittenhouse
Schmitt Joseph, machinist, 337 Callowhill, h 10th ab Pleasant
Schmitt & Rutschman, machinists, 337 Callowhill
Schmitz Adolph, prof. of music, 11 S Sch 8th
Schmitz M. artist, 142 Chestnut
SCHMOELE H., M. D., 11th and Mulberry
Schmoele William, M. D., 11th and Mulberry
Schmucker George A. locksmith, Robb's ct
Schnabel Ellis B. atty. & coun., Beach ab Maiden (K)
Schnabel Gotlieb, carp., 81 G T road (K)
Schnabel John L., hatter, 7th ab Poplar
Schnaitmann Isaac, optitian, 178 N 3d, h rear 40 St. John
Schnatz Frederick, baker, 174 S 3d, h 218 S 2d
Schnebly & Co., dry goods, 392 High, h 368 Chestnut
Schnebly & Co., furniture store, 507 High
Schnebly H. C., fur. & carpets, 172 N 2d
Schnebly Misses, teachers, 368 Chestnut
Schneck Daniel, printer and stationer, N W 2d and Sassafras
Schneider Caspar, carp., rear 18 New Market
Schneider Francis, cordw., 469 N 4th
Schnider Charles B. engraver, 4 S 5th
Schnider Fred., baker, 5th & Noble
Schnider Wm. B. Masonic Hall, 3d St
Schnitzel Christian, drayman, 462 N 5th
Schnitzel Jacob, tailor, 1 Linden's ct
Schnitzel John, shoemr., 278 N Front
Schoales Marcus, M D., 686 N 2d

Scholas John, tailor, Franklin bel 2d (K)
Scholefield John, S E 6th & Mulberry
Scholefield John, carpet weav., 539 N 5th
Scholefield Jos. & Sons, agency, 42 Commerce
Scholefield Wm., shoemr., rear 124 Queen
Scholl John, baker, 5 Blackhorse al
SCHOMACKER J. H. & Co., pianos, 47 S 8th
Schoneman Joseph, mer., 65 N 3d, h 312 N 5th
Schonleber Jacob, turner, 8 St Stephen's pl
School Bernard, weav., Cadwalader ab Jefferson
School & Faurest, marble masons, c Broad and Cherry
School Henry, cabmr., rear 73 N 5th
School John, stone cutter, Broad and Cherry, h Vine n Sch 7th
Schooley Mary, washer, 9th and Carpenter
Schooley William M., h 22 New Market
Schoolman C. coachmr. Elizabeth ab Poplar
Schoot H., 112 Swanson
Schopffel Lewis, cabinetmr., 1 Horstman
Schott & Alexander, mers., 28 Church alley
Schott G. Bryan, atty. at law, 141 Walnut
Schott Hanse J. cabinetmr. Juniper bel Walnut
Schott Jacob, 475 Vine
Schott James, mer, 24 S Front, h Filbert West of Broad
Schott & M'Calla, com. mers., 7 Walnut
Schott William, mer., 7 Walnut, h 35 S 13th
Schowerer V. engrav. St John bel G T road (K)
Schrack Abraham, coal agent, N E 13th & Willow, h S W 13th & James
SHRACK CHRISTIAN, varnish manuf. and paints, 80 N 4th, h 23 Branch.
Schrack G. H., druggist, 147 Coates
Schrack H. & S., saddlers, Margaretta & 2d
Schrack John H. currier, 25 Margaretta
Schrack Joseph, carpenter, Naglee's ct
Schrack Saml, saddler, 277 N 2d, h 55 Franklin
Schrader Fred., dealer, Penn bel Maiden (K)
Schrader J. H., machinist, 185 Callowhill
Schrank George, brickmr. Sch 5th & Barker
Schranz Peter, bootmr., 6 Cresson's al
Schreiber Francis, printer, 22 Cherry
Schreiber John C., painter, 46 Perry
Schreiber Theodore, painter and glazier, 16 Parker
Schreiber W. F., painter, 54 Perry
Schreiner Chas.W., carp., 8 Gebhard
SCHREINER EDWARD, coal mer., Broad & Callowhill, h Sch 8th ab Mulberry
Schreiner Eliza, 4 Charlotte

Schroyer Philip, tavern, G T road ab 6th
Schruchman Abraham, shoemr., Hope above Master (K)
Schryer George, 333 Callowhill
Schueler Jacob, barber, 363 N 3d
Schuelermann John Charles, printer, rear 81 N 5th
Schughart Albert, lab., 44 Rose al
Schuler John, wheelwright, Edward n William (K)
Schultz Frederick, patternmr., 14 Vine
Schumer Wm., carp., Palm ab Brown
Schummer John G., weav., 5th ab Jefferson (K)
Schunknacht Jacob bootmr., 12 S 6th
Schur F., dyer, 193 N 9th
Schurch Peter, quill manuf, 182 Marshall
SCHURCH SAML., quill manuf., 91 Sassafras
Schureman Abm., chairmr., 65 St. John
Schurman Henry, tailor, rear 126 Queen
Schuyler Charles, drayman, rear F road above Bedford
Schuyler John, tailor, 19 S 3d
Schuyler Philip R., undertaker, 4th & Beaver
Schuyler Philip R. jr., framemr., Culvert ab 4th
Schuyler Wm., lab., 4 Rihl's ct
Schwaab Joseph, carter, West and Cherry
Schwabe Sigmund, tobacco, 142½ N 2d
Schwable Caspar, lab., Palmer ab Franklin (K)
Schwable Michael, basketmr., Bryan's ct
Schwacke John H., printer, 226 & 248 N 3d
Schwartz C. G., M. D., 77 N 5th
Schwartz George C., intelligence off., 3 Library
Schwartz Gustavus, M. D., 415 Sassafras
Schwartz Hubert, teacher, Sch 8th ab Vine
Schwarz Jacque, turner, 84 N 5th
Schwartz John, blacksmith, Olive ab 13th
Schwartz John M., baker, 74 New Market
Schwartz John T., chemist, West above Hanover (K)
Schwartz Lewis, cordw., 662 N 2d
Schwartz Margaret, Shackamaxon and Bedford (K)
Schwartz Samuel, patternmr., Marshall above Poplar
Schwarz C. F., baker, 227 S 4th
Schwarz Gotleib, gent., 87 New Market
Schwazwaelder Daniel, cabinetmr. 99 S 2nd
Schweikert Gotleib, brewer, 178 St John
Schweikert Gottleib, vict., Brown ab 12th
Schweikert John, lab., 3 Moore's ct (S G)
Schweitzer John, drayman, rear Shackamaxon bel Franklin (K)
Schweizer John G., pianomr., 3d bel Beaver
Schwekert B., locksm., 9th bel Catharine
Schweppenheiser Catharine, shop, St John & Beaver
Schweppenheiser George N., carp., St. John ab Beaver (K)
Schweppenheiser Wm., carp., Brown ab 12th
Schwise John, cordw., 350 O Y road
Scofield Geo. S., 146 Chestnut, h N W 8th and Chestnut
Scofield James, lab., Carlton ab Sch Front
Scofield Lane, city commissioner, h 81 S 12th
39

Scofield Robert, weaver, Duke ab F road (K)
Scoffin F., M. D., 57 Almond
Scollin Mary, teacher, 30 Powell
Scot Robert, collector and clerk, 13 Marshall
Scott Amos, labourer, 110 Washington av
Scott Amos, jr., trunkmr., 402 N Front
Scott Andrew, grocer, 9th and Ogden
Scott Andrew, printer, 115 Chestnut, h 2 N 9th
Scott Ann, grocer, Poplar and Ontario
Scott Archibald, weaver, rear G T road below Master (K)
Scott Austin, dry goods, 34½ N 2d, h 296 N 7th
Scott & Baker, dry goods, 150 High
Scott Benjamin, jr., mer., 39 N 2d
Scott Catharine, 194 Christian
Scott Catharine, b h, 511 High
Scott David, glass blower, Union above Franklin (K)
Scott Eliza A., rear 527 N 4th
Scott Elizabeth, Sch 7th and Spruce
Scott Esther J. 493 Sassafras
Scott Freeman, 10th and Poplar
Scott George, tavern and oysters, 10 Mulberry
Scott George, lab., 13th ab Fitzwater
Scott George, cordw., Oldham's ct
Scott George, cordw., Catharine ab Morris
Scott George A., clerk, Filbert n Sch 5th
Scott Hamilton J., shipwright, 80 Catharine
Scott Hannah, 101 N 3d
Scott Harriett, milliner, S W 2d & Plum, h 10 German
Scott Hugh, weaver, Callowhill bel Sch 2d
Scott Hugh, fire proof chest mr. S E Front and Mead h 25 Mead
Scott Hugh, labourer, Cedar bel 13th
Scott James, blacksm., Carlton bel Sch 2d
Scott James, lab., 12 Division
Scott James, seaman, 97 German
Scott James, flannel carder, 4th bel Franklin, h 5th bel Camac
Scott James, trimmings, 89 Cedar
Scott James, waiter, rear 9 Maria
Scott James, grocer, Wood and Sch 7th
Scott James, lab., Bedford ab 6th
Scott James B., machinist, Crown bel Franklin
Scott James B., cooper, Clark ab 3d
Scott James M., actor, Sch 8th bel Cherry
Scott Jane, weaver, Front ab Phoenix
Scott Jane A., teacher, rear 229 Mulberry
Scott John, weaver, Richard n Sch 6th
Scott John, carp., Citron bel 13th
Scott John, shuttle manuf., 529 N 4th
Scott John, carpet manuf., Callowhill ab Sch Front
Scott John, blacksmith, rear 483 S Front, shop 505 S Front
Scott John, 40 Bread
Scott John, trunkmr., Court al
Scott John, capt., 66 Catharine
Scott John, manuf., 50 Almond
Scott John, seaman, 3 Southampton ct
Scott John, proof chestmr., 19 Bread, h 50 Almond
Scott John A., carpet weaver, 4th bel Poplar

Scott John C., mer., 150 High, h 10th ab Pine
SCOTT JOHN M., att'y & coun., Washington sq bel Locust
Scott John R., carp, rear 339 S 5th
Scott John R., ladies' shoemr., 173 N 4th
Scott John T., blacksm., Sch 5th ab Callowhill
Scott John T., plasterer, Lemon ab 12th
Scott Jonathan, tailor, Orchard & Rawle
Scott Joseph, lab. 98 W Cedar
Scott Julia, 20 Elizabeth
Scott Levi Rev. 44 Plum
Scott Lewis A., att'y. & coun., Washington sq. bel Locust
Scott Marshall, manuf., Sch 2d bel Callowhill
Scott Michael, cordw., Poplar ab Apple
Scott Nixon, machinist, Charles and Willow
Scott Robert, cordw., 4th n Carpenter
Scott Robert, book seller, S W 11th and High, h Bedford bel 13th
Scott Robert, lab., 12 Division
Scott Robert, mer., 153 High, h 13 Marshall
Scott Robert, tailor, 13th ab Catharine
SCOTT ROBERT & Co., boots and shoes, 153 High
Scott Robert B. wheelwright, Spruce ab Sch 7th h Sch 7th bel Spruce
Scott Robert M., agent, Franklin ab Union (K)
Scott Rosanna, milliner, 7 S 8th
Scott Ruth, washer, N E Pine & Juniper
Scott Saml., brass melter, Shackamaxon below Franklin (K)
Scott Samuel, cordw., Cedar ab 12th
Scott Samuel, lab. Dorothy W Sch 4th
Scott Samuel, carpet manuf., Washington bel Church
Scott Sarah, dressmr., 549 Vine
Scott Sarah L., dry goods, 3 N 12th
Scott Solomon Rev., 12 Collins' al
Scott & Taylor, flannel manfs., 4th bel Franklin
Scott Thos., furniture store, Sch 5th bel High.
Scott Thos., cabmr., Pine & Pratt
Scott Thos., shoemr., Oliver pl
Scott Thomas M., capt., Franklin and Union (K)
Scott Walter, lab., P road bel Marriott
Scott Walter, porter, Shippen ab 12th
Scott Walter, mariner, 13 Reckless
Scott William, dealer, 9 Acorn al
Scott William, tailor, 190 Queen
Scott Wm., blacksmith, 115 Cherry
Scott Wm., drayman, rear Pleasant bel 12th
Scott Wm., bootmr., 2 Hyde's ct
Scott Wm. & Co., embroiderers, 23½ S 2d
Scott Wm. H. tailor, 5 S 13th
SCOTT WM. H. & CO., hatters, 76 S 3d
Scott Wm. R. & Brother, boots & shoes, 286½ High
Scott William R., trunk and collar maker, 11 Bread, h 4 Christian
Scotten Elizabeth, 8 Tiller's ct
Scotton John, stockingmr., Howard bel Master (K)
Scottron S. J., barber, 320 S 6th
Scoular James, weaver, Fulton ab 12th
Scout Jonathan, trunkmr., 86 Callowhill
Scranton Edw., silversm., Elizabeth ab Poplar

Scravendyke James, soap boiler, 16 Relief
Scravendyke John, grocer, 246 S 2d
Scriminger Mary, 22 Castle
Scroggy John, cordw., 5 Sailor's ct
Scroggy Mary Ann, Sycamore ab Locust
Scull & Co., Wood mer., Noble st whf
Scull David, mer., 91 High, h 225 Vine
Scull Edwin, mer., 4 N 3d
Scull Ellen, teacher, 156 Wood
Scull Gideon, grocer, 47 N Water, h 60 Pine
Scull Gideon D., mer., 91 High, h 225 Vine
Scull Jasper, tinman, Schleisman's ct
Scull Peter H., news paper carrier, h Swanson bel Almond
Scull Rachel G., gentw., 436 N 13th
Scull, Rex & Rocap, wood mers., Noble st whf.
Scull & Thompson, grocers, 21 N whfs and 47 N Water
Scull William, gardener, 7 Winter's ct
SCULL, WILLIAMS & Co., dry goods, 91 High
Scully John, cordwainer, William ab Otter (K)
Scurrah Ann, 13 Jefferson row
Seacon Allen, carp., Pearl ab Sch 6th
Seagrove Matthew, weav., Hanover bel F road
Seal Elizabeth, 8 Spring Garden Retreat
Seal Joseph H., mer., 20 Chestnut, h 55 Marshall
Seal Thomas F., mer., 41 High
Sealman Jos., lab., Parham st
Seaman Eben. C., ice cream manuf., 316 S 3d
Seaman John, waterman, rear 33 Plum
Search Christian, skin dresser, 43 Coates
Search Elias, printer, 64 Dock
Search E. & O. I., printers, 64 Dock
Search Jacob, silk & cotton cord manuf., 8th & Washington, h Christian ab 4th
Search Joshua, cotton cord, 5th and Marriott
Search O. I., printer, 64 Dock
Searin Philimon F., furniture car; 20 Sarah (K)
Searl Clinton, bricklayer, Melon ab 9th
Searl Francis, bricklayer, Melon ab 9th
Searl John, printer, Dickerson's ct
Searl Joseph, silver plater, 128 N 13th, h Callowhill bel 13th
Searl Robert, carp., York ct
Searles James, drayman, Franklin and Dunton
Searles Mary, sempstress, Franklin ab Hanover
Sears Benj., waiter, 36 Burd's ct
Sears David, lab., rear 512 N Front
Sears Samuel, jeweller, 320 S 4th
Seaver Wm. R., com. mer., 35 S Front
Sebold Solomon, cordw., rear Poplar ab 3d
Sechenheimer H., groc., St John & George (K)
Seckel Frederick, brewer, c 5th and Minor, h 164 S 9th
Seckel George D., 45 S 13th
SECKEL GEO. L., atty. & coun., rear 392 Sassafras
Seddinger Henry, oysterman, 10th & Christian
Seddinger John, bitmr., St. John ab Beaver (K)
Seddinger J. L. milliner, 52 Mulberry
Seddinger Matthias, silver plater, 18 Lagrange, h 52 Mulberry
Seddinger Wm. J., carter, Bedford & Crown (K)
Sedgwick T., gentw., 29 Flower

Sedniger Jos., patternmr., Hallowell n 7th
See Abraham S., mer., 70 High, h 493 Mulberry
SEE, BROTHER & CO., mers., 70 High
See Colhoun R., mer., 70 High h 333 Spruce
See James P., tailor, 417 S Front
See Samuel, cooper, Federal ab 2d
See Wm., tobacconist, 417 S Front
Seebeth Wm., biscuit baker, Pearson's ct (K)
Seed Isaac, weaver, 2 Fox ct
Seed Thomas, 1 Sheaff
Seed William, painter, Pine ab 13th
Seeders Philip, lab., Higgins' ct
Seeds Christiana, 7 Flower's al
Seeds Mary, shop, ½ road ab Reed
Seeger Ann N 12th ab Cherry.
Seeger C. F., silver plater, 44 S 6th
Seeger Jacob, shoemr., 121 Queen
Seeger Wm., cabinetmr., 276 S 5th
Seel Joseph, lab., 3 Linden ct
Seeler Godfrey T. shoemr. 35 Cherry
Seeler Harman, lab., 268 Shippen
Seeler Samuel N., 325 N 8th
Seeley Caroline, Flower al
Seeley E. M., ivory black manuf., 2d and Montgomery, h 660 N 2d
Seeley Wm., weaver, Howard bel Master (K)
Seeley Wm., tailor, 27 Merchant, h 140 Green
Seery John, shop, Sch 8th and Willow
Seery Owen, baker, 140 N Front
Sees Geo., machinist, rear Pleasant ab 12th
Seffarlen Jacob, baker, Apple and George
Seffert John, baker, 225 Walnut
Segerlen Rachel, Washington bel 4th
Seher Lewis, cordw., Franklin & O'Neil
Seiberlich Alborn, machinist, Broad and Poplar
SEIBERLICH A., bootmr., 2 Exchange pl, h 19 Carter's al
Seiberlich F., tailor, Poplar ab 3d
Seiberlich John, tailor, 127 N 2d
Seidel John P., cabtmr., 1 Library
Seidenbach & Brother, dry goods, 16½ S 2d
Seidenbaugh Jonas, coal, 68 N 4th
Seidinsticker George, ed. German Dem., 52 O Y road
Seidle Godfrey, vict., G road & 4th (K)
Seidler Ferd., druggist, 2d & Edward (K)
Seidler Lewis, lab., rear 128 Beach (K)
Seilhimer Henry, tinman, 21 Carter's alley
Seiliez Lewis, cook, 7 Elbow la
Seip Peter, manuf., rear 465 St John
Seiser John, tailor, 66 N 2d
Seiser John, jr., mer., 15 N 3d, h 66 N 2d
Seithers Jos., barber, Poplar & New Market
Seittery Fred., Brown ab Cherry (K)
Seittery Wm., blacksm., Vienna bel Duke (K)
Seitz John, baker, P road bel Christian
Seitzinger Wm. F. trimmings, 373 S 2d
Sekro William C. silver plater, h 10 Parker
Selby James, capt., Church ab Washington
Selby Lawrence, cordw., Hallowell
Selby Mary, b h, 219 Spruce
Selby Samuel, grocer, R road bel Broad
Selby William, match factory, Prune ab 5th, h 376 S Front

Selby W. B. R. hatter, 324 High, h 7th ab Catharine
Seldener Richard, vice cons., Norway & Sweden, 87½ S Front, h 117 Lombard
Seldener Richard, jr., M. D., 117 Lombard
Selfridge John, stone cutter, Ruddach's ct
Selfridge Robert, manuf. Shippen ab 12th
Selfridge Robert, bootmr., 2 Boyd's av
Selfridge Wm. lab. Shippen ab 12th
Selfridge Wm., carp., Buttonwood ab 12th
Selkirk Wm., suspender mr., Sch 7th & High
Sell Abraham, hatter, Perry bel Master (K)
Sell Joseph, corn broker, Bedford bel Hanover
Sell Manasseh, crockery, 142 N 3d
Sell Solomon, tailor, Bedford ab Union (K)
Sell Thomas, lab., Dewitt's av (K)
SELL & WALTER, crockery, 142 N 3d
Sell Wm., plasterer, Wallace bel Broad
Sellers Abraham, mer., 141 Chestnut, h Chesnut ab Sch 6th
Sellers C. B. acct. 198 Noble
Sellers David, mer. 231 High, h 23 N 12th
Sellers, Davis & Co., grocers, 111 N 3d
Sellers Edwin M., mer., 143 High, h 47 Marshall
Sellers Jacob M., saddler, 50 High
Sellers James, sailmr. Farie's ct
Sellers James, mer., 231 High
Sellers Jesse, mer., 111 N 3d
Sellers Joel, confect., 113 N 3d, h 97 Dillwyn
Sellers Joel J. & Co. grocers, 219 N 2d
Sellers John, carpet weaver, 7 Passmore's pl
Sellers Joseph, silver plater, 27 N 7th, h 10th ab Catharine
Sellers J. & D. wire work. and fire hose manufs. 231 High
Sellers & Leidigh, grocers, 175 N 3d
Sellers Levi, mer. 3d ab Vine, h 27 Magnolia
Sellers Lewis, lab., rear Centre bel Parrish
Sellers M., baker, 12th & Pearl
Sellers & Pennock, machine card manufs. 231 High
Sellers Robert B. mer. 111 N 3d, h 140 Marshall
Sellers Samuel, carpenter, 13th and Pleasant, h Callowhill ab 13th
Selman Wm. millwright, 370 N 3d
Selybron Casson, dealer, 211 S 6th
Seltzer J. V. R. grocer, 240 N 2d, h 108 St John
Selzor Wm. stonecutter, 16 Perry
Semler Adam, book binder, Haines' ct
Semple Margaret, widow, Division bel 12th
Semple Catharine, Shackamaxon n Franklin (K)
Senat P. L., cdm., mer., h 4 City row
Senatz G. J., machinist, 4 Weccacoe
Senderling Charles, carp., School n Edward (K)
Senderling George, tailor, 10th ab Poplar
Senderling Jacob, lab., 25 Charlotte
Senderling Jacob, jr., boot fitter, rear Orchard ab Rawle
Senderling John C. carp. Lewis ab Poplar
Senderling M. Z., druggist, Union and Franklin (K)
SENDOS & KELSH, lookingglasses, 156 N 2d
Senior David, shoemr. 607 N 2d
Senior Joseph, tinner, Beaver bel 4th

Senn George, bricklayer, 565 N 3d
Senn John J., baker, Poplar bel 4th
Senn Peter, brickmr., Elizabeth ab Poplar
Senn Thomas, grave digg., rear Parrish ab 10th
Senn Wm., combmr., 151 Green
Senneff George, carp., 100 S 12th
Senneff Jacob, shuttlemr., 26 Howard
SENNEFF JACOB, reed manuf., 165 N 2d
Senseman S., piano-forte maker, 180 N 8th
Sensenbacker Jacob, cordw. 240 Wood
Sensenderfer George, tailor, 360 Coates
Sensenderfer James, carp. rear Vernon ab 10th
Sentman G. W. hatter, 147 N 3d
Seppel Philip, shoemr., Pleasant ab 10th
Serat John, jeweller, 2d and Marion
Sergeant Alexander F., carp. 450 N 4th
Sergeant Elizabeth B., 82 S 12th
SERGEANT JOHN, couns., 91 and h 89 S 4th
Sergeant J. Dickinson, atty and coun. 47 S 5th, h Sch 8th ab Pine
Sergeant Thomas, atty. & coun., h 377 Spruce
Sergeson Ed., blacksm., 498 Callowhill ab 13th
Sergeson Elizabeth, Culvert ab 3d
Sergeson Henry, shuttle maker, 98 Charlotte
Sergeson Wm. shuttle mr. George ab 4th, h Elizabeth ab Poplar
Serine Naylor, carp. Walter's ct
Serjuble George, stone cutter, Ogden bel 11th
Serrill Henry, dry goods, 148 N 3d, h 93 Crown
Serrill Isaac S., att'y. & coun., 10 Sansom
Serrill Thomas A. currier, Rush's ct
Server Allen, carp., 6 Nectarine
Server C. C., rags and paper, 278 S 7th, h 10th and La Fayette
Server F. A., paper mer., 16 Commerce, h 354 Pine
Server F. A. & Co., paper mers., 16 Commerce
Service Catharine, tailoress, 175 S 11th
Servoss Charles, hatter, rear 175 Cherry
Servoss Joseph S. lookingglasses & fancy hardware, 69 N 2d
Setgie John, lab. 5th bel. Franklin (N L)
Seth Wm. H., clothing, 95 S 2d
Setl y Abram, grocery, R. road ab Sch. 7th
Setley Adam, trimmings, 312 N 2d
Setley George, mer., 23 N 3d
Setley & Sevening, importers, 23 N 3d
Setman George, cooper, Higgin's place
Setterberg Charles, book binder, S E 5th and Walnut
Settle George, watchman, George n Sch 3d
Seubert C. F. lace weaver, G T road ab Jefferson (K)
Sevelinge Eliza, 13 Powell
Severn Charles, combmr., Clinton ab Poplar
Severn Benjamin, boilermr. Alien ab F road
Severn Louisa, Charlotte ab Culvert
Severn Wm. comb mr. B. ab 2d

Sewall Benjamin T., tanner, Willow bel 8th
Sewall Scipio, waiter, N W 2d & Walnut, h Middle al
Sewall Wm. seaman, 45 Quince
Seward Thomas, porter, rear 6 E North
Sewell Horatio, dentist, 6 M'Leod place
Sewold Lewis, wheelwrt., Dunton bel Otter (K)
Sexes Joseph, paper carrier, 516 S Front
Sexton E. Mrs., gentw., 50 Pine
Sexton James, sail maker, 120 N 11th
Sexton John W., mer., 5 S 4th, h 13 Scheetz
Sexton Martin, cordw., Carbon place
Sexton Michael, lab., 33 S Juniper
Sexton Patience, shop, 13th bel Coates
Seybert Elizabeth, 185 St John
Seybert Fred. P., mer., 43 N Wharves
Seybert Henry, S W 11th and Chestnut
Seybert William, baker, 13th & Melon
Seybold John, lab., Sch. Bank and Lombard
Seyferheld George, harness mr. Almira pl
Seyferhelt David, brushmr. 22 Mintzer
Seyfert Anthony, printer, 43 Gaskill
Seyfert Charles, bookbinder, 74 N 6th, h 10 Lodge pl
Seyfert John, blacksmith, Poplar ab 9th
Seyfert John H., blacksmith, 1 Sansom's al, h 99 St. John
Seyfert Thomas, printer, 6 Howard
Seyman Marg., 179 N 10th
Seymour Daniel, moulder, G T road ab 6th
Seymour James, tailor, 30 N 13th
Seymour John, cattle dealer, Mantua Village
Seymour John, porter, Centre ab 12th
Seymour Joseph, waiter, 18 Mercer
Seymour Nicholas, carter, rear 5 Ogden
Seymour Patience, washer, Pryor's ct
Seyhs Wm., carpet weaver, G. T. road bel 4th
Shabinger John, baker, 324 S 5th
Shackelford H. A., mer., 103 High, h 124 S 8th
Shaclett Benj. C., mer, 130 Marshall
Shadd Ann, 5 Kneass' ct
Shade Ann, tailoress, 345 S 5th
Shade And., 84 F. road (K)
Shade Franklin, blacksmith, 3 Lafayette pl
Shade Isaac, shoemr., Nectarine ab 10th
Shade John, painter, N E 9th and Buttonwood, h 10th bel Parrish
Shade John V., watchmr. 37 N 4th
Shadhaffer Jacob, lab., Perry bel Master (K)
Shadrach John, block cut., Carleton bel Sch. 3d
Shadrach Wm., Rev., 8 Morgan
Shuer Sarah, milliner, 256 Callowhill
Shaffer Adam, carter, George bel Charlotte
Shaffer Catharine, Naglee's ct
Shaffer Charles, carp., 12th ab Brown
Shaffer Chas. coachmr. 9th bel Green, h Pleasant ab 12th

Shaffer Henry, cordw. 341 S 5th
Shaffer Henry, musician, 7 Pegg
Shaffer Jacob, oysterman, Hallowell
Shaffer Jacob, vict. Philip ab Jefferson
Shaffer Jacob, cabtnr., 2 Marion
Shaffer Jacob, stevedore, Stevenson's ct
Shaffer James, carter, 6th bel Carpenter
Shaffer John, bricklayer, 401 N 3d
Shaffer John, cordw., Marriott bel 5th
Shaffer John, lime dealer, Franklin and Cadwalader (K)
Shaffer Joseph, carp., Sch. 2d and Lombard
Shaffer Joseph, carp. 341 S 5th
Shaffer Martin, morocco dresser, Mintzer's ct
Shaffer Mary, widow, rear 331 N 3d
Shaffer Michael, 356 N 5th
Shaffer Samuel, carter, Clare
Shaffer Wm., rear 99 O. Y. road
Shaffer Wm., lab., Brooks' ct
Shaffer Wm., chairmr., Duke bel Wood (K)
Shaffer Wm., waterman, 2 Lily al
Shaffer Wm. S., pap. hang., Buttonwood n 13th
Shaffner John, mer., 17 N 4th, h 8th n Coates
SHAFFNER & ZIEGLER, varieties, 17 N 4th
Shanes Patrick, lab., Filbert and Sch. 3d
Shaley J. T. cordw. Clawges' ct
Shallcross Leonard, gent., 107 Prime
Shallcross M. C., M. D., 191 Walnut
Shalock James, lab., Murray n Sch. 2d
Shane Ann, Budden's al
Shane Benjamin, clerk, 64 Gaskill
Shane Edward, salesman, 1 Howard place
Shane Eve, school, 240 St. John
Shane John B. bookbinder, 6th bel Carpenter
Shane Morris, lab., Coates n Fairmount
Shane Wm., lab., Alder ab Poplar
Shane Wm., shoemr., 24 S 7th, h 294 High
Shaner Jacob, combmr., Sheppard's ct
Shankland Ann, cook, 24 St. Mary
Shankland Charles H., sea capt., 474 S Front
Shankland John R., tailor, 3d bel Christian
Shankland Joseph W., hatter, Paul ab 6th
Shankland Robert, sailor, 45 Catharine
Shankland Wm., shipmr., 444 S Front
Shanks Abraham, tailor, 266 St John
Shannessy James, flower dealer, 15 Pleasant
Shannon Ann, gentw , 277 S Front
Shannon Catharine A. milliner, 21 Elizabeth
SHANNON ELLWOOD, tea dealer, 63 Chestnut, h 86 S 11th
Shannon Henry, lab. Oak (W P)
Shannon Jacob B., locksmith, 54 N 6th, h 37 Castle
Shannon James, capt., 147 Poplar
Shannon James, lab., 20 Mary (S)
Shannon Jane H., milliner, 2d ab Phoenix (K)
Shannon John, painter, Sch 6th bel George
Shannon John, shop, 221 Cherry
Shannon Mary A., dressmr., 129 N 6th
Shannon Patrick, weaver, Cedar n Sch 2d
Shannon Richard, sailor, Beaver ab 2d (K)
Shannon Wm. weaver, 2d ab Montgomery
Shapleigh M. S., mer., 110 High, h 216 Cherry
Shapley David E., boat builder, Washington (W P)

Sharbinier Henry, rear 128 S 2d
Sharer Charles, paper hanger, Queen ab Shackamaxon
Sharer & Green, paper hangers, Queen ab Shackamaxon
Sharer John, skindr., Apple bel George
Sharker George, Mechanic ab George
Sharker Henry, machinist, rear Apple ab George
Sharkey Bernard, rear Amber ab Phoenix
Sharkey Edward, Marble ct.
Sharkey Henry, porter, Trotter's al
Sharkey Hugh, weaver, Jefferson ab 2d (K)
Sharkey John, weaver, Fitler ab 2d (K)
Sharkey Thomas, weaver, Hope ab Master
Sharkey Wm., manuf., 2d n Jefferson (K)
Sharp Ann, Queen bel 2d
Sharp Anthony, carp., Rittenhouse
Sharp B. W., confec., 290 Pine
Sharp Catharine, 38 Zane
Sharp Charles, tailor, P road bel Marriott
Sharp Edwin, machinist, Whitehall bel 13th
Sharp Elizabeth, 8 Mineral place
Sharp Fred., 4 Franklin (K)
Sharp Geo., silver smith, Rittenhouse
Sharp George W., carpet weaver, 265 St John
Sharp G. L., tailor, 150 S 6th
Sharp Hester, 7 Rogers' ct
Sharp James, printer, 279 N 2d, h 5 Ellen
Sharp John, carp., rear Union ab Franklin (K)
Sharp John, lab., Orange and Melon
Sharp John, mer., 37 N Front, h 71 Lombard
Sharp John, tobacconist, 6 Mechanic
Sharp John, mer., 1 S 4th & S E 13th & High
Sharp John L., lab., 24 Strawberry
Sharp John, lab., 17 Queen
Sharp John B., saddler, rear 75 N 8th
Sharp Joseph, 15 S 2d, h 197 Mulberry
Sharp Lewis, tanner, Ellis ab Washington
SHARP, LINDSEY & HAINES, importers, 13 S 2d
Sharp Mahlon, carp., 14 N 8th
Sharp Mary, Penn ab 13th
Sharp Mary-Ann, dressmr., 54 Chester
Sharp Richard R., carp., Washington ab M road, h 515 S Front
Sharp Robert, carter, St John & Martin's ct
Sharp Samuel, salesman, 5 Federal
Sharp Samuel, tinsmith, 163 Shippen, h Russell and Shippen
Sharp Thomas, tailor, 269 N 3d
Sharp Wm. jeweller, 19 Howard
Sharp Wm., keeper M. Prison, 10th bel Federal
Sharp William R., carpenter, 454 S Front
Sharp William W., carpet weaver 8 Charlotte
Sharp Wm. W., shoemr., R hl's ct & Charlotte
Sharpe Jacob L., grocer, 273 High, h 453 Mulberry
Sharpe Jacob L. & Co., grocers, 273 High
Sharpe William, M. D., 265 S Front
Sharpe William H., gent., 85 Buttonwood
Sharpless Alfred, mer., Broad & Sassafras
Sharpless Charles L., mer., 32 S 2d, h 233 Mulberry
Sharpless David, paper mr., Perry ab Franklin (K)

Sharpless Henry G. mer. 32 S 2d, h 187 Mulberry

Sharpless John, reedmr., G. T. road ab Phœnix

SHARPLESS JOHN M., dye stuffs, 47 N Front

Sharpless John T., M. D., 127 Mulberry

Sharpless Joseph, 74 N 4th

Sharpless J. J., gent., 151 N 4th

Sharpless Saml., wheelwright, Queen bel Marlborough (K)

Sharpless Saml. J., mer., 32 S 2d, h 358 Walnut

Sharpless Townsend, mer., 32 S 2d, h 187 Mulberry

SHARPLESS TOWNSEND & SONS, dry goods, 32 S 2d

Sharpless Wm., printer, 75 Crown

Sharpless Wm P., mer., S E Broad and Sassafras h 2 Palmyra row

SHARPLESS WM. P. & A., forwarding and com. mers., S E Broad & Sassafras

Sharpley Ann, 9 Carberry's ct

Sharpley John, lab., Lane's ct

Sharpley William, cordw., 1 Charlotte ab George

Sharpsheer Jason, bootmr., 14 Allen (K)

Sharratt Charles, silk reeler, 30 Dock,

Sharrer Jacob, porter, Stever's ct

Sharswood George, judge, 124 N 7th

Sharswood William, gent., Vine ab 12th

Sharry Edward, weaver, Phillip above Jefferson (K)

Shattisck Orville Wm., 5 Benezet ct

Shattuck A. L., grocer, c Sch. 7th and Vine

Shaughney James, 33 S Sch 6th

Shaughney Wm. gardener, Sch 8th bel High

Shauvin Louis, printer. Paul ab 6th

Shaw Ann, Harmony st

Shaw A. R., machinist, 185 Christian

Shaw A., tavern, Julianna ab Callowhill

Shaw Catharine R., bonnetmr., 62 Mulberry

Shaw Charles, agent and collector, 215 Spruce

Shaw David, coachmr., Sch Front n Mulberry

Shaw Edward, lab., Penn ab Marsh (K)

Shaw Elizabeth, 167 N 9th

Shaw Elizabeth, crockery, 15 N 7th

Shaw Elizabeth, 123 Christian

Shaw Elizabeth P., 7th ab S Garden

Shaw Hiram, whip mr., 205 G T road (K)

Shaw Isaac F., waterman, rear 164 Swanson

Shaw James, law, Middle al

Shaw James, carp. 2d bel Phoenix

Shaw James, cordwainer, 5th bel G T road (K)

Shaw James, cabinetmaker, 591 Poplar

Shaw James A. B., confect., 4 N 8th

Shaw James M., carter, Crown bel West, (K)

Shaw James M., stone cutter, 430 N 13th

Shaw Jos. E., shoemr., rear Shackamaxon abov Bedford (K)

Shaw Margaret, shop, S W 8th & Wood

Shaw Mary, 73 Christian

Shaw Mary, washer, rear 64 Catharine

Shaw Mary, 115 S 12th

Shaw Mary, Apple bel George

Shaw Nicholas, shoemr., 199 N Water

Shaw Randolph, wheelwright, G T road above Laurel

Shaw Richard, wheelwright, G T road ab Laurel, h St John bel George (K)

Shaw Richard, lab., St John bel George (K)

Shaw Robt., 9 Carleton

Shaw Samuel, bootmr., Lombard n Sch. 7th

Shaw Thos., brushmr., 13 Short ct

Shaw Thomas, corder, Lombard ab Sch 5th

Shaw Travis, cordw., rear 132 Coates

Shaw Wm., weaver, 13th n Fitzwater

Shaw William, M. D., 112 Green

Shay Andw., weaver, Mariner

Shay John, porter, 3 College pl

Shay Park, gent., 14 Morgan

Shay Shepherd, waiter, 10th bel Lombard

Shea Albert, lab., rear Wood ab Broad

Shea Mary, 17 Jacoby

Sheaff David W., painter, 106 N 10th

Sheaff George, office, 7 S 5th

Sheaff John D., gent., 162 Mulberry

Sheaffer John, tavern, Callowhill & Water

Shearer George, bookbinder, 122 German

Shearer Henry, clerk, 135 S 4th

Shearer Henry, tinsmith, S E 4th & Brown

Shearer Isaac, carp., 375 N 4th

Shearer Matt., drayman, Filbert n Sch 5th

Shearrad Robert, machinist, St John above George (K)

Shears Isaac, porter, Front & Shippen

Sheats George, waterman, 86 Swanson

Sheble Charles, hardware, 676 N 2d

Sheble D. B., tailor, 8 Richard

Sheble Jacob B., grocer, N W Penn and Maiden (K)

Sheble Jacob, hardware, 463 N 2d

Sheble John J. furniture, 51 Brown

Sheble J. D. coach trimmer, Lewis ab Poplar

Sheble R. & J. J., furniture, 465 N 2d

Sheble S. & J. A., hardw., 200 N 2d, h 17 Brown

Shedaker Edwin G., clerk, 141 Spruce

Shedaker H. G., coal mer., 29 S 5th, h Vine ab Sch 8th

Shedden John, tailor, 67 Buttonwood

Sheddick Thomas, carp., 7th bel Christian

Shee Bartley, mer. 20 N ...

Sheerer Isaac, saddler, George's ab 3d (K)
Sheets Adam, supt. gas works, S. G., 318 Coates
Sheets Caspar, moulder, Duke n Wood (K)
Sheets Christian, turner, Palmer n F road (K)
Sheets Jacob, lab., rear 408 N 3d
Sheets Jacob, confect. N W 4th & Green
Sheets John, carpenter, 19 Orleans
Sheets John, brickmr., Olivet pl
Sheets Josiah, carp. Hope bel Master (K)
Sheets Peter, brickmr., Locust bel Sch 2d
Sheets Reuben, potter, 614 S Front
Sheets Samuel, bricklayer, West ab Cherry (K)
Sheets Sarah, rear Vienna ab Queen (K)
Sheetys Mary, pedler, 424 N 4th
Sheetz Mary, Vienna and Duke
Shelady Samuel, cupping and bleeding, Sch 8th
    bel Vine
Sheldon A. grocer, Front & Mary
Sheldon Jane, shop, 4 St Mary's ct
Shell E. sempstress, 40 Gaskill
Shell Lawrence, cordw., Charlotte & Franklin(K)
Shellady Levi B., shoemr., 131 S 4th
Shellen John, brickmr., Hammell's ct
Shellcup Geo., shoemr., rear Rachel ab Poplar
SHELLENBERGER H., hatter, 143 N 4th, h
    18 Wallace
Shellenberger & Reed, hatters, 317 N 2d
Sheller Conrad, brickmr., 5 W Cedar
Shelly Augustus, tailor, Miller ab 13th
Shelly Edmund Y. printer, 2d & Tammany, h
    154 Coates
Shelly Geo., machinist, Buttonwood ab 13th
Shelly Henry, waiter, 32 Paschall's al
Shelmire Mary, b. h., S E Duke and 2d
Shenck John, diaphragm fitters, 79 Walnut
Sheneman Benj., planemr., 291 High
Sheneman Jones, tavern, 4 N 10th
Shenfelder Geo., printer, 5 Charles pl
Sheperla Joseph, chairmr., Union ab Franklin
Shepherd Ann, 29 Brandywine st
Shepherd Catharine, 99 O Y road
Shepherd Chas., ladies shoemr., 362 N 6th
Shepherd Francis, cooper, rear 452 Callowhill
Shepherd Francis, rigger, Collins' al
Shepherd George, ship carp., Hanover below
    Franklin
Shepherd Geo. boat builder, Penn ab Poplar h
    Penn bel Maiden (K)
Shepherd George M., ornamental engraver, 7½
    Bread
Shepherd G. F. & Co., straw goods, 183 High
Shepherd Jacob, jr., Beach ab Palmer (K)
Shepherd Jacob, caulker, Marlboro' bel Frank-
    lin.
Shepherd Jacob S., combmr., Shaffer's ct
Shepherd James, carp., rear Court al
Shepherd James M., mer., 12 N 5th, h 16 Pal-
    myra row
Shepherd John, cooper, Sarah ab Queen
Shepherd John, mach't., Sch 8th ab Callowhill
Shepherd John J., gunsm., 135 Green
Shepherd Leonard, locksm., Hanover n Duke(K)
Shepherd Martin, porter, Wood ab Sch 8th
Shepherd Robt., driver, Paul bel 7th
Shepherd Robt., ladies' shoemr., Weeks' ct

Shepherd R. T., clothing, 95 Chestnut & 40 S 3d
Shepherd Stephen, lamp mr., 17 Perry
Shepherd Thos. jr. bricklayer, 3 Wheelock's pl
Shepherd Thos., gent., 27 Madison
Shepherd William, whip mr. Queen ab Bishop
    (K)
Shepherd Wm., morocco fin., Dunton n Frank-
    lin (K)
Shepherd Wm., jr., grocer, 244 S 4th
Sheppard Augustus, lab., Pleasant ab 11th
Sheppard Charles, 71 Cherry
Sheppard Daniel H., glass blower, rear Vienna
    ab Queen (K)
Sheppard Geo. L., silversm., 2 Pleasant Retreat
Sheppard Henry, victualler, Powel and Vineyard
    (F V)
Sheppard John, vict., Powell n Vinegar
Sheppard John, machinist, Rye ab Reed
Sheppard John, weaver, Benton ab School (K)
Sheppard Julia, tailoress, 10 Hampton st
Sheppard J. F., dry goods, 550 High
Sheppard Margaret, gentw., 235 Vine
Sheppard Robt., butcher, Fraley's al (K)
Sheppard Robert K., carpenter, 36 Rittenhouse
Sheppard Samuel, vict., Franklin ab Hanover
Sheppard Samuel C., druggist, 107 S 9th
SHEPPARD THOMAS R., mer., 27 High
Sheppard Wm., carter, 30 Brown (N L)
Sheppard Wm., cooper, 5 Mary
Sheppard Wm. M., engineer, 658 N 2d
Shepperd Benj. L., chairmr., Lewis n Sch 6th
Sherborne Thomas P., cabinetmr., 127 Walnut, h
    150 Queen ab 4th
Sherer Ann, Willow ct
Sherer Hannah, Harmony bel 5th
Sherer Isaac, carp., 375 N 4th
Sherer Jacob, 38 Madison
Sherer John, cooper, 2 Steinmetz's ct
Sherer Wm., paper mr., 8th ab Wallace
Sherick John, bookbinder, Elm bel Franklin (K)
Sheridan James, tailor, 16th S 9th, h 12th ab
    Buttonwood
Sheridan John, lab., Haydock n Front
Sheridan & Kellogg, livery stable, 11 Filbert
Sheridan Nicholas, lab., Filbert n Sch 3d
Sheridan O., livery stable, 11 Filbert
Sheridan Philip, weaver, 3d ab Franklin (K)
Sheridan P. F. Rev. Lebanon ab Christian
Sheridan Thomas, labourer, G T road n Jefferson
Sherker Mary, 9 M'Duffie
Sherlock Dorcas, 26 M'Duffie
Sherlock Joseph, lab., 10th and Fitzwater
Sherman C., printer, 19 St. James, house 203 S
    5th
Sherman Joseph, carp., 20 Decatur
Sherman Rebecca, b h. 45 Sassafras
Sherman S. G., bookseller, 3 Hart's buildings
Sherman & Turner, carps., 20 Decatur
Sherman Wm. E., ship master, 170 S 9th
Shermer Anthony, cabmr. 44 Brown
Shermer George, cooper, rear 10 Washington
    Market pl
Shermer Henry, tavern, c Warren & Queen (K)
Shermer James, carver & gilder, 16 Perry
Shermer James M. gilder, 225 Mulberry

Shermer John, 10th bel Catharine
Shermer John, shoemaker, 218 S 7th
Shermer John F. bricklayer, Cedar bel 8th
Shermer Joseph, shoemaker, N E 8th and Cedar
Shermer Wm., carver & gilder, 30 Mulberry
Shern Patrick, stone cutter, 671 N 2d (K)
Sherrer Eliza, tailoress, Jones W of Sch 5th
Sherrerd Henry D., sec. N. A. Ins. Co., h 56 S 2d
Sherrerd Mary, 169 Cherry
Sherrerd Michael, messenger, Perry & Adams
Sherrerd William D., com. agent, 108 High, h 6 Lodge
Sherron Patrick, weaver, M'Mackin's ct
Sherron Sarah L., 55 M road
Sherry Bridget, dressmr., Cadwalader bel Master
Sherry James, manuf., G T road, ab Master
Sherry John, farmer, Johnson's la ab 4th
Sherry John, lime burner, Sch Front bel Lombard
Sherry Michael, cordw, 6th & Elizabeth
Sherry Patrick, weaver, Brinton ab 13th
Sherry Sarah, 8 W Cedar
Sherwood Samuel, seaman, 246 S Front
Sherwood Wm., combmr., Brown bel 11th
Shettsline John, shoemr., Brown bel 13th
Shetzline Abm., glass bl., Wood bel Duke (K)
Shetzline Baker, glass bl. rear Cherry ab Queen (K)
Shetzline Conrad, Palmer n F road
Shetzline David, gent., 248 Christian
Shetzline Elizabeth, trimmings, P road and Carpenter
Shetzline Jacob, lab., Wood ab Franklin (K)
Shetzline John, huckster, Jackson (S G)
Shetzline Michael, carter, Newmarket ab Laurel
Shetzline Michael, drayman, 4 Stewart's pl
Shew T. B., photographist, 116 Chestnut
Shewell Geo. E., R road ab Buttonwood
Shewell Linington, dry goods, 127½ N 3d, h 44 Lombard
Shewell Rachel, R road ab Buttonwood
Shewell Thomas, mer., 151 Filbert
Shewell William M., mer., 23 N 4th, h Washington ab 10th
Shewmon Elizabeth, Marlboro' ab Duke
Shibe John, ship carp., Marlboro' bel Duke
Shibe John, bookbinder, 21 opp Beaver (K)
Shibe John D., whipmr., Thompson ab 4th
Shibe Sarah, baker, 511 N 2d
Shibe Wm., ship wright, 182 Swanson
Shick Jacob, jr., tailor, 6th and Buttonwood
Shick John, matches, St John n Beaver (K)
Shick Peter, cordw., 3 Orchard
Shields Ann, gentw., Sch 6th n Summer
Shields Ann M., teacher, Sch 7th ab Wood
Shields Deborah, tailoress, 184 Christian
Shields Eliza, 155 N 7th
Shields Elizabeth, Sch 7th bel Callowhill
Shields George, cordw., 5 Madison

Shields Joseph R., variety store, 378 N 2d
Shields Mary, Sassafras ab 13th
Shields Mich., chandler, 2 Martin's ct (K)
Shields & Miller, hardware, 79 N 3d
Shields Richard, plasterer, George E Sch 6th
Shields Sarah, b. h., 23 Brandywine st
Shields Susan, Queen bel 3d
Shields Thomas, lab., Catharine bel Flower
Shields Thomas, brickmr., Lombard W Ashton
Shields Washington, tailor, 26 Charlotte
Shields Wm., weaver, Philip ab Jefferson (K)
Shields Wm. J., mer., 57 Jones' al, h Hamilton ab Sch 3d
Shierman Hannah, shop, 25 Magnolia
Shiffler Fredk., saddler, 44 Beck st
Shifler John, clerk, Llweyln's ct (K)
Shifler John, clerk, St John bel Beaver (K)
Shilky John, weaver, 18 Harmstead
Shilling Wm., currier, rear 468 N 3d
Shilling Wm., lab., Wiley's ct
Shillinglaw Wm., baker, Spruce ab Sch 5th
Shillingford Henry H., mer., 147 High, h 3d n Washington
Shillingsburg Jno., carp., Benton ab School (K)
Shillingsburg M., wid., Benton ct and School
Shillingsburg Saml., cooper, 12 Montgomery
Shillingsford Michael, blacksm., 10 Carberry's ct
Shillingsforth James, caulker, Cherry ab Queen
Shillingsforth Jas., carp., Cherry ab Queen (K)
Shimpf John, carp., Dunton bel Otter (K)
Shinaberrier Thos., lab., Jackson ct (N L)
Shindler John, sail maker, N whfs n Vine, h 23 Callowhill
Shineberger Nicholas, soap maker, 267 N 3d
Shingle John, vict., Front ab Franklin (K)
Shingles J., umbrella mr., 211 N 8th
Shinkle Christ., shoemr., 15 Farmer
Shinkle John, weaver, 5 Bell's ct
Shinkle John W., coal, 31 S 3d
Shinkle & Shivers, coal mers., 31 S 3d
Shinn Asa, bricklayer, Elizabeth bel Poplar
Shinn Charles, butcher, Front ab Franklin (K)
Shinn Earl, measurer, 136 Pine
Shinn Hester, 9 Elliott av
Shinn Isaac L., shoemr., 7th and Hallowell
Shinn Richard, carp., Elizabeth ab Parrish
Shinn Stacy, blacksm., Front ab Reed
Shinn Wm. H., grocer, Rose ab School (K)
Shinnewald And., cooper, Wood bel Duke (K)
Shinnick Lewis, brickmr., 400 Coates
Shipley Augustus B., mer., 71 High, h 304 N 6th
Shipley John, weaver, Carroll bel 13th
Shipley Lydia, 11th ab Sp Garden
Shipley Thomas, conveyancer, 16 N 7th
Shipley & Warner, hardware, 71 High
Shipman Jacob, porter, 24 Bread
Shipman Joseph J., mer. & notary public, 46½ Walnut, h 266 N 6th
Shippen Eliza I., 211 Spruce

Shirey John, tobacconist, 12th & Pearl
Shirley John, shoemr., 15 Harmony st
Shirkey Ann, 171 Shippen
Shirkey Wm., ship carp., Crown ab Bedford (K)
Shisler Caroline, 321 St John
Shissler John P., weaver, Front bel Master (K)
Shissler Saml., drayman, 91 G T road (K)
Shive David, tailor, 269 N 3d
Shiveley Matthias, vict., 7th and Brown
Shively Mich., blacksm., Cherry n Duke (K)
Shivers Ann, 53 W Cedar
Shivers Charles, druggist, N E 7th & Spruce
Shivers James K., M. D., 97 Locust
Shivers Josiah A., coal, 31 S 3d, h Sp Garden ab 12th
Shivers J. K., wood dealer, Callowhill st whf., h 18 Laurel st (N L)
Shivers Thomas, gent., 97 Locust
Shober, Bunting & Co., mers., 14 S whfs
Shober Geo., fisherman, Vienna bel Franklin
Shober H. Regina, 254 Cherry
Shober John B., mer., 14 S whfs, h 106 S 8th
Shober S. L., mer., 14 S whfs, h 106 S 8th
Shoch David, tobacconist, G T road bel 6th
Shoch Edwin, cordw. h Hanover ab Bedford(K)
Shoch G. P., accountant, 78 Brown
Shoch Margaret, gentw., 78 Brown
Shoch Samuel P., cordwainer, 4 R road
Shock Jacob, cordw., Brown bel Front
Shock James, shoemr., 7 Smith (N L)
Shock Jos., buck sk. dress, 3d ab Franklin (K)
Shockcor Jos., cordw., Mechanic ab George
Shockcor Martha, 39 Charlotte
Shockcor Mary, Charlotte bel Poplar
Shockley Henry, lab., 587 S 2d
Shoden Patrick, lab., Jones n Sch 8th
Shoefner Andrew, locksm., rear 13th bel Brown
Shoemaker Abby, 89 Wood
Shoemaker Adam H., clerk, G T road & 2d (K)
Shoemaker Allen, printer, 278 Marshall
Shoemaker Benj. A., carter, Marshall bel Poplar
Shoemaker Charles, tailor, 29 N 6th
Shoemaker Charles, cordw., 538 N 2d
Shoemaker Chas., lab., Ann bel Sch 4th (F V)
Shoemaker Chas., carp., 100 Marshall
Shoemaker Comly, carp., Poplar & Marshall
Shoemaker Daniel, lastmr., 155 Poplar
Shoemaker Ferd., carter, Hanover bel F road (K)
Shoemaker Gotleib, lithographer, 11 Charlotte (K)
Shoemaker Gottlieb, hackler, Philip ab Master (K)
Shoemaker Hannah, 280 Walnut
Shoemaker Harman, cordw., 5 Stearley's ct
Shoemaker John J., tobacconist, 452 High, coal, S E Lombard and Broad
Shoemaker Jonathan, 25 N 12th
Shoemaker Jonathan, ex-broker, 46½ Walnut
Shoemaker Jacob, carp. weav., Crown ab Duke (K)
Shoemaker Margaret, rear 13th bel Buttonwood
Shoemaker Mary Ann, Queen ab Palmer (K)
Shoemaker Mary, 13th bel Wood
Shoemaker N., M. D., 226 Mulberry
Shoemaker Robert, druggist, 2d & Green

Shoemaker Robert, lab., Wiles' row
Shoemaker, S. P., druggist, 335 N 2d
Shoemaker Wm., black & white sm., 5 Brandywine st
Shoemaker, Wm. K., bricklayer, 10th ab Parrish
Sholl John, shoes, 85 R road
Shone John, tailor, rear 3 Eutaw
Shoppe Geo., drover, 122 Catharine
Shorday Christopher J., morocco dress., 3 N 3rd, h N 2d opp. Beaver.
Shore Edward, weaver, Hanover ab Franklin (K)
Short H. B., carpenter, 36 Perry
Short Jacob, sawyer,
Short Jane, St Joseph's av
Short Leonard, cabinetmr., 9 Faries' ct
Short Martha, washer., Dyott's ct (K)
Short Patrick, shop, 20 Spafford's ct
Short Rebecca, gentw., 189 S 6th
Short Spencer, porter, 43 Quince
Short Wm., tailor, Teas' ct
Short Wm., gent., 145 Walnut
Shorter Ann, whitewasher, Edward n School (K)
Shorter S. S., milliner, 181 Lombard
Shortridge John H., mer., 233 S 9th
Shorts Shadrach, lab., 9 Middle al
Shote Geo., carp. weav., Apple bel Franklin
Shotwell Reb., Filbert E of Sch 6th
Shourds D. H., shoemaker, 157 N 2d
Shourds Francis, rags, 261 Shippen
Shourds Marg., R road ab Washington
Shourds Martha C., 163 N 4th
SHOURDS WM. C., grocery, N E 4th & Cedar
Shourds Wm. H., ladies' shoemr., 194 St John
Showaker Catharine, Coates bel 10th
Showaker Isaiah, shop, 11th and Wood
Showaker Jacob, carp., Coates bel Broad
Showaker John G., combmr., 467 N 3d
Showaker Samuel, cooper, Olive ab 12th
Showers Fredk., Sch 8th ab Cherry
Showers John, lab., George n Sch 2d
Showers Nathan, driver, 1 St Joseph's av
Showwaker Charles, cooper, Wood bel 13th
Shrank Geo. J., brickmr., 52 W Cedar
Shreck Sarah, washer, Palmer & Franklin (K)
Shreeve Barbara, gentw., 23 Penn ab Poplar (K)
Shreeve Elizabeth, 399 N Front
Shreeve G. P., dry goods, S E Marshall & Callowhill
Shreeve Jacob R., tobacconist, 486 Sassafras
Shreeve John, port. painter, 82 Mulberry, h 25 Linden (K)
Shreeve John, stone cutter, Willow ab Front
Shrekagast Abraham, lab., rear 20 Lily al
Shreeve Ann, shop, Olive n 12th
Shriver Wm., victualler, Green & Franklin
Shriver William J., victualler, 345 Callowhill
Shryock Augustus, clerk, 13th bel Buttonwood
Shryock Wm. C., painter, 2 Westford av
Shubert Alphonso, stone cutter, Sch 7th below Pine
Shubert Benjamin F., wheelwright, 6 Carlton
Shubert Isaac, carp., Shippen ab Shippen la.
Shubert John, shoemr., Tamarind bel Coates
Shubert John, fisherman, Allen bel Palmer (K)

40

Shubert Saul, machinist, Nectarine bel 11th
Shubert Wm., carp., 22 Federal
Shuff Andrew, blindmr., 172 S 5th
Shuff Eliza, gentw., Wood n 8th
Shuff William, cabinetmr., Peach n Coates
Shugard Simon, harnessmr., Sp Garden bel 9th, h 9th & Washington
Shugart Caspar, carpet weav., R road bel Wallace
Shugart George, carp. weav., R road bel Wallace
Shugart George S., hardware, 385 N 2d
Shugart Simon, carp., 1 Townsend's av
Shugrue John, hatter, 10th and Nectarine
Shuler John, blacksm., Marshall and Willow
Shuler Philip, skin dress., Franklin ab 4th(K)
Shuler Theodr., shop, St John, bel G T road(K)
Shull Anthony, blacksmith, rear 12 Rachel (N L)
Shull Edwin, mer., 4 N 3d, h 21 Branch
Shull Jno., tobac. Queen bel Shackamaxon(K)
Shull Nancy, 120 New
Shull Philip, lab., Wistar's ct (K)
Shults Catharine, rear 120 Dillwyn
Shults Charles, cordw., 312 S 6th.
Shults Clayton, ropemr., Franklin bel Cherry (K)
Shults Philip M., cordw., 312 S 6th
Shultz Ann, 294 S 6th
Shultz Bernard, cabinetmr., F road bel Faanklin
Shultz Charles, shipwright, Concord bel 3d
Shultz Frederick, cabinetmr., 38 Queen
Shultz Gabriel, labourer, Brown n Washington av
Shultz Geo., engineer, Marlboro' bel Bedford(K)
Shultz Jacob, baker, Apple ab Poplar
Shultz Jacob S., carp., Shield's al., h Green ab 9th (K)
Shultz John M., baker, 182 Locust
Shultz Martin, mer., 77 S Front
Shultz Robert E., carpenter, 349 Cedar
Shultz Wm., cordw., Nectarine bel 11th
Shultz Wm. S., carp., 49 Commerce, h 301 Callowhill
Shulze F. S., 75 S 4th
Shuman Abrm. B., clerk, 421 N 6th
Shuman Cath., rear Marshall ab Poplar
Shuman Frederick, grocer, S W 7th & Coates
Shuman Geo., starchmr., James ct (K)
Shuman Joseph, vict., Charles bel Buttonwood
Shuman J., blacksm., 276 S 7th
Shuman Wm., dealer, 42 George (S)
Shuman Wm., grocer, 7th & Brown
Shumway W. A., mer., 7 High, boots, &c., 2d and Pine, h 4th & Gaskill
Shunk F. R., M. D., 35 Palmyra sq
Shunk Isaac, measurer, 35 Palmyra sq
Shupard G., dressmr., 12 Dillwyn
Shurdy Richard, weav., 4 Richardson's ct
Shurlock Parkhurst, chairmr., House of Refuge, 13th bel Coates
Shurlock William, paint. & glaz., F road above Phoenix

Shuster Henry, carpenter, 17 Spring Garden
Shuster Jacob, cabinetmr., 5 Wallace
Shuster Jacob, gauger and cooper, 75 N Water, h 30 Vine
Shuster Jacob, jr., guager and cooper, 75 N Water, h 32 Elfreth's al
Shuster John, lab., Nectarine bel 11th
Shuster John, cordw., 158 N 13th
Shuster John, oak cooper, 557 N 3d
Shuster Jos., provision, 331 Vine
Shuster Lawrence, gent., 22 Franklin.
Shuster Lawr'e., jr., vict., Franklin ab Callowhill
Shuster Martha, 293 S 3d
Shuster Peter, victualler, 32 Franklin.
Shuster Peter A., carp., Clinton ct
Shuster & Robinson, blacksms., Front ab Mary
Shuster Samuel, tavern, Sp Garden ab 9th
Shuster Saml., blacksm., Carlton ab Sch 6th
Shuster Saml., vict., Brooke ab Coates
Shuster Thos. F., carp., Buttonwood bel 9th
Shuster Wm., blacksmith, Front & Mary, h 111 Queen
Shuster Wm. D., stone cutter, 9th n Buttonwood
Shuster Wm. H., plasterer, Hazel
Shuster Wm. H., house & sign paint., 32 Franklin
Shute James C., grain and feed, 39 Cedar, h 24 Shippen
Shutretter Anthony, cordw., rear Orchard ab Rawle
Shutt John, cordw., 21 Chester
Sibbald Chas. F., mer., 15 Walnut, h Spruce bel 11th
Sibbet Wm., baker, rear 9 Shackamaxon(K)
Sibbs Joseph, framemr., 4 Exchange pl., h 68 Garden
Sibert Catharine, shop, 145 Cherry
Sibert Danl., shoemr., 3 Garrigue's ct
Sibert Elizabeth, 525 N 4th
Sibert Geo., cabinetmr., Linden ab Sch 7th
Sibley Elizabeth, wid., rear 109 Queen
Sibley John, mer., 116 High, h 34 Palmyra sq
Sickel Horatio, blacksm., 462 N 2d
Sickel John, bookseller, 8 N 6th
Sickel John D., jeweller, 5 John
Sickel Thomas H., blacking manuf., 89 F road
Sickels Mahlon, cabinetmr., Poplar ab Lewis
Sickels Wm. H., clerk, Paul ab 6th
Sickey Jos., ship carp., Monroe ab Palmer(K)
Sickfrit Joseph, ship carp., Elm below Franklin (K)
Sickler Martha, rear Marshall ab Poplar
Sickler Richard M., tailor, 145 N 3d
Sickler Vinicomb, cabman, 55 M road
Siddall Joseph, watchcase mr., 6 Laurel (C)
Siddall Jos. glass mer., 124 Franklin
Siddall Jos., clerk, 10th ab Poplar
Siddall

Siddons John, jeweller, Washington bel 4th
Siddons John, tailor, 22 Strawberry
Siddons Joseph, tailor, 12 Chatham
Siddons Jos., coal, 13 Exchange pl, h 191 N 8th
Siddons Josiah C., hatter, Jenning's row
Siddons Wm., carp., 159 Christian
Sides Joseph, shoemr., 3 Passmore's pl
Sides Wm., cordw., rear 176 Poplar
Sidleman Thomas, cooper, 7 Jenning's row
Sidman Charles, tailor, 14 Poplar
Sidman Mary, tailoress, Green's ct
Siebeling Henry, bootmr., 21 James (S G)
Siedenstricker Bedwick, provision, 3d & German
Sieger Michael, mer., 49 N 3d
Sieger Peter, mer., 49 N 3d, h 287 N 6th
Siegrist Frederick, confect., 4 Sp Garden
Siemen Charles, hair dresser, c 12th and Graff
Siemers Fredk. M., cooper, Rye bel Marion
Sien George, 7 Pearl ab 12th
Sifer Wm., machinist, Carroll bel 13th
Sigfried Susannah, 20 Bread
Sigler Amos, gunsm., rear 144 St John
Sigler Amos, silversm., Shields
Sigler Jacob, baker, Front bel Master (K)
Sigmound Jacob, lab., rear 5th ab Christian
Sigmound John L., shoemr., rear 5th ab Christian
Signs Saml., oak cooper, 2d bel Oxford(K)
Sigoigne A Mrs., teacher, 7 Washington sq
Sikes Dudley, sashmr., Cedar ab 7th, b 26 Harmony ct
Silbert Dorothy, grocer, Parker & Carpenter
Silbert Eliza, gentw., 97 Fitzwater
Silbert Rosanna, 328 S 5th
Silcox Wm., mat weaver, 23 S 9th, h 29 S 10th
Silence Catharine, Melon bel 13th
Siler Henry, carter, 7 Elbow la
Sill Geo., oyster house, 49 N whfs
Sill Hiram, tailor, Marion opp Rye
Sill Israel, chairmr., 17 Rachel
Sill Joseph, fan. dry goods, 185 Chestnut
Sill J. & Co., fancy dry goods, 185 Chestnut
Silladay Joseph, shoemr., 3 Adams
Sillick Crosby, cordw., 31 Mary (S)
Sillvers David, carp., George ab Sch 7th
Siloy Abrm., sea capt., 97 Gaskill
Silva Francisco, gent., 10 Plum
Silver Charles, seaman, Queen bel Front
Silvernail Elizabeth, washer, 6th bel Poplar
Silvers Addison, 7th & Callowhill
Silvers E C., rear 17 Brook
Silvers Wm., lab., rear Marshall ab Brown
Silverthorn John, glass blower, Dyott's ct (K)
Silvis Benjamin, mer., 108 N 3d, h 112 St John
Silvius John, ironmonger, Clark bel 4th
Silvy & Kochersperger, grocers, R road & Melon
Silvy William, grocer, Melon & R road
Simcox Robert, saddler, rear 19 Castle
Simes James W., druggist, 459 High
Simes Margaret, Clinton bel Parrish
SIMES SAMUEL, druggist, N W 12th and Chestnut
Simes Samuel, baker, High n Sch 3d
Simler George, 14 Gebhard
Simler John, baker, 174 N 13th

Simmelwright Henry, lab., Mechanic bel George
Simmons Ann, gentw., 341 Vine
Simmons A. H., S W 3d & Chestnut, h Mulberry n Juniper
Simmons A. H. & Co. pubs. Dollar Newspaper, S W 3rd & Chestnut
Simmons David P., real estate agent, 431 N 6th
Simmons Edw., mer., Filbert E of Sch 6th
Simmons Edward S., lumb. mer., 197 N Water, h 201 Mulberry
Simmons E., 88 Spruce
Simmons George, shoemaker, Carlton ab 12th
Simmons Henry, coachman, 3 Poplar
Simmons Henry, blacksm., Bedford ab 6th
Simmons James, carp., 235 S 6th
Simmons John, teacher, Locust ab 8th, h Noble ab 8th
Simmons John P., hatter, 6 Elder
Simmons J., dentist, 161 Mulberry
Simmons Makenzie, 3 Hurst
Simmons Mary, Mulberry bel Juniper
SIMMONS MRS., wid. of Stephen, 251 Vine
Simmons Samuel, bricklayer, 9 Rittenhouse
Simmons Stephen H., chair maker, 41 Spruce
Simmons William H., salesman, 89 Franklin
Simmons W. R., clerk, 66 Christian
Simms Jane, 174 Callowhill ab Sch 6th
Simon Christian, tanner, rear Charlotte n Culvert
Simon Christ., lab., rear Crown ab Franklin(K)
Simon David, ship carp., Marlboro' ab Queen(K)
Simon Edw., printer, 8 Harmony ct
Simon George, 264 S 5th
Simon James K., bookbinder, 141 S 5th, h 483 S 2d
Simon John H., bookseller, 114 N 3d, h 237 N 3d
Simon Mary, Queen bel Shackamaxon
Simon Susannah, 18½ Bread
SIMONS CHARLES W., oil, 32 S Water, h Callowhill n Sch 5th
Simons Danl., cordw., Ellis ab Washington(S G)
Simons Edward, lab., Wood ab Sch 4th
Simons Geo., Marriott and 6th
Simons George W., thimble mr., 115 Chestnut, h 192 S 2d
Simons Henry, wheelwright, 117 New Market, h Washington av ab Noble
Simons Henry, lab., Franklin bel Vienna(K)
Simons James, tobacconist, 199 Lombard
Simons James, cordw., Barber's row
Simons John, weaver, Stewart and Catharine
Simons John, shoemr., 47 Commerce
Simons John, shoemr., Palmer ab Duke (K)
Simons John, coachmr., School
Simons John, blacksm., Lister's pl
Simons John P., acct., 8 Elfreth's al
Simons M. P., case mr., 100 Chestnut
Simons Samuel, acct., 11 North
Simons Sarah, washer, St Mary ab 7th
Simons William, bricklayer, 226 S 3d
Simons Wm., fisherman, Vienna ab Queen(K)
Simpins R. G., tailor, Broad ab Race
Simpson Abraham, ship carpenter, Crown ab Queen.
Simpson Alex., seaman, Little Water ab Cedar

Simpson Ambrose, tobacconist, 527 N Front, h Allen ab F road
Simpson Ann, 25 Barron
Simpson & Bro., watch case mr., 21 Franklin pl
Simpson Bushrod W., engineer, 13th ab Coates
Simpson Catharine, shop, 189 Cherry.
Simpson David, tavern, 102 Cherry
Simpson David, silver plater, Hope bel Master (K)
Simpson David, carp., 5 Pratt st
Simpson & Dessau, wines and liquors, 96 N 3d
Simpson Edward, plasterer, Washington (W P)
Simpson Elias, merchant, 96 N 3d, h Callowhill n 8th
Simpson Elias, 276 Callowhill
Simpson Emery, lab., 58 St Mary's st.
Simpson E. A. & F., milliners, 67 S 11th
Simpson Francis, skin dresser, 21 Linden (K)
Simpson George, wool dealer, 475 and 477 and h 471 N Front
Simpson Geo., lab., 37 Prosperous al
Simpson Hannah, trimmings, 318 Vine
Simpson Harriet, gentw., 67 Pine
Simpson Henry, mer., Buttonwood ab 12th
Simpson Henry L., cordw., Marion & Lancaster
Simpson Hood, manuf., High W Sch 7th
Simpson H., 174 N 4th
Simpson Isaac, cabtmr., 72 E South
Simpson Isaac, cordw., Cherry n F road (K)
Simpson James, boat builder, 10 Somers' ct
Simpson James, tailor, 8th bel Carpenter
Simpson James, trimmings, 2d and Prime
Simpson James, 90 S 4th
Simpson James, ship carpenter, marine rail way, h 456 S Front
Simpson James, tailor, 83 Mulberry
Simpson James, grocer, S E Sch 7th and Sassafras
Simpson James, lab., 15 Flower
Simpson James H., merchant, 90 S 4th
Simpson James & T., dry goods, S E 4th and Lombard
Simpson John, tailor, 98 Filbert
Simpson John, chaplain at Alms House, (W P)
Simpson John, shop, 143 Cherry
Simpson John, Hallowell n 7th
Simpson John, dry goods, 71 E Cedar
Simpson John, watchman, Richard n Sch. 6th
Simpson John, hatter, 103 & h 70 Chestnut
Simpson John W., jeweller, 8th bel Carpenter
Simpson Joseph A., comb manf., 17 Bank, h Orleans & Lombard
Simpson J. L. & T. B., dry goods, High W of Sch 7th
SIMPSON J. & NEILL, ship builders, Marine Railway
Simpson Mary, 21 Morgan
Simpson Mary Ann, washer, rear 296 S 8th
Simpson Mehitable, b h., Front and Green
Simpson Peter, chair mr., Allen ab F road (K)
Simpson Philip, basket mr., 458 N 2d
Simpson Reuben, waiter, Washington ab 11th
Simpson Robert F., carp., 634 S 2d
Simpson Robert G., shipwright, 123 Queen
Simpson Samuel, acct., 404 N 10th.

Simpson Samuel, basketmr., 18 Brown
Simpson Samuel, carp., 12 Hampton
Simpson Sandy, labourer, Carpenter ab 8th
Simpson Sarah, eating-house, rear 6 Blackhorse alley
Simpson Soby, Hines' pl
Simpson Stephen, Sch 4th n Chestnut
Simpson, furniture, 72 Cedar
Simpson Thomas, lab., Jones ab Sch 8th
Simpson Thomas, combmaker & dry goods, 296 Pine
Simpson Thomas, tallow chandler, 21 Lily al
Simpson Thompson, Sch 5th bel Spruce
Simpson Thompson, pedler, George n Sch 2d
Simpson William, cordw., 27 Garden
Simpson William, nailer, Rugan ab Callowhill
Simpson Wm., tavern, Washington, (W P)
Simpson Wm., weaver, Otter ab Front
Simpson Wm., provisions, Coates bel 11th
Simpson Wm., bricklayer, 326 S 6th
Simpson Wm., lab., rear 4th ab Beaver
Simpson Wm., salesman, 26 Rittenhouse
Simpson Wm., oil cloth mr., Franklin ab Front
Simpson William R., cordw., Coates bel 11th
Simpson W. H., tailor, 154 S 6th
Sims Abigail, huckster, rear 76 S 2d
Sims Anthony, tavern, N E Federal & M road
Sims Dorcas, eating house, 10 Letitia ct
Sims John C., gent., 188 Spruce
Sims John M., att'y at law, 46 S 6th
Sims Wm., ropemr., M road & Wharton
Sinclair Kennedy, cabinetmr., 179 S 2d
Sinclair Margaret, Jackson (S G)
Sinclair Thomas, lithographer, 79 S 3rd, h 319 S 5th
Sinclair Thomas, carp., 210 S 4th
Sinclair W. J., b h., N W Swanson and Prime
Siner David S., brass founder, 161 Apple
Siner Elizabeth, Vienna ab Queen (K)
Siner Elizabeth, widow, 536 N 4th
Siner Hannah, tobacconist, 65 N 6th
Siner Henry, brickmr., Orchard ab George
Siner James, glass cutter, Wood and Duke
Siner Jacob, gent., Franklin & Marlboro' (K)
Siner John, senr., brass founder, 40 Apple
Siner John, jr., brass founder, Orchard above George
Siner John H., brickmaker, 2d ab Montgomery, h 496 N 3d
Siner John T., gunsm., Charlotte ab George (N L)
Siner William, tavern, 4th & George
Siner Wm., brass founder, Orchard ab George (N L)
Sines Hiram L., clocks and shoes, 164 N 2d
Sines Thos., lab., Otter n Front (K)
Sinex John, bookbinder, Charlotte bel Beaver
Sinex Robert H., carp., Centre bel 13th
Sinex Thomas, printer, Apple ab Culvert
Sinexon Hannah, gentw., 56 Gaskill
Singer John, gent., Spruce ab Broad
Singer Richard S., gent., 12th ab Brown
Singer Theodore, waiter, 49 Quince
Singer Thomas, cotton mer., 51 N Front, h 178 S Front

Singers Mary, rear Beck's ct bel 2d
Singerly George, dealer, 400 N 3d
Singerly Thos., cordw., St. John ab Tammany
Singleton George, waiter, 14 Middle al
Singleton Horatio G., bricklr., Carpenter n P road
Singleton James, ship carp., 95 Prime
Singleton John, 7 Lagrange pl
Singleton John S., suspender manuf., Beach bel Marlboro'
Singley Hannah, b h, 243 N 6th
Sink Ann, Vine n Sch 8th
Sink Charles, tailor, 14 New Market
Sink Charles, musician, 206 R road
Sink C., lab., Prime below Front
Sink C. jr., paper hanger, 206 R road
Sink Lewis, tobacco, Callowhill ab Sch 8th
Sinkler Henry H., military mount., Claire al
Sinkler Wm. S., boots & shoes, 448 Vine
Sinn Davis N., mer., 197 High, h 42 Buttonwood
Sinnickson Chas., coal, 44 Walnut, h 209 S 8th
Sinnickson Thomas, mer., 75 High, h 79 Pine
Sipe Frederick, cordw., Lily alley ab Green
Sipe Jacob, bootmr., 222 S 3d
Sipher Sarah, huckster, Brown bel 13th
Sipler Geo., blacksm., 31 Farmer, h 142 Poplar
Siples Conrad, cordw., 18 Pratt
Sipple James, tailor, Lancaster bel Reed
Sipple Stephen, clothes, 82 N 2nd, h 279 S 3d
Sipple Thomas, lab., Carpenter ab 8th
Sipps Peter, brickmr., Ann W Sch 4th
Sipps Wm., brickmaker, 15 Sch. 5th
Sipps Wm. F., brickmr., Ann W Sch 4th
Sirrel Henry, mer., 93 Crown, h 85 Wood
Sisco Wm. driver, Lemon ab 11th
Sisty B. P., pocket book manuf., 52½ Chestnut
Sisty John Rev., 284 N 7th
Siter Edward, mer., Mulberry and Broad, h 9 Montgomery
SITER JAS. & CO., forward. & co. mer., Broad ab Mulberry
Siter Jno., mer., 133 High, h Mulberry ab Broad
SITER, PRICE & CO., importers, 133 High
SITER, STAUFFER & CO., com. mers, 41 N whfs & 83 N Water
SITES GEO. F., chair mr., N W Front & Sasfras, & 94, and h 122 N Front
Sites Joseph, M. D., 3 Linden pl
Sithens Isaac, corder, Front & Mary
Sitler H. D., paint., Shackamaxon ab Allen (K)
Sitley John, hatter, 120 Buttonwood
Siveris Peter, beer house, 14 Coombe's al
Sivil Charles, mer., Spruce bel 11th
Sixmuth John, glassbl., Queen opp Cherry (K)
Sixte Francis, bricklay., Olive bel 12th
Sixte Joseph A., silversmith, Linden n Sch. 7th
Skaats Rinier, capt., 273 S Front
Skay James, weaver, Pine n Sch Front
Skerrett Catharine, 13 Rittenhouse
SKERRETT DAVID C., M. D., proth'y District Court, h 285 Spruce
Skerrett George A., bookbinder, 98 Locust
Skerrett James, machinist, Clinton ab Franklin (K)
Skerrett Joseph, jeweller, 5 M'Manamy's ct

Skerrett Rebecca S., 144 S 9th
Skerrett William A., Lombard ab Juniper
Sketchley George, tinsm., 205 Callowhill
Sketchley Wm., lampmr., Palm bel Brown, shop 5th & Callowhill
Skidmore Charles, cutler, 4 Hermitage pl
Skill John, painter, 137 Spruce, h 78 Fitzwater
Skillington George, tailor, 131 S 4th
Skillington, H., sea captain, 52 Wood
Skillman Ann, tobacconist, Brown n Washington av
Skillman Thomas A., blacksmith, 7 Nectarine ab 8th
Skillman Wm. G., acct. 19 Wallace
Skilton A. & G. B., dry goods, 260 S 2d
Skilton Oliver, porter, Knight's ct
Skilton Robert, weaver, 626 N 3d
Skilton Samuel, weaver, Lombard E Sch 6th
Skilton Thomas, weaver, 8 Barber row
Skinader Matthew, lab. rear 25 Ogden
Skinader Thomas, lab. rear 23 Ogden
Skinner Charles B. varnisher, 12 Cypress st
Skinner E. H., painter, 366 N 3rd
Skinner John C. drayman, Hope bel Master (K)
Skinner Peter, grinder, 3 Charles pl
Skinner Smith, tinsmith, 80 Brown
Skipton Valentine, car., rear 441 Vine
Skivington Mary, Palmer opp Allen (K)
Slack Abner, printer, 46 Almond
Slack Anthony T., drayman, Hope bel Phoenix (K)
Slack Anthony W. mer. 46 N 2d, h 35 N 10th
Slack Benjamin, lab., Lafferty's ct
Slack Charles, bricklayer, 9th ab Carpenter
Slack Cornelius, lab., R road ab Broad
Slack Daniel, wharf builder, 17 F road
Slack Henry, clerk, 350 N 4th
Slack James T., coach trimmer, 35 Marriott
Slack Maria, stockmr., 424 S 4th
Slack Mary, dressmr., 35 N 10th
Slacum Benjamin, tavern, 5th & Carpenter
Slade Alfred, mer., 36 S Front, h 413 Chestnut
Slade John S., mer. 14 S Front
Slaght James C., coal mer., Sch 8th ab Cherry
Slahter Samuel, tobacconist, 203 High
Slamman Mary, Howard & School (K)
Slater Charles, lab., rear 5th bel Christian
Slater Jas., distiller, 12 Marriott
Slater Thomas, dyer and scourer, Beach n Maiden (K)
Slater Thos B., bell roller manf.
Slater Walter, saw grinder, Wayne ab Washington
Slater William, ship wright, Beach ab Shackamaxon
Slater Wm., saw grinder, Ontario ab Poplar
Slater William, shoemr., 376 N 2d
Slatter Richd. H saddler, Otter bel William (K)
Slatter Thomas, confect., N E 7th & Walnut, & 174 S 6th
Slaugh Bartholomew, grocer, 10th & Parrish
Slaugh Catharine, tailoress, Charlotte ab Beaver
Slaugh John, cordw., Beaver & Poplar
Slaughter Chas. C. paper stainer, 20 Howard
Slaughter Frederick, rear 2d ab Phoenix (K)

Slaughter Peter C., carp., 4 S 13th
Slaughter Samuel, ropemr. 9th ab Carpenter
Slaven John, clerk, rear 380 S 3d
Sleaven John, weaver, 11th ab Carpenter
Sleaven Patrick, weaver, Phoenix ab 2d (K)
Slavin Ann, shop, Broad ab Race
Slavin Henry, lab., Murray & Sch 3d
Slavin Patrick, stone mason, George n Sch 2d
Slaw Ann, 3d bel Carpenter
Slaw Geo. E., clerk, Charlotte ab Beaver
Slaw Richard, Fitler st (K)
Slaw Wm., carp., Law's ct
Slaymaker Richard, 4 Wood
Sleavan Daniel, weaver, 11th ab Carpenter
Sleavan Patrick, weaver, 11th ab Carpenter
Sleeper Deborah, Chatham bel Green
Sleeper Edward E., tailor, 18 S 3d
Sleeper Edwin, 25 Chatham
SLEEPER & FENNER, umbrella manufs., 126 High
Sleeper James, bellows mr., c Front & Elfreth's alley
Sleeper John L. & Sons, tailors, 18 S 3d, h 210 N 4th
Sleeper J. C., tailor, 18 S 3d, h 210 N 4th
Sleeper Martha, 383 N 4th
Sleeper Sharon, umbrella manuf., 344 High
Sleeper Vincent, acct., 45 Duke
Sleeper Wm., umbrella manuf., 126 High, h 390 N 6th
Sleeper Wm. H., confect., 121 N 2d, h Allen ab Shackamaxon (K)
Sleeth Eliza, spooler, Fulton and 13th
Slemmer J. C., druggist, G T road & 2d
Slemmer Matthias, cabinetmr., 29 Apple
Slemmer Wm., carp., Lydia ab School (K)
Slendarke Geo. H. A., coach lace weaver, Cadwalader bel Phoenix (K)
Slesser Wm., lab., G T road ab Front
Slessman Jacob, lab., Wood ab Franklin (K)
Slevin Dennis, lab., 1 Bryan's ct
Slevin Jas., mer., 403 Mulberry
Slevin John, dealer, 418 High
Slifer Samuel, carp., Brown ab 10th
Slinger Henry, plast., rear Fitler ab 2d (K)
Slingluff Sarah, 410 N 3d
Sliver Toman, shop, G T road & St John (K)
Sloan Benjamin, lab., West ab Walnut
Sloan & Blayney, shoemrs., 602 N 2d (K)
Sloan Catharine, milliner, 94 N 5th
Sloan Charles, carp., Sch 3d bel Lombard
Sloan Eliza, sempstress, 7 Ogden
Sloan Elizabeth, b. h., 157 E Cedar
Sloan George W., waterman, Lancaster & Keefe
Sloan Hector, shoemr., Cadwalader above Phœ-

Sloan John P., tailor, 5 and h 2 N 8th
Sloan Joseph, waterman, Washington av below Brown
Sloan Joseph, weaver, Phillip ab Jefferson (K)
Sloan Malachi W., carter, Sch 5th ab High
Sloan Mary, Sch 4th n Barker
Sloan Mary, huckster, 10 Washington Market p
Sloan Robert, printer, 400 S 3d
Sloan Robert, tavern, c 2d and G T road
Sloan Samuel, contractor, 95 German
Sloan Susan, teacher, 16 Stamper's al
Sloan Thomas, weaver, Jefferson ab 2d
Sloan Warner, shoemr., 2 Salem al
Sloanaker Samuel, agt., Coates n Fairmount
Sloanaker Wm., agt., 129 Chestnut, h 135 N 12th
Sloat Geo. B., planing mill, Sch 8th & Hamilton, Beach n Hanover, h Broad ab Wallace
Sloat Jonas, millwright, Broad ab Wallace
Slocomb James, grocer, S W 2d and Queen, h Sutherland
Slocomb Riley, grocer, 164 Swanson
Slocum Charles M., dentist, 130 Mulberry
Slocum John R., rear 71 Christian
Slocum Peter, morocco dresser, rear 110 Washington av
Sloss Jos., weaver, 560 N Front ab Otter
Slote Wm. S., stereotyper, George bel 5th
Slough Jesse, bootmr., 476 Sassafras
Slough Nicholas, morocco dr., Poplar ab 9th
Slover Benj., carter, St John n Bridge (K)
Slover Stephen, shoemr., 61 N 8th
Slusmon John, seaman, 24 Beck (S)
Slyhoff Godfrey, lab., G T road bel Rose
Slyhoff John, farmer, 21 F road
Slyhoff James, cordw., Naglee's ct
Small Adam, cigar mr., Green's ct
Small A. E., M. D., 275 Race
Small John, baker, 552 S Front
Small Josiah, waterman, Collins' al
Small Robert H., law bookseller, 25 Minor, h 415 Spruce
Small Wm. B., M. D., Callowhill n Sch Front
Small Wm. F., att'y., Front bel Otter (K)
Smalley Henry L., mer., 279 N 8th
Smalley Samuel, Brown ab 4th
Smallwood Joseph, hair dresser, Race & 11th
Smart Alfred, fly lath maker, 199 G T road
Smart Chas., lab., 26 St Mary's st
Smart David, weaver, Amber ab Phœnix (K)
Smart Ismay, porter, Stanley st
Smart James, typecaster, 2 Skerrett's ct
Smart James, pearl button mr., 362 N 3d
SMART JOHN, watchmr., 306 High
Smart Nathaniel, dealer, 1 Stanley st

SMETHURST ROBERT, conveyancer, 51 N 6th, above stairs, h 54 S 2d
Smethurst Wm., machinist, S E 4th & Tammany
Smick Andrew, blacksm., R road ab Wallace, h Parrish ab Sch 8th
Smick John, combmr., Queen bel Crown (K)
Smick Peter, watch case maker, Monroe n Palmer (K)
Smick Wm., barber, 567 S 2d
Smiley Matthew, cordw., Lombard n Sch 7th
Smiley Peter, clothing, 253 Cedar
Smiley Rosanna, tailoress, 58 Chester
Smiley Thomas T., M. D., 217 S 5th
Smiley T. J. L., 217 S 5th
Smith Aaron, carp., 25 Beaver (K)
Smith Aaron D., mer., 13th and Pleasant
Smith Abel, blacksm., Beach ab Marlboro'
Smith Abraham C., tailor, 62 N 4th
Smith Absalom H., boots and shoes, 20 High
Smith Acy, provision, S E 7th and Shippen
Smith Adam, morocco dresser, Schleisman's al, h 243 N 3d
Smith Adam, cabinetmr., 3d bel George
Smith Adolphus, painter, Mary n F road (K)
Smith Albert O., blacksm., 8 Juniper al
Smith Alex., lab., Lombard n Sch 5th
Smith Alex., tailor, Coates bel 11th
Smith Alex. C., tailor, 19 S 5th, h 6th below Parrish
Smith Alex., clerk, Sch 2d ab Lombard
Smith Alfred, Perry & Spruce
Smith Alice, store, 54 Vine
Smith Allen, brushmr., 134 St John
Smith Allen T., dentist, 241 Spruce
Smith Andrew, lab., 2 Marshall's ct
Smith Andrew, grocer, 13th & Pine
Smith Andrew, cordw., 83 German
Smith Andrew, printer, 50 N 6th, h 60 Wood
Smith Andrew, weaver, Harmstead st
Smith Ann, b. h., 294 Walnut
Smith Ann, washer, 6 Eutaw
Smith Ann, b. h., 433 Chestnut
Smith Ann, tobacconist, 236 Callowhill
Smith Ann, cook, 305 E Pine
Smith Ann C., b. h., 182 S 11th
Smith Ann J., milliner, 14 S 12th
Smith Archibald, lab., Dugan bel Spruce
Smith Arch'd, lab., 8 Helmuth
Smith Aubrey H., atty. and counseller, office 53 S 5th
Smith & Austin, hatters, 48 Noble
Smith Azariah, dry goods, 13th and Brown
Smith A. B., carter, F road opp Allen
Smith A. M. & R. B., trimmings, 115 Spruce
Smith, Bagaley & Co., grocers, 221 High
Smith & Barr, dry goods, 33 N 2d
Smith Benj., coal mer., Wallace bel 10th
Smith Benj. W., carp., 11th bel Coates
Smith, Brother & Co., hardware, 188 High
Smith & Brown, pattern mrs., 15 Crown
Smith B., Secretary Penn. Fire Insur. Co., 134 Walnut
Smith Caroline, 242 Filbert
Smith Catharine, 113 Vine
Smith Catharine, 160 Lombard

Smith Catharine, Carpenter bel P road
Smith Charles, grocer, 12 Decatur
Smith Charles, farmer, G T road bel 7th
Smith Charles, shoemr., 25 P road
Smith Charles, coachman, Locust n Broad
Smith Charles, black and whitesm., Dillwyn bel Noble, h 136 Dillwyn
Smith Charles, carpet weaver, Mechanic above George
Smith Charles, stocking weav., Bond's ct (N L)
Smith Charles, carp., Lombard ab 13th
Smith Charles, flour and feed, High & Sch Front
Smith Charles, lab., rear 5th bel Christian
Smith Charles B., printer, Watson's al
Smith Charles B., grocer, S E 3d & Noble, h 70 Noble
SMITH CHARLES B. & BROTHER, grocers, S E 3d & Noble
Smith Charles C., baker, R road bel Broad
Smith Charles F., cordw., back 118 N 11th
Smith Charles H., mer., 42 Commerce
Smith Charles J., paper hanger, N W 9th and Lombard
Smith Charles M., clerk, 86 Charlotte
Smith Charles R., watchmr., 143 S 5th
Smith Charles S., Treas. Girard Trust, 9 S 5th, h 13th bel Locust
Smith Charles S., flour, 25 Lily al
Smith Charles W., mer., 103 N Front, h 251 Mulberry
Smith Christian, lab., 68 Zane
Smith Christian A., carp., 6 Chatham
Smith Christian L., piano mr., 23 Walnut
Smith Christine, Sassafras n Sch 7th
Smith Christopher, ship carp., Wood ab Franklin (K)
Smith Christ., potter, 11 New Market
Smith Clement, cabinetmaker, Rittenhouse W Sch 6th
Smith Clifford, mer., 188 High, h 244 Spruce
Smith Conrad, carp., rear Wood ab Franklin
Smith Conrad, lab., Cherry bel West (K)
Smith C. Stephen, 174 S Front
Smith C W. & J. R., mers., 103 N Front
Smith Daniel, manuf., 8 Linden st (K)
Smith Daniel, currier, 70 New
Smith Daniel, clothing, 187 Shippen
Smith Daniel, jr., mer., 81 S Front, h 11th and Clinton
Smith Daniel, currier, 57 Garden st
Smith Daniel, Perry and Adams
Smith Daniel B., grocer, Pleasant bel 13th
Smith Daniel L., car, Sergeant, h 4 Madison
Smith David, waiter, 305 S 8th
Smith David, capt., 21 Brown
Smith David, paper stainer, Reeves ab Sch 2d
Smith David, 26 Perry
Smith David, lab., Marriott bel 3d
Smith Diana, teacher, Prosperous al
Smith Danl. B, druggist, N E 6th and Mulberry 101 N 10th
Smith Edward, flour and feed, 257 S 5th
Smith Edward, gent., 144 Mulberry
Smith Edward, shop, h 49 Penn
Smith Edward, ink manuf., 159 N 3d

Smith Edward, sign painter, 74 N 6th, h 70 S 3d
Smith Edward, confec., Vine bel Sch. 2d
Smith Edward G., M. D., Vine and Franklin
Smith Edward P., carp., Perry ab Franklin (K)
Smith Elijah, porter, rear of 16 Little Pine
Smith Elina, Steam Mill alley
Smith Eliza, teacher, Brown bel 10th
Smith Eliza, washer, Middle alley
Smith Elizabeth, trimm store, 30 E Lombard
Smith Elizabeth, 225 Christian
Smith Elizabeth, dry goods, 421 N 2d
Smith Elizabeth, 23 Dyott's ct
Smith Elizabeth, shop, High W Sch. 4th
Smith Elizabeth, shop, 2d bel Reed
Smith Elizabeth, tavern, 55 Green
Smith Elizabeth, 135 Queen
Smith Elizabeth, Franklin ab Palmer (K)
Smith Elizabeth & Son, dry goods, 467 N 2d
Smith Ellwood M., grocer, S E 3d and Noble, h 134 Dillwyn
Smith Enoch, 162 S 10th
Smith Erastus, stencil cutter, 9th ab Coates
Smith Ernest C., hatter, 31 Marshall, h 222 Noble
Smith Estill, Mrs., 161 S 5th
Smith Eugene, teacher, Federal ab 10th
SMITH EVI & SON, grain and lime, 252 and h 234 N Front
Smith Ezra W., carp., 51 S Juniper
Smith E. E., glassware and china, 7 S 4th, h 30 Washington sq
Smith E. F., 5 Portico sq
SMITH & FIELD, com. mers., 81 S Front
Smith Francis, coachmr., 45 S 4th
Smith Francis, bricklayer, G T road ab Thompson (K)
Smith Francis, vict., rear G T road bel Jefferson
Smith Francis, 7th ab Christian
Smith Francis Gurney, mer., 37 S Front, h 42 Lombard
Smith Francis G. jun., M. D., 291 Spruce
Smith Franklin D., bricklayer, Baker ab 7th
Smith Frederick, baker, P road ab Federal
Smith Frederick, tinman, 3 Gebhard
Smith Frederick, coachmr., 11 Plum
Smith Fred'k C., barber, 10 S 6th, h 53 Wood
Smith Frederick G., brewer, 18 Dillwyn
Smith Frederick H., casemr., 118 Chestnut, h 8 Castle
Smith Frederick S., segar store, N E 8th and Green
Smith F., sea capt., Church ab Prime
Smith F. G., barber, 63 Wood
Smith Garretson, pattern maker, Lily alley
Smith George, 75 George
Smith George, bootmr., 209 N 3d
Smith George, caulker, Otter n G. T. road
Smith George, glass blower, Dyott's ct (K)
Smith George, dealer, George n Sch. 6th
Smith George, cordw., Franklin bel School (K)
Smith George, lab., rear 433 N 3d
Smith George, ship carp., Palmer ab Queen (K)
Smith George, lab., Juniper ab Pine
Smith George, stone mason, 565 N 3d
Smith George, jeweller, 108 S 2d
Smith George, lab., Carlton E of Sch. 2d

Smith Geo., Bickham W of Sch. 8th
Smith George A., coach trimmer, 436 S 6th
Smith George B., driver, 107 Christian
Smith George C., weav., George ab St John (K)
Smith George D., chairmr., 403 N 2d, h 8th bel Wallace
Smith Geo. D., currier, 240 N 3d, h 183 N 7th
Smith Geo. F., dry goods, Callowhill and Marshall
Smith George F., 301 S 10th
Smith George K., druggist, 296 N 2d bel Noble h 214 N 4th
Smith George L., oyster house, Franklin and Union
Smith George M., jeweller, 10 Jones W Sch 8th
Smith George M., brushmr., Parrish bel 11th
Smith George R., gent., 487 Mulberry
Smith George R., hatter, 178 N 5th
Smith George W., shoemr., 121 M. road
Smith George W., auctioneer, 77 Cedar, h 41 George (S)
Smith George W., 29 N 7th
Smith George W., atty. at law, 3 Dugan row
Smith George W. jr., mer., 184 N 2d
Smith Gertrude, washer, 21 Prosperous alley
Smith Grace, 8th n Sp. Garden
Smith Grizilla, 233 Vine
Smith G. Castor, engineer, Washington n 10th
SMITH G. ROBERTS, atty. and coun., 61 S 4th, h Walnut ab Broad
Smith Hancock, mer., 8 S Front, h Sch. 8th bel Spruce
Smith Hannah, 40 S 6th
Smith Harman, glass manuf., 192 N 2d
Smith Harrison, mer., 76 High, h 413 Spruce
Smith Henderson, carp., Barker W of Sch. 5th
Smith Henry, pedler, 4 Maria
Smith Henry, agent, rear 465 St. John
Smith Henry, moulder, Cadwalader ab Franklin
Smith Henry, morocco and linings, G. T. road and Otter
Smith Henry, waiter, 162 Lombard
Smith Henry, lab., Melon bel 12th
Smith Henry, cordw., Rose alley ab Green
Smith Henry, cook and waiter, Callowhill above 13th
Smith Henry, barber, 1 S 7th
Smith Henry, oysters, Grubb st
Smith Henry, drayman, 6th ab Franklin
Smith Henry, umbrella manuf., Carlton ab Sch. 8th
Smith Henry, lab., Palm ab Brown
Smith Henry, jr., cordw., 56 Green
Smith Henry E., butcher, Catharine ab 6th
Smith Henry F., constable, George ab 4th (N L)
Smith Henry G., barber, N W 2d and Walnut, h 7 Norris' alley
Smith Henry G., clerk, Cherry ab Franklin (K)
Smith Henry H., mer., 175 N 2d
Smith Henry H., M. D., 117 S 9th
Smith Henry L., acct., 509 S Front
Smith Henry M., barber, 121 S 5th
SMITH & HODGSON, druggists and chemists, N E 6th and Mulberry
Smith, Hoppel & Jones, F. Mt. finishing works
Smith Horace P., druggist, 213½ High

Smith Horatio Sidney, carp., 4 S Rittenhouse
Smith Horatio S., conveyancer, Callowhill ab Sch. 5th
Smith Houston, alderman, Johnson's lane & 3d
Smith Hugh, dry goods, Front bel Master
Smith Hugh, provisions, 208 S 6th
Smith Hugh, clerk, rear 2 S 13th
Smith Hugh, carpet weaver, 84 S 2d, h 49 George (S)
Smith Hugh, lumb. mer., c O Y road and Brown
Smith Hugh, painter, 17 Farmer
Smith Huston, 297 N 6th
Smith Isaac, button maker, 248 Catharine
Smith Isaac, iron roller, Beach and Fraley's ct
Smith Isaac, carp., 135 Carpenter
Smith Isaac, lab., 7 Scott's ct
Smith Isaac jr., flour mer., Pine st. whf., h 303 S Front
Smith Isaac D., carp., 563 N 3d
Smith Isaac R., oysterman, 22 Mary (S)
Smith Isaac R., mer., 221 High, h 276 Walnut
Smith Isabella, gentw., 4 M. road
Smith Isacher, blacksm., Apple ab George
Smith Israel A., cordw., 2 Northampton ct
Smith Jacob, ven. blinds, 182 S 4th
Smith Jacob, tobacconist, 569 N 3d
Smith Jacob, glass blower, Dyott's ct (K)
Smith Jacob, machinist, 10th and Nectarine
Smith Jacob, shoemr., Shields' alley
Smith Jacob, lab., Queen ab Palmer
Smith Jacob, turner, Hanover bel West (K)
Smith Jacob, cordw., rear 326 S 5th
Smith Jacob, carp., Wharton ab 4th
mith Jacob, cordw., rear 6 Charlotte
mith Jacob, fisherman, 9 Wood (K)
mith Jacob C., jeweller, Wood bel Sch. 7th
mith Jacob R., mer., 103 N Front, h 253 Mulberry
mith Jacob R., auctioneer, 75 Gaskill
mith James, coachmr., 8 Boyd's av
mith James, grocer, High bet Ashton & Front
mith James, lab., Otter bel G. T. road
mith James, vict., Charlotte ab Culvert
mith James, shop, Lombard n Sch. 4th
mith James, grocer, Logan and Sp. Garden
mith James, engineer, Beach ab Poplar (K)
mith James, plasterer, Jones W Sch. 6th
mith James, tinsmith, 339 S 2d
mith James, nailer, Carlisle ct
ith James, shoemr., Wharton ab 4th
ith James, stone mason, Lebanon ab Christian
th James Rev., Queen ab Marlborough
th James Rev., 30 N 11th
ith James, brass founder, St John ab George
ith James, weaver, Marlborough ab Franklin (K)
ith James, lab., 293 S 6th
ith James, Brown's ct
ith James, dyer, Spruce n Front
ith James, carp., Jefferson n Sch. 6th
ith James, carter, Jones n Sch. 8th
ith James, waterman, 120 Washington av
ith James, skin dresser, rear 6th ab Poplar
ith James, shoemr., 168 Shippen
ith James B., calico printer, Francis (F V)
    41

Smith James B., bookbinder, 23 S 8th and 8 Lodge alley
Smith James & Breinig, provisions, 50 Tammany and 76 Callowhill
Smith James & Co., machine card manufs., 16 Commerce, factory c Marshall and Willow
Smith James E., cutlery, 175 S 2d
Smith James L., bricklayer, 13th and Carlton
Smith James L., corder, 4 Short ct
Smith James M., seaman, 32 Coates' alley
Smith Jas. M., grocer, 7 N Water, h 120 Spruce
Smith James O., driver, Sch. 4th ab George
Smith James P., min. painter, 72 S 11th
Smith James R., mer., 107 High, h 7 Montgomery sq
Smith James R., cordw., Gilbert bel 10th
SMITH JAMES S., Sec. and Treas. Phila. Contributionship, 96 S 4th
SMITH JAMES S., clock maker, 82 N 3d, h 36 Marshall
Smith James S., cash. South. Bank, h 272 N 2d
Smith James W., book bind., George bel Apple
Smith Jane, Perry ab Franklin (K)
Smith Jane, sempstress, 1 Clark
Smith Jane, Broad bel Vine
Smith Jane, 122 Prime
Smith Jeremiah, coach painter and carriage repository, 27 and 42 Dock, h 38 Walnut
Smith Jeremiah, coachman, 4 Osborn's ct
Smith Jeremiah H., plumber, 5 Assembly Buildings, h Fitzwater ab Irish Tract Lane
Smith Jesse E., com. mer., 34 High
Smith Jesse H., flour and feed, G T road ab Camac
Smith Job, shop, 9th bel Coates
Smith Joel B., mer., 32 Commerce, h 451 N 6th
SMITH JOHN, Prot. ct. Com. Pleas, h Franklin ab Palmer (K)
Smith John, lab., Callowhill E Sch. 2d
Smith John, grocer, Apple and Culvert
Smith John, lab., Stoy's ct (K)
Smith John, hosier, 2d bel Franklin (K)
Smith John, copper smith, 4th bel George
Smith John, tavern, Sch. 8th and High
Smith John, distiller, High n Sch. 4th, h Filbert n Sch. 5th
Smith John, lab., 9 Gray's alley
Smith John, cooper, 9th bel Poplar
Smith John, fisherman, Wood bel Franklin (K)
Smith John, harness maker, G T road ab 6th
Smith John, carp., Duke n Vienna (K)
Smith John, weaver, Perry's ct
Smith John, vict., Sassafras n Sch. 7th
Smith John, sea capt., Washington bel Front
Smith John, distiller, Wood n Sch.
Smith John, carp., Plynlimmon place
Smith John, manuf. lenses, 14 Bread
Smith John, lab., Henk's ct
Smith John, shoemr., Perry bel Master (K)
Smith John, 3d bel Thompson
Smith John, carver, Walnut n Sch. 3d
Smith John, cordw., Parrish bel Broad
Smith John, dealer, 342 N Front
Smith John, carter, O Y road bel Coates
Smith John, hosier, Perry ab Franklin

Smith John, boatman, Sch 2d n Wood
Smith John, Adams and Jackson
Smith John, F road ab Franklin (K)
Smith John, cabman, George n Sch 7th
Smith John, chandler, 248 S 4th
Smith John, lab., 4 Poplar pl
Smith John, susp. weav., Palmer bel Duke (K)
Smith John A., tailor, Parrish bel 12th
Smith John A., upholsterer, 64 S 4th
Smith John A., carver, Ellis ab Washington (8 G)
Smith John B., gent., Christian bel 8th
Smith John C., tobacconist, James ab 10th
Smith John C., 15 Vernon
Smith John C., jeweller, Taylor's al, h 30 Scheetz st
Smith John C., ladies' shoemr., 21 Clair
Smith John C., mer., 81 N 3d
Smith John C., Chatham ab Buttonwood
Smith John F., cupper & leecher, 75 N 4th
Smith John F., 8th bel Wallace
Smith John F., stone cut., Buttonwood bel 11th
Smith John F., type founder, 6 George
Smith John G., blacksm., Cherry bel Duke (K)
Smith John G., tobacconist, 36 Dillwyn
Smith John G., currier, Willow al
Smith John H., chairmr., 38 Mead
Smith John H., tailor, Ontario bel Poplar
Smith John J., morocco dr., Front bel Master
Smith John J., dyer, 44 N 7th
Smith John Jay, Librarian Phila. Library, h 7 Franklin row (9th st)
Smith John K., druggist, 296 N 2d, h 180 N 4th
Smith John K. & Co., druggists, 296 N 2d
Smith John L., printer, 4th and Appletree al, h 32 N 5th
Smith John L., tobacconist, rear 26 N 6th
Smith John L., engineer, 175 G T road (K)
Smith John L., upholsterer, 70 S 12th
Smith John M., fisherman, Allen bel Palmer (K)
Smith John M., shoemr., 266 S 4th
Smith John M., grocer, Franklin ab 4th (K)
Smith John M., carp., Brown ab 8th
Smith John P., cabinetmr., rear 99 O Y road
Smith John S., painter, R road bel Melon
Smith John T., tanner, St John ab Beaver, h 497 N 4th
Smith John T., carp., (W P)
Smith John W., shoemr., 213 Queen
Smith John W., plasterer, Sch 8th n Cherry
Smith John W., sheet iron worker, Fraley's ct (K)
Smith John W., hatter, 58 Cedar, h 21 German
Smith Johnson, bleacher, S W 13th and Filbert
Smith Jonathan, tailor, N W 6th and Chestnut, h 40 Marshall
Smith Jonathan A., shoemr., 268 S 2d
Smith Jonathan C., pianos, 215 Chestnut
Smith Jonathan H., mer., 147 High
Smith Jos., moulder, Cadwalader ab Franklin
Smith Joseph, paint manuf., Parrish bel Broad
Smith Jos., barber, Brown's ct
Smith Jos., carp., rear 37 Apple
Smith Joseph H. jr., 244 N Front

Smith Joseph, shoemaker, Pine ab Willow, h Christian ab 7th
Smith Joseph, ship carp., Allen ab Shackamaxon
Smith Joseph, carp., 230 F road n Master
Smith Joseph, gent., Apple ab George
Smith Joseph, barber, 15 Arcade
Smith Joseph, 151 S 2d
Smith Joseph B., broker, 75 Dock, h Broad ab Pine
Smith Jos. B., barber, R road bel Broad
Smith Joseph C., hatter, 48 Noble, h Green ab Front
Smith Joseph E., jeweller, 26 N 13th
Smith Joseph H., waterman, 7 Burd (S)
Smith Joseph H., tailor, Culvert ab 4th
Smith Joseph H., acct., 1 Schriver's ct
Smith Joseph L., shoemr., 329 S 2d
Smith Joseph M., carp., 9 Mead
Smith Joseph P., 435 Mulberry
Smith Josiah, carp., G T road ab Camac (K)
Smith Julia, shop, 90 Poplar
Smith Julia, Lisle st bel Shippen
Smith J. B., file manuf., 71 New
Smith J. Gates, clerk, 465 S Front
Smith J. Greendell, florist, O Y road and 5th
Smith Mrs. J. George, 284 N 5th
Smith J. Milderberger, 235 S 9th
Smith J. R. C., gent., Waluut bet Sch. 6th and 7th
Smith J. Somers, atty. and coun., 65 h 96 S 4th
Smith J. W., dentist, 37 George
SMITH KENDERTON, atty. and coun., 112 Walnut
Smith Lawrence, lab., 8 North
Smith Lawrence, suspender mr., Cherry below Duke (K)
Smith Leonard, Hooven's ct
Smith Leopold, weaver, Elk st (K)
Smith Lewis, 42 St John
Smith Lloyd P., publisher, 19 St James
Smith Louis, saddler, 40 Coates' al
Smith Lucy, 6 Wagner's al
Smith Lucy Ann, rear 101 Dillwyn
Smith Margaret Jane, trimmings, 176 N 13th
Smith Marg., tailoress, Brown's ct
Smith Maria, 2 Crown
Smith Maria, gentw., Spruce ab Sch 7th
Smith Maria, gentw., Myrtle
Smith Marshall, lab., Marshall ab Poplar
Smith Martha, tailoress, 9 Rose al (N L)
Smith Martha, corset mr., 169 Mulberry
Smith Martha, S E 11th and Pine
Smith Martha, 73 Cherry
Smith Mary, b. h., 184 Chestnut
Smith Mary, Wood ab Franklin (K)
Smith Mary, Franklin ab Palmer (K)
Smith Mary, bel Washington ab 8th
Smith Mary, tailoress, 65 E Catharine
Smith Mary, 64 Franklin
Smith Mary, rear Carpenter bel 8th
Smith Mary, 3 Wilson
Smith Mary, Ann (F V)
Smith Mary Ann, 8th bel Carpenter
Smith Mary A., dry goods, 261 N 7th
SMITH R. RUNDLE, atty. and coun., 65 S 4th

Smith Mary R., 473 N 5th
Smith Matilda W., 413 Spruce
Smith Matthias, vict., 7th ab Poplar
Smith Michael, carter, Mifflin ab Perry
Smith Milton, mer., h Filbert bel Sch 7th
SMITH, MURPHY & CO., mers., 97 High
Smith Mrs., wid. of Benjamin P., h 257 Pine
Smith Nathan, plasterer, 145 N 13th
Smith Nathan S., cordw., 466 N 4th
Smith Newberry, gent., 227 Vine
Smith Newberry A., mer., 113 High, h 12 Girard
Smith Nicholas, shipwr., Franklin bel Palmer
Smith Noah, Sch 8th n Vine
Smith Owen, cordw., 144 Locust
Smith Owen, lab., rear Palmer ab Beach (K)
Smith Owen, miller, 5 Franklin row
Smith Patrick, mason, Philip ab Master (K)
SMITH PATRICK, tavern, N E Front and Mulberry
Smith Patrick, coachman, 9 Pleasant av
Smith Patrick, hatter, 9 Spafford st
Smith Patrick, lab., William ab Otter (K)
Smith Pemberton, mer., 298 High, h 23 S 10th
Smith & Peters, printers, 50 N 6th
Smith Phebe, widow, 104 N 7th
Smith Philip, watch case mr., 5 Drinker's al
Smith P. Jenks, mer., 67 High, h 117½ S 3d
Smith Rachel, tavern, Nixon & Callowhill
Smith Rachel L., 104 N 2d
Smith Ralph, acct., 134 Dillwyn
Smith Rebecca, Franklin and Union
Smith Rebecca, tailoress, 37 Queen
Smith Reuben, tobacconist, 149 Green
Smith Richard A., carp., 7 Miller's ct
Smith Richard H., acct., 92 S Front
Smith Richard M., printer, High E Sch 5th
Smith Richard S., Prest. Union Mutual Ins. Co., 6 Exchange, h 22 Clinton
Smith Robert, porter, Gilles' al
Smith Robert, lab., Locust n Beech
Smith Robert, carver, S E 8th and Coates
Smith Robert, cordw., Queen ab 2d
Smith Robert, brewer, c 5th and Minor, h 191 N 7th
Smith Robert, editor of the Friend, 50 N 4th, h 258 Cherry
Smith Robt., drayman, Hamilton's ct
Smith Robt., lab., 6 Humphrey's ct
Smith Robt., Sch 8th bel High
Smith Robert A., boxmr., 7th and High, h 22 Morgan
Smith Robert C., printer, Christian ab 3d
Smith Robert H., city clerk, h 3 S Sch 7th
Smith Robert J., printer, 3 Wall
Smith Robert L., clerk, 426 N 5th
Smith Robert P., printer, 144 Chestnut
Smith Robert W., vict., 18 P road
Smith Roderick D., jeweller, 21 Franklin pl, h 133 Wood
Smith Rowen, cabmr., Depot bel 9th
Smith Rudolph, cooper, Franklin ab 3d (K)
Smith Rufus, mer., 12 Commerce, h 292 N 7th
Smith R. Mrs., ladies' shoes, 21 N 6th
Smith R. P., milliner, 142 Cedar

Smith R., Sheaff, land agent, 15 N 13th
Smith Samuel, cordwainer, 2 Nicholson
Smith Samuel, tobacconist, 104 P road
Smith Samuel, drayman, 4th ab Carpenter
Smith Samuel, drayman, Jones W Sch 5th
Smith Samuel, sexton, Ohio
Smith Samuel, plast., Pleasant ab 13th
Smith Samuel, distiller, Sch 6th n Summer
Smith Samuel B., bookseller, 4th and Mulberry, h Sch 4th ab Vine
Smith Saml. E., Front ab Franklin
Smith Samuel F., Pres. Phila. Bank, h Walnut ab Broad
Smith Samuel F., turner, Sch 6th ab Vine
Smith Samuel S., engineer, 148 S 5th
Smith Sarah, Atherton
Smith Sarah, 42 S 13th
Smith Sarah, wid of Wm., Burd bel Catharine
Smith Sarah, Plum st
Smith Sarah Ann, b. h., 94 Walnut
Smith Sarah G., 169 Spruce
SMITH & SECKEL, brewers, c 5th and Minor
Smith Seth, 11th and Green
SMITH SIDNEY V., atty. and coun., Walnut ab 6th
Smith Silas, planemr., 114 New Market
Smith Solomon, mer., 97 High, h 115 S 3d
Smith Sommers, ship joiner, 11 Clark st
Smith Steph., lumber mer., Lombard ab 9th
SMITH & SWIFT, tailors, N W 6th and Chestnut
Smith S. Decatur, mer., 35½ S Front, h 42 Lombard
Smith Teresa, 45 Pegg
Smith Terence, carter, 4 Fitzwater
Smith Thomas, weav., Lombard, E of Sch 6th
Smith Thomas, gent., 13 N 12th
Smith Thomas, weav., Fulton ab 12th
Smith Thomas, shoemr., 13th and Pearl
Smith Thomas, shoemr., 1 Magnolia
Smith Thomas, dyer, Adams bel 13th
Smith Thos. & Ogden, rolling mill, Landing st ab Coates, Fairmount
Smith Thomas B., mer., 159 High, h Richmond
SMITH THOMAS D., alderman, 5th and Library, h 139 Walnut
Smith Thomas E., manuf., Jackson and Adams
Smith Thomas L., carpet store, 19 S 2d
Smith Thomas M., confect., 61 Cedar
Smith Thomas M., iron mer., 62 N Front, h 357 Mulberry
SMITH THOMAS S., atty. & coun. Walnut ab 6th, h 72 S 11th
Smith Thomas W., cordw., 2 Orchard
Smith Townsend, brickmr., 7th bel Poplar
SMITH T. B., pickles, 152 and h 328 S Front
Smith Valentine, lab., Beech ab Spruce
Smith Wade T., mer., 79 S 3d, h Summer near Sch 6th
Smith Waterman, jr., agent, Callowhill n Sch Front
SMITH & WAY, mers., 67 High
Smith Wm., machinist, 424 Coates
Smith Wm., carp., Filbert n Sch 4th
Smith Wm., weaver, Amber ab Phœnix

Smith Wm., ladies' shoemr., 15 Little Water
Smith Wm., machinist, Jacoby & Cherry, h 13 Jacoby
Smith Wm., porter, 14 Franklin pl
SMITH WM., atty & coun., 81 Walnut
Smith Wm., tailor, 469 N 3d
Smith Wm., distiller, N E 12th & Lombard
Smith Wm., lab., 8 Bell's ct
Smith Wm., broker, 37 N 5th
Smith Wm., grocer, 23 Elizabeth
Smith Wm., furniture car, Loud ab 9th
Smith Wm., ship carp., 28 Dyott's ct (K)
Smith Wm., morocco dress., 10 Margaretta
Smith Wm., bricklayer, Lombard E Sch 7th
Smith Wm., Coates ab 13th
Smith Wm., bricklayer, 16 Flower
Smith Wm., stonecutter, Sycamore ab Locust
Smith Wm., carter, rear Pleasant bel 13th
Smith Wm., drayman, Drinker's ct
Smith Wm., Dr., 97 Bedford
Smith Wm., engineer, Alton ct
Smith Wm., cedar cooper, 224 Coates
Smith Wm., manuf., Pine ab 12th
Smith Wm., wheelwt., 184 Queen
Smith Wm., trader, 10 Benton
Smith Wm. B., sea capt., Keefe ab Lancaster
Smith Wm. B., founder, 617 N 2d (K)
Smith Wm. C., morocco dresser, New Market ab Noble
Smith Wm. C., fisherman, Queen & Bishop (K)
Smith Wm. Earle, window shades, 92 Walnut
Smith Wm. E., carp., 9th ab Coates
Smith Wm. F., dry goods, 421 N 2d
Smith Wm. G., cooper, Willow bel Garden
Smith Wm. G., cedar cooper, 224 Coates
Smith Wm. G., atty and coun., 28 and h 186 S 5th
Smith Wm. H., sugar refiner, 71 Vine
Smith Wm. H., plasterer, 13th bel Melon
Smith Wm. H., veterinary surgeon, Miller's al
Smith Wm. H. & Brother, sugar refin., 71 Vine
Smith Wm. J., machinist, Beach bel Palmer, h Queen ab Warren
Smith Wm. J., weaver, Lombard ab Sch 2d
Smith Wm. K., shoemr., Cedar ab 9th
Smith Wm. M., painter, G T road op 5th
Smith Wm. P., 240 S 10th
Smith Wm. R., clerk, 13th bel Green
Smith Wm. S., mer., 80 S whfs., h 131 Pine
Smith Wm. S., tailor, 6 China
Smith Wm. S. & Co., com. mers., 80 S wharves, & 161 S Water
Smith Wm. W., mer., 76 High, h 413 Spruce
Smith W. E., leather & findings, 136 N 3d
Smith W. C. & S., leather dealers, N W 2d &

Smitson John, stonecut., Vienna & Franklin (K
Smitten R. T., watchmr., Thompson ab 13th
Smitten Workman, merchant, 163 Queen
Smoker John, silversm., Thompson ab Broad
Smothers Dicina, washer, 174 N 8th
Smucker Gotlieb, lab., rear 527 N 4th
Smullen Hugh, lab., 3 Baxter's ct
Smullen Lewis, lab., Wood ab Sch 7th
Smullen Wm., clerk, 19 Noble
Smulling John, blacksmith, Shackamaxon above Queen
Smulling Mary, shoes, 39 Mary
Smulling Wm., clerk, 122 New Market
Smylie John, saddler, 388 High, h Washington n 10th
Smyth James, vict., 24 Charlotte
Smyth John, printer, Shack n Bedford (K)
Smyth Lindley, sugar refiner, 27 Church al, h 299 Spruce
Smyth Thos., tavern, 107 G T road
Snagg Margaret, Plei's ct (K)
Snare Jacob, framemr., 474 N 4th, h 8th below Poplar
Snare Stephen, lab., Chester ct
Snavoinger L., tailor, 409 N Front
Snearinger Susanna, gentw., 448 N 3d
Sneck Charles, vict., Sch 4th ab Vineyard
Sneck Geo. victual. Vineyard n Sch 4th (F V)
Sneck Thos., vict., Sch 4th n Vineyard
Sneethen John, cordw., 239 Vine
Snell Benj., sea captain, 367 S 3d
Snell Caroline, tailoress, rear 535 Vine
Snell George, lab., Lombard E Sch 4th
Snell Lewis, tavern, N W Crown & Callowhill
Snell Sarah, 16 Morgan
Snellbaker Edward, boots and shoes, 131 Mulberry
Snellbaker P. A., shoemr., 118 New
Snellbaker Vincent, chair painter, 2 Charles pl
Sneller Jacob, blindmr., 518 N 2d (K)
Snellgrove George, baker, 6th bel Carpenter
Sneyd Elizabeth, 111 Buttonwood
Snider George, clerk, 142 N 8th
Snider George, bookbinder, 210 Cherry
SNIDER JACOB, jr., wine mer., 76 Walnut, h Sch 8th bel Pine
SNIDER JACOB, alderman, 70 N 8th
Snider Samuel, carp., 73 Penn
Snider Wm. M., machinist, Morris ab Lombard
Snode John, carp., 4th bel Franklin (K)
Snodgrass Andrew, clerk, Sch 8th n Sassafras
Snodgrass Joseph, pilot, 452 S Front
Snodgrass Joseph, lab., Spruce & Ashton
Snodgrass M., milliner, 5th & Green
Snodgrass Robert, drayman, Sch 2d

Snowden John, carter, Essex
Snowden Joseph, clerk, 408 S 3d
Snowden Joseph S, lumber mer., Snowden's whf., h 4th & Washington
Snowden Thomas, surg. instr. maker, 15 N 5th, h 430 Sassafras
Snowden Wm., painter and glazier, 39 Filbert
Snowdon Beulah, 27 New
Snowdon Edward, china ware, 34 N 3d
Snowdon Joseph, Friends' book store, 84 Mulberry ab 3d, h 250 N 5th
Snyder Abraham H., grocer, G T road ab 6th
Snyder Ann, 140 Spruce
Snyder Anthony F., 45 German
Snyder Barbara, 352 S Front
Snyder & Brothers, jewellers, 140 S 2d
Snyder Catharine, 55 S 13th
Snyder Catharine, Crown bel Duke (K)
Snyder Charles, carp., 147 Coates
Snyder Charles, ship carp., Union ab West
Snyder Charles H., agent, 4 Butz's ct
Snyder Chas. T., grocer, S W 13th & Olive
Snyder Christian, grocer, 215 N 3d
Snyder Daniel, carter, 4 Callowhill
Snyder David, turner, 2d ab Greenwich
Snyder Edwd., tailor, 15 Wood
Snyder Edward, cabinetmr., Logan bel Wallace
Snyder Edward F., cutler, 22 S 7th, h 238 Catharine
Snyder Elias, carp., Apple bel George
Snyder Elizabeth, Buttonwood bel 12th
Snyder Francis, machinist, Charlotte ab Poplar, h Porter's ct
Snyder Francis, turner, 3 Porter's ct
Snyder Frederick, oyster house, R road below Pleasant
Snyder Frederick, b h, 25 Branch
Snyder Frederick, baker, 518 High
Snyder Garrett, carp., Melon ab 13th
Snyder Geo., carp., George ab 3d (N L)
Snyder Geo., painter, Clinton ab Brown
Snyder Geo., brickmr., Gray's Ferry road bel South, h 12th bel Spruce
Snyder Geo., combmr., Front ab Oxford (K)
Snyder Geo., fruiterer, 4 Cherry
Snyder Geo., painter, Carlton ab 12th
Snyder Geo., manuf., 198 Christian
SNYDER GEO. A., botanic physician, 5th and Powell
Snyder Geo. C., teller Southwark Bank, h 354 S 3d
Snyder Geo. P., hatter, 7 St James
Snyder Henry, painter, S E Front and Almond, h Washington ab 3d
Snyder Henry, blockmr., William opp Benton
Snyder Henry, feed store, Garden and Noble
Snyder Henry, carp., Melon n R road
Snyder Henry, blacksm., Jackson (8 G)
Snyder Henry C., 122 F road (K)
Snyder Henry C., dep. supt. M Prison, h 3d ab Federal
Snyder Horatio, lab., School (N L)
Snyder Jacob, cordw., Allen ab Shackamaxon
Snyder Jacob H., 346 Vine
Snyder Jacob W., tailor, 146 N 8th

Snyder Jesse H., cordw., 62 N 3d, h 266 Coates
Snyder John, carman, rear 448 N 4th
Snyder John, carman, St John & George (K)
Snyder John, jr., grocer, 182 Callowhill, h 410 N 9th
Snyder John, carp., Pleasant bel 12th
Snyder John, engineer, Carlton E Sch 7th
Snyder John, combmr., Brown ab 10th
Snyder John, jr. & Carlisle, 182 Callowhill
Snyder John G., hatter, 5 Laurel (C)
Snyder John H., com. mer., 4 Commerce, h 372 N 5th
Snyder John M., polisher, Wistar ab 11th
Snyder Joseph, fancy chair and looking glass manuf., 105 Walnut
Snyder Joseph, tailor, Palmer ab Franklin (K)
Snyder Joseph A., builder, Sassafras ab Sch 8th
Snyder Joseph F., clerk, 220 S 4th
Snyder Josiah, tinsmith, 2 Raspberry
Snyder J. M., oak cooper, 3 Flower
Snyder Margaret, rear 340 Coates
Snyder Mark, carp., Carlton bel Sch 2d
Snyder Mary, b. h., 81 N 7th
Snyder Mary E., grocer, N E 9th & Fitzwater
Snyder & Master, cabtmr., 87 W Callowhill
Snyder Michael, tavern, 98 N 4th
Snyder & Ovenshine, omnibus keepers, Vine & Broad
Snyder Peter, mason, Wood bel Sch 6th
Snyder Peter, cabtmr., Union ct
Snyner Peter, visiter of poor, 29 N Sch 6th
Snyder Peter, segarmr., Ross n Queen (K)
Snyder Peter, cooper, 5 Sansom al
Snyder Peter L., clerk, 3 Ellen (N L)
SNYDER PHILIP F., conveyancer, 115 S 6th, h 171 Christian
Snyder Simon, mer., 96½ High, h 26 Merchant
Snyder Simon, bookbinder, 1 Frank's ct
Snyder Thos., cabtmr., Clair bel Carpenter(S)
Snyder Thos., tailor, 308 N 2d, h 59 Apple
Snyder Thos. H., painter, 4 Lyndall's al
Snyder Uriah C., machinist, 58 Green
Snyder White M., coal office, S E 10th and Sergeant, h Wood ab Sch 8th
Snyder Wm., driver, 3 Dilk's ct
Snyder Wm., wheelwrt., Carpenter ab 5th
Snyder Wm. A., shipsm., Shackamaxon ab Bedford
Snyder Wm. D., clerk, 29 Sansom, h 169½ Christian
Snyder Wm. G., ship carp., Hanover ab Queen (K)
Snyder Wm. P., hinge and boltmr., Swanson ab Christian, h Washington ab Swanson
Sobbe Wouter, painter, 128 Plum
Soby David, tobacconist, 64 N 6th
Soby Jas. O., tobacconist, 445 N 6th
Soby Wm., tobacconist, 227 N 3d
Sockum Stephen, carter, Marriott la bel P road
Soffee John, sen., High n Sch 8th
Soffee John, jr., High n Sch 8th
Soffee Wm., shoe store, High ab Broad
Soistman C., turner, 68 N 4th
SOLIS & BROTHERS, furriers, 86 Mulberry
Solis Daniel, vict., 7th ab Poplar

Solis D. H., furrier, 86 Mulberry
Solis Solomon, furrier, 86 Mulberry
Solley Wm., painter, Sp Garden bel 9th, h 9 Linden
Solliday Daniel H., watchmr., 186 Callowhill
Solliday Elizabeth, 167 Coates
Solly John, shoemr., Reiff's ct (K)
Solly Obadiah, cordw., Reiff's ct (K)
Solly Robt., cordw., Brown bel Vienna (K)
Solms S. J., mer., 22 Penn, (C) bel Pine, h 237 S Front
Solms John B., mer., 241 S 9th
Solms Joseph, 218 S Front
Solomon Absalom, cordw., Haydock bel Front
Solomon & Bro., fancy goods, 34 Bank
Solomon G. F., mer., 34 Bank
Solomon John, painter, High n Ashton
Solomon J. J., barber, F road ab Maiden (K)
Solomon Saml. M., acct., 2 Carrolton sq
Solomon T., gunsmith, Washington (W P)
Solts Alex., tavern, St John and Poplar
Solts Catharine, distiller, S W 2d and Prime
Soly Wm. jr., tobac., Elizabeth ab Franklin
Somers Chalkley, mer., N E 2d and High, h 77 Filbert
Somers Elizabeth, trimmings, S W Noble and Marshall
Somers Jacob, 6 New Market
Somers Lewis S., M. D., 256 N Front
Somers M. L., gentw., 194 N 5th
Somers Rachel, 119 N 7th
Somers & Snodgrass, cloths, &c., N E 2d & High
Somers Wm. C., carp., 10 Mary (S)
Somerville John, baker, Broad ab Coates
Sommerman G. E., baker, Callowhill ab Sch 8th
Sommers Alexander, grocer, 134 N 13th
Sommers Jacob, carp., Parrish ab 7th
Sommers John, butcher, 36 Queen
Sommers John F., gold heater, 36 Dock
Sommersett Jacob, coffinmr., 152 S 5th
Songo Isaiah, lab., 11 Griswold al
Songster Robt., weaver, 36 Cedar
Songster Thos., lab., 20 Harmstead
Sontag Charles, manuf., 231 High

Souder Henry, shoemr., N Market & Young's al
Souder Jacob, blacksm., 337 N 3d
Souder Jacob, bricklayer, 10th n Brown
Souder Jacob W., tailor, 350 & 366 High
Souder John, confect., Logan bel Wallace
Souder John, lastmr., Sarah bel Bedford
Souder Joseph, seaman, rear 116 Brown
Souder Joseph W., mer., 11 High, h 149 N 2d
Souder & Middleton, boots and shoes, 11 High
Souder Nathaniel, cabinetmr., 95 & 97 N Front
Souder & Warren, cloths, 358 & 368 High
Souder Wm., carp., Wood ab Sch 8th
Souder Wm., patternmr., Marlboro' ab Queen
Souder Wm. M., planemr., h 28 O Y road
Souders Hannah, wid., G T road ab Franklin (K)
Souders John, vict., Franklin ab Marlboro'
Soulier Mary, gentw., 132 S 5th
Soumeillan James, baker, 334 N 2d
Sourin Edward J. Rev., St John's, 13th st
Sourwalt Wm., bookbinder, 109 Dillwyn
South Wm., jeweller, 147 S 3d
Southern Adam, crockeryware, 248 S 2d & 274 Chestnut
Southern James, tavern, 8th and Catharine
Southgate Robt., copper, tin & sheet iron worker, 55 Walnut, h 61 Pine
Southgate Robert & Son, copper and sheet iron works, 55 Walnut
Southwick Lucinda, Smith's ct
Southwick Sarah, carter, 2 Marion
Southworth Delas P., clerk, 60 N 4th
Southworth G. W., agent, 60 N 4th
SOUTTEN & BROUGHTON, com. mers., 38 N whfs.
Soutter Robert jr., com. mer., 38 N whfs., h 21 Girard
Sowden John T., packer, Wood bel Duke (K)
Sowden Wm., grocer, Franklin and Wood (K)
Sower J. R., mer., 36 N 3d
Sower Peter, lab., West ab Walnut
Sowerby Sarah, milliner, 73 N 6th
SOWERS & BOLDIN, hardware, 141 High
Sowers Catharine, huckster, Schleisman's al
Sowers Daniel, carp., Vine n Sch
Sowers David, carter, Franklin ab Willow

Spain George, cooper, Parrish ab 13th
Spaker Lawrence, lab., Vienna bel Duke
Shang Samuel, fishing tackle, &c., 94 N 3d, h 82 Dillwyn
Spang & Wallace, sporting store, 94 N 3d
Spangenberg Mary B., tailoress, Court al
Spangler Christian E., mer., 128 N 3d, h 149 O Y road
Spangler George, tailor, Wallace bel 9th
Spangler George, 250 S Front
Spangler H L., carp., 49 New Market, h 512 N 5th
Spanier M., dealer, La Fayette
Sparhawk John, merchant, 124 High, h 9th bel Lombard
Sparhawk Thos. P., mer., h 246 Spruce
Sparks Jacob F., shot manuf., 11 Queen
Sparks Julia, milliner, 341 N 2d
Sparks Peter, dry goods, 48 S 2d, h 7 North
Sparks P., wid. 8 Almond
Sparks Robert, painter, rear 264 S 5th
Sparks Samuel A., dry goods, N W 5th and Sassafras
Sparks Samuel M., ship carp., 1 John (S)
Sparks Sarah, shop, 10th and Washington
Sparks Thos, shot manuf., 35 Walnut, h 130 S 3d
Sparks T. jr., mer., 35 Walnut, h 237 Spruce
SPARKS T. & T. jr., shot manuf., 35 Walnut & John (S)
Speace Michael, stone cut., Bonsall and 10th
Speacht Wm., shoemr., George n Beach
Speak John F., saddler, Linden n Green
Speakman Abigail, rear 3 Paschal al
Speakman Geo., drayman, Stackhouse ct
Speakman John, successor to J. B. Wickersham, wire worker, 249 High, h 188 Pine
Spear Daniel, cooper, Carroll ab 13th
Spear George, lime, P road and 6th
Spear John, lab., Collins's ct
Spear John D., Chemist, 12½ and h 14 Filbert
Spear Samuel, weaver, Crown bel Duke (K)
Spear Thos., cordw., 480 Callowhill
Spear Thos. G., printer, 40 S 3d, h 544 High
Spear Wm. M., medicines, 383 Callowhill
Spear Wm. W. Rev., Chestnut n Sch 5th
Spearing Saml., carp. weaver, 322 Vine
Spearing Saml., coppersm. Federal ab 2d
Spearman Wm. D., com. mer., 100 S whfs
Specht C. F., brewer, 58 Shippen, h 66 Shippen
Specht Lawr'e., blacksm., Thompson ab Sch 8th
Speck A. C., tavern, Crown and Vine
Speck Charles T., tailor, Washington ab 3d
Speck Charles W., baker, Washington ab 3d
Speel Adam, cabmr., 27 O Y road
SPEEL & DONOHUE, bookbinders and stationers, 18 N 5th and 5th and Cherry
Speel Henry W., printer, 43 Almond
Speel Jos. A., bookbinder, N W 5th & Cherry, h 179 N 8th
Speer Andrew, grocer, 65 Fitzwater
Speer John, printer, back 130 Sassafras
Speight Charles S., salesman, 20 S Front, h 180 Queen
Speilberger Lewis, butcher, St John ab George (K)

Spelbrink Barnard, bootmr., 196 S 5th
Spelbrink Herman, sugar ref. 171 Queen
Spence Gabriel, lab., 8 Vaux's ct
Spence George, carter, Beach ab Shackamaxon
Spence James K., collector, 48 S 6th
Spence Robert, lab., Filbert E Sch 3d
Spence Robert, weaver, Poplar st
Spence Thos., lab., Cedar bel 12th
Spence Wm., Helmuth n Sch 6th
Spence Wm., watchman, Filbert E Sch 3d
Spenceley James, plasterer, Washington ab 13th
Spencer Ann, washer, rear 18 Acorn al
Spencer Asa, engrav., 95½ Walnut, h 15 S 10th
Spencer Charles, manuf., 14 N 8th
Spencer C. Mrs., b h, 95 S 3d
Spencer Edmund M., coachmr., 13th & Cherry, h 9 Perry
Spencer Elizabeth, dressmr., Ross' ct
Spencer George, lab., 9th ab Carpenter
Spencer George H., boot fitter, Church av
SPENCER HENRY W., 113 Pine
Spencer Howard, gent., 53 N Water, h S W 11th & Spruce
Spencer, Hufty & Danforth, bank note engravers, 95½ Walnut
Spencer James, jr., butcher, 2d bel Wharton
Spencer James, sen., drover, 113 M road
Spencer James H., M D, 668 N 2d (K)
Spencer Jas. S., grocer, S W 2d & Cedar
Spencer Jas. S., 53 N Water, h S W 11th and Spruce
SPENCER JAMES S., jr., iron store, 53 N Water, h S W 11th & Spruce
SPENCER JAMES S. & CO., grocers, S W 2d and Cedar
Spencer John, captain, 384 S 5th
Spencer John, cordw., rear P road
Spencer Joseph, 7th ab Coates
Spencer J. Austin, atty. & coun., 216 N 6th
Spencer Lydia, tailoress, 1 Concord ct
Spencer Oliver, jeweller, Sch 6th ab Filbert
Spencer Peter, shoemr., S E 6th & Mulberry
Spencer Robert, machinist, Otter bel G T road
Spencer Sophia, whitewasher, 24 Burd's ct
Spencer Thomas, machinist, rear G T road ab 2d (K)
Spencer Wm., brushmr., 6 Howard's pl
Spencer Wm. M., mer., 53 N Water, h S W 11th and Spruce
Spering Charles C., boots and shoes, 73 N 3d, h 4 Noble
Spering Chauncey, clerk, 4 Noble
Spering, Good & Co., dry goods, 138 High
Spering Joshua, mer., 125 High
Spering Joshua, mer. atty. & coun., 61 S 4th, h Sp Garden bel 12th
Spering Matthew, lab., rear Jackson ab Apple
Spering Nathan, trunkmr., 24 N 4th, h 21 Chatham
Spering Wm., mer., 138 High, h 8th n Coates
Sperry H. N., turner, 83 Sassafras
Sperry John J., clerk, Sch 8th n Sassafras
Sperry William, mer., 101 S Front, h 447 Chestnut
Sperry Wm., clockmr., 254 Wood

Spicer Geo. F. cabinetmr., Charlotte ab Culvert
Spicer Jacob, 354 Coates
Spicer Mary, gentw., 387 Vine
Spicer Wm. P., dentist, 65 S 11th
Spiece Henry, com. mer., 103 Dillwyn
Spiegel John R., combmr., School st
Spielberger David, vict., 613 N 2d
Spielberger John, vict., 537 N 3d
Spielberger Joseph, vict., 153 Poplar
Spieler Wm., photographist, 97 Chestnut, h Jay bel Coates
Spielman Jacob, shop, Sch 2d & Vine
Spies Christ., lab., Palmer n Duke (K)
Spies Wm., cordw., Duke ab Hanover (K)
Spiese & Maurer, flour & feed store, 261 N 3d
Spiggle Isaac, potter, Brown bel Vienna (K)
Spildinger Henry, reedmr., 43 New Market
Spilman Charles, dentist, 554 N 2d
Spilman Henry C., barber, 554 N 2d
Spink Wm., dry goods, Beach bel Maiden (K)
Spinkle Charlotte, Queen ab Bishop (K)
Spinney Joseph, seaman, 100 Carpenter
Spire Willard, cordw., Apple ab Poplar
Spiskey Anthony, carman, 59 Sassafras
Spittall J., engraver, 27 Prune
Spittall Wm., grocer, Beck pl
Splane Richard, lab., 203 N Front
Spoerer Theodore, painter, rear 352 N Front
Spofford Wm. E., Locust ab Broad
Spohn Elizabeth, 212 Sassafras
Spooner David C., manuf., 116 Chestnut, h 5th bel Franklin
Spooner Edwin, mer., 242 N 3d, h 299 N 6th
Spooner John H., variety store, 129 High, h 278 N 6th
Spooner Wm., mer., 242 N 3d, h O Y road bel Green
Spooner Wm. & Son, mers., 242 N 3d
Sprague Edward, U S Mint, h 15 Madison
Sprague J. H., druggist, 33 N 4th, h 434 Sassafras
Sprague Susan, milliner, 132 N 11th
Spratt John W., trunkmr., 28 Charlotte
Sprigs Margaret, rear 6 Rose al
Sprikleboch Cath., Hanover below Franklin (K)
Spring Charles, machinist, Marlboro' ab Beach
Spring Charles E., fur'r., Garden n Buttonwood
Spring Henry, baker, Cedar ab 11th
Springer Alfred, Green bel 13th
Springer And., 7th bel Paul
Springer B. H., coal mer., 48 Walnut bel Dock, h 17 Sansom
Springer Emanuel, Noble ab 8th
Springer E., mer., 10 Bank, h Noble ab 8th
Springer Geo. H., miller, 13th ab Willow
Springer H. M., secy. Wash. Mut. Insur. Co., 48 Walnut, h Green ab 11th
Springer Israel R., chairmr., Berks' ct
Springer Jacob, chairmr., Elizabeth ab Poplar

Springer Lewis R., engineer, 8 State
Springer Maria, milliner, 331 N 2d
Springer Rachel, 128 Walnut
Springer W. F., carp., 194 Queen
Springfield Morris, shoemr., 8 Gabell's ct
Springs Fred., coachman, Pryor's ct
Springs W. L., mer., 167 High
Springsteen Benjamin R., mer., Ogden ab 10th
SPRINGSTEEN & Co., brooms & wooden ware, 122 N 3d, h Ogden n 10th
Sproat Maria, 62 N Juniper
Sprogell Marshall, atty. and coun., 40 S 6th, h 188 S 9th
Sprole Wm., cooper, Wheat ab Keefe
Sproul James, lab., Shippen ab 13th
Sproul Joseph, tailor, Sheaff's al
Sproul Mary Ann, milliner, Sch 7th bel Pine
Sproul Wm. A., gent., Shippen ab 13th
Sproull George, carp., 7th & Christian
Sproulls M., gentw., 48 Lombard
Sprowl David, bootmr., 7 E Almond
Sprowl Wm., cordw., Filbert E Sch 3d
Sprowl Wm., weaver, rear G T road ab 5th
Sprowls Israel, bricklayer, Wood bel 12th
Spry Joshua G., mer., 84 High, h 11 Palmyra row
Squafold Wm., spinner, Montgomery bel Front
Squibb Edward R., M D, 294 Walnut
Squibb Robert, tanner, St John bel Beaver, h Edward bel 2d (K)
Squire Francis, 7 Montgomery
Stabler Henry, blacksm., 5th ab Jefferson (K)
STACKHOUSE AMOS, stovemr., 389 High, h 11th n Division
Stackhouse A., potter, 3 Melon pl
Stackhouse Chas., painter, 25 N 5th, h 3 Flower ct
Stackhouse Charles C. P., crockery, Sp Garden bel Franklin
Stackhouse Chas. P., grocer, 227 Christian
Stackhouse David, cordw., rear 250 St John
Stackhouse James, clerk, 5th ab Buttonwood
Stackhouse John P., mer., 20 S Front, h 137 Dillwyn
STACKHOUSE POWELL, stove manuf., 167 N Front, h Plynlimmon pl
Stackhouse Robert, clerk, 398 Coates
Stackhouse Saml. P., collector, 177 N 2d
Stackhouse Wm., carp., Crown ab Bedford (K)
Stadler Christian, beer maker, 312 N Front
Stafford John, trimmings, 178 S 5th
Stafford John S., constable, 35 R road
Stafford Margt., Crown ab Queen
Stafford Thos., cordw., Otter ab Dunton (K)
Stafford Wm., waiter, 243 S 7th
Stafford Wm., lab., Sch 3d bel Chestnut
Stagers Charles, tailor, 8th & Fitzwater
Stagers Cornelius, keeper N prison, S W 8th & Fitzwater

Stahl Jacob, baker, 61 Franklin
Stahler Daniel, carp., Poplar ab 2d
Staiblin Geo. J., blacksm., Olive ab 13th
Stainrook David, jr., 5th ab Buttonwood
Stainrook John, painter, Centre ab Brown
Stainrook John, painter, rear Willow bel 8th
Stainrook Thos., blacksm., Duke bel Marlboro' (K)
Stainrook Wm., bricklayer, 4 Wagner's ct
STAIT W., Eagle city post, at Adams' exp. off. 80 Chestnut
Stalder John B., carp., 19 Quince
Staley Andrew, mer., N E 5th & Commerce
Stalhoeber Christine, rear Apple bel Franklin
Stall Daniel, tailor, Apple ab Culvert
Stambach George G., hatter, 400 N 2d
Stamford John, steel manuf., 5 Mintzer's ct
Stanbrough Ann, b h, 223 S 5th
Stancliff John, keeper of E. State Peniten. Callowhill ab Sch 5th
Stancliff Wm., painter, Decatur bel Corn
Standbridge Geo. L., music, 7 Benezet
Standbridge John C., gent., 7 Benezet
Standbridge J. C. B., prof. of music, 101 Filbert
Standring John, wool sorter, 2d & Montgomery (K)
Standring Mary Ann, Locust n Sch 3d
Stanert Francis C., carp., 9th ab Coates
Stanford & Brainard, clothing, N W 2nd and Spruce
Stanford Hannah, shop, 30 Dyott's ct
Stanford Stephen V., N W 2d & Spruce, h 8 Little Pine
Stanford Wm., carp., 4th & Federal
Stanley James F., acct., 8 S 12th
Stanley Job S., carp., Sch 5th & Carlton
Stanley Norris, gent., 9 Pine
Stanley Wm., drover, 294 St John
Stanmire George, brickmr., 2d ab Montgomery (K)
Stanmire George, brickmr., Beaver bel 4th
Stanmire Jacob, brickmr., 8th ab Master
Stanmire Thos., brickmr., 6th bel G T road
Stannert Hannah, dressmr., bel Parrish
Stansberry Elias, mor. dresser, 4 Union ct
Stansbury Wm., carter, 1 Tarr al
Stanton Jacob C., cordw., Smith's ct, Pearl ab 12th
Stanton John, druggist, N W Sch 2d and Chestnut
Stanton Lewis, ship carp., Bond's ct
Stanton Sophia, 1 Warren's ct
Stanton Thos., seaman, 76 Penn st
Stapleton John, tavern, 28 Penn sq
Stapleton Margaret, 27 Garden
Stapleton Wm., carp., 27 Garden
Stappen H. T., shoes, 167 N 3d
Stark Cath., milliner, 59 Pine
Stark James, lab., 13th n Cedar
Stark James, tailor, 42 S 4th
Stark Peter, cedar cooper, 330 S 5th
Starkey Abel, hatter, 16 New
Starkey Charles, baker, Miller's al
Starkey Jas., mariner, 450 S Front

Starkey Nathan, cabinet and portable desk mr., 66 S 4th
Starn Beulah, Shackamaxon and F road (K)
Starne Henry, carp., Jackson (S G)
Starne Joseph, combmr., rear 8 New Market
Starr Edward, bootmr., 3 Leiper
Starr Edwin, type founder, 97 Chestnut, h 6th bel Wall
Starr E. & Son, typefounders, 97 Chestnut
Starr Henry, cordw., 24 Clare
Starr Isaac, Spruce ab Broad
Starr James, shoemr., Sch 8th n Willow
Starr Jeremiah, grocer, High W Sch 7th, h Sch 6th and High
Starr John, broker, 24 Arcade, h 250 N 7th
Starr Nathan R., tailor, Filbert E of Sch 7th
Starr Samuel, acct., 12th & Callowhill
Starr Thomas W., type founder, 97 Chestnut, h 8 N 9th
Starrett Rebecca, huckster, Steward ab Christian
Staten Hannah, rear Front bel Phœnix
States Daniel, cordw., Amber ab Phoenix (K)
States Owen, brickmr., rear 9 Lisle st
Staton Caroline, Bledisloe pl
Statzell P. M., watchmr., 172 N 2d
Stauderman Henry, brewer, Wood ab 10th
Stauffer Jacob, merchant, Broad ab Mulberry Cherry ab 13th
Stauffer Jacob, cordw., Clinton ab Brown
Stauffer Jesse, grocer, 95 Green
Stauffer John, carp., P road bel Green
Stauffer J. K., tailor, R road ab Green
Staunton Richard, hat presser, 108 N 8th
Stavely & M'Calla, publishers Episcopal Recorder, 12 Pear
Stavely Wm., publisher, 12 Pear
Stead G. W., canes & cigars, 8 Nectarine above 9th
Stead James, weaver, Hancock ab Norris (K)
Steadman Reuben, machinist, 3 Parker av
Stearly C., combmr., 31 Apple
Stearly Jacob, mer., 17 Commerce, h 136 Coates
Stearly Jacob & Son, paper warehouse, 17 Commerce, and sugar refs., 140 Coates
Stearly Wilson H., mer., 17 Commerce, h 427 N 6th
Steck Jacob, baker, Tomlin's ct
Steck John, baker, Francis & James (F V)
Steck John, jr., baker, 106 New Market
Steck John H., custom house, 25 S Sch 6th
Stecker Henry L., machinist, 8th bel Poplar
Stedfold James, clerk, 131 Christian
Stedman Joseph, rag dealer, Apple & Culvert
Stedman Wm., paper and rags, 5th & Catharine
Steeb Frederick, boot crimper, 42 Pegg
Steedman Charles, 200 S 9th
Steel Anson, cloth mer., 506 Vine
Steel A., cabinetmr., 354 Callowhill
Steel Canby, hatter, 101 Noble
Steel Catharine, Scott's ct
Steel Charles W., agent, 47 Commerce
Steel Christopher W., starch manuf., 2d & Jefferson
Steel Deborah, 65 Carpenter (S)

42

Steel Edwin R., clerk, 65 Carpenter
Steel Eliza, b. h., 254 High
Steel Elizabeth, 7 Workman's ct
Steel E. Mrs., 29 Walnut
Steel Francis J., M. D., 511 N Front
Steel Henry, clothing, rear Maria ab 4th
Steel Henry A., clerk, 13th ab Buttonwood
Steel James, com. mer., S W Cherry and Broad, h Callowhill bet 10th & 11th
STEEL JAMES & CO., forwarding, S W Broad and Cherry
Steel James R., ship chandler, 84 Swanson, h 32 Christian
Steel Jane, George bel Sch 6th
Steel John, carpet weaver, West and Union
Steel John, cabinetmr., 8 Washington Market pl
Steel John, cordw., Fraley's ct (K)
Steel John & Co., balance manufs., 31 Farmer
Steel Juliet Ann, tailoress, 3 Eutaw
Steel J. W., engraver, 80½ Walnut, h 40 Sansom
Steel Keziah, gentw., 15 German
Steel Lewis, hat finisher, 3 Sheaff
Steel London, lab., 52 Quince
Steel Richard W., com. mer., 81 N 10th
Steel Robert, blacksm., 3d ab Federal
Steel Robert, weaver, rear Fitler bel Harrison
Steel Samuel, lab., rear 25 Ogden
Steel Samuel, weaver, Ann ab 13th
Steel Samuel, weaver, Hope bel Master
Steel Samuel, weaver, White's ct
Steel Sam'l, furniture car, F road n Franklin(K)
Steel Sarah Ann, 45 N 8th
Steel & Sharp, dry goods, 45 N 8th
Steel Thomas S., ship master, 19 Moyamensing road
STEEL THOS. S. & BROTHER, ship chandlers, 85 Swanson
Steel Wm., mer., 16 Norris' al, h 7 Union
Steel Wm., weaver, Jefferson ab Front
Steel Wm. J., grocer, Water & Mulberry, h 111 Vine
Steel Wm. W., stove finisher, 72 N 6th, h 9th bel Buttonwood
Steel W. H., ship chandler, h Federal ab 7th
Steele Joseph, crockery, 129 S 11th
Steele Robert, custom house, h 66 S 5th
Steele Wm., weaver, Franklin bel School (K)
Steele Wm. S., cabinet mr., 18 St John
Steelman Apsley, capt., 170 Christian
Steelman Edmund, wood mer., Vine st whf., h 80 Crown
Steelman Hester, 332 S 5th
Steelman James S., lastmr., 44 Union
Steelman Jonathan, lab., Rex ct
Steelman L., waterman, 18 Mead al
Steelman & Mead, wood, Vine st whf
Steelman Risley, trader, 599 N Front (K)
Steen James, carp., 13 Fetter la, h Parker ab Washington
Steen James, rear 39 New Market
Steen John, tavern, 219 S 6th
Steen John L., builder and carpenter, 14 S 13th
Steen Robert, mer., 186 High, h Walnut above Broad
Steen Robert, painter, 10th and Green

Steen Robert & Co., grocers, 186 High
Steetz John, susp. weav., Palmer ab Franklin(K
Steever Edgar Z., plumber, S E 11th and Sassafras
Steever George W., acct., 50 & 52 N Front, h 312 N 3d
Steever Henry D., accountant, 422 N 5th opp Parrish
Steever James G., carp., Jackson pl
Steever Samuel K., clerk, 90 N 9th
Steffan Martin, machinist, 179 St John
Steffe Jacob, stove and patternmr., 118 N 2d
Steiger John M., tailor, 527 N 4th
Stein Abraham, tobacco, 228 Chestnut, h 16? Wood
Stein Abraham G., china ware, 206 N 3d, h 188 Dillwyn
Stein Harman, carp., rear 152 Poplar
Stein Simon, clothier, 176 Cedar
Steinbach Albert, 30 Cresson's al
Steinbach Andrew, cordw., Lewellen's av (K)
Steinberger A., coal mer., office N E 9th and Willow, h N E Wood & Marshall
Steinberger David, 319 Willow st
Steinberger Michael, glue boiler, 5th ab Camac
Steinberger Louis, shop, St John bel Beaver(K
Steinbrenner Anette, 219 Pine
Steiner Henry J., baker, 10 Mary's ct
Steiner Jacob, mer., 75 N 3d, h 63 O Y road
STEINER JOHN CONRAD, tobacco, 150 N 3d
Steiner John P., mer., 75 N 3d, h 59 O Y road
STEINER J. & J. P., fancy goods, 75 N 3d
Steinert John, cordw., St John ab Brown
Steinfeltz Sarah, washer, rear Nectarine above 10th
Steinhaur John, cordw., rear 113 Green
Steinhour Wm., gent., 446 N 3d
Steinman C. F., hardware, 3d & Franklin, h 4th ab George (N L)
Steinman John, blacksm., 22 Green
Steinman John W., clerk, Franklin and 3d
Steinmetz A., stone cutter, R road ab Willow, h 155 Buttonwood
Steinmetz Christian, garden, F road opp Norris
Steinmetz Daniel, mer., N W 5th & Commerce, h 7 S Sch 7th
Steinmetz Elizabeth, Rugan ab Callowhill
Steinmetz Elizabeth, shop, 33 Franklin
Steinmetz Elizabeth Miss, 270 Chestnut
Steinmetz Geo., brushmr., 265 High, h Queen ab Hanover (K)
Steinmetz George, shop, Parrish ab 9th
Steinmetz G. P., 33 Franklin
Steinmetz Jacob, lab., 7th ab Poplar
Steinmetz John, drayman, Mechanic bel George
Steinmetz John, brushmr., F road opp Marlboro
Steinmetz & Justice, hardware, N W 5th and Commerce
Steinmetz Robert, carter, 72 Christian
Steinmetz Wm., locksm., 21 Franklin pl
Steitz Jacob, cabinetmr., Sp Garden & Franklin
Stelfox John, tinsmith, 98 N 11th
Stelle Joseph W., hatter, Linden bel Front
Stelle J. C., clerk market, 24 State
Steller Eliza, dressmr., Western pl

Stellwagen Charles K., watchmr., 223 Chestnut, h 131 S 9th
Stellwaggen Charles, provisions, 143 S 9th
Stelzer John, vict., Mary n F road (K)
Stem Henry, carp., 2d bel Phoenix (K)
Steman Peter, com. mer., Front and Willow, h 80 Dillwyn
Stemmil Charles, fancy goods, 207 Chestnut
Stenchfield Ephraim, Lancaster Pike (W P)
Stephel George, baker, Sch 2d bel Callowhill
Stephens Abijah E., mer., 10 City row
Stephens Ann, washer, Wood ab Queen (K)
Stephens Edmund, tailor, 65 Walnut
Stephens Elizabeth, Madison ct
Stephens George, bootmr., 94 Sassafras
Stephens Henry, lab., 7 Lily al
Stephens James R., millinery, 63 Cedar
Stephens Robt., stone mason, Higgins' ct
Stephens William, gent., 268 Lombard
Stephens Wm. J., cordw., Church av
Stephens W. M., cordw., 6 Short ct
Stephenson John, stone cutter, Jones n Sch 4th
Stephenson Samuel, D. D., Sch 3d bel Callowhill
Steretz John G., trunkmr., 104 New Market
Sterling Gilbert S., mer., 37 S wharves
Sterling James T., Front and Mead
Sterling James T., 4th and Master (K)
Sterling John, sailmr., Prime ab Swanson
Sterling Samuel, carp., 3 Beck
Sterling Sarah, milliner, 191 S 6th
Stern Chas., Torr's al bel R road
Stern Fred'k., dry goods, 482 N 2d
Stern Henry, tobacconist, 104 Callowhill
Stern Henry & Co., tailors, 398½ N 2d
Stern Jacob, hatter, 25 Duke st
Stern Lewis, printer, Carroll ab 13th
Stern Menko, trader, 295 N 2d
Stern S., pedler, 36 Pegg
Sternberger Solomon, furnishing store, 320 Sassafras
Sterne Margaret, Beck n Front
Sterne Wm., clerk, P. O., 275 Green
Sterr George, sr., livery stable, Lodge al, h Franklin & Noble
Sterr Mary, dry goods, Franklin and Noble
Sterret Esther, trimmings, Lombard above Sch 7th
Sterrett Anthony, cordw., 76 New Market
Sterrett Ezekiel, vinegar, 32 Jacoby
Sterrett Francis, weaver, Union ab West (K)
Sterrett James B., machinist, 159 Green
Sterrett John, lab., Budden's al
Sterrett John T., chairmr., 173 Green
Sterrett Jos., brushmr., Catharine ab 9th
Sterrett Margaret, 159 Green
Sterrett Mary, tailoress, 83 Bedford
Sterrett Sarah, Sch 7th bel Sassafras
Sterrett Sarah, 90 N 11th
Stetler John, tinwr., Sp Garden and Franklin
Stetler Philip, blacksm., 3 Little Willow
Stetson B. D., Phila. Tattersalls, 137 Filbert bel 13th
Stettler W., grocer, 229 Shippen
Stetzell George, huckster, 135 G T road
Stetzell Jacob, baker, Federal ab 2d

Stetzenberg George, paper hanger, Otter bel G T road
Stevens Albert G., tailor, 4 Richard
Stevens & Brothers, tobacconists, 413 High
Stevens B. F., tinman, 15 Benton
Stevens Catharine, 69 Coates
Stevens Daniel, blacksm., 143 N road
Stevens Edward, hatter, 164 S Front
Stevens Edwin D., mer., 33 Church al
Stevens Eliza, 539 N 5th
Stevens Elizabeth, Burd's ct
Stevens Elizabeth, 5 Powell
Stevens Erastus, M. D., 150 S 5th
Stevens George, silver plater, James & R road
Stevens Hannah, dressmr., Poplar bel Rachel
Stevens Henry A., atty., Vine ab 12th
Stevens & Huston, com. mers., 33 Church al
Stevens Isaac A., letter carrier, 44 Barker
Stevens James, mer., 21 S Water
Stevens James H., tailor, 158 S 3d
Stevens Jeffery C., carp., St Paul's av
Stevens John, lab., Mark's la
Stevens John B., shipping office, 19 Penn
Stevens Joseph, chairmr., Culvert bel 4th
Stevens Joseph, seaman, 3 Wale's av
Stevens Louisa, washer, Lemon
Stevens Rhoda, 4 Wall
Stevens Thomas, blacksm., Wheat ab Reed
Stevens Uriah S., tailor, 471 High
Stevens Wm., cordw., 6th bel Christian
Stevens Wm., cooper, 190 S Front
Stevens Wm., actor, James ab 10th
Stevens Wm., boot black, 17 S 7th, h 44 Currant al
Stevens Wm., waiter, 27 Washington
Stevens Wm. N., variety store, S E 3d & Mulberry, h 84 Dillwyn
Stevenson Andrew, lab., Culvert ab 3d
Stevenson Ann, b h, 9 N 8th
Stevenson Augustin, mer., 225 N 3d, h 108 Callowhill
Stevenson Augustin, jr., mer., 225 N 3d, h 10 Callowhill
Stevenson A. M., auctioneer, 68 High, h S E 11th and Spruce
Stevenson & Co., blindmrs. Washington bel 7th
Stevenson Cornelius, city treasur., 5th & Chestnut, h 296 Walnut
Stevenson Daniel, waterman, Hallowell n 7th
Stevenson Daniel, carter, Palm bel Brown
Stevenson Daniel, cabinr., rear 7 Bread
Stevenson Edward, carp., P road ab Washington
Stevenson Edward, cooper, 73 Penn
Stevenson Eliza, Oliver pl
Stevenson & Harned, blindmrs., 386 N 2d
Stevenson Hugh, lumber mer., N W 13th and Locust, h 9th and Cedar
Stevenson James, founder, School ab Otter (K)
Stevenson James, blindmr. 386 N 2d, h Bedford ab Crown (K)
Stevenson James, lab., 2 Harrison's ct (K)
Stevenson James, grocer, 9th & Callowhill
Stevenson James, carp., Keefe and Wheat, h 404 S 3d
Stevenson James, tailor, 64 Sassafras

Stevenson James, weaver, rear G T road below Jefferson
Stevenson James, lab., Lombard n Sch 8th
Stevenson James, cooper, Orchard ab Rawle
Stevenson Jane, chandler, 223 S 6th
Stevenson John, lab., Harris' ct
Stevenson John, baker, 97 S 8th
Stevenson John, N W 2d & Coates
Stevenson John B., grocer, 228 N 3d, h 147 Dillwyn
Stevenson Johnson, porter, rear Barker near Sch 5th
Stevenson Joshua, Parrish bel 7th
Stevenson J. B., mer., Sp Garden bel 10th
Stevenson Margaret, dry goods, 221 S 5th
Stevenson Margaret, shop, 333 Vine
Stevenson & Maris, lumber mers., N W 13th & Locust
Stevenson Mary, b h, N W 2d & Pine
Stevenson Mary, gentw., 375 Walnut
Stevenson Mary, O Y road bel Coates
Stevenson Samuel, coachmr., 24 Maiden (K)
Stevenson Samuel, merchant, 167 High, h 163 N 9th
Stevenson Saml., brickmr., Shackamaxon near Bedford
Stevenson Sarah, Nectarine ab 9th
Stevenson Theodore, hatter, rear 615 N Front
Stevenson Thomas, R road bel Buttonwood
Stevenson Thomas S., carp., Pearl ab Sch 8th
Stevenson Wm., waiter, 66 German
Stevenson Wm., mer., 250 & h 252 N 3d
Stevenson Wm., cordw., 6th bel Christian
Stevenson Wm., weaver, Amber ab Phoenix
Stevenson Wm., waiter, Caroline pl
Stevenson Wm. & Benjamin, leather, 250 N 3d
Stevenson Wm. G., gent., 17 Powell
Steward Ann D., trimmings, 123 Sassafras
Steward Arch., hair dresser, Sch 2d & High
Steward David T., regulator of weights, N W 13th & Filbert
Steward George, waiter, 20 Acorn al
Steward George W., wigmr., 147 S 6th
Steward Job, sailmr., rear School
Steward John, carp., 86 Poplar
Steward John, jr., locksm., 90 Cherry, b Poplar ab 7th
Steward John, car driver, George n Sch 7th
Steward & O'Hare, locksmiths, 90 Cherry
Steward Sarah, shop, 258 S 5th
Steward Wm., lab., rear 319 Shippen
Stewardson Anna, wid. of Thomas, 90 Mulberry
STEWARDSON GEORGE, mer., 90 Mulberry
Stewart Agnes, Pearl ab 13th
Stewart Alex., gent., 325 S 6th
Stewart Alexander, 373 S 3d
Stewart Alex., lab., Filbert n Sch 4th
Stewart Amanda M., dry goods, 40 N 8th
Stewart Ann, Carpenter & 3d

Stewart Charles, mer., 331 E Lombard
Stewart Charles, stonecut., 129 W Sassafras
Stewart Charles, carp., Robeson's ct
Stewart Charles, carp., Charles ab Noble
Stewart Charles, weav., Hanover ab Duke (K)
Stewart Charles, lab., 45 W Cedar
Stewart Charles H., waterman, Paul n 7th
Stewart Daniel, barber, 11th bel Pine
Stewart Daniel, pawn broker, 262 S 7th, h 328 E Cedar
Stewart Mary, 28 Barker
Stewart David, iron found., 332 Sp Garden
Stewart Dugald, bricklayer, 7 Orleans
Stewart Edward, tinsmith, 101 Cedar
Stewart Eliza, washer, Centre ab 12th
Stewart Eliza, tailoress, Adams and 13th
Stewart Elizabeth, 394 Sassafras
Stewart Emeline, wid of John, 1 School
Stewart Esther, N E Sch 8th & Walnut
Stewart E. & F., art. flowers, 29 S 4th
Stewart Francis, 373 Sassafras
Stewart Francis, gent., 2 Madison
Stewart George, M. D., Filbert E of Sch 6th
Stewart George, carp., Cherry and Brown
Stewart George, tailor, 10th & Pleasant
Stewart Hen., fisherman, Cherry ab. Queen (K)
Stewart Henry, lab., 6 Osborn's ct
Stewart Henry H., eating h, 10 N 5th
Stewart Hugh, cabmr., 16 Benton
Stewart H., dealer, 26 Queen
STEWART H. B., morocco dresser, St. John and Willow, h 234 N 6th
Stewart James, stonecutter, 343 E Lombard
Stewart James, keep. pris., Bushhill
Stewart James, weaver, George E Sch 6th
Stewart James, weaver, Lombard n Sch 7th
Stewart James, lab., 33 M'Duffie
Stewart James, lab., 7 Washington ab 11th
Stewart James, cabinetmr., 1 Southampton ct
Stewart James, ship carpenter, Queen below Cherry (K)
Stewart James, grocer, 104 Christian
Stewart James, carp., 17 Plum
Stewart James, 6 Wells' pl
Stewart James A., grocer, 10th ab Buttonwood
Stewart Jas. M., carp., 102 Filbert, house Perry
Stewart James W., mariner, Cox bel 2d
Stewart James W. Rev., Juniper bel Pine
Stewart Jane, 10 S Penn sq
Stewart Jane H., Noble ab Franklin
Stewart Jefferson D., 170 S Front
Stewart John, hatter, 306 N Front
Stewart John, carp., 2 Lebanon row
Stewart John, blacksm., Carlton ab Sch 3d
Stewart John, chairmr., Edward bel G T R (K)
Stewart John, stonecutter, Winter ct
Stewart John, tinsmith, R road ab Wallace
Stewart John, tavern, 315 N 3d

Stewart John, merchant, 103 S wharves, h 206 Spruce
Stewart John A., Apple ab Brown
Stewart John M., acct., Green ab 13th
Stewart Jos., lab., Penn bel Shackamaxon (K)
Stewart Joseph, weaver, Rose ab 13th
Stewart Joseph D., M. D., 193 N 7th
Stewart J., jr., locksm., Poplar ab 7th
Stewart J. H., manuf., 68 & 70 Dillwyn
Stewart Louisa M., Shackamaxon ab Queen
Stewart Margaret, 10 Jackson's ct
Stewart Martha, art. flowers, 21 S 4th
Stewart Martha, Ball alley
Stewart Mary, dry goods, 528 High
Stewart Mary, dry goods, 115 N 10th
Stewart Mary, weaver, rear Philip above Jefferson (K)
Stewart Mary A., milliner, 140 S 5th
Stewart Matthew, sen., 142 Sassafras
Stewart Matthew, jr., tin ware and stoves, 126 Sassafras
Stewart Moses, watchman, Sch 2d ab Vine
Stewart & Newman, mers., 89 S Front
Stewart Paul, lead factory, 11 Helmuth
Stewart Peter, teacher, 12th ab Division
Stewart Peter, waiter, 7 Pryor's ct
Stewart P. Mrs., 113 Swanson
Stewart Rachel, 3 Gray's al
Stewart Robert, drover, 472 S Front
Stewart Robert, gent., 243 E Cedar
Stewart Robert, grocery, 13th & Pine
Stewart Robert, weaver, Elme's ct
Stewart Robert, carp., Crawford's ct
Stewart Robert R., gent., 249 Walnut
Stewart Samuel, carp., Pleasant and 10th
Stewart Saml., clothier, Cedar ab 11th
Stewart Samuel, porter, rear 332 S 2d
Stewart Sarah, b h, High E of Sch 3d
Stewart Sarah, 15 Coates al
Stewart Sarah, school, 3 Chatham
Stewart Sarah, 52 Perry
Stewart Sidney, waterman, 25 Harmony
Stewart Stephen, machinist, 107 St John
Stewart S., Dr., N W 3d & Queen
Stewart Thos., gent., 7 Lodge
Stewart Thos., cabinetmr., Yhost, h 182 Queen
Stewart Thos., cordw., 420 S Front
Stewart Thos., customhouse, h Sch 8th below Spruce
Stewart Thos., carp., Coates ab 11th
Stewart Thomas, weaver, rear G T road below Master
Stewart Thomas S., chairmr., 150 N Front
Stewart Thomas S., lumber mer., Brown n 4th, h 276 Marshall
Stewart T. S., architect, 10th ab Shippen
Stewart Victor, soap boiler, 40 Fitzwater
Stewart, Walters & Co., ship yard, foot Hanover (K)
Stewart Wm., cordw., Sch 6th n Callowhill
Stewart Wm., lab., M'Bride's ct (K)
Stewart Wm., gardener, 14 Franklin pl
Stewart Wm., shop, 126 S 6th
Stewart Wm., 20 Queen
Stewart Wm., plasterer, Chancellor bel Sch 6th

Stewart Wm., baker, 430 High
Stewart Wm., weaver, West bel Hanover (K)
Stewart Wm., weaver, Franklin ab Front (K)
Stewart Wm., Shippen bel 9th
Stewart Wm., lab., Bishop bel Queen
Stewart Wm., C., seaman, 79 Swanson
Stewart Wm. H., mer., 311 Sassafras
Stewart W. H., mer., 89 S Front, h 249 Walnut
Stichter Henry, stovemr., 78 N 6th
Stickler Peter, lab., Court al
Stickney David, carp., Otter bel G T road
Stickney W. L., tailor, 291 N 2d
Stief R. F., coach painter, 5 Turner
Stieff Andrew, baker, 17 N 5th
Stieff Ed., cordw., Kline's ct
Stieff John, baker, 17 N 8th
STIERLEY JOHN, tobacconist, N E 2d and Union, h Washington ab Swanson
Stiloman Richard, blacksmith, G T road bel 2d, h William bel Edward (K)
Stiles Ann, shop, 8 Callowhill
Stiles Benj., gent., Poplar & Broad
Stiles & Buchart, druggists, 226 N 3d
Stiles Edward, grocer, S E 3d & Union
Stiles Edward, teacher, 154 Marshall
Stiles Edward J., 310 Walnut
Stiles Henry, 189 N 5th
Stiles Jacob, lumber mer., Marlboro' ab Beach (K)
Stiles James, waiter, 8 Osborn's ct
Stiles James H., confect., 492 N 2d
Stiles John E., confect., 5 Melon pl
Stiles John H., tailor, 211 N 3d, h 25 Coates
Stiles John L., carp., 14 Centre
Stiles Robt., upholst., 162 S 3d
Stiles Samuel, stage offi., Walnut & Sch Beach
Stiles Surmon, blacksmith, 38 Pratt
Stiles Valentine H., dyer, 325 Sassafras
Stiles Wm., upholsterer, Assembly Bui., h 13th ab Sp Garden
Stiles Wm. C., 262 N 4th
Stiles Wm. M., dyer, 91 N 6th
Stiles Wm. S., confect., 158 N 3d
Still Francis, porter, 3 Middle al
Still Francis, tinpl. work., 98 Washington av
Stille Alfred, M D, 365 Walnut
Stille Benj., mer., 317 Chestnut
Stille Catharine, Walnut bel Sch 8th
Stille Charles J., atty. & coun., 152 Walnut, h Chestnut bel Broad
Stille John A., printer, Clark ab 3d
Stille Maria Mrs., 367 Wood
Stilley James, ladies' shoemr., 523 S 2d
Stillie Mary, gentw., 247 S 3d
Stillman John, bootmr., 28 Bank
Stillman Lawrence, port. house, R road & 13th, h Washington ab R road
Stillwell Daniel D., cordw., rear 16 Rachel
Stillwell Davis B., cooper, 13th and Willow, h Wood ab Sch 6th
Stillwell Joseph, shoemr., 5 St Stephen's pl
Stiltz E. & C., dry goods, 117 N 10th
Stiltz & Hartley, tailors, 420 N 2d
Stultz John D., 117 N 10th

Stilz Christian, shoemr., 128 Coates
Stilz John, tailor, 420 N 2d
Stilz Margaret, wool dealer, G T road n Otter
Stilz Michael, shoemr., 486 N 2d
Stimble Benjamin B., bricklayer, O Y road bel Green
Stimble Edwin D., carp., 153 O Y road
Stimble George S., bricklayer, 153 O Y road
Stimmel Hiram, lab., Brinton bel 11th
Stimmel Maria, Caledonia ct
Stimmel R., printer, 90 Christian
Stimpson Stephen, waterman, Church bel Christian
Stinchman Caspar, Hanover ab Queen (K)
Stine George, carp., 18 Clare
Stine John, cedar cooper, 5 Rudolph's ct
Stine John, brickmr., George n Sch 2d
Stine Matt., cordw., Apple bel George
Stinebaker John, carp., Palmer ab Franklin (K)
Stines Isaac B., carp., 13th bel Green
Stinger Charles, brushmr., Wood bel 4th
Stinger Elizabeth, 10 Pennsylvania av
Stinger Geo. R., bricklayer, 14 Starr al
Stinger Joseph, hatter, 416 High
Stinger Simpson, lab., Duke ab Hanover
Stinger S. & C., dressmrs., 138 Chestnut
Stinnel Hiram, clerk, Norman's al
Stinnel Thos., sawmr., Norman's al
Stinsman Bishop, lab., Bethesda row
Stinsman George, ladies' shoemr., 509 S 2d
Stinsman Peter, lab., Church bel Greenwich
Stinsman Westley, clerk, Reed ab 2d
Stinson Alex., tailor, 12 Dannaker's av
Stinson Ann, grocer, Marlboro' n Duke
Stinson David, lab., Jefferson ab Front
Stinson Hugh, weaver, G T road ab Franklin
Stinson James, grocer, Fitler bel Harrison (K)
Stinson James, weaver, Perry bel Master
Stinson John, lab., 1 Richardson's ct
Stinson John, weaver, Fitler ab Harrison (K)
Stinson Mary, 244 Catharine
Stinson Robt., lab., 56 St John
Stinson Thos., weaver, Hancock bel Master
Stinson Thos., manuf., Charlotte bel George
Stirk Wm., carp., rear Poplar ab 9th
Stirling Wm., carp., 19 Hunter, h 311 Cherry
Stiteler J. B. Rev., 529 N 5th
Stites & Cooper, patternmrs., Hope ab Phoenix (K)
Stites Daniel, pilot, M road bel Marion
Stites George, looking-glass mr., Beach below Maiden (K)
Stites Noah, lab., 155 Swanson
Stitt Alex. A., printer, 2 Bonsall
Stitt John W., mer., 28 N Front
Stitt S. B., mer., 15 N Front, h 99 New
Stitt Wm., lab., Washington ab 11th
St Jean Anna C., gentw., 139 N 11th
St John James, cordw., 422 S Front
ST. JOHN & GODDARD, exchange brokers, 31 S 3d
St John Wm., sutler, Noble ab 8th

Stock Frederick, gent., 83 Tammany
Stock Frederick, carp., 319½ High
Stock Jacob, cordw., 1 Charles
Stock John, tailor, rear 447 N 4th
Stockdale Geraldus, 8 Plum
Stockdale Geraldus B., teacher, 367 S 5th
Stockdale G. T., printer, 6 Plum
Stockdale Jacob, grocer, N E 7th & Catharine
Stockdale Percival, clerk, 25 Mary (S)
Stocker Anthony, N D, 345 Spruce
Stocker Caroline, widow of J. C., gentw., 54 Walnut
Stockley Chas. T., 77 S whfs
Stockley Cornelius, tailor, 53 N 6th
Stockley N. & C. T., grocers, 77 S whfs
Stockley Wm., tailor, 53 N 6th
Stockly Levi, barber, 12th and Cedar, h 191 N 9th
Stockman George, saw mill, Beach ab Palmer
Stockman Jacob, thimble and pencil maker, 66 Chestnut
Stockson Caroline, 4 Lemon
Stockton Abraham, tanner, 8 Poplar
Stockton Charles, shoemr., rear 8 Mark's la
Stockton Chas. M., tailor, 428 N 2d, h 449 N 6th
Stockton Daniel, lab., rear 71 Beach
Stockton Daniel, stonecut., 131 New Market
Stockton Eliza P., 227 Filbert
Stockton Hugh H., mer., 9 N Front, h 154 S 11th
Stockton Joseph, tailor, rear 176 Poplar
Stockton Owen J., tailor, 663 N 2d (K)
Stockton R. F., capt. U S Navy, 383 Walnut
Stockton Samuel W., manufac. incor. teeth, 116 Chestnut, h 139 O Y road
Stockton Stacy, Madison house, 39 N 2d
Stockton S. W. & Co., manufs. incorrupt. teeth, 116 Chestnut
Stockton T. H. Rev., 154 N 11th
Stockton Wm., mer., 7½ N Front
Stockton Wm. R., dry goods, Buttonwood and 11th
Stockton Wm. S., publisher, 126 Mulberry
STODDART CURWIN, dry goods, 280 N 2nd, h Franklin ab Sassafras
Stoddart Elizabeth, 82 Catharine
Stoddart Isaac, bookseller, 8th & Chestnut, h 79 Buttonwood
Stoddart John, coal office, 8 S 7th, h 101 N 7th
Stoddart Joseph M., dry goods, 282 N 2d
Stoeckel Theobald, cabinet mr., 271 N 2nd, h Adelphi al ab Pegg
Stoecklin John, barber, 169 Green
Stoecklin Matthew, upholsterer, 169 Green
Stoever Frederick, wine mer., 43 S Front
Stoever Wm. H., acct. W Bank, 250 N 4th
Stokeley Charles, lab., 6 Caroline pl
Stokely David, chairmr., 45 E Catharine
Stokely Eliza, 230 Christian
Stoker Jane, dry goods, Sch 8th & George
Stokes Alice, dressmr., 407 Sassafras
Stokes Charles, tailor, 296 High, h 79 Franklin

Stokes Granville, tailor, 262 High, h Cherry n Broad
Stokes Hannah A., dressmr., 10th ab Wood
STOKES HARVEY, lime mer., N W Front and Callowhill
Stokes Herbert N., 127 S 2d
Stokes James V., carp., 43 Chester
Stokes John, auctioneer, 22 N 2d, h 74 Marshall
Stokes John, carp., Warner's ct
Stokes John, confectioner, 124 Dillwyn
Stokes John W., tailor, 194 High, h 148 Marshall
Stokes Joseph, cordw., Carlton bel Sch 2d
Stokes Joshua, carp., 16 Green
Stokes Joshua, cooper, Sheaff's al
STOKES J. W. & E. D., tailors, 194 High
Stokes L. B., carp., Fries' ct, h 489 Vine
Stokes Maria, shop, Sheaff al
Stokes R., dry goods, S W 9th and Vine, h 16 Green
Stokes Samuel E., mer., 10 & h 170 N Front
Stokes Sarah, confect., S E Vine & Chester
Stokes Thomas, plasterer, 11th & Pearl
Stokes Thomas, shoemaker, 11 N 6th, and carp. 28 Jones' al, h Wood ab 12th
Stokes Thomas, turner, Franklin bel 2d (K)
Stokes T. J. P., M D, Spruce W Sch 3d
Stokes U. W., mer., N E 8th and Spruce
Stokes Wm., dry goods, 91 S 6th
Stokes Wm., carp., 28 Jones' al, h 288 High
Stokes Wm., lab., rear 13 Eutaw
Stokes Wm., jr., clerk, Washington (W P)
Stokes Wm. A., atty. & coun., 77 S 5th
Stokes Wm. C., cordw., 24 Parker
Stokes Woolman, tailor, 69 Chestnut
Stokley Wm. S., confec., 66 Zane
Stoll Daniel, baker, Benton ab School (K)
Stoll Reinhardt, ostler, 14 New Market
Stolte C. F., musician, Rittenhouse n Sch 6th
Stone Amasa, hemp hose manuf., Quarry near Bread, h Washington ab 10th
Stone Ann, 6 Reed's av
Stone Charles H., mer., 45 S 2d, h 152 Pine
Stone Charlotte, b h, 426 High
Stone Esther, teacher, 65 S 7th
Stone Henry, bell hanger, 69 S 5th, h 4th below Catharine
Stone Isaac, painter, Williamson's ct
Stone James N., mer., 45 S 2d
Stone John, mer., 45 S 2d, h 3 Sansom
Stone John & Sons, silk mers., 45 S 2d
Stone J. E., mer., 36 S Front, h N E 13th and Spruce
Stone Samuel, tinsmith, 57 N Front
STONE, SLADE & FARNHAM, mers., 36 S Front
Stoneman Joseph, plasterer, 185 Brown
Stonemetz Jacob, millwright, Wood ab 13th
Stones Jos., lab., 30 Queen (S)
Stones Saml. M. D., N W Pine and Juniper
Stones Samuel, 252 N 7th
Stones Thos., weaver, Duke bel Palmer (K)
Stong Abm., cordw., Robb's ct
Stong Ambrose, packer, Church av
Stong Joseph, ladies' shoemr., Robb's ct
Stong Philip, carp., 9th bel Poplar

Stoop Andrew, grave digger, Palmer n F road
Stopp Thomas, grocer, George and Charlotte
Stoppart Wm., engineer, Beach bel Maiden (K)
Storath Wm., beer house, 76 Browne
Storer Abigail, b. h., 27 S 10th
Storey Thos., shop, 213 S 3d
Stork Elizabeth, milliner, 47 Pine
Stork Jonathan, lab., rear, 2 Rose al
Storms Henry C., mer., 75 High
Storms Phebe, shop, 458 S Front
Storner Andrew, baker, 151 Catharine
Storrs George Rev., 18 Chester
STORRS GEO. F., druggist, S E 8th and Vine
Story Ann, shop, 227 S 5th
Story Benj., drayman, 8 Faries' ct
Story Edward, mariner, 47 Carpenter
Story George P., bookbinder, 12 Pear, h 157 Queen
Story George W., copper pl. printer, rear 347 S 3d
STORY JOHN, tavern, 71 N whfs
Story John, coach trim., rear 450 S Front
Story Samuel, tobacconist, 380 S 2d
Story Wm., weaver, 21 W Cedar
Story Wm. A., 158 S 4th
Stotesbury & Ayres, iron foundry, Beach ab Maiden (K)
Stotesbury & Ayres, hardware, 42 N 3d
Stotesbury F. P., grocery, 29 Madison
Stotesbury Richard G., hardware, 42 N 3d, h 10th bel Cedar
Stothard John, Cherry bel Broad
Stotsenberg Philip, lab., Wharton ab 4th
Stott Elizabeth, N E 12th & Mulberry
Stott Thos., pickler, 89 Swanson
Stott Wm., lithographer, 42 Walnut
Stoud Chas. M., cordw., rear 153 Green
Stouse Daniel, 18 George
Stout Anna J., shop, 125 Coates
Stout Benj., carp., 9th and Parrish
Stout Charles, cooper, St John and George (K)
Stout Elizabeth, George ab Sch 8th
Stout George, whip factory, 3 N 3d, h 62 Wood
Stout Geo., porter house, Thompson ab Broad
Stout George & Co., whip manufs., 3 N 3d
Stout Henry, whipmr., 128 New Market
Stout Jacob, carter, Ball's ct
Stout John jr., dentist, 14 City row
Stout John, saddle and harnessmr., S W 6th and Catharine
Stout John, whipmr., 3 Wallace
Stout John L., carp., 5 Sp Garden
Stout Lewis, segarmr., 21 Perry
Stout Mary, 440 N 4th
Stout Saml., watchmr., 492½ N 2d
Stout Simpson, tailor, 157 E Lombard
Stout Thos., machinist, Crown and Bedford (K)
Stovell John, dentist, 102 Mulberry
Stovell T. B., druggist, N E 13th and Walnut
Stover George, lab., Locust n Beach
Stover Wm., grocer, N E 3d and Wood, h 9th ab Coates
Stover Wm. & Sons, grocers, N E 3d and Wood
Stow John P., cordw., Barker's ct (K)
Stow Margaret, rear Harriet ab Ross (K)

Stowe Thomas, 77 Plum
Stowman George W., cordw., Rachel ab Poplar (N L)
Stowman Timothy M., corder, Rachel ab Brown
Stowman Wm., cooper, 181 Brown
Stoy Daniel, shipwright Queen bel Hanover
Stoy Daniel, shoemr., Shackamaxon bel Allen
Stoy Frederick G., capmr., Sch 8th n Vine
Stoy Henry, shipwr., Beach ab Shackamaxon
Stoy Henry B., shoes, Queen ab Shackamaxon
Stoy Thos., ship joiner, Bedford ab Crown (K)
Stoy W. G., acct., 6 Lybrand
Strach David, bricklr., Filbert n Sch Front
Stradling John, carp. weav., 5 S 3d, h 15 North
Stradling T., painter, 25 N 4th
Strafford C. M., druggist, 6th and Wall
Strafford J. B., M. D., 6th opp Queen (S)
Strahan W. H., machinist, 199 S 4th
Strain John, lab., Beach bel Chestnut
Strain Neal, lab., Cooper n Sch 3d
Strain Thomas, fancy soap, Preston
Straley Joseph, stone mason, Oldham's ct
Stran Jas., quilt mr., rear Marriott bel 6th
Stranaghan James, trimmings, 63 S 8th, h Cedar ab 11th
Stranahan Andrew, grocer, 2d and Federal
Stranahan A., grocer, N W Mead and Swanson
Stranahan James, tavern, 245 Shippen
Straney Mary, dressmr., Cuskaden's ct
Strang Isaac, carp., Rye bel Marion
Straser Geo., blacksm., Marlboro' bel Duke (K)
Strattan Benj., ladies' shoemr., 7 Ranstead pl
Strattan Jacob, mer., 70 High, h 425 Sassafras
Strattan Mary, trimmings, 12th ab Sassafras
Stratton Alby, lab., F road opp Allen
Stratton Ann, Prosperous al
Stratton Austen S., cake baker, Garden bel 10th
Stratton Benj., hatter, 6 N 6th, h Julianna and Wood
Stratton Chas. S., painter, 2d bel Phœnix (K)
Stratton Ebenezer, tailor, 46 Wood
Stratton Elias, bricklr., 1 Diamond
Stratton Enoch, bricklr., 7th and Brown
Stratton Enos, glass bl., Queen ab Vienna (K)
Stratton George, starch fact., Hancock ab Phœnix (K)
Stratton George & Samuel, starch manufs., Hancock ab Phoenix (K)
Stratton G., Fisher's pills, 181 S 9th
Stratton Henry, dyer, 612 N 3d
Stratton Jacob, plasterer, Alden ab Poplar
Stratton John, gardener, 234 N 7th
Stratton John, painter, 251 Green
Stratton John, painter, 6th ab Callowhill, h 251 Green

Stratton S. C., Sch 6th and Vine
Stratton Wm., driver, F road opp Master
Stratton Wm., gas fitter, 87 Franklin
Stratton Wm., cordw., 477 N 2d
Stratton Wm., oak cooper, 13th and Melon
Stratton Wm. A., forwarding mer., 276 High, h 98 N 9th
Stratton Wm. B., pattern mr., Elk ct (K)
Straube August, printer, rear Hanover bel Duke (K)
Strauss M. J., tailor, 340 N 2d
Strauss Simon, shop, N 4th ab Callowhill
Strawbridge Ann, gentw., Melon ab 10th
STRAWBRIDGE & BORDEN, dry goods, 43 High
Strawbridge George, mer., 43 High, h 25 N Sch 8th
Strawn Daniel, livery stable, 109 Callowhill, h 145 Sp Garden
Strawn J. J., M. D., 145 Sp Garden
Strecker Ferdinand H., marble carver, R road bel Sp Garden, h Buttonwood bel 13th
Strecker Fred., tailor, rear 83 Brown
Streeper David, plasterer, 8 Chatham
Streeper George, blacksm., Berk's ct
Streeper John jr., carp., 526 N 5th
Streeper John K., whipmr., Davis' ct
Streeper Jos., bootmr., Beaver and Charlotte
Streeper Mary, Streeper's ct
Streeper Mary, shop, 196 S 3d
Streeper Nicholas, oyster house, F road bel Master
Streeper O. G., shop, G T road and Rose
Streeper Wm., ladies' shoemr., Marble pl
Streeper Wm., flour inspector, Davis' ct
Street Anderson, oysterman, Marriott ab 4th
Street Catharine, 4th ab Christian
Street Emanuel, bricklr., 283 N 7th
Street F. R., painter, 1 Bank al, h 102 German
Street George, boots and shoes, Shackamaxon and Queen
Street Isabella, shop, 10 Cresson's al
Street James, weaver, Perry ab Phoenix
Street John, books and stationery, 456 N 2d
Street John F., minister, 127 O Y road
Street & M'Nichol, painters, 1 and 2 Bank al
Street Rachel, 7th ab Coates
Street Robert, port. and historical painter, 486 Coates
Street Thomas, blacksmith, 91 New Market
Street Thomas, bootmr., 108 N 2d
Street W. P., mer., N E Water and High, h 119 Vine
Streeton Friend J., carp., Wesley ab 3d
Strehle H., dressmr., 13 Laurel (C)

Strickland John, lab., Sassafras ab Sch 3d
Strickland Levi, acct., Sch 3d ab Callowhill
Strickland Marg., Sassafras ab Sch 3d
Strickland Simeon, gent., Powell & Ann (F V)
Strickland Thomas, seaman, 15 New Market
Strickland Thos., gardener, Sassafras ab Sch 3d
Strickler Jacob, shipsm., Allen ab Shackamaxon
Strien Catharine, 496 S 2d
Strien Michael, carter, Wesley ab 3d
Strien Wm., contractor, Wesley ab 3d
Strigel John, tailor, 41 Green
Strike Chas., lab., 351 E Lombard
Strike Saml., weigher, Claskey's ct
Strine Chas., segar store, 24 Hurst st
String David A., ship master, Beach bel Maiden
String Joseph, corder, Shippen st whf, h 517 S Front
String Peter, waterman, 10 York ct
String Saml., waterm., Vienna bel Franklin (K)
Stringer Jacob, tavern, Fairview and Sch 8th
Stringer John, brushmr., rear 317 N 3d
Stringer J. F., bootmr., Parrish bel 10th
Stringfield John, plasterer, Lewis ab Poplar
Stringfield Samuel, plasterer, Lewis ab Poplar
Strobel George Rev., 116 S 4th
Stroble C., carter, Conrad's ct (N I.)
Strock Daniel, combmr., Elizabeth ab Franklin
Strock Ephraim, bootmr., 3 Jackson
Strock Jas. T., brushmr., Elizabeth ab Franklin
Strock John, carp. weav., Crown ab Duke (K)
Strock Jos., lab., Palmer ab Duke (K)
Strock Joseph, salesman, New Crown
Strock Louisa, gardener, Palmer ab Franklin
Strockbine Geo., waterman, Brook ab Coates
Strockbine Henry, cordw., Weeks' ct
Strode A. J. Mrs., milliner, O Y road ab Callowhill
Strodeck Henry, confect., 127 Sassafras
Stroh Christian F., wool dealer, Front bel Otter (K)
Strong Frances, gentw., 9 Washington sq
Strong George, varieties, 16 S 2d
Strong Nathan, atty. and coun., 141 Walnut
Strong Saml., cabinetmr., 387 S Front
Strong S. E., gentw., 36 N 10th
Strosser John, machinist, Grier's ct
Stroub Richard, hat dyer, Clinton bel Poplar
Stroud Edward, carp., 27 Elfreth's al
Stroud George M., atty. and coun., 5th and Library, h R road n College
Stroud James, merchant, 47 S Water, h 172 N Front
Stroud Jane, Ann and Sch 6th
Stroud John, painter, Amber ab Phœnix (K)
Stroud Tacy Ann Mrs., 491 Mulberry
Stroud Thos., lock tender, Fairmount
Stroud Wm., lab., 4 Sailor's ct
Stroud Wm., boot fitter, 4 Mary's ct
Stroup Abraham, shoemr., Clay av (K)
Stroup George, tailor, 4 N Water, h 11 Morgan
Stroup George, cordw., Fraley's al (K)
Stroup Jas. H., mer., 12 N whfs
Stroup John, mer., 12 N whfs
Stroup Margaret, 8 Palmyra sq
Stroup Samuel, shoemr., 6 Vaux's ct

43

Stroup Wm. J., mer., 12 N whfs. & 21 N Water, h 8 Palmyra sq
Strouse Jacob, lab., Duke ab Cherry (K)
Strouse Lewis, pedler, 72 Apple
Strouse Mary, 3 Poplar ct
Strowhouer John, cordw., 83 Apple
Strunk George, lab., Fraley's al (K)
Strunk George, lab., Poplar bel 8th
Strunk George, carter, Clinton bel Poplar
Strunk John, lab., 22 Maiden (K)
Strunk Wm., lab., Allen ab F road (K)
Struthers Alex., watchman, George E Sch 6th
Struthers John, marble mason, 360 High, h 21 S Penn sq
STRUTHERS JOHN & SON, marble masons, 360 High
Struthers Wm., marble mason, 360 High, h 3 S 11th
Stryker John B., dry goods, 12 Bank
Stryker John P., cabinetmr., N E M road and Federal
Stuard Henry D., undertaker, 113 W High
Stuard Margaret A., Jones n Sch 4th
Stuard Wm., cabinetmr., 366 Coates
Stuart Albert F., engraver, 20 S 6th
Stuart & Brothers, importers, 6 & 8 Church al
Stuart Charles, carpetings, 203 S 2d, h Quince and Lombard
Stuart Charles, cordw., Juniper ab Cherry
Stuart George, dentist, 467 Chestnut
Stuart George H., importer, 6 and 8 Church al, h Locust W of Broad
Stuart Hugh, cabinetmr., 34 N 12th
Stuart Isabella, dry goods, 85 Shippen
Stuart James, gent., 59 Lombard
Stuart James, watchmr., 231 High, h 41 Wood
Stuart James, acct., 361 S 3d
Stuart John, cordw., Say ab Sch 8th
Stuart Robert, oak cooper, Melon and 13th
Stuart Thos., lab., 3 Elmslie's al
Stuart Wm. P., weaver, Front ab Master
Stubbelfine Jas., pedler, Fraley's ct (K)
Stubbs Charles, sea capt., 15 Beck pl
Stucke J., cordw., 313 N 3d
Stuckert Catharine, 155 S 10th
Stuckert David, 304 N 3d
Stuckert Geo. T., 165 Locust
Stuebgen Henry G., fancy goods, 301 Mulberry
Stugert Veldine, tailor, 354 N Front
Stukey John M., 346 S 5th
Stull Adam, vict., 159 Buttonwood
Stull George W., provisions, Poplar and Alder
Stull Henry, instrument mr., 2 Pennsylvania av
Stull John, 13 Franklin
Stull John, jr., Willow bel Garden
Stull Peter, shipwrt., rear Beach ab Hanover (K)
Stull Saml., engraver, 75 Dock
Stull Wm., musician, Westford av
Stulz Rheinard, lab., rear 40 Charlotte
Stump John F., weigh master, 30 S whfs, h 104 S 12th
STURDIVANT JOHN, Congress Hall, 57 S 3d and 83 Chestnut
Sturdivant Joseph, seaman, 28 Almond st
Sturgeon & Hunter, dry goods, 193 High

Sturgeon Jane, weaver, 2d and Phœnix (K)
Sturgeon Richard, mer., 193 High, h 186 S 9th
Sturgeon Wm., lab., Willow W Sch 3d
Sturges Geo., clerk, 2 Rittenhouse
Sturges John, lab., Beach ab Poplar (K)
Sturges Lemuel, cordw., rear 143 Franklin
Sturges Stephen, acct., 218 S 8th
Sturges Thomas, acct., 241 S 9th
Sturges Thomas T., cordw., 9 Turner
Sturgeus Sarah, Pearl bel Sch 7th
Sturgis John, carp., Chestnut (W P)
Sturgis Joshua C., tavern, 87 Washington av
Sturtevant Lewis, mer., 21 Mer. Exc., h 9th n Pine
Stutz Henry, blacksm., Benfer's ct (K)
Stutzenburg Geo., brickmr., Pine ab Sch 3d
Styan Thos., tinsm., 43 Apple
Styer Chas., moulder, Carlton bel Sch 2d
Styer Henry, coal mer., Noble ab 9th, h 340 Callowhill
Suber George, lab., Rihl's ct
Suber Jacob, blacksm., St John ab George (K)
Subers Abner, cordw., Fraley's al (K)
Subers Burrows, cop. plate printer, 4th ab Washington
Subers Catharine, rear 2 Heinzel's ct
Subers Robert, carp., Wood bel 13th
Subers Theodore, gunsm., 368 N 4th
Subers T. B., blacksm., Fetter's la, h 304 N 8th
Subers Worthington, tailor, 133 S 10th
Suddards Wm. Rev., 224 Cherry
Sudler Henry, oysterman, 157 Catharine
Sudler Wm., lab., rear Marriott bel 6th
Sugden J., cabinetmr., 122 S 2d
Sugg Wm., ladies' shoes, 34 N 13th
Suker Jacob, fisherman, Dyott's ct (K)
Sulger Isaac, attorney, 161 Mulberry
Sulger Jacob, jr., 218 Mulberry
Sulger James E., painter & glazier, Maria ab 4th
Sulleberger Jane, dressmr., N E 9th & Filbert
Sullender James, hatter, 6 S 6th
Sullender & Paschal, hatters, 6 S 6th
Sullivan Abraham, clothing, 69 S 2d, h 10th bel Lombard
Sullivan Barth., lab., Webb's al
Sullivan Barth., dealer, George ab 10th
Sullivan Danl., cabinetmr., 9 Plum
Sullivan David, S W 3d and German
Sullivan Dennis, lab., 194 N Water
Sullivan Dennis, tavern, 6 Stamper's al
Sullivan Dennis, printer, 9 Pratt's ct
Sullivan Ellen, shop, 8 Lagrange
Sullivan Ezekiel, clothing, 106 Lombard

Sullivan John, lab., 2 Farmer's row
Sullivan John, lab., Bedford ab 12th
Sullivan John, lab., 2 Lagrange
Sullivan John H., grocer, N E 9th & Christian
SULLIVAN JOHN T. S., atty., 128 Walnut
Sullivan Louisa, 6 Cedar row
Sullivan Mary, milliner, 4 N 12th
Sullivan Patrick, 9 Bonsall
Sullivan Thomas, porter, Centre ab 12th
Sullivan Thomas H., painter, 66 Union
Sullivan Timothy, porter, 14 Boyd's av
Sullivan Timothy, lab., 166 N Water
Sully & Earle, artists' gallery, 169 Chestnut
Sully Thomas, artist, 11 S 5th
Sully Thomas, jr., artist, 169 Chestnut
Sulzberger Levi, pedler, 1 Paschal's al
Summerill F., dentist, 303 Sassafras
Summerfield Alex., mach'st., Ashton ab Spruce
Summergilll John, carder, Philip bel Jefferson
Summers Ann, George ab Sch 8th
Summers David, rear 22 Brown
Summers & Elliott, milliners, 18 N 12th
Summers Geo., U S Mint, h Lombard E Sch 6th
Summers Geo., com. mer, 39 Crown
Summers Henry, S W Sch 8th & Vine
Summers Jesse, ropemr., 6th bel G T road
Summers John, trader, 6th bel G T road
Summers John, capt., 11 Beck pl
Summers Philip H., acct., N Market ab Coates
Summers Sarah, tailoress, 93 N Juniper
Summers Samuel, ropemr., G T road ab 5th
Summers Stephen F., trunkmr., 51 S 3d
Summers Thos., currier, 6 Dillwyn's pl
Summers Wm., cordw., Hallowell ab 6th
Summers Wm., tailor, Chestnut bel Sch 3d
Summers Wm., carter, rear Lemon bel 11th
Sunderland Peter, tailor, 12th bel Coates
Sunderland Robt. H., shoemr., High n Sch 7th
Sunderland Thos., huckster, Robert's ct
Super Jane, dry goods, 21 N 9th
Super Wm., P T Bank, h 286 Coates
Suplee Albert H., dry goods, 43 N 8th
Suplee Chas., carp., Parrish ab Sch 8th
Suplee David E., plasterer, 275 Wood
Suplee Elizabeth, Passmore pl
Suplee E. H. carp., S E North, h 37 George
Suplee Jonas, b h., 41 N 8th
Suplee Lydia, b h., 105 Mulberry
Suplee Sarah, dry goods, 41½ N 8th
Suplee Thomas B., mer., 85 High, h 112 Franklin
Supple Elizabeth, 4 Wood bel Sch 6th
Supple Mary, dry goods, 19 N 8th
Supplee Samuel, carp., Citron n Orange

Sutliff George, dyer, 3d ab Franklin (K)
Sutphin Luke V., carp., Queen and Wood
Sutter Charles J., tobacconist, 98 Callowhill
Sutton Bartholomew, brickmr., Crown ab Queen
Sutton Benj., oysterman, 4 Hurst
Sutton Charles, carp., G T road bel Phoenix
Sutton Daniel D., shipwrt., Crown ab Bedford
Sutton Edward, brickmr., rear Hanover above Franklin (K)
Sutton James C., ship carp., 480 N 2d
Sutton James T., Franklin Iron Works, Franklin ab Front, h Marlboro' ab Queen (K)
Sutton John, brickmr., Wood bel Duke (K)
Sutton John, tinsm., 29 Brown
Sutton John J., brushmr., 14 Hamilton pl
Sutton John N., ship carp., 32 Charlotte
Sutton Jonathan, wheelwrt., Mary ab West(K)
Sutton Samuel, refectory, 131 N 4th
Sutton Sarah, rear Hanover ab Franklin (K)
Sutton Thomas, bookseller, 3d and Vine
Sutton Thomas, carp., 185 N 13th
Sutton Wm., M. D., 183 S 7th
Sutzer R. M., dressmr., 218 N 5th
Swagar Jane, gentw., 252 N 7th
Swaim James, M. D., N E 7th and George, h 396 Mulberry
SWAIN, ABELL & SIMMONS, publishers of Public Ledger, S W 3d and Chestnut
Swain Eben, umbrellamr., 20 N 9th
Swain Ely, 184 Carpenter
Swain Jesse, weav., rear Hanover bel Duke(K)
Swain Joel, car, Peach
Swain John L., mer., Spruce n Sch 6th
Swain J. W., umbrella mr., 37 N 3d
Swain Mary, wid., 244 Wood
Swain Moses, blacksm., Walnut W Sch 3d
Swain Robert, chairmr., rear 102 Christian
Swain Robt., ropemr., 24 Clair
Swain Sophia, 514 N 2d bel Beaver (K)
Swain S. C., Mrs., 514 N 2d bel Beaver
Swain Thomas E., dentist, 501 S 5th
Swain Wm. H., tailor, 314 N 2d
Swain W. M., publisher, S W 3d and Chestnut, h Washington and 4th
Swan Alex., printer, 74 Queen
Swan Joseph, carter, 7 Pratt
Swan Robert, stone cutter, 1 Marble place
Swank Ann, rear 13th bel Brown
Swank Matt., machinist, Parrish ab 10th
Swanson Edward, tobacco, M'Duffie n Sch 2d
Swartz Anna, carpet weaver, 66 Noble
Swartz Augustus S., stove store, 101 N 2d
Swartz Catharine, wid. of Daniel, 118 St. John
Swartz Fred., book binder, Cherry n Duke (K)
Swartz George & Son, tailors, 190 N Water
Swartz John, dealer, 508 N 2d (K)
Swartz Joseph, ship joiner, Union bel Franklin (K)
Swartz Joseph, carpet factory, 519 N 3d

Swayne Joel W., Filbert n 13th
Swear Henry, cordw., Steam Mill alley
Sweatman John, cordw., rear 72 Catharine
Sweed John, tobacconist, Willow and 8th
Sweeds Henry, biscuit baker, 157 N Front
Sweeney Ann, P. road ab German
Sweeney Daniel, hatter, Ball bel Cedar, h 90 Cedar
Sweeney Dennis, gent., 127 Shippen
Sweeney Edw., lab., 97 O Y road
Sweeney Edward, lab., Carpenter ab 8th
Sweeney Ellen, store, 396 Front
Sweeney James, lab., 10 Atherton
Sweeney James, lab., Pine ab Willow
Sweeney John, cordw., Phoenix ab Front (K)
Sweeney John, lab., Murray n Sch. 2d
Sweeney John, lab., Pearl ab Sch. 8th
Sweeney John, lab., 20 Boyd's av
Sweeney Joseph, butcher, Washington (W P)
Sweeney Matthew, drayman, 6 John's ct (N L)
Sweeney Miles, hatter, 80 E Lombard
Sweeney N., lab., 9 Swanson
Sweeney Patrick, lab., 9th bel Marriott
Sweeney Peter, lab., 144 S 5th
Sweeney Samuel, printer, 7th n Washington
Sweeney Thomas, grocer, Lombard and Carbon Sch.
Sweeney Wm., printer, Brinton bel 11th
Sweeney Wm., shoemr., Murray n Sch. 3d
Sweeny Alex., dry goods, 299 Walnut
Sweeny Ann, shop, Callowhill n Sch. 3d
Sweeny Ann M'T., teacher, 72 Almond
Sweeny Conrad, cordw., Edward n G T road
Sweeny Daniel, stone mason, Ann n Sch. 3d
SWEENY & DAVIS, eating house, 43 Walnut
Sweeny Dennis, lab., Callowhill ab Sch. 2d
Sweeny George, potter, R. road ab 13th
Sweeny. Geo. F., 43 Walnut
Sweeny Hugh, cabman, Marble ab 10th
Sweeny James, carter, Clare (S)
Sweeny Martha, Dean and Locust
SWEENY MYLES D., tavern, 98 S 2d
Sweeny Paul, lab., 7 Norris' ct
Sweet Hiram, carp., Wood ab 12th, h 16 Montgomery
Sweet Joseph, lab., rear Ontario ab Poplar
Sweet P. F., doctor, 332 N 3d
Sweeten Jesse, cordw., Smith's ct ab 12th
Sweeton Amos, lab., 19 Vernon
Sweeton Joseph H., cordw., 1 Stanley
Sweetser Edward F., mer., 73 S Front
SWEETSER SAMUEL JR., mer. broker, N W Water and Chestnut
Sweetwood J. B., trader, 103 Walnut
Sweigart John, 12 Emlen's ct
Sweiser Peter, lab., West and Palmer (K)
Sweitzer Geo., whipmr., Charlotte ab Thompson
Sweitzer Michael, segarmr., Charlotte ab Brown
Sweney Thos. W., mer., 143 High

Swift Lewis, pianomr., Lybrand ab Race
Swift Mary, Spruce ab Broad
Swift Matilda, wid. of Francis, tavern, 62 Penn
Swift Paul, M. D., 436 Sassafras
Swift R., toys, &c., 312 High, h c 11th and Filbert
Swift Thomas, lab., Filbert bel Sch. 5th
Swift Thos. H., tailor, 8th ab Christian
Swift Wm., mer., tailor, N W 6th and Chestnut
Swift Wm., 75 Locust
Swimley & Bailey, grocers, 13th and Coates
Swindle Elizabeth, Federal ab 4th
Swink John, grocer, Hanover and F road
Swinsberg Geo., lab., Franklin bel Hanover
Swint Charles, ladies' shoemr., 2 Friendship ct
Swire Elias, cordw., 199 Callowhill
Switzer John, lab., 4th bel Master (K)
Swope Benj., turner, 299 S 3d, h 26 Beck (S)
Swope Charles, dry goods and turner, 299 S 3d
Swope David, grocer, 332 High
Swope George, gent., 351 N 6th
Swope Jacob, drayman, Elizabeth ab Poplar
Sword Sarah D., Walnut n Sch. 7th
Swygert John, tailor, Green's ct
Swyler Selina, gent., 28 Green
Syberg Arnold, artist, 83 N 5th
Syers Catharine, 100 Dillwyn
Syfritt Jacob, Pearl ab Sch. 6th
Sykes Anna, b. h., W Cedar n Sch. 2d
Sykes Benjamin, tavern, 84 Sassafras
Sykes Robert W., gent., 334 Chestnut
Sykes Wm., painter, Elmes' ct
Sylvester Everhart, French crimper and tobacconist, 30 Beach (K)
Sylvester Francis, soap boiler, 247 S 6th
Sylvester Frederick, boot crimper, Maiden ab Beach (K)
Sylvester Frederick J., broker, 1 Merchants' Exchange, h Locust W Sch. 6th
Sylvester Samuel, bootmr., 109 N 7th
Symington Alexander, gent., 364 Walnut
Symington Wm., stone mason, 13th bel Cedar
Synnamon James, carp., P. road ab Carpenter
SYZ, IRMINGER & CO., mers., 6 Chestnut
Syz John, mer., 6 Chestnut, h 183 Walnut

———

Taber George, saddler, 18 Decatur, h 118 North 10th
Taber G. H., mer., 55 High, h 317 Sassafras
Taber John C., mer., 55 High, h 147 N 9th
TABER J. C. & G. H. & CO., mers., 55 High
Taber Mary H., milliner, 33 N 10th
Taber Wm. E., mer., 55 High, h 33 N 10th
Tack John, tailor, 172 S 3d
Tack John C., tailor, Twelve foot al
Tack Nicholas, tailor, 45 Pine
Tackman Wm. C., oak cooper, Parrish ab 10th

Tage Charles, tailor, 8 S 3d
Tage Sarah, gents. furnishing store, 98 N 4th
Tage Wm. & Son, tailors, 8 S 3d
Tagert Jos., prest. F & M Bank, h 76 S 6th
Tagg George H., dry goods, S E 10th & Pine
Taggart Benj., lab., Haydock n Canal
Taggart Daniel, lab., Mariner ab 13th
Taggart E. Roner, 142 High
Taggart J. W., gentlemen's furnishing store, 3 N 6th, h 17 Sergeant
Taggart Mary, 28 Rittenhouse
Taggart Michael, lab., Sch 7th ab Locust
Taggart Robert, 181 S 11th
Taggart Wm., weaver, Perry ab Phoenix
Taggert John H., printer, 319 S 6th
Taggert Rose, shop, 4th & Carpenter
Taggert Wm., engineer, Coates ab 11th
Tague Edward, weaver, Carpenter bel 11th
Tague Hugh, ostler, Linden ab Sch 7th
Tague James, carter, Poplar bel Broad
Tague John, weaver, Milton ab 11th
Tague Peter, ostler, Centre ab 12th
Taigue Charles, ostler, Zane bel 8th
Tait Samuel, 211 Pine
Talbert Alfred, bricklayer, Prime ab Front
Talbott James, grocer, S E Prime & 2d
Talley Alexander H., carp., 1 Clinton av
Talley Benjamin, carp., Ulrich's al
Talley Henry, stereotyper, Queen bel Shackamaxon (K)
Talley James, weaver, Perry bel Master (K)
Talley James S., carp., 6 Washington row
Tallman Abbey A., 137 O Y road
Tallman Adam, blacksmith, Federal bel 2d
Tallman Elizabeth, gentw., 25 N 5th
Tallman George, grocer, 52 S whfs, h 262 N Front
Tallman John, hatter, 341 N 4th
Tallman J., ship chandler, 50 S wharves, h 352 S 3d
Talmadge William, cordw., 14 Branner's al
Tams Edwin, mer., 217 High, h 64 N 11th
Tams James, mer., 217 High
Tams James & Co., impor. china & queensware, 217 High
Tams John, mer., 217 High, h 4 N 11th
Tams Samson, mer., 227 High, h Washington sq
Tams Wm., gent., 504 Vine
Tancare Francis, waiter, 128 Cherry
Taney Wm., tavern, 480 Coates
Tanguy John, mer., 369 High
Tanier John, ropemr., 521 S 2d
Tanner Benjamin, gent., 12th & Montgomery
Tanner John, hatter, 11 Pearl
Tanner Robt., grocery, Sch 7th n Rittenhouse
Tanner Wm., cordmr., 523 S 2d
Tapper Charles, calico printer, R road n F M
Tapper Thomas, carp., Palm bel Brown
Tardif Wm., painter, Sanders' ct (K)
TARR A. DE KALB, atty. & coun, 42 S 5th

Tasker Thos. T., iron founder, S E 3d & Walnut, h 23 Wharton ab 2d

Tate Alexander, chair ornamenter and painter, 161 Christian

Tate Arthur, porter, 229 Lombard

Tate Catharine, nurse, 8 Sterling al

Tate James, trunkmr., High W of Sch 5th, h Barker W of Sch 6th

Tate John, Crabb bel Shippen

Tate Thomas, weaver, Lombard n Sch 4th

Tatem Alfred, druggist, S E 11th & Vine

Tatem Allen W., cabinetmr., 83 and h 113 N Front

Tatem Jackson, captain, 214 Pine

Tatem Joseph B., sailmr., Swanson bel Christian, h ᵃ road bel Marion

Tatem R. S. M., 201 S 7th

Tatem Thos. J., chairmr., 81 and h 113 N Front

Tatem Wm. E., plumber, 60 Dock, h 3 Laurel (C)

Tatham Benjamin jr., manuf. 1st whf bel Cedar

TATHAM & BROTHERS, manufacturers of sheet lead and pipes, 1st whf bel Cedar

Tatham George N., 1st whf bel Cedar

Tatham Henry B., 1st wharf bel Cedar, h 196 S 9th

Tatham Robert, blacksmith, Bevan's ct

Tatham Wm. P., 1st whf bel Cedar

Tatlow Edward, clerk, 2d & Master (K)

Tatman James P., 105 High, h 167 N 4th

Tatum Daniel O., mer., 18 N Front

Tatum D. O. & J., com mers., 18 N Front

Tatum E. & A., teachers, Clover ab 12th

Tatum John, mer., 18 N Front

Tatum Josiah, pub. Farmers' Cabinet, 50 N 4th, h 260 Cherry

Taws F., engineer, Rittenhouse ab Sch 5th

Taws Henry, machinist, 1 Gebhard

Taws Lewis, engineer, S W Sch 7th and High, h Cherry ab Sch 7th

Taxis Samuel, framemr., S E Apple & Culvert

Taylor Alex., 474 S Front

Taylor Ann, milliner, 1½ N 10th

Taylor Ann Eliza, 126 S 3d

Taylor Amos, mer., 43 N Water, h 353 Walnut

Taylor Benj., brush finisher, 159 Marshall

Taylor Benjamin, brush maker, 5 N 3d, h 2 Montgomery sq

TAYLOR BENJ. & SON, brush manufs., 5 N 3rd

Taylor Boyd & Co., grocers, 7 and 9 S Water

Taylor Catharine, gentw., 25 Clinton

Taylor Catharine, nurse, 38 Beck (S)

Taylor Charles, 20 Washington sq

Taylor Charles B., waterman, 14 Parham

Taylor Charles H., M D, 436 N 4th

Taylor Charles M., coal mer., Callowhill above 13th, h Sch 7th ab Filbert

Taylor Charlotte, Crown ab Duke (K)

Taylor Crispin, mer., 33 Carter's al, h 24 Madison

Taylor C., 18 Montgomery

Taylor Damon, currier, Garden ab Willow

Taylor Daniel, shoemr., 246 Sassafras

Taylor David B., mer., 7 & 9 S Water, h 25 Spruce

Taylor David B., lumb. mer., Coates st whf, h 489 N 4th

Taylor Eber, watchman, Cherry n Sch 7th

Taylor Edward T., mer., 200 High

Taylor Elisha R., tobacconist, 123 S 6th

Taylor Elizabeth, 7 Gay's ct (N L)

Taylor Elizabeth, G T road ab Otter

Taylor Elizabeth, dressmr., Wood bel Sch 6th

Taylor Ellen, wid. of Geo., Palmer bel Franklin

Taylor Ellen, 87 Tammany

Taylor Ellen, 16 New

Taylor Emeline bel M road

TAYLOR ENOCH, coun. & atty., 135 N 6th

Taylor & Eveland, morocco manufs., S E 3d & Willow

Taylor Felix, lab., Lloyd bel Shippen

Taylor Francis, carp., 7th ab Poplar

Taylor Francis J., oil cloth manuf., G T road op 5th

Taylor Francis J. & Co., oil cloth manufs., G T road opp 5th

Taylor Franklin, atty. & coun., 100 Walnut

Taylor George, shoemr., 21½ Spruce

Taylor George, lab., rear 16 Little Pine

Taylor George, shipping master, 52 Penn

Taylor George, gent., S E Marshall and Buttonwood

Taylor George, cake baker, 9 Bank

Taylor George, 4 Howard's ct

Taylor George, refectory, S W Cedar & S whfs.

TAYLOR GEORGE W., agent Friends' Bible Association, 50 N 4th, h N E Broad and Spruce

Taylor Geo. W., thimble manuf., 94 Chestnut

Taylor Gideon, watchman, Mary bel 2d

Taylor G. E., mer., 129 N 3d, h 76 Franklin bel Buttonwood

Taylor G. W., mer., 168 High, h 123 Pine

Taylor G. W. & L. B., mers., 168 High

Taylor Harriet, dressmr., 53 Coates

Taylor Henry, printer, 121 German

Taylor Henry, carp., 7th ab P road

Taylor H. P. & W. C., fancy soap manufs., Logan ab Wallace

Taylor Isaac, cordw., 124 German

Taylor Isaac, tobacconist, 261 S 6th

Taylor Isaac W., leadworker, Allen ab Hanover (K)

Taylor Israel, coal mer., 501 Callowhill, h Sch 7th ab Filbert

Taylor Jacob, West & Cherry (K)

Taylor Jacob R., druggist, N E Broad & Spruce

Taylor James, carp., G T road and Otter (K)

Taylor James, bird stuffer, 36 N 13th

Taylor James, waiter, 17 Mercer

Taylor James, cordw., c 4th & Carpenter

Taylor James, seaman, 228 E Lombard

Taylor James, tavern, c Penn & Lombard

Taylor James, sea captain, 91 Catharine

Taylor James, painter, 3 Rule's ct

Taylor James, sr., carp., Carpenter ab 4th

Taylor James H., tailor, Willow ab Charles

Taylor James L., grocer, 32 Walnut

Taylor Jane, 38 Chatham
Taylor Jeremiah, saddler, 8 Broad n Chestnut
Taylor Jesse, machinist, 61 G T road (K)
Taylor Jesse W., cabtmr., 8 Noble
Taylor John, lab., Lombard n Sch 5th
Taylor John, gent., 250 N 4th
Taylor John, coal mer. 17 S 6th, h 153 Catharine
Taylor John, trea. dist. K., h Beach ab K Market
Taylor John, machinist, 102 Swanson
Taylor John, stevedore, rear 164 Catharine
Taylor John, starchmr., West bel Cherry (K)
Taylor John, cordw., Paschall's al
Taylor John, millwright, Howard pl
Taylor John, machinist, 26 N 13th
Taylor John, coach painter, Pleasant bel 10th
Taylor John, blacksm., Wharton bel M road
Taylor John, bootmr., 5 Reckless
Taylor John, carder, Front bel Phoenix
Taylor John, Cottage Recess Garden, Callowhill n Sch 3d
Taylor John, b h, 16 N 12th
Taylor John, carp., Beach
Taylor John, paper stain., Carlton ab Sch 2d
Taylor John D., carp., 503 N 4th
Taylor John E., druggist, 157 Poplar
Taylor John E., ship master, 23 Scheetz
Taylor John E., M. D., 157 O Y road
Taylor John G., provisions, 8 S Water, h 388 S 3d
Taylor John H., seaman, 13 John (S)
Taylor John J., lab., Union and West (K)
Taylor John L., gardener, Chancellor below Sch 6th
Taylor John M., mer., 96 High, h 337 Walnut
Taylor John M., vict., 87 M road
Taylor John S., Rev., 40 Almond
Taylor John W., carp., 612 S Front
Taylor & Jones, clothing, 264 High
Taylor Joseph, sailor, 14 Almond
Taylor Joseph, weaver, Harmstead ct
Taylor Joseph, carder, 4th bel Franklin (K)
Taylor Julianna, 38 Swanson
TAYLOR J. & C. M., coal deal., 501 Callowhill
Taylor J. H., com. mers., 102 High
Taylor & Lawrie, silversmiths, 25 Library
Taylor Leah T., wid., Front bel Catharine
Taylor Leonard, shoemr., 16 Plum
Taylor Levi, mer., 7 and 9 S Water, h 188 S Front
Taylor Lewis B., 168 High, h 127 Pine
Taylor Lorenzo D., cordw., 10 Marble pl
Taylor Louisa, 172 N 13th
Taylor Louisa, tailoress, 12 Mary's ct
Taylor L. B., mer., 168 High, h 127 Pine
Taylor L. S., milliner, 521 N 2d
Taylor Margaret, Cedar n 12th
Taylor Maris, carp., Crown n West
Taylor Martha, dressmr., 170 S 3d
Taylor Mary, shop, 455 S 2d
Taylor Mary, dry goods, 95 W Callowhill
Taylor Mary E., b h, 88 N 9th
TAYLOR MORDECAI, atty. and coun: 50 N 7th
Taylor Morris, butcher, rear 196 Prime

Taylor N., cordw., 11 Tammany
TAYLOR N. & G., tin plate and copper, 129 N 3d
TAYLOR & PAULDING, mers., 96 High
Taylor Prudence, 223 Swanson bel Christian
Taylor Ralph, twister, Leopard ab Franklin
Taylor Richard, 111 N 5th
Taylor Richard M., brewer, N E 8th & Vine, h 239 Vine
Taylor Robert, machinist, Wood bel Sch 6th
Taylor Robert, shoemr., 170 Cable lane, h 8th ab Noble
TAYLOR ROBERT, mer., 32 Walnut, h 233 Spruce
Taylor Robert, silversm., 25 Library, h Willow ab 5th
Taylor Robert C., brushmr., 5 N 3d
Taylor R. C., pres. Dauphin & Susq. Coal Co., 48 S 4th, h 100 S 9th
Taylor Samuel, collect., 343 N 3d
Taylor Samuel H., carp., 2 Steward above Catharine
Taylor Slater C., carman, Ann n Sch 3d
Taylor Stacy, carp., 13th ab Willow, h Pleasant bel 13th
Taylor Thos., mer., 248 S Front
Taylor Thos., blacksmith, Concord ab 2d
Taylor Thomas, lab., 83 N Juniper
Taylor Thos. A., mer., 73 High, h 94 New
Taylor Thos. B., acct., N E Broad & Spruce
Taylor Thos. C., coachsm. Crown ab Duke (K)
Taylor Thos. H., 96 S 8th
Taylor Thos. R., paper & rags, 13 Minor, h 373 Pine
Taylor Thos. S., acct., 7 S Penn sq
Taylor T. R. & Co., paper & rags, 13 Minor
Taylor Wm., mariner, Christian & Front
Taylor William, b h, 272 S Front
Taylor William, brass finisher, 94 Catharine
Taylor Wm., trunkmr., 50 Laurel
Taylor Wm., locksm., rear 64 Catharine
Taylor Wm., gent, 161 N 6th
Taylor Wm., bricklr., Catharine bel 10th
Taylor Wm., bonnet presser, 16 Lagrange pi
Taylor Wm., plumber, 28 Parham
Taylor Wm., mer., 27 & 29 S Water, h 265 S 3d bel Shippen
Taylor Wm., hatter, 48 Sassafras
Taylor Wm. B., tailor, 331 S 3d
Taylor Wm. C., fancy soap manuf., 6 Marshall row
Taylor Wm. & Co. previsions, 27 & 29 S Water
Taylor Wm. H., b h, 208 High
Taylor Wm. M., chairmr., 460 N 3d
Taylor Wm. P., carp., 8 Linden (S G)
Taylor Willis, tailor, S E 2d & Spruce, h 358 S 3d
Taylor Wilson, chemist, Duke n Hanover (K)
Taylor Zachariah, 254 Filbert
Tea George, carp., Olive n 13th
Tea Richard, carp., h 26 Magnolia
Teal David, capt., 58 Christian
Teal George, blacksm., Robinson's ct (S G)

Teal Joseph, seaman, 88 S Front
Teal Levi, mariner, China ab Front
Teal Peter, machinist, Sch 7th bel Vine
Teale Theodore D., pump and blockmaker, 27 Reckless
Teamer Andrew, ship carp., Marlborough ab Bedford
Teamer Richard, boat builder, Prime bel 3d
Teamer Wm., patternmr., Marlborough above Bedford (K)
Teany Wm., stone mason, Ogden bel 10th.
Teany Wm., carp., 13th ab Washington
Tear Philip, custom h. off., 29 Cox's al
Teeple John, shoemr., rear 161 Christian
Tees Anna Maria, Helmuth n Pine
Tees Chas., shipcarp., Cherry ab Duke (K)
Tees Jacob, shipwr., Beach bel Hanover (K)
Tees John, ship carp., Beach ab Palmer (K)
Tees Lewis, ship carp., Allen ab Marlboro' (K)
Tees Peter, ship carp., Crown bel Franklin (K)
Tees Samuel, ship carp., Queen below Hanover (K)
Tees Wm. ship carp. Franklin ab Hanover (K)
Teese George, saddler, 4 S 4th, h 108 Franklin
Teese Jane, 161 N Front
Teese Lewis, cabman, Sch 7th ab Chestnut
Teese Wm., weaver, M'Mackin's ct
Teesseire E. C., 294 Chestnut
Teill Geo., mer., 1½ N 3d, h Ogden bel 11th
Telford Ann, 29 Beaver (K)
Telford R. M., milliner, 497 N 2d
Tempelton James, tailor, Centre ab 12th
Tempest Robert, jeweller, 87 S 2d, h 22 Lombard
Temple, Barker & Evans, dry goods, 161 High
Temple James, bootmr., Shippen ab 7th
Temple Joseph E., mer., 161 High
Temple Thomas, collector, 355 Cherry
Templin Hannah, St. John ab Poplar
Tenbrink Elizabeth, 1 Oliver pl
Tenbrook Philip H., mer., 17 S Water, h 234 N 6th
Tenbrook Wm. E., mer, 17 S Water, h Sch 5th & Barker
TENER HUGH W., atty., 4 George
Tener Robert jr., salesman, 175 High
Ten Eyck Peter, 17 Catharine
Tennant James, mer., 93 High, h N W 13th & Mulberry
Tennant Marg., 4 Clymer
Tennent Henry, tin worker, 20 S 4th, house 8 German
Tennent John, agent Penn. Canal Co., 110 S 3d
Tennent Susan, 11 Jacoby
Tenny John, boatbuilder, Vine ab Nixon
Terrill John, machinist, Maiden bel Front
Terry Ann, nurse, 7 Short ct
Terry Asaph, dry goods, Summer ab Sch 8th
Terry David, watchman, 185 O Y road
Terry Harvey, dry goods, 55 N 2d
Terry Wm., house carp., School n Franklin (K)
Test Alex., printer, Queen ab Sarah (K)
Test Clayton, clerk, Sch 2d ab Wood
Test C. H., brushmr., Beach ab Maiden (K)
Test John M., brushmr., 22 Maiden (K)

Test Middleton, carver and gilder, Beach near Maiden (K)
Test R. W., druggist, 169 N 2d
Test Sarah, shoe binder, 2 Freed's av
TETE FRANCIS, mer., 28 Walnut, h 208 Spruce
Teuful Christian, printer, 28 Franklin pl
Tevis Benj. Mrs., gentw., 384 Walnut
Tevis Joshua, mer., 10 Bank, h 10 W Walnut
Tevis, Scott & Tevis, mers., 10 Bank
Tewksbury Elizabeth, wid. of Jes. 5 Wharton
Thacher Arthur, mer., 177½ High, h 42 Palmyra row
THACHER CHAS. F., shoes, 38 N 3d, h Callowhill ab 11th
Thacher Geo., bricklayer, Apple bel Franklin
Thacher Oliver N., hatter, 2½ N 8th
Thackara Benj., pianomr., 231 Christian
Thackara Benj., clerk, 176 Chestnut
Thackara Francis, wid. of Wm., b h, 22 S 6th
Thackara Marg., gentw., 3 road bel Prime
Thackara Marmaduke, drayman, Bedford and Elm (K)
Thackara Samuel, plasterer, 7 Sansom
Thackara Saml. W., conveyancer, 114 S 3d
THACKARA S. W & YARDLEY J. S., conveyancers, 114 S 3d
Thackray Isaac, 211 S 3d
Thackray Mark, tailor, 211 S 3d
Thackston C. A., tobacco mer. & importer of cigars, 15 S 4th
Thalabas John, ladies' shoemr., 1 Sheldon row
Thatcher Arthur, clerk, 11th bel Callowhill
Thatcher C., hatter, 345 Callowhill
Thatcher G. W., blacksm., Ann n Sch 3d
Thatcher Joseph, carp., Powell (F V)
Thatcher S. D., mer., 3 Church al
Thatcher Thos., lab., rear 482 N 3d
Thaw Chas., pen maker, Cantrell's ct
Thaw Wm., carp., Ogden ab 10th
Thaw Wm., cashier Mech. Bk., h 23 S Sch 7th
Thawvarth Samuel, cordw., 78½ Green
THAYER & COWPERTHWAITE, boots & shoes, 139½ High
Thayer Edward N., comedian, 372 Cedar
Thayer J., shoemr., 247 N 3d
Thayer Martin, mer., 48 S 4th, h 23 Girard
Thayer M. R., atty & coun., 48 S 4th
Thayer Z., boots and shoes, 139½ High, h 37 Crown
Theilacker G., baker, P road op German
Theobald A., shoemr., 33 Sassafras
Theveny Lewis, cabinetmr., George bel 5th
Thibault Francis, jeweller, 5 Bank al, h 61 Pine
Thibault Fredk., broker, 87 Swanson
Thibault Mary, dressmr., 3 Mayland
Thiele Edward, tailor, 550 N 2d
Thiell Maria, dry goods, 127 Locust
Thieson Chas. F., messenger, 9 M road
Thirion Lewis, jeweller, 8 Franklin pl
Thisselwood E., lab., Reckless ct
Thoborn Hannah T., b h, 23½ S 2d
Thody Elizabeth, 8 Tammany ct
Thom Geo., Shackamaxon n Bedford (K)
Thom Wm., millwt., Wood ab 13th

Thomman Samuel, gas fitter, Parrish ab 13th
Thomas Alice, dry goods, 10th ab Parrish
Thomas Amos. lab., 19 Watson's al
Thomas Ann, Culvert bel 5th
Thomas Ann, Filbert & Sch 7th
Thomas Asa, shoe store, 123 N 2d
Thomas Asy, drayman, 5th and Franklin
Thomas Aymer, tailor, 46 Walnut
Thomas Benj., waiter, 32 Burd's ct
Thomas Benj., silver pl., Duke ab Palmer (K)
Thomas Benj. F., lab., Jackson (S G)
Thomas B., ropemr., Spruce st whf., h Johnson's la bel 5th
Thomas Catharine, 8th bel Catharine
Thomas Cecilia, huckster, Noble bel 3d
Thomas Charles, lab., Poplar st
Thomas Charles, clerk Bank U. S., h 101 N 5th
Thomas Charles, machinist, N W cor. 3d and Washington
Thomas Charles, brewer, 6 City row
Thomas Charles J., brewer, 10th n George, h 61 City row
THOMAS, COWPERTHWAIT & CO., booksellers, 253 High
Thomas Daniel, cab mr., 3 R road
Thomas Daniel J., mer., 26 S 4th
Thomas Daniel J., mer., 149 Marshall
Thomas David, gent., 338 N 5th
Thomas David, lab., Lloyd bel Shippen
Thomas David B., sawyer, Parrish bel Broad
Thomas David B., druggist, 81 W Callowhill
Thomas Edward, waterman, Walter's ct
Thomas Edward H., tinsm., Fraley's ct
Thomas Eli H., tobacconist, G T road below St. John
Thomas Elizabeth, shop, 7 Prune
Thomas Elizabeth, 32 Blackberry al
Thomas Evan, blacksm., Hope bel Phœnix (K)
THOMAS & EVANS, china ware, 26 S 4th
Thomas Ezekiel, stove moulder, 240 N 13th
Thomas F. C., druggist, 6th and Sp Garden
Thomas F. W., printer, 105 Callowhill
Thomas George, 195 Mulberry
Thomas George, engraver, 20 S 4th
Thomas Geo. S., cedar cooper, Orchard above Rawle
Thomas & Glause, carp., Vine bel 13th
Thomas Harriet, vest mr., 278 Green st
Thomas Henrietta, sempstress, rear 137 Green
Thomas Henry Rev., Carpenter ab 12th
Thomas Henry, lab., St John bel G T road
Thomas Henry, milliner, 105 Cedar
Thomas Jacob, gent., 25 S 10th
Thomas Jacob, carp., 11th bel Cedar
Thomas Jacob M., merchant, 10 N Front, h 362 Mulberry
Thomas Jacob V., 30 Logan's sq
Thomas James, pawnbroker, S W 3d & Cedar
Thomas James, lagger, 277 N Front

Thomas Jesse, mer., 402 Vine
Thomas Joel, lace imp., 24 Pratt
Thomas John, mer., 10 N Front, h 312 N 6th
Thomas John, confect., 19 Barron
Thomas John, plasterer, Lemon bel 11th
Thomas John, wheelwright, Sch 8th ab Sassafras
Thomas John Dover, auct., 93 Walnut, h Sch 8th bel Spruce
Thomas John D., M. D., 6th and Spring Garden
Thomas John G., M. D., 518 Vine
Thomas John G., dry goods, 120 High
Thomas John M., druggist and apothecary, S W cor. Cedar and 7th
Thomas John P., hair dresser, 149 Chestnut, h 13 Laurel
Thomas John W., dry goods, 265 N 2d
Thomas Jonathan, bricklayer, 45 Duke
Thomas Jonathan, exchage broker, 30 Federl
Thomas Jonathan, morocco fin., rear 493 N 3d
Thomas Joseph, tailor, Elizabeth ab Poplar
Thomas Joseph, Marshall ab Brown
Thomas Joseph, lab., Apple bel George
Thomas Joseph, miller, 236 N 2d
Thomas Joseph C., shoemr., 78 Catharine
Thomas Joseph M., carp., 7th ab Poplar
Thomas Joseph M., mer., 253 High, h Penn sq
THOMAS JOSEPH T., attorney and coun., 66 S 6th
Thomas Josiah, boot and shoemr., 44 George (S)
Thomas Julia, washer, 39 Currant al
Thomas J. M., 84 Noble
Thomas Lavinia, washer, 322 Cedar
Thomas Levi, lab., 7 Middle al
Thomas Lewis, baker, 8 Madison
Thomas Lewis B., collector, York pl
Thomas Margaret, Wood ab R road
Thomas Margaret Ann, 5 M'Leod pl
Thomas Martin, turner, 382 High, h 8 Madison
THOMAS & MARTIN, com. mers., 10 N Front
Thomas Mary, Brown and Apple
Thomas Mary, dressmr., 3 N Sch 7th
Thomas Mary, milliner, 159½ S 2d
Thomas Mary Ann, trimmings, 151 N 11th
Thomas Mary A., millinger, 165 S 2d
Thomas Michael, barber, 1 S Front
Thomas & Mink, shoe manuf., 511 High
Thomas Morgan, barber, Broad above Wood, h Pearl bel Broad
Thomas Morgan J., teacher, 13 Union sq
Thomas Moses, auctioneer, 93 Walnut, h Sch 7th ab Spruce
THOMAS MOSES & SON, auctioneers, 93 Walnut
Thomas N. D., cordw., 18 Mary (S)
Thomas Paul, cabinetmr., P road bel Cedar
Thomas Phebe, gentw., Filbert ab Broad
Thomas Philip, porter, 14 Burd's ct
Thomas Philip, barber, 13 Laurel

homas Robert, ropemr., 480 S 4th
HOMAS R. S., tailor, 19 S 5th, h 303 Mulberry
homas Samuel, carp., 5 Shepherd's al
homas Samuel S., pawn broker, 5th & Cedar
homas Seth, blacksm., 80½ Locust
homas Simon, barber, 3 N 10th
homas Stephen N., machinist, Allen's ct
homas Susan, widow of William, Orchard
homas Tarleton, grocer, N W 10th & Ogden
homas Thomas, tavern, 208 S 5th
HOMAS & TWITCHELL, brewers, 10th & George
homas William, barber, 61 S 8th
homas William, waiter, 125 N 2d
homas Wm., lab., Milton n 11th
homas Wm., cedar cooper, Stout's al
homas Wm., mer., 49 S whfs., h 242 N 5th
homas Wm., 282 Coates
homas Wm., lab., F road ab Palmer
homas Wm. A., grocer, High & Howard
homas Wm. B., miller, N W 13th and James, h Buttonwood bel 13th
homas Wm. R., undertaker, St John ab Beaver (K)
homas Wm. R., carp., 1 York pl
homas Wm. S., ship joiner, 75 Plum
homas Wm. S., hatter, Hanover ab Bedford(K)
homas Wm. S., barber, Baker ab 7th
homas W. W., tailor, 49 O Y road
homason John, tinman, 8 S 2d, h 67 N 6th
homason Wm. J., tinsmith, 8 S 2d, h 11 New
homen A., baker, 277 S 4th
hommason Augustus A., machinist, Steward ab Christian
hommason John, grocer, Steward ab Christian
hompson Aaron, atty. & coun., 103 Walnut
hompson Abigail, 159 N Front
hompson Alexander, chairmr., 88 S 5th
hompson Alex., weaver, Sassafras n Sch 7th
hompson Alex., lab., Rye ab Wharton
homyson Alex., clerk, 25 P road
hompson Alex. M., shoemr., 1 Monroe's ct
hompson Ambrose, carp., Poplar ab 13th
hompson Ambrose W., stationer, 30 N 4th, h 19 Girard
hompson Amelia, Walnut bel Sch 8th
hompson Andrew, capt., 8 Beck pl
hompson Ann, 59 Queen
hompson Ann, wid. of Samuel, Melon below R road
hompson Ann M., 14 Dean
hompson Arable, lab., rear 27 High
hompson Benj., lab., Carleton ab Sch 3d
hompson Benj., tailor, Carpenter ab 6th

Thompson Daniel, blacksm., 34½ Elfreth's al, h 3 James
Thompson David, salesman, 7 Greswald al
Thompson David, carp., Carleton bel Sch 5th
Thompson David, hatter, 6 Fetter la
Thompson David, bootmr., 3d ab Marriott
Thompson David E., printer, S W 7th & High
Thompson Deborah, b. h., 521 Coates
Thompson Delia, Sassafras and Juniper
Thompson Edward, lab., rear 83 New Market
Thompson Edward, lab., 7th and Willow
Thompson Edward B., gent., Callowhill above Broad
Thompson Eliza, 2 Pearl ab 12th
Thompson Eliza, porter house, 91 Shippen
Thompson Elizabeth, 19 Willow st
Thompson Elizabeth, 92 Mulberry
Thompson Enoch, blacksm., Green ab 9th
Thompson Enos, shoemr., 16 Burd's ct
Thompson Ephraim B., cordw., 12 Bank, house Washington ab 4th
THOMPSON GEORGE, manuf., 20 Walnut, h 219 Walnut
Thompson George, porter, 4 Eagle ct
Thompson George, mariner, 32 Mead
Thompson George, cordw., Willow bel 4th
Thompson George C., gent., 4th above Washington
Thompson George S., 474 Callowhill
Thompson Gilbert, Bucks Co. hotel, 397 N 2d
Thompson Hannah, 28 Mead
Thompson Harman, ship carp., Beach ab Palmer (K)
Thompson Harman, carp., 29 Apple
Thompson Henry, watchmr., Sch 3d and Cedar
Thompson Henry, feed, 278 Cedar
Thompson Hugh, miller, 250 St. John
Thompson Isaac, coachmr., Ruddach's ct
Thompson Isaac, blacksm., Beach ab Maiden(K)
Thompson Isaac, mer., h 113 Mulberry
Thompson Isaac, baker, N W 11th and Vine
Thompson Isaac, confectioner, 366 High
Thompson Isaac, jr., dry goods, 14 Bank
Thompson Isaac R., portrait paint., Beaver above 2d (K)
Thompson Isaiah, porter, 15 Parker st
Thompson I. H., M. D., 113 Mulberry
Thompson James, waiter, rear 27 High
Thompson James, ropemr., rear Cherry above Queen (K)
Thompson James, brushmr., 379 N 2d, h Noble bel 8th
Thompson James, enginemr., Duke below Palmer (K)
Thompson James, grocer, 643 N 2d

THOMPSON JOHN, corder, Dock st wharf, h 20 Catharine

THOMPSON JOHN, alderman, 401 High

Thompson John, N W Lynn & Nixon (F M)

Thompson John, clerk Qr. Ses. 13 St. House, h 274 S 4th

Thompson John, turner, Green n Pine, h 258 Catharine

Thompson John, machinist, Littleboy's ct

Thompson John, blacksmith, rear 6 Carpenter

Thompson John, shoemr., Sch 4th ab Cedar

Thompson John, weaver, Lemon st

Thompson John, dentist, Mifflin n 13th

Thompson John F., clerk, 91 Gaskill

Thompson John G., atty. and coun., 55 S 5th

Thompson John H., stove finisher & sheet iron worker, 158 Christian

Thompson John H., carp., Dorothy n Sch 4th

Thompson John J., 219 Walnut

Thompson John L., plasterer, rear Irvine st

Thompson John P. Rev., Bledisloe pl

Thompson John R., bar tender, Beaver above 2d (K)

Thompson John R., pilot, Washington ab Noble

Thompson John W., barber, 104 Sassafras, h N E 8th & Bedford

Thompson Jonah, mer., 18½ Walnut

Thompson Jonathan, lab., 14 Burd's ct

Thompson Joseph, lab., Stevenson's ct

Thompson Joseph, paper hanger, 151 S 3d

Thompson Joseph, plasterer, Juniper bel Pine

Thompson Joseph, huckster, 18 Stamper's al

Thompson Joseph, lab., 3 Gray's al

Thompson Joseph, lab , Liberty

Thompson Joseph, cordw., 4th & George

Thompson Jos. H., mer., 60 High, h 148 N 10th

Thompson Jos. H., currier, Willow ab 2d, h 200 Callowhill

Thompson Jos. W., carp., 13th bel Melon .

Thompson Josiah B., mer., 14 Commerce, h 474 Callowhill

Thompson Karan H., 5th bel George (N L)

Thompson Lewis, 68 Dock & 11th & R road, h 11th ab Washington

Thompson Lewis, printer, 11 Carter's al., h 31 N 5th

Thompson Lydia, rear of 28 St John

Thompson Lydia P., 221 Walnut

Thompson Margaret, cloak and dressmr., Broad ab Shippen

Thompson Margt., gentw., 142 S Juniper

Thompson Mark, carp., Scott's ct (N L)

Thompson Martha, 186 S Front

Thompson Mary, Little Pine

Thompson Mary, shop, Christian n 9th

Thompson Mary, tavern, N W Brown and 6th

Thompson Mary Ann, gentw., 119 N 11th

Thompson Matthew, pavier, 10th & Catharine

Thompson Matthew, lab., Richard n Sch 6th

Thompson Matthew, stone mas., Jackson (S G)

Thompson Maxwell, carver, 332 S Front

Thompson M. La Rue P. Rev., S E Sch 6th and Mulberry

Thompson Mrs., hat mr., High and Sch Front

Thompson N. B., mer., 47 N Water, h 167 S 5th

Thompson Oscar, clerk, Washington ab 3d

Thompson Oswald, atty and coun., 35 S 5th, h 218 Pine

Thompson Peter, mariner, Church bel Christian

Thompson Peter, silversm., 142 N 8th

Thompson Philip, waiter, 3 Twelve Foot al

Thompson Phoebe, b. h., 16 Branch

Thompson Rachel, 3 Gray's al

Thompson Rachel, teacher, Sch 7th n Vine

Thompson Robert, stone cut., Pearl ab 12th

Thompson Robt., lab., Lombard & Sch Front

Thompson Robt., blindmr., 330 S 2d

Thompson Robt., paver, 137 S 11th

Thompson Robt., whf. build., 8th bel Christian

Thompson Robt., lab., Carlton bel Sch 7th

Thompson Robt., lab., Rugan ab Callowhill

Thompson Robt., baker, 225 S 5th

Thompson Robt., trunkmr., St Joseph's av

Thompson R., mer., 74 S Front, h 95 S 4th

Thompson Saml., lab., Lombard n Sch 7th

Thompson Sarah, Poplar and Mechanic

Thompson Sarah, 8 Wells' row

Thompson Sarah, West Philadelphia

Thompson Sarah L., 12 Montgomery sq

Thompson Solomon, lab., Carpenter ab 13th

Thompson S. C., cordw., 59 S 4th

Thompson Thomas, grocer, Sch 6th & Wood

Thompson Thomas, lab., Richard

Thompson Thos., sea capt., Marlboro' ab Franklin (K)

Thompson Thos., 11th bel Buttonwood

Thompson Thos. R., painter, F road bel Frankl.

THOMPSON T. & L., cabinet findings, mahogany, 68 Dock, & marble steam saw-mill, 11 R road

Thompson Viney, washer, Steel's ct

Thompson & West, blacksm., 34½ Elfreth's al

Thompson Wm., shoemr., Morris bel Fitzwater

Thompson Wm., stone cut., 5 Lisle

Thompson Wm., cordw., 115 Buttonwood

Thompson Wm., waiter, Centre n 13th

Thompson Wm., carp., Sch 6th ab Mulberry

Thompson Wm., porter, 23 Hurst

Thompson Wm., porter Bank U S, h 158 Christian

Thompson Wm., plasterer, Winter

Thompson Wm., carter, Jones n Sch 5th

Thompson Wm., grocer, Wiley's ct

Thompson Wm., furniture, G T road

Thompson Wm., 32 Logan's sq

Thompson Wm. D., mer., 40 High, h 32 Logan sq

Thompson Wm. E., mer., 7 Commerce

Thompson Wm. H., clerk, 75 Catharine

Thompson W. & Son, grocers, 264 S 2d

Thompson W. R., mer., 74 & 76 S Front, h 268 Spruce

THOMPSON W. R. & Co., grocers, 74 and 76 S Front

Thomson Edward, gent., 338 N 6th

Thomson Eliza, widow, 14 Dean

Thomson George, cooper, 65 S Water

Thomson George, carp., 76 George

Thomson James C., tavern, S W 10th & Filbert

Thomson John, cooper, 25 Penn, h N E Front and Lombard

Thomson Peter, bookseller, N W 6th & Mul. berry, h 2 Thompson's ct
Thomson Peter, druggist, 40 Sassafras
Thomson Wm., gent., 80 S 11th
Thomson Wm. W., cooper, 65 S Water, h 176 S Front
Thomson Wm. W. & Geo., coopers, 65 S Water
Thorman Charles C., tailor, 647 N 3d
Thorn Ann, b. h., 24 New Market
Thorn & Brothers, painters, 5½ N 8th
Thorn Catharine, wid. of John, 502 N 5th
Thorn Catharine, widow of George, 5th below George (N L)
Thorn Daniel, carp., 133 S 11th
Thorn David, bricklayer, Garden bel Willow
Thorn David C., bricklr., Juniper ab Pine
Thorn Enoch, carp., 338 Pine
Thorn Enoch, jr., carp, 17 Mifflin
Thorn George W., brickmr., 502 N 5th
Thorn Joel T., painter, 28 N 12th, h Vine ab 12th
Thorn John, ropemr., R road ab Wallace
Thorn Lewis, cabinetmr., 8 Paschal's al
Thorn N., cabinetmr., Brown's ct (N L)
Thorn Wm., agent, 12 Christian
Thorn Wm. F., bricklr., 336 Pine
Thorne C. H., painter and glazier, 74 and h 123 Callowhill
Thorne Franklin M., mer., 10 High
Thorne Hannah, b. h., 197 Cherry
Thorne Rich., turner, 267 N 5th, h 30 Chatham
Thorne Thomas, tailor, 7 S 9th
Thorne Wm., morocco dr., Parrish bel 6th
Thorne Wm., ladies' shoes, 138 Mulberry
Thornhill Patrick, 200 Queen
Thornley Anthony, coff. roast., Newton
Thornley Edwin, plumber, Hallowell's ct
THORNLEY JESSE O., coffee roaster, M road bel Federal
THORNLEY JOHN, India rubber goods, 135 & h 110 Chestnut
Thornley Thomas, carter, Locust n Sch 3d
Thornley Wm., gardener, Square bel Corn
Thornley Wm., eating house, 17 Jones al
Thornley Wm., coffee roaster, Bevan's ct
Thornton Daniel, agent, 8 N 8th
Thornton Esther, 46 Dock
Thornton Henry, soap manuf., Horstman's ct
Thornton James, machinist, Bedford n Elm (K)
Thornton John, salesman, 16 Union (S)
Thornton John, silver plater, 9th ab Carpenter
Thornton Lewis M., carp., Hughes' ct
Thornton Martha M., stockmr., 277 S 5th
Thornton Patrick, weaver, Bedford ab 12th
Thornton Robt., M road bel Prime
Thornton Thomas, blacksm., 79 G T road
Thornton Thos., weaver, Helmuth
Thornton Thomas B., carp., Sch 8th n Vine
Thornton Wm., mariner, Concord
Thornton Wm., coachman, 2 Mercer
Thornton Wm., mariner, 10 Reckless
Thorp Elizabeth, confec., 156 S 5d
Thorp John, shoemr., Jenning's row
Thorp Joseph, whitesm., 168 N 4th
Thorp Joshua, tavern, 295 N 3d
Thorp Wm. A., 57 Union

Thorp Wm. N., shoemr., Pleasant row
Thorspecken F. & Co., importers, 41 High
Thouron Augustus E., mer., 83 High
Thouron H. E., mer., 83 High, h 83 S 6th
Thouron Ns., mer., 83 High, h 83 S 6th
Thouron Ns. & Sons, com. mers., 83 High
Thrasher G. F., printer, 303 Callowhill
Throckmorton & Green, dry goods, 41 High
Throckmorton Joseph W., mer., 41 High, h 73 N 9th
Throne Robt., grocer, N E 10th and Parrish
Throp Thos., carp., 19 Parker
Thudium C. A., mer., 75 N 3d
Thum Charles D, brushmr., 86 N 3d
Thum Margaret Mrs., gentw., 126 New Market
Thumlert George, undertaker, 52 Apple
Thumlert Geo., plasterer, Crown bel Franklin
Thurber S. Mrs., b. h., 216 N 5th
Thurlo Paul, mer., 172½ High, h 34 Branch
Tibbels Thos. B., 14 Lagrange pl
Tibbett Deborah, 10th and Nectarine
Tice Jacob, tailor, 1 Elizabeth (N L)
Tice Otho S., carp., 109 Lombard
Tice Upton, carp., 109 Lombard
Ticker Jacob, basketmr., 489 N 3d
Tickner Geo., farmer, Sch Front n Vine
Tickner Perger, paint. & glazier, Sch 8th bel High, h Sch Front bel Vine
Tickner Robt., painter, Wood ab Sch 3d
Tiel Jacob, cabtmr., 27 N 4th
Tiel Samuel, millwrt., Haydock bel Front, h 27 Linden
Tielitz John F., fruiterer, 84 N 6th
Tieman Christian W., chemist, Cherry above Franklin (K)
Tiernan Mrs., b. h., 90 Lombard
Tiernan Patrick, lab., 4 Brook's ct
Tierney David, provision, 295 Vine
Tierney Simon, lab., 254 N Water
Tiers Arundius, founder, Beach ab Marsh, (K) h 8th bel Coates
Tiers Cornelius, manuf., 521 Chestnut
Tiers F. H., mer., S E Chestnut and Front, h 4 Boston row, Chestnut
Tiers John, mer., S E Chestnut and Front, h 120 S 8th
TIERS JOHN & CO., importers & tea dealers, S E Chestnut and Front
Tiers Joseph, mer., S E Chestnut and Front, h Walnut E Sch 7th
Tietz Christian, glass cut., Sterling al Franklin bel Cherry (K)
Tilburn Richard H., grocer, S W Front and Almond
Tilden Abram., cabinetmr., 423 S Front
Tilden Enos, tailor, S E 3d and Noble, h 2 N 5th
Tilden Hiram B., clerk, Franklin bel Green
Tilden Howard, N E Broad and Brown
Tilford John W., broker, 79 S 3d, h 6 Clinton sq
Tilford Sophia, shop, George n Beach
Tilge Henry, furrier, 140 N 3d, h 88 New
Tilghman Ann, rear 124 Dillwyn
Tilghman Benj., atty. & coun., 10 Prune
Tilghman B. C., atty. & coun., 10 Prune
Tilghman Henry, seaman, Poplar n Broad

Tilghman Perry, coachman, 8th bel Cedar
Tilghman Sarah, P road bel Marriott
Tilghman Wm. M., atty. & coun., 32 Sansom
Till Andrew, porter, Shippen ab 12th
Till Catharine, b. h., 1 N 9th
Till Elizabeth, 1 Benezet
Till Henry, lab., 47 Quince
Till Isaac, St Mary ab 7th
Till John, huckster, rear 482 N 3d
Till John, porter, Griffith's ct
Till John, currier, Bevan's ct
Till John, oysters, 12 High, h New Market bel
   Green
Till Wm., ship carp., Vienna bel Franklin (K)
Tiller Fred. W., cop. pl. print., 9th ab Parrish
Tiller Samuel, cop. pl. printer, 39 Carter's al, h
   203 Locust
Tilley Eliza, gentw., 7th ab Coates
Tilley Henry, drug., N E 3d and Pine
Tilley Hugh, queensware, 28 P road
Tillinghast Jos., inst. mr., Sch 4th bel High
Tillison Joseph, lab., 24 Nectarine
Tillman Henry, waiter, 178 Pine
Tillman Peter, hatter, Marlboro' bel Franklin
Tillman Peter, coachman, 9 Wiley's ct
Tillman Rebecca, 149 Brown
Tillotson John, tailor, 61 S 8th
Tilton Matilda, washer, Eagle ct
Timbers Charles, lab., Ogden bel 11th
Timbers Geo., cordw., Amber ab Phoenix (K)
Timbers Jonathan, lab., R road ab 8th
Timewell John H., cabinetmr., 114 German
Timmins Bartholomew, lab., 9 Elbow la
Timmins B., tailor, 56 Lombard
Timmins Francis, tailor, 165 S Front, h 12
   Spruce

Tipton John, blacksm., Allen ab Shackamaxon
Tipton Wm., shoemr., 375 S Front
TISDALL CHAS., weigh master, 136 S Front
   and surveyor, 22½ Walnut, h 124 Christian
Titgen Martin, boxmr., 6 Littleboy's ct
Titlow & Fry, silversmiths, rear 71 S 2d
Titlow John, driver, G T road and Little Popl.
Titlow Joseph, drover, G T road and Mud la
Titlow J., silversm., rear 71 S 2d, h 19 Shippen
Titreville Sarah, b. h., Callowhill bel Sch Front
Tittermary J. V., crier Common Pleas, h 139
   Catharine
Tittermary Miss, seminary, Queen op Crown (K)
Tittermary Robert C., collector, 6th bel Car-
   penter
Tittermary Susanna, Mechanic's ct (N L)
Tittermary Thos. J., carp., Traquair's ct
Tittle Chas. T., silversmith, 136 Christian
Tittle James H., typefounder, 136 Christian
Tittle Moses, bootmr., 136 Christian
Titus John, cooper, 30 Commerce, h 201 Mar-
   shall
Titus John, atty. & coun., S E 5th and Library
Titus Maria, rear 15 Strawberry
Tizard Richard, rigger, Mead al whf, h Suther-
   land
Tizler Frederick, spooler, Steam Mill al
Tobey Saml. C., mer., 22 S whfs, h 19 S 10th
Tobey S. & C. S., com. mers., 22 S whfs
Tobias & Co., liquors, 278 Callowhill
Tobias David, porter, Eagle ct
Tobias David, broker, 161 Vine
Tobias Solomon & Son, wine and liquor, 66 and
   68 N 3d
Tobiason A. L., confectioner, 106 S 2d
Tobin Edward, dealer, N E 5th and High, h 1

Todd Wm., stamp cut., 4½ and h 131 S 9th
Todd Wm., shoemr., Walnut n Sch 3d
Todhunter & Sill, com. mers., 12 S Front
Todhunter Wm., com. mer., 12 S Front, h 68 S 5th
Toffart Benj., paint., 97 S 8th, h rear 216 N 8th
Tolan Enos, grocery and flour, N E Noble and Garden
Toland Geo. W., Pres. Reliance Mut. Ins. Co., S W 5th and Walnut, h 178 Mulberry
Toland Henry, porter, 104 Lombard
Toland Robert, mer., 180 High, h 302 Walnut
Toland Wm. S., umbrella mr., 426 N 4th
Tolbert Eliza, dressmr., Howard's av
Tolbert Henry, clothing, 113 N 2d
Tolbert Sarah, gentw., Pine ab 13th
Tolbert Wm., oysterm., rear Washington ab 6th
Tolene J. B., tavern, S E Dock and Water
Tolin John, weaver, Carter st
TOLMAN JOHNSON, shoes, 70 N 2d
Tolman Saml., bootmr., 24 N 4th, h 181 Spring Garden
Tolman Thos., bootmr., 24 N 4th, h 22 New
Tolson Wm., lab., Square bel Corn
Tomalty Michael, weav., c 10th and Milton
Tombleston Nathan, block and pumpmr., Davis' landing
Tomer Henry W., 29 North
Tomkins Benj., carter, Carleton ab 12th
Tomkins Chalkley, carp., Ogden ab 12th
Tomkins Ely, cordw., Jackson (N L)
Tomkins Gideon, mason, 2 Moore's ct
Tomkins Isaac, shovelmr., Concord st
Tomkins Isaac, gent., 169 Sp Garden
Tomkins Joseph M. G., painter, rear 7 Rachel
Tomkins Saml., bricklr., rear Pearl ab Sch 6th
Tomkins Wm., carp., 10th ab Poplar
Tomkins Z. S., carp., Ogden ab 12th, h S W Poplar and 12th
Tomlin Brazilla, carp., F road opp Otter
Tomlin Charles S., wheelwr., Shackamaxon ab Queen (K)
Tomlin Eliza A., milliner, 461 N 2d
Tomlin Jane, 2d and Mary
Tomlin Samuel, painter, 36 Laurel n Rachel
Tomlin Saml., cooper, 101 S Water, h 41 Penn
Tomlin Stephen, tin pl. work., Davis' ct
Tomlin Stokes, cooper, 14 Little Water, h 39 Penn
Tomlin Wm., carp., Reed bel Front
Tomlin W. W., wheelwright, Shackamaxon ab Queen (K)
Tomlinson Benjamin, carp, Shippen ab 10th, h Washington ab 6th
Tomlinson Eliza, milliner, 112 S 10th

Tomlinson Saml. S., cabinetmr., Coates ab 11th
Tomman Frederick, clerk F. and M. Bank, 344 N 10th
TOMPKINS A. W., confectioner, 308 Chestnut
Tompkins David, tailor, Bread and Quarry
Tompkins John, collector, rear 38 Laurel st
Tompkins John B., collector and agt., William bel Edward
Tompkins John B., whipmr., 8 Smith's pl
Tompkins Jona, machinist, Parrish n 13th
Tompkins Jos., salesman, 3 John st (S)
Tompkins Nathan, ladies' shoemr., Buttonwood and Chatham
Tompkins Saml., cedar cooper, 297 High, h 8th ab Green
Tompkins Sarah, 30 Washington sq
Tompkins Susan, widow, 6th bel Hallowell
Tompkins S. A., milliner, 13th bel Wood
Toms Benj., carp., 7 Townsend's av
Tonello C., cabinr., Pleasant and Hay's ct
Toner Charles, bottler, 44 Quince
Toner Edwd., boatman, 44 Quince
Toner James, lab., Carpenter bel 9th
Toner John, lab., Sch 2d and M'Duffie
Toner John, weaver, rear Carpenter bel 9th
Toner Owen, lab., 4th bel Jefferson
Toner T., boot and shoemr., 422 High
Tong Thos., manuf., Hanover ab Duke (K)
Tong Wm., weaver, Duke bel Palmer (K)
Tonge Wm., weaver, F road n Bedford (K)
Toole Francis, lab., Lewis bel Sch 5th
Toole Mary, b. h., 205 S 6th
Toole Patrick, lab., Filbert n Sch 3d
Tooley Wm., tailor, Hay's ct
Tooley Wm., tailor, rear 195 Noble
Toomay James, weaver, 10 Pratt's ct
Toomey Dennis, lab., Linden bel Sch 6th
Toomey Patrick, weaver, 6 Pratt's ct
Toone Jonathan, stock. weav., 148 Poplar
Tooney Michael, stovemr., rear 17 Farmer
Topham John, scrivener, 26 S 7th, h 12th ab Spruce
TOPPAN, CARPENTER & CO., bank note engravers, 76½ Walnut
Toppan Charles, engraver, 76½ Walnut, h 103 Locust
Toppin George W., saddler, 12th ab Vine
Toppin Henry, weaver, Hanover ab Duke (K)
Toppin Samuel, book binder, 51 Franklin
Toram Francis, carp., Sch 7th bel Walnut, h Sch 3d ab Filbert
Toram Stephen, bottler, 41 Cedar, h 382 S 5th
Torbert A. W., tailoress, 25 Franklin
TORBERT JAMES, Bull's Head, 397 High
Torbert Susan, b. h., 15 Sansom

Torr Josiah N., printer, 351 Callowhill
Torr Martha, R road ab Wood
Torr Wm. S., mer., 12 S Front, h Mantua vil
Torrence Abraham, lab., Sch 6th bel High
Torrence John R., paint., 76 N 4th, h 73 Franklin
Torrens Daniel, carter, Rugan ab Callowhill
Torrens James, P road opp Plum
Torrens Wm., tailor, 10th ab Federal
Torrens Wm., china store, 224 S 5th
Torrens Wm. & J., feed store, 222 S 5th
Torrey Hamilton, lab., Wood bel 13th
Torrey Mary A., Wood bel 13th
Torry Allen, carp., 51 Perry
Tothera H., tinsmith, N E 4th and Catharine
Totten Henry, painter, 9th bel Coates
Totter Wm. H., bricklayer, 6th ab Poplar
Toulon Edw., lab., rear Christian bel 9th
Tourtelot A. Mrs., milliner, 80 S 8th
Tovaunte Anna, dressmr., 2 Benton
Towar Alexander, late bookseller, 13 N 7th
Towell James, brushmr., 4th ab Carpenter
Towell John, constable, Carpenter ab 4th
Town Benj., chairmr., S E Sch 5th and High
Town Gustavus V., printer, 30 S 4th, h 180 S 11th
Town John, sailmr., 33 & 34 S whfs, h 45 Carpenter
Town Joseph, shipwt., Hanover ab Franklin
Town J. Hen., founder, Prime bel 5th, h S 11th ab Pine
Town Matt., mariner, Marriott ab 5th
Town Robert, chairmr., S E Sch 5th & High, h 8 Howard
Town Theodore N., printer, 30 S 4th, h Callowhill ab 12th
Town Thos. B., printer and stationer, 35 S 3rd, h 13th and Sp Garden
Town Thos. H., printer, Ex building
Town T. & G., print. & stationers, 30 S 4th
Towne John, gent., Walnut W Sch 7th
Townrow Sarah, trimmings, 337 S 4th
Towns Wm., moroc. dresser, 21 Charlotte
Townsend Arabella, b h, 98 N 4th
Townsend Chas., carp., 12 Centre
Townsend Chas., watchmr., 49 & h 138 S 10th
Townsend Charles, jr., watchmr., 29 Dean
Townsend Cornelius, shoemr., 386 S 2d
Townsend Edward, dentist, h 254 N 4th
Townsend Elisha, dentist, Broad bel Walnut
Townsend George C., mer., 48½ High
Townsend Henry C., att'y., 309 Mulberry
Townsend James, lab., rear Orchard bel Rawle
Townsend John, carpet weaver, 502 N 2d
Townsend John, waterman, Walter's ct
Townsend John, collector, 151 S 13th
Townsend John K., dentist, 79 N 9th
Townsend Joseph B., att. at law, 309 Mulberry
Townsend Lydia, gentw., 86 N 5th
Townsend Mary, b h, 223 Spruce
Townsend Ogden, 50 High, h 32 Buttonwood
Townsend R. H., M D, 345 N 6th
Townsend Samuel, dyer, F road bel Franklin (K)
Townsend Saml., mer., 35 S 2d, h 101 Mulberry

Townsend Saml., waterman, rear 2 Union (S)
TOWNSEND SOLOMON, shoes & bonnets, 21 N 3d, h 97 Pine
Towson & Hines, carvers, N W 2d and Dock
Towson Wm. H., musician, 118 N 8th
Toy Amy, 336 Vine
Toy Andrew, surg. inst. maker, 13 Mary (S)
Toy Andrew, bone cutter, 25 Reckless
Toy Jacob, wheelwright, Garretson's row
Toy Nich., shipwright, 475 S Front
Toy Nicholas, jr., carver, 142½ S 2d, h 111 Carpenter
Toy Wm. J., shoemr., 4 Seiser's ct
Tozar Elias, waterman, 8 Walter's ct
Tozer John, dealer, Ann ab R road
Tozer John, ostler, 25 Blackberry al
Tracy Charles, watch casemr., 106 Chestnut, h 2 Prospect al
Tracy C. & E., watch casemrs., 106 Chestnut
Tracy Edward, 427 Chestnut
Tracy E., jeweller, 106 Chestnut, h Broad & S Penn sq
Tracy George, bootmr., 66 Chestnut, h 17 Carter's al
Tracy Joseph, cordw., Marriott ab 4th
Tracy Martin, blacksmith, R road n 10th
Tracy Mary, Leiper's ct
Tracy Michael, confectioner and fruiterer, 241 High
Tracy Michael, tailor, 292 High
Tracy Wm., watchmr., 1 Adams
Trader Parker, waterman, 34 Beck st
Traenor Wm., musician, 9 De Witt's av
Trabn Peter C., clockmr., Hanover n F road
Trailer John, lab., Haydock bel Front
Trainer Catharine, Marion ab 2d
Trainer Eliza, 61 Carpenter
Trainer James, bootmr., 106 Locust
Trainer James Mrs., tavern, S W c Broad and Cedar
Trainer John, drayman, Hazzard pl
Trainer Patrick, weaver, Crown bel Duke
Traner Joseph, lab., Washington ab Wood
Tranfried Nich., cordw., 438 N 3d
Trank P., shoemr., rear 26 Charlotte
Trank Thomas, lab., rear 468 N 3d
Trappe Cath. Mrs., Filbert n Sch Front
Traquair Adam, prest. city commissioners, h 49 N 11th
Traquair James, 143 High, h 49 N 11th
TRAQUAIR SAMUEL H., att'y. and couns. 5 Franklin row
Trautwine J. C., architect, 11 S 7th, h 253 N 6th
Travers John, waterman, 460 S 2d
Travers Margaret C., 2 Pleasant av
Travilla Jacob, shoemr., 8 N 5th
Travillar Ann Mrs., Hughes' ct (S)
Treadly John, lab., Llewellyn's av (K)
Treadway Ann shop, 2d n Edward (K)
Treadway Timothy, mariner, 68 M road
Treadwell Oren B., clockmr., 82 N 7th
Tredemicks John, cordw., rear Allen ab F road (K)
Tredwell M. H., mer., 50 High, h 282 Sassafras
Tree Mrs., gentw., 158 S Front

Treffenger Jacob, vict., Apple bel George
Trefts Adam, printer, 72 New Market
Trefts Jacob, lab., 3 Poplar
Trefts John, lab., Dyott's ct (K)
Trefz Geo., victualler, G T road bel Jefferson
Trego Charles B., gent., 186 Pine
TREGO F. AUGUSTUS, collector, 26 S 7th, h 186 Pine
Treichel Cha., dep. collector customs, C house, Chestnut st
Treichel Geo., acct., 7 Nectarine st
Trembel Jos., pedler, Murray & Sch 3d
Trenaman John, groc., Vienna ab Queen (K)
Trenchard & Campbell, feed store, Brown and Lombard
Trenwith Richard, lab., 145 S Front
Tresler Benj., vict., Orchard bel Rawle
Treston Owen, lab., Hays' ct (K)
Trevor J. B., cashier Phila. Bank, h 4 Girard
Trevor J. B., jr., 4 Girard
Trewend Theo., ironfounder, River st, h 25 S Sch 7th
Trewendt Theodore, com. mer., 53 N whfs and 111 N Water, h 25 Sch 7th
Trexler & Bush, tobacconist, 230 N 3d
Trexler & Co., tobacc., 165 Poplar
Trexler Henry, cooper, Haig's ct (K)
Trexler Henry, shoemr., 72 Maiden
Trexler Jacob, cordw., Union ab Franklin (K)
Trexler James E., tobacconist, 230 N 3d, h 102 Noble
Trexler John, carter, George n Sch 3d
Trexler John T. confectioner, Poplar & Apple
Trexler Manasses, tobacconist, N W 12th and Coates
Trexler Maria, Howard ab Master (K)
Triall Thos. M., weaver, rear 5 Gebhard
Tribbitt Wm., teamster, Wharton ab 4th
Tribu Wm., lab., 12 Eagle ct
Trick John, baker, 247 Wood bel 13th
Tricket Wm., moulder, Spruce n Sch 5th
Triebel Charles H. R., hatter, 377 N 2d
Triebels Peter W., hatter, 44 Noble, h 387 N 2d
Triesbach Elizabeth, shop, Phoenix bel G T road
Trimbey Ralph, artist, Morris st
Trimble Edman, acct., 22 Wallace
Trimble James, weaver, Master bel Hancock
Trimble & Johnson, com mers, 61 N whfs and 127 N Water
Trimble Robert, sr., Franklin ab Noble
Trimble Robert, jr., clerk, Franklin ab Noble
Trimble Wm., mer., 61 N whfs
Trimmer Edward, livery stable, Prune bel 6th, h 8 Prune
Trimnel Cornelius, seaman, 14 Blackberry al
Trinkle B. J., bookbinder, Poplar ab 9th
Trinkle John, bookbinder, Dean ab Bedford
Trinkle John, currier, Poplar ab 9th
Trinkle Wm., bookbinder, 65 Noble
Triol Manuel, painter, 253 Broad
Tripler Jacob, grocer, 4 N Water, h Green bel 10th
Tripner George, vict., Brown & 12th
Tripner George, rear 20 James

Tripner Jacob, shoe dealer, S W 8th & High, h 10 Sergeant
Tripple Anthony, cordw., 58 N 5th
Tripple James, harness maker, 591 Front (K)
Tripple John, cordw., Juniper ab Locust
Tronner Henry, scale manuf., 196 High, h 2 Pleasant Retreat
Troll Jacob, barber, 462 S Front
Trollinger Jacob, stonemas., Clinton bel Poplar
Trost Wm., tobacconist, rear Beach ab Hanover (K)
Troth Ann B., dry goods, 324 Sassafras
Troth Gilman, ship joiner, Allen bel Shacka. maxon (K)
Troth H. Mrs., 30 Girard
Troth J., wood & lumb. yard, Beach ab Warren (K)
Troth Paul, bricklayer, 2 Wile's row
Troth Samuel F., druggist, 224 High, h 102 N 9th
Troth Saml. F. & Co., druggists, 224 High
Troth Wm., lampmr., Nectarine bel 11th
Troth Wm. P., druggist, 224 High, h 36 Girard
Trott Geo., jr., mer., 45 Dock, h 389 Walnut
Trotter Chas., hatter, Brown ab 8th
Trotter & Dixon, coal mers., Maiden ab Beach (K)
Trotter Edward H., merch., 36 N Front, h 10 Franklin
Trotter Elizabeth, variety store, 79 Locust
Trotter George, mer., 36 N Front
Trotter Jas., weav., rear Perry ab Franklin (K)
Trotter John R., tailor, 660 N 2d
Trotter Joseph, president of Bank Penn., h 258 N 4th n Green
Trotter Joseph H., mer., h 258 N 4th
Trotter Nathan, mer., 36 N Front, h 256 N 4th
Trotter Nathan & Co., mers., 36 N Front
Trotter Philip, carp., Washington bel 8th
Trotter Samuel H., mer., 26 & h 258 N 4th
Trotter Wm., mer., 17 N Water, h 215 N 4th
Trotter Wm. H., mer., 35 Chestnut, h 256 N 4th
Troubat Francis J., atty., 6 Library, h 11th ab Pine
Troubat Raymond, M. D., N W Sch 6th and George, h 11th ab Pine
Trough Henry, tinsmith, 3d bel Marriott
Trough & Lemmens, tinmen, 241 S 2d, and 168 S 3rd
Trout Catharine Mrs., Buttonwood ab 10th
Trout Jacob, carter, Franklin ab Palmer
Trout Jeremiah, vict., 12th bel Brown
Trout John, Wood bel 12th
Trout Joseph, vict., Parrish bel 12th
Trout Lydia, 24 Currant al
Trout Michael, carp., Harriet bel Ross (K)
Trout Saml. B, acct., 13th ab Whitehall
Trout Wm., capt., 494 N 4th
Trout Wm. W., carp., Parrish bel 12th
Trout W. B., vict., James ab 10th
Troutman Christiana, 12th bel Cherry
Troutman George M., cashier Western Bank, h Mulberry n Sch 6th
Troutman Henry C., merch., 120 High, h 230 N 5th

Troutman John H., mer., 183½ High, h N W 12th & Washington
Troutman L. M., grocer, 237 High, h 12th ab Mulberry
Troutman Wm., Callowhill ab 12th
Troxell John, printer, 370 N 5th
Troxell John, blacksm., 146 F road (K)
Truan Robert, lab., Sch 5th ab Spruce
Truckass Wm., confect., 458 N 3d
Trucks John & Co., grocers, 17 N 5th
Trucks John, grocer, 17 N 5th, h 8 N 7th
Trucksass John, baker, 584 N 3d
Truet James B., U. S. N., h 2d ab Greenwich
Truitt Allen T., cabinetmr., 4 Lee's ct
Truitt Charles, clerk, 299 E Lombard
Truitt Charles B., hardware, 169 High, h Sch 5th ab Mulberry
Truitt Joseph, lab., rear Church bel Christian
Truitt, Pendleton & Truit, hardware, 169 High
Truitt R. W. D., mer., 169 High
Truitt Wm., waterman, 56 3 road
Truelender Joseph, drayman, Hope bel Master (K)
Truefitt Lewis A., broker, 10 Bank al
Truefitt H. P., brok., 11 Bank al, h 182 Spruce
Trull Mary, Mrs., 19 Mead
Trullender Casper W., shoemr., Shield's al
Truman A. S., hardware, 321 Callowhill
Truman Evan, cabinetmr., Parker & Carpenter
Truman Geo., dentist, 102 N 7th
Truman George S., soap and candles, 323 Callowhill
Truman Hannah, gentw., 45 George (S)
Truman Joseph M., tin plate worker, 325 Callowhill
Truman Sarah, Noble ab 7th
Trumbower Jacob, huckster, 2 Tammany ct
Trump Daniel, mer., 420 N 5th
Trump Edward D., lumb. mer., 56 Coates
Trump Jacob, rag store, 409 High
Trump John W., mer., 62 New
Trump Michael, lumb. mer., 129 Dillwyn
TRUMP M. & SONS, lumber mers., 1st wharf bel Coates
Trump Simeon, blacksm., 3d bel Prime
Trumpah Alfred, apothecary, 540 N Front
Trusty Delia, washer, 11 Wagner's al
Trusty G. W., hod carrier, Lemon
Trusty Jacob, lab., 16 Poplar ct
Trusty Patience, fruiterer, 10th bel Lombard
Trusty Perry, mariner, 5th bel Christian
Truxton Isabella Mrs., 50 N 8th
Triday G. H., carver, 60 Dock, h 14 Melon
Tryon Edward K., combmr., Queen n Shackamaxon
Tryon Edward K., rifle manuf., 134 N 2d
Tryon George K., iron store, 116 N 2d, h 147 Vine
Tryon G. W., pres. Fire Association, S W 5th & North, h 147 Vine

Tuchner Jacob, mer., 61 N 2d
Tucker B., lab., Mayland and Mulberry al
Tucker B. J., mer., 23 N whfs., h 168 Chestnut
TUCKER B. J. & OUTERBRIDGE, com. mers. 78 S whfs.
Tucker Christopher, clerk, 6 Magnolia
Tucker Daniel, bootmr., 201 N 3d, h 28 O Y road
Tucker D. H., M. D., N E Juniper & Chestnut
Tucker E., cordw., Marriott la bel 6th
Tucker George, 13 Girard
Tucker Geo. W. carp. Howard & Franklin (K)
Tucker Isaac T., cordw., Barber's row
Tucker John, mer. 18 Chestnut, h 341 Chestnut
Tucker John B., agent, 7 Gray's al
Tucker Mary, 413 Mulberry
Tucker Samuel, M D., 212 Walnut
Tucker Thomas, mer., 41 S whfs., h 37 N 11th
Tucker Wm. E., engraver, S W 5th & Walnut
Tuder Catharine, widow of Samuel, 8th below Christian
Tuder John, ropemr., 8th n Carpenter
Tuder Samuel jr., 8th n Carpenter
Tuder Wm., ropemr., 110 Carpenter
Tudor John, cordw., 1 Fetter la
Tuft John, corder, Sch 3d ab Lombard
Tuft John, tavern, 216 S Water, h Poplar
Tuft John, capt., 29 Queen
Tuft Vining, corder, Sch 3d ab Lombard
Tull James, machinist, 109 Buttonwood
Tull James, vict., rear West bel Hanover (K)
Tull John P., patternmr., Allen and Shackamaxon (K)
Tull Richd. ship build. Beach bel Maiden (K)
Tull Samuel, ship carp., Crown ab Queen (K)
Tuller Charles, mer., 76½ S Front
TULLER & COX, wine & liquors, 76½ S Front
Tully Anthony, 4 Washington Market pl
Tully Berget, washer, 20 Cypress
Tully David, carter, Ann E Sch 4th
Tully John, tailor, Spruce ab Sch 7th
Tully Miles M., inspector customs, 99 S Whfs., h 290 S 3d
Tully Thomson, cabinetmr., 24 Harmony ct
Tully Thomas, shoemr., 13 Parker
Tully Wm., carp., 269 S 4th
Tumbleson Samuel, ivory blackmr., 2d ab Montgomery (K)
Tumbleston Abigail, 114 S Front
Tunis Ann Eliza, 3 S Broad
Tunis Elizabeth, gentw., 254 Chestnut
Tunison Henry, clerk, 8 Butler's av
Tunnel Abner, carp., Russel bel Shippen
Tunnell James, lab., Pascal al
Tunnell Peter, tanner, 200 Coates
Tunnelty Duffy, weaver, Carpenter ab 10th
Tupman George & Son, hosiers, 79 N 8th
Tupman John, leather store, 5th & P road
Tupman Wm., hosier, 79 N 8th
Turbenson Thomas, watchmaker, 21 S 3d

Turley Sarah, Pearl ab Nixon
Turnbridge John, hair dresser, 55 N 6th
Turnbull Edward, weaver, Marlborough above Franklin (K)
Turnbull George, cabinetmr., 68 Shippen
Turnbull Geo., gent., 173 Coates
Turnbull James, shoemr., 20 Dean
Turnbull John, moulder, 273 S 3d
Turnbull Laurence, M. D., 385 Spruce
Turnbull Robert, mahogany sawyer, 170 Cherry
Turner Catharine, china store, Shackamaxon ab Queen (K)
Turner Cecilia, Eagle ct
Turner Edward, confect., 104 S 2d
Turner Edw., saw manuf., rear 96 Cherry, h 133 Cherry
Turner Edw., carp., 163 N 10th
Turner Edward B., confec. Fisher ab Carpenter
Turner & Fisher, stationers, 15 N 6th
Turner Francis, chairmr., rear 263 St John
Turner Francis, shoemr., 21 N 13th
Turner Frederick, stationer, 15 N 6th
Turner Geo., carp., 20 Decatur
Turner George, chairmaker, 108 N Front, h 8 Drinker's al
Turner Grace, 238 Lombard
Turner Henry, printer, 84 N 4th
Turner Henry, grocer, 64 Vine
Turner Henry, porter, Apple ab Brown
Turner Henry E., clerk, Spruce ab 13th
Turner Jacob, waiter, rear 7 Lisle
Turner James, lab., Apple ab Brown
Turner Jas., saw manuf., 2d ab G T road (K)
Turner Jas. A., druggist, 201 High, h 162 S 9th
Turner Jane, 10 Parham
Turner Jesse, bootmaker, 60 S 2d, h Hallowell ab 6th
Turner Jesse, waiter, Buckley n 11th
Turner Jesse, carp., 1 Swanson ct
Turner John, lab., Marriott bel 6th
Turner John, lab., Beach ab Spruce
Turner John, porter, Deal's av
Turner John S., trunkmr., 9th bel Poplar
Turner Jonathan, saw manuf., rear 50 N 2d, h R road ab Wood
Turner Joseph, bricklayer, Lane's ct
Turner Jos. machinist, Beach ab Marshall (K)
Turner Julia A., dressmr., Olive ab 12th
Turner Levi, pilot, rear 92 Christian
Turner Marg., 21 Beach
Turner Nathaniel, whitesm., Rose & School (K)
Turner Patrick, 7 Loxley's ct
Turner Rebecca, 53 Currant al
Turner Reuben, lab., 34 Paschall's al
Turner Richard, taylor, 18 Boyd's av
Turner Robert, carp., 22 Paschall's al
Turner Robert, brassfound., Prime & Church
Turner Robert, pawnbrok., S E 10th & Cedar
Turner Robert C., provision dealer, 163 Car-

Turner Wm., stove finisher, Dunton near Franklin (K)
Turner Wm., jeweller, 4th bel Carpenter
Turner Wm., sailor, St Mary
Turner Wm. W., clerk, 98 Green
Turney Ann, trimming store, Franklin & Callowhill
TURNPENNY JOSEPH C., druggist, N E 10th and Spruce
Turnpenny Tabitha, N E 10th and Spruce
Turpin George, waiter, 5 Painter's ct
Tussey Wm., carp., 12th ab Buttonwood, h 12th ab Vine
Tustin Adam, lab., Fitler bel Harrison (K)
Tustin James J. mer., 19 N 6th
Tustin John, Black Bear, 5th & Merchant
Tustin & Pennypacker, grocers, 19 N 6th
Tustin Thos., mer., 29 N Sch 8th
Tustin Wm., cabinetmr., William n Otter (K)
Tute Patrick, salesman, Parrish bel Broad
Tuthill John, lab., 68 Apple
Tutifer Sarah, Pryor's ct
Tuttle Edward, 19½ Cresson's al
Tuttle John, fisherman, Wood ab Queen (K)
Tutton Jenkins P., clerk, Franklin bel Coates
Tutum James, weaver, Mariner & 13th
Twaddell Charles, bricklayer, Hope bel Phœnix (K)
Twaddell Edward, shoe store, High ab Sch 5th
Twaddell John, weav., Shippen la ab Catharine
Tweed Columbus, carp., Callowhill bet Sch 4th and 5th
Twelves Richard, drug grinder, Front ab Otter
Twelves Samuel, carter, Hope bel Phœnix (K)
Twelves Sarah W., 269 Chestnut
Twesten August., tobacconist, High bet Sch Front & Ashton
Twibill G. W., pocket book manuf., 34 S 6th
Twining John, Crown bel Franklin (K)
Twitchell G. S., brewer, 31 S 10th
Tyer Charles, grocer, M road bel Washington
Tyer Mary, 3d ab Beaver
Tyler Ann, huckster, 1 Taylor's ct
Tyler Charles, cabinetmr., Christian bel 9th, h 44 Lebanon
Tyler Elizabeth, b h, 163 Chestnut
Tyler Henry, 479 High
Tyler Jerred, saddler, Rye bel Wharton
Tyter Joseph, hat finisher, 35 Union (S)
Tyler Joseph, carpet weav. 3d ab Franklin (K)
Tyler Robert, atty. & coun., 10 S 7th
Tyler Wm., currier, 165 N 3d, h 76 Lombard
Tyndale Cornelius J., stovemr., 97 S 2d, h 368 Cedar
Tyndale Hector, 219 Chestnut
Tyndale Henry, machinist, S W Front & Green
Tyndale Mary, china, 46 S 2d
TYNDALE & MITCHELL, chinaware, 219 Chestnut

Tyson Ann, 494 Chestnut ab Broad
Tyson Ann, gentw., 494 Chestnut
Tyson Charles, wood mer Swanson n Washington, h 12 Catharine
Tyson Charles M., mer., 140 High, h 113 S 8th
Tyson Comly, clerk, 13 Turner
Tyson David, cordw. Hanover ab Franklin (K)
Tyson Edmund J., clerk, 361 N 2d
Tyson Edward T., grocer, G T road and 6th
Tyson Elijah, lumb. yard, Hanover n West (K)
Tyson Geo., lab., Hanover ab Franklin (K)
Tyson George F., lumber mer., Hanover below West (K)
Tyson Henry, grocer, 8 Duke
Tyson Henry, lab., rear Hanover bel Duke (K)
Tyson James, grocer, 5th ab George
Tyson Jesse, cooper, 130 St. John (K)
TYSON JOB R., atty. & coun., 4th and Prune, office 2 Prune
Tyson John C., photographist, 313 High
Tyson John K., salesman, 360 N 10th
Tyson Leach, machinist, rear 130 Sassafras, h 13 Ellett's av
Tyson Oswald, plasterer, 88 Apple
Tyson Peter, cabinetmr., 19 Lily al
Tyson Samuel, hatter, Wood ab Sch 4th
Tyson Samuel H., inspector customs, h Chestnut n Sch 2d
Tyson Sarah K., dry goods, G T road & 6th (K)
Tyson Seth, gent., 360 N 10th
Tyson S. & M. A., milliners, 215 N 2d

———

Jber David, vict., Lemon n 10th
Uber David, carp., 21 Maria
Uber David M., grocer, R road ab Sp Garden
Uber Geo. F., collector, 79 R road

Ulrick Wm , lab., Washington ab 3 road
Umberger Jas. C., tailor, 192 High, h 43 Filbert
Umphent Jacob W., printer, 3d and Clark
Umsted Arnold, blacksm., Beckett st
Umsted Catharine, wid., 202 Wood
Umsted Jacob, mer., 448 High, h 278 N 7th
Umsted Thomas, combmr., Schleisman's al
Underdown Isaac, oil-cloth clothing, 206 S Water, h 454 S Front
Underhofler Daniel, grocer, 102 Callowhill
Underhofler Israel, 22 Dillwyn
Underkofler Daniel, grocer, 240 N 2d, h 102 Callowhill
Underkofler Jacob, trader, Rose al ab Green
Underwood Elizabeth, milliner, 374 Walnut
Underwood Henry, brickmr., 341 Brown
Underwood Henry, bootmr., Bedford ab 12th
Underwood Thomas, engraver, 31 N 11th
Ungerer Henry, shop, P road and Fitzwater
Unkel Susan, 459 N 3d
Unruh John, trunkmr., N E 7th and High, and 142 Chestnut, h 27 Logan
Unruh Nicholas B., saddler, 212 N 2d
Unverzagt H. W., baker, 103 Coates
Updegrave Allen, carp., Apple ab George (N L)
Updike Benj. M., tailor, Reid's av
Updike Corsham, cordw., 1 Rittenhouse
Upjohn Jared, tailor, Parrish ab 9th
Upperman Adam, fisherm., Vienna bel Franklin
Upperman Chas., fisherman, Vienna bel Franklin (K)
Upperman John, fisherm., Vienna bel Franklin
Upperman John A., vict., Hope ab Oxford (K)
Upton John, eating house, 66 Dock bel Pear
Upton Wm., livery stable, h 3 Chancery la
Uram Simon, mer., 169 Vine
Urick John, porter, Caroline pl
Urie Wm. Rev., Catharine ab 5th

Valentine & Thomas, iron, 125 N Water
Valentine Tilghman, lab., 30 Morris st
Valentine Wm., waiter, Eagle ct
Valerette John, weaver, Carlton bel Sch 2d
Vallance Isaac J., tailor, Marriott ab N road
Vallance Wm., weaver, Pearl ab Nixon
Valleny John, lab., Reeves n Sch 3d
Vallee Mary Ann, 19 Keefe st
Vallee Michael, cordw., 25 Castle
Vallette Eugene, printer, Prospect al
Vallette Henry M., pub. notary, 147 Chestnut
Vallette Sarah Mrs., 7 Strawberry
Vallette Washington, printer, 91 Dillwyn
Vallier James, M. D., 66 Lombard
Value Victor, teacher, 350 Walnut
Vanaken Wm., cabinetmr., 33 N 7th
Van Arkey Johnson, coachman, 20 Raspberry
Van Arkey Simon, porter, 8 Barkley
Vanarsdale C. C., D. D., N W 13th and Walnut
Vanarsdalen Richard, collector, 176 Queen
Vanarsdall A. S., ladies' shoemr., 108 N 6th
Van Artsdalen John, driver, 9th bel Poplar
Vanback Wm., cabmr., 80 Gaskill
Van Beil David, gents. furn. store, 152 S 2d
Van Beil H., pawn broker, S E 3d and Cedar
Van Beil & Son, shirt mrs., 152 S 2d
Van Blunk Peter C., collector, 440 S 4th
Van Brackle James, shoemr., 118 Locust
Van Brackle Samuel, cabmr., 123 Locust
Van Brunt & Fitzgerald, provision dealers, 23 S Water and 508 N Front
Van Brunt J., provision dealer, 149 N Front, & h 194
Van Brunt Tunis, provision dealer, 23 S Water and 508 N Front
Van Buren T. G., atty. and coun., 324 Walnut
Vance Arthur B., shoemr., Federal bel 2d
Vance Chas., cordw., Lydia and School (K)
Vance James, waterman, Burchell's ct
Vance James M., hardware, 59 High, h 5 Noble
Vance John, porter, 174 N 8th
Vance John S., tavern, 501 N 2d
Vance Thos., painter, 178 N 8th
Vance Wm., ship carp., 35 E Catharine
Vancleve Noah, grocer, Coates and Fairmount
Vancollem Myer A., 318 S 2d
Vancollum Miss, furnishing store, 318 S 2d
Vancord Hall, carp., rear 135 Carpenter
VANCOURT J., printer, c Bread and Quarry, h 94 St John
Vandegriff Mary, 25 Cresson's al
Vandegriff Samuel, hatter, M'Avoy's ct
Vandegrift David C., carp., Coates bel 10th
Vandegrift Horatio, plasterer, 2 Railroad ct
Vandegrift Middleton, tailor, 4 S 6th
Vandegrift Wm., carp., Franklin ab Front (K)
Vandel John, 33 Garden st
Vanderbeck Aaron, lab., 5th bel Christian
Vanderbelt John, livery stable, N E Callowhill and Kunckle, h 3 Kessler's ct
Vanderbilt John, marble cutter, 11th and Race, h 208 N 11th
Vandergrift Abraham, carp., 138 Coates
Vandergrift Mordecai, carp., Nectarine ab 9th
Vanderhule Ransom, lab., Fraley's ct (K)

Vanderburchen Wm., hatter, Marlborough bel Duke (K)
Vanderkemp J. J., agent Holland land company, 132 Walnut
Vanderslice Anthony, cordw., Robinson's ct (K)
Vanderslice Dr. A. J., 210 S 3d
Vanderslice E., dentist, 135 Mulberry
Vanderslice Henry, cordw., Jefferson pl
Vanderslice Henry, moroc. dress., Franklin bel Union (K)
Vanderslice Isaac, cordw., 14 Poplar
Vanderslice Jacob, cordw., Beach bel Warren (K)
Vanderslice Jacob, gunsmith, 175 Green
Vanderslice Jacob F., shoemr., 575 S 2d
Vanderslice James, cordw., Fraley's al (K)
Vanderslice James, oak cooper, 175 Green
Vanderslice Jane, b. h., 107 Mulberry
Vanderslice John, fisherm., Charlotte ab Poplar
Vanderslice Maria, Goldsmith's ct
Vanderslice Moses I., clothes, 190 Cedar
Vanderslice Samuel, oak coop., 350 N Front
Vanderslice Sarah, widow, Crown bel Franklin
Vanderslice Wm. H., paper hanger, Centre ab Brown
Vanderveer David jr., lumber, 12th bel Sp Garden
Vanderveer David, gent., Coates ab Broad
Vanderveer Wm., lumber mr., Broad bel Coates, h 12th ab Buttonwood
Vanderveer Wm., lumber mer., 334 N 13th
Vanderveer W. & D., lumber, Broad bel Coates
Vanderver Jos., blacksm., rear 33 Vine
Vandeveer Jos., moulder, 4 Pt. Pleasant ct (K)
Vandeventer David, carp., 54 Allen
Vandeventer Thomas, tav., Beach & Marsh (K)
Vandever Elwood & Co., bookbinders, N E 6th and Chestnut
Vandeyer Thomas, mariner, rear 366 N 6th
Vandusen John, shipwr., Hanover & Beach (K)
Vandusen Joseph P., ship carp., Marlborough ab Beach (K)
Vandusen Matthew jr., ship builder, Beach ab Hanover (K)
Vandusen Matthew Sr., ship builder, Beach ab Hanover (K)
Vandusen Sam. B., mer., 159 High, h 177 Vine
Vandusen Thomas, lab., St John ab George (K)
Vandusen Thos., tobacconist, S W 4th & Noble
Vandusen Washington, shipwright, Hanover ab Beach (K)
Vandike Wm. & Son, grocers, 330 N 2d
Vandyke Chas., plasterer, 336 Pine
Vandyke Fredk., tailor, Sp Garden bel 8th
Van Dyke Fredk., clerk Farm. and Mechs. Bk., h Mulberry n Sch 8th
Van Dyke Frederick A., M. D., 26 Montgom. sq
Vandyke John, saddler, Front and Maiden
Vandyke John S., stone cutter, Sch 4th ab Callowhill
Vandyke John S., harness mr., 6th bel Parrish
Van Dyke Joseph, plasterer, 332 Pine
VAN DYKE J. C., atty. and coun., 140 Walnut
Vandyke Nicholas, carter, Emerald n Sch 6th
Van Dyke Rush, M. D., S E 2d and Pine

Vandyke Wm., tailor. 6 Sch av
Van Gelder Susan, 59 Union
Van Gilder John, cordw., 490 S 2d
Vangunter John, tailor, Clinton bel Parrish
Vanharlingen J. M., dry goods, 1 S 9th, h 23 Logan's sq
Vanhist Rineir, sawyer, 3 Miller's ct
Vanhook E., mer., 194 N 2d
Vanhook Wm. F., 194 N 2d
Vanhorn Benj., carp., Cox ab Sch 6th
Vanhorn Chas., stockmr., 18 S 6th
Van Horn Chas., hatter, Domsler's ct (K)
Van Horn Christian, cordw., 154 F road
Van Horn Elizabeth, huckster, 17 Chatham
Van Horn George, stone mason, Vernon ab 10th
Van Horn Israel, bricklr., 13th ab Callowhill
Van Horn John, stone mason, Hamilton Village
Van Horn J. D., carp., 7th ab Poplar
Van Horn Lewis, acct., Ross and Harriet
Van Horn Martha, Parrish ab 13th
Van Horn Phillips, blacksm., 9 Jackson ct
Van Horn Sarah, 16 York ct
Van Horn Thos., blacksm., Lewis n Sch 6th
Vaniderstine John, cordw., Hallowell
Vankampin John, corder, rear 433 N 3d
Vankirk Aaron, carp., Lewis ab Poplar
Vankirk G., cordw., 502 S 7th
Vankirk Manning F., engineer, Perry ab Franklin (K)
Vankirk Wm. J., carp., Wallace bel 10th
Van Leer George R., livery stable, 106 S 10th
Van Leer Jos. W., dentist, 106 S 10th
Vanloan David, tailor, 198 Cedar
Vanloan John, nailor, George ab 2d (K)
Vanloan Schuyler, brassfounder, rear 180 Poplar
Vanloan Saml., photographist, 140 Chestnut, h Powell (F V)
Vanloan Wm., cordw., 2 Hartshorn's ct
Vanmeter Henry, biscuit baker, 346 N Front
Vanmeter John, paper hanger, 54 Chestnut, h Heverford R (M V)

Vansandt Charles, bootmr., Sch 7th bel Pine
Vansant Alfred D., shoemr., Mechanic
Vansant Julia Ann, dry goods, Sch 8th bel Callowhill
Vansant J. S., grocer, 195 N 2d, h 39 Vine
Vansant J. S., mer., 195 N 2d, h 106 Callowhill
Vanschoick B. H., furniture, 143 N 2d
Vansciver Budd, cordw., 297 Callowhill
Vansciver Bernard, lab., 21 Prime
Vansciver Catharine, Coates n Fairmount
Vansciver Isaac, coach manuf., 5 and 7 Branch, h Sp Garden bel 11th
Vansciver Joseph, coachmr., 4 Margaretta pl
Vansciver Saml. A., 3 Shippen
Vansciver & Son, coachmts., 5 and 7 Branch
Vansciver Wm. S., carpt., 191 N Front
Vansickel C., cordw., 16 Gebhard
Vanstavoren Chas., bricklr., rear Hope ab Otter
Vanstavoren Cornelius, carp., 169 N 11th
Vanstavoren Jackson, M. D., 51 George
Vanstavoref James, b. h., 51 George
Vanstavoren Samuel, blacksmith, Melon bel 11th road, h 12th bel Sp Garden
Vansycle Elijah, wine mer., 136 N 2d, h 180 Mulberry
VANSYCLE & SON, wine-mers., 136 N 2d
Vantine John L., watchmr., 3d and Brown
Vantine Washington, ship carp., 96 Carpenter
Vantine Wm., mariner, rear 75 Christian
Van Trump Elizabeth, 125 Callowhill
Vanvleit Wm., dry goods, 128 S 2d and 274 High
Van Winckle John, cordw., Wistar's ct (K)
Van Winckle John W., dry goods, S E 8th and Mulberry, h 87 Buttonwood
Van Wyck C. C., M. D., 96 S 8th
Vanzant Garret, shoe dealer, 221 N 2d
Vanzyle Mary, gentw., 103 German
Vanzyle Wm., clerk, 103 German
Vare Aug., coal mer., 11 E Shippen
Vare Henry, charcoal, 24 Vernon

Vaughan Patrick, lab., rear 1 Bread
Vaughan Samuel, ship builder, whf. foot of Warren, h Queen ab Vienna (K)
Vaughan Thos., ship carp., c Queen and Marlborough (K)
Vaughan Thos. T., ship carp., Queen ab Shackamaxon (K)
Vaughan Thos. W., druggist, Bedford ab Shackamaxon
Vaughan Wm., collector, 9th ab Ogden (N L.)
Vauhhan Wm., cordw., rear Carlton bel Sch 2d
Vaughan Wm., lab., Catharine and Grubb
Vaughan Wm. jr., ship carpenter, Queen below Bishop (K)
Vaughan Wm. B., shipwrt., Queen and Shackamaxon
Vaux E. H., wid. of George, 145 Mulberry
Vaux Margt., wid. of Roberts, 346 Mulberry
Vaux Richard, Recorder of Philadelphia, 4 State House row, h Walnut W Sch 8th
Vaux Wm. S., gent., 145 & h 479 Mulberry
Veacock Ann, gentw., 111 Lombard
Veacock J., gent., S W Pine and Front
Veal Moses, waterman, rear 137 Green
Veder Daniel R., capmr., Harrison
Veder John, grocer, 387 S Front
Vellegreen Mrs., toy shop, 51 S 2d
Veloker Nicholas, lab., Lewis ab Poplar
Velthoven Elizabeth, 19 Dugan
Venable John, 49 Christian
Venai Catharine, shop, S W Sch 7th & George
Venai John, tinsm., Sch 7th & George
Venning Edward, carp., 8 Bonsall
Venning John, carp., 14 Barley
Venning Louisa, 32 Burd's ct
Venning Luke, shoemr., 87 S 2d, h Barley ab 10th
Verdries Sarah, dressmr., 9 Elliott av
Vernon Robert H., shoemr., Brinton bel 11th
Vernon Samuel, wheelwrt, 99 Filbert
Vernon Theodore, shoemr., 92 Christian
Vernou Eliza, 3 S Front
Vernou Joseph, mer., 3 S Front
Vernou Wm. C., marble & mahogany, 93 S 2d, h 11 Norris' al
Veron A. P., gentw., 98 Fitzwater
Verree John, rolling-mill, Penn bel Maiden
Vert Edw., engineer, Palmer bel Franklin (K)
Vesey Edward, clothing cellar, N 2d ab Sassafras, h 191 S 4th
Vessels John S., bricklr., 6th ab Poplar
Vethake Henry, professor, 32 Girard
Vetter Andrew, shoemr., 73 N 5th
Vetter Rebecca, 1 Goodwill ct
Vetterlein Theodore H., mer., 259 N 2d, h 34 Callowhill
VEZIN CHARLES, mer., 50 S Front, h Pine bel 3d
Viall James W., carp., 19 Cox, shop cor Swanson and Shippen
Vicary John, mer., Filbert n Sch 7th
Vice David, brickmr., Mechanic ab George

Vickers Jacob, engineer, Penn ab Maiden (K)
Vickers Jane, S W 7th and Sansom
Vickers M. P., gentw., 165 Wood bel 11th
Vickers Robert, P road bel Federal
Vickery Benj., tobacconist, 163 Lombard
Vickery Benj., cordw., 116 Green
Vickery Joseph, weaver, 13th n Shippen
Vierick Frederick, tailor, 4 Orange
Vierick John C., musician, 13th bel Locust
Vigor Henry, tailor, 65 Walnut
Viguers Charles, cordw., Wheat ab Wharton
Vincent Eliza, Lombard bel 12th
VINCENT FREDERICK, atty. and coun., 104 S 3d
Vincent George W., lab., 14 Union (S)
Vincent John, cordw., 11th bel Cedar
Vincent Robert, porter, Lombard W Sch 7th
Viney Patience, Mark's la ab 11th
Vinson John, blacksm., 1 Little Willow
Vinton Charles A., mer., 4 Sansom
Vinyard James, sailmr., 406 N 5th
Vinyard & Shindler, sailmrs., N whfs bel Vine
Vinyard Wm., timber insp., office Navy Yard, h 140 Catharine
Virden Isaac, brickmr., Spruce W Sch 5th
Virden James, brickmr., Cox st
Virden Sarah, wid. of John, Braley's ct
Virtue Edward, tailor, 241 Cedar
Vogdes Israel, carp., Washington (W P)
Vogdes Jesse, sen., carp., Washington (W P)
Vogdes John R., atty., 56 S 6th, h 346 Chestnut
Vogdes & Phillips, att'ys., 56 S 6th
Vogdes William, att'y. at law, 11 State House, h 335 Sassafras
Vogel Chas., carter, 4 Sailor's ct
Vogel Chas. B., grocer, 487 Vine
Vogel John, lab., Ash bel Duke (K)
Vogel John, mer., 7th ab Brown
Vogel John, currier, 63 Tammany
Vogel Joseph P., ship builder and lumber mer., Ogelby's whf., h 47 Lombard
Voght Louis, carp. weaver, Pike
Vogle Albert, clerk, 7th ab Parrish
Vogle Chas., tailor, 439 N 3d
Vogle Frederick, 245 N 6th
Vogle John L., baker, 81 Christian
Voglebach Chas. F., tailor, 176 Poplar
Vogt Charles, M. D., 91 Lombard
Vogt Frederick K., 1 Faries ct
Vogt George, locksm., rear Beck's ct
Vogt Henry, framemr., Shafer's ct
Voight Louis, agent for sale of glass, 4 Branch, h 27 Wood
Voight Maria, wid., 40 Buttonwood
Voigt Edward P., acct., 319 N 6th
Voigt E., locksm., 311 N 3d
Volans Samuel, gent., 324 Mulberry
Volier Ferdinand, baker, Parkcrab Washington
Volk Frederick, lab., Poplar bel 4th
Volk John Charles, carp., 30 Charlotte
Volkmar Henry, gent., 4 Duke
Volkmar Henry, jr., gratemr., 121 S 3d, h 84

Vollmer Christian G., baker, 190 St John
Vollmer Gotlieb, upholsterer, S E 11th and Chestnut
Vollmer & Montre, upholsterers, S E 11th and Chestnut
Vollum Edward P., currier, 168 S 13th
Vollum Henry, carp., 19 Dean
Vollum Wm. P., carp., Dean and Lyndall al, h 21 Orleans
Vondersmith Daniel, 200 S 3d, h 10th & Loud
Vondersmith S. P., druggist, S W 7th and Sassafras
Vonpool & Shannon, sailmrs., 53 N whfs
Vonnieda Daniel, tobac., Charles ab Willow
Vonnieda Jacob, trader, 13th ab Callowhill
Vonpul Catharine, 62 N 8th
Voorhees Allen, constable, 56 Duke
Voorhees Franklin, tailor, 66 Washington av (N L)
Voorhees Peter, cordw., 3 Clare al
Voorhees Peter, bootmr., 14 Swanson
Vorhees Eliza, tailoress, rear 30 Sheaff
Vork Wm., confect., 146 Lombard
Vottier Wm., plasterer, 446 S 4th
Voute L. C., watchmr., S E High and Strawberry, h 19 Branch

———

Waaser Chas., skin dresser, 589 N 3d
Wachmouth Fredk., scalemr., rear 156 Poplar
Wachsmuth Vincent F., 248 High
Waddell Thos., weaver, Hope bel Master
Waddington Henry, weaver, Carpenter ab 13th
Waddington James S., dry goods, Sch 3d ab Cedar
Waddle Harlan, cordw., 75 Noble
Waddle Robt., Dorothy n Sch 4th
Wade Francis, clerk, 8th ab Christian
Wade Geo. C., printer, 8th ab Christian
Wade Hannah, gentw., 8th ab Christian
Wade Joseph B., 256 S Front
Wade Julia, 32 Marion
Wade Lewis, segarmr., 63 Apple
Wade Martha, 76 Union
Wade Patrick, lab., S 8th bel Shippen
Wade Robt., mer., 24 Commerce, h Sch 7th ab Spruce
Wadleigh L. F., teacher, rear 229 Mulberry
Wadlow Jane, 7 Jones' al
Wadlow Moses, combmr., 58 Brown
Wadlow Samuel, variety store, 214 Callowhill

Wagner Chas. I., carp., 14 Rachel
Wagner Charles F., vict., Benton n School
Wagner Charles M., atty. & coun., 207 N 6th, h 110 Chestnut
Wagner Christian, baker, 75 S 5th
Wagner Christopher, blacksmith, Franklin and School (K)
Wagner David G., carp., 10th ab Poplar
Wagner Frederick, tailor, 484 N 2d & 361 N Front
Wagner Fredk., P., hairdresser, 335 N 3d
Wagner F. P., stovemr., 260 N 3d
Wagner Geo., fisherman, Cherry ab Queen (K)
Wagner Geo., shop, 6 Rachel
Wagner Geo., farmer, 7 Nectarine
Wagner Geo., shoemr., Wheat bel Wharton
Wagner Geo., shoemr., 18 Cresson's al
Wagner Geo. L., moroc. dresser, Warner's ct
Wagner G. Xav., professor, 523 N 4th
Wagner Jacob, wheelwrt., Mechanic ab George
WAGNER JACOB, tavern, 102 New Market
Wagner Jacob, lime mer., Noble bel O Y road, h 210 Noble
Wagner Jacob, baker, 259 N 7th
Wagner Jacob, wheelwrt., 135 Brown, h 5 Orchard
Wagner Jacob, awningmr., 3 N 7th, h 26 N 6th
Wagner Jacob F., moroc. dresser, 3 Seybold's ct
Wagner John, sen., Palmer bel Queen (K)
Wagner John, fisherman, Bishop bel Queen (K)
Wagner John, bookbinder, 219 Cedar
Wagner John, blacksm, Brown ab 4th, h Apple ab George
Wagner Joseph, cordw., 134 Brown
Wagner Joseph, blacksm., R road ab Wood, h N W 10th and Pearl
Wagner J. B. & G. M., hardware, 173 Callowhill and 332 N 3d
Wagner Margaret Mrs., 420 N Front
Wagner Mary Ann, rear 121 O Y road
Wagner Mary A., Pleasant bel 13th
WAGNER & M'GUIGAN, lithographers, 116 Chestnut
Wagner Peter, printer, 2 Branch al
Wagner Philip, conveyancer, Green ab 7th, h 420 N Front
Wagner Reuben C., cordw., Marriott bel 6th
Wagner Samuel, 252 Mulberry
Wagner Sebastian, sugar baker, 20 Branner's al
Wagner Solomon, carp., 657 N 2d
Wagner & Stuart, engravers, 20 S 6th

Wainwright & Gillingham, saw mill, Beach bel Hanover

Wainwright Isaac, oysterman, Head Quarters, h 13 Franklin pl

Wainwright Isaac H., roll. mill, foot Marlboro' st (K)

Wainwright John, umbrella mr., 7th ab Poplar

Wainwright Jonathan, steam saw mill, Beach bel Hanover (K)

Wainwright Wm., grocer, N E 2d & Mulberry, h 228 Sassafras

Wainwright William J., mer., 152 High, h 279 N 6th

Wait John, weaver, Jefferson & Hope (K)

Waite George, jeweller, 352 S 5th

Waiter Joshua, dealer, 223 G T road (K)

Waith William, druggist, 56 S Front, h 12th ab Cedar

Waitham Bennett, pilot, Wharton ab 3d

Waitham James, capt., Franklin ab Palmer (K)

Waitt Frederick, jeweller, 11 Exchange pl, h 22 Carter's al

Wake Christopher, cordw., Melon ab 9th

Wakeham Thos., G T road ab 5th

Wakely Charles, stovemr., 17 Harmony ct

Wakely Jesse, cabman, Goodwill ct

Wakely Wm., carman, 4 Howard

WALBORN CORNELIUS A., stock & gentlemen's furnishing store, 7 & 9 and h 25 N 6th

Waldie W. S., clerk, 295 Callowhill

Waldire Joseph, lab., rear 64 Catharine

Waldraven Lydia, gentw., N E 6th and Parrish

Waldron Nathan'l, mer., High st whf., h 1 S 11th

Waldron Oliver P., chairm., George ab Broad

Waley Eliza, Hines' pl

Waley Theodore, lab., rear 102 Carpenter

Walford James, shoemr., c 7th and Noble

Walker Abm., trimmings, High n Sch 5th

Walker Alex., tailor, Jones W of Sch 5th

Walker Ambrose, printer, 179 Catharine

Walker Amor, carp., Callowhill n Sch 3d

Walker Andrew, furniture car, 6 Traquair's ct

Walker Andrew C., dry goods, 67 Cedar

Walker Ann, b. h., 91 S 8th

Walker A. M., gent., 221 S 9th

Walker Catharine, confectioner, 104 N 8th

Walker Daniel, cigar mr., Fisher

Walker David, shoemr., Sassafras n Sch 7th

Walker Elizabeth, shop, Sch 6th ab Vine

Walker Elizabeth Y., 20½ Sassafras

Walker Elizabeth, 287 St John

Walker Francis, barber, 16 N 12th

Walker George, cordw., Edward bel 2d (K)

Walker George, combmr., 287 St John

Walker George, store, 372 N 6th

Walker George, baker, Willow bel Garden

Walker George M., cordw., 12 Parker

Walker George R., salesman, 225 N 9th

Walker James R., confect., 246 N 2d

Walker John, weaver, Howard bel Master

Walker John, cordw., Marriott's la bel 6th

Walker John, constable, 352 Pine

Walker John, weaver, Amber ab Phoenix

Walker John, carp., Reed ab Rye

Walker John, weaver, Higham's ct (K)

Walker John, gent., 424 N 4th

Walker John, mason, Carlton ab Sch 3d

Walker John, tailor, Pearl ab Sch 6th

Walker John F., acct., 245 Marshall

Walker Joseph, 224 N 6th

Walker Joseph, porter house, 272 S 7th

WALKER LEWIS, flour mer., 400 High, h 63 N 11th

Walker Margaret, gentw., 182 N 11th

Walker Mary Ann Mrs., Filbert ab Sch 7th

Walker Matthew, spinner, Franklin and Noble, h 13th bel Green

Walker & Miller, grocers, Vine bel 12th

Walker Ralph, lab., rear 511 N 3d

Walker Richard B., trunk mr., Crown ab Bedford (K)

Walker Robert, grocer, G T road ab 2d

Walker R. B., carp. store, 25 N 2d, h 223 Coates

Walker Samuel, weaver, 18 Helmuth

Walker Samuel, baker, 2d ab Master (K)

Walker Samuel, morocco dr., 544 N 2d (K)

Walker S. J., druggist, 184 High, h 70½ N 11th

Walker Solomon B., varnisher, 3 Warner's ct

Walker Thomas, potter, Amber ab Phoenix

Walker Thomas, stone cut., Vaughan ab Locust

Walker Thomas, weaver, Wagner's al

Walker Thomas, engineer, 14 York ct

Walker Thomas, tailor, 16 Dannaker's av

Walker & Wallace, grocers, S E Front & Coates

Walker Wm., lab., Milton ab 10th

Walker Wm., weaver, Franklin ab Front (K)

Walker Wm., confectioner, 87 S 2d

Walker Wm., cordw., Poplar bel New Market

Walker Wm., tailor, Baker bel 8th

Walker Wm., cordw., R road bel Sch 7th

Walker Wm. H., cordw., rear 441 Vine

Walker Wm. J., wooden ware, 267 Spruce

Walker Wm. J., leather and finds., 466 N 2d, and 368 N 3d

Walker Wm. M., refectory, 2d bel Oxford (K)

Walker Wm. W., bookseller, 28 N 3d, h Juniper ab Pine

Walker Wm. W., music store, 120 Walnut

Walkinfear Wm., baker, Brown ab Cherry (K)

Wall Elizabeth, 23 Coombes' al

Wall Geo., wool dealer, 15 N Front, h 99 New

Wall Helmsley R., carp., Clare

Wall Henry, carp., Brown bel 10th

Wall James, machinist, Whitehall

Wall John, stocking weaver, rear 455 N 3d

Wall John C., druggist & keeper of prison, 272

Wall Philip, carp., Duke n Wood (K)
Wall Samuel E., cordw., 182 Christian
Wall S., house painter, 214 N 6th
Wall Wm., tailor, 55 Plum
Wall Wm., brushmr., 18 Starr al
Wall Wm. H., carp., Union ab F road (K)
Wall Willis D., carp., 3 Baxter's av
Wallace Allen, constable, 56 Duke
Wallace Andrew, weaver, Mariner
Wallace Catharine, 12 Chancery la
Wallace Cesar, carter, 85 Bedford st
Wallace Charles, carp., Helmuth st
Wallace C. Mrs., shop, Church bel Christian
Wallace Daniel, carp., Filbert n Sch 4th, h Lombard n Sch 2d
Wallace Eleazer, saddler, 143 N 10th
Wallace E., M. D., 39 S 10th
Wallace Frederick, hats & caps, 122 N 2d
Wallace Frederick, mer., 10½ High, h 252 N 2d
Wallace George, vict., Sch 7th n Vine
Wallace George, tinman, 21 Howard
Wallace Henry, cordw., Queen bel Shackamaxon (K)
Wallace Henry, painter, Vine ab Sch 2d
Wallace Henry E., att'y & coun., 177 Sassafras
Wallace Horace B., att'y & coun., S E 6th and Walnut, h 284 Spruce
Wallace Isaac, vict., Buttonwood ab 10th
Wallace James S., editor, h 1 York
Wallace Jane, dressmr., 19 Mulberry
Wallace John, clerk, 83 Penn st
Wallace John, carter, Ashton ab Pine
Wallace John, coal dealer, 13 Hamilton pl
Wallace John, printer, Vienna ab Queen (K)
Wallace John, tavern, c Broad & Shippen
Wallace John, sr., vict., Sch 7th n Vine
Wallace John, grocer, S E 3d and Lombard
Wallace John, carp., Cedar ab 12th
Wallace John F., coal yard, Willow ab Broad
WALLACE JOHN WILLIAM, att'y & coun., S E 6th & Walnut, h 284 Spruce
Wallace Joshua M., M. D., 1 Monroe pl
WALLACE J. WILSON, attorney and coun.,

Wallace Samuel, tailor, 11 Lagrange pl
Wallace Samuel, tin mr., 119 S 12th
Wallace Sarah, 184 Carpenter
Wallace Thomas, lab., Jones W Sch 5th
Wallace Thomas, jr., clerk, Callowhill ab 11th
Wallace Thomas, ship carp., Union ab Franklin (K)
Wallace Thomas, stationer, rear 13 Minor, h 55 N 11th
Wallace Thomas, R road ab Ann
Wallace Thomas, weaver, Mariner
Wallace Thomas, potter, New Market ab Laurel
Wallace Thomas K., city commissioner, h 11 S Sch 7th
Wallace Wm., jr., coal mer., 48 Walnut, h S W 11th and Washington
Wallace Wm., chandler, 10th bel Sp Garden
Wallace Wm., shoemr., Beach ab Poplar (K)
Wallace Wm., blacksm., Carlton bel Sch Front
Wallace Wm., wines and liquors, 127 W High
Wallace Wm., gent., 248 Cedar
Wallace Wm., Sec. & Treas. Little Sch Nav. R. R. & Coal Co., 80 Walnut, h 7 S 11th
Wallace Wm., weaver, Higham's ct
Wallace Wm. B., potter, 5th bel Washington
Wallace William & Co., coal yard, Broad below George
Wallace Wm. H., mer., 94 N 3d, h 18 Palmyra square
Wallace Wm. J., gent., Sch 5th bel Lombard
WALLACE WILLIAM & NEPHEW, coal dealers, 48 Walnut bel Dock
Wallace Wm. W., att'y and coun., S E 5th and Library
Wallace Wilson, lawyer, 9th ab Catharine
Wallen John, car driver, 8 Baker's ct
Wallen Wm., lab., Murray n Sch 2d
Wallen Wm., weaver, 8 Pleasant row
Wallens Joseph S., printer, 365 S Front
Wallens Miles, mer., 64 N 2nd
Wallens & Moore, boots & shoes, 64 N 2d
Waller Frederick W., gold beater, 60 Dock, h 21½ Spruce

Walls Levin, blacksm., 21 Prime

Walls Sol., lab., rear 89 Swanson

Walls Thomas, weaver, G T road bel Master

Walls William, porter, ab Cherry

Walmsley Joseph, gent., 208 N 4th

Walmsley Samuel, engraver, Montgomery bel Front (K)

Walmsley Thos., starch manuf., Jefferson and Hancock, h Hanover ab West (K)

Walmsley Wm., mer., 15 Church al

Waln Edward, atty. and coun., 177 Walnut

Waln Jacob S., gent., 257 Walnut

Waln & Leaming, mers., 28 S Front

Waln Lewis, mer., 28 S Front, h 250 Walnut

WALN S. MORRIS & CO., mers., 35 and 36 S whfs

Walnut John, carp., 8 Carpenter (S)

Walnut Thos., barber, 65 Shippen, h 96 S 11th

Walnut Thomas, carp., 19 Mead al

Walpole Mary A., Washington & Swanson

Walpole Samuel, tavern, 62 Shippen

Walraven Henry, blksm., Franklin ab Front (K)

Walraven John J., variety store, 263 S 2d, h 6th bel Washington

Walraven Lewis Y., dry goods, 28 N 9th

Walsh Andrew, machinist, 10th ab Carpenter

Walsh Christ., gent., Sch 8th bel George

Walsh Christopher, jr., acct., 45 Buttonwood

Walsh Dennis, ropemr., 137 N road

Walsh James, lab., 24 Gray's al

Walsh John, agent, 119 S Front, h 9 Walnut

Walsh Mary, 320 Vine

Walsh Michael, painter, Christian bel 9th

Walsh Nicholas, grocer, 18 Flower

Walsh Robert F., mer., 38 S Front, h 5 Girard

Walsh R. I. & M. R., teachers, 29 Strawberry

Walshaw Ann, G T road ab Franklin (K)

Walter Adam, porter cellar, 123 Mulberry

Walter Adam, carter, 3d ab Poplar

Walter Adam B., engraver, 8th and Green

Walter & Berghauser, importers, 30 Church al

Walter Charles, cordw., 409 S 2d

Walter David C., carp., rear Marshall ab Brown

Walter Edwin, secretary Lehigh coal and navigation Co., 82 S 2d, h 132 N 12th

Walter George, snuff manuf., 11th bel Coates

Walter George, shoemr., Beach below Maiden (K)

Walter Geo. F., tailor, 222 High, h 163 N 10th

Walter Hannah, washer, Mulberry al

Walter Hebman, carp., 11 E Cedar

Walter Henry, printer, 5 James

Walter Israel H., 12th and Whitehall

Walter Jacob F., baker, 27 Strawberry

Walter Jacob L., porter, 9 Hamilton pl

Walter James, 70 S 2d

Walter John, gluemr., G T road and Camac (K)

Walter Joseph, lab., 8th and Green

Walter Jos., cop. pl. printer, 26 Howard

Walter Joseph S., builder, 53 N 11th

Walter Joseph S. Mrs., Green ab 11th

Walter J. F., 205 Noble

Walter J. J., tin plate worker, 13 M'Duffie

Walter Mary, dry goods, 352 N Front

Walter Matthias, jr., shoes, 235 Vine

46

Walter Philip D., baker, John and N road

Walter R. and Ann, variety store, 123 Mulberry

Walter Theodore, mer., 30 Church al, h 36 Callowhill

Walter T. U., architect, Locust n Sch 8th

Walter Wm. P., hardware, 469 High

Walters A. B., George n Broad

Walters A. G., incr., 3 Dock, h Chestnut (W P)

Walters Benj., chairmr., 129 E Pine

Walters Corn. C., shoemr., Penn bel Maiden (K)

Walters Edward, jeweller, Dorothy n Sch 4th

Walters Francis, baker, George ab Sch 7th

Walters George, ship carp., Hanover bel Franklin (K)

Walters George A., cordw., 496 S 2d

Walters George F., currier, 11 Jackson's ct

Walters Hannah, gentw., Sch 7th ab Pine

Walters Hannah, Beach ab Maiden (K)

Walters Henry, carp., Beach ab Shackamaxon

Walters Jacob, tobacconist, 28 Cherry

Walters James, tailor, 3 Callowhill

Walters James, butcher, Depot bel 9th

Walters Jeremiah, buttonmr., rear 461 N 3d

Walters John, conf., 25 R road

Walters John C., copperplate printer, Carlton ab 13th

Walters Peter, plast., Carpenter ab 8th

Walters Robt., lab., Sch 5th ab Spruce

WALTERS & SOUDERS, mers., 3 Dock st. wharf

Walters Wm., cordw., Wood ab Sch 6th

Walters Wm. W., mer., 16 S 4th, h 20 Chatham

Walthour Gustavus, bandbox mr., 2 Derringer's court

Waltman Ann E., 163 Locust

Waltman Geo., flour & feed, P road & Marriott

Waltman John, huckster, Duke and Wood (K)

Waltman Susanna, store, Carpenter bel 10th

Walto Barbara, Brown ab Cherry

Walton A., trader, Cherry bel Franklin (K)

Walton Benj., bonnets, 61 & h 159½ S 2d

Walton Chas., dentist, 175 Sassafras

Walton Chas. J., hatter, 107 N 2d, h 314 S 4th

Walton Coates, mer., 14½ S 4th, h Sch 8th ab Pine

Walton David G., plasterer, 462 N 4th

Walton Dennis, porter, Cherry n Broad

Walton Edith, huckster, Vernon pl

Walton Edward, Washington & Third

Walton Ed. H., mer., 29 N 2d, h 5 Palmyra row

Walton Edwin, machinist, Sch 5th bel Barker

Walton Enoch, carp., 184 S 4th

Walton & Evans, dry goods, 33 N 2d

Walton George, carp., 94 New Market

Walton George, segarmr., 7 Smith's al

Walton George H., dry goods, Callowhill above Franklin

Walton Hannah, b h, 37 N 10th

Walton Isaac, mer., 28 N 3d

Walton Isaiah, plasterer, 22 Rose al

Walton James, cordw., Poplar ab 10th, h Vernon ab 10th

Walton Jeremiah, 314 S 4th

Walton Jesse, Sch 5th bel Filbert

Walton John D., printer, 78 Buttonwood

Walton Joseph, coal mer., 39 S 2d, h 134 Marshall

Walton John T. bonnets and shoes, 103 N 2d

Walton Jos. R., clerk, 18 Vernon (S G)

Walton J., importer of needles, 72½ High, h Washington ab 10th

Walton Lewis, Chestnut n Sch 4th

Walton Mary C., milliner, 56 Mulberry

Walton Mordecai, Washington st (W P)

Walton Penelope, 47 Filbert

Walton Priscilla, 102 Lombard

Walton Richard, ½ D, 78 Buttonwood

Walton R. M., dress and cloak maker, 102 Lombard

Walton Salem, tavern, 247 N 2d

Walton Samuel, carter, 8 Rachel

Walton Saml., hatter, 61 & h 312 S 3d

Walton S. D., hatter, 61 S 3d, h 312 S 4th

Walton S. D. & Co., hatters, 61 S 3d

Walton Thos., alderman, 490 N 3d

Walton Thos. C., carter, rear Orange ab Washington

Walton Wells, constable, 20 S 7th

Walton Wm., printer, 75 Franklin

Walton Wm., shoemr., 223 Christian

Waltz Benj., printer, rear 76 Sassafras

Waltz John, baker, 31 Apple

Walz George, tailor, 10th ab Ogden

Walz John, tailor, rear 5 Ogden

Walz John, jr., bootmr., 10th ab Ogden

Wanamaker G. W., watchman, 3 Helmuth

Wanck Elizabeth, Hanover bel Franklin (K)

Wandell Adam John, tavern, 5th and G T road (K)

Wandell Charles, baker, 35 Coates

Wandell John, 149 N 4th

Wandell John, jr., mer., 76 High

Wands Alex., shoemr., Fitzwater ab 8th

Wands W. W., printer, 95 Fitzwater

Wannaker Samuel R., brickmr., 382 N 4th

Ward James, carp., Carlton bel Sch ?

Ward Jane, Lemon ab 12th

Ward Jehu, watchmr., 106 Chestnut

Ward John, cordw., 3 Catharine

Ward John, paper hanger, 301 High, ab Sassafras

Ward John, agent, 30 S 2d, h Reakir

Ward John, basketmr., 12 Pear

Ward John B., cabtmr., 338 S Front

Ward John P., mer., 5½ N 2d

Ward Joseph, ladies' shoemr., 8½ S 8

Ward J. & W. L., watches and jewe Chestnut

Ward Margaret, shop, Jefferson n Br(

Ward Mark, blacksm., Callowhill n S(

Ward & M'Cormick, cloths, 5½ N 2d

Ward Patrick, lab., 2 Elmslie's al

Ward Perry, lab., 7 Richards

Ward Peter, carter, Federal ab 7th

Ward Robert H., tinsm., P road bel C

Ward Saml. A., pub. fashions, 62 Wal

Ward Saml. L., mer., 448 High, h 171

WARD S. A. & A. F., pubs. Phila. fa Walnut

Ward Townsend, bookseller, 45 S 4th

Ward Ursula Mrs. 60 S 5th

Ward Walter, M. D., 129 N 9th

Ward Wm., tailor, 22 Almond

Ward Wm., bootmr., Wharton ab Ree

Ward Wm. L., jeweller, 106 Chestnt 6th and North

Wardel R. C., engraver, 5th and Wal

Wardell John A., cordw, Cobb's ct

Wardell Jos. D., fish dealer, G T roa((K)

Wardell Philip, bookbinder, 3 Brook

Wardell Wm., tobacconist, 25 Laurel

Warden Abijah B., jeweller, S E 5th ₛ nut, h 238 N 5th

Warden David A., vocalist, 9 Cadꞷⁿ

Warfield Joseph, eating house, S E Dock and Walnut
Warfield Risin, lab., Flower ab Christian
Wark John, lab., Beach ab Locust
Warley Henry, grocer, S E 2d & Brown, h 177 St John
Warley Henry, weaver, 177 St John
Warley & Landy, grocers, S E 2d & Brown
Warman Edward, 32 R road
Warne E. S., dry goods, 225 N 3d, h 73 Marshall
Warne Jesse, b. h., N W 4th & Spruce
Warne Mahlon, harnessmr., 152 Chestnut, h 416 Poplar
Warner Ann G., 7 Prospect al
Warner Augustus, vict., Ogden ab 12th
Warner Chas., cigar mr., 13th ab Poplar
Warner Chas., plumber, Shackamaxon n Franklin (K)
Warner Cuthbert, watch casemr., 4 Hudson's al, h Melon ab 9th
Warner Daniel, painter, R road ab Callowhill
Warner Edward, combmr., Poplar bel 4th
Warner Eliza, 187 Queen
Warner Eliza, variety store, Sch 8th n Vine
Warner E. W., mer., 29 S whfs., h 395 Spruce
Warner Francis B., lumber mer., 361 N 6th
Warner Fred'k, tobacconist, Beach n Maiden
Warner F. V., lumber mer., Sch 8th & Sassfras, h 543 Vine
Warner George, shoemr., 9 Knight's ct
Warner George, iron founder, 14 Eutaw
Warner Geo., baker, 100 Christian
Warner George W., mer., 377 High
Warner Gilbert, capt., 69 E Lombard
Warner & Gravel, grocers, N W R road & Callowhill
Warner H. Mrs., 125 Melon bel R road
Warner John, carp., 116 Catharine, h 30 Pine
Warner John, vict., 8th & Callowhill
Warner John, jr., vict., 4 Miller's ct
Warner Joseph, silversm., 16 & h 22 Merchant
Warner Joseph, 171 High, h 225 N 4th
Warner J. A., mer., S E 2d & Callowhill
Warner Lewis, drover, 8th ab Parrish
Warner Mary, b. h., 14 N 10th
Warner Noah, lab., 19 Acorn al
Warner Philip, bootmr., 109 N 9th
Warner Rachel, 6 Sterling
Warner Redwood F., mer., 71 High, h 5 Clinton
Warner Robert B., carp., 2 Warner's ct
Warner R. P., watch casemr., 4 Hudson's al, h 12 Franklin
Warner Sarah, 518 S Front
WARNER, VETTERLEIN & CO., tobacco warehouse, 2d and Callowhill
Warner Wm., engraver, 80½ Walnut
Warner Wm., carpet weaver, 337 S 2d
Warner Wm., cordw., 42 Mead al
Warner Wm., china packer, Front and Queen
Warner Wm., tobacconist, 69 Tammany
Warner Wm. & Co., watch casmrs., 4 Hudson al
Warner Wm. H., painter, 22 Montgomery
Warnick Chas. W., founder, G T road ab 6th, h 6th & G T road

Warnick Chas. W. & Co., Philada. stove works, G T road ab 6th
Warnick Francis, carp., Olive ab 10th
Warnick James, plasterer, 7 Parham st
Warnick Nicholas P., lab., 180 Carpenter
Warnock Abigail, confect., 61 N 10th
Warnock David, weav., Benton bel William (K)
Warnock James, U. S. Mint, Sch 5th ab Wood
Warnock Jane, 37 Filbert
Warnock Mary Ann, Carbon pl
Warnock Robert, dry goods, 39 N 8th
Warnock Robert & Wm., dry goods, 39 N 8th
Warnock Wm., mer., 39 N 8th, h 40 Filbert
Warr John, engraver, 9 Hart's buildings, h 452 Callowhill
Warr Lydia, 218 N 9th
Warr Mary, tavern, Garden & Vine
Warr Mary, cigar mr., 16 Star al
Warr Samuel, tailor, Lewis ab Poplar
Warr Thomas, lab., Cooper n Sch 3d
Warren Ann, importer, 21 Pear
Warren Catharine, Ontario ab Poplar
Warren Charles, clerk, Wood & 10th
Warren C., 181 Pine
WARREN DAVID, tavern, N W 4th & Gaskill
Warren Deborah, b. h., 463 Vine
Warren Geo. S., tailor 358 & h 320 High
Warren Henry, landscape painter, 146 N 8th
Warren Jabez, importer, 48½ High, h 508 Vine
Warren James, moulder, Filbert n Sch 4th
Warren James T., clerk, Buttonwood bel 8th
Warren John, cordw., Wood ab 13th
Warren John F., blacksm., Mechanic bel George
Warren Jos., lab., Bank ab Lombard
Warren Jos., provision, William ab Vine
Warren Mary M., washer, Dean ab Locust
Warren Nathaniel, chairmr., 78 N 7th
Warren Philip, carter, 43 Coates
Warren Robert G., 132 Franklin
Warren S., lumber mer., Washington av below Coates, h 24 Green
Warren Thomas, lab., 3 Osborn's ct
Warren & Townsend, importers of trimmings, 48½ High
Warren Uriah, oysters, 9th ab Green, h Brown and Centre
Warren Wm., 24 Franklin
Warren Wm., cordw., rear 7 Otter ab School (K)
Warren Wm., cotton spinner, G T road above Otter (K)
Warrin Jas., clerk, Cherry n Sch 6th
Warrin S. & A., corsets and toys, 281 Walnut
Warrington Benj. B., cordw., Reakirt's ct (K)
Warrington Deborah, bonnetmr., 52 Mulberry
Warrington Isaac D., combmr., 27 John
Warrington John, carter, Poplar bel Broad
Warrington Joseph, M. D., 229 Vine
Warrington Samuel R., watchmaker, 58 High, h 159 N 6th
Warrington S. R. & Co., watches, &c., 58 High
Warrington Thos., carp., 130 S 2d
Wartham M. P., drayman, 96 Coates
Wartham Sam'l, drayman, S E Apple & George
Warthman Adam, jr., drayman, 614 N 3d
Warthman Anthony M., drayman, 5th ab George

Warthman Charles, butcher, Marriott ab 4th
Wartman Abraham, Garden ab Noble
Wartman Abraham, vict., Parrish ab 10th
Wartman Edward, vict., Buttonwood ab 5th
Wartman Mary, Willow ab 8th
Wartman Michael, tobacconist, 173 N 3d, h 17 Dillwyn
Wartman Michael D., vict., 10 Callowhill street Market, h Garden ab Noble
Warwick Charles F., trimmings, N E Sch 7th and Lewis
Warwick Edw., furniture, 439 High, h 20 Perry
Warwick Lucretia, milliner, 326 Sassafras
Warwick Samuel, 9th and Willow
Warwick & Worrell, furniture, 439 High
Washburn L., Queen ab Shackamaxon
Washington C., 16 Marshall
Washington George, boot black, 75 Chestnut, h 162 S 5th
Washington H., doctor, 10 Little Pine
Washington John, carter, 15 Little Oak st
Wasson Mary, rear 13 Ogden
Waterfield Richard, druggist, 2 Young's pl
Waterford Chas., porter, White's ct
Waterford Joseph, sailmr., 8th bel Catharine
Waterhouse Elbridge G., printer, 214 S 9th
Waterman A. G., 56 Walnut, (above stairs,) h S W 11th and Spruce
Waterman & Ghalfant, tavern, 329 High
Waterman Isaac S., tavern, 329 High
Waterman Isaac S., merchant, 290 N 2d, h 247 Vine
Waterman John, lampmr., 31 Vernon
Waterman John, lumb. insp., Federal ab 2d
WATERMAN JOSEPH, Western Exch., High W Sch 8th
Waterman Lewis, measurer, M road bel Prime
Waterman Mary, Front and Margaretta
Waterman & Osbourn, grocers, N W 2d & Mulberry
Waterman Robert H., carp., Hudson's al, h 21

Waters Wm., waiter, 36 Bonsall st
Watford Eli, porter, 2 Burd's ct
Watford T. B., sexton, Union n F road
Watkin Catharine, dressmr., 15 Elfreth al
Watkins Benj. A., turner, 28 Dock, h 40 Catharine
Watkins David, moulder, Juniper & Lawrence
Watkins Jos., moulder, Allen above Shackamaxon (K)
Watkins Julianna, 98 Catharine
Watkins Sam'l P., jr., mer., 38 Bank, h Scheetz bel 2d
Watkins Thomas, lab., Marlboro' bel Beach
Watkins Thomas W., sailmr., 527 N 3d
Watkins Wm., cabinetmr., 606 S 2d
Watkins Wm., pedler, Hay's ct (K)
Watkins William B., mer., 36 Bank, h 98 Catharine
Watkinson & Hall, dry goods, 7 S 2d
Watkinson Richard, tailor, 140 Chestnut, house Chestnut (W P)
Watkinson R., grocer, Washington (W P)
Watkinson Wm., 215 N 9th
Watkinson W. E., mer., 7 S 2d, h 215 N 9th
Watling James, silversmith, 14 Nectarine
Watmore Chas., hay mer., 566 N 2d
Watmough Edmund C., att'y & coun., 18½ & h 309 Walnut
Watson Amor, watchman, Melon ab 9th
Watson Amos, flour store, 177 O Y road
Watson Ann, Parrish ab 5th
Watson Ann, teacher of music, 142 S 11th
Watson A., b. h., 162 N 2d
Watson Benj. R., lab., 2 Bickham's ct
Watson Brock, cabinetmr., 68 Callowhill, h 38 Dillwyn
Watson Cato, Gilles' al
WATSON CHARLES C. & SON, tailors, 92 Chestnut
Watson & Cox, wire workers, 48 N Front
Watson David, 266 Lombard

Watson James, watch maker, 72 High, h 527 Chestnut

Watson James H., bootmr., 30 & h 367 S 6th

Watson James S., wood wharf, 1st wharf above Green, h 16 Laurel (N L)

Watson James V., carp., 345 N 7th

Watson Jesse, 4 Green

Watson Johannas, iron chest mr., 76 S 3d, h 107 Lombard

Watson John, weaver, Brazier ab Lloyd

Watson John, cordw., Bedford ab 12th

Watson John, carp., 7th ab Poplar

Watson John, weaver, Master bel 2d (K)

Watson John, waiter, 359 Lombard

Watson John, boot black, 40 Blackberry al

Watson John, sailmr., Wheat ab Wharton

Watson John W., waterman, Higgins' ct (S)

Watson Joseph T., barber, 176 Sassafras

Watson J. F., lithographer, 80½ Walnut

Watson Margaret, widow, Spruce n Sch 5th

Watson Marmaduke, tavern, 193 N 2d

Watson & Rennels, fruiterers, 267 High

Watson Robert, shoemr., 236 Catharine

Watson Robert, jeweller, 104 Locust, h Marriott bel 3d

Watson Samuel, porter, rear Poplar ab 9th

Watson Samuel, blacksmith, Path

Watson Samuel, engineer, Union ab F road (K)

Watson Samuel F., teacher, 128 Catharine

Watson Samuel H., plumber, 152 S 4th, h Tanner ab Wharton

Watson Thomas, wire worker, 48 N Front, h 110 St John

Watson Washington, N W 13th & Walnut

Watson Wm., porter, 4 Deal's ct

Watson Wm., weaver, Front and Oxford

Watson Wm., carter, 378 S 5th

Watson Wm., 31 S 10th

Watson Wm., carp., Nectarine bel 11th

Watson Wm., brushmr., 313 S 6th

Watson Wm., capt., 49 Almond

Watson Wm., ladies' shoemr., rear 119 Queen

Watson Wm., mer., 36 N whfs, h 40 Almond

Watson Wm. B., tailor, 349 N 6th

Watson Wm. J., Spruce n Sch 8th

Watson Wm. S., mer., 267 High

Watt Alex., manf., 13th ab Cedar

Watt Ann, tailoress, 80 Apple

Watt David, manuf., Pine E Sch 3d, h 348 Pine

Watt Edith, mantuamr., Callowhill ab 11th

Watt George L., gunsm., h 99 W High

Watt Jas., basketmr., Vienna ab Queen (K)

Watt John, manf., 13th ab Cedar

Watt John M., saddler, Ailen n F road

Watt Joseph, tinman, Callowhill ab Nixon

Watt Joseph, cordw., 353 N Front

Watt Mary, tailoress, Adams bel 13th

Watt Moses, weaver, Hope ab Master (K)

Watt Nicholas, lab., Palm ab Brown

Watt Wm. W., manf., Pine E Sch 3d, h George ab Sch 6th

Watt Wm., manuf., Sch 3d and Pine, h Sch 5th bel Spruce

Watters Wm., shoemr., 3 Benton's av

Wattles Andrew D., port. paint., 323 Vine

Watts Anna, 1 Federal

Watts Benj., lab., Corn ab Reed

Watts Daniel, lab., Corn n Reed

Watts Edw., contractor, Dorothy n Sch 3d

Watts E., lab., Corn ab Reed

Watts George, importer, 11 S 2d, and S W 2nd and High

Watts George, cordw., Abraham's ct (K)

WATTS HENRY M., att'y and counsellor, 148 Walnut

Watts James, silversmith, 7 Lodge al, house 27 Blackberry al

Watts Jas., lab., Sch 4th ab George (F V)

Watts John, cutler, 82 F road (K)

Watts John, weaver, Howard bel Master (K)

Watts Jos. G., oyster h, 82 F road (K)

Watts Wm., silversm., 21 Franklin pl., h P road bel Christian

Wattson Edw. F., clerk, 151 Dillwyn

Wattson Edwin, biscuit baker, 129 N Front, h 22 Sassafras

Wattson Thomas, biscuit baker, 129 & h 164 N Front

Wattson Thomas B., biscuit baker, 129 N Front h 324 N 6th

WATTSON THOMAS & SONS, biscuit bakers 129 N Front

Waud Lavinia, Olive ab 10th

Waugh S. B., port. paint., S E 9th and Chestnut

Wauhope Chas., soap manuf., Shippen ab 12th

WAY A. H. & CO., gents. furnishing store, 161 Chestnut

Way Elizabeth Mrs., Chancellor n Sch 6th

Way Francis D., mer., 18 S Front, h N W Juniper & Walnut

Way G. H., carp., Christian bel 7th

Way Joseph, pilot, 127 Lombard

Way Jos., jr., tailor, rear Carpenter bel 8th

Way J. T., mer., 67 High, h 342 N 6th

Way Wm., lab., Washington av

Wayman Alex. Rev., Hurst st

Wayne Anthony, hardware, 2d & Almond

Wayne Caleb P., hardware, S W 4th & High, h 55 N 4th

Wayne Charles, mer., Buttonwood ab 8th

Wayne Charles S., hatter, 19 N 4th, h Washington ab 10th

Wayne & Co., hatters, 19 N 4th

WAYNE C. P. & SON, hardw. & look. glasses S W 4th & High

Wayne Daniel, cabtmr., rear 9 St James

Wayne Edward F., clerk, 25 Logan sq

Wayne E. C., hardware, S W 4th and High, h Washington

Wayne Wm. H., Cherry ab Sch 6th
Waytts Chas., whitewash., 11th bel Cedar
Weaber Geo. J., tailor, Hanover bel Bedford
Weadley Wm., bricklayer, Ellis st
Wear Hugh, lab., Washington ab 13th
Wear Judah, Brown ab 6th
Wear & Wood, wood mers., wharf 219 N Water
Wearmouth Michael, tailor, Nectarine bel 11th
Wears Isaiah, hair dresser, Poplar ab 5th
Weart John A., stage office, 45 S 3d
Weatherby Cavalier, gent., S 7th ab Catharine
Weatherby Mary, 5th ab Coates
Weatherly David, jr., convey., 19 S 3d, h 50 N 10th
Weatherly D., watchmr., 150 N 10th
Weatherstine Saml., brickmr., Poplar bel 2d
Weaver Adam, cooper, Sch 6th, bet Market & Chestnut, h 14 Howard
Weaver Albert, ropemr., Franklin and Shackamaxon
Weaver Albert, segars, 4 Smith's al
Weaver Alexander, Buttonwood & 5th
Weaver Caroline, widow of Jacob, 11 Wagner's court
Weaver Catharine, Apple ab George (N L)
Weaver Chas., currier, rear 527 N 4th
Weaver Chas., locksm., 9 Freed's av
Weaver Chas., bookbinder, Wistar ab 11th
Weaver Cromley P., carp., Sch 6th ab Thompson
Weaver Daniel, iron work., Filbert n Sch 5th
Weaver David, Charlotte ab Culvert
Weaver D. J., carp., George bel 11th
Weaver Edward, carp., rear 360 S 2d
Weaver Edw. H., plumber, N W 12th & Locust
Weaver Elijah, stationer, 55 N Front, h 76 Dillwyn
Weaver Elijah, stove finisher, Carpenter bel 3d
Weaver Frederick, weaver, rear Hanover below Franklin
Weaver Fredk., machinist, Elizabeth ab Poplar
Weaver Geo., coachmr., 157 Pine
Weaver George, brickmaker, rear Marshall ab Poplar
Weaver Geo. I., ship chandler, 19 N Water and 11 N whfs, h 412 N Front
Weaver Geo. P., agent, Alice ct
Weaver G., shop, 9th & Callowhill
Weaver Henry, brickmr., Pleasant ab 11th
Weaver Henry, stove finisher, Fralcy's ct (K)
Weaver Henry, combmr., 85 N Juniper
Weaver Henry, vict., Loud bel 10th
Weaver Henry C., fruiterer, 227 Walnut
Weaver H. E. Mrs., milliner, 499 N 2d
Weaver Isaiah, barber, Coates bel Broad
Weaver Jacob, grate manufact., 121 S 8d, h 56 Union
Weaver John, Leiper's ct

Weaver Peter, rag dealer, Apple bel George
Weaver Reuben S., M. D., 219 N 6th
Weaver Reynolds, bootmr., Orchard bel Jackson
Weaver Samuel, oak cooper, Washington below 13th
Weaver Thos., lab., 189 Lombard
Weaver Valentine, cordw., R road ab Ann (F V)
Weaver & Volkmar, grate and fender mrs., 121 S 3d
Weaver Wm., sexton, Centre bel 13th
Weaver Wm., paper & rags, St John ab Popla:
Weaver Wm. F., mer., 12 N 3d, h 14 Clinton
Weaver Wm. W., bricklayer, Sch 7th ab Vine
Webb Albert, carp., 19 Franklin pl
Webb Ann, 63 S 11th
Webb Burkitt, grocer, S E Front and Queen, h 32 Catharine
Webb Charles, grocer, N W 7th and High
Webb Charles R., grocer, S E Front & Queen, h 12 Queen
Webb Edward G., printer, 6 N road
Webb Elizabeth, N road bel Christian
Webb George, grocer, 130 N 11th
Webb George, blacksm., Jackson (N L)
Webb Greenleaf S. Rev., 201 Queen
Webb Hiram, tailor, 6 S 3d
Webb Isaac L., trunkmr., 14 Ellen
Webb Jas. L., cur'er, 50 N 4th, h 229 Marshall
WEBB JAMES R., grocer, S W 2d and Dock, h 24 Sansom
Webb John, 39 George (S)
Webb John, tavern, 16 N 3d
Webb John, cabtmr., c Culvert and Mechanic
Webb John, 214 N 5th
Webb John, painter, Callowhill ab Sch 6th
Webb Joseph, lab., 32 Mayland
Webb Joseph, lab., Court al
Webb Joshua, currier, 2 Wallace
Webb L., shipwright, 75 German
Webb & Norton, tailors, 6 S 3d
Webb Rebecca, 443 S 2d
Webb Rebecca N E P road and Washington
Webb Reuben, grocer, 50 N 4th, h 244 Green
Webb Reuben & Son, curriers, 50 N 4th
Webb Saml., tanner, Williams' ct
Webb Samuel, gent., 60 New
WEBB SAMUEL, conveyancer, 58 S 4th, h 16 Logan sq
Webb Thos., carp., 36 Beck (S)
Webb Thos. S., Eagle Hotel, 139 N 3d
Webb Thos. W., druggist, N W 3d & Shippen
Webb Wm., 349 N 6th
Webb Wm., waterman, Miles' ct
WEBB WILLIAM B. & CO., druggists, S W 10th and Sp Garden
Webb Ziba, mer., Callowhill ab Nixon
Webber Benj. Rev., Ogden bel 10th

Weber Henry, lab., Senneff's ct
Weber Henry, pianomr., 208 Cherry
WEBER JACOB, druggist, S E Shippen & 9th
Weber Jacob, cordw., Duke ab Cherry (K)
Weber John C., mer., 96½ High
Weber Matthias, tailor, 4th bel G T road
Weber Wm, mer., 4 Commerce, h St John n Bridge
Weber Wm. & Co., paper and rags, 4 Commerce
Webster Chauncey Rev., 329 Pine
Webster Daniel, seaman, 13 Plum
Webster David, atty. and coun., 1 State House, h 145 N 9th
Webster Jarvis, 120 N 4th
Webster John R., bricklayer, 145 N 9th
Webster Joseph, dealer, 162 Swanson
Webster Joseph, boat builder, Beach ab Warren, h Queen ab Palmer
Webster Osgood R., shoe store, 277½ N 2d, h 1 Jay (S P)
Webster & Patterson, brickmrs., Cedar n Sch 3d
WEBSTER THOMAS, Jr., tobac. mer., 54 S Front, h 145 N 9th
Webster Wm., farmer, Cedar n Sch 2d
Webster Wm., bricklayer, Brook ab Coates
Webster Wm. K., cabinetmr., German bel 4th
Weckerly Abr'm., vict., O Y road n Poplar
Weckerly Daniel, shoemr., 226 Callowhill
Weckerly Daniel L., druggist, c G T road and Otter
Weckerly Elizabeth, rear Mechanic ab Culvert
Weckerly Elizabeth, widow, 157 Coates
Weckerly Elizabeth, sempstress, rear 73 G T road (K)
Weckerly George, brickmr., 270 Coates
Weckerly Jacob, vict., 265 N 8th
Weckerly John, vict., 157 Buttonwood
Weckerly John, vict., 123 Coates
Weckerly Joseph, vict., Apple ab George
Weckerly Peter, vict, Vinyard (F V)
Weckerly Peter, vict., 333 N Front
Weckerly Sarah, G T road and Otter (K)
Weckert Geo., lab., Ogden's ct
Weed Joseph, manuf., Bedford bel Crown
Weed Mrs. E., 172 S 3d
Weed Wm., Robert Morris House, Fairmount
Weeks Andrew, botanic med., Poplar ab 12th
Weeks Christian, lab., 7th ab Little Poplar
Weeks Christian Mrs., Shackamaxon n Bedford
Weeks Edo., tailor, Ogden n 10th
Weeks E., lab., Queen ab 2d
Weeks Jeremiah, shingle dr., Miller's ct (N L)
Weeks Joel, feed store, 225 E Cedar
Weeks John, cordw., Shackamaxon n Bedford (K)
Weeks John, saw filer, 449 S Front
Weeks Joseph, ladies' shoes, Linden bel Benton
Weeks Joshua, sheet iron work, Rachel n Laurel
Weeks Josiah, shoemr., Tammany ab 2d
Weeks Nathaniel, shoemr., 15 Helmuth
Weeks Severn, lab., George n Sch 7th
Weeks Wm., mariner, 26 Catharine
Weeks Wm. W., fancy goods, 96 N 6th, h 1 Haines

Weer Samuel W., painter, 21 S 8th, h 147 N 12th
Wehmeyer Frederick, baker, 422 N 4th
Wehner B. J., cordw., 230 Vine
Wehrung Nicholas, cabinetmr., 136 Brown
Weibel John, tailor, 398 N 2d
Weibel Robert, lab., Hay's ct (K)
Weichselbaum L., musician, rear 17 Lily al
Weidel Earnest F., cordw., Callowhill ab 13th
Weidle Andw., baker, 290 St John
Weidler John, bootmr., 79 Callowhill
Weidley Henry, tinman, 12 Gebhard
Weidling Harman J., cabmr., 407 N 4th
Weidner David, stationer, 412 N 6th
Weidner George P., carman, rear 308 St John
Weidner L. F., toolmr., rear 76 N 6th
Weidershiem Wm., tea and coal, 396 N 3d
Weigel F., baker, 59 St John bel George (K)
Weightman Jno., shovelmr., Washington (W P)
Weighton John, rear 452 Callowhill
Weikel Hannah, shop, N E Beaver & St John (K)
Weikel Peter, segars, 80 N 3d
Weil Abraham, pedler, 59 N Market
Weil Benjamin, pedler, 59 New Market
Weil H. J., box manuf., 190 N 5th
Weil Simon, b. h., Sassafras bel 2d
Weiland F., music teacher, 208 Cherry
Weiler David, trader, 19 Tammany
Weiller Herman, clothing, 78 N 2d
Weilman F., tailor, Poplar bel 4th
Weiner Wm., pedler, 515 St John
Weinert J. F., boot and shoemr., Front & Coates
Weingartner Andrew, cordw., rear 21 Charlotte
Weingärtner Mary, Pleis' ct (K)
Weir Chas., bookbinder, F road opp Otter
Weir Charlotte, 140 S 11th
Weir & Jack, grocers, Sch 5th and High
Weir Margaret, Sch 4th n Dorothy
Weir Robert, cordw., 252 S 5th
Weirman John, tailor, 68 N 10th, h Nectarine bel 11th
Weirman Saml., cordw., 273½ N Front
Weirman & Swanger, tailors, 86 N 10th
Weiseman Samuel, butcher, 230 N 9th
Weiser Geo., lab., Hummel's row
Weisgarper Frederick, moroc dress., 49 Duke
Weisman Edwd., printer, 4 Deinger's ct
Weisman Jacob, tobacconist, F road bel Queen
Weisman Wm., ropemr., Washington ab R road
Weiss Chas., coal yard, 9th ab Poplar
Weiss Ernest, drug importer, 43 N Front
Weiss Geo., silversm., 399 N Front
Weiss Geo. E., grocer, Beaver, Palmer ab Duke
Weiss John, sugar boiler, Piper's ct
WEISS & SCHIVELY, drugs, 43 N Front
Weisz & Kipp, tailors, 299 N 3d
Weitzell Jacob W., ladies' shoes, 79 N 8th
Weixelbaum Abraham, optician, rear 17 Lily al
Weixelbaum Isaac, musician, Sansom al
Welch Benj., manuf., 10th ab Poplar
Welch Francis, lab., Sch 3d bel George
Wessman Frederick, tailor, rear 118 Brown
Welch George, shoemr., Wallace ab R road
Welch Henry D., cordw., 10th ab Poplar

Welch James C., atty. and coun., S E 5th and Library
Welch John C., dentist, 116 N 7th
Welch John H., barber, Front and Sassafras
Welch Mary, 359 S 3d
Welch & Walter, engravers, 112 Union
Welch Wm. M., provisions, 343 Spruce, h Sycamore ab Spruce
Wellbank John, tavern, Rugan and Callowhill
Wellbank Sarah, wid. of Henry, James and Willow
Weld H. H., editor, Green bel 10th
Welden Elizabeth, Hope bel Master (K)
Welden James, weaver, Brinton ab 12th
Welden John, fisherman, rear Palmer op Allen
Welden Obed, cordw., 27 Cresson's al
Welding Charles, painter, 5 Elfreth's al
Weldon Alex., framemr., 4th bel Franklin
Weldon Lawrence J., fisherman, Beach above Hanover
Weldon Wm., ship carp., Cherry ab Queen
Welien Andrew, tailor, 104 New Market
Weller Fredk., drayman, 1 Young's al
Weller Jesse, agt. R. R., State ab 5th 8th
Weller Samuel, carter, Division bel 12th
Welling Chas. H., mer., 22 Chestnut
Welling Sarah H., b. h., 161 Chestnut
Wellington John, scourer, 42 Gaskill
Wellington John B., cordw., Reckless ct
Wellington Mary, nurse, 6 College pl
Wellington Richard T., tobacconist, 62 Sassafras, h 130 N 2d
Wellington Wm., printer, 130 N 2d
Wells Ann, nurse, William n Sch 3d
Wells Ann, Cob's ct
Wells Catharine, 83 St John
Wells Ellen, wid. of Elisha, 128 Franklin
Wells Eliza, tailoress, 7 Skerrett's ct
Wells Emanuel, lab., Taylor's ct
Wells F. S., gent., Charlotte ab Poplar
Wells Israel, printer, Tyler st
Wells Jacob, lab., 46 Quince
Wells James, cordw., 12 Myer's ct
Wells Jas., cordw., Duke n Cherry (K)

Welsh Henry, bootmr., 362 N 4th
Welsh Henry, naval officer, Custom House
Welsh Henry, tobacconist, 202 S 6th
Welsh Henry J., bootmr., 143 Green
Welsh Jacob, carp., 8th bel Coates
Welsh James, tea store, 192 N 2d
Welsh James, weaver, Crown ab Franklin (K)
Welsh James, shoemr., 319 S 3d
Welsh James, printer, 261 S 3d
Welsh John, plasterer, Buttonwood rear 13th
Welsh John, slater, Ontario bel Poplar
Welsh John, plasterer, 11th & Christian
Welsh John, mer., 51 S whfs, h 91 Pine
Welsh John, weaver, Baker's ct
Welsh John, weaver, Cadwalader bel Jefferson
Welsh John, jr., mer, 50 S whfs, h 402 Spruce
Welsh J. R., 64 O Y road
Welsh Lewis, weaver, rear G T road ab Master (K)
Welsh Michael, wheelwrt., 26 Pegg
Welsh Orlando, cordw., N W Crown & Callowhill
Welsh Patrick, porter, 8 Little Pine
Welsh Patrick, weaver, Cadwalader ab Phœnix
Welsh Patrick, weaver, rear G T road ab Master (K)
Welsh Richard, drayman, Lombard ab Sch 7th
Welsh Richard E., collector, 117 Lombard
Welsh Robert, weaver, Cadwalader ab Master
Welsh Saml., mer., 50 S whfs, h 8 Portico sq
Welsh Saml. M., sea capt., Catharine bel 2d
Welsh Samuel & William, mers., 50 S whfs
Welsh Thos., blacksm, Kneass' ct
Welsh Thos., cabman, Jones n Sch 5th
Welsh Walter, ropemr., Wheat and Corn
Welsh Walter, 6th bel Shippen
Welsh Wm., shoemr., rear 198 Sassafras
Welsh Wm., mer., 50 S whfs, h 400 Spruce
Welsh Wm., lab., Ann E Sch 3d
Welsh Wm. H., cooper, rear Beck bel 2d
Welsor Edwin H., chairmr., 241 Cedar
Wemmer N. J., carpet manf., High n Sch Front, h 193 Locust
Wenban James, tavern, 153 S Front
Wendel John, dealer, 115 Poplar

Wentz Hannah, 262 N 7th
WENTZ WM. K., auctioneer, 279 High, h 262 N 7th
Wentzell Lewis J., wheelwr., 6 Pleasant Retreat
Wenzell A., boot and shoemr., 597 N 2d
Wenzell Geo., wheelwr., William n Edward
Wenzell John W., tailor, Ogden bel 10th
Wenzell Samuel, joiner, Queen ab Palmer (K)
Weper Henry, baker, Crown bel Duke (K)
Werber Joseph, shop, S W Pegg & N Market
Werner George C., torpedo mr., 10 Hickory ct
Wernly Chas., vict., 591 N 3d
Wernwag Wm., baker, 555 Chestnut
Wert Peter, whipmr., Marlborough bel Franklin
Wesby John, cooper, 15 Jones' al, h Catharine ab 7th
Wesby & M'Donald, coopers, 15 Jones' al
Wescott Deborah, 25 Linden st (K)
Wesley Ann, 4 Quarry
Wesley John, drayman, 3 Mechanic's av
Wesley Michael, iron moulder, rear Wood ab Broad, h Burr's ct
West Abigail, gentw., 49 Spruce
West Abraham, blacksm., 34½ Elfreth's al, h 108 Crown
West Anna, gentw., 143 N 7th
West Arthur, porter, Lisle bel Shippen
West Benj., bricklr., Poplar bel 9th
West Charles C., gent., 45 Marshall
West Charles E., umbrellamr., George & Charlotte
WEST & COX, coal mers., 86 S 3d
West Dennis, lab., Orchard and Rawle
West Eliza, 372 Walnut
West Elizabeth, 3 Starr al
West F. jr., M. D., office 119 Walnut, h 108 S Front
West George, baker, 490 S 2d
West George, carter, 94 Bedford
West George G., clerk Phila. Bank, h N E 3d and Christian
West Hannah, druggist, Queen ab Hanover (K)
West Hannah, dressmr., 52 Logan
West Henry, cordw., Cedar bel 10th
West Henry, brassfounder, West ab Marlboro'
West Isaac, waiter, 5 Blackberry al
West James, gent., 366 Walnut
West James, blacksmith, Filbert bel 9th, h 42 Filbert
West James, shoemr., 164 S 11th
West James, lab., Lisle ab Fitzwater
West James, shoemr., Blight
West John, provision store, 47 Currant al
West John, janitor, 31 S Juniper
West John, waterman, 55 Mead al
West Joseph, lab., Herrigues' ct
West Joseph, ——, ———— 3d and Wood

West Richard, brass founder, Perry ab Franklin (K)
West Richard L., 316 S 2d
West Robert, gent., 537 Chestnut
West Robt., lab., rear Marriott bel 6th
West Samuel, hatter. Benton's av
West Samuel C., boot and shoemr., 347 Pine
West Sarah, Sch 8th ab Mulberry
West Thomas, hatter, rear 196 Christian
West Tobias, dealer, 2 S 8th, h 12 Barley
West Washington, ship carp., Allen bel Marlborough
West Wm. jr., coal mer., 86 S 3d, h 82 Lombard
West Wm., ship master, 10th n Shippen
West Wm., lab., 2 Warren
West Wm., dry goods, 279 S 2d
West Wm. M., tobacconist, George bel 3d (K)
West Wm. P., bootmr., 184 E Pine
West Wm. R., carp., Citron bel 13th
Westcott Augustus, waterman, Sarah n Bedford (K)
Westcott Giles, plumber, 298 Sassafras, h Winter ab Sch 3d
Westcott G. G., mer., 107½ High, h 268 Pine
Westcott Joseph, waterman, Court al
Westcott Joseph jr., waterman, 26 Coates
Westcott Richard, lab., Winter st
Westcott Thompson, atty. & coun., 24 George, h rear 23 N 6th
Westenberger Jacob, gent., 362 S 4th
Wester Andrew J., grocer, Hanover and Franklin (K)
Wester Eliz'th., Franklin bel Union (K)
Wester E. H., painter, 3 F road, h Allen below Hanover (K)
Wester Isaac, barber, 517 High, h Sch 3d n Pine
Wester Mary, tailoress, rear 468 N 3d
Westerhood B. H., city watch, 2 Walnut al
Westerhood Lewis D., tailor, 19 Queen (K)
Westerfield Henry, tailor, rear 126 Queen
Westford Sarah, washer, 20 Elizabeth
Westhoff Chas., weaver, 1 Pearl st
Westley Richd., pilot, Bevan's ct
Westner Robt., blacksm., Brown bel Front
Westney Mary, 53 Queen
Weston Elizabeth, 25 Benton
Weston John M., herb doctor, 4 S 7th, h 61 N 7th
Westphal Harriet, nurse, rear 77 George
Wetherald Haworth, clerk, 22 Prune
Wetherby E., bricklayer, 301 Lombard
WETHERILL & BROTHER, druggists, 65 N Front
Wetherill Charlotte Miss, 12th ab Mulberry
Wetherill Christopher, mer., 56 N Front, h 20 Mulberry

Wetherill John M., lumb. mer., S W Sch 5th & Mulberry, h Sch 4th ab Chestnut
Wetherill John P., druggist, 65 N Front, h 13th bet Cherry and Mulberry
Wetherill John Price & Wm., white lead and chemicals, 12th and Cherry
Wetherill John P. jr., 13th ab Mulberry
Wetherill Joseph, dry goods and trimmings, 324 S Front
Wetherill Marg. S. Mrs., 461 Mulberry ab 12th
Wetherill Mary, gentw., 170 S 4th
Wetherill Rachel A., dry goods and trimmings, 343 S 2d, h 324 S Front
Wetherill Wm., M. D., 65 N Front
Wetherill Wm. H., mer., 56 N Front
Wetherly Henry, musician, 71 Carpenter (S)
Wething Priscilla, sempstress, 170 Locust
Wethington Joseph, musician, 30 Quince
Wethman James, Bacon's ct
Wetter Henry, blacksm., Bedford opp Union
Wetter John, cabinetmr., 59 Garden
Wetter John H., boot crimper, Shackamaxon bel F road
Wetter Philip, weaver, Bedford opp Union
Wetzell Charles S., carp., Beach ab Marlboro'
Wetzell John, button mr., Fitler ab 2d (K)
Wetzell Paul, cordw., Hope ab Otter
Wetzell Peter, carp., Shackamaxon bel Franklin
Wevill George, upholsterer, 52 S 5th
Wex Hannah, Cadwalader bel Phoenix
Weyand Joseph, cordw., Front bel Phoenix (K)
Weyant Geo. W., boiler mr., Sarah n Queen (K)
Weyant John, carp., 2 Mechanic (N L)
Weyant Peter, collector, 446 N 4th
Weyant Samuel, alderman, office F road and Allen, h 86 F road (K)
Weygand Henry, clerk, 20 Chatham
Weygand Philip, oysterhouse, High st ferry, h 20 Chatham
Weygandt Conrad, sugar refiner, rear 100 St John
Weygant Thomas J., musical instrument mr., 10 N 8th
Weyl Henry G., bleeder and cup., 366 Coates
Weyman Christian, tobacconist, 22 N 6th
Weyman Daniel, 24 Mintzer
Weyman Elizabeth, 308 N Front
Weyman George, awning mr., rear 19 Noble
Weyman Margaret, b. h., Jones' al
Weymer Jacob W., tinsmith, 10½ N 6th
Weymer Samuel, tinsmith, 10½ N 6th
Weymer Samuel & Son, stoves, 10½ N 6th
Weyser C., dyer, 10th bel Buttonwood
Whaland Thomas, baker, 21 Ellen
Whale Henry, dancing school, Assembly Build.
Whan John, weaver, G T road bel Jefferson (K)
Whartenby Geo., cordw., Carpenter bel 10th
Whartenby James, silversmith, 211 Mulberry
Whartenby John, cooper, rear 4 Burd st
Whartenby Joseph, tailor, Carpenter bel 10th
Whartenby Thos., silver ware manuf., 211 Mulberry, h 12th ab Callowhill
Whartenby Thomas & Co., silver ware manufs., 211 Mulberry
Wharton Ann, 87 Pine

Wharton & Bard, carps., Dillwyn ab Tammany
Wharton Benj., saddler, 119 Noble
Wharton Benj. D., mariner, 20 Parham
Wharton Carpenter, bookseller, 174 Buttonwood
Wharton Charles W., merchant, 29 N 3d, h 130 Spruce
Wharton Daniel C., mer., 6 S Front, h Spruce n Broad
Wharton Elisha, mariner, rear 92 Christian
WHARTON FRANCIS, atty. & coun., 150 and 152 Walnut
Wharton Francis R., gent., 322 Chestnut
Wharton F., real est. brok., 47 S 4th, h 13th bel Green
Wharton George F., shoemr., Beaver ab 2d (K)
Wharton G. M., atty. and coun., 13 Prune
Wharton G. W., carp., 8th bel Cedar, h 200 S 4th
Wharton Hannah, gentw., 304 Walnut
Wharton James D., cordw., 6 Wood (K)
Wharton Jas. S., coal deal., Broad and Mulberry
Wharton John, carp., Melon bel 13th
Wharton John, cordw., 13 Dyott's ct (K)
Wharton Joseph, carp., 7 Union ct
Wharton Keziah, 11 Lombard ct
Wharton Mahlon, 7th ab Poplar
Wharton Mary M., milliner, S E 5th & Chestnut
Wharton Misses, gentw., 197 Spruce
WHARTON RODMAN, white lead manuf. 101 S Front, h 130 Spruce
Wharton Thos., clerk, Filbert W of Sch 7th
Wharton Thomas F., gent., 154 S 10th
WHARTON THOMAS I., atty. and coun., 150 Walnut
Wharton Wm., gent., 130 Spruce
Wharton Wm. D., cordw., 8th bel Parrish
Wheaton Amos, machinist, Vine bel 13th
Wheaton Isaac, carp., Penn bel Shackamaxon
Wheaton Joseph, shoemr., Lawrence's ct (K)
Wheaton Richard, grocer, 340 N Front
Wheaton Samuel, blacksm., Beach ab Marlborough (K)
Wheeler Ann F., 48 Crown
Wheeler Baltis, chairmr., 264 Mulberry
Wheeler Charles, atty. and coun., S E 5th and Library
Wheeler Jonathan Jones, ship master, 95 Vine
Wheeler John, blacksm., 46 N 8th, h 196 Locust
Wheeler John, gentw., Hamilton village
Wheeler John J., coal mer., Broad ab Cedar
Wheeler John R., shower baths, 64 & h 21 Dock
Wheeler Stephen, 9th bel Catharine
Wheeler Thomas, carp., Chancellor n Sch 6th
Wheeler U. H., M. D., dentist, 18 S 12th
Wheeles John H., atty & coun., 52 N 6th
Wheelhouse Elizabeth, 17 Linden (K)
Wheeling John, lab., Pearl ab Broad
WHELAN EDWARD, gas fitter & lampmr., 6 S 7th, h 75 Filbert
Whelan John G., mer., 158 High, h F road
Whelan Martin, lab., Ann n Sch 3d
Whelan Timothy, tanner, rear 238 St John
Whelan Timothy, weaver, Murray n Sch 3d
Whelan Timothy, dealer, P road bel Marriott
Whelan Townsend, broker, Spruce bel Sch 8th

Whelan Wm., carp., 24 Garden
Whelan Wm., 187 Spruce
Whelan Wm., weaver, Murray n Sch 3d
Whelan Wm. E., mer., 158 High, h 124 S 3d
WHELAN W. E. & J. G., shoes, caps & bonnets, 158 High
Whelen Edward S., stock & exch. broker, 9 S 3d, h S side Spruce ab Broad
Whelen Mary, Sch 8th ab Pine
Whenner Harriet, Clinton bel Poplar
Whetham John W., com. mer., 78 N whfs., h N W 13th and Green
Whetham Joseph, 42 N whfs., h N W 13th and Green
Whetham J. D., ship chandler, 5 N Water and R road ab Green
Whetham J. & J. D., ship chandlers, 5 N Water & 42 N whfs.
Whetstone Abraham, plasterer, Johnson's lane ab 3d
Whetstone Catharine, gentw., 6th bel Christian
Whetstone Samuel, shoemr., Green & 13th
Whillden Seth, cordw., 545 S 2d
Whilldin Alex., mer., 19 N Front, h 20 Pine
Whilldin Oliver, shoe store, 113 & h 350 S 2d
Whilldin Washington, 22 Pear
Whilldin Wilmon, jr., capt., 224 S Front
Whilldin Wilmon, sen., capt., 224 S Front
Whinna Ann, F road ab Phœnix (K)
Whipper Alfred, clothing, 12 N 2d
Whipple George P., bricklayer, 4 Reckless
Whipple Job, grocer, Coates n Fairmount
Whipple Mary, b h, 15 Scheetz
Whipple Wm., capt., 8th & Wallace
Whistler Isaac, coachman, 221 St John
Whisler Jacob, lab., 175 Green
Whisnor John, pol. off., Atherton
Whistell Wm., lab., rear 265 St John
Whister Peter, cordw., Edward bel Germantown road (K)
Whitaker Ephraim, cabinetmr., R road below Broad
Whitaker Frances M., washer, rear 129 Walnut
Whitaker Joseph, clerk, Noble bel 8th
Whitaker Mary, 264 Coates
Whitall & Brother, druggists & glassw. 70 N 3d
Whitall Hannah A. & Deborah, 238 N 4th
Whitall Henry, pedler, Sch Front & Lombard
Whitall John M., mer., 70 N 3d, h 185 N 7th
Whitall Joshua, 6 Linden (K)
Whitall Joshua, M. D., druggist, Queen opp Cherry
Whitall Joseph, teacher, Vine ab 4th, h N E Buttonwood & Marshall
Whitall Tacy P., 31 N 10th
Whitcraft Abner, rigger, Brown & Franklin (K)
White Albert, tailor, Ross ab Queen (K)
White Albert, barber, S W. 6th & Cherry
White Alex., tobacconist, 396 N 2d
White Alphonso, carp., rear 43 Cherry, h 3 Crown
White Ambrose, gent., 363 Mulberry
White Ann, Logan bel Sp Garden
White Ann, washer, Allen's ct
White Arthur, distillery, Sch 3d ab Lombard

White Arthur, weaver, Wagner's al
White Arthur, lab., Stephens' ct
White A. J., mer., 11 S Water, h 9th bel Fitzwater
White & Bacon, conveyancers, 206 Mulberry
White Benj., machinist, Palmer n Franklin (K)
White Benj., lab., Fox's ct
WHITE & BROTHER, hardware, 127¼ N 3d, h 283 S 10th
White Catharine, 179 Coates
White Charles, waiter, 7 Mercer
White Charles, weaver, rear F road bel Master
White Charles, painter & glazier, Sch 7th bel Sassafras
White Charles H. cabinetmr. 199 Walnut, h 283 S 10th
White Charles R., mariner, 8 Reckless
WHITE C. H. & J. F., cabinetmrs., 109 Walnut
White Daniel, cordw., 21 Hazel
White David, drayman, Cherry & Sch 3d
White David, tailor, S W Water & Mulberry, h 47 Sassafras
White David, carp., 308 Pine
White David H., mer., 29 S whfs., h Walnut n Sch 8th
White David W., acct., New Crown bel Green
White Deborah, gentw., 4 Swanson
White Douglas, tavern, Bushhill
White Edward, eating house, 44 Arcade
White Edward, inst. mr., 20 S 4th, h Logan bel Sp Gar de n
White Edward, grocer, N W 4th & Coates, h Coates ab 4th
White Elisha, drayman, F road bel Oxford
White Eliza N., 48 St John
White Elizabeth, Hope bel Master (K)
White Emma, 31 Elizabeth
White Francis, lab., Murray
White George, findings, 497 High
White George, chairmr., 382 N 2d
White George, porter, 122 Lombard
White George C., hatter, 10 Smith's pl
White George M., bricklayer, 2 Short ct
White Hannah, shop, New Market and Laurel
White & Fellner, painters, 311 N 2d
White Francis, mariner, 6 Reckless
White George, carter, 321 St John (K)
White George, navy off., Sch 6th & Chestnut
White George C., plumber, 71 S 11th
White Henry, confectioner, Cedar ab 11th
White Hen., mer., 21 S Water, h 16 W Walnut
White Hen. G., manuf., Q Y road & Callowhll
White Hiram, oysters, 216 High, h Caroline pl
White Hugh, weaver, West bel Hanover
White Isaac, tavern, 4 Martin's ct
White Jacob C., barber, 100 O Y road
White James, cabinetmr., Hallowell
White James, painter, Lewis ab Poplar
White James, blacksm., Alder ab Poplar
White Jas., weaver, Quince n Lombard
WHITE JAMES, grocer, N W Marshall and Coates
White James, acct., 216 Green
White Jas. E., brassfound., rear G T road & 5th
White James, cabmr., 4 Morris

White James M., hair dresser, 15 S 4th
White James R., carp., 355 E Lombard
White James S., dry goods, 174 Sassafras
White Jane, 31 Chatham
White Jane, Maiden ab F road
White Jasper, Essex
White Jesse, mer., 11 Marshall
White Joel M., shoemr., Perry & Spruce
White John, lab., 2 Grape
White John, com. mer., 13th bel Green
White John, mer., 523 Chestnut
White John, porter, 2 Norris' ct
White John, weaver, F road op Queen
White John, variety store, 179 N 2d
White John, gent., Front & Duke
White John, grocer, 17 Beaver (K)
White John, weaver, Higham's ct (K)
White John, blacksm., Shippen ab Broad
White John, baker, 7 Gray's al
White John, butcher, rear 62 Catharine
White John, biscuit mr., Relief ct
WHITE JOHN A., alderman, 75 Locust, h Locust ab Juniper
White John F., cabmr., 107 Walnut
White John F., barber, Front and Vine, h 203 S 7th
White John J., atty. & coun., 206 Mulberry
White John P., mer., 124 High, h 109 S 8th
White John R., Pres. Mt. Carbon Railroad Co., & Del. Coal Co., 78½ Walnut, h 20 Clinton
White Jonas H., waterman, 17 Federal (S)
White Joseph, grocer, N W 8th & Buttonwood
White Joseph, broker, 23 Arcade, h 552 High
White Joseph, cabinetmr., 326 S 3d

White Robert, porter, 1 Osborn's ct
White Robert, furniture, 192 Cedar
White Robert, printer, 6 Paynter's ct
White Robert M., barber, 30 S 7th
White Samuel, coach driver, R road ab Francis
White Samuel, cabinetmr., 45 Cedar
White Samuel, carriage repos., 38 & 40 Dock
White Samuel C., flour store, 6th and Noble, h 268 N 6th
White Samuel F., seaman, Huling's ct
White Samuel G., brewer, 24 S 6th, h N W 9th and Mulberry
White Samuel M., postoffice, h 24 Powell
White Samuel S., dentist, 273 Race
White Sarah, b'h, 35 Dock
White Shadrach, porter, rear 153 Lombard
White, Stevens & Co., grocers, 21 S Water
White Thomas, bonnet manuf., 41 S 2d
White Thomas, bookbr., 7 Carberry ct
White Thomas, cordw., F road bel Bedford
White Thos., grocer, Poplar & Apple
White Thos., weaver, Benton bel William (K)
White Thos. E., seaman, M'Kean's ct
White Thomas H., N W 9th and Spruce
White Thomas H., lab., 4 Kelley's av.
White Thomas J., carp. New Market ab Laurel
White, Warner & Co., com. mers., 29 S whfs., & 49 S Water
White Wm., seaman, 7 Mead al
White Wm., shoemr., 10 Almond
White Wm., waterman, Mead al n 2d
White Wm., saddler, Gray's ct.
White Wm., waterman, Burd n Catharine
White Wm., atty. &

Whitehead Wm., shoemr., 34 Coates' al
Whitehouse Jane, widow, 390 N 3d
Whitely Richard, oyster house, 334 High
Whiteman Benj., lab., Stilt's ct
Whiteman Chas., skin dresser, Abraham's ct (K)
Whiteman Chas., shoemr., Marriott bel 4th
Whiteman Clarence, clerk, 135 N 11th
Whiteman David, carter, c 3d & George (N L)
Whiteman David, grocer, N W 11th & George
Whiteman Isaac A., carp., 12 Maiden (K)
Whiteman Jacob, baker, 40 Union
Whiteman Jacob, oyster house, S E 6th & Sassafras, h 16 Pennsylvania av
Whiteman Jacob, butcher, 5 Culvert
Whiteman John, lab., rear Carlton n Sch 5th
Whiteman John, 1st teller P. B'k, h 136 N 11th
Whiteman John, plumber, 195 Walnut
Whiteman Joseph, lab., Duke ab Wood
Whiteman Michael, clerk P. Bank, h 149 N 11th
Whiteman Peter, ladies' shoemr., 66 N 9th
Whiteman Peter, carter, Franklin ab Willow
Whiteman Rachel, trimmings shop, 117 Green
Whiteman Sarah, Wood bel Sch 5th
Whiteman Thomas, plasterer, Court al
Whiteman Wm., tanner, 543 N 2d
Whiteman Windell, cordw., Wood ab 13th
Whiteman Windell, gent., Wood bel Sch 7th
Whitemore Chas., 126 Franklin
Whiteside Geo., lab., 2 Hampton
Whiteside James, lab., 1 Hampton
Whiteside Jas., weav., Howard bel Franklin (K)
Whiteside Justus, druggist, 90 Crown
Whiteside Mark, carter, 13th ab Cedar
Whiteside Rush J., Short ct
Whitham Wm., jeweller, Hoovel's ct
Whiting Jos. P., baker, 227 S 6th
Whitingham Sarah, dry goods, 352 Callowhill
WHITMAN E. S., coal dealer, Broad and Sassafras
Whitman L. P., mer., 2 Chestnut
Whitman Misses, seminary, 122 S 5th
Whitman Nathan, 122 S 5th
Whitman Stephen F., fruiterer, 426 High
Whitman Wm. E., att'y & coun., office 49 S 5th
Whitney Alfred, blacksm., Queen bel Shackamaxon
Whitney Ann R., grocer, 25 Strawberry
Whitney Asa, machinist, Broad & Hamilton, h Sch 5th bel Cherry
Whitney & Brothers, glass manufs., 38 N Front
Whitney E. D., mer., 24 S Front
Whitney John J., mer., 32 S 4th
Whitney P. S., 117 S 3d, h George n Sch 6th
Whitney, Schott & Co., American dry goods, 24 S Front
Whitney Stillman, shoe store, Lister's pl
Whitney Wm., shipmaster, 83 Christian
Whitney Wm., mer., 24 S Front
Whitson Deborah, dry goods, 23 S Sch 6th
Whitson James, machinist, 20 John (S)
Whittaker Samuel, hatter, 429 N Front
Whittaker Sarah, tavern, Tammany & St John
Whittaker Wm., hatter, Weccacoe bel Catharine
Whittel Elizabeth, widow, G T road ab Franklin (K)

Whittelsey Mary Ann, widow, 352 N 3d
Whitten Wm., manuf., Lombard n Sch 2d
Whittington A., waiter, 18 Little Pine
Whittington Benj., cutter, 262 Sassafras
Whittington Ebenezer, lab., Pearl ab 13th
Whyte Isaac H., gent., 252 Filbert
Wiand Wm., confec., rear 23 John (S)
Wiatt Solomon, bookbinder, 171 High, h 6 Lfreth's al
Wiatt Wm. N., bookbinder, Beach bel Maiden
Wibberly James, shoemr., High n Sch 4th
Wible John, glass cutter, Quarry n Bread, house Union bel Franklin (K)
Wible Martin, cordw., Thomas al
Wible Rebecca, shop, 306 N Front
Wich Michael, lab., 6 Margaretta place
WICHT & LANKENAU, importers, 28 Chestnut
Wicht Wm. V., mer., 28 Chestnut, h 66¾ S 4th
Wick David, coal dealer, 15 Queen
Wickersham John B., wire worker, 223 High
Wickersham Morris S., broker, 78 S 3d, h 6 S Penn sq
WICKERSHAM & SON, stock br., 78 S 3d
Wickersham Thomas, broker, 73 S 3d, h S W Broad & Pine
Wickersham Wm. M., wire worker, 313 High, h 5 N 9th
Widdifield Abigail, supt. Wills' Hospital
Widdifield Hannah, conf., 151 S 9th
Widdifield Wm., mer., 71 N 10th
Widdifield Wm. A., acct., 223 Cherry
Widdons Mary, b. h., 11 Marriott
Widdows Chas., carp., 2 Truxton
Widdows Wm. P., clerk, 4 Swarthouse pl
Wideman Paul, bitmr., Marlboro' ab Bedford
Widener John, brickmr., 408 Coates
Widener Michael, carp., Olive bel 12th
Widener Wm., cordw., rear 119 Queen
Widman F. W., sword mr., 98 N 3d
Widmer Charles, shoemr., 12 S 2d
Wiedersum George, tinsm., Queen ab Shackamaxon
Wiegand George, inspector gas fittings Philadelphia gas works, h 10 Castle
Wiegand John, surg. inst. mr., 15 N 5th, h 432 Sassafras
Wiegand Joseph, baker, 52 Swanson
WIEGAND & SNOWDEN, surgical inst. mrs., 15 N 5th
Wieghtman Wm., chemist, 8th ab Brown
Wiegner Henry, carp., Lily al & Green
Wiegner Jacob, carp., 554 N 3d c Culvert
Wieland Augustus, rear 154 St John st
Wieland Jacob, jr., wheelwt., Bedford n Elm, h Clinton ab Parrish (K)
Wiener Heinrich, importer, 36 Chestnut, h 279 Sassafras
Wier J. & Sons, tailors, 227 Wood
Wiese John, shoemr., 3 Rodolph's ct
Wietezeli Conrad, carp., Filbert n Sch Front
Wiggins Charles, tavern, 322 N 2d
Wiggins Jacob P., tavern, 108 Plum
Wiggins Theodore, shoemr., 184 S 4th
Wight Andw., mer., 198 Chestnut, h 43 Clinton

Wight Charles, cordw., 11th ab Vernon
Wightman Aurelia, George n Sch 8th
Wightman Charles G., mer., 8 Commerce
Wightman Nathan, shoemr., 28 Quince
Wightman & Willcox, mers., 8 Commerce
Wignall Frances, Warren bel Queen (K)
Wikoff Peter, gent., 80 S 12th
Wilcocks Alex., M. D., 96 S 11th
Wilcocks Sarah, widow, 311 Walnut
Wilcox Augustin, mer., Rittenhouse ct
Wilcox David L., ship master, 17 Pine
Wilcox Edmund, merchant, 145 High, h 429 Walnut
Wilcox Elizabeth, 301 Spruce
Wilcox Frances E., stone cutter, 4 Madison
WILCOX, MARIS & CO., dry goods, 145 High
Wilcox Richardson, smith, Crown bel Franklin
Wilcox Wm., leghorn & straw hats, 7 S 3d, h 343 S 2d
Wild John, carrier, 15 Marion
Wild Sam'l, spinner, Franklin ab Marlboro'(K)
Wilde Eliza, china store, F road n Franklin (K)
Wilde Joseph, manuf., F road bel Franklin
Wilde S. E. Mrs., Sch Front & Vine
Wildemuth Gotlieb, lab., M'Bride's ct (K)
Wildenmuth Wm., carter, rear 97 N Market
Wildes James, cotton-spinner, Mary Sch
Wildes Samuel, tailor, Marriott ab 6th
Wildin Henry, capt., Front bel Wilson
Wildley Geo., plasterer, 26 Parham st
Wildman E., M. D., dentist, 8 N 11th
Wildy Jonathan shoe store, 510 N 2d (K)
Wildy Richard, carter, F road opp Marlboro'
Wildy Richard, jr., carman, West ab Marlborough (K)
Wile Charles, tobacconist, 226 Vine
Wile George, cabinetmr., Broad ab Wallace

Wiley Robert, weaver, Philip ab Jefferson
Wiley Robert, weaver, Dugan n Pine
Wiley Robert, watchman, Sch 4th bel High
Wiley Robert, jr., tailor, Chancellor n Sch 6th
Wiley Samuel, carter, Penn ab Maiden (K)
Wiley Samuel, weaver, Perry bel Phoenix (K
Wiley Samuel, weaver, Howard ab Phoenix
Wiley Thomas, weaver, Howard ab Phoenix(K)
Wiley William, brickmr., 35 N 12th
Wilgus John, clerk, Poplar ab Lewis
Wilgus John T., tailor, Lewis ab Poplar
Wilgus Josias, cordw., Sanders' ct (K)
Wilgus Richard, grocer, N E 4th and Culvert
Wilhelm Charles, lamp mr., Wood bel Sch 7th
WILHELM FREDERICK, confectioner, 23 High, h 32 Vine
Wilhelm John L., carp., Juniper ab Locust
Wilke Henry, huckster, Pleasant ab Charles
Wilkee Fred'k W., tinsmith, 630 N 3d
Wilkey Samuel, tallow chandler, 530 N 2d
Wilkins Aaron, F road n Franklin (K)
Wilkins Abraham, broker, 3 Arcade
Wilkins Benj., 481 Vine
Wilkins B. W., shop, 185 Lombard
Wilkins Constantine, corder, Cedar st whf, h 13 Swanson
Wilkins Edw., bricklayer, Dunton ab Otter (K)
Wilkins Harriet, dressmr., 186 Coates
Wilkins Henry, sea capt., 17 German
Wilkins Henry, city watch, 13th ab Mulberry
Wilkins Jacob, carp. Marriott ab 4th, h 21 Clark
Wilkins John, ship carp., Oliver pl
Wilkins John, lab., York ct
Wilkins John S., store, 25 Apple
Wilkins Joseph D., constable, 131 Marlborough
Wilkins Joseph R., acct., 1 Noble
Wilkins Mary, sempstress, rear 392 Sassafras

Wilkinson Wm., b h, 31 Union (C)
Wilkinson Wm., atty. & coun., 158 Coates
Wilkinson Wm. D., flour, 4th & George, h Apple ab George
Wilkinson Wm. S., dentist, 88 Mulberry
Wilkinson W. C., stone cut., F road bel Green, h 284 Sassafras
Wilks Benj. G. S., musician, 2 Castle
Will Elizabeth, shoes, F road ab West
Will John, shoemr., rear Marlborough ab West (K)
Willaner Jacob, tailor, Front ab Otter
Willaner John, tailor, Front ab Otter (K)
Willard Catharine, 567 S Front
Willard Charles, wheelwright, Sch 3d bel Callowhill
Willard Frederick, point cut., St John & Brown
Willard Joseph, driver, Prime ab Front
Willard Martha, Richard n Sch 6th
Willcox Augustine, mer., 8 Commerce, h 27 N Rittenhouse
WILLCOX JAMES M. & CO., paper warch., 7 Minor
Willcox John, mason, 11th bel Pine
Willcox John, cot. deal., Otter n Front (K)
Willette Edw., seaman, 4th bel Wharton
Willetts John, wheelwright, Wood ab Sch 4th
Williams Abraham, cordw., Orchard ab Rawle
Williams Ann, rear 110 Catharine
Williams Ann, Poplar bel 3d
Williams Ann, washer, 14 Pine al
Williams Ann, Emeline
Williams Ann C., blacksmith, Queen ab 2d, h 328 S 4th
Williams Anna Maria, 495 Mulberry
Williams Anna M., 260 N 7th
Williams Anthony, cordw., 27 Vernon (S G)
Williams Anthony, porter, Gale's ct
Williams Arthur, 12th and Wood
Williams A., photographist, 136 Chestnut, h 27 S Sch 6th
Williams Benj., mason, Carlton ab Sch 3d
Williams Benj., milkman, St Andrew's st
WILLIAMS BENJ. J., painter and ven. blind mr., 12 N 6th and 143½ S 2d, h 311 Lombard ab 9th
Williams & Brother, oil and candle manufs., Granite buildings, Broad st
Williams & Brother, com mers, 22 N Front
Williams B. P., mer., 14 S 4th, h 159 N 9th
Williams B. P. & Co., shoe warch., 14 S 4th
Williams Cath., 11 Mary (S)
Williams Charles, lab., 141 Cherry
Williams Charles, bootmr., 10th & Catharine
Williams Charles, gent., 215 Walnut
Williams Charles, gent., 282 N 5th
Williams Charles, gauger, rear 6 S whfs, h Julianna and Vine
Williams Charles, whitewasher, 9th and Christian
Williams Chas. Rev., D D, Spruce ab Sch 8th
Williams Charles B., mer., 91 High
Williams Charles B., tanner, 7th ab Willow, h 7th ab Parrish
Williams Charles V., ship carp., 4 Wharton

Williams Christiana, Ontario ab Poplar
Williams C. C., dentist, 120 Mulberry
Williams Daniel, Garden bel Buttonwood
Williams David, framemr., 452 N Front
Williams David E., lumb. mer., Sch 6th & Pine, h 215 Walnut
Williams Draper, lab., 313 Cherry
Williams Edward, stove manf., 206 Cedar
Williams Edward, carp., 64 Christian
Williams Edward, auct., Sch 4th ab Vine
Williams Edward, stone cutter, rear 19 Sterling al
Williams Edward W., tailor, Carlton ab 12th
Williams Elijah B., foreman, Wistar ab 11th
Williams Elizabeth, 28 Coates
Williams Ellen, 6 Webb's al
Williams Esther, Green n Spruce
Williams Evan, tailor, 3d and Noble
Williams Francis, cordw., rear Vienna ab Franklin (K)
Williams Frederick, clerk, Sch 7th ab Filbert
Williams Frederick G., agent, 136 Chestnut
Williams Garrett, carp., 345 N 8th
Williams George, seaman, 17 Parham
Williams George, jeweller, 25 Clark
Williams George, gent., 71 N 7th
Williams Geo., lum. mer., 11th ab Washington
Williams Geo., jr., mer., 44 N 2d, h 357 N 6th
Williams Geo., jr., mer., 269 N 6th
Williams Geo. G., 256 N 5th
Williams George W., morocco and linings, 69 G T road
Williams Georgiana, widow, Frazier's ct
Williams Gottleib, victualer, Buttonwood below 10th
Williams Harriet, 138 Wood
Williams Harrison, barber, 221 S 6th
Williams Henrietta, 49 Quince
Williams Henry, shoe store, 114 W High
Williams Henry, cordw., rear Elizabeth below Poplar
Williams Henry, blacksm., rear 15 Mead al
Williams Henry, collector, rear 176 Shippen
Williams Henry J., atty. & coun., 7 York build's
Williams Henry T., tailor, 8 Sp Garden
Williams Hester, tailoress, Apple ab Poplar
Williams Hetty, washer, Green's ct
Williams & Hinds, stovemrs., 398 High
Williams Hiram, hatter, 5 Spragg's av
Williams Hope, mer., 144 Chestnut
Williams Howard, lumber merch., h Mulberry Sch 8th
Williams Huey, lab., 4 Crabb st
Williams Isaac, mariner, Higgins' ct
Williams Isaac, porter, 150 Locust
Williams Isaac, b h, 413 High
Williams Isaac, cordw., Brook bel Brown
Williams Isaac, lab., Beach bel Poplar
Williams Isaac, lab., Beach n High bridge
Williams Isaac, barber, 9th and Washington, h Smith's ct
WILLIAMS ISAAC S., imp. and manuf. tinw., 256 and h 258 High
Williams Isaiah, porter, Bell's ct
Williams Jacob, baker Carpenter n Broad

Williams Jacob P., tailor, 469 Vine
Williams Jacob T., lard oil, 71 N Water, h 161 N 9th
Williams James, lab., Paschall's ct
Williams Jas., framemr., rear 465 St John
WILLIAMS JAMES, hotel, 68 S Front
Williams James, weaver, Fox's ct
Williams James P., bricklayer, 206 Lombard
Williams James W., min. painter, 41 N 6th
Williams Jane, widow, Sch 4th n High
Williams Jesse, dry goods, 209 Coates
Williams Jesse M., shoe store, 546 High
Williams John, lab., 5 Spafford st
Williams John, lab., 6 Mineral pl
Williams John, lab., McIntyre's al (K)
Williams John, carp., Pearl ab Sch 8th
Williams John, bricklayer, 9th ab Carpenter
Williams John, painter, h 3 Franklin row (S G)
Williams John, lab., Lombard ab Sch 7th
Williams John, grocer, Front and Laurel, h 137 Franklin
Williams John, lab., Duke bel Vienna (K)
Williams John, carp., 112 Catharine
WILLIAMS JOHN, coal mer., Locust & Broad, h Juniper ab Pine
Williams John, tavern, 13th and Lombard
Williams John, gardener, Parrish ab Sch 8th
Williams John, Lombard E Sch 6th
Williams John, tavern, 85 Penn st
Williams John, lumber mer., Green ab 9th
Williams John C., tailor, 330 High, h 13th and Carroll
Williams John L., cordw., 7th bel Carpenter
Williams John & Son, lum. mers., N E 10th and Green
Williams Joseph, stonecutter, 296 S 10th
Williams Joseph, gent., 544 N 5th
Williams Joseph, cordw., 19 Chatham
Williams Joseph, cordw., 7th bel Carpenter
Williams Joseph, weaver, Benton n School
Williams Joseph, collarmr., rear 108 F road
Williams Joseph D., tanner, Poplar ab Marshall
Williams Joseph K., livery stable, Juniper and Broad, h 116 Marion
Williams Joseph J., lum. mer., R road & Green, h Mulberry n Sch 8th
Williams & Lasher, dry goods, 44 N 2d
Williams Lavinia, dressmr., Lombard ab 7th
Williams Lewis, lab., Bedford bel Broad
Williams Margaret, washer, 31 Quince
Williams Margery, 34 Prune
Williams Mary, 59 Middle al
Williams Mary, washer, 290 E Lombard
Williams Mary, S W 11th and Chestnut
Williams Mary A., trimming store, 95 P road
Williams Mary R., 69 Locust
Williams Matilda, dressmr., 204 Cherry
Williams Matt'w, merch., 32 N Front, h 10th ab Catharine
Williams Michael J., porter, 6 Lagrange
Williams Moses R., cap manufac., 61 S 3d, h 5 Beck pl
Williams Nathan W., teacher, rear St Stephen's

Williams Paul, lab., 8 Raspberry
Williams Peter, lab., Wood bel Sch 7th
Williams Phebe, 95 Plum
Williams Priscilla, washer, Eagle ct
Williams Rebecca, washer, rear 30 Cherry
Williams Reed A., lum. mer., R road & Green, h 421 Sassafras
Williams Richard, coachm, Currant al ab Locust
Williams Richard, dry goods, High W of Sch Front
Williams Richard, N W O Y road & Coates
Williams Richard, mer., 26 Chestnut, h 169 S 5th
Williams Richd. T., carman, 629 S 2d
Williams Rynear, cabmr., 111 W High, n Sch 7th
WILLIAMS R. A. & J. J. & CO., lumber mers. R road and Green
Williams Samuel, tavern, 235 S 7th
Williams Samuel, grocer, Poplar and 8th
Williams Samuel, cordw., Vine ab Sch 8th
Williams Samuel, jr., merchant, 14 S 4th, h 441 Walnut
Williams Samuel, barber, Juniper al
Williams Samuel T., printer, 264 Chestnut
Williams Sarah, gentw., 215 Walnut
Williams Sarah, Lombard n Sch 7th
Williams Sarah, 1 Maple
Williams Sarah, 9th ab Carpenter
Williams Seth, cordw., Church and Reckless
Williams Solomon S., woollen factory, Willow ab Sch 6th
Williams Thos., tailor, 32 S 7th
Williams Thos., grocer, Cherry bel Franklin (K)
Williams Thos., blacksm., Front and Brown
Williams Thos., lab., Paschall's ct
Williams Thos. jr., lum. mer., S W Sch 6th and Pine, h 88 S 12th
Williams Thos. F., stovemr., 398 High, h 323 Cherry
Williams Thos. R., 103 N 10th
Williams Wm., grocer, 104 Swanson
Williams Wm., seaman, 17 Cox
Williams Wm., oysterman, Higgins' ct
Williams Wm., lab., rear 50 Logan
Williams Wm., watchman, 70 Almond
Williams Wm. A., carp., 7th and Washington (S)
Williams Wm. P., morroc. dr., Kienzle ct
Williams Wm. P., hair dress., S 5th & Shippen
Williams Wm. R., rigger, 28 Union (S)
Williams Wm. S., 297 High
Williamson Abraham, tavern, S E Cedar and Swanson
Williamson Abraham, lab., Ross n Queen
Williamson Ann R., b. h., 16 Elfreth's al
Williamson Benj. H., sailmr., 11 Arcade, h Carlton ab 12th
WILLIAMSON, BURROUGHS & CO., dry goods, 73 High
Williamson Chas., carter, Mechanic ab Culvert
Williamson David, boilermr., S 7th bel Catharine
Williamson David, mer., 14 N 2d
Williamson David F., mer., 14 N 2d

Williamson Emeline, Sarah bel Bedford
Williamson Ephraim B., currier, rear 450 N 4th
Williamson & Evans, carps, Centre bel 13th
Williamson Garret P., carp., 46 N 8th, h Parrish ab 7th
Williamson George, glass blower, Palmer bel Queen (K)
Williamson George A., chairmr., Rachel above Laurel
Williamson Henry B., Carlton ab 12th
Williamson Henry B., carp., 351 S 3d
Williamson Henry W., bookbinder, 9 Kelly's av
Williamson Jas., grocer, Front and Otter (K)
Williamson Jane, milliner, N W 9th & Filbert
Williamson Jesse, carp., 10th bel Parrish
Williamson Jesse, 22 German
Williamson John, lab., Jackson bel Budd
Williamson John, machinist, Haydock bel Front
Williamson John, weaver, 22 Brinton
Williamson Joseph, jr., carter, Mechanic below George (N L)
Williamson Joseph D., carver and gilder, 94 Walnut
Williamson Lewis, cordw., Howard bel Franklin (K)
Williamson Mahlon, jr., dry goods, 73 High, h 111 Mulberry
Williamson Passmore, conveyancer, S W 7th & Mulberry
Williamson Robert, planing mill, Mechanic bel George
Williamson Robert, grocery, 10th and Wallace
Williamson Samuel driver, Apple ab George
Williamson Silas, carter, rear 83 New Market
Williamson & Son, druggists, 298 S 2d, h 296 S 2d
Williamson Samuel, carp., 290 Sassafras, h 209 Cherry
Williamson Sarah Jane, dressmr., 29 N 9th
Williamson Sidney, gentw., 117 N Front
Williamson Thos., weaver, Lloyd ab Fitzwater
WILLIAMSON THOMAS & SON, conveyancers, S W 7th and Mulberry
Williamson Walter, M. D., 80 N 11th
Williamson Wm. S., carp., Centre bel 13th, h 333 Pine
Willig George, music store, 171 Chestnut
Willik Adam, porter, Paschal's al
Willing Charles, gent., 17 Clinton
Willing Rebecca, 331 Chestnut
Willing Richard, Pres. Mut. Assurance Co., 54 Walnut, h 105 S 3d
Willing Thos. M., 6 Washington sq
Willingmire John, cordw., 541 N 5th
Willis Arthur H., teacher, 114 W High
Willis B. B., clerk, 41 N 4th
Willis Charles E., saddler, 330 N 5th
Willis David, 49 Pine
Willis Edw., carp., Sch 2d bel Cedar
Willis George, lab., 14 St Mary
Willis Geo. jr., porter, 10 Little Pine
Willis Isaac, marketman, Logan ab Green
Willis Jacob, lab., Washington ab 11th
Willis James, ladies' shoemr., 241 Mulberry
Willis Mark T., tailor, 2 Union

Willis Mary Ann, gents. furnishing store, 127 Chestnut
Willis Misses S. & L., 34 S 13th
Willis Smith, tailor, 5 Fetter la
Willis S. D., morocco casemr., 17 S 5th, h 368 S 5th
Willits Aaron, lab., Paschal's al
Willits Ann Mrs., 2 Union
Willits Ebenezer, Franklin & Hanover (K)
Willits E., grocer, Front and Wharton
Willits Jas., book st., 294 Wood bel 13th
Willits John, bricklayer, 16 W North
Willits John, carp., 11th ab Vine
Willits John F., bricklayer, 138 N 13th
Willits John H., teacher, 38 Franklin
Willits Joseph B., bricklayer, 398 Vine
Willits Peter, bricklayer, 38 Sheaff
Willits Wm. R., wheelwrt., Vienna ab Franklin (K)
Willoughby Samuel, waterman, School
Wills David, wheelwrt, 13 Sommer's ct
Wills George, combmr., 8 Cobb's ct
Wills George, barber, 55 S 4th, h 165 Carpenter
Wills Isaac, carp., 143 St John
Wills James, acct., Marshall ab Parrish
Wills Joseph G., carp., 13th ab Poplar
Wills Nichols, carp., 564 S 2d
Wills Sarah, spooler, Philip bel Jefferson
Wills Thos. E., Bank Pennsylvania, Washington ab 12th
Wills Wm., rear Beach ab Poplar (K)
Wilmer Ann E., 32 S 13th
Wilmer & Brother, combmrs., 121 High
WILMER & CANNELL, importers, 8 N Front
Wilmer, carter, Beach ab Maiden (K)
Wilmer Catharine, 5th bel Franklin (N L)
Wilmer John, combmr., 121 High, h 117 New
Wilmer John R., mer., 20 S Front, h 410 Spruce
Wilmer J. Ringgold, mer., 8 N Front, h Spruce bel 12th
Wilmer L. A., editor, Hallowell n 7th
Wilmer Margaret, 498 S 2d
Wilmer Rebecca, 114 St John
Wilmer Thos., mer., 121 High, h 213 Coates
Wilmore Charles, porter, Baker ab 7th
Wilmore Wm., porter, 28 Paschal's al
Wilmott Margaret, wid. of Lewis, grocer, Vienna and Franklin
Wilshine Chas., driver, Coates ab 12th
Wilson Absalom, grocer, 526 N 3d
Wilson Adam, carter, 281 Marshall
Wilson Alexander, stone cutter, 10 Ellet's av
Wilson Alexander, M. D., Cedar ab 11th, and drugs, 13th and Shippen
Wilson Alex., weaver, Wood ab Sch Front
Wilson Alice, washer, 2 Liberty ct
Wilson Allen, stove dealer, 401 N Front
Wilson Andrew, jeweller, 428½ High
Wilson Andrew A., cordw., 2 N road, h 76 Christian
Wilson Ann Jane, milliner, 28 Strawberry
Wilson Ann, wid., nurse, 1 Conkle's ct
Wilson Ann, teacher, 43 Chestnut
Wilson Anna, teacher, Callowhill ab Sch Front
Wilson Asa, blacksm., Pt Pleasant retreat

48

Wilson Austin, clerk, 10th bel Cedar
Wilson Benj., porter, 9 Green (C)
Wilson Benj., attendant, 4 Linden ct (K)
Wilson Benj., porter, rear 160 Queen
Wilson Benj., cordw., rear 15 Browne
Wilson Bennet C., cordw., Turner
Wilson Bennett, cordw., Shippen bel P road
Wilson Catharine, wid. of James, George bel St John (K)
Wilson Catharine, 68 N 8th
Wilson Charles, carp., 522 N 5th
Wilson Charles A., cordw., 29 Mechanic
Wilson Charles C., reporter, 542 S Front
Wilson Charles T., mer., 8 S Water, h 296 N 6th
WILSON CHARLES T. & CO., provis., 8 S Water
Wilson, Childs & Co., wheelwrts., 305 N 3d
Wilson Clayton, cordw., O'Neill bel Franklin(K)
Wilson Clement A., acct., 26 S 3d, h 310 N 8th
Wilson C. S. Mrs., ship colourmr., 114 S Front, h 73 S 8th
Wilson Daniel, lab., Lawrence ct (K)
Wilson Danl., tavern, N W Queen & Swanson
Wilson David, tailor, Carlton ab Sch 6th
Wilson David, cabman, Lewie ab Poplar
Wilson David, machinist, Jefferson ab Front(K)
Wilson David G., stone cut., Buttonwood bel 11th
Wilson David G., wheelwrt., 305 N 3d, h 86 Dillwyn
Wilson David H., oak cooper, Mechanic
Wilson David E., mer., 5 Walnut
Wilson Edward, collector, 114 W Lombard
Wilson Edward, dealer, Sutherland
Wilson Edward, watchman, Richard
Wilson Elizabeth, rear 123 Christian
Wilson Elizabeth, 10 Morgan
Wilson Elizabeth, dressmr., Perry ab Franklin
Wilson Ephraim, soap chandler, 641 N 2d
Wilson Ephraim, ship carp., Church bel Washington
Wilson E., M. D., S E 7th and Green
Wilson Francis C., publisher, 98 Chestnut, h 4 Fayette
Wilson Franklin S., tailor, 109 Chestnut
WILSON F. C. & CO., publishers, 98 Chestnut
Wilson George, boot and shoe manuf., 6 Bank, h 57 Mulberry
Wilson George, marble yard, R road bel Sp Garden
Wilson George, acct., 253 S Front
Wilson George, porter, 33 Mar., (S)
Wilson George, gent., 77 N 5th
Wilson George, jr., grocer, N 5th and Noble
Wilson Geo. W., grocer, N W Brown and 12th
Wilson G. C., bootmr., 28 Bank, h 402 N 6th
Wilson G. V., mer., 122 High, h 245 N 7th
Wilson Hamilton D., hair dresser, 5½ S 10th, h 75 N 10th
Wilson Hannah, shop, 251 S 5th
Wilson Harriet, wid. of Henry, Garden ab Callowhill
WILSON HAWKSWORTH MOSS & ELLI

Wilson Henry, tailor, 9th bel Coates
Wilson Henry, lab., Wood ab 13th
Wilson Henry, cabinetmr., 9th bel Carpenter
Wilson Henry, weaver, Phoenix bel G T road
Wilson Henry W., tailor, 24 Lombard
Wilson Horace, waiter, 125 N 2d, h Little Pine n 7th
Wilson Howard, clerk, 12 Buttonwood
Wilson Hugh, lab., Palmer ab Duke (K)
Wilson Isaac, blacksmith, 5th ab Franklin
Wilson Isabella, dressmr., 223 S 5th
Wilson Isabella, dry goods, 138 N 8th
Wilson Jacob, lab., 3 Cauffman's ct
Wilson Jacob B., brush maker, 438 N 2d, h 15 Pratt's ct
Wilson James, weaver Sch 4th opp Barker
Wilson James, dairyman, 639 N 2d
Wilson James, oysters, 129 Cherry
Wilson James, pilot, Washington ab M road
Wilson James, mer., Pine bel 10th
Wilson James, mer., 49 N 3d, h 264 Chestnut
Wilson James, carp., Lewis ab Poplar
Wilson James, grocer, S E 6th and Coates
Wilson James, shoemr., Harriet and Ross (K)
Wilson James, boat builder, Callowhill n Fairmount
Wilson James, Poplar bel 7th
Wilson James, lab., rear 6 Locust
Wilson James, brickmr., Gulielma
Wilson Jas., F road ab Franklin
Wilson James Henry, saddler, Broad ab Sassafras
Wilson Jas. M., Rev., 8 W North
Wilson Jane M., 52 Shippen
Wilson Jesse, waiter, Allen's ct
Wilson Jesse, waiter, 24 Mayland
Wilson Job S., capt., Fraley's al (K)
Wilson John, mariner, 31 Marriott
Wilson John, stone cutter, O'Neal (K)
Wilson John, mer., 45 N Front
Wilson John, clerk, 11th ab High
Wilson John, tavern, Beach opp K Bank (K)
Wilson John, painter and glaz., 182 S 9th
Wilson John, cordw., Otter n School
Wilson John, shoemr., Catharine bel Lebanon
Wilson John, capt., 13th ab Cedar
Wilson John, carp., Hunter bel 11th, h Lewis ab Thompson
Wilson John, pilot, 12 Beck (S)
Wilson John, painter, 243 S 6th
Wilson John, carter, Seller's ct
Wilson John, weaver, Spruce n Sch 4th
Wilson John A., cordw., Benton ab School (K)
Wilson John G., cordw., 97 N 13th
Wilson John G. Rev., Hanover ab West (K)
Wilson John H., cordw., Otter n G T road (K)
Wilson John M., carp., Lewis ab Poplar
Wilson John M., clerk, 296 S 5th
Wilson John M., mer., 140½ High, h N W 10th and Pine
Wilson John M., clerk, 28 Magnolia

Wilson John T., tailor, 9 Beck pl
Wilson John V., mer., 122 High, h 118 Franklin
Wilson Joseph, blacking and ink, 105 Catharine
Wilson Joseph T., tailor, Christian ab 3d
Wilson Levi H., tailor, 190 N 10th
Wilson Margaret, 1 Shield's al
Wilson Margaret, spooler, Harmony ct (K)
Wilson Maria, variety store, 268 S 6th
Wilson Mary, gentw., Sp Garden bel 12th
Wilson Mary, Charlotte bel Franklin (K)
Wilson Mary Ann, 17 Chatham
Wilson Mary M., bonnetmr., 66 Mulberry
Wilson Minard W., mer., 265 N 7th
Wilson Oliver H., sign painter, 262 N 3d, h 5th ab Brown
Wilson Oliver H., mer., 73 High, h 12 Button-wood
Wilson Peter H., brushmr., 6 Gulielma
Wilson Phœbe, 35 Prime
Wilson Rachel, huckster, 45 Franklin
Wilson Richard, carter, 195 Lombard
Wilson Richard, weaver, F road ab Franklin
Wilson Robert, carpet weav., Hanover ab West
Wilson Robert, manuf., Gabell's ct
Wilson Robert, shop, Vine n Schuylkill
Wilson Robert, carp., 156 N Juniper
Wilson Robert, carp., Juniper ab Cherry
Wilson Robt., manuf., Jones W of Sch 7th
Wilson Robt., waterman, rear 106 New Market
Wilson Robert S. & Co., painters, 65 Dock
Wilson R., lab., 5th bel Franklin
Wilson R. S., bootmr., 59 Mulberry
Wilson Samuel, carter, 428 N 5th
Wilson Samuel, weaver, Cadwalader ab Phœnix
Wilson Saml., cabs, Lewis ab Poplar
Wilson Saml., lab., Pearl ab Nixon
Wilson Samuel, carp., 1 Harmony ct
Wilson Samuel, cooper, Reeves n Sch 2d
Wilson Saml., wheelwr., George n Sch 3d
Wilson Saml., skin dress., rear 12 Shivers' ct
Wilson Sarah Ann, trimmings, 4th and Culvert
WILSON, SIEGER & BROTHER, dry goods, 49 N 3d
Wilson Silas, carp., 8 Lodge al, h 125 Button-wood
Wilson Silas, pedler, 217 N 9th
Wilson Silas C., dry goods, N W 12th & Vine
Wilson Susan, widow, 296 N 6th
Wilson S. D., port. painter, 8 N 5th
Wilson Tamar, shoe br., 1 Roberts' ct
Wilson Theodore, clerk, 214 Noble
Wilson Thomas, lab., School ab Rose (K)
Wilson Thomas, blacksm., Perry bel Phœnix
Wilson Thomas, sea capt., 16 Union
Wilson Thomas, bootmr., 24 Carter's al
Wilson Thomas, weaver, rear West bel Hano-ver (K)
Wilson Thomas, Madison and Sassafras
Wilson Thomas, lab., Penn bel Maiden (K)
Wilson Thos., lab., Olive bel 12th
Wilson Thos., tobacconist, 57 P road
Wilson Thos. A., carp., 440 S Front
Wilson Thos. W., painter, 4 Jacoby
Wilson Wm., oysterman, Prospect pl
Wilson Wm., blacksm., Marriott bel 3d

Wilson Wm., hatter, 50 N 2d
Wilson Wm., silversmith, 5th and Cherry, h 77 Cherry
Wilson Wm., mer., 14 S 6th, h Spruce ab 7th
Wilson Wm., watchman, Cedar n Sch 4th
Wilson Wm., marble yard, G T road opp New Market
Wilson Wm., carp., Elm bel Franklin
Wilson Wm., printer, Sutherland
Wilson Wm., lab., Crown bel Duke
Wilson Wm., stone cutter, rear 10th ab Poplar, h 4th ab Beaver
Wilson Wm. B., ship carp., 25 Prime
Wilson Wm. B., M. D., 163 Mulberry
WILSON WM. & CO., grocers, 14 S 6th
Wilson Wm. D., cotton mer., 91 S Front, h Sp Garden bel 11th
Wilson Wm. F., carp., 35 Commerce
Wilson Wm. H., coach painter, Broad & Wood, h Carpenter and M road
Wilson Wm. H., 1 S 10th, h 30 S 13th
Wilson Wm. W., Vernon ab 10th
Wilson W. H., hardware, 9 N 3d, h 10 Button-wood
Wilstach Wm. P., saddlery hardware, 28½ N 3d, h 18 Montgomery sq
Wilt Abraham, carter, Coates ab 9th
Wilt Alpheus, carp., Marlborough ab Bedford
Wilt Catharine, rear 513 N 3d
Wilt George, carter, Jackson (S G)
Wilt Henry, machinist, Porter's ct
Wilt Jacob, ship carp., Sarah bel Bedford
Wilt James, machinist, rear 494 N 3d
Wilt Wm., carter, Palm bel Brown
Wiltbank John, M. D., 194 Mulberry
Wiltbank Peter W., bookseller, Sch 7th ab Fil-bert
WILTBANK SAMUEL P., mer., 14 Commerce, h 116 N 8th
Wiltberger C. sen., Washington and Till (W P)
Wiltberger Eliza, 197 Noble
Wiltberger Eliza E., Flibert ab Sch 8th
Wiltberger Theod. M., acct., Washington (W P)
Wiltner Jas., bootmr., Moon's ct
Wimer James, printer, 166 E Pine
Wimer John, cooper, Broad ab Sassafras, h Sch 8th ab Wood
Wimer Joseph, plasterer, German bel 5th
Wimer Thomas, 163 Buttonwood
Wimley Catharine, widow, 16 Tammany
Wimley John, cordw., 81 New Market
Wimley Wm., S E 7th and George
Wims George, couch painter, 7 Hickory
Winams Elihu, tin smith, Church al
Winberg Wm., confect., 475 N 2d
Winch A., bookseller, 116 Chestnut
Winchell Edwin, dealer, Washington bel 6th
Winchester Martha, 142 S 10th
Winder John, lab., 67 Beach (K)
Winder Samuel, carp., 106 S 12th
Winder Wm. H., mer., 76½ Walnut
Windle Wm., patternmr., Marlboro' ab Queen
Winebrener David, gent., Sch 5th and Locust
Winebrener David S., mer., 70 N 3d, h 100 N 9th
Winey Geo., tobacconist, rear 308 St John

Winfield Charles, ship joiner, 14 China
Winfield Saml., ship joiner, 67 Queen
Winfield Wm. jr., printer, 483 S Front
Wingate Charles, mer., 18 N 4th
Wingate George, baker, 169 Shippen
Wingate P. B., mer., Fitzwater bel 9th
Wingate Sarah, 96 Christian
Winger Moses, tobacconist, High W of Sch 6th
Winhultz Henry, upholsterer, 19 Nectarine
Winkler August, ropemr., G T road ab 5th
Winkler Fedeli, weaver, rear Clinton bel Parrish
Winkley H., mer., 63 S Water
Winkworth Thomas A., boot fitter, Perry ct
Winn Anthony, block and pump mr., Stout's al
Winn Michael, tavern, 19 Walnut
Winn Samuel, carter, Carpenter ab 8th
Winn Sarah, gentw., Kirkpatrick's ct
Winn Thos., brass founder, 4 Elizabeth (N L)
Winnemore Henry, sea capt., 520 S 2d
Winnemore Jacob, lab., State st
Winnemore Maria A., widow of Isaac, Ann ab Sch 6th
Winnemore Philip, carver, 8 State
Winner Jon., weaver, rear G T road ab Master (K)
Winner Joseph, weaver, 50 Dyott's ct
Winner Joseph, music store, 348 N 3d
Winner Lewis, cabinetmr., rear Charlotte ab Poplar
Winner Mary, Charlotte bel Franklin (K)
Winner S., combmr., 7 S 2d, h 4 Morgan
Winner Wm. E., portrait painter, 95 Wood
Winning James G., carp., 2 Quince
Winning Margaret, dressmr., 131 S 11th
Winning Robert, machinist, Newton
Winrow Jno., shop, 213 Walnut, h 126 Lombard
Winship W. S., copper plate printer, 26 George
Winslow Eliza, 380 S 3d
Winslow Geo., grocer, S W Queen and Swanson
Winslow H. G., M. D., 143 N 9th
Winslow Isaac, silver spoon manf., 115 N Water
Winslow Robert, china store, 269 Cedar
Winslow Seth E., clerk, Franklin bel Palmer
Winsmore James, mariner, 1 Burd (S)
Winston John, lab., 9th bel Christian
Winsud Sidney, 123 S 9th
Winter Bernard, 81 George
Winter Charles, printer, 10 Freed's av
Winter & Co., coal gratemrs., 50 S 10th
Winter Gilly, iron worker, Sch 8th ab Chestnut
Winter Jacob, tailor, Parrish bel Broad
Winter John, bonnet presser, 105 N 5th
Winter Joseph, tailor, Wallace bel 13th
Winter Wm., coal grat. mr., 50 S 10th
Winterbottom John, tailor, 16 Cox's al
Winterbury Henry, 47 Juhanna
Winterhalter Bernard, carpet weav., 146 Coates
Winters Charles, carp., Bottonwood n 13th
Winters Henry, lab., rear 190 Carpenter (S)
Winters Isaac, watcher, 419 and h 173 N 2d
Winters Jacob, widow bel 9th
Winters James, lab., Small bel 6th
WINTERS JOHN S. & CO., hardwa., 250 N 2d
Winters Mary, 10 Wood

Winters Nicholas, saddler, N E Charles & Willow
Winters Wm., bleacher, Mechanic ab Poplar
Winters Wm., dealer, 382 S 2d
Winters Wm. W., carter, 313 Cherry
Winther Ernest, cabtmr., 540 N 2d (K)
Wiper Susan, Hanover ab Queen
Wire George, provision store, 12th and Buttonwood, h Callowhill ab 12th
Wireman Henry, ladies' shoes, 6th and Buttonwood
Wirt Jas., lab., rear Poplar bel Mechanic
Wirth Jacob, dry goods, 205 O Y road
Wirts W., teacher, 93 N 9th, h Buttonwood ab 8th
Wisanor F., M D, 2d ab Jefferson (K)
Wise Ann, widow, 23 Beck
Wise Chas., coal dealer, 7th ab Poplar
Wise Chas., dry goods, 154 High, h 31 N 5th
Wise Christian, lab., 2 Lagrange pl
Wise Christ., baker, 488 N 3d
Wise George, boots and shoes, 1 N 5th, h 113 N 5th
Wise George K., silversm., 20 Library, h 399 N Front
Wise Jacob, flour mer., S E 4th and Vine
Wise Jas. E., chandler, Francis n Sch 5th
Wise John, painter, Pearl ab Sch 8th
Wise John, mer., 154 High, h 159 O Y road
Wise John, carv. & gild., New Market & Pegg
Wise John, varnisher, rear 114 Plum
Wise Mary, Washington bel 6th
Wise Michael, mer., Spruce st whf, h 3 Lodge
Wise Peter, lab., 40 Currant al
Wise, Pusey & Wise, dry goods, 154 High
Wise Thomas, carp., 8 Beck (S)
Wise & Thomas, ship chandlers, Spruce st whf
Wise Wm., mariner, Marriott bel 6th
Wiseman Catharine, 111 S 10th
Wiseman Jacob, ropemr., 83 M road
Wiseman John, ropemr., 2 Jones' ct
Wiseman Samuel, ropemr., 2 Jones' ct
Wiser Daniel, carp., Parrish n Broad
Wiser Gustavus, acct., Shaffer's ct and Rawle
Wiser Jacob, cedar cooper, Haydock bel G T road
Wiser Willoughby, carp., 3 Hight's ct
Wisham Samuel, provisions, 470 Vine
Wishart Cincinnatus, confect., 112 Washington avenue
Wishart Mary, burnisher, rear 133 Green
Wisinger Wm., chairmr., 79 N Front
Wismer Jacob, dealer, 113 Apple
Wisner Catharine, 12th n Pine
Wisner Jahyl, plumber, Yhost ct
Wispert Wm., carp., Duke bel Palmer
Wistar B. Wyatt, mer., h 259 Mulberry
Wistar Casper, M D, 184 Mulberry
Wistar Henry L., bootmr., Wistar's ct (K)
Wistar Maria, widow of Peter, 3d bel Thompson (K)
Wistar Mifflin, M D, 16 Washington sq
Wistar Richard, gent., 11 Clinton sq
Wistar Sarah, gentw., 157 Filbert
Wistar Susan N., 496½ Chestnut

Wistar Thomas, gent., 383 High
Wister Barbara, Perry ab Franklin (K)
Wister Caspar, M D 29 N 10th
Wister Wm., bootmr., Perry ab Franklin (K)
Wister Wm. W., brewer, N W 10th and Filbert, h 26 N 10th
Witchel Wm. H., carp., Brown bel Broad
Witcraft Wm., shuttlemr., Mechanic bel Culvert
Witham E., jeweller, 3 Franklin pl, h 372 N Front
Witham & Newman, jewellers, 3 Franklin pl
Witham Sarah, shop, 252 S Front
Witheat Henry, rigger, 20 Union (S)
Witherup Alex., brushmr., Ogden bel R road
Withers Geo. W., dry goods, 13th bel Callowh'l
Withers Hanson L., mer., 74 High, h 31 N 12th
Withers John H., mer., 81 N 3d
WITHERS JOHN H. & CO., dry goods, 81 N 3d
Withers Jos. N., mer., 110 High, h N E 13th & Mulberry
Withey B. Martin, combmr., 491 Poplar
Withington Ralph, machinist, Phoenix bel G T road
Withington Samuel, coal dealer, 115 Filbert
Witley Norris, carp., rear Beach ab Poplar (K)
Witman Caspar, lacemr., Gatchell's av
Witman Charles, ship carp., China ab Front
Witman Mary, b h, 114 N 4th
Witman Mortimer, ship carp., China ab Front
Witmer Ann, shop, 89 S Water
Witmer Elam F., forw and com mer, Broad bet Sassafras and Vine, h 27 N 13th
Witmer Jacob, grocer, 408 and 410 High, h N W Filbert and Broad
Witmer Jacob & Son, forw. and com. mers., 408 and 410 High
Witmer Samuel L., 408 and 410 High
Witmer Theodore B., atty., 141 Walnut
Witmier John, tanner, rear 288 N Front
Witmor W. H., medicines, 10 N 6th
Witsell Hannah, shop, Beaver bel Charlotte
Witsil Albert G., cordw., Van Buren pl
Witsil Chas. W., chairmr., Vernon bel 11th
Witsil John, cooper, 9 Well's row
WITTE W. H., variety, 126 N 3d, h 77 New
Witter Henry, blacksm., 31 Otter (K)
Witters Wm. C., com mer, 19 N 4th, h 34 Union
Wittich D., shoemr., 5 Myers' ct
Wittich John G., tavern, G T road and Jefferson
Wittich Paul, shoemr., 298 S 4th
Wittig Charles, M D, 218 N 4th
Witzeman John, baker, 508 Callowhill
Witzeman M., milliner, 508 Callowhill
Wize John, furniture, 495 High
Woddrop Robert S., M D, Callowhill ab 11th
Woelpper David, vict., 50 Franklin
Woelpper George, Bridge st (M V)
Woelpper Geo., victualler, 44 Franklin
Woelpper Mrs., wid. of David, 18 Franklin
Woelpper Wm., boat builder, High n Sch Front
Woglom Catharine, 149 N 9th
Wohlleben B. Mrs., 260 Mulberry
WOLBERT C. J., auct'r., 51 High, h 102 Marshall

Wolbert F., gentw., 406 N 2d
WOLBERT & HERKNESS, aucts., Carpenter's court
Wolbert John, cordw., St John and Tammany
Wolbert Jonathan, cordw., rear Melon bel 12th
Wolbert Julia, ice office, 37 Shippen
Wolbert Rebecca, 6 Elizabeth, (N L)
Wolcott R. W., machinist, 26 Parham
Wolf Abraham S., mer., 25 N 3d, h 84 Vine
Wolf Cath., Week's ct
Wolf Cæsar, seaman, Poplar n Broad
Wolf Charles, tobac., G T road opp 5th
Wolf Conrad, cordw., Front bel Phoenix (K)
Wolf David, cordw., 11 Brooke
Wolf David, carp. & ship joiner, 13 Queen (K)
Wolf Elizabeth, b h, 5 Friendship ct
Wolf E., bookbinder, Ann ab Powell (F V)
Wolf George, shoemr., Apple ab Brown
Wolf George, carp., Union ab Franklin (K)
Wolf George, oyster house, Manderson ab Market (K)
Wolf Hannah, 5 Little Willow
Wolf Henry, butcher, 68 German
Wolf Henry, butcher, Palmer ab Franklin (K)
Wolf Henry, cabinetmr., 56 Callowhill
WOLF ISAAC, dentist, 27 Brown (N L)
Wolf Jacob, tavern, 50 Callowhill
Wolf John, butcher, Front ab Otter (K)
Wolf John F., cabinetmr. 59 M road
Wolf John G., shoe store, 413 N 2d
Wolf John G., tailor, Nectarine bel 10th
Wolf Lewis, cordw., h 404 N 3d
Wolf Lewis, bootmr., 13 York ct
Wolf Martin, stonecutter, R road ab Girard av
Wolf Mary, wid. of David, N 2d opp Beaver
Wolf Mordecai, waiter, 2 White's ct
Wolf Peter, cordw., 5 Almira pl
Wolf Saml., lab., Loud ab 9th
Wolf Sarah Ann, cupper and leecher, 27 Brown
Wolf Wm. C., carp., rear F road ab Bedford (K)
Wolf Wm. W., printer, 12th ab Washington
Wolf Z., paper-hanger, N W Green and St John
Wolfe E. D., mer., 89 N High, h 155 Mulberry
Wolfe Henry, butcher, 70 German
Wolfe Jacob P., constable, 58 Union
Wolfe Jacob R., gent., Spruce ab Sch 8th
WOLFE & PEYTON, dry goods, 89 High
Wolfe Sarah, 10 German
Wolfe Wm. B., hardware merch., S W 5th and High, h 437 Sassafras
Wolfer George J., boxmr., 42 Sassafras
Wolfersberger Philip, varie. store, 59 Sassafras and 145 N 2d
Wolff Abm., cordw., 90 Cherry
Wolff John, agent, Traquair's ct
Wolff Joseph M., printer, 11 Jefferson row
Wolff J. & W., paper hangings, 270 N 3d
Wolff Nicholas, merch., 20 Church alley, h 248 Mulberry
Wolff & Rautenberg, importers, 20 Church al
Wolff Susan, 75 S 12th
Wolff Susan, washer, 11 Mary's ct
Wolff S. M. D., 118 S 4th
Wolff Wm., baker, 188 St John
Wolford Peter S., watchman, 149 Cherry

Wolgamuth Francis F., clerk, 75 Franklin
Wollaston Geo. W., atty. and coun, S W 3d and Willing's al
Wollenweber Louis, printer, 277 N 3d
Wolsieffer Philip M., teach. music, 36 Madison
Wolverton John, painter, Duke ab Hanover (K)
Wolverton Wilson, machinist, 22 Parker
Womellsdorff Wm., 5 Oldham's ct
Womelsdorff Henry, drayman, Mechanic below George (N L)
Womrath Geo. K., mer., 15 N 4th
Womrath G. F., furrier, 13 N 4th, h Frankford
Womrath & Neville, fringes, &c., 15 N 4th
Wonch Frederick, baker, Callowhill ab 6th
Wonderly Alfred, tailor, Hutchinson ab Poplar
Wonderly Catharine, 44 Chester
Wonderly David, 15 Sassafras
Wonderly Elizabeth, R road bel Sp Garden
Wonderly Francis, tailor, Hutchinson ab Poplar
Wonderly George, carter, Gabel's ct (N L)
Wonderly John, Wood bel 12th
Wonderly Jos., gent., 262 E Lombard
Wonderly J. S., mer., 5 N 4th, h 69 Crown
Wonderly Mary, rear 357 N 3d
Wonderly Samuel, mer., 5 N 4th, h 286 N 6th
Wonderly S. & Son, combs & fancy goods, 5 N 4th
Wonderly Wm. K., vict., 4 Locust
Wood, Abbott & Co., mers., 127 High
Wood Abraham, shoemr., Parrish ab 7th
Wood Adam, lab., St John ab George
Wood Alan, iron mer., 3 N 5th, h 201 N 4th
Wood Alice, 4 Jackson's ct
Wood Ann, 152 S 9th
Wood Ann, 7 Reckless
Wood Ann, Parrish and Clinton
Wood Austin W., baker, 275 Callowhill
Wood Benj., flour and feed, 10th and Locust
Wood Cable, grocery, h 56 Gaskill
Wood Charles J., hatter, 297 S 10th
Wood Charles S., mer., 131 High, h 326 Mulberry
Wood David E., mer, 255 N 7th
Wood David L., 269 Green
Wood D. C., iron master, 13 N Front
Wood Edward, weaver, Fitler (K)
Wood Edward G., constable, 28 Cresson's al
Wood Edward L., mer., 157 High, h 31 N 10th
Wood Elizabeth, Miss, Chancellor n Sch 6th
Wood & Erringer, com. mer., 37 Chestnut
Wood Firman, Brown bel 10th
Wood Francis, driver, 10th bel Spring Garden
Wood George, baker, M'Christies' ct
Wood George, waiter, Cedar ab 11th

Wood Horatio C., mer., 37 Chestnut, h 210 Sassafras
Wood Isaac, boat build., Allen bel Hanover (K)
Wood Isaac, flour dealer, 16 Logan
Wood Jacob, saw sharpener, Brown ab 4th
Wood Jacob, cordw., 438 N 5th
Wood James, confect., 440 N 5th
Wood James, sen., iron mer., 159 N 2d
Wood James & Sons, iron mers., 159 N 2d
Wood John, dry goods, 174 Locust
Wood John, machinist, 7 M'Leod pl
Wood John, mer., Mulberry n 3d, h 7th above Green
Wood John, tobac. Queen ab Shackamaxon (K)
Wood John, millwt., Sch 2d ab Wood
Wood John, lab., Gorrell's ct
Wood John, lab., 3 Hummell's row (K)
Wood Jonathan, weav., Jefferson ab Front (K)
Wood Jos., painter, 538 N Front
Wood Jos. jr., mer., 122 High, h 146 Mulberry
Wood Joseph, mer., N W 4th & High, h 146 Mulberry
Wood Joseph, reporter, N W 4th & Library, h Parrish bel 7th
Wood Josiah, cook, Gilles' al n Cedar
Wood Josiah, flour inspec., 25 Noble
Wood J. & T., millwts., Wood ab Sch 2d
Wood Margaret, 435 Sassafras
Wood Margaret, 55 Coates
Wood Maria, 15 Elfreth's al
Wood Mary, Otter bel G T road (K)
Wood Mary Ann, mantuamr., 3 Tammany ct
Wood Michael, gent., 9 Hampton
Wood Michael, lab., 300 Shippen
Wood Nathan P., tailor, 237 Green
WOOD & OLIVER, mers., 131 High
Wood Peter, seaman, Salem al
Wood Philip, soap & candlemr., 12th & Carpenter, h 71 S 12th
Wood Philip W., tavern, Coates & 9th
Wood Richard D., mer., 127 High, h 421 Mulberry
Wood Richard G., chairmr., rear 114 German
Wood Robt., manuf., M'Duffy n Sch 2d
Wood Robert, blacksm., R road bel Sp Garden, h Buttonwood ab R road
Wood Robert, cordw., 77 Christian
Wood Robert M., cabman, 1 Benton
Wood Samuel, tailor, 561 N 3d
Wood Samuel, watchman, 12th ab Vine
Wood Samuel B., wood dealer, 219 N Water, h 188 Apple
Wood Samuel C., car., 11 Harmony ct
Wood Samuel C., mer., 1 S 4th

Wood Thomas R., cordw., Parrish ab 7th
Wood Wm., comedian, 5 Dannaker's av
Wood Wm., shoemr., 106 Prime, h 562 S 2d
Wood Wm., engineer, Hope ab Master (K)
Wood Wm., cabinetmr., 224 S 3d
Wood Wm., wheelwright, 467, and h 538 N Front
Wood Wm., saddler, 35 New
Wood Wm., 5 Montgomery
Wood Wm., lab., 79 G T road
Wood Wm., cord., Wood ab Sch Front
Wood Wm. S., oysters, Washington (W P)
Wood Wm. W., mer., 36 Buttonwood
Wood Wm. W., teacher, 2 Union sq
Wood Wm. W., cabman, 611 N 2d
Wood Wm. W., lab., 4 Rogers' ct
Wood & Wilson, dry goods, 122 High
Wood & Yerkes, lime mers., 9th & Willow
Woodburn R., lab., 59 Palmyra sq
Woodbury Thos., com. mer., 24 N whfs, h 16 Buttonwood
Woodelton Geo., lab., Dyott's ct (K)
Wooders Moses, wheelwright, Bedford ab Marlborough
Woodfall James, Sch 2d ab Vine
Woodfall Thomas, printer, Tyler
Woodhead Joseph, stocking manuf., Perry bel Master
Woodhouse George, clerk, 12 Short ct
Woodhouse Wm., gent., Hutchinson ab Poplar
Woodlen Lewis, coachman, Watson's al
Woodley Wm. M., brickmr., Jefferson
Woodman John, blacksmith, 14 Short ct
Woodman Margaret, Carroll ab 12th
Woodruff Abigail D., 8 Franklin row
Woodruff A. L., cap manuf., 129 N 2d
Woodruff Edmund D., police officer, 70 Lombard
Woodruff Edward E., mer., 116 High, h 155 N 7th
Woodruff Jas., stocking weav., Reakirt's ct (K)
Woodruff James, carp., Poplar bel 7th
Woodruff John, bonnets and caps, 25 N 6th, h 3 Lybrand
Woodruff Margaret, 463 N 4th
Woodruff Mary, Fraley's ct (K)
Woodruff Moses M., grocer, S W Front & Sassafras
Woods Aaron, clerk, Callowhill n F M
Woods Adam, lab., Brown bel 13th
Woods Ann, 161 Buttonwood
Woods Barney, weaver, Harmony ct (K)
Woods Charles E., boat builder, Penn above Poplar, h 21 Penn ab Poplar
Woods Daniel B., teacher, 3 Sumner
Woods Edward, carp., William below Edward (K)
Woods Edward, 36 P road
Woods Harris, clothing, 187 S 6th
Woods James, carp., William & Edward (K)
Woods Jane, washer, rear 115 Queen
Woods John, lab., St Andrews
Woods John, bookseller, 13 S 8th
Woods John, weaver, 4th & Master (K)
Woods Michael, weaver, G T road ab Master

Woods Oliver E., livery stable, 26½ N 3d, h 353 Sassafras
Woods Patrick, lab., Lombard ab Sch Front
Woods Peter, tavern, S E 5th & Lombard
Woods Robert, lab., Brazier ab Lloyd
Woodside A., portrait painter, 88 N 5th
Woodside Caroline, 10 Cresson's al
Woodside James, grocer, S W 4th & Queen
Woodside James, weaver, Marlboro' ab Duke
Woodside John, carp., Moore's ct (S G)
Woodside John A., painter, 88 N 5th
Woodside Wm., tea dealer, 4th & Queen
Woodside Wm., cordw., 243 Christian
Woodson Frederick, waiter, 17 Lisle
Woodson Frederick, shop, 210 S 6th
Woodthrift George W. cordw., Duke n Marlborough (K)
Woodward Ann, widow of Saul, 6 Franklin sq.
Woodward & Brinckle, mers., 15 S Front
Woodward & Brothers, tobacconists, 73 N 3d
Woodward Charles, gent., 44 Crown
Woodward Charles, jr., tobacconist, 73 N 3d, h 104 St John
Woodward C. & Co., tobacconist, 73 N 3d
Woodward Eliza M., b h, 3 Virginia row
Woodward E. F., engraver, 46½ Walnut
Woodward Gavin H., tobacconist, 73 N 3d, h 133 Franklin
Woodward Isaac, carter, 14 Fothergill
Woodward James S., mer., 15 S Front, h 14 Palmyra sq
Woodward John, lab., rear 265 S 7th
Woodward J. F., coal yard, foot of Linden (K)
Woodward J. J., publisher, h Locust and Mary (W P)
Woodward Mary, b h, 59 N 4th
Woodward M. Wallis, cashier Manu. and Mech. Bank, h 274 N 6th
Woodward Thomas W., mer., 17 S 4th
Woodward Wm. watchman, Jefferson ab Broad
Woodward W. H., mer., 221 High
Wooldridge J. B., harnessmr., 217 Christian
Wooldridge J. W., painter, 10 N 10th
Wooldridge Wm. B., printer, 148 Carpenter (S)
Wooldridge M. Mrs., tailoress, 80 Apple
Wooley Jordan, gent., 20 Laurel
Woolf John L., 82 Marshall
Woolf Thomas J., clerk, 202 Marshall
Woolley Adam, sailmr., rear 61 Garden
Woolley Edw., carp., Dunton bel Franklin
Woolley Elizabeth, 7th bel Parrish
Woolley John, paper hangings, 432 N 13th
Woolley John, cooper, Turner
Woolley John N., trader, Warren bel Queen
Woolley Samuel P., blacksm., 10th ab Poplar
Woolley Wm., machinist, Say ab Sch 8th
Woolley Wm. H., yarn manufacturer, Front bel Phoenix
Woolman Hannah, confectioner, 156 S 4th
Woolman James, machinist, 10th ab Poplar
Woolman Mary M., 8th ab Green
Woolman W. U., paper hanger, rear 10th above Coates
Woolmer Margaret, dry goods, 291 Callowhill
Woolsey Sarah, 89 Walnut

Woolson Alex., shoe manufac., 371 S 3d
Woolson John, Rev., 17 Shippen
Woolson John, butcher, Shippen ab 11th
Woolson Richard J., painter, 11 Short ct
Woolston Thomas L., gent., 114 Franklin, off. 3 Sp. Garden
Wooster George, cordw., 8 Cadwalader (K)
Wootten Chas. H., com. mer., 63 S Front, h Buttonwood ab 8th
Wootten John, manuf. of whalebone, 94 Spruce
Word Henry. lab., rear 482 Coates
Worden James, barber, 467 N 4th
Work F. K., carp., 277 S 3d
Work George, printer, 4th bel Carpenter
Work John W., printer, 6 Somers' ct
Work Samuel, carp., Callowhill ab Sch 5th
Work Samuel, clerk, 271 S 3d
Workman & Eustis, com. mers., 15 S Water
Workman H. Weir, mer., 15 S Water
Workman John, mer., 28 Walnut
Worl A. J., tobacco, Poplar ab 10th
Worl Sarah, b h, 8th bel Parrish
Worley Joseph, printer, 382 Coates
Worley Joseph, printer, rear 130 Sassafras
Worley Phœbe, gentw., N E 12th & High
Worman Lewis H., mer., 235 N 3d, h 229 Mulberry
Wormsley Robert, weaver, Palmer near West (K)
Wormsley Wm., weaver, Palmer n Duke (K)
Worn Catharine, 470 S 2d
Worn Philip, tavern, 95 N 4th
Worne Eliza, 55 Buttonwood
Worne Philip, brushmr., 6 Branner's al
Worrall E. P., dentist, 237 Mulberry
Worrall Nathaniel, mer., 29 N Front, h 280 Green
Worrell Ann, William's ct
Worrell Ann, gentw., 66 S 6th
Worrell A., mer., 26 Church alley, h Filbert ab Broad
Worrell Charles, 15 Magnolia
Worrell Elizabeth, rear 20 Rose al
Worrell Goodwin, jeweller, 195 St John
Worrell George P., piano mr., 439 High, h 13th bel Wood
Worrell Isaac J., musician, 198 N 10th
Worrell James C., mer., 13 Church al
Worrell John R., mer., 13 Church al, h Chestnut ab Juniper
WORRELL JOHN R. & SON, importers, 13 Church al
Worrell Ralph C., cordw., 6 Mechanic's court (N L)
Worrell Stephen, miller, Carroll ab 13th
Worrell Wm., coppersm., 178 N 2d
Worrell Wm., mer., 26 Church al, h 22 Montgomery sq
WORRELLS, COATES & CO., importers, 26 Church al
Worsley Thos., perfumer, 65½ S 3d, h Cherry ab Queen (K)
Worste Mary, milliner, Queen n Shackamaxon
Worton G. W., barber, Shackamaxon n Bedford (K)

Wortz Edward, ship carp., Palmer bel Franklin (K)
Worth J. L., coal mer., Shackamaxon above Franklin
Worthington Allen, book agt., Crown n Franklin (K)
Worthington & Crew, druggists, N W 5th and Callowhill
Worthington Henry, grocer, 3d & Catharine
Worthington Henry W., druggist, N W 5th and Callowhill
Worthington Hugh, engineer, 17 Dyott's ct (K)
Worthington John, gent., 4th bel Franklin (K)
Worthington John, oyster house, Queen above Crown (K)
Worthington Lewis, carp., 7 Charlotte
Wosten James, cotton spinner, Mary st n Beach
Wray Alexander, mer., 14 Church al, h 15 Palmyra sq
Wray Andrew, gent., 349 N 7th
Wray Andrew, bricklayer, 4 Jones' al
Wray Chas., chairmr., Elizabeth bel Parrish
Wray & Coates, stone cutters, R road & Washington
Wray Frisby, lab., Burrler's av
Wray & Graham, importers, 14 Church al
Wray Isabella, b. h., 335 N Front
Wray Jas., mer., 41 Chestnut, h 10th bel Spruce
Wray James, dyer, 4th bel Franklin (K)
Wray James, blacksm., Pearl bel Sch 8th
Wray James A., carp., 7 Hamilton pl
Wray John, tailor, Green bel R road
Wray Mary, George n Sch 7th
Wray Matthew, carp., Allen bel Marlboro' (K)
Wray Moses, porter, rear 99 Mulberry
Wray M. Mrs., cupper & bleeder, 157 Vine
Wray Wm., bricklayer, rear 45 Duke
Wray Wm., weaver, Charlotte bel Thompson
Wray Wm., tailor, 157 Vine
Wray Wm., keeper prison, Bush Hill
Wray Wm. A., stone cutter, R road and Washington, h 1 Brandywine
Wreaks Joseph, gent., 122 N 10th
Wriggins Wm., grocer, Queen and F road
Wright Abigail, glove manuf., 169 S 2d
Wright Alfred J., carp., Franklin bel Palmer(K)
Wright Andrew, dry goods, S E 8th & Chestnut, h 43 Clinton
Wright Archibald, mer., N E Vine and Water, h 232 N 4th
Wright A. F. W., principal model school, 411 N 2d
Wright A. & Nephew, salt mers., N E Vine and Water
Wright Benj., wheelwr., Washington (W P)
WRIGHT & BROTHERS, umbrella mrs., 114 High
Wright Catharine, wid. of James, 13th & Penn
Wright Charles, baker, G T road n 4th
Wright Charles F., carp., 188 N 13th
Wright Christian, cordw., 12 Dyott's ct (K)
Wright Christopher, cordw., 78 Catharine
Wright Crispus S., 3d ab Federal
Wright C. S., livery stable, 11 and h 3 Comptroller st

Vright Daniel, currier, rear 41 Duke
Vright Deborah, rear 2d ab Otter (K)
Vright Edward N., mer., 259 High
Vright Elizabeth, trimmings, Marlboro' below Franklin
Wright Enos, tailor, 9 Sheaff's al
Vright E., upholsterer, Fairmount st
Vright E. L. Mrs., 265 S 10th
Wright Fred'k, upholsterer, R road ab Ann (F V)
Vright George, grainer, 6 Fetter la
Vright Geo., plasterer, Carlton ab Sch 3d
Vright Geo., lab., Otter n F road
Vright Geo. A., importer, 23 S 4th
Wright Geo. P., tailor, 528 Vine
Vright Hannah, widow, rear 365 S 5th
Vright Harriet, 31 Sansom
Vright Henry, washer, Centre ab 12th
Vright Hiram, wheelwr., 5 Wells' row
WRIGHT & HUNTER, plumbers and gas fitters, 14 S 8th
Vright H. Mrs., 39 E Pine
Wright Isaac, grocers, 29 Coates
Wright Isaac K., tailor, 50 N 6th, h 8th above Green
Wright Isaac K., coal dealer, Catharine st whf., h 9 Catharine
Wright Israel, 26 Elfreth's al
Wright Jacob H., watchman, 195 N Sch 7th
Wright James, weaver, G T road ab Master(K)
Wright James, tailor, Prime bel 2d
Wright James A., mer., 259 High
Wright James, weaver, O'Neal st (K)
Wright John, seaman, Deal's av
Vright John, umbrella maker, 114 High, h 81 Wood
Vright John, mer., N E Vine and Water, h 175 N 7th
Vright John, dyer, 13th ab Shippen
Vright John, jeweller, Ogden's ct
right John, tobacconist, 222 E Cedar
right John, carp., 282 Wood
right John, gent., 281 S Front
right John K., agent, 10th bel Wallace
right John S., grocer, Green & Logan
right Jonathan, shoemr., 54 New Market
right Joseph, umbrella mr., 114 High, h 171 Callowhill
right Joshua, grocer, Franklin and Sp Garden, h 221 N 9th
right J. & J., grocers, c Spring Garden and Franklin
right J. M., 76 Walnut, h 192 S 9th
right Keziah, 74 Catharine
right, Large & Lottimer, agency, 47 High
right Lorenzo D., shoemr., Carpenter ab 10th
right Martha, 8 Elder
right Mary, milliner, 19 N 12th
right Nathan, carp., 42 N 5th
right Peter, book-keeper, Marlborough above Franklin
right Peter, mer., 259 High, h 3 Girard
right Peter & Sons, chinamrs., 259 High
right & Pike, china ware, 29 N 3d
ight Richard, importer, 23 S 4th
49

Wright Robert, mason, 134 S 12th
Wright Robert, mer., 114 High
Wright Robert, gardener, 117 E Plum
Wright Robert E., cabinetmr., 134 S 12th
Wright Robert H., bricklayer, Pine ab Sch 3d
Wright Robert K., mer., 29 N 3d
Wright R. C. L., tailor, 190 Noble
Wright R. & G. A., importers, 23 S 4th
Wright R. L., tailor, 59 S 3d, h 134 S 12th
Wright Samuel, mer., 114 High
Wright Samuel, tailor, 202 N 11th
Wright Samuel, shoemr., Vine n 13th
Wright Samuel, lab., rear Orchard bel Rawle
Wright Samuel S., carp., 35 Castle
Wright Sarah, bonnet mr., 43 N 5th
Wright Sarah, 119 Vine
Wright Thomas, boat builder, 26 Dyott's ct (K)
Wright Thomas, warper, c Dugan and M'Makin court
Wright Thomas A., salesman, rear 106 S 3d
Wright Wm., clerk, 44 Dillwyn st
Wright Wm., gas fitter and plumber, 14 S 8th, h Pine ab Juniper
Wright Wm., hat blockmr., Hudson's al & Harmony ct, h 14 Perry
WRIGHT WILLIAM, medicines, 169 Sassafras, h 7th ab Parrish
Wright Wm., shoemr., 156 Christian
Wright Wm., engineer, 1 Wallace
Wright Wm., lab., 5th ab Buttonwood
Wright Wm., milkman, Centre bel Parrish
Wright Wm. H., upholsterer, 147 S 11th
Wrighter John, carp., 1 Diligent av
Wrighter Reading, 10 Diligent av
Wrigley James, weaver, Bank ab Pine
Wrigley Susan, 19 Benton
Wucherer John R., Pres. Phoenix Ins. Co., 52 Walnut, h 428 Spruce
Wunder George, vict., Front ab Oxford (K)
Wunder Jacob, viet., Cherry bel Franklin (K)
Wunder Jacob, vict., Miller's row (K)
Wunder Jonathan, weaver, F road ab Phoenix
Wunder Paul, butcher, Palmer bel West (K)
Wunder Samuel, vict., Oxford ab Front (K)
Wunder Susan, George & St John (K)
Wunder Wm., vict., Hanover bel West (K)
WUNDERLICH & GRIER, ford. & com. mers., 272 High
Wunderlich John, carp., 127 G T road (K)
Wunderlich John, mer., 272 High
Wuneder Wm., blacksm., Hanover bel Duke(K)
Wurfflein Andrew, gunsm., 335½ N 3d
Wurmser & Co., cake baker, 337 N 2d
Wurst John, confec., 126 N 5th
Wurts Charles, mer., 175 High, h 115 S 8th
Wurts Charles S., mer., 175 High, h Sch 6th & Walnut
Wurts Joseph, lab., Marshall ab Poplar
WURTS, MUSGRAVE & WURTS, dry goods, 175 High
Wurts Wm., mer., 175 High, h 4 York Build'gs
Wurtz John, vict., 224 N 9th
Wurz John, shoemr., 97 Callowhill
Wyand Daniel, ladies' shoemaker, 11th ab Carpenter

Wyand Jacob, japanner, 158 Sassafras, h 298 Vine
Wyand John, watchmr., rear 210 Cherry
Wyant Samuel, 86 F road (K)
Wyatt Elizabeth, 183 Lombard
Wyatt Hannah, 183 Lombard
Wyatt Samuel, grocer, 20 Cedar
Wyeth John, gent., 77 Wood
Wyeth S. D., stereotype foundry, 7 Pear
Wyle John, capt., 5 Union sq
Wyley Amanda, sewer, St Joseph's av & Sch 5th
Wylie Geo., manuf., 10th & Carpenter
Wylie Hugh, shoemr., Sassafras W Broad
Wylie Samuel B. Rev., professor and vice provost of Penn Univer. Ann bel Sch 4th, (F V)
Wylie Samuel O. Rev., 31 S Sch 6th
Wyman Jonas, gent., 429 Sassafras
Wynkoop Abraham, 137 N 11th
Wynkoop Benjamin N., mcr., rear 83 High, h 137 N 11th
Wynkoop Henry, teacher, 6th st M village
Wynkoop Matilda, 4 Ferris' ct
Wynkoop Wm. T., Filbert ab 11th
Wyseiser Wm., baker, 96 Washington av
Wythes Joseph, bonnet manuf., 138½ S 2d
Wythes Walter, coffee roaster, Phoenix below G T road (K)

———

Yans Christian, combmr., 231 St John
Yapp Seneca, waterman, Simmon's ct
Yapp Thomas, brass fin., Simmon's ct
Yard Edmund, mcr., 109 High, h 119 S 3d
Yard Edmund J., collector, 23 Spruce
Yard Edmund S., collector, 23 Spruce
Yard Eliza, dry goods N E 8th & Walnut
YARD, GILMORE & CO., silk goods, 109 High
Yard John, wheelwright, Mary ab West (K)
Yard John, jr., tax collector, 1 Montgomery
Yard Pearson, dry goods, 12 N 9th
Yard Thomas W., mcr., 125 High
Yardley Eliza, Olive ab 10th
Yardley John S., conveyancer, 114 S 3d, house 6 Logan
Yardley Joshua, carp., 9th ab Parrish
Yardley Rachel, 32 Madison
Yardley Samuel, broker, S 3d, h 125 Wood
Yardley Theo., bricklayer, Powell bel Sch 4th
Yardley Thomas, clerk, 13th ab Callowhill
Yardley Thomas H., M. D., 264 N 4th
Yardley Wm., gent., 125 Wood
Yarly Conrad, cordw., Ontario bel Poplar
Yarger Samuel, carp., 10th bel Parrish
Yarnall A. H., druggist, Sch 3d and Lombard
Yarnall B. H., mcr., 16 S 4th, h 402 Mulberry
Yarnall Charles, druggist, 39 High, h 30 S 12th
Yarnall David D., mcr., 287 High
Yarnall Edward, druggist, 39 High, h S W 12th

Yarnall Wm., mcr., 14½ S 4th, h Sch 7th below Mulberry
Yarnall Wm., mason, Brown bel Broad
Yarnalls & Walton, hardware, 14½ S 4th
Yarrow John, mcr., 127 High, h 17 Montgomery square
Yasley Pascal, bricklayer, 1 Madison
Yates Abraham, capt. watch, Filbert n Sch 8th
Yates David W., sailmr., Cherry ab 13th, h Penn ab 13th
Yates Edman, tinsmith, 164 S 6th, h 48 S 6th
Yates Edwd., mariner, Hallowell
Yates Edward D., bootmr., 30½ S 6th
Yates Emma, b. h., 25 Sansom
Yates Evan, weaver, Roney's ct (K)
Yates George W., tailor, 100 German
Yates John W., draym., rear Cherry bel Franklin (K)
Yates Washington, undertaker, 465 Vine
Yates Wm., girth webb mr., rear 262 High, h 72 Franklin
Yates Wm., saddler, 6 Lombard ct
Yeager Benj., victualler, 9th bel Noble
Yeager Casper jr., cop. pl. mr., North n 11th
Yeager Catharine, Depot ab 8th
YEAGER & CHAMBERLAIN, combs, &c., 135 High
Yeager Daniel, carp., 9 Boyd's av
Yeager David B., vict., Sch Front ab Coates
Yeager Edward, engraver, Walnut ab 6th
Yeager George, whip braider, 68 Noble
Yeager Geo. W., machinist, 575 N Front
Yeager Henry, lab., Harriges' ct (N L)
Yeager Henry, vict., Crown bel West (K)
Yeager Henry, butcher, Sch 3d ab Callowhill
Yeager H. S., carver and gilder, 94 Walnut, h 235 N 9th
Yeager Jacob, wheelwr., 73 G T road (K)
Yeager Jacob R., saddler, 71 E Shippen
Yeager Jeremiah, 141 S 11th
Yeager Jeremiah, hatter, Poplar bel 9th
Yeager John, carter, Herriges' ct
Yeager John, moroc. fin., Rachel bel Laurel
YEAGER JOHN C., hatter, 163 N 3d
Yeager Joseph, engraver, 30 Palmyra sq
Yeager Joseph, gent., 326 Cedar
Yeager Jos., seaman, Prime ab Swanson
Yeager J. P., brushmr., 67 Gaskill
Yeager Lewis, cordw., rear 1 Orchard
Yeager Mary, gentw., 309 E Pine
Yeager Peter, tavern, 68 N 6th
Yeager Wm., cordw., Sch 8th n Vine
Yeager Wm., dealer, 8 Chester
Yeager Wm. E., brush maker, 81 E Cedar, h 67 Gaskill
Yeager Wm. W., mcr., 135 High, h 253 N 7th
Yeakle Wm., chairmr., 106 N 13th
Yearsley Geo., plasterer, 9 Blunston's av
Yearsley Rebecca, Steward bel Catharine

Yerkes Charles T., clerk, New Market ab Noble
Yerkes Geo., brushmr., 337 N 2d, h New Market ab Noble
Yerkes Harman, agent, 138 N 8th
Yerkes Jonathan, Sup. Frank. Square, h 3 Sergeant
Yerkes Silas, livery stab., 45 Noble, h 339 N 2d
Yerkes Wm., lime, 9th and Willow, h 9th and Nectarine
Yerkess H. H., tobacconist, 212 N 8th
Yetter Ann, rear Hanover bel Duke (K)
Yetter George, brickmr., Sch 5th ab Spruce
Yetter Willian, bricklayer, Nectarine n 11th
Yhost Mary Ann, gentw., Carpenter bel 7th
Yocom James, stovemr., N E 2d and Sassafras, h 117 Wood
Yocom & Wilson, leather and findings, 225 N 2d
Yocum Andw., cabinetmr., Jefferson n G T road
Yocum David, trunkmr., 392 Sassafras
Yocum Jacob H., gratemr., Juniper bel Walnut
Yocum John, stone cut., 7th bel Washington
Yocum Peter, shoemr., Shield's ct
Yoerg Fred K., furniture car, rear 31 Otter (K)
Yohe Daniel, mer., 74 Franklin
Yohn Philip, drayman, 10th ab Coates
Yohn W. H., shoe mr., Pegg al
Yomer Wm., tailor, Wharton ab 4th
Yons Daniel, blacksm., Eyres' ct (K)
York Elizabeth, widow, rear 110 Catharine
York Henry, cabinetmr., 138 Christian
York Thos., seaman, Fitzwater ab 13th
Yorke James, carp., Shippen ab 13th
Yorke Lewis S., com. mer., 43½ N whfs, h S E 8th and Buttonwood
Yost Alexander, weav., Montgomery bel Front
Yost Caleb, weaver, Montgomery bel Front (K)
Yost Peter, candy manuf., 52 F road
Yost Sarah, dressmr., 114 E 5th
Yost Zebulon, weaver, Cherry and Monroe (K)
Youcom James, 117 Wood
Youker Francis, grocer, 379 N Front
Youker Jacob, wheelwright, Taylor's ct (K)
Young Adam, baker, Carpenter bel 5th
Young Adam, lab., 3 Washington ct
Young Alexander, distiller, S W Cedar & Crabb, store 10 P road, h 12 P road
Young Alexander, weaver, Shippen bel Broad
Young Alexander K., 98 S 12th
Young Alfred D., chair paint., 21 Parker
Young Andrew, brassfound., Hope bel Phoenix
Young Andrew, 260 Pine
Young Andrew, carp., 543 Chestnut
Young Andrew, carter, rear Poplar ab 6th
Young Andrew S., capt., 15 Somer's ct
Young Armar, dry goods, 19 Bank
Young A. D., dressmr., 177 S 11th
Young Benj., biscuit baker, 24 Brown
Young Benj., carp., Shackamaxon and Bedford (K)
Young Catharine, Christian n 6th
Young Cath., widow, Palmer n F road (K)
Young Charles, pedler, George E Sch 3d
Young Charles, mér., 290 N 2d, h 204 N 4th
Young Charles, weaver, Shippen la n Fitzwater
Young Chas. E., tailor, rear Penn bel Broad

Young Charles M., tailor, Sp Garden bel 9th, h 8th ab Buttonwood
Young Charles W., toys & varieties, h 259 S 2d
Young Clayton, shopkeeper, N W Tammany & Dillwyn
Young Creighton, carp. weav., Front and Jefferson (K)
Young Daniel L., bricklr., School ab Rose (K)
Young David, chemist, lab., 11 M'Duffie
Young David, pumpmr., Washington ab 6th
Young David, clerk, Lewis ab Poplar
Young David, cooper, 85 S Water, h 68 Almond
Young David, lab., Marriott ab 5th
Young David, engineer, Haydock ab Front
Young Dilworth, cardw., Lemon n 11th
Young Edmund, coach and engine painter, 11 North ab 10th, h Division ab 11th
Young Edmund, blacksm., 9 Green (C), h Carpenter ab 6th
Young Edwd, turner, 1 Fetter la, h 1 Mineral pl
Young Edward, chairmr., 117 Green
Young Elizabeth, wid., Elizabeth ab Franklin
Young Elizabeth, Sch 5th bel Spruce
Young Ezekiel J., collector, 327 S 3d
Young Frederick W., conf., 145 S 10th
Young Geo., grocer, S E Steward & Catharine
Young George, lab., Hanover ab Bedford (K)
Young George, carp., 5 Brinton
Young Geo., collector, 3 Pearl n Sch 7th
Young Geo., brickmr., 6th ab Master (K)
Young Geo., weaver, Amber ab Phoenix
Young Geo., oysters, 347 N Front
Young Geo., painter and glazier, 318 S 5th
Young George J., carp., Brandywine ab 13th
Young Hannah, nurse, 71 Mulberry
Young Henry, printer, Shippen bel P road
Young Henry, blacksm., 28 Farmer
Young Henry, tavern, S E Sch 8th & Callowhill
Young Henry, clerk, 154 S John
Young Henry J., carp., 568 S 2d
Young Hugh, lab., Thompson bel Sch 7th
Young Israel, bonnet presser, 215 S 2d
Young Jacob, blacksmith, 9 Green (C), h 186 S 9th
Young Jacob, printer, 27 North
Young Jacob, tailor, 34 Pegg
Young Jacob, cordw., 3 Short ct
Young Jacob B., dealer, 31 Prosperous al
Young Jacob S. ladies' shoemr., rear 306 St John
Young James, warper, Fairview (F M)
Young Jas., lab., 2 Abbott's ct
Young Jas., mer., 74 & 76 S Front, h 156 S 13th
Young James, dry goods and collector, N E 3d and Catharine
Young James, lieut. of police, Mayor's office, h 117½ Filbert
Young James, lab., Wood W Sch 8th
Young James, weav., Front bel Jefferson (K)
Young James, grocer, 210 & h 208 N 3d
YOUNG JAMES, printer, 5 Harmony ct, h 122 S 4th
Young James, bookbinder, Concord st
Young James H., engraver, 222 S 4th
Young Jas. S., mer., 96½ High
Young John, dealer, Front bel Master (K)

Young John, mer., 26 S whfs
Young John, lab., Aspen ab Spruce
Young John, tavern, 11th and Buttonwood
YOUNG JOHN, printer, 3 Black Horse al
Young John, painter, Hallowell
Young John, weaver, Patterson's ct
Young John E., lum. mer., Sch 7th and High, h Vine n Sch 8th
Young John G., stone cut., 89 Dillwyn
Young John G., 145 S 10th
Young John H., sea capt., 130 Catharine
Young John L., hatter, Sch Front and High
Young John W., watchman, 11th and Coates
Young Joseph, bricklayer, Cherry ab Duke
Young Joseph, butcher, F road n Palmer
Young Joseph, weaver, rear 463 N 4th
Young Joseph P., bootmr., 140 Chestnut
Young Joseph S., agent, 18 N 12th
Young Lewis, collector, 121 Christian
Young Margaret, 23 Montgomery
Young Margaret, washer, 25 Mechanic
Young Marg., F road ab Palmer (K)
Young Marian, 118 Catharine
Young Martha, bandbox mr., 122 New
Young Martha, 156 S 13th
Young Mary, Faries' ct
Young Mary, washer, Prospect al
Young Michael, lab., Franklin ab Palmer (K)
Young Montgomery P., atty., 333 S 6th
Young Moses, 25 Paschall's al
Young Nathan, clerk, 90 Dillwyn
Young Oliver P., tailor, 4 S 5th and h 21 Parker
Young Peter, sen., baker, Poplar ab 10th
Young Peter, coppersm., 565 S Front
Young Peter K., boot polisher, Lewis ab Poplar
Young Philip, wheelwright, 21 Parker
Young & Randolph, lumber mers. High & Sch 7th
Young Richard, lab., Paschall's al
Young Richard, 66 S 11th
Young Richard, lab., George ab R road (F V)
Young Richard, gilder, 409 High, h 4 Ann W Sch 4th
Young Ridgway, waiter, 10 Currant al
Young & Roark, blacksmiths, 6 New Market
Young Robert, stone agent, Kensington av
Young Robert, weaver, Filbert n Sch 3d
Young Robert, moulder, Washington bel 6th
Young Robert, drover, R road ab Wallace
Young Samuel, tavern, Lewis & Girard av
Young Samuel, painter, 25 Cresson's al
Young Samuel, plasterer, 6 Ronaldson st
Young Samuel, confectioner, 185 N 2d
Young Samuel, tobacconist, 200 Noble
Young Saml. B., tobacconist, Hallowell's ct
Young Sarah, 7 Lawrence
Young Sarah, shop, F road bel Franklin (K)

Young Wm., M. D., infirmary and chemist, 153 Spruce
Young Wm., weaver, Front ab Jefferson (K)
Young Wm., tailor, 38 Catharine
Young Wm., porter, 3 Pine al
Young Wm., combmr., Palmer n F road (K)
Young Wm., tailor, 486 Coates
Young Wm. J., bookbinder, Rex ct
Young Wm. J., math. inst. mr., 9 Dock, h 473 S Front
Young Wm. S., printer, 50 N 6th, h 173 Sassafras
Young W. S., U. S. Navy, Filbert n Sch 6th
Young Zebulon, confect., Howard n Franklin
Younger Casper, saw frame mr., N E Front and Green
Younger Ed., harnessmr., George ab Mechanic
Younghanns Fredk. cabmr. rear 29 Cherry
Yous Danl., blacksm., Montgomery ab F road
Yunger E., umbrellamr. 63 N 4th, h 23 Wood

———

Zah Frederick, cordw., Charlotte bel Poplar
Zane Abigail, gentw., 325 S Front
Zane Andrew, wood wharf, Beach ab Shackamaxon
Zane Charles, carp., rear 9th ab Coates
Zane & Downer, 6½ N whfs
Zane Elizabeth, 80 Penn
Zane Henry, shoemr., 558 S 2nd
Zane Jesse S., mer., 77 S Front, h 23 Mulberry
Zane Joel, weigher, 6½ N whfs.
Zane John, gent., Bridge (M Village)
Zane John, carp., 64 S Swanson
Zane Robert, 2 Miller's ct
Zane Simeon E., blacksm. h Sheaff ab 12th
Zane Simeon T. blacksm., 14 Logan
Zane Thos., hatmr., 80 Penn st
Zane Wesley, bricklayer, 128 Beach
Zane Wm. B., 77 S Front, h 380 Sassafras
Zaner Philip, porter, Lemon st
Zantzinger George, wine mer., 113 Chestnut, h S E 13th and Locust
Zantzinger Henry, atty. & coun. 51 S 5th
Zantzinger Wm., M. D., Sch 7th ab Spruce
Zaun Jacob, bootmr., 399 N 3d
Zebley Benj. F., carp. 31 Montgomery
Zebley Jacob, blacksm., 8 Drinker's al, h 18 Bread
Zebley Jacob S., 76 S 11th
Zebley John, clerk, 249 S 9th
Zebley Joseph P., shoemr., 8 Madison
Zebley & Mervine, blacksms., 8 Drinker's al
Zederick Peter, mariner 37 Penn

Zell John F., marble mason, 9th & Coates, h 374 Coates

Zell & Smith, hardware, 298 High

Zell Thomas, mer., 298 High

Zell Thomas M., flour and feed store, High and Sch 5th

Zellender Reuben, painter, Lewis ab Poplar

Zeller Elizabeth, gentw., 10th ab Parrish

Zeller George, lab., Stearly ct

Zeller Henry, tailor, 2 Charlotte

Zeller Wm., jeweller, 157 Buttonwood

Zelley Henry B., cordw., 2 Maria

Zelley John G., tailor, 53 New

Zellner Enoch, cordw., 61 St John bel George (K)

Zellner Susan, 61 St John bel George (K) .

Zelner Charles, cordw. 6 Weaver's ct (N L)

Zelner Charles, bootmr., 353 N 3d

Zelner Elizabeth, 447 N 3d

Zelner W., cigarmr., 445 N 3d

Zendt John, carp. Palmer bel West (K)

Zener James, shoemr., 1 Lily al

Zentler Conrad, printer, rear 104 N 2d

Zentner Lorentz, mason, 6th bel G T road

Zepp Daniel, carp. 454 N 4th

Zepp Jacob, carp. Nectarine ab 9th, h 13 Nectarine

Zepp Philip, cabtmr., rear Hanover ab Franklin

Zepp Saml., jeweller, 79½ N 2d, h 25 Race

Zerman Francis, druggist, 9th & Catharine

Zern Geo., lime dealer, rear 261 St John

Zernow Fredk. lab., Culvert & Mechanic

Zettler George, furniture car, Washington bel R road

ZIEBER GEORGE B., periodical agency, S W 3d & Chestnut, h 184 Chestnut

Ziegefuss Abraham, tavern, 216 N 3d

Ziegler Charles, mer., 17 N 4th, h 22 Branch

Ziegler George K., clerk, 388 N 4th

Ziegler Geo. J., dentist, 150 Mulberry

Ziegler Jacob, carp., 113 Melon

Ziegler John, shoemr., 38 Queen

Ziegler John, carpet weaver, 149 Poplar

Ziegler John E., grocer, 261 N Front

Ziegler John G., tavern, N E Callowhill and Crown

Ziesel Anthony, tobacco, store and house 288 N Front

Zimmer Jacob, baker, 309 S 2d

Zimmer Joseph, lab., Keyser's row (K)

Zimmerling Charles, sugar refiner, Zane ab 7th, h 282 N 7th

Zimmerman Ann, layer out of dead, 72 Coates

Zimmerman Charles W., Pine ab 12th

Zimmerman Christian, baker, 149 Spruce

Zimmerman J., hair cutter, 344 Callowhill

Zimmerman Margaret, 373 N 4th

Zimmerman Sarah, gentw., 8th ab Parrish

Zimmerman Thomas, tailor, 100 Prime

Zimmerman & Wilts, grain and flour, Cedar ab 13th

Zink George, carp., Ann (F V)

Zinser John, grocer, S E Coates & New Market

Zippler John, cabinetmr., Poplar bel 9th

Zippra Philip, huckster, Jones' al (N L)

Zittler Richard, rigger, F road n Franklin (K)

Zoll John M., vict., 5th ab Jefferson (K)

ZOLL JOSEPH, boot and shoemr., 36 S 3d

Zollickoffer Henry M. druggist, N E 6th & Pine

Zollikofer Werner, mer., 16 N 4th

Zolls John, cordw., 592 N 3d

Zorns Joseph, cooper, 130 St John

ZORNS J. S., M D, 91 Green

Zuigner Lorentz, beer house, 278 N 3d

Zuntle Christian, ashman, Hope ab Phoenix

CAMDEN, NEW JERSEY.

Abbott Robert T., farmer, Washington bel 4th | Allen Joseph B., steersman, 3d ab Mark +

Atkinson Josiah, justice of the peace, 3d above Plum
Atkinson Thomas, South Camden

Babington Robert, shoemr., 2d and Federal
Ballinger Mary, cooper ab 4th
Balser Wm., trader, Plum bel 2d
Barker Wm., farmer, 7th and Federal
Barns Geo. W., painter, Plum ab 3d
Barrett Mrs., grocer, 2d and Plum
Bartlett Seth, blacking manf., Federal ab 4th
Bate Wm. J., farmer, c 5th and Market
Bates Benjamin, blacksmith, Federal
Bates Thos., captain, Federal ab 2d
Baxter John, tailor, Market bel 3d
Baxter Mrs., 2d ab Plum
Baxter Thos. H., cabtmr., Lanning's row
Bayley E., bleeder, Pine bel 3d
Beagary Benj., carp., Federal ab 4th
Beck John, baker, Federal ab 3d
Bender Peter, sausagemr., 2d ab Plum
Bender Wm., carp., 4th ab Plum
Beneman Daniel, ladies' shoemr., Plum ab 3d
Bennett Abraham, carp., 2d ab Pine
Benson John, agent, Railroad bel 3d
Bernard J., ladies' shoemr., Pine ab 3d
Biddle W. & J., hardware, 3d and cooper
Boardman H., coachmr., Plum ab 3d
Boardman Thos. coachmr. Plum ab 3d
Bodine James, Federal ab 2d
Boggs Isaac, lab., Plum ab 3d
Bowlby Charles, agent, Federal ab 4th
Boyd Harriet, Plum ab 5th
Bozorth Richard, vict. 4th bel Cooper
Braddock Saml., carp., 3d and Market
Bradshaw Wm., turner, 2d ab Line
Branan John, marketman, Pine bel 3d
Bremin George, mer., Cooper and 6th
Brinnisholtz Jacob, tobacconist, 2d ab Line
Brown David, baker, Federal ab 3d
Brown J. A. boot fitter, Cooper bel 6th
Brown Wm., mer., Federal bel 4th
BROWNING ABRAHAM, atty. and coun., c 2d and Market, h Market n 2d
Browning Benj., dealer, Federal ab 3d
Browning B. Mrs., S W 5th and Market
Browning Edw. and Bros., drug mill, Front and Market
Browning Hannah, Federal ab 2d
Browning Jacob, clerk, Federal ab 4th
Browning John, lum. mer. Front ab Market
Buck Joshua, lab. 2d ab Market
Burkhardt M., chairmr., Cooper ab Front
Burr & Grave, grocers, 3d and Plum
Burrough Joshua, mer. English's ferry, h 2d bel Cooper
Burrough Mark, weaver, Federal ab 3d
Burroughs Benjamin, Cooper's Point
Burroughs Mrs., b h., 2d and Market
Burt Wm., bookbr., Pine ab 3d

Cake Richard C., Ferry House, Federal
Campion Stacy B., Cooper's Ferry
Capewell and Bro., glass works, Kaighn's pt
Carpenter G. W. steam mill, Cooper ab 3d

Carter Daniel, sausages, Market ab 3d
Carter Jeremiah, sausage mr. Cooper and 2d
Casner Jacob, carp., Federal & 4th
Casner Joseph, tobacconist, Federal ab 2d
Caum Arthur, pilot, 2d bel R road
Caum James, engineer, Plum bel 3d
Chapman Henry, tinman, 3d and Federal
Chapman J. & H. tin smiths, Market bel 2d
Chapman Sorbet, tinsmith, Market bel 2d
Charlton Wm., tailor, Pine ab 2d
Clark John, wheelwright, Cooper and 4th
Cole & Elfreth, ice dealers, Market ab 2d
Cole Isaac, coachmr. Front, h Plum ab Front
Cole Jesse, ice mer. 2d bel Cooper
Collings J. S. coachmr. Front ab Market
Cook Charles, trader, Front bel Market
Cooley John, trader, Plum bel 4th
Coombs John, gent., Federal ab 3d
Cooper Hannah, widow, Cooper's Point
Cooper Joseph W. gent. Cooper's Point
Cooper Mary, Cooper ab Front
Cooper R. M., M. D., Cooper ab Front
Cooper William, gent. Cooper's Point
Cooper Wm. D. attorney, office 2d bel Market, h Cooper ab Front
Cowperthwaite J. K. justice of the peace, N E Federal and 2d
Crawford John, lab., 4th bel Plum
Crutchley S., dyer, Plum bel 2d

Daugherty Edward, provisions, 3d and Railroad
Davis Benjamin, lab. Plum bel 4th
Davis Benjamin T. turpentine distiller, Front ab Market, h Cooper ab Front
Davis D. M., M. D., Front ab Plum
Davis Elijah, mer., S Camden
Davis Ephraim, barkeeper, Cooper ab 2d
Davis Nathan, mer., Federal st wharf, h Market ab 2d
Dawson John, coachmr. Plum ab 3d
Dayton James B., att'y, Market bel 2d
De Lacour Joseph C., druggist, N W 3d and Plum, h Federal ab 2d
Devenney Wm., tobacconist, Federal and Front
Dobbins D., blacksm., Cooper and Front
Dorsey Daniel, carp. Federal bel 4th
Doughty Samuel, capt. Federal bel 3d
Dudley Thomas H., att'y, 2d ab Plum, h Railroad bel 3d
Duer James, shoemr. Plum ab 4th
Duffell Edward, coachmr., Plum ab 3d

Eastlack Rebecca, Plum ab 3d
Elder Joseph, book binder, Plum ab 4th
Elfreth John R., wheelwright, Market ab 2d
Elfreth Samuel D., smithery, Front ab Market, h 2d ab Market
English Israel, tavern, Cooper's ferry
Evans J. U. coachmr. Market bel 2d
Everell Charles, dry goods, Cooper and 2d
Everett Wm., gunsm., Federal ab 3d
Elwell James, Railroad Hotel

Fakler Charles, baker, Plum bel 3d
Ferguson Franklin, printer, Front & Market

Fetter John, carp., Broadway ab Spruce
Fetters Richard, florist, 3d ab Market
Feuring Wm. piano mr. 6th and Market
Fine John, R R ag't, R road bel 4th
Fisher Saml., carp., Federal ab 4th
Fisler Lorenzo F., M. D., Federal bel 3d
Fitzerald Wilson, cooper, Federal ab 2d
Flanegan & Carpenter, steam mills, Front ab Cooper
Follansbee John, shoemr., Federal ab 3d
Forman S. S. blacksmith, 2 Plum
Fortiner William, bricklayer, Federal ab 3d
Fox John, sawyer, Front ab Cooper
Fox Wm., lab., Plum ab 3d
Frick Benjamin, lab. 3d ab Market

Gahan James, lab., Pine ab 2d
Gant Mrs., Kaighn's pt
Gardiner Thos. W., mer., Cooper bel 6th
Garrett Charles S., saddler, 6 Lanning's row
Garrett Samuel W. coach trimmer, 2d above Market
Garwood Danl., lab., 2d ab Market
Gayhart S., clockmr., 4th and Market
Giford Wm. S., lab, Line ab Oak
Gill John, president Camden Bank
Gilmore James, trader, 3d bel Plum
Githen Josiah, butcher, Plum ab 3d
Glover Samuel, coachmr., 3d and Pine
Goforth Catharine, Federal ab 2d
Goldsmith Nathan, lab. Plum ab 3d
Goldsmith Stephen, lab. 2d ab Plum
Gray Philip J., publisher Camden Mail, Front n Federal, h 4th n Market
Gregory David H., engineer, 6th and Cooper
Gregory J. G. & Co. lottery managers, 1 Lanning's row
Gregory Wm. trader, Federal ab 3d

Haines Aaron N., mer., R road bel 3d
Haines Mordecai, gent. Market ab 3d
Hale Levi, carp. Cooper and 5th
Hall Jesse, carp., Pine bel 3d
Hamilton Wm., carver, Kaighn's pt
Hammell Benjamin A., huckster, Cooper's hill
Hammeth Hepzibah, 2d ab Plum
Hannold S., oysterman, 2d bel Pine
Harrison R., Plum bel 4th
Hart Samuel, gent., Camden, (N J)
Hartsgrove B., refectory, Plum bel 4th
Hatch Wm. J. shoe store, 6th and Cooper
Hawkins Jonathan, segars, Federal ab 2d
Hawley, Lemuel, coachmr., Federal ab 2d
Heiners Charles, confect., Front ab Plum
Helings Elizabeth, Smith's row
Hervey Robt., acct., Kaighn's pt
Hess Daniel, grocer, 4th and Walnut
Heyl Elizabeth, Columbia Gardens
Hickman Reuben, sausage mr. Plum ab 3d
Hillman Mary, Market ab 3d
Hinkle H., bookbinder, 2d bel Pine
Hoagland John, coach trimmer, Cooper ab Front
Hooy John W. boot fitter, 3d ab Market
Holby Joseph, stone cutter, Pine bel 3d
Holl J. G., baker, Pine bel 4th

Hollis C. J., engraver, 6th bel Cooper
Hope A., manf., Plum bel 5th
Hope William M., vict., Cooper ab Front
Horner Isaac, ferryman, 2d ab Plum
Howe Wm. C., agent, 2d ab Line
Howell Richard W., att'y & coun., off. Front n Federal, h Market ab 3d
Hoy Thomas, trader, Plum and 4th
Hoyt Abraham, lab., Cooper ab 5th
Hood George, fireman, Plum bel 2d
Hughes Wm. W., stovemr., Federal ab 4th
Humphreys Francis, engraver, Pine ab 4th
Humphreys C. S. painter, 5 Lanning's row
Hunt Benj. I., bootmr., Federal ab 2d
Huston Thos., shoemr., Plum ab 5th
Huston Wm. coachsmith, 2d ab Plum
Hutchinson A., tobacconist, Mulford's ct ab 2d

Igley Geo., weaver, Market bel 3d
Inman Saml., grocer, Pine and 3d

Jackson Joseph, oysters, 2d bel Cooper
Jackson Joseph, oysters, Market ab 2d
Jeffers William N., attorney and counsellor, off. Plum and Front, h Plum ab 2d
Jinkins Andrew, watchman, Plum bel 5th
Jones Amy, 2d ab Plum
Jones Burden, waterman, Federal ab 2d
Jones Geo., waterman, Oak bel Line
Jones R. B., bricklayer, Pine bel Broadway
Jones Wm., waterman, Kaighn's pt
Jones W. T. & Co., whip & cane manuf., Broadway and Line
Kahl Lewis, barber, 3 Lanning's row
Kaighn Charles, farmer, Kaighn's Point
Kaighn Elias, smithery, Kaighn's Point
Kaighn's Misses, Kaighn's pt
Kay Elizabeth, Railroad bel 3d
Kelly Isaac, carp. Plum ab 3d
King S., Cooper n 5th
Kurtz Henry, painter, Market ab 3d

Lafetra Samuel, butcher, Federal ab 3d
Lanning Paul C., Plum ab 2d
Lare J., wood corder, Federal bel 6th
Lawrence John, constable, Market ab 2d
Lawrence Wm., clerk, Cooper ab Front
Lawrence Wm. P., agent, Cooper ab 2d
Leake Saml., grocer, Plum bel 4th
Lees S., superintendent, Cooper ab Front
Lewis Charles S., mer., Front ab Plum
Lippincott John, blacksmith, Cooper ab 2d
List Lewis, machinist, Plum ab 4th
Long John, blacksm., Front bel Cooper's ferry
Lord John, oyster house, 2d bel Cooper
Lummis Samuel, saddler, Cooper's ferry, Market and 4th
Lustre Seth, lab. Plum ab 3d
Lutton Robert, gent., Plum ab 2d
Lybrand Jos. M. Rev., Cooper ab 2d
Lyle Thos., gent., 5th and Cooper

Madara Thomas, clerk, Plum bel 4th
Manley Mrs., Plum ab 2d
Mansell S. E., grocer, c 2d bel Federal

Mansfield Robert, dealer, Plum bel 3d
Martin Alfred, tailor, 3d and Federal
Mason S. Rufus, 3d & Cooper
Matlack Chas., pilot, Plum ab Front
Matlack Seth, mer., 3d and Market
Matthews James F., ship carp., Cooper's ferry
Matthews M., ship carp., Cooper's ferry
McCalla Aulay, cashier Camden Bank, h Cooper ab Front
McClain Samuel, clerk, South Camden
McCreedy Thomas, livery stable, Federal ab 3d
McCully Catharine, Federal ab 2d
McDonald Philip, miller, Cooper and 3d
McGonagle Mrs., Plum bel 3d
McGrath John, tailor, Market bel 6th
Mellier A., clerk, 3 Smith's row
Mickle Ann, 2d ab Plum
Mickle Isaac, atty., Bridge av
Mickle John, capt. Railroad ab 2d
Mickle John W., gent., Bridge av
Middleton Amos, farmer, Cooper's Point
Middleton B., painter, 2d ab Market
Middleton B., wharf tender, 4th bel Market
Middleton Joseph, lab. Plum ab 4th
Middleton Timothy, dealer, Plum ab 2d
Miller Evan, plasterer, 4th bel Chestnut
Miller Matthew, coal mer., Federal n 3d
Millington Mathias, printer, Broadway & Pine
Mills Alfred, stone mason, Oak bel Line
Mills W., lab., Pine ab 2d
Mitchell Stephen, book-keeper, Federal ab 2d
Montgomery Robt., clerk, Kaighn's pt
Moore H., fireman, Kaighn's pt
Moore James, hatter, 2d ab Line
Moore J. J., tailor, Chestnut ab 4th
Moore S., engraver, 2d ab Plum
Morgan Edward, constable, Plum ab 2d
Morgan John, silver plater, 2d and Plum
Morgan John, silver plater, 4th and Cooper
Morgan R., grocer, Federal ab 3d
Mulford Isaac, M. D., Federal ab 2d
Mulford Thos. W., atty., 2d bel Plum
Mumford E. W. engraver, Market bel 3d
Murray John, lab., Plum bel 5th
Muschamps, Edwd., carp., Federal ab 2d
Myers Albert G., silversm., Federal ab 3d

Newton Hannah, Market bel 6th
Newton John, marketman, 3d bel Pine
Nicholas Peter, painter, Federal bel 4th
Nichols E., painter, Market ab 4th

Osborn David, waterman, Oak bel Line
Osborn James, waterman, Pine bel 3d

Pedder James, farmer, Plum ab 4th
Peel Wm., variety store, Plum bel 4th
Perkins Wm., machinist, Cooper ab Front
Perry Sarah, 5th and Market
Peters Mrs., Federal ab 3d
Pfeifer G. C. tailor, 2d and Plum
Phillips Stephen D. confectioner, 4th bel Market
Pierce Samuel, tinsmith, Federal ab 2d
Pimlott Jas., shoemr., Pine bel 4th
Pine Daniel, farmer, Federal bel 4th
Pinyard Wm. coach trimmer, 3d ab Federal
Plum Wm. ostler, Plum bel 3d
Plum Wm., slip tender, 3d bel Pine
Porter Henry, butcher, Front ab Market
Porter Isaac, miller, Cooper ab 2d
Porter J. H., bar keeper, Cooper ab 2d
Poulson Josh. R., broker, Cooper ab 2d
Pusey Joshua, currier, Plum bel 3d

Read John S. paper hanger, Plum ab 2d
Reed Richard Y., Plum bel 4th
Richards John, peddler, Cooper ab 3d
Richmond Geo. B., tailor, Federal ab 2d
Robbins E., silver smith, Plum ab 2d
Roberts Azael, shoes, 2d and Federal
Roberts Azael, shoemr., Federal ab 2d
Roberts Caleb, cabinetmaker, 3d & Federal
Robinson John, trader, 4th and Federal
Rodgers John, coal dealer, R road ab 3d
Roseman Geo., butcher, Plum ab 3d
Ross James, carpets, Pine bel 5th
Ross John, tailor, 4 Lanning's row
Ross Samuel, hair cloth manuf. c 4th & Federal, h 4th and Plum
Roth Fred capt. Plum bel 4th
Rudderow Rebecca T., Federal ab 2d
Russell Benj., pilot, Mulford's ct ab 2d

Sage Miles, carp. 4th & Cooper
Sagers Wm., painter, Pine bel 5th
Sands J., cordw., Plum & 2d
Sapp John, barkeeper, Federal ab 4th
Saunders Alex., clerk, Federal ab 2d
Sautter John, grocer, Pine bel 3d
Sawn Josiah, cooper, Pine ab 2d
Schwarz Dr., Market bel 5th
Scott E. & S., dry goods, Federal ab 2d
Scull Joab, mer., c 2d and Federal
Sexton Charles, painter, Plum n 2d
Shane John, cotton factory, 3d & Federal
Sharp Richard, fireman, Plum ab 2d
Shaw Edwd., carp., Pine ab 3d
Sheaffer

Simons J. B., lab., Chew ab 4th
Simpkins R. G., tailor, 4th bel Walnut
Sivil Nathan, dealer, Federal ab 4th
Slaghter A., grocer, 2d & Market
Sloan James W., Recorder of the City of Camden and justice of the peace, off. 2d bel Federal, h Kaighn's Point
Sloan Jas., shop, Plum ab 3d
Sloan John, butcher, Federal ab 4th
Sloan Wm. trader, Plum ab 4th
Smallwood Manly, blacksm., Pine bel 3d
Smith Abraham, butcher, South Camden
Smith A. F., grocer, Kaighn's pt
Smith Jacob, baker, 3d & Market
Smith James, gent. 2d ab Plum
Smith Jas., gent., 4th and Plum
Smith Jesse, judge, Federal bel 3d
Smith John, moulder, Spruce ab 4th
Smith John, carp., Chestnut ab 4th
Smith J., waterman, Spruce ab 4th
Smith S. R., lab., Plum ab 2d
Smith Mrs., Plum bel 3d
Snider & Co., cordw., Kaighn's pt
Southwick Charles, superint. Railroad bel 3d
Spikeman Arthur, blacksm., Line & Oak
Sparks A., carter, Spruce bel 4th
Spracklin Peter, machinist, Line ab 3d
Steeling Jas. M., dentist, Federal and 3d
Steeling Wm., M. D., Federal and 3d
Stetser Joseph, blacksmith, 1 Plum
Starr John, machinist, Federal ab 4th
Steinmetz Geo., glass blower, 4th bel Chestnut
Sterling H., cooper, 2d ab Market
Stevens James, sawyer, Front bel Cooper
Stiles Levi, coal, Front bel Market
Stockham George, lumb. mer., Front ab Cooper
Stone Ephraim, printer, South Camden
Stone Joshua, steersman, Kaighn's pt
Stone J., capt., Kaighn's pt
Stow Wm., mer., Federal ab 4th
Street A. K. Rev., Plum ab 2d
Stow H., carp., Plum ab 3d
Subers Aaron, engineer, 2d ab Market
Subers Benj., oysterman, Line ab 3d
Surann David, lathe cutter, Line n Broadway
Sweeten Andrew, carp., Market ab 3d
Sweeten Samuel, carp., West bel 4th
Swop E., carter, 4th bel Spruce
Swope John, butcher, Market bel 2d

Taylor Abraham, mason, S Camden
Taylor D., oyster house, Market ab 3d
Taylor Joseph, boat builder, Front, h 3d and Market
Taylor Thos. R. Rev. 5th bel Market
Thompson John, collar maker, Plum ab 3d

Thompson Joseph S. supert. Federal ab 3d
Thoompson Thomas, harness mr. Market ab 4th
Thorn John, gent., Federal & 4th
Thorn John, tavern, Kaighn's pt
Thorn Thomas, moulder, Plum ab 2d
Toole Ebenezer, tavern, Kaighn's pt
Trueax Clayton, shoemaker, c 3d and Market
Tucker Ephraim, trader, Federal ab 3d
Tyre Richard, lab. Cooper's Point

Vanneman Daniel, shoemr., Plum ab 3d
Vansciver A., blacksm., Market ab 2d
Vernon Jackson, engineer, Willow ab 2d

Wainwright Thos. B., gent., Federal ab 3d
Ware Geo. C., Federal bel 3d
Ward Isaac B., butcher, Plum bel 2d
Ward R. J. grocer, 3d and Federal
Ward Thos. H., butcher, Federal ab 3d
Weatherby Joseph, Railroad Garden
Welcher S., liquor, Federal & 3d
Welden John A., seaman, Willow ab 2d
Wescott John, engineer, Federal ab 3d
Weston Samuel, Market ab 4th
White John, shoemr. Plum bel 4th
Whitecar James A. corder, Market bel 3d
Wilkins Isaac, Market and 3d, h 3d and Cooper
Wilkins Richard, carter, 3d bel Pine
Williams Geo., grocer, 2d bel Line
Williams James, toolmr., Line ab 3d
Williams Joseph, mason, 2d bel Line
Williams Mrs., 4th bel Market
Wills J., carp., Plum bel 5th
Wilson James H., Washington Hotel, S Camden
Wilson Richard, lab., 2d bel R. road
Woodruff Leonard, constable, 2d ab Plum

Youndt Chas., engineer, 2d bel Federal
Young John D., grocer, Federal & 2d

Zimmerman G., Columbia garden, 5th & Market

PUBLIC BUILDINGS.

ACADEMY, Market ab 5th
BAPTIST CHURCH, 4th bel Market
CAMDEN BANK, N W 2d and Market
COURT HOUSE, Federal ab 11th
EPISCOPAL CHURCH, Market ab 4th
FRIENDS' MEETING HOUSE, Market by Cooper
METHODIST CHURCH, 3d bel Federal
PRESBYTERIAN, 5th bel Cooper.

LIST OF

Councils, Police, Clerks, Inspectors, Custom House, Libraries, &c.

CORPORATION OF THE CITY OF PHILADELPHIA.

John Swift, Mayor, office c 5th & Chestnut.

Richard Vaux, Recorder, office State House row.

Cornelius Stevenson, Treasurer, office c 5th and Chestnut.

Robert H. Smith, City Clerk, office c 5th and Chestnut.

Edward Olmsted, Solicitor, S 5th ab Walnut.

Clerk of Police—Orrin Bailey.

Lieutenant of Police—James Young.

2d do. do. J. Henry Bulkley.

Special Constable—William Russell.

MEMBERS OF COUNCIL.

SELECT COUNCIL.

President—Wm. M. Meredith.

John P. Wetherill, William Morris, Chas. Gilpin, Robert Toland, John Trucks, Joseph R. Chandler, Jas. J. Boswell, Algernon S. Roberts, Job R. Tyson, Abraham J. Lewis, Isaac Elliott. —Clerk, Henry Helmuth.

COMMON COUNCIL.

Samuel Norris, President.

Thos. Snowden, Henry C. Corbit, George Campbell, Jacob Amos, Daniel L. Miller, J. Rodman Paul, Edmund Wilcox, Edmund A. Souder, Wm. G. Mentz, J. C. Davis, C. A. Poulson, B Orne, G. R. Fisher, Robert Hutchinson, Jesse Godley, Wm. Divine, Joshua

CLERKS OF HIGH STREET MARKET.—Peter Conrad, James Glading.

CLERK OF SECOND STREET MARKET.—Henry B Gillingham.

CLERK OF HIGH STREET MARKET, WEST OF TENTH—James Stille.

CITY AND COUNTY.

Henry Lelar, Sheriff.

N. B. Leidy, M. D., Coroner.

COUNTY COMMISSIONERS.

Wm. Vanosten, Thomas D. Grover, John Burk.

John Miller, Clerk.

John H. Dohnert, County Treasurer.

A. R. Peale, Joseph Gatchel, jr., Allen Rutherford, Auditors.

DISTRICT OF NORTHERN LIBERTIES.

Mayor, Mr. Belsterling.

Treasurer, Jacob S. Mintzer.

Clerk, S. Snyder Leidy.

SPRING GARDEN DISTRICT.

Treasurer, Henry F. Bowen.

Clerk, Samuel Sappington.

MOYAMENSING.

Treasurer, James M'Cann.

Clerk, J. M. Raybold.

KENSINGTON DISTRICT.

Treasurer, John Taylor.

Clerk, Jacob Dietz.

William Vodges and E. Otis Kendall. Professors in the Department of Mathematics.

F. A Bregy. Professor in the Department of French and Spanish Languages.

Henry McMurtrie, M. D. Professor in the Department of Natural History.

Henry Haverstick. Professor of Latin and Greek Languages.

M. Boyé. Professor of Natural Philosophy and Chemistry.

George J. Becker. Professor of Drawing and Writing.

CUSTOM HOUSE,

Chestnut above Fourth.

Collector.—James Page.
Deputy do.—Chas. Treichel.
Do. do.—Richard L. Howell.
Naval Officer.—Henry Welsh.
Deputy do.—John D. George.
Surveyor.—John Davis
Deputy do.—Jno. W. Forney.

DIRECTIONS.—The Desks are numbered from 1 to 11, and the business done at each Desk is as follows :

Office hours from 9 A. M. to 2 P. M.
No. 1. Fees and cash duties received.
    Counter. Deputy Collector's.
    Counter. Deputy Naval Officer's.
No. 2. Debenture coastwise, and estimating and liquidating duties.
No. 3. Impost book-keeper.
No. 4. Disbursements
No. 5. Export, Debenture, Bounty, &c.
No. 6. Weigher.
No. 7. Bonds and permits.
No. 8. Naval officer. Duties, exports, &c.
No. 9. Invoices, protections, and Marine Hospital.
    Counter. Entrance and Clearance of vessels.
No. 10. Registers, enrolments and licenses.
No. 11. Miscellaneous.

INSPECTORS OFFICES.

Office for the northern district on Wright's wharf above Race street. The northern district extends from the north side of Market street to Gunner's Run.

Office for the middle district N. E. corner of Walnut and Front street. The middle district extends from the south side of Market street to the north side of Spruce street.

Offices for the southern district N. W. corner of Lombard street, on the wharf, and Penn near Lombard street. The southern district extends from the south side of Spruce street to the Navy Yard.

WARDENS OF THE PORT.

Master Warden, Patrick Hays, office 33 Walnut.

Harbour Master, A. L. Roumfort, 5 S wharves.

PHILADELPHIA LIBRARY COMPANY,

Corner S Fifth and Library.

INCORPORATED BY WILLIAM PENN.

Shares $40. Annual subscription $4.

John J. Smith, Librarian and Treasurer.

ATHENÆUM,

Sixth and Adelphi.

Shares $25. Stockholders' Annual Payments, 5 dolls.—Visiters, 10 dolls.

Samuel Breck, L. L. D., President.
Quintin Campbell, Treasurer.
William M'Ilhenney, Secretary.

OFFICE OF THE GUARDIANS OF THE POOR—19 South 7th.

The Board consists of the following members, viz.

CITY OF PHILADELPHIA.

William S. Hansell, 28 High
George W. Jones, 223 Chestnut
John Price Wetherill, 13th above Mulberry
John F. Gilpin, 307 Spruce
Reese D. Fell, 62 Chestnut
William Abbott, 189 S. 3rd.

DISTRICT OF SOUTHWARK.

Frederick Plummer, N E Shippen & Vernon.
Wm. G. Flanagan, 39 Almond.

NORTHERN LIBERTIES.

Thomas Holloway, 25 Ellen.
Daniel S. Beiderman, Green street wharf.

KENSINGTON DISTRICT AND UNINCORPORATED NORTHERN LIBERTIES.

Peter Fisher, Shackamaxon near Franklin (K)
Michael Day, Marlboro' ab Queen street

SPRING GARDEN AND PENN TOWNSHIP.

Christopher Mason, 162 N 12th, Thomas Robinson, 17 Palmyra Square.

TOWNSHIP OF MOYAMENSING.

Samuel F. Reed, 234 South 6th.

President, Wm. G. Flanagan, 39 Almond.
Treasurer, William Abbott, at the office of the Guardians.
Secretary, Samuel J. Robbins, 19 South 7th.
Solicitor, James Hanna, 11 Prune
Steward, Daniel Smith.

The Board meets at the Alms House, Blockley, every Monday afternoon at 3 o'clock, where applicants for apprentices, with the children to be bound, must attend. The committee on the Alms House attend there every Wednesday and Friday, at 3 o'clock, P. M.

N. B. All applications for temporary relief must be made to the Visiters of the City or Districts in which the applicant resides. Office of the Secretary, Visiters of the City, and out-door Agent, No. 19 South 7th street.

Office hours from 8 until 1 o'clock, and from 3 until sunset.

VISITORS.

For the City.—Peter Snyder, N. Sch 6th st.; D. A. Cornog, No. 12 Madison st.

For the District of Southwark.—James R. Nelson, 5 Cox.

For the Northern Liberties.—Samuel Engard, Mayor's office, Third near Green.

For Unincorporated Northern Liberties.— John Mann, Heart lane near Rose Hill

For Kensington District.—Daniel Hughes, Shackamaxon next door to the cor. of Franklin street.

For Spring Garden.—Wm. Harwood, 1 Ridge road.

For Penn Township.—Francis D. Mower, Hart's Lane near R road.

For Moyamensing.—John D. Neff, 207 S. 6th

PHILADELPHIA COLLEGE OF PHARMACY.

Hall in Zane street.

President—Daniel B. Smith. Vice-President—George B. Wood, M. D. Secretary—Charles Ellis. Corresponding Secretary—Elias Durand. Treasurer—J. C. Turnpenny.

UNIVERSITY OF PENNSYLVANIA.

MEDICAL DEPARTMENT.

Founded 3d of May, 1765.

Fees $120. Matriculation fee, payable only once, $5.

Session commences the first Monday in November, and continues until the middle of March ensuing.

PROFESSORS.

N. Chapman, M. D., Practice of Medicine.
Robt. Hare,   "   Chemistry.
Wm. Gibson,   "   Surgery.
Wm. E. Horner,   "   Anatomy.
Saml. Jackson,   "   Institutes of Medicine.
Geo. B. Wood,   "   Materia Medica.
Hugh L. Hodge,   "   Obstetrics.

WM. E. HORNER. Dean

Treasurer. John J. Thompson, Secretary. J. Cox, Librarian.

THE AMERICAN PHILOSOPHICAL SOCIETY.

Sixth and Adelphi.

N. Chapman, President.

Robert M. Patterson, Franklin Bache, and Alex. D. Bache, Vice Presidents.

J. K. Kane, Alfred L. Elwyn, Robley Dungleson, Secretaries.

George Ord, Treasurer.

HISTORICAL SOCIETY OF PENNSYLVANIA.

The council meets on the 4th Monday of every month, and the society on the 1st Monday of Feb. May, Aug. and Nov. at Philosophical Hall, 115 S 6th street.

President, Hon. Thos. Sergeant.

Vice Presidents, Thomas M. Pettit, Job R. Tyson, William Rawle, A. Langdon, Elwyn.

Recording Secretary, Edward Armstrong.

Foreign Corresponding Secretary, D. J. Desmond.

Domestic Corresponding Secretary, John Jordan, jr.

FRANKLIN INSTITUTE.

Meetings: Institute, Quarterly, 3d Thursday in the month. Conversation, monthly, 3d Thursday in the month. Board of Managers, 3d Wednesday in the month.

Samuel V. Merrick, President.

Abraham Miller, Thomas Fletcher, Vice Presidents.

Isaac B. Garrigues, Recording Secretary.

Jno. F. Frazer, Corresponding Secretary.

Frederick Fraley, Treasurer.

Wm. Hamilton, Actuary.

FUEL SAVING SOCIETY

Schuylkill, Rev. B. R. Loxley, Ashton and Lombard

West Kensington, Rev. Frederick Ketcham, Hancock ab Franklin (K)

Broad st. Rev. J. L. Burrows, c Broad & Brown

CATHOLIC.

St. Augustine's, Rev. Jno. P. O'Dwyer, 4th opp New

St. Joseph's, Rev. I. J. Barbelin, Willing's al

St. Mary's, Rev. C. J. H. Carter, 4th ab Spruce

St. John's, Bishop Kenrick, 13th below High

Holy Trinity, Rev. Nicholas Perrins, 6th and Spruce

St. Michaels, Rev. Wm. Loughram, 2d, W Kensington

St. Francis Xavier, Rev. P. Rafferty, near Fair Mount

St. Patricks, Rev. D. F. Devitt, Sch. 3d above Spruce

St. Philip de Neri, Rev. N. Cantwell, Queen ab Second.

St. Peter's, Rev. Joseph Fey, 5th & Franklin

St. Paul's, Rev. P. F. Sheridan, Christian below 10th

CHRISTIAN CHAPEL.

Rev. Frederick H. Plummer, Christian bel 6th

COLORED.

First Presbyterian, Rev. Charles W. Gardner, 7th below Shippen

Second Presbyterian, Rev. Benj. F. Templeton, St. Mary ab 6th.

Central Presbyterian, Rev. S. Gloucester, Lombard near 9th.

Bethel, 6th ab Lombard

Bethel Union, Coates bel O Y road

Brick Wesley, Lombard bel 6th

Little Wesley, Hurst below Lombard

First Baptist, 11th & Pearl.

Union Baptist, Rev. Daniel Scott, Little Pine above 6th

Shiloh, Rev. J. Durham, Clifton and Cedar.

St. Thomas', Rev. William M. Douglass, 5th bel Walnut

Little Union, Little Pine bel 7th

DISCIPLES OF CHRIST.

Fifth and Gaskill, Elders Taylor, Hall & Rowzee

DUTCH REFORMED.

First, Rev. C. C. Vanarsdale, Crown ab Sassafras

Third, Rev. G. W. Bethune, D. D., c 10th and Filbert

EPISCOPAL.

Christ Church, Rev. B. Dorr, D. D., 2d ab High

St. James', Rev. Henry J. Morton, 7th ab High

St. Peter's, Rev. Wm. H. Odenheimer, 3d & Pine

St. Luke's, vacant, 13th bel Spruce.

St. Philip's, Rev. Edward Neville, Vine bel 8th.

Epiphany, Rev. James H. Fowles, D. D., Sch. 8th and Chestnut

Grace, Rev. William Suddards, 12th and Cherry

St. Matthew's, Rev. Geo. E. Hare, Francisville

Trinity, Rev. John Coleman, D. D., Catharine above 2d

Gloria Dei, Rev. J. C. Clay, D. D., Swanson near Navy Yard

Church of the Ascension, Rev. Frederick Ogilvie, Lombard ab 11th

Church of the Evangelists, Rev. Thos. H. Quinan, 5th ab Catharine

Emanuel, Rev. J. Maxwell, Marlboro' ab Franklin (K)

All Saints, Rev. Henry Major, Fitzwater and Shippen lane

Church of the Nativity, Rev. N. Sayre Harris, 11th and Washington

Advent Church, Rev. John Kerr, O Y Road ab Tammany

Church of the Redemption, Rev. G. Durborrow, Callowhill and Sch 2d.

FRIENDS' MEETING HOUSES.

S E 4th and Mulberry, S W 5th and Mulberry, Washington sq, S 12th bel High, c 9th & Spruce, S W 6th & Noble, Cherry n 5th, c Green & 4th

GERMAN REFORMED.

Rev. J. F. Berg, Sassafras bel 4th

Rev. R. C Evans, School and Edward

Rev. Henry Bibighaus, D. D., St. John below Green

INDEPENDENT.

Rev. John Chambers, S Broad bel Chestnut

JEWS' SYNAGOGUES.

Isaac Leeser, Cherry n 3d

————, Adelphi street.

LUTHERAN.

St. Michael's, Rev. Gabriel A. Reichert, 5th and Apple Tree alley

Zion, Rev. C. R. Demmé, D. D., 4th and Cherry

St. Paul's, Brown and St. John

St. John's, Rev. P. F. Mayer, D. D., Sassafras ab 5th

St. Matthew's, Rev. Theophilus Storke, New below 4th

METHODIST EPISCOPAL.

St. George's, 4th below Vine

St. John st, St. John ab Beaver

Ebenezer, Christian bel 4th

Kensington, Queen and Marlboro'

Salem, Juniper and Lombard

Union, 4th ab High

Twelfth st, 12th near Poplar
Wharton st., Wharton ab 3d
Independent, Rev. J. Keller, Sch 6th and St.
   Joseph avenue
Sanctuary, 5th above George
Cohocksink, G. T. road and 5th
Bethlehem Home Mission, Callowhill bet Sch.
   3d and 4th

METHODIST PROTESTANT

First, Rev. Thos. H. Stockton, 11th and Wood
Ebenezer, Marlboro' and West (K)
Brickmakers', Sch. 3d ab Chestnut
Southwark Mission, 4th and German

MORAVIAN.

Rev. Emmanuel Rondthaler, Bread & Sassafras

MARINERS'.

Bethel, (Methodist) Shippen and Penn.
Mariners', (Eastburn) Rev'd. Orson Douglas,
   Water n Chestnut

NEW JERUSALEM.

Fourth street, bel German

PRESBYTERIAN.

First, Rev. Albert Barnes, Washington sq
Second, Rev. C. C. Cuyler, D. D., N 7th n Mul-
   berry
Third, Rev. Thomas Brainerd, 4th & Pine
Fourth, 12th & Lombard
Fifth, M. La Rue P. Thompson, Mulberry ab 10th
Sixth, Rev. Jos. H. Jones, Spruce n 6th
Seventh, Rev. Willis Lord, Broad ab Chestnut
Scots, Rev. Alexander Macklin, Spruce ab 3d
Ninth, Rev. Archibald Tudehope, Sch. 7th and
   George
Tenth, Rev. Henry A. Boardman, 12th & Walnut
Eleventh, Rev John L. Grant, Vine bel 13th
Twelfth, Rev. Wm. Ramsey, Cedar ab 11th

Central, (vacant) 8th and Cherry
Central, (N L) Rev. Anson Rood, Coates ab 3d
Cumberland, Rev. H. S. Porter, 7th above Wood
Western, (vacant) Sch 6th & Filbert
First, (N L) Rev. Ezra Stiles Ely, Buttonwood
   n 6th
North, Rev. Thomas L. Janeway, 6th ab Green
First, (S) Rev. Robert Adair, German ab 2d
Fairmount, Rev. Charles Brown
Cohocksink, Rev. Dan'l. Gaston, G. T. R. ab 6th
Union, Rev. James W. Stewart, 13th below
   Spruce
Clinton st., Rev. Joel Parker, D. D., 10th and
   Clinton
First Associate, Rev. Chauncey Webster, Wal-
   nut ab 4th
First Reformed, Rev. Samuel B. Wylie, D. D.,
   and Rev. T. W. J. Wylie, 11th bel High
Second Reformed, Rev. Samuel Stevenson, Fair
   Mount
Reformed, Rev. James M. Willson, Cherry near
   11th
Reformed, S. O. Wylie, Sch 6th ab Cherry.
First Associate Reformed, Rev. J. B. Dales, 13th
   ab High
Second Associate Reformed, Rev. J. B. Scouller
   Lombard bet Sch. 3d & 4th
Third Associate Reformed, Rev. Jos. T. Cooper,
   Franklin ab Green
Third Associate, Rev. J. C. Lyons, F road above
   Franklin (K)
Spring Garden, Rev. John M'Dowell, 11th ab
   Spring Garden

UNITARIAN.

First, Rev. W. H. Furness, 10th and Locust

UNIVERSALIST.

First, Asher Moore, Lombard ab 4th
Second, C. C. Burr, Callowhill bel 5th
Third, Phœnix ab F. road

COURTS IN PENNSYLVANIA.

SUPREME COURT.

The Supreme Court holds six terms for arguments, &c., in the Five Districts of the State, and
adjourned Courts as they may deem necessary. The regular Terms are—

For the Eastern District, composed of the City and County of Philadelphia, and the Counties
of Delaware, Chester, Montgomery, Bucks, Northampton, Lehigh, Wayne, and Pike, at Philadelphia, in March, to continue two weeks, and 2d Wednesday in December, to continue three weeks.
The last Monday in July is the return day for July term, but no court is then held.

For the Lancaster District, composed of the Counties of Lancaster, York, Dauphin, Lebanon,
Schuylkill, and Berks, at Lancaster, 2d Monday in May.

For the Middle District, composed of the Counties of Northumberland, Union, Columbia,
Centre, Mifflin, Juniata, and Huntingdon, McKean, Clearfield, Lycoming, Potter, Tioga, Bradford,

LIST OF PUBLIC INSTITUTIONS.

Academy of Natural Sciences, N W George and Broad

Academy of Fine Arts, 311 Chestnut

Alms House, Schuylkill, (west side)

Alms House, (Friends) Walnut ab 3d

American Philosophical Society, S W 5th and Chestnut

American Sunday School Union, 146 Chestnut

Apprentices' Library, c 5th and Mulberry

Arch st Theatre, 219 Mulberry

Artists' Fund Hall, Chestnut ab 10th

Association for the Supply of Teachers, 144 Chestnut

Asylum for Lost Children, Commerce ab 5th

Asylum Magdalen, c Sassafras and Sch. 2d

Athenæum, 6th and Adelphi.

Athenian Institute and Philosophical Hall, S 6th and Adelphi.

Bricklayers' Hall, N E 13th and Sassafras

Callowhill Market, from 4th to 7th

Carpenters' Hall, N W 13th and Sassafras

Chestnut st Theatre, 201 Chestnut

Christ Church Hospital, 8 Cherry

City Hospital, Sch. 4th n Coates

City Tobacco Warehouse, Dock and Spruce

City Water Works, Fairmount, office 200 Cherry

City Commissioners' Office, S W 5th & Chestnut

City Treasurer's Office, S W 5th and Chestnut

City Watering Committee, office S W Chestnut and 5th, above stairs

Clarkson Hall, 103 Cherry, ab 6th

College and Medical Hall, 9th n High

College of Pharmacy, Zane ab 7th

Commissioners' Hall, S Garden, 309 Vine

Commissioners' Hall, N Liberties, 281 N 3d

Commissioners' Hall, (S) S 2d n Christian

Commissioners' Hall, (K) Master and Front

Commissioners' Hall, (M) Christian ab 9th

Corporation School of Friends, Pine bel 2d

County Commissioners' Office, State House, W wing, above stairs

Custom House, Chestnut ab 4th

Dispensary, 41 S 5th

Fair Mount Water Works, ab Upper Bridge

Fish Market, from Water to wharf, in High

Franklin Institute Hall, 9 S 7th

Franklin Square, bet Sassafras and Vine and N 6th and Franklin

Girard Trust Treasurer's office, S 5th ab Chestnut

Guardians of the Poor, office 19 S 7th

Health Office, c 6th and George

High st Market, from the Delaware to 8th

House of Refuge, c R road and Coates

Historical Society of Penn., Philosophical Hall

Home Missionary Society, N E 8th & Buttonwood

House of Industry, 7 Ranstead place

Jefferson Medical College, 56 S 10th

Library of Foreign Literature and Science, Philosophical Hall, 5th bel Chestnut

Logan Square, bet Sassafras and Vine and Sch 3d and 5th

Marine Hospital, ab Gray's Ferry

Marshall's office, State House, above stairs Chestnut

Masonic Hall, S 3d bel Walnut

Masonic Hall, (old) Chestnut ab 7th

Mayor's office, S W 5th and Chestnut

Medical Institute, Locust ab 11th

Menonists, Crown bel Callowhill

Mercantile Library, 5th and Library

Monument Cemetery, Broad ab Master

Museum Building, 9th bel Chestnut

Musical Fund Hall, 60 Locust

Navy Agent's Office, 98 Chestnut

National Theatre, Chestnut n 9th

Navy Yard and Offices, S E Front and Prime

New County Prison and Debtors' Apartment, P road bel Federal

New House of Correction, Bush Hill

New Market, from Pine to Cedar in 2d

New Penitentiary, Coates W of House of Refuge

Northern Dispensary, 1 S Garden

Northern Liberties Gas Works, Maiden below N Front

Northern Liberty Hall, 322 N 3d

Northern Liberty Market, from Coates to Poplar

Odd Fellows' Hall, 6th & Haines

Orphan's Asylum, (coloured) 13th ab Callowhill

Orphan Asylum, St. Joseph's, S W Spruce & 7th

Orphan Asylum, St. Mary's, 5th n Pine

Orphan Asylum, St. John's, Chestnut ab 12th

Old Academy, 42 N 4th

Penn Square, N and S of High, W of Juniper

Penn's Treaty Monument, Shackamaxon, (K)

Pennsylvania Medical College, Filbert above 11th

Pennsylvania State Arsenal, 29 S Juniper

Philadelphia Dispensary 5th bel Library

Philadelphia Circus, Walnut ab 8th

Philadelphia Exchange, N E c 3d and Walnut

Philadelphia Gas Works, Sch. Front n High, Office Franklin Institute, S 7th

Philadelphia Library, N E 5th and Library

Philadelphia Museum, Chestnut ab 7th

Philadelphia Orphan's Asylum, N E Sch. 5th & Cherry

Philosophical Hall, 6th and Adelphi

Post Office, Merchants' Exchange

Post Office, Kensington, Maiden n Market

Post Office, Spring Garden, Callowill n 8th

Preston Retreat, Hamilton n Sch. 3d

Public High School, Juniper n High

Public School, Sch., Ashton ab Lombard

Public School, New Market ab Noble

Public School, Zane ab 7th

Public School, 11th & Buttonwood

Public Model School, Chester & Maple

Public School, Sassafras ab Broad

Public School, c 8th & Fitzwater

Public School, W Kensington, N 2d and Master

Public School, Northern Liberties, 432 N 3d

Public School, Catharine ab 3d

Public School, Callowhill n F 3

Public School, Coates bel 13th

Public School, O Y road ab Poplar

Public School, South Eastern, Front bel Pine

Public School, S E 2d and Reed

Public School, 5th bel Prime

Public School, (coloured) 6th n Lombard

Recorder's Office, 3 State House, E wing

Rittenhouse Square, bet Walnut and Spruce and Sch. 3d and 6th

School of St Peter's Church, 79 Lombard

Seaman's Friend Society, or Girard House, 23 N Water

Seminary of St Charles Borromeo, Sch 5th and Sassafras

Sheriff's Office, State House, W wing

Southern Dispensary, 98 Shippen

Southwark Library, S 2d bel Plum

Southwark Market, 3 rd fr Prime to Washington

State House, Chestnut bet 5th and 6th

State Armory, c Juniper and Penn Square

Union Benevolent Society, Office S W 8th and Lodge

Union Canal Company, office 6 Carpenter's ct

Union Glass Works, Beach n Warren

Union Temperance Hall, Christian ab 9th

United States Arsenal, Gray's ferry road n Federal

United States Naval Asylum, Gray's ferry road n U S Arsenal

United States Mint, c Chestnut & Juniper

University of Pennsylvania, S 9th n High

Walnut Street Theatre, N E 9th & Walnut

Washington Square, S side of Walnut ab 6th

Wharton Market, bet Prime & Washington

Widows, Indigent, & Single Women's Asylum, Cherry E of Sch. 5th

Wills' Hospital, for the Lame and Blind, Sassafras W of Sch. 5th

LIST OF

STREETS, LANES, ALLEYS, COURTS, AVENUES, AND ROADS

In the City and Liberties of Philadelphia.

Abbott's ct, S from Killpatrick's al bel 6th
Abraham ct, (K) E from St John ab Beaver,
Academy st, W fr 10th, bet Mulberry & Cherry
Acorn al, from 52 Locust to Spruce
Adams st, from Fitzwater, ab 6th
Adams st, from 12th to 13th, bet. Spruce & Pine
Adelphi Avenue, from Pegg to Noble
Adelphi st, fr 5th to 6th bet Walnut and Prune
Agnew's ct, N from Race bel 8th
Alban st, from Norman to Clare al
Albert's av. S from Palmer ab Franklin (K)
Albertson's ct, N from John
Alder st. N from Poplar ab 10th (S G)
Alice ct, N from George ab 10th
Allen st, from F road to Palmer, E & W (E K)
Allen's al, from 159 S 6th
Allen ct, E from 159 S 6th
Allen's ct, W from 84 N Front
Allen's ct, S from 150 Spruce
Almira pl, W from 404 N Front
Almond st, from Delaware to 315 S 2nd
Alton ct. S from 12 Richard
Amber st, N fr Phœnix E of F road
Anderson row, S from Washington bet 10th & 11th
Ann st, (N L) from 57 Vine to Callowhill
Ann st, fr S 12th to 13th bet Lombard & Cedar
Ann st, from Wissahicon to Charles st, bet Francis and Vineyard
Ann st, fr Sch. 3d E to Sch. 7th, bel Rittenhouse
Apollo st, (continued) fr Cedar to Gaskill W of 4th st
Apple st, S from George bet 4th and O Y road
Appletree st, from 50 N 4th to 35 N 5th
Apricot al, from Currant to Poplar al
Arcade ct, N fr Shippen bel 9th
Arch, or Mulberry st, from Delware to Sch., N of High
Armstrong's ct, N fr 9 Prune, rear of 106 S 4th
Arrison's ct, W from Sch. 8th n. Chestnut
Arsenal st, from Gray's Ferry road to Federal al
Ash st, E from Duke ab Wood (K)
Ash al, from Sch. Front to 2nd, bet High and Chestnut
Ashland st, from Union to Spruce, bet 2d & 3d
Ashton st, N and S from High, E of Sch. Beach
Aspen al, from Aspen ct to Lombard
Aspen ct, S from Ash al
Aspin st, N from Spruce bet Sch. 2d & Front

Assembly Buildings, S W 10th & Chestnut
Asylum st. fr Broad to Sch. 8th bet Spruce & Pine
Atherton st. leading from Carpenter to Marriott's, bet 5th and 6th
Atkinson's ct, N from 153 Lombard
Austin st, from Federal to Moy. prison ab 10th
lane, bet 5th and 6th
Aydelott's ct, N from Parham bel Front

Bache's ct, W from 180 Marshall
Bache st, N from Cherry ab Broad
Bacon's ct, E from 25 New Market
Badger's ct, from 147 Coates
Bagges' ct, from 11 John (S)
Baird's ct, N from Brown bel Bread
Baker st, E and W from Sch. 7th, bet Fitzwater and Shippen
Baker's al, from 55 New to 70 Vine
Baker's ct, E from O Y road to New Crown
Baker's ct, E from 49 New Market
Baker's ct, rear 8th bet Fitzwater and Shippen
Baker's ct, (K) W from Cadwalader bel Phœnix
Baker st, W from Spafford
Ball al, from 120 Cedar to 77 Shippen
Ball's al, from Delaware river to 391 N Front
Ball's ct, W from 514 N Front
Bank al, from S 2nd, S side of the Bank of Pennsylvania, to 67 Dock
Bank pl, S W 4th and Chestnut
Bank st, from 70 High to 69 Chestnut
Bank st, N from Pine to Cedar, E of Sch. Water
Barclay's al, from 190 S 6th
Barker's ct, S from Crown ab Queen (K)
Barker's st, from Sch. 3d to 7th bet High and Chestnut
Barker st, from Carpenter to Prime bet 5th and 6th
Barley st, from 10th to 11th, bel Pine
Barrington's ct, N from Spruce, bet Sch. 4th and 5th
Barron st, from 24 Gaskill to 75 Cedar
Barber's ct, N from Melon ab 11th
Barber's row, N from Melon ab 11th
Bauersach's ct, W from Front bel Master (K)
Baxter's av, from George (S), bet Shippen and Plum
Baxter's ct, S from 120 German
Beach st, from K High Bridge to Bishop
Beam's ct, E from 217 St. John
Bearsticker's ct, W from 68 N 6th
Beaver ct, N from 37 Cherry

51

Beaver st, from N 2nd to N 3rd bet Poplar and George (N L)

Beck st, from 172 Swanson to 453 S Front

Beck's ct, N from 59 Coates

Beck's ct, N from 41 Beck

Beck st, W from P road near the intersection of 6th

Beck place, from Front to Sutherland, bet Christian and Queen

Becket st, W from Sch 7th bel Coates

Bedford st, from 12th bel E Cedar

Bedford st, (K) from F road to Hanover

Beach st, Sch. from the Permanent Bridge to Cedar

Belin's row, from 468 Sassafras to Walnut st

Bell's (Wm.) ct, W from Bingham's ct

Bell's (Henry) ct, N from Marshall's al

Belmont pl, Spruce, S side bel Broad

Benezet st, W from 24 N 11th to 12th

Benfer's ct, fr St. John, of Beaver

Benner's al, from 85 Elm to Vine

Benner's ct, N from 59 Cherry

Benton st, from School to William, E and W, (W K)

Benton ct, S from 98 Prime

Benton's av, W from Flower ab Catharine

Berger ct, Frankford road near Otter (K)

Berk's ct, rear 69 Apple

Bethesda row, Corn fr Square to Mackey

Bevan's ct, N from Washington ab M road

Bickham st, Sch. from Sch. N 7th to 8th bet Filbert and Mulberry

Bickham's ct, W from 256 S Front

Biddle st, E fr William (F M)

Biddle's al, from 78 High to 9 Elbow lane

Billing's ct, W from 110 N 8th

Binder's ct, W fr Queen ab Cherry

Bingham's ct, N from 69 Spruce

Bishop st, from the head of Beach to Queen (K)

Blackberry al, from Walnut to Spruce and from Pine to Lombard, bet S 8th and 9th

Black horse al, from 29 S Front to 19 S 2nd

Black horse al, from 202 Cedar to Small

Black horse ct, N from 171 High

Black's ct, W from 180 Marshall

Bladen's ct, bet Elfreth's al. and Mulberry and 2d and Front

Bladen's ct. S from Spruce below Little Dock

Bledisloe pl. W of Marshall ab Poplar

Bloom al, see Carlton

Blythe st, fr Pine to Budd bet Juniper & Broad

Bnivvier's ct, 1st bel G T road in Otter (K)

Boehm's ct, N from 402 N 2nd to 207 St. John

Bond's ct, from 15 Laurel

Bond st. fr W 10th to 11th bel Spruce

Bonsall st, fr 9th to 10th bet Lombard and Cedar

Boston Row, Chestnut ab 12th, N side

Bowdoin st, from 12th to 13th bet Mulberry and Cherry

Bowman's al, from 460 N 4th

Boyd's al, from rear 119 N 11th, to Wiley's ct

Boyd's ct, E from 3 S 10th

Boyd's av, N from middle of North to Vine

Boyd's ct, S from Cedar to Small

Boyle's ct, N from 25 Sugar al

Boyle's ct, E from 79 P road

Braceland's ct, W from Front ab Christian

Bradford's al, from 246 S 7th to 8th

Branch st, fr N 3d to 4th bet Sassafras & New

Branch al, E fr 5 Madison, forms elbow to Graff

Brandywine st, from 13th to Broad, bet Spring Garden and Green.

Branner's al, S from 176 Vine

Brasier st, W from Lloyd bel Shippen

Brasier's ct, Pascal's al ab 4th

Bread st, N from 77 Mulberry to 76 Sassafras

Bridgewater st. S from Washington ab Bridge

Brighton st, W fr Broad to Sch. 8th, bet Walnut and Locust

Briley's ct. E from Lisle

Brinton's al, E from 11th to R road ab Callowhill

Brinton st, from 12th to 13th bel Shippen

Britton's al, S from Bedford to Shippen bel 8th

Britton's al, E from 205 N Water

Broad st, N and S from High, W of Juniper

Broadbent's ct, rear 37 New Market

Brook's ct, W from 126 N Front

Brook's ct, W fr. St. Joseph's av, W of Sch 5th

Brook st, N from 101 Coates

Brown's ct, N from 93 Sassafras

Brown's ct, N from Carlton, bel Broad

Brown st, N L and Spring Garden, from High Bridge to Broad, N of Coates

Brown st, N from Budden's to Walnut al bet 13th & Juniper

Brown st. K, from Cherry to Vienna, bet Prince and Duke

Browne's ct, N L, E from 19 Budd

Brusstar's al, from Beach to Queen n Shackamaxon

Bryan's ct, S from 102 Cherry

Buck road, S E from United States Arsenal and Gray's Ferry road

Buckley st, E from 127 S 6th

Budd st, from 67 Green to G T road

Budd st, from S 12th to S 13th, bet Spruce and Pine

Budden's al, from Juniper to 12th bet Cherr and Mulberry

Buist's row, S from Fitzwater bet 12th and 13th

Burchell's ct, E from 3rd ab Christian

Burr's ct. W from Hanover bet Duke & Prince

Burd st, (S) from 78 Catharine to Queen

Burd's al, from Raspberry to Watson's al

Burd's ct, S from 124 Locust

Burd's row, N and S, rear 40 Currant al

Burk's ct, W from 230 S 11th

Burns' ct, W from 292 S 7th

Butlar's av, E from Juniper ab Pine

Buttonwood al, from N 13th to Juniper n High

Buttonwood st, from O Y road to Broad, bet Callowhill and Spring Garden

Butz's ct, E from 131 St. John

Cadwalader st, bet 2nd and G T road ab Master

Cake's ct, from 31 Coates' al

Calbraith's ct, E from New Market n Noble

Caldwell's row, bet Pearl & Wood, W side 13th

Caldwell st, E from Sch. Beach, bet Walnut and Locust

Caledonian ct, N from Filbert ab 10th

Callowhill st, from the Delaware to Schuylkill N of Vine

Camac st, W from N 2nd n Mud l

Campbell's ct, W from Sch. 4th n Carpenter

Campbell's ct, N from 71 German

Canal st, N W fr Coates, near Sch river

Canal st, N from Master, n High Bridge

Cantrell's ct, W from 504 S 2nd

Carberry's ct, S from 230 Catharine

Carbon pl, S from Sassafras, W of Broad

Carbon st, N from Shippen to Cedar ab 10th

Carlisle ct, S from 224 Coates

Carlisle st, N fr Parrish bet Sch 8th and Broad

Carlton sq, Callowhill between N 11th & 12th S side

Carlton st, from N 11th to Sch. Front, bet Wood and Callowhill

Carolina pl, S from Barley st ab 10th

Caroline st, N from Wharton, bet 4th and 5th

Carpenter's al, (S) N from 105 Catharine

Carpenter's ct, S bet 116 and 118 Chestnut

Carpenter st, W from S 6th to 7th, bet High and Chesnut

Carpenter st, (S) W from N road opp John to Shippen l

Carroll st. W from 12th ab Poplar

Carrol's ct, enters N 4th n G T road

Carrolton sq, 10th from Green to Spring Garden

Carson st, bet Vine and Callowhill and bet Sch. 8th and Broad

Carter st. N from Carpenter bel 11th

Carter's al, from 65 S 2nd to 55 S 3rd

Carter's al, (P Township) E from 13th n Wood

Carver st, E fr 319 S 5th

Castle st, from N 10th to 11th bet North and Sassafras

Catharine st, from Delaware to Shippen lane bet German and Queen (S)

Cauffman's ct, E from 147 N 2nd

Cauffman's ct, S from 14 Cherry

Cedar, or South, from Delaware to Sch. S of Pine and S boundary of the city

Cedar row, W fr 11th to 12th of Cedar st

Centre st, from S 12th to S 13th, bet Lyndall al and Locust

Centre st. N from Brown bel 9th & 10th (N L)

Centre al, from S 11th to Quince, bet Walnut and Locust

Chancellor st, from Sch. 6th to 7th bel Walnut

Chancery la, S from 32 Arch to 15 Coombe's al

Chandler's ct, N fr Palmer ab Queen

Charles pl, Willow ab Charles st

Charles st, N fr Cedar ab 4th

Charles st, from 335 Callowhill to Buttonwood

Charles st, fr Francis l to George st, Francisville

Charlotte st, N to Master, from 121 Brown

Chatham st, N fr Sch. 6th to 7th bet Chestnut and George

Chatham st. N from Buttonwood to Green, bet 5th and 6th

Cherry st, from 74 N 3rd to Schuylkill

Cherry st, (K) from Queen to Mary

Chestnut st, from Delaware to Schuylkill bet High and Walnut

Chester ct, from 11th bel Coates

Chester st, N from Sassafras to Vine bet 8th & 9th

Chew's ct, E from 281 S 5th

China row, W from 4th ab Master (K)

China st, W from 516 S Front

Christian st, from Delaware to Irish track lane bet Queen and Prime

Christian's ct, W fr 382 S Front

Church al, from 20 N 2nd to 11 N 3rd

Church al, from Mulberry to 142 Cherry

Church av, E from Broad bel Brown

Church st, S from 22 Christian to Prime (S)

Church st. S from bel N. Yard to South. Canal

City row, N from 136 N 11th

Clair st, S from Carpenter opp Atherton

Clare al, from N 13th to Juniper bet Lambert and Vine

Clare's ct, S fr Washington ab 6th

Clark st, from 13th to Juniper bet Walnut and Locust

Clark st, W fr 3d bel Carpenter. (S)

Clawges' ct, N from Mulberry al

Clay av, N fr. Hanover bel Franklin (K)

Clay st, from Sch. Beach n Pine to Wharves.

Clifton st, S from Cedar n S 11th

Clinton av, W fr 8th ab Coates

Clinton ct, E from Lawrence ab Noble

Clinton st, from 9th to 11th bet Spruce and Pine

Clinton st, from Franklin to Master N & S (E K)

Clinton st, (S G) N fr Brown bet 8th and 9th

Clinton sq, Chestnut W from Broad to Sch. 8th

Clover st, from S 12th to S 13th bet High and Chestnut

Clymer st, (K) N fr Mud Lane, bel G T road

Clymer st, E & W from 6th bel Fitzwater

Coates' al, from 134 N Front to 151 N 2nd

Coates' ct, E from 31 New Market st

Coates' st, from Delaware to Schuylkill N of Green

Cobb's ct, W from N 4th S of Poplar

Cobb st, fr 236 Catharine to Queen

Coburn st, N from Cedar ab 2nd

Cochran st, N from Fitzwater bel 13th

Coffee's ct, from 180 N 8th

Coffin's ct, S from 14 Cherry

Colladay's ct, E from 137 N 8th

Collard's al, from Beach to Allen N & S (E K)

College av, E from S 10th n High

College av, from Coates to the front of Girard College

College pl, S from College avenue

College row, R road ab 11th to Buttonwood

Collin's al, from 403 S Front to Swanson

Collins' ct, W fr Nixon (F M)

Colonnade row, Chestnut st W from Sch. 8th to Sch. 7th

Columbia row, N fr William ab Morris (F M)

Comptroller st, from 37 Union to Spruce

Commerce st, from 4th to 6th ab Market

Concord st, from 2nd to 3rd bet Catharine and German

Conkle's ct, N from 133 Green

Conrad's ct, N from Poplar ab Front

Coomb's ct, N from 35 German

Coombe's al, from 44 N Front to 51 N 2nd
Cooper st, W from Sch. 3d, S of Walnut
Cooper's ct, N fr Shippen bel 9th
Cooper's ct, (N L) from 408 N Front
Cordwainer's al, now called Fothergill st, from Pine to Lombard bet 9th and 10th
Corn st, S from Marion to Reed bel M road
Cornelius' ct. E from Queen n Bishop (K)
Court al, S from Brown, bet Front and Oak
Courtlin pl, W from 6 New Market n Vine
Cox's st, from 300 S Front to 323 S 2d
Cox's st, from Sch. 5th to 6th, bel Spruce
Crabb st, from Gaskill to Shippen, bet S 4th and S 5th and from Shippen to Plum
Craig's ct, from St. John ab Poplar
Crans' ct. S from Christian bel 9th
Crane's ct, S from Mead bel 2d
Crawford's ct, W from Front ab Noble
Cressman's ct, from 125 Charlotte
Cresson's al, from 96 N 5th to 91 N 6th
Cresson's ct, N from 61 Cherry
Crockett's ct, from 5th ab Chestnut
Crooked Billet, opens at 21 S Water
Crown st (New) runs N from Tammany n O Y road to Green
Crown st, from 155 Race to O Y road and Willow
Crown st, (K) from Queen to F road, bet Shackamaxon and Marlboro'
Culvert st, fr 3d to O Y road N of Beaver
Cumming's Row, Poplar E from N 7th
Cunston's R. av, W from Sch 5th bet Barker & Chestnut
Currant al, from Walnut to Spruce bet S 10th and S 11th
Currie's ct, N from Shippen ab 11th
Cuskaden's ct, S from 118 German
Curtis' ct. S from Union ab Franklin (K)
Cypress st, from 144 S 3d to 79 S 4th

Dannaker's av, E fr N 3d ab Sassafras
Darby road, see Woodland
Davies' pl, N from Great bel 12th
Davis's or Davison's al, from S 13th to Juniper, bet Chestnut and High
Davis's ct, W from O Y road ab N 5th
Davis's or Whitebread's ct, S from 72 Christian
Davis's ct, S from Coates bel Marshall

Dewee's ct, W from 29 Prime
Diamond st, N fr Fitzwater bel 13th
Diamond st, from 13th to Juniper, bet Broad & Chestnut
Dickerson ct, N from Olive bel Broad
Dickson's al, W from 7th bet Shippen & Fitzwater
Dickson's ct, E fr G T road ab 4th
Diligent av, S fr Buttonwood bel 10th
Dilk's ct, Wood ab R road
Dilwyn place, S from Willow bel 4th
Dillwyn st, N from Vine above 3d to Green
Division row, E from N 12th ab Callowhill
Division st, from 11th to 12th, ab Callowhill
Division st, N from Ann st, Francisville
Dock st, from 158 S Front to 67 S 3d, opposite Girard Bank
Doman's place, N fr 131 Christian
Domsler's ct, (K) W from Cadwalader above Franklin
Donaldson's st, from Gray's ferry road to Federal al, bet Arsenal and Buck road
Donnegan's ct, opens at 215 St. John
Dorothy st, E fr Sch. 3d, bet High and Mulberry
Dorr's ct, N fr Pleasant bel 11th
Drinker's al, from 108 N Front to 119 N 2d
Drinker's ct, S from 66 Union
Duffy's ct. S from Fitzwater, bet 6th and 7th
Dugan st, from Spruce ab Sch. 8th to Pine
Dugan's Row, Spruce st from Dean to 13th
Duke st, (N L) from 242 N Front to 363 N 2d
Duke st (K) N E fr Palmer, bet Franklin and West
Duncan's ct, S from 108 Shippen
Dungan's av, G T road to 2d ab Otter
Dunton's st, from Otter to Phœnix N & S (W K)
Dutch ct, E from Beach n Locust, Sch
Dutton's ct, S from Washington bet. 6th & 7th
Duval's ct, W from 36 Ann (N L)
Dyott's ct, E from Franklin ab Vienna (K)

Eagle ct, fr Haliberton's ct across Currant al
Earl st, from Duke to West N & S bet Hanover and Palmer (E K)
Ebenezer pl, N from Catharine bet 3d and 4th
Eckfeldt's ct, N from Commerce ab 5th
Edward st, from 2d to School E & W (W K)

Elm st, fr Franklin ab Hanover (K)
Elmes' ct, N from Vine n Sch.
Elmslie's al, W from 118 S 2d to Laurel, S of the Custom House
Elmyra row, E from 13th bel Vine
Ely's av, S from Carpenter (S) n 5th
Emeline st, W from 8th bel Cedar
Emerald st, from Sch. 6th to 7th, bet Chancellor and Locust
Emlen's al, S from Clever al to 5 Powell
Emlen's ct, from Pegg or Willow to 4 Noble
Engard's ct, E from 443 N 3d .
Eppright's ct, bet Front and Lancaster below Reed
Erie st, S from Shippen ab 10th
Esher's av, from Coates ab 12th
Essen st, from Catherine to Christian, between 8th and 9th
Etris' ct, W from 128 N 5th
Eutaw st, N fr 135 Cherry
Evans' ct, E from 163 N 6th
Evans' st, S from Prime bet 3d and 3 road
Everhart's ct, N from Sassafras n 8th
Ewing's ct, from George st (S), bet Shippen & Plum
Exchange st, S from 72 Chestnut
Eyre's ct. W from Beach ab Warren (K)

Factory st, E fr Sch, wharf, bet Spruce & Clay
Fairmount av, N William ab Callowhill
Fairmount st, ftom Callowhill to Coates, W rom Sch. Front
Fairview st, E from Sch. 4th to Broad
Faries' ct, N from North st above N 10th
Faries ct, W from 148 N Front
Farmer's Row, E from 41 Dock
Farmer st, (Sugar alley) W from 32 N 6th to 23 N 7th
Farr st, from 14 Mulberry al to Vine, bet 5th & 6th
Fayette st, from 53 Filbert N to 262 Mulberry
Fayette av, from 34 Julianna
Farries' ct, W from 148 N Front
Federal al, from Federal road to Arsenal
Federal st and road, from S Front to Schuylkill, bet Prime and Wharton
Feinour's place, W from 72 Swanson
Fetter lane, from 85 N 3d to Bread
Fifth st, N and S from High, W of 4th
Fifth st, (Schuylkill) N & S fr High W of Broad
Filbert st, from 22 N 8th to Sch, bet High and Mulberry
Filbert av, S from 1 Filbert st
Fisher st, S from 258 Catharine to Queen
Fisher's ct, W fr 6 Rachel
Fisher's ct, E from 13 Laurel
Fisher's ct. W from Palmer bet Prince & Queen
Fisher st, N fr Carpenter ab 3d
Fitler st, N fr 2d and Montgomery .
Fitzwater st, W from Passyunk road to Gray's

Flower's st, from Fitzwater ab Hubbell
Flower's al, W from 44 New Market
Fontanell's ct, N fr 79 Poplar ab 3d
Fordham's ct, W fr Beach ab Warren (K)
Fothergill st, N fr 319 Lombard bet. 9th & 10th
Fourth st, N and S from High, W of 3d
Fourth st, (Sch.) N and S from High, W of Broad
Fox's ct, N from Cedar, bet 12th and 13th
Fraley's al, from Allen to Queen N and S, (E K)
Fraley's ct, bet Shackamaxon st & F road, & Allen & Beach (K)
Francis st, from R road to Charles, bet Francis' lane and Ann (F V)
Frankford road N from Maiden (K)
Franklin pl. from High to Chestnut, N of 3d
Franklin pl, E from 9th ab Coates
Franklin Row, Coates W from N 10th
Franklin Row, W side of S 9th, bet Walnut and Locust
Franklin Square, from Sassafras to Vine
Franklin st (S) W from M road bel Greenwich
Franklin st, from Sassafras to Coates, W of Franklin square
Franklin st. (E K) N E from F road to Hanover, bet Duke and Bedford
Franklin st (N L) fr N 3d to N 4th n G T road
Frank's ct, E from Franklin ab Noble
Fraser's ct, E from Carpenter (S) ab 4th
Frazier's lane, W from 6th bel Christian
Freed's av. from 262 Sassafras to 147 Cherry
Freeman's ct, from 7th bel Coates
Freeston's place, E from 51 M road
Freytag's al, S from Bedford to Shippen, bet 5th and 6th
Fries' ct, W from 2 N 11th
Friendship ct, E from 195 St. John
Fromberger's ct, W from 34 N 2d
Fromberger's ct, W from Ann (F V)
Fromberger's ct, W from 30 St John
Front st, N and S from High, W of Water
Front st, (Sch.) N and S from High, bet Ashton and Sch. 2d
Fuller's al, from Swanson to 403 S Front
Fulton st, W fr 12th bel Fitzwater
Furlong's ct, N from 127 Cherry W of 7th

Gabell's ct, S from Lombard n Sch 5th
Gabel's ct, S from 66 Brown (N L)
Galbraith's ct, N from 119 Queen
Galbraith's ct, E from 103 New Market
Gale's ct, E from 89 P road
Gamphire's ct, N from 255 Catharine
Garden st, from 305 Vine to Buttonwood
Garrett's ct. N from 17 Sergeant
Garretson's ct, E from 3d, between Queen and Christian
Garretson's Row, E from 3d ab Christian
Garrigues' ct, N from 213 Sassafras n N 6th .
Garrill's ct. S 5th opp 317
Gaskill Place, S bet Sch. 5th and 6th.

Gebhard st, from Cherry to Sassafras bet Sch. 7th and 8th

Geddes' st, N fr Johnson's lane ab 4th

Gentener's ct, S from 118 Brown

George's al, from New to Vine, bet 2d and 3d

George st, from S 9th, opp Sansom to Sch., bet Walnut and Chestnut, (see Little George)

George st, (N L) from n 550 N 2d to N 6th

George st, (S) from 82 Cedar to 27 Plum

George st, S fr R. road to Charles, N of Francisville

German st, from 334 S 2d to P road, (see Little German)

Germantown road, begins at the intersection of N Front and Maiden

Gideon's ct, opposite 104 Wood ab 8th

Gilbert st. E from 10th to Kessler

Gilbert's ct, E from 103 N Market

Giles' al, from 181 Cedar to 136 Lombard

Gilliam's ct, N from 33 Mulberry

Girard st, from 11th to 12th, bet High and Chestnut

Girard av. W from Broad ab Poplar

Girard's Wharf, ab High, N Wharves

Girl's st, W fr 318 S 5th

Glenat's ct, back of Poplar ab Beach (K)

Goddard's al, from 2 New Market, to 211 N 2d

Goldsmith's ct, E from Rachel, bet Poplar and Brown

Goldsmith's ct, W from New Market n Baptist church

Goodwill al, S fm Sassafras bel Juniper to Cherry

Goodwin's Row, Catharine from Morris to Lebanon

Gorrel's ct, W from 318 S 5th

Govett's ct, N from 9 Bonsall

Graff's al, N from 57 Sassafras

Graff st, fr 11th to 12th S of Vine

Graham's ct, from Bedford ab 12th

Granite Buildings, Broad bet Sassafras & Vine

Grape ct, N from Lodge ab 8th

Grape al, from Ann to George, bet Powell and R road (F V)

Grape st, from 24 S 8th to 13 S 9th

Gravel's ct, S fr Olive ab 13th

Gray's al, from Front to 2d, bet Walnut and Chestnut

Gray's al, fr N 11th to Faries' ct bet Vine & North

Gray's ct, N from Poplar n Budd

Gray's ct, E from 157 N 11th

Gray's ct, E from 13th n Coates.

Gray's Ferry road, from Cedar n Sch. Front S W to Sch. at Gray's Ferry bridge

Grear st, (now Pleasant) W from 11th n R road

Greble's ct, S from 130 Brown n 2nd

Greenleaf's ct, W bet 10 and 12 S 4th

Green st, from 358 N Front to Broad st, S of Coates

Green st, (city) from 127 Pine to 152 Spruce

Green st, W from Cadwalader (K)

Green's ct, S from 248 Shippen

Green's ct, W from 36 Apple to Orchard

Greenwich st, W from Delaware bel Jarvis' la

Greenwood pl, from 201 Noble

Greswold's al, from Little Oak to Fitzwater

Grible's ct, N fr 117 Christian

Grier's ct, W from 13th ab Coates

Grim's ct, S from Poplar n 2d

Grim's row, W fr 6th ab Poplar

Grindstone al, from N 81 High to Church al

Grover st, S from Queen to Christian, bet Sutherland and Front

Grubb st, S from Catharine ab 6th

Gurther's ct, E from 512 N Front

Gulielma st. W from Broad to Sch 8th, bet Cedar and Lombard

Haas' ct, E from 391 N 3d

Hagerty's ct, E from 7th N of Walnut

Haines st, W from 102 N 6th

Hallowell's ct. S from Poplar ab 7th

Hallowell's ct, N from Paschall al ab 4th

Hallowell st, W from 6th bel Carpenter

Hamilton ct, rear Linden ab Spring Garden

Hamilton pl, N from Callowhill ab 13th

Hamilton st, from Upper Ferry road to Broad, N of Callowhill

Hamilton st, from Cedar to Washington, bet. 11th and 12th

Hamilton's ct, S from 76 German ab 3d

Hamilton's ct, W from 4th ab Carpenter

Hampton st, from Sch 2d to 3d, bet Pine & Lombard

Hancock st. W from Franklin bet 2d & Front

Hank's ct, rear 7 Budd. (N L)

Hank's ct, from 18 Rachel

Hanly's ct, E from Wall ab P road

Hanover st, from the Delaware to F road bet Marlborough and Palmer (K)

Hansel's ct, W from 326 S 5th

Harberger's row, S fr Jones W of Sch 6th

Harmony or Cake's ct, N from 27 Coates' al

Harmony ct, from 76 S 3d to 47 S 4th above Walnut

Harmony ct. from Shippen to Small

Harmony ct, E fr 327 S 4th

Harmony st, W from 327 S 4th

Harmony ct, W from Cadwalader ab Jefferson

Harmstead st, E from Sch. 2d ab Cedar

Harper's al, from 83 S Water

Harriet st, runs from Ross ab Queen (K)

Harris' ct, W from 8 Lætitia ct

Harrison pl, N from Coates below 2d

Harrison pl. N from Parrish bel 11th

Harrison st from F road to G T road E and W (W K)

Harrison st, S from Locust, bel Sch. 5th

Harrison's ct. N from G T road to William, bet Otter and Rose (K)

Harrison's av, fr N. Market, between Coates and Green

Hart's ct, E from 57 New Market

Harthorne's ct, W from 178 Marshall

Hartnet's ct. E from Lisle

Hartung's al, W from 26 N 2d to 31 N 3d

Hatter's ct, from Vine N near Sch Front

Hatter's row, bet Spring Garden and James n Sch. 8th

Hause's ct, N from Cherry E of 9th

Harvey's ct, (K) E from St John ab Beaver

Haydock st, from G T road ab Maiden E t Canal

Hay's ct, from Pleasant to James ab Charles .
Hay's ct, N from Penn to Beach bel Maiden. (K)
Hazel st, W from Front bel Greenwich
Hazel st, from 11th to 12th bel Poplar
Hazelhurst's ct, E from S 10th bet High and Chestnut
Hazzard's ct, E from 7th ab Shippen
Headman's place, S from Shoemaker bel 8th
Heiberger's ct, E from St. John bel Beaver
Helmuth st, W from Sch. 7th ab Lombard
Hemphill's ct, from Pleasant ab 10th
Henderson's ct, W from 7th bel Coates
Hermitage pl, E from 3d opp Branch
Herriges' ct, W from Rachel ab Brown
Hewson st, from Prince to Queen N & S (E K)
Hiberger's ct, N from 311 Poplar
Hickory ct, N from Callowhill ab 6th
Higgin's ct, N from 29 John (S)
Higgin's pl, S fr. Carpenter ab 3 road
High (Market) st, from Delaware to Schuylkill, bet Mulberry and Chestnut
High's ct, 2d ab Laurel (K)
Higham's ct, W from Cadwalader, bet Phoenix and Master
Hight's ct, N from Pleasant bel 10th
Hight's ct, from Willow N ab 8th
Hilliard's ct, from Ogden n 9th
Hincle's ct, from Pleasant bel 10th
Hindes' ct, N from 23 Filbert
Hines' ct, from 106 Christian (S)
Hinkel's ct, N from 207 Sassafras to Bryan's al
Hinkel's ct, (N L) N from 249 Vine
Hodges' Wharf, opens at 85 N Water
Hooting's ct, S from Cedar to Bedford
Hooven's ct, W from 448 N 4th
Hoffman's al, S from 176 Sassafras
Hog al, E from 163 S 6th
Holloway pl, W from N Front n Laurel
Holmes' al, E from 211 N 2d to New Market
Hope st, from Otter to Phoenix N and S (W K)
Hope st, from 2d to Front ab G T road
Hopkins' ct, N E from William bet Otter and Rose
Hoppel's ct, W from Brooks bet Coates & Brow
Horstman's ct. S from 76 German
Horter's block, W from Broad bet Morris and Fair Mount
Howard place, S from Washington, between 8th and 9th
Howard place, W fr Quince bet Spruce & Pine
Howard place, N from R road ab Coates
Howard's ct, W from Laurel bel Pear
Howard st, from School to Franklin N and S E of Hope. (W K)
Howard's ct, S from 268 Sassafras
Howard's ct, N from Hamilton bel Sch 6th
Howard's pl, N from Baker (S) bet 7th and 8th
Howard st, S from High, W of Sch. 8th
Howe's ct, from 14 Julianna
Howell's ct, N from Noble ab 4th
Hubbell st, S from Fitzwater, bet 8th and 9th
Huddel's ct, E from 91 Swanson
Hudson's al, from 112 Chestnut to Harmony ct
Hudson's lane, W from P road n Christian

Hughes' ct from Federal to Marion bel 3 road
Hughes' ct, lane or alley, from M road bel Carpenter to 3d
Hughe's ct, N from Carpenter ab 6th
Huling's ct, W from Wheat ab Rule
Hummell's Row, St John bel G T road (N L)
Hummell's Row, N 10th bel Buttonwood (S G)
Hummell's ct, E from 525 N 3d
Humphrey's ct, N from Filbert ab Sch. 8th
Hunter's ct, E from N 11th, bet High & Filbert
Hunter st, from Broad to Fairmount, bet Morris and St. Andrew
Hurst st, from 146 Lombard to 191 Cedar
Hutchinson st. N from Poplar, bet 9th and 10th
Hutchinson's ct, W fr F road bel Otter
Hyde's ct, N from 23 Filbert

Increase ct, fr George to Juniper al, W of S 10th
Irish Tract lane, S from Cedar ab Broad to Buck lane
Irvine st, from 13th to R road, ab Sp Garden

Jackson's av, from Front to F road bel Master
Jackson ct, S from Maiden n N Front
Jackson ct, N fr Baker
Jackson ct, S from 336 Vine bet 9th & 10th
Jackson pl, N fr. Jackson st, bel 5th (N L)
Jackson st, (S G) fr Brown to Parrish, bet 11th and 12th
Jackson st, S from Budd to Adams, bet Spruce and Pine and Perry and 13th
Jackson st. W from Palmer ab West (K)
Jackson st, from Apple to Old York road bel Poplar
Jackson st from Marriott to Carpenter ab 3d
Jacoby st, S from Montgomery, bet 12th and 13th
James' ct, N from Bedford ab 12th
James ct, from Front to Hope E and W (W K)
James st, from Maple to Lemon
James st, from 9th to Broad bet Callowhill and Buttonwood
Janney's ct, from Marshall bel Coates
Jarvis lane, W from Delaware bel Reed
Jay st, fr. Wallace to Coates bet 8th & 9th
Jefferson Row, south side of Lombard from 9th to 10th
Jefferson avenue, W from Broad n Walnut
Jefferson st, from Sch. 5th to 6th, S of Locust
Jefferson st, from Harrison to Sch. 6th bet Locust and Rittenhouse
Jefferson st, W from F road bet Oxford an Master
Jefferson Place, W from 468 N Front
Jenning's-row, N from Catharine, bet 3d & 4th
John st, from 466 S Front to M road
John's ct, E from 2nd ab High
John's ct, S from 10 Willow
Johnson's lane, W from 3 road bel Wharton
Johnston's ct, E from Parker's al
Johnston's ct, E from 13th ab Cedar
Johnston's ct, W fr Penn n Maiden
Johnston's ct. E from 81 P road
Joint al, E from Sch. 8th ab Chestnut
Jones' al, W from 14 N Front to 17 N 2d

Jones' al, N from 15 St. Mary's al
Jones' al, W from Lilly al ab Green
Jones' al, (N L) S from Brown bet 2d and Budd
Jones' ct, W from Front bel Master
Jones' ct, E from 491 S 2d
Jones' st, fr Sch. 4th to 6th, bet High & Filbert
Joseph's al, from Montgomery to Marion ab 12th
Julianna st, N from 175 Vine to N of Callowhill
Julianna street, (now Chatham) N from Button-
wood, E of 6th to Green
Juniper al, from S 10th n Walnut to Juniper la
Juniper la, fr George to Walnut bet 10th & 11th
Juniper st, N & S from High bet 13th and Broad
Justice ct, rear 314 N 2d

Karney's ct, W from Nixon (F M)
Kean's ct, E from 25 New Market
Keefe st, W f Front, bet Marion and Wharton
Keenan's ct, E from G T road bel Jefferson (K)
Kelley st, W from 26 S 13th to Juniper
Kelley's av, E from N 13th bel Vine
Kelley's ct, N from Kelley st bel Juniper
Kelley's ct, E from 295 S 5th
Kelly's ct, N from German bet 3d and 4th
Kelly's ct, N from Washington
Kennedy's ct, W from 450 N Front
Kenworthey's ct, N from 145 Cherry
Kepler st, N from Coates bet 9th and 10th
Kern's ct, rear Poplar n Marshall
Kessler's ct, E from N 4th n Coates
Kessler's st, N from 147 Coates
Key's al, from 160 N Front to 183 N 2d
Keyser's Row, W from Apple bel Master (K)
Kienzel's ct, rear of 46 Green
Kimsli's ct, rear 43 Duke
Kinley's ct, S fr Lombard ab Sch. 7th
King st, from Murray to Sch 8th, bet Pine and
Lombard
King st, fr. Sassafras to. Cherry, bet Sch 8th and
Broad
Kirkpatrick's al, E from 243 S 6th
Kline's ct, from 110 Christian (S)
Kline's ct, W fr 492 N 3d
Kneass's ct, runs S from George bet 10th and
11th
Knight's ct, S from 194 Cherry
Knoodle's ct, (Vaughn) fr Walnut to Locust bet
Sch 7th and 8th
Korndaffer's ct. N from Marriott ab M road
Krider's al, N from 70 Swanson to Front
Krider's ct, W from Krider's al, bet Almond &
Mead
Krider's ct, N from Bedford ab 7th
Kugler's ct, opens at 130 Sassafras
Kunckle's ct, from Green ab 3rd
Kurtz st, N of Poplar bet 11th & 12th

Lætitia ct, from 30 High to Black horse al
La Fayette st, W from 9th ab Federal
La Fayette pl. N from Coates ab 13th
La Fayette ct, fr N side of Cedar bet 4th & 5th
Lagrange place, W from 34 N 2d
Lagrange st, W from 26 N 2d
Lambert st, from N 13th to N Juniper bet Nor-
man and Clare al
Lancaster ct, E from Lancaster bel Wharton

Lancaster st S from Marion ab Front
Landall's ct. W from Fraley's ct to Queen
Landing st. N W from Coates to Lemon Hill
Lane's ct, S from Lombard, bet 13th and Broad
Laurel ct, rear of Laurel st. (C)
Laurel st, from 29 Spruce to Pear
Laurel st, (N L) fr N Front opp Maiden to N 2d
Lawrence ct, N from Julianna bel Green
Lawrence's ct. W from Penn ab Marsh
Lawrence st, W from N 12th to Juniper bet
High and Filbert
Law's ct, S from 102 Christian
Lawson ct, bet George and Walnut, running
from 12th
Leadbeater's av, from Lybrand to Juniper, bet
Race and Vine
Lebanon st, fr Fitzwater ab Morris to Christian
Lebanon row, Shippen fr 10th to 11th
Lee's ct, W from 302 St. John
Leech's ct, S from 156 Spruce
Leed's av, S of Vine, bet Broad and Sch 8th
Leed's al, S of Vine bel Sch 8th
Leiper's ct, E from 33 N 11th
Leiper al, fr Vine to North st W of 10th
Leiper st, E from 13th ab Chestnut
Lemon st, W from Sch. 6th ab Pine
Lemon st, from 156 N 8th to Chester
Leopard st, from Phœnix to Franklin N and S
(W K)
Lewis' al, from 24 Small to Plum al
Lewis' ct. N from St. Mary ab 6th
Lewis's ct, N from 297 Callowhill
Lewis st, W from Sch. 8th, opp. Jefferson av
Lewis st, N from Poplar ab 10th
Leyden's ct, E from 117 N 10th
Liberty al, from 9 Duke to 10 Green
Liberty ct, E from N 10th bet Morgan and Vine
Liberty ct, W from 2 N 9th
Library st, from 62 S 4th to 35 S 5th
Lily al, from Tammany n N 2d to n Coates
Linden Place, south side Spruce from 11th to
Quince
Linden ct, W from 3rd bel Green
Linden st, from Spring Garden to Green bet 9th
and 10th
Linden st, from Sch. 6th to 8th bet Chestnut &
Barker
Linden st, E from Front ab Maiden
Linn st, fr Sch Front to William S of Hamilton
Linn's Row, W from Columbia Row
Lisle st, from Fitzwater ab 8th to Shippen
Lister's place, S from Shippen bel 4th
Little Dock st, S from 50 Spruce to 177 S 2d
Little George st, W from 59 S 6th to 91 S 7th
Little Green st, from 2d to G T road E and W
(W K)
Little German st, W from 99 Swanson to 377
S Front
Little Oak st, W from Twelve feet al, bet Ship-
pen and Fitzwater
Little Pine st, from S 6th to S 8th bet Pine
and Lombard
Little Poplar, W from G T road bet 5th & 6th
Little Washington st, from S Front to S 2d bel
Federal

Little Water st, from 1 Lombard st to Cedar
Littleboy's ct, opens at 48 Mulberry
Lloyd's ct, E from G T road ab Phœnix
Lloyd's st, S from Shippen ab Broad
Locust st, from 6th c Washington sq to Sch.
Lodge al, from 16 S 7th to S 8th rear of the Masonic Hall
Lodge st, W from S 2d N of the Bank of Pennsylvania to Exchange st
Lodge place, N from Lodge al ab 7th
Logan st, fr Buttonwood to Green bet Franklin and 8th
Logan square, Vine from Sch 3d to 5th
Logan's ct, E from St John ab Beaver (K)
Lollar's ct, W from 328 N Front
Lombard st, from Delaware to Sch. bet Pine & Cedar
Lombard ct, W from 4th bet Pine and Lombard
Lombard Row, S from 222 Lombard
Long lane, S from Cedar n Sch. 7th
Loud st, from 9th to 10th, between Carpenter and Christian
Lowery's ct. W from Beach ab Poplar
Lowry's ct, W from R road bel Callowhill
Loxley's ct, N from 115 Mulberry
Loxley's ct, S from 30 Spruce
Lugar's Row, enters 2d N of Beaver
Lybrand st, N from Sassafras n Broad
Lydia st, fr Front to William N of Rose
Lyndall al, from S 12th to S 13th bet Walnut & Centre
Lyndall ct, E from 10th bel Pine
Lytle's ct, E from 363 S 2d
Lytle's ct, E from 2d bel Mead

Mackey st, fr 2d to Corn bet Reed and Wharton
Macleod pl, from 156 Sassafras
Madison av, E from 13th ab Willow
Madison ct, N from 23 St. Mary
Madison st, from Sassafras W of 11th to Vine
Magnolia st, N from Noble E of N 6th'
Maiden's Row, N from Catharine bet S Front & S 2d
Maiden st, from Delaware to the intersection of N Front and G T road
Malt al, from Nicholson's ct to 206 Sassafras
Manderson st, from Beach to F road ab the Market (K)

Marker st, from S 2d to R road bel Greenwich
Market al, E Sch 7th ab Callowhill
Marlborough st, from the Delaware to F road
Marriott's la. W from 4th to P road bel Christian
Marriott st, from R road to 4th, bel Christian
Marsh st, from the Delaware n the High bridge to Front
Marshall's ct, from 122 S 4th to S 5th
Marshall's ct, (K) W from G T road ab 5th
Marshall's ct, E from 239 S 2d
Marshall st, 8th st, N from Wallace, bet Green and Coates
Marshall st, N from Vine W of N 6th
Marshall st, W fr S 4th ab Wharton
Martin's ct, St. John's bel Beaver (K)
Mary's al, from 27 Gillis' al to S 6th
Mary st, K from Cherry to F road
Mary st, S from 406 S Front to 505 S 2d
Mary st, W fr Sch Beach to Willow ab Spruce
Mary's ct, N from 149 Cherry
Mary's ct, E from 239 S 2d
Master st, W fr F road to R road n Phœnix. (K)
Matlack's ct, S from 12 Spruce
Maxwell's ct, from 116 Christian (S)
Mayland st, from 190 Sassafras to Mulberry al
M'Afee's ct, S from Cedar ab 5th
M'Atee's ct, W fr Cadwalader ab Jefferson (K)
M'Allister's ct, F road near Queen (K)
M'Avoy's ct, E from 15 Charlotte
M'Bride's ct, E from 555 N 4th
M'Cloud's ct, opens at 154 Sassafras
M'Clugn's ct, W fr. Orange ab Washington (S G)
M'Coy's ct, E from 385 S Front
M'Coster's ct, bet Sch 5th and 6th and Pine and Spruce
M'Crelish ct, E from 337 N 3d
M'Dermott's ct, S from 247 Shippen
M'Duffie st, W from Sch. 4th bel Lombard
M'Ginley's ct. W from Swanson bel Washington
M'Ginnel's ct, E from 7 Vernon
M'Intire's ct. W from Marlboro' bel Allen
M'Kean's ct, S from 4 Locust
M'Mackin's ct, W from Dugan ab Pine
M'Manemy's ct, S from German bet 4th & 5th
M'Mullen's ct, rear 62½ S 4th
Mead al, from S 2d opp. German to Swanson
Mechanic's av, N from Lawrence ab 12th
Mechanic ct, S from 70 Maiden
Mechanic st, N from Linn (E M)

Mifflin's ct, W from 318 S Front
Mifflin st, from 12th to 13th, bet Pine & Lombard
Miles' Row, n Rose and William
Miles' al, W from 102 S 10th
Miles' ct, from Rose to Willow, N School (K)
Miller's al, E from 87 S 6th
Miller's al, E from Sch. 8th ab Sassafras
Miller's ct, (N L) W from 314 N 2d
Miller's ct, E from N 4th ab Branch
Miller's ct, rear 217 St. John
Miller's ct, (N L) N from 45 Green
Miller's ct, from Garden N of Willow
Miller's ct, S from 260 Sassafras
Miller's st, S fr. 13th bet Parrish and Brown
Milton st, W from 10th bel Christian
Mineral pl. E from Bread ab Mulberry
Minor st, from 4 South 5th to 3 S 6th
Minor st, N from Coates n Fairmount
Mint-ct, West from Raspberry lane bet Cherry
　　and Sassafras
Mintland's ct. N from 125 Plum
Mintzer's ct, W from 244 N 2d
Mintzer st, from Brown to Coates, bet. 3d & 4th
Moliere's ct, S from 42 Shippen
Moffatt's ct, W from 138 N 2d
Monmouth ct, S from the middle Jones' al
Monroe ct, S from Lawrence bel Juniper
Monroe place, from N E 8th & Locust to Wash-
　　ington sq
Monroe st, W from Cherry to Palmer bel Duke
　　(K)
Montgomery square, from N E Cherry and 10th
　　round to S E 11th and Sassafras
Montgomery st, W from 12th to 13th bet Sassa-
　　fras and Vine
Montgomery st, E fr Black Horse, F road to G
　　T road
Moore st, E from Church bel Greenwich
Moore's al. N from Say bet Sch. 6th and 7th

Mulberry al, W from N 5th bet Sassafras & Vine
Mulberry, (Arch) from the Delaware to Sch. bet
　　High and Sassafras·
Murphy's ct, W from 254 N Front
Murray st, bet Spruce and Locust and Sch. 2d
　　and 3d
Murray st, from Pine to Lombard, bet Broad &
　　Sch 8th
Murray's ct, from 338 S Front
Mustin's ct, E from 9 Elder alley
Myers' ct, N from 221 Sassafras
Myers' ct, E from 123 N 3d
Myers' ct, E from Sch 8th bel Vine
Myer's place, S from Mulberry al, n 6th
Myrtle st. E from 12th bet Parrish and Poplar

Naglee's ct, E from 251 St. John
Nectarine st, from 8th to 11th bet Buttonwood
　　and Spring Garden
New st, from 160 N 2d to n 93 N 4th
New Market st, from 19 Vine to 52 Green
Newton st, S from Carpenter bet 4th and 5th
Nicholas ct, W from St. John n Franklin
Nicholson st, from 113 Cherry to Sassafras
Ninth st, N and S from High W of 8th
Nixon st, N from Vine to Coates ab Sch Front
Noble st, W from Delaware to N 9th
Nonnater's ct, S from 280 Mulberry
Norman al, from S 13th to Juniper bet Sassafras
　　and Lambert
Norris' al, from 68 S Front to 87 S 2d
Norris ct, N from Carpenter (S) n 4th
Norris's ct, E of New Market bet Vine and Cal-
　　lowhill
Norris Row, E from Cadwalader bet Phoenix
　　and Master
North st, (E) from 35 N 5th to 39 N 6th
North st, (W) from N 10th to N 11th S of Vine
North st W from 816 N 2d

Lombard, bet 12th | Perkenpine ct, E from 43 Budd
Perry ct, W from 58 N 8th
erry al bel Walnut | Perry ct, N from Cedar n 13th
Queen to N 2d | Perry st, from 466 Vine S to Sassafras
adwalader E and W | Perry st, S from Spruce bet 12th and 13th to Lombard
Perry st, from Franklin to Master bel Canal
l near Fairmount | N and S (W K)
3 bet 9th and 10th | Peter st, from Sch. 2d to 3d bel High
Orange, bet Hanover | Peters' al, from Charlotte to Brown n N 4th
Petticoat ct, E from Water ab Callowhill
es at N W Vine and | Pfeiffer's al, from 22 New Market to 235 N 2d
way bet 11th & 12th, | Pfeiffer's ct, E from N 2d to G T road
E direction until it | Phœnix st, W from F road bet Master and Franklin
and 10th | lin (K)
road bet Filbert and | Philip st, N from Master n 2d
Pickam's ct, N W from 354 S Front
on to 395 S Front | Pierce's ct, E from 297 N 4th ab German
l Locust | Pike st. from Cherry to Margaret bel 13th
3d | Pine al, from Ball al to 241 S 4th
ater al) from Wash- | Pine st, from Delaware to Sch. bet Spruce and Lombard
Pink st, from Master to Jefferson N and S above
r (S) bet 5th & 6th | G T road (W K)
er between 5th and | Piper's ct, E from 185 St John
Pitt st, from Cohocksink creek to G T road bet
the Mutual Burying | N 2d and N 3d
Plain st, from Lancaster to Wheat, bet Reed and
road bet Brown and | Wharton
Pleasant avenue, fr 235 Lombard to Little Pine
O Y road bet Green | Pleasant st, from Charles to Broad, bet James and Buttonwood
lotte n Cohocksink | Pleasant Retreat, W from N 7th bel Coates
173 Cedar, boundary | Pleasant ct, from N side of Lawrence, bet 12th
yamensing | and 13th and bet High and Filbert
ine ab Sch. 8th | Pleasant Row, N fr. Spruce W of Sch 3d
Washington (S) | Pleis' ct, S from Poplar ab 3d
nt | Pleis' ct, E from St John ab Beaver (K)
an bet 4th and 5th | Pleis' ct, W from Garden bel Callowhill
Oak bet 5th & 6th | Plum st, from 320 S 2d to P road
oates bet 2d & New | Plum al, from Greswold's al to S 6th
Plumber's ct, from 21 German
ab Crown. (K) | Plynlimmon pl, W from 144 N Front
of St. James' Church | Point Pleasant ct. W from Penn n Maiden
S 3d | Polard st, fr G T road to Budd N of Laurel
Vine to William bet | Poplar al, N fr Locust, bet Currant al and S 11th
mount to G T road | Poplar ct, from Rose, al to Miles al
to 299 N 2d | Poplar pl, S from Poplar bel 3d
Vine | Poplar st, from 13th to Broad bet Carpenter and Mariner
road (K) | Poplar st, from 440 N Front to Ridge Road
W of Juniper, | Poplar st, (Little) E fr G T road bet 5th & 6th
le to Buttonwood | Poplar sq, N from Parrish to Poplar N 9th
lmond | Porter's ct, W from 532 N 3d
to Beach along the | Portico sq, Spruce bet 9th and 10th
Portland lane, from 152 S 6th to S 7th
oates | Potter's ct, S from Lombard W of 13th
bel 3d

Pottery al, from 8 Small to Little Oak

Powell's Row, Keefe st from c Lancaster

Powell st, from 100 S 5th to 133 S 6th

Powell st, W fr Francis. (F V)

Pratt st, from Spruce ab Sch. 7th to Pine

Pratt's ct, from 396 N Front

Pray's ct, W from 50 Charlotte

Presbyterian (Bryan's) ct, W from 170 S 4th

Preston st, from Melon to Wallace ab 9th

Price's ct, S from bet 66 and 68 Lombard

Prime st, (called also Washington) from Delaware to A road, bet Carpenter and Federal

Prince st, N E from the end of Franklin (E K)

Prospect al, E from 27 N 13th

Prospect ct, E fr N 11th bet Filbert & Mulberry

Prospect pl. S from 230 Christian

Prosperous al, S fr Locust bet S 11th & S 12th

Prosperous al, W from Spafford bel Shippen

Providence ct, N from 15 Sergeant

Prune st, from 110 S 4th W to S 6th

Pryor's ct, from 165 S 10th to Raspberry al

Pump al, W from Spafford bel Shippen

Quarry Row, N of Callowhill (F M)

Quarry st, W from 96 N 2d to 101 N 3d

Queen st, (S) from P road bet Catharine and Christian to the Delaware

Queen st, (Point-no-point) N E from F road n Otter to Gunner's run (K)

Querville's ct, S from Tammany ab 4th

Quigg's ct, N from Catharine ab 3d

Quince st, from Walnut to Lombard, bet 11th and 12th

Race st, (see Sassafras) from Delaware to Sch. N of Mulberry

Rachel row, rear 113 Dillwyn

Rachel st, N from Brown to Laurel, (N L) bet Budd and N 2d

Radford's row, fr 13th & Shippen to Fitzwater

Rafferty ct, N from Carpenter, bet 8th and 9th

Railroad ct, W from Jay bel Coates

Randall's ct, W from Blackberry al ab Locust

Randolph's ct, W from 126 N 2d

Ranstead place, N from 26 S 4th

Rapin's ct, S from 102 High

Raspberry st from Walnut to Spruce, bet S 9th and S 10th

Raspberry lane, from 173 Cherry to 286 Sassafras

Rawle st, from O Y road to Apple

Read's al, from 190 Cedar

Reakirt's ct, S from George ab 2d

Reckless st from 529 S Front to Church

Reckless ct, W from Church ab Reckless st,

Redwood st, W from 4th bel Federal

Reed st, W from Delaware river bel Wharton

Reeves st, from Sch. 2d & Wood & Vine

Reid's st, N from 107 German

Reid's ct, E from 5th bel Christian

Reid's av, W from Flower bet 8th and 9th

Reiff's ct, E from N Front ab Otter

Relief al, from Carter's al to Dock

Relief place, from 19 Relief st

Relief st, from 218 S Front to 227 S 2d

Renfer's ct, E from St. John ab Beaver

Rex's ct, W fr Weaver ab Green

Rex's ct, W fr Marshall bel Poplar

Richard st, W from Sch. 7th ab Lombard

Richards st, W from 96 N 9th

Richardson's ct, N from 159 Sassafras

Rickard's ct, from George ab 2d. (K)

Ridgeway's ct W from 110 N 8th

Ridgeway's Row, Callowhill ab William

Ridge Road, N W from the c of Vine and N 9th

Rigler's ct, from F road bel Franklin (K)

Rihl's ct, W from 526 N 3d

Rihle's ct, N from 79 Poplar

Rihle's ct, W from 250 St. John

Ritner st, fm Sch 7th to 8th bet Spruce & Locust

Rittenhouse st, from Sch. 3d to 6th bel Locust

Rittenhouse st, from Sch. 7th to 8th ab Sassafras

Rittenhouse place, N side of Locust bet S 9th and S 10th

Rittenhouse Row, Chestnut bet 12th and 13th

Rittenhouse square, from Locust to Spruce, bet Sch. 4th and 5th

Roach's ct. S from Union ab Bedford

Robb's ct, W from R road ab 13th

Robenson ct, N fr. Spruce bet Sch 4th and 5th

Roberts' ct. N from Mark's la. bet 11th & 12th

Roberts' ct, N from 53 Mead

Robeson's ct, from Vine ab Broad

Robinson's ct, N from 299 Callowhill

Robinson's ct. W from Penn n Maiden (K)

Robinson's ct, fr 5th bel Coates

Rodger's ct, rear 12 Emlen's ct

Roger's ct, N from Pegg

Rollins' Row, Brinton st, E from 13th

Ronaldson's Row, S from S E Cedar, and 9th to N E Shippen

Ronaldson st. from Cedar to Shippen bet 9th & 10th

Rooney's ct, W from St. John, n C Creek

Rose al, (K) from Rose to Lydia, bet School & William

Rose al, (N L) from Tammany n N 3d to Coates

Rose al, (C) N from 127 Locust

Rose la, from G T road, 1st ab Mud lane

Rose st, N E from G T road, bet Otter & N 2d

Rose st, W fr S 13th, bet Shippen & Fitzwa

Rose st, fr G T road to School E and W (W K)

Ross' ct, S from 25 Concord

Ross' ct. N from Little Oak

Ross st, from Queen to Prince N and S (E K)

Rowlinson's ct, E from 169 N 2d

Roy's ct, N from Shippen ab 5th

Ruddach ct, N from James bel 10th

Rudolph's ct, S from 266 Sassafra

Rugan st, from 345 Callowhill to James

Rule's ct, E from 291 S 5th

Rule st, W from Lancaster to Wheat

Runkle's ct, N from 233 Green

Rush's ct, N from 211 Cherry ab 9th

Russell's ct, n Sch Front and Callowhill

Russell st, from Shippen to Fitzwater, bet 8th and 9th

Rutter's ct, N fr 46 Federal, bet 2d and M road

Rye st, from Marion to Reed ab 2d

Rye st, (C) from Graff street South, forming an elbow out to Madison street

Sailor's ct, S fr. Willow ab 13th
Salem al, W from 12th ab Lombard
Sanderson ct, E fr. Eliza bel Parrish
Sansom's al, from Willow to Noble, bet St John and N 3d
Sansom's Row, N side of Walnut, bet Swanwick and S 8th
Sansom st, W from S 7th to S 9th, bet Chestnut and Walnut
Sarah st, from Queen (K) n F road to Bedford
Sassafras st, (or Race) from Delaware to Sch N of Mulberry
Sassafras al, from 190 Sassafras st to Mulberry al
Saunder's ct, E from Pitt n Beaver
Savage's Row, from 12th to 13th in Locust, S side
Say's al, from Sch. 7th to Sch. 8th, bet Race and Vine
Say's al, from Cherry to walnut W of 13th
Say's ct, W from 36 N 3d
Scattergood's Block, rear 308 St. John
Scattergood's ct, W from 408 N Front
Scheaff st, W from 12th bet High and Mulberry
Scheme (Vine al) from N 15th to Broad ab Vine
Scheetz st. E from 331 S 2d to Front
Schively's al, from 138 N 5th to 141 N 6th
Schlessinger's ct, E from N 3d bet Poplar and Beaver
School av, S from Union n S 2d
School st, E from 54 Apple (N L)
School st, from Otter to Franklin N & S (W K)
Schrader's ct, W fr Apple to ab George (N L)
Schriver's ct, E from 57 N 8th
Schuylkill av, from 11th to Quince, bet Spruce and Pine

Schuylkill la, W from 11th bet Spruce & Pine
Scott's al, from 379 High to Filbert
Scott's ct, S from 14 Poplar
Scott's ct, W from 342 S Front
Scott's ct, N from 153 Cedar
Scott's ct. E from 4th bel George
Second st, N and S from High W of Front
Second st, (Sch.) N & S from High W of Sch 3d
Seiser's ct, S from 56 Sassafras
Sellers' ct, N from Carlton ab 13th
Senniff's ct, N fr. George bet Ashton and Sch Beach
Seneca ct, W from Samson's alley near Noble
Sergeant st, from N 9th bet Sassafras and Morgan, to N 10th
Seventh st, N and S from High W of 6th
Seventh st, (Sch.) N & S fr High W of Sch. 8th
Seybold's ct, fr. Noble ab 3d
Shackamaxon st, from the Delaware to the F road, bet. Sarah and Crown
Shafer's ct, from 21 Garden
Shafer's ct, S from Nectarine bel 10th
Shaffer's ct, fr R road ab 13th
Shaffer's ct, S from Apple near Apple
Sharpless' ct, N fr. St. Joseph's av. bel Sch 5th
Sheaff's al fr N 11th n Sassafras, W to N 12th
Sheldon Row, from Walnut to Good Water al, in 8th
Shephard al, fr Mulberry to Cherry bet 7th & 8th

Shepherd's ct, W from 36 N 3d
Shepherd's ct, S from 355 Coates ab 11th
Sherborne's ct, S from Poplar bel 6th
Sherker's al, 3 from Shippen bel 6th
Shied st, from Front to 2d, between Almond & Catharine
Shield's al, from 140 S 9th to Raspberry al
Shield's al, from Prosperous al, to Quince st
Shield's ct, S from Relief al bet Front & 2d sts
Shippch lane, from Cedar n Broad to Federal
Shippen st, from Delaware to Broad S of Cedar
Shippen's ct, S from Pearl bet. 12th and 13th
Shirker's al, S from Bedford to Shippen, bet 5th and 6th
Shoemaker st, E from 13 S 8th to Lodge place
Shoemaker's ct, W from N Front, bet Nos. 10 and 12
Short's ct, E from N 12th ab Sassafras
Shuster's ct, rear 198 N 8th
Sibert st, E & W from Sch 7th ab Thompson
Silvas, from Plum ab 2d
Sim's al, from S wharves to S water n High
Simmon's ct, W from 216 N Front
Simmon's ct, E from 29 New Market
Simpson's ct, rear 62 Catharine
Simpson,s ct, N fr 119 Queen
Singler's Row, W from N 2d ab Phoenix
Sixth st (Sch.) N and S fr High, W of Sch. 7th
Skerret's ct, S from Shield's al ab 9th
Slessman st, from 507 N 3d to Cohocksink
Small st. West, bet Cedar & Shippen from 5th st
Smith's al, from n 219 S 3d to Gaskill
Smith's al, (N L) from 119 Green to 128 Coates
Smith's ct. N from (Allen's ct) Front st
Smith's ct, S from High n Sch. 8th
Smith's ct, E from 117 N 5th
Smith's ct, W from 172 N 8th
Smith's ct, W from rear 88 N Front
Smith's ct, E from St John n Globe Mill
Smith's ct, S from Gaskill bel 3d
Smith's ct, N from Bedford bel 8th
Smith's ct, from Pearl ab 12th
Smith's ct, S fr. Linden ab Sch 8th
Smith's pl, from 8 Linden bel Green
Sinneff's ct, N from George ab Sch Beach
Sixth st, N and S from High, W of 5th
Snider's ct, E from Rye bel Wharton
Sober's al, from 129 Walnut towards Library
Somer's ct, W from S 2d ab Christian
South st, (Cedar) from Delaware to Schuylkill, the S boundary of the city proper
South al, (Commerce st,) from 5th to 6th, N of High
South Avenue, along Schuylkill ab Catharine
South ct, rear 214 N 8th
South row, W from Sch 4th ab Hamilton
Southampton ct, E from 25 Laurel
Southwark Rail Road, a continuation of the Columbia Rail Road at its termination c Broad and Chestnut, along Broad to Prime, down Prime to 4th and Washington, along Washington to Swanson, and along Swanson to Cedar
Spafford st, from 50 Bedford to Fitzwater
Spragg's av, S from 64 Christian

Spring st, W from Sch. 7th bet Sassafras & Vine

Spring Garden retreat, N from S Garden bel 13th

Spring Garden st, (120 feet wide) from 6th to Broad, bet Buttonwood and Green

Springmill ct, William ab Linn (F M)

Spruce st, from Delaware to Schuylkill, bet Walnut and Pine

Square st, from Rye to Corn, bet Mackey and Wharton

St Andrew's st, from Sch. Front to Broad, bet Hunter and Coates

St. Bernard's ct, from 360 S 2d

St. George's al, from 55 New to Vine

St. James st, E from 7 N 7th

St. John st, Vine between 2d & 3d to G T road

St. Joseph's avenue, from Sch. 5th to Sch. 6th, bet High and Chestnut

St. Mary's al. N from Gilles' al ab Cedar

St. Mary st, from 220 S 6th W to S 8th

St Paul's av, E from 7th ab Catharine

St. Stephen's place, from 322 High to College av

Stable al, from opp 46 S 8th to S 7th

Stackhouse ct, W fr Front ab Race

Stall's ct, from 203 Sassafras to Bryan's al

Stamper's al, from 208 S 2d to 163 S 3d

Stanbury st, W fr Broad to Sch. 8th S of Filbert

Stanley st, from 3d to 4th, bet Plum and German

Starr al, S from 188 Sassafras

State st, from Sch. 7th to 8th ab Sassafras

Steam Mill al, E from St John ab Willow

Stearly's ct, W from Smith's al, Coates

Steel's ct, N from St Mary ab 6th

Steel's ct, N from 13 German

Steele's ct, N from 269 Cedar

Steinmetz's ct, E from 93 N 4th

Steinmetz's ct, (N L) from Buttonwood n N 5th

Steinmetz ct, (S G) N from Pleasant ab 12th

Stephen's ct, W from 404 N Front

Sterling's al, from 15 Cherry to 118 Sassafras

Stevenson's ct, E from 5th, bet Christian and Marriott's la

Steward st, S from Fitzwater to Christian, bet 9th and 10th

Stewart's ct, from Cherry to 394 Sassafras

Stewart pl, S fr. Ogden ab 9th

Stewart's ct, W from N 11th n Sassafras

Stewart's ct, from 92 Gaskill

Stiles' ct opens at 110 Washington

Stiles' ct, E from Beach bel Maiden (K)

Stillhouse al, W from 330 N Front

Stilz's ct, E from Charlotte ab Beaver

Stoke's ct, E from 13th n Broad

Stout's al, from 127 Coates to Brown

Stoy's ct, from Beach to Queen N and S above Shackamaxon (E K)

Strahan's ct, W from Flower

Stranahan's ct, S from 258 Shippen

Strawberry st, from 58 High to 56 Chestnut

Strener's ct, E from Charlotte n Beaver

Sun ct, S fr. Ogden ab 9th

Sutherland av, from Cedar along Sch river

Sutherland st, from Christian to Queen, bet 2d and Grover

Swain'a ct, N from 137 Christian

Swanson st, from 10 Cedar to the Navy Yard

Swanson ct, W from Swanson bet Queen and Christian

Swanwick st, from Little George to 153 Walnut

Swarthmore place, fr, 2d E bet Sassafras & Vine

Swede's al, commencement of Church from 22 Christian

Swede's ct, E from 463 S 2d

Sweney's ct, E from 321 S 3rd

Sycamore st, S from Walnut to Spruce, bet Juniper and Broad

Tamarind st, N from Green ab Front

Tammany ct, S from Tammany st, ab 4th

Tammany st, E from 318 O Y road to N 2d, bel Noble and Green

Tanner st, N fr Wharton to Federal

Taper al, N from 53 Green

Tariff place, W from 10th bel James

Taylor's al, from 58 S Front to 73 S 2d

Taylor's ct, E from St John ab Beaver (K)

Taylor's ct, E from Barron ab Cedar

Teas' ct, S from Olive ab 13th

Temperance st, (see Gebhard) from Cherry to Sassafras, bet Sch. 7th & 8th

Tenfeet al, N from Middle al, bet 6th and 7th

Tenth st, N and S from High W of 9th

Third st, N and S from High W of 2d

Third st, (Sch.) N and S from High W of Sch 4th

Thirteenth st, N and S from High W of 12th

Thomas's al, from 116 Oak to 415 N Front

Thompson st, from intersection of 3d and G T road to 6th E and W bel Master (W K)

Thomson ct, S from 34 Sassafras

Thorn's ct, N fr. Melon bet 11th and 12th

Thorn's ct, W from N 4th n George (N L)

Thorn's ct, from 9th n Coates

Tidmar's st, from P road facing Carpenter (S) to Shippen's la

Tiller's ct, E fr Vaughan, bet Walnut & Locust

Timber lane, from F road ab Shackamaxon to Turner's lane

Tomlin's ct, E from Rachel n Laurel

Ton al, from 57 S Water

Torr's ct, fr 9th W to Ridge road S of Callowhill

Townsend's av, from 118 Budd to Rachel

Townsend's ct, S from 84 Spruce

Traquair's ct, E from 11 N 10th

Travis ct, rear 202 Cedar

Trimble's ct, from 510 N Front

Trinity pl, E from 7th ab Brown

Trotter's al, from 32 S 2d W to Strawberry

Trusty's ct, from 6 Locust

Truxton ct, S from Budd to Adams, bet Spruce

Tyler st, W from Fisher to 4th, bet Carpenter and Marriott (S)

Type al, (Pearl) W fr 10th N of Vine to William bet Vine and Wood

Ulrich row, (K) W from 2nd ab Phœnix

Ulrick's al, N from Coates bel 8th

Union ct, (K) from Bedford to Prince bet Marl borough and Hanover

Union ct, from 150 Wood ab the R road

Union Place, S W Lombard and Ashton Sch

Union sq, George st, from Sch. 7th to 8th

Union st, from Bedford to F road N and S (E K)

Union st, from 165 S Front to 79 S 4th

Union st, from 180 Swanson to 463 S Front

Unity ct, S from 16 Little Pine

Upper Ferry road, (now part of Callowhill) from intersection of Callowhill and Nixon to the Upper Bridge

Vail's ct, from Pearl n Sch.

Valley ct, E from 3 Wagner's al

Van Buren ct, rear N side Parrish bel 11th

Van Buren ct, W fr Cadwalader ab Jefferson

Vanzyke's ct, N from 103 German

Vaughn st, fr Walnut to Locust, W of Sch. 7th

Vaux's ct, E from 293 S 10th

Venango st, W from 12th to Dean bel Locust

Vernon st, from 44 Cedar to 29 Shippen

Vernon st, from N 10th to 11th, bet Parrish and Brown

Vernon pl. S from Vernon bet Shippen and Almond

Vicker's ct, N from Barker ab Sch. 6th

Videll's ct, W from 58 S 2nd

Vienna st, from Queen to West, bet Cherry and Wood (K)

Vine al, from N 10th to Broad ab Vine

Vine ct, N from Vine bel 12th

Vine st, (the N boundary of the city) from the Delaware to Schuylkill, bet Sassafras and Callowhill

Vineyard st, from R road to Charles bet Ann and George. (F V)

Virginia row, E from 13th in Walnut

Vollum st, rear of Venango n 66 S 12th

Wager st, E from G T road & 5th (K)

Wager st, (N L) W from 5th between Poplar and Franklin

Wager's ct, S from Crocket's ct

Wagner's al, (M) from Fitzwater to Brinton bet 12th and 13th

Wagner's al, from 135 Cherry N to 252 Sassafras

Wagner's ct, W from N 5th ab Noble

Wagner's ct, N from 5th ab Noble to Dean

Wagner's ct, W fm Sch 8th bet Sassafras & Vine

Wales' av. S from 116 German

Walker's ct, E from 239 N 2nd

Walker's ct, rear G T road and 2d (K)

Walker's ct, S from Willow ab 6th

Wall st, from P road to 7th, opp Queen

Wall's Elbow, from Emlen's ct to Roger's ct

Wallace's ct, in rear Ann st (F V)

Wallace's ct, W from 10 N Front

Wallace ct, W from Church bel Christian

Wallace st, from 7th W to Broad bet Green an Coates

Walnut al, from N 13th W to N Juniper, bet Cherry and Sassafras

Walnut st, W from Delaware to Schuylkill bet Chestnut and Spruce

Walter's ct, N Front ab Noble

Warder place, N from Duke ab Front

Warner's ct, W from 534 N 4th

Warner's ct, from 118 Catharine

Warner's ct, S from 230 Shippen to German

Warner's ct. S from Stanley to German

Warner's ct. S from 234 Shippen

Warren's ct, N from 5 Sugar al

Warren st, from Dean to Quince ab Spruce

Warren st, (K) from Beach to Queen bet Hanover and Bishop

Washington ct, W fr Washington av ab Green

Washington av, (N L) from Willow N to Brown, bet Front and Delaware river

Washington ct, N from 230 Lombard

Washington market-place, 120 feet in width, extending from 3rd st to P road at the distance of about 400 feet S of Cedar

Washington place, S from 109 West Filbert

Washington road, bet Green and Hickory

Washington row, W from 130 Apple

Washington sq, fr Walnut bel 8th S & E to 7th

Washington st, (See Shippen)

Washington st, High continued from the Permanent Bridge through Hamilton village

Washington st, from Master N ab 2d to Montgomery (W K)

Washington st, (S) from Delaware to Broad bet Christian (being part of line of the (S) Rail road)

Washing tonst, (S Garden) from 9th to Broad bet Green and Wallace

Washington st, N from Otter bet William & Front

Washington st, N fr 11th bet Lombard & Cedar

Washington st, W from 8th bel Prime

Water st, Sch. W of Sch. Front

Water st, from High N to Willow, and S to Pine, E of Front

Watkin's al, from 22 Bread to 85 N 3rd

Watman's ct, W from 5th ab Noble

Watt st, from Sch. 3d to 4th, bet Pine and Lombard

Watts' ct, William bel Morris

Watson's al, from Branch to New

Watson's al, S from 104 Locust

Wayne st, from Washington to Wallace, bel 10th

Weaver's ct, S from 76 German

Weaver's ct, rear 337 N Front

Weaver's ct, E from 337 N 2d

Weaver's row, E from G T road to Cadwalader n Camac

Weaver st, N from Green to Coates ab O Y road

Webb's al, from 221 Cherry to 336 Sassafras

Webb's al, from Oak (N L) to 371 N Front

Webster's ct, W from 26 P road

Weccacoe av, S from 12 Christian

Weccacoe st, N from 183 Queen to Catharine

Weeks' ct, N from Rachael ab Poplar

Welling st, from Mulberry to Cherry, above Sch Front

Wells' row, S from S E 8th and Green

Wesley st, W fr 3d, bet Wharton & Johnson's l

Wesley st., from 3 road, W

West ct, E from 29 N Market

West st, from F road to Wood (K) ab Duke

West st, bet Sch Front & Beach, from Walnut

West st, E from 233 N 2d

Western av, from Sch 8th ab Sassafras to Pearl

Westford av. S fr. Noble ab 8th

Westmoreland st, from Broad to Sch. 8th, bet Locust and Spruce

Wharf st, from Cedar along the wharves

Wharton st, from the Delaware to P road bel Federal

Wheat st, S from Marion, bet S 2nd and Front

Wheeler's place, S from Coates bel Broad

Whetstone ct, S from the c 6th & Christian

Whillden's ct, E from Rye opp Square

Whitaker's ct, W from 66 S 5th

White's ct, S fr Cedar bet 12th and 13th

White's ct. S from Bedford bet Shippen la and Broad

Whitehall st, from 12th to Broad, bet Buttonwood and Spring Garden

Whitehead's ct, W from 294 S 4th

Wickecoe av, S from Christian n Swanson

Wiggins' ct, S from 62 Cherry

Wiles' row, N from Wallace bel Broad

Wiley's ct, S from Castle n 10th

Wiley's ct. N from 35 Plum

Wiley's ct. W from 120 N 11th

Williams' ct. E from Vaughan bel Locust

Williams' ct, fr 262 Cedar to 71 Bedford. (M)

Williams' ct, N from Pleasant bel 10th

William's st, N from 343 Callowhill

William st, W fr. Sch 3d bel Locust

William st, from Otter to Rose (K)

William st, from Vine to Coates

William st, from Coates to Vine W of Sch Front

William st, fr Sch. 5th to 4th bel Cedar

William st, from Otter to Edward N & S (W K)

Williamson's ct, from Concord bel 3rd

Willing's al, from 98 S 3rd to 75 S 4th

Willing's st, N fr. Mulberry bet Sch Front and Ashton

Willis ct, E from 9 Crown

Willow al, from Willow ab 2nd

Willow ct, from Vine W of 6th

Willow st, S from Pine ab Sch. 6th

Willow st, Sch., from Locust to Cedar, bet Schuylkill and Beach

Willow st, from the Delaware W to 9th, N of Callowhill

Willow st, S from Wood bel 12th to Pearl

Wilson's ct, rear of 3 Poplar

Wilson's ct, rear 132 Buttonwood

Wilson's ct, N from Carpenter, bet 8th and 9th

Wilson st, bet Reckless & Christian & Front & Swanson

Wilts' ct, S from Brown n 10th

Winter's ct, S from Montgomery

Winter st, W from 3d bet Race and Vine

Winter st. N from George ab 3d (N L)

Wirtz ct, S from 116 Brown

Wistar st, S from Washington bel 7th

Wistar st, E from 12th ab R road

Wistar's ct. S from Phœnix bel G T road

Wistar's ct, S from Vine, E of Broad

Witman's al, from Kunckle, bel Callowhill to N 4th

Witman's ct, W from 400 N 2nd

Wolgam's ct, E from 75 N 8th

Wolf's ct, S from 68 German

Wood's ct, E from Garden bel Callowhill

Wood ct, E from Swanson n Prime

Wood st, (N L & S G) from 2nd st W to the Sch. bet Vine and Callowhill

Wood st, (K) from Queen n Gunner's run to West

Work's ct. E from 275 S 3d

Woodland st, W of Permanent Bridge, (West Philad.)

Workman's ct, W of Front ab Mead

Wright's al, from Miller's al to Vine bet Sch 8th and Broad

Wyatt st, E from Wistar to 7th

Yeager's ct, N fr Shippen bel 7th

Yeager's ct, N from Carlton bel Broad

Yhost st, fr 158 Catharine to Queen

York buildings, Walnut bet Washington sq and S 8th

York ct, E from 37 Budd

York st or ct, from 103 S 3rd E to Laurel

York pl, E from 5th bel Poplar

Young's alley, W from New Market above Willow

Young's pl, N from 111 Queen (S)

Zachary's ct, N from 31 Walnut

Zane st, from 32 N 7th W to N 8th

417

BANKING INSTITUTIONS.

BANK OF THE UNITED STATES.

(CLOSED.)

Chestnut and Fourth.

Chartered February 18, 1836.

JAMES ROBERTSON, *President.*

HERMAN COPE—*Superintendent of Suspended Debt.*

BANK OF PENNSYLVANIA.

Incorporated March 30th, 1793.—Capital $2,500,000.—Shares, $400.

Dividends declared on the first Wednesdays in January and July.

Discounts—Wednesdays and Saturdays.

JOSEPH TROTTER, *President.*   GEORGE PHILLER, Cashier.

Directors for 1847. *Election in Feb'y.*

Joseph Trotter,	R. M. Lewis,	W. E. Hacker,	Wm. V. Anderson,
Jacob R. Smith,	Mordecai D. Lewis,	Gideon Scull,	Jacob M. Thomas,
Horatio N. Burroughs,	Wm. H. Dillingham,	Wm. Geisse,	Levi Taylor.

A. B. CUMMINGS, *Notary.*

PHILADELPHIA BANK.

South-west Fourth and Chestnut.

Incorporated 1804.—Capital $2,000,000.—Paid in $1,800,000.

SAMUEL F. SMITH, *President.*   JOHN B. TREVOR, *Cashier.*

Directors.

Samuel F. Smith,	Joshua Longstreth,	Robert Patterson,	E. M. Lewis,
John Welsh,	William Worrell,	Quintin Campbell,	John W. Claghorn,
Samuel W. Jones,	John Devereux,	Richard D. Wood,	Henry C. Corbit,
Joseph R. Evans.			

Discount—Mondays and Thursdays.—EDWARD HURST, *Notary.*

GIRARD BANK.

South Third near Dock.

Charles S. Boker,	Edmund Wilcox,	John Bingham,	Wm. M. Muzzey,
James Harper,	John G. Whelan,	W. H. Reed,	S. C. Ford,
Samuel Hood,	Reuben Lukens,	Thomas Prichett,	A. H. Julian,
Edwin Coolidge.			

Chartered 1832—Extended, and Capital increased, 1836.

FARMERS' AND MECHANICS' BANK.

Chestnut Street, West of Fourth, (North side.)

Incorporated 1824.—Capital $1,250,000.—Discount—Tuesdays and Fridays.

JOSEPH TAGERT, *President.*   WILLIAM PATTON, Jr., *Cashier.*

Directors.

418

SCHUYLKILL BANK.

(CLOSED.)

S. E. Sixth and High. . . . Chartered 1814.—Capital $1,000,000.

JOHN PRICE WETHERILL, *President.*

Election—First Monday in November.

BRANCH—PORT CARBON, SCHUYLKILL COUNTY.

BANK OF NORTH AMERICA.

Chestnut Street, West of Third, (North Side.)

Chartered by Congress, 1781.—Capital $1,000,000.—Discount, Mondays and Thursdays.

J. RICHARDSON, *President.*   J. HOCKLEY, *Cashier.*

Directors.

John Richardson,	Hugh Elliott,	A. J. Lewis,	Thos. Robins,
Benjamin S. Curtis,	John H. Brown,	Paul W. Newhall,	Thomas M. Smith,
Thomas Allibone,	Jacob P. Jones,	John B. Budd,	Wm. W. Keen.

SAMUEL BADGER, *Notary.*

MANUFACTURERS' & MECHANICS' BANK, N. L.

North-west corner of Vine and North Third.

Chartered 1832.—Capital $600,000.—Discount—Tuesdays and Fridays.

JOHN FARR, *President.*   M. W. WOODWARD, *Cashier.*

Directors.

John Farr,	Frederick Gaul,	Wm. C. Kent,	Nathaniel Randolph,
Jos. H. Seal,	Wm. P. Cresson,	John Welsh, Jr.,	A. W. Adams,
Geo. R. Graham,	Francis Jordan,	Henry Conrad,	Geo. W. Carpenter.
Edwin Spooner,			

SAMUEL BADGER, *Notary.*

419

BANK OF THE NORTHERN LIBERTIES.

North side of Vine, near North Third.

Chartered 1813.—Capital $500,000.—Discount—Tuesdays and Fridays.

R. L. PITFIELD, *President.* S. W. CALDWELL, *Cashier.*

Directors.

Robert L. Pitfield,	Joshua Lippincott, Jr.,	Peter A. Keyser,	Jno. Patterson,
Jos. T. Mather,	Thomas Hart,	Samuel Grant,	John Taylor,
M. Magrath,	C. Koons,	John Naglee,	Joseph R. Jenks.
Benj. Baker,	A. C. Barclay,	David Kirkpatrick,	

JOHN H. FRICK, *Notary.*

MECHANICS' BANK,

OF THE CITY AND COUNTY OF PHILADELPHIA.

South Third street below High, (West side.)

Chartered 1814.—Capital $1,400,000.—Discount.—Tuesdays and Fridays.

JOSEPH B. MITCHELL, *President.* WILLIAM THAW, *Cashier.*

Directors.

J. B. Mitchell,	Archibald Wright,	Philip S. Justice,	James Dunlap,
James H. Hart,	Charles Leland,	William M. Clark,	Robert Steen,
Jas. S. Woodward,	William Richardson,	Geo. D. Rosengarten,	F. N. Buck.
Wm. R. Thompson,			

F. J. TROUBAT, *Notary.*

STATE BANK, AT CAMDEN, N. J.

Office, 12 Church Alley, Philadelphia.

Chartered 1812.—Capital $300,000.—Discount—Wednesdays and Saturdays.

JOHN GILL, *President.* A. M'CALLA, *Cashier.*

Directors.

John Gill,	J. J. Spencer,	Samuel C. Champion,	Charles Reeves.
Jas. W. Cooper,	Samuel R. Lippincott,	Richard Fett,	

420

BANK OF PENN TOWNSHIP.

North-west corner of Sixth and Vine streets.

Chartered 1826.—Capital $250,000.—Discount—Wednesdays and Saturdays.

ELIJAH DALLETT, *President.*　　　　　　JAMES RUSSEL, *Cashier.*

Directors.

Elijah Dallett,	Lawrence Shuster,	John D. Ninesteel,	Benjamin Davis,
Daniel Deal,	James H. Stroup,	Wm. C. Ludwig,	D. B. Hinman,
John Woertz,	Elijah Dallet, Jr.,	John H. Campbell,	Samuel Bispham.
Peter Maison,			

WM. O. KLINE, *Notary.*

SOUTHWARK BANK.

South Second street, below Cedar, (West side.)

Chartered 1825.—Capital $250,000.—Discount—Mondays and Thursdays.

T. SPARKS, *President.*　　　　　　JOSEPH S. SMITH, *Cashier.*

Directors.

Thomas Sparks,	John Thompson,	John C. Allen,	Lewis Clark.
Peter Williamson,	Louis Robert,	Samuel Castner,	Thomas D. Grover,
Robert Burton,	John Baker,	Wm. Clark,	Thomas Barnett.
Walter Thompson,			

JOHN W. NESBITT, *Notary.*

KENSINGTON BANK.

Re-chartered for fifteen years from November, 1836.—Capital $250,000.

Discount—Tuesdays and Fridays.

JONATHAN WAINWRIGHT, *President.*　　　　　　CHARLES KEEN, *Cashier.*

Directors.

Jonathan Wainwright,	Charles Edwards,	Alexander Peterson,	Saml. Megargee,
Jacob P. Donaldson,	John Landell,	Henry Crilley,	Geo. J. Weaver,
Michael Day,	James Keen,	Lewis Shinneck,	Hugh Smith.
Joseph Baker,			

FRAN. J. TROUBAT, *Notary.*

THE PHILADELPHIA SAVING FUND SOCIETY.

Incorporated February 25, 1819.—Open for Deposits and Payments on Mondays and Thursdays only, between the hours of 9 A. M. and 1 P. M., and 3 and 7 P. M.

Office, 68 Walnut street, above Third.

CLEMENT C. BIDDLE, President.　　　　　　GEORGE GREINER, Treasurer.

Managers.

J. J. Vanderkemp,	Francis Gurney Smith,	John Bacon,	George Campbell,
Lawrence Lewis,	Samuel Grant,	Thomas C. Rockhill,	Lewis Waln,
John R. Neff,	Thomas H. White,	Tobias Wagner,	Jacob R. Smith,
Quintin Campbell,	William Davidson,	John Keating,	William Platt,
John A. Brown,	William Smith,	James Dundas,	H. J. Williams.
Caleb Cope,	Samuel W. Jones,	Charles Vezin,	Thos. Robins.

Interest—Four per cent. per annum.

421

THE PHILADELPHIA LOAN COMPANY.

Office 6 Minor street.

WILLIAM ALMINDINGER, President.   THOMAS J. HEMPHILL, Secretary.

SOUTHERN INSURANCE AND TRUST COMPANY.

Office S. W. corner of Second and Spruce street. Capital, $125,000. Incorporated 1836.

GEORGE K. CHILDS, President.   WILLIAM W. SMITH, Cashier.

Directors.

G. K. Childs,	Martin J. Croll,	John Reynolds,	James M'Cann,
Zebulon Locke,	Wm. J. Savage,	Jno. Leadbeater, sr.,	Charles H. Rogers,
Joseph Feinour,	Anson Steel,	Saml. Reckless,	Robert S. Wilson.
Joseph Murry,			

GLOBE INSURANCE AND TRUST COMPANY.—Office 435 North Second street.

OSMON REED, President.   JONATHAN ALDEN, Cashier.

Directors.

George Butz, Jr.,	Elijah Tyson,	Bowers Lowber,	Jacob Harman, Jr.,
Osmon Reed,	Elisha R. Johnston,	Peter Fisher,	John Haines.

JOHN SMITH, (Pronth'y.)

INSURANCE COMPANIES.

FIRE AND MARINE.

NORTH AMERICA.—Office on the S. W. corner of Walnut and Dock streets. Chartered 1794. Capital $300,000. Shares $5. Dividends January and July.

ARTHUR G. COFFIN, President.   HENRY D. SHERRERD, Secretary.

INSURANCE COMPANY OF THE STATE OF PENNSYLVANIA.

Office, 4 Exchange.

Capital $200,000. Shares $200 Dividends February and August.

SIMEON TOBY, President.   WILLIAM HARPER, Secretary.

DELAWARE MUTUAL SAFETY INSURANCE COMPANY.

Office (Gowen's Building) S. E. Dock and Third streets.

WILLIAM MARTIN, President.   WM. EYRE, Jr., Vice-President.

RICHARD S. NEWBOLD, Secretary.

MARINE RISKS and RISKS by STEAMBOATS, RAIL-ROADS, RIVERS and LAKES insured on the most favourable terms. Losses will be liberally and promptly adjusted.

FIRE RISKS on Merchandise, Buildings, and other property insured, either in town or country, for a limited time or permanently.

COLUMBIA.—Office 5 Exchange. Charter perpetual.

C. N. BUCK, President.   R. S. HAMILTON, Secretary.

MARINE.

UNION MUTUAL.—Office, No. 6 Exchange Buildings.

Capital $300,000. Shares $60. Dividends January and July.

RICHARD S. SMITH, President.   GEORGE LEWIS, Secretary.

422

PHŒNIX MUTUAL.—Office, No. 52 Walnut street.
Capital $120,000. Shares $40. Dividends June and December.
JOHN R. WUCHERER, President. DAVID LEWIS, Secretary.

DELAWARE.—Office 3 Exchange Buildings.
Capital $200,000. Shares $40. Dividends June and December.
JOSHUA EMLEN, President. JOHN DONNALDSON, Secretary.

AMERICAN MUTUAL.—Office N. E. corner of Third & Walnut st., Exchange Building.
WILLIAM CRAIG, President. JOSHUA P. HAVEN, Secretary.

WASHINGTON MUTUAL INSURANCE COMPANY.—Office 48 Walnut street.
CHARLES S. RICHE, President. HENRY M. SPRINGER, Secretary.

FIRE.

PHILADELPHIA CONTRIBUTIONSHIP.—Office No. 96 South Fourth street.
Incorporated March 25, 1752.
JAMES S. SMITH, Treasurer and Secretary,

MUTUAL ASSURANCE.—Office No. 54 Walnut street.
RICHARD WILLING, Pres't. LAWRENCE LEWIS, Treasurer and Sec.

AMERICAN.—Office No. 72 Walnut street. Capital $500,000.
WILLIAM DAVIDSON, President. FREDERICK FRALEY, Secretary.

PENNSYLVANIA FIRE INSURANCE.—Office 134 Walnut street.
Capital $400,000. Charter perpetual.
QUINTIN CAMPBELL, President. BEATON SMITH, Secretary.

FRANKLIN.—Office 163½ Chestnut street.
Capital $400,000, paid in. Shares $100. Dividends April and October. Charter perpetual.
CHARLES N. BANCKER, President. CHARLES G. BANCKER, Secretary.

FIRE ASSOCIATION.—Office No. 34 North Fifth street.
GEORGE W. TRYON, President. ANDREW BUTLER, Treasurer and Sec.

COUNTY FIRE.—Office 248 North Third street.
Capital, $400,000. Charter perpetual. Dividends January and July.
AUGUSTIN STEVENSON, President. JACOB F. HŒCKLEY, Secretary.

CITY AND COUNTY MUTUAL INSURANCE.—Office No. 74 Walnut street.
Capital authorized by law. $400,000. Charter perpetual. Dividends January and July.
GEORGE M. HICKLING, President. JOHN McCOLLOM, Secretary.

SPRING GARDEN MUTUAL.—Office No. 196 North Sixth street, N. W. corner Wood.
Charter perpetual.
CHARLES STOKES, President. LEWIS KRUMBHAAR, Secretary.

RELIANCE MUTUAL.—Office S. W. corner Walnut and Fifth street.
GEORGE W. TOLAND, President. B. M. HINCHMAN, Secretary.

LIVES AND ANNUITIES.

THE PENNSYLVANIA COMPANY FOR INSURANCES ON LIVES AND
GRANTING ANNUITIES.—Office 66 Walnut street.
Capital $500,000. Shares $100. Dividends January and July. Charter perpetual.
HYMAN GRATZ, President. WM. B. HILL, Actuary.

423

THE GIRARD LIFE INSURANCE, ANNUITY AND TRUST COMPANY OF PHILADELPHIA.

Office No. 159 Chestnut street.   Capital $300,000.   Charter perpetual.

B. W. RICHARDS, President.   JOHN F. JANES, Treasurer and Actuary.

ASSOCIATION FOR THE RELIEF OF DISABLED FIREMEN.

CHARLES SCHAFFER, President.

GEORGE W. TRYON, Vice-President.   ANDREW BUTLER, Secretary.

EDMUND A. SOUDER, Treasurer.   JOHN RUTHERFORD, Assist. Secretary.

BOARD OF HEALTH, 1846-'47.

CITY.—Robert Donnell, N. W. Eighth and Walnut.

Samuel W. Weer, No. 147 North Twelfth street, and No. 68 Chestnut street.

Edward Duff.

John A. Elkinton, M. D., No. 102 North Fifth street.

Jos. M. Thomas, 70 North Eleventh, and 253 High.

John Lindsay, No. 8 Belmont Place.

SOUTHWARK.— { George G. West. / Benjamin E. Martin.

NORTHERN LIBERTIES.— { Benjamin E. Carpenter, No. 215 Coates street. / Richard L. Lloyd, No. 359 North Sixth street.

SPRING GARDEN.—Amos Phillips.

MOYAMENSING.—John D. Hoffner, No. 229 South Sixth street, below Shippen.

KENSINGTON.— { J. E. Eldridge. / J. Bethell.

OFFICERS OF THE BOARD.

President—John Lindsay, 8 Belmont Place.

Secretary—Benjamin E. Carpenter, 215 Coates.

Treasurer—Richard L. Lloyd, 359 North Sixth.

Solicitor—J. A. Phillips, No. 56 South Sixth street.

Clerk of the Board—Samuel P. Marks, Shippen street, above Tenth.

Steward of Lazaretto—John J. Garvin.

Matron of City Hospital—Mrs. P. Altemus, Hospital.

Messenger—Charles F. Thiesen, No. 9 Moyamensing road.

Assistant Messenger—Thomas Bedford, Eighth above Coates street.

Physician of City Hospital—F. W. Sargent.

Runner—David Brown.

EXECUTIVE OFFICERS.

HEALTH OFFICER—Wm. Loughlin, 215 South Sixth.

PORT PHYSICIAN—H. D. Dietrich, M. D., 159 North Tenth.

LAZARETTO PHYSICIAN—Joshua Y. Young. M. D., Lazaretto.

QUARANTINE MASTER—Alexander McKeever, Lazaretto.

424

GOVERNMENT OF THE UNITED STATES.

JAMES K. POLK, President.
GEORGE M. DALLAS, Vice President.
JAMES BUCHANAN, Secretary of State.
ROBERT J. WALKER, Secretary of the Treasury.
W. L. MARCY, Secretary of War.
JOHN Y. MASON, Secretary of the Navy.
NATHAN CLIFFORD, Attorney General.
CAVE JOHNSON, Post Master General.

GOVERNMENT OF PENNSYLVANIA.

EXECUTIVE.

FRANCIS R. SHUNK, Governor.
JESSE MILLER, Secretary of State.
JOHN BANKS, Treasurer.
BENJAMIN F. CHAMPNEY, Attorney General.

MINISTERS AND CONSULS FROM FOREIGN POWERS RESIDENT AT PHILADELPHIA.

FROM AUSTRIA.
Daniel J. Desmond, Vice Consul, 99 Spruce.

FROM BAVARIA
C. F. Hagedorn, Consul, 67 S 4th

FROM BELGIUM.
A. E. Borie, Consul, 45 Dock.

FROM BRAZIL.
Edward S. Sayres, Vice Consul, 15 Walnut

FROM BREMEN.
C. F. Plate, Consul, 29 Church alley.

FROM GREAT BRITAIN.
William Peter, Consul, 152 S 3d.

FROM BUENOS AYRES.
Nalbro Frazier, Consul, 5 Walnut.

FROM DENMARK.
John Bohlen, Consul, 67 S 4th.

FROM EQUADOR,
Samuel Sweeter, 79 S Front.

FROM WIRTEMBERG.
Fred. Klett, 2d & Callowhill.

FROM FRANCE.
Baron D'Auterive, Consul, 8 Sansom.

FROM HAMBURG.
Charles N. Buck, Consul General, 5 Exchange.

FROM HANOVER.
John Leppien, Consul, 29 Church alley.

FROM MEXICO.
Felix Merino, Vice Consul, 5th and Powell.

FROM THE NETHERLANDS.
Henry Bohlen, Consul, 69 S 4th.

FROM PORTUGAL:
Daniel J. Desmond, 99 Spruce.

FROM PRUSSIA.
J. C. Lang, Consul, 67 S 4th.

FROM ROME.
Daniel J. Desmond, Consul General.

FROM SARDINIA.
Daniel J. Desmond, Consul.

FROM SAXONY.
R. Ralston, Consul, 4 S Front.

FROM SICILY.
D. J. Desmond, 99 Spruce.

SPAIN.
Geo. Chacon, Consul General, 95 N Water.

SWEDEN.
R. D. Seldner, Vice Consul, 68 S Front.

FROM SWITZERLAND.
John Syz, 6 Chestnut.

FROM TUSCANY.
Daniel J. Desmond, Consular Ag't, 99 Spruce.

FROM URAGUAY.
Benjamin W. Frazier, Vice Consul.

FROM VENEZUELA.
William M'Ilhenney, Esq., Consul, Athenæum

425

GENERAL COURT DIRECTORY.

COMPILED EXPRESSLY FOR THIS WORK.

UNITED STATES CIRCUIT COURT.

President Judge.....The Honourable Robert C. Grier, one of the Associate Justices of the Supreme Court.

Associate Judge.....The Honourable John K. Kane.

Meets on the 11th of April and the 11th of October, in each year, except those dates should fall on Sunday, and then on the day following.

Clerk, George Plitt.

UNITED STATES DISTRICT COURT.

Judge.....The Honourable John K. Kane.

Meets on the third Monday of February, May, August and November.

COURT OF ADMIRALTY.

Judge.....The Honourable John K. Kane.

This Court is considered as always open, the adjournments being at the option of the Judge.

COURT OF BANKRUPTCY.

Judge.....The Honourable John K. Kane.

This Court is considered as always open, the adjournments being at the option of the judge.

The above are all held in the western room of the second story of the centre building of the State House.

Clerk.....Francis Hopkinson, Esq.

Marshal.....George M. Keim, Esq.

SUPREME COURT OF PENNSYLVANIA.

Chief Justice.....The Honourable John Bannister Gibson.

Associate Justices.....The Honourable Molton C. Rogers, Thomas Burnside, Thomas S. Bell and Richard Coulter.

The Eastern District is composed of the City and County of Philadelphia, and of the Counties of Delaware, Chester, Montgomery, Bucks, Northampton, Lehigh, Monroe, Pike, Carbon and Schuylkill.

The jurisdiction in all those counties is appellate, except in the City and County of Philadelphia, where, besides appellate jurisdiction, there is original jurisdiction in all cases where the amount in controversy is five hundred dollars and upwards.

There are two terms for the Eastern District, holden at Philadelphia on the third Monday of December, continuing three weeks; on the second Monday of March, continuing two weeks. These terms are continued, by adjournment, for a longer period. The first and last days of each term are return days. The last Monday of July is also a return day, when the Court is opened for motions, and so forth. The first Monday of each month is also a return day for all process, original, mesne or final. The Court has power to fix special return days.

54

NISI PRIUS COURT.

There are three sessions of the Nisi Prius holden by the judges of the Supreme Court—the judges alternating—commencing on the first Mondays of November, January and March, in each year. Each session is divided into two periods of at least three weeks each, for jury trials. The remainder of the sessions is appropriated to equity cases and arguments in this court. The first Monday in every month is a return day for original process.

The judge at Nisi Prius hears and determines all cases in equity brought in the Supreme Court.

The act of Assembly usually termed the affidavit of defence law, has been extended to this Court. The arbitration act is also in force.

Prothonotary of the Eastern District.....Joseph Simon Cohen, Esq.

DISTRICT COURT.

President Judge.......The Honourable Joel Jones.

Associate Judges.....The Honourable John K. Findlay and George Sharswood.

There are three terms for jury trials in each year, commencing on the first Monday of March, September, and December. The first four weeks of each are devoted to motions and arguments, and the nine weeks following to jury trials.

The June term is entirely for motions and arguments, and commences on the first Monday of June, and continues 4 weeks.

There are four terms in each year for process: the first Monday in every month being return day. The March term commences after the first Monday of February; the June term commences after the first Monday of May; the September term commences after the first Monday of August; the December term commences after the first Monday of November.

Meets in the south room of the second story, and in the north room of the first story of the County Court House.

Prothonotary.....David C Skerrett, M. D.

COURT OF COMMON PLEAS.

President Judge.....The Honourable Edward King.

Associate Judges.....The Honourable John Richter Jones, James Campbell and Anson V. Parsons.

The regular terms commence on the first Monday of March and June, the third Monday of September, and the first Monday of December. The first Monday of each month is a return day for all process except foreign attachments and subpoenas for divorce. No jury trials are held in the June term; but at each of the other terms, seven weeks are set apart for trials by jury; and the remainder of the term is de

voted to arguments in the equity and others branches of the Court.

The March term commences after the first Monday of December; the June term after the first Monday of March; the September term after the first Monday of June; and the December term after the third Monday of September.

Prothonotary......John Smith.

ORPHANS' COURT.

Same Judges......Is in session on the first and third Friday in every month.

Clerk......David Hanley.

INSOLVENT COURT.

Same Judges......Held four times in the year, a day of hearing being fixed by the Court. Continues in session until all the cases are disposed of.

Prothonotary......John Smith.

REGISTER'S COURT.

Same Judges, with the Register of Wills..... I held whenever there is a disputed case before the Register, and it is brought up for adjudication.

Prothonotary......John Smith.

COURT OF OYER AND TERMINER.

Same Judges, by virtue of the Constitution of Pennsylvania.

Clerk......John Thompson.

COURT OF QUARTER SESSIONS.

Same Judges......Is held six times in the year. Stated periods being set apart in each term for granting Tavern Licenses, disposing of the Road cases, and the other business of that Court.

Clerk......John Thompson.

The Court of Oyer and Terminer and Quarter Sessions meet in the south room of the first story of the County Court House.

The Court of Common Pleas, Orphans, Insolvent and Register's Courts, meet in the west room of the State House, first story.

LEGAL RATES OF INTEREST,

AND PENALTIES OF USURY,

IN THE DIFFERENT STATES AND TERRITORIES.

Maine, 6 per cent., forfeit of the claim.

New Hampshire, 6 per cent., forfeit of thrice the amount unlawfully taken.

Vermont, 6 per cent., recovery in action and costs.

Massachusetts, 6 per cent., forfeit of thrice the usury.

Rhode Island, 6 per cent., forfeit of the usury and interest on the debt.

Connecticut, 6 per cent., forfeit of the whole debt.

New York, 7 per cent., usurious contracts Mississippi, 8 per cent., by contract 10, usury recoverable in action for debt.

Louisiana, 8 per cent., Bank interest, 6, contract 10, beyond contract void.

Tennessee, 6 per cent., usurious contracts void.

Kentucky, 6 per cent., usury recoverable with costs.

Ohio, 6 per cent., usurious contracts void.

Indiana, 6 per cent., a fine of double the excess.

Illinois, 6 per cent., by contract 12, beyond

427

BENEVOLENT INSTITUTIONS IN PHILADELPHIA.

ʂᴛʟᴜᴍ ·ꜰᴏʀ Lᴏsᴛ Cʜɪʟᴅʀᴇɴ—19 South Seventh.

.ᴍᴇʀɪᴄᴀɴ Sᴜɴᴅᴀʏ Sᴄʜᴏᴏʟ Uɴɪᴏɴ.—F. W. Porter, Cor. Sec. Herman Cope, Treas. The So. y's House, 146 Chestnut. Anniversary meeting, Tuesday after the third Thursday in May.

.ᴍᴇʀɪᴄᴀɴ Bᴀᴘᴛɪsᴛ·Pᴜʙʟɪᴄᴀᴛɪᴏɴ ᴀɴᴅ Sᴜɴᴅᴀʏ-sᴄʜᴏᴏʟ Sᴏᴄɪᴇᴛʏ.—Rev. J. M. Peck, Cor. Sec. ʳ. B. R. Loxley, Asst. Treasurer. Depository, 31 N 6th.

ɪᴏᴀʀᴅ ᴏꜰ Pᴜʙʟɪᴄᴀᴛɪᴏɴ.—Under the care of the General Assembly of the Pres. Church. ᴡ. Mitchell, M. D., Treasurer. Jos. P. Engles, Publishing Agent. Office corner of George . Seventh street.

ᴘʜɪʟᴀᴅᴇʟᴘʜɪᴀ Tʀᴀᴄᴛ Sᴏᴄɪᴇᴛʏ.—D. W. Prescott, Treas. Depository, 6th street near Chest. . A. Flint, Agent. Anniversary, 4th Tuesday in September.

ꜰɪʀsᴛ Dᴀʏ ᴏʀ Sᴜɴᴅᴀʏ Sᴄʜᴏᴏʟ Sᴏᴄɪᴇᴛʏ. Fred. Erringer, President. John Farr, Vice Pre. ᴇɴt. Clement A. Wilson, Secretary. Charles J. Sutter, Treasurer.

ᴘʜɪʟᴀᴅᴇʟᴘʜɪᴀ Sᴀʙʙᴀᴛʜ Assᴏᴄɪᴀᴛɪᴏɴ.—144 Chestnut. President, John A. Brown. Secretary, ʀtin Buehler, 195 High. O. S. Powell, 20 Pine, General Agent.

ᴘᴇɴɴsʏʟᴠᴀɴɪᴀ Bɪʙʟᴇ Sᴏᴄɪᴇᴛʏ.—144 Chestnut. President, Ashbel Green, D. D. Jacob Lex, ɪas. Jos. H. Dulles, Cor. Sec. Anniversary meeting, 1st Wednesday in May.

ᴘʜɪʟᴀᴅᴇʟᴘʜɪᴀ Bɪʙʟᴇ Sᴏᴄɪᴇᴛʏ.—Office 144 Chestnut. President, Jas. Bayard. Cor. Sec'y., ᴇodore Cuyler. Treasurer, Geo. B. Reese. Gen Agent, Wilfred Hall.

ɪᴏᴀʀᴅ ᴏꜰ Mɪssɪᴏɴs.—Under the care of the General Assembly of the Presbyterian Church. ʳ. Wm. A. McDowell, Cor. Sec. Office 29 Sansom.

ᴅᴏᴍᴇsᴛɪᴄ ᴀɴᴅ Fᴏʀᴇɪɢɴ Mɪssɪᴏɴᴀʀʏ Sᴏᴄɪᴇᴛʏ.—Of the Episcopal Church. Thomas Robins ᴀsurer.

.ᴍᴇʀɪᴄᴀɴ Bᴏᴀʀᴅ ᴏꜰ Cᴏᴍᴍɪssɪᴏɴᴇʀs ꜰᴏʀ Fᴏʀᴇɪɢɴ Mɪssɪᴏɴs.—Agency Offi. 142 Chestnut. Hen. Perkins, Agent. Rev. David Malin, General Agent for States of Pennsylvania, New Jer. Delaware and Maryland.

ᴘʜɪʟᴀᴅᴇʟᴘʜɪᴀ Hᴏᴍᴇ Mɪssɪᴏɴᴀʀʏ Sᴏᴄɪᴇᴛʏ—Auxiliary to the American Home Missionary So. ʏ, embracing the States of New Jersey, Pennsylvania, Delaware and Maryland. Rev. E. R. ʀchild, Cor. Sec. Office, 142 Chestnut, house 79 Locust.

ᴘʜɪʟᴀᴅᴇʟᴘʜɪᴀ Cɪᴛʏ Mɪssɪᴏɴ.—Rev. Thomas G. Allen, General Agent. Office Lombard ab 9th.

ᴅᴏᴀʀᴅ ᴏꜰ Eᴅᴜᴄᴀᴛɪᴏɴ.—Under the care of the General Assembly of the Pres. Church. J. B. ᴛhell, Treas. Office 29 Sansom.

ᴘʜɪʟᴀᴅᴇʟᴘʜɪᴀ Eᴅᴜᴄᴀᴛɪᴏɴ Sᴏᴄɪᴇᴛʏ.—Rev.—Ray, Cor. Sec., 142 Chestnut. George W. M'Clel. , Treas., 100 Market street.

ɴɪᴏɴ Bᴇɴᴇᴠᴏʟᴇɴᴛ Assᴏᴄɪᴀᴛɪᴏɴ.—Captain Wm. E. Sherman, Agent. Office S W 8th & Lodge.

ᴜᴇʟ Sᴀᴠɪɴɢs Sᴏᴄɪᴇᴛʏ ᴏꜰ ᴛʜᴇ Cɪᴛʏ ᴀɴᴅ Lɪʙᴇʀᴛɪᴇs ᴏꜰ Pʜɪʟᴀᴅᴇʟᴘʜɪᴀ.—Instituted May 21, .. Incorporated May 11, 1837. Officers—Prescott, President, Townsend Sharpless. Vice-Presidents, ᴇl McCurdy, (one vacancy.) Treasurer, Blakey Sharpless. Secretary, Wm. Robinson.

ᴇʀᴍᴀɴ Sᴏᴄɪᴇᴛʏ ꜰᴏʀ ᴛʜᴇ Rᴇʟɪᴇꜰ ᴏꜰ Gᴇʀᴍᴀɴ Eᴍɪɢʀᴀɴᴛs.—Frederick Erringer, President.

428

SEAMEN'S FRIEND SOCIETY.—Captain Reynolds, Treas.   R. S..H. George, Sec., 26 S 5th.

INSTITUTION FOR THE INSTRUCTION OF THE BLIND.—N. W. Sch. 3d and Sassafras.

WILLS HOSPITAL.—J. Rodman Paul, M. D., Pres. Charles Ellis, Sec.   A. Widdifield, Steward.

PENNSYLVANIA COLONIZATION SOCIETY.   Joseph R. Ingersoll, President.   Stephen Caldwell, Treasurer.   Office Walnut above Sixth.

PENNSYLVANIA ANTI-SLAVERY SOCIETY.   J. Miller M'Kim, Pub. Agent.   Office 31 N 5th.

DAILY NEWSPAPERS.

THE UNITED STATES GAZETTE, 66 Dock
THE PENNSYLVANIAN, 70 Dock
THE PENNSYLVANIA INQUIRER & NATIONAL GAZETTE, 57 S Third
THE AMERICAN SENTINEL, 79 Dock
THE NORTH AMERICAN, N E 4th and Chestnut
THE PUBLIC LEDGER, (Penny paper) S W Third and Chestnut
THE SPIRIT OF THE TIMES, (Penny) 32 S. Third
THE DAILY CHRONICLE, (Penny) Franklin Place
THE DAILY SUN, (Penny) 65 South 3rd.
THE NATIVE EAGLE AND ADVOCATE, (Penny) 83 Dock.
THE DAILY KEYSTONE, (Penny) 85 Dock.

WEEKLY NEWSPAPERS.

THE SATURDAY COURIER, 97 Chestnut
UNITED STATES SATURDAY POST, Third and Chestnut

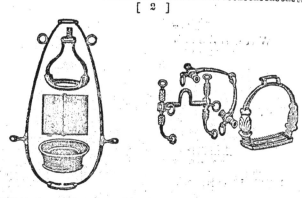

CIRCULAR.

The Subscriber respectfully informs his customers, and the public in general, that he has, at considerable expense, obtained the method of making nearly all the

ENGLISH VARNISHES

AND

BLACK OIL JAPANS

Now used in London, and has lately added to the above some cheap Coach and Cabinet Varnishes:

Superior Pale Coach Body Varnish.
Coach Body Varnish, No 1.
Carriage   "   "   1.
Carriage   "   "   2.
Carriage   "   "   3.
Superior Cabinet Varnish, for polishing Furniture.
Superior Cabinet Varnish, for finishing Furniture after the grain is filled up.
Copal Varnish, for Japanners.
Superior Pale Copal Varnish, for Japanners and Scrap Work.
Various kinds of cheap Varnishes,

Red Varnish, for Trunks,
Transferring Varnishes, with directions for use.
Patent-Polish Varnish.
Drying Japan and Gold Lacquer Varnish.
Superior Adhesive Black Oil Japan, for Castors, Buttons, Umbrella Brasses, Buckles, &c.
Brunswick Black Oil Japan, No. 1, for Locks and particular Iron Work, Leather, Paper, &c.
Brunswick Black Oil Japan, No. 2 & 3, for Umbrella Makers, &c.

LEWIS FATMAN & Co.

MANUFACTURERS OF

STEAM FRICTION MATCHES

AND

OIL PASTE BLACKING,

AND

MATCHES WITHOUT BRIMSTONE.

No. 41 NORTH FRONT STREET,

ABOVE MARKET,

PHILADELPHIA.

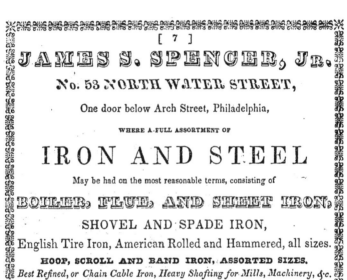

ROBERT JOHNSTON'S

Stock, Bank Note Exchange, and

COLLECTION OFFICE,

IS REMOVED FROM No. 11 TO

No. 24 SOUTH THIRD STREET,

OPPOSITE TO CONGRESS HALL, PHILADELPHIA,

Where the different branches of the BANK NOTE, STOCK and COLLECTION BUSINESS, will be conducted on the most liberal terms.

Uncurrent Bank Notes bought and sold.

Drafts, Notes and Bills, on the various sections of the United States, collected with despatch.

Every description of Stocks, Loans, &c., &c., bought and sold on Commission, at the Board of Brokers.

PHILADELPHIA

WATCH & JEWELRY STORE,

NO. 96 NORTH SECOND STREET,

CORNER OF QUARRY.

The following articles are kept constantly on hand, and will be sold below usual prices :

Gold and Silver Lepine Watches, plain extra and full jewelled.

Gold and silver Lepine Watches.

" " plain English, Swiss and French Watches.

Silver Quartier Watches, fine quality.

Imitation " " "

Quartiers, small size, very fine, warranted.

Gold Guard Keys, various styles.

Gold Fob Chains, " "

Gold Curb Guard Chains, "

Silver " " "

Silk Guards.

Fine Gold Jasroon Chains.

Gold Lockets and Snaps, various styles.

Gold Medallions, all sizes.

" Padlocks.

Gold and Silver Pencils, all sizes and styles.

Gold and Silver Spectacles, with white and coloured glasses. concave, convex, plain and perifocal.

Gold and Silver Thimbles.

Silver Table Spoons.

" Tea Spoons.

" Salt Spoons.

" Mustard Spoons.

" Forks.

" Butter Knives.

" Sugar Tongs.

" Cups.

" Nurse Tubes.

" Napkin Rings.

" Scissor Hooks.

" " Chains.

JAMES S. MASON,

)NTINUES THE MANUFACTURE OF HIS UNEQUALL
AND INIMITABLE

HALLENGE BLACKING

ALSO, OF HIS

Imperishable Black Copying Ink,

AND

BLUE WRITING FLUID INK,

STORE 192 NORTH THIRD STREET,

PHILADELPHIA.

----

l of the above articles are offered by the manufacturer of them with the utmost confi
eir superiority; and he feels assured that a whole book of certificates and puffs woul
ilt so convincing that his manufactures are really what he warrants them to be, as th
there is hardly a city, town, or village of any importance in the United States, in v
SON'S BLACKING and INK are not only known, but esteemed as sta:

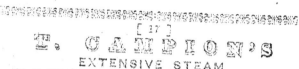

THE

PENNSYLVANIA COMPANY

FOR

INSURANCES ON LIVES,

AND

GRANTING ANNUITIES;

INCORPORATED MARCH 10, 1812,

WITH A PERPETUAL CHARTER;

OFFICE NO. 66 WALNUT STREET,

PHILADELPHIA.

CAPITAL $500,000,

INVESTED IN WELL-SECURED

MORTGAGES AND GROUND RENTS.

HYMAN GRATZ, *President.*

DIRECTORS.

PENNSYLVANIA LIFE INSURANCE COMPANY.

This Company enter into the various contracts dependent upon the contingencies of human life, such as

TO MAKE INSURANCES ON LIVES, by Land or Sea, temporary, or for whole term of life.

GRANT ANNUITIES, immediate or contingent.

SELL ENDOWMENTS.

PURCHASE LIFE INTERESTS, &c.

ALSO, RECEIVE IN TRUST

MONIES in suit in Court, payable upon the decision and order of court.

MONIES from Executors and Administrators of persons deceased, to accumulate at interest and payable to heirs.

MONIES on deposit from individuals, for stated periods, or payable on demand, with Interest, &c., &c.

Their terms are as liberal as those of any office in this country, and are about the same as those of the best English offices; and from the long experience they have had, the satisfaction they have given by the prompt settlement of all claims, and the security afforded by their AMPLE CAPITAL AND RESERVED FUNDS, they hope for a still further increase of their business.

Rates of Premiums for Insuring One Hundred Dollars on a Single Life, the assured participating in the profits, yet not liable for losses.

Age.	Premium for One Year.	Annual premium for seven years.	Annual premium for whole Life.	Age.	Premium for One Year.	Annual premium for seven years.	Annual premium for whole Life.
14	69	75	1.44	38	1.48	1.70	3.02
15	72	79	1.49	39	1.57	1.76	3.11
16	76	82	1.54	40	1.69	1.83	3.20
17	80	86	1.59	41	1.78	1.83	3.31
18	84	90	1.64	42	1.85	1.89	3.40
19	88	94	1.59	43	1.89	1.92	3.51
20	90	95	1.75	44	1.90	1.94	3.63
21	92	97	1.81	45	1.91	1.96	3.73
22	94	99	1.87	46	1.92	1.98	3.87
23	97	1.03	1.93	47	1.93	1.99	4.01
24	99	1.07	1.93	48	1.94	2.02	4.17
25	1.00	1.12	2.04	49	1.95	2.04	4.49
26	1.07	1.17	2.11	50	1.96	2.09	4.60
27	1.12	1.23	2.17	51	1.97	2.20	4.75
28	1.20	1.23	2.24	52	2.02	2.37	4.90
29	1.28	1.35	2.31	53	2.10	2.59	5.24
30	1.31	1.36	2.36	54	2.18	2.39	5.16
31	1.32	1.42	2.43	55	2.32	3.21	5.63
32	1.23	1.46	2.50	56	2.47	3.56	5.90
33	1.34	1.48	2.57	57	2.70	4.01	6.13
34	1.35	1.50	2.64	58	3.14	4.22	6.37
35	1.36	1.53	2.75	59	3.37	4.44	6.62
36	1.39	1.57	2.81	60	3.14	4.67	6.88
37	1.43	1.53	2.89				

Pamphlets with Tables of the various rates of Premiums and other particulars, will be furnished at the Office.